For Students

STUDYSPACE
wwnorton.com/studyspace

This free student Web site provides a rich array of multimedia resources and review materials within a proven, task-oriented study plan. Each chapter is arranged in an effective Organize, Learn, and Connect structure, with review materials such as chapter outlines, flashcards, quizzes and ebook links. The Norton Quiz+ Assessment Program gives students customized chapter-by-chapter study plans that target specific content areas for review. The StudySpace also offers:

- **Chapter Audio Podcasts** that serve as chapter overviews and discussions of key concepts. The content is chapter-specific and is organized around the key Learning Objectives.
- **Animations** that cover more topics and psychological processes in the text. They can be accessed on StudySpace and launched from the ebook.
- **Drag-and-Drop Labeling Exercises** that use the line art from the text to help students understand key diagrams and complex structures.
- **Visual Quizzes** that integrate the revised art program from the text to help students review the details of important figures and diagrams.
- A regularly updated **Psychology in the News** feed.
- **Video exercises** introduce students to the latest research trends in psychology.

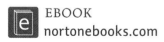

EBOOK
nortonebooks.com

Same great content, half the price!
The ebook links to StudySpace and offers many useful electronic tools, such as highlighting and sticky notes.

STUDY GUIDE

by Susan Oestreicher (University of Wisconsin at Oshkosh) and Edgar E. Coons (New York University)

This Study Guide provides additional opportunities for self-testing and study suggestions. Each chapter contains a concept map showing the linkage of ideas, learning objectives, practice questions with answers, a self test, and keywords from the text.

ZAPS
wwnorton.com/zaps

The Norton Psychology Labs (produced by the psychology departments at the University of Twente and the University of Rotterdam) are a collection of interactive online labs that allow students to participate in classic psychological studies.

EIGHTH EDITION

Psychology

HENRY GLEITMAN

JAMES GROSS

DANIEL REISBERG

W · W · NORTON & COMPANY

New York · London

W. W. Norton & Company has been independent since its founding in 1923, when William Warder Norton and Mary D. Herter Norton first published lectures delivered at the People's Institute, the adult education division of New York City's Cooper Union. The firm soon expanded its program beyond the Institute, publishing books by celebrated academics from America and abroad. By mid-century, the two major pillars of Norton's publishing program—trade books and college texts—were firmly established. In the 1950s, the Norton family transferred control of the company to its employees, and today—with a staff of four hundred and a comparable number of trade, college, and professional titles published each year—W. W. Norton & Company stands as the largest and oldest publishing house owned wholly by its employees.

Copyright © 2011, 2007, 2004, 1999, 1995, 1991, 1986, 1981 by W. W. Norton & Company, Inc.

All rights reserved
Printed in Canada

Editor: Sheri L. Snavely
Associate editor: Sarah England
Editorial assistants: Wamiq Jawaid and Josh Bisker
Project editor: Rebecca A. Homiski
Production manager: Chris Granville
Marketing manager: Amber Chow
Design: Antonina Krass
Photo editor: Trish Marx
Illustrations: Dragonfly Media Group
Composition: Preparé
Manufacturing: Transcontinental Interglobe

Library of Congress Cataloging-in-Publication Data
Gleitman, Henry.
    Psychology / Henry Gleitman, James Gross, Daniel Reisberg. — 8th ed.
      p. cm.
    Includes bibliographical references and index.

    ISBN 978-0-393-93250-8 (hardcover)

1. Psychology—Textbooks. I. Gross, James J., Ph. D. II. Reisberg, Daniel. III. Title.
    BF121.G58 2010
    150—dc22   2009042599

W. W. Norton & Company, Inc., 500 Fifth Avenue, New York, NY 10110
www.wwnorton.com
W. W. Norton & Company Ltd., Castle House, 75/76 Wells Street, London W1T 3QT
2 3 4 5 6 7 8 9 0

HENRY GLEITMAN is Professor of Psychology and the former chair of the department at the University of Pennsylvania. He is the recipient of the American Psychological Foundation's Distinguished Teaching in Psychology Award (1982) and, from the University of Pennsylvania, the Abrams Award (1988) and the Lindback Award (1977). He has served as President of the APA's Division 1: General Psychology and Division 10: Psychology and the Arts. Most importantly, Professor Gleitman has taught introductory psychology for five decades to over 40,000 students.

JAMES GROSS is Professor of Psychology at Stanford University and Director of the Stanford Psychophysiology Laboratory. Professor Gross's research focuses on emotion and emotion regulation processes in healthy and clinical populations. His 150 or so publications include *The Handbook of Emotion Regulation* (Guilford, 2007), and he has received early career awards from the American Psychological Association, the Western Psychological Association, and the Society for Psychophysiological Research. Professor Gross is also an award-winning teacher, a Bass University Fellow in Undergraduate Education, and the Director of the Stanford Psychology One Teaching Program. His teaching awards include Stanford's Dean's Award for Distinguished Teaching, the Stanford Phi Beta Kappa Teaching Prize, Stanford's Postdoctoral Mentoring Award, and Stanford's highest teaching prize, the Walter J. Gores Award for Excellence in Teaching.

DANIEL REISBERG, author of the bestselling *Cognition: Exploring the Science of the Mind*, Fourth Edition (Norton, 2010), is Professor of Psychology and chair of the department at Reed College in Portland, Oregon. Professor Reisberg has over two decades of experience in teaching Psychology's Intro course, and also teaches a popular course in Cognition; he teaches advanced seminars on Thinking and on Psychology & The Law. His research has focused on the nature of mental imagery as well as on people's ability to remember emotionally significant events. He has served on the editorial boards of many of the field's journals, and also serves as a consultant for the justice system, working with police and the courts to improve the quality of eyewitness evidence.

To all the people who have made this book possible—
Our teachers, our colleagues, our students, and our families.

Contents in Brief

Contents

CHAPTER 1

CHAPTER 4

SENSATION 132

CHAPTER 5

PERCEPTION 180

CHAPTER 6

CONSCIOUSNESS 218

CHAPTER 13

SOCIAL PSYCHOLOGY 504

CHAPTER 14

DEVELOPMENT 544

TREEATMENT OF MENTAL DISORDERS 676

Preface

From one end to the other, psychology is an exciting field. It's a field that addresses questions that have intrigued humanity for ages—including what it is that all humans have in common, distinguishing us from other species, and also how it is that humans differ from each other. It's a field that addresses deep philosophical issues—like the nature of consciousness, or the degree to which each of us is in control of our own actions. But it's also a field that addresses practical problems—such as how to help the mentally ill, how to raise our children, or even how, in general, to make people happier.

The excitement attached to these questions is what originally motivated us to join the field of psychology, and it is what continues to motivate us as teachers and researchers. It is, of course, also what motivated us in writing this book. But the drive to write this book was further enhanced by another consideration, namely that psychology is also a *dynamic* field, with new ideas and new data emerging at a remarkable pace. For this reason, any description of the field—such as the coverage in a textbook—will soon need updating, and so, in each revision of this text, we've introduced our field's new discoveries, addressed new issues and new problems, and also benefitted from the insightful suggestions offered by our readers, both students and colleagues.

NEW IN THIS EDITION

This is the eighth edition of *Psychology*, and it is our most ambitious revision so far. We have—of course—added an enormous amount of new content, ranging from new discoveries about the neural bases of pleasure and pain to new insights into how to treat serious illnesses such as depression. But we've also changed the book in deeper ways. The table of contents itself is revised, with new chapters on research methods (Chapter 1), genetics and the evolutionary roots of behavior (Chapter 2), and consciousness (Chapter 6). To allow for this crucial new material, we've also reorganized other sections of the book (Chapters 13 and 14), integrating material that had been previously covered in separate chapters, allowing us to highlight important linkages and bring key themes into greater prominence. We've also shifted the sequence of chapters, to emphasize (among other points) the links between our understanding of thinking in general (Chapter 9) and our understanding of how people differ in their intellectual abilities (Chapter 11).

We've also made significant changes inside the chapters. This edition, like every prior edition, has been guided by a profound sense of respect both for our field and for our readers: We are certain that readers both want and deserve a sophisticated treatment of our field, one that conveys the substance of our field and captures the methodological power of our science. At the same time, we want the book to be as accessible as it is sophisticated, and so we've revised the prose throughout the book with the goal of making the text both intellectually intriguing and also fun to read. We've also added a new art program and a collection of new features—special figures to highlight research methods; margin definitions to highlight key terms; concrete vignettes to invite readers into each chapter—all of which, we hope, will make the book a more pleasurable read!

THE UNITY OF PSYCHOLOGY

As you will see in the chapters that follow, the field of psychology covers an extraordinary range of topics, and tackling these topics demands a remarkable diversity of methods and intellectual perspectives. We have done all we can to convey this diversity, so that readers can see the full richness of our field. At the same time, psychology is a coherent intellectual enterprise, with many strands uniting the various types of work that psychologists do and the broad range of issues that psychologists care about. In writing *Psychology*, we have tried to convey both the field's breadth and its unity, so that readers can understand how the various elements of our field form a rich, cohesive fabric.

One of the principal ways we do this is by showcasing the methods of psychology. Psychology tackles a diverse set of issues and employs many different methods. As a result, the exact procedures we use in, say, a study of how the brain makes vision possible are quite different from the procedures we use in, say, a study of whether a particular form of psychotherapy is effective. No matter what the issue, though, and no matter what the procedure, psychology insists on the logic and rigor of the scientific method, guaranteeing that our claims are always well-rooted in fact.

We showcase the scientific method throughout this text. Chapter 1, for example, puts psychology's use of the scientific method in plain view right at the start; illustrations of method—and the safeguards needed to ensure good science—then echo throughout the entire book. Many of these illustrations are presented graphically—in special *Scientific Method figures*—to capture as clearly as possible how psychologists do their work.

Why this focus on methods? There are three reasons. First, the issues in play throughout this book are deep and often consequential: How should we think about human nature? How should we raise our children? What is "mental health," and how can we promote it? With issues as important as these, it's essential that we provide solid, fully justified, fully defensible claims, claims that are as accurate as we can possibly make them. The scientific method is our best bet of reaching that goal.

The second reason is straightforwardly educational. In our own classrooms and in our writing, we want to make sure students understand the field of psychology. This understanding has to include both *what* we know and also *how* we know it, because our methods are, in truth, a significant part of what defines the modern field of psychology. Indeed, our methods are a central part of what makes our field different from the other endeavors seeking to understand and explain human behavior—the study of history, for example, or the claims made in novels or religious texts. As a result, we would argue that anyone hoping to "know psychology" simply has to understand our field's methods, and so methods must be showcased in the text.

The third reason is also educational—but in a different sense. Much has been written about the importance of "critical thinking," and the need to train students to be better critical thinkers. We happily note, therefore, that several lines of evidence indicate that this training can be provided by education in psychology—especially if that education emphasizes psychology's methods. And, in truth, this should not be surprising: We've already noted that psychology tackles real world problems, and, in our science, we carefully test our claims. We pay close attention to whether our sample of data is large enough and representative of broader patterns. We seek out alternative explanations of the observations we've made so far. Surely these methodological steps, applied to day-to-day issues, are part of what we mean by (and hope for!) in critical thinking. This makes it entirely reasonable that scientific training in psychology can build critical thinking habits in students—and this in turn provides powerful motivation for our showcasing of methods in this text.

THE DIVERSITY OF PSYCHOLOGY

Even as we appreciate the unity of psychology, it is also important to understand the diversity within our field—in the topics covered, the methods used, and the perspectives taken. The need for multiple perspectives in our field is especially clear when we consider the rich interplay between psychological issues, concerned with our feelings, beliefs, and actions, and biological issues, concerned with the functioning of the nervous system. Philosophers, for example, ask how our conscious awareness is made possible by the roughly three pounds of organic material that make up the brain. Parents ask themselves how much of their child's personality should be attributed to genetic influences. Clinicians ask whether our best option for treating depression might be some adjustment in the brain's physiology.

We'll tackle all of these issues in this text, and, in the process, explore how exactly we can use a biological perspective to address psychological questions. Indeed, this is a prominent feature of the Eighth Edition, and virtually every chapter offers examples of how, in the last decade or two, studies of the nervous system, genetics and evolution have provided numerous—and often surprising—insights into psychology.

This emphasis on the underlying biology is one of the reasons why we have added a new chapter (Chapter 2) focused specifically on genetics and evolution. Among other considerations, this chapter allows us to explain why it's pointless to pursue a "clean separation" between biological and psychological accounts, and likewise impossible to separate issues of "nature" and "nurture." In tackling this crucial issue, we'll end up with a more sophisticated understanding of why our psychological functioning is as it is.

Indeed, this rejection of dichotomies—like the one between "nature" and "nurture"— is another important theme in this edition, and brings us again to the diversity of our field. Time and again in this text, we'll find that we need to walk away from the easy dichotomies that theorists sometimes offer: Are mental disorders such as depression or schizophrenia best thought of as medical problems or mental problems? Are people at root really all the same, so that we can meaningfully talk about "human nature," or are people (in different cultures, perhaps, or even within a culture) fundamentally different from each other? Are someone's actions shaped more by who she is, or by factors in her circumstances? When people reach foolish conclusions or do bad things, is the problem in their thinking or in their emotions (so that, somehow, their feelings are pulling their thoughts "off track")? Each of these questions offers a crucial distinction, but, nevertheless, these questions are all misleading. That is because, in each question, *both* of the proposals that are offered are correct, and so we need to acknowledge the importance of both poles of each dichotomy. We'll meet this point again and again in this book, and it will provide an important organizing theme for our coverage.

THE RELEVANCE OF PSYCHOLOGY

The field of psychology touches on many aspects of our (and our readers') lives. As an academic matter, psychology is, in an important way, a "hub discipline," one that unites many different concerns, many intellectual traditions. Thus, psychology is sure to make solid contact with the readers' other intellectual interests—whether the reader is a scientist or in the humanities, focused on biology or sociology, economics or aesthetics.

Psychology also touches our lives in another—and more direct—way. After all, psychology deals with the nature of human experience and behavior, the hows and whys of what we do, think, and feel. How could an exploration of these topics not be relevant to someone's life? Our obligation as authors, though, is to keep these links to daily living in full view as we move through the text. To make sure we meet this demand, we've tried throughout to be guided by the questions we hear, year after year, from our own students: "Why is it that I remember yesterday's conversation one way, but my girlfriend remembers it differently?" "Why do I get nervous whenever I have to stand up and give a presentation in front of a group?" "Why is it that she has such an easy time in math, while I slog through every assignment?" "Why do some children seem so cheery all the time, while others seem gloomy?" These are literally the sorts of questions we hear, and they provide clear (and fascinating) bridges between psychological science and every day life. We've kept these questions in our thoughts as we've written, and we frequently mention such questions as we proceed. In this way, the relevance of the text to reader's life is essentially guaranteed!

Overall, then, we hope it's clear that we've been trying to juggle many goals in designing, and then writing, this book. Throughout, though, our most important guide has been our experience as teachers (with a combined total of roughly 100 years in the classroom!). This experience leaves us with no doubt that one of the best ways of learning something is to teach it, because in trying to explain something to others we first have to clarify it for ourselves. And, if there's a gap in our own understanding, student questions are sure to expose that gap. This is true for every course we have ever taught, but most especially for the introductory course, because students in that course ask the toughest—and the best—questions of all.

This edition, as well as its predecessors, reflects our attempts to answer their questions, and to answer them not only to satisfy the students but also to satisfy ourselves.

ACKNOWLEDGMENTS

Finally, there remains the joyful task of thanking the friends and colleagues who helped so greatly in the writing of this book. Many, many individuals offered their time and expertise in the first seven editions of this book. Some read parts of the manuscript and gave valuable advice and criticism. Others talked to us at length about various issues in the field. We are grateful to them all.

We wish to offer special thanks to those who reviewed or offered invaluable advice on the Eighth Edition:

David H. Barlow, *Boston University*

Bruce G. Berg, *University of California, Irvine*

Jennifer L. S. Borton, *Hamilton College*

Gwen J. Broude, *Vassar College*

David Carroll, *University of Wisconsin–Superior*

Janet Chang, *Trinity College*

Susan C. Cloninger, *The Sage Colleges*

Edgar (Ted) E. Coons, *New York University*

Kelly Cotter, *Sacramento State University*

Rachel Dinero, *Cazenovia College*

Wendy Domjan, *University of Texas at Austin*

Brent Donnellan, *Michigan State University*

C. Emily Durbin, *Northwestern University*

Howard Eichenbaum, *Boston University*

Naomi Eisenberger, *University of California, Los Angeles*

Donald Ernst, *Hillsdale College*

Russel K. Espinoza, *California State University, Fullerton*

Betty Jane Fratzke, *Indiana Wesleyan University*

David Funder, *University of California, Riverside*

Preston E. Garraghty, *Indiana University*

George W. Gilchrist, *The College of William and Mary*

John T. Green, *University of Vermont*

Bruce C. Hansen, *Colgate University*

Lisa A. Harrison, *California State University, Sacramento*

Carl L. Hart, *Columbia University*

Raymond C. Hawkins II, *University of Texas at Austin*

Terence Hines, *Pace University*

Scott Huettel, *Duke University*

Linda A. Jackson, *Michigan State University*

Hendree E. Jones, *Johns Hopkins University*

Steve Joordens, *University of Toronto, Scarborough*

Katherine A. Kaplan, *University of California, Berkeley*

Scott Kaufman, *Yale University*

Ann Kring, *University of California, Berkeley*

Michael Kubovy, *University of Virginia*

Robert Kurzban, *University of Pennsylvania*

Alan Lambert, *Washington University*

Barbara Landau, *Johns Hopkins University*

Patricia Lindemann, *Columbia University*

Paul A. Lipton, *Boston University*

Mika MacInnis, *Brown University*

Etan Markus, *University of Connecticut*

Michael E. Martinez, *University of California, Irvine*

Tim Maxwell, *Hendrix College*

Kelly McGonigal, *Stanford University*

Matthias Mehl, *University of Arizona*

Douglas G. Mook, *University of Virginia*

Beth Morling, *University of Delaware*

Aaron J. Newman, *Dalhousie University*

Baron Perlman, *University of Wisconsin, Oshkosh*

Steven J. Robbins, *Arcadia University*

Juan Salinas, *University of Texas at Austin*

Catherine A. Sanderson, *Amherst College*

Asani H. Seawell, *Grinnell College*

Marc M. Sebrechts, *The Catholic University of America*

Colleen Seifert, *University of Michigan*

Kennon Sheldon, *University of Missouri*

Rebecca Shiner, *Colgate University*

Carol Slater, *Alma College*

Andra Smith, *University of Ottawa*

David M. Smith, *Cornell University*

Susan South, *Purdue University*

Robert Sternberg, *Tufts University*

Megan S. Steven, *Dartmouth College*

Dawn L. Strongin, *California State University, Stanislaus*

Karen K. Szumlinski, *University of California at Santa Barbara*

John Trueswell, *Institute for Research in Cognitive Science*

Kristy vanMarle, *University of Missouri–Columbia*

Jonathan Vaughan, *Hamilton College*

Simine Vazire, *Washington University in St. Louis*

Jeremy M. Wolfe, *Harvard Medical School*

Charles E. Wright, *University of California, Irvine*

Nancy Yanchus, *Georgia Southern University*

David Zehr, *Plymouth University*

We also want to thank Ted Coons at New York University for all of his dedication to our book, and his detailed reviews and work on the student materials that support the book. Ted Wright at UC Irvine was also an enormously helpful advisor for the cognition chapters.

Lila R. Gleitman coauthored Chapter 10, "Language," and we are grateful for her expertise, clarity, and humor. She has read every chapter of the book, and the current edition still shows many benefits of her counsel on the book's substance, style, and elegance.

Paul Rozin has long been a friend of this book and his insightful and wide-ranging comments testify to his extraordinary breadth of knowledge and depth of thought, and continue to influence us. As a dedicated teacher at the University of Pennsylvania, he has helped us see many facets of the field in a new way, especially those that involve issues of evolutionary and cultural development.

Further thanks go to the many people at W. W. Norton & Company: Chris Granville, who skillfully managed the production of the book; Antonina Krass, whose brilliance as a book designer continues to astound us; Development Editor Sarah Mann, who worked tirelessly on the book from start to finish and played an enormous role in improving our prose; Associate Editor Sarah England, who shepherded the fine new drawings and Scientific Method illustrations created by Dragonfly Media Group; Trish Marx, for leaving no stone unturned in researching new photos for this edition; Rebecca Homiski, for quadruple-checking every element of the book, while working diligently with an optimistic spirit to keep the whole project on schedule; Chris Thillen and Ellen Lohman, for their remarkable service in copyediting; Alana Conner, for her lively contributions to the chapter-opening vignettes; Wamiq Jawaid and Josh Bisker, who performed their multifarious duties as editorial assistants with skill and speed; Marian Johnson, for her calm and steady manuscript expertise; media editor Dan Jost, who created and refined a media program that supports both instructors and students; and Matthew Freeman, who is guiding our ancillary team in their substantive revisions. Finally, we also thank Ken Barton, whose input and ongoing efforts have contributed to our success in the UK and Europe; and also our marketing manager, Amber Chow, for her tireless efforts to market this new edition throughout North America.

We are also deeply grateful to our Norton editors, most recently Jon Durbin and Sheri Snavely. They have both poured boundless energy into this project, and the book is much improved for their efforts. We also want to express our gratitude to Roby Harrington, head of Norton's college division, and Drake McFeeley, president of W. W. Norton.

Our final thanks go to Norton's former chairman of the board, Donald Lamm, who was responsible for bringing Henry Gleitman and W. W. Norton together many, many years ago. As Gleitman put it in a previous edition, "Age has not withered nor custom staled his infinite variety. His ideas are brilliant and outrageous as ever; his puns are as bad as ever. And my esteem and affection for him are as great as ever." We all remain greatly indebted to him.

Merion, Pennsylvania
Portland, Oregon
San Francisco, California
January 2010

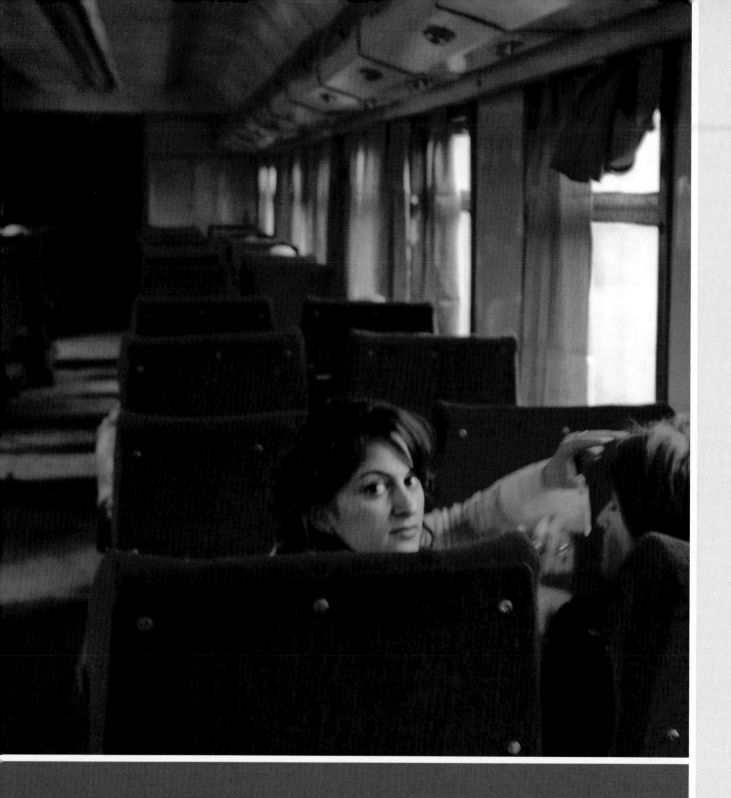

Prologue: What Is Psychology?

Why do we do the things we do? Why do we feel the things we feel, or say the things we say? Why do we find one person attractive and another person obnoxious? Why are some people happy most of the time, while others seem morose? Why do some children behave properly, or learn easily, while others do not?

Questions like these all fall within the scope of psychology, a field defined as the *scientific study of behavior and mental processes*. Psychology is concerned with who each of us is and how we came to be the way we are. The field seeks to understand each person as an individual, but it also examines how we act in groups, including how we treat each other and feel about each other. Psychology is concerned with what all humans have in common, but it also looks at how each of us differs from the others in our species—in our beliefs, our personalities, and our capabilities. And psychologists don't merely seek to *understand* these various topics; they are also interested in *change:* how to help people become happier or better adjusted, how to help children learn more effectively, or how to help them get along better with their peers.

This is a wide array of topics; and, to address them all, psychologists examine a diverse set of phenomena—including many that nonpsychologists don't expect to find within our field! But we need this diverse coverage if we are to understand the many aspects of our thoughts, actions, and feelings; and, in this text, we'll cover all of these points and more.

THE BREADTH OF PSYCHOLOGY'S CONTENT

As a means of introducing this text—and our field—let's consider some examples that convey the broad scope of psychology. We'll start by considering the range of *contents* or *topics* psychology examines and then we'll turn to some examples that illustrate the range of *methods* and *perspectives* psychologists employ.

Morality and the Brain

Why is it that some people—Mahatma Gandhi, Mother Teresa—find the moral courage to devote their lives to good causes, while others—Adolf Hitler, Saddam Hussein—are capable of horrific offenses against humanity? On a much smaller scale, why is it that ordinary people sometimes choose to do the right thing, and sometimes choose morally questionable paths? The answer has many elements, including each person's beliefs and how individuals evaluate their options when confronting a moral choice. But just as important is the person's *emotional* response to a moral problem—confirming the age-old notion that moral behavior depends as much on the "heart" (feelings) as on the "head" (rational weighing of options).

We can confirm this claim in several ways, including close examination of the brain. This research depends on *neuroimaging* techniques, developed in the last few decades, that let investigators monitor, moment by moment, the level of metabolic activity in different parts of the brain (i.e., which brain sites are at that moment using more oxygen or more glucose—the brain's "fuel"—than usual; Figure P.1). Neuroimaging allows the researcher to ask which brain regions are especially active when someone is in a particular mental state—such as trying to make a decision, or feeling embarrassment, or wrestling with a moral dilemma.

In one study, healthy volunteers had to evaluate three types of questions. The first type didn't involve moral issues (e.g., choosing which of two coupons to use at a store). A second type involved a moral issue that seemed (by comparison) impersonal; an

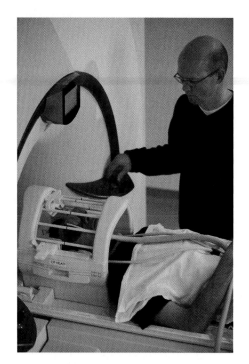

P.1 How does brain imaging work? One commonly used type of brain imaging, functional magnetic resonance imaging (fMRI), allows researchers to assess the blood's oxygen level (a good indicator of brain activity) at specific sites. fMRI shows different "slices" through the living brain, highlighting more active regions in different colors.

(A)

Imagine you're waiting near the track for a trolley to arrive. Suddenly, you notice a runaway trolley car speeding forward, out of control. You realize that if the trolley isn't stopped, it will run over and surely kill five people. But then you see a track switch. If you throw it, the trolley will turn onto another track, where it will hit (and kill) only one person. Would you throw the switch?

(B)

Imagine you're standing on a footbridge above a trolley track, and you see a runaway trolley car speeding forward. You realize that if the trolley isn't stopped, it will run over and surely kill five people. But another person is standing next to you on the bridge. If you push him off the bridge, the trolley will hit him, and his dead body will stop the trolley, saving the other five. Would you push him?

P.2 Making moral decisions

example is shown in Figure P.2A. The final type involved a similar issue, but cast in a way that is much more personal; an example is shown in Figure P.2B.

The two moral dilemmas described in Figure P.2 are obviously similar; in both cases, the question boils down to whether someone is willing to sacrifice one life to save five. But people respond to these dilemmas quite differently. They're far more likely to throw the switch (see Figure P.2A) than to push the other person off the footbridge (see Figure P.2B). What causes this difference? Is it linked to how people reason about these two scenarios? Studies of the brain suggest otherwise: The researchers found relatively few differences between the pattern of brain activation for people solving "impersonal" moral dilemmas (like the one in Figure P.2A) and people solving nonmoral practical problems (like the question about coupons). Both types of problems were associated with increased activity in the brain's prefrontal and parietal areas—brain areas thought to be involved in the active processes of reasoning. This finding suggests that, for both of these types of problems, people were thinking things through, weighing their options, and trying to make the most reasonable choice.

The pattern of brain activation was quite different, though, for people considering the personal dilemmas like the one in Figure P.2B. These people showed increased activity in the medial frontal gyrus, the posterior cingulate gyrus, and the angular gyrus—all areas strongly associated with emotional responses (Green, Sommerville, Nystrom, Darley, & Cohen, 2001; Greene & Haidt, 2002; Figure P.3). The same areas are also especially active when we are reacting to others in a social setting. Data like these— and many other results as well—support the claim that moral decisions are not just a matter of rational calculation, but also are powerfully shaped by emotional and social considerations. The brain data strongly suggest, in other words, that what made Mahatma Gandhi and Mother Teresa special may have been their ability to rely on *feelings* as much as *reasoning*, on *compassion* as much as *intellectual beliefs*, in guiding their moral choices.

P.3 **Brain activity in moral decision-making** These fMRI images were produced by *subtracting* the brain activation levels when people were making impersonal decisions from the activation levels when people were making personal decisions (as in Figure P.2). The colored areas, therefore, show sites within the brain that were more active for the personal decisions. The three images all show the same brain, but each image shows a different "slice" through the brain; the number above each image is a measurement (in a standardized system) of how "high" in the brain the slice is—and so the leftmost image shows a slice roughly at the center of the head; the middle image shows a slice 10 mm closer to the top of the head, and the rightmost image shows a slice 10 mm higher still.

The Broad Effects of Brain Damage

In the previous section, we considered data that involved brain activation: Which parts of the brain are especially active when someone is contemplating *this* sort of moral dilemma, or *that* sort? We can learn just as much, though, from data involving the opposite shift—that is, from cases in which brain areas are not contributing to a task at all, because the relevant brain sites have been damaged by injury or disease.

Brain damage can cause profound—and often tragic—life changes, but its effects can also provide important insights into how the brain functions. For example, people who have suffered damage to brain sites crucial for establishing new memories seem literally unable to learn anything new. Studies of these patients have taught us a great deal about the biological basis for memory; these studies can also teach us about the broad function of memory in our day-to-day lives—including some unexpected ways that memory guides our behavior.

One study examined two patients who suffered from profound memory disruption. At the normal lunchtime for these patients, the researcher set a full meal in front of each patient and commented, "Here's lunch." When the patients had eaten, the plates were removed; and after a few minutes of conversation, the patients had completely forgotten their recent meal. This is, of course, what we would expect, based on the patients' overall diagnosis. But then, after a few more minutes, the researcher brought them another meal and made the same comment, "Here's lunch" (Rozin, Dow, Moskovitch, & Rajaram, 1998).

At this point, one might think the patients would feel that their bellies were full and therefore would decide not to eat any more. Remarkably, though, both of the patients readily ate the second lunch—and, a few minutes later, a third. Apparently, the memory that you have just eaten is one of the factors controlling your food intake. When the memory is absent, your control over your own eating is impaired, and you are heavily influenced by cues such as the sight of available food.

It's also important to know that, just after eating their first lunch, these patients were asked how hungry they felt. Even though they had just eaten, they reported being fairly hungry. This response is in clear contrast to the pattern observed in people with intact memories; they reliably report feeling less hungry right after finishing a meal. It seems, then, that the feeling of hunger is not just the result of our having an empty stomach. Instead, the feeling of hunger is also shaped by memory—specifically, by the recollection of how long it has been since our last meal.

Decision Making

The examples we have sketched so far reflect psychology's roots in biology—and thus how much we can learn about the mind by studying patterns of brain activity or brain damage. Other aspects of psychology, in contrast, focus on the processes and capacities of the mind and pay much less attention to the neural underpinnings of these processes. Consider, for example, the way people make choices—not the sort of difficult moral decision involved in the trolley problem (see Figure P.2), but the sort of decisions that people have to make all the time, as part of their everyday lives.

Our lives are, in truth, filled with decisions. In the store, we choose which brand of toothpaste to buy, or whether to buy corn flakes or granola. Other decisions are less frequent, but more important: We choose a college major, or which apartment to rent, or what city to live in. Still other decisions can be deeply consequential—for example, when we choose which candidate to vote for, or which course of medical treatment to pursue.

What guides each of these decisions? Some of the factors are not surprising. Decisions are, for example, obviously influenced by your values and expectations: You value chocolate ice cream, but not strawberry, and so you choose according to this preference. You expect that the surgery will cure your back pain, and you value being free of pain; thus, you decide to go ahead with the surgery.

Decisions can also be influenced by someone's personality. Some people are comfortable taking risks, while others stick to safer options—whether they're choosing a romantic partner or deciding which dessert to order. Similarly, some people constantly seek new and varied experiences, while others prefer more familiar pleasures, and these personality traits also guide their decision making.

Other factors, however, are less obvious—including the specific way a decision is *framed*. For example, which would you trust more—a new medication that has been successful in 50% of its clinical trials, or a medication that has failed in 50% of its clinical trials? Would you rather buy meat that is 80% lean or meat that is 20% fat? In each case, these differences in description should not affect your decisions—because, after all, 50% success *is exactly the same as* 50% failure, and 80% lean *is identical to* 20% fat. Nonetheless, people are heavily influenced by these differences in how their options are described. If we offer one group of people a treatment "with a 50% success rate," and offer a second group a treatment "with a 50% failure rate," people in the first group are much more likely to accept the treatment. Likewise, a group of shoppers presented with 80% lean meat is more likely to buy than a group offered meat that is 20% fat (Figure P.4; Keren, 2007; Levin, Gaeth, Evangelista, Albaum, & Schreiber, 2001).

What's more, these data have a consistent pattern: Across a wide range of circumstances, people are far more sensitive to negative outcomes than positive ones, more sensitive to *losses* than they are to corresponding *gains*. So when patients hear of a treatment's 50% failure rate, they are impressed—and alarmed—by this outcome, and they refuse the treatment. Likewise, when the disadvantages of a product are prominent (20% fat), this knowledge too has a potent effect.

We can find the same pattern in another setting. In one study, researchers asked some volunteers how much they would be willing to pay for a subscription to Magazine One. A second group was offered Magazine Two, and asked how much they'd be willing to pay. A third group was offered both magazines, and asked how much they would be willing to pay for each one. The third group of participants quite naturally tried to compare the magazines, weighing their pluses and minuses. But, in line with the pattern

P.4 Effects of framing Across a wide range of circumstances, people are heavily influenced by whether their options are described in positive or negative terms. In this study, people evaluated beef that was described as either "80% lean" or "20% fat." Study participants judged the beef described as 80% lean as being of higher quality and tasting better.

already described, these people were more impressed by the negative features of the magazines than the positives, more influenced by each magazine's limitations than its strengths. In effect, then, the comparison led them to emphasize what they didn't like about each magazine. As a result, these participants set a markedly lower value on the magazines than did the participants in the first two groups (the people who had evaluated just one of the options).

Innate Tendencies

We mentioned earlier that *personality* influences our decision making—some people are more comfortable with risk, some people are more attracted by novelty, and so on. But where do these differences in personality come from? Part of the answer, of course, is experience—each of us has been shaped by our parents, our friends, our successes, and our failures. But part of the answer involves tendencies that are largely independent of experience.

Even in the uterus, babies behave differently from each other. Some babies kick and move around in the uterus more than others, and these differences in activity level typically continue after birth. Likewise, at birth and beyond, some babies are easily upset; others seem far calmer. Some babies are fearful when they encounter a novel stimulus; others seem to be constantly seeking out new stimulation.

According to many theorists, these differences in behavior provide the core of the infant's developing personality. This claim is supported by the fact that these traits, visible in the first weeks of life, are linked in several ways to the child's personality in the years to come. For example, infants who are easily upset are likely to be more anxious as preschoolers and, later, as adolescents. Likewise, infants who are more sociable usually grow up to be more outgoing a decade (or more) later. So it seems that each infant's temperament really does establish a trajectory that continues in later years. In addition, these early differences among babies seem heavily influenced by genetics. We know this because identical twins, who have the same genes, tend to have very similar temperaments even if they are raised in different families; fraternal twins, who share only half their genes, tend to be less similar in temperament (Buss & Plomin, 1984).

Animals at Play

So far, our examples have dealt with human behavior. However, psychologists also study the behavior of other animals. This research is important for many reasons, including the direct comparison it allows between humans and other species—a comparison that can provide crucial insights into the functions of our behavior, as well as its evolutionary roots.

For example, human children spend a lot of time playing, and a lot of this play takes the form of imitating adult behaviors. It's also striking that, across a wide range of cultures, the pattern of play among young boys often differs from the pattern among young girls: Young boys engage in much more "mock combat," and generally engage in rougher, more physical playtime than girls do (Figure P.5A–B).

To what extent do children play in these ways because of encouragement from their parents? If this influence is large, then our explanation of these play activities will need to emphasize the cultural values and expectations of the children's mothers and fathers. At the same time, to what extent is the pattern of the play also shaped by biological forces—forces that might operate in other species, and might be independent of what the parents do or do not value?

(A) (B) (C)

P.5 **Play across cultures and species** In virtually all cultures—and in most animal species—the young engage in various forms of play. In all settings, rough, physical play is much more common among males.

Studying other species is one way that psychologists can address these questions. It turns out that many species—young chimpanzees, wolf pups, and even kittens—engage in activities that look remarkably like human play (Figure P.5C). And, in many of these species, we see clear differences between male and female play—the playful activities of the young males are more physical, and contain more elements of aggression, than the activities of females.

As these points suggest, there are surely biological influences on our play activities—and, in particular, biological roots for the sexual differentiation of play. More broadly, the widespread occurrence of play raises interesting questions about what the function of play might be, such that evolution favored playtime in so diverse a set of species.

Social Behavior in Humans

Animal playtime shares many features with human play, including the central fact that play behavior is typically *social,* involving the coordinated activities of multiple individuals. Social interactions of all sorts are intensely interesting to psychologists: Why do we treat other people the way we do? How do we interpret the behaviors of others around us? How is our own behavior shaped by the social setting?

Many studies indicate, in fact, that we are often powerfully influenced by the situations we find ourselves in. One striking example concerns people who confess to crimes—including such horrid offenses as murder or rape. Evidence from the laboratory as well as the courts tells us that some of these confessions are false—meaning that people are admitting to hideous actions they actually didn't commit. In some cases, the false confessions are the product of mental illness—they come from people who have lost track of what is real and what is not, or people who have a pathological need for attention. But in other cases, false confessions are produced by the social situation that exists inside a police interrogation room (Figure P.6): The suspect is confronted by a stern police officer who steadfastly refuses the suspect's claims of innocence. The suspect is also

P.6 **The influence of the situation** This scene from *Law and Order: Criminal Intent* provides a realistic view of the setting for police interrogations. The room is bare and windowless, so that the person being questioned feels isolated, has no distraction, and can lose track of time. The police officer can then arrange various pressures to persuade the suspect that he has just two options—confess, or not confess but be convicted anyway. This setup is effective at drawing confessions from actual criminals—but, unfortunately, is also effective at drawing false confessions from people who are innocent!

isolated from any form of social support—and so the interview continues for hours in a windowless room, where the suspect has no contact with family or friends. The police officer controls the flow of information about the crime, shaping the suspect's beliefs about the likelihood of being found guilty, and describing the probable consequences of a conviction. With these factors in place, it's surprisingly easy to extract confessions from people who are, in truth, entirely innocent (Kassin & Gudjonsson, 2004).

It should be said, though, that the police in this setting are doing nothing wrong. After all, we do want genuine criminals to confess; this will allow the efficient, accurate prosecution of people who are guilty of crimes and deserve punishment. And, of course, a criminal won't confess in response to a polite request from the police to "Please confess now." Therefore, some pressure, some situational control, is entirely appropriate when questioning suspects. It is troubling, though, that the situational factors built into this questioning are so powerful that they can elicit full confessions from people who have committed no crime at all.

PSYCHOLOGY'S DIVERSE METHODS AND PERSPECTIVES

All of these illustrations reflect the enormous diversity in the *content* of psychology. But how should we study these various topics? Across much of the 20th century, psychology was dominated by a small number of well-defined theoretical perspectives; we will look more closely at these perspectives in later chapters, defining each approach and exploring its strengths and limitations. For now, though, we simply note that no single approach dominates modern psychology. Instead, a defining element of this field is its diverse perspectives. In other words, there is not only variety in *what* psychologists study, there is also great diversity in *how* psychologists investigate the various phenomena of interest to them.

The need for a diverse set of perspectives makes sense when we consider that psychology approaches topics as different from each other as the social influences on confession and the cognitive control of eating. But the need for diverse approaches is evident even when we consider how psychologists approach a single phenomenon. Even for a single topic, psychologists draw on a range of different methods and different types of analysis, and then seek some means of unifying what they have learned from all of their efforts. To illustrate this point, let's look at some of the ways psychologists approach just one topic: how people remember the important, sometimes life-changing, emotional events they experience.

The Neural Basis of Emotional Memory

High-school graduation. The death of a beloved pet. A particularly romantic evening. For most people, events like these—events that were *emotional* when they occurred—can be recalled in vivid detail even years later. Why is this? Why are these emotional events so well remembered?

The answer to these questions has several elements, one of them involving specific brain mechanisms (Figure P.7): One structure within the brain—the *amygdala*—seems to function more or less as an alarm system, evaluating the content of various inputs (or ideas or memories), and detecting whether that content is emotionally significant. If emotional content is detected, then various processes inside the amygdala activate

P.7 Some of the brain structures crucial for emotional memory
This diagram shows the brain as if semitransparent, so that we can peer inside and see the location of the amygdala and hippocampus.

Amygdala   Hippocampus

other brain sites, including sites within the *hippocampus* that are crucial for establishing long-term memories. Thus, emotional arousal leads—via the amygdala, modulating the activity of the hippocampus—to more complete and longer-lasting memories (McGaugh, 2003; Reisberg & Hertel, 2004).

Evidence for these claims comes from several types of research. In some cases, we can use brain scans to assess the moment-by-moment activity levels in the amygdala while someone is witnessing an emotional event. These scans show that the more activated the amygdala is during the event, the more likely the person is to have strong memories of the experience later on (Cahill, Babinsky, Markowitsch, & McGaugh, 1996).

Conversely, we can study the memories of people who have suffered damage to the amygdala—damage that causes a disorder known as Klüver-Bucy syndrome. These individuals seem overall to be less emotional—less likely to show fear, less likely to be aggressive, and so on—thus confirming the role of the amygdala in shaping our emotional lives. But, in addition, these individuals do not show the enhancement of memory for emotional events that we can so easily observe in most other people. Without the amygdala, the processes that produce this enhancement cannot function; individuals with Klüver-Bucy syndrome thus show little difference between how they remember significant emotional episodes and how they remember much more mundane events (Buchanan & Adolphs, 2004).

The Evolutionary Basis for Emotional Remembering

It seems, then, that the structure of the brain provides one reason that people remember emotional events so well—our memory for these events is directly shaped by a specific interaction among the brain's parts. This aspect of the brain's "wiring" is part of our biological heritage and is well established at birth—and so, apparently, it's specified largely by the blueprint laid out in our genes. But where does this blueprint come from? The answer, in brief, is evolution: Our ancient ancestors varied somewhat in their biological traits; and, thanks to this variation, some of our ancestors were better suited to their environment than others. These better-suited ancestors were therefore more likely to survive than their less well-adapted neighbors, and so they were more likely to reproduce and so more likely to pass on their genetic material to the next generation. As this process then repeated itself, generation after generation, the genetic pattern passed onward by these better-adapted ancestors became more and more common in our species. Consequently, modern humans are likely to have inherited this genetic pattern as well as the traits that it produces.

Why might evolution have shaped our memory for emotional events? One answer to this question starts with the sorts of emotional events our ancient ancestors were likely to experience. Encounters with dangerous predators would probably have filled our ancestors with fear, and they would surely have considered these encounters worth remembering so they could avoid facing the predator again. Likewise, the discovery of a site with especially plentiful berries might have been exciting—and this discovery, too, would be worth remembering, so that these ancient humans would be able to find the berries again. Examples like these remind us that it's often useful to remember emotional events, because they typically involve experiences and information that truly matter for us. It seems plausible, therefore, that those of our ancestors who were especially able to remember emotional events might have gained a survival advantage—a key element in evolution by natural selection.

In fact, evolution might have tuned our capacity to remember in fairly specific ways. To understand this point, consider a procedure known as *fear conditioning*: An organism is given a warning stimulus (a bright light, perhaps, or a tone) and then, a few seconds later, is presented with some noxious stimulus (e.g., the sight of a predator, or a painfully loud noise). With this setup, the organism quickly learns the significance of the warning stimulus, and becomes fearful the moment it begins. This is a good thing, because the signal—and the organism's understanding of the signal—gives the animal time to prepare (or to flee) before the noxious stimulus arrives.

Not surprisingly, fear conditioning is slower if the organism has suffered damage to the amygdala—confirming the importance of this brain structure in supporting emotional memory. For present purposes, though, the crucial thing is that the speed of fear conditioning depends on the nature of the warning stimulus. A range of organisms, including humans, show faster learning if the warning stimulus is a picture of a snake than if it's a picture of, say, a mushroom (Figure P.8). In other words, the pairing of "see picture of snake, then receive electric shock" produces more rapid learning than a pairing of "see a picture of a mushroom, then receive shock." This pattern holds even if the

P.8 Fear conditioning Fear conditioning is more rapid if the "warning stimulus" is a picture of a snake, presumably because many organisms are—for evolutionary reasons—prepared to associate bad consequences with this visual stimulus.

individual organism has never in its life seen a snake. It seems, then, that some organisms are prepared, in advance of any learning, to associate bad consequences with the sight of a snake. This response is almost surely a result of our evolutionary past, in which rapid learning about snakes mattered for survival.

Amazingly, this pattern of faster learning in response to snake pictures remains in place even if the snake picture, as the warning stimulus, is flashed so quickly on a computer screen that it's virtually unrecognizable. This finding suggests that it's not just learning that prepares us for these stimuli, but perception—which allows us to detect these (apparently threatening) creatures even from a split-second view.

Cognitive Influences on Emotional Memory

It is clear, then, that our understanding of emotional memory must include its biological basis—the neural mechanisms that promote emotional memory, and the evolutionary heritage that makes it easier for us to form some memories than others. But our theorizing also needs to include the ways that people *think about* the emotional events they experience: What do they pay attention to during the experience? How do they make sense of the emotional event, and how does this interpretation shape their memory?

The role of attention is evident, for example, in the fact that emotional memory tends to be uneven—some aspects of the event are well remembered, other aspects are neglected. Thus, during a robbery, witnesses might focus on the robbers themselves—what they did, what they said (Figure P.9). As a result, the witnesses might remember these "central" aspects of the event later on but might have little memory for other aspects of the event—such as what the other witnesses were doing. In this regard, memory is very different from, say, the sort of record created by a videocamera. If the camera is turned on and functioning properly, it records everything in front of the lens. Memory, in contrast, is selective; it records the bits that someone was paying attention to, but nothing more. As a result, memory—for emotional events and in general—is invariably incomplete. It can sometimes omit information that is crucial for some purposes (e.g., information the police might need when investigating the robbery).

Memory is also different from a videorecord in another way. A videocamera is a passive device, simply recording what is in front of the lens. In contrast, when you "record" information into memory, you actively interpret the event, integrating information gleaned from the event with other knowledge. Most of the time, this is a good thing because it creates a rich and sophisticated memory trace that preserves the event in combination with your impressions of the event as well as links to other related episodes. However, this active interpretation of an event also has a downside: People often lose track of the *source* of particular bits of information in memory. Specifically, they lose track of which bits are drawn from the original episode they experienced and which bits they supplied through their understanding of the episode.

In one study, for example, people spent a few minutes in a professor's office; then, immediately afterward, they were taken out of the office and asked to describe the room they had just been in. Roughly a third of these people clearly remembered seeing shelves full of books, even though no books were visible in the office (Brewer & Treyens, 1981). In this case, the participants had "supplemented"

P.9 The role of attention in memory How well do witnesses or victims of crimes remember what they saw? Can we count on the accuracy of their testimony? The answer depends, in part, on exactly what the witnesses paid attention to during the crime (the weapon? the robbers' faces?) and on how the witnesses were questioned.

their memory of the office, relying on the common knowledge that professors' offices usually do hold a lot of books. They then lost track of the source of this "supplement"—and so lost track of the fact that the books came from their own beliefs and not from this particular experience.

How does this pattern apply to emotional memories? We have already said that emotional events tend to be remembered vividly: Often, we feel like we can "relive" the distant event, claiming that we recall the event "as though it were yesterday." But as compelling as they are, these memories—like any memories—are open to error. In one study, researchers surveyed college students a few days after the tragic explosion of the Space Shuttle *Challenger* in 1986. Where were the students when they heard about the explosion? Who brought them the news? Three years later, the researchers questioned the same students again. The students confidently reported that, of course, they clearly remembered this horrible event. Many students reported that the memory was still painful, and they could recall their sense of shock and sadness upon hearing the news. Even so, their recollections of this event were, in many cases, mistaken. One student was certain she was sitting in her dorm room watching TV when the news was announced; she recalled being deeply upset and telephoning her parents. It turns out, though, that she had heard the news in a religion class when some people walked into the classroom and started talking about the explosion (Neisser & Harsh, 1992).

Similar results have been recorded for many other events. For example, surveys of current college students usually show that they vividly remember where they were when they heard the news, of the September 11, 2001, attacks on the United States and how they heard it. When we take steps to check on these memories, however, we often find substantial errors. Many of the students are completely confident—but mistaken—about how they learned of the attacks, who brought them the news, what their initial

P.10 **Even vivid memories are subject to error** Most Americans can vividly recall where they were when they first heard the news about the 9/11 attacks—but careful checks show that these memories often contain errors! Even President Bush seemed to have trouble recalling when and how he heard the news; in the days after the attack, he gave the media three different accounts of how he'd heard.

responses were (e.g., P. Lee & Brown, 2004; Pezdek, 2004). Similar memory errors can be documented even in George W. Bush, U.S. president at the time of the attacks (Figure P.10). Bush confidently recalled where he was when he heard the news, and what he was doing at the time—but his recollection turned out to be mistaken (D. Greenberg, 2004). Being president, it seems, is no protection against memory errors.

What's going on in all of these cases? When we experience a traumatic event—like the *Challenger* explosion, or the September 11 attacks—we're likely to focus on the core meaning of the event and pay less attention to our own personal circumstances. This means that we will record into memory relatively little information about those circumstances. Later, when we try to recall the event, we're forced to reconstruct the setting as best we can. This reconstruction process is generally accurate, but certainly open to error. As a result, our recollection of emotional events can be vivid, detailed, compelling—and wrong.

Social Influences on Emotional Memory

Memories are also different from videorecords in another way: Once a videorecord is established (on tape, or on a DVD), it remains in storage, ready for playback. The videorecord may fade, or get erased, but it is unlikely to change in any way. Not so for memories. There are several reasons for this, including the ways that people share their memories with others—a sharing that happens particularly often with memories of emotional events.

Each person's memory is, of course, their own, and they can keep their recollection private if they wish. But memory also has a social function: We exchange memories to instruct or amuse each other. We exchange memories as a means of creating a social bond—"That's amazing, because the same thing happened to me!" We report on our past to help other people understand our actions, and perhaps to lead them to like us more, or to gain their trust or respect.

It turns out, though, that this exchange of memories is not just a matter of reporting. Instead, we often reshape a memory so that it will better serve our social goals. The event as we've now described it then becomes woven into (or replaces) the memory we began with. In this way, sharing a memory with others can, in fact, change how we remember the past.

In one study, for example, people viewed a movie clip and then, two days later, were interviewed by the experimenter about the movie. During the interview, the experimenter led participants to describe entire episodes that hadn't appeared in the movie at all (e.g., a practical joke, played on one of the movie's main characters). The participants knew they were "describing" nonexistent episodes, reporting on things they hadn't seen at all. Several weeks later, though, when participants were asked to recall what they had seen in the movie, almost half of them included in their recall the episodes that they had themselves fabricated (Chrobak & Zaragoza, 2008; also see Coman, Manier, & Hirst, 2009; Weldon, 2001). Apparently, the participants' conversation with the experimenter about the movie changed how they remembered the film's plot—to the point of adding entire fictitious events.

The Cultural Setting of Emotional Memory

Thus we've seen that emotional memories—like all memories—can be shaped by the process of telling and retelling, and this process depends in important ways on the social situation. We're likely to recall a memory differently if talking with a friend as opposed to a police officer; we're likely to recall a memory differently if talking with a child as opposed to an adult. And, in each situation, the style of telling we adopt is likely to influence how we remember the original event later on.

Similarly, the way an emotional event is recalled, and the way the event is remembered, can be shaped by the culture a person lives in. For example, in some Asian cultures, it is considered inappropriate for people to display strong emotion in public (Figure P.11). This social convention shapes how people relate their emotional experiences to others, which in turn shapes the way they remember these experiences. In most Western cultures, on the other hand, displays of emotion are common; women in particular are often encouraged to "share their feelings." This convention, too, shapes how events are described—and thus how they are remembered.

These differences from one culture to the next can have a powerful effect on how people think about the past. For example, we've already mentioned the attacks of September 11, 2001, and the vivid memories that most Americans (and many outside of the United States) have of these events. As we discussed, some aspects of these memories may be mistaken—including the details that individuals recall about when and how they heard the news and how they reacted. Even so, these memories powerfully influence the way Americans think about the threat of terrorism and the politics of the Middle East. In these ways, the memories help shape the culture.

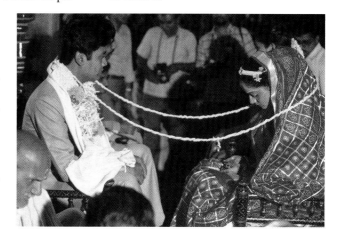

P.11 The role of cultural context
Each culture has rules for public behavior, including public displays of emotion. These rules influence how people describe their past—which in turn can shape what people remember.

The reverse, however, is also true: Our shared culture shapes what we remember. In America, daily news reports often contain reminders of September 11—specific mentions of the attacks, comments about the threat of terrorism, and so on. Television shows and movies often contain references to the attacks. These (and other) reminders—all part of our cultural surrounding—virtually guarantee that the attacks will be frequent in people's thoughts and remain prominent in their memories.

Other examples are easy to find, and shared memories of important episodes are transmitted from generation to generation in many countries. For example, the violence in the Balkans, the Middle East, or Somalia is fueled by deeply rooted hostility between different ethnic or religious groups. The hostilities in turn are often justified on the basis of long-past events that one side of the conflict perceives as horrific offenses or deep injustices and the other side views as benign or legitimate. In each case, the cultural surround contains frequent references to these events, guaranteeing that the events—no matter how long ago they occurred—remain fresh in each person's memory and continue to guide their thinking about these horrible conflicts.

A Developmental Perspective on Emotional Memory

Clearly, then, if we are going to understand how people remember emotional events, we need to consider many factors and take several different perspectives. Some of these perspectives are biological, including a microscopic view of specific changes taking place in the brain when memories are formed and a macroscopic view emphasizing the influence of evolution on brain function. A cognitive perspective focuses on which aspects of a situation people pay attention to and what kinds of knowledge they merge with their memories of an experience. A social perspective leads us to ask how and why people share their memories, and how such interactions affect what is remembered. We also need to think about the ways that the cultural context influences the sharing of memories and shapes how someone reacts to (and recalls) the target event.

Yet another perspective is *developmental*: How do children learn to recall emotional events? How do they learn the appropriate way, in their culture, to report on events? How accurate or complete is their recollection? These questions have significant scientific interest as well as considerable practical importance. It's increasingly common for children to provide evidence for legal disputes, including divorce proceedings or trials involving allegations of child abuse. In these settings, it is crucial to have some guidelines about how best to draw accurate information from children—and how to evaluate the information children provide.

Fortunately for the courts, children's memories of events are often quite accurate and relatively complete. But children are also highly suggestible—so, when asking them about past events, it is crucial not to convey expectations that could influence their answers. In many cases, children also do not understand which aspects of an event are likely to be relevant to their audience, so they often need guidance in choosing what to report.

One line of research, for example, has examined how children remember events that are not just emotional, but traumatic. Obviously, we cannot create these events in the laboratory—that would be ethically repugnant. But outside of the lab, children sometimes need medical procedures that can be deeply upsetting or uncomfortable—including procedures that involve medical professionals closely examining and manipulating the young child's genitals. How will they remember these procedures later?

Evidence suggests that children generally remember these medical procedures quite well. If questioned carefully and neutrally, they can report many aspects of the event.

The one group of children least likely to recall the event is, not surprisingly, those who are very young—for example, children under three years old. These children probably lack the intellectual and neural capacities to establish clear and explicit memories of any sort; and so, inevitably, they cannot recall medical trauma.

However, these painful memories are susceptible to the same influences as other memories. With time, even traumatic memories fade and, as a result, are more and more open to errors. The child may even recall elements of the event that never happened at all. Likewise, if a child is questioned in a suggestive manner, her recollection can be substantially altered—aspects of the event may change, or new (fictional) experiences might be introduced into the episode.

Disorders of Emotional Memory

Each perspective on emotional memory contributes to our overall understanding, and each approach can be informed by the others. But there is still one more perspective we need to consider: Throughout psychology, we must understand the ways that people are alike, and also the ways they differ. Some of the differences among people can be understood as variations within the range considered healthy or "normal"; these include differences in personality, aptitudes, beliefs, and more. But some differences among people—including their responses to emotional events—take us outside of the range that we can call "healthy."

Consider, for example, people who have witnessed a violent car crash. As we have discussed, various mechanisms promote memory for this sort of emotional episode. But, for some people, these mechanisms seem *too* effective. They seem to end up with "too much memory" of the crash, and they cannot get the disturbing scene out of their heads.

Similar descriptions apply to a soldier who has been through a horrible battle, or a woman who has been raped. In these cases, it is important that there be some memory. The soldier often needs to report to his officer what happened, so that the next step in the battle can be planned (Figure P.12). The woman needs to remember her ordeal so that she can give evidence to the police that will lead to the prosecution of the rapist. Even so, the soldier and the rape victim eventually need to move on with their lives, and put the horrors of their experiences behind them. But this may not be possible, because the painful memory may stay with them more than they would wish.

P.12 **Disorders of emotional memory** Many mechanisms make it more likely for us to remember emotional events. In some cases, however, these mechanisms seem to be *too* effective—and so people are sometimes haunted by vivid recollection of horrific events they have experienced. This is an all-too-common problem for soldiers returning from war and for women who have suffered sexual assault.

In such cases, the neural and cognitive mechanisms that support emotional remembering seem to produce a cruel enhancement of memory. This horrific memory can, in turn, contribute to the condition known as *post-traumatic stress disorder*, or *PTSD*. Be aware, though, that not all soldiers, and not all rape victims, develop PTSD—and we need to ask why this is. Part of the explanation lies in biology: Some people seem genetically at greater risk for this disorder, plausibly because their nervous systems are especially reactive to whatever stressful events they encounter. Cognitive mechanisms are also relevant, because the emergence of PTSD depends to some extent on a person's beliefs and expectations—in particular, what the person *feared* would happen at a moment of crisis, rather than what actually happened. Social mechanisms are also pertinent; studies indicate that telling others about the trauma, or even just writing about the trauma in a diary, can help defuse the emotional response to the trauma and thus make PTSD less likely (e.g., Pennebaker, 2004).

WHAT UNITES PSYCHOLOGY?

It's clear, then, that if we are going to understand emotional memories—including why they are so vivid, why they are sometimes inaccurate, why they can sometimes contribute to PTSD—we need to study these memories from many perspectives and rely on many different methods. And what holds true for these memories also holds true for most other psychological phenomena. They too must be viewed from many perspectives because each perspective is valid, and none is complete without the others.

With all this emphasis on psychology's diversity, though, both in the field's content and in its perspectives, what holds our field together? What gives the field its coherence? The answer has two parts: a set of shared themes, and a commitment to scientific methods.

A Shared Set of Thematic Concerns

As we have seen, psychologists ask questions that require broad and complex answers. But, over and over, a small number of themes emerge within these answers. These themes essentially create a portrait of our science and are a central part of the answer to the broad question "What has psychology learned?" These themes also highlight key aspects of psychology's *subject matter* by highlighting crucial points about how the mind works and why we behave as we do.

MULTIPLE PERSPECTIVES

One of these recurrent themes has already entered our discussion—namely, that the phenomena of interest to psychology are influenced by many factors (Figure P.13). As we have seen, this interaction among multiple factors forces the field to draw on a variety of perspectives, methods, and types of analysis. But, along with this methodological point, there's an important lesson here about the nature of the mind, and the nature of behavior: We are complex organisms, sensitive to many different cues and influences, and any theory that ignores this complexity will inevitably be incomplete. This is, by the way, why the modern field of psychology has largely stepped away from the all-inclusive

Cognitive
perspective

Developmental
perspective

Neural
perspective

Individual

Evolutionary
perspective

Social
perspective

Cultural
perspective

P.13 Multiple influences on an individual

frameworks that once defined our field—such as the framework proposed by Sigmund Freud, or the one proposed by B. F. Skinner. (We'll return to both of these perspectives in later chapters.) The problem is not that these frameworks are wrong; indeed, these scholars made enormous contributions to the field. The problem instead is that each of these frameworks captures only part of the puzzle, and so our explanations will ultimately need to draw on multiple types of explanation.

THE LIMITED VALUE OF DICHOTOMIES

Another theme is related to the first: It concerns the interplay between our biological heritage, on the one side, and the influence of our experiences, on the other. It's sometimes easy to think of these influences as separate. We might ask, for example, whether a particular behavior is "innate" or "learned," whether it is rooted in "nature" or "nurture." Similarly, it's easy to ask whether a particular action arises from inside the organism or is elicited by the environment; whether your roommate acted the way she did yesterday because of her personality or because of aspects of the situation. As our discussion of emotional memories has indicated, though, these "either-or" dichotomies often pose the issue in the wrong way, as though we had to choose just one answer and dismiss the other. The reality instead is that we need to consider nature *and* nurture, factors inside *and* outside the organism. And—above all—we need to consider how these various influences interact. Emotional memories, for example, are influenced by a rich interaction between factors inside the organism (like our genetic heritage, or the functioning of the amygdala, or the individual's personality or prior beliefs) and factors in the situation (like cultural expectations, or situational pressures). The same is true for most other behaviors as well.

WE ARE ACTIVE PERCEIVERS

A third theme has also already come up in our discussion: We do not passively absorb our experience, simply recording the sights and sounds we encounter. We have mentioned that our memories integrate new experiences with prior knowledge, and that we seem to "interpret as we go" in our daily lives and then store in memory the product of this interpretation. These ideas, too, will emerge again and again in our discussion, as we consider the active nature of the organism in selecting, interpreting, and organizing experience.

THE INEVITABILITY OF TRADE-OFFS

A fourth theme is related to the third: Our activities, in interpreting our experience, both help us and hurt us. They help by bringing us to a richer, deeper, better organized sense of our experience, thus allowing us to make better use of that experience. But these same activities can hurt us by leading to inaccuracy—if our interpretation is off, or if our selection leads us to overlook or forget bits of the experience that we may need later. A similar kind of trade-off was relevant to our discussion of PTSD: The biological mechanisms that promote emotional memory ensure that we will remember the important events of our lives. But these same mechanisms can burden us with memories that are more vivid and longer-lasting than we might sometimes wish. Trade-offs like these, in which generally useful mechanisms sometimes have undesirable consequences, are evident throughout the study of psychology. In other words, we'll see over and over that some of the undesirable aspects of our perception, memory, emotions, and behavior may just be the price we pay for mechanisms that, in a wide range of circumstances, serve us very well.

Broad themes like these (and we will discover other themes, in other chapters) bring a powerful coherence to the field of psychology, despite its diversity of coverage and methods. As we'll see, there are important consistencies in how we behave and why we do what we do, and these consistencies provide linkages among the various areas of psychology.

A Commitment to Scientific Methods

Along with this set of thematic concerns, another factor also unifies our field: a commitment to a *scientific* psychology. To understand the importance of this point, let's bear in mind that the questions occupying psychologists today have fascinated people for thousands of years. Novelists and poets have plumbed the nature of human action in countless settings. Playwrights have pondered romantic liaisons or the relationship between generations. The ancient Greeks commented extensively on the proper way to rear children, and philosophers, social activists, and many others have offered their counsel regarding how we should live—how we should eliminate violence, treat mental illness, and so forth.

Against this backdrop, what is distinctive about psychology's contribution to these issues? A large part of the answer is that psychologists, no matter what their perspective, work within the broad framework of science—by formulating specific hypotheses that are open to definitive testing and then taking the steps to test these hypotheses. In this fashion, we can determine which proposals are well founded and which are not, which bits of counsel are warranted and which are ill advised. Then, when we are reasonably certain about which hypotheses are correct, we can build from there—knowing that we are building on a firm base.

Scientific research methods have served psychology well. We know a great deal about emotional memories, and why we sometimes forget things, and how children develop, and why some people suffer from schizophrenia, and much more. But what is the scientific method, and how is it used within psychology? This is such an important question for the field that it demands thorough coverage, and so it will be our focus for all of Chapter 1. By exploring these methodological points, we'll see how psychologists develop their claims. We'll also learn why these claims must be taken seriously and how they can be used as a basis for developing applications and procedures that can, in truth, make our world a better place.

1 Research Methods

For at least 10,000 years, humans have been manipulating their own brains by drinking alcohol. And for at least the last few decades, researchers have wondered whether alcohol had a positive effect on physical health. Study after study seemed to suggest that people who imbibed one alcoholic beverage per day—a 12-ounce beer, a 6-ounce glass of wine, or a 1.5-ounce shot of spirits—had healthier hearts than did people who abstained from drinking altogether. A drink a day, it seemed, kept the cardiologist away.

Yet these studies may be flawed. When Kaye Fillmore, a researcher at the University of California, San Francisco, and her team analyzed 54 published studies on how moderate drinking affects the heart, they found that most of the drink-a-day studies had not used random assignment, a technique described in this chapter. In studies with random assignment, researchers use coin tosses or the like to decide into which condition—the control group or various experimental groups—each study participant should go. By letting chance dictate who goes into which group, researchers are more likely to end up with truly comparable groups.

Instead of randomly assigning participants to drinking and nondrinking groups, though, 47 of the 54 studies compared people who were already having one drink daily to people who were already teetotaling. Why is this design a problem? Think about it: In the United States, where most of these studies took place, it's fairly normal to have a drink occasionally. Usually, people who never drink abstain for a reason, such as religious or moral beliefs or medical concerns.

In fact, Fillmore and her team found that many of the nondrinkers in these studies were abstaining from alcohol for medical reasons, including advanced age or a history of alcoholism. In other words, the nondrinking groups in most of the studies included more unhealthy people *to begin with*, compared to the drinking groups. As a result, these studies didn't show that drinking alcohol led to better health. Instead, they showed that better health often leads to, or at least allows, a moderate level of alcohol consumption.

Fillmore and her colleagues also highlighted seven studies that avoided this methodological shortcoming by excluding participants with a history of certain medical problems. These studies found that the drinkers were no healthier than longtime nondrinkers—evidence against the drink-a-day hypothesis. But because this conclusion rests on very few studies, researchers can't yet say whether a drink a day is good for your heart.

Why didn't all 54 studies use random assignment to avoid these complications? The investigators were simply coping with the realities of human research. To conduct an experiment with random assignment, a researcher would have to convince some wine lovers to give up their daily Bordeaux and persuade some teetotalers to abandon their objections to alcohol. This job would be hard enough, but ethical concerns would still remain: What if alcohol really did damage the drinkers' hearts or, alternatively, what if the nondrinkers suffered from not tossing back their daily dram?

In all of their research, psychologists have to address these issues of scientific rigor, cost, and ethics—and they do so with careful attention to research methods. In this chapter, we'll introduce the basics of collecting, analyzing, and interpreting the data of psychological science. We'll start by describing how psychologists make observations and how they make sure their data are reliable and unbiased. We'll then turn to how psychologists summarize what they've observed and use the data to draw conclusions. We'll also look at the two major types of research—observational studies and experimental studies. And we'll discuss how psychologists balance the demands of scientific research with ethical concerns, to protect the rights and dignity of research participants.

With our arsenal of sound research methods, you'll be ready to test your own ideas about how, why, and what people sense, perceive, think, and act. And with some practice, you too, can begin contributing to the field of psychological science.

MAKING OBSERVATIONS

variable Any characteristic whose values can change.

In many regards, the science of psychology works the same way as any other science. Like physicists, chemists, or biologists, psychologists make careful measurements, using well-chosen instruments. Like scientists in any domain, we look for patterns within our observations—**variables** that seem linked to each other and (often just as interesting) variables that turn out to be independent of each other. When we find those patterns, we run carefully controlled experiments to investigate the patterns— that is, to learn what's causing the patterns we've detected.

But how exactly does psychology proceed? After all, many of the events we hope to understand cannot be observed directly (because they involve thoughts or feelings "hidden" in each person's mind). And many of the phenomena we hope to study are difficult to measure. (How does one measure an attitude, for example, or a preference?) Let's look at how the scientific method unfolds in psychology, beginning with the broad question of how psychologists describe the phenomena they observe.

Defining the Question

Science begins with observation—but *what* should we observe? If we are interested in, say, how young children play together (Figure 1.1), it's just not possible to observe everything about their playtime. *Everything* (if interpreted literally) would include each child's every blink, every breath she takes, every time she scratches her ear or touches her hair, and much, much more. A lot of this information is unlikely to be of interest to our study, and so we'd be buried under an avalanche of unnecessary details that might make us lose track of the more useful information.

It seems, therefore, that we need to choose which aspects of the children's behavior we care about and which aspects we can ignore. In making this choice, we're usually guided by the *questions* we hope to address through our observations: Is a child's behavior influenced by the size of her playgroup? If so, we need to count how many children are involved in the group. Does the weather shape the child's style of play? To find out, we'd need to note the weather and somehow describe the "style."

Moreover, it's not enough just to have a question. We also need to formulate the question in a way that leaves no doubt about how we're going to link the question to the evidence we collect. To make this idea concrete, imagine that we wanted to ask: Which sex is more aggressive in its playtime—boys or girls? In tackling this issue, we'd need to be clear from the start about what sorts of actions would count as "aggressive." Otherwise, we might observe children for hours and still have no way to answer our question.

This requirement to be specific is usually met by making sure that any research project begins with a **testable hypothesis**—a specific claim about the facts, framed in a way that will allow an unambiguous test. Testability, in turn, is guaranteed by ensuring that the hypothesis is *falsifiable*—stated so that we're clear at the start about what pattern in the evidence could show the hypothesis to be false.

We can see how important these ideas are by considering hypotheses that are *not* testable. Think about the forecasts that astrologers offer (Figure 1.2)—for example, "There will soon be major changes in your life." This prediction is open-ended in ways that prevent any linkage to specific observations: What exactly is meant by *soon,* or *major changes*? There's plenty of room for debate about how these terms should be defined, and so there's room for debate about what sorts of observations would or wouldn't falsify the forecast. As a result, we have no way to check the forecast against the facts, no way to tell if the claim is right or wrong. For scientific purposes, this situation is unacceptable.

This example also makes it clear that a testable hypothesis requires well-defined terms (Figure 1.3). To see how this plays out, let's press on with the question about whether the sexes differ in their aggression on the playground. To address this question, we'll need to develop an **operational definition**—one that translates ("operationalizes") the variable we want to assess (aggression) into a specific procedure or measurement. We'll also need the

1.1 **How do young children play together?** The number of observations we *might* make about these children is huge. For purposes of research, therefore, we need to specify what aspects of the children's behavior are likely to relate to the questions we're hoping to address.

testable hypothesis A prediction that has been formulated specifically enough so that it is clear what observations would confirm the prediction and what observations would challenge it.

operational definition A definition that translates the variable we want to assess into a specific procedure or measurement.

1.2 **Testable hypotheses?** Astrologers and newspaper tabloids often predict the future, but the phrasing of these predictions is usually so open-ended that we can't test the claims in any rigorous way.

"I think you should be more explicit here in step two."

1.3 Testable claims A scientific claim must be specific enough to be testable; vague claims cannot be tested.

dependent variable The variable that is measured or recorded in an experiment.

independent variable The variable that the experimenter manipulates as a basis for making predictions about the dependent variable.

operational definition to have *construct validity*—that is, it must truly reflect the variable named in our hypothesis. Thus, for example, we wouldn't operationalize aggression on the basis of how often someone frowns. This wouldn't be valid, because sometimes people frown for reasons other than aggression and sometimes they don't frown when they're being aggressive. So it would be better to operationalize aggression as a count of actions like kicks, punches, and bites. This would count as an operationalization because these behaviors can be directly observed in the data.

These points about operationalization and validity are concerns about how we define our **dependent variable**—so called because the investigator usually wants to find out whether changes in this variable *depend* on some other factor. In our case, we want to know whether a child's aggression levels depend—at least partly—on his or her sex; so the dependent variable would be our measure of aggression. The **independent variable**, in contrast, is the factor whose effects we hope to examine. If we're asking how boys and girls differ in their aggression, then we have a single independent variable—sex—that can take either of two values (male or female).

In many studies, the dependent variable is operationalized in terms that can be easily and objectively measured. If, for example, we're measuring someone's memory capacity, our dependent variable might be the percentage of correct answers on some test. If we're studying how sensitive someone's hearing is, we might count the number of faint tones that person can detect. A quality like aggression, though, might require a different sort of yardstick because deciding whether an act is aggressive can be a subjective matter. (Was that shove playful, or was it a hostile push? Was that kick deliberate, or just an accident?) In dealing with this subjectivity, our best option is to use a panel of judges who assess the study's participants on the relevant dimension. We could, for example, videotape the children at play and then show the recording to the judges. They would rate each child's aggression on, say, a 7-point scale where a rating of 1 means "not at all aggressive," and 7 means "extremely aggressive."

By using a panel of judges, we can check on the subjectivity of the assessment (Figure 1.4). If a child's play seems aggressive to one judge but not to another, it confirms the concern that this is a subjective matter. In that case, we can draw no conclusions from the study; we'll need to find some other way to measure our dependent variable. But if the judges agree to a reasonable extent, then we can be confident that their assessments are neither arbitrary nor idiosyncratic—and this would allow us to use the results of judges' assessments as the study's dependent variable.

1.4 Panels of judges If a study's dependent variable involves subjectivity, it's useful to rely on a *panel* of judges to assess the variable. To ensure that the judgments are neither arbitrary nor idiosyncratic, investigators will use these assessments as research data only if the judges are reasonably in agreement with each other.

Systematically Collecting Data

Suppose we've defined our question and figured out how to measure our dependent variable. What comes next? In everyday life, people often try to answer empirical questions by reflecting on their personal experience. They'll try to recall cases that seem relevant to the issue being evaluated, and say things like, "What do you mean, boys are more aggressive? I can think of three girls, just off the top of my head, who are extremely aggressive."

This sort of informal "data collection" may be good enough for some purposes, but it's unacceptable for science. For one thing, the "evidence" in such cases is being drawn from memory—and, as we'll discuss in Chapter 8, people's memories aren't always accurate. Another problem is that memories are often *selective*. In Chapter 9, we'll consider a pattern known as *confirmation bias*. This term refers to people's tendency to recall evidence that confirms their views more easily than they can recall evidence to the contrary. So if someone happens to start out with the idea that girls are more aggressive, confirmation bias will lead them to supporting evidence—whether their initial idea was correct or not.

More broadly, scientists refuse to draw conclusions from *anecdotal evidence*—evidence that involves just one or two cases, has been informally collected, and is now informally reported. There are many reasons for this refusal: The anecdotes are often drawn from memory; and, for the reasons just described, that by itself is a problem. What's more, anecdotes often report a *conclusion* drawn from someone's observations, but not the observations themselves, and that invites questions about whether the conclusion really does follow from the "evidence." For example, if someone reports an anecdote about an aggressive girl, we might wonder whether the girl's behavior truly deserved that label—and our uncertainty obviously weakens the effect of the anecdote.

Perhaps the worst problem with anecdotal evidence, though, is that the anecdotes may represent exceptions and not typical cases. This is because, when reporting anecdotes, people are likely to overlook the typical cases precisely because they're familiar and hence not very interesting. Instead, they'll recall the cases that stand out either because they're extreme or because they don't follow the usual pattern. As a result, anecdotal evidence is often lopsided and misleading.

If we really wanted to compare boys' and girls' aggression, then, how could we avoid all these problems? For a start, we need to record the data in some neutral and objective way, so there's no risk of compromising the quality of our evidence through bias or memory errors. Second, our data collection has to be systematic (Figure 1.5). We might want to collect observations from all the boys and all the girls at a particular playground; or perhaps, just to keep our project manageable, we might observe every tenth child who comes to the playground. Notice that these will be firsthand observations—we're not relying on questionable anecdotes. Notice also that our selection of which children to observe ("every tenth child") is not guided by our hypothesis. That way, we can be sure we're not just collecting cases that happen to be unusual, or cases that support our claim. This sort of data collection can be cumbersome, but it will give us data that we can count on in drawing our conclusions.

Defining the Sample

Often, psychologists want their conclusions to apply to a particular **population**—all members of a given group. In our discussion of aggression, for example, we've been considering a claim that potentially applies to all children. In other cases, we might be concerned with a narrower population—all 3-year-olds living in urban environments, or all

1.5 The right method Scientific data must be collected systematically—and, of course, the method of data collection must be appropriate for the specific questions being investigated.

population The entire group about which the investigator wants to draw conclusions.

patients suffering from schizophrenia, or all white-collar workers. Whatever the population we're aiming at, though, we almost never draw data from the entire population. Instead, investigators study only a **sample**—a subset of the population they are interested in.

Why should we care about this distinction between sample and population? Imagine that an investigator studied aggression in a sample of children from wealthy families, and drew conclusions about boys and girls in general. These conclusions might be misleading because it's possible that wealthy children behave differently from other children. Perhaps wealthy children are spoiled by their parents, so they're less well behaved; or perhaps wealthy children are better educated, so they're *better* behaved. In any case, these children might be different from their less wealthy peers; studying them might tell us a lot about this particular subset of our population, but it might not tell us much about others.

For these reasons, choosing a sample is a critical step in data collection. And, like most steps in a research project, the choice must be guided by the research question. If the question concerns a broad population ("How do boys in general differ from girls in general with regard to their aggression?"), then investigators need to select a sample that reflects this broader group. If the question is more specific ("How do Canadian boys differ from Canadian girls with regard to their aggression?"), the sample must be adjusted appropriately.

We also need to keep in mind that in any population, each person is different in some ways from every other. Some people are outgoing, some are more restrained; some are energetic, some are relaxed. How can we deal with this diversity and still make sure that our sample represents the broader group? A crucial tool for this purpose is **random sampling**—a procedure in which every member of the population has an equal chance of being picked to participate in the study. Random sampling helps investigators ensure that their sample mirrors the diversity of the overall population, so they can be more confident that their sample really does inform them about the properties of the population at large.

Random sampling is an important tool, but it's not the only approach to sampling. In some settings, for example, a research question isn't focused on what is *common* or *typical* in a population. Instead, researchers want to ask what's *possible* in that population, or they want to examine directly how *diverse* the population is. For these purposes, the researcher might use the strategy of *maximum variation sampling*—a strategy of deliberately seeking out the unusual or extreme cases.

In addition, psychologists sometimes find it useful—and even *necessary*—to study single individuals rather than a broader sample. In these analyses, known as **case studies**, investigators report data on one person—one case—in great detail. Case studies have played an enormous role in the history of psychology. Many of Sigmund Freud's claims were based on case studies—his analyses of the patients he saw in his clinical practice (Chapter 15). Likewise, Jean Piaget's influential theorizing about child development was based initially on the study of just three children—his own (Figure 1.6). Piaget and his followers then went on to test his claims with larger groups of children (Chapter 14).

Case studies play a particularly important role in the study of the brain—specifically, in efforts to understand how the brain functions by examining cases of brain damage. One example is the case of a man called H.M. (1926–2008), whose memory deficits—resulting from neurosurgery for seizures—were severe and intriguing (Chapter 8). H.M. was possibly the most studied person in the history of psychology, and his pattern of deficits offered crucial insights into how memory functions. Similarly, the case of Phineas Gage (1823–1860) has influenced our understanding of the functions of the brain's frontal lobes. Phineas suffered damage to the frontal lobe when a construction

sample The subset of the population that the investigator studies in order to learn about the population at large.

random sampling A procedure in which every member of the population has an equal chance of being picked to participate in a study.

case study An intensive study of one person.

1.6 Jean Piaget and his "test subjects" Most of Piaget's initial theorizing was based on careful study of his own three children.

accident forced a piece of iron through his head. His case was one of the first to inform psychologists about how damage to specific portions of the brain can change someone's personality. (For more on Gage, see Chapter 3.) Examples like these remind us that case studies are indeed an important part of the psychologist's tool kit.

Assessing External Validity

Clearly, then, different studies rely on different sorts of data—sometimes a random sample, sometimes a maximum variation sample, sometimes a single case. There is similar diversity in the *situations* that studies examine. In some studies, we want the situation to be representative of the broader world; for example, we hope our study of aggression on the playground will tell us about aggression in other settings. In other studies, though, there's no need for representativeness because our hypothesis can be tested only by examining some unusual or even artificial circumstance—one in which we can observe patterns that would otherwise be hidden.

If we do want our study to reflect the broader world, we need to ensure its **external validity**—that is, to make sure the study does represent the world as it exists outside of our investigation. To ensure external validity, we obviously need the sample of people in the study to be representative of the broader population. We also need to make sure the circumstances of the study accurately reflect those in the broader world. Imagine, for example, that while studying aggression in children, we observe the children's behavior when they're tired and cranky at the end of a long, hard school day. In this setting, we might get a distorted picture of the children because in this situation they're quite likely to misbehave. As a result, we probably shouldn't draw conclusions from the study about how children behave in other circumstances (Figure 1.7).

External validity also depends on what's being investigated. An investigator interested in the human visual system can probably study American college students and draw valid conclusions about how vision works in all humans. This extrapolation from the data would be valid simply because the properties of the visual system are rooted in the biology of our species, so we can generalize widely from a relatively narrow data set. But we'd have to be much more cautious in our generalizations if we studied the same college students in hopes of learning about, say, human romantic fantasies. In that case, our results might tell us little about anyone other than the particular group studied.

Be aware, however, that questions of external validity need to be resolved through research. For example, consider laboratory studies of memory. These studies often involve college students memorizing either lists of words or brief stories. Can we draw conclusions from these participants, and this task, about how (for example) eyewitnesses will recall a crime or how medical patients will remember a doctor's instructions? To find out, we might need to study actual eyewitnesses or patients and see if the principles derived from the laboratory studies apply to these samples as well. This analysis would then help us decide, in future studies, whether we could generalize from laboratory findings.

Monitoring Demand Characteristics

External validity also depends on another consideration: We need to make sure that our study itself doesn't affect the behaviors we hope to examine. One concern here is that people's behavior sometimes changes when they know they're being observed. They may be trying to present themselves in the best possible light, or maybe they're just feeling self-conscious about being observed and act differently as a result.

external validity The degree to which a study's participants, stimuli, and procedures adequately reflect the world as it actually is.

1.7 **External validity** How children play depends on the circumstances, and so the level of physical aggression likely on the football field (A) is markedly different from the level that's likely while sitting in church (B). If we want to make claims about children's behavior, we need to be alert to these points and not draw general conclusions from an atypical situation.

demand characteristics The cues in a study that might tell a research participant what behaviors are expected or desirable in that setting.

double-blind design The technique of assigning participants to experimental conditions while keeping both the participants and the researchers unaware of who is assigned to which group.

DOUBLE BLIND STUDY...

1.8 Double-blind testing Unlike the effort shown here, double-blind testing doesn't involve experiments done by pairs of blindfolded researchers. Instead, it involves studies in which neither the person tested nor the person conducting the test knows the experimental hypothesis, and neither of them knows which participants are in which comparison group.

descriptive statistics Mathematical procedures that allow a researcher to characterize a data pattern; these procedures include measures of central tendency and of variability.

inferential statistics Mathematical procedures that allow a researcher to draw further claims from a data pattern, including claims about whether the pattern observed in the sample is likely to be observed in other samples.

A study's **demand characteristics** can also alter people's behavior. This term refers to any cues in a situation that make participants think one response is more desirable than another. Sometimes the demand characteristics are communicated in the way questions are phrased ("You do brush your teeth every morning, don't you?"). Sometimes they're conveyed more subtly—perhaps without realizing it, the investigator smiles and is more encouraging when the participants answer in one way rather than another.

In some studies, demand characteristics influence an entire data pattern. For example, how often do people drive their cars through red lights? To find out, we might collect responses on a questionnaire that asks people directly about their driving habits. ("In the last month, how often have you . . .") But the results from this study would surely underestimate the frequency of this traffic violation: we're asking about an illegal activity, so people are likely to give us a less candid but more "desirable" response ("I *never* run red lights.").

In other cases, demand characteristics can create artificial differences between the groups being compared. Imagine that an investigator is comparing the problem-solving skills of American and Japanese students, but he's warmer and more encouraging to the Japanese participants than to the Americans. In this situation, any differences we observe between the groups might be due to the students' country of origin, or they might be due to this differential treatment. Because of this ambiguity, we could draw no conclusions from these data.

Investigators take several steps to minimize a study's demand characteristics. First, they try to phrase questions and instructions as neutrally as possible, so that participants can't identify any response as preferred or "better." If questions are likely to be embarrassing or provoke anxiety, the investigators do everything possible to diminish these concerns and guarantee that all information gained from the participant will remain confidential. Investigators are also careful to treat all study participants alike. In many studies this equal treatment is guaranteed by the use of a **double-blind design,** in which neither the person who actually collects the data nor the study participants themselves know the nature of the hypotheses at stake—or, in some studies, the nature of the groups being compared (Figure 1.8). This approach ensures that the investigators treat the various groups of participants alike and that participants in the various groups have similar expectations about the procedure.

WORKING WITH DATA

After we've defined a question, chosen a sample, and collected the data—what's next? To address this question, let's press on with our earlier example. Imagine that some researchers have measured the aggressiveness of a group of boys playing together and a group of girls playing together, so they now have an "aggression score" for each person. This leaves the researchers with two lists of numbers, as shown in Table 1.1. (The data in the table are fictional, but we'll describe the real outcome of this sort of comparison before we're done.)

In most studies, the researchers' next step would involve some sort of statistical analysis of the data. Broadly speaking, this analysis will have two parts: First, the researchers will rely on **descriptive statistics** to summarize the data. Second, the researchers will use **inferential statistics** to ask how confident they can be in drawing conclusions based on their sample. This is, of course, usually the step that tells the researchers whether the data support their hypothesis or not.

TABLE

1.1

Aggression Scores among Children

BOYS				GIRLS			
Name	Score	Name	Score	Name	Score	Name	Score
Andrew	16	Don	22	Lauren	5	Enriqueta	6
Aaron	17	David	29	Kristen	22	Lila	9
Colin	16	Juan	26	Katherine	11	Sue	2
Henry	22	Ming	7	Jessica	15	Gail	8
Ryan	9	Ben	23	Anna	9	Carol	10
Dan	25	Peter	13	Jenny	2	Judy	27
Matt	5	Dave	11	Lilly	7	Anne	13
Jake	17	Jaime	21	Miriam	21	Julia	18
Sol	15	George	21	Liz	17	Maureen	19
Bo	20	Jim	18	Tanya	15	Mary	13
Fred	29	Rick	12	Cathy	20	Susan	23
Paul	3	Bob	19	Kris	16	Paula	10
Mark	27	Noah	13	Jennifer	17	Rosa	16
Michael	20	Sid	19	Dell	12	Sonya	18
Jess	9	Jon	18	Jen	14	Friderike	13
Rob	13	Derek	28	Maggie	14	Sam	11

Descriptive Statistics

In Table 1.1, it's difficult to see any pattern at all. Some of the boys' numbers are high, and some are lower; the same is true for the girls. With the data in this format, it's hard to see anything beyond these general points. The pattern becomes obvious, however, if we summarize these data in terms of a *frequency distribution* (Table 1.2)—a table that lists how many scores fall into each of the designated categories. The pattern is clearer still if we graph the frequency distributions (Figure 1.9). Now we can easily see that the most common scores (in these fictional data) are between 16.1 and 20 for the boys and between 12.1 and 16.0 for the girls. As we move further and further from these central categories (looking either at higher scores or lower), the number of people at each level of aggression drops.

MEANS AND VARIABILITY

The distribution of scores in Table 1.1 yields a graph in Figure 1.9 that is roughly bell shaped. In fact, this shape is extremely common when we graph frequency distributions—whether the graph shows the frequency of various heights among 8-year-olds, or the frequency of going to the movies among college students, or the frequency of particular test scores for a college exam. In each of these cases, there tends to be a large number of moderate values and then fewer and fewer values as we move away from the center.

To describe these curves, it's usually enough to specify just two attributes. First, we must locate the curve's center. This gives us a measure of the "average case" within the data set—technically,

TABLE

1.2

Frequency Distribution for Aggression Scores among Children

Aggression score	Number of boys with scores in this range	Number of girls with scores in this range
0–4	1	2
4.1–8.0	2	4
8.1–12.0	4	7
12.1–16.0	6	9
16.1–20.0	8	6
20.1–24.0	5	3
24.1–28.0	4	1
28.1–30.0	2	0

1.9 The likelihood of aggressive behaviors in boys and girls These (*fictional*) data provide a frequency distribution, depicting the results shown numerically in Table 1.2. In this format, it's easy to see that the most common score for girls is between 12.1 and 16.0; the most common score for boys is higher, between 16.1 and 20.

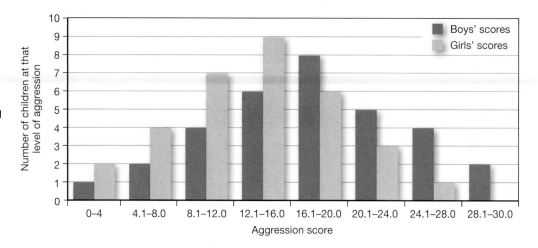

we're looking for a *measure of central tendency* of these data. The most common way of determining this average is to add up all the scores and then divide that sum by the number of scores in the set; this process yields the **mean.** But there are other ways of defining the average. For example, sometimes it's convenient to refer to the **median,** which is the score that separates the top 50% of the scores from the bottom 50%.

The second characteristic of a frequency distribution is its **variability,** which is a measure of how much the individual scores differ from one to the next. A highly variable data set includes a wide range of values and yields a broad, relatively flat frequency distribution like the one in Figure 1.10A. In contrast, a data set with low variability has values more tightly clustered together and yields a narrow, rather steep frequency distribution like the one in Figure 1.10B.

We can measure the variability in a data set in several ways, but the most common is the **standard deviation.** To compute the standard deviation, we first locate the center of the data set—the mean. Next, for each data point, we ask: How far away is this point from the mean? We compute this distance by simply subtracting the value for that point from the mean, and the result is the *deviation* for that point—that is, how much the point "deviates" from the average case. We then pool the deviations for all the points in our data set, so that we know overall how much the data deviate from the mean. If the points tend to deviate from the mean by a lot, the standard deviation will have a large value—telling us that the data set is highly variable. If the points all tend to be close to the mean, the standard deviation will be small—and thus the variability is low.

mean (M) A measure of central tendency computed by calculating the sum of all the observations, then dividing by the number of observations.

median A measure of central tendency taken by putting the data values in order and finding the value that divides the distribution in half.

variability The degree to which scores in a frequency distribution depart from the central value.

standard deviation (SD) A measure of the variability of a data set, calculated as the square root of the variance (V).

(A) High variability

(B) Low variability

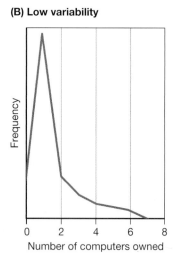

1.10 Frequency distributions with high or low variability These (*fictional*) data provide examples of frequency distributions with high and low variability. (A) People vary enormously in how many CDs they own; some own only 1 or 2, and some own hundreds. (B) There is relatively little variability in how many computers a family owns. Many families own one computer; some own none; a few own 2 or 3.

CORRELATIONS

In describing the data they collect, investigators also find it useful in many cases to draw on another statistical measure: one that examines **correlations.**

Returning to our example, imagine that a researcher examines the data shown in Table 1.1 and wonders why some boys are more aggressive than others, and likewise for girls. Could it just be their age—so that, perhaps, the older children are better at controlling themselves? To explore this possibility, the researcher might create a *scatter plot* like the one shown in Figure 1.11. In this plot, each point represents one child; the child's age determines the horizontal position of the point within the graph, and his or her aggression score determines the vertical position.

The pattern in this scatter plot suggests that these two measurements—age and aggression score—are linked, but in a negative direction. Older children (points to the right on the scatter plot) tend to have lower aggression scores (points lower down in the diagram). This relationship isn't perfect; if it were, all the points would fall on the diagonal line shown in the figure. Still, the overall pattern of the scatter plot indicates a relationship: If we know a child's age, we can make a reasonable prediction about her aggression level, and vice versa.

To assess data like these, researchers usually rely on a measure called the **correlation coefficient,** symbolized by the letter *r*. This coefficient is always calculated on *pairs* of observations. In our example, the pairs consist of each child's age and his or her aggression score; but, of course, other correlations involve other pairings. Correlation coefficients can take any value between +1.00 and −1.00 (Figure 1.12). In either of these extreme cases, the correlation is perfect. For the data shown in Figure 1.11, a calculation shows that *r* = −.60. This is a reasonably strong negative correlation, but it's obviously different from −1.00, thus confirming what we already know—namely, that the correlation between age and aggression score is not perfect.

correlation The tendency of two variables to change together. If one goes up as the other goes up, the correlation is positive; if one goes up as the other goes down, the correlation is negative.

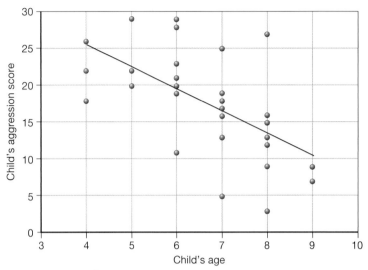

1.11 Scatter plot In this example, each point in the plot represents the aggression score for one child. Superimposed on the plot is a "trend line," which represents a mathematical summary of the data pattern.

correlation coefficient (*r*) A number that expresses both the size and the direction of a correlation, varying from + 1.00 (perfect positive correlation) to −1.00 (perfect negative correlation).

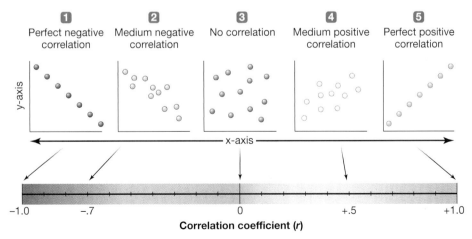

1.12 Correlation coefficients Correlation coefficients (values for *r*) range from –1.0 (a perfect negative correlation) to +1.0 (a perfect positive correlation). Shown here are some intermediate values, including the pattern of no correlation (*r* = 0.00).

Many of the relationships psychologists study yield *r* values in the ballpark of .40 to .60. These numbers reflect relationships strong enough to produce an easily visible pattern in the data. But, at the same time, these numbers indicate relationships that are far from perfect—so they certainly allow room for exceptions. To use a concrete example, consider the correlation between an individual's height and his or her sex. When examined statistically, this relationship yields a value of $r = +.43$. The correlation is strong enough that we can easily observe the pattern in everyday experience: With no coaching and no calculations, people easily detect that men, overall, tend to be taller than women. But, at the same time, we can easily think of exceptions to the overall pattern—women who are tall or men who are short. This is the sort of correlation psychologists work with all the time—strong enough to be informative, yet still allowing relatively common exceptions.

Let's be clear, though, that the strength of a correlation—and therefore the consistency of the relationship revealed by the correlation—is independent of the sign of the *r* value. A correlation of $+.43$ is no stronger than a correlation of $-.43$, and correlations of -1.00 and $+1.00$ both reflect perfectly consistent relationships.

CORRELATIONS AND RELIABILITY

In any science, researchers need to have faith in their measurements: A physicist needs to be confident that her accelerometer is properly calibrated; a chemist needs a reliable spectrometer. Concerns about measurements are particularly salient in psychology, though, because we often want to assess things that resist being precisely defined—things like personality traits or mental abilities. So, how can we make sure our measurements are trustworthy? The answer often involves correlations—and this is one of several reasons that correlations are such an important research tool.

Imagine that you step onto your bathroom scale, and it shows that you've lost 3 pounds since last week. On reflection, you might be puzzled by this; what about that huge piece of pie you ate yesterday? For caution's sake, you step back onto the scale and now it gives you a different reading: You haven't lost 3 pounds at all; you've gained a pound. At that point, you'd probably realize you can't trust your scale; you need one that's more reliable.

This example suggests one way we can evaluate a measure: by examining its **reliability**—an assessment of how *consistent* the measure is in its results, and one procedure for assessing reliability follows exactly the sequence you used with the bathroom scale: You took the measure once, let some time pass, and then took the same measure again. If the measure is reliable, then we should find a correlation between these observations. Specifically, this correlation will give us an assessment of the measure's *test-retest reliability.*

A different aspect of reliability came up in our earlier discussion: In measuring aggression, we might worry that a gesture or a remark that seems aggressive to one observer may not seem that way to someone else (Figure 1.13). We thus need to guard against the possibility that our data are idiosyncratic—merely reflecting what one person regards as aggressive. To deal with this concern, we suggested that we might have a panel of judges observe the behaviors in question and that we'd trust the data only if the judges agree with each other reasonably well. This procedure relies on a different type of reliability, called *inter-rater reliability,* that's calculated roughly as the correlation between Judge 1's ratings and Judge 2's ratings, between Judge 2's ratings and Judge 3's, and so on.

reliability The degree of consistency with which a test measures a trait or attribute.

1.13 What counts as "aggression"? One test of reliability is *inter-rater reliability*—a measure of whether different judges agree with each other. We might need to check on this point in a study of aggression because it's often unclear whether a behavior is truly aggressive. For example, are the women on the left sharing secrets, or is the one leaning forward being aggressive? Are the two men just chatting, or is the man on the right raising his eyebrows to indicate a bit of aggressive sarcasm?

VALIDITY OF A MEASURE

Imagine that no matter who steps on your bathroom scale, it always shows a weight of 137 pounds. This scale would be quite reliable—but it would also be worthless, and so clearly we need more than reliability. We also need our dependent variable to measure what we intend it to measure. Likewise, if our panel of judges agrees, perhaps they're all being misled in the same way. Maybe the judges are really focusing on how cute the various boys and girls in the study are, so they're heavily biased by the cuteness when they judge aggression. In this case, too, the judges might agree with each other—and so they'd be reliable—but the aggression scores would still be inaccurate.

These points illustrate the importance of **validity**—the assessment of whether the variable measures what it's supposed to measure. There are many ways to assess validity, and correlations play a central role here too. For example, intelligence is often measured via some version of the IQ test, but are these tests valid? If they are, then this would mean that people with high IQ's are actually smarter—so they should do better in activities that require smartness. We can test this proposal by asking whether IQ scores are correlated with school performance, or with measures of performance in the workplace (particularly for jobs involving some degree of complexity). It turns out that these various measures are positively correlated, thus providing a strong suggestion that IQ tests are measuring what we intend them to.

validity The extent to which a method or procedure measures what it is supposed to measure.

Inferential Statistics

The statistics we've considered so far allow us to summarize the data we've collected, but we often want to do more than this. We want to reach beyond our data and make broader claims—usually claims about the correctness (or the falsity) of our hypothesis. For this purpose, we need to make inferences based on our data—and so we turn to inferential statistics.

TESTING DIFFERENCES

In the example we've been discussing, we began with a question: Do boys and girls differ in how aggressive they are? This comparison is easy for our sample because we know that in the (fictional) data we've collected, the boys' mean level of aggression is 17, and the girls' mean is 12. Obviously, the boys' scores are higher—providing a clear answer to our question *for this sample*. Ultimately, though, the sample isn't our concern. Instead, we want to make claims about a broader population; and so we still want to ask: Are boys in general (i.e., boys outside of our sample) more aggressive than girls in general?

To answer this question, we need to make some estimates based on our sample. Researchers use specific calculations for this purpose, but leaving the details aside, these calculations center on three points. First, how big a difference is found in the sample? In our example, the **effect size**—the difference between the groups—is 5 units (this is the difference between the boys' average, 17, and the girls' average, 12). In general, the larger the effect size, the more likely it is that the result can be taken at face value.

Second, how great is the *variability* of the data? The logic here is straightforward: If the variability in our sample is low, essentially this means that we kept seeing the same scores again and again. In that case, we're likely to continue getting the same scores if we look beyond our sample—and so we should be more comfortable in extrapolating from our sample. If, on the other hand, the data in our sample are highly variable, then we know that the broader population is diverse—so if we looked beyond this sample, we might find much higher scores or much lower ones. In this case, we'd have to be much more cautious in drawing conclusions from our sample.

Third, how many observations does the data set include? All things being equal, the greater the number of observations, the more likely the sample is to reflect the properties of the broader population. Thus, the greater the number of observations, the more trust we can put in our results.

Let's be clear, though, that these three factors—effect size, variability, and number of observations—can trade off against each other. If, for example, the effect size is small, then we will draw conclusions from our data only if we're certain that our measurements are quite accurate—and so we will insist on a low level of variability and a large number of observations. Similarly, if the variability is very low, then there's no reason to collect a huge amount of data—this would simply give us the same observations, over and over. Therefore, with low variability, we need relatively few data points.

These trade-offs are, in fact, built directly into the calculations researchers use to evaluate the **statistical significance** of a result. This calculation takes as its input the effect size, the variability, and the number of observations; and ultimately, its output is something called a *p-value*. This value is literally the probability of getting the data pattern we did purely by accident. After all, we know that peculiar accidents can happen: Sometimes, when you toss a coin, you get five "heads" in a row, entirely by chance. When you're rolling dice, you might—just by luck—go 30 or 40 rolls without rolling a seven. Our calculations tell us whether the result in our experiment is a similar sort of fluke—a chance occurrence only.

What could "chance" mean in the context of our comparison between boys and girls? Bear in mind that some boys are simply more aggressive than others, and likewise for girls. So it's possible that—just by luck—our sample of boys happens to include a couple of particularly aggressive individuals who are driving up the group's average. It's also possible that—again, just by luck—our sample of girls includes several especially well-behaved individuals who are driving the group's average down. This is the sort of possibility that our statistics evaluate—by asking how consistent the results are (measured by the variability) as well as how likely it is that just a few chance observations (e.g., a few misbehaved boys or a few especially docile girls) could be causing the difference we've observed between the groups (i.e., the effect size).

If the p-value we calculate is high, then we've observed an outcome that could easily occur by chance. In that case, we would cautiously conclude that our result might have

effect size The magnitude of the difference between groups in a study, often computed by subtracting the mean of one group's scores from mean the other's scores.

statistical significance A calculation central to inferential statistics that describes the likelihood that the results of a study happened by chance.

Method

1. Children filled out a survey about how often they engaged in or were the victims of various types of aggressive behaviors: physical (hits, kicks), verbal (threats, insults), and indirect (gossiping, deliberate exclusion).

2. Researchers collected data in Finland, Israel, Italy, and Poland, allowing a cross-cultural comparison.

Results

Boys and girls reported involvement in about the same number of aggressive behaviors. In all of the cultures studied, however, girls were much less likely to be involved in physical aggression, but much more likely to participate in indirect/social aggression.

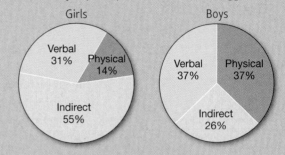

CONCLUSION: Neither sex is "more aggressive" overall. Because the sexes tend to show aggression differently, a great deal depends on how you define and measure aggression.

SOURCE STUDY: Oesterman et al., 1998

been a random fluke, and so we should draw no conclusions from our data. If the p-value is low (i.e., we observe an outcome that would rarely occur by chance), we conclude the opposite—the outcome is likely not the product of chance and should be taken seriously.

In most cases, psychologists use a 5% rule for making this determination—usually expressed with the cutoff of $p < .05$. In other words, if the probability of getting a particular outcome just by chance is less than 5%, then we conclude that the particular result we observed is unlikely to be an accident. Let's note, though, that there's nothing sacred about this 5% rule. We use other, stricter rules when evaluating especially important results or when considering *patterns* of evidence rather than just a single result.

So, with all of this said, what's the actual difference between boy's and girl's aggression—with real data, not the fictional data we've been considering so far (Figure 1.14)? The answer, with carefully collected data, turns out to depend on how exactly we define the dependent variable. If we measure *physical* aggression—pushing, physical intimidation, punching, kicking, biting—then males do tend to be more aggressive; and it doesn't matter whether we're considering children or adults, or whether we assess males in Western cultures or Eastern (e.g., Geary & Bjorklund, 2000). On the other hand, if we measure *social* aggression—ignoring someone, gossiping about someone, trying to isolate someone from their friends—then the evidence suggests that females are, in this regard, the more aggressive sex (Oesterman et al., 1998). Clearly, our answer is complicated—and this certainly turns out to be a study in which defining the dependent variable is crucial.

OBSERVATIONAL STUDIES

We've now explored some fundamental tools for psychology research—statistical tools, principles that govern the definition of variables, and procedures for selecting a sample. But what can we do with these tools? How do we go about setting up a psychological study? The answer varies considerably, and psychological studies come in many different forms. In some cases, psychologists observe conditions as they already exist in the world. Our main example so far—comparing boys and girls in their level of aggression—has been in this category. This sort of study is referred to as a **quasi-experiment**—a comparison of two or more groups that we did not create; the groups already existed in the world quite independent of our study.

In other cases, we do **correlational studies**—we collect multiple bits of information about each research participant and then examine the relationships among these bits of information. For example, how important is it, as we walk through life, to have good self-control—an ability to rein in our impulses and govern our own thoughts and emotions? One study addressed this broad question by asking people to evaluate various aspects of their own self-control. Specifically, the participants had to decide how well certain statements applied to them: "I am good at resisting temptation," "I am always on time," and so on. The investigators also collected other pieces of information about these same individuals and then looked at the relationships among these various measures. The data indicated that higher levels of self-control were associated with better grades in school, fewer symptoms of mental disorder, less binge eating, and better social relationships (Tangney, Baumeister, & Boone, 2004). All in all, the study indicated the advantages of self-control and, more broadly, illustrated the sorts of things we can learn from a correlational study.

Quasi-experiments and correlational studies are different in important ways (e.g., they usually require different types of statistical analysis). They are alike, however, because they both involve data from a natural situation, one that the researcher did not create. On this basis, we can think of them both as types of *observational studies*—studies that observe the world as it is. In a different type of research, though, psychologists do create (or *alter*) situations in order to study them. If, for example, we wanted to ask whether stern warnings about aggression caused a decrease in bad behaviors, we could give the stern warning to some children and not to others and then see what happens. In this case, we're not studying a previously existing situation; we are adding our own manipulation—the warnings—to see what this does to the data. Studies of this sort, involving a change or manipulation, are called *experiments*.

Ambiguity about Causation

Psychologists often want to study the effects of factors they cannot control. The independent variable in our aggression example—sex—is a good illustration. If we want to learn about the effect of sex on aggression, therefore, we need to do an observational study, not an experiment.

Other illustrations are easy to find. For example, some authors have proposed that birth order is a powerful influence on personality and that compared to later-born children, firstborn children are more likely to identify with their parents and less likely to rebel. To test this claim, we'll once again need to study the world as it is rather than doing an experiment. Plainly, a wide range of issues call for the use of observational studies; and these studies, when properly designed, are an important source of evidence for us.

But let's be clear that observational studies have an important limitation—their ability to tell us about cause and effect. Here's an example: Suppose a researcher hypoth-

quasi-experiment A comparison that relies on already-existing groups (i.e., groups the experimenter did not create).

correlational studies Studies in which the investigator analyzes the relationships among variables that were in place before the study, without manipulating those variables.

esizes that *clinical depression* leads to a certain style of thinking in which the person constantly mulls over unhappy occasions. To verify this hypothesis, the researcher tests two groups—people who are depressed and people who are not—and has the participants in each group fill out questionnaires designed to assess their thought habits. Let's suppose further that the researcher finds a difference between the groups—the participants suffering from depression are more likely to ruminate on their life difficulties.

How should we think about this result? It's possible that depression encourages the habit of rumination; that would explain why rumination is more likely among people with depression. But, it's also possible that cause and effect are the other way around—and so a tendency toward mulling over life's problems is actually causing the depression. That interpretation also fits with the result; but it would have very different implications for what we might conclude about the roots of depression as well as how we might try to help people with depression.

In observational studies, researchers are often uncertain about which variable is the cause and which is the effect. Worse, sometimes there's another possibility to consider when interpreting observational data: Perhaps a third factor, different from the two correlated variables, is causing both. This is the **third-variable problem** (Figure 1.15). For example, a number of studies have suggested that students who take Latin in high school often get above-average grades in college, and there's an obvious cause-and-effect interpretation for these data: Background in Latin gives students insight into the roots of many modern words, improving their vocabulary and thus aiding college performance (Figure 1.15A).

third-variable problem The possibility that two correlated variables may be changing together only due to the operation of a third variable.

Scenario A: Two variables

Scenario B: The third variable problem

Scenario C: An alternate version of the third variable problem

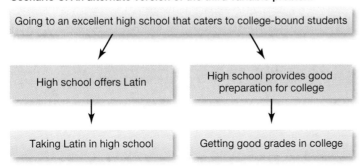

1.15 The third-variable problem Students who take Latin in high school get better grades on average than do their college classmates who didn't take Latin. Is Latin the cause of collegiate success (A), or is there some other underlying factor? (B) Maybe what matters is the type of student who takes Latin. (C) Alternatively, maybe what matters is the type of school where Latin is offered. Because any of these possibilities are compatible with the observation that taking Latin and better grades go together, the observation is ambiguous; no conclusions can be drawn from it.

This explanation of the data certainly seems plausible—but it may not be right, and there are surely other ways to think about the evidence. For example, what sorts of students typically choose to take Latin in high school? In many cases, they're students who are academically ambitious, motivated, and able. And, of course, students with these same traits are likely to do well in college. Thus, these students have distinctive characteristics—motivation and aptitude—that become the "third variable," which leads to taking Latin and to getting better grades in college (Figure 1.15B). On this basis, taking Latin would be associated with good college grades, but not because one caused the other. Instead, both effects might be the products of the same underlying cause. (Figure 1.15C illustrates yet another possibility—and a different notion of what the third variable might be in this example.)

These complications—identifying which factor is the cause and which is the effect, and dealing with the third-variable problem—often make it difficult to interpret observational data. Researchers often summarize this difficulty with a simple slogan: *Correlation does not imply causation.* Of course, sometimes correlations do reflect causality: Smoking cigarettes is correlated with, and is a cause of, emphysema, lung cancer, and heart disease. Being depressed is correlated with, and is actually a cause of, sleep disruption. But correlations often do not imply causes: The number of ashtrays an individual owns is correlated with poor health, but not because owning ashtrays is hazardous. Similarly, there's a correlation between how many tomatoes a family eats in a month and how late the children in the family go to bed—but not because eating tomatoes keeps the kids awake. Instead, tomato eating and late bedtimes are correlated because they're both more likely to occur in the summer.

How can we address these problems? Sometimes we can disentangle cause and effect simply by collecting more observational data. For example, in the study of depression and thinking style, we might be able to determine which of these elements was on the scene first: Were the people depressed before they started to ruminate? Or were they ruminating before they became depressed? Here, we're exploiting the simple logic that the causes must be in place before the effects. In other cases, though, it's just not possible to draw conclusions about cause and effect from observational data, and so we need to turn to a different type of research—one that relies on *experiments*.

ESTABLISHING CAUSE AND EFFECT: THE POWER OF EXPERIMENTS

In ordinary conversation, people use the word *experiment* when referring to almost any sort of test. ("Would a bit of oregano make this stew taste better? Let's experiment and find out!") In the sciences, though, **experiment** has a more specific meaning: It is a test in which the investigators manipulate some variable in order to set up a specific comparison. Let's look at what this means and why it's so important—including why experiments allow us to make cause-and-effect claims.

experiment A study of causal relationships in which the researcher manipulates an independent variable to examine its effect on a dependent variable.

Experimental Groups versus Control Groups

In an observational study, the researcher simply records what she finds in the world. In a scientific experiment, in contrast, the researcher deliberately changes something. She might change the nature of the test being given, or the circumstances, or the instructions. This change is usually referred to as the **experimental manipulation**—and the point of an experiment is to ask what results from this change. To see how this plays out, let's consider a new example.

Many companies sell audio recordings that contain subliminal messages embedded in background music. The message might be an instruction to give up smoking or curb overeating, or it might be designed to build self-esteem or overcome shyness. The message is played so softly that you can't consciously detect it when listening to the recording; still, it's alleged to provide important benefits.

Anecdotal evidence—reports from various people announcing, "Hey, I tried the tapes, and they really worked for me!"—sometimes suggests that these subliminal messages can be quite effective. However, we've already discussed the problems with relying on such anecdotes; and so, if we want a persuasive test of these messages, it would be best to set up an experiment. Our experimental manipulation would be the presentation of the subliminal message, and this would define our study's independent variable: message presented versus message not presented.

What about the dependent variable? Suppose we're testing a tape advertised as helping people give up cigarette smoking. In that case, our dependent variable might be the number of cigarettes smoked in, say, the 24-hour period after hearing the tape. In our study, we might ask 20 students—all longtime smokers—to listen to the tape; then we'd count up how many cigarettes they each consume in the next 24 hours. However, this procedure by itself tells us nothing. If the students smoke an average of 18 cigarettes in the 24-hour test period, is that less than they would have smoked without the tape? We have no way to tell from the procedure described so far, and so there's no way to interpret the result.

What's missing is a basis for comparison. One way to arrange for this is to use two groups of participants. The **experimental group** will experience the experimental manipulation—their tape contains the subliminal message. The **control group** will not experience the manipulation. So, by comparing the control group's cigarette consumption to that of the experimental group, we can assess the message's effectiveness.

But exactly what procedure should we use for the control group? One possibility is for these participants to hear no recording at all, while those in the experimental group hear the tape containing the subliminal message embedded in music. This setup, however, once again creates problems: If we detect a contrast between the two groups, then the subliminal message might be having the predicted effect. But, on the other hand, notice that the subliminal message is embedded in music—so is the experimental group being influenced by the music rather than the message? (Perhaps the participants find it relaxing to listen to music and then smoke less because they're more relaxed.) In this case, it helps to listen to the recording; but the result would be the same if there had been no subliminal message at all.

To avoid this ambiguity, the procedures used for the control group and the experimental group must match in every way except for the experimental manipulation. If the experimental group hears music containing the subliminal message, the control group must hear the identical music without any subliminal message. If the procedure for the experimental group requires roughly 30 minutes, then the procedure for the control participants should take 30 minutes. It's also important for the investigators to treat the two groups in precisely the same way. If we tell members of the experimental group they're participating in an activity that might help them smoke less, then we must tell members of the control group the same thing. That way, the two groups will have similar expectations about the procedure.

experimental manipulation The deliberate alteration of the independent variable in an experiment in order to learn about its effects on the dependent variable.

experimental group The group within an experiment that experiences the researcher's manipulation of the independent variable.

control group A group within an experiment that does not experience the experimental manipulation.

Random Assignment

As we have just described, it's crucial for the experimental and control group procedures to be as similar as possible—differing only in the experimental manipulation itself. It's also essential for the two groups of participants to start out the procedure being well matched to each other. In other words, there should be no systematic differences between the experimental and control groups when the experiment begins. Then, if the two groups differ at the *end* of the experiment, we can be confident that the difference was created during the experiment—which, of course, is what we want.

How can we achieve this goal? The answer is **random assignment**—the process of using some random device, like a coin toss, to decide which group each participant goes into. According to some descriptions, this is the defining element of a true experiment. Random assignment is based on the simple idea that people differ from each other. Some people are anxious and some are not; some like to race through tasks while others take their time; some pay attention well and others are easily distracted. There's no way to get around these differences—but with random assignment, we can be confident that some of the anxious people will end up in the experimental group and some in the control group; some of the attentive people will end up in one group and some in the other. Random assignment doesn't change the fact that participants differ from one to the next, but this procedure makes it very likely that the *mix* of participants in one group will be the same as the mix in the other group. As a result, the groups are matched overall at the start of our experiment—and that's exactly what we want.

Notice that we've now solved the concerns about cause and effect. Thanks to random assignment, we know that the groups started out matched to each other before we introduced the experimental manipulation. Therefore, any differences we observe in the dependent variable weren't there *before* the manipulation, and so they must have arisen *after* the manipulation. As we mentioned earlier, this is just the information we need in order to determine which variable is the cause and which is the effect.

Random assignment also removes the *third-variable problem*. The issue there was that the groups being compared might differ in some regard not covered by the variables being scrutinized in our study. Thus, students who take Latin in high school might also be more motivated academically, and the motivation (not the Latin) might be why these students do especially well in college.

This problem wouldn't arise, however, if we could use random assignment to decide who takes Latin classes and who doesn't. Doing so wouldn't change the fact that some students are more motivated and others are less so; but it would guarantee that the Latin takers included a mix of motivated and less motivated students, and likewise for the group that does not take Latin. That way, the groups would be matched at the start—so if they end up being different later on, it must be because of the Latin itself.

Within-Subject Comparisons

Random assignment thus plays a central role in justifying our cause-and-effect claims. But the psychologist's tool kit includes another technique for ensuring that the experimental and control groups match each other at the start of the experiment. This technique involves using the *same people* for the two groups, guaranteeing that the two "groups" are identical in their attitudes, backgrounds, motivations, and so forth. An experiment that uses this technique of comparing participants' behavior in one setting

random assignment In an experimental design, the random placement of participants in either the experimental or control groups, ensuring that the groups are matched at the outset of the experiment.

to the same participants' behavior in another setting is said to use **within-subject comparisons.** This kind of experiment differs from the other designs we've considered so far, which use **between-subject comparisons.**

Within-subject comparisons are advantageous because they eliminate any question about whether the experimental and control groups are fully matched to each other. But within-subject comparisons introduce their own complications. For example, let's say that participants are first tested in the proper circumstances for the control condition and then tested in the circumstances for the experimental condition. In this case, if we find a difference between the conditions, is it because of the experimental manipulation? Or is it because the experimental condition came second, when participants were more comfortable in the laboratory situation or more familiar with the experiment's requirements?

Fortunately, we can choose from several techniques for removing this sort of concern from a within-subjects design. In the example just sketched, we could run the control condition first for half of the participants and the experimental condition first for the other half. That way, any effects of sequence would have the same impact on both the experimental and control data, so any effects of sequence could not influence the comparison between the conditions. Techniques like this enable psychologists to rely on within-subject designs and can remove any question about whether the participants in the two conditions are truly comparable to each other.

Internal Validity

You may have detected a theme running through the last few sections: Over and over, we've noted that a particular procedure or a particular comparison might yield data that are open to more than one interpretation. Over and over, therefore, we've adjusted the procedure or added a precaution to avoid this sort of ambiguity. That way, when we get our result, we won't be stuck in the position of saying that maybe *this* caused the result or maybe *that* caused the result. In other words, we want to set up the experiment from the start so that, if we observe an effect, there's just one way to explain it. Only in that situation can we draw conclusions about the impact of our independent variable.

How have we achieved the goal? The various steps we've discussed all serve to isolate the experimental manipulation—so it's the only thing that differentiates the two groups, or the two conditions, we are comparing. With random assignment, we ensure that the groups were identical (or close to it) at the start of the experiment. By properly designing our control procedure, we ensure that just one factor within the experiment distinguishes the groups, Then, if the two groups differ at the end of the study, we know that just one factor could have produced this difference—and that's what allows us to make the strong claim that the factor we manipulated did, indeed, cause the difference we observed.

These various steps (random assignment, matching of procedures, and so on) are all aimed at ensuring that an experiment has **internal validity**—it has the properties that will allow us to conclude that the manipulation of the independent variable was truly the cause of the observed change in the dependent variable. If an experiment lacks internal validity, it will not support the cause-and-effect claims that our science needs.

Beyond the Single Experiment

So far, we've considered the many elements needed for a proper experiment. But we should also realize that the scientific process doesn't end once a single experiment or observational study is finished (Figure 1.16). As one further step, the research must be

within-subject comparisons Within a study, comparing the data about each participant in one situation to data about the same participant in another situation.

between-subject comparisons Within a study, comparing one group of individuals to a different group.

internal validity The characteristic of a study that allows us to conclude that the manipulation of the independent variable caused the observed changes in the dependent variable.

1.16 Science takes a long time Any scientific achievement builds on the work of other, earlier scientists.

replication A repetition of an experiment that yields the same results.

meta-analysis A statistical technique for combining the results of many studies on a particular topic, even when the studies used different data collection methods.

evaluated by experts in the field to make certain it was done properly. This step is usually achieved during the process of publishing the study in one of the scientific journals. Specifically, a paper is published *only* after being evaluated and approved by other researchers who are experts in that area of investigation. These other researchers provide *peer review* (i.e., the paper's authors and these evaluators are all "peers" within the scientific community), and they must be convinced that the procedure was set up correctly, the results were analyzed appropriately, and the conclusions are justified by the data. It's only at this point that the study will be taken seriously by other psychologists.

Even after it's published, a scientific study continues to be scrutinized. Other researchers will likely try to replicate the study—to run the same procedure with a new group of participants and see if it yields the same results. A successful **replication** assures us that there was nothing peculiar about the initial study and that the study's results are reliable. Other investigators may also run alternative experiments in an attempt to challenge the initial findings.

This combination of replications and challenges eventually produces an accumulation of results bearing on a question. Researchers then try to assemble all the evidence into a single package, to check on how robust the results are—that is, whether the results are consistent even if various details in the procedure (the specific participants, the particular stimuli) are changed. Sometimes, this pooling of information is done in a published article—called a *literature review*—that describes the various results and discusses how they are or are not consistent with each other. In addition, researchers often turn to a statistical technique called **meta-analysis.** This is a formal procedure for mathematically combining the results of numerous studies—so, in effect, it's an analysis of the individual analyses contained within each study. (For more on meta-analysis, see Chapter 17.) Meta-analysis allows investigators to assess the consistency of a result in quantitative terms.

It's only after all these steps—the result has been replicated, has survived scrutiny and challenge, and has been corroborated through other studies brought together in a review or meta-analysis—that we can truly consider the original results persuasive and the conclusions justified. Now we can say that the original hypothesis is *confirmed*—that is, well supported by evidence. Notice, however, that even after all these steps, we do not claim the hypothesis is *proven*. That's because scientists, in an open-minded way, always allow for the possibility that new facts will become available to challenge the hypothesis or show that it's correct only in certain circumstances. On this basis, no matter how often a scientific hypothesis is confirmed, it is never regarded as truly "proven." But, of course, if a hypothesis is confirmed repeatedly and withstands a range of challenges, scientists regard it as extremely likely to be correct. They then conclude that, at last, they can confidently build from there.

We should also mention the other possible outcome: What if the study is properly done and the data aren't consistent with the authors' original prediction? In that case, the hypothesis is *disconfirmed*, and the scientist must confront the contrary findings. Often, this means closely scrutinizing these findings to make certain the study that is challenging one's hypothesis was done correctly. If it was, the researcher is obliged to tune the original hypothesis—or set that hypothesis aside and turn instead to some new proposal. What the scientist cannot do, though, is simply ignore the contrary findings and continue asserting a hypothesis that has been tested and found wanting.

Finally, with all of these safeguards in place, what about our earlier example? Are recordings containing subliminal suggestions an effective way to give up smoking or to increase your attractiveness? Several carefully designed studies have examined the effects of this type of recording, and the results are clear: The messages do seem to work, but this effect almost certainly involves a placebo effect—that is, an effect

1.17 **Placebos** Placebo effects can be quite powerful and must be controlled for (typically by a double-blind design) to ensure that the experimenter's manipulation—not merely the participants' expectations about that manipulation—is having an effect.

produced by the participants' positive expectations for the procedure and not the procedure itself (Figure 1.17). Once the investigator controls for the participants' expectations about the recordings, the subliminal messages themselves produce no benefit (Greenwald, Spangenberg, Pratkanis, & Eskenazi, 1991).

RESEARCH ETHICS

We're almost finished with our broad tour of how scientific research proceeds. However, one last issue demands comment. It's not about how research is carried out or how findings are interpreted. Instead, it's about what research can and cannot be done.

As we've seen, the external validity of an investigation depends on the relationship between a study and its real-world context. This, in turn, requires us to study real people and real animals. And this requirement brings with it a demand that psychological research be conducted ethically, using methods that protect the rights and well-being of the research participants.

Psychologists are serious about research ethics. Virtually every institution sponsoring research—every college and university, every funding agency—has special committees charged with the task of reviewing research proposals to make sure the procedures adequately protect human and animal participants. Researchers who study laboratory animals must protect the animals' health and provide adequate housing and nutrition. In the United States, psychological research with human participants must also follow the guidelines established by the American Psychological Association (1981, 1982), one of psychology's most prominent professional organizations. The U.S. government also has regulations governing research with human participants. Institutions failing to observe these regulations are ineligible to receive grants from federal agencies, such as the National Science Foundation or the National Institutes of Health. Similar guidelines to protect research participants are in place in many other countries; for example, the Council for International Organizations of Medical Sciences published a set of international guidelines for research ethics in 2002. And, independent of international boundaries, most psychological research journals require that when publishing research, authors clearly state that their study observed all the rules protecting the participants.

Human participants must not only be protected physically; we must also respect their privacy, autonomy, and dignity. Accordingly, an investigator must guarantee that the data are collected either anonymously or confidentially and that participants are not treated in any way they might find objectionable. Before the study begins, the investigator must give participants as much information as possible about what their task will involve, inform them of any risks, and assure them they can leave the study at any time. Based on that information, the participants can decide for themselves whether they'll continue in the study—and so the procedure is run and the data collected only after participants have given their **informed consent.**

Then, at the end of the experiment, the investigator must **debrief** the participants—that is, explain to them what the experiment involved and why. If the experiment involved any deception or hidden manipulation, this must be revealed. If the study involved any manipulation of beliefs, mood, or emotion, the investigator must attempt to undo these effects. Ideally, participants should leave the study with some understanding of how the research, and their participation in it, may benefit psychological knowledge and human welfare.

Be aware that these ethical protections—especially the need to obtain informed consent—can conflict with the procedures needed to ensure the study's validity. In some cases, for example, the validity of a study requires keeping research participants somewhat uninformed about the study's design. Participants in a control group usually aren't told they're in a control group, because hearing this might erode their motivation to perform well on the experimenters' tasks. In the same way, subliminal self-help recordings are alleged to work through unconscious mechanisms. Thus, it may be important to keep the person who will hear the recording from knowing in advance exactly what message will be (subliminally) contained within the recording.

How can investigators resolve these conflicts between ensuring experimental validity and continuing to honor ethical standards? Overall, the ethical considerations must be the greater priority. Investigators must do everything they can to minimize the use of deception and guard against risks to research participants. If any risk remains, the investigators must clearly and persuasively argue that the information to be gained from the experiment truly justifies the risk. Similarly, if an experiment involves deception, the investigators must explain how the scientific value of the experiment justifies that level of deception.

These decisions about risk or deception are sometimes difficult; indeed, the history of psychology includes many conflicts over the ethical acceptability of psychological studies (e.g., Baumrind, 1964; Hermann & Yoder, 1998; Korn, 1997; Milgram & Murray, 1992; Savin, 1973; Zimbardo, 1973). This is one reason that decisions about ethical acceptability usually aren't made by the investigators themselves, but by a multidisciplinary supervisory committee—usually called an *institutional review board*, or *IRB*—assigned the task of protecting research participants.

Moreover, the requirement to protect human and animal rights simply prohibits some studies—no matter how much we might learn from them. For example, how does child abuse affect a child's later social or emotional development? This deeply important question cannot be studied experimentally, because no researcher would physically abuse participants to study the outcomes. If we want to learn more about the effects of abuse, we need to find other means (such as a quasi-experimental design, in which the researcher evaluates children who—sadly—have already been abused).

informed consent A research participant's agreement to take part in the study, based on full information about what the experiment will involve.

debriefing A step at the end of an experiment in which the researcher explains the study's purpose and design to each participant and undoes any manipulations to participants' beliefs or state.

Throughout this chapter, we've emphasized the power of science. But we must not forget that our science involves living creatures—including our fellow human beings—who must always be respected and protected. We therefore need to ensure that our science is as humane as it is rigorous.

THE POWER OF SCIENCE

The commitment to scientific inquiry has served psychology remarkably well. Psychologists know an enormous amount about human behaviors, feelings, and thoughts, and we know how humans differ from other species as well as how we resemble them. Moreover, we're quite certain about these things—our claims are not matters of conjecture or opinion, but assertions rooted in well-established facts.

Before leaving this chapter, though, we should point out that the scientific method, with all of its controls and precautions, is also useful in other domains. Specifically, the logic of science can also help people to draw more sensible conclusions from their everyday experiences.

Consider Jesse, who always takes a large dose of vitamin C when she feels a cold coming on. Jesse has noticed that her colds are usually mild and brief, and she concludes that the vitamins help her (Figure 1.18). Or think about Sol, who checks his horoscope online every morning and believes that the forecast is usually correct: Whenever the stars indicate that he's going to have a day filled with new opportunities, he does! Likewise, Julie had been hoping for months that Jacob would show some interest in her. After suspecting that he was turned off by her shyness, she tried to act less timid when he was around—and now they're great friends. Julie concludes that her shift in approach was a success. In all of these cases, people are drawing conclusions based on their experiences. Are their conclusions justified?

Notice that Jesse always takes vitamin C when she's coming down with a cold. As a result, she has an experimental "group" (herself) that takes the pill, but no control group (people who take no vitamins). It's possible that her colds would be just as mild without the vitamins, and so her conclusion that the vitamin C helps is unwarranted.

Sol does have a basis for comparison—days with a certain astrological prediction (such as the promise of new opportunities) versus days with a different prediction.

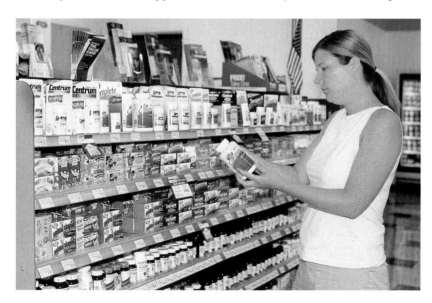

1.18 **Evaluating evidence outside the lab** Do vitamins and diet supplements provide a real benefit? Answering everyday questions like this one requires roughly the same logic that scientists use in testing their hypotheses.

Even so, there's a flaw in Sol's reasoning. Notice that he reads his horoscope every morning, so he starts each day with expectations based on the astrological forecast he has read. Perhaps he's more likely to notice his opportunities whenever the forecast has alerted him to look for them. In this case, the pattern Sol has observed might support the power of positive expectations, but it says nothing about the accuracy of astrology.

Julie's comparison (acting timid versus acting bold) is also problematic. Maybe Jacob is just slow in noticing people; so it wasn't her boldness, but merely the passage of time, that made the difference.

As these examples show, the scientist's concerns also apply to cases of common-sense reasoning. In the laboratory and in life, comparisons are needed if we hope to draw convincing conclusions. In both arenas, we need to rule out sources of ambiguity if we wish to be certain about the factors leading to a particular outcome. In these ways, the logic of scientific investigation turns out to have a use outside of the laboratory. What's more, by using this logic, we can avoid drawing unwarranted conclusions and end up with a clearer, more accurate understanding of our personal and social environment.

The methods of science can apply to our daily lives in another way: Scientists take evidence very seriously, and they don't continue to make claims that are contradicted by the evidence. To be sure, scientists often hesitate to abandon their theories; and so they carefully scrutinize challenges to their beliefs. But when the evidence makes it plain that a particular belief is mistaken, then the belief must be set aside.

empirical claims Claims that can be true or false depending on the facts.

The same attitude would serve people well in many daily activities. Of course, each of us holds many beliefs that depend on our values rather than facts, and these beliefs are not subject to scientific testing. But when our beliefs do rest on **empirical claims**— i.e., claims that can be true or false, depending on the facts—it is surely unwise to ignore the facts. As one example, for many years—and despite compelling scientific evidence—policy-makers denied a connection between cigarette smoking and health problems. The cost of this failure to take the evidence seriously is plain. Likewise, the evidence that human activities contribute to global warming is now overwhelming; but for years, many politicians chose to ignore this evidence and offered policies that increased the damage to our planet's climate systems. Examples like these are powerful reminders of the value of science—not just as a source of specific information, but as a broader model of the steps we need to take (and the honesty we need to display) to keep our beliefs in line with the facts.

SOME FINAL THOUGHTS: METHODOLOGICAL ECLECTICISM

Questions about human behavior and mental processes are among the most interesting questions we can ask, and people have been trying to answer them for thousands of years. One of psychology's great contributions has been the application of the scientific method to these questions—with great benefit, because we have learned an enormous amount.

In this chapter, we have tried to sketch what the scientific method involves in psychology. We've emphasized the points that apply to all research, such as the importance of systematic data collection and the need to remove ambiguity or to minimize a procedure's demand characteristics. But, along with these methodological similarities, we've also mentioned the diversity of research. We have emphasized random samples as well as the value of case studies. We have also talked about the contrast between observational studies and experiments.

With an eye on this diversity of research types, it's important to emphasize that each type has its advantages, and none is better than the others. A random sample allows us to study a small group and then draw broad conclusions from it. Even so, case studies are sometimes appropriate or even necessary. Suppose, for example, an investigator is studying an individual (perhaps someone with brain damage) who truly is unique; in a situation like this, a larger-scale study of multiple participants is just not possible. Often, the case study provides insights or suggests effects that can then be pursued with a larger group—but sometimes the case study is by itself deeply and richly instructive. This feature is, by the way, not unique to psychology: Geologists routinely report "case studies" examining a single volcano; oceanographers study single tsunamis. In both of these disciplines, the investigators understand that they're "merely" describing a single case, but they proceed because they know that a single case can offer powerful insights into more general issues and phenomena.

Similarly, observational studies are immensely valuable because they allow us to learn about events or behaviors that we couldn't possibly manipulate. Besides that, they're often done in natural settings that allow us to observe events ranging from how children behave in an actual school setting to how wolves behave in their normal habitat. But, as we've discussed, observational studies are also limited. Because they usually cannot inform us about cause-and-effect relations, observational studies are weaker in this specific regard than experiments are.

Experiments, in turn, are immensely valuable because they allow us to untangle cause-and-effect relationships. But experiments aren't always possible. In many situations, manipulation of a variable—or random assignment—is either logistically impossible or forbidden by ethical constraints. When random assignment *is* possible, it provides a powerful benefit: It virtually guarantees that the two groups being compared were matched to each other at the outset, so that changes between them can be attributed to the experimental manipulation. But this benefit has a cost attached: Randomly assigning participants or holding all the variables in a situation constant except the experimental manipulation requires an experimenter to be in control of the research situation. Gaining that control typically means introducing some artificiality into the setting. The artificiality, in turn, raises questions about external validity—that is, questions about whether the experiment accurately mirrors the real-world phenomenon that the investigator hopes to understand.

How do researchers manage these trade-offs, or decide which method to use? They make the decision case by case; but for most circumstances, their preferred approach is to use multiple methods in the hope that the different methods will converge on the same answer. In this way, each of the methods complements the other, and the particular strengths of each method can help address concerns that might have been raised by the weaknesses of other methods. This strategy gives researchers a powerful means of arguing that the results are not some peculiar by-product of using this or that research tool; instead, they're telling us about the world as it truly is.

Psychological claims are typically claims about *facts*, and to check on these empirical claims, psychologists rely on the methods of science.

MAKING OBSERVATIONS

- Scientific observations typically begin with a question or hypothesis. The hypothesis must be specific enough to be *testable*, so that it will be clear what results might falsify the hypothesis. This requirement for testability usually calls for an *operational definition* of the key terms in the hypothesis, in order to specify the study's *dependent variable*. The data for a study must also be systematically collected, and so researchers usually ignore anecdotal evidence.

- Based on their observations of a *sample*, psychologists want to draw conclusions about a broad *population*. In *random sampling*, every member of the population has an equal chance of being picked to participate in the study. Researchers sometimes turn to other procedures, including *case studies*.

- Often, researchers want their study to mirror the circumstances of the broader world; in this case, they need to ensure the study's *external validity*. This validity depends on many factors, including the requirement that the study itself not change the behaviors the researchers hope to understand. One concern here involves the study's possible *demand characteristics*—cues that can signal to the participants how they're supposed to behave. One way of avoiding this problem is to use a double-blind design.

WORKING WITH DATA

- Researchers use *descriptive statistics* to summarize the data from their studies. These include measures of central tendency of the data, often computed as the *mean*, and measures of the *variability*, often assessed by the *standard deviation*.

- Researchers also use *correlations* to summarize the pattern of their data, asking whether changes in one measurement are somehow linked to changes in some other measurement. These linkages are often summarized via a *correlation coefficient*, *r*. Correlations can be used to check on the *reliability* of the measurements, and they're also one way to assessing the measure's *validity*.

- Researchers use *inferential statistics* to make inferences based on their data. This process often involves testing a difference between two groups, and it typically provides an assessment of a result's *statistical significance*—ultimately expressed as a p-value, the probability of getting the data pattern just by chance.

OBSERVATIONAL STUDIES

- Observational studies are crucial for psychology, but they're often uninformative about causation. In some observational studies, we can't be sure which observation is the cause and which is the effect; in other cases, we need to worry about the *third-variable problem*—the idea that some other (i.e., third) variable is influencing both the variables observed in our study.

ESTABLISHING CAUSE AND EFFECT: THE POWER OF EXPERIMENTS

- To assess cause and effect, researchers typically turn to experiments in which they deliberately change some aspect of a situation and observe the results. It's crucial for investigators to treat the *experimental group* and *control group* exactly the same in every way except for the *experimental manipulation* itself.

- The two groups must also be matched at the outset of the experiment. In many cases, researchers use *random assignment* to ensure matching groups. In other cases, researchers use a *within-subject comparison,* although they must then take other precautions to address problems that might be created by the sequence of conditions in the procedure.

- Scientific conclusions rarely rest on a single experiment. Instead, the experiment must be scrutinized by other researchers and usually *replicated* through subsequent studies. Only then can we confidently say that the original hypothesis has been confirmed or disconfirmed.

RESEARCH ETHICS

- Researchers must take precautions to protect the study participants' physical well-being as well as their privacy, autonomy, and dignity. If these ethical requirements collide with procedures needed to ensure a study's validity, then all risks to the participants must be minimized. Any remaining risks must be fully justified on scientific grounds.

THE POWER OF SCIENCE

- The methods of science can also be used to evaluate claims in everyday life. People can apply these methods to help ensure their conclusions are warranted. Relying on the methods of science can also help politicians make certain their policies are in line with the best available evidence.

ONLINE STUDY TOOLS

Go to StudySpace, **wwnorton.com/studyspace**, to access additional review and enrichment materials, including the following resources for each chapter:

Organize
- Study Plan
- Chapter Outline
- Quiz+ Assessment

Learn
- Ebook
- Chapter Review
- Vocabulary Flashcards
- Drag-and-Drop Labeling Exercises
- Audio Podcast Chapter Overview

Connect
- Critical Thinking Activity
- Studying the Mind Video Podcasts
- Video Exercises
- Animations
- **ZAPS** Psychology Labs

The Genetic and Evolutionary Roots of Behavior

Some of the best ideas in the world have the worst reputations. Take global warming, for example. When scientists in the mid-20th century began to worry that humans' carbon-spewing, forest-clearing ways were heating up the planet, many people scoffed that the scientists were just tree huggers. Much of the public could not believe that actions as mundane as driving cars and cutting down trees might eventually lead to cataclysmic results. And yet a few decades later, the data are rolling in and the word is getting out: It's getting hot in here.

Evolution is another good idea that gets a bad rap. For many years, people mocked evolutionists for asserting that humans and apes have a common ancestor. They rejected the notion that the world's beauty and complexity could be the result of random trial and error—in which the better adapted variations survived, and the less successful ones simply died off. Many people were offended by the idea that natural laws rather than divine direction shaped living organisms.

And yet the data keep rolling in and the word keeps getting out: Evolution and genetics are engines of nature that drive the shapes, sounds, and actions of life everywhere. These truths apply just as surely to humans as they do to orangutans, silverfish, and decorative ferns.

Granted, evolution and genetics have earned some of their infamy. First of all, early versions of evolutionary theory had a few kinks. Because they didn't know about genes, many evolutionists believed that parents could pass on traits they had gained over the course of a single lifetime to their offspring. According to this theory, say, a giraffe that had to reach for higher and higher leaves would develop a longer and stronger neck, which its calves would then inherit. Even Darwin believed a version of this theory, despite the evidence that it simply was not true.

The study of genetics also suffered from unsavory applications. In the early 20th century, for example, eugenicists and so-called social Darwinists used a corrupted version of evolutionary theory to justify sterilizing, euthanizing, and even murdering people who allegedly carried socially undesirable genes. But in the second half of the 20th century, scientists began to redeem evolutionary theory and genetics research by using them to promote and protect human rights rather than dismantle them. Researchers repeatedly showed that race and ethnicity are to a large extent social constructions, not genetic facts. They demonstrated that genes are only part of the story of development and behavior; the remaining part involves social and environmental conditions—many of which we help to create. And they explained that part of the strength of our species lies in the variability of its members, not in the reproductive success of a few people with a particular set of traits.

Evolution is one of science's best established, best confirmed theories, and thousands of researchers have built on this framework in powerful ways. These advances have been crucial for psychology—and an understanding of evolution and genetics has become an integral part of the field. We are incorporating genetics into our explanations of why some people respond well to antidepressant medication and some do not, and why some individuals are introverted while others are outgoing. An evolutionary perspective has provided insights into why people find some types of reasoning problems difficult and others a breeze, or why men and women tend to react differently to a partner's sexual infidelity.

As we consider how biological factors shape psychological functioning we'll start by asking *how* genes influence us. We'll need to work through what genes are, how they shape development, and how they eventually influence behavior. Second, we'll ask how the genes got to be the way they are. This question will lead us to a discussion of evolution by natural selection, which is the mechanism responsible for adaptive genetic changes. Third and most important, we'll ask how we study the genetic or evolutionary roots of a behavior.

By the end of this chapter, you'll be able to share the amazement that many psychologists feel when they see that a few molecules, a few simple rules, and a few million years provide the biological roots for reasoning, talking, learning, planning, empathizing, and everything else we do. Evolution and genetics are not just good ideas; they are foundations of life.

GENETICS AND DNA

People often speak of the "genes for obesity," or the "genes for depression." But what exactly is the linkage between the complex molecules we call *genes* and these large-scale observable traits? Let's start by taking a look at what genes are and how they operate.

Living things are all made of cells, and the *diversity* of cells is immense. For example, Figure 2.1 shows just three of the cell types found in the human body—each cell type

2.1 Cell types (A) Red blood cells contain large amounts of a protein called hemoglobin. Hemoglobin picks up oxygen when red blood cells pass through the lungs and then drops off the oxygen when these cells pass through the body's other tissues. (B) Goblet cells, found in the lining of the small intestine, manufacture granules of a protein called mucigen. When a goblet cell releases mucigen granules into the intestine, they combine with water to make mucin, a component of the mucus that lubricates the intestine. (C) Rod cells, which serve as light detectors in the eye, contain a protein called rhodopsin that absorbs light.

with a different size, shape, and function. What makes these cells so different is the proteins each type contains, with each cell producing the specific proteins necessary for its role in the body. But what governs the production of proteins? The answer lies in the cell's genes.

With just a few exceptions, all cells in a plant or animal contain a *nucleus*—essentially the biological control center for the cell (Figure 2.2). Within the nucleus are the cell's **chromosomes,** complex structures that each contain a single long molecule of **DNA (deoxyribonucleic acid).** The DNA, in turn, governs the cell's structure and its chemical processes by providing a set of detailed instructions for making the structural proteins that give each cell its shape and for making the proteins called enzymes that govern the cell's functioning.

Genes

A DNA molecule is constructed like a twisted ladder, forming a shape known as a double helix. The rungs in the DNA ladder are made up of chemical subunits typically referred to by their single-letter abbreviations: A (adenine), T (thymine), C (cytosine),

chromosomes Structures in the nucleus of each cell that contain the genes, the units of hereditary transmission. A human cell has 46 chromosomes arranged in 23 pairs.

DNA (deoxyribonucleic acid) The complex molecule that is the constituent of genes.

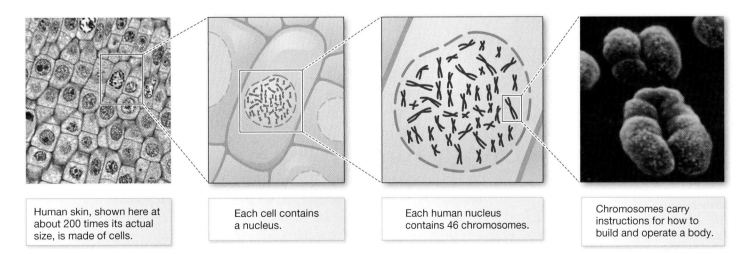

Human skin, shown here at about 200 times its actual size, is made of cells.

Each cell contains a nucleus.

Each human nucleus contains 46 chromosomes.

Chromosomes carry instructions for how to build and operate a body.

2.2 The cell's control center Cells contain nuclei, which contain chromosomes, which contain DNA.

| Chromosome | Chromosomes are made up of coiled strands of DNA. | The DNA molecule has a double helix shape. | The rungs of the double helix are made up of complementary chains of adenine (A), thymine (T), guanine (G), and cytosine (C). |

2.3 A DNA molecule The production of proteins is governed by the sequence of subunits on the DNA molecule. The sequence (for example, CAGGTC or TCCA) determines the structure of the protein that will be produced as well as when, where, and in what amount the protein will be made.

gene A section of a DNA molecule that contains instructions for how and when to assemble a protein. Genes are located on chromosomes.

and G (guanine). Each rung consists of a *pair* of these subunits: A always pairs with T, and C always pairs with G.

The A–T and C–G pairs can be placed in any sequence along a DNA molecule, just as beads of different colors can be strung in any order along a necklace. This feature of DNA enables the molecule to carry instructions for building proteins. If we read along one of the uprights of the ladder, we encounter a sequence of letters (Figure 2.3; from top to bottom along the right side of the molecule, the sequence is CAGGTC). The machinery inside each cell "reads" this molecular sequence in sections; some of the sections describe the structure of a protein, while other sections control when, where, and in what amount each protein will be made. The section of a DNA molecule that describes the structure of a protein, together with its control sequences, is called a **gene**.

The DNA in each chromosome encodes instructions for building hundreds of different proteins. In organisms that reproduce sexually, these chromosomes come in pairs (Figure 2.4). Human cells have 23 pairs, for a total of 46 chromosomes per cell; and each human cell contains between 20,000 and 30,000 protein-coding genes (Stein, 2004; Venter, Adams, Myers, Li, Mural et al., 2001). This count has astonished many scientists, who had anticipated a number four or five times larger! Indeed, the numbers surely seem small when we compare these counts to the 20,000 or so genes in a simple roundworm (*C. elegans*) cell. It's important to bear in mind, though, that very few traits are specified by single genes. Instead, what matters is the combination of genes, and our (roughly) 25,000 genes allow for a lot of combinations.

2.4 Human chromosomes The human genome consists of 23 pairs of chromosomes; these together contain roughly 25,000 genes. One pair of chromosomes (the so-called *sex chromosomes*) is either XX or XY; this pair determines whether the person is genetically female or male. The other 22 pairs are called *autosomes*.

Gene Expression

Virtually every cell in a person's body contains a copy of the same 46 chromosomes, collectively called the person's *genome*. Why then do the cells, all containing the same DNA, end up different from each other in their structure and functions (see Figure 2.1)? The answer lies in the fact that within each cell, the genes are not all active all the time. Instead, some genes in each cell are *expressed* and some are not. In fact, the process of *gene expression* is quite intricate, controlled by the interaction of an enormous variety of factors. In all cases, though, these factors work by modifying the biochemical environment inside the cell, and it's this intracellular environment that turns specific genes "on" or "off."

One of the variables that can alter the biochemistry within a cell is the environment just *outside* of the cell—and so whether a gene will be expressed (and thus how the cell will grow) often depends on what other cells are nearby. Another variable is timing—and so some genes are active early in an organism's development, but not later. Still other variables depend on the organism's overall environment and its behavior. For example, *temperature* influences gene expression, and so does sheer stimulation—so that for some genes, expression in a complex, engaging environment will be different from the expression in an impoverished environment with little stimulation. Still other key factors are (perhaps surprisingly) lodged in the social world—so that in some cases, gene expression depends on the people you're with and how you're interacting with them (e.g., Cole, 2009). Other aspects of the organism's behavior also matter: For example, extensive exercise will cause a person to build larger muscles because exercise triggers biochemical changes in the body that activate certain genes. These genes then produce the proteins that become the building blocks of larger, stronger muscles.

Notice, therefore, that how (or whether) genes will be expressed depends on both the environment and experience. As a result, it makes no sense to talk about "purely" genetic effects. We need instead always to emphasize the *interaction* between genetic factors and the context, and we also need to bear in mind that the interaction involves effects in both directions: As we've just seen, the environmental setting and the organism's experiences have a huge impact on gene expression; therefore, factors of experience shape how the genes operate. At the same time, genetic factors lead an organism to a certain pattern of sensitivities and a certain capacity to remember. Therefore, genetic factors shape what the organism experiences. As a result of all this, the often-mentioned "nature/nurture" distinction, cleanly separating genetic from environmental effects, is misleading. Neither type of influence operates without the other.

This interaction between environment and genes also leads to another lesson: People often seem to assume that an organism's genes determine its destiny; a particular genetic pattern, they believe, will govern how the organism turns out. Instead, an organism's genes define only its **genotype**—the specific sequence of genes on each of its chromosomes. In contrast, the organism's traits and capacities define its **phenotype**—what the organism is actually like. And the phenotype is a product of *both* the genotype *and* the environmental context, interacting in the ways we've discussed. Thus, the organism's genotype provides a crucial starting point, but does not by itself specify how the organism will end up.

genotype The complete set of an organism's genes.

phenotype The overt characteristics and behaviors of an organism.

Gene Transmission

Why does an organism have the genes that it does? The immediate answer lies in biological inheritance, because organisms inherit their genotype from their parents. Bear in mind here that chromosomes come in pairs, and, in most cell growth, all the pairs are copied into the new cells. However, when women make egg cells and men make sperm cells, each egg or sperm receives just one chromosome from each pair. Thus, in humans, each egg and each sperm contains 23 chromosomes rather than the normal complement of 46 (i.e., 23 pairs). When egg and sperm combine, the resulting cell ends up with two sets of 23—one from the egg (and so from the mother) and one from the sperm (and so from the father), and thus the correct number of chromosomes (Figure 2.5).

2.5 Parents' chromosome pairs combine to create a child's Cells in the human body generally contain 46 chromosomes—that is, 23 pairs. When females produce an egg, however, the egg contains just 23 chromosomes—one from each of the mother's pairs. The same is true when males produce sperm cells—they contain just one chromosome from each of the father's pairs. (For explanatory simplicity, the chromosomes in the second row are shown as they appear in prophase II of meiosis.) When egg and sperm combine, the baby ends up with the appropriate number of chromosomes.

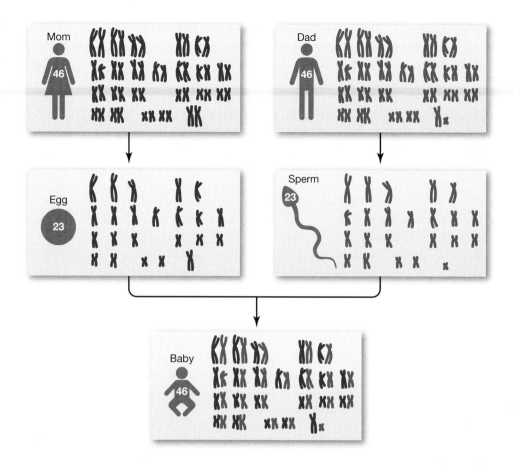

It's a matter of chance, however, which of the mother's chromosomes (i.e., which chromosome from each of her pairs) go into each egg, and this allows for a lot of possible combinations (more than 8 million). As a result, each egg is likely to be different from every other. The same is true for the father—again it's a matter of chance which chromosome from each of his pairs ends up in a particular sperm cell. Then, it's also largely chance that determines which of the father's sperm fertilizes which of the eggs. As a result of all of these chance occurrences, each offspring is likely to represent a new combination of genes—a new play in the genetic lottery we call sexual reproduction.

Interactions among Genes

Scientists are just beginning to understand exactly how genes lead to a particular structure—whether the structure is a human heart with its four chambers, a human eye, or a human brain ready to learn language. We do, however, know a lot about the broad patterns of inheritance, and our modern understanding grows out of work done more than a century ago: In the mid-1800s, a Moravian monk named Gregor Mendel (Figure 2.6) was cultivating pea plants in a monastery garden in Brünn (now Brno, Czech Republic). Mendel carefully observed the results of cross-fertilizing one variety of plant with another, and from his observations he worked out some basic laws of genetic inheritance. Mendel presented his ideas in 1865 and 1866, first in a pair of lectures at the Brünn Natural History Society and then in a paper published in the Brünn Society's Proceedings. However, his work was not widely appreciated, and Mendel's extraordinary achievement was not recognized until after 1900 (see Provine, 1971).

Let's start, therefore, with the same kind of case that Mendel started with: a characteristic shaped largely by variation in just one gene. (We mentioned earlier that the huge

2.6 Gregor Mendel (1822–1884) Our modern understanding of genetics grows out of Mendel's pioneering work 150 years ago.

majority of genetic influences are more complex than this and depend on an intricate interaction among many genes; still, a discussion of the single-gene case will allow us to get some important fundamentals out in view.) We have said that chromosomes come in pairs, and since genes are located on chromosomes, genes also come in pairs: Each gene occupies a specific position within its chromosome—called the gene's *locus*—and for each gene, there is a partner gene located at the corresponding locus on the other half of the chromosomal pair. The two genes in each pair—one on the chromosome contributed by the father, and one on the chromosome contributed by the mother—may be identical, or they may differ. If the paired genes are identical, we say that the individual is *homozygous* for that gene; if the two are different, the individual is *heterozygous* for the gene. In all cases, though, the variations of a specific gene are referred to as **alleles** of that gene.

How do things unfold if a person is heterozygous—having one allele of a particular gene on one chromosome and a different allele of that gene on the other chromosome? The simplest result is a relationship of *dominance*. As an illustration, consider *dimples*, one of the few human traits largely determined by variation in just one gene (Figure 2.7). If someone inherits from both parents the allele that favors dimples, then the person is virtually certain to end up with dimples. And if the person doesn't inherit this allele from *either* parent, then she won't have dimples. But what if the person inherits the allele that favors dimples from one parent, but not from the other? In this case, the person will probably still have dimples because the allele for dimples is **dominant:** it will exert its effect whether the other member of the gene pair is the same or not. In contrast, other alleles are **recessive:** A recessive allele will affect the phenotype only if it matches the allele of its partner gene.

A handful of other human traits are also based on a single gene pair; the list includes baldness, red-green color blindness, and high susceptibility to poison ivy (all recessive). Notice, though, that these examples all involve normal variations among genes. Sometimes, however, a person inherits a rare malfunctioning gene that can cause serious medical and psychological problems. One example is the gene (on chromosome 12) that causes a disorder known as *phenylketonuria* (*PKU*). This single (recessive) gene can lead to profound mental retardation.

In fact, the linkage between PKU and retardation is well understood. Because of the defective gene, someone with PKU produces far too little of a specific digestive enzyme. As a result, the person is unable to metabolize phenylalanine, a common amino acid. This leads to a buildup of undigested phenylalanine in the body and causes severe problems in brain development.

The treatment for PKU is straightforward: If we ensure that there is little phenylalanine in the person's diet, then his inability to digest this chemical doesn't matter at all. In that case, the inherited disorder is inconsequential and the person develops normally. Notice, then, that the PKU *genotype* may or may not lead to the *phenotype* of retardation; it all depends on the person's diet. (We'll have more to say about this disorder in Chapter 11.)

The alleles of a gene can also interact in other ways. In some cases, the alleles are *codominant*—a relationship in which both genes in the pair affect the phenotype. A common example is blood type: If the person inherits the allele favoring blood type A from one parent and the allele favoring blood type B from the other parent, the person will end up with type AB—expressing both genes.

In other cases, the alleles are in a relationship of *incomplete dominance*, so that a person with two different alleles will have a phenotype that's intermediate between the types favored by each allele on its own. An important example concerns the *serotonin*

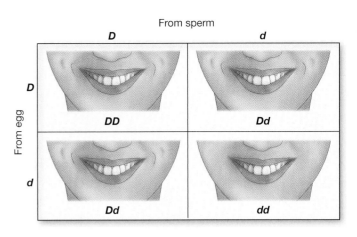

From sperm

From egg

2.7 **Inheritance of dimples** Dimples are one of the few traits largely determined by variation in just one gene. If someone inherits the allele that favors dimples from both parents (and so the person's genotype is *DD*), the person will almost certainly have dimples. If someone inherits this allele from *neither* parent (genotype *dd*), then dimples are unlikely. What if the person is heterozygous? The allele favoring dimples is *dominant*, and so the genotype *Dd* usually leads to dimples.

allele An alternative form of a specific gene.

dominant A term for a gene that directs the development of a particular characteristic even when the corresponding gene on the other chromosome is different—i.e., some other allele.

recessive A term for a gene that directs the development of a particular characteristic only if the corresponding gene on the other chromosome matches it—i.e., is the same allele.

transporter gene, located on chromosome 17. Serotonin is one of the chemicals that nerve cells use to communicate with each other, and it plays a role (among other functions) in regulating our emotions. (For more on this chemical communication, see Chapter 3.) Nerve cells that use serotonin also make a protein, called the serotonin transporter, whose job it is to mop up serotonin after it has been used to send a message. The gene that controls the production of this protein has two alleles that differ in the length of one part of the gene. An individual can have the longer allele on both of their copies of chromosome 17 (and so their genotype is described as *l/l*), or the short allele on both (a genotype of *s/s*), or the short allele on one and the long allele on the other (*s/l*).

The long allele of this gene is *incompletely* dominant over the short allele. As a result, people with the *l/l* genotype produce more serotonin transporter than do people with the *s/l* genotype; they, in turn, produce more serotonin transporter than do people with the *s/s* genotype. How does this matter for the individual? Studies have indicated that people who produce less of the serotonin transporter are at greater risk for both depression and anxiety and may react differently to antidepressant medication. Because these claims have been controversial (Arias, Catalán, Gastó, Gutiérrez, & Fañanás, 2003; G. Brown & Harris, 2008; Caspi, Sugden, Moffitt, Taylor, Craig et al., 2003; Lesch, Bengel, Heils, Sabol, Greenberg et al., 1996; Munafo, Durrant, Lewis, & Flint, 2009; Risch, Herrell, Lehner, Liang, Eaves et al., 2009), it's plain that more studies are needed. Even so, there's no question that serotonin plays a key role in regulating our moods, appetites, and sleep schedules—facts that guarantee continued research on the serotonin transporter gene.

Polygenic Inheritance

We have discussed several examples of variations in a single gene, and we've also looked at some of the ways that the alleles of a gene can interact. But keep in mind that the vast majority of an organism's traits are influenced by *many* genes, through a pattern known as **polygenic inheritance.** Examples here include bipolar disorder and schizophrenia. Both disorders are much more likely if a person inherits a certain genetic pattern, but the pattern includes many genes, each playing a part in creating the disease risk. (For more on these disorders, see Chapter 16.)

The logic of polygenic inheritance is, however, the same as the logic we've been discussing: The genes that are part of the polygenic pattern come in pairs, and the genes within each pair may have the same alleles or different ones. If the genes are different, then one allele may be dominant or (more likely) incompletely dominant or codominant. And, above all, the way that the genotype is reflected in the person's phenotype will depend on an interaction between the genetic pattern and numerous factors in the person's environment and experience.

polygenic inheritance A pattern in which many genes all influence a single trait.

proximate cause The influences within an organism's lifetime that led to its particular traits or behaviors.

ultimate cause The reasons why, over many years of evolution, a particular trait or behavior helped members of a population to survive and reproduce.

EVOLUTION BY NATURAL SELECTION

Each of us—as a human, or as a specific individual—is significantly shaped by our genetic pattern. That pattern, in turn, is inherited from our parents—half from our fathers and half from our mothers. But where did *their* genetic pattern come from? More broadly, why is the human genome as it is? Questions like these shift our focus from **proximate causes**, the mechanisms, within the organism's lifetime that led its phenotype, to **ultimate causes**, the reasons why, over many years of evolution, a particular trait or behavior would have helped members of a population to survive and reproduce.

The Principles of Natural Selection

Much of what we know about evolution grows out of the pioneering work of Charles Darwin. Charles Darwin (1809–1882; Figure 2.8) was an English naturalist who, from an early age, was so engrossed in outdoor pursuits that he habitually neglected his schoolwork. "To my deep mortification," Darwin later recalled (1887, p. 32), "my father once said to me, 'You care for nothing but shooting, dogs, and rat-catching, and you will be a disgrace to yourself and all your family.'"

Darwin's father, Robert, tried sending Charles to the University of Edinburgh for medical school (Desmond & Moore, 1991). Robert was a graduate himself, as was his own father. Charles, however, was bored by the lectures and horrified by the violence and gore of surgery, which in those days was performed without anesthesia.

Robert next sent Charles to Christ's College, Cambridge, to study for a career as a clergyman. There, Charles discovered a new hobby: beetle collecting. It seemed, yet again, that his father's worst fears were being realized. But Charles had by then become a promising student of natural history. He sufficiently impressed his botany instructor, John Steven Henslow, that Henslow recommended him for the position of captain's companion on a voyage to South America aboard the HMS *Beagle*, a ship surveying the coast of South America for the British Royal Navy. Against his better judgment, Robert let Charles go. On that voyage Darwin made observations that led, in 1859, to his publication of an extraordinary and world-changing book, *On the Origin of Species*.

Across the 19th century, it had become clear to scientists that the creatures populating the planet were markedly different from those that had been around in earlier epochs; the fossil record told them this. But what had produced the change? Darwin's thinking about this issue was shaped by the diversity of creatures he observed during the *Beagle's* voyage—and, in particular, the diversity of creatures he saw on the Galápagos Islands, off the coast of Ecuador. There he noticed, for example, that the local finches varied considerably in the sizes and shapes of their beaks.

In reflecting on the finches, Darwin began to develop the first of his great ideas: the descent of all life from a common origin. He hypothesized that all of the finch species on the islands were descendants of a single type of finch that had colonized the islands long ago. This led him to consider a broader notion—that *all life* on Earth had a shared origin, so that all creatures had descended from an ancient common ancestor. In this view, modern species had emerged—through some process of modification—from this shared ancestor. But how did this modification take place?

The answer to this question—the notion of evolution through natural selection—was Darwin's second great idea, but it didn't occur to him until years later, when he read the works of the English economist Thomas Malthus (1776–1834). Malthus noted that living things reproduce rapidly enough so that populations are always growing—and, crucially, growing more rapidly than the food supply is. As a result, shortages of resources are inevitable; the consequence is that some individuals will survive, but others will not. That, for Darwin, was the key.

Which individuals would do well in this competition for resources, and which would do poorly? Darwin realized that the answer was linked to his observations of how individuals in a species differed from each other. A finch with a wide bill might be better able to crack open seeds than its narrow-billed fellow, and so a wide-billed finch would have an advantage in the competition for food. This advantage wouldn't matter when food was plentiful, but it would be crucial when—as Malthus had noted—the shortage inevitably arrived. In that circumstance, the wide-billed finch would be more likely to survive and eventually to reproduce. Darwin also knew that offspring tend to

2.8 Charles Darwin (1809–1882)
Darwin's theory of evolution by natural selection has dramatically changed the way scientists think about life on Earth. Here Darwin is shown at about 30 years old, in a watercolor by George Richmond.

resemble their parents in many ways (although he did not know the mechanism of this transmission), and so the wide-billed finch was likely to have wide-billed progeny. A narrow-billed finch, on the other hand, might not survive long enough to reproduce; so obviously, it would not contribute any narrow-billed descendants to the next generation. The upshot of all this is that the next generation would contain more wide-billed birds, and fewer narrow-billed birds, than the generation before.

Of course, the same logic would also apply to other populations of organisms. For example, fish vary in their coloration, and those that are slightly darker in color might be better camouflaged against the river's bottom—and so they're more likely to escape predators. Again, this would help the darker-colored fish survive long enough to reproduce, so they could leave behind offspring that would inherit their coloration. In this way, there would be a greater number of dark-skinned fish, and fewer light-colored ones, in the next generation.

Darwin called this process **natural selection**, and he realized that the process, if repeated generation after generation, could produce large changes in a population. Darwin termed these changes *transmutation*, but they are now called *evolution*. Thus, if dark-colored fish are more likely to reproduce in this generation and the next, and the next after that, eventually many (and perhaps most) of the surviving fish will be the descendants of dark-colored ancestors and probably will be dark-colored themselves. In this way, a trait that renders some members of a population better adapted to survive and reproduce in their particular environment will become more and more common— leading, over the generations, to a change in the entire population.

In these examples, variations in a population of animals (bill width in the finch, or coloration of the fish) give some members a survival advantage that allows them to have more offspring than others do. But not all variations have this effect, and which variations are beneficial depends largely on the organism's environment. If, as we noted, food is plentiful, then it may not matter how wide the finch's bill is. Likewise, if there are few predators, the light-colored fish may fare as well as the dark ones. Even if predators are numerous, the dark-colored fish will benefit only if the river bottom is dark. If the river bottom is sandy, then the light-colored fish might be better camouflaged. Notice, then, that we cannot think of this selection process as favoring the "better" or "more advanced" organism. Instead, evolution favors the organism that is better adapted to survive and reproduce within the environment currently in place. If the environment changes (e.g., a sandy river bottom becomes muddy), then the pattern of selective advantages will change as well.

This last point is important enough to deserve special emphasis. In thinking about evolution, it's important to avoid the **naturalistic fallacy**—the idea that anything "natural" is "good"—or the (related) idea that more recently evolved traits are "better" than those that evolved earlier, so that natural selection "improves" or "advances" a species (Figure 2.9). These ideas are mistaken. As we've just discussed, natural selection depends only on whether an organism is well suited to its current environment. The mechanisms of evolution certainly have no way to peer into the future, to know which traits will serve the organism well in environments to come. Indeed, sometimes natural selection can favor traits that confer an advantage within one environment but later can *harm* the organism when the environment changes. (We'll consider several examples later in the chapter.)

We need to be clear, therefore, that the process of evolution has no foresight and has no value judgments attached to it. Evolution is a matter of survival and reproduction—and that is all. Even so, evolution is a process that powerfully and consistently shapes all life on earth.

natural selection The mechanism that drives biological evolution. It refers to the greater likelihood of successful reproduction for organisms whose attributes are advantageous in a given environment.

naturalistic fallacy The (mistaken) idea that anything "natural" must be "good."

2.9 Naturalistic fallacy

YOU ARE HERE

Genes and Evolution

Darwin's deeply important conception boils down to three principles. First, there must be variation among the individuals within a population. Second, certain of the variants must survive and reproduce at higher rates than others. Third, the traits associated with this superior survival and reproduction must be passed from parents to offspring.

There are, to be sure, many variations between individuals that do not meet these conditions. As we've discussed, not all variations contribute to survival; nor are all of the traits in parents passed on to their young. But when these three conditions are met, Darwin argued, the composition of a population will necessarily change from one generation to the next. And if this process continues for many generations, the population will evolve.

These basic ideas seem so straightforward that one of Darwin's colleagues, Thomas Henry Huxley, reported feeling "extremely stupid not to have thought of that" on his own (Darwin, 1887, p. 197). Perhaps Huxley should have been easier on himself, though, because Darwin needed to get past two substantial obstacles in his thinking: He didn't know why organisms within in a population differed from each other, and he also didn't know how traits could be transmitted from one generation to the next. Of course, he did know that both of these conditions were often met: Plant and animal breeders had been developing new varieties for years—selectively breeding the biggest, healthiest cows in the herd to produce the best possible offspring; carefully crossing different varieties of corn to obtain a new hybrid with certain desirable qualities. But what was the mechanism? Why were some cows bigger than others, and why were some traits—but by no means all—passed from one generation of corn plants to the next?

The answers to these questions, we now know, hinge in large part on the organism's genome. Of course, individuals differ in their phenotypes for many reasons (different experiences, different exposure to nutrients, and more), but another reason for these differences is variation in the genotype. And it's differences in genotype that are transmitted from one generation to the next.

In thinking about these issues, let's keep in mind that all the individuals in a species actually have enormously similar genomes. Indeed, this genome is a large part of what *defines* the species, and it's why members of the species all have roughly the same anatomy and physiology. But against this backdrop of uniformity, individuals do vary in their genotype; and we've already noted one of the reasons—the random element that's involved in sexual reproduction. Thanks to this random element, each individual inherits a new combination of alleles, inevitably introducing some variation into the population.

Another reason for variations in genotype involves the process of reproducing chromosomes. This process is *usually* accurate, but it isn't perfect, and sometimes **mutations** occur—errors in replicating the DNA—so that the chromosomes in the father's sperm or the mother's egg are not exact copies of the chromosomes governing the father's biology or the mother's. Mutations can happen randomly, and most mutations either have no effect or *harm* the organism. But some mutations do confer an advantage for survival and reproduction—and, in all cases, mutations contribute to the genetic diversity within a species, which in turn contributes to the phenotypic diversity that is the raw material for natural selection.

Clearly, then, our knowledge of genetics fills in some gaps in Darwin's account—helping us to understand both the variations within a population and how these variations can be transmitted to the next generation. This emphasis on genes also allows us to address a common misunderstanding of how evolution proceeds: Evolution is often described as "survival of the fittest," but this phrase is actually misleading because

mutations Errors in the replication of DNA.

2.10 The broken-wing display When a predator approaches the plover's nest, the mother flies a short distance away and drags a wing, as if she were injured. The predator is likely to turn away from the nest and pursue the (apparently vulnerable) mother. This behavior is easily understood in Darwinian terms—but only if we emphasize the survival of the mother's genes, and not the mother herself.

survival itself is not all that evolution is about. Personal survival does matter, of course, but only insofar as it enables the organism to reproduce and pass along its genes to the next generation.

To see the importance of this emphasis on genes, consider a behavior observed in many birds, such as the piping plover: When a predator approaches the plover's nest, the mother bird flies a short distance away from her young, lands, and hops around, dragging one wing in a way that suggests she's injured and unable to escape (Figure 2.10). The predator spots this (seemingly) easy target and turns away from the young, pursuing the apparently injured mother instead. In this way, the mother can lead the predator away from her chicks; then, once her brood is safe, she reveals that in fact she is perfectly healthy and flies swiftly away.

This behavior protects the bird's young but puts the mother plover at substantial risk. When feigning injury, she's highly vulnerable to the approaching predator; she would surely be safer if she immediately flew to safety. Still, the evolutionary basis for this behavior is easy to understand: The mother herself would survive if she immediately flew to safety, but in that case the predator would probably eat her chicks. As a result, the mother bird would have fewer offspring to whom she has passed her genes. Let's also assume that the plovers' genome helps to shape her maternal behavior—and, in particular, plays a role in determining whether the mother plover puts herself at risk to protect her brood, or abandons the nest to save her own skin. We can now see that if an individual plover happens to have genes favoring a self-protective response, she's more likely to survive, but less likely to contribute copies of those genes to future generations. As a result, any genes promoting self-protection would become less common in the population. Natural selection would therefore end up favoring the protective mother—or, more accurately, would favor the genes that help shape this protective behavior—and so this behavior would become the dominant pattern in the population.

A similar argument applies to cases in which an organism protects individuals that are not its offspring. For example, if a Belding's ground squirrel sees a predator, it gives a cry of alarm. The cry warns other ground squirrels so that they can scurry to safety. But, by sounding the alarm, the first ground squirrel gives away its location and so puts itself in danger. If we focus on individual survival, therefore, this behavior makes no evolutionary sense. Once again, though, we need to think in terms of the *genes'* survival, not the individual's. The other squirrels protected by the alarm call share many of the first ground squirrel's genes, and so by protecting these other individuals, the squirrel protects its genes—including the genes that promoted this helpful behavior. The genes that favor this behavior will then be more likely to be passed along to the next generation—and the genes, as always, are what evolution is about.

Evidence for Evolution by Natural Selection

Since Darwin's day, thousands of evolutionary biologists have contributed to the development of modern evolutionary theory. Yet, around the globe, many nonscientists have misgivings about evolution. According to one recent survey, only 40% of the people surveyed in the United States said it's true that "human beings, as we know them, developed from earlier species of animals." About a third of the people questioned flatly rejected this statement (J. Miller, Scott, & Okamoto, 2006; for a glimpse of the data in other countries, see Figure 2.11).

The situation is entirely different, however, within the scientific community: Virtually every modern scientist regards evolution as one of science's best-documented, most firmly established theories. Why are they so convinced? Scientists point to numerous lines of evidence: We know (as Darwin did) that organisms can be transformed by selective breeding; this is the way that botanists create new hybrid plants and farmers create new breeds of cow. We understand in impressive detail how genetic mutations arise, how genes are transmitted from generation to generation, and how genes influence an organism's traits. In addition, the fossil record provides ample confirmation of evolution's claims, with the bones of ancient species providing clear evidence for the various intermediate organisms that existed during the process in which one lineage evolved into another (Figure 2.12). Moreover, in many cases we can find anatomical leftovers in modern species that reveal the evolutionary past of the species—for example, the remnant hip and leg bones inside whales tell us that whales descended from mammals that lived on land, and the human coccyx strongly indicates that humans are descended from ancestors who had tails (Gingerich, Ul-Haq, Von Koenigswald, Sanders, Smith et al., 2009). We can also examine the molecular structure of the genome in various organisms; this examination confirms the pattern of relatedness among species and, indeed, lets us map out the likely "family tree" of modern species.

We can also watch the process of evolution unfolding in various populations. As one example, Lake Washington (just east of Seattle) was cloudy and green for many years, thanks to the exuberant growth of algae fed by treated sewage dumped into the water by surrounding cities. This situation had a significant effect on the threespine stickleback, a small fish living in the lake, because the murky water made it difficult for predators—mostly cutthroat trout—to locate (and eat) the sticklebacks (Kitano & Bolnick, 2008; also Hagen & Gilbertson, 1972; Wallace, Gilbert, & King, 2001). During the 1960s, the cities around the lake began to divert their sewage elsewhere, and by 1976 the water had cleared, putting the sticklebacks at much greater risk of being eaten.

This change in circumstances had a powerful impact on the sticklebacks. These fish vary in how much protective "body armor" they carry: Some individuals have strong, bony

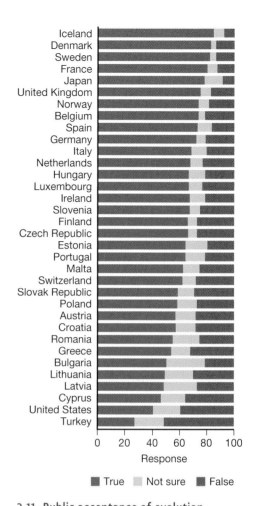

True ■ Not sure ■ False ■

2.11 Public acceptance of evolution Despite overwhelming evidence for the theory of evolution, many Americans remain skeptical about it. In a 2005 survey, only in Turkey did a larger group of people express reservations about the statement that "human beings, as we know them, developed from earlier species of animals." This statement—almost universally endorsed by scientists—was much more favorably received in most European countries and in Japan.

2.12 Fossilized remains supporting evolution The four-winged dinosaur (*Microraptor gui*) has flight feathers on its arms and its legs. This is compelling evidence that this dinosaur is one of the ancient ancestors of modern birds.

2.13 Natural selection in the modern world In the 1950s, the murky waters of Lake Washington hid the stickleback from predators' view. Now that the water has cleared, trout are more easily finding and eating the sticklebacks. The result has been a striking change in the number of sticklebacks with bony plates on their sides—plates that serve as armor, protecting the fish from the trout.

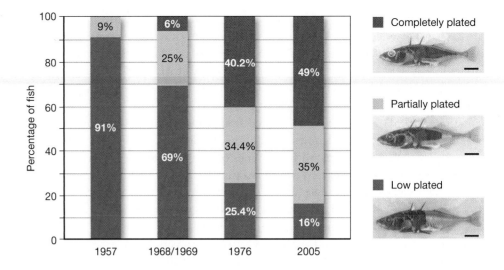

plates on their sides, and others have much lighter plates (Figure 2.13). In the mid-1950s, there was little predation (because the trout couldn't see their prey in the murky waters), with the result that the sticklebacks in Lake Washington needed little armor—and in fact most of them had only light armor. As the waters cleared, though, these unprotected fish became highly vulnerable to predators and fewer of them survived long enough to breed. In contrast, the few fish that were more heavily armored were much more likely to survive a predator's attack, and so they lived long enough to pass to their offspring the genes that had produced the heavy armor. This is why a 2005 survey showed that almost all of Lake Washington's sticklebacks were either heavily or moderately armored; in contrast, the lightly armored individuals—the clear majority 50 years ago—had become more rare.

The Unity of Life

As we have seen, Charles Darwin deserves credit for two great ideas. We've looked closely at his idea of natural selection, the process that changes the traits of a population over time and may eventually create entirely new species. His other idea concerns the *starting point* for this process—namely, that all modern organisms descended, with modifications over time, from a common ancestor. Darwin was correct about this point as well—and as we'll see, this idea has important implications for psychology.

Evidence in support of this shared ancestry comes from the many (and sometimes surprising) commonalities among species. For example, close examination of the genomes of birds and crocodiles tells us that they have an enormous amount in common—in fact, they're genetically more similar to each other than either of them is to any other animal group (Janke, Erpenbeck, Nilsson, & Arnason, 2001). Birds and crocodiles, therefore, are each other's closest living relative; and this helps us understand the various traits they share, such as building nests, laying hard-shelled eggs, and caring for their young. Similar commonalities confirm that the closest living relatives of the whales are the even-toed, hoofed mammals, including the hippos (Geisler & Theodor, 2009; Thewissen, Cooper, Clements, Bajpai, & Tiwari, 2009). Our own closest living relatives—a fact evident in shared anatomy, shared behaviors, and very similar genomes—are the common chimpanzee and the bonobo.

In fact, this sharing of attributes extends quite a long way—because ultimately, *all* of Earth's living things are derived from a common lineage. This extraordinary unity of life is evident in some remarkable similarities among our planet's creatures. Here's a demonstration: Crystal jellyfish have a gene enabling them to make a substance called green fluorescent protein, and this protein makes the jellyfish glow green in the blue light of the ocean. Genetic engineers recently took a copy of the jellyfish's gene and inserted it into the chromosomes of rhesus monkey egg cells (Yang et al., 2008). The scientists fertilized the egg cells in a dish and then implanted them in a surrogate mother monkey. The mother gave birth to baby monkeys that make green fluorescent protein—and so, under blue light, the monkeys emit a bright green glow (Figure 2.14).

Genes transferred between species can not only grant novel functions, they can also restore functions lost as a result of genetic defects. Fruit flies have a gene called *apterous* that plays a variety of crucial roles in the development of the adult fly. Flies that lack functional copies of this gene have, among other defects, no wings. However, when given the *human* version of the gene (called *hLhx2*), the flies develop normally (Rincón-Limas, Lu, Canal, Calleja, Rodríguez-Esteban, et al., 1999).

These results provide powerful evidence that diverse species are indeed descended from common ancestors. After all, the fact that a jellyfish gene works just fine inside the cells of a monkey indicates that monkeys and jellyfish are related. Likewise, the fact that a human gene can substitute for one in the fruit fly shows that humans and flies are kin.

The unity of life is essential to psychology. Because of our shared ancestors, we have much in common with other species; and this is why we can learn a great deal about *us* by studying *them*. Thus, we can gain an understanding of human memory by studying learning in sea snails; we can learn about the genetic roots of ADHD through studies that involve genetic engineering in mice; and we can develop new medications for mental illness by studying the effect of these pills on laboratory rats. All of these advances rest on the strong biological resemblance between humans and other animals, which is a result of our common ancestry.

2.14 The unity of life These baby monkeys make green fluorescent protein because they carry genetic instructions borrowed from a jellyfish. This result is an extraordinary confirmation that the biochemical mechanisms inside these animals' cells are quite similar.

THE GENETICS AND EVOLUTION OF BEHAVIOR

Darwin firmly believed that all of his claims about natural selection applied both to organisms' structural traits (like a finch's bill width, or a fish's coloration) and to its behavior traits (like being a protective parent or a skilled problem solver). Indeed, the evolutionary logic is the same whether we're considering an animal's anatomy or its behaviors, capacities, and preferences. For behaviors just as for physical traits, evolution requires the same three conditions: variation among individuals; a higher rate of reproductive success for individuals with some of the variations; and some means of passing the successful variation from one generation to the next. If this selection process continues generation after generation, eventually the advantageous traits or behaviors will characterize the entire species.

But *how* does evolution shape behaviors, or capacities, or preferences? We've suggested the answer in some of our earlier examples: Psychological traits, just like physical features, are part of an animal's *phenotype*. If this phenotype makes it more likely that the animal will survive and reproduce, then the animal's *genes* will be well represented in the next generation. And to the extent that an animal's behaviors, capacities, and preferences are shaped by those genes, then these traits also are likely to be well represented in the next generation.

2.15 Evolutionary influence on behavior
In some cases, evolution has guided organisms toward specific, well-defined behaviors—like the weaver bird's specific style of nest building.

niche construction The process in which organisms, through their own behaviors, alter the environment and create their own circumstances.

Of course, the genotype does not produce these traits directly. Instead, the genes (as always) guide the production of proteins, which in turn, lead to the construction of a nervous system with a specific design. It's then the nervous system, modulated by other signaling systems (e.g., hormones) and various environmental influences, that makes the behaviors (or capacities or preferences) more likely.

In fact, many behaviors in many organisms have been shaped in exactly this way—and this point leads us to another common misunderstanding about evolution: Some people have the idea that natural selection would lead to rigidly defined behaviors—favoring organisms that always produce the same (presumably adaptive) responses to a predator, or to a mate, or to their young. If we observe flexibility in a response, therefore, or if we see that a behavior is shaped by learning, we conclude that the behavior depends on the organism's experience, not evolution.

Once again, though, this view is mistaken. To be sure, evolution has in many cases guided an organism (human or otherwise) toward relatively well-defined behaviors, like a particular courtship dance or a specific style of nest building repeated season after season (Figure 2.15). Even in these cases, though, evolution has favored mechanisms that produce *flexibility* in how an animal acts.

To understand this point, bear in mind that virtually all species evolved in changing environments. In some cases, the organism encountered changes from one day to the next, so that the berry bush that was filled with fruit yesterday is empty today; the predator that lurked by the water hole just a day ago has now moved to other hunting grounds. In other cases, the changes were slower paced—climatic conditions might vary from one year to the next, and food supplies that were available in some seasons might disappear in others. In any of these settings, animals that always behaved in the same manner would fare poorly. As a result, natural selection would favor individuals that could *shift* their behavior in response to new circumstances and that could rapidly deploy new skills appropriate for an altered setting.

This need for flexibility in an animal's behavior is amplified by the process of **niche construction**—a process in which organisms, through their behaviors, alter their environments and thus create their own circumstances. In biology, a *niche* refers to all of the factors in an organism's environment that have the potential to affect its life. Animals can and do alter these factors; and by doing so, they alter the opportunities and challenges they face.

These considerations are especially important for humans, because our ancestors were quite skilled in niche construction—building new shelters, finding (or developing) new sources of food, and creating social alliances that favored individuals with communication skills. Because of changes like these, ancient humans would have had a substantial survival advantage if they were flexible in their behavior, responsive to new cues in the environment, and able to share information with others. Thus, natural selection would, in many cases, have favored *innovators, learners,* and probably *teachers* (Csibra & Gergely, 2009; Tomasello, 2000).

Evolution therefore favors flexibility and learning—in part because environments inevitably vary, and in part because organisms end up changing their environment and need to cope with those changes. But can we be more specific about the origins of particular human behaviors? As we'll see throughout this text, we can often draw important lessons from considerations of the proximate causes of a behavior, with an emphasis on genetics; just as often, we can draw insights by asking about ultimate causes, with an emphasis on evolution. Let's develop these points by considering three extended examples.

The first case we'll consider involves the *expression of emotions*—and smiles in particular. Here we'll see what can be learned by comparisons across cultures and species. The second case involves *intelligence* and illustrates how research can illuminate the proximate causes of a complex capacity. Our third case involves a topic that's central to natural selection—sexual reproduction. How do we choose our partners? Why do we choose to be loyal to our partner (or not)? Research in the last few decades has made it clear that an evolutionary perspective on these questions can be enormously useful.

The Biological Roots of Smiling

All animals interact with other members of their species, whether as mates, parents, offspring, or competitors. And these interactions, in turn, usually depend on some kind of communication as each animal lets the other know about its status and intentions. Sometimes, the style of communications is **species specific**—pertaining to just one species—but often the communication involves signals shared by many types of animals. Thus, many mammals use the same "surrender" display to end a fight: They lie on their backs, exposing their bellies and their throats, as a way of communicating (roughly) "I know I've lost the fight; I'm giving in, and making myself completely vulnerable to you. Let's not fight any more."

Humans, too, have various ways of communicating their status and intentions. In many circumstances, of course, we use language—and so we can, with enormous precision, convey our message to a conversational partner. We also communicate a great deal by our body position—how close we stand to another person, how we hold our arms, how we orient our bodies, and so on. Our faces convey still more information—including the various facial displays that express emotion.

THE ORIGINS OF SMILING

Virtually all babies start smiling at a very young age. The first smiles are detectable in infants just 1 month old; smiles directed toward other people are evident a month or so later. One might think that babies *learn* to smile by observing others and imitating the facial expressions they see, but evidence argues against this proposal. For example, babies who are born blind start smiling at the same age as sighted babies, and—just like sighted babies—they're most likely to smile when interacting with others and when they're comfortable and well fed. Likewise, one study compared the facial expressions of three groups of athletes receiving their award medals at the 2004 Paralympic Games (Matsumoto & Willingham, 2009). One group had been blind since birth; a second group had some years of visual experience but was now fully blind; a third group had normal sight. The study showed essentially no difference among these groups in their facial expressions.

Apparently, then, the behavior of *smiling* is something that humans do without a history of observational learning. On this basis, we might expect to find smiles in all humans in all cultures—and we do. In other words, the behavior of smiling is **species general**—observable in virtually all members of our species. In one study (that we'll discuss in more detail in Chapter 12), American actors were photographed while conveying emotions such as happiness, sadness, anger, and fear. These photos were then shown to members of an isolated tribe in New Guinea, and individuals there were asked to pick the emotion label that matched each photograph. Then the procedure was reversed: The New Guinea tribesmen were asked to portray the facial expression appropriate to specific situations, such as happiness at the return of a friend or anger at the start of a fight. Photographs of their performances were shown to American college students, who were asked to judge which situation the tribesmen had been trying to convey in each photo (Ekman & Friesen, 1975).

Performance in these tasks was quite good—the New Guinea tribesmen were generally able to recognize the Americans' expressions, and vice versa. Importantly,

species specific Pertaining to just one species.

species general Pertaining to all organisms in a species.

performance varied from one emotion to the next, with (for example) disgust and fear more difficult to recognize than sadness. The expression producing the most accurate identification, though, was happiness. Smiles are apparently a universal human signal (Ekman, 1994; Izard, 1994).

SMILES IN OTHER SPECIES

The behavior of smiling is not just shared across cultures; it is also shared across *species*. In other words, we find similar emotional expressions in animals with genomes similar to ours. Thus, smiling is *species general* (found in the entire species), but it is not *species specific* (found only in one species).

Darwin himself was especially interested in this point and drew evidence from several sources, including his own observations of animals at the London Zoo. He eventually published his findings in a book entitled *The Expression of the Emotions in Man and Animals* (Darwin, 1872). Darwin's observations made it clear to him that there were different types of smiles—a point that has been well confirmed in more recent research. The smiles can be differentiated in terms of the situations that elicit them; they can also be differentiated by their exact appearance. And, remarkably, the various types of smiles can be identified as readily in other species as they can in humans.

One type of smile seems straightforwardly *expressive* of your inner state, and it's produced when you feel happy. This smile will be produced even if no other people are around, and it involves both a change in mouth shape (the corners of the lips are pulled upward) and a shift in the muscles of the upper face, surrounding the eyes. The latter shift creates the pattern often called *crow's feet*—lines that radiate outward from the eyes (Figure 2.16).

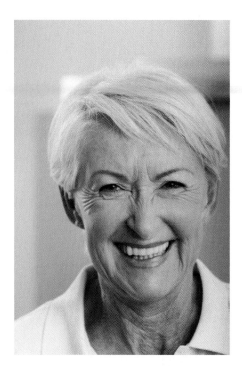

2.16 The expressive smile The expressive smile involves both changes in mouth shape and a shift in the muscles surrounding the eyes. The shift creates the pattern known as "crows' feet," radiating outward from the eyes.

The expressive smile obviously occurs in humans when events or stimuli please us, or when we hear a good joke. A similar expression occurs in young monkeys in the midst of play; many observers interpret it as a signal between monkeys that their pushing and tumbling is playful rather than aggressive. Smiles in humans also promote cooperation: A smile on someone's face often signals their intention to cooperate and, at the same time, the sight of a smile tends to evoke positive feelings in the perceiver, making cooperation more likely.

A different sort of smile seems more *polite* in nature, and it's rarely produced without an audience. In this smile, one pulls the corners of one's lips upward but with little movement of the eyes. This sort of smile seems to function as a greeting and also as a means of defusing situations that otherwise might be tense or embarrassing (Goldenthal, Johnston, & Kraut, 1981). It's also a smile people use when they wish to simulate happiness (e.g., when pretending to have fun at a dreadful party, or when trying to persuade someone they're amusing when they are actually boring).

This polite smile can also be found in nonhuman primates, where it generally takes a form of drawing back the lips and revealing the teeth, but keeping the teeth plainly closed. In monkeys, this smile may be a gesture of submission at the end of a conflict, or it may be intended to *avoid* a conflict. It's as if one monkey is saying to another, "Look—my teeth are closed; I'm obviously not preparing to bite you or fight you. So be good to me" (Figure 2.17).

2.17 The polite smile This form of smile involves lips drawn back, revealing the teeth—but with the teeth plainly closed. This smile may be a gesture of submission or a means of avoiding conflict.

What does all of this imply about the *origins* of smiling? The fact that smiles emerge with no history of learning (e.g., in individuals blind since birth) tells us that this behavior is strongly shaped by inborn (genetic) factors. This claim is certainly consistent with the universality of smiling (across cultures and across species), which suggests an ancient origin for this behavior: It's likely that the smiles evident in American college students, in New Guinea tribesmen, or in playful monkeys were shaped by natural selection long ago, in the ancestors shared by all of these modern primates. Moreover, the obvious function of smiles in modern creatures supplies an important clue as to *why* the behavior of smiling served our ancestors well—by providing a signal about emotions and intentions that facilitated social interactions. These observations in turn provide a clear indication of why this behavior was promoted and preserved by natural selection. All of these are key points whenever we try to establish—whether we're focusing on smiles or any other trait—how and why the trait evolved.

The Genetics of Intelligence

In our discussion of smiles, we drew on several types of evidence: observations of individuals in special circumstances (e.g., people blind since birth) as well as comparisons across cultures and across species. These various forms of evidence all point toward the conclusion that smiles have ancient evolutionary roots. But there is another source of information that's just as important for inquiries into the biological roots of a behavior or capacity: a comparison among family members. This point is well illustrated by the study of the ways in which humans differ in their levels of intelligence.

Broadly put, *intelligence* refers to the capacity that allows people to acquire new knowledge and use it to draw conclusions, solve problems, and adapt to new circumstances. Researchers have devised various intelligence tests and found that people vary considerably in how much of this capacity they have. We need to acknowledge the considerable debate about these tests (e.g., whether they are fair to all groups) and about the definition itself (e.g., whether there are intellectual skills left out of the definition, and thus left out of the tests). Nonetheless, there are many indications that the tests, refined over the last century, are valid. For example, the measurements line up well with our commonsense notions of intelligence (and so people you think of as "smart" are likely to do well on the measurements). The measurements also allow us to predict how well people will perform in a range of activities that seem in obvious ways to require intelligence.

We'll have more to say about these issues in Chapter 11, but in the meantime we can ask: Where do these measured differences come from? As is usually the case, the answer has several parts. For a start, a number of environmental variables influence intelligence, and so (for example) many factors associated with poverty impede intellectual growth and thus undermine a person's intellectual potential. Conversely, lifting someone out of poverty and into a healthier, more enriched environment can increase intelligence. Moreover (and encouragingly!), spending time in *school* seems to increase intelligence. But, in addition, the evidence is clear that these environmental factors interact with genetic factors that also matter for intelligence. Let's look at the evidence.

COMPARISONS AMONG RELATIVES

We mentioned earlier that all members of a species resemble each other genetically, and this point applies to humans just as it applies to any other creatures; this is why we all have bodies of a distinctly human shape, internal organs that are unmistakably human, and so on. But, even though we have the same human genome, each of us has our own pattern of alleles for these genes, half inherited from our mother and half from our father. Because of this legacy, there's a 50% overlap between each child's genetic pattern and the pattern of each parent. By similar logic, there's also 50% overlap, on average, between each child's pattern and the pattern of his or her biological siblings.

What about twins? Here it's crucial to distinguish two types of twins: Typically, a woman releases one egg per month, and it's either fertilized or not. Occasionally, the woman releases *two* eggs in the same month, and each egg may be fertilized by one of

2.18 Monozygotic and dizygotic twins

Sometimes a woman releases two eggs in the same month, and both are fertilized. The result is dizygotic twins—conceived at the same time, born on the same day, but with only 50% overlap in their genotypes (the same overlap as for ordinary siblings). Sometimes a woman releases a single egg that is fertilized and then splits into two. This sequence results in monozygotic (identical) twins with 100% overlap in their genotypes.

Two sperm fertilize two eggs… which become two zygotes.

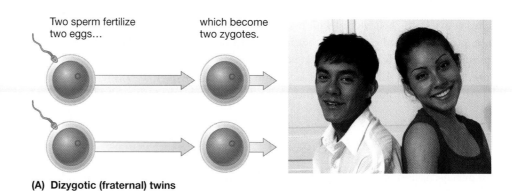

(A) Dizygotic (fraternal) twins

One sperm fertilizes one egg… and the zygote splits in two.

(B) Monozygotic (identical) twins

dizygotic (DZ) Twins that develop from two different eggs that are simultaneously fertilized by two sperm. Like ordinary siblings, they share 50% of their genes.

monozygotic (MZ) Twins that develop from a single fertilized egg that then splits in half. These twins are genetically identical.

the father's sperm. This sequence of events results in **dizygotic** twins (sometimes called DZ or fraternal twins): siblings who are conceived at the same time, develop in the uterus together, and are born on the same day. But, just like any other siblings, DZ twins grow from distinct eggs and distinct sperm cells, and so the genetic relatedness between them is the same as it is for other siblings—a 50% overlap in the genome (Figure 2.18).

In other cases, the mother releases just one egg and it is fertilized by one sperm; but then the egg splits into two, so that a pair of fetuses develop from the same (fertilized) egg. This results in **monozygotic** (MZ or identical) twins. Since both MZ twins developed from the same egg and the same sperm, they have a 100% overlap in their genomes.

We can attempt to tease out the influence of genes on intelligence by comparing the similarities between DZ twins as opposed to MZ twins in intelligence tests. If genes influence test scores, then the resemblance within monozygotic twin pairs (with 100% overlap between the patterns of their alleles) should be stronger than the resemblance within dizygotic twin pairs (50% overlap). For that matter, the resemblance within dizygotic pairs should be greater than the resemblance between pairs of randomly chosen (not related) individuals (who have 0% overlap in the pattern of their alleles). All of these predictions are correct: Monozygotic twins resemble each other closely in their intelligence levels, and so the correlation between their intelligence scores is an impressively high .86 (again, see Chapter 11 for more on these data). If we examine pairs of dizygotic twins, we still find resemblance, but less so than with monozygotic twins; and the correlation between their scores is roughly .60. And, if we choose individuals at random (no overlap in genome), we find little resemblance between their scores—often a correlation of zero. (Figure 2.19).

2.19 Genetic relatedness and intelligence Monozygotic twins tend to resemble each other in intelligence, whether the twins are raised together or not; dizygotic twins show less resemblance, although they resemble each other more than do randomly selected individuals.

But there's a complication in these data: Monozygotic twins grow up in virtually identical environments. (After all, people often can't tell the twins apart, and so of course end up treating them in the same way!) Dizygotic twins are likely to be treated a bit differently from each other, but they usually grow up in the same home with the same parents, the same resources, and the same schooling. If we examine random individuals, in contrast, they are sure to have grown up in different environments—and so they experienced different levels of stimulation, different types of education, different levels of encouragement by their parents, and more. Thus, perhaps the pattern in intelligence scores—great resemblance among monozygotic twins, less among dizygotic twins, less among random individuals—can be explained without reference to genetics. Perhaps the data are telling us instead that people who grow up in *similar environments* tend to end up with similar levels of intelligence.

Researchers have several ways of addressing this issue, including the study of children who have been adopted and raised by adults who are not their biological forebears. This situation allows us to examine the resemblance within pairs of identical twins who were adopted by different families and so raised in different households. Under these conditions, we can study the effect of the twins' shared genetic pattern when they're exposed to different environmental influences. Even in this situation, the resemblance between the monozygotic twins is quite strong (a correlation of .75; again, for all of these data, see Chapter 11).

In the same spirit, we can compare the intelligence scores of adopted children to the scores of the adults who *raised* them, and we can also compare these scores to those of the children's biological parents. The data show a much stronger resemblance between each child and his or her biological parents than between the child and the adopted parents—another way of showing the power of genetic factors.

HERITABILITY

We noted earlier that various environmental factors influence intelligence. Some factors (e.g., poverty) undermine intelligence, and other factors (e.g., schooling) lift it. But the comparisons among relatives make it clear that intelligence is also shaped by each person's genotype; we see this in the fact that individuals who resemble each other genetically also resemble each other in intelligence scores—even if they live in different settings.

heritability ratio (H) A measure that describes, for a given population in a given environment, what proportion of the variance of a trait is due to genetic differences.

Is there some way to combine these findings to ask, in essence, *to what extent* genetic factors are responsible for the differences between individuals, as opposed to the effect of environmental influences? Researchers usually address this question by asking about *variance*, a statistic that quantifies variation. More specifically, researchers compute a **heritability ratio**—a statistic summarizing how much of the variance in a population can be attributed to genetic differences among individuals. To compute this ratio, researchers begin by asking, for a particular trait and a particular population: *How much phenotypic variance is there in this group?* They then ask: *How much of that phenotypic variance is caused by differences in the genome?* These two numbers are then combined in a ratio:

$$\text{Heritability} = \frac{\text{Genetic variance}}{\text{Total phenotypic variance}}$$

This ratio can take a value between 0 and 1, where 0 indicates that *none* of the phenotypic variability is attributable to the genome, and 1 indicates that *all* of the phenotypic variability is attributable to the genome.

Let's be very clear that a heritability estimate tells us only about the causes of variation within the population studied, and it applies only to the particular environment in which the population was studied. Indeed, this point is built into the measurement. We start by asking: How much do the individuals' phenotypes vary *in the group that we're examining, in their current environment?* Then we ask: *How much of this variability can be attributed to genetic factors?* Unmistakably, therefore, the measurement is defined from the start for a specific group in a specific environment. The measurement will likely change if we consider a different group (or the same group in a different environment).

It's also important to remember that heritability estimates tell us nothing about the genetic influence on an *individual's* traits. As we've discussed, within each individual, the effects of genes and environment are inseparable. A heritability ratio is a description of a *group*—and it tells us what proportion of the total variation within that group is attributable to genetic differences between the group's members.

Researchers have given various estimates for the heritability of intelligence; in one study (McClearn, Johansson, Gerg, Pedersen, Ahem et al., 1997), the estimates ranged from .29 to .75, suggesting that 29% to 75% of the differences between individuals' levels of intelligence are due to genetic differences. Within this range, though, the most commonly mentioned heritability for intelligence is .60 or about 60%.

The wide range of estimates for the heritability of intelligence provides a useful reminder that heritability depends on the group and the environment being considered. To see how important this is, consider a study that examined intelligence scores in two groups of people: a group of middle-class individuals and a group of people with low socioeconomic status (SES) (Turkheimer, Haley, Waldron, D'Onofrio, & Gottesman, 2003). For the middle-class group, the study estimated the heritability of intelligence to be roughly 70%. For the low-SES group, in contrast, the estimated heritability was close to *zero*.

Why should this be? One interpretation is that the human genome provides a *potential* for developing intellectual skills, but this potential will emerge only if the person receives adequate nourishment, decent health care, and appropriate intellectual stimulation. Without these ingredients, that person's potential will never be realized—and so the influence of the genes (which define the potential at the outset) will never become visible. This may be why, in a low-SES environment, the genes (setting the potential) have a much weaker effect on intelligence.

As a different example, consider the effects of *age*. One might expect that the heritability of intellectual skill would be higher in young children than in older individuals because, as time goes by, the person is exposed to more and more environmental influences that can potentially offset or eclipse the influence of genetic factors. In truth, though, the opposite is the case; the heritability of many psychological traits—including intelligence, but also including various measures of personality—tends to *increase* with age (Bergen, Gardner, & Kendler, 2007). One likely explanation is that individuals with different genotypes choose different life experiences; in particular, they may seek out experiences that *amplify* whatever genetic differences they started with. As a result, those genetic differences grow more visible as the years go by (Kendler & Baker, 2007).

THE EVOLUTION OF INTELLIGENCE

We can draw many lessons from our discussion of intelligence so far. First, we've seen the power of some research tools—such as the comparison of monozygotic and dizygotic twins, and the need to examine both the effects of shared genome and those of shared experience. Second, we've considered an important form of measurement—the heritability ratio—but also discussed the limitations of that measurement. Third, we've once again seen the importance of the interaction between genes and environment (this was crucial for the notion, just mentioned, that experience can *amplify* genetically rooted traits). And, fourth, we've encountered new reminders of the need to distinguish genotype and phenotype (e.g., the genotype seems to have little impact on the phenotypic intelligence of low-SES individuals).

All of these issues speak to the *proximate* cause of intelligence. What about the ultimate cause? What can we say about the broad evolution of intelligence? Claims about ultimate cause focus on the *function* of a trait, asking how the trait might have promoted the survival and reproductive success of our ancient ancestors. Sometimes, we can address this issue by considering the function of the trait in the current environment—how does the trait help us *now*? What we need to work toward, however, is an account of the trait's function in the **environment of evolutionary adaptiveness (EEA)**, the environment that was in place when the trait was evolving. This earlier environment is a key consideration because—as mentioned earlier—natural selection has no way to peer into the future. The process depends only on whether an organism's traits help it to survive and reproduce in its current environment.

Sometimes the function of a trait is obvious; sharp claws and camouflage are fairly easy to understand. But often careful experiments are needed to discern why a particular trait or behavior is in place. To illustrate this point, let's step briefly away from the topic of intelligence and consider the study described in Figure 2.20. Researchers wanted to find out why burrowing owls engage in the puzzling (and somewhat bizarre) behavior of collecting animal dung and spreading it around the entrances to their burrows. One possible explanation is that the stench of the dung around a burrow might repel predators and thereby protect the eggs and chicks inside. Owls that festoon their burrows with dung would thus see more of their chicks survive than would owls that prefer a clean front porch. A second hypothesis is that the owls use the dung as bait to attract the dung beetles that they eat, and so the owls can feed themselves while continuing to guard their nests. When the researchers tested both claims, they found strong evidence that owls collect dung because it attracts food. This example shows that we can often test hypotheses about a behavior by examining the behavior's contemporary function, taking care to rule out alternative explanations.

environment of evolutionary adaptiveness (EEA) The environment that was in place when a trait was evolving.

2.20 SCIENTIFIC METHOD: Why do burrowing owls spread dung around the entrances to their nests?

Method

1. Researchers removed dung from around the owls' nests.

2. They placed cow pies around half the burrows (group A), but not the other half (group B).

3. They analyzed the pellets of indigestible remains that the owls regurgitated after eating to monitor the owls' diet.

4. Then they reversed conditions by removing dung from group A's burrows and placing dung around group B's burrows.

5. Again, they monitored what the owls ate.

Results: Owls with cow pies around their burrows ate ten times as many dung beetles as when their burrows were bare.

CONCLUSION: The dung owls place around their nests attracts beetles, which the owls eat.

SOURCE STUDY: Levey, Duncan, & Levins, 2004

Let's now return to the topic of intelligence, and ask: Why did humans evolve to be so smart? We've already mentioned that our ancient ancestors would have benefited from flexibility in their behavior and from being able to solve problems, detect patterns, and draw conclusions. It seems likely that these skills would have led to a reproductive advantage—and, if so, natural selection would have favored individuals with these skills. The result, over many generations, would be that levels of these skills would have increased in the population at large.

But why do individuals *differ* in their level of intelligence? What's the ultimate cause of the *differences* in intelligence from one person to the next? The answer, in brief, is that we do not know, and, in thinking about this issue, it's important to keep in mind that some of an organism's traits—including traits significantly influenced by the genome—may not be a product of natural selection.

To make this point clear, we need to bear in mind that some traits improve an organism's chances of surviving and reproducing; other traits undermine the organism's chances; and still other traits *don't matter for survival.* Evolution, of course, will work to promote the first type of (helpful) traits, and will work to eliminate the second (harmful) type. But the forces of natural selection will have no impact on the third type of traits, and so these traits will simply remain in place, unaffected by evolution.

As one example, consider the fact that people differ in whether their earlobes are detached from their heads or not (Figure 2.21). This variation is clearly rooted in the genes, but it seems highly unlikely that this trait had any impact on our ancestors' chances of surviving and reproducing. As a result, evolution favored neither attached earlobes nor loose ones, and so both genotypes remained in place for our species—commonly occurring variations on the human genome.

2.21 Not all heritable traits have functions Some people have earlobes that dangle off the bottom of their external ears; some people have earlobes that do not dangle, but are attached to the upper neck. This trait is highly heritable; in fact, it's almost entirely determined by a single gene. But the trait has no apparent function, and thus serves as a reminder that some phenotypic differences are merely the results of random variation in the human genome.

Of course, there are many differences between ear lobe shape and intelligence. Among other points, earlobe shape is governed almost entirely by genetic factors; intelligence, in contrast, depends—as we have seen—on a rich interaction between genetics and a person's circumstances. Even so, the two cases may be alike in one crucial regard: Our ancient ancestors needed to be smart enough to handle life's challenges, and so evolution did favor individuals who had some intelligence. However, in the environment of evolutionary adaptiveness, there may have been no payoff to being "somewhat smarter than average," and no disadvantage to being "slightly less smart than average." Hence these differences would have been irrelevant to natural selection, with the result that person-to-person differences in intelligence may (just like the differences in earlobe shape) simply be a consequence of the ordinary random variation in the human genome.

The Evolution of Mating Patterns

In the case of intelligence, our main emphasis was on proximate causes and, in particular, the relatively high heritability of intelligence in many circumstances. In other cases, we know much less about proximate causes but more about *ultimate* causes—the function of a behavior and the reasons it evolved. Some of the clearest examples in this latter category concern an important topic for natural section—selecting and attracting a mate.

MATING SYSTEMS

In many species, the partners remain together after mating for a breeding season or even longer. In some species, the resulting relationship is **monogamy**—a reproductive partnership between one male and one female. In other species, the arrangement involves **polygamy;** that is, several members of one sex mating with one individual of the other. This arrangement can involve either *polygyny,* several females mating with one male, or *polyandry,* several males mating with one female.

What accounts for these different mating systems? A clue comes from a difference in the patterns found in mammals and in birds. Some 90% of birds form enduring social bonds with just a single mate. In contrast, more than 90% of mammals are polygamous: one male

monogamy A mating pattern in which one male and one female form an enduring reproductive partnership.

polygamy Any mating system in which a member of one sex mates with several members of the opposite sex.

mates with a number of females, or (in some species) one female mates with several males. These observations can easily be understood in terms of ultimate (i.e., evolutionary) causes, which hinge on what an organism can do to maximize its reproductive success.

Let's start with the problem faced by birds. In many species, successful incubation of the eggs requires both parents—one to sit on the eggs and keep them warm, and the other to forage for food to nourish the bird that's sitting. Then, after the hatching, finding food for a nestful of hungry chicks may still require the full-time efforts of both birds. Under these circumstances, monogamy makes reproductive sense for both the male and female. Each parent needs its partner's continuing help; otherwise, no chicks—and so none of their genes—will survive.

The situation is quite different for most mammals. Here there's no issue of tending the nest, because there is no nest. Instead, the fetus grows within the mother's uterus, allowing her to continue foraging for food during the offspring's gestation. Then, after birth, only the mother can secrete the milk needed to feed the young. Thus, strictly in terms of physical needs, the father is unnecessary after conception. The young can often survive under the mother's care alone, and so the male's genes will be carried into the next generation whether he's in attendance or not.

Let's also bear in mind that the more offspring a creature has that survive to maturity and reproduce, the better represented its genes will be in the next generation. By this logic, "success" in an evolutionary context often means having as many surviving offspring as possible. Therefore, to maximize his reproductive success, the male mammal should mate with one female and move swiftly to the next, operating on the idea that the more females he mates with, the more children he's likely to father. There's no need to stick around after mating, to care for his offspring, because the young will probably survive without him.

Females need a different approach to mating to make sure their genes are transmitted into the next generation. They don't have the option of having dozens of offspring, because they need to invest considerable time and resources carrying and then nursing each of their progeny. As a result, females maximize their reproductive success by mating just a few times during their lives—but ensuring the health and well-being of each of their young. From an evolutionary perspective, this is a key reason females usually prefer fewer partners than males do.

This logic allows us to explain the mating patterns of walruses, bison, wolves, and most other mammals—in each case, the males choose to mate with multiple females, while females prefer few partners, and perhaps just one. Does the same logic apply to humans? If it does, then humans should also have a tendency toward polygyny—and they do. One survey examined 185 different cultures worldwide. Only 16% of these required monogamous marital arrangements (for the classic data, see Ford & Beach, 1951). The vast majority of traditional, unindustrialized cultures allow (or even encourage) polygyny.

It does seem plausible, then, that evolutionary pressures have selected for the sexes' different attitudes toward mating. Perhaps the difference between the sexes is then reinforced by learning, and also shaped by cultural norms. After all, young boys in many cultures are taught that sexual conquests prove their "manliness," while girls are taught to value home, family, and a dependable partner. This, too, might explain why men end up preferring more partners than women do.

Thus, we might have an evolved tendency supported by learning—so that each mechanism reinforces the other. In addition, we need to ask why the cultural pattern takes the form that it does: Why do cultures convey certain expectations to boys and different expectations to girls? Our explanation will likely draw us once again to considerations of natural selection. Clearly, the evolutionary account—describing the ultimate cause of these mating preferences—is likely to be a key part of how we think about this comparison between the sexes.

WHICH MATE DOES THE CHOOSING?

The process of natural selection has other implications for mating. For example, in most species of mammals, it's usually the female who makes the final choice of whether to mate or not. The biological reasons for this pattern are straightforward: Reproduction puts a huge burden on a mammalian female—something that we can measure either in terms of the energy cost of carrying and then nursing her offspring or in terms of sheer amount of time she must invest in her young. For a doe's offspring to survive, for example, she has to devote an entire breeding season to carrying the young and then nursing them. As a result, she can have only one or two fawns per year—and so she has only one or two chances each year to transmit her genes to the next generation (Figure 2.22).

2.22 **The cost of reproduction** For mammalian females, reproduction has serious costs. A doe must devote an entire breeding season to carrying the young and then nursing them, or the offspring will not survive.

On this basis, evolution would have favored females who were quite careful in their choice of reproductive partners. For them, reproduction is a serious business with heavy biological costs; they need to get it right and choose a mate who will be the best father possible—one who will contribute healthy genes and provide resources and support, thus making it much more likely that the young will survive.

What about the male's point of view? In most species, he needs only a few minutes for mating with the female and must commit just a few easily replaced sperm. Then he can unconcernedly go about his business, perhaps to impregnate the next female a short time later. For males, reproduction is not costly—and so it matters less whether they choose their partners carefully. Indeed, if they want to maximize their *number* of partners, males cannot be too selective.

This line of thinking suggests that natural selection would have favored females who were extremely careful about their mate choices and males who were not. And this is the pattern of the data—because, as we've said, in many species it's the female who chooses whether to mate or not. As it turns out, there are exceptions to this broader pattern—but these too can be understood in evolutionary terms. For example, consider the sea horse, whose young are carried in a brood pouch by the male. Since the male makes the greater reproductive investment, he correspondingly exhibits greater sexual discrimination than the female. The same story applies to phalaropes—arctic seabirds whose eggs are hatched, and whose chicks are fed, by the *males*. For these birds, a greater part of the biological burden falls on the male. We should expect males to show a corresponding increase in sexual choosiness—and that's just what happens. Among the phalaropes, the female does the wooing and the male does the choosing (G. Williams, 1966).

2.23 **Males, females, and courtship** In most species, it's the female who decides whether to mate or not, causing the male to do some self-promotion.

A related evolutionary argument applies to the difference between males' and females' roles in *courtship*. If it's the females who do the choosing, then the burden falls on the males to attract and persuade their potential partners. This explains why, in many species, the male is brightly colored while the female's fur or plumage is relatively drab; similarly, in many animals the male has conspicuous anatomic features (such as striking antlers or an extraordinary tail) that the female lacks. Since the female makes the decision, the male needs to do some self-promotion (Figure 2.23).

Females take notice of these various displays and structures because they show off the males' size, health, and strength. In fact, many studies confirm that the males' displays really do persuade females. For example, in one species of widow birds, the males have tail feathers that are up to 20 inches long. To study the importance of this trait, an unsympathetic investigator cut the tails on some males and placed feather extensions on others. After a suitable period, the investigator counted the number of nests in each bird's territory. The males whose tails were cosmetically extended had more nests than did the unaltered males, who in turn had more nests than their unfortunate fellows whose tails had been shortened (Andersson, 1982). It does pay to advertise.

HUMAN MATE CHOICE

In our species, both males and females are selective in choosing their sexual partners, and mating happens only when both partners consent. However, the two sexes differ in *how* they make their choices. Data indicate that while both sexes value physical appearance, on average, men care more than women do about their partner's attractiveness. Conversely, women typically care more than men do about their partner's social status—women prefer higher-status males. Men also tend to prefer women younger than themselves, while women tend to prefer men who are slightly older. The data also indicate that these male–female differences are found throughout the world in countries as diverse as China, India, France, Nigeria, and Iran (Figure 2.24; D. Buss, 1989, 1992; D. Buss & Barnes, 1986). Quite interestingly, though, the two sexes agree on one point: Across cultures, both men and women value kindness and intelligence in their prospective mates (D. Buss, 1992).

According to David Buss, the investigator who uncovered many of these results, the best explanation is evolutionary—hinging, once again, on the ultimate causes of these behaviors. Specifically, if our male ancestors preferred attractive women, Buss argues that this preference would have increased their reproductive success because attractive women are likely to be healthy and fertile. As a result, natural selection would have favored males with this preference, and so the preference would have become widespread among the males of our species. Likewise, the younger a woman is, the more reproductive years she's likely to have ahead of her. A male who selects a younger partner is therefore likely to end up with more offspring. Again, this preference would increase the male's reproductive success—and so the preference would have been favored by natural selection and thus would become more common for the species.

The female's preferences are also easy to understand from this perspective. Because of her high investment in each child, the female's best bet is—as we've said—to have just a few offspring and to do all she can to ensure each child's survival. Having a healthy mate would be helpful on this score—so women too should seek out attractive partners, based on the idea that attractiveness is often an indicator of health. Crucially, though, women should also prefer higher-status mates, based on the expectation that these mates will be more likely to provide the food and other resources the women's children will need. Thus, there's a reproductive advantage associated with a preference for such a male, so that over time, genes promoting this preference would become increasingly common among females in the species (Bjorklund & Shackelford, 1999; D. Buss, 1992).

There are, to be sure, other influences on sexual behavior and mate choice, and we'll return to this topic in Chapter 12. Still, across a wide range of cultures, each of the sexes shows great consistency in the attributes they seek in a mate—exactly as predicted by an evolutionary perspective.

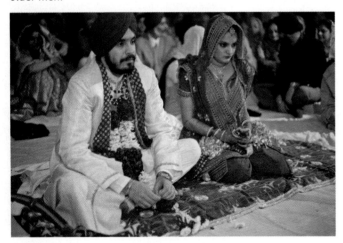

2.24 Male preference for younger women In a wide range of cultures, men prefer partners who are younger than they are; women prefer high-status, slightly older men.

JEALOUSY

We've discussed several intriguing claims about how natural selection has shaped human mating, but we should note that these claims have been controversial. When Richard Alexander (in 1974) and Edward O. Wilson (in 1975) began applying evolutionary logic to human behavior, their work—then called *sociobiology*—attracted both enthusiastic adherents and vehement critics. The debate has continued regarding more recent work within a perspective called *evolutionary psychology*, which has impassioned advocates (D. Buss, 2009; Pinker, 2003; Tooby & Cosmides, 1990) as well as harsh critics (e.g., Buller, 2005; for a glimpse of the debate between these views, see D. Buss & Haselton, 2005; Cosmides, Tooby, Fiddick, & Bryant, 2005; Daly & Wilson, 2005; Delton, Robertson, & Kenrick, 2006).

Let's be careful, however, not to overstate the disagreements. In particular, we need to avoid the trap of "either-or" thinking—explaining a behavior either in terms of evolution (ignoring cultural influences) or in terms of culture (ignoring evolution). Instead, we need to remember always that human behaviors are influenced *both* by factors rooted in our genes (and so shaped by evolution) and by factors rooted in our experience (and so shaped both by culture and by our individual circumstances). Moreover, these two broad categories of influence are—as we've repeatedly said—interdependent: Gene expression is influenced by our environment and experience, and the impact of experience is dependent on the genetically shaped sense organs that let us perceive the experience and on the genetically shaped brains that let us understand and remember the experience.

Even taking these complexities into account, it's undeniable that an emphasis on natural selection has been fruitful for psychologists and has led to a host of new hypotheses about why we act as we do. Many of these hypotheses have been powerfully confirmed through careful data collection. For some further illustrations, let's look at the findings concerned with *jealousy* and *fathering*.

Jealousy is, of course, found in men (as in Shakespeare's *Othello*) and women (as in the saying, "Hell hath no fury like a woman scorned"). But the basis for jealousy in romantic relationships may be different in the two sexes. According to several studies, men care more about sexual loyalty than emotional loyalty; they think it's worse for their partner to sleep with someone else than to be emotionally engaged with someone else. For women, the data indicate, the pattern reverses; women show greater concern about emotional disloyalty than about sexual transgressions (D. Buss, Larsen, Westen, & Semmelroth, 2001; also Schmitt & Buss, 2001; for some concerns about these findings, see Harris, 2002; DeSteno, Bartlett, & Salovey, 2002).

Once again, this pattern makes sense in evolutionary terms. From this perspective, a woman may have less reason to care if her mate has sex with others. For purposes of transmitting her own genes into subsequent generations, all she needs is a single one of her partner's sperm cells to launch her pregnancy; once she is pregnant, it won't matter how the male distributes his "surplus" sperm. What the female does need from the male are the resources he provides to nourish both her and her young. Without the resources, her young might perish—and, in evolutionary terms, this would be a calamity. This is why a female feels deeply threatened when her partner starts devoting his resources to other women (and their offspring), and it's why the female wants an *emotional* commitment from her mate—so that he remains loyal to her and focused on her needs. Hence it is her mate's emotional disloyalty, not his sexual wanderings, that is most threatening to the woman's evolutionary self-interest.

What about men? If a man devotes his resources to a woman and her children, he needs to be sure that these children carry his genes and not someone else's; otherwise, he's spending his resources to promote another male's legacy. On this basis, it should be very troubling for a male if his mate is sexually unfaithful; that would create doubts about the paternity of her offspring. Her emotional infidelity, on the other hand, is less worrisome: It is okay if his mate loves someone else, provided that her love doesn't lead her to have sex with that someone else.

PATERNITY

A woman always knows for certain that the babies she gives birth to are her biological offspring. Men, on the other hand, don't share this certainty and may sometimes question whether a baby is their child (Figure 2.25). As we've seen, this point has implications for men's jealousy; it also has implications for how fathers care for their young. For example, Platek and colleagues (Platek, Burch, Panyavin, Wasserman, & Gallup, 2002; Platek, Raines, Gallup, Mohamed, Thomson et al., 2004) photographed the faces of 20 undergraduate men and 20 undergraduate women. They then used a photo-morphing computer program to blend each volunteer's face with that of an unrelated infant. The result was an image of a child that roughly simulated what the volunteer's own baby might look like.

The researchers then presented each participant with photos of five children's faces. None of the volunteers knew that one child's face was a blend with their own face; the other four faces were blends with other adults' faces. The researchers then asked, among other questions, "Which one of these children would you adopt?"

From an evolutionary perspective, men should be quite sensitive to issues of paternity; and so they should have a preference for babies who resemble them, because the resemblance would suggest biological relatedness. And in fact, 18 of the 20 men tested picked "their" child—the photograph that had been morphed with their own face. Women, on the other hand, should be less sensitive to biological relatedness because, as we have described, this has not been a concern for them over the course of human evolution. The study results were consistent with this idea; only 7 of the 20 women picked "their" child.

Another result is more dramatic and—potentially—deeply consequential. From an evolutionary perspective, males should take care of their own young (and so protect their genetic legacy) but should not take care of other men's young—including others' young that might be raised by their mates. In the modern world, therefore, we would expect an evolved tendency for males to favor their biological children over their stepchildren. This favoritism might, in many fathers, be overruled by other considerations; and so many stepfathers will be loving, generous, and supportive to their adopted children. Even so, the biologically rooted tendency should still be detectable in a variety of ways. Indeed, let's look at the extreme: What if the father is inclined to violence? If, as a horrific prospect, he harms his children, which ones will he harm?

Daly and Wilson (1988) gathered data on the most extreme, most horrible parental crime: infanticide. They examined cases of this offense in Canada between 1974 and 1983 and found that children under the age of 2 were killed by stepparents at 70 times the rate they were killed by biological parents. To be sure, the *overall* rate of infanticide was quite low, and very few stepparents committed this terrible crime. Still, the probability of this crime was much higher for stepparents than for biological parents.

Once again, though, we need to acknowledge the room for debate. The intriguing finding that men preferred "their own" baby's photo far more often than women did comes from a study of a small sample of college students. It would surely be helpful to know whether results from much larger groups and across cultures support the evolutionary interpretation of the data. Likewise, the

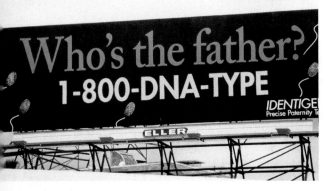

2.25 DNA testing Modern biotechnology now makes it easy to compare the DNA of two individuals—and thus to estalish who an infant's father is.

Daly and Wilson data have been controversial (for reviews, see Daly & Wilson 2001, 2005, 2007). Among other issues, the findings are observational, not experimental, and (for the reasons highlighted in Chapter 1) this makes it difficult to establish cause and effect. We therefore need a bit of caution in interpreting these findings; but this takes nothing away from the fact that the evolutionary perspective, here and in many other realms, has uncovered some truly striking results. It's now up to subsequent researchers to nail down our best explanation of these findings.

SOME FINAL THOUGHTS: THE STRENGTHS AND THE LIMITS OF EVOLUTIONARY THEORIZING

There's no question that human behavior, thoughts, and feelings are shaped by human biology; and human biology, in turn, includes the genetic blueprint that each of us inherits. It's plain, therefore, that to understand who we are, we need to understand that blueprint. And in fact researchers have already identified many traits—ranging from specific behaviors to broad learning capacities—that are powerfully shaped by the particular pattern of alleles each of us has inherited. These findings leave no doubt that the human genome matters enormously for human psychology.

Indeed, we should celebrate the enormous progress researchers have made in their explorations of the human genome and how it influences both biological and psychological functioning. We are, for example, starting to identify specific gene patterns that contribute to anxiety, and we are identifying particular alleles that can make someone more or less sensitive to antipsychotic medication. We're also making great progress in understanding the specific neural mechanisms, shaped by the genes, that produce a wide range of psychological outcomes.

We've also learned a great deal by asking *why* the human genome is as it is, and why our phenotypes are as they are. Clearly, then, the evolutionary perspective has great value for psychology—helping us understand the function of a wide range of behaviors and drawing our attention to key comparisons with other species and comparisons across cultures.

However, we've also offered some words of caution in this chapter, concerned with ways in which a genetic or evolutionary account is sometimes overinterpreted. For example, we've warned against either-or thinking that presumes genetic influences could be cleanly separated from environmental factors. Instead, the opposite is the case—these two types of influence are constantly interacting. Likewise, we've emphasized that a genetic pattern does not establish someone's destiny; a genotype does not in any way guarantee a particular phenotype.

In our discussion, we've also warned against the common idea that evolution makes organisms "better," so that any attribute emerging from natural selection must be "good" or "desirable." Instead, we've seen that natural selection works simply by favoring traits *if those traits help the organism survive and reproduce in its current environment*. Natural selection also has no way to determine, or be influenced by, whether those traits will be helpful in the future—and there's no guarantee that they will. In fact, some of the traits that likely helped our ancient ancestors may, in our current environment, actually be harmful.

One example (which we'll return to in Chapter 12) is our genetically rooted capacity to store, as bodily fat, the excess calories we ingest. In ancient times, this mechanism would have helped our ancestors survive because, when food was scarce, they could draw on these earlier-established deposits of fat. In much of the modern world, in contrast, food supplies are plentiful; and in this setting, the same save-for-later pattern is contributing to a worldwide epidemic of obesity: People's bodies are storing the excess calories but then not drawing on these deposits, so that many people end up being burdened by the numerous problems associated with being overweight.

Similarly, consider our response to *threat*. Our ancient ancestors responded to threat by activating their bodily systems in a way that prepared them for strong physical action. That way, they were all set if they needed to deal with the threat either by running away at top speed or by fighting. In the modern world, however, most of the threats we encounter do not invite a physical response—but we're still stuck with the same reaction pattern; and it takes a heavy toll on us, causing many of the medical and psychological difficulties associated with *stress*. (For more on this issue, see Chapter 12.)

We must not think of evolution, therefore, as some sort of wise or benevolent guide, always finding ways to improve a species. Rather, through natural selection, organisms that are better suited to their current environment flourish. This is the heart of Darwin's remarkable proposal, a proposal that has been repeatedly confirmed and impressively elaborated by more recent researchers. This process has led to the incredible diversity of creatures on this planet, and to the enormous complexity we see in them—including the complexity that will be our subject matter throughout this text.

SUMMARY   CHAPTER 2

GENETICS AND DNA

- The *nucleus* of each biological cell contains *chromosomes,* which each contain a single molecule of *DNA.* Within this molecule, specific sections called *genes* govern the cell's functioning by providing detailed instructions for making proteins. Humans have 23 pairs of chromosomes and roughly 25,000 protein-coding genes; these are collectively called the person's *genome.*

- In each cell, some genes are *expressed* at any point in time and others are not. Gene expression is controlled by the biochemical environment inside the cell, which in turn is influenced by many factors, including the organism's overall environment, its experience, and its behavior. An organism's genome therefore specifies only its *genotype;* the overt traits and behaviors of the organism define its *phenotype,* which is the product of the genotype and experience in constant interaction.

- Most characteristics are influenced by the action of many genes. Each gene, though, is paired with another gene; the pairs are located at corresponding positions on the pairs of chromosomes. The genes may be the same *allele* or not; and if they are different, one gene may be *dominant* and the other *recessive,* or the genes may be *codominant,* or one may be *incompletely dominant.*

EVOLUTION BY NATURAL SELECTION

- Charles Darwin hypothesized that all modern organisms are descended from a small set of shared ancestors and have emerged over time through the process of evolution. An enormous amount of evidence has confirmed these proposals. The key mechanism is *natural selection*: If individuals with certain traits are more likely to survive and reproduce, then their genes will be better represented in the next generation; and if the genes gave rise to the advantageous traits, then those traits will be more common in the next generation.

- It is important to avoid the *naturalistic fallacy,* however—the idea that evolution somehow improves organisms, or that anything natural is good.

- Darwin's broad proposal boils down to three principles: there must be variation among the individuals within a population; certain of the variants must survive and reproduce at higher rates than others; the traits associated with this advantage must be passed from parents to offspring. Both the variation itself and the transmission of traits, across generations, depends on the organism's genome.

- The emphasis on the survival of genes helps explain a number of behaviors, including behaviors in which organisms endanger their own survival to protect their offspring or relatives. These behaviors are best understood in terms of the survival of genes, rather than the survival of individuals.

- The evidence for modern evolutionary theory comes from many sources, including the fossil record as well as the examination of the resemblance between the genomes of various organisms. We can also document the unfolding of evolution in some modern organisms. The shared ancestry for many organisms is evident in the extraordinary unity of life we can document in many ways.

THE GENETICS AND EVOLUTION OF BEHAVIOR

- Evolution by natural selection has shaped behaviors just as it shapes an organism's physical traits. In many cases, this natural selection has favored flexibility in an organism's behavior, and so organisms have evolved mechanisms through which they can alter their responses and learn new skills.

- The behavior of smiling seems to be *species general* for humans, but is not *species specific*. The behavior is also evident in individuals blind since birth, making it clear that this behavior does not depend on a history of learning.

- Examination of humans and other primates indicates that there are at least two types of smiles: One type is expressive of an individual's inner state, and is produced even if no other people are around; the other type is more social and functions as a greeting or a means of defusing tense situations. All of these points provide powerful indications that smiles have ancient roots, and were selected by evolution as a means of communication, allowing others to read our inner states and intentions.

- An individual's level of intelligence is influenced by genetic factors; we can see this in the fact that individuals who resemble each other genetically (identical twins) tend to resemble each other in their intelligence, even if the twins were reared separately. Intelligence is also influenced by environmental factors, and researchers use the *heritability ratio* as a summary of the effect of genetic differences within a given population and environment.

- The value of the heritability ratio depends on the group being examined. In lower-SES groups, the heritability may be zero; the heritability also increases with a person's age, plausibly because each person chooses environments that amplify the individual's genetic potential.

- Human intelligence was favored by natural selection because our ancient ancestors had a reproductive advantage if they could communicate, solve problems, and draw conclusions. However, it's unclear, from an evolutionary perspective, why humans *vary* in their intelligence—reminding us that not all

inherited characteristics are the direct result of natural selection.

- Most mammals are polygynous, and this pattern is easily understood in evolutionary terms. To maximize their reproductive success, most male mammals should mate with as many females as possible; female mammals, in contrast, maximize their reproductive success by mating just a few times during their lives, but taking steps to ensure the well-being of each of their progeny.

- This logic helps explain why human males express a desire for multiple partners, and why it's usually the female, in most species, that makes the choice of whether to mate with a particular male or not. By the same logic, natural selection explains why it's usually males who take the larger role in courtship, seeking to attract the female.

- Human males seem to care more about their partner's appearance than females do; women seem to put greater weight on their partner's social status than males do. Natural selection likely favored these tendencies, based on the idea that a partner's appearance indicates health and fertility; a partner's status indicates the likelihood that he will provide resources needed to raise the young.

- An evolutionary perspective also leads to the expectation that men will be more distressed by sexual infidelity in their partners than by emotional infidelity; women should show the reverse pattern.

 ONLINE STUDY TOOLS

Go to StudySpace, **wwnorton.com/studyspace**, to access additional review and enrichment materials, including the following resources for each chapter:

Organize
- Study Plan
- Chapter Outline
- Quiz+ Assessment

Learn
- Ebook
- Chapter Review
- Vocabulary Flashcards
- Drag-and-Drop Labeling Exercises
- Audio Podcast Chapter Overview

Connect
- Critical Thinking Activity
- Studying the Mind Video Podcasts
- Video Exercises
- Animations
- **ZAPS** Psychology Labs

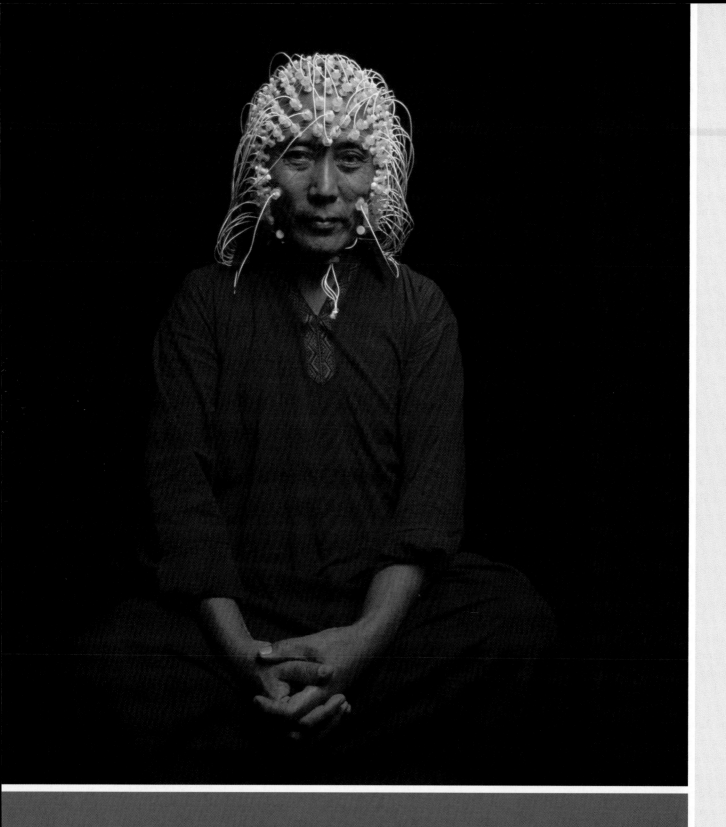

3

The Brain and the Nervous System

All too often, you don't know what you've got until it's gone. And so it goes with brains: Much of what we know about this magnificent organ comes from studying what happens when it is damaged. Because the resulting problems depend on where the damage is located, we have evidence that the brain is made up of specialized regions. The achievements that we can easily observe—thinking, feeling, or acting—require exquisite coordination among these areas. To begin describing these diverse regions, let's briefly tour your cerebral cortex, the brain's outermost layer.

Place your fingertips on your forehead. A few centimeters beneath your skull, the frontal lobes serve as the brain's executive center—essentially the CEO of your mind. These lobes are crucial for many human feats: our capacities to plan for the future, think abstractly, and control impulses. Right up front in your skull, they are especially vulnerable to impact. What can damage here do?

Phillipa, a 35-year-old teacher living near Auckland, New Zealand, suffered a terrible transformation after a burglar broke into her home and, while attacking her, bludgeoned her head. Once a calm professional and devoted mother, Phillipa became wild and unpredictable—undressing in front of strangers, swearing at passersby, and sobbing at the slightest provocation. Heartbroken, Phillipa's husband eventually placed her in an institution. These days, she is usually happy to see her family but never seems to miss them. In fact, she curses and yells at them when they stay too long.

Now walk your fingers to the crown of your head. Directly below, your parietal lobes weave together sensory information to create your sense of spatial layout. They represent this information via a succession of maps. One map describes the space around you; another corresponds to your skin, so you can distinguish a touch on your leg from one on your arm; yet another tracks your body position.

If any of the maps are disrupted, the effects can be bewildering. Consider Arthur (a pseudonym), a physician in the Midwest. Arthur's body map lacks the brain cells that should represent his right leg, below the mid-thigh. As a result, his brain can't integrate sensations coming from this portion of his leg—and he has always struggled with a disconcerting desire to have his lower leg amputated. If asked, he calmly traces a line with his finger exactly where he'd like the surgeon to cut.

Now drop your fingers to your temples. Just beneath them, the temporal lobes interpret sounds, including speech. The effects of damage here are evident in the case of J. S., whose temporal lobe damage, following severe viral encephalitis, drastically altered his language and memory abilities. When shown pictures of objects, for instance, J. S. labels them with numerals. He can form sentences of no more than three words and often misunderstands what others say. Still, many of his other capacities remain intact—so he can easily do math and abstract reasoning problems.

To complete this tour, walk your fingers to the back of your head. Here your occipital lobes interpret visual information arriving from your eyes. Different sections of these lobes are each responsible for a certain type of analysis. One region determines the colors in the input; another interprets motion, another assesses shapes, and so on. Damage to any of these areas causes a corresponding visual deficit. Some people are unable to see color: To them, the world looks covered in ash. Others can't perceive movement: They see the bus is here, and know it used to be over there—but never sense its motion.

We have mentioned only a few functions of the four lobes; many more brain structures regulate everything from appetite to anger, from learning to liking. In this chapter, we'll consider many of these structures—where they are and how they contribute to our overall functioning. Throughout, we'll view the brain essentially as a piece of biological machinery—a very modern perspective. The idea that thoughts and feelings had a physical origin was regarded for millennia as deeply heretical, and we'll start by setting some historical context for modern inquiries into the biology of the mind. Our inquiry then turns to the neurons—the cells that make up the nervous system—and the way they process and transmit information. Of course, neurons function within a large system, so we turn next to the brain. We'll explore the architecture of the nervous system, and then zoom in to examine the cerebral cortex, including the functions mentioned above.

As you master the brain's intricate parts, try not to lose sight of the miraculous whole: Your brain weighs about three pounds, maybe 2% of your body weight, but it generates your beliefs, personality, habits, skills, emotions, memories, and hopes. How this is possible is one of modern science's great mysteries. We'll return often in this text to this remarkable intersection of body and mind, cells and self.

THE ORGANISM AS A MACHINE

The idea that human behaviors, thoughts, and feelings are a product of the *brain* is usually attributed to the philosopher René Descartes (1596–1650; Figure 3.1). Before Descartes' time, people in the Western world generally regarded human behavior as complex and mysterious but, in any case, best understood as the result of the soul's directives and certainly not the product of some mere machinery.

3.1 René Descartes (1596–1650)
Descartes, a philosopher and mathematician, argued that much of human behavior can be understood in mechanical terms.

Descartes' new perspective, however, was encouraged by the times in which he lived. After all, the 1500s and 1600s saw enormous scientific advances: Kepler and Galileo were developing ideas about the movements of the stars and planets visible in the night sky, and their observations were part of the intellectual growth that led to Isaac Newton's formulation of the laws of motion, summarized in 1687 in his extraordinary book *Principia Mathematica*. These new views of the universe suggested that natural phenomena could be understood through relatively straightforward principles of acceleration, inertia, and momentum—principles that could be described precisely with simple mathematical laws. These laws, in turn, could explain a huge range of phenomena—from the drop of a stone to the motions of planets. Indeed, the same laws could be seen operating—rigidly, immutably—in the workings of ingenious mechanical contrivances that were all the rage in the wealthy homes of Europe: cuckoo clocks that sounded on the hour, water-driven gargoyles with nodding heads, statues in the king's garden that bowed to visitors who stepped on hidden springs. The turning of a gear, the release of a spring—these simple mechanisms could cause all kinds of clever effects.

With these intellectual and technical developments in place, and with so many complex events that could be explained in such simple terms, it was only a matter of time before someone asked the crucial question: Could human actions be explained just as mechanically?

Descartes' answer to this question, as well as his view of action in general (whether the action of a human or some other animal), was radical and straightforward. He proposed that every action by an organism is a direct response to some event in the world: Something from the outside excites one of the senses; this, in turn, excites a nerve that transmits the excitation to the brain, which then diverts the excitation to a muscle and makes the muscle contract. In effect, the energy from the outside is "reflected" by the nervous system back to the animal's muscles, a conception that gave rise to the term *reflex* (Figure 3.2).

Seen in this light, human and animal actions can certainly be regarded as the doings of a machine. But Descartes also understood that he needed some account of the *flexibility* in our behavior. After all, the sight of food might trigger an action of reaching toward the food if we are hungry, but it triggers no action at all if we're not. In Descartes' terms, therefore, it seemed that excitation from the senses could be reflected to one set of muscles on one occasion and to an entirely different set on another—as though the reflex mechanisms included some sort of central switching system that controlled which incoming signal triggered which outgoing one.

How could Descartes explain this switching system? He knew that a strictly mechanical explanation would have unsettling theological implications: If all human action was caused by some sort of machinery, what role was left for the soul? Descartes also knew that Galileo had been condemned by the Inquisition because his scientific beliefs threatened the doctrines of the Catholic Church. Perhaps it's no surprise, then, that Descartes proposed that the centralized controller of human behavior was not a machine at all. Many processes within the brain, he argued, did function mechanically; but what truly governed our behavior, what made reason and choice possible, and what distinguished us from other animals, was the *soul*—operating through the brain, choosing among nervous pathways, and controlling our bodies like a puppeteer pulling the strings on a marionette.

In the following decades, though, theology's grip on science loosened and other thinkers went further. They believed that the laws of the physical universe could ultimately explain all action, whether human or animal, so that a scientific account required no further "ghost in the machine"—that is, no reference to the soul. They therefore extended Descartes' logic to all of human functioning, arguing that humans differ from other animals only in being more finely constructed mechanisms.

Of course, the ultimate question of whether humans are just machines is as much a question about faith as it is about science. In Descartes' time, this question centered on whether

3.2 Reflex action as envisaged by Descartes In this sketch, drawn by Descartes himself, the heat from the fire (A) starts a chain of processes that begins at the affected spot of the skin (B) and continues up the nerve tube until a pore of a cavity (F) opens. Descartes believed that this opening allowed the animal spirits in the cavity to enter the nerve tube and eventually travel to the muscles that pull the foot from the fire.

neuron A specialized cell in the nervous system that accumulates and transmits information.

dendrites The branched part of a neuron that receives impulses and conducts them toward the cell body.

cell body The portion of the neuron containing the metabolic machinery that keeps the cell alive and functional.

axon The part of a neuron that transmits impulses to glands, muscles, or other neurons.

Neuron A

Dendrites

Nucleus

Cell body

Neural impulse

Axon

Nodes of Ranvier

Myelin sheath

Axon terminals

Neuron B

our behavior could be explained entirely in terms of fluid pressures or gears; in more modern terms, this question focuses on whether our behavior can be explained entirely in terms of chemical and electrical signals within the brain. In either case, the problem is the same: No one has the slightest idea of how to test for the existence of an intangible soul; thus, the question of whether we are machines, or machines with souls, is not something that can be determined by science. Even so, no one can deny that the strategy of regarding humans as machines—omitting all mention of a soul in our scientific theorizing—has fostered dramatic breakthroughs in understanding ourselves and our fellow animals.

BUILDING BLOCKS OF THE NERVOUS SYSTEM

Descartes' views were based largely on conjecture, because in his time scientists knew little about how the nervous system functions. Today, roughly five centuries later, we know far more and our theorizing can be correspondingly more sophisticated. In fact, the data and research tools now available have allowed the development of a new and rapidly growing field called *neuroscience*—a multidisciplinary effort that seeks to understand the nature, function, and origins of the nervous system. Neuroscience draws some of its insights from psychology but also draws on biology, computer science, medicine, and other fields. The subject matter of neuroscience is similarly broad, ranging from fine-grained research projects that scrutinize molecular interactions inside individual nerve cells to much broader efforts asking how large tracts of neural tissue give rise to conscious experience.

Let's be clear from the start that studying the brain is, to say the least, an enormously daunting task. Within the human brain, the total number of **neurons**—the individual cells that act as the main information processors of the nervous system—has been estimated to be as high as 100 billion, roughly the number of stars in the Milky Way, and each of these neurons connects to as many as 50 thousand others (Nauta & Feirtag, 1986). The brain also contains another type of cell, glia, whose function we're just beginning to understand. In some parts of the brain, glia outnumber the neurons by 10 to 1. All these cells, and all their interconnections, are contained within an organ that weighs only 3 to 4 pounds—leading many writers to suggest that the human brain is the most complex object in the universe.

As a first step in understanding this complexity, let's look at the basic building blocks of the nervous system—the neurons and glia. We'll then turn to the *nerve impulse*—the means through which individual neurons communicate with each other.

The Neuron

The neuron is a cell that specializes in sending and receiving information. Neurons typically have three main parts: the **dendrites**, the **cell body** (or *soma*), and the **axon** (Figure 3.3). The dendrites, the "input" side of the neuron, receive signals from many other neurons. In most neurons, the dendrites are heavily branched, like a thick and tan-

3.3 The neuron A schematic diagram of the main parts of a neuron. Part of the cell is myelinated—its axon is covered with sets of segmented, insulating sheaths formed by encircling glial cells.

3.4 Different kinds of neurons It's important to remember that while the text discusses the structure of a "typical" neuron, neurons actually come in various shapes and sizes. Pictured here are neurons from (A) the spinal cord (stained in red), (B) the cerebral cortex, and (C) the cerebellum.

gled bush. The cell body contains the neuron's nucleus and all the elements needed for the normal metabolic activities of these cells. The axon, finally, is the "output" side of the neuron and sends neural impulses to other neurons. The axon usually extends outward from the cell body like a wispy thread, and it may fork into several branches at its end.

Neurons come in many shapes and sizes (Figure 3.4). Their cell bodies vary from 5 to about 100 microns in diameter (1 micron = 1/1,000 millimeter). In comparison, the average human hair has a diameter of about 100 microns. Neurons' dendrites are typically short—say, a few hundred microns. Axons, however, can be much longer. For example, the longest axons in humans are those of the *motor neurons,* which transmit neural impulses from the brain to the muscles. The motor neurons that allow us to wiggle our toes are, in most people, more than a meter long. As a result, these particular neurons, with their small cell bodies connected to very long axons, have roughly the same proportions as a basketball attached to a garden hose a mile and a half long.

The motor neuron carries an **efferent** signal that allows the brain to control the muscles. Efferent neurons in general carry information from the brain to some destination outside the brain. Other neurons convey information inward; these **afferent neurons** keep the nervous system informed about both the external world and the body's internal environment (Figure 3.5 on page 90).* Some of the afferent neurons are attached to specialized receptor cells that respond to external energies such as pressure, chemical changes, light, and so on. These receptor cells translate (more technically, *transduce*) the physical stimuli into electrical changes, which then trigger a nervous impulse in other neurons.

It turns out, though, that roughly 99% of the brain's nerve cells are neither afferent nor efferent neurons. Instead, they're neurons that make connections *within* the central nervous system, and they're divided into two types: The *projection neurons* link one area of the central nervous system to some other (perhaps distant) area; to perform this function, these nerve cells typically have long axons. The **interneurons,** in contrast, make "local" connections within the nervous system and usually have either very short axons or none at all. (Be aware that some neuroscientists use the term *interneuron* to refer to both of these nerve cell types—e.g., Kolb & Whishaw, 2009.)

efferent neurons Nerves that carry messages outward from the central nervous system.

afferent neurons Nerves that carry messages inward toward the central nervous system.

interneurons Neurons that are neither afferent nor efferent, but instead carry information from one neuron to another.

---

*To remember the terms *efferent* and *afferent*, bear in mind that efferent neurons carry information exiting from the brain, and afferent neurons carry information arriving in the brain. Efferent neurons (i.e., carrying information out the exit) are also the means through which we effect changes in the world; afferent neurons (carrying the arriving information) are the means through which we are affected by our experiences.

3.5 Afferent and efferent neurons

Afferent neurons carry information into the central nervous system (CNS); interneurons make connections *within* the CNS; efferent neurons carry information outward from the CNS. For many simple reflexes, this circuit is completed within the spine, with no need for connections in the brain. This allows rapid responses to urgent inputs.

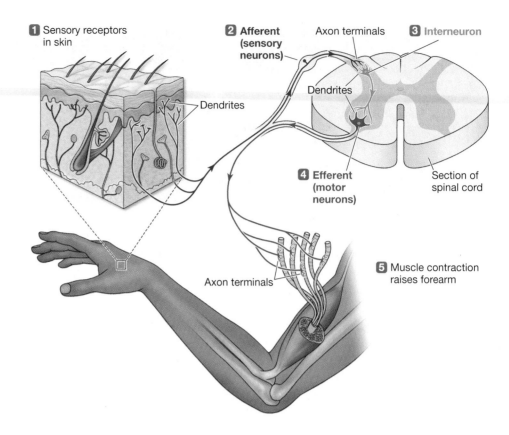

1 Sensory receptors in skin

Dendrites

2 Afferent (sensory neurons)

Axon terminals

3 Interneuron

Dendrites

4 Efferent (motor neurons)

Section of spinal cord

Axon terminals

5 Muscle contraction raises forearm

Glia

What about the other type of cells that make up the brain—the **glia** (Figure 3.6)? For many years, scholars thought the glia played only a few roles—holding the neurons in place and supplying them with nutrients and oxygen. Indeed, this second-class status is reflected in the word *glia* itself, which comes from the Greek for "glue" or "slime."

It turns out, however, that glia have a rather broad set of crucial functions. First, as we've long supposed, glia do provide the nourishment for the neurons—but we've also learned that glia play a key role in *controlling* the nutrient supply. For example, the sugar *glucose* is the main fuel for the nervous system, but most of the energy neurons need does not come from glucose directly. Instead the glia convert the glucose into another molecule, called lactate, that feeds the neurons. The glia are also sensitive to the activity level in each neuron and increase the blood flow (providing more oxygen and fuel) whenever the neurons in the brain region become more active (Rouach, Koulakoff, Abudara, Willecke, & Giaume, 2008).

The glia also play a central role in the brain's *development*. Before birth and in the months afterward, the human brain grows at a remarkable rate as its cells rapidly reproduce and differentiate. The newly created neurons then migrate from one position in the brain to another, moving at a speed of up to 1 millimeter each day. This migration is guided by glia, acting as guidewires—much like beanpoles guiding the growth of bean shoots in the garden. Then, once the neurons have reached their destinations and established the appropriate connections, the glia produce chemicals that help to shut down the process of neural growth. In this way, the glia ensure a relatively stable pattern of connections (McGee, Yang, Fischer, Daw, & Strittmatter, 2005; G. Miller, 2005a; for more on these processes of brain development, see Chapter 14).

3.6 Glial cells These glial cells are from a rabbit brain.

glia A type of cell in the nervous system long believed to provide a "support" function for neurons; recent research indicates that glia provide many other functions as well.

myelin A fatty substance that makes up some types of glial cells; these cells wrap around the axon of some neurons, providing an insulating "myelin sheath" around these neurons.

3.7 Myelin For neurons with long axons (A), the axon is covered with a succession of myelin cells. These cells form an insulating sheath (B) around the axon, but with gaps—the nodes of Ranvier—in between the myelin cells. These sheaths are formed early in neural development (C) as the myelin cell first encloses the axon and then wraps around and around it. The photomicrograph (D) shows the actual appearance of the myelin; the axon is shown in yellow and the (many) layers of myelin are in green.

Yet another function of glial cells is to increase the speed of neuronal communication. The glia that accomplish this are mostly made of a fatty substance known as **myelin;** and soon after birth, these glia start to wrap themselves around the axons of neurons—especially the longer axons that span greater distances and thus need greater transmission speed (Figure 3.7). Each of the "wrappers" in this *myelin sheath* covers a portion of the axon, and soon the entire length of the axon is covered by a series of these wrappers. Crucially, though, there are gaps—called the *nodes of Ranvier*—between the successive wrappers, and it's this combination of wrappers and gaps that speeds up the nerve impulses traveling along these *myelinated axons.* (We'll discuss later *why* the myelination speeds up the impulse.)

Myelin is white—which explains why, when you look at a brain, you'll see a mix of white matter and gray matter (Figure 3.8). The *white matter* consists of the myelinated axons traversing long distances either within the brain or to and from the body. Conversely, *gray matter* consists of cell bodies, dendrites, and the unmyelinated axons.

3.8 Coronal section distinguishing gray and white matter This vertical slice through the brain shows that the brain tissue includes so-called white matter, which mostly consists of myelinated axons and gray matter (shown in beige here), which is made up of cell bodies, dendrites, and unmyelinated axons.

The glia may also have other jobs to do. For example, several recent studies suggest that glia can "talk back" to the neurons, sending signals that help regulate the strength of connections between adjacent neurons. In some circumstances, glia can also release chemicals that increase the reactivity of neurons. This is usually helpful—it makes the nervous system more sensitive to important inputs—but, unfortunately, this same mechanism can sometimes make the neurons too reactive. In the extreme, this increased reactivity may be the source of so-called neuropathic pain—a condition in which people suffer extreme pain in response to even a mild touch—and it may also play a role in the development of epilepsy and several other illnesses (G. Miller, 2005a).

Still other evidence suggests that the glial cells themselves may constitute a separate, slow signaling system within the brain. Glial cells are known to respond to various electrical, chemical, and mechanical stimuli. They also form networks that communicate with each other and that may modulate the activity level of neurons nearby. The extent to which these networks of glia interact with neurons in the brain has not yet been determined, but it may be considerable (Bullock et al., 2005; Gallo & Chitajallu, 2001; Newman & Zahs, 1998; Verkhratsky, 1998).

COMMUNICATION AMONG NEURONS

There's no question that the main signaling within the body is done by the neurons. But how do these cells perform their function? In tackling this crucial question, we'll proceed in three steps: First, we'll look at the functioning of individual neurons and ask what it is about these cells that allows them to "respond"—i.e., to change their functioning in response to stimulation. We'll also consider how the response is transmitted *within* the neuron—usually from the dendrites (where the input signal first arrives) to the axon and then down the length of the axon. Second, we'll discuss how information travels between neurons—that is, from the axon's ending to the next neuron in the chain. As we'll see, communication within the neuron (i.e., from one end to the other) involves *electrical* signals; but communication between neurons (i.e., from one neuron to another) involves an entirely different system that relies on *chemical* signals. Third, we'll then want to take a closer look at these chemical signals. Among other things, this step will allow us to ask how neurons differentiate between *types* of signals as well as how they manage to integrate information received from many sources at once. This discussion also has a crucial implication because an understanding of this chemistry allows us to explain why many drugs work the way they do.

Activity and Communication within the Neuron

The neuron is, in many respects, just a cell. It has a nucleus on the inside and a cell membrane that defines its perimeter. In the middle is a biochemical stew of ions, amino acids, proteins, and DNA along with a collection of smaller structures that provide for the metabolic needs of the cell itself. What makes a neuron distinctive, though, is the peculiarity of its cell membrane. The membrane is highly sensitive to stimulation. Poke it, stimulate it electrically or chemically, and the neuronal membrane actually changes its structure, producing a cascade of changes that can eventually lead to an electrical signal called an **action potential.** This signal—sent from one end of the neuron to the other—is the neuron's main response to input as well as the fundamental information carrier of the nervous system.

action potential A brief change in the electrical charge of a neuronal membrane; the physical basis of the signal that travels the length of the neuron.

3.9 Recording the voltage within a neuron A schematic drawing of how the impulse is recorded. One electrode is inserted into the axon; the other records from the axon's outside. When the neuron is at "rest," these electrodes will detect a −70-millivolt difference between the cell's interior and its exterior. When the neuron "fires," however, the voltage will briefly shift, although the −70-millivolt difference is soon restored.

At its heart, the action potential involves electrical changes. To study these changes, we can begin by inserting one microelectrode into a neuron's axon and placing a second electrode on the axon's outer surface (Figure 3.9). This setup allows us to measure electrical activity near the cell's membrane. It also tells us that even when the neuron is not being stimulated in any way, there's a voltage difference between the inside and the outside of the cell. Like a miniature battery with a positive and a negative connection, the inside of the axon is electrically negative relative to the outside, with a difference of −70 or so millivolts (a standard AA battery, at 1.5 volts, has over 200 times this voltage). Because this small voltage difference occurs when the neuron is stable, it's traditionally called the neuron's **resting potential.**

How does this situation change when the neuron is stimulated? To find out, we can use a third microelectrode to apply a brief electrical pulse to the outside surface of the cell. This pulse reduces the voltage difference across the membrane. If the pulse is weak, it may reduce the voltage difference a little bit, but the neuron's membrane will maintain its integrity and quickly work to restore the resting potential of −70 millivolts. But if the pulse is strong enough to push the voltage difference past a critical **excitation threshold** (about −55 millivolts in mammals), something dramatic happens. In that region of the cell, the voltage difference between the inside and outside of the membrane abruptly collapses to zero and, in fact, begins to reverse itself. The inside of the membrane no longer shows a negative voltage compared to the outside; instead, it suddenly swings positive—up to +40 millivolts. This momentary change in voltage, the action potential, is crucial for the functioning of the neuron. This change is short-lived, and the resting potential is restored within a millisecond or so.

resting potential The voltage difference between the inside and the outside of a neuronal membrane when the neuron is not firing.

excitation threshold The voltage difference between a neuron's interior and exterior that, if exceeded, causes the neuron to fire.

Explaining the Action Potential

We've just described the action potential in terms of electrical measurements, but what lies behind these measurements? What is going on inside the neuron—and, crucially, at the neuron's cell membrane—that causes this momentary change in the neuron's electrical state? The answers lie in the movements of ions through the neuron's membrane. Ions are molecules (or single atoms) that have a positive or negative electrical charge. When a neuron is at rest (i.e., not stimulated), the inside of the cell contains both positive ions and negative ones, and the same is true for the fluid outside the cell membrane. What's crucial is the *concentration* of each ion type, and these concentrations are different inside the cell than they are outside.

What governs the ion concentrations? As one factor, the cell's membrane contains mechanisms called *ion pumps* that—as their name implies—actively pump ions into or out of the cell. For the most part, these pumps work to move sodium (Na+) *out* of the cell and potassium (K+) *into* the cell, but they do so unevenly: three sodium ions move out for every two potassium ions that move in.

In addition, the cell membrane contains *ion channels*—actual passageways through the membrane. When open, these channels allow certain ions (but not others) simply to pass through. In other words, the channels work roughly like bouncers at a party or a bar—they let desired guests pass through unchallenged but block undesired visitors.

When a neuron is at rest, sodium ions are barely able to pass through these channels, but potassium ions flow through freely. We need to bear in mind, though, that (thanks to the ion pumps) there are more potassium ions inside the cell than outside, and (as a general fact of chemistry) ions tend to move from areas of higher concentration to areas of lower concentration. Therefore, the dominant movement of potassium through these channels is outward—out of the cell interior and into the extracellular fluid. This creates a surplus of positive ions outside of the cell, and this is the main source of the resting potential—again: the voltage difference across the neuron's membrane, with the cell interior electrically negative relative to the cell exterior.

The situation changes dramatically when some portion of the membrane is stimulated in some way (mechanically, electrically, or chemically). In this case, a new set of ion channels—ones that allow sodium to pass—spring open and so sodium ions flood into the cell (Figure 3.10). This process leads to an excess of positively charged particles on the inside of the membrane, and this is why our electrodes detect a sudden swing toward a positive voltage. Immediately after, though, the membrane returns to its original status: The sodium pumps resume their evacuation of sodium to the outside of the

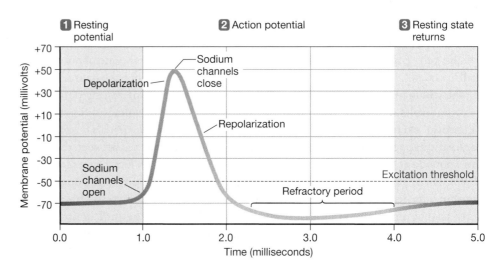

3.10 The action potential Action potential recorded from the squid's giant axon. This simplified diagram omits many of the other chemical changes (i.e., other ion flows) involved in this sequence.

neuron, and the sodium channels slam shut to keep it out. This process reestablishes the membrane's stability and restores the resting potential.

This restoration is fast, but it does take a moment; and during this restoration process, there is still an imbalance of ions. This is why, during this brief interval, it is much more difficult to launch a new action potential. This interval is referred to as the **refractory period**—the time after an action potential during which the cell membrane is unprepared for the next action potential. Once the refractory period is done, however—a time span of just a few milliseconds—the membrane is back to its resting state and ready for the next input.

Propagation of the Action Potential

So far, we have considered the ion flow at just one point on the neuron's membrane: When the membrane is perturbed at that location, the ion channels there open, sodium ions rush in, and the cell interior at that region briefly loses its negative charge. We said earlier, though, that the neuron doesn't just respond to an input; it also *transmits* this response from one end of the neuron to other. Specifically, the neuron sends a signal down its axon, where it will eventually launch a new series of events triggering the *next* neuron. How does this transmission work?

As we've just noted, when a neuron's membrane is disturbed, it is briefly **depolarized**— that is, it loses the electrical charge that normally exists across the membrane. This depolarization takes place at a particular location; but it spreads because depolarization at one point on the membrane causes other nearby ion channels to open, and so sodium rushes into the cell at those locations as well. Of course, the resting potential is quickly restored at *those* locations, but—for a brief moment—a new portion of the cell's membrane has been depolarized. This depolarization causes the next set of ion channels to open, which causes the next set to open, and so on in a domino-like sequence as the action potential at one site triggers an action potential at the next. In this way, the depolarization moves down the entire length of the axon and throughout the rest of the neuron as well. This sequence of events is known as the **propagation** of the action potential. The whole thing is like a spark traveling along a fuse—except that whereas the fuse is consumed by the spark, the ion channels rapidly reclose and the membrane restores itself (i.e., reestablishes the resting potential; Figure 3.11).

One might worry that this process could continue infinitely—as one region of the membrane depolarizes its neighbor, which in turn causes a new depolarization of the first region, which then depolarizes the neighbor again, and on and on. This back-and-forth disruption is prevented by the refractory period at each area of the membrane. Thanks to the refractory period, the area of membrane that was depolarized first is unresponsive when, a moment later, its neighbor is depolarized. As a result, the action potential is propagated in one direction only and thus works its way down the axon.

The flow of ions in or out of the neuron is, as we've said, quite rapid. Even so, the propagation of the action potential is surprisingly slow—it travels at about 1 meter per second, roughly the walking speed of an average adult. If this was top speed for neural signals, it would be disastrous for most organisms; fast-paced actions would be impossible. This problem is solved, however, by an anatomical feature we've already mentioned: the myelin layers that wrap around an axon and—crucially—the gaps between the myelin wrappers.

If an axon is myelinated, ions can move into or out of the axon only at the nodes of Ranvier. At all other locations, the axon is enclosed within its myelin wrapper, and this blocks ion flow. In essence, therefore, the action potential has to skip from node to

refractory period The time after an action potential during which a neuron's cell membrane is unprepared for the next action potential.

depolarize In the nervous system, to lose the charge that normally exists across the neuronal membrane.

propagation The spread of the action potential down an axon, caused by successive changes in electrical charge along the length of the axon's membrane.

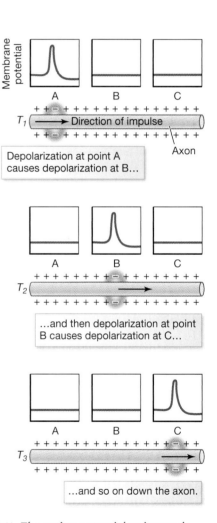

3.11 The action potential as it travels along the axon The axon is shown at three different moments—T_1, T_2, and T_3— after the application of a stimulus. The voltage inside the membrane is shown at three different points along the axon—A, B, and C.

node; and thanks to these jumps, it moves relatively quickly: Myelinated axons can propagate their action potentials at speeds up to 120 meters per second (about 260 miles per hour).

To appreciate the huge importance of the myelin, consider the deficits someone suffers when myelination breaks down in the brain. This happens in *multiple sclerosis* (MS), a disease in which the body's immune system mistakenly regards the myelin as an intruder and attacks it. The manifestations of MS are variable but severe, and they can include such serious maladies as total blindness and paralysis.

All-or-None Law

all-or-none law The law that all action potentials have the same strength and speed regardless of the triggering stimulus.

If a stimulus is strong enough to destabilize the neuronal membrane, the neuron produces an action potential; in that case, we say the neuron has *fired*. The action potential will be the same size and is propagated at the same speed, regardless of whether the stimulus just meets threshold or exceeds it by 2, 3, or 20 times. This phenomenon is sometimes called the **all-or-none law.** Just as pounding on a car horn won't make it any louder, a stronger stimulus won't produce a stronger action potential. A neuron either fires or it doesn't—there's no in between.

Obviously, though, we need some way to differentiate the weak signals from the strong. Otherwise, we'd have no way to tell apart the buzz of a mosquito and the roar of a jet engine, the light of a distant candle and the full illumination of a sunny day. If neurons can't vary the strength of their response, how do we make these differentiations?

Part of the answer is that more intense stimuli excite greater numbers of neurons. This happens because neurons vary enormously in their excitation thresholds. As a result, a weak stimulus stimulates only neurons with relatively low thresholds, while a strong stimulus stimulates all of those neurons plus others whose threshold is higher.

It's also important to realize that when neurons are bombarded with a sustained stimulus, they do not just fire once and then stop. Instead they generate a whole stream, or "volley," of action potentials by means of repeated cycles of destabilization and restabilization. Of course, the all-or-none law applies within the volley, so the size of each action potential is always the same. Even so, neurons can vary the *rate* of their firing in the volley; and in most cases, the stronger the stimulus, the more often the neuron will fire. This pattern holds until we reach a maximum rate of firing, after which further increases in stimulus intensity have no effect (Figure 3.12). Different neurons have different maximum rates, and the highest in humans are on the order of 1,000 impulses per second.

At threshold

Firing frequency

Time

At 160% of threshold intensity

At 270% of threshold intensity

500 msec

3.12 Stimulus intensity and firing rate Responses of a crab axon to an electrical stimulus at three levels of current intensity. *Threshold* refers to the lowest intensity that will trigger a response. The time scale used here is compressed, and so the action potentials show up as single vertical lines or "spikes." Notice that increasing the current intensity has no effect on the height of the spikes (as we would expect, based on the all-or-none law), but it leads to a marked increase in the frequency of spikes per second.

The Synapse

The propagation of the action potential moves a signal from one end of an axon to the other. But how is the signal then passed to the next neuron, so that the message can continue traveling toward its destination? For many years, no one saw this as a problem. Descartes, for example, believed that reflexes were formed from a long, continuous strand of nervous tissue—in essence, one neuron. According to this view, the incoming sensory information triggers a response at one end of this neuron. The signal is then propagated down the length of the cell and eventually triggers a response at the end of the same neuron. But this view (and several variations of it) soon faced a major problem: If myelinated neurons can send a signal at 120 meters per second, then how long should it take someone to withdraw their hand if they happen to touch a hot stove? The sensation of heat would have to travel from fingertips to brain and then get back out to the arm muscles to produce the movement—in all, a distance of less than 2 meters. Based on a signal speed of 120 meters per second, we can predict that the person will respond in less than one-hundredth of a second. But in fact, the response is likely to be 20 times *slower* than that (roughly 200 milliseconds).

By the end of the nineteenth century, therefore, most researchers were convinced that the neuronal transmission must involve some intervening steps and that these steps slow things down. Today we know that this conjecture was correct; the lines of neuronal communication depend on a *succession* of neurons, not just on one long neuron that somehow reaches from the sensory input all the way to the muscles that produce the response. Within this succession of neurons there's a small gap between adjacent neurons, so the neural signal has to move down a neuron's axon, jump across the gap and then trigger the next neuron's response, move down its axon, and so on. This gap between neurons is called the **synapse.**

Transmission across the synapse does slow down the neuronal signal. But it's a tiny price to pay, because this setup yields a huge advantage: Each neuron receives information from (i.e., has synapses with) many other neurons, and this allows the "receiving" neuron to integrate information from many sources. Among other benefits, this pattern of many neurons feeding into one makes it possible for several weak signals to add together, eliciting a response that any one of the initial signals could not trigger on its own. In addition, communication at the synapse is *adjustable:* As we'll discuss in Chapter 7, the strength of a synaptic connection can be altered by experience; this is essential for learning because adjustments at the synapse allow the organism to store new knowledge and gain new skills.

synapse The small gap between two adjacent neurons, consisting of the presynaptic and postsynaptic neurons' membranes and the space between them.

The Synaptic Mechanism

So far, we've suggested that communication across the synapse (communication *between* neurons) functions differently from—and is slower than—the transmission of information within a neuron. But how exactly do neurons communicate across the synapse? The answer turns out to be *chemical*—the neuron on the "sending" side of the synapse releases certain molecules that drift across the synapse and trigger a response on the "receiving" side. This process is entirely different from the electrical signaling that takes place within a single neuron.

Early insight into these points came in 1921 from an experiment by Otto Loewi, who later earned the Nobel Prize for his work. Loewi knew that activity in the *vagus nerve* causes the heart rate to slow down, and he hypothesized that the nerve communicates with the heart by releasing a certain chemical. To test this hypothesis, he dissected two frogs and removed their hearts. He placed each of the hearts, with nerves still attached, in a separate container filled with fluid. He then electrically stimulated one of the vagus nerves and—not surprisingly—the attached heart immediately slowed its rate of beating. Loewi then took a sample of the fluid from that container and dripped it into the separate container holding the second heart. What should happen? If the signal from the vagus nerve was electrical or mechanical, then this signal would not change the fluid in the first container; and so shifting the fluid into the *second* container should have no effect. But if the signal was chemical, then some of the relevant molecules would probably diffuse out into the fluid of the first container and be carried along when the fluid was dripped into the other container. As a result, the fluid (with these molecules) should slow the second heart, just as it slowed the first. This is exactly what happened; so apparently, the signal was chemical (Figure 3.13 on page 98).

3.13   SCIENTIFIC METHOD: What kind of signal do neurons use to communicate: electrical, mechanical, or chemical?

PREDICTION: If the signal from the vagus nerve to the heart is either *electrical* or *mechanical*, then activity in this nerve, and the sending of the signal, won't affect the fluid surrounding the heart. But if the signal is *chemical*, some of the signaling substance might diffuse into the fluid.

Method

1. Loewi placed two still-beating frog hearts (with vagus nerves attached) into jars of saline solution, A and B.

2. With an electrode, he stimulated the vagus nerve of the heart in Jar A to slow its beating.

3. To see whether Jar A's fluid now contained traces of a chemical signal from the nerve, he transferred a sample of Jar A's fluid into Jar B. He observed its effect on the second heart.

Vagus nerve

A   B

Stimulating electrode

A   A

Fluid from Jar A

B   B

Results

The heart in Jar B beat slower when he added fluid from Jar A to its bathing solution.

CONCLUSION: The vagus nerve sends *chemical* signals to the heart.

SOURCE STUDY: Loewi, 1921

---

neurotransmitters Chemicals released by one neuron (usually the presynaptic neuron), which trigger a response in another neuron (usually the postsynaptic neuron); the chief means of communication among neurons.

3.14 The synapse Electron micrograph of the knoblike axon terminals, which contain the synaptic vesicles.

In Loewi's procedure, the output from the vagus nerve was a chemical that influenced the muscle tissue in the heart. In many other contexts, the output from a neuron is a chemical that triggers a response in another neuron. But how exactly do these chemical messages work? Let's focus on what happens when one neuron is sending a signal to another neuron. The cell that sends the message is called the *presynaptic neuron* (it's the one "before the synapse"), and the actual transmission process begins in the tiny *axon terminals* of this cell. Within these swellings are many tiny sacs, or *synaptic vesicles* ("little vessels"), that are like water balloons filled with **neurotransmitters**—the chemicals that will, when released, influence other neurons.

When the presynaptic neuron fires, some of the vesicles literally burst. They eject their contents into the gap separating the presynaptic cell from the cell that will receive the signal—the *postsynaptic neuron* (the one "after the synapse"). The neurotransmitter molecules diffuse across this gap and latch onto *receptors* on the membrane of the postsynaptic cell (Figure 3.14; Figure 3.15A and B). This sequence causes certain ion channels in the postsynaptic membrane to open or close.

As we'll see, there are several types of neurotransmitters, and each type has different effects on the postsynaptic cell. For example, some neurotransmitters open the channels to (positively charged) sodium ions (Figure 3.15C and D). This flow of ions will decrease membrane's voltage difference, but if the voltage change is small, the membrane may be able to compensate and thus restore the resting potential.

It's important to realize, though, that this postsynaptic cell is probably receiving inputs from other presynaptic cells: They're also releasing neurotransmitters that latch onto the cell's receptors. This activity causes a further flow of sodium into the postsynaptic neuron, driving its voltage farther and farther from the resting level. Eventually, the voltage difference for the postsynaptic cell may reach the cell's excitation threshold. This triggers an action potential in this cell that will speed down this neuron's axon, causing it to release neurotransmitters of its own.

In other cases, the neurotransmitters latching onto the receptors can have the opposite effect—they can make the postsynaptic cell *less* likely to fire. Specifically, at some synapses, the presynaptic cell releases transmitter substances that lead to an *increased* voltage difference across the membrane of the postsynaptic neuron. This can happen, for example, if the transmitters cause the opening of channels that let chloride ions (Cl^-) enter the postsynaptic cell. These ions make the inside of the postsynaptic cell even more negatively charged than it was at the start. The heightened voltage difference moves the cell *away* from its excitation threshold, making it less likely to fire.

Most neurons have synaptic connections with neurons that excite them (i.e., that depolarize the membrane, making an action potential more likely), as well as with others that inhibit them (by *hyper*polarizing the membrane, making an action potential less likely). We can think of these inputs as "yes" votes and "no" votes, and the response of the postsynaptic cell will depend

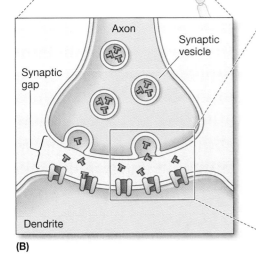

3.15 Schematic view of synaptic transmission (A) Neuron 1 transmits a message across the synaptic gap to neuron 2. (B) The events in the axon terminal. (C) The vesicle bursts, and neurotransmitter molecules are ejected toward the postsynaptic membrane. (D) Neurotransmitter molecules settle on the receptor site, an ion channel opens, and Na+ floods in.

on a final tally of the votes—the balance of excitatory yeas and inhibitory nays. If the net value is excitatory, and if this value exceeds the threshold, the cell will fire—that is, produce an action potential.

What happens to the transmitter molecules after they've affected the postsynaptic neuron? They can't just stay where they are, because they might continue exerting their effects long after the presynaptic neuron has stopped firing, thus making any input permanent. To avoid this problem, some transmitters are inactivated shortly after they've been discharged; this is done by special "cleanup" enzymes that break them up into their chemical components. More commonly, though, neurotransmitters are not destroyed but reused. In this process, called **synaptic reuptake,** the neurotransmitter molecules (after they've had their effect on the postsynaptic cell) are ejected from the receptors, vacuumed up by molecular pumps back into the presynaptic axon terminals, and repackaged into new synaptic vesicles.

synaptic reuptake The presynaptic neuron's process of reabsorbing its own neurotransmitters after signaling so that they can be released again the next time the neuron fires.

Neurotransmitters

On the face of it, the nervous system might seem to need only two transmitters: an excitatory one that makes the postsynaptic cell more likely to fire and an inhibitory one that makes the cell less likely to fire. But the reality is different; there are actually a great number of transmitter substances. About a hundred have been isolated so far, and many more are sure to be discovered. (A few of these neurotransmitters are listed in Table 3.1.)

Why does the nervous system need so many signal types? For one thing, the variety helps the nervous system to keep separate the different types of information being passed back and forth. The key idea here is that individual neurons are selective in what neurotransmitters they will respond to. Many neurons are responsive to more than one transmitter; but even so, each neuron has its own pattern of sensitivities. For example, a neuron inhibited by GABA will respond differently—or perhaps not at all—to molecules of serotonin that happen to float by. Thus, in each part of the brain, the nervous system can use one transmitter to send one type of message and a different transmitter to send a different type of message.

TABLE 3.1	Neurotransmitters	
	Neurotransmitter	**Functions and characteristics**
	Acetylcholine (ACh)	Released at many synapses and at the junction between nerves and muscles; the release of ACh makes the muscle fibers contract.
	Serotonin (5HT, after its formula 5-hydroxy-tryptamine)	Involved in many of the mechanisms of sleep, mood, and arousal.
	Gamma-amino butyric acid (GABA)	The most widely distributed inhibitory transmitter of the central nervous system.
	Glutamate	Perhaps the major excitatory transmitter in the brain; plays a crucial role in learning and memory.
	Norepinephrine (NE)	Helps control arousal level; influences wakefulness, learning, and memory.
	Dopamine (DA)	Influences movement, motivation, emotion.

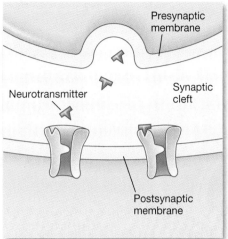

3.16 Lock-and-key model of synaptic transmission Transmitter molecules will affect the postsynaptic membrane only if their shape fits the shape of certain receptor molecules in that membrane—much as a key has to fit into a lock. The diagram shows two kinds of transmitters and their appropriate receptors.

How do neurons manage to be selective in this way? The answer, which depends on the exact shape of the receptors on the postsynaptic neuron, is sometimes described in terms of the *lock-and-key model* of transmitter action. This theory proposes that transmitter molecules will affect the postsynaptic membrane only if the molecule's shape fits precisely into the receptor, much as a key will work only if it has exactly the right shape for that lock (Figure 3.16).

Let's be clear, though, that the lock-and-key model provides a highly simplified account of the dynamics linking transmitters to receptors. Thus, our ultimate theory will need to include a number of significant complications (e.g., Bullock et al., 2005). Even so, the notion of receptors being selective in their response, and the idea of different neurotransmitters providing different signals, are key elements in controlling the complex flow of information throughout the brain.

Drugs and Neurotransmitters

Research on neurotransmitters has been crucial for neuroscience and has allowed enormous progress in our understanding of how the nervous system functions. In addition, this research has produced another benefit: Discoveries about neurotransmission have taught us a lot about how various drugs—legal and illegal—exert their effects.

In general, there are various ways either to enhance or impede the actions of a neurotransmitter. Chemicals that enhance a transmitter's activity are called **agonists**— a term borrowed from Greek drama, in which the agonist is the name for the hero. Drugs that impede such actions are **antagonists,** a term that refers to the hero's opponent (so to speak, the villain; Figure 3.17 on page 102).

Agonists and antagonists exert their influence in many ways. Some agonists actually mimic the transmitter; so, on their own, they can activate the receptors. Other agonists block the reuptake of the transmitter into the presynaptic cell, and still others work by counteracting the cleanup enzyme that breaks down the transmitter after it has triggered a response. Both of these mechanisms have the effect of leaving more transmitter within the synaptic gap; this increases the transmitter's opportunity to influence the postsynaptic membrane and so ends up increasing both the strength and duration of the transmitter's effect. Still other agonists work by promoting the production of the transmitter, usually by increasing the availability of some "ingredient" needed for the transmitter's chemical manufacture. This increased availability allows the body to produce more of the transmitter, so that more can be released upon stimulation.

agonists Drugs that enhance a neurotransmitter's activity.

antagonists Drugs that impede the activity of a neurotransmitter.

Agonists

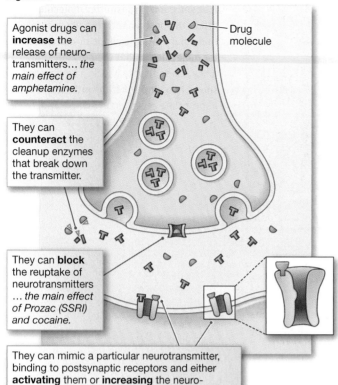

Agonist drugs can **increase** the release of neuro-transmitters... *the main effect of amphetamine.*

They can **counteract** the cleanup enzymes that break down the transmitter.

They can **block** the reuptake of neurotransmitters ... *the main effect of Prozac (SSRI) and cocaine.*

Drug molecule

They can mimic a particular neurotransmitter, binding to postsynaptic receptors and either **activating** them or **increasing** the neuro-transmitter's effects... *the main effect of nicotine.*

Antagonists

Antagonist drugs can **block** the release of neuro-transmitters... *the main effect of AMPT.*

Drug molecule

They can **destroy** neurotransmitters in the synapse.

They can mimc a particular neurotransmitter, binding to postsynaptic receptors enough to **block** neurotransmitter binding... *the main effect of propranolol (beta-blocker) and Haldol (antipsychotic drug).*

3.17 Agonists and antagonists Some drugs serve as agonists and can promote neuro-transmission in a variety of ways. Other drugs have the opposite effects and work as antagonists, diminishing or disrupting the effects of the neurotransmitters.

Antagonists work through similar mechanisms, but with the opposite effect. Thus, some antagonists prevent the transmitter from working by binding themselves to the synaptic receptor and blocking off the transmitter—essentially serving as a kind of putty in the synaptic lock. Other antagonists operate by speeding up reuptake, and others by augmenting cleanup enzymes.

Many of the agonists and antagonists identified by neuroscience depend on *endogenous* substances. These substances are produced naturally within the body, and they provide a way for the nervous system to modify and control its own functioning. One example is the *endorphins*—a family of chemicals, produced inside the brain, that powerfully influence how we perceive and cope with pain (Hughes et al., 1975). These naturally produced painkillers influence the brain in much the same way that morphine does. In fact, much of what we know about endorphins comes from parallels with our understanding of how drugs like morphine or heroin influence the body.

In other cases, neurotransmission can be modified by *exogenous* agonists or antagonists—chemicals introduced from outside the body. Getting these agents into the brain can be difficult: The cells that make up the nervous system are extremely sensitive to toxins, and so they're protected by the **blood-brain barrier**—a layer of tightly joined cells that surrounds the blood vessels in the brain and literally acts as a filter to prevent toxins from reaching the central nervous system (Mayhan, 2001). This barrier obviously evolved to keep out toxic substances, but it's also an obstacle to medications. As a result, investigators trying to develop medicines aimed at brain cells need to design an effective medication as well as ensure that it will pass through the barrier and reach the target cells.

blood-brain barrier Specialized membranes that surround the blood vessels within the brain and filter harmful chemicals out of the brain's blood supply.

Once in the brain, these medications have their influence by altering neurotransmission—some working as agonists, others as antagonists. Cocaine, for example, is an agonist; it works by blocking the reuptake of dopamine, norepinephrine, and epinephrine into the presynaptic molecules. The effect is arousal throughout the body, restlessness, and in some cases euphoria. Many antidepression medications—including Prozac, Zoloft, and Paxil—work in roughly the same way but specifically block the reuptake of serotonin. Still other drugs are antagonists. Some of the medications used for schizophrenia, for example, block postsynaptic receptors and seem effective in helping patients control psychotic thinking and restore normal functioning in their lives. (For more on the therapeutic effects of various drugs, see Chapter 17; for more on the mind-altering effects of drugs, see Chapter 6.)

COMMUNICATION THROUGH THE BLOODSTREAM

We're almost done with our discussion of how the nervous system manages its communication. But we need to touch briefly on one more aspect of this communication; namely, the signals that are transmitted by means of chemical messages mixed into the blood and thus distributed throughout the body. This type of communication is, in important ways, very different from the one we've been considering. Still, there are also important parallels between signaling from neuron to neuron, across the synapse, and signaling across much greater distances, via the bloodstream.

In the brain and throughout the body, the circulation of blood serves many purposes. Blood delivers oxygen and nutrients and carries away the waste products created by ordinary cell metabolism. This supply of nutrients is, of course, crucial for all cells; but it's especially important for the nervous system because neurons are energy gluttons. Although the human brain averages just 2 or 3% of our body weight, it burns up roughly 18% of the calories we take in; it uses a similarly high proportion of the total oxygen taken in by our lungs.

TABLE	The Main Endocrine Glands and Some of Their Functions	
3.2	**Gland**	**Function(s) of the released hormones**
	Anterior pituitary	Often called the body's master gland because it triggers hormone secretion in many of the other endocrine glands.
	Posterior pituitary	Prevents loss of water through kidney.
	Thyroid	Affects metabolic rate.
	Islet cells in pancreas	Affects utilization of glucose.
	Adrenal cortex	Has various effects on metabolism, immunity, and response to stress; has some effects on sexual behavior.
	Adrenal medulla	Increases sugar output of liver; stimulates various internal organs.
	Ovaries	One set of hormones (estrogen) produces female sex characteristics and is relevant to sexual behavior. Another hormone (progesterone) prepares uterus for implantation of embryo.
	Testes	Produces male sex characteristics; relevant to sexual arousal.

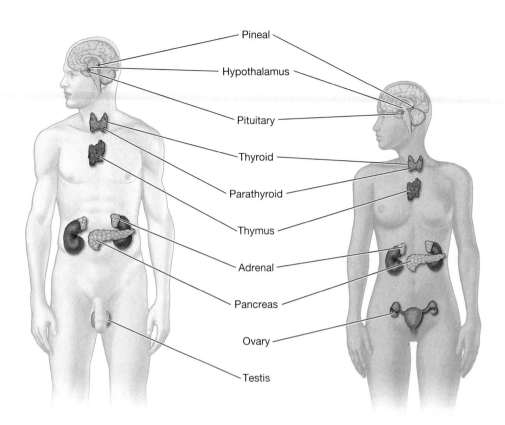

Pineal
Hypothalamus
Pituitary
Thyroid
Parathyroid
Thymus
Adrenal
Pancreas
Ovary
Testis

3.18 Location of major endocrine glands and hypothalamus

endocrine system The system of glands that release secretions directly into the bloodstream and affect organs elsewhere in the body.

hormone A chemical released by a gland. Hormones travel through the bloodstream and influence functions such as metabolic rate, arousal level, and the liver's sugar output.

The circulation of blood also provides a means of sending signals from one location to another. This other means of internal communication is called the **endocrine system** (Table 3.2 and Figure 3.18). In this system, various *glands* release chemical secretions called **hormones** into the bloodstream and in this way affect structures that are often far removed from their biochemical birthplace. As an example, take the pituitary gland. One of its components secretes a hormone that tells the kidney to decrease the amount of water excreted in the urine—a useful mechanism when the body is short of water. Or consider the adrenal glands, positioned on top of the kidneys. These glands produce several chemicals that govern the body's response to fear or stress; we'll have much more to say about these two glands and their functioning in our later discussion of motivation (Chapter 12).

At first glance, the communication provided by the endocrine glands seems very different from that provided by the nervous system. Neurotransmitters only have to cross the synaptic gap, which is less than 1/10,000 of a millimeter wide, and their effects are virtually immediate. The transmitters are then quickly reabsorbed or destroyed, and so their effects are quite brief. In contrast, the chemical messages employed by the endocrine system often have to travel great distances within the body, and so their effect is inevitably slower but also longer lasting.

Despite these differences, the two communication systems have a lot in common. Endocrine messages are launched into the bloodstream and thus travel everywhere the blood travels, reaching virtually all parts of the body. Still, these messages are detected only by specialized receptors at particular locations; in this way, endocrine messages have well-defined targets just like the neurotransmitters do.

Neurotransmission and the endocrine system are also alike because both systems rely on chemical substances as their messengers. Indeed, they often use the *same* substances because a number of chemicals serve both as hormones and as neurotransmitters.

Norepinephrine, for example, is one of the hormones secreted by the adrenal gland; and it's also an important neurotransmitter. Moreover, the effects produced by norepinephrine as a hormone overlap substantially with the effects produced by activating the neurons that use norepinephrine as their transmitter. Relationships like these suggest that neurons and the cells of the endocrine glands may have evolved from a common origin— an ancestral signaling system from which both our endocrine and nervous systems are derived (LeRoith, Shiloach, & Roth, 1982).

METHODS FOR STUDYING THE NERVOUS SYSTEM

Individual neurons—activated by neurotransmitters binding to their receptors and then sending signals down their axons, causing the release of more neurotransmitter— are the building blocks of the nervous system. But how are these building blocks assembled to create a system that can control the beating of our hearts, the temperature of our body's core, or the rhythm of our sleeping and waking? Indeed, how are these building blocks assembled into a system complex enough to make possible our emotions, thoughts, and actions?

We've made enormous progress in understanding these issues, thanks partly to the extraordinary research tools that have become available to neuroscientists in the last few decades. Let's pause to examine some of these tools and then turn to what we've learned by using them.

Recording from Individual Neurons

As we have already seen, it's possible to record the activities of a single neuron; it's also possible to stimulate the neuron and observe the result. So far, we've focused on what these recordings can tell us about neurons in general—for example, how the flow of ions can produce an action potential. Similar methods, however, can be used to study how specific neurons function in a particular setting.

For example, the technique of *single-cell recording* has told us a great deal about the brain mechanisms crucial for *vision,* and we'll rely heavily on evidence drawn from single-cell recording in Chapters 4 and 5. In a typical study using this procedure, researchers monitor the moment-by-moment activity of individual neurons in the brain while placing various stimuli in front of the animals' eyes. The data indicate that some cells function as "motion detectors"; they fire rapidly when a moving stimulus is in view, but not when the stimulus is stationary. Other cells seem to function as "shape detectors," firing more rapidly whenever a particular form is in view. Still other cells have their own specialties. Overall, though, the data obtained through single-cell recording allow us to identify the apparent function of each neuron, and so guide us toward a broader understanding of how individual cells contribute to the overall processes of visual perception.

It's also possible to collect single-cell data from many individual neurons at the same time—through a procedure known as *multi-unit recording.* This procedure uses microelectrodes to record the activity of individual cells and then relies on computer analyses to examine patterns of activity across the entire collection of cells. Studies of this sort can record from hundreds of neurons simultaneously, providing information about how each cell is influencing the others as well as information about the aggregate pattern of responding (e.g., Lebedev & Nicolelis, 2006). As one example, multi-unit recordings have been used to monitor activity in brain areas that animals ordinarily use to control their limbs, and then the recordings have been used to control *artificial* limbs. This extraordinary advance may soon lead to technology in which humans who have been paralyzed can control robotic arms and legs simply by thinking about the relevant movements!

Studying the Effects of Brain Damage

In many cases, we gain further insights into brain functioning by asking what happens if the brain is somehow *changed*—either deliberately in our research or through accident or injury. For example, in the laboratory, we can use chemicals or weak applications of electricity to stimulate particular brain areas and then observe the resulting changes in behavior. Likewise, we can use different chemicals, or slightly stronger electric currents, to create a *brain lesion*—damage to the brain cells—at a particular site and then compare how the brain functions with this damage to how it functions when the site is unharmed. Alternatively, we can disrupt the flow of information into or out of an area by cutting—technically, *transecting*—the relevant pathways and then observing the result (Figure 3.19).

Although each of these techniques has been a valuable source of new knowledge, it should be obvious that these procedures, which involve altering the brain of another living creature, raise some ethical questions. In some cases, the ethical concerns can be weighed against the direct medical benefits of a procedure. (Lesions or transections are sometimes used to treat extreme cases of epilepsy; even though these procedures are carried out for therapeutic purposes, we can still gain valuable information by studying the results.) In other cases, the brain manipulation is done not for medical treatment but as

3.19 Brain lesioning All animal strategies, including those aimed at creating a brain lesion, rely on special apparatus that allows precise measurement and precise placement of electrodes.

part of a scientific study; here, the ethical concerns must be weighed against the study's potential scientific benefits. These benefits are, however, often large; for example, studies of brain lesions have allowed enormous progress in our understanding of Parkinson's disease, multiple sclerosis, and Alzheimer's disease. This progress will undoubtedly contribute to new forms of treatment for these conditions.

NEUROPSYCHOLOGICAL STUDIES

Outside of the laboratory, people sometimes suffer disease or injuries that can cause damage to the brain. These naturally occurring cases are tragic, but they can provide information useful both for researchers and for those involved in treating the afflicted individual. The study of these cases defines the special field of *neuropsychology*—the effort to gain insights into the brain's function by closely examining individuals who have suffered some form of brain damage.

Early studies in neuropsychology relied on clinical observation of patients with brain damage or disease: What were their symptoms? How was their behavior disrupted? For example, consider the grisly case of Phineas Gage, who in 1848 was working as a construction foreman. Gage was preparing a site for demolition when some blasting powder misfired and launched a 3-foot iron rod into his cheek, through the front part of his brain, and out the top of his head (Figure 3.20). Gage lived, but not well. As we'll discuss later, he suffered intellectual and emotional impairments that gave researchers valuable clues about the roles of the brain's frontal lobes (Valenstein, 1986).

In Gage's case, the brain damage was clear; the task for investigators was to define the consequences of the damage. In other cases, the situation is reversed: The behavioral effects are obvious, but the nature of the brain damage needs to be discovered. As one example, later in the chapter we'll consider cases of *aphasia*—disruption of language use caused by brain damage. More than a century ago, physicians were able to describe the disruption itself—the difficulties their patients had in speaking or understanding. It was not until years later that they identified the affected brain regions—regions that we now know are crucial for language.

3.20 **Phineas Gage** (A) A photograph of Phineas Gage and the actual rod that passed through his brain. (B) A computer reconstruction showing the path of the rod.

In more recent studies, neuropsychologists have moved beyond clinical observation. Now they often do fine-grained experiments to find out exactly what a brain-damaged individual can and cannot do. These experiments are usually combined with the neuroimaging techniques we'll describe in a moment, so that the investigators can match a precise picture of the person's brain damage with an equally precise assessment of her deficits.

TRANSCRANIAL MAGNETIC STIMULATION STUDIES

Over the past 25 years, investigators have developed a new experimental technique that can produce *temporary* brain disruption and allow investigators to perform experiments that would otherwise not be possible. This technique—**transcranial magnetic stimulation (TMS)**—involves creating a series of strong magnetic pulses at a particular location on the scalp (Figure 3.21). At certain intensities and frequencies, these pulses *stimulate* the brain region directly underneath that scalp area; thus, investigators can use TMS to activate otherwise sluggish brain regions.

At other intensities, though, TMS has a different effect: It creates a temporary disruption in the brain region just beneath the scalp—allowing investigators to "turn off" certain brain mechanisms for a brief period of time and observe the results (Fitzgerald, Fountain, & Daskalakis, 2006). This technique obviously presents an enormous range of experimental options and lets investigators examine in detail the function of this or that brain region. However, TMS does have limits as a research tool: It influences only structures near the surface of the brain (i.e., immediately inside the skull). Even so, TMS is a powerful addition to the neuroscientists' tool kit.

We should also mention that TMS is more than just a research tool, because investigators are also exploring its therapeutic potential (e.g., Gershon, Dannon, & Grunhaus, 2003). Some uses are already in place: In late 2008, the U.S. Food and Drug Administration approved the use of TMS as a therapeutic procedure for some

transcranial magnetic stimulation (TMS) The technique of applying repeated magnetic stimulation at the surface of the skull to temporarily stimulate or disable a target brain region.

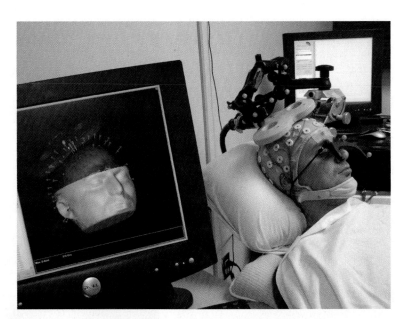

3.21 Transcranial magnetic stimulation (TMS) At low intensities, TMS is used to stimulate specific brain regions. At higher intensities, TMS causes a temporary disruption.

cases of clinical depression. We'll return to this technique, and its potential uses, in Chapter 17.

Recording from the Whole Brain

Neuroscientists also rely on techniques that can provide detailed portraits of the whole brain—without in any way disrupting the brain's functioning. There's actually a wide array of such techniques, each with its own strengths and limitations: Some tell us the exact shapes and positions of brain structures but give no information about how active those brain sites are at the moment; others do the reverse—they provide information about activity levels but not about the exact anatomy. Some techniques are exquisitely accurate in locating *where* the brain is especially active, but they're less exact about *when* exactly the activity is occurring. Other techniques reverse this pattern and give us temporal information, but not spatial.

RECORDING THE BRAIN'S ELECTRICAL ACTIVITY

As we've discussed, communication from one neuron to the next typically relies on chemical signals. However, communication within each neuron (e.g., communication down the axon) relies on an electrical signal. The amount of current involved here is minute—but, of course, many millions of neurons are all active at the same time, and the current generated by all of them together is great enough to be detected by sensitive electrodes placed on the surface of the scalp. This is the basis for *electroencephalography*—a recording of voltage changes occurring at the scalp that reflect activity in the brain underneath. The result of this procedure is an **electroencephalogram, or EEG** (Figure 3.22).

EEGs tell us, for example, that there is often a detectable rhythm in the brain's electrical activity—a rhythm that results from many, many neurons all firing at more or less the same rate. We'll have more to say about these rhythms in Chapter 6, when we consider the changes that we can observe in brain activity when someone is falling asleep.

To detect the brain's rhythms, we need to record the brain activity over a period of several seconds or longer. Sometimes, though, researchers want to ask how the brain responds electrically to a specific event that takes place at a particular moment in time. In this case, we can measure the changes in the EEG in the brief period just before, during, and after the event. These changes are referred to as an **event-related potential (ERP)**.

Let's be clear that an EEG is a record of activity throughout the brain. The EEG therefore includes the brain's response to our experimental stimulus, but it also includes the electrical result of all of the brain's other activities—for example, the brain's control of heart rate during the experimental procedure, the brain's monitoring of body temperature, and so on. How can we remove this "background noise" from the EEG to reveal just the bit of brain activity we're interested in—namely, the brain's response to our experimental stimulus? We do this by presenting the stimulus over and over, and collecting ERPs from each presentation. We can then average together the results of all these recordings, based on the idea that this will "cancel out" all of the brain's background activities and thus isolate the brain's response to our signal. In this way we can measure rather precisely the pattern of electrical changes in the brain caused, say, by listening to a musical phrase or deciding to launch a particular movement.

3.22 Recording brain waves The overall electricity of the brain can be measured via electrodes placed on the surface of the scalp.

electroencephalogram (EEG) A record of the brain's electrical activity recorded by placing electrodes on the scalp.

event-related potential (ERP) Electrical changes in the brain that correspond to the brain's response to a specific event; measured with EEG.

Our understanding of the linkage between brain and behavior has been revolutionized by the development of *neuroimaging techniques*. These provide remarkable three-dimensional portraits of the brain's anatomy and functioning, with absolutely no invasion of brain tissue and with the brain's owner awake and fully conscious throughout the procedure.

One technique for imaging brain anatomy is the **CT (computerized tomography) scan,** also known as a *CAT (computerized axial tomography) scan* (Figure 3.23A). In this technique, researchers take a series of X-ray pictures of the brain, each from a different angle, and then use a computer to construct a detailed composite portrait from these images. These scans, which yield precise information about the exact shape and position of structures within a brain, are immensely useful for medical diagnosis (e.g., in detecting tumors or structural abnormalities) and for research (e.g., for locating the brain damage that is the source of a patient's behavioral or cognitive difficulties).

A more widely used neuroimaging technique is **magnetic resonance imaging (MRI).** MRI scans are safer than CT scans because they don't involve X-rays. Instead, the person is placed in a strong magnetic field; this aligns the spinning of the nuclei of atoms that make up the brain tissue. Then a brief pulse of electromagnetic energy (a radio wave) is used to disrupt these spins. After the disruption, the spins of the nuclei shift back into alignment with the magnetic field; as this shift happens, the atoms give off electromagnetic energy. This energy is recorded by detectors arrayed around the person's head, analyzed by a computer, and assembled into a three-dimensional representation of the brain that can show the healthy tissue as well as tumors, tissue degeneration, and the blood clots or leaks that may signal strokes (Figure 3.23B).

CT and MRI scans provide precise anatomical depictions; but they cannot tell us about the brain's moment-by-moment functioning, including which areas of the brain are particularly active at any point in time and which are less active. To record this kind of brain activity, experimenters use other techniques, including **positron emission tomography (PET) scans.** In a PET scan, the participant is injected with a safe dose of some radioisotope—often an isotope of a sugar that resembles glucose, the brain's

CT (computerized tomography) scan A technique for examining brain structure by constructing a composite of X-ray images taken from many different angles.

MRI (magnetic resonance imaging) A neuroimaging technique that documents the effects of strong magnetic pulses on the molecules that make up brain tissue. A computer then assembles this information into a picture of brain structure.

PET (positron emission tomography) scan A technique for examining brain function by observing the amount of metabolic activity in different brain regions.

3.23 Brain scans The CT scan (A) shows the brain of an 85-year-old woman. The MRI scan (B) shows more detail. The dark regions are actually open spaces (called ventricles) within the brain, filled with fluid. The distinction between the brain's white matter and gray matter is also visible.

metabolic fuel. The PET scan then keeps track of how this radioactivity is distributed across the brain. The key idea here is that the brain cells that are more active at any moment will need to use more glucose and so, in this setup, will absorb more radioactivity. By keeping track of the pattern of radioactivity, we can know where the glucose is being used, and hence we can know which regions within the brain are particularly active.

A newer technique called **functional MRI (fMRI) scanning** adapts standard MRI procedures to study brain activity (Figure 3.24). In most cases, fMRI scans rely on the fact that hemoglobin—the molecule that carries oxygen in the bloodstream—is less sensitive to magnetism when it is actually transporting an oxygen molecule than when it is not. By keeping track of the hemoglobin, therefore, detectors can measure the ratio of oxygenated to deoxygenated blood; this ratio yields a measurement called the *blood-oxygenation-level-dependent signal,* or *BOLD signal.* When neural regions are especially active, this ratio increases because the active tissue is demanding more oxygen. By tracking the BOLD signal, therefore, we can measure activity in the brain.

One advantage of fMRI scans over PET scans lies in their spatial precision, and fMRI scans can identify locations within 3 or 4 millimeters. A larger advantage, though, lies in fMRI's ability to tell *when* the brain activity took place. PET scans summarize the brain's activity level over a period of 40 seconds or so; and they cannot tell us when, within this time window, the activity took place. The BOLD signal, in contrast, provides measurements across just a few seconds; and this greater temporal precision is one of several reasons that fMRI scans are used far more often than PET. (We should note that an EEG record yields even more precise information about timing, but—unlike an fMRI—it cannot tell us exactly where in the brain the activity is taking place.)

Whether we're relying on PET scans or fMRI scans, though, we need to keep a complication in view: The entire brain is active all of the time—its cells are always using glucose and always needing oxygen. This is because neurons are living cells and require energy to sustain themselves and, in particular, to maintain their resting potential. What PET and fMRI seek to measure, therefore, are the *increases* beyond this constant state of activity. In other words, the measurement is not "which areas are active when someone is (say) listening to music?" Instead, the measurement is "which areas become *more* active when someone is listening to music?" These increases are typically assessed by a process that, in the end, resembles simple subtraction: Researchers measure the brain's activity when someone is engaged in the task that's being investigated, and they subtract from this value a measurement of the brain's activity when the person is not engaged in the task. Of course, it's important to design this baseline measurement carefully, so that (like any control condition) it is identical to the experimental condition in all ways except for the factor that the researchers are especially interested in. Thus, careful design of the control condition becomes part of the craft of using neuroimaging techniques.

The Power of Combining Techniques

The techniques we've described are each quite powerful; but as we've noted, each has its own limitations—some techniques provide information about structures but not activities, while others tell us *where* the activity took place but not *when,* and so on. In addition, PET scans and fMRI scans can tell us what brain areas are activated during a particular process, but this by itself doesn't tell us whether those areas are actually needed for the process. Perhaps the brain activity we're observing is a *consequence* of

functional MRI (fMRI) scan A technique for examining brain function by measuring blood flow and oxygen use within the brain.

3.24 Functional MRI Using functional magnetic resonance imaging, researchers can produce precise summaries of brain activity. In this image, the data from fMRI scans have been assembled into a 3D and show activation levels for a person inspecting faces; activation is especially high in an area known as the fusiform face area (FFA). This view shows the brain from behind and slightly above; the back half of the brain is not included so we can see structures deep in the brain that would be hidden otherwise.

the process, much like sweating is a consequence of (and not a cause) of physical activity. In that case, the brain activity would be *correlated* with a mental process but would not play a role in guiding or supporting that process.

How can we get past these various limitations? The answer draws on a strategy commonly used in psychology: We seek data from multiple sources, so that we can use the strengths of one technique to make up for the shortcomings of some other technique. Indeed, by collecting data of many different types, we gain the advantages of all the types—and so end up with a compelling package of evidence.

Thus, for example, some studies combine EEG recording with fMRI scans, so that we can learn from the EEG exactly *when* certain events took place in the brain, and learn from the scans *where* the activity took place. Likewise, some studies combine fMRI scans with CT data—the first procedure tells us about blood supplies (and therefore brain activity) and the second provides a detailed portrait of the person's brain anatomy. Together, these techniques can give us enormous precision in identifying exactly which regions of the brain are involved in a particular task.

In addition, neuroscientists often combine neuroimaging with studies of brain damage, basing this approach on the logic that if damage to a brain site disrupts a function, this is an indication that the site does play a role in supporting the function. In the same way, TMS allows us (temporarily) to "turn off" a particular brain site. If doing so causes a disruption in some process, this too indicates the site plays a role in supporting that function. Data like these allow us to go beyond claims about correlation and make stronger claims about cause and effect. The key, though, is that we rely on a variety of techniques and draw our conclusions only from a convergence of evidence gathered from many paradigms.

THE ARCHITECTURE OF THE NERVOUS SYSTEM

By using the tools we've just described, researchers have gained a detailed understanding of the structure and functioning of the nervous system. No matter what part of the nervous system we consider, however, one theme quickly emerges—a theme of *functional specialization:* Each part of the brain—indeed, each part of the nervous system throughout the body—performs its own job, and the functioning of the whole depends on an exquisite coordination among these various elements. As a result, we need to understand the nervous system with reference to some anatomy—so that we'll know what the various parts are, and approximately where they are. On this basis, let's start by taking a broad tour of the nervous system.

The Central and Peripheral Nervous Systems

central nervous system (CNS) The brain and spinal cord.

peripheral nervous system (PNS) The afferent and efferent nerves that extend from the brain and spinal cord to connect them with the organs and muscles.

At the most general level, the nervous system can be divided into several parts (Figure 3.25). The **central nervous system** (**CNS**) includes the brain and spinal cord, working as an integrated unit. All nerves elsewhere in the body are part of the **peripheral nervous system** (**PNS**), and virtually all of the nerves in the peripheral nervous system connect to the CNS via the spinal cord. This is part of the reason why damage to the cord is so dangerous, and why the cord is protected by the bones and connective tissue of the spine. Of course, the brain, too, is well protected. It's covered, first, in a shell of bone (the skull) and three layers of tough membranes (the

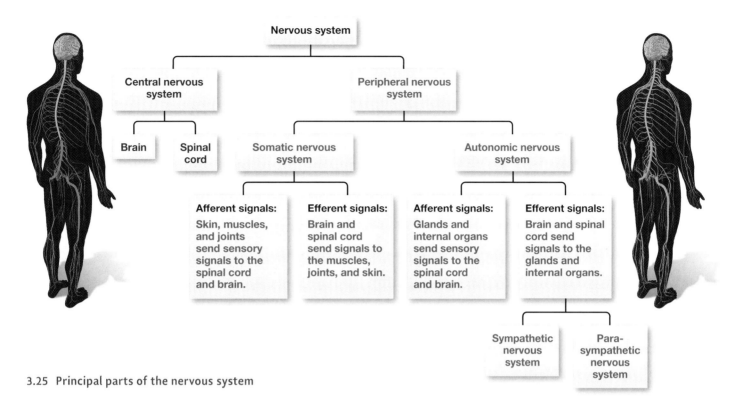

3.25 **Principal parts of the nervous system**

meninges). It's also floating in a bath of *cerebrospinal fluid* that (among other things) acts as a shock absorber when the head moves abruptly this way or that.

The peripheral nervous system itself has two distinguishable parts. The **somatic nervous system** (**SNS**) includes all the (efferent) nerves that control the skeletal muscles as well as the (afferent) nerves that carry information from the sense organs to the CNS. The other division—the **autonomic nervous system** (**ANS**)—includes all the (efferent) nerves that regulate the various glands in the body as well as those that regulate the *smooth muscles* of the internal organs and blood vessels. (The name "smooth muscles" refers to how these muscles look when observed under a microscope; this is in contrast to the skeletal muscles, which look striped.) The ANS also includes (afferent) nerves that bring the CNS information about these various internal systems.

Finally, the autonomic nervous system is itself divided into two parts: the **sympathetic branch**, which tends to "rev up" bodily activities in preparation for vigorous action, and the **parasympathetic branch**, which tends to restore the body's internal activities to normal after the action has been completed (Figure 3.26 on page 114).* These divisions of the ANS act reciprocally; excitation of the sympathetic branch leads to an increased heart rate, while excitation of the parasympathetic branch leads to cardiac slowing. Sympathetic activation produces a slowing down of peristalsis (rhythmic contractions of the intestines), so that we're not using energy for digesting when we're on the run; parasympathetic activation does the opposite—it speeds up peristalsis. We'll have much more to say about these systems in later chapters, when we discuss motivation (in Chapter 12) and when we discuss the effects of *stress* on health.

somatic nervous system (SNS) The division of the peripheral nervous system that controls the skeletal muscles and transmits sensory information.

autonomic nervous system (ANS) The division of the peripheral nervous system that receives information from and controls the internal organs.

sympathetic branch The division of the autonomic nervous system that mobilizes the organism for physical exertion.

parasympathetic branch The division of the autonomic nervous system that restores the body's normal resting state and conserves energy.

---

*For this pair of terms, it may help to bear in mind that the **s**ympathetic branch provides a **s**urge of energy when the organism needs it. In contrast, the **p**arasympathetic branch is activated when there's no emergency—in other words, in times of **p**eace.

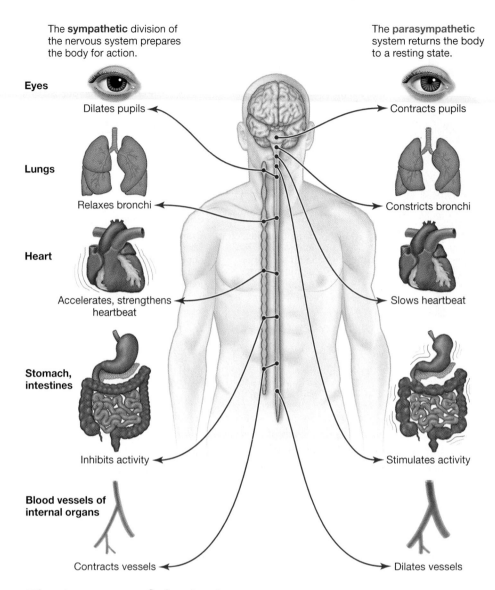

The **sympathetic** division of the nervous system prepares the body for action.

The **parasympathetic** system returns the body to a resting state.

Eyes — Dilates pupils / Contracts pupils

Lungs — Relaxes bronchi / Constricts bronchi

Heart — Accelerates, strengthens heartbeat / Slows heartbeat

Stomach, intestines — Inhibits activity / Stimulates activity

Blood vessels of internal organs — Contracts vessels / Dilates vessels

brain stem The brain region at the top of the spinal cord that includes the medulla and the pons.

cerebellum The part of the brain that controls muscular coordination and equilibrium.

cerebral cortex The outermost layer of the forebrain.

cerebral hemisphere One-half (left or right) of the cerebrum, the topmost part of the brain.

frontal lobe The area at the front of each cerebral hemisphere; includes tissue crucial for many aspects of planning and controlling thoughts and behavior.

parietal lobe The area in each cerebral hemisphere that lies between the frontal and occipital lobes; includes tissue crucial for receiving information from the skin senses.

temporal lobe The areas in each cerebral hemisphere lying below the temples; includes tissue crucial for hearing and many aspects of language use.

occipital lobe The rearmost area of each cerebral hemisphere; includes tissue crucial for processing visual information.

The Anatomy of the Brain

The peripheral nervous system is crucial. Without it, no motion of the body would be possible; no information would be received about the external world; the body would be unable to control its own digestion or blood circulation. Still, the aspect of the nervous system most interesting to psychologists is the central nervous system. It's here that we find the complex circuitry crucial for perception, memory, and thinking. It's the CNS that contains the mechanisms that define each person's personality, control his or her emotional responses, and more.

The CNS, as we've seen, includes the spinal cord and the brain itself. The spinal cord, for most of its length, actually does look like a cord; it has separate paths for nerves carrying afferent information (i.e., information *arriving* in the CNS) and nerves carrying efferent commands (information *exiting* the CNS). Inside the head, the spinal cord becomes larger and looks something like the cone part of an ice cream cone. Structures at the very top of the cord—looking roughly like the ice cream on top of the cone—form the **brain stem** (Figure 3.27). The *medulla* is at the bottom of the brain stem; among its other roles, the medulla controls our breathing and blood circulation. It also helps us maintain our balance by controlling head orientation and limb positions in relation to gravity. Above the medulla is the *pons*, which is one of the most important brain areas for controlling the brain's overall level of attentiveness and helps govern the timing of sleep and dreaming.

Just behind the brain stem is the **cerebellum** (Figure 3.28A). For many years, investigators believed the cerebellum's main role was to control balance and coordinate movements—especially rapid and carefully timed movements. Recent studies confirm this role, but suggest that the cerebellum also has a diverse set of other functions. Damage to this organ can cause problems in spatial reasoning, in discriminating sounds, and in integrating the input received from various sensory systems (J. Bower & Parsons, 2003).

Sitting on top of the pons are two more structures—the *midbrain* and *thalamus* (see Figure 3.27). Both of these structures serve as relay stations directing information to the forebrain, where the information is more fully processed and interpreted. But these structures also have other roles. The midbrain, for example, helps regulate our experience of pain and plays a key role in modulating our mood as well as shaping our motivation.

On top of these structures is the *forebrain*—by far the largest part of the human brain. Indeed, photographs of the brain (Figure 3.28B) show little other than the forebrain because this structure is large enough in humans to surround most of the other brain parts and hide them from view. Of course, we can see only the outer surface of the forebrain in such pictures; this is the **cerebral cortex** (*cortex* is the Latin word for "tree bark").

The cortex is just a thin covering on the outer surface of the brain; on average, it is a mere 3 mm thick. Nonetheless, there is a great deal of cortical tissue; by some estimates, the cortex constitutes 80% of the human brain (Kolb & Whishaw, 2009). This considerable volume is made possible by the fact that the cortex, thin as it is, consists of a very large sheet of tissue; if stretched out flat, it would cover roughly 2.7 square feet (2,500 cm^2). But the cortex isn't stretched flat; instead, it's crumpled up and jammed into the limited space inside the skull. This crumpling produces the brain's most obvious visual feature—the wrinkles, or convolutions, that cover the brain's outer surface.

Some of the "valleys" in between the wrinkles are actually deep grooves that divide the brain into different anatomical sections. The deepest groove is the *longitudinal fissure,* running from the front of the brain to the back and dividing the brain into two halves—specifically, the left and the right **cerebral hemispheres.** Other fissures divide the cortex in each hemisphere into four lobes, named after the bones that cover them—bones that, as a group, make up the skull. The **frontal lobes** form the front of the brain, right behind the forehead. The *central fissure* divides the frontal lobes on each side of the brain from the **parietal lobes,** the brain's topmost part. The bottom edge of the frontal lobes is marked by the *lateral fissure,* and below this are the **temporal lobes.** Finally, at the very back of the brain—directly adjoining the parietal and temporal lobes—are the **occipital lobes.**

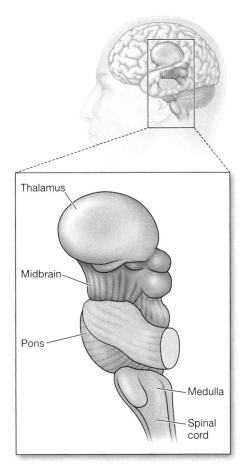

3.27 The brain stem The brain stem, consisting of the structures at the very top of the spinal cord, includes the pons and the medulla.

(A) **(B)**

3.28 The cortex of the cerebral hemispheres (A) Side-view diagram of the brain's convolutions, fissures, and lobes. The cortex hides most of the brain's other parts from view, although the cerebellum and brain stem are visible. (B) An actual human brain, shown from the side; the front of the head faces left.

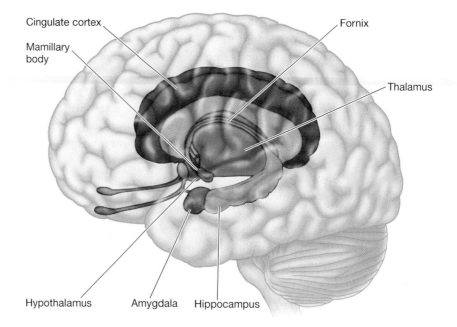

3.29 The limbic system This system is made up of a number of subcortical structures.

Cingulate cortex

Mamillary body

Fornix

Thalamus

Hypothalamus   Amygdala   Hippocampus

As we'll see, the cortex—the outer surface of all four lobes—controls many functions. Because these functions are so important to what we think, feel, and do, we'll address them in detail in a later section. But the structures beneath the cortex are just as important. One of these is the **hypothalamus,** positioned directly underneath the thalamus and crucially involved in the control of motivated behaviors such as eating, drinking, and sexual activity (see Chapter 12). Surrounding the thalamus and hypothalamus is a set of interconnected structures that form the **limbic system** (Figure 3.29). This system—especially one of its parts, the **amygdala**—plays a key role in modulating our emotional reactions and seems to serve roughly as an "evaluator" that helps determine whether a stimulus is a threat or not, familiar or not, and so on. Nearby is the **hippocampus,** which is pivotal for learning and memory as well as for our navigation through space. (In some texts, the hippocampus is considered part of the limbic system, following an organization scheme laid down more than 50 years ago. More recent analyses, however, indicate that this earlier scheme is anatomically and functionally misleading. For the original scheme, see MacLean, 1949, 1952; for a more recent perspective, see Kotter & Meyer, 1992; LeDoux, 1996.)

Lateralization

The entire human brain is more or less symmetrical around the midline, so there's a thalamus on the left side of the brain and another on the right. There's also a left-side amygdala and a right-side one. Of course, the same is true for the cortex itself: There's a temporal cortex in the left hemisphere and another in the right, a left occipital cortex and a right one, and so on. In almost all cases—cortical and subcortical—the left and right structures have roughly the same shape, the same position in their respective sides of the brain, and the same pattern of connections to other brain areas. Even so, there are some anatomical distinctions between the left-side and right-side structures. We can also document differences in function, showing that the left-hemisphere structures play a somewhat different role from the corresponding right-hemisphere structures.

The asymmetry in function between the two brain halves is called **lateralization,** and its manifestations influence phenomena that include language use and the per-

hypothalamus A subcortical structure that plays a vital role in controlling many motivated behaviors, like eating, drinking, and sexual activity.

limbic system A group of interconnected structures (including the hypothalamus, the amygdala, and others) that are crucial for emotion, motivation, and many aspects of learning and memory.

amygdala An almond-shaped, temporal lobe structure that plays a central role in emotion and evaluating stimuli.

hippocampus A temporal lobe structure that plays a pivotal role in learning and forming new memories.

lateralization Functional differences between the two cerebral hemispheres. E.g., in most right-handers, the left hemisphere is specialized for language, while the right hemisphere is better at some visual and spatial tasks.

corpus callosum The thick bundle of fibers connecting the cerebral hemispheres.

ception and understanding of spatial organization (Springer & Deutsch, 1998). Still, it's important to realize that the two halves of the brain, each performing somewhat different functions, work closely together under almost all circumstances. This integration is made possible by the *commissures*—thick bundles of fibers that carry information back and forth between the two hemispheres. The largest and probably most important commissure is the **corpus callosum,** but several other structures also ensure that the two brain halves work together as partners in virtually all mental tasks (Figure 3.30).

In some people, these neurological bridges between the hemispheres have been cut for medical reasons. This was, for example, a last-resort treatment for many years in cases of severe epilepsy. The idea was that the epileptic seizure would start in one hemisphere and spread to the other, and this spread could be prevented by disconnecting the two brain halves from each other (Bogen, Fisher, & Vogel, 1965; D. Wilson, Reeves, Gazzaniga, & Culver, 1977). The procedure has largely been abandoned by physicians, who are turning to less drastic surgeries for even the most extreme cases of epilepsy (Woiciechowsky, Vogel, Meyer, & Lehmann, 1997). Nonetheless, this medical procedure has produced a number of "split-brain patients"; this provides an extraordinary research opportunity by allowing us to examine how the brain halves function when they aren't in full communication with each other.

This research makes it clear that each hemisphere has its own specialized capacities (Figure 3.31). For most people, the left hemisphere has sophisticated language skills and is capable of making sophisticated inferences. The right hemisphere, in contrast, has only limited language skills; but it outperforms the left hemisphere in a variety of spatial tasks such as recognizing faces and perceiving complex patterns (Gazzaniga, Ivry, & Mangun, 2002; Kingstone, Freisen, & Gazzaniga, 2000).

3.30 Corpus callosum In this drawing, the two halves of the brain are shown as if pulled apart, revealing the corpus callosum, one of the main bundles of fibers carrying information back and forth between the hemispheres.

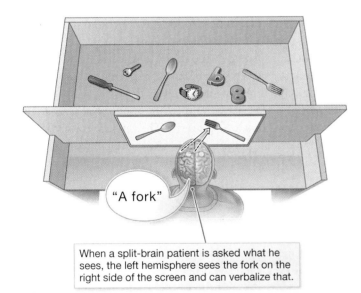

"A fork"

When a split-brain patient is asked what he sees, the left hemisphere sees the fork on the right side of the screen and can verbalize that.

The right hemisphere sees the spoon on the screen's left side, but it cannot verbalize that. However, if the patient reaches with his left hand to pick up the object, he does select the spoon.

3.31 The split-brain patient In this experiment, the patient is shown two pictures, one of a spoon and one of a fork. If asked what he sees, his response is controlled by the left hemisphere, which has seen only the fork (because it's in the right visual field). If asked to pick up the object shown in the picture, however, the patient—reaching with his left hand—picks up the spoon. That happens because the left hand is controlled by the right hemisphere, and this hemisphere receives visual information from the left-hand side of the visual world.

These differences between the left and right cerebral hemispheres are striking, but they're clearly distinct from many of the conceptions of hemispheric function written for the general public. Some popular authors go so far as to equate left-hemisphere function with Western science and right-hemisphere function with Eastern culture and mysticism. In the same vein, others have argued that Western societies overemphasize rational and analytic "left-brain" functions at the expense of intuitive, artistic, "right-brain" functions.

These popular conceptions contain a kernel of truth because, as we've seen, the two hemispheres are different in several aspects of their functioning. But these often-mentioned conceptions go far beyond the available evidence and are sometimes inconsistent with it (Efron, 1990; J. Levy, 1985). Worse, these popular conceptions are entirely misleading when they imply that the two cerebral hemispheres, each with its own talents and strategies, endlessly compete for control of our mental life. Instead, each of us has a single brain. Each part of the brain—not just the cerebral hemispheres—is quite differentiated and so contributes its own specialized abilities to the activity of the whole. But in the end, the complex, sophisticated skills that we each display depend on the whole brain and on the coordinated actions of all its components. Our hemispheres are not cerebral competitors. Instead, they pool their specialized capacities to produce a seamlessly integrated, single mental self.

THE CEREBRAL CORTEX

All parts of the brain are important—and there's no truth at all to the often-quoted claim that we "use only 10% of our brain" (Figure 3.32). (The evidence is clear, for example, that damage virtually anywhere in the brain causes some form of disruption. This fact alone tells us that the entire brain is needed for one function or another!) One brain region, however, holds special interest for psychologists: the cerebral cortex. Here we find the brain tissue that is pivotal in our ability to perceive the world and to understand what we perceive. Here also is the brain tissue we need for planning our movements, producing and comprehending language, and carrying out the broad set of functions that we call "thinking"—whether we're thinking about abstract matters or concrete issues, pragmatic problems or social concerns. The cerebral cortex is also the portion of the brain that supports the pattern of beliefs and preferences that give each of us our unique personalities and values. Let's examine this essential (and large) section of the brain.

"You know, scientists claim we use only 10% of our brain!"   *"Gee, think of how much smarter we'd be if we used the other 60%!"*

3.32 Two underused brains?

Projection Areas

Many researchers divide the cortex into three broad types of tissue. *Sensory areas* receive and interpret information from the eyes, ears, and other sense organs. The *motor areas* control our behaviors—our movements through the world. The remaining areas are typically called *association areas* and are said to be involved in the complex processes broadly referred to as thinking.

The sensory areas are divided by modality, and so the brain region needed for vision is located in the occipital cortex, and the region needed for hearing is in the temporal cortex (Figure 3.33). Within each of these modality-specific areas, we find **projection areas**—areas where the brain tissue seems to form a "map" of the sensory information. (The term *projection* is borrowed from mapmaking.) Thus, for the visual projection

projection areas Areas in which the brain tissue seems to form a "map" of sensory information.

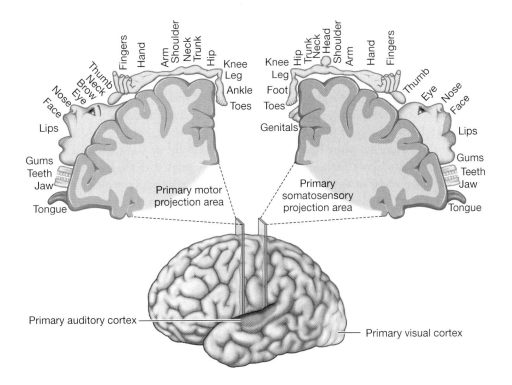

3.33 The primary motor and somatosensory projection areas The primary motor projection area is located at the rearmost edge of the frontal lobe, and each region within this projection area controls the motion of a specific body part, as illustrated on the top left. The primary somatosensory projection area, receiving information from the skin, is at the forward edge of the parietal lobe; each region within this area receives input from a specific body part. The primary projection areas for vision and hearing are located in the occipital and temporal lobes, respectively. These two areas are also organized systematically. For example, in the visual projection area, adjacent areas of the brain receive visual inputs that come from adjacent areas in visual space.

areas, adjacent sites in the brain represent adjacent locations in the external world. For the auditory projection areas, adjacent sites in the brain represent similar pitches.

As it turns out, the brain has multiple projection areas—multiple maps—for each sense modality. The term *primary projection area* is therefore used to designate the initial receiving station for information arriving from the sense organs—and so there's a primary projection area for vision, one for hearing, and one for information arriving from the skin.

We also find projection areas in the motor areas of the cortex. In that case, adjacent sites in the brain usually represent adjacent parts of the body. And there, too, we find a primary projection area—the departure point for signals that exit the cortex and ultimately result in muscle movement.

PRIMARY MOTOR AREAS

The discovery of the primary motor projection area dates back to the 1860s, when investigators began to apply mild electric currents to various portions of the cortex of anesthetized animals. The effects were often quite specific. Within the frontal lobe, stimulating one point led to a movement of the forelimb; stimulating another point made the ears prick up. These early studies also provided evidence for the pattern of **contralateral control,** in which stimulating the left hemisphere led to movements on the right side of the body and stimulating the right hemisphere caused movements on the left.

Similar results have been obtained with humans. Canadian neurosurgeon Wilder Penfield, for example, collected data from his patients who were undergoing surgery for epilepsy. The surgery was intended to remove diseased tissue; and, as is common in neurosurgery, the patients were awake during the procedure. (Because the brain itself has no pain receptors, neurosurgery is often performed with only local anesthesia that is required just to allow the surgeon to penetrate the scalp and skull.) In the surgeries, Penfield confirmed that stimulating the motor area in the frontal lobe led to movement

contralateral control The typical pattern in vertebrates in which movements of the right side of the body are controlled by the left hemisphere, while movements of the left side are controlled by the right hemisphere.

of specific body parts—much to the surprise of the patients, who had no sense of willing the action or performing it themselves.

Systematic exploration persuaded Penfield that for each portion of the motor cortex, there was a corresponding part of the body that moved when its cortical counterpart was stimulated. These findings are often summarized with a "motor homunculus," a schematic picture showing each body part next to the bit of the motor projection area that controls its movement (Figure 3.33, top left).

As Figure 3.33 makes plain, equal-sized areas of the body are not controlled by equal amounts of cortical space. Instead, the parts that we can move with the greatest precision (e.g., the fingers, the tongue) receive more cortical area than those over which we have less control (e.g., the shoulder, the abdomen). Evidently, what matters is function—the extent and complexity of that body part's use (Penfield & Rasmussen, 1950).

PRIMARY SENSORY AREAS

Methods similar to Penfield's revealed the existence of sensory projection areas. The *primary somatosensory projection area* is directly behind the primary motor projection area, in the parietal lobe (see Figure 3.33, top right). This area is the initial receiving area for sensory information arriving from the skin senses. Patients stimulated at a particular point in this area usually report tingling somewhere on the opposite side of their bodies. (Less frequently, they report experiences of cold or warmth.) The somatosensory projection area resembles its motor counterpart in several ways. First, it shows an orderly projection pattern in which each part of the body's surface sends its information to a particular part of the cortical somatosensory area. Second, the assignment of cortical space is not in proportion to the size of each body part. Instead, the space corresponds to the sensitivity of each region; the parts of the body that are most sensitive to touch (such as the index finger, lips, and tongue) receive more cortical space (Figure 3.34). Finally, sensation—like motor control—is contralateral. That is, sensory information from each part of the body proceeds to the brain hemisphere on the side opposite to it—so that (for example) sensations from the right thumb arrive in the left hemisphere, sensations from the left shoulder are sent to the right hemisphere, and so on. (Information from the trunk of the body close to the body's midline is represented in both hemispheres.)

The brain has similar primary projection areas for vision and for hearing, and they're located in the occipital and temporal lobes, respectively (see Figure 3.33). Patients stimulated in the visual projection area report optical experiences, vivid enough but with little form or meaning—flickering lights, streaks of color. When stimulated in the auditory area, patients hear things—clicks, buzzes, booms, and hums.

As we noted earlier, the visual and auditory areas are—like the somatosensory area—well organized spatially. In the occipital lobe, especially the area known as the visual cortex, adjacent brain areas represent adjacent locations in visual space. In the temporal lobes, adjacent areas represent similar ranges of pitch. The visual area also respects the principle of contralateral input: Objects seen (by either eye) to the left of a person's overall line of sight are processed by the right visual area, and objects seen on the right are processed by the left visual area. The auditory projection area, in contrast, provides a rare exception to the brain's contralateral wiring, because both cerebral hemispheres receive input from both ears.

3.34 The sensory homunculus An artist's rendition of what a man would look like if his appearance were proportional to the area allotted by the somatosensory cortex to his various body parts.

Association Areas

The projection areas take up less than one-fourth of the human cortex. The remaining areas were traditionally called "association areas" and were implicated in higher mental functions like thinking, remembering, and speaking. The idea behind the "association" label was that these areas provided the links—the associations—making these higher functions possible.

More recent research confirms that these regions are involved in higher mental functions but has made it clear that we need to subdivide the association areas. We also now know that some sites within the cortex's association areas function as additional projection areas, over and above those we've just described.

For example, in front of the primary motor projection area, *nonprimary* motor areas appear critical for initiating and coordinating complex, skilled movements. On the sensory side, each sensory modality may have dozens of secondary projection areas located in the temporal and parietal lobes. What's more, each of these areas shows its own mapping and is involved in the processing of different aspects of sensation. Indeed, the cortex seems to have at least 25 nonprimary projection areas for vision, each specialized for a different visual quality such as form, color, or movement (Gazzaniga et al., 2002).

The Results of Cortical Damage

We mentioned earlier that our understanding of any brain region depends on multiple sources of data. For studies of the association cortex, however, neuropsychological studies (studies of brain damage) have often been our earliest indicators of a brain region's function. Let's therefore take a closer look at the association cortex through the lens provided by brain damage.

DISORDERS OF ACTION

Lesions in the cortex of the frontal lobe sometimes produce **apraxias**—serious disturbances in the initiation or organization of voluntary action. In some apraxias, the patient cannot perform well-known actions such as saluting or waving good-bye when asked to do so. In other cases, seemingly simple actions become fragmented and disorganized. When asked to light a cigarette, the patient may strike a match against a matchbox and then keep striking it after it's already burning; or, he may light the match and then put it into his mouth instead of the cigarette. These deficits are not the result of simple paralysis, since the patient can readily perform each part of the action by itself. His problem is in initiating the sequence or in selecting the right components and fitting them together.

Some apraxias may represent a disconnection between the primary and nonprimary motor areas. The primary motor area is responsible for producing the movements of individual muscles, but the nonprimary motor areas must first organize and initiate the sequence. Indeed, evidence suggests that the neurons in the nonprimary areas fire almost a full second before the actual movement occurs; this confirms the role of these areas in preparing the action (Deecke, Scheid, & Kornhuber, 1968). In short, the nonprimary areas seem to be responsible for "Get ready!" and "Get set!" Then, at the "Go!" signal, the primary motor area takes over (Bear, Connors, & Paradiso, 1996; Roland, Larsen, Lassen, & Skinhøj, 1980).

apraxia A serious disturbance in beginning or carrying out voluntary movements.

In other disorders, the patient suffers a disruption in the way she perceives the world. Some patients (for example) lose the ability to perceive motion, and so they cannot tell the speed or direction of a moving object. As one patient put it, "When I'm looking at the car first, it seems far away. But then when I want to cross the road, suddenly the car is very near" (Zihl, Von Cramon, & Mai, 1983). Other patients suffer brain damage that disrupts their ability to perceive color; they describe the world as clothed only in "dirty shades of gray" (Gazzaniga, Ivry, & Mangun, 2009).

Other patients seem able to see, but they can't recognize what they see. This pattern is referred to as **visual agnosia** and is usually produced by damage to the occipital cortex or the rearmost part of the parietal cortex. A patient with agnosia can often describe the shape, color, and texture of an object before her eyes; but can recognize the object only through means other than vision. For example, a patient shown an ordinary fork might describe it as "points on top of a stick," but she would not be able to name the object or describe how to use it. However, the moment the patient feels the fork in her hands, she easily identifies it.

Agnosia is a problem in recognition, not in seeing. This is made especially clear by a case in which a patient was shown a glove and asked what it was. The patient described the glove as "a continuous surface infolded in itself ... [with] five outpouchings, if this is the word" (Sacks, 1985, p. 14). Perhaps, the patient thought, it might be a "change purse ... for coins of five sizes." Plainly, there's nothing wrong with this person's vision (or his verbal fluency!), but it's clear that he had no clue about what the glove actually was.

One subtype of agnosia, known as *prosopagnosia*, usually involves damage to areas in both the temporal and parietal lobes. Patients with prosopagnosia have trouble recognizing faces—even immensely familiar faces. In one often-quoted case, a person suffering from prosopagnosia complained to a waiter that another patron in the restaurant was rudely staring at him while he ate. It turned out, however, that this prosopagnosic diner was looking into a *mirror* on the restaurant wall and had failed to recognize his own reflection.

In some cases, the difficulties associated with prosopagnosia can spread beyond faces: A farmer who developed prosopagnosia lost the ability to tell his individual cows apart; a prosopagnosic bird-watcher lost the ability to distinguish different types of warblers (de Renzi, 2000; Farah & Feinberg, 2000). In one remarkable case, a prosopagnosic patient lost the ability to tell cars apart; she could locate her own car in a lot only by reading all the license plates until she found her own (A. Damasio, H. Damasio, & Van Hoesen, 1982).

In still other disorders, the patient's problem is one of attention, so that the patient seems utterly oblivious to certain aspects of the world. A striking example is the so-called **neglect syndrome**, which typically results from damage to certain areas on the right side of the parietal lobe. A patient with this disorder seems not to realize that the left-hand side of the world exists. If asked, for example, to read compound words like *toothpick* or *baseball*, the patient reads *pick* and *ball*. When asked to draw the face of a clock, he squeezes all the numbers onto the clock's right side (Figure 3.35). When eating, he selects and eats food only from the right side of his plate. When dressing, he ignores the left shirt sleeve and pants leg; when shaving, he leaves the left side of his face unshaven (Awh, Dhaliwal, Christensen, & Matsukura, 2001; Duncan et al., 1999; Rafal & Robertson, 1995; Robertson & Manly, 1999).

visual agnosia The inability to recognize a visual stimulus despite the ability to see and describe it.

neglect syndrome The result of certain right parietal lobe lesions that leave a patient completely inattentive to stimuli to her left, including the left side of her own body.

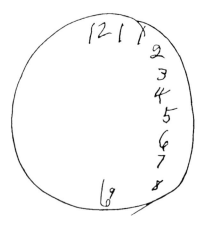

3.35 Neglect syndrome A patient with damage to the right parietal cortex was asked to draw a typical clock face. In his drawing, the patient seemed unaware of the left side; but he still recalled that all 12 numbers had to be displayed. The drawing shows how he resolved this dilemma.

Broca's area

Wernicke's area

(A)

(B)

3.36 **Areas of the brain crucial for language** (A) Many sites in the brain play a key role in the production and comprehension of language. In right-handed people, these sites are located in the left hemisphere, generally at the lower edge of the frontal lobe and the upper edge of the temporal lobe. Broca's area, long thought to play a central role in speech production, is located near the areas that control speech muscles; Wernicke's area, which plays a central role in our comprehension of speech, is near other areas that play a key part in audition. (B) This photo shows the brain of Broca's actual patient, preserved from the 19th century.

aphasia Any of a number of linguistic disorders caused by injury to or malformation of the brain.

DISORDERS OF LANGUAGE

Other lesions in the cortex lead to disruptions of the production or comprehension of language. Disorders of this kind are called **aphasias,** and they're almost always produced by lesions (strokes, typically) in the left hemisphere.

Early studies suggested that aphasias could be divided into two broad types: one that seemed primarily to involve the production of speech, and one that seemed primarily to involve the comprehension of speech. Aphasias of speech *production* were often referred to as *nonfluent aphasias* and typically involved lesions in a region of the left frontal lobe, called *Broca's area* after the French physician Pierre-Paul Broca, who in 1861 first predicted its relation to speech (Figure 3.36). The result of this disorder may be mute silence, or speech that resembles a staccato, spoken telegram: "Here ... head ... operation ... here ... speech ... none ... talking ... what ... illness" (Luria, 1966, p. 406).

A different pattern is associated with the so-called *fluent aphasias*—cases in which patients seem able to produce speech but don't understand what is said to them, though they usually answer anyway. Unlike patients with nonfluent aphasias, those with fluent aphasias talk freely and rapidly; but while they utter many words, they say very little. The sentences they produce are reasonably grammatical, but they're "word salad"—largely composed of the little filler words that provide scant information. A typical example is, "I was over the other one, and then after they had been in the department, I was in this one" (Geschwind, 1970, p. 904). Fluent aphasias are usually associated with damage to a brain site known as *Wernicke's area*—a region that borders on the auditory primary projection area and is named after the nineteenth-century neurologist Carl Wernicke.

This distinction—between disorders of speech production associated with damage to Broca's area and those of comprehension associated with damage to Wernicke's area—works as a coarse characterization of aphasia. But to capture the real nature and the full range of types of aphasia, we must considerably refine the distinction. The reason is simple: Like most mental activities, speech production and comprehension involve the coordination of many different steps, and many different processes. These include processes needed to "look up" word meanings in one's "mental dictionary," processes needed to figure out the structural relationships within a sentence, processes needed to integrate information gleaned about a sentence's structure with the meanings of the words within the sentence, and so on (Chapter 10). Since each of these processes relies on its own set of brain pathways, damage to those pathways disrupts the process. As a result, the disruption observed in aphasia is often quite specific—it involves impairment to a particular processing step, which then leads to disruption of all subsequent processes that depend on that step. In many cases, this disruption seems mostly to affect speech production; in other cases, the disruption is primarily visible in comprehension; and in still other cases, the disruption is clear in both activities (see Cabeza & Nyberg, 2000; Demonet, Wise, & Frackowiak, 1993; Grodzinsky & Santi, 2008; Habib, Demonet, & Frackowiak, 1996).

DISORDERS OF PLANNING AND SOCIAL COGNITION

Earlier, we referred to the famous case of Phineas Gage. After an iron rod was driven through his head, Gage could still speak and move fairly normally. But something subtler had changed. A medical report on Gage put it this way:

> He is fitful, irreverent, indulging at times in the grossest profanity (which was not previously his custom), manifesting but little deference for his fellows, impatient of restraint or advice when it conflicts with his desires, at times pertinaciously obstinate, yet capricious and vacillating, devising many plans of future operation, which are no sooner arranged than they are abandoned in turn for others appearing more feasible. Previous to his injury . . . he possessed a well-balanced mind . . . was energetic and persistent in executing all his plans of operation. In this regard his mind was radically changed, so decidedly that his friends and acquaintances said he was "no longer Gage." (Valenstein, 1986, p. 90)

Gage's symptoms fit reasonably well with other things we know about the effect of damage to the frontmost part of the frontal lobe—the **prefrontal area** (Bradshaw, 2001; Lichter & Cummings, 2001; Milner & Petrides, 1984). In general, damage here seems to disrupt the person's **executive control** over her own thinking—and so she loses the capacity to set priorities, override habits, make plans, choose a strategy, ignore a distractor, and more.

This disruption shows up in many aspects of the person's behavior. Outside the laboratory, she is unable to control her own impulses. She is likely to give in to habit and seize on whatever temptation a situation offers. In the lab, we can document this disruption with the *Wisconsin Card-Sorting Task.* In this task, the person is given a deck of cards, with symbols on each card; the cards vary in the number, shape, and color of the symbols. Initially, the person has to sort the cards according to (say) the color of the symbols; midway through the task, however, the rule is changed. Now he has to sort according to the symbols' shape. Patients with frontal lobe damage have enormous difficulty with the task and typically show a pattern of **perseveration**—continuing to sort according to the initial rule despite explicit feedback that they're now doing the task incorrectly (e.g., Goldman-Rakic, 1998).

A related pattern is revealed when patients with frontal lobe damage are asked to make a copy of a drawing. For example, when asked to copy Figure 3.37A, a patient

prefrontal area The frontmost portion of the frontal lobes, involved in working memory, strategy formation, and response inhibition.

executive control Processes such as making plans or overriding habitual responses that let the brain direct its own cognitive activities.

perseveration The tendency to repeat a response inappropriately; often a result of deficits in executive control caused by prefrontal lesions.

3.37 Drawings by patients with prefrontal brain damage A patient with damage to the prefrontal cortex was asked to copy the figure shown in (A). The result is shown in (B). The sketch is reasonably accurate, but it was plainly drawn feature by feature with no overall plan in mind.

(A)

(B)

produced the drawing shown in Figure 3.37B. The copy preserves many features of the original, but close inspection makes it clear that the patient drew the copy with no particular plan in mind. The large rectangle that defines much of the shape was never drawn; the diagonal lines that organize the figure were drawn in a piecemeal fashion. Many details are correctly reproduced but were not drawn in any sort of order; instead, these details were added whenever they happened to catch the patient's attention (Kimberg, D'Esposito, & Farah, 1998; for more on the brain's processes of executive control, see Duncan, 1995; Gilbert & Shallice, 2002; Kane & Engle, 2003; Stuss & Levine, 2002).

PLASTICITY

Overall, then, it should be clear that the brain—indeed, the entire nervous system—contains many distinct regions. Each region has its own job to do, and so we can understand the nervous system only by keeping track of the various parts—where each is, what it does, and how each contributes to a person's overall functioning.

But there's one more layer of complexity that we need to confront, because the functioning and arrangement of the brain can *change* during our lifetimes. Neurons can change their pattern of connections—so that, in effect, the brain gets new "wiring." And there is increasing evidence that the brain can grow new neurons in certain circumstances. These changes are fascinating on their own—but they also hold out a promise of enormous importance: Perhaps we can harness this potential for change in order to *repair* the brain when it has been damaged through injury or disease. Let's look at the nature of **brain plasticity**—the brain's capacity to alter its structure and function.

brain plasticity The capacity for the brain to alter its structure and function.

Changes in Neuronal Connections

Each day brings us new experiences, and through them we learn new facts, acquire new skills, and gain new perspectives. Our reactions to the world—indeed, our entire personalities—evolve as we acquire knowledge, maturity, and maybe even wisdom. These various changes all correspond to changes in the nervous system, making it clear that the nervous system must somehow be *plastic*—subject to alteration.

In fact, the nervous system's plasticity takes many different forms. Among other options, individual neurons can alter their "output"—that is, can change the amount of neurotransmitter they release. On the "input" side, neurons can also change how *sensitive* they are to neurotransmitters by literally gaining new receptors. Both of these alterations play a pivotal role in learning, and we'll return to these mechanisms—and fill in some details about how they function—in Chapter 7 as part of a broader discussion of learning.

Neurons can also create entirely new connections, producing new synapses in response to new patterns of stimulation. The changes in this case seem to take place largely on the dendrites of postsynaptic cells. The dendrites grow new dendritic spines—little knobs attached to the surface of the dendrites (Figure 3.38; Kolb, Gibb, & Robinson, 2003; Moser, 1999; Woolf, 1998). These spines are the "receiving stations" for most synapses; so growing more spines almost certainly means that, as learning proceeds, the neuron is gaining new synapses—new points of communication with its cellular neighbors.

3.38 Photomicrograph of dendritic spines

Cortical Reorganization

Plasticity in the nervous system can also lead to larger-scale changes in the brain's architecture. In one study, investigators trained monkeys to respond in one way if they heard a certain musical pitch and in another way if they heard a slightly different pitch (Recanzone, Schreiner, & Merzenich, 1993). We know from other evidence that—just as in humans—the monkeys' projection areas for sounds are organized in maps; different sites on the monkey's cortex are responsive to different frequencies of sound. After training, though, the map of the monkey's auditory projection area was reorganized, so that much more cortical area was now devoted to the frequencies emphasized during training.

Can the same plasticity be demonstrated in humans? One research team used neuroimaging to examine the somatosensory projection areas in a group of highly trained musicians, all of whom played string instruments; a comparison group consisted of nonmusicians (Elbert, Pantev, Wienbruch, Rockstroh, & Taub, 1995). The results showed that in the musicians' brains, more cortical area was dedicated to the representation of input from the fingers—suggesting that because of their instrumental training, the musicians' brains had been reorganized to devote more tissue to skills essential for their playing.

A related result comes from a study of London cabdrivers. These drivers need sophisticated navigation skills to find their way around London, and they become more and more skillful as they gain experience. This skill, in turn, is reflected directly in their brain structure: Studies show that these cabdrivers have enlarged hippocampi—and the hippocampus, you'll recall, is a brain structure crucial for navigation. Further, the more years of cab-driving experience an individual had, the greater the degree of hippocampal enlargement (E. Maguire et al., 2000).

Even more evidence comes from research with the blind. In one study, investigators used neuroimaging to compare the brain activity in blind and sighted research participants who were exploring a surface with their fingertips (Sadato et al., 1996). The sighted participants showed the expected pattern of increased activity in somatosensory areas as they felt the target surface. In contrast, during this task the blind participants showed increased activity in the *visual cortex*. Apparently, for these individuals, this brain area had taken on a new job. No longer occupied with visual information, this area of cortex had shifted to the entirely new task of processing information from the fingertips (also see Kauffman et al., 2002).

Thus it seems that the brain is plastic both at the microscopic level, where it involves changes in how neurons communicate with each other, and at a much grander level. If a person receives a lot of practice in a task, more brain tissue is recruited for the task—presumably because the tissue has been "reassigned" from some other task. Likewise, sensory cortex that was initially sensitive to one modality can apparently be reassigned to an entirely different modality.

New Neurons

The last form of plasticity we'll look at has been controversial because a long-held doctrine in neuroscience was that, at birth, the brain has all the neurons it will ever have. As a result, plasticity during the organism's lifetime must be due to changes in these neurons. However, neuroscientists have been expressing reservations about this doctrine for years (e.g., Ramón y Cajal, 1913), and it turns out that those reservations were justified. There is now clear evidence that new neurons continue to develop throughout an organism's lifetime and that this growth is promoted by learning and enriched experience (Eriksson et al., 1998).

The evidence suggests, however, that *neurogenesis*—the birth of new neurons—is very slow in the adult human brain; and it seems that most of these new neurons don't survive for long (Scharfman & Hen, 2007; Shors, 2009). It's also unclear whether neurogenesis occurs in all parts of the adult brain—and, in particular, whether it occurs in the cerebral cortex (Bhardwaj et al. 2006). If it doesn't, this may be a regard in which humans are different from many other species.

In some ways, these results seem backwards. One would think that the creation of new neurons would allow flexibility for the organism and so would contribute to learning—and therefore would be most prominent in species (including humans!) that are capable of especially sophisticated learning. Yet it seems that we may be the species for which cortical neurogenesis is *least* likely. What explains this pattern? One hypothesis is that human intellectual capacities depend on our being able to *accumulate* knowledge, building on things we have already learned. This in turn may require some degree of biological stability in the brain, so that we do not lose the skills and knowledge we've already acquired. For this purpose, we may need a permanent population of cortical neurons—and this means *not* introducing *new* neurons. From this perspective, the absence of neuronal growth might limit our flexibility; but it might nonetheless be a good thing, helping to sustain long-term retention of complex knowledge (Rakic, 2006; Scharfman & Hen, 2007).

Repairing Damage to the Nervous System

Notice, then, that plasticity has its advantages and disadvantages. On the positive side, plasticity makes it possible to "rewire" the nervous system in response to new information and new experience. On the negative side, plasticity may in some circumstances undermine the stability of a pattern of neural connections and thus may be disruptive. So perhaps it's not surprising that different species have evolved to have different degrees of plasticity, with the pattern presumably dependent on that species' need for flexibility or for longer-term retention.

There's one arena, though, in which plasticity is certainly desirable: If the nervous system is damaged through injury or disease, the effects can be disastrous. It would be wonderful, therefore, if the nervous system could repair itself by growing new neurons or reestablishing new connections. This sort of self-repair is often possible in the peripheral nervous system; there, neurons can regenerate their axons even after the original axon has been severed. Unfortunately, this sort of regrowth after damage seems not to occur in humans' central nervous system, and here, once nerve fibers are damaged, they generally stay damaged. (For some of the mechanisms blocking this self-repair, see W.-Y. Kim & Snider, 2008.)

Is there some way, however, to use the processes of plasticity observed in healthy brains to restore damaged brains? If so, we might be able to repair the damage created by injury—such as the spinal injury suffered by actor Christopher Reeve, well known for his role in the *Superman* movies (Figure 3.39). After his injury, Reeve spent the rest of his life paralyzed but devoted his energy and talent to encouraging research on spinal cord injuries and other nerve damage. A means of restoring damaged brains might also give hope to those suffering from Alzheimer's disease or Parkinson's disease, both of which involve the destruction of brain tissue (Figure 3.40).

Researchers are actively exploring these issues; some of their efforts are focused on encouraging the growth of new neurons (e.g., W.-Y. Kim & Snider, 2008), and other research

3.39 Repairing damage to the nervous system Christopher Reeve's fame grew with his starring role in the *Superman* movies. He was paralyzed by a spinal cord injury and spent the rest of his life (and his considerable talents) in encouraging research on spinal cord injuries.

3.40 Hope for brain repair? Michael J. Fox (left) has devoted enormous energy to promoting research that might lead to treatment for Parkinson's disease, from which he suffers. Ronald Reagan (right), the 40th president of the United States, was diagnosed with Alzheimer's disease 5 years after leaving office; he died 10 years later.

is seeking to implant new tissue into the brain in order to replace the damaged cells. Some of the most exciting work, however, is in a third category and involves a mix of implanting tissue and encouraging growth. Specifically, this effort involves implanting, into an area of damage, the same sorts of *stem cells* that are responsible for building the nervous system in the first place. Stem cells are, in general, cells that are found in early stages of an organism's development and that have not yet begun to specialize or differentiate in any way. The idea in using these cells is that we would not be replacing the damaged brain tissue directly. Instead, the stem cells would, once in place, serve as precursors of the cells the brain needs—so the brain could, in effect, grow its own replacements.

Preliminary studies in animals suggest that when stem cells are injected into a patch of neurons, the cells are—as we would hope—induced to turn into healthy neurons just like their neighbors, taking the same shape, producing the same neurotransmitters, and filling in for dead neurons (Holm et al., 2001; Isacson, 1999; Philips et al., 2001; Sawamoto et al., 2001). Thus it seems plausible that stem-cell therapy may provide a means of treatment for various forms of brain injury—and so far the results have been quite encouraging (Kondziolka et al., 2000; Veizovic, Beech, Stroemer, Watson, & Hodges, 2001). In one remarkable study, researchers inserted human stem cells into the damaged spines of laboratory rats. The rats, which had been paralyzed at the study's start, recovered well enough so that they could walk again (Cizkova et al., 2007).

Research in this domain continues. In early 2009, the U.S. Food and Drug Administration gave permission for the first clinical trials for stem-cell therapy in humans who had suffered spinal cord injury. However, the progress of research in this arena has been slow—largely due to an ethical debate over where the stem cells usually come from. As part of a fertility treatment, a woman's ova are sometimes removed, fertilized in a laboratory, and allowed to develop into large masses of cells. One of these masses is then placed back into the woman in hopes that it will implant in the uterus and develop into a normal pregnancy. The other masses—the ones not implanted—were for many years the main sources for stem cells, and there lies the problem: In principle, these other masses might also have been implanted and might also have developed into a human fetus. On that basis, some people have argued that use of these cells for any other purpose is essentially a form of abortion and thus is unacceptable to anyone who opposes abortion.

This issue led President George W. Bush to limit the use of federal research money for studies relying on embryonic stem cells. Early in 2009, President Barack Obama reversed that policy—so we can now expect the pace of research to accelerate. Meanwhile, investigators are also seeking to develop alternative sources of stem cells; this may allow us to avoid the ethical debate altogether. One way or another, stem cell research is certain to continue; and in light of the evidence so far, this research holds enormous promise for treating—and perhaps reversing—a range of profoundly disabling diseases as well as helping people who have suffered tragic injuries.

SOME FINAL THOUGHTS: DO ALL PSYCHOLOGICAL QUESTIONS HAVE BIOLOGICAL ANSWERS?

Psychologists assume that all psychological events—our thoughts, desires, attitudes, and values—are made possible by activity in the nervous system. Therefore, at least in principle, it should be possible to describe any specific event in terms of its underlying biology. Indeed, our examination of the biological basis of behavior in Chapters 2 and 3 has brought us handsome dividends. We've learned a great deal at a microscopic level (e.g., knowledge about individual neurons) and on a larger scale (e.g., knowledge about entire brain areas). The knowledge has allowed sophisticated theorizing and has supported useful applications (e.g., the development of new antidepressants; potential treatments for Alzheimer's disease).

Does all of this imply that answers to all psychological questions should be phrased in terms of action potentials and neurotransmitters? The answer is no. One reason is simply *impatience*. Neuroscientists have made enormous progress in understanding the brain, but we're still many decades away from understanding how, say, your memory of last summer's vacation is recorded in your brain cells, or what it is in the brain that makes one person sociable and another an introvert. As we'll see in upcoming chapters, though, we can say a lot about these and other questions without referring to the underlying biology. Thus, for at least the next century, it will be psychology and not neuroscience that illuminates many aspects of our behavior, thoughts, and feelings.

There's a second reason the answer is no. Although neuroscience can provide exquisite detail about exactly how a process unfolds in the brain, sometimes, for some questions, we don't want this detail. Instead, what we want is a broader view of the "big picture." Imagine, for example, that a professor wants to know whether a particular student recalls the material covered in class yesterday. At least in theory, she could check on the status of the students' trillion or so brain neurons to make certain they're in a configuration that reflects good, accurate memory. But this strategy would be incredibly cumbersome. Besides, how would the professor decide if the neurons were in the proper configuration? Presumably, she would need to know whether this configuration adequately represents the *meaning* of the class materials. So her analysis might initially focus on the nervous system; but then she needs to "translate" this level of analysis into a different one that focuses on concepts and definitions rather than synapses and neurotransmitters. In other words, the professor's assessment would end up asking about the student's *knowledge* and *beliefs* and so, ultimately, would involve a psychological analysis, not a biological one.

Let's take this a step further and imagine that the professor wants to *improve* the student's understanding—correcting an error, perhaps, or filling a gap. In this effort, the professor would certainly be guided by her grasp of the student's beliefs and knowledge. She would surely be less helped by knowing that Neuron number 24,732,118 is firing more often than it should, or that Neuron number 116,219,301 is firing but should not be. Plainly, to help this student, it is the psychological analysis that we need.

Overall, then, it's self-evident that neuroscience—its methods and its explanations—will be enormously useful and wonderfully instructive for many purposes. It will certainly allow us to answer a broad range of important questions. But this same sort of analysis will be less helpful for other purposes and other questions. This is why psychologists often rely on neuroscience explanations—but not always. Insights from neuroscience, in other words, are an essential part of psychological explanation and will inform our discussion throughout this text. But it's important to remember that we also need insights from other perspectives and other types of analysis. What these insights involve, and how other sorts of psychological explanations are formulated, are the topics of subsequent chapters.

THE ORGANISM AS A MACHINE

- Many scientists have tried to explain human and animal behavior in mechanistic terms. For Descartes, this definition involved the reflex concept: A stimulus excites a sense organ that transmits excitation upward to the brain, which in turn relays the excitation downward to a muscle or gland and so produces action.

BUILDING BLOCKS OF THE NERVOUS SYSTEM

- The basic unit of communication in the nervous system is the *neuron.* Each neuron typically has *dendrites,* a *cell body,* and an *axon.* The vast majority of neurons are *interneurons* that connect to yet other interneurons.

- The nervous system also contains *glia.* These cells have many functions, both during development and in supporting the function of the mature nervous system. The glia may also constitute a separate, slow signal system.

COMMUNICATION AMONG NEURONS

- When the neuron's membrane is stable, an excess of positively charged ions are on the outside, resulting in the negative voltage difference of the *resting potential.* When the membrane is sufficiently stimulated, though, ion channels in the membrane spring open. This change allows ion movement that leads to an excess of positively charged particles inside the membrane and produces the positive voltage swing of the *action potential.* The excitation spreads to neighboring regions and leads to the *propagation* of the action potential along the axon. This propagation is much faster if the axon is *myelinated,* which causes the *depolarization* to proceed down the axon by means of a number of skips or jumps. In all cases, though, the action potential obeys the *all-or-none law:* Once the action potential is launched, further increases in stimulus intensity have no effect on its magnitude.

- Communication between neurons is made possible by the release of *neurotransmitters.* The transmitters cross the *synapse* and latch onto receptors on the postsynaptic cell, potentially triggering a response in that cell. Some transmitters are inactivated shortly after being discharged by "cleanup" enzymes. More commonly, neurotransmitters are reused by a process of *synaptic reuptake.*

- The lock-and-key model proposes that transmitter molecules will affect the postsynaptic membrane only if the molecule's shape fits into certain synaptic receptor molecules. However, drugs called *agonists* can enhance a neurotransmitter's effect; *antagonists* impede its effect. Some agonists enhance a transmitter's effect by blocking its synaptic reuptake; others act by counteracting the cleanup enzyme. Yet other drugs affect the synaptic receptors by mimicking the transmitter's action.

COMMUNICATION THROUGH THE BLOODSTREAM

- Blood circulation not only brings energy to the nutrient-hungry brain but also aids communication by carrying hormones secreted by the *endocrine glands* to various target organs throughout the body. Despite some important points of contrast, the endocrine system has much in common with the chemical communication between neurons, suggesting a shared evolutionary origin for these two types of communication.

METHODS FOR STUDYING THE NERVOUS SYSTEM

- One source of data about the nervous system comes from single-cell recording, which can be done for an individual cell, or, in multi-unit recording, with a number of cells. Another source of data focuses on cases of brain damage. In some animal studies, this damage is produced in the laboratory; but neuropsychologists often study naturally occurring cases of brain damage. In still other cases, scientists can study the effects of temporary brain damage by using the technique of *transcranial magnetic stimulation (TMS).*

- A variety of techniques are used to study the whole brain. Electroencephalography is a procedure that uses sensitive electrodes, placed on the scalp, to measure voltages produced by ordinary brain activity. Neuroimaging techniques are used to study the living brain. Some of these techniques (*MRI* and *CT scans*) study the brain's anatomy—the size and location of individual structures. Other techniques, such as *PET* and *fMRI scans,* reveal which brain locations are particularly active at any moment in time. All of these techniques make it clear that most mental activities rely on many brain sites, so that activities like reading or making decisions are supported by the coordinated functioning of many different parts of the brain.

THE ARCHITECTURE OF THE NERVOUS SYSTEM

- The nervous system is divided into the *central nervous system* (the brain and spinal cord) and the *peripheral nervous system,* which includes both *efferent* and *afferent* nerves. The peripheral nervous system is divided into the *somatic nervous system* and the *autonomic nervous system.*
- The very top of the spinal cord forms the *brain stem,* which includes the *medulla* and the *pons,* and just behind these structures is the *cerebellum.* The midbrain is on top of the pons, and on top of all is the forebrain. The outer surface of the forebrain is the *cerebral cortex.* The cortex is a large, thin sheet of tissue, crumpled inside the skull. Some of the folds—or *convolutions*—in the cortex are actually deep grooves that divide the brain into sections, such as the *frontal lobes,* the *parietal lobes,* the *occipital lobes,* and the *temporal lobes.*
- The entire brain is roughly symmetrical around the midline, so that most structures come in pairs—one on the left side, one on the right. The left and right structures are generally similar, but they can be distinguished both anatomically and functionally. Crucially, the two halves of the brain work as an integrated whole.

THE CEREBRAL CORTEX

- *Localization of function* refers to the task of determining the function of each brain area. In the cortex, some parts serve as *projection areas*—they are the first receiving stations for information coming from the sense organs and the departure points for signals going to the muscles. Most projection areas have a *contralateral organization.* Each area is organized so that (for example) adjacent areas in the motor projection area represent adjacent parts of the body, and adjacent areas in the visual projection area represent adjacent regions of space.

However, the assignment of cortical space is disproportionate, so that (for example) parts of the body that are most sensitive to touch receive more cortical space.

- We have learned much of what we know about other parts of the cortex by studying cases of brain damage. Damage at identifiable sites can produce *apraxias* (disorders in action), *agnosias* (disorders in perception), or *aphasias* (disorders of language). Still other forms of brain damage produce disorders of planning or social cognition.

PLASTICITY

- The nervous system is *plastic*—subject to alteration in the way it functions. Some of this plasticity involves changes in how much neurotransmitter a presynaptic neuron releases. Neurons can also change how sensitive they are to neurotransmitters. Moreover, by growing new *dendritic spines,* neurons can create entirely new connections.
- Plasticity can also involve larger-scale changes, including changes in the brain's overall architecture. The central nervous system can grow new neurons, although it appears unable to do so in cases of cortical injury. This promotes stability in the brain's connections, but obviously it can be an obstacle to recovery from brain damage.

 ONLINE STUDY TOOLS

Go to StudySpace, **wwnorton.com/studyspace**, to access additional review and enrichment materials, including the following resources for each chapter:

Organize
- Study Plan
- Chapter Outline
- Quiz+ Assessment

Learn
- Ebook
- Chapter Review
- Vocabulary Flashcards
- Drag-and-Drop Labeling Exercises
- Audio Podcast Chapter Overview

Connect
- Critical Thinking Activity
- Studying the Mind Video Podcasts
- Video Exercises
- Animations
- **ZAPS** Psychology Labs

CHAPTER 4

Sensation

Katie Callahan has three secrets: "I don't like chocolate. I don't like coffee. And I don't like beer. They all taste like burnt dirt to me."

"But when I tell people this, they think I'm prissy, or boring, or anorexic," says Katie. "It really throws a wrench in your social life. And so I learned in college to keep my food aversions to myself."

In her late twenties, Katie figured out why her friends' cravings left her gagging: She's a supertaster. While her friends savor chocolate, cheese, and chilies, to her they taste like dish soap, salty baby oil, and acid.

"My tongue has about 100 times more taste buds than normal tasters'," Katie explains, and she's not alone. According to one estimate, 25% of Americans are supertasters, while 50% are normal tasters. The remaining 25% are nontasters, who cannot sense certain bitter chemicals. While nontasters live in a pastel world of taste, supertasters live in a neon world, says Linda Bartoshuk, a psychologist who studies supertasters. Bartoshuk, a nontaster, confesses that she regularly sweetens her wine with sugar.

Genetics research suggests that Katie owes her sensitive tongue to her parents. They both dislike strong flavors, although neither has dietary displeasures as severe as their daughter's. The strength of Katie's aversions suggests that she received a double dose—one from each parent—of the allele that codes for supertasting.

Because the insides of their mouths are easily overwhelmed, supertasters tend to eat less sugary and fatty food. This often keeps them thin and lowers their risk of heart disease. But supertasters also tend to eat fewer vegetables with cancer-fighting flavonoids (which taste too acrid to them), so they may be more vulnerable to certain cancers. How can our tiny taste buds so powerfully shape our behavior and potentially our health? The first step in tackling this question is to ask how our tongues—or, more broadly, our sense organs—funnel the outside world into our bodies and minds. These questions are central to the psychology of sensation.

Katie's case also reminds us that our senses shape our daily existence. Of course, someone who's blind can have a full, rich life—but nonetheless, walking down a hallway or crossing a street are much more challenging than for someone sighted, and some activities (like driving) are out of the question. Likewise, deaf people live perfectly normal lives in most respects; but they can't respond to the smoke alarm's shriek or the wail of a police siren, and they can converse with only a limited number of people. (Roughly 2 million people are proficient in American Sign Language worldwide; but compare that to, say, the world's 400 million English speakers.) Things are more extreme for individuals lacking other senses—including people who can't sense pain. As we'll see, these people are at risk for many injuries, including biting their tongues while chewing or leaning on a hot stove without realizing it.

Our dependence on the senses raises a question: How reliable are they? You've likely had the experience of spotting a friend in a crowd—only to discover that the person is someone else altogether. You've probably heard someone calling you, but then realized you imagined it. And surely at some point you've failed to hear someone speaking to you. Is it possible that our sensory experiences are often inaccurate or incomplete—so that the world we sense differs from the world as it is?

The world certainly poses a challenge for our sensory apparatus: This page is now in front of your eyes—but you also see your hands, others in the room, the table surface, and more. Your eyes take in a wealth of information from each of these objects—and your eyes and brain constantly collect, encode, interpret, and act upon what you see, even as you simultaneously make sense of an influx of other sensory information.

In this chapter, we'll examine how our senses function, beginning with the questions that launched scientific inquiry in this domain: How accurate and complete are our sensory experiences? And how objective is our perception of the world? We'll then turn to psychologists' methods for addressing these questions. With that base, we'll survey the senses, starting with properties they all have in common and then considering each sense separately.

You may not be a supertaster or have especially acute hearing; you may not be nearsighted or color-blind. But this chapter will help you appreciate the complexity of what may seem to be the simplest of functions—seeing, smelling, hearing, tasting, and feeling the world around us.

THE ORIGINS OF KNOWLEDGE

Where does human knowledge come from? One possibility is that our knowledge comes directly from the world around us, and that our eyes, ears, and other senses are simply collecting the information the world provides. According to this view, our senses faithfully receive and record information much as a camera receives light or a microphone receives sound, and this implies that our perception of the world is a relatively passive affair. After all, a camera doesn't choose which light beams to receive, nor does it interpret any of the light it detects. Instead, it simply records the light available to it. Likewise, a microphone doesn't interpret the speech or appreciate the music; again, in a passive way, it simply receives the sounds and passes them along to an amplifier or recording device. Could this be the way our vision and hearing work?

The Passive Perceiver

Advocates for the philosophical view known as *empiricism* argued that our senses are passive in the way just described. One of the earliest proponents of this position was the 17th-century English philosopher John Locke. He argued that at birth, the human mind is much like a blank tablet—a *tabula rasa*, on which experience leaves its mark (Figure 4.1).

4.1 **John Locke (1632–1704)** English philosopher and one of the first advocates for empiricism.

> Let us suppose the mind to be, as we say, a white paper void of all characters, without any ideas:—How comes it to be furnished? Whence comes it by that vast store which the busy and boundless fancy of man has painted on it with an almost endless variety? Whence has it all the materials of reason and knowledge? To this I answer, in one word, from experience. In that all our knowledge is founded; and from that it ultimately derives itself. (Locke, 1690)

To evaluate Locke's claim, however, we need to be clear about exactly what information the senses receive. What happens, for example, when we look at another person? We're presumably interested in what the person looks like, who he is, and what he's doing. These are all facts about the **distal stimulus**—the real object (in this case, the person) in the outside world. (The distal stimulus is typically at some distance from the perceiver, hence the term *distal*.)

But it turns out that our information about the distal stimulus is indirect, because we know the distal stimulus only through the energies that actually reach us—the pattern of light reflected off the person's outer surface, collected by our eyes, and cast as an image on the retina, the light-sensitive tissue at the rear of each eyeball. This input—that is, the energies that actually reach us—is called the **proximal (or "nearby")** **stimulus.**

distal stimulus An object or event in the outside world.

proximal stimulus The energies from the outside world that directly reach our sense organs.

The distinction between distal and proximal stimuli is crucial for hearing as well as vision. We hear someone speaking and want to know who it is, what she's saying, and whether she sounds friendly or hostile. These are all questions about the speaker herself, so they're questions about the distal stimulus. However, our perception of these points must begin with the stimulus that actually reaches us—the sound-pressure waves arriving at our eardrums. These waves are the proximal stimulus for hearing.

The distinction between distal and proximal stimuli is a problem for empiricists. To see why, let's look at the concerns raised by another empiricist philosopher, George Berkeley. As Berkeley pointed out, a large object that's far away from us can cast the same-size image on our retina as can a small object much closer to us (Figure 4.2). Retinal-image size, therefore, doesn't tell us the size of the distal object. How, then, do we tell the large objects in our world from the small? Berkeley also knew that the retina is a two-dimensional surface, and that all images—from near objects and far—are cast onto the same plane. He argued, therefore, that the retinal image cannot directly inform us about the three-dimensional world. Yet, of course, we have little difficulty moving around the world, avoiding obstacles, grasping the things we want to grasp. How can we explain these abilities in light of the limitations of proximal stimuli?

4.2 **Distal and proximal stimuli** When this person looks out on the world, the retinal image cast by his hand will be roughly the same size as the image of the car. But one of these images obviously represents a much larger object! Clearly, then, retinal-image size (the proximal stimulus) alone cannot tell us the size of the distant object (the distal stimulus).

4.3 Distance cues in Renaissance painting This painting by Paris Bordone (1500–1571) shows how distance cues can create a vivid sense of depth on a flat canvas.

4.4 Immanuel Kant (1724–1804) German philosopher who advocated for innate categories of experience.

The empiricists' answer to these questions boils down to a single word: *learning*. We can perceive and move around in the three-dimensional world, they argued, because our *experience* has taught us how to interpret the two-dimensional proximal stimulus. To see how this interpretation unfolds, consider the role of *depth cues* contained within the retinal image. These cues include what's called *visual perspective*—a cue used to convey depth in many paintings (Figure 4.3). The empiricists argued that, in many circumstances, we see the pattern of visual perspective and a moment later reach for or walk toward the objects we're viewing. This experience creates an association in the mind between the visual cue and the appropriate movement; and because this experience has been repeated over and over, the visual cue alone now produces the memory of the movement and thus the sense of depth. (For more on distance cues, see Chapter 5.) In this way, our perception is guided by the proximal stimulus *and* the association.

The Active Perceiver

Other philosophers soon offered a response to the empiricist position, arguing that the perceiver plays a much larger role than the empiricists realized. In this view, the perceiver does far more than supplement the sensory input with associations. In addition—and more important—the perceiver must categorize and interpret the incoming sensory information.

Many scholars have endorsed this general position, but it's often attributed to the German philosopher Immanuel Kant (1724–1804; Figure 4.4). Kant argued that perception is possible only because the mind organizes the sensory information into certain preexisting categories. Specifically, Kant claimed that each of us has an innate grasp of certain spatial relationships, so that we understand what it means for one thing to be *next to* or *far from* another thing, and so on. We also have an innate grasp of temporal relationships (what it means for one event to occur *before* another, or *after*) as well as what it means for one event to cause another. This basic understanding of space, time, and causality brings order to our perception; without this framework, Kant argued, our sensory experience would be chaotic and meaningless. We might detect the individual bits of red or green or heavy or sour; but without the framework supplied by each perceiver, we'd be unable to assemble a coherent sense of the world.

Notice that, in Kant's view, these categories (Kant called them "forms of apperception") are what make perception possible; without the categories, there can be no perception. The categories must be in place, therefore, before any perceptual experience can occur, so they obviously can't be *derived from* perceptual experience. Instead, they must be built into the very structure of the mind, as part of our biological heritage.

PSYCHOPHYSICS

The debate just described was a debate among philosophers, and it made few appeals to any sort of scientific evidence. Ultimately, though, the questions at stake could be understood as questions about whether our perceptions of the world reflect reality as it truly is, or instead reflect reality as it has been interpreted and categorized by us. These seem like questions that should be open to scientific scrutiny, and so it's not too surprising that this dispute prodded investigators to explore in a more systematic way just how the senses function.

At the most basic level, this scrutiny must begin with the relationship between the physical inputs we receive—the stimuli—and the psychological experiences these stimuli give rise to. How closely do our experiences correspond to the inputs? Which inputs give rise to which experiences? The area of research that charts these relationships, linking psychological experiences to physical stimuli, is called **psychophysics**—an enterprise that asks questions like these: What will change in our perception of a sound as the frequency of the sound waves changes? What change in the physical attributes of light corresponds to the change from perceiving red to perceiving green? They might seem technical, but such questions are crucial if we are to understand the relationship between the objective, physically defined stimuli we encounter and the subjective, psychological world of our conscious experience. In other words, we're trying to understand the relationship between the world as it actually is and the world as we perceive it to be.

Sensory Thresholds

We can apply the methods of psychophysics to several different questions as well as a wide range of stimuli. Picture this: You're in a restaurant, eating a particularly tasty fish. Knowing you'd like to re-create the dish in your own kitchen, you might ask, "What's the source of that distinctive flavor?" Here you're asking a psychophysical question—what was it in the physical stimulus that led to a particular sensation, a particular taste? You might realize that the flavor came from adding a tiny bit of saffron to the fish, and so you decide to use saffron in your own cooking. But saffron is the world's most expensive spice, so you'd like to add as little as possible. How much saffron do you need—so that people tasting the fish will just pick up the hint of saffron? This is a psychophysical question about people's ability to detect an input. And perhaps you try the dish once, and decide that next time the saffron flavor could be a tiny bit stronger. How much saffron should you add to produce that stronger flavor? This, too, is a psychophysical question—about the ability to detect differences.

Let's start our examination of psychophysics, therefore, with the issue of *detection:* To continue the example, when we try to determine the smallest amount of saffron you can use (so that you get the effect of the spice without straining your budget), we're asking a question about an **absolute threshold**—the smallest quantity of an input that can be detected. The absolute threshold is assessed in precise physical terms—the number of strands of saffron needed; or the amount of light, measured in quanta, needed for someone to see the light; or the loudness, measured in sound pressure levels, needed for someone to hear a sound. However, we can translate these thresholds into common-sense terms—and when we do, it's clear that our thresholds for many stimuli are very low indeed (Table 4.1).

Our cooking example also highlighted a different type of detection—namely, the detection of differences. If we add two more strands of saffron, can we detect this alteration in the stimulus? How about five more grains, or ten? These are questions about someone's **difference threshold**—the smallest *change* in an input that can be detected. When a stimulus is changed by this minimal amount, psychophysicists call it a **just-noticeable difference**, or **jnd.**

We can measure thresholds for many different sensory dimensions—flavors, brightness, loudness, smells, heaviness, pressure, and more. Across all of these dimensions, difference thresholds show a consistent property: They depend on *proportional*

psychophysics An approach to perception that relates the characteristics of physical stimuli to the sensory experiences they produce.

absolute threshold The smallest quantity of a stimulus that an individual can detect.

difference threshold The smallest amount that a given stimulus must be increased or decreased so that an individual can detect the difference.

just-noticeable difference (jnd) The smallest difference that an organism can reliably detect between two stimuli.

TABLE 4.1	Absolute Thresholds	
	Modality	Example of minimal stimulus that can be detected
	Vision	A candle flame 30 miles away on a dark, clear night
	Hearing	A ticking watch 20 feet away with no other noises
	Taste	A teaspoon of sugar in 2 gallons of water
	Smell	A drop of perfume in 3 rooms
	Touch	The wing of a fly falling on your cheek from a height of 3 inches

Source: Galanter, 1962.

differences, and not *absolute* differences. To illustrate, let's say that you can tell the difference between a backpack filled with 25 pounds of camping gear and one that contains a half-pound more—and so 25.5 pounds. This does not mean that, in general, you're sensitive to half-pound differences. What matters instead is the proportional change—in this case, a difference of 2%. Thus, you probably would not be able to distinguish between a backpack filled with 50 pounds of gear and one that contains 50.5 pounds. This is still a half-pound difference, but only a 1% change. But you would be able to distinguish 50 pounds from 51, or 75 pounds from 76.5—in each case a 2% difference.

This important role for proportions, first documented by the 19th-century physiologist E. H. Weber, is known as **Weber's law.** Put algebraically, this law is written as

$$\frac{\Delta I}{I} = c$$

In the equation, I is the intensity of the standard stimulus, the one to which comparisons are being made; ΔI is the amount that must be added to this intensity to produce a just-noticeable increase; c is a constant (in our example, it was .02, or 2%). The fraction $\Delta I / I$ is referred to as the *Weber fraction*.

Weber's law is important for several reasons, including the fact that it allows us to compare the sensitivities of different sensory modalities. Suppose we want to know whether the eye is more sensitive than the ear. We cannot compare jnds for brightness and loudness directly; the first is measured in millilamberts, the second in decibels, and there's no way to translate the one into the other. But we can compare the Weber fractions for the two modalities. If the fraction for a specific sense modality is small, then we know that the modality is able to make fine discriminations; that is, it will detect even small percentage changes. And, of course, the smaller the Weber fraction, the more sensitive the sense modality. Using these comparisons, we can show that we are much keener at discriminating brightness (we're sensitive to differences of merely 1.6%) than weight (2%), and more sensitive to differences in weight than we are to differences in loudness (10%). The Weber fractions needed for this comparison, and fractions for other sense modalities, are presented in Table 4.2.

Weber's law also helps us solve a further puzzle: The measurement of difference thresholds tells us whether the perceiver can detect a *change* or not. Often, though, we want to know more than this. We want to know about the perceiver's experience—how bright does the light seem to the perceiver, or how loud does the sound seem? Then we

Weber's law The observation that the size of the difference threshold is proportional to the intensity of the standard stimulus.

TABLE 4.2	Representative (Middle-Range) Values for the Weber Fraction for the Different Senses		
	Sensory modality	Weber fraction ($\Delta I/I$)	Weber fraction as a percentage
	Vision (brightness, white light)	1/60	1.6%
	Kinesthesia (lifted weights)	1/50	2.0%
	Pain (thermally aroused on skin)	1/30	3.3%
	Hearing (tone of middle pitch and moderate loudness)	1/10	10.0%
	Touch (cutaneous pressure "spot")	1/7	14.2%
	Smell (odor of India rubber)	1/4	25.0%
	Taste (table salt)	1/3	33.3%

want to link these measurements to the stimulus, so that we can specify the correspondence between the intensity of the stimulus and the intensity of the experience.

More than a hundred years ago, Gustav Fechner was able to address this issue mathematically, building on Weber's law. His result, often referred to as **Fechner's law,** describes the relationship between the physical intensity of a stimulus and the psychological intensity of the experience produced by that experience. The law states that the strength of a sensation increases logorithmically with the intensity of the stimulus. Formally, the law is written:

$$S = k \log I$$

In the equation, S stands for psychological (i.e., subjective) magnitude; I is the physical intensity of the stimulus; and k is a constant whose value depends on the value of the Weber fraction.

In the years since Fechner we've learned that, in truth, this law does not hold up perfectly in all circumstances. (For example, the perception of *pain* does not show the pattern predicted by Fechner's law; for pain, a very small increase in the stimulus causes a large increase in the sensation—a pattern that's useful in compelling us to deal with pain when it arises.) For our purposes, though, the law does hold in a wide range of settings and with a diversity of stimuli. It offers a reasonably accurate characterization of the relationship between stimulus intensity and subjective impression.

Fechner's law The observation that the strength of a sensation is proportional to the logarithm of physical stimulus intensity.

Detection and Decision

Sensory thresholds are defined in terms of stimulus intensities—how much intensity do we need before we can detect the stimulus? How much of a change in intensity do we need to detect that two stimuli are different? It turns out, however, that these intensities are not the only factors determining how someone responds in a psychophysical experiment. Indeed, even this early in our description of the sensory processes, we need to realize that we're not trying to understand how light meters or audiometers work. Instead, we're discussing the capacities and behaviors of living organisms—and that introduces some complications.

perceptual sensitivity An organism's ability to detect a signal.

decision criteria An organism's rule for how much evidence it needs before responding.

signal-detection theory The theory that perceiving or not perceiving a stimulus is actually a judgment about whether a momentary sensory experience is due to background noise alone or to the background noise plus a signal.

To illustrate, imagine a pair of research participants, Matt and Fiona. Matt says, "Yes, I heard that one," in response to most of the barely audible tones being presented by the experimenter. Fiona, in contrast, says yes to only a few of the tones, and she insists that she couldn't hear anything at all on the remaining test trials. One interpretation of this pattern is that Matt has more acute hearing than Fiona does; they differ, in other words, in their **perceptual sensitivity**. A different possibility, though, is that Matt and Fiona differ only in their **decision criteria**—that is, in the "cutoff" they use for deciding when to say yes and when to say no. Maybe Matt is a bit of a risk taker. Or perhaps he has always thought of himself as having acute hearing, and this leads him to put more trust in the vague feeling that he might have just heard the tone. For either of these reasons, Matt may—without even realizing it—adopt an attitude of "When in doubt, say 'Yes, I heard that one.'" Fiona, on the other hand, might be more cautious; or she might be worried that the experimenter will think she's careless if she says yes too often. To avoid this danger, she slips into a more conservative attitude: "When in doubt, say 'No, I didn't hear that one.'" If any of these interpretations are correct, then the difference between Matt's and Fiona's responding might not reflect a difference in their hearing; instead, it shows only that they handle uncertainty in different ways.

SIGNAL-DETECTION PROCEDURES

Variations in decision criteria add a layer of extra complexity to our discussion of sensory thresholds, but **signal-detection theory** allows us to deal with this complexity. In a signal-detection procedure, the experimenters present a faint target stimulus on some trials but no stimulus on other trials. This procedure allows the experimenters to ask how often the participant gives each of the four possible types of response. One response type is a *hit*—the participant says, "Yes, I detected the target" when there really was one. A second type is a *false alarm*—the participant says, "Yes, I detected the target" when there was none. A third response type is a *correct negative*—saying "No target" when this is in fact the correct answer. The final type is a *miss*—saying "No target" even though one was actually presented (Figure 4.5).

To see how this information can be used, let's continue with the example of Matt and Fiona. We've already said that Matt has a higher *hit* rate than Fiona does, and we've noted that this observation is, by itself, ambiguous: Perhaps Matt's hearing is more sensitive than Fiona's, or maybe he's just more casual in his responding and relies on a relatively loose criterion. Based on hit rates alone, there's no way to tell these possibilities apart. A signal-detection experiment, though, provides other information, and this allows us to figure out what's going on with these two participants. Let's say that, in fact, Matt does have a low criterion for responding, and that's why he usually says yes to each of the faint signals. The same low criterion, though, will encourage Matt to say yes even when no signal is presented; those trials, too, will often satisfy his rule of "When in doubt, say 'Yes, I heard that one.'" So Matt will, as we've said, have a high hit rate; but he'll also have a relatively high false-alarm rate. His responses, in other words, will tend to be in the two cells in the left-hand column of Figure 4.5.

In contrast, let's suppose that Matt's hit rate is high because he really does have excellent hearing and can detect each of the subtle signals. In that case, Matt probably won't be fooled by the stimulus-absent trials; his acute hearing will allow him to realize that these trials contain no stimulus, and so he'll correctly respond "no" to these trials. Therefore, his false-alarm rate will be low, and his responses overall will accumulate in the top left and bottom right cells of Figure 4.5.

Response given

		Yes	No
Stimulus	Present	Hit	Miss
	Absent	False alarm	Correct negative

4.5 The four possible outcomes of the detection experiment In a signal-detection procedure, the experimenters present a target stimulus on some trials but no stimulus on other trials. This allows them to ask how often the participant gives each of the four possible types of response.

These points set the pattern for a signal-detection analysis. In general, if individuals differ in how sensitive they are to the signal, then they'll differ in their proportions of correct and incorrect responses—their total number of hits and correct negatives relative to their total number of misses and false alarms. But if individuals differ in their response criterion (e.g., whether they say yes when in doubt, or no), then they'll differ in their proportions of yes and no responses. (Of course, it's possible for participants to differ in *both* their sensitivity *and* their criterion; but, with a bit of algebra, we can disentangle these effects from the signal-detection data.) By looking at all of the numbers, therefore (i.e., by looking at hits, misses, false alarms, and correct negatives), we can calculate two measures for each person. We can, first, measure the person's *sensitivity* to the input—and, for most purposes, this is the measure we want. Second, we can measure the person's *criterion*—and so gain a measure of how much information the person needs before saying, "Yes, I heard it" (or saw it or smelled it or whatever).

People differ in their sensitivity for various reasons: For example, a 20-year-old's hearing is typically more sensitive than a 50-year-old's because of the age-related decline in hearing. A 20-year-old who listens to a lot of loud music will have less sensitive hearing than someone who listens to quieter music, because the ear is damaged by overstimulation. And so on.

Why do people have different response criteria? The answer involves several different factors—some of them enduring traits of the person, some of them tied to the specific circumstances. We considered some examples in our discussion of Matt and Fiona—for example, the possibility that Matt might just be a risk taker, or that he's guided by his self-confident belief that he has good hearing. Just as important is a person's belief about the *frequency* of signals. (If, for example, you believe that signals will be presented on 98% of the trials, it makes sense to adopt a rule of "When in doubt, say 'I heard it'"—because this rule will lead to a correct response most of the time. If you believe, in contrast, that signals will be presented on only 1% of the trials, it makes sense to adopt the opposite rule.) Also crucial is the **payoff matrix**—the pattern of benefits and costs associated with each type of error. Imagine Matt was trying to impress the experimenter with his fine sense of hearing. In that case, Matt would put special weight on the benefits associated with a hit and the costs associated with a miss. This approach would encourage a lower criterion. Suppose Fiona, on the other hand, is worried about appearing careless; she might emphasize the costs associated with a false alarm, thus leading her to use a higher criterion.

IMPLICATIONS OF SIGNAL DETECTION

Signal-detection analysis is a valuable research method with applications in a wide range of settings. Researchers have used signal detection to study cases as diverse as the memory effects of hypnosis and the decisions made by college admissions officers. As just one example, consider the case presented in Figure 4.6. Here a doctor who is seeking to diagnose cancer is trying to decide whether a "signal" (the illness) is present in that patient or not, and, with the problem laid out in this way, the resemblance between the doctor's task and, say, Matt's or Fiona's—as in Figure 4.5—should be obvious. Suppose we want to evaluate this doctor's performance—maybe we're trying to decide how much we can trust this particular doctor, or whether the doctor needs more training. In all cases, we'd need to measure the doctor's *sensitivity* to this "signal," and we'd need to separate that sensitivity from the doctor's criterion. To see how important this is, imagine a doctor who diagnoses cancer in patient after patient. This might mean the doctor is especially astute and can detect this serious problem whenever he encounters

payoff matrix The pattern of benefits and costs associated with certain types of responses.

(A)

Diagnosis

	Cancer	No cancer
Present	Correct diagnosis	Miss
Absent	False alarm	Correct diagnosis

Cancer

(B)

4.6 Signal-detection analysis applied to medicine The decision options in B obviously resemble those in Figure 4.5, and so we can think of a doctor's task in reaching a diagnosis as similar to the task of someone in a sensory test. Thus, we can use the logic of signal detection theory to assess the doctor's performance.

it; this sounds like a doctor one should seek out. But it might also mean the doctor has a lax criterion and offers this horrible diagnosis based on relatively thin evidence; now this sounds like a doctor to be avoided! It would obviously be useful to know which of these descriptions is correct, and of course this is precisely the information provided by signal-detection analysis. (For details on how signal detection has been applied to other domains, including medical diagnosis, see, for example, McFall & Treat, 1999; Swets, Dawes, & Monahan, 2000.)

Signal-detection analyses highlight another crucial point: We often make decisions with imperfect information, so it's inevitable that we'll make some errors. What can we do about this? If we are especially concerned about *false alarms* (a cancer test that says someone has the disease even though she doesn't, or a jury that votes "guilty" even though the defendant is innocent), we can take steps to raise the response criterion. This adjustment will decrease the number of false alarms, but it's likely to increase the number of misses (failing to detect an actual tumor, or acquitting someone who is actually guilty). On the other hand, we could shift in the opposite direction—to a lower criterion—but this would lead to the opposite pattern of benefit and risk: Lowering the criterion will decrease the number of misses but increase the number of false alarms.

How should we think about these issues? That depends on the specific case—and, in particular, the potential consequences of a miss or false alarm. Overall, though, when we make decisions (or develop a cancer test, or instruct a jury), it's important to remember that this trade-off between misses and false alarms is in place. If we want to evaluate anything from a cancer test or a jury instruction to the memory effects of hypnosis or the police department's decision about whether to take a bomb threat seriously, signal-detection analyses can provide separate measurements of sensitivity and criterion—information that allows us to ensure that these decision processes are well tuned to our goals.

A SURVEY OF THE SENSES

Psychophysics allows us to specify the correspondence between physical stimuli and psychological experiences, but this is just the first step of our inquiry. We also want to understand *why this correspondence is as it is.* Let's say, for example, that we've learned from psychophysics that placing a particular molecule on the tongue leads someone to say, "Yeah, I can detect a taste—and it's sweet. It's chocolate!" What are the steps that bring us from the molecule to this recognition? As our first question, we might ask how the molecule manages to trigger a response in the nervous system at all. We'd also want to ask why the molecule leads to a sensation of sweet, while some other molecule might lead to a sensation of salty. And once the molecule has triggered a response in the nervous system, how does this response lead to the conscious experience of tasting a delicious bit of chocolate?

To answer questions like these, notice that we need to begin with the physics of the stimulus. From there we'll move to electrochemistry, to examine how physical inputs trigger events in our bodies. Next we need to ask how the nervous system analyzes and then recognizes these incoming signals. Then, finally, we can zero in on our ultimate target—an explanation of the conscious experience of the "chocolate" sensation; or, with a different stimulus, the conscious experience of seeing a beautiful shade of blue.

Let's pause to appreciate the extraordinary ambition of this project. We're seeking to build a bridge from events that are microscopic and objective to events that are large scale and entirely subjective. We're trying to specify the connections that will let us move seamlessly from a discussion of physics at one end of the process to comments about conscious experience at the other end. Seems ambitious, doesn't it? Maybe so, but we've made enormous progress on this project. In the rest of this chapter, we will survey some of what we've learned. We begin with some considerations that apply to all of the sense modalities. Next we turn to our vestibular sensation (roughly, our sense of up and down and of whether we are moving or still) and then to the sensations of touch, pain, taste, and smell. Near the end of the chapter, we explore the two sense modalities that are unquestionably the most important sources of information for us—namely, hearing and vision.

Sensory Coding

Each of the sense modalities has its own properties and follows its own rules. For some modalities (vision, hearing, taste, and smell), we have specialized organs that collect, concentrate, and amplify the incoming stimulus information. In other cases (the various skin senses), we simply accept the input, unamplified, as it arrives. For some senses, the crucial input consists of some form of energy—a mechanical push against the eardrum in the case of hearing; a photon striking the back of the eyeball for vision. For other senses, the key input is chemical—a molecule on the tongue or in the nose. Some senses (vision, hearing, smell) can respond to stimuli that are far away from us; others (touch, taste) respond only to nearby inputs.

Even with these differences, the various senses have some crucial features in common. In all cases, the physical stimulus must be converted into a neural signal; this is the step of **transduction.** Then, once the stimulus is transduced, the nervous system needs somehow to represent the various qualities of the input. At the coarsest level, the nervous system must register the fact that we saw the pizza but did not taste it, or that we heard the approaching car but did not see it. What's more, the nervous system must somehow represent differences within each sensory system—that the pizza was salty, not sweet; or that the car was remarkably loud. These are all issues of **sensory coding**—how the qualities of the input are translated into specific representations within the nervous system.

One aspect of sensory coding involves *psychological intensity*—the difference between a bright light and a dim one, or a subtle scent of cinnamon in contrast to a dense cloud of the smell. In most cases, the nervous system codes stimulus intensity via the rate of firing by the neurons in a sensory system: the more intense the stimulus, the greater the rate of firing. Stimulus intensity is also encoded via the sheer number of neurons that are triggered by the stimulus: the more intense the stimulus, the more neurons it activates, and the greater the psychological magnitude.

The second aspect of coding is *sensory quality*—how the nervous system represents the difference between, say, vision and hearing; or within a modality, how it represents the difference between, for example, a high-pitched note and a low one, or the difference between a sweet taste and a bitter one. The first of these sensory quality issues—the difference *between* modalities—is straightforward. Almost 200 years ago, Johannes Müller argued that the key lies simply in which nerves are being stimulated. Stimulation of the optic nerve (whether from light or some other source) causes the sense of seeing; this is why strong pressure on the eyeballs leads us to see rings or stars (to the dismay of boxers and the delight of cartoonists; Figure 4.7). Similarly, stimulation of the auditory nerve—whether it's from a sound or something else—causes the sense of hearing. This is why people sometimes experience "ringing in their ears" in the absence of any environmental sound—some illness or injury is causing stimulation of the auditory nerve.

transduction The process through which a physical stimulus is converted into a signal within the nervous system.

sensory coding The process through which the nervous system represents the qualities of the incoming stimulus—whether auditory or visual, for example, or whether a red light or a green one, a sour taste or a sweet taste.

4.7 Seeing stars Whether it comes from light or some other source, stimulation of the optic nerve causes the sense of seeing. This is why boxers sometimes "see stars." The punches they receive cause the head to move abruptly, making the eyeballs press briefly against their eye sockets. This pressure mechanically stimulates the optic nerves and makes the stars appear.

4.8 Pattern coding Researchers recorded the response from receptors in a monkey's tongue when the monkey was given a taste of sodium chloride (NaCl, or table salt), which humans regard as salty-tasting, or a taste of highly dilute acid, which humans regard as sour-tasting. All four taste receptors responded to the acid, and three responded to the salt. Notice in addition that the response from the salt-preferring receptors was very similar for the two tasks. Results like these make it plain that tastes are not encoded simply by which receptors are responding—because generally all of them are—nor by the strength of response from a single receptor type. Instead, individual tastes are represented within the nervous system only in the pattern of responding across the receptor types.

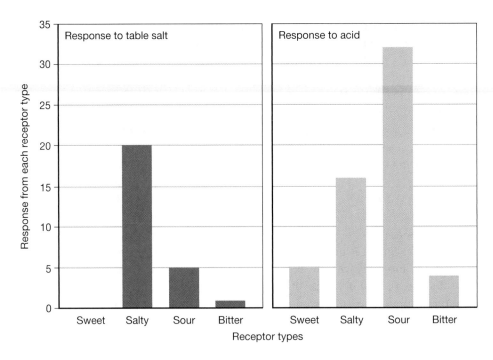

specificity theory The proposal that different sensory qualities are signaled by different quality-specific neurons. This theory is correct in only a few cases (e.g., pain).

pattern theory The proposal that different sensory qualities are encoded by specific *patterns* of firing among the relevant neurons.

What about differences *within* a sense modality? For example, blue, green, and red are all visual sensations, so they all involve activity in the optic nerve. But of course each color is qualitatively different from the others. Likewise, sweetness and saltiness are both tastes; but they're plainly distinct for the perceiver. How are differences like these encoded? One hypothesis stays close to Müller's insight and is often referred to as **specificity theory.** This proposal suggests that different sensory qualities (sweet versus sour, red versus green) are signaled by different neurons, just as the different sense modalities (vision versus pressure) are signaled by different nerves. In this conception, the nervous system acts as if these quality-specific neurons were somehow "labeled" with their quality, so that the nervous system registers the presence of "red" whenever there's an incoming signal in the "red neurons," registers the presence of "hot" whenever there's a signal coming from the "hot neurons," and so on.

This proposal turns out to be correct in some cases—for example, specific neurons do seem to convey the sensation of pain. More commonly, though, the data demand a different explanation—usually called **pattern theory** (Figure 4.8). According to this view, what matters for sensory quality is not which neurons are firing. Instead, what allows us to identify the input is the overall *pattern* of activation—which neurons are firing more, and which less, at any given moment.

We'll have much more to say about pattern theory in our discussion of the specific modalities. For now, let's just note that there's no single answer to the question of how sensory coding is achieved. The difference among senses (e.g., taste versus sight, hearing versus smell) is certainly signaled by "labeled lines," so activity in the optic nerve causes the sensation of seeing, activity in the auditory nerve causes the sensation of hearing, and so on. Some specific sensations (e.g., pain) may also be signaled by labeled lines; but more commonly, the nervous system uses a pattern code to distinguish the qualities within each sensory modality.

Sensory Adaptation

One further consideration is also relevant to all the sensory systems. Of course, our sensory responses are influenced by the physical magnitude of the stimulus—and so the taste buds respond more powerfully to a concentrated sugar solution than a weak one; the eye responds more strongly to a bright light than a dim one. But our sensory responses are also influenced by *changes.* Thus, a sugar solution will taste much sweeter if you've just been tasting something salty; a blast of room-temperature air will feel quite warm on your skin if you've just come in from the cold.

The importance of change in shaping our sensations shows up in many settings—including the phenomenon of **sensory adaptation.** This term refers to the way our sensory apparatus registers a strong response to a stimulus when it first arrives, but then gradually decreases that response if the stimulus is unchanging. Thus, when we first walk into a restaurant, the smell of garlic is quite noticeable; but after a few minutes, we barely notice it. Likewise, the water may feel quite hot when you first settle into the bathtub; a few moments later, the sensation of heat fades away.

Sensory adaptation is easily documented both in the lab and informally. Here's an example: Stare at the dot in the center of Figure 4.9, trying not to move your eyes at all. After 15 or 20 seconds, the gray haze surrounding the dot will probably appear to shrink and may disappear altogether. (The moment you move your eyes, the haze is restored.)

What's happening in this case? The gray haze is initially a novel stimulus, so it elicits a strong response from the visual system. After a moment or two, the novelty is gone; and, with no change in the input, the response is correspondingly diminished. It's important for this demonstration, though, that the haze has an indistinct edge. While looking at the figure, your eyes will tremble just a bit, so the image of the haze will shift slightly from one position on your eye to another. But, because the edge of the haze is blurred, these shifts will produce very little change in the stimulation—so the haze slowly vanishes from view. (With more sharply defined contours, small changes in eye position will cause large changes in the visual input. As a result, even the slightest jitter in the eye muscles will provide new information for the visual system. This helps us understand why you can stare out the window for many minutes, or stare at a computer screen, without the input seeming to vanish!)

What do organisms gain by this sort of sensory adaptation? Stimuli that have been around for a while have already been inspected; any information they offer has already been detected and analyzed. It's sensible, therefore, to give these already checked inputs less sensory weight. The important thing is change—especially sudden change—because it may well signify food to a predator and death to its potential prey. Adaptation is the sensory system's way of ensuring these priorities by pushing old news off the neurophysiological front page.

The Vestibular Sense

We've now looked at several of the themes shared by the various sense modalities. But, as we said earlier, the senses also differ in important ways. Let's turn, therefore, to a brief tour of the various senses and see how each one functions.

It's often said that humans have five senses—vision, hearing, taste, smell, and touch. However, we can't take this count seriously for several reasons, including the fact that it doesn't include some of the senses. One is **kinesthesis,** the name for sensations coming from various receptors in the muscles, tendons, and joints. Kinesthesis informs us about our movements and the orientation of our body in space. Another is the **vestibular sense,** which signals movements of the head, whether produced by deliberate motion or by an external force. This sense helps us know which way is "up" and which is "down," and it also tells us whether we're moving at a constant velocity or accelerating. The receptors for the vestibular sense are in the *semicircular canals,* located within the inner ear

sensory adaptation The process by which the sensitivity to a stimulus declines if the stimulus is presented for an extended period of time.

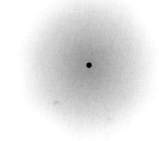

4.9 **Sensory adaptation** Keep staring at the black dot. After a while, the gray haze around it will appear to shrink.

kinesthesis The sensations generated by receptors in the muscles, tendons, and joints that inform us of our skeletal movement.

vestibular senses The sensations generated by receptors in the semicircular canals of the inner ear that inform us about the head's orientation and movements.

(A)

(B)

4.10 The vestibular sense (A) The location of the inner ears, which are embedded in bone on both sides of the skull. (B) It's the vestibular sense that informs us about our position relative to gravity, and also tells us whether we're accelerating or not. Of course, amusement park rides give this sense modality an extreme workout.

(Figure 4.10). The canals contain a thick liquid that moves whenever the head moves. This motion bends hair cells located at one end of each canal; and when they're bent, these hair cells give rise to nervous impulses. Together, the impulses from each of the canals provide information about the nature and extent of the head's movements.

People become keenly aware of the vestibular sense whenever it isn't working properly. This is the plight, for example, of someone who has consumed too much alcohol: Even when lying quietly in bed, the person is likely to complain that the world is "spinning around." The spinning effect occurs because alcohol, once in the bloodstream, diffuses into the inner ear and changes the density and viscosity of the fluid inside the semicircular canals. This change disrupts the normal functioning of the vestibular system, and dizziness is the result (e.g., Karch, 2007).

Far more important, though, is the functioning of the vestibular sense in ordinary circumstances. For example, one function of this sense is to provide a firm base for vision. As we move through the world, our heads move continually. To compensate for this endless rocking, our eyes have to move accordingly. This adjustment is accomplished by a reflex system that's coordinated by the cerebellum but initiated by messages from the vestibular sense. In this way, the visual system is effectively stable and operates as if it's resting on a solid tripod.

The Skin Senses

skin senses The group of senses, including pressure, warmth, cold, and pain, through which we gain information about our immediate surroundings.

The Greek philosopher Aristotle believed that all of the senses from the skin were encompassed in the broad category of *touch*. Today we know that the so-called **skin senses** include several distinct subsystems, each giving rise to a distinct sensation—including pressure, temperature, and pain (Figure 4.11). Not surprisingly, some parts of the body have greater skin sensitivity than others—it's especially high in the hands and fingers, the lips and tongue, and the genital areas.

(A)

Skin surface

Texture and pattern receptors

Pain receptor (free nerve endings)

Ruffini endings

Low-frequency vibration receptor

Duct of sweat gland

Fat cells

High-frequency vibration receptor

(B)

4.11 Skin senses The skin includes distinct types of receptors associated with the various skin senses, such as pressure, temperature, and pain. The temperature sense, in turn, is linked to other mechanisms (like the control of sweating) that help us maintain a consistent body temperature.

Among the various senses, the skin senses may be the best example of specificity coding (or "labeled lines"), whereby distinct types of receptors are associated with different sensations. Some of the receptors respond to sustained pressure or very low-frequency vibration. A second type of receptors respond to faster vibrations. Yet another type, called the Ruffini endings, respond to sustained downward pressure or stretching of the skin; among other functions, these latter receptors probably play a key role in helping us monitor and control our finger positions.

Still other receptors are responsible for our sensitivity to temperature—and even here, we encounter specialization. One type of receptor fires whenever the temperature increases in the area immediately surrounding the receptor; a different (and more numerous) type of receptor does the opposite—firing in response to a drop in skin temperature. It turns out that, in most cases, neither of these receptor types is especially active. This is because many mechanisms inside the body work to maintain a constant body temperature, and so neither receptor type is triggered. But if you move close to the radiator or step into cold water, these receptors immediately respond, informing you about these events.

Pain

One of the skin senses deserves special mention—our sense of pain. Pain usually begins with activity in the **nociceptors**—receptors in the skin that have bare nerve endings and that respond to various forms of tissue damage as well as to temperature extremes. These receptors come in two types: *A-delta fibers* allow rapid transmission of information and are responsible for the pain you experience when you're first injured.

nociceptors Receptors in the skin that give rise to the sense of pain; they respond to various forms of tissue damage and to temperature extremes.

The *C fibers,* in contrast, are unmyelinated and therefore slower in their transmission; they're the source of the dull ache that remains long after the injury occurs.

Activity in the nociceptors is aversive—obviously, we'd prefer to avoid pain! But pain plays a crucial role for us—as evident in the rare individuals who have medical conditions making them insensitive to pain (Melzack & Wall, 1982). These individuals are constantly at risk: They can't feel the pain of resting a hand on a hot stove, so they're in danger of burning themselves. They can't feel the irritation of an object caught in the throat, so they don't cough—creating a danger of choking. They don't notice if they bite their own tongues while chewing food. These (and many other) examples remind us that pain is *useful*—helping us to avoid a wide range of hazards. Without this "alert system," our likelihood of serious injury would be a lot greater and our life expectancies much shorter.

Let's be clear, though, that the experience of pain depends on far more than the nociceptors themselves because there are circumstances in which people appear to feel no pain despite activity in these receptors. The classic examples come from soldiers who appear not to notice their wounds until the battle ends, or athletes who don't feel a sprained ankle, or even a broken rib, until the excitement of the game subsides.

How should we think about these observations? Part of the answer involves substances, produced by our bodies, that function as internal medications. These substances—which we first met in Chapter 3—are chemically quite similar to drugs like morphine or codeine, and they interfere with the neurotransmission involved in pain sensation. These natural internal painkillers, called endorphins, help us in many circumstances to continue functioning despite a seemingly painful injury.

Pain sensations can also be blocked via a different mechanism: According to the **gate control theory,** pain sensations must pass through a neural "gate" to reach the brain and can be blocked at that gate by neurons that inhibit signals from the nociceptors, so that these signals are never transmitted to the brain. The gate neurons that provide this inhibition can be triggered in several ways, including *counterirritation*. This term refers to the phenomenon in which painful sensations from one part of the body trigger the gate neurons and thus decrease the sensitivity to pain elsewhere in the body (e.g., Motohashi & Umino, 2001).

We also know that the experience of pain is influenced by someone's beliefs and emotions. However, these cognitive factors may be affecting the emotion that accompanies pain rather than the sensation of pain itself (Melzack & Casey, 1968). These two aspects of pain—the sensation and the emotion—can be distinguished subjectively. They can also be distinguished functionally—so that hypnosis (for example) seems to alter the emotional response to pain without decreasing the actual intensity of the sensation. These two aspects of pain can also be distinguished by brain activity—the sensation corresponds mostly to activation in specific areas of the somatosensory cortex, and the emotion corresponds more closely to activity in the anterior cingulate cortex (Rainville, Duncan, Price, Carrier, & Bushnell, 1997; for more on pain as a source of *motivation*, see Chapter 12).

Smell

Smell may be the sense modality that we understand least (for recent surveys, see A. Gilbert, 2008; Zarzo & Stanton, 2009). Still, some basic facts are clear: Complex molecules drift through the air, and some are drawn up the nose to a mucous membrane called the **olfactory epithelium**—it's located at the top of the nasal cavity, a little less than three inches up from the nostrils' opening. The epithelium in each nostril contains roughly 10 million olfactory receptor neurons. Some of the molecules that reach

gate control theory The proposal that pain sensations must pass through a neural "gate" in order to reach the brain and can be blocked at that gate by neurons that inhibit signals from the nociceptors.

olfactory epithelium A mucous membrane at the top of the nasal cavity; contains the olfactory receptor neurons that respond to airborne molecules called odorants.

(A)

Nasal passage

Odorants

Glomerulus

Olfactory bulb

Olfactory sensory neurons

(B)

4.12 The sense of smell Molecules in the air, called odorants, are drawn up into the nose and pass through the nasal cavity to receptors that trigger the sense of smell.

these neurons bind to these receptors, changing their membrane structure and thus triggering an electrical response. The molecules that can produce a response in these receptors are called *odorants* (Figure 4.12).

The axons from the receptors exit the nasal cavity through a thin layer of bone and reach upward into the olfactory bulb, a brain structure above the nasal cavity and just beneath the frontal lobes. Within the olfactory bulb, the axons converge at sites called **glomeruli.** The nose contains roughly 1,000 types of receptors, and each glomerulus receives input from just one of these receptor types. Because each type of odorant binds more easily to some types of receptors than others, we can think of each type of receptor as having a "preferred" odorant. Then, with each glomerulus receiving inputs from just one type of receptor, this preference for certain odorants is inevitably passed along from the receptors to the glomeruli.

It's not clear, however, how the many glomeruli give rise to the various odors that humans can discriminate (Axel, 1995). We've already mentioned the roughly 1,000 types of receptors—and therefore 1,000 types of glomeruli—but in fact humans can distinguish roughly 10,000 different odors. Right away, these numbers tell us that our sense of smell does not rely on a one-glomerulus-per-scent coding—we don't rely on "labeled lines" that use one neural pathway for each scent. Instead, it must be that each odor we can distinguish produces some unique pattern of activation in the various glomeruli. What this pattern is—and so exactly how the nervous system distinguishes, say, the smell of roses from the smell of vanilla—remains a topic for research (for a recent exploration of these issues, see Khan et al., 2007).

The sense of smell has many functions. Smell helps many animals to locate food—think of a bear managing to find the ripe berries, or a dog hunting for a rabbit. Smell also helps animals avoid danger; it's why predators usually approach their prey from downwind, so that the prey won't pick up the predator's scent. Smell also contributes heavily to our sense of *flavor*—partly because air carrying odorants can reach the nasal cavity through either the nose or an opening at the back of the mouth. In fact, a large part of what we call flavor—and thus a large factor in our selection (and enjoyment!) of

glomeruli Sites in the brain's olfactory bulb where signals from the smell receptors converge.

foods—is really smell. This point is evident whenever someone has a head cold that impairs their sense of smell. In that situation, most foods taste incredibly bland—strong testimony to just how much flavor involves the way something smells, rather than how it tastes. You can test this point without having a head cold: Pinch your nose closed, shut your eyes, and have someone feed you either a small bit of an onion or a small bit of apple. Without visual or smell cues, you won't be able to tell which bit is which. Indeed, in the laboratory, people with their nostrils blocked seem unable to tell apart flavors as diverse as grape, coffee, chocolate, and garlic (Mozel, B. Smith, P. Smith, Sullivan, & Swender, 1969).

Smell also has important social functions. For some animals, smell allows one individual to recognize other individuals—so that infant rats can recognize their mothers via smell, and their mothers can recognize them the same way. In addition, smell can serve a communicative function by alerting other individuals to the whereabouts or the status of other individuals from that species. This is, of course, why many animals mark their territories by rubbing against trees, or by depositing small splashes of urine at various landmarks within their domain. These activities leave scent traces that announce the scent donor's "ownership" of that bit of real estate.

Smell-based communication within a species usually involves specialized chemicals called **pheromones**—biologically produced odorants that convey information to other members of the species. Some pheromones simply identify the species: "Know by this smell that a fellow cat is nearby." Other pheromones convey information about the donor's current state. For instance, some pheromones serve as alarm signals—when an animal is frightened, its sweat includes chemicals that can be detected by other members of that species, putting them on alert that some threat is at hand (e.g., Brechbühl, Klaey, & Broillet, 2008). Other pheromones play a role in mating—for example, helping males of the species to locate sexually receptive females (e.g., Michael & Keverne, 1968).

There has been considerable debate about the role of pheromonal communication in humans—especially in human mating. We do know that human parents can sniff a T-shirt and tell by the scent which of their children wore the shirt (R. Porter & Schaal, 1995; Wallace, 1977). We also know that human infants just a week old can distinguish between their mother's scent and the scent of another lactating woman (Macfarlane, 1975; Cernoch & Porter, 1985). But what about a role for pheromones in selecting a mate, or in sexual arousal itself? Many laboratories are exploring this issue, often with the hope of identifying some sex attractant—and, as Figure 4.13 suggests, often with funding from the perfume industry! However, the results of this research have been inconclusive at best (McClintock, 2000). Even so, there's no question that at least some aspects of human reproductive behavior are influenced by scent. We find some evidence for this point among young women who live together; they tend to have synchronized menstrual cycles, ovulating and menstruating on the same days. More, this synchrony is established relatively quickly—after the women have lived together for just 3 months (McClintock, 1971).

What causes this menstrual synchrony? The answer turns out to be scent. In a number of experiments, investigators have collected perspiration from the underarms of one group of women and then wiped these secretions under the noses of a different group of women who've never met the scents' donors. This communication via smell is enough to establish the synchrony (Stern & McClintock, 1998)—a powerful indicator that some aspects of our reproductive systems are, in fact, governed by odor cues.

pheromones Biologically produced odorants that convey information to other members of the species.

4.13 Pheromones

Taste

For the sense of taste, just as for the sense of smell, the proximal stimuli are molecules of particular shapes that react with receptor cells. But there are many differences between taste and smell. For smell, the molecules we call *odorants* are carried through the air and so can reach the receptors from a considerable distance. (You can, for example, smell the garlic cooking in the kitchen the moment you enter the house; and you can smell smoke from a fire when you're still miles away from the flames.) In contrast, the molecules called *tastants* are carried by fluids, not by air. Tastants cannot easily travel from one place to another; this is why we can't taste the cookie even if it's just inches away from us.

Another difference between taste and smell concerns the location of the receptors themselves. The smell receptors are located, as we've discussed, in the olfactory epithelium at the top of the nose. The taste receptors are located primarily on the tongue, although many are found on the roof of the mouth and the upper throat. So, to taste something, we need to place it into our mouths. Specifically, when we eat or drink something, the tastant molecules are carried to the **papillae** that cover our tongue (Figure 4.14). Each papilla contains hundreds of taste buds, and each taste bud contains a hundred or so receptor cells. At these receptors, the molecules trigger a response that ultimately leads to the sensation of taste. However, these counts (the number of taste buds per papilla, or the number of receptors per taste bud) are only rough approximations, because many factors can change the counts. One factor, for example, is *age*. Evidence suggests that a young child may have twice the number of taste receptors that a 20-year-old has; the elderly have even fewer taste receptors (Herness & Gilbertson, 1999).

A further difference between taste and smell lies in the sheer complexity of these senses. For smell, there are roughly 1,000 receptor types. For taste, there are just five types evenly distributed over the whole tongue (Bartoshuk & Beauchamp, 1994). In fact, scientists believed for many years that the sense of taste was even simpler—they identified just *four* types of taste receptors, each type especially sensitive to one of four basic tastes: *salt, sour, bitter,* and *sweet*. It's now clear, however, that there's a fifth type of receptor, and it's especially sensitive to a flavor called by its Japanese name: *umami* (pronounced "oo-MA-me"; Kurihara & Kashiwayanagi, 1998). Umami, often described as "savory," is the flavor that characterizes many high-protein foods, including meat and cheese. It also turns out to be the taste produced by the flavor enhancer monosodium glutamate (MSG).

Each receptor type responds, at least to some degree, to all tastants. Thus, the sweet-preferring receptors respond most strongly to molecules we taste as sweet, but these same receptors also respond (although less strongly) to molecules we taste as salty or bitter (see Figure 4.8). The same is true for the other receptor types: they too are especially sensitive to inputs of just the right sort, but they will respond somewhat to most other inputs. The upshot is that activity by any one of the receptor types is ambiguous. If there's a weak response from, say, the salty-preferring receptors, is it because the input was sour or because the input was salty and highly diluted? The only way to know is by comparing activity in the salt-preferring receptors to activity in the other types of receptors: A weak response from salt-preferring receptors occurring simultaneously with a strong response from sour-preferring receptors suggests that you may be sucking on a lemon. A weak response from the salt-preferring receptors occurring simultaneously with an even weaker response from the other receptor types suggests that you're tasting lightly salted water.

papillae Structures on the tongue that contain the taste buds, which in turn contain taste receptors.

4.14 The sense of taste When we eat or drink something, molecules called tastants trigger responses in receptors located on the taste buds, which are in turn located on the papillae—visible here as pink disks. This photo shows the surface of the tongue at roughly 100× magnification.

What are the physical stimuli that produce each of the basic taste qualities? We do not have a full answer. We know that the sour taste is associated with acids, and that salty tastes emanate from sodium-sensitive receptors. The story is more complicated for sweet and bitter sensations. Both are generally produced by complex organic molecules, but there are no clear-cut rules summarizing the relationship between a molecule's structure and the resulting taste. Thus, sweet tastes are produced by various sugars; but they're also produced by several different artificial sweeteners, some of which have chemical structures very different from sugar.

Whatever their physical basis, though, it's clear that tastes often have a special biological role. For example, many nutritive substances contain some form of sugar, and so natural selection would have favored organisms with a preference for sweets—which would have led these organisms to a high-calorie diet, helping them survive. This helps us understand why most animals, shaped by natural selection, are strongly attracted by sweet tastes. (Whether a preference for sweets is still healthy in the modern world—where high-calorie foods are so readily available to us—is another matter.) On the other hand, many toxic substances are bitter, and so natural selection would likely have favored organisms that avoided bitter tastes. This helps us understand why most animals do avoid bitter flavors and, if they ingest something bitter, respond by gagging or vomiting.

These evolutionary claims obviously suggest that some of our taste preferences are shaped by our genetic heritage. As a result, we should be able to document taste preferences in newborns—and in fact we can: The newborns of many species (including humans) have strong taste preferences; they respond positively to sweet tastes but grimace and gag in response to bitter tastes (Figure 4.15).

Our genes also influence our sense of taste in other ways. People differ in their pattern of taste sensitivities; some individuals are especially sensitive to some flavors, other people are more sensitive to other flavors. At least some of this variation seems to be shaped by genetic factors, a point that's well documented for the so-called *supertasters*. These are people who seem enormously sensitive to certain tastes, probably because they literally have more papillae than other people do. We can identify supertasters by placing on their tongue a bit of paper impregnated with the chemical compound *propylthiouracil (PROP)*. For roughly 75% of our species, this chemical has either no detectable taste or only a mild taste; for the supertasters, though, this chemical has an extremely bitter taste. Happily, supertasters are unlikely to encounter PROP (and the horrid taste it produces for them) outside of the lab. Even so, their sensitivity still shapes the everyday experience of supertasters: They generally dislike—and avoid—some relatively common foods, including brussels sprouts and other forms of cabbage; coffee; spinach; and various soy products (Bartoshuk, 2000; Bartoshuk, Duffy, & Miller 1994; Mennella, Pepino, & Reed, 2005).

Other taste preferences, though, are more heavily influenced by learning. In some cases, learning can create a *conditioned taste aversion* in which an organism, due to a specific experience, comes to associate a particular taste with illness—and from then on seems to find that flavor repulsive. (We'll have more to say about conditioned taste aversion in Chapter 7.) In other cases, the learning may simply involve a matter of familiarity. Many adults can, for example, name certain "comfort foods"—foods that somehow make them feel safe and comfortable—and, in most cases, these are the familiar foods of childhood. Familiarity also plays a key role in defining a culture's *cuisine*—people in Greece are familiar with, and generally like, foods carrying the flavors of olive oil, tomato, and cinnamon; people in China are familiar with, and generally like, foods carrying the flavors of soy and ginger;

4.15 Babies' innate responses to bitter and sweet Many animals show strong taste preferences from a very young age. The baby in (A) is showing her displeasure after tasting a bitter leaf of arugula; the baby in (B) is enjoying the sweet taste of a fortune cookie.

(A)   (B)

people in the Middle East have the same response to lemon and parsley, and so on (E. Rozin, 1973). Still other taste preferences are also shaped by learning, but the nature of the learning is simply unclear. Why do some people learn to love tofu, while others have the opposite reaction? Why do some people learn to enjoy beers—perhaps a dark beer in particular, or an especially bitter one—while others do not? These are simply questions for further research.

HEARING

Our survey so far has deliberately held two senses to the side—namely, hearing and vision. This is because humans rely on these two senses more than any of the others, justifying more extensive coverage of how we hear and how we see. Without question these are the two sense modalities that we use for the vast majority of our communication, and that provide our main guidance as we move around. Let's therefore examine how these two essential modalities function, starting with our sense of hearing.

The Stimulus: Sound

What is the stimulus for hearing? Outside in the world, some physical object is moving—perhaps an animal scurrying through the underbrush, or a set of vocal cords vibrating. This movement agitates the air particles that surround the moving object, causing these particles to jostle other particles, which in turn jostle still other particles. The actual movement of these particles is slight (about one-billionth of a centimeter) and short-lived; the particles return to their original position in a few thousandths of a second. But the motion is enough to create a momentary pressure that pushes outward from the moving object in a pattern similar to the ripples that are set in motion by a stone thrown into a pond.

If the movement continues for even a short time, it will create a series of pressure variations in the air. When these **sound waves** hit our ears, they initiate a set of further changes that ultimately trigger the auditory receptors. The receptors in turn trigger neural responses, which eventually reach the brain and lead to the experience of hearing.

Sound waves vary in many ways; but, in the simplest case, they take the form shown in Figure 4.16. This is, for example, the pattern that would result if a tuning fork were

sound waves Successive pressure variations in the air that vary in amplitude and wavelength.

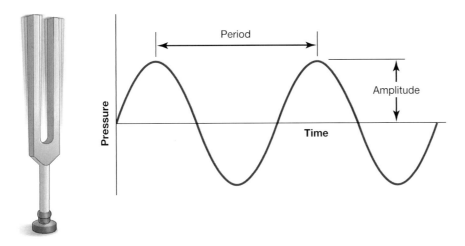

4.16 **The stimulus for hearing** A vibrating object creates a series of pressure pulses in the molecules surrounding it. To describe the pattern this produces, it's useful to measure the air pressure at a single point in space. The pressure of a sound wave rises and falls, as shown here. The extent of the pressure determines the height (amplitude) of the wave; the timing between points of maximum pressure determines the period.

vibrating back and forth, pushing on the air molecules next to it each time the vibration moves the fork in one direction, and then pulling back on the same air molecules a moment later when the vibration moves the fork in the other direction. That's why the pressure rises and falls as time goes by, in correspondence to the pushes and pulls the tuning fork is creating. (A vibrating guitar string or a vibrating clarinet reed have roughly the same effect, although these instruments produce a more complex pattern than the one shown in the figure; other movements—like the sound of a voice—would produce still more complex patterns.)

The pattern shown in Figure 4.16 is produced by a physical vibration and corresponds exactly to the plot of the trigonometric sine function, so this wave can be accurately labeled a *sine wave*. To describe the wave more precisely, we need to specify two things. First is the **amplitude**—the amount of pressure exerted by each air particle on the next. As the figure shows, this pressure is constantly changing as the air molecules vibrate toward each other, then away, then toward again. Thus, the amplitude we actually measure is the *maximum* pressure achieved at the crest of the sound wave. Second, we need to specify how widely spaced these pressure crests are. We could do this in terms of *wavelength*—a measurement of the distance between one crest and the next—or in terms of *period*, a measure of how much time elapses between one crest and the next. When measuring sounds, it's usually more convenient to take the inverse of the period; so, instead of measuring seconds per crest, we measure crests per second, which is the **frequency** of the wave. This means our measure is literally a count of how many times in each second the wave reaches its maximum amplitude (Figure 4.17).

Amplitude and frequency are physical dimensions of the sound wave itself, but they correspond reasonably well to the psychological dimensions of loudness and pitch. Roughly speaking, a sound will be heard as louder as its amplitude increases. It turns out that humans can respond to an enormous range of amplitudes, so investigators find it useful to measure these intensities with a logarithmic scale, which compresses the range into a more convenient form. Specifically, sound intensities are measured in *decibels*, and they're always assessed in relation to some standard. A standard of zero decibels is often assumed to be the average detection threshold for an adult with normal hearing. Loudness doubles each time the intensity of a sound increases by 10 decibels (Stevens, 1955).

The frequency of a sound wave is measured in cycles per second, or *hertz* (named after the 19th-century physicist Heinrich Hertz). As frequency increases, the subjective pitch of the sound goes up. Middle C on a piano generally has a frequency of 261 hertz; the C an octave higher has a frequency of 522 hertz. (In general, a doubling of frequency produces the experienced pitch difference of one octave.) The frequencies associated with other musical tones are shown in Table 4.3. Young adults can hear tones as low as 20 hertz and as high as 20,000 hertz. As people get older, their sensitivity to sound declines—especially at the higher frequencies. For this reason, sometimes there's little point for a

amplitude The height of a wave crest, used (in the case of sound waves) as a measure of sound intensity.

frequency The number of wave peaks per second. In sound, frequency governs the perceived pitch of the sound.

Frequency: A physical measure of the number of wave crests per second.

Low frequency (low-pitched sound)　　High frequency (high-pitched sound)

Amplitude: A measure of the amount of pressure exerted by each air particle on the next.

High amplitude (loud sound)　　Low amplitude (soft sound)

4.17 Simple waveforms vary in frequency and amplitude The two sine waves at the top of this figure have the same amplitude, but differ in frequency. The two waves shown at the bottom of the figure have the same frequency, but differ in amplitude.

TABLE 4.3	Sound Frequencies of Some Musical Tones	
	Sound	Frequency (hertz)*
	Top note of grand piano	4,244
	Top note of piccolo	3,951
	Top range of soprano voice	1,152
	Top range of alto voice	640
	Middle C	261
	Bottom range of baritone voice	96
	Bottom range of bass voice	80
	Bottom note of organ (can be felt but not heard)	16

*Note that some orchestras, and some musicians, choose to tune their instruments differently. Middle C, for example, is sometimes tuned to a frequency of 256 hertz, or one as high as 264.

30- or 40-year-old to buy expensive stereo equipment, since what makes the equipment expensive is often its exquisite ability to reproduce high frequencies accurately! In many cases, the middle-aged stereo buyer will be deaf to these frequencies and so probably won't be able to tell the difference between the expensive stereo and a cheaper one.

So far, we've been talking only about sine waves; but we rarely encounter sine waves in our everyday lives. Instead, the sound waves we usually experience are far more complex. Figure 4.18A, for example, shows the moment-by-moment changes in air pressure produced by a few seconds of music; Figure 4.18B shows the moment-by-moment pressure changes produced by a bit of ordinary speech.

The mathematician Joseph Fourier was able to show that these complex waves are actually just the sum of simpler components—in particular, the sum of a series of sine waves. Essentially, we can think of sine waves as the "ingredients" that combine to produce more complicated sounds. The "recipe" for creating the more complex sound must

(A) Music

(B) Speech

4.18 **Complex sounds** (A) The opening few chords of Margie Adam's piano solo, "Whimsy Salad." (B) The sound pattern produced when someone utters the words, "This is what speech looks like." Both patterns, complex as they are, can be understood as a composite of simple sine waves.

identify which ingredients are to be used (i.e., which frequencies) and how much of each ingredient is needed (i.e., how much amplitude for each of the frequencies is mixed into the whole). But once that's done, we can use the recipe to create any sound we choose from sine-wave ingredients. Psychologists as well as physicists, audio engineers, and many others routinely use Fourier analysis to describe in detail the sounds we encounter in our day-to-day experience.

From Sound Waves to Hearing

So far, our discussion has described only the physics of sound waves—the stimulus for hearing. What does our ear, and then our brain, do with this stimulus to produce the sensation of hearing?

GATHERING THE SOUND WAVES

Mammals have their receptors for hearing deep within the ear, in a snail-shaped structure called the **cochlea**. To reach the cochlea, sounds must travel a complicated path (Figure 4.19). The *outer ear* collects the sound waves from the air and directs them toward the **eardrum**, a taut membrane at the end of the *auditory canal*. The sound waves make the eardrum vibrate, and these vibrations are then transmitted to the **oval window**, the membrane that separates the *middle ear* from the *inner ear*. This transmission is accomplished by a trio of tiny bones called the **auditory ossicles**—the smallest bones in the human body. The vibrations of the eardrum move the first ossicle (the malleus), which then moves the second (the incus), which in turn moves the third (the stapes). The stapes completes the chain by sending the vibration pattern on to the oval window, which the stapes is attached to. (The ossicles are sometimes referred to by the English translations of their names—the *hammer,* the *anvil,* and the *stirrup,* all references to the bones' shapes.) The movements of the oval window then give rise to waves in the fluid that fills the cochlea, causing (at last) a response by the receptors.

Why do we have this roundabout method of sound transmission? The answer lies in the fact that these various components work together to create an entirely mechanical—but very high-fidelity—amplifier. The need for amplification arises because the sound waves reach us through the air, and the proximal stimulus for hearing is made up of minute changes in the air pressure. As we just mentioned, though, the inner ear is (like most body parts) filled with fluid. Therefore, in order for us to hear, the changes in air pressure must cause changes in fluid pressure—and this is a problem, because fluid is harder to set in motion than air is.

To solve this problem, the pressure waves have to be amplified as they move toward the receptors; this is accomplished by various features of the ear's organization. For example, the outer ear itself is shaped like a "sound scoop" so it can funnel the pressure waves toward the auditory canal. Within the middle ear, the ossicles use mechanical leverage to increase the sound pressure. Finally, the eardrum is about 20 times larger than the portion of the oval window that's moved by the ossicles. As a result, the fairly weak force provided by sound waves acting on the entire eardrum is transformed into a much stronger pressure concentrated on the (smaller) oval window.

TRANSDUCTION IN THE COCHLEA

For most of its length, the cochlea is divided into an upper and lower section by several structures, including the **basilar membrane.** The actual auditory receptors—the

cochlea The coiled structure in the inner ear that contains the basilar membrane.

eardrum The taut membrane that transmits the vibrations caused by sound waves from the auditory canal to the ossicles in the middle ear.

oval window The membrane separating the middle ear from the inner ear.

auditory ossicles The three bones of the middle ear that transmit the vibrations of the eardrum to the oval window.

basilar membrane A membrane running the length of the cochlea; sound waves cause a deformation of this membrane, bending the hair cells in the cochlea and thus stimulating the auditory receptors.

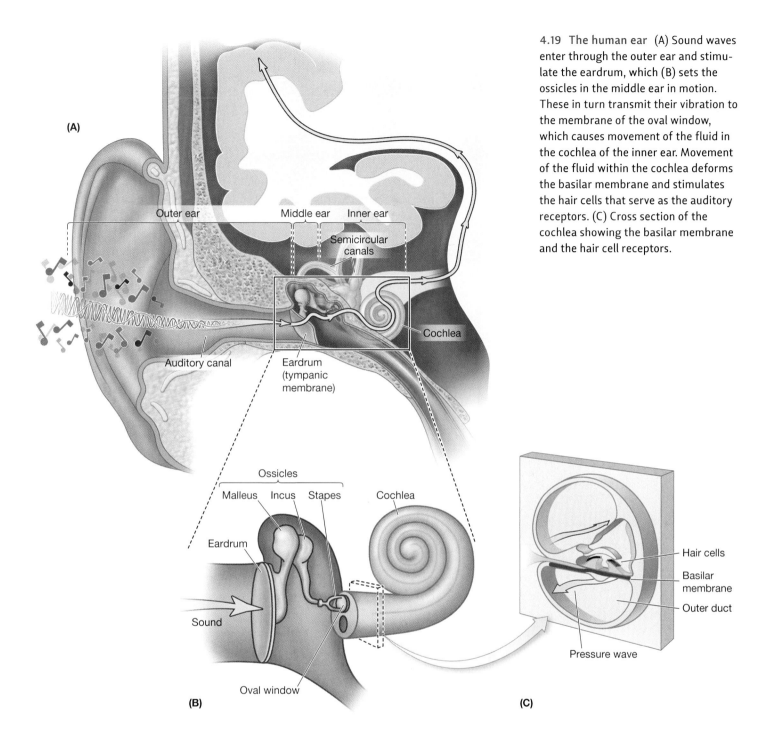

(A)

Outer ear   Middle ear   Inner ear

Semicircular
canals

Cochlea

Auditory canal

Eardrum
(tympanic
membrane)

Ossicles

Malleus   Incus   Stapes   Cochlea

Eardrum

Sound

Oval window

(B)

Hair cells

Basilar
membrane

Outer duct

Pressure wave

(C)

4.19 **The human ear** (A) Sound waves enter through the outer ear and stimulate the eardrum, which (B) sets the ossicles in the middle ear in motion. These in turn transmit their vibration to the membrane of the oval window, which causes movement of the fluid in the cochlea of the inner ear. Movement of the fluid within the cochlea deforms the basilar membrane and stimulates the hair cells that serve as the auditory receptors. (C) Cross section of the cochlea showing the basilar membrane and the hair cell receptors.

15,000 **hair cells** in each ear—are lodged between the basilar membrane and other membranes above it (Figure 4.19c).

Motion of the oval window produces pressure changes in the cochlear fluid that, in turn, lead to vibrations of the basilar membrane. As the basilar membrane vibrates, its deformations bend the hair cells; this bending causes ion channels in the membranes of these cells to open, triggering the neural response. Sound waves arriving at the ear generally cause the entire basilar membrane to vibrate, but the vibration is not uniform. Some regions of the membrane actually move more than others, and the frequency of the incoming sound determines where the motion is greatest. For higher frequencies, the region of greatest movement is at the end of the basilar

hair cells The auditory receptors in the cochlea, lodged between the basilar membrane and other membranes above.

4.20 **Hermann von Helmholtz** (1821–1894) Proponent of the place theory of pitch perception.

membrane closer to the oval window; for lower frequencies, the greatest movement occurs closer to the cochlear tip.

More than a century ago, these points led Hermann von Helmholtz (Figure 4.20) to propose the **place theory** of pitch perception. This theory asserts that the nervous system is able to identify a sound's pitch simply by keeping track of where the movement is greatest along the length of the basilar membrane. More specifically, stimulation of hair cells at one end of the membrane leads to the experience of a high tone, while stimulation of hair cells at the other end leads to the sensation of a low tone (Figure 4.21).

There's a problem with this theory, though. As the frequency of the stimulus gets lower and lower, the pattern of movement it produces on the basilar membrane gets broader and broader. At frequencies below 50 hertz, the movement produced by a sound stimulus deforms the entire membrane just about equally. Therefore, if we were using the location of the basilar membrane's maximum movement as our cue to a sound's frequency, we'd be unable to tell apart any of these low frequencies. But that's not what happens; humans, in fact, can discriminate frequencies as low as 20 hertz. Apparently, then, the nervous system has another way of sensing pitch besides basilar location.

(A)

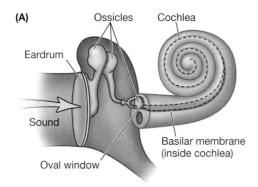

(B) Cross section of the cochlea (if it were unrolled)

4.21 **The deformation of the basilar membrane by sound** As shown in (A), the cochlea is a coiled structure; the basilar membrane wraps around and around within this coil. In (B) we've shown what the cochlea would look like if it were somehow uncoiled; now the basilar membrane can be depicted as (roughly) a rectangular sheet. This allows us, in (C), to show the relation between sound frequency and the location of the peak of the basilar membrane's deformation. The peak of the deformation is located at varying distances from the oval window. As the figure shows, the higher the frequency of the sound, the closer to the oval window this peak will be.

(C)

Low-frequency sound

Medium-frequency sound

High-frequency sound

This other means of sensing pitch is tied to the firing rate of cells in the auditory nerve. For lower-pitched sounds, the firing of these cells is synchronized with the peaks of the incoming sound waves. Consequently, the rate of firing, measured in neural impulses per second, ends up matched to the frequency of the wave, measured in crests per second. This coding, based on the exact timing of the cells' firing, is then relayed to higher neural centers that interpret this information as pitch.

Note, then, that the ear has two ways to encode pitch: based on the location of maximum movement on the basilar membrane, and based on the firing rate of cells in the auditory nerve. For higher-pitched sounds, the location-based mechanism plays a larger role; for lower-pitched sounds, the frequency of firing is more important (Goldstein, 1999).

FURTHER PROCESSING OF AUDITORY INFORMATION

Neurons carry the auditory signals from the cochlea to the midbrain. From there, the signals travel to the geniculate nucleus in the thalamus, an important subcortical structure in the forebrain (see Chapter 3). Other neurons then carry the signal to the primary projection areas for hearing, in the cortex of the temporal lobe. These neurons and those that follow have a lot of work to do: The auditory signal must be analyzed for its **timbre**—the sound quality that helps us distinguish a clarinet from an oboe, or one person's voice from another's. The signal must also be tracked across time, to evaluate the patterns of pitch change that define a melody or to distinguish an assertion ("I can have it") from a question ("I can have it?"). The nervous system must also do the analysis that allows us to identify the sounds we hear—so we know that we heard our cell phone and not someone else's, or so we can recognize the words someone is speaking to us. (For more on the recognition of speech, see Chapter 9.) Finally, the nervous system draws one other type of information from the sound signal: Pretty accurately, we can tell where a sound is coming from—whether from the left or the right, for example. This *localization* is made possible by several cues, including a close comparison of the left ear's signal and the right ear's, as well as by tracking how the arrival at the two ears changes when we turn our head slightly to the left or right.

Let's keep our focus, though, on how we can detect a sound's pitch. It turns out that each neuron along the auditory pathway responds to a wide range of pitches, but even so, each has a "preferred" *pitch*—a frequency of sound to which that neuron fires more vigorously than it fires to any other frequency. As in the other senses, this pattern of responding makes it impossible to interpret the activity of any individual neuron: If, for example, the neuron is firing at a moderate rate, this might mean the neuron is responding to a soft presentation of its preferred pitch, or it might mean the neuron is responding to a louder version of a less preferred pitch.

To resolve this ambiguity, the nervous system must compare the activity in each of these neurons to the level of activity in other neurons, to determine the overall pattern. So the detection of pitch, just like most of the other senses, relies on a "pattern code." This process of comparison may be made easier by the fact that neurons with similar preferred pitches tend to be located close to each other on the cortex. This arrangement creates what's known as a *tonotopic map*—a map organized on the basis of tone. For example, Figure 4.22 on page 160 shows the results of a careful mapping of the auditory cortex of the cat. There's an obvious ordering of preferred frequencies as we move across the surface of this brain area.

place theory A proposal about pitch perception stating that regions of the basilar membrane respond to particular sound frequencies, and the nervous system interprets the excitation from different basilar regions as different pitches.

timbre The quality of a sound apart from its pitch or loudness; timbre enables us to distinguish a clarinet from an oboe, or one person's voice from another.

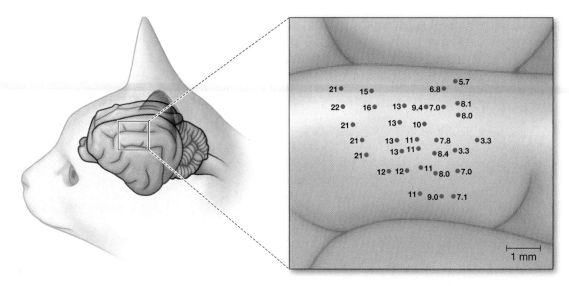

4.22 Tonotopic map Cells close to each other on the auditory cortex respond to similar auditory frequencies. In this figure, the numbers represent the preferred frequency (in kHz) for cells at each position. Cells shown on the right respond to lower frequencies; as we move to the left, we find cells that respond to higher and higher frequencies.

VISION

Vision provides us with an enormous amount of information. It tells us about shapes and colors, about spatial arrangements, and about objects both near and far away. We also tend to put great trust in our vision—it's why we say things like "seeing is believing." And it's easy to document this trust in vision. We can, for example, arrange things so that you *see* a person speaking off to the left but *hear* their voice from your right. In this setting, you're likely to believe what you see and thus (mis)perceive the voice to be coming from the left. Common experience confirms this point: In large lecture halls, the speaker's voice sounds like it's coming from the front of the room—where the plainly visible lecturer is standing. But in many cases, the sound waves are actually reaching you from loudspeakers positioned around the room; you can check this by closing your eyes and paying careful attention to where the sounds are coming from. The moment you open your eyes, though, the sounds again seem to be coming from the front of the lecture hall—the visual information is overruling the evidence you receive from your ears.

How does vision function? In tackling this broad question, we'll focus on three issues. First, what are the structures for gathering the stimulus, and how do they work? Second, what is the nature of the transduction process that converts the physical energy of the stimulus into a neural signal? Third, what are the coding processes that allow us to discriminate—and then recognize—the millions of shapes, colors, and patterns of movement that make up our visual world?

The Stimulus: Light

Many objects in our surroundings—the sun, candles, lamps, and so on—produce light that's then reflected off most other objects. It's usually reflected light—from this book page, for example, or from a friend's face—that launches the processes of vision.

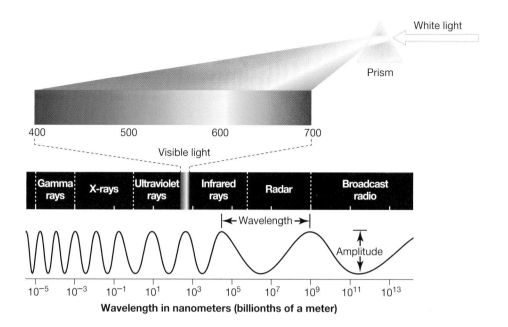

Whether it's emitted or reflected, the stimulus energy we call "light" can be understood as traveling in waves. Like sound waves, these light waves can be described in terms of two measurements. First, light waves can vary in amplitude, which is the major determinant of perceived brightness. A light wave's amplitude is measured as the "height" of the waves, starting from the wave's baseline. Second, light waves vary in frequency—how many times per second the wave reaches its maximum amplitude. As it turns out, these frequencies are extremely high because light travels so swiftly. It's more convenient, therefore, to describe light waves using the inverse of frequency—wavelength, the distance between the crests of two successive waves. Wavelengths are measured in nanometers (billionths of a meter) and are the major determinant of perceived color.

The wavelengths our visual system can sense are only a tiny part of the broader electromagnetic spectrum (Figure 4.23). Light with a wavelength longer than 750 nanometers is invisible to us, although we do feel these longer infrared waves as heat. Ultraviolet light, which has a wavelength shorter than 360 nanometers, is also invisible to us. That leaves the narrow band of wavelengths between 750 and 360 nanometers— the so-called *visible spectrum*. Within this spectrum, we usually see wavelengths close to 400 nanometers as violet, those close to 700 nanometers as red, and those in between as the rest of the colors in the rainbow.

Be aware, though, that the boundaries of the visible spectrum are not physical boundaries indicating some kind of break in the electromagnetic spectrum. Instead, these boundaries simply identify the part of the spectrum that human eyes can detect. Other species, with different types of eyes, perceive different subsets of the broader spectrum. Bees can perceive ultraviolet wavelengths that are invisible to us; other mammals, including some types of monkeys, can tell apart wavelengths that look identical to us.

Gathering the Stimulus: The Eye

Eyes come in many forms. Some invertebrates have simple eyespots that merely sense light or dark; others have complex, multicellular organs with crystalline lenses. In vertebrates, the actual detection of light is done by cells called **photoreceptors.** These cells are located

photoreceptor A light-sensitive cell located on the retina that converts light energy into neural impulses.

retinal image The image of an object that is projected on the retina. Its size increases with the size of that object and decreases with the object's distance from the eye.

on the retina, a layer of tissue lining the back of the eyeball. Before the light reaches the retina, however, several mechanisms are needed to control the amount of light reaching the photoreceptors and to ensure a clear and sharply focused **retinal image.**

The *iris* is a smooth, circular muscle surrounding the pupillary opening—the opening through which light enters the eye. Adjustments in the iris are under reflex control and cause the pupil to dilate (grow larger) or contract, thus allowing considerable control over how much light reaches the retina.

In the mammalian eye, the *cornea* and the *lens* focus the incoming light just like a camera lens does (Figure 4.24). The cornea has a fixed shape, but it begins the process of bending the light rays so they'll end up properly focused. The fine-tuning is then done by adjustments of the lens, just behind the cornea. The lens is surrounded by a ring of ligaments that exert an outward "pull," causing the lens to flatten somewhat; this allows the proper focus for objects farther away. To focus on a nearby object, contraction of a muscle in the eye reduces the tension on the ligaments and allows the lens to take on a more spherical shape.

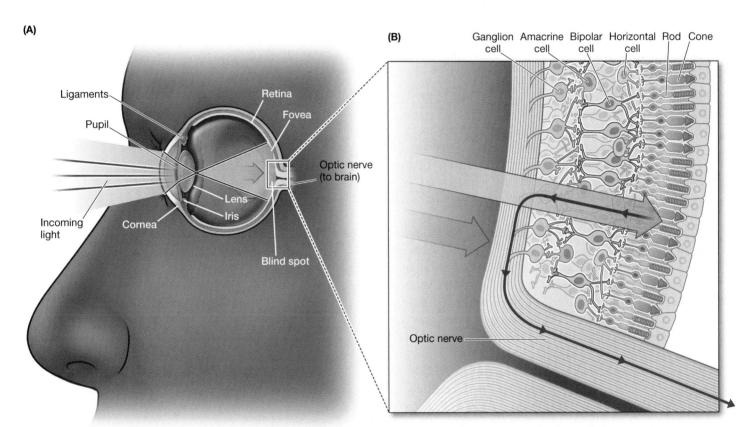

4.24 The human eye (A) Light enters the eye through the cornea, and the cornea and lens refract the light rays to produce a sharply focused image on the retina. The iris can open or close to control the amount of light that reaches the retina. (B) The retina is made up of three main layers: the rods and cones, which are the photoreceptors; the bipolar cells; and the ganglion cells, whose axons make up the optic nerve. Two other kinds of cells, horizontal cells and amacrine cells, allow for lateral (sideways) interaction. You may have noticed that the retina contains an anatomical oddity: the photoreceptors are at the very back, the bipolar cells are in between, and the ganglion cells are at the top. As a result, light has to pass through the other layers (they're not opaque, so this is possible) to reach the rods and cones, whose stimulation starts the visual process.

(A)

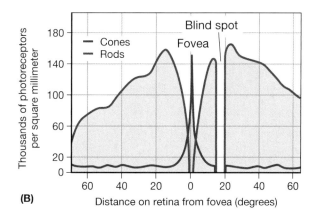

(B)

4.25 Rods and cones (A) Rods and cones are receptor cells at the back of the retina that transmit the neural impulses of vision. In this (colorized) photo, cones appear green; rods appear brown. (B) Distribution of photoreceptors. Cones are most frequent at the fovea, and the number of cones drops off sharply if we consider locations away from the fovea. In contrast, there are no rods at all on the fovea. There are neither rods nor cones at the retina's blind spot.

The Visual Receptors

Once light reaches the retina, we leave the domain of optics and enter that of neurophysiology, because it is at the retina that the physical stimulus energy is transduced into a neural impulse. The retina contains two kinds of receptor cells, the **rods** and the **cones;** the names of these cells reflect their different shapes (Figure 4.25). The cones are plentiful in the **fovea,** a small, roughly circular region at the center of the retina; but they become less and less prevalent at the outer edges of the retina. The opposite is true of the rods; they're completely absent from the fovea but more numerous at the retina's edges. In all, there are some 120 million rods and about 6 million cones in the normal human eye.

The rods and cones do not report to the brain directly. Instead, their message is relayed by several other layers of cells within the retina (see Figure 4.24). The receptors stimulate the *bipolar cells*, and these in turn excite the *ganglion cells*. The ganglion cells collect information from all over the retina, and the axons of these cells then converge to form a bundle of fibers that we call the **optic nerve.** Leaving the eyeball, the optic nerve carries information first to the *lateral geniculate nucleus* in the thalamus and then to the cortex (Figure 4.26). (Notice that this pathway resembles the one for auditory signals, which go from the ear to a different section of the geniculate nucleus and then to the cortex.)

rods Photoreceptors in the retina that respond to lower light intensities and give rise to achromatic (colorless) sensations.

cones Visual receptors that respond to greater light intensities and give rise to chromatic (color) sensations.

fovea The area roughly at the retina's center where cones are plentiful and visual acuity is greatest.

optic nerve The bundle of fibers that proceeds from each retina to the brain.

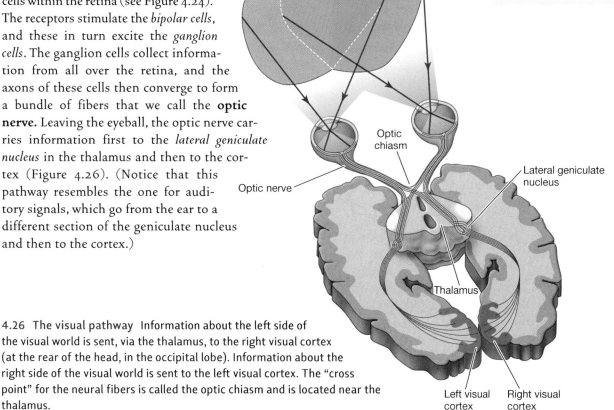

4.26 The visual pathway Information about the left side of the visual world is sent, via the thalamus, to the right visual cortex (at the rear of the head, in the occipital lobe). Information about the right side of the visual world is sent to the left visual cortex. The "cross point" for the neural fibers is called the optic chiasm and is located near the thalamus.

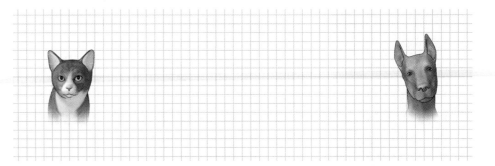

4.27 The blind spot Close your right eye and stare at the picture of the dog. Can you see the cat without moving your eye? Move the book either closer to you or farther away. You should be able to find a position (about 7 inches from your face) where the cat's picture vanishes when you're looking at the dog. That's because, at that distance, the cat's picture is positioned on the retina such that it falls onto the blind spot. Note, though, that the grid pattern seems continuous. With this sort of regular pattern, your visual system is able to "fill in" the gap created by the blind spot.

This anatomical arrangement requires a space at the back of each eyeball to enable the axons of the ganglion cells to exit the eye on their way to the thalamus. These axons fill this space entirely, leaving no room for rods or cones. As a result, this region has no photoreceptors and is completely insensitive to light. Appropriately enough, it's called the *blind spot* (Figure 4.27).

Rods and cones differ in their structure, number, and placement on the retina; they also differ in their function. The rods are the receptors for night vision; they operate at low light intensities and lead to *achromatic* (colorless) sensations. The cones serve day vision; they respond at much higher levels of illumination and are responsible for sensations of color.

Why do we need two types of photoreceptors? The answer is clear when we consider the enormous range of light intensities encountered by organisms like ourselves as we go about our business during both day and night. In humans, the ratio in energy level between the dimmest stimulus we can detect and the brightest we can tolerate is roughly 1:100,000,000,000. Natural selection has allowed for this incredible range by a biological division of labor—so we have two separate receptor systems, one for vision in dim light and the other for vision in bright light.

The enormous sensitivity of the rods comes at a price: The same traits that make the rods sensitive to low levels of light also make them less able to discriminate fine detail. As a result, *acuity*—the ability to perceive detail—is much greater in the cones. This is the major reason why we point our eyes toward any target that we'd like to perceive in detail. This action positions our eyes so that the image of the target falls onto the fovea, where the cones are most closely packed and visual acuity is greatest.

Be aware that the differences between rods and cones also create situations in which we want to rely on the rods. That's why it's sometimes helpful to look at something "out of the corner" of your eye. Sailors and astronomers have known for years that when you're trying to find a barely visible star, it's best not to look directly at the star's location. By looking slightly away from the star, you can ensure that the star's image falls outside of the fovea and onto a region of the retina that's dense with the more light-sensitive rods. This strategy limits the ability to discern detail; but, by relying on the rods, it maximizes visual sensitivity to faint stimuli.

Rods and cones can also be distinguished in one further way—their chemistry. Inside each photoreceptor is a **photopigment**, a light-sensitive chemical pigment that allows the transduction of light energy into a neural signal. When light enters the receptor, the light energy changes the chemical form of the photopigment, setting off a chain of events that ultimately leads to an electrical signal. In this way, the light energy is translated into the electrochemical language of the nervous system. Inside the receptor, the pigment itself is then reconstituted so that it will be ready to react with light again when the next opportunity arises.

Rods and cones contain different photopigments. The rods contain *rhodopsin,* a pigment that breaks down more readily in response to light than the cone pigments do.

photopigment A chemical in the photoreceptors that changes its form in response to light, producing an electrical change that signals to the nervous system that light is present.

4.28 Brightness contrast Four (objectively) identical gray squares on different backgrounds. The lighter the background, the darker the gray squares appear.

Rhodopsin is part of the reason that rods can function at lower light levels. There are three different cone photopigments, and each cone contains one of the three types. The differences among the three pigments are crucial to the cones' ability to discriminate colors—a topic we'll turn to shortly. Rods, which contain just one pigment, are sensitive to differences in brightness (white versus gray, or a strongly illuminated red versus a weakly illuminated one); but they cannot discriminate among different hues. So, for example, the rods will respond in exactly the same way to a patch of red and an equally bright patch of blue. In effect, this response makes each of us nearly "color blind" at the visual periphery—that is, rather poor at telling colors apart if they fall on a retina position far enough from the fovea so that the position contains mostly rods and very few cones.

Contrast Effects

Earlier in the chapter, we discussed the fact that our sensory systems are keenly sensitive to *differences*—and so a noise sounds louder if it occurs in an otherwise quiet room; a room feels particularly warm if you've just come in from the cold. Similar effects can easily be documented for vision.

Notice, though, that these examples all involve changes as time goes by—so that the stimulus *now* is different from the one you experienced a moment ago. It turns out that the visual system is also sensitive to spatial contrast—the differences between the stimulus in view *here* and the one in view *there*. This is evident, for example, in *brightness contrast*—the effect that makes a stimulus look much brighter on a dark background than on a bright one (Figure 4.28). Brightness contrast can be documented in many settings, and so it plays a role in creating some illusions (Figure 4.29) as well as certain artistic effects.

Contrast effects have an extremely important consequence: They make it easier for us to identify the objects we encounter. This point grows out of the fact that the objects we see are usually viewed against backgrounds that are at a different brightness level than the target object; hence, a change in brightness—from darker to lighter, or vice versa—typically marks a visual boundary, a point where one object stops and another begins. And, of course, these boundaries are immensely important for the visual system because they define the object's *shape*—and shape, in turn, is the information we generally use to identify an object.

Perhaps it's not surprising, then, that the visual system does more than just detect brightness boundaries. It actually *amplifies* them by a process often called *edge enhancement* which relies on brightness contrast and allows us to see the edges between objects more clearly. This exaggeration of edges happens with virtually all stimuli, but it's

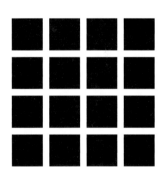

4.29 The effect of distance between contrasting regions The white lines in this grid are the same color throughout, but they don't appear to be—each "intersection" seems to contain a gray spot. The uneven appearance of the white strips is caused by contrast. Each strip is surrounded by a black square, which contrasts with it and makes it look brighter. But this is not the case at the intersections, where the strips touch the black squares only at their corners. As a result, there's less contrast in the middle of the intersections and we see gray spots there.

4.30 Mach bands (A) These gray strips are arranged in ascending brightness, from left to right. Physically, each strip is of uniform light intensity, as shown graphically in red in (B), which plots position against physical light intensity. But the strips don't appear to be uniform. For each strip, contrast makes the left edge (next to its darker neighbor) look brighter than the rest, while the right edge (next to its lighter neighbor) looks darker. The result is an accentuation of the contours separating one strip from the next. The resulting appearance—the way the figure is perceived—is shown in blue in (B).

(A)

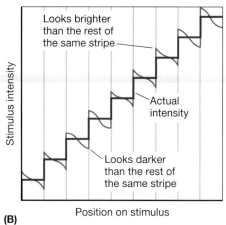

(B)

lateral inhibition The pattern of interaction among neurons in the visual system in which activity in one neuron inhibits adjacent neurons' responses.

particularly obvious in the illusion we call *mach bands* (Figure 4.30A). In this figure, each separate strip of gray is uniform in its brightness. That is, the figure shows a homogenous dark strip, then a uniform slightly lighter strip, then another uniform slightly lighter strip, and so on. However, most people don't perceive the strips as uniform. Instead, they perceive each strip as being slightly darker along its right-hand edge, where it meets its brighter neighbor. They also perceive each strip as slightly brighter along its left-hand edge, where it meets its darker neighbor. The resulting pattern is summarized in Figure 4.30B.

This illusion is produced by contrast effects like those we've already described. Specifically, when a light region borders a dark region, contrast between the two makes the light region look even lighter and makes the dark region look darker still. By accentuating the difference between the two adjacent regions, the contrast highlights the edge where the two regions meet.

We can take our explanation of this effect one step further because we can specify the events in the nervous system that lead to brightness contrast. The key is **lateral inhibition**—a pattern of interaction among neurons in which activity in one neuron actually decreases the responses in adjacent neurons. This is, in other words, inhibition exerted sideways. We can document this effect at many levels of the visual system; for example, recordings from single cells in the retina confirm that activity in one cell actually causes the immediately adjacent cells to fire *less* than they otherwise would.

To see how this pattern of interaction leads to edge enhancement, consider two cells, each receiving stimulation from a brightly lit area (Figure 4.31). One cell (Cell B in the figure) is receiving its stimulation from the middle of the lit area. It is strongly stimulated, but so are all of its neighbors, creating a situation in which all of the cells in this area are inhibiting each other. As a result, Cell B's activity level is *increased* by the stimulation but also *decreased* by the lateral inhibition it's receiving from nearby cells—including (in the figure) Cells A and C. This combination leads to only a moderate level of activity overall in this cell—and so the signal Cell B sends to the brain is weaker than it would have been without the inhibition.

In contrast, another cell (Cell C in the figure) is receiving its stimulation from the edge of the lit area. Cell C is therefore strongly stimulated, and so are its neighbors *on one side*. As a result, this cell is receiving inhibition from one side (by Cell B) but not from the other (Cell D), so it will be less inhibited than Cell B (which is receiving inhibition from all sides).

What's the result of all this interaction? Cells B and C initially receive the same input, but C is less inhibited than B, so it ends up firing more strongly than B and

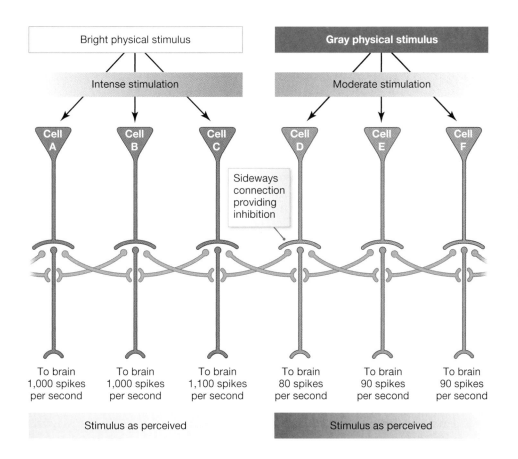

Bright physical stimulus			Gray physical stimulus		
Intense stimulation			Moderate stimulation		
Cell A	Cell B	Cell C	Cell D	Cell E	Cell F

Sideways connection providing inhibition

To brain 1,000 spikes per second	To brain 1,000 spikes per second	To brain 1,100 spikes per second	To brain 80 spikes per second	To brain 90 spikes per second	To brain 90 spikes per second

| Stimulus as perceived | | | Stimulus as perceived | | |

4.31 Response pattern to different colors: Lateral inhibition Cells B and C receive the same input. Cell B, however, is inhibited by its neighbors on both sides; Cell C is inhibited by neighbors on only one side. As a result, Cell C will send a stronger signal to the brain, emphasizing the "edge" in the stimulus. Likewise, Cells D and E receive the same input, but Cell D receives more inhibition. This cell will send a weaker signal to the brain, again emphasizing the edge of the dark gray patch. The spikes per second for each neuron are hypothetical figures, but they illustrate the sort of differences in firing rate that lateral inhibition can produce.

thus sending a stronger signal to the brain than B does. Of course, the same is true for all of the other cells (like Cell C) that receive their input from the edge of a surface, and for all cells (like B) that receive their input from the middle of the surface. The result is that all the cells detecting the edge of a bright surface end up producing a stronger response than that of the cells detecting the middle of the surface. This pattern will then lead to an exaggerated response along the surface's edges, making these edges easier to detect.

The reverse happens for cells being stimulated by a patch that's not as bright. Cells D and E both receive the same (weak) input. Cell E, though, is surrounded by cells that are only mildly activated, so it receives only gentle inhibition from its neighbors. Cell D, in contrast, has at least one very excited neighbor (Cell C), so it receives a large dose of inhibition. As a result, Cells D and E both receive the same input, but Cell D (because of the inhibition it receives) ends up firing less strongly than Cell E. Again, this leads to an exaggeration of the edge; and the weakest signal is coming from the cell at the edge of the dark patch.

These interactions among cells indicate exactly how the visual system enhances the brightness of boundaries it encounters—and, with that, why Mach bands appear as they do. Besides that, these mechanisms illustrate another important point. At the very beginning of this chapter, we asked whether we can think of the sensory mechanisms as passive recorders of the stimulus input or as mechanisms that somehow organize and interpret the input. The answer to these questions should be clear by now—and will become clearer as our discussion continues. Thanks to lateral inhibition, the visual system seems to be refining the stimulus information from the very start, emphasizing some aspects of the input (the edges) and understating other aspects (the areas being uniformly stimulated).

400 nm   500 nm   600 nm   700 nm

4.32 Hues The visible spectrum consists of light waves from about 400 to 700 nanometers.

Lateral inhibition arises from mechanisms just a synapse or two into the visual system; but even at this early level, the nervous system is "cleaning up" the input and doing far more than merely "receiving and recording" the incoming stimulus.

Color

Clearly, then, interaction among sensory elements can shape the sensory input. In particular, this process can highlight elements such as boundaries and moments of change that are of particular interest to the organism. This pattern of interaction is also evident when we consider a different aspect of vision—namely, the perception of color.

A person with normal color vision can distinguish over 7 million shades of color. But fortunately, this staggering number of colors can be classified in terms of just three dimensions. First, *hue* is the attribute that distinguishes blue from green from red; it's also the attribute shared by, say, a bright orange, a middle orange, and a dark orange. This dimension corresponds closely to the way we use the word *color* in everyday life. Hue varies with wavelength (Figure 4.32), so that a wavelength of 465 nanometers is perceived as *unique blue*, a blue that's judged to have no trace of red or green in it; a wavelength of about 500 nanometers is perceived as *unique green* (green with no blue or yellow); and a wavelength of 570 nanometers is perceived as *unique yellow* (yellow with no green or red).

Second, *brightness* is the dimension of color that differentiates black (low brightness) from white (high brightness) and distinguishes the various shades of gray in between. Black, white, and all of the grays are the *achromatic colors;* they have no hue. But brightness is also a property of the *chromatic colors* (purple, red, yellow, and so forth). Thus, ultramarine blue is darker (i.e., has a lower brightness) than sky blue, just as charcoal gray is darker than pearl gray (Figure 4.33).

4.33 Brightness and saturation Colors can be arranged according to their brightness. This dimension is easiest to recognize when looking at a series of grays (as in the leftmost column of this grid), which are totally hueless and vary in brightness only. But chromatic colors can also be classified according to their brightness, as in the other columns. As you move from left to right in this grid, brightness stays the same but saturation increases.

High brightness

Low brightness

Less saturation (achromatic) ← → More saturation (chromatic)

The third dimension, *saturation*, is the "purity" of a color—the extent to which it is chromatic rather than achromatic. The more gray (or black or white) that's mixed with a color, the less saturation it has. Consider the bottom row of the grid shown in Figure 4.33. All five of these squares have the same hue (blue), and all have the same brightness. The patches differ only in one way: the proportion of blue as opposed to that of gray.

The Neural Basis of Color Vision

What is the neural basis of color vision? The answer turns out to have two parts: how the retina itself functions, and how the nervous system handles the information received from the retina.

COLOR RECEPTORS

More than 200 years ago, Thomas Young hypothesized that humans have three types of color receptors; and he offered a theory of color vision building on these three elements. In 1866, Hermann von Helmholtz offered some refinements of this view. Today we know that, at least in broad outline, the *Young-Helmholtz theory* was essentially correct. Human color vision is **trichromatic**—based on three elements, each tied to one type of *cone*.

What are these "elements"? We've already mentioned that each of the three cone types contains a different photopigment. Each of these photopigments is sensitive to a broad range of wavelengths, but their patterns of sensitivity are plainly distinct (Figure 4.34). One pigment, and so the cones containing that pigment, is most sensitive to wavelengths in the short-wave region of the spectrum. Consequently, this pigment is sensitive to many inputs but especially sensitive to wavelengths typically perceived as blue. A second pigment is especially sensitive to wavelengths in the middle range (wavelengths typically perceived as green), and the third to wavelengths in the long range (typically perceived as orange or red; Bowmaker & Dartnall, 1980; MacNichol, 1986).

It's important to realize that due to the broad sensitivities of these pigments, all three types of cones respond to most of the wavelengths in the visible spectrum. It's therefore impossible to discriminate among wavelengths simply by noting which

trichromatic color vision The principle underlying human color vision. Color vision occurs through the operation of three sets of cones, each maximally sensitive to a different wavelength of light.

4.34 **Sensitivity curves of three different cones in the primate retina** The retinas of humans and monkeys contain three different kinds of cones, each with its own photopigment that differs in its sensitivity to different regions of the spectrum. One type of cone absorbs more of the shorter wavelengths (so it's more sensitive to light in this spectral region); its sensitivity is shown as a solid line. A second cone type absorbs more of the middle wavelengths (dashed line), and a third (dotted line) absorbs more of the longer ones.

cones are responding, because generally all of them are. So once again, it appears that the nervous system relies on pattern coding; the input's wavelength is being specified by the relative rates of response by all three cone types. For an input of 480 nanometers, for example, the "short-preferring" and "middle-preferring" cones will respond equally, and their response will be about double the response of the "long-preferring" cones. This pattern of response specifies this particular wavelength. Likewise, an input of 580 nanometers will produce a response in the long-preferring cones that's roughly double the response in the middle-preferring cones, and there will be virtually no response from the short-preferring cones. This pattern identifies this specific wavelength. And so on for the millions of other response patterns, each of which identifies a specific wavelength.

Of course, many of the colors you encounter involve a mix of several different wavelengths; but that's not a problem. Each of the wavelengths contained in this mix will trigger the neural response that would result if that wavelength were presented on its own, and so the total response for each cone type will simply be the sum of that cone's responses to each ingredient—each wavelength—in the mix. Here's an example: If the input contains wavelengths A, B, and C, the short-preferring cones' response to this stimulus will simply be the total of those cones' response to A when it's presented alone, plus their response to B when it's presented alone, plus their response to C. (And so if, say, the light is at an intensity in which wavelength A on its own would trigger the receptor to fire 70 times per second, and B on its own would trigger the receptor to fire 30 times per second, and C would trigger the cell to fire 10 times per second, the mix of A, B, and C will cause the cell to fire roughly 110 times per second.) The same goes for the middle-preferring and long-preferring cones; their responses, too, will simply be the sums of their responses to each of the individual ingredients in the mix.

Be aware, though, that it's the total response that matters—not how the total was achieved. Thus, if three wavelengths together cause the short-preferring cones to fire 110 times per second, it doesn't matter if the wavelengths on their own would have produced rates of 70, 30, and 10 (as in the previous paragraph), or if they would have produced rates of 20, 60, and 30 or 37, 15, and 58. All that matters is the sum. And this is crucial, because it's almost always possible to find different mixes of wavelengths that will produce the same three totals (again, one total for each of the cone types). This explains why artists can mix their pigments to produce virtually any color, and it's how a television or computer monitor produces the various colors that appear on the screen. In both of these cases, we're combining wavelengths so that we'll get the three totals we need to produce the desired perception.

COMPLEMENTARY HUES

The trichromatic analysis of color vision is consistent with many facts—including the central observation that there are just three cone types, each with its own photopigment. Other observations, however, don't seem to fit with the trichromatic view—such as the fact that, in important ways, colors seem to come in pairs. This pairing is evident, for example, in *simultaneous color contrast*—the chromatic counterpart of brightness contrast. Color contrast refers to the tendency of any chromatic region in the visual field to induce a *complementary color* in adjoining areas. For example, a gray patch tends to look bluish if it's surrounded by yellow, and yellowish if surrounded by blue; likewise, a gray patch looks reddish if surrounded by green, and greenish if surrounded by red (Figure 4.35). In this way, then, blue and yellow are "paired," as are red and green.

Color contrast can also be demonstrated in temporal relationships rather than spatial ones. Suppose that you stare at a green patch for a while and then look at a white wall. You'll see a *negative afterimage* of the patch—in this case, a reddish spot (Figure 4.36). In the same way, staring at a red patch will produce a green afterimage; staring at something blue will produce a yellow afterimage; and staring at yellow will produce a blue afterimage. In all cases, the afterimage has the complementary hue of the original stimulus. This effect again emphasizes the apparent pairing of colors—a pairing that trichromatic analyses leave completely unexplained.

Another way to appreciate the importance of complementary colors is by mixing together colored lights. In these mixtures, "paired" colors seem to cancel each other; thus, if we mix blue and yellow lights, we produce a hueless white. The same is true if we mix red and green lights, or purple and yellow-green, or orange and blue-green. Here, too, it appears that colors are paired, such that each color has an "opposite" that cancels it—a relationship that, again, has no explanation in trichromatic theory.

As an aside, note that color mixing works differently when we mix *paints* or other pigments rather than lights (as in Figure 4.37). Why? Because of the physics. Here's an example: If a blue light is shining on a white surface, then the surface will reflect the wavelengths contained within that blue light. If a yellow light is also shining on the surface, then its wavelengths will be reflected too. So the full set of wavelengths reflected will be those from the blue light *plus* those from the yellow—which is why this is called an *additive color mixture*. In contrast, when white light shines on a *pigment*, only a certain band of wavelengths is reflected; the remaining wavelengths are absorbed by the pigment. Thus blue paint reflects the wavelengths between 420 and 520 nanometers, but it absorbs wavelengths outside this range; and so these other wavelengths are removed or "subtracted" from the reflected light. Yellow paint reflects wavelengths above 480 nanometers, and it absorbs those below. If the two paints are mixed together, then the only wavelengths reflected by the combination are those that aren't absorbed (i.e., not subtracted from the input) by *either* ingredient. This mixture turns out to be just the wavelengths above 480 nanometers and below 520; and that band of wavelengths is seen as green.

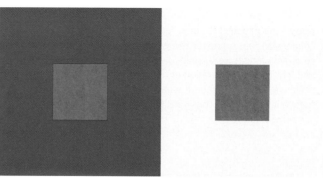

4.35 Color contrast The gray patches on the blue and yellow backgrounds are physically identical, but they don't look that way. To begin with, there's a difference in perceived brightness; the patch on the blue looks brighter than the one on the yellow—a result of brightness contrast. There's also a difference in perceived hue; the patch on the blue looks somewhat yellowish, while that on the yellow looks bluish. This is color contrast, a demonstration that hues tend to induce their antagonists in neighboring areas.

4.36 Negative afterimage Stare at the center of the figure for a minute or two, and then look at a white piece of paper. Blink once or twice; the negative afterimage will appear within a few seconds, showing the flower in its correct colors.

4.37 Different ways to mix color In subtractive color mixing, each constituent—here, each filter—subtracts certain wavelengths from the total light. In additive mixing, each constituent contributes wavelengths. Thus, in (A), subtractive mixing of three primaries yields black; in (B), additive mixing yields white.

opponent-process theory A theory of color vision that proposes three pairs of color antagonists: red-green, blue-yellow, and white-black. Excitation of neurons sensitive to one member of a pair automatically inhibits neurons sensitive to the other member.

THE OPPONENT-PROCESS THEORY

How should we think about the fact that colors seem to come in pairs? The answer lies in the **opponent-process theory**, first suggested by Ewald Hering but then developed by Leo Hurvich and Dorothea Jameson. This theory begins with the undeniable fact that we have three cone types, but it argues that the output from these cones is then processed by another layer of neural mechanisms that recode the signal on the basis of three pairs of colors—red versus green, blue versus yellow, and black versus white. These pairs are said to involve an "opponent process" because the two members of each pair are antagonists—that is, excitation of neurons on one side of these mechanisms automatically inhibits cells on the other side (Figure 4.38). As a result, each of the opponent-process mechanisms can be thought of as a balance—and if one arm of the balance goes down, the other necessarily goes up (Hurvich & Jameson, 1957).

How do these mechanisms shape our perception of color? According to the opponent-process theory, the psychological experience of hue depends on two of the opponent-process pairs—red-green and blue-yellow. If, for example, the input tips the red-green balance toward red and the blue-yellow balance toward blue, the perceived hue will be violet. If the input contains neither red nor green (so the red-green pair stays in balance) and the blue-yellow system tips toward blue, we perceive a pure blue. If both hue systems are in balance, there will be no hue at all, and the resulting color will be seen as achromatic (i.e., without hue).

This conception easily explains the apparent pairing of colors, because the pairing is built into the opponent processes themselves. It also explains why, according to most observers, there appear to be four primary colors (red, green, blue, and yellow)—even though, without question, our retina has only three cone types. But, in addition, evidence has directly confirmed the claims of the opponent-process theory by documenting that many of the neurons in the visual system behave exactly as the theory proposes. For example, certain cells increase their firing rate if the retina is stimulated by green light, but they decrease their rate if the retina is stimulated by red light. Other cells show the opposite pattern (increase for red, decrease for green). Still other cells show a similar pattern of responses for blue and yellow light (Figure 4.39; De Valois, 1965). All of this is exactly what we might expect if these cells embody the mechanisms proposed by the opponent-process theory.

(A) Blue-yellow opponent process

(B) Red-green opponent process

4.38 From receptors to opponent-process pairs A simplified presentation of a neural system in which the three receptor elements feed into two color opponent-process pairs. (A) The blue-yellow system is excited by the short-wave receptors and inhibited by the medium- and long-wave receptors. (B) The red-green system is excited by the short-wave and long-wave receptor elements, and it's inhibited by the medium-wave elements.

4.39 Opponent-process cells in the visual system of a monkey The figure shows the average firing rate of blue-yellow cells in response to light of different wavelengths. These cells are excited by shorter wavelengths and inhibited by longer wavelengths, analogous to the cells in the human system that signal the sensation "blue."

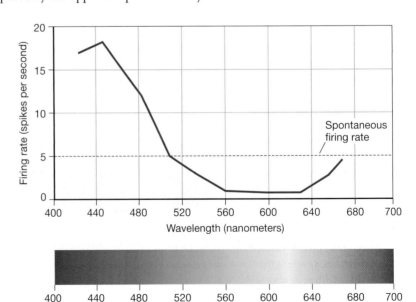

COLOR BLINDNESS

Not everyone responds to color like most of us do. Some form of color-vision defect is found in 8% of Caucasian males (but only 0.03% of females; the rate of color blindness is lower in other races). The deficiencies in color vision come in various forms. The great majority of people identified as color blind are actually missing one of the three visual pigments (and so they're "dichromats," not "trichromats"). Other forms of color blindness can involve a defective opponent process or a malfunction in brain circuitry needed for color vision (Hurvich, 1981). Most common is a confusion of reds with greens; least common is total color blindness, in which no hues can be distinguished at all. Interestingly, though, most of these problems are rarely noticed in everyday life, and color-blind people can spend many years without even realizing they're color blind. They call stop signs "red" and grass "green," just like anyone else does. And, presumably, they spend much of their lives believing that others perceive colors the same way they do. Their color blindness can be confirmed only with special tests like the one shown in Figure 4.40.

Color blindness can result from various injuries to the eye or brain, but this condition most commonly has a genetic origin. It's also much more frequent in humans than it is in other primates with color vision similar to our own. This finding has led some scholars to explore the evolutionary origins of color blindness. They argue that this supposed "defect" might actually have benefited some of our evolutionary ancestors—for example, in certain situations a color-blind hunter can spot prey that others might miss. (Because hues that appear "matched" to someone with normal color vision sometimes don't appear matched for someone who is color blind, some forms of camouflage—when the prey seems to be the same hue as the background foliage—will fail with someone who is color blind.) These situations might have produced a reproductive advantage for our color-blind ancestors, leading to an increased frequency in the relevant human genes.

Recent studies indicate that the genetics of color blindness are relatively complex and that many genes, on at least 19 different chromosomes, can contribute to color blindness. One of the genetic causes involves a gene mutation on the X chromosome, and this finding explains why color blindness is much more common in men than in women. Women have a pair of X chromosomes, so at least one of the chromosomes in this pair is likely to have a normal version of the relevant gene—leading to normal color vision. Men have an XY genetic pattern, and so only one X chromosome. If this chromosome contains the mutated gene, men have no "backup" gene on another chromosome—and color blindness is the result.

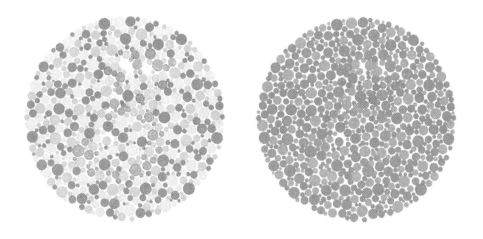

4.40 **Testing for color blindness** Plates used to test for color blindness. To pick out the number in the plate on the left, you must be able to discriminate certain hues. Those with normal color vision can do it and will see the number 3; color-blind people would see the version on the right.

How does the world look to someone who is color blind? For a long time, this question seemed impossible to answer, since most color-blind individuals have no way to compare their experience to that of an individual with normal color vision, and so no way to describe the difference. However, researchers discovered one unusual person (one of the rare women with a color-vision defect) who was red-green color-blind in one eye but had normal color vision in the other. She was able to describe what she saw with the defective eye by using the color language she had learned to use with her other eye. As she described it, with the color-blind eye she saw only grays, blues, and yellows. Red and green hues were altogether absent, as if one of the opponent-process pairs were missing (Graham & Hsia, 1954).

Perceiving Shapes

The perception of color enhances our appreciation of art and, more practically, allows us to distinguish a ripe fruit from a green one. Other aspects of vision are far more important. After all, a color-blind individual can live a perfectly normal life. But the same can't be said for an individual who can't tell a square from a circle, and can't tell whether the shape in front of her is that of an apple or that of a banana. These individuals (known as *visual agnosics*) are dramatically impaired in their functioning. We therefore need to ask how the visual system manages the perception of shape. This achievement turns out to be quite complex; so we'll begin addressing it in this chapter and then return to it in Chapter 5.

FEATURE DETECTORS

Recordings from individual nerve cells have allowed electrophysiologists to examine how particular cells in the visual system respond to certain stimuli. In these studies, researchers place a microelectrode into the optic nerve—or, in many studies, into the brain of an anesthetized animal. The animal's well-being is carefully monitored, both for ethical reasons and to allow the investigators to assess how neurons function in an intact, healthy organism. The animal's eye is then stimulated by visual inputs of varying brightness and different shapes, arriving at the eye from different locations (Figure 4.41). In this way, the investigator can learn which stimuli evoke a response from that cell.

Results from these studies show that the cells in the visual system—whether we're considering the rods and cones themselves, neurons in the optic nerve, or neurons in the brain—all have a preferred target, a certain type of stimulus that's especially effective in causing that cell to fire. We can think of the cells, therefore, as "detectors," each one tuned for (and so likely to detect) its own set of targets.

What sorts of detectors does the visual system rely on? The answer depends on the species. Frogs, for example, need only a few bits of information about the world: "What's that large shape moving toward me? Just in case it's a predator, I'll take a leap to safety." "What's that small, dark shape moving around? It might be a fly, so I think I'll flick my tongue at it." Because they need so little information to survive, frogs have just a few detector types—and they're located on the retina, so the frog can quickly analyze the input and act on it (Lettvin, Maturan, McCulloch, & Pitts, 1959).

Unlike frogs, most animals—including the mammals—need more detailed information about the world around them. Their visual systems perform a more complex analysis, supported by a greater variety of detector types, located in the cortex as well as on the retina. Most of what we know about this visual analysis comes from the work

receptive field For a particular cell in the visual system, the pattern of retinal stimulation that most effectively causes the cell to fire. For some cells, this pattern is defined simply in terms of a retinal location; for others, the most effective input has a particular shape, color, or direction of motion.

feature detectors Neurons in the retina or brain that respond to specific attributes of the stimulus, such as movement, orientation, and so on.

Method

1. An anesthetized cat has one eye propped open so that a series of visual stimuli—e.g., lines with different orientations—could be directed to particular regions of its retina.

2. A microelectrode was implanted in its visual cortex to monitor a single cell's firing rates in response to the lines.

Stimulus projected on screen

Micro-electrode

Amplifier   Oscilloscope

3. When the cell fired, its neural impulses were amplified, then displayed on an oscilloscope. (The procedure was repeated to monitor many individual cells' responses.)

Results

| Some cells fired more rapidly in response to a vertical line. | These vertical-preferring neurons fired at only a moderate rate in response to a tilted line. | These cells didn't increase their firing rate at all in response to a horizontal line. |

Image on screen

Neuron firing rate

CONCLUSION: Each neuron in the visual cortex has a "target" stimulus that evokes especially rapid firing. These targets include low-level features, such as arcs or lines of a specific orientation.

SOURCE STUDIES: Hubel & Wiesel, 1959, 1968

---

of David Hubel and Torsten Wiesel, who won a Nobel Prize for their research (Figure 4.42). Working first with cats and then with primates, these investigators confirmed that each cell in the visual cortex responds to stimuli in only a limited region of space—or, equivalently, each cell in the retina responds to stimuli on only a limited region of the retina. This region defines that cell's **receptive field** (Figure 4.43). More important, this research made it plain that cells differ in the types of detectors they are. Some cells have receptive fields of a special size, location, *and shape*—and so they fire at their maximum rate only when the visual input is a line of a specific orientation at a specific retinal position. One such cell might respond to a vertical line at one position in the visual field, while another cell might respond to a line tilted to 45 degrees at the same position; still another cell might respond to a vertical line at some other position. In this way, and because the visual field is blanketed by receptive fields, lines of any orientation at any position will be detected by the appropriate type of cell (Hubel & Wiesel, 1959, 1968).

Other cells in the visual cortex are a bit more sophisticated. They also fire only in response to a line or edge of a particular orientation, but they're largely indifferent to the line's specific location within the visual field (see Figure 4.41). Cells like these serve as **feature detectors**, detecting certain elements within the visual pattern. Other cells, deeper within the visual system, presumably then assemble these now detected elements in order to detect larger configurations and more complex patterns.

Consistent with this suggestion, Hubel and Wiesel were able to locate other cells that responded only to more complicated inputs. For example, some cells responded maximally to corners or particular angles. Other cells responded to movement patterns, firing maximally only when they detected movement of the appropriate velocity and direction.

4.42 Torsten Wiesel and David Hubel Hubel and Wiesel won the Nobel Prize in 1981 for their groundbreaking work exploring the function of individual cells in the visual system.

4.43 Receptive fields on the cat's visual system Using the setup shown in Figure 4.41, stimuli are presented to various regions of the retina. The data show that different cells show different patterns of responding. For example, parts (A) through (D) show the firing frequency of a particular ganglion cell. (A) This graph shows the baseline firing rate when no stimulus is presented anywhere. (B) The cell's firing rate goes up when a stimulus is presented in the middle of the cell's receptive field. (C) In contrast, the cell's firing rate goes *down* if a stimulus is presented at the edge of the cell's receptive field. (D) If a stimulus is presented both to the center of the receptive field and to the edge, the cell's firing rate does not change from its baseline level. Cells with this pattern of responding are called "center-surround" cells, to highlight their opposite responses to stimulation in the center of the receptive field and the surrounding region.

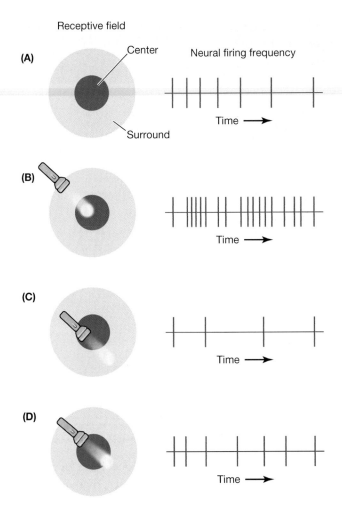

DETECTORS FOR COMPLEX FORMS

It's easy to see how feature detectors might be useful. Let's say that a pattern of visual input reaches your retina and triggers a "horizontal-line detector" and a "vertical-line detector." When these two detectors fire at the same time, this event might trigger a response in a "right-angle detector." If at the same time you've also detected three other right angles, this combination might trigger a response from your "square detector." Activity in this detector might then combine with activity in other detectors and eventually lead you to say, "Oh, look—there's my Intro Psych textbook."

In this way, the feature detectors we've just discussed might be the starting point for a hierarchy of detectors that leads, step-by-step, from simple features to slightly more complex shapes to still more complex shapes. And eventually, the steps will lead to detectors that fire only in response to the sight of a complex object in the world—such as the letter *Q*, or your mother's face, or a sports car.

Is this explanation plausible? Could we have specific detectors for each of the countless things we recognize? For some targets, these detectors do exist—and, no surprise, they're usually detectors for stimuli that are especially significant for a species. For example, certain cells in a monkey's cortex have been shown to respond to pictures of a monkey's face, but not at all to pictures of other parts of a monkey's body. Other cells seem to respond almost exclusively to pictures of a monkey's hand—whether the hand has an open palm or clenched fist or the fingers are pointed up or down (Desimone, Albright, Gross, & Bruce, 1984).

Still, it seems highly unlikely that such built-in mechanisms could account for all the forms that higher animals—especially humans—perceive and recognize. Simple creatures like frogs are able to recognize only a few patterns, so it's reasonable to think they might have specialized detectors for each one. In contrast, humans easily discriminate among a multitude of patterns; and this simple fact speaks powerfully against the idea that we might have specialized detectors for each of them—triangles, squares, apples, apple pies, champagne bottles, cabbages, kings—the list is endless. We know that the perception of any kind of form begins with a feature analysis; this process is plain in the functioning of the detector cells. But how do we integrate these features to create more complex forms? The answer to this question is surprisingly complex, and it's one of our main concerns in Chapter 5.

SOME FINAL THOUGHTS:
THE ACTIVE PERCEIVER

Obviously, there's still much to say about how we come to know the world around us. We've looked at how sensory systems transduce the proximal stimulus, and how they code the incoming message into the various dimensions of our sensory experience. But we still need to ask how we come to recognize the various objects and events that we encounter every minute of our lives.

Even at this early stage of our discussion, though, we've answered a question we asked at the very start: When perceiving things, do we simply open our eyes and receive the information the world provides for us, recording this information faithfully and passively the way a camera does? Or do we take a more active role of shaping the input and interpreting and organizing it? By now it's clear that the evidence favors the second view: The complexities of signal detection remind us that even when detecting a simple stimulus—a light, a tone, a scent—we must often make a judgment, a decision about whether we detected an input or not. Likewise, thanks to mechanisms like lateral inhibition, it seems that we do shape the inputs we receive. We accentuate the most crucial bits (namely, edges) and deemphasize the less important bits. In a similar way, the detectors in our visual systems respond only to those aspects of the input that are likely to be useful. Creatures as simple as frogs need relatively little visual information, so their visual system is designed to pick out only a few features. As a result, they're essentially blind to any aspects of the input other than those few bits they must have. Our needs are more complicated; but even so, our visual system is attuned to an identifiable set of features. So, inevitably, our subsequent analyses are based on precisely this feature information. In these and other ways, our visual system does shape the visual input from the very start by selecting and emphasizing the aspects we're especially interested in.

As we'll see in Chapter 5, this is just the beginning of the active role we take in perceiving the world around us. At the most basic levels, our sensory systems are active receivers of information. And the level of activity involved in shaping and interpreting the input simply increases as we go deeper into the processes that make perception possible.

THE ORIGINS OF KNOWLEDGE

- The study of sensory processes grew out of questions about the origin of human knowledge. The empiricists argued that all knowledge comes through stimuli that excite the senses. However, the only way to get information about *distal stimuli* (the objects or events in the world) is through the *proximal stimuli* (the energies that impinge on a sensory surface). The empiricists therefore argued that much of perception is built up through learning by *association*.

PSYCHOPHYSICS

- Research in *psychophysics* seeks to relate the characteristics of the physical stimulus to both the quality and intensity of the sensory experience. One psychophysical measurement is the *absolute threshold*. Another measurement is the *difference threshold*, producing a *just-noticeable difference (jnd)*. According to *Weber's law,* the jnd is a constant fraction of the intensity of the comparison stimulus. Building on this principle, *Fechner's law* states that the strength of a sensation grows as the logarithm of stimulus intensity.

- Data in psychophysical procedures are influenced by a perceiver's sensory *sensitivity* as well as her *decision criteria*. These two factors can be assessed separately, though, via a *signal-detection* procedure.

A SURVEY OF THE SENSES

- *Sensory codes* are the rules by which the nervous system translates the properties of the proximal stimulus into neural impulses. Psychological intensity is usually coded by the rates of firing by the neurons and by the sheer number of neurons triggered by the stimulus.

- Other codes are for *sensory quality*. In some cases, qualitative differences within a *sensory modality* are best described by *specificity theory*—that different *sensory qualities* (e.g., red versus green) are signaled by different neurons, just as the different sense modalities are signaled by different nerves. More commonly, sensory coding is best described by *pattern theory*, which holds that certain sensory qualities arise because of different patterns of activation across a whole set of neurons.

- Certain properties can be observed in all of the sensory systems—including the phenomenon of *adaptation*—the tendency to respond less to a stimulus that has been around and unchanging for some time.

- The *vestibular sense* signals movements of the head, and helps us know which way is "up" and which is "down." The receptors for this sense are in the semicircular canals in the inner ear.

- The *skin senses* include several distinct subsystems, and lead to the separate sensations of pressure, temperature and pain. Even within these systems, we must distinguish different types of receptors—for example, one type that fires when the temperature rises, and another that fires in response to a drop in skin temperature.

- The sense of *pain* depends on specialized receptors that respond to various forms of tissue damage and temperature extremes. However, the experience of pain is also influenced by other mechanisms, including the endorphins, and by neural circuits that provide a "gateway" blocking the transmission of some signals from the nociceptors.

- The sense of *smell* is triggered by receptors in the *olfactory epithelium,* which then send their neural signals to *glomeruli* in the olfactory bulb. The experience of a specific smell is coded by a pattern of activity across the glomeruli. Smell has many functions—helping animals to find food and avoid predators, and, in many circumstances, providing a means of communicating within a species. The chemicals used for these communications are called *pheromones*.

- The receptors for *taste* are located on the *papillae* found primarily on the tongue. There are five types of receptors, and each type is sensitive to a wide range of inputs. Once again, therefore, the qualities of taste (sweet vs. salty, sour vs. bitter) are coded by a pattern of responding across the five receptor types.

HEARING

- *Sound waves* can vary in *amplitude* and *frequency,* and set up vibrations in the eardrum that are then transmitted by the *auditory ossicles* to the *oval window,* whose movements create waves in the *cochlea*. Within the cochlea is the *basilar membrane,* which contains the auditory receptors that are stimulated by the membrane's deformation. According to the *place theory*, the experience of pitch is based on the place of the membrane that is most stimulated; each place is especially responsive to a particular frequency and generates a particular pitch sensation. According to the *frequency theory,* the experience of pitch depends on the firing frequency of the auditory nerve. Evidence suggests that both theories are correct—the perception of higher frequencies depends on the place stimulated on the basilar membrane, and the perception of lower frequencies depends on firing frequency.

VISION

- Vision is our primary distance sense. Its stimulus is light, which can vary in *intensity* and *wavelength.* Some structures of the eye, such as the iris and the lens, control the amount of light entering the eye and form a proper proximal stimulus—the *retinal image*. Once on the retina, the light stimulus is transduced by the *rods* and *cones*. Acuity is greatest in the *fovea*, where the density of cones is greatest.

- Rods and cones differ markedly in function. The rods operate at low light intensities and are insensitive to differences in hue. The cones function at much higher illumination levels and are responsible for sensations of color.

- The various components of the visual system interact constantly, and these interactions actively shape and transform the stimulus input. One kind of interaction involves *contrast effects*, including brightness contrast. These effects serve to accentuate edges—as in the case of Mach bands. The physiological mechanism underlying this effect is *lateral inhibition*, a clear example of how the visual system refines the stimulus information by emphasizing some aspects of the input and understating others.

- Visual sensations vary in *color;* and color sensations can be ordered on the basis of their hue, brightness, and saturation. Normal human color vision is *trichromatic*, depending on three cone types. However, some facts do not fit with this trichromatic conception, because colors come in pairs—as shown by the phenomena of complementary colors, color contrast, and negative afterimages.

- *Opponent-process theory* proposes that the output of the cones serves as input for a further layer of mechanisms that recode the signal into three opponent-process pairs: *red-green, blue-yellow,* and *black-white*.

- Shape perception depends on specialized *detector cells* that respond to certain characteristics of the stimulus, such as curves and straight edges. The optimal input for each cell—that is, a stimulus of a certain shape and size at a certain position—defines the cell's *receptive field*. In cats and monkeys, *feature detectors* seem to respond maximally when a line or edge of a specific orientation is in view. Other cells, deeper within the visual system, assemble these elements in order to detect larger configurations and more complex patterns.

Ⓢ ONLINE STUDY TOOLS

Go to StudySpace, **wwnorton.com/studyspace**, to access additional review and enrichment materials, including the following resources for each chapter:

Organize
- Study Plan
- Chapter Outline
- Quiz+ Assessment

Learn
- Ebook
- Chapter Review
- Vocabulary Flashcards
- Drag-and-Drop Labeling Exercises
- Audio Podcast Chapter Overview

Connect
- Critical Thinking Activity
- Studying the Mind Video Podcasts
- Video Exercises
- Animations
- **ZAPS** Psychology Labs

Perception

Should you find yourself at a karaoke party, performing a song that you think you know by heart, be careful: You might end up falling prey to a mondegreen.

Mondegreens are misperceptions of common phrases, especially from poems and songs. Thousands of people are convinced, for example, that Creedence Clearwater Revival is crooning, "There's a bathroom on the right." The actual lyric is "a bad moon on the rise." Likewise, when country star Crystal Gale proclaims, "Don't it make my brown eyes blue?" legions of fans think she's singing, "Doughnuts make my brown eyes blue." Even religious music is open to these errors. Countless church-goers unknowingly change "Gladly the cross I'd bear" into a hymn to visually challenged wildlife: "Gladly, the cross-eyed bear."

Mondegreens reveal how *active* and *interpretive* perception is. Although perception feels effortless, much of the sensory information we receive is incomplete and ambiguous—so we have to supplement and interpret that information in order to understand what's going on around us. In many mondegreens, the acoustic input is truly ambiguous—the sound waves that reach you when someone says "the cross I'd bear" are virtually identical to the sound waves that comprise "the cross-eyed bear." You have to interpret the input. Other mondegreens don't match the stimuli as closely, showing that people do more than interpret the sensory information; some-times, they actually *overrule* it. This is true of the mondegreen that gave the phenomenon its name. As a girl, the American writer Sylvia Wright loved the 17th-century Scottish ballad "The Bonnie Earl O' Murray," which she perceived as saying:

> They hae [have] slain the Earl Amurray,
> And Lady Mondegreen.

"I saw it all clearly," Wright recalls in a *Harper's Weekly* article: "The Earl had yellow curly hair and a yellow beard and of course wore a kilt. ... Lady Mondegreen lay at his side, her long, dark brown curls spread out over the moss." This is a wonderfully romantic image but, it turns out, not what the balladeers intended: Wright may have *heard* "And Lady Mondegreen," but the stanza actually ends "And laid him on the green."

As we'll see, errors like mondegreens are relatively rare—perception is generally accurate. However, these errors plainly reveal that perception involves interpretation. After all, if you weren't interpreting to being with, how could you ever misinterpret?

In this chapter, we'll examine this interpretation process, looking at how it leads to accurate perception of the world, and also how it occasionally leads to perceptual error. We'll focus on humans' most important source of perceptual information—our sense of *vision*—starting with the crucial question of how we recognize objects. We'll then turn to how variations in our *circumstances* affect perception. Finally, we'll consider one last layer of complication: It's not enough just to see what something is; we also need to know what it is doing. We'll therefore examine how we perceive *motion*.

Perception feels easy and immediate: You open your eyes and recognize what you see. You understand sounds the second they reach your ears. In truth, perception only *seems* simple because you're extraordinarily skilled at it. In this chapter, we'll explore just how complex the perceptual process really is.

FORM PERCEPTION: WHAT IS IT?

The ability to recognize objects is, of course, enormously important for us. If we couldn't tell a piece of bread from a piece of paper, we might try to write on the bread and eat the paper. If we couldn't tell the difference between a lamppost and a potential mate, our social lives would be strange indeed. So how do we manage to recognize bread, paper, mates, and myriad other objects? In vision, our primary means of recognizing objects is through the perception of their form. Of course, we sometimes do rely on color (e.g., a violet) and occasionally on size (e.g., a toy model of an automobile); but in most cases, form is our major avenue for identifying what we see. The question is *how*? How do we recognize the forms and patterns we see in the world around us?

The Importance of Features

One simple hypothesis regarding our ability to recognize objects is suggested by data we considered in Chapter 4. There we saw that the visual system contains cells that serve as *feature detectors*—and so one of these cells might fire if a particular angle is in view; another might fire if a vertical line is in view; and so on. Perhaps, therefore, we just need to keep track of which feature detectors are firing in response to a particular input; that way, we'd have an inventory of the input's features, and we could then compare this inventory to some sort of checklist in memory. Does the inventory tell us that the object in front of our eyes has four right angles and four straight sides of equal length? If so, then it must be a square. Does the inventory tell us that the object in view has four legs and a very long neck? If so, we conclude that we're looking at a giraffe.

Features do play a central role in object recognition. If you detect four straight lines on an otherwise blank field, you're not likely to decide you're looking at a circle or a picture of downtown Chicago; those perceptions don't fit with the set of features presented to you by the stimulus. But let's be clear from the start that there are some complexities here. For starters, consider the enormous variety of objects we encounter, perceive, and recognize: cats and cars, gardens and gorillas, shoes and shops; the list goes on and on. Do we have a checklist for each of these objects? If so, how do we search through this huge set of checklists, so that we can recognize objects the moment they appear in front of us?

Besides that, for any one of the objects we can recognize there is still more variety. After all, we recognize cats when we see them close up or far away, from the front or the side, and sitting down or walking toward us (Figure 5.1). Do we have a different feature checklist for each of these views? Or do we somehow have a procedure for converting these views into some sort of "standardized view," which we then compare to a checklist? If so, what might that standardization procedure be? We clearly need some more theory to address these issues. (For more on how we might recognize objects despite changes in our view of them, see Tarr, 1995; Vuong & Tarr, 2004.)

Similarly, we often have *partial views* of the objects around us; but we can recognize them anyway. Thus, we recognize a cat even if it's sitting behind a tree and we can see only its head and one paw. We recognize a chair even when someone is sitting on it, blocking much of the chair from view. We identify the blue form in Figure 5.2 as a square, even though one corner is hidden. These facts, too, must be accommodated by our theory of recognition.

The Importance of Organization

It seems, then, that we'll need a great number of feature lists (due to the sheer number of objects we can recognize). We'll also need flexibility in how we use the feature lists (to address the diversity of views we get of each object, and the problem of partial views). But there's still another problem for us to confront: It turns out that the catalog of features we rely on—and so the starting point for our recognition of objects in the world—depends on how we *interpret* the visual input.

This role for interpretation can be demonstrated in several ways. One is that we choose to ignore many of the features available to our visual system, basing our recognition only on a subset of the features that are actually in view. To make this idea concrete, consider Figure 5.3. The pattern in the man's shirt contains many lines and angles, but we give them little priority when analyzing the scene. Instead, we focus on the features defining the outline of the man's body and telling us that this is, in fact, a picture of a man wearing sunglasses. Likewise, we ignore the outline of the shadows cast by the trees because we realize that the features making up this outline don't tell us much about the identity of the objects in the picture. It seems, then, that we somehow choose which features "matter" for our recognition and which features are incidental.

5.1 The variability of stimuli we recognize We recognize cats from the side or the front, whether we see them close up or far away.

5.2 Recognizing partially occluded figures We recognize the blue form as a square even though it doesn't have the right inventory of features—thanks to the fact that one of its corners is hidden from view.

5.3 The complexity of real-world scenes Our recognition of objects depends only on a well-chosen subset of the features that are in view. So, for example, we recognize the man's shirt by paying attention to its outline; we're not misled by the lines that form the pattern in the fabric, or by the edges of the shadows. Instead, we manage to zoom in on just those features that define the shapes we're interested in.

5.4 A hidden figure At first the figure seems not to contain the features needed to identify the various letters. But once the figure is reorganized with the white parts forming the figure and not the dark parts, its features are easily detected. So it seems that the analysis of features depends on a preliminary step in which the viewer must organize the figure.

Figure 5.4 illustrates a different type of interpretation. These dark shapes seem meaningless at first, but after a moment most people find a way to reorganize the figure so that the familiar letters come into view. But let's be clear about what this means. At the start, the form doesn't seem to contain the features we need to identify the *L*, the *I*, and so on—and so we don't detect these letters. Once we've reorganized the form, though, it does contain the relevant features and so we immediately recognize the letters. Apparently, therefore, the catalog of features present in this figure depends on how we interpret its overall form. Based on one interpretation, the features defining these letters are absent—and so we can't detect the letters or the word *LIFT*. With a different interpretation, the features are easily visible and we can immediately read the word. It seems, then, that features are as much "in the eye of the beholder" as they are in the figure itself.

As a related example, consider Figure 5.5. Here, most people easily perceive two complete triangles—one on the orange background, one on the green. But again, the features of these triangles aren't present on the page; specifically, the *sides* of the triangle aren't marked in the figure at all. However, the perceiver organizes the overall form so that the missing sides are filled in—she's essentially creating the features for herself. Once that's done, she can clearly perceive the triangles.

PERCEPTUAL PARSING

The previous examples powerfully suggest that the perception of form depends both on feature input—that is, what's actually in front of your eyes—and on how you organize and interpret the form. But what exactly does it mean for a perceiver to "interpret" a form, or to find an "organization" within a figure? And why do you end up with one interpretation and not another? Why, for example, do most people decide that Figure 5.5 should be organized in a way that connects the angles so that they become parts of a single form rather than treating them as separate forms?

Questions like these were crucial for **Gestalt psychology**, a school of psychology that emphasized that organization is an essential feature of all mental activity: We understand the elements of the visual input as linked to each other in a certain way, and the identity of these elements depends on the linkage. (That's why in Figure 5.5, we perceive the round elements as intact circles, each partially hidden by another form, rather than as a series of "Pac-Man" figures.) Likewise, we appreciate a work of music because we perceive the individual notes as forming a cohesive whole. Similarly, our thoughts have meaning only in relationship to each other. In all cases, the Gestalt psychologists wanted to ask how this organization was achieved, and how it influenced us. (The word *Gestalt* is derived from a German word meaning "form" or "appearance.")

Gestalt psychologists described several aspects of this organization and identified several principles that guided it. Some of the principles are concerned with the way you *parse* the input—that is, how you separate a scene into individual objects, linking together the parts of each object but not linking one object's parts to some other object. To make this idea concrete, consider the still life in Figure 5.6. To make sense of this picture, your perception must somehow group the elements of the scene appropriately.

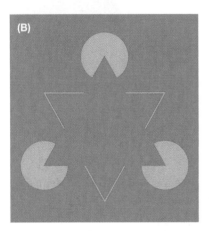

5.5 Subjective contours In (A) we see an orange triangle whose vertices lie on top of the three green circles. The three sides of this orange triangle (which looks brighter than the orange background) are clearly visible, even though they don't exist physically. In (B) we see the same effect with green and orange reversed. Here, the green triangle—which looks darker than the green background—has subjective green contours.

Gestalt psychology A theoretical approach that emphasizes the role of organized wholes in perception and other psychological processes.

(A)

(B)

5.6 Perceptual parsing (A) A still life. (B) An overlay designating five different segments of the scene shown in (A). To determine what an object is, the perceptual system must first decide what goes with what: Does portion 2 go with 1 or with 3, 4, or 5? Or does it go with none of them?

Portion 2 (part of the apple) must be united with portion 5 (more of the apple), even though they're separated by portion 4 (a banana). Portion 2 should not be united with portion 1 (a bunch of grapes), even though they're adjacent and about the same color. The bit of the apple hidden from view by the banana must somehow be filled in, so that you perceive an intact apple rather than two apple slices. All of these steps involved in deciding which bits go with which other bits fall under the label of parsing.

What cues guide you toward parsing a stimulus pattern one way rather than another? The answer involves both feature information and information about the larger-scale pattern. For example, we tend to interpret certain features (such as a T-junction—Figure 5.7) as indicating that one edge has disappeared behind another; we interpret other features differently. In this way, "local" information—information contained in one small part of the scene—helps guide our parsing. But "global" information—information about the whole scene—is also crucial. For example, perceivers tend to group things together according to a principle of **similarity**—meaning that, all other things being equal, they group together figures that

similarity In perception, a principle by which we tend to group like figures, especially by color and orientation.

T-junction   **Y**-junction

5.7 How features guide parsing We noted earlier that feature analysis depends on a preliminary step in which the viewer organizes the overall figure. But it turns out that the opposite is also true: The features determine how the viewer organizes the figure. For example, viewers usually interpret a T-junction as one surface dropping from view behind another. They usually interpret a Y-junction as a corner pointing toward them.

A Similarity
We tend to group these dots into columns rather than rows, grouping dots of similar colors.

B Proximity
We tend to perceive groups, linking dots that are close together.

C Good continuation
We tend to see a continuous green bar rather than two smaller rectangles.

D Closure
We tend to perceive an intact triangle, reflecting our bias toward perceiving closed figures rather than incomplete ones.

E Simplicity
We tend to interpret a form in the simplest way possible. We would see the form on the left as two intersecting rectangles (as shown on right) rather than as a single 12-sided irregular polygon.

5.8 Other Gestalt principles

proximity In perception, the closeness of two figures. The closer together they are, the more we tend to group them together perceptually.

good continuation A factor in visual grouping; we tend to perceive contours in a way that alters their direction as little as possible.

subjective contours Perceived contours that do not exist physically. We tend to complete figures that have gaps in them by perceiving a contour as continuing along its original path.

5.9 Figure and ground (A) One of the early steps in seeing a form is to segregate it from its background. If we perceive the figure in part (A) as a blue rectangle with a hole in it (B), the edge marks the contour of the hole. The situation is reversed in (C). Now the edge marks the white blob, not a break in the blue background. In this sense, the edge belongs to the figure, not the ground. As it turns out, the perception in (C) is much more likely.

resemble each other. So in Figure 5.8A, we group blue dots with blue dots, red with red. Perceivers are also influenced by **proximity**—the closer two figures are to each other, the more we tend to group them together perceptually (for more on these principles of perceptual organization, see Figure 5.8; Palmer, 2002; Wertheimer, 1923).

Parsing is also guided by several other principles, including **good continuation**—a preference for organizations in which contours continue smoothly along their original course. This helps us understand why portions 2 and 5 in Figure 5.6 are grouped together as parts of a single object; but good continuation can also be documented in much simpler stimuli (Figure 5.8C). Good continuation is also relevant to Figure 5.5. Some theorists interpret the **subjective contours** visible in this figure as a special case of good continuation. In their view, the contour is seen to continue along its original path—even, if necessary, jumping a gap or two to achieve this continuation (Kellman & Shipley, 1991; Kellman, Garrigan, & Shipley, 2005).

FIGURE AND GROUND

Another part of visual organization is the separation of the object from its setting, so that the object is seen as a coherent whole, separate from its background. This separation of *figure* and *ground* allows you to focus on just the banana in Figure 5.6, treating everything else in the scene as merely the backdrop for the banana. But the separation of figure and ground is just as important with simpler and entirely unfamiliar figures. In Figure 5.9A, the white splotch appears to most people as the figure and is

Which is figure, which is ground?

(A)

Alternative ways of organizing this stimulus

(B)

(C)

perceived as closer to the viewer than the blue region (which is seen as the ground) as shown in 5.9c. The edge between the blue and white regions is perceived as part of the figure, defining its shape. The same edge does not mark a contour for the blue region but merely marks the point at which the blue region drops from view.

Of course, you can usually identify a figure so quickly and easily that it feels like this specification is somehow specified by the stimulus itself and is not an element of your interpretation. But the fact remains that identifying the figure, like all aspects of perceptual organization, is up to you. This is most evident whenever you realize there's more than one way to interpret a given stimulus—as in Figure 5.10, which can be seen either as a white vase or as two blue faces in profile. This **reversible figure** makes it clear that the stimulus itself is neutral in its organization. What is figure and what is ground, it seems, depends on how we look at it.

Other examples point to the same broad conclusion and highlight the perceiver's active role in interpreting the input. Is Figure 5.11A—the Necker cube—aligned with the solid cube shown in Figure 5.11B, so we're viewing it from above? Or is it aligned with the cube shown in Figure 5.11C, so we're viewing it from below? Most people can organize the Necker cube in either way, so they first perceive it to have one orientation and then the other. Apparently, then, the organization is not specified by the figure itself but is instead up to the perceiver.

All of these observations suggest that perception is less "objective" than one might suppose, because what we perceive is, it seems, often determined by how we interpret or organize the input. At the same time, it's important to realize that perceivers' inferences and interpretations tend to be neither foolish nor random. Quite the contrary: Our interpretations of the sensory input are, first of all, shaped by our experience; and they're correct far more often than not (Enns, 2004). Likewise, the interpretations themselves tend to be quite logical, as if our visual system always follows certain rules. We've already mentioned some of these rules—a preference for grouping *similar* things together, for example, or a preference for parsing the input so that it creates smooth contours. But other rules also guide us: For example, we seem to prefer perceptual interpretations that explain *all* the information contained within the stimulus, and so we avoid interpretations that would explain only bits and pieces of the stimulus. We also seem to avoid interpretations that would involve some contradiction, such as perceiving a surface to be both opaque and transparent. What's more, we seem to avoid interpretations that depend on accident or coincidence. ("This is what the form would look like if viewed from exactly the right position.") Of course, no one claims that the perceptual apparatus is literally proceeding through a sequence of logical steps, weighing each of these rules in turn. Still, our perception does seem guided by these principles, so that our interpretations of the input will be logical and usually correct (Figure 5.12).

5.10 Reversible figure-ground pattern This figure can be seen as either a pair of silhouetted faces or a white vase.

reversible figure A visual pattern that easily allows more than one interpretation, in some cases changing the specification of figure and ground, in other cases changing the perceived organization in depth.

(A) The Necker cube

Alternative ways of perceiving this stimulus
(B)   **(C)**

5.11 The Necker cube The ambiguous Necker cube, shown in (A), can be perceived as aligned with either the cube shown in (B) or the one in (C).

5.12 Impossible figures We've mentioned how "logical" the perceptual system seems to be, but it's important to realize that this logic has limits. As an example, consider these so-called impossible figures. We perceive them as if they show three-dimensional objects, although contradictions within each figure guarantee that they can't be three-dimensional.

(A)   **(B)**   **(C)**

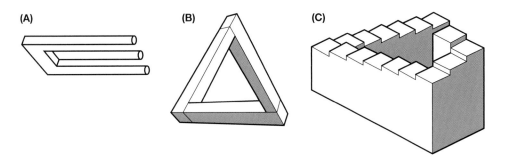

NETWORK MODELS OF PERCEPTION

The last few pages have created a new question for us. We've been focusing on the interpretive nature of perception, and we'll keep doing that throughout this chapter. In all cases, people don't just "pick up" and record the stimuli that reach the eye, the way a camera or videorecorder might. Instead, they organize and shape the input. When they encounter ambiguity—and they often do—they make choices about how the ambiguity should be resolved.

But how exactly does this interpretation take place? This question needs to be pursued at two levels. First, we can try to describe the sequence of events in functional terms—first, *this* is analyzed; then *that* is analyzed—laying out in detail the steps needed to accomplish the task. Second, we can specify the neural processes that actually support the analysis and carry out the processing. Let's look at both types of explanation, starting with the functional approach.

Feature Nets

Earlier in this chapter, we noted some complications for any theorizing that involves *features*. Even with these complications, though, it's clear that feature detection plays a central role in object recognition. We saw in Chapter 4 that the visual system does analyze the input in terms of features: Specialized cells—feature detectors—respond to lines at various angles, curves at various positions, and the like. More evidence for the importance of features comes from behavioral studies that use a **visual search** procedure. In this task, a research participant is shown an array of visual forms and asked to indicate as quickly as she can whether a particular target is present—whether a vertical line is visible among the forms shown, perhaps, or a red circle is visible amid a field of squares. This task is easy if the target can be distinguished from the field by just one salient feature—for example, searching for a vertical among a field of horizontals, or for a green target amidst a group of red distracters. In such cases, the target "pops out" from the distracter elements, and search time is virtually independent of the number of items in the display—so people can search through four targets, say, as fast as they can search through two, or eight as fast as they can search through four (Figure 5.13, part A or B; Treisman, 1986a, 1986b; Wolfe

visual search A task in which participants are asked to determine whether a specified target is present within a field of stimuli.

5.13 Visual search In (A), you can immediately spot the vertical, distinguished from the other shapes by just one feature. Likewise, in (B), you can immediately spot the lone green bar in the field of reds. In (C), it takes much longer to find the one red vertical, because now you need to search for a *combination* of features—not just for red or vertical, but for the one form that has both of these attributes.

(A)   (B)   (C)

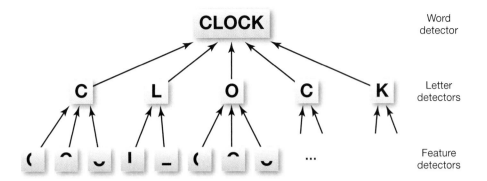

Word
detector

Letter
detectors

Feature
detectors

5.14 How a feature net guides identification An example of a feature net. Here the feature detectors respond to simple elements in the visual input. When the appropriate feature detectors are activated, they trigger a response in the letter detectors. When these are activated, in turn, they can trigger a response from a higher-level detector, such as a detector for an entire word.

& Horowitz, 2004; we'll have more to say about visual search later in the chapter). These results make it clear that features have priority in our visual perception. We can detect them swiftly, easily, and presumably at an early stage in the sequence of events required to recognize an object.

But how do we use this feature information? And how, knowing about the complications we've discussed, can we use this information to build a full model of object recognition? One option is to set up a *hierarchy* of detectors with detectors in each layer serving as the triggers for detectors in the next layer (Figure 5.14). In the figure, we've illustrated this idea with a hierarchy for recognizing *words*; the idea would be the same with one for recognizing *objects*. At the lowest level of the hierarchy would be the feature detectors we've already described—those responsive to horizontals, verticals, and so forth. At the next level of the hierarchy would be detectors that respond to combinations of these simple features. Detectors at this second level would not have to survey the visual world directly. Instead, they'd be triggered by activity at the initial level. Thus, there might be an "L" detector in the second layer of detectors that fires only when triggered by both the vertical- and horizontal-line detectors at the first level.

Hierarchical models like the one just described are known as **feature nets** because they involve a network of detectors that has feature detectors at its bottom level. In the earliest feature nets proposed, activation flowed only from the bottom up—from feature detectors to more complex detectors and so on through a series of larger and larger units (see, for example, Selfridge, 1959). Said differently, the input pushes the process forward, and so we can think of these processes as "data driven." More recent models, however, have also included a provision for "top-down" or "knowledge-driven" processes—processes that are guided by the ideas and expectations that the perceiver brings to the situation.

To see how top-down and bottom-up processes interact, consider a problem in word recognition. Suppose you're shown a three-letter word in dim light. In this setting, your visual system might register the fact that the word's last two letters are *AT;* but at least initially, the system has no information about the first letter. How, then, would you choose among *MAT, CAT,* and *RAT?* Suppose that, as part of the same experiment, you've just been shown a series of words including several names of animals (*dog, mouse, canary*). This experience will activate your detectors for these words, and the activation is likely to spread out to the memory neighbors of these detectors—including (probably) the detectors for *CAT* and *RAT.* Activation of the *CAT* or *RAT* detector, in turn, will cause a top-down, knowledge-driven activation of the detectors for the letters in these words, including *C* and *R* (Figure 5.15).

feature net A model of pattern recognition involving a network of detectors and having feature detectors as the network's starting point.

(A) Top-down processing

Formulate hypothesis about the identity of the stimulus.

Thoughts about *animal*

MAT   CAT   RAT

Select and examine relevant aspects of the stimulus to check the hypothesis.

M   C   R

(B) Bottom-up processing

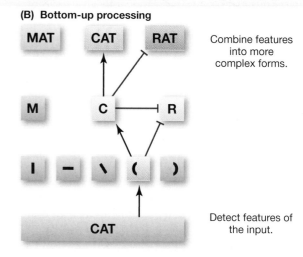

Combine features into more complex forms.

MAT   CAT   RAT

M   C   R

CAT

Detect features of the input.

5.15 Bidirectional activation (A) Thoughts about the concept *animal* activates the words *CAT* and *RAT* (among others), which then activate their constituent letters, including the first-position letters *C* and *R*. This process also inhibits incompatible words, such as *MAT*. Activation is indicated with arrows; inhibition in red. (B) Some milliseconds later, further perceptual analysis of the first letter of the stimulus word has activated the feature curved-to-the-left, which partially activates the letter *C*. This process adds to the activation of the word *CAT* and inhibits the letter *R* and the word *RAT*. Thus, the word *CAT* is more intensely activated than all other words. To keep things simple, many other connections (e.g., between the words *CAT* and *RAT*) are not shown in the figure.

While all this is going on, the data-driven analysis continues; by now, your visual system has likely detected that the left edge of the target letter is curved (Figure 5.15B). This bottom-up effect alone might not be enough to activate the detector for the letter *C*; but notice that this detector is also receiving some (top-down) stimulation (Figure 5.15A). As a result, the *C* detector is now receiving stimulation from two sources—from below (the feature detector) and above (from *CAT*), and this combination of inputs will probably be enough to activate the *C* detector. Then, once this detector is activated, it will feed back to the *CAT* detector, activating it still further. (For an example of models that work in this way, see McClelland, Rumelhart, & Hinton, 1986; also Grainger, Rey, & Dufau, 2008.)

It's important, though, that we can describe all of these steps in two different ways. If we look at the actual mechanics of the process, we see that detectors are activating (or inhibiting) other detectors; that's the only thing going on here. At the same time, we can also describe the process in broader terms: Basically, the initial activation of *CAT* functions as a knowledge-driven "hypothesis" about the stimulus, and that hypothesis makes the visual system more receptive to the relevant "data" coming from the feature detectors. In this example, the arriving data confirm the hypothesis, thus leading to the exclusion of alternative hypotheses.

With these points in view, let's return to the question we asked earlier: We've discussed how the perceptual system *interprets* the input, and we've emphasized that the interpretation is guided by rules. But what processes in our mind actually do the "interpreting"? We can now see that the interpretive process is carried out by a network of detectors, and the interpretive "rules" are built into the way the network functions. For example, how do we ensure that the perceptual interpretation is compatible with all the information in the input? This point is guaranteed by the fact that the feature detectors help shape the network's output, and this simple fact makes it certain that the output will be constrained by information in the stimulus. How do we ensure that our perception contains no contradiction (e.g., perceiving a surface to be both opaque and transparent)? This is guaranteed by the fact that detectors within the network can inhibit other (incompatible) detectors. With mechanisms like these in place, the network's output is sure to satisfy all of our rules—or at least to provide the best compromise possible among the various rules.

From Features to Geons to Meaning

The network we've described so far can easily recognize targets as simple as squares and circles, letters and numerals. But what about the endless variety of three-dimensional objects that surround us? For these, theorists believe we can still rely on a network of detectors; but we need to add some intermediate levels of analysis.

A model proposed by Irving Biederman, for example, relies on some 30 geometric components that he calls **geons** (short for "geometric ions"). These are three-dimensional figures such as cubes, cylinders, pyramids, and the like; nearly all objects can be broken down perceptually into some number of these geons. To recognize an object, therefore, we first identify its features and then use these to identify the component geons and their relationships. We then consult our visual memory to see if there's an object that matches up with what we've detected (Biederman, 1987; Figure 5.16).

In Biederman's system, we might describe a lamp, say, as being a certain geon (number 4 in Figure 5.16) on top of another (number 3). This combination of geons gives us a complete description of the lamp's geometry. But this isn't the final step in object recognition, because we still need to assign some meaning to this geometry. We need to know that the shape is something we call a *lamp*—that it's an object that casts light and can be switched on and off.

As with most other aspects of perception, those further steps usually seem effortless. We see a lamp (or a chair, or a pickup truck) and immediately know what it is and what it is for. But as easy as these steps seem, they're far from trivial. Remarkably, we can find cases in which the visual system successfully produces an accurate structural description but fails in these last steps of endowing the perceived object with meaning. The cases involve patients who have suffered certain brain lesions leading to visual agnosia (Farah, 1990). Patients with this disorder can see, but they can't recognize what they see (Chapter 3). Some patients can perceive objects well enough to draw recognizable pictures of them; but they're unable to identify either the objects or their own drawings. One patient, for example, produced the drawings shown in Figure 5.17. When asked to say what he had drawn, he couldn't name the key and said the bird was a tree stump. He evidently had formed adequate structural descriptions of these objects, but his ability to process what he saw stopped there; his perceptions were stripped of their meaning (Farah, 1990, 2004).

(A) Some of the geons

(B) Some objects that can be created

5.16 Some proposed geometric primitives Part (A) shows some of the geons (geometric ions) that our perceptual system uses in its analysis of complex forms. Part (B) shows how geons are assembled into objects—so that geon 5 side-attached to geon 3 creates the shape of a coffee cup.

geons (geometric ions) Simple geometric figures, such as cubes, cylinders, and pyramids, that can be combined to create all other shapes. An early (and crucial) step in some models of object recognition is determining which geons are present.

(A) Original   **(B) Copy**

5.17 Drawings by a patient with associative agnosia The left column shows the forms shown the patient; the right column shows the patient's drawings. While the patient could see the models well enough to reproduce them accurately, he was unable to recognize these objects.

THE NEUROSCIENCE OF VISION

Where are we so far? We started by acknowledging the complexities of form perception—including the perceiver's need to interpret and organize visual information. We then considered how this interpretation might be achieved—through a network of detectors, shaped by an interplay between bottom-up and top-down processes. But these points simply invite the next question: How does the nervous system implement these processes? More broadly, what events in the eye, the optic nerve, and the brain make perception possible?

The Visual Pathway

As we saw in Chapter 4, the rods and cones pass their signals to the bipolar cells, which relay them to the ganglion cells (Figure 4.26). The axons of the ganglion cells form the optic nerve, which leaves the eyeball and begins the journey toward the brain. But even at this early stage, the neurons are specialized in important ways, and different cells are responsible for detecting different aspects of the visual world.

The ganglion cells, for example, can be broadly classified into two categories: the smaller ones are called **parvo cells,** and the larger are called **magno cells** (*parvo* and *magno* are the Latin for "small" and "large"). Parvo cells, which blanket the entire retina, far outnumber magno cells. Magno cells, in contrast, are found largely in the retina's periphery. Parvo cells appear to be sensitive to color differences (to be more precise, to differences either in hue or in brightness), and they probably play a crucial role in our perception of pattern and form. Magno cells, on the other hand, are insensitive to hue differences but respond strongly to changes in brightness; they play a central role in the detection of motion and the perception of depth.

This pattern of neural specialization continues and sharpens as we look more deeply into the nervous system. The relevant evidence comes largely from the single-cell recording technique that lets investigators determine which specific stimuli elicit a response from a cell and which do not (see Chapter 4). This technique has allowed investigators to explore the visual system cell by cell and has given us a rich understanding of the neural basis for vision.

PARALLEL PROCESSING IN THE VISUAL CORTEX

In Chapter 4, we noted that cells in the visual cortex each seem to have a "preferred stimulus"—and each cell fires most rapidly whenever this special stimulus is in view. For some cells, the preferred stimulus is relatively simple—a curve, or a line tilted at a particular orientation. For other cells, the preferred stimulus is more complex—a corner, an angle, or a notch. Still other cells are sensitive to the color (hue) of the input. Others fire rapidly in response to *motion*—some cells are particularly sensitive to left-to-right motion, others to the reverse.

This abundance of cell types suggests that the visual system relies on a "divide-and-conquer" strategy. Different cells—and even different areas of the brain—each specialize in a particular kind of analysis. Moreover, these different analyses go on in parallel: The cells analyzing the forms do their work at the same time that other cells are analyzing the motion and still others the colors. Using single-cell recording, investigators have been able to map where these various cells are located in the visual cortex as well as how they communicate with each other; Figure 5.18 shows one of these maps.

parvo cells Ganglion cells that, because of their sensitivity to differences in hue, are particularly suited to perceiving color and form.

magno cells Ganglion cells that, because of their sensitivity to brightness changes, are particularly suited to perceiving motion and depth.

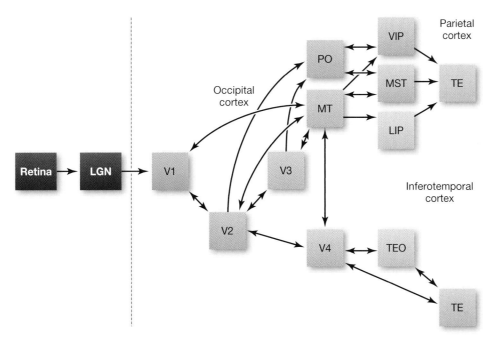

5.18 The visual processing pathways Each box in this figure refers to a specific location within the visual system; the two blue boxes at the left refer to locations outside the cortex; all other boxes refer to locations on the cortex. Notice two key points: First, vision depends on *many* different brain sites, each performing a specialized type of analysis. Second, the flow of information is complex—so there's surely no strict sequence of "this step" of analysis followed by "that step." Instead, everything happens at once and there's a great deal of back-and-forth communication among the various elements.

Why this reliance on parallel processing? For one thing, parallel processing allows greater speed, since (for example) brain areas trying to recognize the shape of the stimulus aren't kept waiting while other brain areas complete the motion analysis or the color analysis. Instead, all types of analysis can take place simultaneously. Another advantage of parallel processing lies in its ability to allow each system to draw information from the others. Thus, your understanding of an object's shape can be sharpened by a consideration of how the object is moving; your understanding of its movement can be sharpened by noting what the shape is (especially the shape in three dimensions). This sort of mutual influence is easy to arrange if the various types of analysis are all going on at the same time (Van Essen & DeYoe, 1995).

The parallel processing we see in the visual cortex also clarifies a point we've already discussed. Earlier in the chapter, we argued that the inventory of a figure's features depends on how the perceiver organizes the figure. So, in Figure 5.4, the features of the letters were absent with one interpretation of the shapes, but they're easily visible with a different interpretation. In Figure 5.5, some of the features (the triangle's sides) aren't present in the figure but seem to be created by the way we interpret the arrangement of features. Observations like these make it sound like the interpretation has priority because it determines what features are present.

But it would seem that the reverse claim must also be correct because the way we interpret a form depends on the features we can see. After all, no matter how you try to interpret Figure 5.18, it's not going to look like a race car, or a map of Great Britain, or a drawing of a porcupine. The form doesn't include the features needed for those interpretations; and as a result, the form will not allow these interpretations. This seems to suggest that it's the features, not the interpretation, that have priority: The features guide the interpretation, and so they must be in place before the interpretation can be found.

How can both of these claims be true—with the features depending on the interpretation and the interpretation depending on the features? The answer involves parallel processing. Certain brain areas are sensitive to the input's features, and the cells in these areas do their work at the same time that other brain areas are analyzing the larger-scale configuration. These two types of analysis, operating in parallel, can then interact with each other, ensuring that our perception makes sense at both the large-scale and fine-grained levels.

THE "WHAT" AND "WHERE" SYSTEMS

Evidence for specialized neural processes, all operating in parallel, continues as we move beyond the visual cortex. As Figure 5.19 indicates, information from the visual cortex is transmitted to two other important brain areas in the inferotemporal cortex (the lower part of the temporal cortex) and the parietal cortex. The pathway carrying information to the temporal cortex is often called the **"what" system**; it plays a major role in the identification of visual objects, telling us whether the object is a cat, an apple, or whatever. The second pathway, which carries information to the parietal cortex, is often called the **"where" system**; it tells us where an object is located—above or below, to our right or left (Ungerleider & Haxby, 1994; Ungerleider & Mishkin, 1982).

There's been some controversy, however, over how exactly we should think about these two systems. Some theorists, for example, propose that the path to the parietal cortex isn't concerned with the conscious perception of position. Instead, it's primarily involved in the unnoticed, automatic registration of spatial location that allows us to control our movements as we reach for or walk toward objects in our visual world. Likewise, this view proposes that the pathway to the temporal cortex isn't really a "what" system; instead, it's associated with our conscious sense of the world around us, including our conscious recognition of objects and our assessment of what these objects look like (e.g., Goodale & Milner, 2004; also D. Carey, 2001; Sereno & Maunsell, 1998).

No matter how this debate is settled, there can be no question that these two pathways serve very different functions. Patients who have suffered lesions in the occipital-temporal pathway—most people agree this is the "what" pathway—show visual agnosia (see Chapter 3). They may be unable to recognize common objects, such as a cup or a pencil. They're often unable to recognize the faces of relatives and friends—

"what" system The visual pathway leading from the visual cortex to the temporal lobe; especially involved in identifying objects.

"where" system The visual pathway leading from the visual cortex to the parietal lobe; especially involved in locating objects in space and coordinating movements.

5.19 The "what" and "where" pathways
Information from the primary visual cortex at the back of the head is transmitted to the inferotemporal cortex (the so-called "what" system) and to the posterior parietal cortex (the "where" system).

but if the relatives speak, the patients can recognize them by their voices. At the same time, these patients show little disorder in visual orientation and reaching. On the other hand, patients who have suffered lesions in the occipital-parietal pathway— usually understood as the "where" pathway—show the reverse pattern. They have difficulty in reaching for objects but no problem with identifying them (A. Damasio, Tranel, & H. Damasio, 1989; Farah, 1990; Goodale, 1995; Newcombe, Ratcliff, & Damasio, 1987).

The Binding Problem

It's clear, then, that natural selection has favored a division-of-labor strategy for vision: The processes of perception are made possible by an intricate network of subsystems, each specialized for a particular task and all working together to create the final product—an organized and coherent perception of the world.

We've seen the benefits of this design, but the division-of-labor setup also creates a problem for the visual system. If the different aspects of vision—the perception of shape, color, movement, and distance—are carried out by different processing mod- ules, then how do we manage to recombine these pieces of information into one whole? For example, when we see a ballet dancer in a graceful leap, the leap itself is registered by the magno cells; the recognition of the ballet dancer depends on parvo cells. How are these pieces put back together? Likewise, when we reach for a coffee cup but stop midway because we see that the cup is empty, the reach itself is guided by the occipital-parietal system (the "where" system); the fact that the cup is empty is perceived by the occipital-temporal system (the "what" system). How are these two streams of process- ing coordinated?

We can examine the same issue in light of our subjective impression of the world around us. Our impression, of course, is that we perceive a cohesive and organized world. After all, we don't perceive big and blue and distant; we instead perceive sky. We don't perceive brown and large shape on top of four shapes and moving; instead, we perceive our pet dog running along. Somehow, therefore, we do manage to re-integrate the separate pieces of visual information. How do we achieve this reunification? Neuroscientists call this the **binding problem**—how the nervous system manages to bind together elements that were initially detected by separate systems.

We're just beginning to understand how the nervous system solves the binding problem. But evidence is accumulating that the brain uses a pattern of *neural synchrony*—different groups of neurons firing in synchrony with each other—to identify which sensory elements belong with which. Specifically, imagine two groups of neurons in the visual cortex. One group of neurons fires maximally whenever a vertical line is in view. Another group of neurons fires maximally whenever a stimulus is in view moving from left to right. Also imagine that, right now, a vertical line is presented, and it is moving to the right. As a result, both groups of neurons are firing rapidly. But how does the brain encode the fact that these attributes are bound together, different aspects of a single object? How does the brain differentiate between this stimulus and one in which the features being detected actually belong to different objects—perhaps a static vertical and a moving diagonal?

The answer lies in the timing of the firing by these two groups of neurons. In Chapter 3, we emphasized the firing *rates* of various neurons—whether a neuron was firing at, say, 100 spikes per second or 10. But we also need to consider exactly *when* a neuron is firing, and whether, in particular, it is firing at the same moment as other neurons. When the neurons are synchronized, this seems to be the nervous system's

binding problem The problem con- fronted by the brain of recombining the elements of a stimulus, given the fact that these elements are initially analyzed separately by different neural systems.

indication that the messages from the synchronized neurons are in fact bound together. To return to our example, if the neurons detecting a vertical line are firing in synchrony with the neurons signaling movement—like a group of drummers all keeping the same beat—then these attributes, vertical and moving, are registered as belonging to the same object. If the neurons are not firing in synchrony, the features are registered as belonging to separate objects (Buzsáki & Draguhn, 2004; Csibra, Davis, Spratling, & Johnson, 2000; M. Elliott & Müller, 2000; Fries, Reynolds, Rorie, & Desimone, 2001; Gregoriou, Gotts, Zhou, & Desimone, 2009).

PERCEPTUAL CONSTANCY

perceptual constancy The accurate perception of certain attributes of a distal object, such as its shape, size, and brightness, despite changes in the proximal stimulus caused by variations in our viewing circumstances.

We began this chapter by noting that perception seems easy and immediate—we open our eyes and see, with no apparent complexities. But we also said that this intuition is misleading, because perception involves considerable complexities—many steps to be taken, and many points at which the perceiver must play an active role in interpreting the input. This message emerged again and again in our discussion of how we recognize the objects that surround us, and the same broad message—multiple steps, and an active role—emerges when we consider another essential aspect of perceiving: the achievement of **perceptual constancy.** This term refers to the fact that we perceive the constant properties of objects in the world (their sizes, shapes, and so on) even though the sensory information we receive about these attributes changes whenever our viewing circumstances change.

To illustrate this point, consider the perception of size. If we happen to be far away from the object we're viewing, then the image cast onto our retinas by that object will be relatively small. If we approach the object, then the image size will increase. We're not fooled by this variation in image size, though. Instead, we manage to achieve *size constancy*—correctly perceiving the sizes of objects in the world despite the changes in retinal-image size created by changes in viewing distance. Likewise, if we view a door straight on, the retinal image will be rectangular in shape; but if we view the same door from an angle, the retinal image will have a different shape (Figure 5.20). Still, we achieve *shape constancy*—that is, we correctly perceive the shapes of objects despite changes in the retinal image created by shifts in our viewing angle. We also achieve *brightness constancy*—we correctly perceive the brightness of objects whether they're illuminated by dim light or strong sun.

5.20 Shape constancy When we see a door at various slants from us, it appears rectangular even though its retinal image is often a trapezoid.

5.21 **An invariant relationship that provides information about size** (A) and (B) show a dog at different distances from the observer. The retinal size of the dog varies with distance, but the ratio between the retinal size of the dog and the retinal size of the textural elements (e.g., the floor tiles) is constant.

Unconscious Inference

How do we achieve each of these forms of constancy? One hypothesis focuses on *relationships* within the retinal image. In judging size, for example, we might be helped by the fact that we generally see objects against some background, and various elements in the background can provide a basis for comparison with the target object. Thus the dog sitting nearby on the kitchen floor is half as tall as the chair and hides a number of the kitchen's floor tiles from view. If we take several steps back from the dog, none of these relationships changes, even though the sizes of all the retinal images are reduced (Figure 5.21). Size constancy, therefore, might be achieved by focusing not on the images themselves but on these unchanging relationships.

Relationships do contribute to size constancy, and that's why we are better able to judge size when comparison objects are in view or when the target we're judging sits on a surface that has a uniform visual texture (like the floor tiles in the example). But these relationships don't tell the whole story. Size constancy is found even when the visual scene offers no basis for comparison—if, for example, the object to be judged is the only object in view—provided that other cues signal the *distance* of the target object (Chevrier & Delorme, 1983; Harvey & Leibowitz, 1967; Holway & Boring, 1947).

How might our visual system use this distance information? More than a century ago, the German physicist Hermann von Helmholtz developed an influential hypothesis regarding this question. Helmholtz started with the fact that there's a simple inverse relationship between distance and retinal image size: If an object doubles its distance from the viewer, the size of its image is reduced by half. If an object triples its distance, the size of its image is reduced to a third of its initial size. This relationship is guaranteed to hold true because of the principles of optics, and the relationship makes it possible for perceivers to achieve size constancy by means of a simple calculation. Of course, Helmholtz knew that we don't run through a conscious calculation every time we perceive an object's size; but he believed we were calculating nonetheless—and so he referred to the process as an **unconscious inference** (Helmholtz, 1909).

What is the calculation that allows someone to perceive size correctly? It's simply multiplication: the size of the image on the retina, multiplied by the distance between you and the object. (We'll have more to say about how you know this distance in a later section.) Thus, imagine an object that, at a distance of 10 feet, casts an image on the

unconscious inference A process postulated by Hermann von Helmholtz to explain certain perceptual phenomena such as size constancy. For example, an object is perceived to be at a certain distance and this is unconsciously taken into account in assessing its retinal image size, with the result that size constancy is maintained.

If an object moves to a new distance, the size of the retinal image cast by that object changes. A doubling of the distance reduces the retinal image by half. If the distance is tripled, the retinal image is cut to one-third of its initial size.

(A) Closer objects cast larger retinal images

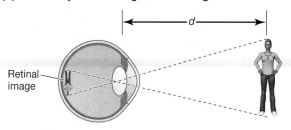

(B) Father objects cast smaller retinal images

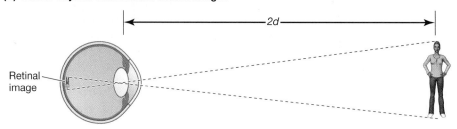

retina that's 4 millimeters across (Figure 5.22). The same object, at a distance of 20 feet, casts an image of 2 millimeters. In both cases, the product—10 × 4 or 20 × 2—is the same. If, therefore, your size estimate depends on that product, your size estimate won't be thrown off by viewing distance—and of course, that's exactly what we want.

What's the evidence that size constancy does depend on this sort of inference? In many experiments, researchers have shown people some object and, without changing the object's retinal image, changed the apparent distance of the object. (There are many ways to do this—lenses that change how the eye has to focus to bring the object into sharp view, or mirrors that change how the two eyes have to angle inward so that the object's image is centered on both foveas.) If people are—as Helmholtz proposed—using distance information to judge size, then these manipulations should affect size perception. Any manipulation that makes an object seem farther away (without changing retinal image size) should make that object seem bigger. Any manipulation that makes the object seem closer should make it look smaller. And, in fact, these predictions are correct—a powerful confirmation that we do use distance to judge size.

A similar proposal explains how people achieve shape constancy. Here, we take the slant of the surface into account and make appropriate adjustments—again, an unconscious inference—in our interpretation of the retinal image's shape. Likewise for brightness constancy: We seem to be quite sensitive to how a surface is oriented relative to the available light sources, and we take this information into account in estimating how much light is reaching the surface. Then we use this assessment of lighting to judge the surface's brightness (e.g., whether it's black or gray or white). In all these cases, therefore, it appears that our perceptual system does draw some sort of unconscious inference, taking our viewing circumstances into account in a way that allows us to perceive the constant properties of the visual world.

Illusions

This process of taking information into account—no matter whether we're taking viewing distance into account, or viewing angle, or illumination—is crucial for achieving constancy. More than that, it's yet another indication that we don't just "receive" visual information, we *interpret* it. The interpretation is always an essential part of our perception and generally helps us perceive the world correctly. But the role of the interpretation becomes especially clear when we *mis*interpret the information available to us and end up misperceiving the world.

Consider the two tabletops shown in Figure 5.23. The table on the left looks appreciably longer and thinner than the one on the right; a tablecloth that fits one table surely won't fit the other. Objectively, though, the parallelogram depicting the left table-top is exactly the same shape as the one depicting the right tabletop. If you were to cut out the left tabletop, rotate it, and slide it onto the right tabletop, they'd be an exact match. (Not convinced? Just lay another piece of paper on top of the page, trace the left tabletop, and then move your tracing onto the right tabletop.)

Why do people misperceive these shapes? The answer involves the normal mechanisms of shape constancy. Cues to depth in this figure cause the viewer to perceive the figure as a drawing of two three-dimensional objects, each viewed from a particular angle. This leads the viewer—quite automatically—to adjust for the (apparent) viewing angles in order to perceive the two tabletops, and it's this adjustment that causes the illusion. Notice then, that this illusion about *shape* is caused by a misperception of *depth*: The viewer misperceives the depth relationships in the drawing and then takes this faulty information into account in interpreting the shapes. (For a related illusion, see Figure 5.24.)

A different example is shown in Figure 5.25. It seems obvious to most viewers that the center square in this checkerboard (third row, third column) is a brighter shade than the square indicated by the arrow. But, in truth, the shade of gray shown on the page is identical for these two squares. What has happened here? The answer again involves the normal mechanisms of perception. Notice, first, that the central square is surrounded by dark squares; this arrangement creates a contrast effect that makes the central square look brighter. The square marked at the edge of the checkerboard, on the other hand, is surrounded by white squares; here, contrast makes the marked square look darker. So for both squares, we have contrast effects that move us toward the illusory perception. But the visual system also detects that the central square is in the shadow cast by the cylinder. Our vision compensates for this fact—again, an example of unconscious inference that takes the shadow into account in judging brightness—and powerfully magnifies the illusion.

5.23 Two tabletops The table on the left looks longer and thinner than the one on the right, but in fact, the parallelograms depicting each tabletop are identical. If you were to cut out the left parallelogram, rotate it, and slide it onto the right parallelogram, they'd line up perfectly. The apparent difference in their shapes is an illusion resulting from the way viewers interpret the figure.

5.24 The monster illusion The two monsters shown here are the same size on the page, but the monster on the right appears larger. This is because the depth cues in the picture make the monster on the right appear to be farther away. This (mis)perception of distance leads to a (mis)perception of size.

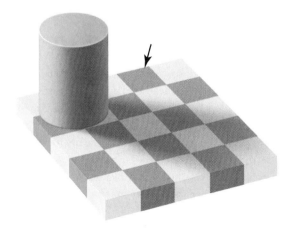

5.25 A brightness illusion Most viewers will agree that the center square in this checkerboard (third row, third column) is a brighter shade than the square indicated with the arrow. But, in truth, the shade of gray shown on the page is identical for these two squares! If you don't believe it, use your fingers or pieces of paper to cover everything in the figure except these two squares.

DISTANCE PERCEPTION: WHERE IS IT?

So far in this chapter, we've emphasized how you recognize the objects you encounter. This focus has led us to consider how you manage to perceive forms as well as how you cope with variations in viewing circumstances in order to perceive an object's shape and size correctly. And once again, this discussion leads to a new question: To perceive *what* something is, you need to achieve constancy. But, to achieve constancy, you need to perceive *where* something is—how far it is from you (so that you can achieve size constancy) and how it is angled relative to your line of view (so that you can achieve shape constancy).

Of course, information about where things are in your world is also valuable for its own sake. If you want to walk down a hallway without bumping into things, you need to know which obstacles are close to you and which ones are far off. If you wish to caress a loved one, you need to know where he or she is; otherwise, you're likely to poke him or her in the eye. Plainly, then, you need to know where objects in your world are located.

How, therefore, do you manage to perceive a three-dimensional world, judging which objects are close and which are far? The answer centers on **depth cues**—features of the stimulus that indicate an object's position. What are these cues?

Binocular Cues

One important cue for distance comes from the fact that our two eyes look out onto the world from slightly different positions; as a result, each eye has a slightly different view. This difference between the two eyes' views is called **binocular disparity,** and it gives us important information about distance relationships in the world (Figure 5.26).

Binocular disparity can induce the perception of depth even when no other distance cues are present. For example, the bottom panels of Figure 5.26 show the views that each eye would receive while looking at a pair of nearby objects. If we present each of these views to the appropriate eye (e.g., by drawing the views on two cards and placing one card in front of each eye), we can obtain a striking impression of depth.

Disparity was the principle behind the stereoscope, a device popular in the 19th century (Figure 5.27), which presented a slightly different photograph to each eye and so created a vivid sense of depth. The same principle is used in 3-D movies, in which two different movies—presenting two slightly different views of each scene—are projected simultaneously onto the theatre's screen. For these movies, viewers wear special glasses to ensure that their left eye sees one of the movies and their right eye sees the other. In this way, each eye gets the appropriate input and creates the binocular disparity that in turn produces a compelling perception of depth.

Monocular Cues

Binocular disparity has a powerful effect on the way we perceive depth. But we can also perceive depth with one eye closed; so, clearly, there must be cues for depth that depend only on what each eye sees by itself. These are the **monocular depth cues.**

One of the monocular depth cues depends on the adjustment that the eye must make to see the world clearly. Specifically, we've already mentioned that in each eye, muscles adjust the shape of the lens to produce a sharply focused image on the retina. The amount of adjustment depends on how far away the viewed object is—there's a lot of adjustment for nearby objects, less for those a few steps away, and virtually no adjustment at all for objects more than a few meters away. It turns out that perceivers

---

depth cues Sources of information that signal the distance from the observer to the distal stimulus.

binocular disparity A depth cue based on the differences between the two eyes' views of the world. This difference becomes less pronounced the farther an object is from the observer.

5.26 Binocular disparity Two images at different distances from the observer will present somewhat different retinal images. In the left eye's view, these images are close together on the retina; in the right eye's view, the images are farther apart. This disparity between the views serves as a powerful cue for depth.

monocular depth cues Features of the visual stimulus that indicate distance even if the stimulus is viewed with only one eye.

(A)

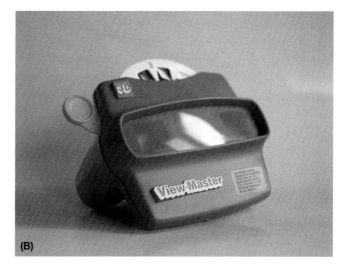

(B)

5.27 Stereoscope and View-Master After their invention in 1833, stereoscopes were popular for many years. They work by presenting one picture to the left eye and another to the right; the disparity between the pictures creates a vivid sense of depth. The View-Master, a popular children's toy, works exactly the same way. The photos on the wheel are actually pairs—at any rotation, the left eye views the leftmost photo (the one at 9 o'clock on the wheel) and the right eye views the rightmost photo (the one at 3 o'clock).

are sensitive to the amount of adjustment and use it as a cue indicating how far away the object is.

Another set of monocular cues have been exploited for centuries by artists to create an impression of depth on a flat surface—that is, within a picture—which is why these cues are often called **pictorial cues.** In each case, these cues rely on straightforward principles of physics. For example, imagine a situation in which a man is trying to admire a sports car, but a mailbox is in the way (Figure 5.28A). In this case, the mailbox will inevitably block the view simply because light can't travel through an opaque object. This fact about the physical world provides a cue we can use in judging distance. The cue is known as **interposition** (Figure 5.28B)—the blocking of our view of one object by some other object. In this example, interposition tells the man that the mailbox is closer than the car.

pictorial cues Patterns that can be represented on a flat surface in order to create a sense of a three-dimensional object or scene.

interposition A monocular cue to distance that relies on the fact that objects farther away are blocked from view by closer objects.

(A)

(B)

5.28 Pictorial cues (A) This man is looking at the sports car, but the mailbox blocks part of his view. (B) Here's how this scene looks from the man's point of view. Because the mailbox blocks the view, we get a simple but powerful cue that the mailbox must be closer to the man than the sports car is.

5.29 Linear perspective as a cue for depth

In the same way, distant objects necessarily produce a smaller retinal image than do nearby objects of the same size; this is a fact about optics. But this physical fact again gives us perceptual information we can use. In particular, it's the basis for the cue of **linear perspective**, the name for the pattern in which parallel lines seem to converge as they get farther and farther from the viewer (Figure 5.29).

One more pictorial cue is provided by *texture gradients*. Consider what meets the eye when we look at cobblestones on a street or patterns of sand on a beach. The retinal projection of the sand or the cobblestones shows a pattern of continuous change in which the elements of the texture grow smaller and smaller as they become more distant. This pattern of change by itself can reveal the spatial layout of the relevant surfaces (Figure 5.30). If these textures also have discontinuities, they can tell us even more about how the surfaces are laid out (Figure 5.31; Gibson, 1950, 1966).

linear perspective A cue for distance based on the fact that parallel lines seem to converge as they get farther away from the viewer.

motion parallax A depth cue based on the fact that, as an observer moves, the retinal images of nearby objects move more rapidly than do the retinal images of objects farther away.

The Perception of Depth through Motion

Whenever you move your head, the images projected by the objects in your world necessarily move across your retinas. For reasons of geometry, the projected images of nearby objects move more than those of distant ones; this pattern of motion in the retinal images gives us yet another distance cue, called **motion parallax** (Helmholtz, 1909).

A different motion cue is produced when we move toward or away from objects. As we approach an object, its image gets larger and larger; as we move away, it gets smaller. The pattern of stimulation across the entire visual field also changes as we move toward an object, resulting in a pattern of change in the retinal stimulation that's called *optic flow*. This flow gives us crucial information about depth and plays a large role in the coordination of our movements (Gibson, 1950, 1979).

5.30 Texture gradients as cues for depth
Uniformly textured surfaces produce texture gradients that give us information about depth: as the surface recedes, the size of the texture elements decreases, and the density of these elements increases.

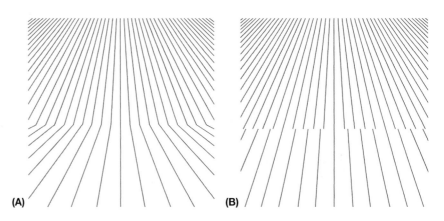

5.31 The effect of changes in texture gradients Such changes provide important information about spatial arrangements in the world. Examples are (A) an upward tilt at a corner; and (B) a sudden drop.

(A)   (B)

5.32 **Monocular cues to depth: light and shadow** Observers are sensitive to many different depth cues, including depth from shading. (A) Eight circular objects. Most viewers will say the object in the middle looks concave (indented), and the other seven look like they're bulging out. (B) The same figure rotated 180 degrees. Now the middle object looks convex, while the other seven seem concave. The reason is the location of the shadows. When the shadow is at the bottom, the object looks convex; when it's at the top, the object looks concave. This makes sense because light almost always comes from above.

The Role of Redundancy

You might think that the various distance cues all end up providing the same information—each one tells us which objects are close by and which are far. On that basis, it might be efficient for the visual system to focus on just one or two cues and ignore the others. The fact is, however, that we make use of all these cues as well as several others we haven't described (e.g., Figure 5.32).

Why did natural selection favor a system influenced by so many cues, especially since these cues often provide redundant information? It's because different distance cues become important in different circumstances. For example, binocular disparity is a powerful cue, but it's informative only when objects are relatively close by. (For targets farther than 30 feet away, the two eyes receive virtually the same image.) Likewise, motion parallax tells us a great deal about the spatial layout of our world, but only if we're moving. Texture gradients are informative only if there's a suitably uniform texture in view. So while these various cues are often redundant, each type of cue can give us information when the others cannot. By being sensitive to them all, we're able to judge distance in nearly any situation we encounter.

MOTION PERCEPTION: WHAT IS IT DOING?

We obviously want to know what objects are in view and where they're located, but we also want to know what these objects are doing. Are they moving or standing still, approaching slowly or rapidly, racing toward the food we wanted for ourselves, or heading off in some altogether different direction? These questions bring us to a different aspect of perception—namely, how we perceive *motion*.

Retinal Motion

One might think that the perception of motion is extremely simple: If an object in our world moves, then the image cast by that object moves across our retinas. We detect that image motion, and thus we perceive movement.

As we'll soon see, however, this account is way too simplistic. Still, it contains a key element of truth: We do detect an image's motion on the retina, and this is one aspect of the overall process of motion perception. More specifically, some cells in the visual cortex respond to image movements on the retina by firing at an increased rate whenever movement is present. However, these cells don't respond to just any kind of movement, because the cells are *direction specific*. Thus, the cells fire if a stimulus moves across their receptive field from, say, left to right; but not if the stimulus moves from right to left. (Other cells, of course, show the reverse pattern.) These cells are therefore well suited to act as **motion detectors** (see, for example, Vaultin & Berkeley, 1977).

Apparent Movement

It's clear, however, that retinal motion is only part of the story. Suppose we turn on a light in one location in the visual field, then quickly turn it off, and after an appropriate interval (somewhere between 30 and 200 milliseconds) turn on a second light in a different location. The result is **apparent movement.** The light appears to travel from one point to another, even though there was no motion and, indeed, no stimulation whatsoever in the locations between the two lights (Figure 5.33). This phenomenon is perceptually quite compelling; given the right timing, apparent movement is indistinguishable from real movement (Wertheimer, 1912). This is why the images in movies seem to move, even though movies actually consist of a sequence of appropriately timed still pictures (Figure 5.34).

Apparent movement might seem like an artificial phenomenon because the objects in our world tend to move continuously —they don't blink out of existence *here* and then reappear a moment later *there.* It turns out, however, that, the motion we encounter in the world is often so fast that it's essentially just a blur across the retina, and so triggers no response from the retinal motion detectors. Even so, we do perceive the motion by perceiving the object first to be in one place and then, soon after, to be somewhere else. In this way, the phenomenon of apparent movement actually mirrors a process that we rely on all the time, thanks to the fact that our eyes often need to work with brief "samples" taken from the stream of continuous motion (Adelson & Bergen, 1985).

motion detectors Cells in the visual cortex that are sensitive to an image moving in a particular direction across the retina.

apparent movement The perception of movement produced by stimuli that are stationary but are presented first at one positions and then, at an appropriate time interval, presented at a different position.

Physical events

Perceptual experience

5.33 **Apparent movement** The sequence of optical events that produces apparent movement. Light A flashes at time 1, followed by light B at time 2, then back to light A at time 3. If the time intervals are appropriately chosen, the viewer will perceive a light moving from left to right and back.

5.34 Apparent movement created by a series of stills A sequence of stills showing a gymnast doing a flip. If the stills are shown in succession, with proper timing, the viewer will perceive smooth movement—even though there's nothing actually moving in the stimulus input.

Eye Movements

As you look around the world, you're constantly moving your head and eyes. This activity creates another complication for motion perception. Each movement brings you a somewhat different view, and so each movement necessarily causes a change in the retinal image. But, despite all this retinal motion, the world doesn't seem to move each time you shift your viewing position. Clearly, it takes more than motion across the retina to produce a perception of motion in the world.

But how do you avoid becoming confused about this retinal motion? How do you manage to separate the retinal motion that's caused by movement in the world from the retinal motion produced by a change in your viewing position? The answer parallels our earlier discussion of constancy. As we've seen, people take *viewing distance* into account when judging *size,* and that's how they achieve size constancy. In the same way, you seem to take *your own movements* into account when judging the *position* of objects in the world, and so you perceive the objects as having *position constancy.* How does this work? Whenever you move your eyes or turn your head, you unconsciously compute the shift in the retinal image that your own motion will produce, and you cancel out this amount of movement in interpreting the visual input (Figure 5.35). The result is constancy.

(A) Objective movement

Eye stationary

Retinal
displacement

(B) Objective world stationary

Eye movement

Retinal
displacement

5.35 Compensation for eye movements In (A), an object has moved from right to left, so its retinal image has shifted from location *a* to location *b.* In (B), there's no motion in the world; instead, the eye has moved from left to right. But here, too, the object's retinal image shifts from location *a* to location *b.* Based only on the retinal information, the displacements in (A) and (B) seem identical. But our brains allow for the displacements caused by changes in eye position. So in (B), the brain would decide that there had been no movement because the motion of the eye was precisely equal (and opposite) to the displacement on the retina.

Here's a specific example. Imagine you're about to move your eyes 5 degrees to the left. Even before making the movement, you know that it will cause the retinal image to shift 5 degrees to the right. You can therefore compare this anticipated shift with the shift that actually occurs; if they match, then you know that you produced all of the retinal motion—and so there was no movement in the environment. In algebraic terms, we can think of this canceling-out process this way: When you move your eyes, there will be a 5-degree shift; but 5 degrees right of anticipated change minus 5 degrees right of actual change yields zero change overall. The zero change, of course, is what you perceive in this situation —no motion (Bridgeman & Stark, 1991).

Evidence for this claim comes from studies in which some heroic experimenters had themselves injected with drugs that temporarily paralyzed their eye muscles. They reported that under these circumstances, the world appeared to jump around whenever they tried to move their eyes—just what canceling-out theory would predict. The brain ordered the eyes to move, say, 10 degrees to the right; and so it anticipated that the retinal image would shift 10 degrees to the left. But the paralyzed eyes couldn't follow the command, so no retinal shift took place. In this setting, the normal cancellation process failed; as a result, the world appeared to jump with each eye movement. (Algebraically, this is 10 degrees left of anticipated change minus zero degrees of actual change, yielding 10 degrees left overall. The visual system interpreted this 10-degree overall difference as a motion signal.) These studies strongly confirm the canceling-out theory (Matin, Picoult, Stevens, Edwards, & MacArthur, 1982).

Induced Motion

Clearly, then, motion perception depends on several factors. Movement of an image across the retina stimulates motion detectors in the visual cortex (and elsewhere in the brain), and this certainly contributes to movement perception. However, activity in these detectors isn't necessary for us to perceive motion; in apparent movement, the detectors are silent but we perceive motion anyhow. Activity in the detectors is also, by itself, not *sufficient* for us to perceive motion: If those detectors register some movement, but the nervous system calculates that the movement was caused by a change in the observer's position, then no motion is perceived.

Even with all of this said, there's a further step in the process of motion perception, because we not only detect motion but also *interpret* it. This interpretation can be demonstrated in many ways, including the phenomenon of **induced motion.** Consider a ball rolling on a billiard table. We see the ball as moving and the table at rest. But why not the other way around? We can definitely see the ball getting closer and closer to the table's edge; but, at the same time, we can see the table's edge getting closer and closer to the ball. Why, then, do we perceive the movement as "belonging" entirely to the ball, while the table seems to be sitting still?

Evidence suggests that our perception in this case is the result of a bias in our interpretation: We tend to perceive larger objects as still and smaller objects as moving. In addition, if one object encloses another, the first tends to act as a stationary frame so that we perceive the enclosed object as moving. These biases lead to a correct perception of the world in most cases, but they can also cause errors. In one study, research participants were shown a luminous rectangular frame in an otherwise dark room. Inside the frame was a luminous dot. As the subjects watched, the rectangle moved upward while the dot stayed in place. But the subjects perceived something else. They described the dot as moving downward, in the direction opposite to the frame's motion. Participants had correctly perceived that the dot was moving closer to the rectangle's bottom edge and farther from its top edge. But they misperceived the source of this change.

induced motion Perceived movement of a stationary stimulus, usually caused by movement of a surrounding framework or nearby objects.

The physical movement of the frame had induced the perceived movement of the enclosed shape.

Similar effects can easily be observed outside of the laboratory. The moon seems to sail through the clouds; the base of a bridge seems to float upstream, against the river's current. In both cases, we see the surrounded object as moving and the frame as staying still—exactly as in the laboratory findings. A related (and sometimes unsettling) phenomenon is *induced motion of the self*. If you stand on the bridge that you perceive as moving, you feel as if you're moving along with it. The same effect can occur when you're sitting in a car in traffic: You've stopped at a red light and then, without warning, the car alongside you starts moving forward. You can sometimes get the feeling that for just a moment, you (and your car) are moving backward—even though you're sitting perfectly still.

The Correspondence Problem

Induced motion provides one illustration of how our perception of motion depends on interpretation. Another illustration, and a different type of interpretation, is involved in the so-called **correspondence problem**—the problem of deciding, as you move from one view to the next, which elements in the second view correspond with which elements in the first view (e.g., Weiss, Simoncelli, & Adelson, 2002; Wolfe, Kluender, & Levi, 2006). To see how this problem can arise, consider the stimulus pattern shown in Figure 5.36. At one moment, you're shown the pattern in panel A; then, a moment later, the pattern in B; then the pattern in A again; and so on back and forth. What will you perceive? With some adjustment of the timing, we can set things up so that this display will produce apparent movement, but what will the movement be? Will you perceive a red dot moving counterclockwise and turning blue, as shown in panel C? Or will you perceive a dot moving clockwise, and changing into a square, as shown in panel D?

correspondence problem As your view changes, the perceptual task of determining which aspects of the current view correspond to which aspects of the view seen a moment ago.

(A) At first you see:

(B) And then you see:

Do you perceive...

(C) a change in position and in color?

(D) a change in position and in shape?

5.36 **The correspondence problem** The viewer is first shown the pattern in (A), and then the pattern in (B), and then (A) again. With appropriate timing, the person will perceive motion, but the direction of motion is ambiguous: Some people will perceive counterclockwise motion (as in C), so that the objects are changing in color; other people will perceive clockwise motion (as in D), so that the objects are changing in shape. Both interpretations fit with the stimulus information.

For the display shown in Figure 5.36, there's no "correct" solution to the correspondence problem. The solutions leading to panel C and panel D both make sense. Thus, the stimuli shown in panels A and B are truly ambiguous; so it's no surprise that some people will perceive the motion illustrated in C and some will perceive the pattern in D. Indeed, an individual can perceive one of these patterns for a while and then abruptly shift her perception and perceive the other.

As we noted in our discussion of apparent movement, many real-world circumstances involve motion that's fast enough to be just a "blur" for the visual cortex's motion detectors. The only way we can detect this motion is to note that the stimuli were first *here*, and then *there*, and to infer from this that the stimuli had moved. It's exactly this situation that creates the correspondence problem—and so we often encounter this problem in our everyday perception of the world. As in many aspects of perception, our decision about the correspondence (i.e., what goes with what) is made quickly and easily; and so we don't realize that we have, in fact, interpreted the input. But the role of our interpretation becomes clear whenever our perception is *mistaken*. This is, for example, why we perceive spirals that are merely spinning as "growing outward" toward us, why we observe rotating barber poles to be moving upward, and why a fast-spinning wagon wheel that's turning clockwise can end up looking like it's actually spinning counterclockwise. In each case, the misperception grows out of an incorrect solution to the correspondence problem, and hence a confusion about which elements in the current view correspond with which elements in the scene just a moment ago.

The correspondence problem is an important aspect of motion perception. But this problem also draws our attention to a crucial theme for this chapter: As we said at the outset, our perception of the world usually seems immediate and effortless. We open our eyes and we see, with no apparent need to interpret or calculate. Even so, our perception of the world does involve a lot of steps and quite a few inferences. We become aware of those steps and inferences when they lead us astray, such as when they lead to an illusion of one sort or another. But it's important to recognize that the illusions arise only because interpretation is always a part of our perceptual process. Otherwise, if the interpretation weren't in place, then there'd be no way for the interpretation to go wrong! Perception, in other words, is always an active process—even if we normally don't detect that activity.

PERCEPTUAL SELECTION: ATTENTION

Our discussion throughout this chapter has been shaped by the challenges we face in getting an accurate view of the world around us. The challenges come from many sides—the enormous number of objects we can recognize; the huge diversity in views we can get of each object as we move around in the world; the possibility of interpreting the sensory information we receive in more than one way. Besides all that, here's another challenge we need to confront: When we look out at the world, we don't just see one object in front of our eyes; instead, we look at complex scenes containing many objects and activities. These many visual inputs are joined by inputs in other modalities: At every moment, we're likely to be hearing various noises and perhaps smelling certain smells. We're also receiving information from our skin senses—perhaps signaling the heat in the room, or the pressure of our clothing against our bodies. How do we cope with this sensory feast? Without question, we can choose to pay attention to any of these inputs—and so if the sounds are important to us, we'll focus on those; if the smells are alluring, we may focus on those instead. The one thing we can't do is pay attention to *all* of these inputs. Indeed, if we become absorbed in the book page in front of our eyes, we may lose track of the sounds in the room. If we listen intently to the sounds, we lose track of other aspects of the environment.

How should we think about all of this? How do we manage to pay attention to some inputs and not others?

Selection

When a stimulus interests us, we turn our head and eyes to inspect it or position our ears for better hearing. Other animals do the same, exploring the world with paws or lips or whiskers or even a prehensile tail. These various forms of *orienting* serve to adjust the sensory machinery and are one of the most direct means of selecting the input we wish to learn more about (Posner & Rothbart, 2007).

For humans, eye movement is the major means of orienting. Peripheral vision informs us that something's going on, say, in the upper-left section of our field of vision. But our peripheral acuity isn't good enough to tell us precisely what it is. To find out, we move our eyes so that the area where the activity is taking place falls into the visual field of the fovea (Rayner, Smith, Malcolm, & Henderson, 2009). In fact, motion in the visual periphery tends to trigger a reflex eye movement, making it difficult not to look toward a moving object (Figure 5.37).

However, eye movements aren't our only means of selecting what we pay attention to and what we ignore. The selective control of perception also draws on processes involving mental adjustments rather than physical ones. To study these mental adjustments, many experiments rely on the *visual search* task we've already discussed. In this task, someone is shown a set of forms and must indicate as rapidly as possible whether a particular target is present. We noted earlier that this task is effortless if the target can be identified on the basis of just one salient feature—if, for example, you're searching for a red circle among items that are blue, or for the vertical in a field of horizontals. We also mentioned earlier that in these situations, you can search through four items as fast as you can search through two, or eight as fast as you can search through four. This result indicates that you have no need to look at the figures on the screen one by one; if you did, then you'd need more time as the number of figures grew. Instead, you seem to be looking at all of the figures at the same time.

It's an entirely different situation when someone is doing a *conjunction search*—a search in which the target is defined by a combination of features. Thus, for example, we might ask you to search for a red vertical among distracters that include green verticals and red horizontals (Figure 5.13C), or to search for a blue circle hidden among a bunch of blue squares and red circles. Now it's not enough to search for (say) redness or for the vertical's orientation; instead, you must search for a target with both of these features. This requirement has an enormous impact on performance. Under these conditions, the search times are longer and depend on the number of items in the display; the more items there are, the longer it takes you to search through them.

What's going on here? Apparently, we don't need to focus our attention when looking for the features themselves. For that task, it seems, we can look at all the items in front of us at once; and so it doesn't matter if there are two items to examine or four or ten. But when we're looking for a *conjunction* of features, we need to take the extra step of figuring out how the features are assembled (and thus

5.37 Eye-movement records when looking at pictures The red track traces the path of the viewer's eye movements while examining this photograph. The numbers indicate the amount of time (in milliseconds) that the eyes spent looking at the points within the picture.

whether, for example, the redness and the vertical are part of the same stimulus or not). And this step of assembling the features is where attention plays its role: Attention allows us, in essence, to focus a mental spotlight on just a single item. Thanks to this focus, we can analyze the input one stimulus at a time. This process is slower, but it gives us the information we need; if at any moment we're analyzing only one item, then we can be sure the features we're detecting all come from that stimulus. This tells us directly that the features are linked to each other—and, of course, for a conjunction search (and for many other purposes as well), this is the key.

Notice, then, that attention is crucial for another issue we discussed earlier in the chapter—the binding problem. This is, you'll recall, the problem of figuring out which elements in the stimulus information belong with which and, several lines of evidence confirm a role for attention in achieving this "binding." In some studies, for example, people have been shown brief displays while they're thinking about something other than the display. Thus, the research participants might be quickly shown a red *F* and a green *X* while they're also trying to remember a short list of numbers they'd heard just a moment before. In this situation, the participants are likely to have no difficulty perceiving the features in the visual display—so they'll know that they saw something red and something green, and they may also know they saw an *F* and an *X*. In a fair number of trials, though, the participants will be confused about how these various aspects of the display were bundled together, so they may end up reporting **illusory conjunctions**—such as having seen a green *F* and a red *X*. Notice, therefore, that simply detecting features doesn't require the participants' attention and so goes forward smoothly despite the distracter task. This finding is consistent with the visual search results as well as our earlier comments about the key role of feature detection in object recognition. But, in clear contrast, the *combining* of features into organized wholes does require attention, and this process suffers when the participant is somehow distracted.

Related evidence comes from individuals who suffer from severe attention deficits because of damage in the parietal cortex. These individuals can do visual search tasks if the target is defined by a single feature, but they're deeply impaired if the task requires them to judge how features are conjoined to form complex objects (Cohen & Rafal, 1991; Eglin, L. Robertson, & Knight, 1989; L. Robertson, Treisman, Friedman-Hill, & Grabowecky, 1997).

But what exactly does it mean to "focus attention" on a stimulus or to "shine a mental spotlight" on a particular input? How do we achieve this selection? The answer involves **priming**—a warming up of certain detectors so they're better prepared to respond than they otherwise would be. Priming can be produced in two ways: First, exposure to a stimulus can cause "data-driven" priming—and so, if you've recently seen a red *H*, or a picture of Moses, this experience has primed the relevant detectors; the result is that, the next time you encounter these stimuli, you'll be more efficient in perceiving them. But there's another way priming can occur, and it's based on *expectations* rather than recently viewed stimuli. For example, if the circumstances lead you to expect that the word *CAT* is about to be presented, you can prime the appropriate detectors. This top-down priming will then help if your expectations turn out to be correct. When the input arrives, you'll process it more efficiently because the relevant detectors are already warmed up.

Evidence suggests that the top-down priming we just described (dependent on expectations rather than recent exposure) draws on some sort of mental resources, and these resources are in limited supply. So if you expect to see the word *CAT*, you'll prime the relevant detectors, but this will force you to take resources away from other detectors. As a result, the priming is selective. If you expect to see *CAT*, you'll be well prepared for this stimulus but less prepared for anything else. Imagine, therefore, that you

illusory conjunction A pattern of errors in which observers correctly perceive the features present in a display, such as color and shape, but misperceive how they were combined. For example, they might report seeing a green *O* and a red *X* when a green *X* and red *O* were presented.

priming The process through which a detector or portion of the nervous system is prepared for an upcoming input, making it easier for the participant to recognize that input.

expect to see *CAT* but are shown *TREE* instead. In this case, you'll process the input less efficiently than you would if you had no expectations at all. Indeed, if the unexpected stimulus is weak (perhaps flashed briefly or only on a dimly lit screen), then it may not trigger any response. In this way, priming can help spare us from distraction—by selectively helping us perceive expected stimuli but simultaneously hindering our perception of anything else.

In the example just considered, priming prepared the perceiver for a particular stimulus—the word *CAT*. But priming can also prepare you for a broad class of stimuli—for example, preparing you for any stimulus that appears in a particular location. Thus, you can pay attention to the top-left corner of a computer screen by priming just those detectors that respond to that spatial region. This step will make you more responsive to any stimulus arriving in that corner of the screen, but it will also take resources away from other detectors, making you less responsive to stimuli that appear elsewhere.

In fact, this process of pointing attention at a specific location can be demonstrated directly. In a typical experiment, participants are asked to point their eyes at a dot on a computer screen (e.g., Wright & Ward, 2008). A moment later, an arrow appears for an instant in place of the dot and points either left or right. Then, a fraction of a second later, the stimulus is presented. If it's presented at the place where the arrow pointed, the participants respond more quickly than they do without the prime. If the stimulus appears in a different location—so that the arrow prime was actually misleading—participants respond more slowly than they do with no prime at all. Clearly, the prime influences how the participants allocate their processing resources.

It's important to realize that this spatial priming is not simply a matter of cuing eye movements. In most studies the interval between the appearance of the prime and the arrival of the target is too short to permit a voluntary eye movement. But even so, when the arrow isn't misleading, it makes the task easier. Evidently, priming affects an internal selection process—it's as if your mind's eye moves even though the eyes in your head are stationary.

Perception in the Absence of Attention

As we've just seen, attention seems to do several things for us. It orients us toward the stimulus so that we can gain more information. It helps bind the input's features together so that we can perceive a coherent object. And it primes us so that we can perceive more efficiently and so that, to some extent, we're sheltered from unwanted distraction.

If attention is this important and has so many effects, then we might expect that the ability to perceive would be seriously compromised in the absence of attention. Recent studies indicate that this expectation is correct, and they document some remarkable situations in which people fail to perceive prominent stimuli directly in front of their eyes.

In one study, participants watched a video showing one group of players, dressed in white shirts, tossing a ball back and forth. Interspersed with these white-shirted players—and visible in the same video—a different group of players, in black shirts, also were tossing a ball. But, when participants were focusing on the white-shirted players, that was all they noticed. They were oblivious to what the black-shirted players were doing, even though they were looking right at them. Indeed, in one experiment, the participants failed to notice when someone wearing a gorilla suit strolled right through the scene and even paused briefly in the middle of the scene to thump on his chest (Figure 5.38; Neisser & Becklen, 1975; Simons & Chabris, 1999).

In a related study, participants were asked to stare at a dot in the middle of a computer screen while trying to make judgments about stimuli presented just a bit off of their line of view. During the moments when the to-be-judged stimulus was on the screen, the dot

5.38 SCIENTIFIC METHOD: Do people reliably see what's right in front of their eyes?

Method

1. Each participant watched a video of a group of players, some in white shirts and some in black shirts, tossing a basketball back and forth. They were instructed to keep track of the number of passes made by the players in white shirts.

2. During the 62-second video, a person in a gorilla suit walked into the middle of the game, turned and faced the camera, and thumped its chest, then continued out of the frame.

3. After the video, participants answered four written questions about whether anything unusual had happened in the film.

© 2005, Daniel J. Simons

Results: Intent on their task, half of the participants failed to see the person in the gorilla suit.

CONCLUSION: We can overlook even large, salient stimuli directly in front of us if we're paying attention to something else.

SOURCE STUDY: Simons, D.J., & Chabris, C. F. (1999). Gorillas in our midst: Sustained inattentional blindness for dynamic events. *Perception, 28,* 1059–1074.

at which the participants were staring changed momentarily to a triangle and then back to a dot. When asked about this event a few seconds later, though, the participants insisted that they'd seen no change in the dot. When given a choice about whether the dot had changed into a triangle, a plus sign, a circle, or a square, they chose randomly. Apparently, with their attention directed elsewhere, the participants were essentially "blind" to a stimulus that had appeared right in front of their eyes (Mack, 2003; Mack & Rock, 1998; also see Rensink, 2002; Simons, 2000; Vitevitch, 2003).

OTHER MODALITIES

We've almost finished our discussion of perception, but before we bring the discussion to a close, there's just one more topic to explore. Throughout this chapter, we've examined visual perception and how we recognize the things we see. What about the other modalities? How do we hear—and understand—the speech that reaches our ears or the music we listen to? How do we perceive smells and tastes? How do we experience the warmth of the sun or the cold of an icy wind?

Of course, the various senses differ in many ways. Still, let's not lose track of how much the different sense modalities have in common. For example, as we noted in Chapter 4, all of the modalities are powerfully influenced by contrast effects, so sugar tastes sweeter after a sip of lemon juice, just as red seems more intense after looking at green. Likewise, each sense is influenced by the *others*—and so what we taste is influenced by the smells that are present, how a voice sounds depends on whether it's coming from a face that looks friendly, and so on.

Many of the phenomena discussed in this chapter also have direct parallels in other senses. For example, we've examined the perceiver's role in organizing the visual input, and similar points can be made for hearing: Just as vision must parse the input, deciding where one object ends and the next begins, our sense of hearing must parse the stream of *sounds,* deciding where one note ends and the next begins or where one word ends and the next begins. And, just as in vision, the input for hearing is sometimes ambiguous—fully compatible with more than one parsing. This was evident, for example, in the mondegreens we discussed at the very start of this chapter—including the celebrated misperception of Jimi Hendrix's song "Purple Haze." The song contained the lyric, "'Scuse me while I kiss the sky," but many people mis-heard the lyric as "…while I kiss this guy." The two key phrases ("the sky" and "this guy") are virtually identical acoustically, and the difference between them is therefore "in the ear of the beholder"; no wonder, then, that the phrase was often misperceived.

Hearing, like vision, also requires us to *group* together separate elements in order to hear coherent sequences. This requirement is crucial, for example, for the perception of music. We must group together the notes in the melody line, perceiving them separately from the notes in the harmony, in order to detect the relationships from one note to the next within the melody; otherwise, the melody would be lost to us.

Likewise, our recognition of sounds seems to begin with the input's acoustic features, just as the recognition of objects begins with the input's visual features. Our analysis of sound features is supplemented by top-down (knowledge-driven) processing, just as it is for vision, and the relevant knowledge for hearing includes the hearer's knowledge about the context as well as her broader knowledge about the world. (For more on speech perception, see Chapter 9.)

And hearing, like vision, is powerfully influenced by attention (Figure 5.39). Indeed, some of the classic work on attention is done with auditory inputs and yields data consistent with the findings we reviewed for vision: When our attention is focused on one auditory input, we hear remarkably little from other inputs. Thus, if we're listening to one conversation at a cocktail party, we'll be able to hear that the unattended voice behind us is loud rather than soft, a male's rather than a female's; but we'll have no idea what the unattended voice is actually saying or even whether the unattended speech

5.39 Attentional limits Attention is crucial for hearing, just as it is for vision. This is evident in the many studies showing that driving performance (e.g., speed of reacting to red lights) is impaired when the driver is on the phone. In one study, some participants were told to drive eight miles down the freeway and exit at a rest stop; during this simple task, they were talking with a passenger in the car. A second group of participants had the same driving task, but they were talking on a cell phone. The results showed a huge difference between the groups. Why? The passenger in the vehicle usually adjusted her conversation to accommodate changes in driving—such as not speaking while the driver navigated an obstruction. In contrast, people talking to the drivers on the cell phone kept talking because they weren't aware when the driving became tricky.

Sucess in simple highway navigation (percentage)

Drive while talking with a passenger

Drive while conversing via cell phone

makes any sense at all. This point has been documented by studies that require participants to pay attention to a voice arriving (through headphones) in one ear, while another (unattended) voice is presented to the other ear. In this setup, participants grasp virtually none of the content of the unattended message. In one classic study, the participants couldn't even tell whether the speaker on the unattended ear was reading the passage backward or forward (Cherry, 1953; Reisberg, 2010).

But let's be clear that participants aren't totally deaf to an unattended message. If, for example, this message contains the participants' own names, a substantial number of participants will detect this significant stimulus (Moray, 1959). Participants may also detect other personally relevant stimuli, such as the name of a favorite restaurant or the title of a book they've just read (Conway, Cowan, & Bunting, 2001; Wood & Cowan, 1995). The reason for this is priming. The participant has presumably encountered these significant stimuli recently, so the relevant detectors are probably still "warmed up" and will respond even to a weak input. Just as in vision, therefore, the perception of a stimulus can be promoted either by expectations or by recent exposure; and either form of priming can offset the significant disadvantages associated with the absence of attention.

In short, then, many of the lessons we've learned about vision can be applied directly to the sense of hearing. This is true for many of our specific claims about vision; it's also true for our methodological claims—particularly the need for multiple levels of description. In hearing no less than in vision, it's immensely useful to approach the problems of perception in more than one way, with a close examination of function (what the processes achieve) and the biology (how the processes are implemented in the nervous system) if we are to understand how people come to know the world around them.

SOME FINAL THOUGHTS: SEEING, KNOWING, AND THE PERCEIVER'S ACTIVE ROLE

We began this chapter by noting the apparent simplicity of perception. The perceiver certainly doesn't feel as if she's doing any work or analysis. She simply opens her eyes and sees, easily recognizing the objects that are in view and instantly seeing where those objects are and what they're doing.

From this chapter and the last, however, we have seen that perception is complex. It demands an active perceiver—one who parses the input, separates figure and ground, makes a series of unconscious inferences, generates expectations with which to prime the relevant detectors, and more. Indeed, all of this activity draws us to one final issue. Common sense tells us there's a difference between seeing and knowing: "I know that shirt is blue, but in this light it looks green." "Those stripes make me look fatter than I really am." In cases like these, there's a clear distinction between appearances and what we know to be real.

In this chapter, though, we have blurred this line between seeing and knowing. We know, for example, that *CAT* is a common word; and this knowledge influences how we perceive the word if it's presented. We believe that most objects we encounter are illuminated from above, and this belief influences how we interpret Figure 5.32. But this pattern of results has its limits, and in some ways what we perceive seems well insulated from what we know or what we expect. This point is evident in the so-called

5.40 Illogical interpretations? The text emphasizes that our visual system seeks a logical interpretation of the sensory input. This effort is so strong that we seem to find "logical" interpretations even for inputs that are actually illogical (i.e., geometrically nonsensical).

impossible figures (Figure 5.12, and also Figure 5.40)—we know these figures can't possibly show three-dimensional forms, but we perceive them as three-dimensional anyhow. Likewise, even though we know the "triangle" in Figure 5.5 isn't really there, we still perceive it.

Plainly, then, there are limits on how knowledge and expectations influence what we see—and that cannot be surprising. After all, the mechanisms of perception evolved to provide us with accurate information about the world around us. To perform this function, perception must largely "stick to the facts" and not be pulled off course by our beliefs or expectations—or for that matter by our wishes and hopes.

However, the need for perception to be accurate takes nothing away from the complex interplay between perception and knowledge. We can appreciate this complexity both in the ordinary workings of perception and in a very special setting— the representation of reality in art. Consider Figure 5.41, a wall painting from Egypt created some 3,000 years ago. Why did the artist depict the figures as he did, with eyes and shoulders in front view and the rest of the body in profile? His fellow Egyptians were surely built like we are, so why didn't he draw them "correctly"? The answer seems to be that Egyptian artists drew not what they could see at any one moment or from any one position, but rather what they believed were their models' most enduring and characteristic attributes. They portrayed the various parts of the human body from the vantage point that shows each part in its most easily identifiable form: the front view for the eyes and shoulders, the profile for the nose and feet. The fact that these orientations are incompatible was evidently of no concern to the artist—what mattered was that he'd drawn all of the parts as he knew them to be (Gombrich, 1961).

This example from the arts reminds us that perception and conception, seeing and knowing—even if different from each other—interact in complex ways. In a real sense, therefore, we must connect our discussion of perception to our discussion of what we've learned over our lifetimes—what we know, what we remember, and how we think.

5.41 Horemhab offering wine to Annubis, ca. 1339–1304 B.C.E. The conventions of Egyptian art required the main parts of the human body to be represented in their most characteristic view. Thus, heads are shown in profile and arms and legs from the side; but eyes are depicted in full-face view, as are the shoulders and chest.

FORM PERCEPTION: WHAT IS IT?

- The recognition of forms begins with the detection of simple *features*; and in fact the rapid detection of features can be demonstrated in *visual search tasks*. However, recognition depends on more than a mere checklist of features. This point is evident, for example, in the fact that the catalog of features contained within a stimulus display depends on how the perceiver has *organized* the display.

- To organize the input, the perceiver must parse the visual scene. This process involves the segregation of figure and ground. These interpretive steps seem broadly logical, and so (for example) cannot contain contradictions and cannot appeal to coincidence.

NETWORK MODELS OF PERCEPTION

- According to many theorists, recognition depends on *feature nets*—networks of detectors with feature detectors serving as the initial level in the network. These networks rely on data-driven and knowledge-driven processes, and interactions within the network guarantee that the network's output will provide the best possible compromise among the various rules governing the network's functioning.

- The recognition of more complex objects may require an extra layer of analysis in the feature network—a layer concerned with the identification of *geons*. Once the viewer has identified the geons and how they're connected to each other, a subsequent step is needed to identify the object that's being perceived. This last step can fail—and this is the problem in *visual agnosia*.

THE NEUROSCIENCE OF VISION

- The neural processes underlying perception involve various specialized subsystems. On the retina, *parvo cells* are sensitive to color differences and seem crucial for the perception of pattern and form; *magno cells* are color blind and play an essential role in motion detection and depth perception. In the visual cortex, different types of cells respond to specific aspects of the stimulus. These different analyses go on in parallel; the cells that analyze the forms within the visual input are doing their work at the same time that other cells are analyzing the motion and still others are analyzing the colors.

- Information from the visual cortex is transmitted to the temporal cortex, in an area called the *"what" system;* and to the parietal cortex, in an area called the *"where" system*. The "what" system is crucial for our identification of visual objects; the "where" system tells us where a stimulus is located.

- How do we integrate the results provided by these different neural subsystems? Some evidence suggests that this *binding problem* is solved, in part, by neural synchrony. If, for example, the neurons detecting a *vertical* line are firing in synchrony with those signaling *movement*, then these attributes are registered as belonging to the same object. Synchronized neural firing, therefore, may be the nervous system's way of representing the fact that different attributes are actually parts of a single object.

PERCEPTUAL CONSTANCY

- People perceive a stable world even though changes in our viewing circumstances cause alteration in the stimuli that reach us. For example, we achieve size constancy even though the sizes of the images cast on our retinas are determined both by the size of the distal object and by viewing distance. We achieve shape constancy even though the shape of the image on our retinas depends on viewing angle.

- Evidence suggests we achieve constancy through *unconscious inference*, which involves taking viewing circumstances (distance, viewing angle, illumination) into account by means of a process that performs the same function as a simple calculation.

- The process of unconscious inference can sometimes lead us astray. If, for example, we misjudge the distance to an object, we'll make a mistaken inference about its size—and so produce an illusion of size caused by an error in perceiving distance.

DISTANCE PERCEPTION: WHERE IS IT?

- Our perception of depth depends on various *depth cues*, including *binocular disparity* and *monocular* (or *pictorial*) *cues* such as *interposition* and *linear perspective*. Another source of information is provided by the perceiver's motion, which produces the depth cues of *motion parallax* and optic flow.

MOTION PERCEPTION: WHAT IS IT DOING?

- It might seem that we perceive movement whenever an image moves across the retina—and in fact some cells in the visual cortex do respond to such movements on the retina. But retinal motion is only part of the story. In *apparent movement*, for example, an abrupt change in location produces a perception of movement even though there has been no actual motion (in the world or on the retina).

- When there is motion across the retina, perceivers need to determine whether the motion was produced by movement in the environment or merely by a change in their viewing position. Further complications arise because we not only detect motion, we also interpret it—as shown by the phenomenon of *induced motion*. The interpretation of motion is also essential in solving the *correspondence problem*.

PERCEPTUAL SELECTION: ATTENTION

- Perception is selective, and the selectivity is produced both by *orienting* and through central adjustments. These adjustments depend in part on our ability to prepare ourselves to perceive a particular stimulus by priming the relevant detectors and processing pathways. Thanks to this priming, perception is more efficient for the attended stimulus. Conversely, perception of unattended (and so unprimed) stimuli may be disrupted altogether, and several studies demonstrate how little we perceive of unattended stimuli.

OTHER MODALITIES

- In this chapter, we've focused on vision. But similar phenomena can be demonstrated in other sense modalities, thus implying that other modalities require explanations similar to those we've considered for vision. Hearing, for example, also seems to involve feature analysis; but it also requires parsing and interpretation of the input. Auditory stimuli, like visual stimuli, are often ambiguous; and in hearing, just as in vision, we perceive relatively little from unattended inputs.

 ONLINE STUDY TOOLS

Go to StudySpace, **wwnorton.com/studyspace**, to access additional review and enrichment materials, including the following resources for each chapter:

Organize
- Study Plan
- Chapter Outline
- Quiz+ Assessment

Learn
- Ebook
- Chapter Review
- Vocabulary Flashcards
- Drag-and-Drop Labeling Exercises
- Audio Podcast Chapter Overview

Connect
- Critical Thinking Activity
- Studying the Mind Video Podcasts
- Video Exercises
- Animations
- **ZAPS** Psychology Labs

6 Consciousness

At the next meeting of your psychology class, take a look at that guy in the last row. You know the one—The Sleeper: slumped over the desk, forehead in palm, eyes twitching beneath heavy lids, mouth emitting a soft snore. Not surprisingly, you might conclude that your slumbering peer is wasting time and money, disrespecting the professor, and distracting his classmates. But startled awake (and having read this chapter), The Sleeper might claim that he's actually been experiencing (and perhaps learning from) another state of consciousness.

If exploring consciousness is his goal, The Sleeper might want to try a path that wouldn't require missing class. He might follow the lead of Buddhist meditators, Hindu yogis, and Christian ascetics, all of whom alter their consciousness through religious practices. Within the secular world, he might alter his consciousness by undergoing hypnosis or having a few beers.

But do these various activities really alter consciousness? And what is consciousness, anyway? The dictionary definition, "a critical awareness of one's own situation and identity," might seem straightforward, but, as you'll see, consciousness is—and will probably continue to be—one of psychology's greatest mysteries.

We'll begin this chapter by discussing one of the reasons that consciousness is mysterious—namely, the difficulties in studying it. We'll start with the most obvious means of studying conscious experience: simply asking people to observe and describe their state of mind. As we'll see, there are important limitations on this research strategy, because much of our mental activity unfolds outside of our conscious awareness, leaving us completely unable to observe it, much less recount it to others.

Indeed, because so much of our cognition proceeds without consciousness, we'll need to ask what the function of conscious experience might be: If we can do so much without consciousness, why do we need it? Put differently, what can we—as conscious beings—do that zombies cannot?

We'll then turn to the question of how activity in the nervous system makes consciousness possible. The puzzle here begins with the fact that the nervous system is a physical object—it has a measurable mass, a particular temperature, and a certain location in space. Our conscious awareness, in contrast, has none of these properties, and so—despite the metaphors—we don't actually weigh more when we're struggling with a "weighty decision," and our temperature doesn't go down when we have a "cool idea." How is it possible for our biological machinery and its properties to give rise to our conscious states and their entirely different properties?

Finally, we'll turn to a broad exploration of different "levels" and "types" of conscious experience, including what happens when we sleep and dream, the effects of hypnosis or of religious experiences, and also the altered states associated with certain drugs.

INTROSPECTION AND THE FUNCTIONS OF CONSCIOUSNESS

consciousness Moment-by-moment awareness of ourselves, our thoughts, and our environment.

introspection The process of "looking within" to observe one's own thoughts, beliefs, and feelings.

The study of consciousness may be psychology's most difficult endeavor. This is not because we are methodologically inept, or lack the right high-tech gadgets. Instead, it is a direct consequence of what **consciousness** is—namely, our moment-by-moment awareness of ourselves, our thoughts, and our environment. Crucially, this awareness is entirely "personalized." As William James put it many years ago: "The universal conscious fact is not 'feelings and thoughts exist,' but 'I think' and 'I feel'" (James, 1890/1980; p. 221). Inevitably, then, this awareness is an entirely private matter. You cannot experience someone else's consciousness, nor they yours, and this raises a thorny issue: How can we find out about the nature or the contents of consciousness? As mentioned above, we'll start with what seems to be the most straightforward procedure, in which we ask people to **introspect**—to look within themselves and then describe their subjective experience.

Introspection is a useful method for psychology, but there are clear limits on what it can tell us. At the same time, though, these limits on introspection are interesting on their own. As we'll see, they provide information about the role of consciousness within the broader fabric of our mental lives. Let's get started by looking at what we *can* learn from introspection. We'll then turn to the limits and find out what we can learn from them.

Translating Thoughts into Words

Introspections are an enormously valuable source of evidence and are used in formal investigations as well as in a range of day-to-day settings. But there are many things that we can't learn by asking people to introspect. In some cases, this is because introspectors may choose not to reveal what they're really thinking. Suppose a friend asks you, "Does this dress make me look fat?" or "Did you like the pie I baked for you?" If you put a higher value on diplomacy than on honesty, your answers will be no and yes—even if that's not what you think (Figure 6.1). In other cases, you may want to be honest in reporting your thoughts and experiences but you simply don't have the vocabulary. For example, imagine you're trying to convey in words exactly what your mother looks like. You're likely to fail in this task because most of us lack the descriptors we might need to capture the exact curve of our mother's chin or the precise shape of her eyes. Likewise, imagine that you've met some poor soul who has never eaten chocolate and you're trying to tell her what chocolate tastes like. You might mention that it's sweet, although usually with bitter overtones; you might mention other foods that taste similar to chocolate. Despite these efforts, though, you might end up saying, "If you want to know what chocolate tastes like, you'll just have to try it for yourself."

In many other settings, people do seem able to find words that can convey their thoughts; but there's still a problem here, one that philosophers sometimes convey by means of the *inverted spectrum*: Imagine that some people are born with a strange mutation that makes their color vision the inverse of yours. When they look at a ripe tomato, they see a color that—if you experienced it—you'd call "violet" (Figure 6.2). Their experience when they look at a banana is the same as the experience that you'd have when looking at a pair of blue jeans. When they look at a clear sky (one that you would consider to be *blue*), they see a color that—if you experienced it—you would count as yellow.

How could we tell whether someone has an inverted spectrum? We could—at least in principle—examine the photopigments in the person's eyes and the neural response in his visual cortex. Perhaps those tests would tell us that biologically, his visual system responds to various wavelengths the same way everyone else's does. But does that mean his *subjective experience* is the same as ours? To answer this question, we'd need to know exactly how biological responses translate into subjective experiences—but we don't. Therefore, we can't rely on someone's biology to tell us if they have an "inverted spectrum" or not.

We also can't rely on someone's *behavior* to tell us whether he suffers from this odd visual problem. After all, from a young age, he'd have learned to call tomatoes *red* and bananas *yellow*—just like we do. He would agree that orange and yellow seem similar to each other (although his inner experience would be what we call blue and purple). He would agree that certain colors seem to be the opposites of each other—red and green, for example (although his inner experience would be what we call violet and green). No matter what test we construct, his responses to color and descriptions of color will match ours.

The inverted-spectrum problem is of course a contrived and peculiar case, but similar problems arise in many other settings. For example, if you say that mosquito bites *hurt,* and I say they *itch,* is this because we have different experiences in response to these bites or because we mean different things by the word *itch*? There's no way to know. Likewise, if you claim that your headaches are excruciating and I don't describe mine that way, does this mean your headaches are worse than mine? Or, perhaps, do you mean something different by the word *excruciating*? Again, there's no way to know.

To put these points more broadly, the problem here is that conscious experiences are *ineffable*—an old-fashioned term meaning "utterly indescribable." The problem exists not because people are shy or somehow oblivious to their own conscious states. Instead, conscious states are ineffable because there's often no way to ensure that your words, in describing your conscious experience, mean the same thing as anyone else's words. Do you mean the same thing by "blue" as they do? How about "itchy" or "excruciating"? With no way to answer these questions, we have to accept that the words themselves will

6.1 Honest reporting? People may shade their reports if asked "Do you like this dress?"

6.2 The inverted spectrum problem Imagine someone was born with a strange mutation that changed their color experience. When looking at pink flowers, they'd see a color that—if you experienced it— you'd call blue. They would still have learned to call this color "pink," however, so it would be impossible to detect the peculiar pattern of their color vision.

forever be inadequate as a way of describing consciousness—a profound limitation on what we can hope to learn from anyone's self-report.

The Cognitive Unconscious

Introspection is limited for another reason: There are many things going on in our minds that we are just not aware of. These unconscious events, by definition, are not detectable through introspection, and so cannot be revealed via self-report.

For example, what was your first-grade teacher's name? Odds are good that the answer to this question just popped into your mind, and that event leads us to ask: How did you manage this memory retrieval? How did you locate this bit of information within the vast warehouse of long-term memory? In fact, we have reason to believe you needed several steps to find this information; but you have no awareness of those steps—all you're aware of is the sought-after name.

Likewise, look around the room in which you're sitting. You can see various familiar objects, and you're immediately aware of the size, shape, and position of each one. As we saw in Chapter 5, however, your perception of the world requires several types of activity on your part—you must parse the input, separate figure from ground, and make inferences about aspects of the environment that are partly hidden from your view. However, you're unaware of all this activity; indeed, we used the term *unconscious inference* to describe some aspects of your perception. What you are aware of is just the "output" from these various processes—the perceptual world as you consciously experience it.

Considerations like these highlight the role of the **cognitive unconscious**—the name given to the considerable support machinery that makes our ordinary perception, memory, and thinking possible (after Kihlstrom, 1987; also Glaser & Kihlstrom, 2005). Let's be careful, though, not to confuse the cognitive unconscious with the idea that many people have of the unconscious mind—an idea derived from the thinking of Sigmund Freud, who we'll discuss at greater length in Chapter 15. According to Freud, the unconscious mind is, in effect, an adversary to the conscious mind: Each of these opponents has its own needs, its own goals, and its own style of operation. The unconscious mind, in this view, is constantly striving to assert itself while the conscious mind is constantly on guard against the unconscious mind's actions.

This Freudian conception is markedly different from the way modern scholars understand the cognitive unconscious. They believe instead that the cognitive unconscious is in no sense an adversary to conscious experience. Indeed, it seems misleading to speak of these as two separate "minds," each with its own identity—although that style of speaking is reasonable when discussing the Freudian view. Instead, the cognitive unconscious is—as we've said—merely the term we give for the broad set of background operations that make our experience possible.

Here's an analogy. Let's say you're sitting at your computer, surfing the Internet, and you click your mouse on a link. Your computer has to translate your mouse click into a numerical address, seek out the content at that address, download the content onto your computer, and then translate the HTML code or Java script to activate pixel patterns on your screen and thus create the images you see on the web page. All of these operations take place "behind the scenes," outside of your awareness. You, the user, are aware of only the initial mouse click and then the resulting images. Put differently, you're completely unaware of the *process* that brings the images to your screen; you're conscious only of the *product* created by that process—the images themselves.

In the same way, you're usually unaware of the processes that make your experience possible. You're aware only of the product created by those processes, and most of the

cognitive unconscious The mental support processes outside our awareness that make our perception, memory, and thinking possible.

time that's exactly what you want. You want to know what objects surround you; you generally have no reason to care about the processes that helped you perceive and identify these objects. You want to recall a past event, and you generally have no reason to worry about exactly how you're gaining that information. In these and many other examples, the cognitive unconscious provides you with the information you need while keeping the support machinery appropriately in the background.

Brain Damage and Unconscious Functioning

The existence of the cognitive unconscious sets limits on what we can learn from introspection: There's no point in asking people to introspect about, say, how their perceptual processes operate or how memory retrieval proceeds. These processes, it seems, take place outside of our awareness and so are invisible to introspection. But, in addition to this methodological point, the cognitive unconscious raises questions for us: How much can the cognitive unconscious accomplish? What sorts of mental operations can go forward without our conscious monitoring or guidance?

Some of the evidence relevant to these questions comes from people who have suffered brain damage. In chapter 8, for example, we'll consider people who suffer from *anterograde amnesia*—a profound disruption of their memories—usually caused by damage in and around the hippocampus. As we'll see, these individuals appear almost normal on tests of *implicit memory*—memory that is separate from conscious awareness. In one study, the patients were first presented with a list of words. Just a few minutes later, they were asked in one condition to recall these words and were given helpful hints: Was there a word on the earlier list that began with *CLA____*? Even with this cue, the patients failed to remember that the word *clasp* was on the earlier list—a result that confirms the diagnosis of amnesia. In another condition, though, the patients were tested differently. After being presented with the initial list, they were asked simply to come up with words in response to cues like this: "Can you think of any word that begins with *CLA____*?" We know that other patients who haven't recently seen the word *clasp* are likely to respond to this cue with words more frequently used in conversation (*class, clash, clap, clam*). However, the patients who had recently seen *clasp* did offer this word in response to the *CLA____* cue.

Notice, then, that these patients have no conscious recollection of the previous list—and so they fail to recall the list, after just a few minutes, even with helpful hints. At the same time, the patients do somehow remember the list; we know this because they're likely to produce the list words when asked to complete these word stems. These patients, in other words, show a pattern often referred to as "memory without awareness": They're influenced by a memory that they don't know they have. Clearly, therefore, some aspects of remembering—and some influences of experience—can go smoothly forward even in the absence of a conscious memory.

Similar conclusions are suggested by studies of a remarkable syndrome known as **blindsight,** which is produced by injuries in the visual cortex. Patients with this sort of brain damage are, for all practical purposes, blind. If asked to move around a room, they bump into objects; they do not react to flashes of bright light; and so on. In one experiment, however, these patients were asked to hold a card so that its orientation matched a "slot" directly in front of them. The patients failed in this task, confirming their apparent blindness. But then the patients were told to put the card into the slot, as if mailing a letter—and they did this perfectly (Figure 6.3; Rees, Kreiman, & Koch, 2002; Weiskrantz, 1986, 1997). Thus it seems that these patients can, in a sense, "see," but they're not aware of seeing—again a powerful indicator of how aspects of

blindsight The ability of a person with a lesion in the visual cortex to reach toward or correctly "guess" about objects in the visual field even though the person reports seeing nothing.

Method

1. The patient was asked to position her hand so that the angle of the card she was holding matched the slot.

Matching, slot at 0°

2. She was also asked to put the card in the slot, as if she were mailing a letter.

Mailing, slot at 0°

3. The researchers compared the patient's performance with that of two sighted control participants. All participants were tested with the slot at six different angles ranging from 0° to 150°.

Results

The circles-with-lines show how the blindsight patient fared at the matching and mailing tasks compared to a sighted control patient.

The blindsight patient's performance on the matching task was highly variable and included larger errors. But on the mailing task she performed as well as the controls.

CONCLUSION: People with blindsight may be able to make accurate, goal-directed movements to a target object, despite being unable to consciously perceive the target's orientation or dimensions.

SOURCE STUDY: Goodale, Milner, Jakobson, & Carey, 1991

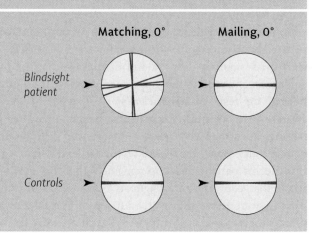

our mental lives can go forward without conscious experience. (For a related case, see Goodale & Milner, 2004.)

Unconscious Attributions

We've now seen that people can remember without realizing they're remembering—and so the processes of memory can to a large extent go forward without consciousness. Likewise, people can perceive without realizing they're perceiving—and so perception, too, can function without consciousness. Other evidence, drawn from people who are neurologically intact, also reveals unconscious mental processing and, intriguingly, documents the sheer complexity of what the unconscious processes can achieve.

In an early experiment by Nisbett and Schachter (1966), participants were asked to endure a series of electric shocks, with each shock slightly more severe than the one before. The question of interest was how far into the series the participants would go. What was the maximum shock they would voluntarily accept?

Before beginning the series of shocks, some of the participants were given a pill and told that it would have several side effects: shaky hands, butterflies in the stomach, irregular breathing, and the like. Of course, none of this was true. The pill was a placebo—a substance that had no medical effects. Even so, this inert pill was remarkably effective: Participants given the pill and told about its side effects were willing to accept a level of shock that was four times the strength of the control participants' maximum.

Why was the placebo so effective? Nisbett and Schachter proposed that their control participants—those who didn't receive the pill—noticed that their hands were shaking, their stomachs were upset, and so on. (These are standard reactions to electric shock.) The participants then used these self-observations as evidence in judging that they were quite uncomfortable in the experiment. It's as if participants said to themselves, "Oh, look, I'm trembling! I guess I must be scared. Man, these shocks must really be bothering me." This thinking led them to terminate the shock series relatively early. Placebo participants, in contrast, attributed these same physical symptoms to the pill. "Oh, look, I'm trembling! That's just what the experimenter said the pill would do. So I guess I can stop worrying about the trembling. Let me look for some other sign that the shock is bothering me." Consequently, these participants were less influenced by their own physical symptoms. They detected those symptoms but discounted them, attributing them to the pill rather than the shock. Essentially, they overruled the evidence of their own anxiety and so misread their own internal state (for related studies, see Bargh, 2005; Nisbett & Wilson, 1977; T. Wilson, 2002; T. Wilson & Dunn, 2004).

In this study, there's no question that the participants who received the pill (and the instructions about its side effects) behaved differently from other participants. It seems clear, therefore, that these participants were thinking about the pill. But they were entirely unaware of this thinking. When specifically asked why they had accepted so much shock, they rarely mentioned the pill. When asked directly, "While you were taking the shock, did you think about the pill at all?" they responded with answers like, "No, I was too worried about the shock to think of anything else."

It seems, therefore, that the participants' thinking about the pill was unconscious; and let's note the complexity of this thinking. The participants are observing "symptoms" (such as their own trembling hands), generating hypotheses about those symptoms, drawing conclusions, and then making decisions (about accepting more shock) based on these conclusions. As it turns out, in this case the participants reached erroneous conclusions because they were misled about the pill by the experimenter. But that takes nothing away from what they're doing intellectually—and unconsciously.

Mistaken Introspections

Let's pause to take stock. Introspections are certainly a valuable source of information, and for some purposes they are the only form of inquiry open to us. At the same time, there are limits on what we can learn from introspection. Some of the limits involve the *communication* of introspections—that is, difficulties in translating introspections into words. Other limits arise because much of our mental life takes place outside of our awareness, so that introspections are almost invariably *incomplete* as a source of information about our thoughts and beliefs.

Worse, our introspections are sometimes *wrong*—they systematically misrepresent our thoughts. This situation is evident in the electric shock experiment just described: Participants who took the pain pill in that study confidently reported that they weren't influenced by the pill, but the data say they *were*. Clearly, then, these participants didn't know what was going on in their own minds.

Related cases, also involving mistaken introspections, are easy to find. In one experiment (Nisbett & Wilson, 1977), shoppers announced that they preferred one nightgown over another because of the feel of the fabric. However, we know this self-report is mistaken because the nightgowns being compared in this study all had the same fabric! Moreover, the study's data tell us that the participants showed a strong preference for the nightgown that was in the rightmost position when the options were presented. But, if researchers asked the participants directly whether they were influenced by the positioning of their choices, they steadfastly insisted they were not. Hence, the participants were *not* influenced by the factor (fabric) they mentioned in their self-reports; but they *were* influenced by a factor (position) that they denied.

How should we think about this pattern? How could people be certain about the source of their own actions—and be *wrong*? One proposal is that the knowledge we each have about ourselves is in many cases the result of an after-the-fact reconstruction, created just moments after we acted in a certain way (or moments after we made a choice or reached a conclusion; Nisbett & Wilson, 1977). In other words, we might think we're recalling why we acted as we did just a few seconds ago; but instead we're (unconsciously) reasoning this way: "I know I did X. I believe that, in general, people do X because of Y. Therefore, I bet I did X because of Y." This process often leads us to correct conclusions because, in many cases, we have sensible beliefs about why people do what they do. Sometimes, though, we have an incomplete or inaccurate understanding of why people act in a certain way. In such cases, our reconstruction will lead us to the wrong conclusion. In this way, our self-understanding may be limited—even when we feel quite certain that we know the sources of our own feelings and behaviors.

The Function of Consciousness

We've now seen several indications of just how much can be accomplished without consciousness, and we've also considered some cases in which people think they know what's going on in their own minds but are wrong. Can we, from this base, gain some insights into when consciousness *is* needed, and what difference it makes if a process unfolds under conscious supervision rather than in the cognitive unconscious?

The answers to these questions hinge on the fact that the cognitive unconscious involves processes that are fast and effortless, but also *automatic* (Figure 6.4). In other words, the cognitive unconscious is not under our direct control. Instead, the cognitive unconscious is, in many settings, simply guided by habit and so performs the same operations now that it has performed in the past. In other settings, the cognitive unconscious is guided by cues in the situation itself—stimuli that indicate what the current response should be.

This absence of direct control is often just what we want, because our habits generally serve us well and we usually do want to respond in a fashion guided by current cues. Moreover, by relying on the cognitive unconscious, we exploit processes that are, as we've said, fast and effortless. But what if, in some circumstances, we want to resist past habits or present temptations? What if our current goals require that we launch some action that's novel? In such cases, we need to exercise *executive control* so that we can inhibit our habits, redirect our thoughts, and reset our priorities. And executive control, it turns out, may require consciousness.

We first discussed the idea of executive control in Chapter 3, and we'll have more to say about it in Chapter 11 when discussing *intelligence*. In that chapter we'll explore the idea that people differ in just how much control they have over their own mental lives—and that this difference, from one person to the next, plays a large part in making some people more intelligent than others. Our point for now is tied to our discussion of consciousness and, specifically, the notion that consciousness may be one of the prerequisites for executive control: To resist habit or temptation, to make sure we're moving toward our goals, we need to be aware of

6.4 Unconscious, automatic processes We're able to accomplish many activities—especially habitual activities—on "autopilot," so we have no need to consciously supervise some of our own actions.

what we're doing, what the situation is, and what our goals require. In other words, we need to be conscious—mindful of our actions and circumstances—in order to take control of our own thoughts, actions, and feelings.

We note, though, that consciousness doesn't guarantee control. Sometimes we are aware of what we're doing and would prefer to do something else, but we still give in to the temptation of the moment. (This is, for just one example, the familiar situation of the dieter who's aware that the second helping of pie is a bad idea but takes it anyhow.) Even so, consciousness is essential for executive control—a necessary first step toward directing our own mental lives.

THE NEURAL BASIS FOR CONSCIOUSNESS

No matter what we claim about the function of consciousness, the simple fact is that we *are* conscious. We each have a stream of inner experiences—and so we know what red looks like, or how it feels to be happy or tired or jittery; we know that we feel good when we're with certain people and uncomfortable when we're with others. What biological mechanisms make these experiences possible? How is it possible for the three pounds of tissue we call the *brain* to support consciousness of the surrounding world and consciousness of ourselves?

The Mind-Body Problem

As we noted at the chapter start, the brain is a physical object: It has a certain mass (about three pounds), a certain temperature (a degree or two warmer than the rest of the body), and a certain volume (a bit less than a half gallon). It occupies a specific position in space. Our conscious thoughts and experiences, on the other hand, are not physical objects and have none of these properties. An idea, for example, does not have mass or a specific temperature. A feeling of sadness, joy, or fear has neither volume nor a location in space.

How, therefore, is it possible for the brain to give rise to our thoughts? How can a physical entity give rise to nonphysical thoughts and feelings? Conversely, how can our thoughts and feelings *influence* the brain or the body? Imagine that you want to wave to a friend, and so you do. Your arm, of course, is a physical object with an identifiable mass. To move your arm, therefore, you need some physical force. But your initial idea ("I want to wave to Jacob") is not a physical thing with a mass or a position in space. How, therefore, could your (nonphysical) idea produce a (physical) force to move your arm?

The puzzles in play here all stem from a quandary that philosophers refer to as the **mind-body problem.** This term refers to the fact that the mind (and the ideas, thoughts, and feelings it contains) is an entirely different sort of entity from the physical body—and yet the two, somehow, seem to influence each other. How can this be? Roughly 400 years ago, the philosopher René Descartes (1596–1650) confronted these issues and concluded that the mind and the body had to be understood as entirely different species of things, separate from each other. The mind, in his view, was defined by the capacity for thought (Descartes' term was *res cogitans*—"thing that thinks"); the body, on the other hand, was defined by the fact that it had certain dimensions in physical space (*res extensa*—"extended thing").

mind-body problem The difficulty in understanding how the mind and body influence each other—so that physical events can cause mental events, and so that mental events can cause physical ones.

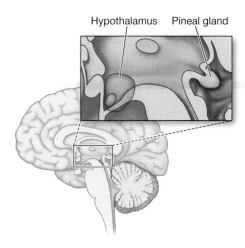

6.5 The mind-body connection?
According to Descartes, the mind and body communicate with each other through the pineal gland; but no modern researchers take this proposal seriously. The pineal gland is located near the center of the brain and just a bit behind the hypothalamus.

Descartes knew, however, that mind and body interact: Physical inputs (affecting the body) can cause experiences (in the mind), and, conversely, thoughts (in the mind) can lead to action (by the body). To explain these points, Descartes proposed that mind and body influence each other through the pineal gland, a small structure more or less at the center of the brain (Figure 6.5). This is the portal, he argued, through which the physical world communicates sensations to the mind, and the mind communicates action commands to the body.

Modern scholars uniformly reject Descartes' proposed role for the pineal gland, but the mystery that Descartes laid out remains. Scientists take it for granted that there's a close linkage between mind and brain; one often-quoted remark simply asserts that "the mind is what the brain does" (Minsky, 1986, p. 287). But, despite this bold assertion, we truly do not know how the physical events of sensation give rise to conscious experiences or how conscious decisions give rise to physical movements. We can surely talk about the *correspondence* between the physical and mental worlds—what physical events are going on when you experience "red" or "sad" or "anxious"—but we do not yet have a cause-and-effect explanation for how these two worlds are linked.

The Many Brain Areas Needed for Consciousness

How do we go about exploring the correspondence between mind and brain, between the mental world and the physical one? One way is to examine the brain status of people who have "diminished" states of consciousness—people who are anesthetized or even in comas. In each case, we can ask: What is different in the brains of these individuals that might explain why they're not conscious?

Research on this topic conveys a simple message: Many different brain areas seem crucial for consciousness, and so we can't expect to locate some group of neurons or some place in the brain that's the "consciousness center" and functions as if it's a light bulb that lights up when we're conscious and then changes its brightness when our mental state changes.

In fact, research in this arena suggests a distinction between two broad categories of brain sites, corresponding to two aspects of consciousness (Figure 6.6). First, there is

6.6 Some of the brain sites crucial for consciousness Consciousness depends on many brain sites, including the reticular formation—a structure that helps regulate the overall level of arousal in the brain—and the thalamus, a structure that seems to be a way station for many types of sensory input. The amygdala also plays a role; this structure seems crucial for regulating our emotional reaction to stimuli or ideas.

the level of alertness or sensitivity, independent of what the person is alert or sensitive *to*. We can think of this as the difference between being dimly aware of a stimulus (or an idea, or a memory) and being highly alert and totally focused on that stimulus. This aspect of consciousness is disrupted when someone suffers damage to certain sites in either the thalamus or the *reticular activating system* in the brain stem—a system that controls the overall arousal level of the forebrain and that also helps control the cycling of sleep and wakefulness (e.g., Koch, 2008).

Second, our consciousness also varies in its content. Sometimes we're thinking about our immediate environment; sometimes we're thinking about past events. Sometimes we're focused on an immediate task, and sometimes we're dreaming about the future. These various contents for consciousness require different brain sites, and so cortical structures in the visual system are especially active when we're consciously aware of sights in front of our eyes; cortical structures in the forebrain are essential when we're thinking about some stimulus that is no longer present in our environment, and so on (Figure 6.7).

In fact, this broad distinction between the degree of awareness or sensitivity and the content of consciousness may be useful for us in thinking about variations in consciousness, as suggested by Figure 6.8 (after Laureys, 2005; also Koch, 2008). In dreaming, for example, we are conscious of a richly detailed scene, with its various sights and sounds and events, and so there's a well-defined content—but our sensitivity to the environment is low. (We'll say more about dreaming later in the chapter.) By contrast, in the peculiar state associated with sleepwalking, we're sensitive to certain aspects of the world—so we can, for example, navigate through a complex environment—but we seem to have no particular thoughts in mind, so the content of our consciousness is not well defined.

Neural Correlates of Consciousness

Further insights into the biological basis for consciousness come from studies of the so-called **neural correlates of consciousness**—specific states of the brain that correspond to the exact content of someone's conscious experience. In one study, for example, the researchers exploited a phenomenon known as *binocular rivalry* (Tong, Nakayama, Vaughan, and Kanwisher, 1998). In the study, one picture is placed in front of one of a person's eyes and another, entirely different picture is placed in front of her other eye. In this setup, the visual system is unable to handle both stimuli at once, or to fuse the stimuli into a single complex perception. Instead, the visual system seems to flip-flop between the stimuli so that, for a while, the person is aware of only one picture, then for a while aware of only the other, and so on. Notice therefore that this is a setting in which the physical situation doesn't change—the two pictures are always present. What is changing is the person's conscious experience—that is, which picture she's aware of. This allows us to ask what changes take place in the brain when the experience changes.

In this study, the researchers placed a picture of a *face* in front one of the participant's eyes and a picture of a *house* in front of the other eye. We know from many other studies that when people are looking at *faces*, neuroimaging reveals high levels of activity in a brain region called the fusiform face area (FFA). We also know that when people are looking at *houses*, there's a lot of activity in a brain region known as the parahippocampal place area (PPA).

6.7 Two separate aspects of consciousness At any given moment, a radio might be receiving a particular station either dimly or with a clear signal. Likewise, at any given moment the radio might be receiving a rock station, or a jazz station, or the news. These two dimensions—the signal sensitivity and the station choice—correspond roughly to the two aspects of consciousness described in the text.

neural correlates of consciousness Specific brain states that seem to correspond to the content of someone's conscious experience.

6.8 Variations in consciousness According to some authors, consciousness has two separable aspects: the level of arousal or overall alertness, and the clarity or specificity of its content.

6.9 Brain activity and awareness (A) An fMRI scan of a subject looking at faces; activation levels are high in a brain area called the fusiform face area (FFA). (B) A scan of the same subject looking at pictures of places; now activity levels are high in the parahippocampal place area (PPA). (C) A comparison of the activity in these two brain areas when a picture of a face is in front of one eye and a picture of a house is in front of the other eye. When the subject becomes aware of the face, activation is higher in the FFA. When the subject becomes aware of the house, activation in the PPA increases. Clearly, the activation level reflects what the subject is aware of and not just the pattern of incoming stimulation.

But what exactly does this brain activity—in the FFA or PPA—indicate? If these brain areas respond simply to the available stimuli, then the pattern of activity should be constant in the Tong et al. procedure. The stimuli, after all, were present all the time. But if these brain areas reflect the participants' conscious perception, then activity should fluctuate—with a change in brain activity each time the binocular rivalry produces a new perception.

In the Tong et al. study, participants pressed buttons to indicate at each moment which picture they were aware of seeing—the house or the face. At the same time, the researchers used fMRI to keep track of the activity levels in the FFA (again, normally responsive to faces) and the PPA (normally responsive to places).

The results are summarized in Figure 6.9. Immediately before the moments in which the participant reported a conscious switch from seeing the face to seeing the house, activity in the FFA went down and activity in the PPA went up. At moments in which the participant reported the reverse switch, the activity levels in these two brain areas showed the opposite pattern.

Apparently, then, activity levels in the FFA or PPA change whenever the participant's conscious experience changes. Put differently, activity in the FFA doesn't indicate "a face is in view." Instead, activity here seems to indicate "the participant is aware of seeing a face." Likewise for the PPA; activity here seems to indicate "the participant is aware of seeing a house." In this fashion, it does seem that that we can use brain scans to identify some of the biological correlates of specific conscious states. (For related results, including some with other species, see Kim & Blake, 2005; Haynes, 2009; Koch, 2008; Logothetis, 1998; Rees & Frith, 2007.)

A different example concerns—remarkably—the conscious sensation of "free will." In a classic study, participants watched a dot moving in a circular pattern on a computer screen, and they were asked to move their hands occasionally (Libet, 1983; also see Haggard & Eimer, 1999; Wegner, 2002). It was up to the participants to decide *when* they would move their hands; but they were asked to note the dot's position at the exact moment when they chose to make this movement, and later they were asked to report this position. This response tells us in essence when the conscious decision to move actually took place, and we can compare that moment to when the movement itself occurred.

Not surprisingly, there was a brief gap—about 200 milliseconds—between the moment of decision and the actual movement. It took a fraction of a second, it seems, to translate the decision into an action (Figure 6.10). The real surprise was that recordings of brain activity showed a marked change—a so-called *readiness potential*—almost a half-second *before* participants reported any awareness of a decision to move. In other words, the participants' brains had launched the action well before the participants themselves felt they had initiated the action. This result seems to imply that the feeling of "I will move my hand now" is not the *cause* of brain activity, as common sense might suggest. Instead, it's the *result* of brain activity—in particular, brain activity in the pre-motor and anterior cingulate cortices (Lau et al., 2004). In other words, the "decision to move" and the initiation of action happen outside of awareness, and the person (consciously) learns only a moment later what they've just decided. (For some complications and possible challenges to this result, see Banks & Isham, 2009; Desmurget et al., 2009; Haggard, 2009; Obhi, Planetta, & Scantlebury, 2009.)

The Global Workspace Hypothesis

The studies we've looked at so far tell us something about where in the brain we can find activity crucial for consciousness; and as we've seen, there plainly is no single brain site that serves as the "seat of consciousness." The studies also tell us something about *when* the brain changes that give rise to consciousness actually occur. However, we want to go beyond merely specifying this where and when. We also want to learn how these brain regions might work together to produce the properties we associate with consciousness and to provide a biological base for the claims we made earlier about the *function* of consciousness.

In approaching these issues, we need to start with some basic facts. As we saw in chapter 3, each area of the brain has a highly specialized function. One brain region is specialized for controlling hand movements, another for processing auditory inputs, and still another for analyzing visual stimuli. Then, within each of these regions, we find further specialization. For example, the various aspects of visual perception depend on distinct brain areas, one specialized for perceiving color, another for perceiving movement, and so on. Each of these areas does its own job, and the activity in each area is highly transient: The neurons respond to the current inputs and then, when their immediate task is done, they cease responding so they're ready for the next input or the next task.

For many purposes, though, we need to sustain the activity in these various systems (e.g., for prolonged scrutiny). We also need to integrate the activity of the various systems into a coherent whole. What makes both of these steps possible is *attention*—probably implemented through mechanisms in the prefrontal cortex, but then influencing activity in many other brain sites (Maia & Cleeremans, 2005). The mechanisms of attention can amplify the activity within a specific neural system, and they can also sustain that activity.

1 Readiness potential   **2** Awareness of decision   **3** Action

−535 msec   −204 msec   0 msec

6.10 The brain basis for the feeling of free will Research participants chose when to move their hand, but noted the dot's position at the moment of their decision. Researchers were, however, able to document a "readiness potential" in the participant's brain way before the (conscious) decision to move.

Attention also seems to link the activity of different neural systems, binding them into a single representation. Thus, for example, a red moving object in front of our eyes will trigger a response in one brain area in which cells are sensitive to motion as well as in an area in which cells are sensitive to color. If we aren't paying attention to this object, these two neural responses will be independent of each other. But if we are paying attention to it, the neurons in these two systems fire in synchrony (see chapter 5). And when neurons fire in this coordinated way, the brain seems to register this as a linkage among the different processing areas. As a result, these attributes are bound together so that we correctly perceive the stimulus as a unified whole.

This coordination of separate neural systems requires communication among distinct brain areas, and this communication is made possible by "workspace neurons" that literally connect one area of the brain to another. However, the communication, and thus the information carried by the workspace neurons, is selective, and so it's certainly not the case that every bit of neural activity gets linked to every other bit. Instead, it's typically the signals from more active areas that are transmitted to other sites. Bear in mind, though, that attention can be used to amplify activity and so can govern which brain areas are more activated and which are less. In this way, the information flow is controllable by virtue of what the person chooses to pay attention to.

These points are the backdrop for the **global workspace hypothesis** about consciousness. According to this hypothesis the integrated neural activity made possible by the workspace neurons provides the biological basis for consciousness. Activity in these neurons does not specify the *content* of consciousness; that content is instead represented in more specialized brain areas. Thus, when you're aware of the blue sky overhead, that "blueness" is represented by the appropriate pattern of firing in your visual cortex; when you're thinking about how cold your toes are, the "coldness" is represented by firing in somatosensory areas. What the workspace neurons do, however, is glue these bits together, creating a unified experience and allowing the exchange of information from one module to the next. (For several variants of this general hypothesis, see Baars, 2002; Baars & Franklin, 2003; Cooney & Gazzaniga, 2003; F. Crick & Koch, 2003; Dennett, 2001; Engel & Singer, 2000; Maia & Cleeremans, 2005; Roser & Gazzaniga, 2004; Tononi, 2004.)

The broad proposal, therefore, is that stimuli or ideas become conscious when they're linked to each other in a dynamic, coherent representation made possible by the workspace neurons and supported by attention. This hypothesis helps us understand why our conscious experience feels unitary and coherent. We aren't, after all, separately aware of redness and movement and roundness. Instead, we're aware of a single experience in which the red apple rolls slowly by. This coherence, of course, is precisely what the workspace allows—one representation, constructed from the coordinated activity of many processing components.

Likewise, we aren't conscious of every aspect of our experience—we can focus on the rose's color and fail to notice its thorns. But, of course, we can usually choose what we're going to focus on (so that, when picking up the rose, we might decide to pay attention to those thorns). These observations are easily accommodated by the workspace hypothesis. As we've said, the information carried by the workspace neurons is selective (so might not carry the information, at least at the start, about the thorns) but is shaped by how someone focuses their attention (and so, with a change in focus, would highlight the thorns).

Also bear in mind that the workspace neurons allow us to maintain a mental representation in an active state for an extended period of time, so that we can continue thinking about a stimulus or an idea after the specific trigger is removed. In this way, we can link the workspace to a form of memory known as *working memory*—the memory that you keep ideas in while you're working with them (chapter 8). We can also link

global workspace hypothesis A hypothesis about the neural basis of consciousness. It proposes that specialized neurons, called workspace neurons, give rise to consciousness by allowing us to link stimuli or ideas in dynamic, coherent representations.

it to the brain areas associated with this type of memory—specifically, the prefrontal cortex (Goldman-Rakic, 1987; also see McIntosh, Rajah, & Lobaugh, 1999).

Finally, the workspace hypothesis may also help with other puzzles—including the *variations* in consciousness that we sometimes experience. For example, when we're asleep (and not dreaming), we aren't conscious of time passing, of any ongoing stream of thought, or of many events taking place in our vicinity. Why is this? Evidence suggests that when we're in sleep (without dreaming), the communication breaks down between different parts of the cortex so that, even though the sleeping brain is intensely active, the various activities aren't coordinated with each other. The suggestion, of course, is that this communication (mediated by the neuronal workspace) is crucial for consciousness, so it makes sense that sleeping people, having temporarily lost this communication, aren't conscious of their state or their circumstances (Massimini et al., 2005).

Likewise, when someone is anesthetized (e.g., before surgery), their brain remains active. Nonetheless, the person is not conscious—after all, that's the *point* of anesthesia! So how should we think about the anesthetized brain? According to one recent review, the "loss of consciousness is associated with a breakdown of cortical connectivity and thus of integration" (Alkire, Hudetz, & Tononi, 2008, pg. 879)—a proposal, again, in line with the idea that consciousness depends on communication and coordination among distinct neural systems.

Overall, then, the global workspace hypothesis—rooted in psychology, philosophy, and neuroscience—links several lines of argument. These include claims about the subjective "coherence" of consciousness, research on the neural correlates of consciousness, and evidence from people who are sleeping or anesthetized. We should acknowledge that there is still controversy about some of these points (e.g., N. Block, 1997, 2001; Chalmers, 1995; Kinsbourne, 2000); but even so, the workspace hypothesis appears enormously promising as an account of how our brains make consciousness possible.

VARIETIES OF CONSCIOUSNESS

The workspace hypothesis, it seems, helps us understand some of the variations in conscious experience. In particular, it explains why we aren't conscious (despite considerable brain activity) during sleep, and likewise why an anesthetized patient isn't conscious. But sleep and anesthesia are just two of the ways our conscious state varies. It's often alleged that *hypnosis* also creates an altered state of consciousness, and that various religious practices can as well. Many drugs—including several drugs taken for recreational purposes—also change a person's conscious state. Let's take a closer look at these variations in conscious experience, starting with the variation that every person experiences virtually every day: the contrast between being asleep and awake.

Sleep

Across the hours of each day, the arousal level of the brain rises and falls. Most of this variation is controlled by a tiny cluster of about 20,000 cells located in the hypothalamus (Mistlberger, 2005). These cells are responsible for controlling many rhythms in the body, including a rhythm of arousal increases and decreases spanning roughly a 24-hour period. This is why the sleep-wake rhythm is called *circadian*—from the Latin *circa* ("nearly") and *dies* ("day") (Figure 6.11).

(A)

6.11 Circadian rhythms (A) When we change time zones, we can get jet lag due to being forced out of one circadian rhythm and into another. Jet lag tends to be worse when traveling from west to east. That's because the body's natural rhythms (B) tend to be somewhat longer than 24 hours. So flying from east to west—say, New York to Chicago—is easier because it lengthens our day by one hour (due to the shift from Eastern to Central time), and this change is in line with the body's natural tendency.

(B)

alpha rhythm A pattern of regular pulses, between 8 and 12 per second, visible in the EEG of a person who is relaxed but awake and typically has her eyes closed.

beta rhythm The rhythmic pattern in the brain's electrical activity often observed when a person is actively thinking about some specific topic.

delta rhythm The rhythmic pattern in the brain's electrical activity often observed when a person is in slow-wave sleep.

SLEEP AND WAKE CYCLES

The rhythm of sleep and wake, as just noted, is controlled largely by circuits in the hypothalamus and mediated by the hormone *melatonin*, produced within the pineal gland (e.g., Zhdanova & Wurtman, 1997). These circuits are in turn controlled by various external influences, including input from the optic nerve that tells the system whether it's day or night (Gooley & Saper, 2005) and also the timing of meals, a further source of regimentation in the body's internal rhythms.

Variations in arousal level are also regulated (indirectly) by the cerebral cortex. This effect is evident in the fact that we often arouse ourselves in response to relatively complex stimuli, such as the sound of our own name or thoughts about a difficult emotional problem. The neurons needed to recognize these stimuli are located in the cortex; but when a significant stimulus is detected, these brain areas send signals to the reticular activating system, promoting arousal throughout the brain.

Whatever the source, we can track the brain's arousal by means of an electroencephalogram, or EEG—a recording of voltage changes occurring at the surface of the scalp. These voltage changes reflect electrical activity in the cortex just beneath the scalp. Figure 6.12 shows an EEG record from a participant who was awake and in a relaxed state with eyes closed; the record shows an **alpha rhythm**—a regular waxing and waning of electrical potential at a rhythm of roughly 8 to 13 cycles per second (Hz). This rhythm is characteristic of the awake-but-resting state and is found in most mammals.

The brain activity changes when someone attends to some stimulus with his eyes open, or when his eyes are closed but he's thinking actively (e.g., doing mental arithmetic). Now the person is likely to show a **beta rhythm**—the voltage is lower and the frequency is higher (14 to 35 Hz); in this state, the pattern of ups and downs in the EEG is difficult to discern.

What about someone who's falling asleep? When you first become drowsy and go to bed, your EEG pattern tends to develop a clear alpha rhythm. You're now likely to fall into a light, dozing sleep from which you can easily awaken if there's some outside noise. You're also likely at this point to experience vivid but fleeting imagery—so-called *hypnagogic imagery*. All of these traits mark what's called the "gateway" to sleep—sleep's stage 1.

After a few minutes in stage 1, your sleep deepens. Over the next hour, you pass through stage 2, which is marked by several distinctive patterns in the brain activity: periods of 1- to 2-second bursts of rapid brain-wave activity, bursts called *sleep spindles,* and very high-amplitude waves known as *k complexes* (Cash et al., 2009). Sleep gets deeper still as you move into stage 3, which is marked by the emergence of slow, large waves in your EEG in a **delta rhythm**—four waves per second (or fewer). Eventually, the delta waves come to dominate the EEG pattern; now you're said to be in stage 4 sleep—and because stages 3 and 4 are both characterized by delta waves, they're often referred to as **slow-wave sleep.** Indeed, stages 3 and 4 are so similar to each other that, in recent years, many sleep researchers have argued that they should be collapsed into one unified stage.

Across all four sleep stages, your heart rate and breathing slow down. Your eyes drift slowly and in an uncoordinated way. By the time you reach stage 4, you're virtually immobile, often curled into a fetal position, and hard to wake up. Indeed, trying to wake someone up from slow-wave sleep takes sustained effort; the person protests, seems disoriented, mumbles incoherently, or thrashes around even if shaken or shouted at. Some people enter this confused half-sleep, half-aware state spontaneously, and this accounts for such sleep disturbances as sleepwalking (Hauri, 1977).

Depending on his or her age, a sleeper typically spends about 20 to 30 minutes in slow-wave sleep. After that, the nature of sleep changes dramatically as the person enters **REM sleep.** His heart rate and respiration rate quicken, almost as if he were awake and exercising. His EEG returns to the high-frequency activity associated with wakefulness (Jouvet, 1967). His eyes start to move in a distinctive way—periodic bursts of jittering back and forth under closed eyelids. These are the rapid eye movements (REM) that give this sleep state its name.

According to nearly all physiological signs, a person in REM sleep seems like he should be awake and alert; an EEG shows an active brain. But even so, the person is sound asleep; in fact, this is the sleep stage in which the person is least sensitive to external stimulation (Williams, Tepas, & Morlock, 1962). Also during this sleep stage, the person's skeletal muscles show a sudden paralysis. In fact, if someone happens to wake up during a REM period, he's susceptible to a frightening but harmless stage known as *sleep paralysis* (Hauri, 1977), in which the muscular paralysis of REM sleep persists for a few moments past awakening, leaving the person conscious but temporarily unable to move.

Notice, then, that REM sleep is characterized by a series of contrasts: The brain is active, but the body is immobile. The cortex is energized, but the skeletal muscles are completely inactive. Because of these contrasts, REM sleep is sometimes also called *paradoxical sleep.*

The first REM period of a night's sleep is the shortest; and once it's complete, people move back through lighter stages of sleep toward deeper stages (Figure 6.13). After

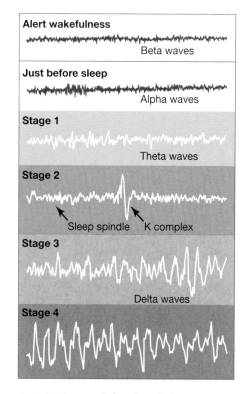

6.12 EEG record showing alpha waves, beta waves, and delta waves We can distinguish the different stages of sleep with EEG recording, which reveals the different patterns of brain activity associated with each stage.

slow-wave sleep A term used for both stage 3 and stage 4 sleep; characterized by slow, rolling eye movements, low cortical arousal, and slowed heart rate and respiration.

REM sleep Sleep characterized by rapid eye movements, EEG patterns similar to wakefulness, speeded heart rate and respiration, near-paralysis of skeletal muscles, and highly visual dreams.

6.13 REM and slow-wave sleep The alternation of slow-wave and REM sleep periods throughout the night (REM periods are in red). Rapid eye movements begin as the person repeatedly emerges from deeper sleep to the level of stage 2. More vivid and visual dreams are recalled after awakening from REM sleep.

another 90 to 100 minutes, a second REM period ensues, and this pattern of alternating REM and non-REM sleep periods continues throughout the night. An average night includes 4 to 5 REM periods, gradually increasing in length, and the final REM period of the night lasts up to 45 minutes (Hobson, 1995).

THE NEED FOR SLEEP

Why does sleep have such a complex architecture, with different stages and different types of activity? What functions do these individual stages serve? Surprisingly, the answers are still unknown.

It is clear that sleep does have some function: If people are deprived of sleep, their alertness decreases, they complain of feeling poorly, their mood suffers, and they do less well on mental and physical tasks (Figure 6.14). They express a desire to get to bed as soon as they can; and when they do get to bed, they rapidly fall asleep (e.g., Dinges, Rogers, & Baynard, 2005).

What's more, people do not just need sleep; they need adequate amounts of both slow-wave and REM sleep. If, for example, people are selectively awakened throughout the night during stages 3 and 4, they spend more time the next night in these sleep stages (Bonnet, 2005; Webb, 1972). Likewise, if they're awakened during REM periods throughout the night, they'll try to make up the lost REM sleep on subsequent nights and spend more and more of the night in REM sleep as the number of days of REM deprivation increases. This pattern of *REM rebound* is also visible in people who have recently stopped taking medications that selectively suppress REM sleep—medications that include some commonly prescribed sleeping pills. When people stop taking these pills, they may sleep less overall (because they're no longer being tugged toward sleep by the pills); but when they do sleep, they're likely to spend an increased number of minutes in REM.

Studies also suggest that sleep deprivation—or even just REM sleep deprivation—leads to a compromised immune system, leaving the organism susceptible to bacterial invasion and therefore more vulnerable to a range of illnesses (Everson & Toth, 2000). Indeed, just several nights of partial sleep deprivation can decrease the body's immune response by half (Spiegel, Sheridan, & Van Cauter, 2002). Sleeplessness also creates other health risks; for example, it's strongly associated with automobile and workplace

6.14 Sleep deprivation Many studies have examined the effects of sleep deprivation, although not using the procedure suggested in the cartoon. In all cases, though, the effects of sleep deprivation are striking—including effects on someone's ability to think well.

6.15 Sleep needs across the life span People differ in how much sleep they need, and this need changes as the person grows and matures. Infants need a huge amount of sleep, much of it REM sleep. The elderly need less sleep and less REM.

accidents (e.g., Walsh, Dement, & Dinges, 2005). Fortunately, though, sleeplessness is easily treated—by letting the person get back to bed! Indeed, even when a person has trouble falling or staying asleep, the problem is easily treatable. Many cases of insomnia respond readily to simple sleep regimens: making the bedroom quiet and dark; keeping bedtimes and waking times constant; refraining from stimulants like caffeine and nicotine after the evening meal; using the bed only for sleep, and getting out of bed if sleep does not come within 15–20 minutes.

How much sleep do we need? The answer varies from person to person, and it certainly varies with age (Figure 6.15; Iglowstein, Jenni, Molinari, & Largo, 2003; Roffwarg, Muzio, & Dement, 1966). Infants take brief naps throughout the day; they average about 16 hours of sleep each day and spend half of that time in REM sleep. As children age, they need appreciably less sleep and spend less time in REM periods and more time in slow-wave sleep, which is apparently important for growth and development. Adolescents average 8 hours per night, 2 of which are REM sleep. Senior citizens average 6 hours per night, of which only 1 hour is spent in REM. Some sleep researchers, however, believe that 6 hours is not enough; they suggest that this amount of sleep—in seniors or anyone—represents undiagnosed yet treatable insomnia (Dement & Vaughan, 1999).

Let's emphasize, though, that these numbers are just averages; some people sleep more and a few sleep much less. People's sleep patterns also differ in another way, because people vary markedly in the timing of their peak alertness during the day. Some people truly seem to be "morning people"; others are "night people" (Duffy, Rimmer, & Czeisler, 2001; May & Hasher, 1998). The so-called early birds differ from the night crew in several ways. The two groups are—as common sense suggests—distinct in when, during each day, they're most alert and when they're most careful in their judgment and reasoning (Bodenhausen, 1990). The groups also differ in how their body temperature, blood pressure, and digestive rhythm fluctuate across a 24-hour period.

Why do people differ in these ways? Part of the reason is biological; this is evident in the fact that the various changes associated with puberty seem to produce a shift in daily rhythms. This is why adolescents usually develop a preference for later bedtimes and later rising times—a preference that lasts into early adulthood (Carskadon, Acebo, & Jenni, 2004; also C. Schmidt, Collette, Leclercq, Sterpenich, Vandewalle et al., 2009). Environmental factors also play a role; these factors include the number of hours of daylight a person is exposed to as well as cultural factors such as the prescribed timing of various meals.

THE FUNCTION OF SLEEP

Sleep-deprivation studies tell us that sleep is necessary, but they don't tell us why. Common sense suggests one hypothesis—the idea that sleep is restorative, allowing us to replace or replenish some substance that's used up when we're awake. This idea is supported by evidence that people do show longer periods of slow-wave sleep under conditions of physical fatigue, when they have a greater need for bodily recuperation (e.g., Youngstedt, O'Connor, & Dishman, 1997). Likewise, marathon runners sleep longer during the nights just after a race, and they spend most of that time in slow-wave sleep (Shapiro, Bortz, Mitchell, Bartell & Jooste, 1981).

Despite these observations, however, it has been difficult to pinpoint exactly what sleep restores. One possibility is that during sleep, our bodies can clear out some of the cellular waste products that are the result of routine metabolic activity (Alanko et al., 2004). A different proposal involves certain growth hormones that our body produces at higher rates when we're asleep. These hormones promote body repair, consistent with the broad idea that sleep is a time of repairing our tissues—whether in response to some injury or just dealing with the ordinary wear and tear in the body caused by daily life (Siegel, 2003).

Other hypotheses about sleep's function are also plausible. One suggestion is that brain activity during REM sustains important brain circuits, based on the notion that synapses need activity to maintain their strength. A different proposal is that sleeping may in effect "reset" overstimulated neurons—perhaps to save energy and perhaps to make sure the neurons aren't firing at their maximum—so they'll be ready to fire in the next day if needed (Figure 6.16; Donlea, Ramanan, & Shaw, 2009; Gilestro, Tunoni, & Cirelli, 2009).

Yet another proposal also focuses on neural activity—but with a different emphasis. This hypothesis suggests that neural activity during both REM and slow-wave sleep helps to consolidate memories gained during the previous day (Dumay & Gaskell, 2007; Hobson, 2002; Rasch & Born, 2008; Stickgold, 2005). Consistent with this proposal, several studies have shown that performance on certain motor tasks (such as rapid tapping in a particular sequence) improves markedly after a period of REM sleep (Mednick, Nakayama, & Stickgold, 2003; Walker, Brakefield, Hobson, & Stickgold, 2003). Likewise, one recent study indicates a linkage between infants' naps and their learning—for example, learning about the patterns of language that they hear (Gómez, Bootzin, & Nadel, 2006; for some challenges to the idea that sleep contributes to memory consolidation, see Miller, 2007; Rickard, Cai, Rieth, Jones, & Ard, 2008).

Obviously, then, researchers still disagree about why we sleep; and many proposals are being discussed. One last proposal offers a very different perspective: Organisms need time each day to digest their food, and this demands that they spend some hours in an inactive state, preferably in a spot sheltered from the weather and away from potential predators. Likewise, animals that locate their food (or mates) by means of vision are limited in what they can do in the dark, and this too demands a period of inactivity, away from danger. It is possible, therefore, that sleep has no function on its own but is simply the way animals spend this inactive time (Figure 6.17)—a period of inactivity imposed by other considerations and

6.16 Sleep and the fruit fly brain These photos compare the brains of well-rested fruit flies (top panel) and flies that have gone 16 hours without sleep (bottom panel). Without sleep, activity levels are much higher at the synapses (indicated by brighter color) —an indication that sleep may allow the neurons to "calm down" after a day's activity, so that (perhaps) they will be ready to go again when needed the next day.

enforced by the circadian rhythm created within the nervous system (e.g., Webb, 1974, 1994). Based on this view, the effects of sleep deprivation may not be the result of missing out on the benefits of sleep. Instead, sleep deprivation may just be the result of an organism fighting against its own natural rhythms—an internal conflict that can by itself be unsettling.

We therefore have many proposals for why we sleep; and so far we have no evidence clearly favoring one proposal over the others. But maybe all of these hypotheses are correct. Maybe, in the end, sleep has all of these functions—thus underscoring the importance of sleep for all animal species.

DREAMS

When we're in slow-wave sleep, we seem to be in a state of diminished awareness. We're certainly not oblivious to the world around us, and stimuli such as loud noises, a firm shaking, or a bright light in our eyes will awaken us. Less intense but meaningful stimuli can also wake us up; the classic example is a mother awakening when she hears her baby cry. Even if we don't wake up, we remain sensitive to some aspects of our environment. Notice, for example, that even though we roll around while sleeping, we manage not to roll out of bed—and so apparently we're somehow sensitive to how close we are to the mattress edges!

There is, however, a part of the sleep state in which we seem acutely aware—but we are aware of events on an internal stage, rather than events from the outside world. We're referring, of course, to *dreams.* Dreaming is strongly associated with REM sleep, and when people are awakened from this stage of sleep, at least 80% (and in some studies more) report that they were just dreaming (e.g., Dement, 1978; Foulkes, 1985). This is true even of participants who claim they have "never dreamed." Apparently these people do dream, even if they typically don't recall their dreams when they wake up.

Plainly, dreaming is strongly associated with REM sleep, but it also seems to occur in other sleep stages. If people are awakened from slow-wave sleep, about half of them report that they had just been dreaming. In talking about these dreams, people use different terms than they do when reporting the dreams associated with REM sleep. The REM sleep reports tend to be pictorial, depicting episodes that include the dreamer as a character and that seem more or less real while the dream is under way. In contrast, when awakened from slow-wave sleep, people tend to give only sparse summaries, noting that they were only "thinking about something" or that their dreams were "boring." They rarely relate the kind of colorful, event-filled drama we usually think of as a dream (Armitage, Hoffmann, & Moffitt, 1992; Cartwright, 1977; Foulkes, 1985).

Does this mean that we actually dream differently in REM sleep than in slow-wave sleep? It's hard to decide, because participants awakened from slow-wave sleep tend to be sluggish and disoriented while those awakened from REM sleep are quickly alert. So it's at least possible that the different kinds of dream reports are reflecting the different states of the just-awakened sleepers rather than the nature of the dreaming itself.

Focusing just on REM dreams, though, what do people dream about (Figure 6.18)? Our evidence comes from the *dream reports* of just-awakened dreamers. The contents of these reports vary enormously, but make it clear that events in dreams do not—as some

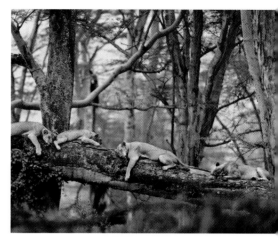

6.17 Another function for sleep Animals need time to digest their food, and perhaps sleep is just the way they spend this time—in an inactive state, sheltered from the weather and away from potential enemies.

6.18 Dreams Dreams ordinarily depict familiar, everyday events—but also include some bizarre elements. For example, dreams about flying are relatively common.

people suppose—flash instantaneously before the dreamer. Instead, events in dreams seem to take about as long as they would in real life. We know this because, when people awake from dreams, we can ask them, as part of their dream report, to estimate how long they had just been dreaming. These estimates tend to be quite accurate—and so someone who recalls, say, 5 minutes of a dream is likely to have just spent 5 minutes in REM sleep; someone who recalls 15 minutes of dream content is likely to have just spent 15 minutes in REM, and so on (Dement & Kleitman, 1957; Dement & Wolpert, 1958).

Dream reports also indicate that dreams tend to showcase a range of relatively ordinary current life preoccupations—including the emotional events of life but also the mundane episodes of one's daily routine (Cartwright, 1994). Dreams likewise tend to include familiar places and objects, people we've recently encountered, or activities we have recently engaged in—including, of course, activities that filled the hours just before sleep. In one study, researchers had people spend several hours playing Tetris before going to bed; many of the participants reported dreaming about blocks falling and rotating, just as they do in the game. It's worth noting, though, that the participants in this study rarely reported dreams about playing the Tetris game itself (Stickgold et al., 2000).

Dreams are not, however, mere replays of daily events. Instead, our dreams often introduce weird or illogical elements. Thus we might dream about being naked in public places, or about flying—without, of course, the aid of an airplane. Despite these peculiar features, though, the dream content seems perfectly natural while it's under way; it's only when we're awake that the dream seems strange.

In addition, people's dreams tend to reveal similar themes from year to year, even over decades (Domhoff, 1996). Some people regularly dream about illness, others dream about fighting, and others dream about romance. But some themes show up in nearly everyone's dreams. For example, for almost everybody, dreams contain bad outcomes more often than good ones, and more negative emotions (fear, worry, embarrassment) than positive ones. Thus, people dream about failed efforts, missing appointments (or exams), or being attacked or chased. Dreams also seem to include more aggressive interactions than friendly ones. In fact, according to one estimate, 2 out of every 100 dream characters are murdered—a proportion far exceeding real-life homicide rates (Hall & Van de Castle, 1966; Hall et al., 1982).

There are also certain themes that are relatively rare in dreams—and perhaps surprisingly so. For example, relatively few of our dreams have detectable sexual content (Domhoff, 2003)—only 10% of the dreams reported by young men and roughly 3% of the dreams reported by women. (But for both males and females, and largely independent of reported dream content, REM sleep is associated with genital arousal—erections in males and vaginal lubrication in females.) However, when we do dream about sexuality, the sex acts are often quite overt—and so the dreamer, the next morning, recalls a dream about wild and passionate intercourse.

WHY DO WE DREAM?

In Western cultures, dreams have historically been considered prophetic; across the centuries, dream analysis has been a standard practice among fortune-tellers. Moreover, people around the world regard their dreams as *meaningful*. In one study, people in countries as diverse as the United States, India, and South Korea said they thought dreams "reveal hidden truths" by allowing "emotions buried in the unconscious" to come to the surface (Figure 6.19; Morewedge & Norton, 2009).

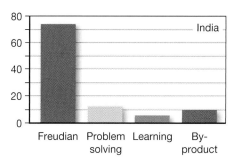

6.19 Dream interpretation and culture Participants in a study that encompassed three different cultures embraced the Freudian view that dreams "reveal hidden truths" by allowing "emotions buried in the unconscious" to come to the surface. People less often endorse the idea that dreams are important for learning or problem-solving, or the idea that dreams are just a by-product of other brain functions. Ironically, it's this last proposal that's best supported by evidence.

Apparently, then, people are ready to endorse a proposal similar to the one suggested by Sigmund Freud in his book, *The Interpretation of Dreams* (1900). Freud argued that we all harbor a host of primitive and forbidden wishes, but we protect ourselves by keeping these wishes out of our conscious thoughts. In dreams, however, our self-censorship is relaxed just a bit, allowing these impulses to break through into our awareness. Even in sleep, though, some of our efforts at self-protection continue; so the forbidden impulses can enter our dreams only in a disguised form. In Freud's view, therefore, the characters that we observe in our dreams, and the actions we witness, are merely the *manifest content* of the dream—the content we're able to experience directly. The real meaning of the dream, in contrast, lies in the dream's *latent content*—the actual wishes and desires that are being expressed (symbolically) through the manifest content. (For more on Freud's theorizing, see chapters 15 and 16.)

Is this proposal correct? At the most general level, Freud is suggesting that dreams usually reflect the sleeper's ongoing emotional concerns; and he was surely correct about this broad point. Thus if you've narrowly avoided a car crash, you're likely to dream about collisions and other accidents; if you're worried about an upcoming exam, you may well end up dreaming about exams or other forms of evaluation. Indeed, in the weeks following the September 11, 2001, attacks, many residents of New York City reported dreams about terrorist attacks (Galea et al., 2002).

There is, however, little evidence to support Freud's more ambitious claim that dream content should be understood in terms of thinly disguised wishes (S. Fisher & Greenberg, 1977, 1996). As one large concern, Freud's own evidence was based on his *interpretation* of dreams, and it's difficult (some would say impossible) to know if the interpretations were correct or not. There's surely nothing inevitable about Freud's interpretations; indeed, some of his followers offered very different interpretations of the same dreams that Freud himself had analyzed. This highlights just how uncertain the interpretation process is, and it reveals that the "evidence" Freud offered for his view is not persuasive in the way science requires.

Modern scholars have therefore turned to a different hypothesis about dream content, one that does not view dreams as having a specific function of their own. Instead, dreams may be just a by-product of other brain activities. Specifically, the **activation-synthesis hypothesis** begins with the fact that during REM sleep, the pons (a structure in the brain stem) produces bursts of neural activity that in turn activate areas in the lateral geniculate nucleus—an important processing center for visual information. This activity then

activation-synthesis hypothesis
The hypothesis that dreams may be just a byproduct of the sleeping brain's activities (activation), which are later assembled into a semicoherent narrative (synthesis).

6.20 Activation in the brain during dreams When a person is dreaming, the pons produces bursts of activity that activate areas in the lateral geniculate nucleus, which leads to activity in the occipital cortex.

Occipital cortex

Lateral geniculate nucleus

Pons

leads to activity in the occipital cortex—the brain area that carries out most of the analysis of visual input. Researchers refer to this neural activity as *PGO waves* because it involves the *pons*, the *geniculate*, and the *occipital* areas (Figure 6.20). These waves are the "activation" part of activation synthesis and give us an immediate explanation for why dreams are filled with vivid visual images—the result of neural activity in brain areas ordinarily involved in processing visual information.

But why do certain images come to mind? The key here is that these brain areas have been primed by other neural activity, activity caused by the person's recent experiences as well as shaped by their recurrent thoughts. It is therefore the combination of PGO activity and this priming that brings certain images—either from the previous day or reflecting broader themes—into awareness. There is, however, no orderly narrative linking the images that come to mind; instead, the sequence is essentially random. Still, the brain does what it can to assemble these images into a coherent plot—this is the "synthesis" part of the activation-synthesis hypothesis. Some of this assembly takes place during the dream itself, but some probably occurs once the person is awake and trying to recall the dream.

Let's be clear, though, that the set of ideas activated in the sleeper's brain is likely to be something of a hodgepodge, since the sequence of these ideas is not constrained by perceptual input or a cohesive set of goals. As a result, the effort toward coherence will often be only partially successful, and this is why dreams are often unrealistic: The shaky plot line is the best the brain can do in weaving together the odd assembly of images that bubble into awareness during REM sleep.

Other aspects of brain activity also play a role in shaping dream content. Several studies have monitored the pattern of blood flow through people's brains while they were dreaming. The data show high levels of activity in the limbic system, a set of structures in the brain—including the amygdala—associated with perceiving and regulating emotion; this result obviously fits with the emotional character of many dreams (Schwartz & Maquet, 2002). The data also show considerable neural activity in the motor cortex—as if the neurons were trying to initiate movements, although other mechanisms (in the brain stem) intercept the signals from the motor cortex and ensure the movements never occur. (This is why, as we mentioned earlier, the body is impressively immobile during REM sleep.)

Brain scans also show *diminished* activity during sleep in some brain areas. These include the prefrontal cortex, a brain region often associated with planning and intelligent analysis. This finding may give us a further clue about why dreams often have peculiar content: When we're in the dream state, the parts of the brain needed to assemble the story elements into an intelligible narrative aren't fully engaged.

SLEEP, DREAMS, AND CONSCIOUSNESS

What can we learn about consciousness by studying sleep and dreams? At the very least, sleep provides a compelling reminder that our conscious state varies—it has different degrees of alertness as a function of our own internal status. Sleep also reminds us that consciousness is intermittent; for some portions of the day, we aren't conscious. This seems to be true during sleep, but it's also true when we're awake. (Consider the relatively common experience of suddenly realizing, after 30 miles of highway driving, that you haven't been aware of the passing miles at all. You were driving on autopilot—steering, maintaining your speed, and so on; but you had "zoned out" and have no recollection of the last half hour.)

Sleep and dreaming also remind us of the sheer difficulty of studying conscious experience. Notice, for example, that we have plausible *conjectures* about why we sleep; but there's no widespread agreement. Likewise, the activation-synthesis notion strikes many researchers as a promising account of why we dream, but the debate continues about whether this proposal is correct. And we still have many unanswered questions about why people's dreams have the contents they do—and why so many people have dreams of flying (for example), appearing naked in public, or being chased.

Why is this research so difficult? It's partly because the study of sleep and dreaming often must depend on what people recall and report about their sleep and their dreams. Self-report data are always worrisome, but the problem is magnified when the self-report is offered by a groggy, disoriented, just-awakened sleeper. What's more, we have powerful reason to be skeptical about this particular self-report because—as mentioned earlier—we know that some people assert they never dream, but these same people reliably report dreams if we manage to awaken them during an interval of REM sleep. In this case, their self-report of never dreaming is patently incorrect, highlighting for us the challenge of relying on people's descriptions of, and their memories of, their mental states in general and their nighttime states in particular.

Hypnosis

Everyone has experienced the altered consciousness associated with sleep. A different form of altered consciousness is less common, but still deeply interesting. This is the altered state that a person reaches when hypnotized. Many myths are associated with hypnosis—including what it is and what it can accomplish. At its essence, though, **hypnosis** is a highly relaxed state in which the participant is extremely suggestible, and the result is that he's likely to feel that his actions and thoughts are happening to him rather than being produced by him voluntarily. But what's the exact nature of this state?

hypnosis A highly relaxed, suggestible state of mind in which a person is likely to feel that his actions and thoughts are happening to him rather than being produced voluntarily.

WHAT CAN HYPNOSIS ACHIEVE?

When German physician Franz Mesmer (1734–1815; Figure 6.21A) first demonstrated his early version of hypnotism, his technique relied on magnets and tanks of water. Mesmer moved around his hypnotic subjects while making complex gestures and passing his

6.21 Hypnosis then and now
(A) Mesmer's original procedure involved an elaborate system of magnets and tubs of water. (B) Hypnosis in the modern world, in contrast, is quite simple and typically involves one person giving instructions to another.

(A)

(B)

hands over their bodies. Most of these details, however, were just theatrics; modern hypnosis procedures are more straightforward (Figure 6.21B). The person being hypnotized sits quietly and focuses on some target—a particular sound, or a particular object that is in view. The hypnotist speaks to the person quietly and monotonously, encouraging her to relax. The hypnotist also offers various suggestions about what will happen—including many things that are just inevitable as the person relaxes: "Your eyelids are drooping downward," or "Your limbs are getting heavy." Gradually, the hypnotist leads the person into a state of deep relaxation and extreme suggestibility.

Extraordinary claims are sometimes made about what people can do while in a hypnotized state, but we need to examine these claims with care. It's true, for example, that people can be led to perform unusual and even bizarre actions; but in many cases, these actions are not the result of the hypnotic state at all. For example, people under hypnosis can be shown fluid and told that it's a powerful acid; they'll then comply with the cruel instruction to fling the "acid" into another person's face. Often, this demonstration is accompanied by the statement that no sane person would perform this act without hypnosis; so, apparently, we're to believe hypnosis can overcome someone's inhibitions and lead them into otherwise unspeakable behavior. It turns out, though, that this argument is mistaken: Exactly the same behavior can be produced by simply asking people to *pretend* to be hypnotized and to act the way they think a hypnotized person would (Orne & Evans, 1965). Clearly, therefore, the hypnosis itself is playing little direct role in producing this behavior.

In chapter 8, we'll also discuss some of hypnosis's alleged effects on memory. For example, in a procedure called *hypnotic age regression*, the hypnotized person is instructed that he has returned to an earlier age—and so is now three years old, for example, or even younger. The hypnotized person will behave appropriately, talking in a child's voice and doing childish things. Even so, the person has not in any real sense "returned" to an earlier age. Instead, he's simply acting like an adult believes a child should. We can obtain similar performances simply by asking people who aren't hypnotized to simulate a child's behavior. In addition, it turns out that adults have a number of mistaken beliefs about how children behave; under hypnosis, the age-regressed person acts in a fashion consistent with the (incorrect) adult notions and thus not like a real child (Silverman & Retzlaff, 1986).

Likewise, many people believe that hypnosis is a powerful way to retrieve lost memories—for example, they think that under hypnosis, a witness to an auto collision can recall precise details of where people were standing at the accident scene, what the cars' license plate numbers were, and more—almost as though hypnosis provided a "rewind" button that allows the person to relive the event and note the details they had neglected in the original episode. None of this is real, however. There's no reason to believe that hypnosis improves memory. Instead, hypnosis may actually undermine memory—making the person more confident in their recollection, whether the recollection is correct or not; and making them markedly more susceptible to leading questions or suggestions that the hypnotist might offer (e.g., Sheehan, Green, & Truesdale, 1992). This is why most American, Canadian, and British jurisdictions forbid courtroom testimony that has been "enhanced" through hypnosis.

At the same time, hypnosis does have some real and striking effects. For example, people under hypnosis can be given various instructions for how they should behave after the hypnosis is done, and in many cases these *posthypnotic instructions* are effective. These instructions can, for example, help people to relax or to eat less (but despite the hype, similar posthypnotic instructions do little to help people give up cigarettes or other drugs; Nash, 2001). Likewise, a hypnotist can produce *posthypnotic amnesia* simply by instructing the hypnotized individual to forget certain events that happened while the person was in the hypnotized state (Kirsch, 2001). The memory for these events, however, is still in place, even if the person can't retrieve it. We know this because the posthypnotic amnesia can be "lifted" with a subsequent hypnotic instruction that allows the lost memories to return.

One of the more dramatic effects of hypnosis, and a powerful indication that hypnosis can create a special state of mind, is the phenomenon of *hypnotic analgesia*—pain reduction produced through hypnotic suggestion (Hilgard & Hilgard, 1975; Patterson & Jensen, 2003; Patterson, 2004). Using this technique, people have undergone various dental procedures and some forms of surgery without any anesthetic, and they report little suffering. In some studies, hypnotized people seem to suffer less than people given various other pain treatments, including acupuncture, aspirin, or even morphine (Stern, Brown, Ulett, & Sletten, 1977).

It's important to mention, though, that not every individual shows the hypnotic analgesia effect, because some people can't be hypnotized. In fact, susceptibility to hypnosis varies broadly. Some people are largely unmoved by a hypnotist's suggestions, and other people—"hypnotic virtuosi"—are powerfully influenced. The degree of susceptibility seems to be linked to how easily the individual can become absorbed in certain activities, such as watching a movie or playing a video game—and the people who are more readily "absorbed" are likely to be more hypnotizable (Barnier & McConkey, 2004; Kirsch & Braffman, 2001; Tellegen & Atkinson, 1974).

THEORIES OF HYPNOSIS

Does hypnosis truly produce an altered state of consciousness, so that a hypnotized person is in a qualitatively different state of mind than someone who's not hypnotized? More broadly, what exactly does hypnosis achieve? Some people argue that hypnosis needs to be understood in relatively mundane social terms—one person (the hypnotist) simply has an enormous influence on another (the person hypnotized). As we'll discuss in chapter 13, social influences can be incredibly powerful, leading us to perform a range of actions that we think we would never do. Perhaps hypnosis can be understood in similar terms—and, if so, then it's more like our ordinary mode of consciousness than one might suppose (e.g., Spanos, 1986; Spanos & Coe, 1992).

We've already seen some of the data consistent with this view. For example, hypnotic age regression isn't a low-tech time machine; instead, the "regressed" individual is simply playing a role as well as she can. Likewise, memories called forth under hypnosis are likely to be constructions—not the result of some highly effective and specialized

(A) Pain reduction

(B)

6.22 The effects of hypnosis (A) Hypnosis does have some remarkable effects—for example, it's effective as an analgesic. (B) The effects of hypnosis are often overstated. For example, under hypnosis, someone can be turned into a "human plank" with their head on one chair, their feet on another, and no support in between. However, the same position is possible (with some effort) by people *not* hypnotized.

process. Similarly, at least some of the remarkable feats associated with hypnosis can also be performed without hypnosis (Figure 6.22), further undermining claims about the special status of the hypnotic state.

A very different proposal, however, is that hypnosis involves a special state of *dissociation* (Hilgard, 1986, 1992), a mental state in which we shift out of our normal "first-person" perspective. We might feel like we're "outside of ourselves," watching ourselves from a detached position. We might also feel like our experiences are happening to someone else and that our actions are controlled by someone else. Some clinical psychologists suggest that dissociation is a powerful means through which each of us can shield ourselves from emotionally painful experiences. The proposal here, though, is that similar mechanisms are involved in hypnosis, so that our conscious control of our thoughts, and our sense of immediate experience, are somehow set aside for as long as the hypnosis lasts.

As one specific version of this hypothesis, consciousness researcher Ernest Hilgard has suggested that hypnosis causes, in effect, a splitting of a person's awareness into two separate streams. One stream is responsive to the hypnotist's instructions, essentially surrendering control to the hypnotist. The second stream of awareness remains in the background as a "hidden observer"—so that the person is alert to the sequence of events—but still leaves the hypnotist in control of what the person does or, to some extent, feels.

Each of these proposals, one emphasizing social influences and one emphasizing dissociation, may capture important truths. And each proposal may explain different aspects of hypnosis. Indeed, some researchers have proposed this sort of hybrid conception of hypnosis by explaining some aspects of the hypnotic state in terms of social factors and other aspects in terms of dissociation (Kihlstrom & McConkey, 1990; Killeen & Nash, 2003). Perhaps, therefore, we can understand *some* of hypnosis's effects as not involving changes in consciousness; but at least some of the effects (e.g., the analgesia) do seem to involve an altered state, so the implication is that hypnosis can actually change someone's conscious status.

Religious States

Altered states of consciousness can also be achieved through some religious practices. Of course, religions vary enormously in their tenets and in their rituals, and that variety is crucial here. In some religions, worship encourages a state of extraordinary excitement in which people shake, or fall on the floor, or shout out in "languages" no human understands. In other religions, worship involves a quiet state that encourages feelings of reverential awe. In still other religions, worship involves special circumstances—deep isolation, or periods of fasting, or even pain—to encourage thoughts about a world filled with supernatural forces.

MEDITATION

Perhaps the most-studied religious state, however, is the one achieved through the religious practice of focused meditation, during which the meditator focuses on a particular chant or perhaps just a syllable. Alternatively, in some traditions, the meditator focuses on a visual target such as a candle in the room or a prayer mandala that is either physically present or called up from memory (Figure 6.23). Practices like these are common in many Asian religions including Hinduism, Taoism, and Buddhism.

6.23 A prayer mandala

In all of these religions, meditators report feeling profoundly relaxed during the meditation exercise and both unresponsive to most external stimuli and simultaneously highly alert to certain ideas. Indeed, in many traditions, the meditators strive to shut out any distracting thoughts while trying to be fully alert to insights that may arise within the meditation.

Notice, then, that there are several parallels between the meditative states and hypnosis: Both are quiet, relaxed states created by close attention to a specific stimulus. In both states, the person is largely oblivious to many stimuli but highly alert to other ideas—the hypnotist's suggestions in the one case and, in the other, thoughts leading to mindfulness, tranquility, and (in some traditions) compassion.

MEDITATION AND THE BRAIN

Meditation has many effects on both mind and body. When compared to nonmeditators, people who meditate seem to have lower blood pressure, lower levels of the body's stress hormones, and enhanced immune response (Barnes, Treiber, & Davis, 2001; Davidson, Pizzagalli, Nitschke, & Kalin, 2003; Infante et al., 2001). Meditation also seems to have a powerful impact on brain activity. One study, for example, used EEGs to assess the brain's state during meditation; the data showed a strong increase in the alpha rhythms associated with a state of relaxation (Lutz et al., 2008).

In another study, the researchers examined a type of meditation in which the person doesn't focus on any particular target. The researchers also used measurement techniques that would be sensitive to faster rhythms in the brain's activity, and they studied meditators with a considerable amount of skill—Buddhist practitioners with at least 10,000 hours of training in meditative practice! In the experiment, the researchers collected EEG data from these adept practitioners while they were in a mental state focused on "unconditional loving-kindness and compassion." For comparison, the study also included a group of control participants who had been given a week to practice meditation. During that week, these control participants were asked at first to think of someone they cared about and to let their mind be filled by a feeling of love or compassion toward this person; later, they were encouraged to let their thoughts be filled with similar feelings toward all sentient beings (Lutz, Greischar, Rawlings, Ricard, & Davidson, 2004).

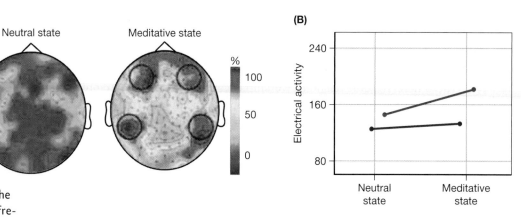

6.24 Meditation and the brain Researchers used EEG measurements to compare well-practiced and novice meditators while they were in the meditative state. (A) The distribution of electrical activity in the so-called gamma frequency—a pattern that indicates organized, coherent activity in the brain. The black circles indicate electrode placements on the scalp. (B) A comparison of the gamma frequency patterns for the two groups. The blue line indicates novice meditators; the red line indicates well-practiced participants.

The EEG records collected during meditation showed several differences between the two groups. One finding was that the brains of well-practiced meditators showed a pattern of neural activity in which brain areas that were anatomically distant from each other were nonetheless firing at the same rhythm and in synchrony. The specific rhythm observed, and the synchrony itself, are both thought to be crucial for the processes that coordinate and integrate brain activity in distinct areas (Figure 6.24). (For more on this issue of how separate brain regions can be "bound" together, see Chapter 5.) The implication, therefore, is that the meditation had created a strongly unified, cohesive experience—an experience, roughly put, of "one-ness." More broadly, this shift in brain activity associated with this type of meditation is certainly consistent with the idea that the meditation does produce a change in the quality of the meditator's moment-to-moment conscious experience.

Drug-Induced Changes in Consciousness

Meditation is one way to change the quality of conscious experience; medication is another. Many psychoactive drugs change aspects of one's experience—so that antidepressants can decrease someone's sense of apathy or sadness; analgesics can decrease how much pain someone is feeling. Other drugs have broader effects and seem to change the very nature of our experience. This is certainly true for many of the illegal drugs taken for recreational purposes; indeed, the change in consciousness is often the reason why people use (and *abuse*) these drugs. In Chapter 3, we discussed some of the biological mechanisms underlying the drugs' effects and noted that these mechanisms all influence information flow at the synapse. Let's now turn to the psychological effects of these drugs by looking first at *depressants* (drugs intended to decrease neural activity) and then at the *stimulants* (drugs that promote neural activity). After that, we'll discuss marijuana as well as the broader set of hallucinogens. And finally, we'll consider the thorny problem of defining "drug dependence" and addiction.

DEPRESSANTS

depressants Drugs that diminish activity levels in the nervous system.

Depressants are broadly defined as drugs that decrease activity in the nervous system. Many depressants are available to us; one is alcohol, a widely used recreational drug in many countries, but also widely used by people as a way of managing their own stress and anxiety. Other depressants are commonly prescribed by physicians; these drugs include medications (e.g., zolpidem) given to people who have trouble sleeping, and drugs (usually benzodiazepines, such as Valium or Xanax) used to treat anxiety. (For more on these drugs, see Chapter 17.)

Depressants are helpful in many circumstances—but if they're misused or overused, they can lead to serious medical and psychological difficulties. For example, both the benefits and the problems associated with alcohol are well documented. At low doses, alcohol produces feelings of pleasure and well-being. But alcohol also depresses activity in neural circuits that ordinarily control our impulses, and when these (inhibitory) circuits are less active, people are likely to engage in a wide range of behaviors they would ordinarily avoid. If provoked, they're more likely to be aggressive. If tempted toward sexual behavior, they're more likely to give in to the temptation. But the same mechanisms can also promote positive behaviors. For example, people asked for charitable donations are more likely to say yes if they've had a drink or two; restaurant customers are more likely to leave generous tips after they've enjoyed a bottle of wine.

This relaxation of inhibition can, of course, create enormous dangers. Thus, people who understand perfectly well the dangers of driving an automobile while drunk may still get behind the wheel of a car—thanks, in large part, to impairment in brain circuits that would ordinarily forbid such behavior. Then, once the person is behind the wheel, alcohol's other effects come into play—slower reaction times, poor coordination, and impaired decision making. All of this makes it easy to understand why, according to annual surveys by the National Highway Traffic Safety Administration, almost half of the deaths from traffic accidents in the United States involve alcohol consumption. Similar data have been reported in many other countries.

Researchers have further suggested that alcohol produces a narrowing of attention, so that people who have been drinking pay attention to a diminished set of cues in the environment and a smaller set of considerations from memory (Steele & Josephs, 1990). As a result, the drinker's thinking is very much tied to the here and now, and he pays little attention to the possible consequences of his actions. This helps us understand why, for example, college students are less likely to use condoms if they've been drinking—apparently, in this setting, students pay less attention to the obvious dangers associated with unprotected sex (MacDonald, Zanna, & Fong, 1996; MacDonald, Cohen, Stenger, & Carter, 2000). This shortsighted thinking may also help explain why, according to one estimate, alcohol is involved in 90% of the rapes and a similar proportion of the violent crimes occurring on college campuses (Wechsler, Davenport, Dowdall, Moeykens, & Castillon, 1994).

We should add, though, that alcohol's effects derive from a mix of the drug's actual impact on brain chemistry and people's *expectations* about its effects. In one study, half of the participants consumed an alcoholic drink and half consumed an alcohol-free drink (Abrams & Wilson, 1983; also see Goldman, Brown, & Christiansen, 1987). In each group, half of the participants thought they had consumed alcohol and half believed there was no alcohol in the drink. (The taste of the drink, for all participants, made it impossible for them to detect the alcohol, and so their beliefs about the drink depended entirely on what the experimenter told them.) All participants were then shown an erotic movie, and those who thought they had consumed alcohol (whether they actually had or not) reported stronger sexual fantasies in response to the film and reported feeling less guilt about these fantasies. Alcohol, it seems, can release someone's impulses through psychological means as well as pharmaceutical ones.

What about the other depressants—sleeping pills or the various antianxiety drugs? These are highly effective if used appropriately, but they can also produce physical and psychological dependence, making withdrawal symptoms after prolonged use quite likely; the symptoms can include enhanced anxiety (a "rebound" effect), insomnia, or even seizures. In addition, people who've been taking these drugs for a long time often become less sensitive to the medication—a pattern known as *drug tolerance*—and so need a higher and higher dose to achieve the same effects. Unfortunately, at higher doses these drugs have further effects: High doses of benzodiazepines, for example, can cause cognitive impairment and, especially if combined with alcohol, can push the person into a coma.

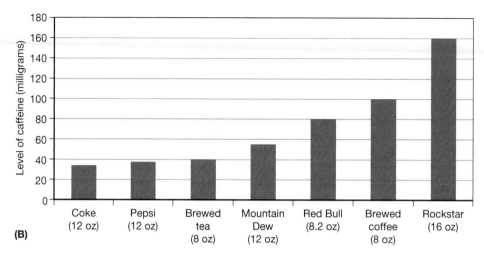

6.25 **The availability of caffeine** Caffeine, a commonly used stimulant, is available from many sources.

STIMULANTS

stimulants Drugs that have activating or excitatory effects on brain or bodily functions.

For medical or recreational reasons, people sometimes turn to **stimulants**—drugs that *stimulate* the nervous system and broadly increase the level of bodily arousal. These drugs raise the person's blood pressure, increase heart and breathing rate, and certainly increase overall alertness. Like the depressants, some of the stimulants are freely available; the most obvious example is *caffeine*, which is found in coffee, tea, various colas, and some of the new energy drinks (Figure 6.25). Other stimulants are more powerful, less available, and in many cases illegal; the list includes cocaine and various forms of amphetamine, such as d-amphetamine, methamphetamine, and MDMA (also known as ecstasy). This list is surely partial, however, because new stimulants are often synthesized to supply an eager market.

Some stimulants have, or once had, legitimate uses. Amphetamines, for example, are sometimes prescribed by physicians to reduce appetite or fatigue, and they're also prescribed as treatment for attention-deficit/hyperactivity disorder (ADHD). Ritalin is another stimulant often prescribed in treating ADHD. (For more on ADHD, see Chapters 16 and 17.) Cocaine was used for many years as a local anesthetic for ear, nose, and throat surgery; it's still used for some surgical procedures. (Novocaine, a more widely used anesthetic, is a close chemical cousin of cocaine.) However, all of these stimulants are often abused as recreational drugs. People use these drugs to boost their energy, mood, and sense of confidence; to decrease the need for sleep; and to improve athletic performance. These benefits may come at a high cost, though, because stimulant use can lead to physical and psychological dependence. What's more, a regular user who abruptly stops using one of these drugs is likely to experience powerful withdrawal symptoms including fatigue, irritability, depression, headaches, and more.

Heavy users of methamphetamine often end up smoking large quantities of this stimulant. They gain a rush of energy and pleasure from inhalation and typically feel elated, confident, and able to stay awake several hours past their usual sleeping time. However, this aroused state is associated with markedly higher blood pressure that can increase the user's risk of heart failure or stroke (Figure 6.26). And, inevitably, the person will reach the end of this aroused period and come crashing down. At that point, the person is likely to become depressed and irritable, and sleep for days.

Cocaine is another commonly used—and abused—stimulant. This drug, derived from the leaves of the coca plant, is usually snorted or inhaled and quickly enters the bloodstream, causing a rush of excitation and euphoria (Figure 6.27). Once again, though, this rush is only temporary. The subsequent crash—as with amphetamines—can involve feelings of fatigue and depression. And here too, long-term abuse can bring with it a set of problems that include risk of dependence, feelings of paranoia, and an array of medical difficulties including cardiac arrest and respiratory problems (Franklin et al., 2002; Gourevitch & Arnsten, 2005).

Another often-abused stimulant is methylenedioxymethamphetamine (MDMA; also known as *ecstasy*). MDMA is a molecule synthesized in the lab; chemically, it resembles another stimulant—methamphetamine—as well as the hallucinogen *mescaline*. MDMA is a drug often taken in social settings (at clubs or a rave) and produces an emotional elevation that involves feelings of pleasure, elation, and warmth. MDMA is also a mild hallucinogen and produces a strong sense of empathy and closeness to everyone who is around.

Once again, though, there's a price to pay for these benefits. When people are using MDMA, they are likely to become dehydrated and to clench their jaws so tightly that they can damage their teeth and jaw muscles. In addition, and like other amphetamines, MDMA users are susceptible to substantial increases in blood pressure, pulse, and body temperature. This situation can put the user at greater risk for cardiac complications (e.g., heart attack) and/or stroke. When the MDMA wears off (typically, after 3 or 4 hours), the person may also experience a kind of rebound that makes him feel sluggish and depressed. And at least some research suggests that continued use of MDMA can create a risk for several other problems (Biello & Dafters, 2001; Morgan, 2000; Pacifici et al., 2001)—including impaired memory, problems in one's body clock that may include sleep difficulties, and weakened immune system function (and so greater vulnerability to illness).

Overall, it seems clear that these stimulants do change a person's conscious experience. Excitement, euphoria, and increased self-confidence all powerfully color his experiences, and the stimulants may produce a sense of enhanced awareness that changes how the world looks, sounds, and feels. The strong sense of empathy produced by MDMA also adds a pleasurable dimension to one's experience. But as we've seen, these drugs expose users to serious health risks including life-threatening medical conditions, a danger of addiction, and a catalog of medical, mental, and emotional difficulties associated with long-term use.

MARIJUANA

Marijuana consists of the leaves, flowers, and buds of the hemp plant (*Cannabis sativa* and also *Cannabis indica*). The active ingredient in marijuana is the chemical *delta-9-tetrahydrocannabinol* (*THC*), which can be introduced into the body in a variety of ways—dried and then smoked, for example, or eaten. The THC can also be concentrated into a form known as hashish. In all cases, marijuana has a range of effects: It relaxes the user, lifts her mood, and (like alcohol) reduces the ability to resist impulses. It also heightens sensations, so it can be considered a mild hallucinogenic.

Like most drugs, marijuana's effects depend on the context, including the user's expectations. If you're surrounded by giggly friends, marijuana is likely to make you giggly as well. If you're alone and anxious, marijuana can magnify these feelings as well.

Marijuana has various therapeutic uses. For many years, it was the best way to control the pain from glaucoma or the nausea from chemotherapy. (Other, more reliable, medications have now been developed for these purposes.) Marijuana also seems to be effective in treating the pain and general discomfort associated with several other medical conditions, including AIDS. This is why marijuana is prescribed

2005© "Faces of Meth"   2.5 Years Later

6.26 Methamphetamine's effects These before-and-after photos dramatically illustrate how the physical damage from methamphetamine can affect appearance.

6.27 An early source of cocaine Early versions of Coca-Cola contained a small quantity of cocaine. However, the amount of the drug was decreased during the years in which the formula for Coke was being "perfected," and the dose was miniscule by 1903; the soda was entirely cocaine free by 1929. Ironically, in 1911 the Coca-Cola Company was sued because of its ingredients—but the lawsuit involved the caffeine contained in the soft drink, not the cocaine!

for medical use in roughly a dozen U.S. states, although each state places its own restrictions on how and by whom the marijuana can be acquired and used.

The risk of addiction or dependence is low for marijuana. Infrequent users seem to suffer few withdrawal problems if they stop using the drug altogether. For more frequent users (e.g., multiple marijuana joints per day), quitting has been shown to produce withdrawal symptoms similar to those of tobacco users when they stop smoking. These symptoms may include sleep difficulties, increased anxiety, and irritability.

In addition—and despite claims to the contrary—marijuana doesn't seem to be a "gateway drug" that leads people to try (and eventually abuse) more potent drugs (Hart, Ksir, & Ray, 2009). There's also little reason to believe the media reports suggesting that marijuana has a long-lasting impact on sexual functioning or fertility (Grinspoon, Bakalar, & Russo, 2005).

Even so, many problems are associated with marijuana use. Marijuana smoke contains cancer-causing substances; in fact, it contains more of these substances than tobacco smoke does. Marijuana intoxication can also undermine a user's judgment, diminish motor coordination, and increase reaction time (Lane et al., 2005)—and so people under the influence of marijuana should certainly not drive or make big decisions of any sort. Marijuana also seems to interfere with memory—both the creation of new memories as well as the recall of older ones—and these effects seem to persist even when the immediate drug effects have worn off (Pope, Gruber, & Yurgelun-Todd, 2001).

How exactly does THC affect the brain? Evidence suggests that this molecule latches onto receptors located especially in the midbrain and in various limbic structures (Devane, Dysarz, Johnson, Melvin, & Howlett, 1988); it seems that all vertebrates may have these *cannabinoid receptors* (Elphick & Egertova, 2001; van Sickle et al., 2005).

These results raise a question, though: Why should the body have receptors that are responsive to THC at all? The answer seems to be that these cells are normally activated by a neurotransmitter called *anandamide* (from the Sanskrit word *ananda*, meaning "bliss"). This transmitter is chemically similar to THC, but it's produced naturally in the body (Devane et al., 1992; Wiley, 1999). Ordinarily, it seems to be involved in a range of functions including mood regulation, appetite control, and pain perception. Marijuana may have its effect, therefore, by triggering some of the same mechanisms.

It turns out that other chemicals also bear some resemblance to anandamide and so may mimic some of its effects. One such chemical is found in chocolate—which may be part of the reason so many people enjoy eating chocolate.

HALLUCINOGENS

So far, we've considered drugs that may change the tone of someone's conscious experience as well as make the person more sensitive to his sensory experiences. A final category of drugs is different: The **hallucinogens** are drugs that powerfully change perception and can also trigger sensory experiences in the absence of any inputs. These hallucinogenic effects are produced by many substances, including LSD (lysergic acid diethylamide, or "acid"), mescaline (from the peyote cactus), psilocybin (from certain mushrooms), and PCP (phencyclidine, often called "angel dust").

All of these chemicals produce enormous changes in how the user perceives the world. They may trigger a sense of seeing fantastic and intricate patterns, an intense kaleidoscope of colors, or a series of meaningful images—some fantasy, some apparently based on the user's emotional experiences. These experiences may trigger or be accompanied by intense emotions, ranging from euphoria in a "good trip" to deep panic or profound paranoia in a "bad trip," with the consequence that one person might be exhilarated by the experience while another is horribly disturbed.

hallucinogens Drugs that powerfully change perception and can trigger sensory experiences in the absence of any inputs.

Hallucinogens seem not to produce dependence. However, due to the unpredictable nature of the experience, users always risk having a hallucination that's deeply distressing. What's more, in the hallucinatory state people often have dreamlike experiences that seem compelling and real; if the person takes these experiences at face value, she can put herself into enormous danger—for example, trying to jump out a window because she's convinced she can fly. In response to these risks, users of hallucinogenic substances often choose to have a support network close at hand— friends who can serve as so-called trip sitters. These are people who aren't using the drug and who stay with the hallucinating person in case the emotions of the trip turn dark or she decides to explore some hazardous activity.

ADDICTION

Our main focus in this chapter has been on the nature of conscious experience, and so our emphasis, in describing various drug states, has been on the experience produced by the drug. However, we've also commented on the dangers associated with these substances. Some of the dangers are medical (e.g., the cardiovascular problems sometimes triggered by stimulants). Some of the problems are psychological (e.g., the panic that can be triggered by a bad trip). Still other dangers concern the bad choices someone makes while under the influence of one of these substances. (Think about the linkage between alcohol use and rape, or the fatalities attributable to drunk driving or the life disruption caused by drugs. Think also about the crimes associated with drug use—for example, when a user can't hold a job because of his drug state, and turns to crime to get the money he needs for the next dose.)

In light of all these dangers, why do people keep using drugs? Common sense provides the answer: In many cases, people put a higher value on the benefits (the drug-created changes in experience) than on the costs. And in many cases, people seem to have no choice: They're dependent on the drug, and so feel a powerful need to use it again and again, regardless of the risks.

This perspective raises another key question: What is dependence? And what do people mean when they say that someone is "addicted" to a substance? Answering these questions is—perhaps surprisingly—extremely difficult.

Researchers and clinicians tend to use the words *dependence* and *addiction* interchangeably and, overall, to define these words based on several attributes. Someone is dependent if, first, he's lost control over his own drug use; this attribute is usually reflected in the fact that the user has a very hard time giving up the drug, even though he would clearly benefit from doing so. Second, people who are dependent tend to show strong **withdrawal** symptoms if they go without the drug—they have strong cravings and exhibit a clear pattern of psychological and medical distress. Third, people who are dependent tend to display a pattern of **drug tolerance**—they have a weaker response to the drug than they did when they first began using it. One frequent result of this tolerance is that as time goes by, the dependent person needs larger and larger doses of the drug to get the desired effect. (For more on mechanisms that lead to withdrawal and tolerance, see Chapter 7.)

This cluster of attributes is clearly in place for some drugs, and some drug users. The most obvious case is probably *heroin.* People addicted to this drug seem unable to give it up, even though their drug use is hugely disrupting their lives (and often the lives of others). Heroin users typically suffer horrible withdrawal symptoms if they don't get their usual dose. And as they continue using the drug, heroin users seem to require larger doses just to maintain the same effect they've gotten in the past. Cases like heroin leave no doubt that addiction is a real and deeply destructive problem.

withdrawal A consequence of drug dependence that occurs when the drug is withheld, such that the person feels strong drug cravings and psychological and medical distress.

drug tolerance The diminished response to a drug that results from extended use, so that over time the user requires larger doses to experience the drug's effects.

But it's easy to find cases in which it's hard to tell if someone has an "addiction" or not. For example, how should we think about cocaine? People do seem to have great difficulty giving up cocaine, once they become frequent users. However, ceasing use of cocaine seems to cause only mild withdrawal symptoms (Kampman et al., 2002). So is cocaine addictive? It shows one of the attributes of addiction, but not another. Or, as a different case, what should we say about habits that show all the characteristics of addiction—but in a relatively mild version? For example, some people spend hours and hours shopping and seem unable to interrupt this habit, even though it's disrupting their lives and their finances. They also seem quite unhappy when they can't go shopping, and so they show a type of *withdrawal.* They also seem to require more and more hours in the mall, as the years go by, to satisfy their desire for shopping. Should we count this habit therefore as a "shopping addiction"?

Some people do seem willing to stretch the term *addiction* to cover these borderline cases—so they talk about someone being addicted to shopping, or sex, or television. Likewise, they use words like *workaholic* or even *soccerholic* to describe people who (allegedly) need a large daily dose of work or soccer, just like an alcoholic needs a large daily dose of alcohol. Most researchers, however, resist this stretching of the terms. To see why, think about the huge amount of life disruption a heroin addict will endure to support her habit, or the horrific suffering of heroin withdrawal. It seems entirely misleading to compare this disruption, or this suffering, to the (much milder) plight of a shopping addict or workaholic; and so it just seems unwise to use the term *addiction* to apply to both cases.

But how should we draw the line that will distinguish a "genuine" addict from these other questionable cases? Some writers make a distinction between *psychological dependence* on a substance (or an activity) and *physical* (or *physiological*) dependence. The general idea is that psychological dependence refers to the intense mental or emotional craving for the addictive substance, whereas physical dependence refers to the medical symptoms we observe during withdrawal. Moreover, genuine addicts show both psychological and physical dependence; the borderline cases are unlikely to show physical dependence.

But this distinction, too, is problematic. Among other concerns, bear in mind that so-called psychological dependence often creates feelings of *stress*—and stress, in turn, shows up in many bodily systems. (When people feel stress, their blood pressure goes up, their blood chemistry changes, and so on.) On this basis, the cravings associated with psychological dependence *cause physical symptoms.* This issue obviously undermines our effort to distinguish these two allegedly different forms of dependence.

In light of all these points, the word *addiction* is truly difficult to define. So perhaps we shouldn't be thinking of addiction as a separate category. Instead, we should think about the issues of substance use in terms of a continuum. At one end of the continuum are the social users of various substances; these are people who have an occasional drink or sometimes take a drug for recreation. Farther along the continuum are people who abuse the substances. They use alcohol or drugs more frequently, and they have at least a few problems because of it. Then, at the far end of the continuum, we find people who are truly dependent—using the substance a lot, experiencing serious problems as a result, and being largely unable to control the use. In this view, addiction is not a distinct state of affairs; instead, it's the extreme end of this range—and a point at which the person needs help in conquering the addiction.

DIFFERENCES AMONG PEOPLE

There's one more approach we might take in defining *addiction* or *dependence.* We might try to define these words by referring to the drugs themselves. For example, we might claim that addiction is what heroin produces; in contrast, mere habit is what marijuana produces. It turns out, however, that this approach doesn't work because, no matter what drug we consider and no matter what definition of addiction we use, not everyone who uses that drug will become addicted (Robinson & Berridge, 2003). Among cocaine users, for example, roughly 1 in 5 becomes a habitual user. Even for heroin, often tagged as the clearest case of an addictive drug, it's just 1 user in 4 who becomes addicted.

This variation from one user to the next certainly adds to our difficulties in defining addiction but is, in addition, an important fact for us to explain. Why do some people become addicted, but not others? As always, the answer has several parts. A direct influence of genetics is likely, so that (for example) someone is more likely to become an alcoholic if one of her biological parents was also an alcoholic (Crabbe, 2002). Personality, which is to some extent shaped by genetics, also plays a role because people differ in their willingness to take risks and their ability to control their own impulses—both factors that can feed into addiction. The environment is also crucial because, in some environments, people have more opportunity to explore various substances and are less discouraged from experimenting with this or that substance (Figure 6.28). A person's life status is also important; substance use is more likely to become substance *abuse*, and the abuse is more likely to become an addiction, if the person has just lost a job or had a close relationship break up. Cultural factors are also relevant; substance use is forbidden or strictly limited by some groups, so that dependence is extremely unlikely among these groups (Trimble, 1993).

A person's *beliefs* about their social surroundings can also play a role. Several studies suggest, for example, that students overestimate how much their friends use alcohol or other drugs (Prentice & Miller, 1993) and that those who most overestimate this usage are most likely to become recurrent users themselves (Graham, Marks, & Hansen, 1991). Unmistakably, therefore, we have many factors to consider when we seek to explain why someone uses a substance, abuses a substance, and may become dependent on the substance. Likewise, we have many options to consider when seeking ways to help people either avoid substance abuse or exit a substance problem they already have.

"Just tell me where you kids get the idea to take so many drugs."

6.28 Environmental influences on drug use

SOME FINAL THOUGHTS: THE UNSOLVED MYSTERIES

Early in the 20th century, American psychologists were convinced that *conscious experience* could not be studied scientifically, and the topic of consciousness was largely absent from the scientific journals. In the years since, we've realized that this early assessment was far too pessimistic, and we now know an enormous amount about consciousness. In this chapter we've discussed a lot of what we know, and other perspectives on conscious experience will appear in other chapters—for example, when we discuss the subjective sense of *familiarity* in chapter 8, or what it actually feels like to be *depressed* in chapter 16.

As we've seen, research has also provided a rich characterization of how much in our minds can proceed *without* conscious awareness, and this has allowed key insights into what consciousness contributes to our mental functioning. These insights in turn are linked to proposals about the biological substrate of consciousness. Our understanding of the neural basis for consciousness can then be linked to a further set of issues—including the altered states of consciousness associated with sleep, for example, or religious meditation.

By any measure, then, we've made enormous progress in our understanding of these incredibly difficult topics. Even so, many puzzles about consciousness remain untouched. Among them, we still have no solution to the mind-body problem. We can specify the locations in the brain and the types of neural activity associated with consciousness; but it remains a mystery how these neural firings give rise to subjective experience. Likewise, in many parts of this chapter, we've focused on what consciousness allows rather than how it feels. We've talked about information flow but said little (for example) about why happiness and sadness feel so different from each other, or whether the way you feel when you're "in love" is the same as the way others feel when they claim to be in the same state.

More than 25 years ago, the philosopher Thomas Nagel captured the essential problem of consciousness in a single question: *What is it like to be a bat?* Nagel's concern, of course, was not with bats but instead with the idea that consciousness is inherently subjective, so that we can count an organism as having "conscious mental states if and only if there is something that it is like to *be* that organism—something it is like *for the* organism" (Nagel, 1974, p. 436). This emphasis on subjective experience has not been our main concern in much of the chapter, and so plainly we've tackled only part of the broader problem of consciousness. In fact, it remains possible that only some aspects of consciousness can be studied by means of data collection and scientific research, while other aspects require other forms of inquiry (e.g., philosophical analysis; for more on this point, see, among others, N. Block, 1997, 2005; A. Damasio, 1999; Dehaene & Chageux, 2004; Jackendoff, 1987; Pinker, 1997).

Even acknowledging these boundaries on what we know, the data we've reviewed— and the conclusions flowing from these data—provide powerful insights into the nature of consciousness, and these data will certainly inform future discussions of this profound and complex issue. This by itself—the mere fact that research can address these extraordinarily subtle issues—has to be a source of great satisfaction for investigators working on these intriguing problems.

SUMMARY   CHAPTER 6

INTROSPECTION AND THE FUNCTIONS OF CONSCIOUSNESS

- The only direct way to study *consciousness* is to have each person look within themselves, or introspect. *Introspection* is a powerful research tool—but limited. People often lack words to report their experiences, and when they have the words, different individuals may use the same words to refer to different inner experiences.

- Introspection is also limited because much of what's going on in our minds happens outside of awareness, in the *cognitive unconscious*—the unnoticed support machinery that makes our perception, thoughts, and memories possible. Many processes of the mind unfold in the cognitive unconscious, but people are aware only of the products that result from those processes.

- The scope of what the cognitive unconscious can achieve is evident in cases of brain damage. From such cases we know that people can remember without being aware they're remembering, and they can even perceive without being aware of their perception. Studies of unconscious attribution also show us the sophistication of the cognitive unconscious—and thus the ability to evaluate and interpret evidence while being unaware of the process.

- Introspections are also sometimes mistaken—when people don't realize what factor has influenced their thoughts or behavior, or when they insist that a factor has influenced them, even though we have reason to believe it hasn't. These cases suggest that introspection often isn't a "readout" of internal processes, but the person's best after-the-fact estimation of why they acted or felt the way they did.

- The cognitive unconscious allows processes that are fast, effortless, and automatic. This suggests that consciousness may be needed whenever we wish to exercise executive control over our own thought processes—rising above habit or resisting the temptation of the moment.

THE NEURAL BASIS FOR CONSCIOUSNESS

- The *mind-body problem* centers on the fact that the conscious mind is a completely different sort of thing than the physical body. This point raises deep questions about how the brain makes consciousness possible and how physical events can cause, or be caused by, conscious thoughts.

- Many brain areas are needed for consciousness. These include areas that seem to govern people's overall level of arousal and alertness; this aspect of consciousness may depend on the thalamus and reticular activating system. The exact content of consciousness depends on diverse brain sites, and depends on what a person is conscious *of*.

- Many studies have examined the *neural correlates of consciousness*. These studies show, for example, that the activity of certain brain sites depends on what visual stimulus the person is currently aware of. Other studies have examined the conscious sensation of "free will" and have identified patterns of brain activity that occur before—and so are plausibly the cause of—this conscious sensation.

- According to the *global workspace hypothesis*, consciousness is made possible by a pattern of integrated neural activity, in turn made possible by the connections provided by the workspace neurons, and controlled by the processes of attention. This hypothesis—while speculative—explains many aspects of consciousness, including its apparent functions.

VARIETIES OF CONSCIOUSNESS

- Our conscious state obviously changes when we're asleep. An important source of evidence about sleep comes from EEG data, which allow us to distinguish the distinct stages of sleep. People seem to need an adequate amount of sleep as well as the right amount of both *slow-wave* and *REM sleep*.

- One hypothesis is that sleep is a time for our bodies to repair themselves or restore substances used up while we're awake. A different hypothesis is that sleep allows neurons to reset their activity levels or consolidate connections made during the day. A third hypothesis is that sleep is merely the state in which animals pass time while digesting, or perhaps it's just time animals spend when unable to find food.

- Dreams are strongly associated with REM sleep. Dream reports suggest that dreams showcase a range of ordinary preoccupations, but they also include weird elements like being naked in public. Many people propose that dreams have hidden meaning; but most researchers suggest that dreams are just a hodgepodge of activated images, woven together into a narrative either by the sleeping brain or perhaps later, when the person recalls the dream.

- *Hypnosis* is another means of altering someone's conscious state. Many extraordinary claims about hypnosis have no basis in fact. Even so, hypnosis can have striking effects, including the powerful influence of hypnotic analgesia. Most current theories emphasize the hybrid nature of hypnosis and describe it as blending the powerful social influence of the hypnotist with the striking effects of dissociation.

- Altered states of consciousness are also associated with some religious practices, including those emphasizing meditation. In the meditative state, the person's brain activity changes—it shows a pronounced alpha rhythm (associated with relaxation) and, in some forms of meditation, a rhythm that's crucial for integrating brain activity in distinct areas.

- Many drugs are also used to alter consciousness. These include *depressants* like alcohol, sleep medications, and antianxiety medications. People also use *stimulants*, including caffeine, cocaine, amphetamine, and MDMA. These drugs decrease the need for sleep and lift a person's energy level and mood, but their many negative effects include substantial risk of dependence as well as psychological and medical problems resulting from drug use.

- Marijuana, another often-used drug, seems to function by activating specialized receptors in the brain that ordinarily respond to a neurotransmitter called anandamide. Marijuana is also considered a mild *hallucinogen*; more powerful hallucinogens include LSD, mescaline, and PCP. These drugs trigger powerful perceptual experiences, but they can also produce a "bad trip" involving panic or profound paranoia.

- All mind-altering drugs have associated risks that range from medical and psychological problems to the dangers of making bad choices when using one of these drugs. Many of these drugs can also lead to dependence or addiction—terms that are defined as points on a continuum ranging from casual and occasional use of the substance to frequent use despite serious problems resulting from that use and a profound inability to control the use.

- People differ in how readily they become dependent on a drug. The difference depends partly on genetic factors and partly on personality, which is itself shaped to some extent by genetics. Drug dependence is also influenced by environmental factors such as social support for (or discouragement of) drug use and whether the person has recently experienced some misfortune.

 ONLINE STUDY TOOLS

Go to StudySpace, **wwnorton.com/studyspace**, to access additional review and enrichment materials, including the following resources for each chapter:

Organize
- Study Plan
- Chapter Outline
- Quiz+ Assessment

Learn
- Ebook
- Chapter Review
- Vocabulary Flashcards
- Drag-and-Drop Labeling Exercises
- Audio Podcast Chapter Overview

Connect
- Critical Thinking Activity
- Studying the Mind Video Podcasts
- Video Exercises
- Animations
- **ZAPS** Psychology Labs

7

Learning

Biologically and psychologically, you have a lot in common with your pet cat, a lowly sea slug, and a tap-dancing chicken. The biological resemblance is evident in the physiology you share with these creatures and the overlap in genetic patterns. But the psychological resemblance is also crucial, and includes an important set of similarities in the way all four of you detect relationships in the world and adjust your behavior accordingly. That is, there's a significant resemblance in the way that you and many other creatures learn.

In simple creatures and complex ones, learning comes in several forms. Both you and the cat look up when your roommate sneezes. But during allergy season, when she's sneezing all the time, you and the cat both learn that sneezes are part of the normal acoustic environment and cease responding to every "a-choo"—a form of learning called *habituation*.

Both you and the sea slug—and virtually every other animal—are also skilled at learning "what goes with what." If, just a couple of times, a light pressure on your skin is followed by a blast of cold air, soon you'll brace for the chill the moment you feel the pressure. Likewise, if the sea slug feels a mild poke and then, a moment later, a slight electric shock, the slug quickly learns to shift into a defensive posture as soon as it feels the poke. This form of learning is called *classical conditioning*.

And what about that dancing chicken? In nature, chickens scratch, peck, and waggle their heads, but they don't dance. Using *operant conditioning*, however, you can transform a chicken's natural antics into stomps, shuffles, and hops. First, identify a reward—such as corn—that your chicken likes. Then, through processes described in this chapter, you initially reward behaviors that vaguely resemble a tap-dance step—say, mere scratching—and then slowly shape these scratches into smooth moves.

You can use similar techniques to train one of your professors to lecture to only one side of the room—an exercise in behavior control cherished by generations of psychology students. In this case, the reward is not food, but the favor of your and your classmates' gaze. The procedure is simple: Conspire with your fellow students to look up with rapt attention whenever your professor addresses one side of the room, and to gaze downward and look bored whenever the prof turns in the other direction. After just a bit of this "training," your professor—like the chicken—will be producing the behavior you've selected.

These simple forms of learning—habituation, classical conditioning, and operant conditioning—are crucial for many aspects of our behavior and emotional responses, as they are for many other creatures on the planet. In this chapter, we'll look at how these types of learning proceed, and consider some of the biological mechanisms that—in you, the cat, the slug, or the chicken—make this learning possible. We'll then turn to some ways in which your learning differs from that of other creatures. For example, animals differ in how well they can learn just by watching their neighbors—and humans are especially skilled in this observational learning. At the same time, other creatures show feats of learning that humans can't match, such as easily learning to navigate in new environments. Why are some forms of learning shared by so many creatures, and why are other forms specific to just a few species? We'll tackle these questions and more in this chapter, as we consider what learning is and how it happens.

THE PERSPECTIVE OF LEARNING THEORY

What exactly is "learning"? In ordinary language, this term is applied to many different cases—the development of new skills, the acquisition of new knowledge, and more. According to some scholars, though, all learning involves the same basic processes.

As we discussed in Chapter 4, empiricist philosophers like John Locke (1632–1704) and George Berkeley (1685–1753) offered a simple account of how we come to understand our world. Perception, they argued, was massively influenced by learning; and (in their view) learning was just a matter of creating *associations* among ideas as a direct result of experience. Thus, for example, the sight of a stove might be followed immediately by the feeling of heat, creating an association between this sight and this feeling; and so you learned that stoves are hot. The sound of the word *flower* might be followed by the sight and smell of the flower, and so these ideas become associated.

But what about more complicated forms of learning? The answer, according to these philosophers, was easy: More complex learning simply involves more associations, built layer upon layer, so that complicated notions—and whole belief systems—are just the result of creating more and more links among individual ideas.

This is an appealing proposal, partly because similar conceptions have fared well in other sciences. Chemistry teaches us that complex molecules are built up by linking relatively simple atoms to each other, and then linking still other atoms to these, continuing in this way until huge combinations are created and the whole has properties that are often strikingly different from those of the individual components. Will a similar proposal work as our basic conception of learning?

A large number of researchers, called *learning theorists*, would answer this question with a firm yes, and in their research, they're guided by a striking implication of this view: If all learning depends on essentially the same mechanisms (i.e., mechanisms of association), then for research purposes it may not matter very much what forms of learning we choose to study, because the lessons we will draw from our research and the principles we will uncover should be the same whether we're scrutinizing simple cases of learning or far more complex ones.

Learning theorists also argue that it's sensible to focus experiments on simple organisms learning simple patterns; that way, the experiments will be easy to do, and the principles we're hoping to uncover should be immediately visible. Thus, rather than studying learning by asking how a college student masters calculus, we might choose to examine how less complicated organisms—rats, for example—form simple associations.

Does this strategy work? Are there uniform principles of learning that will emerge no matter what species and type of learning we examine? We know at the start that all animal species, as diverse as they are, have a lot in common biologically—in the structure of their nervous systems, for example, and in their evolutionary past. On this basis, perhaps all species do learn in essentially the same way; and, if so, we should be able to identify basic laws of learning that apply equally well to a dog learning to sit on command, a fish learning to navigate its way through a dense growth of algae, or a student learning to play a Mozart sonata.

As we'll see, this research strategy—an effort toward understanding *all* learning by studying *simple* learning—has led to many important discoveries. Indeed, in this chapter we'll discuss principles of learning that have amazing generality and apply to many species, situations, and types of behavior. These principles are also the basis for various useful techniques, including procedures used in treating phobias, techniques used to manage prison inmates' behavior, and more.

We'll also see that some forms of learning do not follow these general principles; so our overall discussion of learning will also need to take these distinctive forms of learning into account. Let's look at the data that underlie these important claims.

HABITUATION

Perhaps the simplest form of learning is **habituation**—the decline in an organism's response to a stimulus once the stimulus has become familiar. As a concrete case, imagine someone living in an apartment on a busy street. At first, he finds the traffic noises distracting and obnoxious. After he's lived in the apartment for a while, though, the noises bother him much less—and eventually he doesn't notice them at all. At this point, he's become habituated to the noises (Figure 7.1).

For the city dweller, habituation is obviously important. (Otherwise, with the traffic noise as it is, these people might never get any sleep!) But, more broadly, habituation produces a huge benefit: We want to pay attention to unfamiliar stimuli, because these may signal danger or indicate some unexpected opportunity. But, at the same time, we don't want to waste time scrutinizing every stimulus we run across. How, therefore, do we manage to be suitably selective? The answer is habituation; this simple form of learning essentially guarantees that we ignore inputs we're already familiar with and have found to be inconsequential, and focus instead on the novel ones.

Just as important as habituation is its opposite: **dishabituation**—an *increase* in responding, caused by a change in something familiar. Thus, the city dweller who's

habituation A decline in the response to a stimulus once the stimulus has become familiar.

dishabituation An increase in responsiveness when something novel is presented, following a series of presentations of something familiar.

7.1 Habituation Habituation has both benefits and costs. Thanks to habituation, the bison of Wyoming's Yellowstone Park have grown accustomed to the automobile traffic. This is helpful for the bison—but may be less so for the traffic. Similarly, many city residents have become habituated to the sight of homeless on the street—a sad fact that may undermine people's motivation to help the homeless.

seemingly oblivious to traffic noise will notice if the noise suddenly stops. Likewise, imagine an office worker who has finally gotten used to the humming of the building's light fixtures. Despite her apparent success in ignoring this humming, she's likely to notice immediately when, on one remarkable day, the humming ceases.

Dishabituation is obviously important because a change in stimulation often brings important news about the world. If the birds in the nearby trees suddenly stop chirping, is it because they've detected a predator? If so, the deer grazing in the meadow want to know about this. If the sound of the brook abruptly grows louder, has the water level suddenly increased? This, too, is certainly worth investigating. Thus, dishabituation serves the function of calling attention to newly arriving—and potentially useful—information, just as habituation serves the function of helping you ignore old news.

These simple forms of learning also provide powerful *research tools* for investigators. As one example, consider that adult speakers of Japanese have trouble hearing the distinction, obvious to English speakers, between the words *red* and *led*. This is because there's no equivalent distinction between these sounds in the Japanese language. But how did this perceptual difference between English and Japanese speakers come to be? In one experiment, 4-month-old Japanese infants heard the sound "la, la, la" repeated over and over. At first this sound stream caught their attention, but they soon habituated and stopped responding to the sounds. Then the researcher changed the sound to repetitions of "ra, ra, ra." Would the infants notice the change? In fact, they did: The infants showed immediate dishabituation and once again oriented to the sound. Apparently, Japanese infants heard the distinction between these sounds as readily as infants in English-speaking countries did. This seems, therefore, to be a case of "use it or lose it": All infants, no matter where they're born, can hear this acoustic difference. However, if the sound difference is not relevant to the language in the infant's surroundings (as, for example, in the case of Japanese), the infants stop paying attention to the distinction. By the time they're 12 months old, they've completely lost the ability to tell these sounds apart (for more on this finding, see Chapter 10). This is on its own an important finding, one that sheds light on how perception can change as a result of experience and helps us understand one aspect of language learning. But, for our purposes here, notice that this research relies on habituation and dishabituation as a means of finding out what sounds *different* to an infant and what sounds the *same*. Thus, these simple phenomena of learning provide a straightforward way to explore the perceptual capabilities of a very young (preverbal) child.

CLASSICAL CONDITIONING

Habituation is important, but it tells the organism about only a single stimulus—is the stimulus novel and so worth exploring, or familiar and therefore safe to ignore? Other forms of learning provide more information and, in particular, provide the organism with information about the *relationships* among events in the world.

Relationships come in many varieties. One event might *cause* another; an action might *prevent* some outcome; a certain circumstance might *magnify* an experience; and so on. Overall, though, relationships can usually be understood in terms of associations: Your dog learns to associate the sound of your footsteps with the possibility of a treat; you have learned to associate thunder with lightning; the farmer's cows learn to associate a certain time of day with milking. The importance of these associations was, as we've seen, highlighted by the empiricist philosophers, but the experimental study of these associations did not begin until the end of the late 1800s, when the work of the Russian physiologist Ivan Petrovich Pavlov (1849–1936) made a major contribution (Figure 7.2).

Pavlov and the Conditioned Response

Pavlov's early work, for which he earned the Nobel Prize in medicine in 1904, was not in psychology. Instead, his research was concerned with digestive physiology, and many of his laboratory studies focused on the secretion of saliva in dogs. Pavlov knew from the start that salivation is triggered whenever food (especially dry food) is placed in the mouth. During his experiments, however, a new fact emerged: Salivation could be set off by a range of other stimuli as well, including stimuli that were at first totally neutral. Dogs that had been in the laboratory for a while would salivate in response to the mere sight of meat, or the sight of the dish that ordinarily held the meat, or even the sight of the person who usually brought the meat. Pavlov was intrigued by these effects because he realized that in these cases, the organism seemed to be developing new reflexes and changing its behavior in a fashion directly shaped by learning. He decided to refocus his research program to study this learning.

In his experiments, Pavlov created simple patterns for the animal to detect. For example, he would ring a bell and then give the animal food. Then, after a short wait, he would present another pair of stimuli: bell, then food. After another wait, he presented yet another pairing: bell, then food. After several such pairings, Pavlov observed what happened if the bell was sounded alone, without any food being given (Pavlov, 1927; Figure 7.3). The result was clear: The dog salivated in response to the bell.

To describe this pattern, Pavlov distinguished two types of responses: An **unconditioned response (UR)** was a biologically determined reflex, triggered by a certain stimulus independent of any learning. In Pavlov's terms, the trigger for an unconditioned response was an **unconditioned stimulus (US).** In the procedure described, the unconditioned stimulus (the US) is food in the animal's mouth; the unconditioned response (the UR) is salivation. The linkage that makes the US trigger a UR is something the animal brings into the situation,

7.2 Ivan Petrovich Pavlov (1849–1936) Pavlov (center) in his laboratory, with some colleagues and his experimental subject.

unconditioned response (UR) A response elicited by an unconditioned stimulus without prior training.

unconditioned stimulus (US) A stimulus that reliably triggers a particular response without prior training.

7.3 Apparatus for salivary conditioning Here is an early version of Pavlov's apparatus for classical conditioning of the salivary response. The dog was held in a harness; sounds or lights acted as conditioned stimuli (CS), while meat powder in a dish was the unconditioned stimulus (US). The conditioned response (CR) was assessed with the aid of a tube connected to an opening in one of the animal's salivary glands.

Harness

Salivating (CR)

Meat powder can be delivered to dish (US)

Collecting tube from salivary glands

Measuring cup for saliva

Before conditioning

Food (**unconditioned stimulus**) causes the dog to salivate (**unconditioned response**).

A bell (neutral stimulus) does not cause the dog to salivate.

US   UR

Neutral stimulus   No response

During conditioning trials

During conditioning trials, the ringing bell is presented to a dog along with the food.

then

After conditioning

During critical trials, the ringing bell (**conditioned stimulus**) is presented without the food, and the dog's response is measured.

CS   CR

7.4 Relationships between CS, US, CR, and UR in classical conditioning

---

conditioned response (CR) A response elicited by an initially neutral stimulus—the conditioned stimulus (CS)—after it has been paired repeatedly with an unconditioned stimulus (US).

conditioned stimulus (CS) An initially neutral stimulus that comes to elicit a new response due to pairings with the unconditioned stimulus.

classical conditioning A form of learning in which one stimulus is paired with another so that the organism learns a relationship between the stimuli.

---

and so (in Pavlov's terms) is not a product of the learning process called "conditioning"; that's why the stimulus and response are said to be unconditioned.

The second type of response is a **conditioned response (CR)**, and it is a product of learning. Like the UR, the CR is triggered by a specific stimulus, but it's a stimulus that was neutral at the start of learning. In our example, this neutral stimulus is the bell, and it came to elicit the CR (salivation) only after several presentations in which this stimulus was followed by the US (food in the mouth). In Pavlov's terms, the bell is a **conditioned stimulus (CS)**—a stimulus that's initially neutral but becomes associated with the US during the experiment.

The relationships between US and UR, CS and CR, are summarized in Figure 7.4 and form the basis of the learning studied by Pavlov. In his honor, this type of learning is sometimes called *Pavlovian conditioning*, but it's more commonly known as **classical conditioning.**

Early research on classical conditioning focused on one conditioned response—salivation by dogs—and a narrow range of conditioned stimuli (the sound of bells—or in other experiments, the ticking of metronomes). Subsequent research, however, has made it plain that this form of learning occurs in a remarkable range of species and circumstances. Indeed, classical conditioning can be documented not just in humans but in species as diverse as ants and anteaters, cats and cockroaches, wolves and worms. By using the appropriate US, researchers have conditioned crabs to twitch their tail spines, fish to thrash about, and octopuses to change color. Responses conditioned in studies with humans include changes in heart rate or blood pressure (where the US is typically a loud noise or rap on the knee) and the reflexive eye blink (using a US of a puff of air on the open eye).

Outside of the laboratory, classical conditioning touches many aspects of our lives. We all tend to feel hungry at mealtime and less so in between; part of the reason is a conditioning process in which the CS is a particular time of day and the US is the presentation of food (which normally is paired with that time of day). Our emotional responses to certain songs, or certain smells, or even certain social situations can be understood in similar terms, and the response is likely to be the result of some previous pairing between these stimuli and some emotional experience. This type of learning is, for example, a plausible basis for some forms of anxiety as well as some phobias (Figure 7.5). Yet another example is sexual arousal, which can often be produced by an initially neutral word or gesture that has—through learning—acquired an erotic association. Clearly, then, classical conditioning is a process with wide application and great importance.

The Major Phenomena of Classical Conditioning

As we've seen, classical conditioning can be described in terms of a specific procedure: We need a US and UR that are biologically linked, and then we need a sequence of presentations in which the CS is paired with the US. But we can also describe this form of conditioning in terms of a set of properties that usually characterize this type of learning.

7.5 SCIENTIFIC METHOD: Can classical conditioning establish an emotional response?

Method

1. "Little Albert"—a normal, 9-month-old infant—was presented with a white rat.

2. When Albert reached out to touch the creature, a researcher struck a steel bar with a hammer, producing a loud, startling noise.

3. This pairing (rat + loud noise) was repeated several times.

Results: Little Albert showed intense fear the moment the rat came into view. Albert also exhibited fear of other furry animals, like this rabbit.

CONCLUSION: Classical conditioning can establish strong fearful responses. This may provide insight into how some phobias develop.

SOURCE STUDY: Watson & Rayner, 1920

ACQUISITION OF CONDITIONED RESPONSES

At the start of a conditioning procedure, the conditioned stimulus (CS) does not elicit the conditioned response (CR). In fact, the CS may elicit no reaction at all beyond a general stop-and-look response that organisms produce whenever a new stimulus appears. But after several pairings with the unconditioned stimulus (US), things change, so that a previously neutral CS (say, the sound of a bell) now elicits a CR (salivation).

Let's emphasize, however, that learning doesn't take place all at once. Instead, the learning is gradual, and the strength of the CR slowly grows as the animal experiences more and more pairings of CS and US. This pattern is evident in the data shown in Figure 7.6. Once the CS-US relationship is solidly established, though, the CS can be used in other procedures to establish other conditioned stimuli. As one example, by using meat powder as the US, we can first condition a dog to salivate whenever it sees a light. Once this is done, we can sound a bell and follow that by the light, without ever introducing the food. After enough of these pairings, the bell itself will trigger salivation. In this setting, the bell has become a signal for the light, which we've already established as a signal for the appearance of food. This sequence is called **second-order conditioning**—a procedure in which a neutral stimulus (here, the bell) is paired with some already established CS (like the light), as shown in Figure 7.7.

Second-order conditioning considerably extends the power and importance of classical conditioning. For example, the sight of your dentist is often paired with the discomfort of feeling her drill; as a result, the sight of the dentist (the CS in this case) might become fearful. But other stimuli are in turn associated with the sight of the

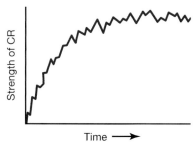

7.6 An idealized learning curve This graph plots CR strength against the number of reinforced (paired) trials. The CR gradually becomes stronger as the number of learning trials increases—but each trial adds less strength than the trial just before it.

second-order conditioning A form of learning in which a neutral stimulus is first made meaningful through classical conditioning. Then, that stimulus (the CS) is paired with a new, neutral stimulus until the new stimulus also elicits the conditioned response.

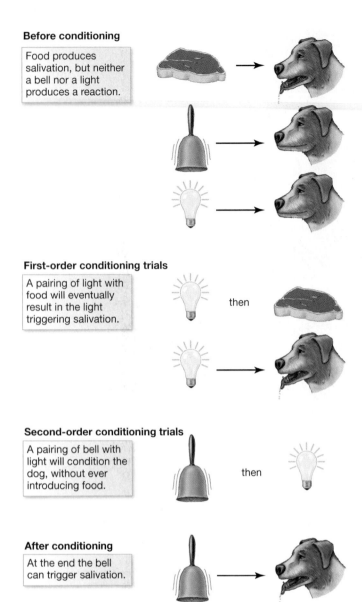

Before conditioning

Food produces salivation, but neither a bell nor a light produces a reaction.

First-order conditioning trials

A pairing of light with food will eventually result in the light triggering salivation.

then

Second-order conditioning trials

A pairing of bell with light will condition the dog, without ever introducing food.

then

After conditioning

At the end the bell can trigger salivation.

7.7 Second-order conditioning Before conditioning, neither the bell nor the light trigger salivation. During *first*-order conditioning, the light is paired with meat, and soon presentation of the light can trigger salivation. During *second*-order conditioning, the bell is paired with the light. As a result, presentation of the bell alone (which has never been paired with meat) will elicit salivation.

extinction The weakening of a learned response that is produced if a conditioned stimulus is now repeatedly presented without the unconditioned stimulus.

dentist—the sight of her office, the sound of her voice, the word *dentist*, and more. Through second-order conditioning, these stimuli, too, can become fearful—potentially leading to a fear of all things related to dentistry. In this way, second-order conditioning can produce widespread effects that, as in this example, can sometimes lead to the highly disruptive fears we call *phobias* (e.g., Gewirtz & Davis, 2000). More generally, though, mechanisms like higher-order conditioning allow the learning process to play a substantial role in shaping key aspects of our emotional lives.

EXTINCTION

Classical conditioning can have considerable adaptive value. Imagine a mouse that has several times seen the cat resting on a kitchen chair. It would serve the mouse well to learn about this association between the cat and a particular location; that way, the mouse will likely feel afraid whenever it nears the kitchen. This fear, in turn, will probably lead the mouse to avoid that room—a habit that could save the mouse's life!

At the same time, it would be unfortunate for the mouse if this association, once established, could never be undone. The cat might lose interest in that resting place or leave the household altogether. Either way, it would be useful for the mouse to lose its fearful response to the kitchen so it can return there to forage for food.

All is well for this mouse, though, because the effects of classical conditioning can be undone through a sequence of events similar to those that established the conditioning in the first place. Pavlov demonstrated that the CR will gradually disappear if the CS is presented several times by itself—that is, without the US. For example, repeated pairings of light plus a blast of cold air will create a conditioned response, so that the animal will shiver (the CR) whenever the light (the CS) is presented. But if the light is then presented several times on its own, the shivering response will be *extinguished*. **Extinction** is the undoing of a previously learned response so that the response is no longer produced (Figure 7.8).

Let's be clear, though, that extinction is not just the result of an animal forgetting what it learned earlier. Of course, animals (including humans) do eventually forget things they once learned, but that is not what's going on in extinction. This point is evident, for example, in the speed of extinction. As Figure 7.8 shows, a response can be extinguished in just a half-dozen trials over a period of only a few minutes. In contrast, forgetting is far slower: To demonstrate this, we can condition an animal, then leave it alone for several weeks, and then test it by presenting the CS. In this cicumstance, we have arranged for no extinction trials, but we have provided an opportunity for forgetting. The result of this procedure is clear: Even after a substantial delay, the animal is likely to exhibit a full-blown conditioned response (B. Schwartz, Wasserman, & Robbins, 2005). It seems, then, that classically conditioned responses are forgotten only very slowly.

The difference between extinction and forgetting is also clear in another procedure. First we condition an animal by repeated pairings of CS and US; then we extinguish the learning by presenting the CS on its own. In a third step, we *recondition* the same animal—by presenting some more learning trials, just like those in the first step of the procedure. What happens? The reconditioning usually takes much less time than the

7.8 Extinction of a classically conditioned response The figure shows the decrease in the amount of saliva secreted (the CR) with increasing number of extinction trials—that is, trials on which the CS is presented without the US. However, if the animal then spends a little time away from the conditioning apparatus, the CR will reappear the next time the animal encounters the CS—a pattern known as spontaneous recovery.

initial conditioning did. The speed of relearning, in other words, is faster than the original rate of learning. Apparently, then, extinction doesn't "erase" the original learning and return the animal to its original naive state. Instead, the animal still has some memory of the learning, and this gives it a head start in the reconditioning trials.

We can draw similar conclusions about extinction from the phenomenon of **spontaneous recovery.** This phenomenon is observed in animals that have been through an extinction procedure and then left alone for a rest interval. After this rest period, the CS is again presented, and now the CS often elicits the CR—even though the CR was fully extinguished earlier (see Figure 7.8).

According to one view of this effect, the extinction trials lead the animal to recognize that a once informative stimulus is no longer informative. The bell initially signaled that food would be coming soon; but now, the animal learns, the bell signals nothing. However, the animal still remembers that the bell was once informative; so when a new experimental session begins, the animal checks to see whether the bell will again be informative in this new setting. Thus, the animal resumes responding to the bell, producing the result we call spontaneous recovery (Robbins, 1990).

Like all aspects of conditioning, spontaneous recovery can easily be observed outside of the laboratory and in humans. For example, various anxiety disorders are often treated via *exposure therapy*—a process modeled after the extinction procedure. In this process, the person is repeatedly exposed to the specific stimulus or the particular situation that has, for that person, been a source of anxiety—heights, say, or enclosed

spontaneous recovery The reappearance of an extinguished response after a period in which no further conditioning trials have been presented.

spaces, or the sight of a snake. (For more on this procedure, see Chapter 17.) During these exposures, the person is kept safe and comfortable—and so there's no fearful US associated with the CS. As we'd expect, this sequence of events leads to extinction of the CR (the feelings of anxiety)—and with each exposure, the person feels less and less anxious.

When exposure therapy ends, however, people often relapse and again become anxious when exposed to the phobic stimulus. This relapse is not a sign that the therapy has failed. It's simply an example of spontaneous recovery of a CR—a sign that more treatment is needed to eliminate the anxiety.

GENERALIZATION

In Pavlov's early experiments, animals were trained with a particular CS—the sound of a bell or metronome, for example—and then later tested with that same stimulus. But Pavlov understood that life outside the lab is more complicated. The master's voice may always signal food, but his tone of voice varies from one occasion to the next. The sight of an apple tree may well signal the availability of fruit, but apple trees differ in size and shape. Because of these variations, animals must be able to respond to stimuli that aren't identical to the original CS; otherwise, the animals may obtain no benefit from their earlier learning.

It's not surprising, therefore, that animals show a pattern called **stimulus generalization**—that is, they respond to a range of stimuli, provided that these stimuli are similar enough to the original CS. Here's an example: A dog might be conditioned to respond to a tone of a particular pitch. When tested later on, that dog will respond most strongly if the test tone is that same pitch. But the dog will also respond, although a bit less strongly, to a tone a few notes higher. The dog will also respond to an even higher tone, but the response will be weaker still. In general, the greater the difference between the new stimulus and the original CS, the weaker the CR will be. Figure 7.9 illustrates this pattern, called a *generalization gradient*. The peak of the gradient (the strongest response) is typically found when the test stimulus is identical to the conditioned stimulus used in training. As the stimuli become less like the original CS, the response gets weaker and weaker (so the curve gets lower and lower).

DISCRIMINATION

Stimulus generalization is obviously beneficial, but it can be carried too far. It's sensible for you to feel fear when someone wearing an angry expression approaches you; and thanks to generalization, you'll feel this fear even if the person's face is a bit different from angry faces you've seen in the past. But if you generalize too much, you might feel fear in response to other facial expressions—and so end up being afraid in many social situations. What you need to do, therefore, is **discriminate**—respond in a way that's guided by the stimuli in your view.

The phenomenon of discrimination is easy to demonstrate. An experiment might, for example, use a loud boat horn as the US; this stimulus reliably produces a startle response when it's sounded. In the first part of the procedure, a red warning light is paired with the boat horn, and after a few pairings, this stimulus will reliably produce a conditioned response—you'll tense your muscles whenever the light appears. Once this CR is established, we proceed to the next step: Now we intersperse trials pairing the red light + horn with other trials in which a new stimulus—say, an orange light—is presented with no US (no boat horn). In this setup, you're likely to generalize at first by

stimulus generalization The tendency for stimuli similar to those used during learning to elicit a reaction similar to the learned response.

discrimination An aspect of learning in which the organism learns to respond differently to stimuli that have been associated with a US (or reinforcement), and stimuli that have not.

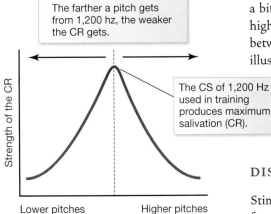

7.9 **Generalization gradient of a classically conditioned response** This figure shows the generalization of a conditioned blinking response in rabbits. The CS during the initial conditioning was a tone of 1,200 hertz, and the US was electric shock. After the conditioned response to the original CS was well established, generalization was measured by presenting various test stimuli and noting the percentage of trials in which the animals produced the CR.

tensing up in response to both the red light (technically referred to as the CS⁺) and the orange light (the CS⁻). As the training continues, however—trials pairing the red light + horn, mixed with trials presenting the orange light alone—you'll learn to discriminate and will cringe only when you see the red light.

In a discrimination procedure you learn, of course, that the CS⁺ signals the approach of the US. What about the CS⁻? In our example, we might think you're learning nothing about the orange light because it's never followed by the horn, and for that matter never followed by any kind of US. Even so, the CS⁻ (again, the orange light) does provide information. When it arrives, this signals a period in which the US is likely *not* to arrive. If the US is the horn, then the CS⁻ indicates that the loud noise is not coming soon. If the US is food, then the CS⁻ signals the start of a period in which no food will be available.

Essentially, then, CS⁻ takes on a meaning opposite to that of the CS⁺. It means "no noise," or "no food," or, in general, "no US." Correspondingly, the animal's response to the CS⁻ tends to be the opposite of its response to the CS⁺. If the US is a noise blast, then the CS⁺ elicits fear and the CS⁻ seems to inhibit fear—and so the animal is *calmer* in the presence of the CS⁻ than it would be otherwise. If the US is food, then the CS⁺ elicits salivation and the CS⁻ causes the animal to salivate less than it ordinarily would. Overall, the CS⁻ takes on the role of **inhibitor**: Whatever the response produced by the CS⁺, the CS⁻ makes that response less likely.

inhibitor A stimulus signaling that an event is not coming, which elicits a response opposite to the one that the event usually elicits.

THE CS AS A "SIGNAL"

In describing discrimination, it seems natural to speak about the CS⁺ and CS⁻ as though they were *signals* for the animal, providing information about things to come. And in fact this way of thinking about the CS helps us understand several aspects of conditioning, including why the rate at which conditioning develops depends on how the CS and US are related to each other in time.

Conditioning happens most efficiently when the CS precedes the US by some optimum interval—usually a half-second or so, or perhaps a few seconds at most. If the interval between the CS and US is increased beyond this optimum, the effectiveness of the pairing drops sharply. But we also don't want the interval between these stimuli to be *too short*. In fact, presenting the CS and US simultaneously is usually ineffective in establishing an association—and the backward procedure, presenting the US *before* the CS, is even worse (Rescorla, 1988; Figure 7.10).

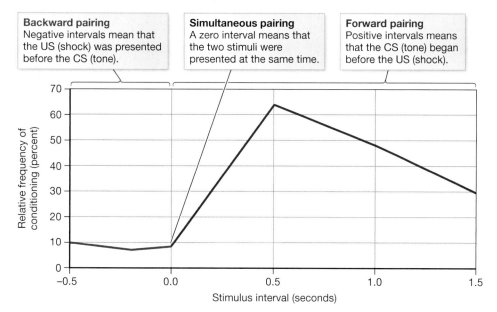

Backward pairing Negative intervals mean that the US (shock) was presented before the CS (tone).

Simultaneous pairing A zero interval means that the two stimuli were presented at the same time.

Forward pairing Positive intervals means that the CS (tone) began before the US (shock).

7.10 The CS-US interval in classical conditioning The figure shows the results of a study of the effectiveness of various CS-US intervals in humans. The CR was a finger withdrawal response, the CS a tone, and the US an electric shock. The time between CS and US is plotted on the horizontal axis; *negative* values indicates that the CS arrived after the US. The vertical axis indicates the strength of conditioning.

These facts make perfect sense if we think of the CS as a signal warning the organism that it should prepare itself for the upcoming US. To see why, imagine a mountain road that has a dangerous hairpin turn. How should drivers be warned about this turn? The best warning would be a "Caution" sign just before the turn (analogous to forward pairing with a short CS-US interval). This sign would be informative, and—crucially—would allow the driver enough time to prepare for the upcoming maneuver. But it's important not to place the sign too far ahead of the turn. Suppose a Caution sign is posted 100 miles before the turn (forward pairing with an extremely long CS-US interval). In that case the driver might not connect the sign with what it signifies—or just as bad, he might have forgotten about the sign by the time he reaches the curve. Things would be worse still, though, if the sign were prominently displayed right in the middle of the hairpin turn (simultaneous pairing), because now the warning comes too late to be of any use. Worst of all, the driver might suspect a degree of malevolence if he discovered the sign placed on the road just beyond the turn (backward pairing), although he'd probably be grateful that he didn't find the sign at the bottom of the ravine.

CONTINGENCY

The CS's role as a signal also has a crucial implication for what *produces* classical conditioning—that is, what the relationship between the CS and the US must be for learning to occur. To understand the issue, consider a dog in a conditioning experiment. Several times, it has heard a metronome and, a moment later, received some food powder. But many other stimuli were also present. At the same time it heard the metronome, the dog heard some doors slamming and some voices in the background. It saw the laboratory walls and the light fixtures hanging from the ceiling. At that moment, it could also feel various bodily sensations. What, therefore, should the dog learn? If it relies on mere contiguity, it will learn to associate the food powder with all of these stimuli—metronomes, light fixtures, and everything else on the scene—since they were all present when the US was introduced.

Notice, though, that many of these stimuli—even if contiguous with the US—give no information about the US. The light fixtures, for example, were on the scene just before the food powder arrived; but they were also on the scene during the many minutes when no food was on its way. So the sight of the light fixtures can't signal that food is coming soon, because the presence of the light fixtures has just as often conveyed the opposite message. Likewise for most of the sounds in the laboratory; they were present just before the food arrived, but they were also present during minutes without food. Therefore, none of these stimuli will help the animal predict when food is coming and when it's not.

To predict the US's arrival, the dog needs some event that reliably occurs when food is about to appear and doesn't occur otherwise. And, of course, the metronome beat in our example is the only stimulus that satisfies this requirement, since it never beats in the intervals between trials when food is not presented. Therefore, if the animal hears the metronome, it's a safe bet that food is on its way. If the animal cares about signaling, it should learn about the metronome and not about these other stimuli, even though they were all contiguous with the target event.

Are animals sensitive to these patterns? Said differently, what is it that leads to classical conditioning? Is it *contiguity*—the fact that the CS and US arrive close to each other in time? Or is it *contingency*—the fact that the CS provides information about the US's arrival? It turns out that contingency is the key, and in fact a CR is acquired only when the CS is informative about things to come.

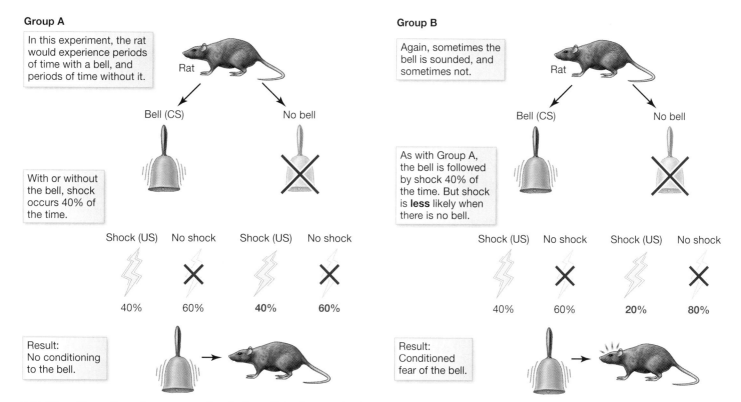

Group A

In this experiment, the rat would experience periods of time with a bell, and periods of time without it.

Rat

Bell (CS)   No bell

With or without the bell, shock occurs 40% of the time.

Shock (US)   No shock   Shock (US)   No shock

40%   60%   **40%**   **60%**

Result: No conditioning to the bell.

Group B

Again, sometimes the bell is sounded, and sometimes not.

Rat

Bell (CS)   No bell

As with Group A, the bell is followed by shock 40% of the time. But shock is **less** likely when there is no bell.

Shock (US)   No shock   Shock (US)   No shock

40%   60%   **20%**   **80%**

Result: Conditioned fear of the bell.

7.11 The effect of contingency on classical conditioning For both groups, there's only a 40% chance that bells will be followed by shock. However, for Group B, shock is *less likely* when no bell is sounded, and, for this group, the bell becomes a fearful stimulus.

In one experiment, rats were exposed to various combinations of a bell (CS) and a shock (US) (Figure 7.11). The bell was never a perfect predictor of the shock, but it did signal that shock was likely to arrive soon. Specifically, presentation of the bell signaled a 40% chance that a shock was about to arrive.

For some of the rats in this experiment (Group A in the figure), shocks also arrived 40% of the time without any warning. For these rats, therefore, the bell provided no information. The likelihood of a shock following the bell was exactly the same as the likelihood of shock in general. And in fact this situation led to no conditioning; instead, the rats simply learned to ignore the tone.

For another group of rats (Group B in the figure), the bell still signaled a 40% chance of shock, and shocks still arrived occasionally without warning. For these animals, though, the likelihood of a shock was only 20% when there was no bell. So in this setting, the bell was an imperfect predictor but it did provide some information, because shock was more likely after the bell than otherwise. And, in this situation, the rats did develop a conditioned response—they became fearful whenever the bell was sounded.

Let's be clear that in this experiment, the two groups of rats experienced the same number of bell-shock pairings, and so the degree of contiguity between bell and shock was the same for both groups. What differed between the groups, though, was whether the bell was informative or not—and it's this information value, not the contiguity, that matters for conditioning. Notice also that the bell was never a perfect predictor of shock: Bells were *not* followed by shock 60% of the time. Even so, conditioning was observed; apparently, an imperfect predictor is better than no predictor at all (Rescorla, 1967, 1988; Figure 7.12).

7.12 An imperfect predictor? The weather forecast is often wrong. Still, the chances of a hot day are greater if the forecast is for heat rather than snow. On that basis, we pay attention to the forecast, even if it's not always correct. Pavlovian conditioning seems to work the same way—and so a somewhat reliable signal seems to be better than no signal at all.

THE ABSENCE OF CONTINGENCY

The importance of contingency is also evident in another way—in an organism's reaction when there's no contingency at all. To explore this idea, let's imagine two different procedures. In both, the animal hears 40 presentations of a tone and receives 20 electric shocks. In the first procedure, these stimuli are presented randomly—and so there's no contingency, no relationship, between hearing the tone and receiving a shock. In the second procedure, the stimuli are arranged so that half of the tones are followed by shock and half are not, and shocks are never presented without a tone preceding them. In this setting, hearing the tone signals a 50% chance that a shock is about to arrive; in the absence of the tone, the chance of shock is zero.

Animals react very differently to these two procedures. In the first, the tone conveys no information—shock is just as likely with a tone as without. Not surprisingly, the tone in this situation does not become a fearful stimulus. Indeed, after just a few presentations of the tone—so that the novelty of this stimulus wears off—the animal's behavior doesn't change at all when the tone is sounded. In the second procedure, in contrast, the tone is informative, indicating that a shock quite likely is about to arrive. It's no wonder that in this case the animal soon shows a fear response whenever the tone is presented.

These two procedures also differ in another way. The first procedure—with its random arrangement of tones and shocks—is far more aversive to animals. This is clear, for example, if we monitor the animals' bodily state (e.g., their heart rates) during both procedures. The comparison tells us that the animals are more stressed in the noncontingent procedure. We can also, in effect, "ask" animals which of these procedures they find worse. We do this using a lab setup in which the animal can enter either of two chambers, one governed by the random procedure we've described and one governed by the contingent procedure. When given these options, animals reliably choose the second procedure.

What's going on here? In the second procedure, there is a clear "danger signal" for the animal (the tone), and this signal reliably produces fear. But this setup also provides a clear "safety signal"—namely, the *absence* of the tone. When the tone isn't sounded, the animal knows no shock is coming and it can relax. In the first (noncontingent) procedure, in contrast, there's never a danger signal, nothing to indicate when a shock is coming, and therefore no specific trigger for fear. But, in this setting, there's also no indication when the animal is safe. As a result, in this procedure the animal is constantly afraid and constantly on guard.

Results like these highlight the importance of contingency—the relations among stimuli that allow us to anticipate upcoming events. When there is some contingency (i.e., one event allows predictions about another event), animals learn this; and it seems to be crucial for classical conditioning. But when there's no contingency, animals learn this, too—and learn that their environment is unpredictable. These points are crucial for, say, dogs in a conditioning experiment, but they're no less important for humans. For example, think about why terrorist activities are so frightening: Terrorists hope to convey the message that they can strike you anytime, anywhere, so that you're never safe. It's this absence of contingency that makes terrorist threats so scary. Similarly—but on a more personal level—think about the distinction between fear and anxiety. According to some theorists, fear is a state triggered by a specific situation or object; anxiety, on the other hand, is chronic, has no object, and occurs in many situations. Some authors suggest that such unfocused anxiety is partly caused by unpredictability—that is, by an absence of safety signals (B. Schwartz et al., 2005; Seligman, 1975).

In the experiments we've been describing, animals seem keenly sensitive to *comparisons among probabilities*. Will a dog learn to salivate in response to a beeper if the sound is followed by food only 30% of the time? The answer is yes, *if* food arrives less than 30% of the time when no beeper is sounded. Will a mouse shiver in response to a tone that, in the past, has been followed only half the time by a blast of cold air? Again, the answer is yes—provided that cold blasts arrive less than half the time without the warning tone.

This sensitivity to probabilities is, in fact, a widespread feature of classical conditioning and can be observed in creatures as diverse as humans and rabbits, pigeons and rats. In all cases, conditioning depends on whether the probability of the US *after* the CS is different from the probability of the US *without* the CS. But how is this possible? The dog and the mouse are obviously not standing by with calculators, computing these probabilities. For that matter, when we study classical conditioning in humans, our participants don't appear to be tallying up the various types of trials and computing the relevant ratios. How, then, are the test subjects influenced by these probabilities?

One proposal starts with the idea that—for any organism, human or otherwise—associations can provide a basis for *expectations,* and learning can then take the form of an *adjustment in expectations whenever a surprise occurs.* To see how this plays out, imagine an animal in a learning experiment. At the very start, there's no association between (say) the sound of the metronome and the delivery of food, and so the animal has no expectation that this CS will be followed by this US. When the food does arrive, therefore, it's a surprise; and this causes the animal to adjust its expectations. Specifically, the surprise leads the animal to a tentative expectation that, in the future, other metronome sounds might also be followed by food. This expectation will be weak at first, and so the next time this CS is followed by the US, the animal will still be a little bit surprised. This will cause another adjustment in the animal's expectation—and so an increase in the strength of association between CS and US.

This process will then be repeated over and over as the learning experiment continues. In each trial, the CS is presented; and this will trigger certain expectations in the animal for what's going to happen next. If these expectations are correct, then the arrival (or nonarrival) of the US will be no surprise, and so there's no reason to adjust the expectations (Figure 7.13). But if the expectations are wrong, then some adjustment is called for. If no US is expected but one arrives anyhow, this surprise will lead to a strengthening of the CS-US association and thus a stronger expectation the next time around. Conversely, if the US is expected but does not arrive, then the CS-US association will be weakened and so there will be a weaker expectation on the next trial.

If things continue in this way, trial after trial, the expectations will be adjusted each time they're out of step with actual events and left alone when they're correct. Put differently, the expectations will be tuned and retuned until they're quite accurate—fully in line with the circumstances. Thus, if the animal is in a situation in which a CS is followed by the US 90% of the time, the animal will end up with strong expectations for what's going to happen next, whenever it

7.13 The role of expectations and surprise This figure shows the (automatic, unconscious) process through which expectations can be adjusted, trial by trial, in a classical conditioning experiment. The one complication not shown here is that bigger surprises (greater departures from expectations) will trigger larger adjustments; smaller surprises will lead to smaller adjustments.

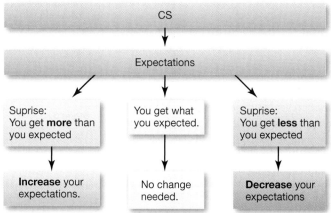

experiences the CS. If the animal is in an environment in which a CS is followed by the US only 80% of the time, or 60%, the animal's expectations will be accordingly weaker.

Notice, then, that we can predict the animal's behavior—in particular, whether the animal will learn or not—by keeping track of the various probabilities in the animal's situation. But the animal has no direct knowledge about these probabilities. Instead, the animal has a set of expectations, based on its experience. The key, though, is that these expectations have been shaped, trial by trial, by an adjustment process that brings the expectations into line with reality, as shown in Figure 7.13. This is the mechanism through which the animal's behavior ends up fully in accord with the probabilities in its environment (Kamin, 1968; Rescorla & Wagner, 1972; but see R. Miller, Barnet, & Grahame, 1995; Pearce & Bouton, 2001).

Is this proposal correct? Is this how classical conditioning proceeds, with a trial-by-trial calibration of expectations? One way to find out is to scrutinize the role of surprise, which—in the account just sketched—plays a crucial role in learning. And in fact the importance of surprise is easily demonstrated. In studies of the **blocking effect**, animals are exposed to a three-part procedure (Figure 7.14). In stage 1, the animals—rats, for example—hear a hissing noise that's followed by a US (let's say, the sight of a sexually receptive mate). As one might expect, this noise becomes a CS for sexual arousal. In stage 2, the hissing sound is still followed by this same US; but now the hissing sound is reliably accompanied by another stimulus—a bright light. The sequence in this stage, therefore, is the "package" of hiss plus light, followed by the sight of the potential mate. Then, in stage 3, it's time for the crucial test: Now we present the light by itself and observe the rat's response.

In stage 2 of this procedure, the light was reliably followed by the US, and we might expect this to produce learning—so that the light will now trigger the CR. But that's not what happens. Instead, the rat doesn't respond to the light at all. This is because in stage 2 the light provided only redundant information. The rat already knew from the hissing noise that the US was about to be presented, and so it wasn't at all surprised

blocking effect A result showing that an animal learns nothing about a stimulus if the stimulus provides no new information.

Stage 1

The hiss is reliably followed by the availability of a sexually receptive mate. A CR is thus quickly established.

Stage 2

The procedure continues, but now a light turns on at the same time as the hiss. The light is thus reliably followed by the availability of a mate. This seems like a CS (light) followed by a US (available mate), so it should therefore produce conditioning.

7.14 The blocking effect procedure What prevented the conditioning in this sequence? In Stage 2, the light provided no new information, because the hiss told the animal that the US would soon arrive. Conditioning does not occur with uninformative stimuli!

Stage 3

Now we see that conditioning has not occured: The animal doesn't respond (produces no CR) to the light.

when the US did arrive. As a result, the rat learned nothing about the light—clear confirmation of the proposal that learning does in fact depend on surprise and, more broadly, on the information value of the stimuli.

The blocking effect can easily be demonstrated in experiments with humans (Beckers, Miller, De Houwer, & Urushihara, 2006; Kruschke & Blair, 2000), and analogous phenomena can be documented outside of the laboratory. In the United States, for example, temperatures are routinely reported in degrees Fahrenheit—unlike the rest of the world, which uses the metric centigrade scale. For some years, weather forecasters tried to teach Americans the alternative scale by routinely describing the temperature with *both* scales: "The high tomorrow will be 75 degrees, or 24 centigrade." "Watch out—it's going to be cold tonight—in the teens, or –10 degrees centigrade." This effort failed—and Americans learned nothing about the metric scale. Why? Because the centigrade number was redundant with the Fahrenheit temperature, and so the centigrade number provided no information, no surprise. As a result, Americans ignored the number—just as a rat in the laboratory ignores the redundant (and therefore uninformative) light.

The Relationship between the CR and the UR

In Pavlov's original studies, dogs salivated both when they heard the CS and when they experienced the US. We might conclude from this that the conditioned response (CR) and unconditioned response (UR) are essentially the same behavior—and simply triggered by different inputs. In truth, though, the CR and UR are rarely identical and are sometimes quite different from each other.

Consider, for example, a rat that has been conditioned to associate a flashing light with electric shock. When the shock is actually presented, the animal jumps and squeals, and its heart beats faster; this is the UR, triggered by the shock itself (the US). When the animal sees the flashing light, though, its response (the CR) is different. The animal freezes and tenses its muscles, and its heartbeat slows. This is not an escape-from-shock reaction; instead, it's a display of fearful anticipation.

From a biological perspective, this result makes sense. A flashing light causes no physical damage, and so there's no need to spend energy escaping from the light. Likewise, an animal can't eat a tone that has been paired with food, so there's no point in opening its mouth and chewing in response to the tone. In these and many other cases, it's sensible for the animal to react somewhat differently to the CS than it does to the US.

So, what is the relationship between the conditioned response (CR) and the unconditioned response (UR)? We've already seen that animals interpret the CS as a signal indicating that the US is about to arrive. Plausibly, then, we can think of the CS as telling the animal to "Get ready!"—and, from this perspective, the CR is just the set of adjustments the animal makes in *preparation* for the US. If the sound of a bell has been reliably followed by food, then the sound now signals that the animal should moisten its mouth so it will be ready to eat when the food arrives. If the sight of a light has been followed by a shock, then the light is a signal that the animal should stop moving around and stay at "full alert" so it will be ready to jump as soon as the shock begins (Domjan, 2005; P. Holland, 1984; Hollis, 1984).

Does this preparation help the animal? It surely does. Evidence suggests, for example, that sexual activity is more likely to lead to offspring if a CS announced the imminent arrival of the US (the sight of a sexually receptive partner). Presumably, this is because the CS allowed the animal to prepare itself for mating (Domjan, 2005). Likewise, digestion is more efficient if a CS announced the imminent arrival of the US (food in the mouth); again, the CS allowed the animal to prepare to ingest and digest the food (Domjan, 2005; Woods & Ramsay, 2000).

Preparation for a US can take many forms. As a remarkable illustration, consider the situation of a heroin addict. The heroin itself is a potent stimulus with many biological effects: It decreases pain sensitivity and lifts the user's mood. It also causes other changes throughout the body, including drying out the mouth and various mucous membranes.

The first few times someone uses heroin, all of these effects are strong. If drug use continues, though, these effects diminish. This phenomenon, which we described in Chapter 6, is called drug tolerance—a decrease in the response to a drug, usually resulting from continued use. If the person wants to keep getting the same impact from the drug, they'll need a larger and larger dose to offset the effect of the tolerance.

Continued use of heroin also leads to *drug dependence* and drug *cravings*—an inability to function without the drug and an overwhelming desire for yet another dose, yet another injection. The cravings are accompanied by their own set of effects—including an *increased* sensitivity to pain, a depression in the person's mood, and an overproduction of fluid in the person's mouth and mucous membranes.

What's going on here? What produces drug tolerance and drug craving? Why does the craving take the form that it does? Answers to these questions turn out to include a key role for classical conditioning. To understand how this works, however, we need to begin with a point we'll discuss more fully in Chapter 12 where we consider the importance of *homeostasis*. This term refers to the remarkably stable environment that exists inside of our bodies—a body temperature that's kept at an almost constant level, a nearly constant pH in the bloodstream, a consistent level of glucose and oxygen in the blood, and so on.

A drug such as heroin changes the body's status in many ways. In other words, heroin disrupts homeostasis; and so, when this drug is present in the body, a range of mechanisms come into play, all seeking to restore homeostatic stability. These mechanisms involve many cellular and biochemical changes throughout the body—all designed to repair the "disruption" caused by the drug.

But, of course, *preventing* a problem is always preferable to solving the problem after it arises; *avoiding* disruption is better than repairing the disruption once it's in place. Rather than waiting until heroin disrupts the body's state and then responding to this disruption, it would be better if the body had a way of dealing with the heroin disruption *as it happens,* so that homeostasis is never lost in the first place. This is where classical conditioning enters the scene: Thanks to conditioning, the body begins a series of adjustments to offset the heroin's effects even before the drug arrives.

Let's put this in concrete terms. For a heroin user, the US is the drug itself; the UR is the body's natural response to the drug (Figure 7.15). The CS is complex and includes all the stimuli that signal the drug is about to arrive—the sight of the needle, thoughts about the drug, possibly the sights and smells of the physical environment in which the drug is injected, and so on. But what is the CR? Here as always, the CR will be a response that prepares the organism for the US, and so we need to ask: What is the right preparation for heroin? If the goal is homeostasis, then the CR should include a depression of mood in order to cancel out heroin's positive effects on mood; it should also include an increase in pain sensitivity to cancel out heroin's analgesic effects; it should include an increase in moisture in the mucous membranes to offset heroin's tendency to dry out these membranes. In point after point, the CR should simply be the opposite of the UR, so that the two will cancel each other out, leaving no overall effect—and thus preserving homeostasis. A CR like this is referred to as a **compensatory response**—one that "compensates" for the effects of the upcoming US.

Of course, when someone is exposed to heroin for the first time, there hasn't yet been an opportunity for learning. Therefore, the US (the heroin) will produce the UR

compensatory response A response that offsets the effects of the upcoming unconditioned stimulus.

Early on in use

At first there's no conditioned response to the conditioned stimulus, and so all we observe is the UR (the response to the molecule itself).

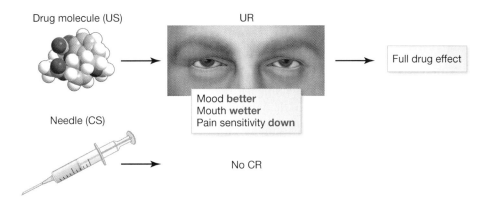

Drug molecule (US)

UR

Mood **better**
Mouth **wetter**
Pain sensitivity **down**

Full drug effect

Needle (CS)

No CR

After repeated uses

The CR is the opposite of the UR: so the two responses cancel each other, thus helping to preserve the body's stable condition.

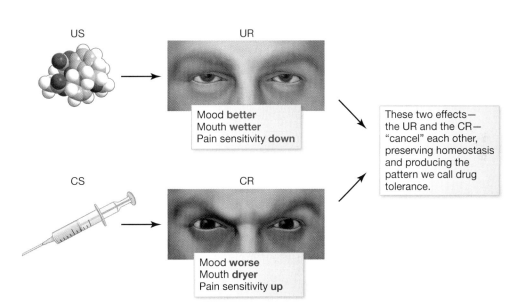

US

UR

Mood **better**
Mouth **wetter**
Pain sensitivity **down**

CS

CR

Mood **worse**
Mouth **dryer**
Pain sensitivity **up**

These two effects—the UR and the CR—"cancel" each other, preserving homeostasis and producing the pattern we call drug tolerance.

If drug isn't available

Here the sight of the needle triggers the CR, but there's no drug present, and so no drug reaction. This leaves the person with the behaviors and feelings we call drug craving—a result, in large part, of the body's compensatory response for heroin, but with no drug to compensate for!

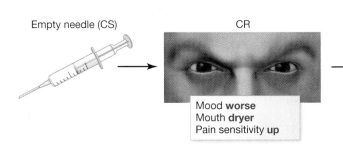

Empty needle (CS)

CR

Mood **worse**
Mouth **dryer**
Pain sensitivity **up**

Craving

7.15 The compensatory response to heroin Early on, the drug user experiences the full effect of heroin. After repeated uses, the sight of the needle (and other stimuli) function as a CS, triggering a compensatory CR—one that is the opposite of the UR (the body's reaction to heroin). The compensatory response "cancels out" the UR, and so helps maintain homeostasis.

(the biological reaction to the drug); but there will be no CR (because no learning has taken place yet). As a result, the person will experience the drug's full effects, and no compensatory response will be in place (Figure 7.15, top panel). After repeated exposures to the drug, though, learning will have taken place. At this point the US still produces the UR; but now, in addition, the CS elicits the compensatory CR. This learned response, we've proposed, functions to "cancel out" the heroin effects and preserve homeostasis. As a result, the UR will be less evident—resulting in the diminished drug response that we call drug tolerance (Figure 7.15, middle panel).

What happens if an addict sees an empty hypodermic needle, or visits the place where he ordinarily buys or injects the drug, but no heroin is available (Figure 7.15, bottom panel)? In these cases the drug-associated signals all indicate that the drug will arrive soon, but then it never arrives—so there's a CS (the signals), but no US (no heroin). With the CS present, the CR will be produced; but with no US, there will be no UR. As a result, the person will experience the CR on its own—and the CR, we've proposed, is the opposite of the UR. Hence the person experiences the depression, the pain sensitivity, and so on—exactly the pattern referred to as drug craving.

Many experiments have confirmed these claims about heroin tolerance and craving. Among other points, the data indicate that tolerance shows not only the pattern of generalization and discrimination that we would expect with classical conditioning but also the familiar patterns of extinction and spontaneous recovery. In other words, tolerance shows the standard profile of classical conditioning, and this is strong support for the account we've just sketched. Moreover, related studies show a similar role for conditioning in tolerance observed with other drugs, including insulin, nicotine, caffeine, and amphetamines (Domjan, 2005; S. Siegel, 1977, 1983; S. Siegel & Allan, 1998; S. Siegel, Kim, & Sokolowska, 2003; Sokolowska, Siegel, & Kim, 2002). Overall, these points provide a powerful argument that the CR is indeed best understood as a *preparation for* the US; but it's important to note that this notion of preparation must be understood broadly.

INSTRUMENTAL CONDITIONING

instrumental conditioning A form of learning in which the participant receives a reinforcer only after performing the desired response, and thereby learns a relationship between the response and the reinforcer.

Habituation and classical conditioning are both general forms of learning that are relevant to many species (including, of course, humans) and many different responses (including a variety of overt behaviors, a range of subjective feelings, and a broad set of bodily responses). An equally important type of learning is **instrumental conditioning** (also called *operant conditioning*). This form of learning involves behaviors that aren't triggered automatically by some stimulus. Instead, instrumental conditioning is concerned with behaviors initiated by—and presumably under the control of—the organism itself. In other words, while classical conditioning essentially involves the creation of new reflexes, instrumental conditioning involves the learning of new voluntary behaviors.

Thorndike and the Law of Effect

The experimental study of instrumental conditioning began a century ago and was sparked by the debate over Darwin's theory of evolution by natural selection. Supporters of Darwin's theory emphasized the continuity among species, both living and extinct: Despite their apparent differences, a bird's wing, a whale's fin, and a human arm, for example, all have the same basic bone structure; this similarity makes it plausible that these diverse organisms all descended, by a series of incremental steps, from common ancestors. But opponents of Darwin's theory pointed to something they perceived as the crucial discontinuity among species: the human ability to think and reason—an ability they claimed animals did not share. Didn't this ability, unique to our species, require an altogether different (non-Darwinian) type of explanation?

In response, Darwin and his colleagues argued that there is, in fact, considerable continuity of mental prowess across the animal kingdom. Yes, humans are smarter in some ways than other species; but the differences might be smaller than they initially seem. In support of this idea, Darwinian naturalists collected stories about the intellectual achievements of various animals (Darwin, 1871). These stories painted a flattering picture, as in the reports of cunning cats that scattered breadcrumbs on the lawn to lure birds into their reach (Romanes, 1882). In many cases, however, it was hard to tell whether these reports were genuine or just bits of folklore. Even if they were genuine, it was unclear whether the reports had been polished by the loving touch of a proud pet owner. What was needed, therefore, was more objective and better documented research—research that was made possible by a method described in 1898 by Edward L. Thorndike (1874–1949; Figure 7.16).

CATS IN A PUZZLE BOX

Thorndike's method was to set up a problem for an animal to solve. In his classic experiments, he placed a hungry cat inside a box with a latched door. The cat could open the door—and escape from the box—only by performing some simple action such as pulling a loop of wire or pressing a lever (Figure 7.17); and once outside the box, the cat was rewarded with a small portion of food. Then the cat was placed back into the box for another trial so that the procedure could be repeated over and over until the task of escaping the box was mastered.

On the first trial, the cats had no notion of how to escape—and so they meowed loudly and clawed and bit at their surroundings. This continued for several minutes until finally, purely by accident, the animal hit upon the correct response. Subsequent trials brought gradual improvement, and the animal took less and less time to produce the response that unlocked the door. By the time the training sessions were completed, the cats' behavior was almost unrecognizable from what it had been at the start. When placed in the box, they immediately approached the wire loop or the lever, yanked it or pressed it with businesslike dispatch, and hurried through the open door to enjoy the well-deserved reward.

If you observed only the final performance of these cats, you might well credit the animals with reason or understanding. But Thorndike argued that the cats solved the problem in a very different way. As proof, he recorded how much time the cats required on each trial to escape from the puzzle box, and he charted how these times changed over the course of learning. Thorndike found that the resulting curves declined quite gradually as the learning proceeded (Figure 7.18). This isn't the pattern we would expect if the cats had achieved some understanding of how to solve the problem. If they had, their curves would show a sudden drop at some point in the training, when they finally got the point. ("Aha!" muttered the insightful cat, "it's the lever that lets me out," and henceforth howled and bit

7.16 Edward L. Thorndike (1874–1949) An important early behaviorist, Thorndike was the first to formulate the law of effect.

7.17 Puzzle box This box is much like those used by Edward Thorndike. By stepping on a lever attached to a rope, the animal releases the latch and so unlocks the door.

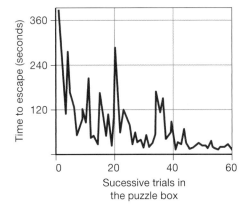

7.18 Learning curve of one of Thorndike's cats To get out of the box, the cat had to move a wooden handle from a vertical to a horizontal position. The figure shows the gradual decline in the animal's response latency (the time it takes to get out of the box). Notice that the learning curve is not very smooth; this feature is common in the learning curves of individual subjects. Smooth learning curves are generally produced by averaging the results of many individual subjects.

no more.) Instead, these learning curves suggest that the cats learned to escape in small increments; they displayed no evidence at all of understanding and certainly no evidence of any sudden insight into the problem's solution.

THE LAW OF EFFECT

In Thorndike's procedure, the cats' initial responses in the puzzle box—biting at the latch, clawing at the walls—all led to failure. As the trials proceeded, though, the cats' tendency to produce these responses gradually weakened. At the same time, the animals' tendency to produce the correct response was weak at first; but, over the trials, this response gradually grew stronger. In Thorndike's terms, the correct response was gradually "stamped in," while futile ones were "stamped out."

But what causes this stamping in or stamping out? Thorndike's answer was the **law of effect.** Its key proposition is that if a response is followed by a reward, that response will be strengthened. If a response is followed by no reward (or, worse yet, by punishment), it will be weakened. In general, the strength of a response is adjusted according to the response's consequences (Figure 7.19). In this view, we do not need to suppose that the cat's performance required any sophisticated intellectual processes. We likewise do not need to assume that the animal noticed a connection between its acts and the consequences of those acts. All we need to assert is that, if the animal made a response and a reward followed soon after, that response was more likely to be performed later.

Notice that Thorndike's proposal suggests a clear parallel between how an organism learns during its lifetime and how species evolve, thanks to the forces of natural selection. In both cases, variations that "work"—behaviors that lead to successful outcomes, or individuals with successful adaptations—are kept on. In both cases, variations that are less successful are weakened or dropped. And, crucially, in both cases

law of effect Thorndike's theory that a response followed by a reward will be strengthened, whereas a response followed by no reward (or by punishment) will be weakened.

Trial 1

The tendency to perform various incorrect responses (biting the bars, jumping up and down) is strong, while the tendency to perform the correct response (pushing the lever) is weak or nonexistent.

Bite at bars

Jump up and down

Meow

etc. ...

Push on lever ———→ Door opens

Later trial

As trials proceed, the strength of the incorrect responses has become weaker and weaker. In contrast, correct response has grown stronger because it has been reliably rewarded.

Bite at bars

Jump up and down

Meow

etc. ...

Push on lever ———→ Door opens

7.19 **The law of effect** A schematic presentation of Thorndike's theory of instrumental learning.

the selection involves no guide or supervisor to steer the process forward. Instead, selection depends only on the consequences of actions or adaptations and on whether these serve the organism's biological needs or not.

Skinner and Operant Behavior

Thorndike initiated the experimental study of instrumental behavior; but, unquestionably, the psychologist who shaped the way most modern learning theorists think about the subject was B. F. Skinner (1904–1990; Figure 7.20). Skinner was one of the first theorists to insist on a sharp distinction between classical and instrumental conditioning. He noted that in classical conditioning, the animal's behavior is elicited by the US. Salivation, for example, is set off by an event outside the organism. But in instrumental conditioning, Skinner argued, the organism is much less at the mercy of external factors. Its reactions are emitted from within, as if they were what we ordinarily call "voluntary." Skinner called these instrumental responses **operants**: They operate on the environment to bring about some change that leads to some consequence. And, in Skinner's view, these consequences are crucial. Like Thorndike, Skinner argued that an operant followed by a positive consequence was more likely to be emitted in the future, while an operant followed by a negative consequence was less likely to be emitted again (Skinner, 1938).

Skinner believed, however, that Thorndike's procedure for studying learning was inefficient. Rather than placing animals in a puzzle box (which required many minutes for each learning trial), Skinner sought a procedure in which the instrumental response could be performed repeatedly and rapidly, so that data could be gathered more easily. Many of his studies therefore employed an experimental chamber (popularly called the Skinner box) in which a rat presses a lever or a pigeon pecks at a lighted key in order to gain a reward (Figure 7.21). In these situations, the animal stays in the chamber for a set interval—perhaps an hour at a time—and during that interval, we track the animal's behavior by recording its *response rate*—the number of lever presses or key pecks per unit of time.

The Major Phenomena of Instrumental Conditioning

As Skinner noted, classical and instrumental conditioning are different in important ways: Classical conditioning builds on a response (UR) that's automatically triggered by a stimulus (US); instrumental conditioning involves behaviors that appear to be voluntary. Classical conditioning involves learning about the relation between two stimuli (US and CS); instrumental conditioning involves learning about the relation between a response and a stimulus (the operant and a reward). Even with these differences, modern theorists have argued that the two forms of conditioning have a lot in common. This makes sense because both involve learning about *relationships* among simple events (stimuli or responses).

It's perhaps inevitable, then, that many of the central phenomena of instrumental learning parallel those of classical conditioning. For example, in classical conditioning, learning trials typically involve the presentation of a CS followed by a US. In instrumental conditioning, learning trials typically involve a response by the organism followed by a reward or **reinforcer.** The reinforcement often involves the presentation of something good, such as grain to a hungry pigeon. Alternatively, reinforcement may involve the termination or prevention of something bad, such as the cessation of a loud noise.

operant In Skinner's system, an instrumental response that is defined by its effect (the way it operates) on the environment.

reinforcer A stimulus delivered after a response that makes the response more likely in the future.

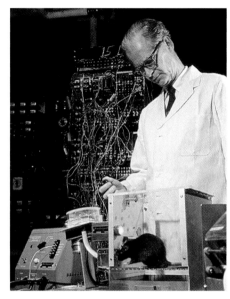

7.20 B. F. Skinner (1904–1990) Unmistakably the most influential of the learning theorists, Skinner made a sharp distinction between classical and operant conditioning.

Lever

Food tray

7.21 Animals in operant chambers This rat is trained to press a lever for food reinforcement. Reinforcement consists of a few seconds' access to a feeder located near the response lever.

In both forms of conditioning, the more such pairings there are, the stronger the learning. And if we discontinue these pairings so that the CS is no longer followed by the US or the response by a reinforcer, the result is extinction.

GENERALIZATION AND DISCRIMINATION

An instrumental response is not directly triggered by an external stimulus, the way a CR or UR is. But that doesn't mean external stimuli have no role here. In instrumental conditioning, external events serve as *discriminative stimuli*, signaling for an animal what sorts of behaviors will be rewarded in a given situation. For example, suppose a pigeon is trained to hop onto a platform to get some grain. When a green light is on, hopping on the platform pays off. But when a red light is on, hopping gains no reward. Under these circumstances, the green light becomes a positive discriminative stimulus and the red light a negative one (usually labeled S^+ and S^-, respectively). The pigeon swiftly learns this pattern and so will hop in the presence of the first and not in the presence of the second.

Other examples are easy to find. A child learns that pinching her sister leads to punishment when her parents are on the scene but may have no consequences otherwise. In this situation, the child may learn to behave well in the presence of the S^+ (i.e., when her parents are there) but not in other circumstances. A hypochondriac may learn that loud groans will garner sympathy and support from others but may bring no benefits when others are not around. As a result, he may learn to groan in social settings but not when alone.

Let's be clear, though, about the comparison between these stimuli and the stimuli central to classical conditioning. A CS^+ tells the animal about events in the world: "No matter what you do, the US is coming." The S^+, on the other hand, tells the animal about the impact of its own behavior: "If you respond now, you'll get rewarded." The CS^- indicates that no matter what the animal does, no US is coming. The S^-, in contrast, tells the animal something about its behavior—namely, that there's no point in responding right now.

Despite these differences, generalization in instrumental conditioning functions much the way it does in classical conditioning, and likewise for discrimination. One illustration of these parallels lies in the generalization gradient. We saw earlier that if an organism is trained with one CS (perhaps a high tone) but then tested with a different one (a low tone), the CR will be diminished. The greater the change in the CS, the greater the drop in the CR's strength. The same pattern emerges in instrumental conditioning. In one experiment, pigeons were trained to peck at a key illuminated with yellow light. Later, they were tested with lights of varying wavelengths, and the results showed an orderly generalization gradient (Figure 7.22). As the test light became less similar to the original S^+, the pigeons were less inclined to peck at it (Guttmann & Kalish, 1956).

The ability to distinguish an S^- from an S^+ obviously allows an organism to tune its behavior to its circumstances. Thus, the dolphins at the aquarium leap out of the water to get a treat when their feeders are around; they don't leap up in the presence of other people. Your pet dog sits and begs when it sees you eating, in hopes that you'll share the snack; but the dog doesn't beg when it sees you drinking. In these and other cases, behaviors are emitted only when the available stimuli indicate that the behavior will now be rewarded.

In fact, animals are quite skilled at making discriminations and can use impressively complex stimuli as a basis for controlling their behavior. In one study, pigeons were trained to peck a key whenever a picture of water was in view, but not to peck otherwise.

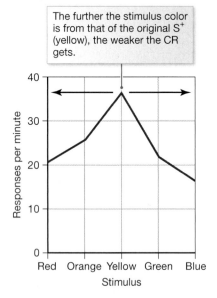

The further the stimulus color is from that of the original S^+ (yellow), the weaker the CR gets.

7.22 Stimulus generalization of an instrumental response Pigeons were originally reinforced to peck at a yellow light. When later tested with lights of various colors, the birds showed a standard generalization gradient, pecking more vigorously at colors more similar to yellow (such as green and orange) than at colors farther removed (such as red and blue).

Some of the water pictures showed flowing streams; some showed calm lakes. Some pictures showed large bodies of water photographed from far away; some showed small puddles photographed close up. Despite these variations, pigeons mastered this discrimination task and were even able to respond appropriately to new pictures that hadn't been included in the training trials (Herrnstein, Loveland, & Cable, 1976). Apparently, pigeons are capable of discriminating relatively abstract categories—categories not defined in terms of a few simple perceptual features. Similar procedures have shown that pigeons can discriminate between pictures showing trees and pictures not showing trees; thus, for example, they'll learn to peck in response to a picture of a leaf-covered tree or a tree bare of leaves, but not to peck in response to a picture of a telephone pole or a picture of a celery stalk. Likewise, pigeons can learn to peck whenever they're shown a picture of a particular human—whether she's photographed from one angle and close up or from a very different angle, far away, and wearing different clothes (Herrnstein, 1979; Lea & Ryan, 1990; for other examples of complex discriminations, see Cook, K. Cavoto, & B. Cavoto, 1995; Giurfa, Zhang, Jenett, Menzel, & Srinivasan, 2001; Lazareva, Freiburger, & Wasserman, 2004; D. Premack, 1976, 1978; A. Premack & D. Premack, 1983; Reiss & Marino, 2001; Wasserman, Hugart, & Kirkpatrick-Steger, 1995; Zentall, 2000).

SHAPING

Once a response has been made, reinforcement will strengthen it. Once the dolphin has leapt out of the water, the trainers can reward it, encouraging further leaps. Once the pigeon pecks the key, food can be delivered, making the next peck more likely. But what causes the animal to perform the desired response in the first place? What leads to the first leap or the first peck? This is no problem for many responses. Dolphins occasionally leap with no encouragement from a trainer, and pecking is something pigeons do all the time. If the trainer is patient, therefore, an opportunity to reinforce (and thus encourage) these responses will eventually arrive.

But what about less obvious responses? For example, rats quite commonly manipulate objects in their environment, and so they're likely to press on a lever if we put one within reach. But what if we place a lever so high that the rat has to stretch up on its hind legs to reach it? Now the rat might never press the lever on its own. Still, it can learn this response if its behavior is suitably shaped. This **shaping** is accomplished by a little "coaching," using the method of *successive approximations*.

How could we train a rat to press the elevated lever? At first, we reinforce the animal merely for walking into the general area where the lever is located. As soon as the rat is there, we deliver food. After a few such trials, the rat will have learned to remain in this vicinity most of the time, so we can now increase our demand. When the rat is in this neighborhood, sometimes it's facing one way, sometimes another; but from this point on, we reinforce the rat only if it's in the area and facing the lever. The rat soon masters this response too; now it's facing in the right direction most of the time. Again, therefore, we increase our demand: Sometimes the rat is facing the lever with its nose to the ground; sometimes it's facing the lever with its head elevated. We now reinforce the animal only when its head is elevated—and soon this, too, is a well-established response. We continue in this way, counting on the fact that at each step, the rat naturally varies its behavior somewhat, allowing us to reinforce just those variations we prefer. Thus, we can gradually move toward reinforcing the rat only when it stretches up to the lever, then when it actually touches the lever, and so on. Step by step, we guide the rat toward the desired response.

shaping The process of eliciting a desired response by rewarding behaviors that are increasingly similar to that response.

7.23 Shaping (A) Nhat, a four-year-old monkey with the Hanoi Circus, was trained using techniques essentially identical to those described in the text—a process of gradual shaping that leads to the desired response. (B) Parents use shaping to teach their children to eat with utensils. As the parents' demands gradually increase, the child's behavior comes closer and closer to the "standard" pattern of using the spoon and fork.

Using this technique, people have trained animals to perform all kinds of complex behavior; many human behaviors probably come about in the same way (Figure 7.23). For example, how do parents in Western countries teach their children to eat with a spoon and fork? At first, they reward the child (probably with smiles and praise) just for holding the spoon. This step soon establishes a grasp-the-spoon operant; and, at that point, the parents can require a bit more. Now they praise the child just when she touches food with the spoon—and, thanks to this reinforcement, the new operant is quickly established. If the parents continue in this way, gradually increasing their expectations, the child will soon be eating in the "proper" way.

Similar techniques are used in therapeutic settings to shape the behavior of the hospitalized mentally ill. Initially, the hospitalized patients might be rewarded just for getting out of bed. Once that behavior is established, the requirement is increased so that, perhaps, the patients have to move around a bit in their room. Then, later, the patients are rewarded for leaving the room and going to breakfast or getting their medicine. In this way, the behavior therapist can gradually lead the patients into a more acceptable level of functioning (see Chapter 17).

WHAT IS A REINFORCER?

We've now said a great deal about what reinforcement does; it encourages some responses, discourages others, and even—through the process of shaping—creates entirely new responses. But what is it that makes a stimulus serve as a reinforcer?

Some stimuli serve as reinforcers because of their biological significance. These *primary reinforcers* include food, water, escape from the scent of a predator, and so on—all stimuli with obvious importance for survival. Other reinforcers are social—think of the smiles and praise from parents that we mentioned in our example of teaching a child to use a spoon and fork.

Other stimuli are initially neutral in their value but come to act as reinforcers because, in the animal's experience, they've been repeatedly paired with some other, already established reinforcer. This kind of stimulus is called a *conditioned reinforcer*, and it works just like any other reinforcer. A plausible example is *money*—a reward that takes its value from its association with other more basic reinforcers.

Other reinforcers, however, fall into none of these categories, so we have to broaden our notion of what a reinforcer is. Pigeons, for example, will peck in order to gain *information* about the availability of food (e.g., G. Bower, McLean, & Meachem, 1966; Hendry, 1969). Monkeys will work merely to open a small window through which they can see a moving toy train (Butler, 1954). Rats will press a lever to gain access to an exercise wheel (D. Premack, 1965; but also Timberlake & Allison, 1974; Timberlake, 1995). And these are just a few examples of reinforcers.

But examples like these make it difficult to say just what a "reinforcement" is, and in practice the stimuli we call *reinforcements* are generally identified only after the fact. Is a glimpse of a toy train reinforcing? We can find out only by seeing whether an animal will work to obtain this glimpse. Remarkably, no other, more informative definition of a reinforcer is available.

BEHAVIORAL CONTRAST AND INTRINSIC MOTIVATION

Once we've identified a stimulus as a reinforcer, what determines how effective the reinforcer will be? We know that some reinforcers are more powerful than others—and so an animal will respond more strongly for a large reward than for a small one. However, what counts as large or small depends on the context. If a rat is used to getting 60 food pellets for a response, then 16 pellets will seem measly and the animal will respond only weakly for this puny reward. But if a rat is used to getting only 4 pellets for a response, then 16 pellets will seem like a feast and the rat's response will be fast and strong (for the classic demonstration of this point, see Crespi, 1942). Thus, the effectiveness of a reinforcer depends largely on what other rewards are available (or have recently been available); this effect is known as **behavioral contrast.**

Contrast effects are important for their own sake, but they may also help explain another (somewhat controversial) group of findings. In one study, for example, nursery-school children were given an opportunity to draw pictures. The children seemed to enjoy this activity and produced a steady stream of drawings. The experimenters then changed the situation: They introduced an additional reward so that the children now earned an attractive "Good Player" certificate for producing their pictures. Then, later on, the children were again given the opportunity to draw pictures—but this time with no provision for "Good Player" rewards. Remarkably, these children showed considerably less interest in drawing than they had at the start and chose instead to spend their time on other activities (see, for example, Lepper, Greene, & Nisbett, 1973; also Kohn, 1993).

Some theorists say these data illustrate the power of behavioral contrast. At the start of the study, the activity of drawing was presumably maintained by certain reinforcements in the situation—perhaps encouragement from the teachers or comments by other children. Whatever the reinforcements were, they were strong enough to maintain the behavior; we know this because the children were producing drawings at a steady pace. Later on, though, an additional reinforcement (the "Good Player" certificate) was added and then removed. At that point the children were back to the same rewards they'd been getting at the start, but now these rewards seemed puny in comparison to the greater prize they'd been earning during the time when the "Good Player" award was available. As a consequence, the initial set of rewards was no longer enough to motivate continued drawing.

Other theorists interpret these findings differently. In their view, results like this one suggest that there are actually two different types of reward. One type is merely tacked onto a behavior and is under the experimenter's control; it's the sort of reward that's in play when we give a pigeon a bit of food for pecking a key, or hand a factory worker a paycheck for completing a day's work. The other type of reward is intrinsic to the behavior and independent of the experimenter's intentions; these rewards are in play when someone is engaging in an activity just for the pleasure of the activity itself.

In addition, these two forms of reward can interfere with each other. Thus, in the study with the "Good Player" certificates, the children were initially drawing pictures for an intrinsic reward. Drawing, in other words, was a form of *play* engaged in for its own sake. However, once the external rewards (the certificates) entered the situation, the same activity became a form of *work*—something you do for a payoff. And once the

behavioral contrast A response pattern in which an organism evaluates a reward relative to other available rewards or those that have been available recently.

activity was redefined in this way, then the absence of a payoff meant there was no longer any point in drawing. (For more on this topic, see Chapter 12.)

Debate continues about which of these interpretations is preferable—the one based on behavioral contrast or the one based on intrinsic motivation. (It also seems plausible that *both* interpretations may capture aspects of what's going on here.) Clearly, there's more to be learned about reinforcement and the nature of motivation. (For further exploration, see Bowles, 2008; Deci, Koestner, & Ryan, 1999a, 1999b; Eisenberger, Pierce, & Cameron, 1999; Henderlong & Lepper, 2002.)

SCHEDULES OF REINFORCEMENT

Let's now return to the issue of how extrinsic reinforcements work, since—by anyone's account—these reinforcements play a huge role in governing human (and other species') behavior. We do, after all, work for money, buy lottery tickets in hopes of winning, and act in a way that we believe will bring us praise. But notice that in all of these examples, the reinforcement comes only occasionally: We aren't paid after every task we do at work; we almost never win the lottery; and we don't always get the praise we seek. Yet we show a surprising resistance to extinction of those behaviors. About some things, we have learned that if you don't succeed, it pays to try again—an important strategy for achieving much of what we earn in life.

This pattern, in which we're reinforced for only some of our behaviors, is known as **partial reinforcement.** In the laboratory, partial reinforcement can be provided according to different **schedules of reinforcement**—rules about how often and under what conditions a response will be reinforced. Some behaviors are reinforced via a **ratio schedule,** in which you're rewarded for producing a certain number of responses (Figure 7.24). The ratio can be "fixed" or "variable." In a "fixed-ratio 2" (FR 2) schedule, for example, two responses are required for each reinforcement; for an "FR 5" schedule, five responses are required. In a variable-ratio schedule, the number of responses required changes from trial to trial. Thus, in a "VR 10" schedule, 10 responses are required *on average* to get a reward—so it might be that the first 5 responses are enough to earn one reward, but 15 more are needed to earn the next.

Other behaviors are reinforced on an **interval schedule,** in which you're rewarded for producing a response after a certain amount of time has passed (Figure 7.25). Thus, on an "FI 3-minute" schedule, responses made during the 3-minute interval aren't reinforced; but the first response after the 3 minutes have passed will earn a reward. Interval schedules can also be variable: For a "VI 8-minute" schedule, reinforcement is available on average after 8 minutes; but the exact interval required varies from trial to trial.

partial reinforcement A learning condition in which only some of the organism's responses are reinforced.

schedule of reinforcement The rules about how often and under what conditions a response will be reinforced.

ratio schedule A pattern of delivering reinforcements only after a certain number of responses.

interval schedule A pattern of delivering reinforcements only after a certain amount of time has passed.

(A) Fixed-ratio schedule

(B) Variable-ratio schedule

7.24 Ratio reinforcement (A) Workers in a garment factory are usually paid a certain amount for each item of clothing completed, so they're rewarded on a fixed-ratio schedule of reinforcement. (B) By law, slot machines pay out on a certain percentage of tries. But these machines pay out at random, so that people feeding coins to a machine are rewarded on a variable-ratio reinforcement schedule.

(A) Fixed-interval schedule

(B) Variable-interval schedule

7.25 Interval reinforcement (A) The behavior of checking the mailbox isn't rewarded until the mail has actually been delivered. Then, the first check of the mailbox after this delivery will be rewarded (by the person actually getting some mail!). This is a fixed-interval schedule of reinforcement. (B) When a wolf prowls through a meadow, the rodents it seeks will all retreat into hiding; so, if the wolf returns soon, he'll find no prey. Eventually, though, the rodents will come back, and then another hunting trip by the wolf will pay off—he'll find his dinner. Therefore, a return visit by the wolf will be rewarded only after some time has passed—and hence this is an interval schedule. But the rodents may sometimes return a little sooner, and sometimes a little later—and so this is a variable interval schedule.

Changing Behaviors or Acquiring Knowledge?

We've almost finished our discussion of instrumental conditioning, except for one crucial question: What is it exactly that animals learn in an instrumental conditioning procedure? The law of effect implies that the learning is best understood as a change in behavior, in which responses are either being strengthened or weakened by the mechanical effects of reinforcement. From the earliest days of learning theory, however, there was an alternative view of conditioning—one asserting that behavior change isn't the key; what matters instead is the acquisition of new knowledge.

One of the most prominent proponents of this alternative view was Edward C. Tolman (1886–1959; Figure 7.26), and many forms of evidence support his position. For example, consider cases of **latent learning**—learning that takes place without any corresponding change in behavior. In one experiment, rats were allowed to explore a maze, without any reward, for 10 days. During these days, there was no detectable change in the rats' behavior; and so, if we define learning in terms of behavior change, there was no learning. But in truth the rats *were* learning—and in particular, they were gaining knowledge about how to navigate the maze's corridors. This became obvious on the 11th day, when food was placed in the maze's goal box for the first time. The rats learned to run to this goal box, virtually without error, almost immediately. The knowledge they had acquired earlier now took on motivational significance, so the animals swiftly displayed what they had learned (Tolman & Honzik, 1930; also H. Gleitman, 1963; Tolman, 1948).

In this case, the knowledge the rats had gained can be understood as a *mental map* of the maze—an internal representation of spatial layout that indicates what is where and what leads to what. Other evidence suggests that many species rely on such maps—to guide their foraging for food, their navigation to places of safety, and their choice of a path to the watering hole. These maps can be relatively complex and are typically quite accurate (Gallistel, 1994; J. Gould, 1990).

CONTINGENCY IN INSTRUMENTAL CONDITIONING

To understand latent learning or cognitive maps, we need to emphasize what an organism *knows* more than what an organism *does*. We also need to consider an organism's cognition for another reason: Recall that, in our discussion of classical conditioning, we saw that learning doesn't depend only on the CS being paired with the US; instead, the CS needs to *predict* the US, telling the animal when the US is more likely and when it's less likely. Similarly, instrumental conditioning doesn't depend only on responses

latent learning Learning that occurs without a corresponding change in behavior.

7.26 Edward C. Tolman (1886–1959) Tolman was an early advocate for the idea that learning involves a change in knowledge rather than a change in overt behavior.

being paired with rewards. Instead, the response needs to predict the reward, so that (for example) the probability of getting a pellet after a lever press has to be greater than the probability of getting it without the press.

What matters for instrumental conditioning, therefore, is not merely the fact that a reward arrives after the response is made. Instead, what matters is the *relationship* between responding and getting the reward, and this relationship actually gives the animal some control over the reward: By choosing when (or whether) to respond, the animal itself can determine when the reward is delivered. And it turns out that this control is important, because animals can tell when they're in control and when they're not—and they clearly prefer being in control.

One line of evidence comes from a study in which infants were placed in cribs that had colorful mobiles hanging above them. Whenever the infants moved their heads, they closed a switch in their pillows; this activated the overhead mobile, which spun merrily for a second or so. The infants soon learned to shake their heads about, making their mobiles turn. They evidently enjoyed this, smiling and cooing at their mobiles, clearly delighted to see the mobiles move.

A second group of infants was exposed to a similar situation, but with one important difference: Their mobile turned just as often as the mobile for the first group; but it was moved for them, not by them. This difference turned out to be crucial. After a few days, these infants no longer smiled and cooed at the mobile, nor did they seem particularly interested when it turned. This suggests that what the first group of infants liked about the mobile was not that it moved, but that they made it move. Even a 2-month-old infant wants to be the master of his own fate (J. S. Watson, 1967; Figure 7.27).

This study with infants illustrates the joy of mastery. Another series of studies demonstrates the despair of no mastery at all. These studies focus on **learned helplessness**—an acquired sense that one has lost control over one's environment, with the sad consequence that one gives up trying (Seligman, 1975).

The classic experiment on learned helplessness used two groups of dogs, A and B, which received strong electric shocks while strapped in a hammock. The dogs in group A were able to exert some control over their situation: They could turn the shock off whenever it began simply by pushing a panel that was placed close to their noses. The dogs in group B had no such power. For them, the shocks were inescapable. But the number and duration of the shocks were the same as for the first group. This was guaranteed by the fact that, for each dog in group A, there was a corresponding animal in group B whose fate was yoked to that of the first dog. Whenever the group A dog was shocked, so was the group B dog. Whenever the group A dog turned off the shock, the shock was turned off for the group B dog. Thus, both groups experienced exactly the

learned helplessness A condition of passivity apparently created by exposure to inescapable aversive events. This condition inhibits or prevents learning in later situations in which escape or avoidance is possible.

7.27 Response control Infants who could make a mobile move smiled and cooed at it; those who had no control over its motion quickly lost interest in the mobile.

same level of physical suffering; the only difference was what the animals were able to do about it. The dogs in group A had some control; those in group B could only endure.

What did the group B dogs learn in this situation? To find out, both groups of dogs were next presented with a task in which they had to learn to jump from one compartment to another to avoid a shock. The dogs in group A learned easily. During the first few trials, they ran about frantically when the shock began but eventually scrambled over the hurdle into the other compartment, where there was no shock. Based on this experience, they soon learned to leap over the hurdle the moment the shock began, easily escaping the aversive experience. Then, with just a few more trials, these dogs learned something even better: They jumped over the hurdle as soon as they heard the tone signaling that shock was about to begin; as a result, they avoided the shock entirely.

Things were different for the dogs in group B, those that had previously experienced the inescapable shock. Initially, these dogs responded to the electric shock just like the group A dogs did—running about, whimpering, and so on. But they soon became much more passive. They lay down, whined, and simply took whatever shocks were delivered. They neither avoided nor escaped; they just gave up. In the earlier phase of the experiment, they really had been objectively helpless; there truly was nothing they could do. In the shuttle box, however, their helplessness was only subjective because now they did have a way to escape the shocks. But they never discovered it, because they had learned to be helpless (Seligman & Maier, 1967).

Martin Seligman, one of the discoverers of the learned helplessness effect, asserts that depression in humans can develop in a similar way. Like the dog that has learned to be helpless, Seligman argues, the depressed patient has come to believe that nothing she does will improve her circumstances. And Seligman maintains that, like the dog, the depressed patient has reached this morbid state by experiencing a situation in which she really was helpless. While the dog received inescapable shocks in its hammock, the patient found herself powerless in the face of bereavement, some career failure, or serious illness (Seligman, Klein, & Miller, 1976). In both cases, the outcome is the same—a belief that there's no contingency between acts and outcomes, and so there's no point in trying. (For more on this theory of depression, see Chapter 16.)*

OBSERVATIONAL LEARNING

We've now considered three types of learning—habituation, classical conditioning, and instrumental conditioning, each of which can be observed in many different species. Indeed, across this chapter we've mixed together examples of how these learning principles apply to humans and how they apply to a range of other organisms. In contrast, a fourth type of learning was for many years regarded as exclusively human; but more recent evidence indicates that this learning, too, can be observed in many

*Before moving on, we should mention that studies of learned helplessness in dogs—like many studies mentioned in this chapter—raise ethical questions. Is it ethically acceptable to deliver electric shock to animals, knowing that the shock produces pain and may produce a depression-like state? These are difficult questions, but the link between these studies and human depression may well help us to understand depression and may lead to more effective forms of treatment for, or even prevention of, this illness. These considerations persuade many investigators that the animal work, as troubling as it is, is necessary to further the goal of diminishing human suffering. In many countries, an Animal Care and Use Committee at each research center weighs these issues before approving any animal experiment, ensuring that every experiment is scrutinized and evaluated with close attention to the protection of animal welfare.

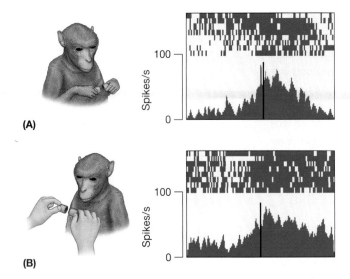

7.28 Mirror neurons Panel A shows the respones of a neuron in a monkey's motor cortex when the animal breaks a peanut. Panel B shows the remarkably similar pattern of activity when the monkey watches someone else open a peanut.

observational learning The process of watching how others behave and learning from their example.

vicarious conditioning A form of learning in which the learner acquires a conditioned response merely by observing another participant being conditioned.

mirror neurons Neurons that fire whenever an animal performs an action, such as stretching out its arm or reaching toward a target, and also whenever the animal watches another performing the same action.

species. At issue here is **observational learning**—a process through which we watch how others behave and learn from their example.

Other species are certainly capable of observational learning (e.g., Bugnyar & Kotrschal, 2002; White & Galef, 1998). For example, monkeys are capable of **vicarious conditioning**—acquiring a fear response, triggered by a specific stimulus, merely by watching another monkey show fear in response to that stimulus (Mineka & Ben Hamida, 1998; Öhman & Mineka, 2001). This learning is probably supported by a specific type of neuron found in the brains of many species: These **mirror neurons** are located in the frontal lobe, near the motor cortex, and fire whenever an animal performs an action such as stretching out its arm or reaching toward a target (Figure 7.28). Remarkably, the same neurons fire when the animal observes someone else performing the same action (Rizzolatti & Craighero, 2004); and several theorists have suggested that these neurons play an essential role both in understanding others' behavior and in imitating that behavior.

Observational learning can also be documented in non-primate species. In one experiment, pigeons were allowed to observe other pigeons getting rewarded either for pecking at a disk or for stepping on a lever. When the "watchers" were then placed in the same experimental chamber, they tended to make the same response—pecking or stepping—they had observed earlier (Zentall, Sutton, & Sherburne, 1996).

Observational learning—and imitation in particular—also plays a central role for humans, even when we're very young (e.g., Bandura, 1977, 1986). Indeed, infants less than a month old imitate the facial expressions of people in their environment (e.g., Meltzoff & Moore, 1977); not much later, they start imitating a range of other behaviors. Sometimes human imitation takes the form of outright mimicry—duplicating, as best we can, the exact behaviors we have observed in others. At other times, the imitation is more sophisticated: We observe others and draw general conclusions about what sorts of behaviors are permissible in that situation.

We can see both forms of imitation at work in a classic study by Bandura (1969, 1977; Figure 7.29). In that study, children watched while an adult punched and kicked a large, inflated doll. Later on, the children were allowed to play in the room with various toys; and those who had observed the adults' aggression tended to mimic it—kicking and punching the doll exactly as the adult had. But these children also showed a broader form of imitation: They became aggressive toward other toys, as if they'd figured out by observation that aggression was permitted and maybe even appropriate in this environment.

As a further illustration of observational learning, consider the impact of media violence—seen on TV or in video games—on children. Research has made it clear that media violence—whether it's watching cartoon characters punch each other or guiding videogame characters as they rip each other apart—does encourage violence in child viewers (e.g., C. Anderson & Bushman, 2002; Bushman & Anderson, 2009; Carnagey & Anderson, 2005; Feshbach & Tangney, 2008), Indeed, the evidence is compelling enough that six major professional societies (including the American Psychological Association and the American Medical Association) issued a joint statement noting that studies "point overwhelmingly to a causal connection between media violence and aggressive behavior in some children" (Joint Statement, 2000, p. 1). This effect probably involves several different mechanisms; still, it's a compelling example of just how important observational learning can be—and it reminds us that this learning can have both good effects (the acquisition of new skills) and bad.

Method

1. Two groups of children were each shown a different short film of an adult playing with a large inflatable "Bobo" doll.

2. In one video the adult played quietly with the doll. In the other the adult hit and kicked the doll.

Results

When children were allowed to play with the doll later, those who had seen the aggressive play were much more likely to hit and kick the doll, as they had seen the adult do.

CONCLUSION: Observational learning can have a powerful effect on aggression.

SOURCE STUDIES: Bandura, 1969, 1977

VARIETIES OF LEARNING

Overall, the attempt to find general principles of learning—principles that apply to virtually all species—has been rather successful. This is why we can gain insights into human depression by studying helplessness in dogs, and it's how we've increased our understanding of human drug addiction—thanks to research on classical conditioning in rats. Other examples of learning phenomena shared across species are easy to find.

We need to acknowledge, though, that there are also important differences from one species to the next in how learning proceeds. These differences are often best understood by taking a biological perspective on learning—a perspective that highlights the actual *function* of learning in each species' natural environment (see, for example, Bolles & Beecher, 1988; Domjan, 2005; Rozin & Schull, 1988).

Biological Influences on Learning: Belongingness

In the early days of learning theory, investigators widely believed that animals (both humans and others) are capable of connecting any CS to any US in classical conditioning, and of associating virtually any response with any reinforcer in instrumental conditioning. A child could be taught that a tone signaled the approach of dinner or that a flashing light or a particular word did. Likewise, a rat could be trained to press a lever to get food, water, or access to a sexually receptive mate.

But a great deal of evidence speaks against this idea; instead, each species seems predisposed to form some associations and not others. The predispositions put *biological constraints* on that species' learning, governing what the species can learn easily and what it can learn only with difficulty. These associative predispositions are probably hardwired and likely to be a direct product of our evolutionary past (Rozin & Kalat, 1971, 1972; Seligman & Hager, 1972).

TASTE AVERSION LEARNING

taste aversion learning A form of learning in which an organism learns to avoid a taste after just one pairing of that taste with illness.

7.30 Taste aversion The text describes taste-aversion learning in the lab, but the same pattern is easily observed in other settings. Young adults often develop a taste aversion to particular forms of alcohol. Usually this is the consequence of a single episode of overindulgence: After drinking far too much vodka, for example, the person ends up quite sick, and that experience can lead to a lifelong distaste for vodka.

A central example of the biological constraints on learning comes from studies of **taste aversion learning.** These studies make it clear that, from the organism's viewpoint, some stimuli belong together and some do not (Domjan, 1983, 2005; Garcia & Koelling, 1966).

To understand this phenomenon, we need to begin with the fact that when a wild rat encounters a novel food, it generally takes only a small bite at first. If the rat suffers no ill effects from this first taste, it will return (perhaps a day or two later) for a second helping and will gradually make the food a part of its regular diet. But what if this novel food is harmful, either because of some natural toxin or an exterminator's poison? In that case, the initial taste will make the rat sick; but because it ate only a little of the food, the rat will probably recover. Based on this experience, though, the rat is likely to develop a strong aversion to that particular flavor, so it never returns for a second dose of the poison.

This sort of learning is easily documented in the laboratory. The subjects, usually rats, are presented with a food or drink that has a novel flavor—perhaps water with some vanilla added. After drinking this flavored water, the rats are exposed to X-ray radiation—not enough to injure them, but enough to make them ill. After they recover, the rats show a strong aversion to the taste of vanilla and refuse to drink water flavored in this way (Figure 7.30).

This learned taste aversion is actually based on classical conditioning. The flavor (here, vanilla) serves as the CS, and the sensation of being sick serves as the US. This is, however, a specialized type of classical conditioning that is distinct from other forms in the sheer speed of learning: One pairing of a taste + illness is all it takes to establish the connection between them. This *one-trial learning* is obviously much faster than the speed of ordinary classical conditioning. What's more, this form of conditioning is distinctive in its timing requirements. In most classical conditioning, the CS must be soon followed by the US; if too much time passes between these two stimuli, the likelihood of conditioning is much reduced (see Figure 7.10). In taste aversion learning, in contrast, conditioning can be observed even if several hours elapse between the CS and the US.

Learned taste aversions are also remarkable for their specificity. In one early study, thirsty rats were allowed to drink sweetened water through a tube. Whenever the rats licked the nozzle of this tube, a bright light flashed and a loud clicking noise sounded. Thus, the sweetness, bright light, and loud noise were always grouped together; if one was presented, all were presented. One group of these rats then received an electric shock to the feet. A second group was exposed to a dose of X-rays strong enough to cause illness.

Notice, then, that we have two different USs—illness for one group and foot shock for the other. Both groups also have received a three-part CS: sweet + bright + noisy. The question is: How will the animals put these pieces together—what will get associated with what?

To find out, the experimenters tested the rats in a new situation. They gave some of the rats sweetened water, unaccompanied by either light or noise. Rats that had received foot shock showed no inclination to avoid this water; apparently, they didn't associate foot shock with the sweet flavor. However, rats that had been made ill with X-rays refused to drink this sweetened water; they associated their illness with the taste (Figure 7.31).

Another group of rats were tested with unflavored water accompanied by the light and sound cues that were present during training. Now the pattern was reversed. Rats that had become ill showed no objection to this water. For them, the objectionable (sweet) taste was absent from this test stimulus, and they didn't associate their illness with the sights and sounds that were present during the test. However, rats that had been shocked earlier refused to drink this water; in their minds, pain was associated with bright lights and loud clicks (Garcia & Koelling, 1966).

Conditioning

The moment the rat sips the sweetened water it also gets the tone and light.

CS: Rat drinks sweetened water

Light

Sound

The US follows shortly thereafter—shocks for some rats and illness for the others.

Shock (US)

Illness (US)

7.31 The specificity of taste aversion Rats that had been shocked associated the shock with the lights and sounds (but not the taste) that had accompanied the painful experience. Rats that had become ill associated the illness with a taste (but not with the lights and sounds).

Experiments

In a subsequent test, rats who had been shocked avoided drinking when they were tested with light and sound but not when they were tested with sweet water. Rats who had become ill avoided drinking when they were tested with sweet water, but not when they were tested with light and sound.

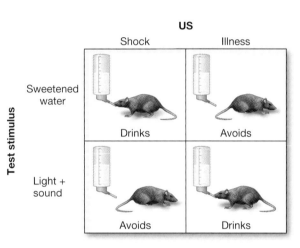

US

	Shock	Illness
Sweetened water	Drinks	Avoids
Light + sound	Avoids	Drinks

Test stimulus

For the rat, therefore, taste goes with illness, and sights and sounds go with externally induced pain. And for this species, this pattern makes biological sense. Illness in wild rats is likely to have been caused by harmful or tainted food, and rats generally select their food largely on the basis of flavor. So there's survival value in the rats being able to learn quickly about the connection between a particular flavor and illness; this will provide useful information for them as they select their next meal, ensuring that they don't resample the harmful berries or poisoned meat.

Using this logic, one might expect species that choose foods on the basis of other attributes to make different associations. For example, many birds make their food choices from a distance, relying on the food's visual appearance. How will this behavior affect the data? In one study, quail were given blue, sour water to drink and were then given a low dose of poison—enough to make them ill, but not enough to harm them. Some of the birds were later tested with blue, unflavored water; others were tested with water that was sour but colorless. The results showed that the quail had developed a strong aversion to blue water but no aversion to the sour water. They learned which water was safe based on its color rather than its taste (Wilcoxin, Dragoin, & Kral, 1971).

Clearly, what belongs with what depends upon the species. Birds are predisposed to associate illness with visual cues. Rats (and many other mammals) associate illness with taste. In each case, the bias makes the animal more prepared to form certain associations and far less prepared to form others (Seligman, 1970).

prepared learning Learning that occurs without extensive training because of an evolved predisposition to the behavior.

7.32 Prepared learning Humans seem prepared to associate aversive outcomes with the sight of snakes. This may be one reason many find the story of the Garden of Eden so compelling.

7.33 The Clark's nutcracker

We should also mention that taste aversion learning, as important as it is, is just one example of **prepared learning** (Figure 7.32). We mentioned a different example in the Prologue: Humans in one experiment were shown specific pictures as the CS and received electric shocks as the US. When the pictures showed flowers or mushrooms, learning was relatively slow. When the pictures showed snakes, learning was much quicker. The implication is that humans (and many other primates) are innately prepared to associate the sight of a snake with unpleasant or even painful experiences (Öhman & Mineka, 2003; Öhman & Soares, 1993; also Domjan, Cusato, & Krause, 2004).

These results may help us understand why so many people are afraid of snakes and why strong phobias for snakes are relatively common. Perhaps it's not surprising that many cultures regard snakes as the embodiments of evil. All these facts may simply be the result of prepared learning in our species—our innate tendencies toward making certain associations but not others.

BIOLOGICAL CONSTRAINTS ON INSTRUMENTAL CONDITIONING

Prepared learning can also be demonstrated in instrumental conditioning because, from an animal's viewpoint, certain responses belong with some rewards and not others (Shettleworth, 1972). For example, pigeons can easily be taught to peck a lit key to obtain food or water, but it's extremely difficult to train a pigeon to peck in order to escape electric shock (Hineline & Rachlin, 1969). In contrast, pigeons can easily be taught to hop or flap their wings to get away from shock, but it's difficult to train the pigeon to produce these same responses in order to gain food or water.

Once again, this pattern makes good biological sense. The pigeon's normal reaction to danger is to hop away or break into flight, so the pigeon is biologically prepared to associate these responses with aversive stimuli such as electrical shock. Pecking, in contrast, is not part of the pigeon's innate defense pattern, so it's difficult for the pigeon to learn pecking as an escape response (Bolles, 1970). Conversely, since pecking is what pigeons do naturally when they eat, the pigeon is biologically prepared to associate this response with food or drink; it's no wonder, then, that pigeons easily learn to make this association in the psychologist's laboratory.

Different Types of Learning

It seems therefore that we need to "tune" the laws of learning on a case-by-case basis to accommodate the fact that a given species learns some relationships easily, others only with difficulty, and still others not at all. This tuning builds some flexibility into the laws of learning; but it allows us to retain the idea that there *are* general laws, applicable (with the appropriate tuning) to all species and to all situations. Other evidence suggests, though, that we must go further than this, because some types of learning follow their own specialized rules and depend on specialized capacities found in that species and few others. On this basis, we need to do more than adjust the laws of learning. We may also need some entirely new laws—laws that are specific to the species that does the learning and to what's being learned (Gallistel, 1990; Roper, 1983).

As one example, consider the Clark's nutcracker, a bird that makes its home in the American Southwest (Figure 7.33). In the summer, this bird buries thousands of pine nuts in various hiding places over an area of several square miles. Then, throughout the winter and early spring, the nutcracker flies back again and again to dig up its thousands of caches. The bird doesn't mark its cache sites in any special way. Instead, it relies on memory to find its stash—a remarkable feat that few of us could duplicate.

The Clark's nutcracker has various anatomical features that support its food-hoarding activities—for example, there's a special pouch under its tongue that it fills with pine nuts when flying to find a hiding place. The bird's extraordinary ability to learn a huge number of geographical locations, and then to remember these locations for the next few months, is probably a similar evolutionary adaptation. Like the tongue pouch, this learning ability is a specialty of this species: Related birds like jays and crows don't store food in this way; and, when tested, they have a correspondingly poorer spatial memory (D. Olson, 1991; Shettleworth, 1983, 1984, 1990).

Many phenomena of animal learning—in birds, fish, and mammals—reveal similar specializations. In each case, the organism has some extraordinary ability not shared even by closely related species. In each case, the ability has obvious survival value and seems quite narrow. The Clark's nutcracker, for example, has no special skill in remembering pictures or shapes; instead, its remarkable memory comes into play only in the appropriate setting—when hiding and then relocating buried pine nuts. Similarly, many birds show remarkable talent in learning the particular songs used by their species. This skill, however, can be used for no other purpose: A zebra finch easily masters the notes of the zebra finch's song but is utterly inept at learning any other (non-musical) sequence of similar length and complexity. Truly, then, these are specialized learning abilities—only one or a few species have them, and they apply only to a particular task crucial for their members' survival (Gallistel, 1990; Marler, 1970).

But what about humans? Throughout this chapter, we've emphasized that a great deal of human behavior—just like the behavior of every animal species—is governed by principles of habituation as well as classical and operant conditioning. But, even so, some of our behavior is the product of distinctly human forms of learning. One example involves the processes through which humans learn language. These processes seem controlled by innate mechanisms that guide the learning and make it possible for us to achieve remarkable linguistic competence by the time we're 3 years old. (We'll say much more about language learning in Chapter 10.) Humans also have remarkable inferential abilities that allow us to gain broad sets of new beliefs, based on events we've observed or information we've received from others; and these new beliefs can profoundly affect our behavior. In these ways, humans are capable of distinctive forms of learning at the same time that they're powerfully shaped by the more general principles discussed in this chapter. (We'll have much more to say about human inferential capacities, and how we're influenced by others, in Chapters 8 and 9.)

Similarities in How Different Species Learn

In short, there are certainly differences—as well as crucial similarities—in how species learn, and, as we've noted, the differences make good biological sense. After all, each species lives in its own distinctive environment and needs its own set of skills, and so it may need to learn in its own ways. But what about the similarities? After all, the rats and pigeons we study in the laboratory don't gather food the way a human does. They don't communicate with their fellows the way a human does. Their nervous systems are much simpler than ours. It wouldn't be surprising, therefore, if they learned in different ways than we do. Yet, as we've repeatedly noted, the major phenomena of both classical and instrumental conditioning apply across species—whether we're considering humans, rats, pigeons, cats, dogs, fish, or even some types of snails (Couvillon & Bitterman, 1980; E. Kandel, 2007).

How should we think about this point? Why do such diverse creatures share certain types of learning? The answer lies in the fact that all of these creatures, no matter what their evolutionary history or ecological niche, share certain needs. For example, virtually all creatures are better off if they can prepare themselves for upcoming events, and to do this they need some way of anticipating what will happen to them in the near future. It's no wonder, then, that many species have developed nervous systems that support classical conditioning.

Similarly, in the world we all inhabit, important outcomes are often influenced by one's behavior, so it pays for all species to repeat actions that have worked well in the past and to abandon actions that haven't succeeded. Hence we might expect natural selection to have favored organisms capable of learning about the consequences of their actions and able to adjust their future behavior accordingly. In other words, we'd expect natural selection to have favored organisms capable of instrumental conditioning.

Of course, people are different from pigeons, and pigeons from sea slugs; no one is questioning these points. Even so, it seems that there are some types of learning that all species need to do. And this is why, in this chapter, we've easily identified principles of learning that apply to an extraordinary range of species and settings.

THE NEURAL BASIS FOR LEARNING

We just suggested that different species all need to learn the same kinds of lessons—including how events in the world are related to each other, and what the consequences are of the organism's own actions. But do all organisms accomplish this learning through the same neural mechanisms? If we zoom in for a closer look, will we find the biology of learning is the same from one species to the next? As is often the case, there are important commonalities between species; but there are also significant differences: The biological mechanisms that allow learning in mammals are somewhat different from the mechanisms crucial for reptiles, amphibians, or invertebrates (Macphail, 1996; Woolf, 1998). Indeed, even within a single species, the biological mechanisms needed for learning can vary and seem to depend on the CS, the US, and the procedure (R. Clark, Manns, & Squire, 2003; Fanselow & Poulos, 2005). Thus, the brain circuits underlying fear conditioning (with electric shock as the US) are centered in the amygdala; the brain circuits underlying eyeblink conditioning (with a puff of air to the eye as the US) are centered in the cerebellum. Conditioning with a long delay between the CS and US typically involves the hippocampus, while conditioning with a shorter delay may not (Berman & Dudai, 2001; Lattal, Honarvar, & Abel, 2004).

Even with these variations, some biological principles do apply to all cases of learning. In all cases, learning depends on *neural plasticity*—the capacity for neurons to change the way they function as a result of experience. In all cases, the plasticity involves changes at the synapse—that is, changes in the way neurons communicate with each other. These changes, in turn, can involve any of three adjustments: Some neurons, after learning, end up sending a stronger signal than they did before. Other neurons become more sensitive to the signals they've been receiving all along. And, third, learning can lead to the creation of entirely new connections among neurons— new synapses—allowing for new lines of communication within the nervous system.

Evidence for these points comes from many sources, including studies of the marine mollusk *Aplysia*. Because the nervous systems of these creatures contain a mere 20,000 neurons, they're good candidates for detailed analysis. Researchers have been able to document that, after conditioning, the *Aplysia*'s sensory neurons—the neurons that receive the CS—literally release more neurotransmitter into the synapse than they did before the conditioning trials. This is a crucial part of why, at the end of learning, these neurons are able to trigger a response—the CR—that they couldn't trigger at the start. This process, which can be documented in many species in addition to *Aplysia*, produces an increase in the neural signal being sent, and is called **presynaptic facilitation** (e.g., Lisman, 2003; Pittenger & Kandel, 2003).

presynaptic facilitation A process, documented in studies of *Aplysia*, that underlies many kinds of learning. It occurs when learning results in an increased release of neurotransmitter into the synapse.

Other forms of neural plasticity, in other organisms, involve postsynaptic changes—that is, they influence the receiving side of the synapse. A particularly important mechanism in this category is **long-term potentiation** (**LTP**; T. Bliss & Lomo, 1973; T. Bliss, Collingridge, & Laroche, 2006; Martinez & Derrick, 1996)—*potentiation* because the mechanism involves an increase in the responsiveness of a neuron (an increase in the neuron's potential for firing) and *long term* because this potentiation lasts for days, perhaps even weeks.

LTP is produced when one neuron activates another neuron over and over. The repeated stimulation causes the postsynaptic neuron to become more sensitive to this input than it was before, so it's more likely to respond to this input in the future. In addition, the increased responsiveness can spread to other nearby neurons. Here's an example: Let's suppose that within some brief period of time neuron A in Figure 7.34 repeatedly causes neuron C to fire. This will cause neuron C to become more responsive to A than it was initially. But, of course, C also has other synapses that receive input from other neurons, such as neuron B in the figure. These receptors too will become more sensitive as a result of neuron A's repeated activity, provided that these other neurons fire at the same time as neuron A. In other words, the spread of potentiation is *activity dependent* and so will spread to neuron B only if B was active at the same time as the neuron that caused the potentiation in the first place—in this case, neuron A (W. Levy & Steward, 1979; McNaughton, Douglas, & Goddard, 1978). In this way, LTP provides a cellular mechanism through which associations—in our example, the association between A's and B's activity—can be detected and recorded in the brain (Fanselow & Poulos, 2005; E. Kandel & Hawkins, 1992; Koekoek et al., 2003; Martinez & Derrick, 1996).

Presynaptic facilitation and LTP both involve changes in how efficiently a synapse functions—the first involves changes in how neurons send signals, and the second involves changes in how neurons receive signals. A third form of neural plasticity involves the creation of entirely new synapses. These changes seem to take place largely on the dendrites of the postsynaptic neurons; as we mentioned in Chapter 3, the dendrites can grow new *dendritic spines* (Moser, 1999; Woolf, 1998). These spines are the "receiving stations" for most synapses; so growing more spines means that, as learning proceeds, the neuron is gaining new lines of communication with its cellular neighbors.

long-term potentiation (LTP)
A long-lasting increase in a neuron's response to specific inputs, caused by repeated stimulation.

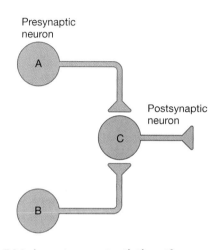

7.34 Long-term potentiation If neuron A repeatedly causes neuron C to fire, the strength of their connection (synapse) will increase (become potentiated).

SOME FINAL THOUGHTS: LEARNING THEORY AND BEYOND

The investigations begun by Pavlov and Thorndike more than 100 years ago have led to many important discoveries, and it's clear that some of the principles they uncovered apply to every species we have studied. We can demonstrate these principles in the laboratory, and we can employ them outside the lab. For example, behavior modification techniques, building on the lessons we've learned in this chapter, are widely used in hospitals for the mentally ill and in one-on-one therapy; many prisons use instrumental conditioning to shape prisoners' behavior; parents employ similar techniques to teach their children good manners, household chores, and interpersonal skills. In short, these principles of learning are extensively used and enormously useful, and they're an effective means of altering or maintaining specific patterns of behavior.

At the same time, we need to place these principles of learning in a broader context. On the one side, we need to connect our understanding of learning to the relevant biology. This allows us to explore the mechanisms that make learning possible—and, with that, to see the *diversity* of mechanisms (even within a single species) that underlie learning. A link to biology also calls our attention to the evolutionary roots of learning, and this helps us comprehend why rats are biologically prepared to associate illness with tastes—and presumably, why humans are biologically prepared to associate snakes with aversive outcomes.

On the other side, we also need to connect our conception of learning to the relevant cognition. As we've seen, learning involves more than a change in behavior; it also involves the acquisition of new knowledge. In classical conditioning, this knowledge involves the relationships among events in the world; that's why the CS serves as a *signal* for things to come. In instrumental conditioning, the knowledge concerns the relationships between one's own actions and events in the world, but it can also include other, broader topics: knowledge about complicated spatial layouts, knowledge about whether an organism has control over its environment or not. But what is this knowledge? How is it stored in memory? How is the knowledge *used* as a basis for solving problems or making decisions? We plainly are not going to understand learning unless we tackle these issues, and this sets part of the agenda for us in the next two chapters.

SUMMARY CHAPTER 7

THE PERSPECTIVE OF LEARNING THEORY

- The empiricist philosophers argued that learning involves the forming of simple associations. More complex learning just involves a great many associations, each layered upon the others. From this perspective, all learning depends on the same mechanisms, and so all learning should be governed by the same principles.

HABITUATION

- The simplest form of learning is *habituation*, a decline in the response to stimuli that have become familiar through repeated exposure. In *dishabituation*, the organism learns that a previously predictable stimulus has now changed, causing the organism to renew its attention to the stimulus.

CLASSICAL CONDITIONING

- In *classical conditioning*, animals learn about the association between one stimulus and another. Before conditioning, an *unconditioned stimulus* (US, such as food) elicits an *unconditioned response* (UR, such as salivation). After repeated occasions on which the US follows a *conditioned stimulus* (CS, such as a buzzer), this CS alone will begin to evoke the *conditioned response* (CR; here again, salivation).
- When a CS-US relationship is well established, the CS can be preceded by a second, neutral stimulus to produce *second-order conditioning*.
- Trials in which the CS is presented without the US lead to *extinction*. However, the phenomenon of *spontaneous*

recovery shows that the CR is masked, not abolished, by extinction.

- Because of *stimulus generalization*, the CR can also be elicited by stimuli that are similar to the CS. To train the animal to *discriminate* among stimuli, one stimulus (CS^+) is presented with the US, while another (CS^-) is presented without the US.

- Several lines of evidence suggest that the CS serves as a *signal* for upcoming events. This fits with the fact that learning is less likely if the CS is simultaneous with the US, or (worse) follows it. The signal value of the CS is also evident because learning occurs only if there is some contingency between CS and US; mere contiguity between these stimuli isn't enough. Animals can also learn about the *absence* of contingency, and animals clearly prefer environments in which stimuli are predictable.

- Animals seem sensitive to relationships among probabilities, but this is not because they're tracking the probabilities directly. Instead, animals develop expectations about upcoming events and adjust their expectations whenever events surprise them. In this way, the expectations are gradually adjusted until they are accurately in tune with probabilities in the environment. The role of surprise is directly evident in the *blocking effect*.

- The CR is not identical to the UR. Instead, the CR seems to be a means of *preparing* for the US. Sometimes the preparation takes the form of a compensatory response, and this point may be crucial in understanding drug addiction and drug tolerance.

INSTRUMENTAL CONDITIONING

- When training an animal using *instrumental* (or *operant*) conditioning, the trainer delivers a reward or *reinforcement* only after the animal gives the appropriate response. According to Thorndike, learning in this situation is governed by the *law of effect*, which states that the tendency to perform a response is strengthened if it's followed by a reward and weakened if it's not.

- *Operants* are voluntary responses, strengthened by reinforcement; but acquiring them may call for some initial *shaping*, through a method of *successive approximations*.

- Some reinforcers are stimuli whose reinforcing power is unlearned. Other conditioned reinforcers acquire their power from prior presentations with stimuli already having that capacity. The magnitude of a reinforcer depends on several factors, including the magnitude of other reinforcers that might be available. This effect, which is reflected in the phenomenon of *behavioral contrast*, may be one source of findings sometimes attributed to *intrinsic motivation*. Many theorists, however, believe that intrinsic motivation involves a separate set of principles, different from those that govern operant conditioning.

- During *partial reinforcement*, the response is reinforced only some of the time. The rule that determines when a reinforcer is given is called a *schedule of reinforcement*. In *ratio schedules*, reinforcement is delivered after a number of responses; the ratio used may be fixed or variable. In *interval schedules*, reinforcers are delivered for the first response made after a given interval since the last reinforcement; this interval, too, can be fixed or variable.

- Learning involves more than a change in behavior; it also involves the acquisition of new knowledge. This principle is evident in many settings, including *latent learning*.

- Operant conditioning results when reinforcement is contingent on a response, not just when reinforcement happens to be contiguous with responding. Organisms' sensitivity to contingency can be demonstrated in the phenomenon of *learned helplessness*, where animals seem to learn they have no control over the events they're experiencing.

OBSERVATIONAL LEARNING

- Many animals can learn simply by watching other individuals and learning from their example. This is evident in *vicarious conditioning*, and it's also clear in learning through *imitation*. However, the impact of media violence reminds us that imitation can be a source of undesired behaviors as well as a source of new skills.

VARIETIES OF LEARNING

- According to the early learning theorists, just about any CS can become associated with any US, and just about any response can be strengthened by any reinforcer. This assertion is challenged by the fact that certain conditioned stimuli are more readily associated with some unconditioned stimuli than with others, as shown by studies of *taste aversion learning*. These studies suggest that animals are biologically prepared to learn certain relations more readily than others. Similar effects occur in instrumental conditioning, where some responses are more readily strengthened by some reinforcers than by others.

- Certain forms of learning are species specific. In humans, specialized forms of learning may include our capacity for learning language as well as our remarkable ability to learn by observing others.

- Animals vary in how (and what) they learn; but in some aspects of learning, diverse species also exhibit striking similarities. These similarities probably arise because all organisms live in the same world, and the nature of the world creates a need in many species for the forms of learning we call classical and operant conditioning.

THE NEURAL BASIS FOR LEARNING

- In recent years, investigators have made considerable progress in understanding the neural bases for learning. These bases involve diverse mechanisms, such as *presynaptic facilitation*, and *postsynaptic changes*, such as *long-term potentiation (LTP)*. Still another mechanism involves the creation of new synapses—made possible by the growth of new dendritic spines, which act as "receiving stations" for synapses and open new lines of communication between cellular neighbors.

 ONLINE STUDY TOOLS

Go to StudySpace, **wwnorton.com/studyspace**, to access additional review and enrichment materials, including the following resources for each chapter:

Organize
- Study Plan
- Chapter Outline
- Quiz+ Assessment

Learn
- Ebook
- Chapter Review
- Vocabulary Flashcards
- Drag-and-Drop Labeling Exercises
- Audio Podcast Chapter Overview

Connect
- Critical Thinking Activity
- Studying the Mind Video Podcasts
- Video Exercises
- Animations
- **ZAPS** Psychology Labs

8 Memory

Genghis Khan got around. At the dawn of the 13th century, the Mongolian warrior conquered the largest empire the world had ever known: an expanse stretching from the Sea of Japan in the east to the Caspian Sea in the west, from Siberia in the north to India in the south. To conquer this territory and then maintain his domination, the emperor had to formulate complex plans. This created a problem: His soldiers were illiterate peasants, scattered over thousands of miles. How could he spread his complicated orders through the ranks quickly, simply, and without error?

His solution: Put the orders in a song. All the Khan's soldiers learned a small set of melodies, which they practiced as they traversed the mountains and steppes. Then, when the time for fighting arrived, commanders would set their orders to the tune of one of these melodies. The soldiers' task was simple: memorize a few new verses for an old song, rather than a series of entirely unfamiliar, abstract instructions. And if any one of the soldiers forgot the lyrics, hundreds of others could sing him the next line. Using this scheme, the soldiers crooned their battle instructions, and large segments of Eurasia fell.

Others in the ancient world also relied on deliberate memorization strategies. The Greeks of classical Athens, for example, put a high value on public speaking, much of which was done from memory. The Greeks therefore developed a number of memorization tricks (some of which we'll discuss later in the chapter) to help them in this endeavor.

Similar mnemonic tactics are used in the modern world. Medical students, for example, have developed strategies that help them memorize anatomy, drug names, and disease symptoms. Thus, they learn the 12 pairs of cranial nerves (olfactory, optic, oculomotor, trochlear, trigeminal, and so on) by taking the first letter of each word and forming a sentence built from new words that start with the same letters. The resulting sentence—"On Old Olympus' Towering Tops A Friendly Viking Grew Vines and Hops"—paints a vivid image that's far easier to remember than the original list.

These examples remind us that—with just a bit of work—we can get enormous amounts of information into our memories, and then recall that information, in detail, for a very long time. But there's also a darker side to memory: Sometimes we remember things that never happened at all. Indeed, far more often than we realize, our memories blend together separate incidents, introduce rogue details, and incorporate others' versions of events into our own recall. In this chapter, you'll learn how these memory errors arise and what they tell us about remembering.

How far off track can memory go? In one study, researchers planted in participants a memory of getting lost in the mall as a child, then being brought home safely by a friendly stranger. Nothing of the sort had happened to anyone in the study, but they came to vividly "remember" it anyhow. Other studies have planted false memories of vicious animal attacks, and even—in one remarkable study—a false memory of a hot-air balloon ride.

How should we put these pieces together? How does memory operate, so that we can easily remember countless episodes, thousands of facts, and the lyrics to hundreds of songs? Why does Genghis Kahn's lyrical trick, or the medical students' sentence-building strategy, help memory? More broadly, what can we do to learn more rapidly and hold on to the information longer? And why do our memories sometimes betray us, leading us to endorse large-scale fictions? We'll tackle all of these questions in this chapter.

ACQUISITION, STORAGE, RETRIEVAL

Each of us has a huge number of memories. We can recall what we did yesterday, or last summer. We can remember what the capital of France is, or what the chemical formula is for water. We remember how to ride a bicycle and how to throw a baseball. These examples—remembering *episodes,* remembering *general facts,* and remembering *skills* or *procedures*—actually draw on different memory systems; but it also turns out that the various types of memory have some things in common, so let's begin with the common elements.

Any act of remembering requires success at three aspects of the memory process. First, in order to remember, you must learn something—that is, you must put some information into your memory. This point seems obvious, but it deserves emphasis because many failures of memory are, in fact, failures in this initial stage of *acquisition.* For example, imagine meeting someone at a party, being told his name, and moments later realizing that you don't have a clue what his name is—even though you just heard it! This common (but embarrassing) experience is probably not the result of ultrarapid forgetting. Instead, it's likely to stem from a failure in acquisition. You were exposed to the name but barely paid attention to it and, as a result, never learned it in the first place.

The next aspect of remembering is *storage*. To be remembered, an experience must leave some record in the nervous system. This record—known as the memory trace—is squirreled away and held in some enduring form for later use. One question to be asked here is how permanent this storage is: Once information is in storage, does it stay there forever? Or does information in storage gradually fade away? We'll tackle these questions later in this chapter.

The final aspect of remembering is *retrieval*, the process through which you draw information from storage and use it. Sometimes, retrieval takes the form of

recall—a process in which you retrieve information from memory in response to some cue or question (Figure 8.1A). Trying to answer a question like "What is Sue's boyfriend's name?" or "Can you remember the last time you were in California?" requires recall. A different way to retrieve information is through **recognition** (Figure 8.1B). In this kind of retrieval, you're presented with a name, fact, or situation and are asked if you have encountered it before. "Is this the man you saw at the bank robbery?" or "Was the movie you saw called *Memento*?" are questions requiring recognition. Recognition can also be tested with multiple items: "Which of these pictures shows the man you saw earlier?" This latter format obviously resembles a multiple-choice exam, and in fact multiple-choice testing in the classroom probes your ability to recognize previously learned material. In contrast, exams that rely on essays or short answers emphasize recall.

8.1 Using memory (A) In this card game, you need to recall which card is in which position; in this case, *position* is the memory cue, and *card identity* is what you're trying to recall. (B) Most standardized tests, in multiple-choice format, rely on recognition. The correct answer is in front of you, as one of your options, and you need to recognize it.

recall A type of retrieval that requires you to produce an item from memory in response to a cue or question.

recognition A type of retrieval that requires you to judge whether you have encountered a stimulus previously.

acquisition The processes of gaining new information and placing it in memory.

intentional learning Placing new information into memory in anticipation of being tested on it later.

incidental learning Learning without trying to learn, and often without awareness that learning is occurring.

ACQUISITION

People commonly speak of "memorizing" new facts or, more broadly, of "learning" new material. However, psychologists prefer the term memory **acquisition** and use it to include cases of deliberate memorization (**intentional learning**) as well as cases of **incidental learning**—learning that takes place without any intention to memorize and often without the awareness that learning is actually occurring. (You know that grass is green and the sky is blue, and you probably can easily recall what you had for dinner yesterday, but you didn't set out to memorize these facts; the learning, therefore, was incidental.)

Memory acquisition is not just a matter of "copying" an event or a fact into memory, the way a camera copies an image onto film. Instead, acquisition requires some intellectual engagement with the material—thinking about it in some way—and it's then the product of this engagement (i.e., what you thought about during the event) that's stored in memory. As we'll see, this simple point turns out to have crucial implications for what you will remember and for how accurate (i.e., true to the actual history) your memory will be.

Working Memory, Long-Term Memory

How does memory acquisition proceed? The answer has to begin with the fact that we have several types of memory, each with different properties, and each type plays its

working memory A term describing the status of thoughts in memory that are currently activated.

long-term memory The vast memory depository containing all of an individual's knowledge and beliefs—including all those not in use at any given time.

primacy effect In free recall, the tendency to recall the first items on the list more readily than those in the middle.

recency effect In free recall, the tendency to recall items at the end of the list more readily than those in the middle.

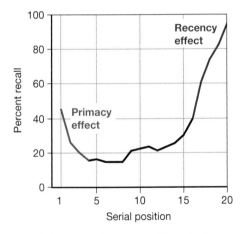

8.2 Primacy and recency effects in free recall Research participants heard a list of 20 common words presented at a rate of 1 word per second. Immediately after hearing the list, participants were asked to write down as many of the words on the list as they could recall. The results show that position in the series strongly affected recall—participants had better recall for words at the beginning of the list (a pattern called the primacy effect) and for words at the end of the list (the recency effect).

own role in the acquisition process. Historically, these different types have been described in terms of the *stage theory of memory,* which proposed (among other points) that memory acquisition could be understood as dependent on three types of memory: When information first arrived, it was stored briefly in *sensory memory,* which held onto the input in "raw" sensory form—an *iconic memory* for visual inputs and an *echoic memory* for auditory inputs. A process of selection and interpretation then moved the information into *short-term memory*—the place you hold information while you're working on it. Some of the information was then transferred into *long-term memory,* a much larger and more permanent storage place (Atkinson & Shiffrin, 1968; Broadbent, 1958; Waugh & Norman, 1965).

This early conception of memory captured some important truths—but needs to be updated in several ways. As one concern, the idea of "sensory memory" plays a much smaller role in modern theorizing and so, for example, many discussions of visual information processing (like our discussion in Chapters 4 and 5) make no mention of iconic memory. In addition, modern proposals use the term **working memory** rather than short-term memory to emphasize the function of this memory: Ideas or thoughts in this memory are currently activated, currently being thought about—and so they're the ideas you are currently *working on.* **Long-term memory,** in contrast, is the vast depository that contains all of your knowledge and all of your beliefs that you happen not to be thinking about at the moment, and this includes your beliefs about relatively recent events. Thus, if just a few minutes ago you were thinking about your weekend plans but now you're thinking about something else, these plans are gone from working memory (because you're no longer working on them); and so, if you can recall your plans, you must be drawing them from long-term memory.

Let's note, though, that what's at stake here is more than a shift in terminology, because the modern view also differs from the stage theory in how it conceptualizes memory. In the older view, working memory was understood broadly as a *storage place,* and it was often described as the "loading dock" just outside the long-term memory "warehouse." In the modern conception, working memory is not a "place" at all; instead, it's just the name we give to a *status.* When we say that ideas are "in working memory," this simply means—as we've already noted—that these ideas are currently activated. This focus on status is also the key to understanding the difference between working memory and long-term memory—the modern conception emphasizes whether the mental content is currently active (working memory) or not (long-term memory), in contrast to older theory's emphasis on time frame ("short term" or "long").

PRIMACY AND RECENCY

Why should we take this broad proposal seriously? Why should we make any distinction between working memory and long-term memory, and why should we think about working memory in the way we've just described? As a first step toward answering these questions, consider the results of studies in which participants hear a series of unrelated words—perhaps 15 words in total, or 20, presented one word at a time. At the end of the list, the participants are asked to recall the items in any order they choose (this is why the participants' task is called *free recall*—they're free to recall the items in any sequence).

In this task, there's a reliable pattern for which words the participants recall and which ones they don't. Words presented at the beginning of the list are very likely to be recalled; this memory advantage for early-presented words is called the **primacy effect.** Likewise, the last few words presented are also likely to be recalled; this is the **recency effect.** The likelihood of recall is appreciably poorer for words in the middle of the list (Figure 8.2).

What creates this pattern? As the to-be-remembered words are presented, the participants pay attention to them, and this ensures the activated status that we call "working memory." There's a limit, however, on how many things someone can think about at once, and so there's a limit on how many items can be maintained in working memory. According to many authors, this limit is seven items, give or take one or two; the capacity of working memory is therefore said to be *seven plus or minus two* items (G. Miller, 1956). As a result, it's just not possible for the participants to maintain all of the list words in their current thoughts. Instead, they'll just do their best to "keep up" with the list as they hear it. Thus, at each moment during the list presentation, their working memories will contain only the half-dozen or so words that arrived most recently.

Notice that, in this situation, new words entering working memory will "bump out" the words that were there a moment ago. The only words that don't get bumped out are the last few words on the list, because obviously no further input arrives to displace them. Hence, when the list presentation ends, these few words are still in working memory—still in the participants' thoughts—so are easy to recall. This is why the participants reliably remember the end of the list; they are producing the result we call the recency effect.

The primacy effect comes from a different source. We know that these early words are not being recalled from working memory, because they were—as we've already noted—bumped from working memory by later-arriving words. It seems, therefore, that the primacy effect must involve long-term memory—and so, to explain why these early words are so well recalled, we need to ask how these words became well established in long-term storage in the first place.

The explanation lies in how participants allocate their attention during the list presentation. To put this in concrete terms, let's say that the first word on the list is *camera*. When research participants hear this word, they can focus their full attention on it, silently rehearsing "*camera, camera, camera, . . .*" When the second word arrives, they'll rehearse that one too; but now they'll have to divide their attention between the first word and the second ("*camera, boat, camera, boat, . . .*"). Attention will be divided still further after participants hear the third word ("*camera, boat, zebra, camera, boat, zebra, . . .*"), and so on through the list.

Notice that earlier words on the list get more attention than later ones. At the list's start, participants can lavish attention on the few words they've heard so far. As they hear more and more of the list, though, they must divide their attention more thinly, simply because they have more words to keep track of. Let's now make one more assumption: that the extra attention given to the list's first few words makes it more likely that these words will be well established in long-term memory. On this basis, participants will be more likely to recall these early words than words in the middle of the list—exactly the pattern of the data.

Support for these interpretations comes from various manipulations that affect the primacy and recency effects. For example, what happens if we require research participants to do some other task immediately after hearing the words but before recalling them? This other task will briefly divert the participants' attention from rehearsing or thinking about the list words—and so the words will be bumped out of working memory. Working memory, in turn, was the hypothesized source of the recency effect, and so, according to our hypothesis, this other task—even if it lasts just a few seconds—should disrupt the recency effect. And indeed it does. If participants are required to count backward for just 30 seconds between hearing the words and recalling them, the recency effect is eliminated (Figure 8.3).

Other manipulations produce a different pattern—they alter the primacy effect but have no effect on recency. For example, if we present the list items more slowly, participants have time to devote more attention to each word. But we've just proposed that attention helps to establish words in long-term memory. We should therefore expect that a slower

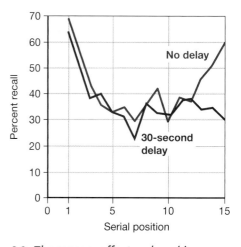

8.3 **The recency effect and working memory** Research participants heard several 15-word lists. In one condition (red), free recall was tested immediately after hearing the list. In the other condition (blue), the recall test was given after a 30-second delay during which rehearsal was prevented. The delay left the primacy effect unaffected but abolished the recency effect, confirming that this effect is based on retrieval from working memory.

(A)

Retrieval from long-term memory specifically activated the hippocampus.

Retrieval from working memory specifically activated the perirhinal cortex.

(B)

8.4 The primacy effect and long-term storage (A) The graph compares free-recall performance when item presentation is relatively slow (2 seconds per item) and fast (1 second per item). Slow presentation enhances the primacy effect but leaves the recency effect unaltered. (B) We can also confirm the distinction between working memory and long-term memory with fMRI scans. These suggest that memory for early items on a list depends on brain areas (in and around the hippocampus) that are associated with long-term memory; memory for later items on the list do not show this pattern (Talmi, Grady, Goshen-Gottstein & Moscovitch, 2005). This obviously provides confirmation that the recency items are coming from a different source than items heard earlier in the list.

presentation will lead to a stronger primacy effect (since primacy depends on retrieval from long-term memory) but no change in the recency effect (because the recency items aren't being retrieved from long-term memory). This is exactly what happens (Figure 8.4).

RECODING TO EXPAND THE CAPACITY OF WORKING MEMORY

As we've mentioned, working memory has a limited capacity. There is, however, enormous flexibility in how we use that capacity—and so, if we can pack the input more efficiently, we can increase the amount of information maintained in this memory.

For example, consider an individual who tries to recall a series of digits that she heard only once:

1776200o1066

If she treats this as a series of 16 unrelated digits, she'll surely fail in her attempt to remember the series. But if she thinks of the digits as years (i.e., the year the U.S. Declaration of Independence was signed; the year of the new millennium; and the year the Normans invaded England), the task becomes much easier because now she has just three items to remember.

Cases like this one make it plain that working memory's capacity can't be measured in *digits,* or *words,* or *kilobytes.* Instead, the capacity is measured in **chunks.** This unscientific-sounding word helps us remember that this is a flexible sort of measurement, because what's in a chunk depends on how the person thinks about, and organizes, the information. Thus, if a person thinks of each digit as a chunk, working memory

chunking A process of reorganizing (or recoding) materials in working memory by combining a number of items into a single, larger unit.

can hold (roughly) seven digits. If *pairs* of digits are chunked together, working memory's capacity will be more than a dozen digits.

To see how important chunking can be, consider a remarkable individual studied by Chase and Ericsson (Chase & Ericsson, 1978, 1979, 1982; Ericsson, 2003). This fellow happens to be a fan of track events, and when he hears numbers, he thinks of them as finishing times for races. The sequence "3, 4, 9, 2," for example, becomes "3 minutes and 49 point 2 seconds, near world-record mile time." In this way, four digits become one chunk of information. The man can then retain seven finishing times (seven chunks) in memory, and this can involve 20 or 30 digits. Better still, these chunks can be grouped into larger chunks, and these into even larger ones. For example, finishing times for individual racers can be chunked together into heats within a track meet, so that, now, 4 or 5 finishing times (more than 12 digits) become one chunk. With strategies like this and with a lot of practice, this man has increased his apparent memory capacity from the "normal" 7 digits to 79 digits!

Let's be clear, though, that what has changed through practice is merely the man's chunking strategy, not the holding capacity of working memory itself. This is evident in the fact that, when tested with sequences of letters rather than numbers—so he can't use his chunking strategy—his memory capacity drops to a perfectly normal six consonants. Thus, the seven-chunk limit is still in place for this fellow, even though (with numbers) he's able to make extraordinary use of these seven slots.

Establishing Long-Term Memories

So far, we've argued for a separation between working memory and long-term memory, and we're starting to see indications of each memory's attributes. Working memory has a small capacity—although it's flexible in what it can hold, thanks to the process of chunking. Long-term memory, in contrast, is vast. After all, the average college student remembers the meanings of 80,000 words, thousands of autobiographical episodes, millions of facts, hundreds of skills, the taste of vanilla and the smell of lemon. All these things and more are stored in long-term memory.

Working memory and long-term memory also differ in how they're "loaded" and "unloaded." To get information into working memory, all you need to do is pay attention to the material; that's built into the definition of working memory. Getting information into long-term storage, in contrast, seems to take some time and effort; that was essential for our discussion of the primacy effect.

We need to fill in some of the details, though, about how this "loading" of long-term memory works. With that, we'll get a clearer picture of why working memory is defined the way it is—as an active process rather than as a mere storage box.

THE IMPORTANCE OF ACTIVE ENGAGEMENT

In explaining primacy, we made a key assumption—namely, that *paying attention* to words on a list helps you establish those words in long-term memory. Presumably the same would be true for other contents, so that, no matter what you're memorizing, attention plays a key role in establishing memories. But is this assumption correct?

Consider people's memory for ordinary coins. Adults in the United States have probably seen pennies, for example, tens of thousands of times; adults in other countries have seen their own coins just as often. But, of course, most people have little reason to pay attention to the penny. Pennies are a different color and size from the other coins, so we can identify them at a fast glance and with no need for further

8.5 An ordinary penny Despite having seen the U.S. penny thousands and thousands of times, people seem to have little recollection of its layout. Test yourself. Which of these drawings is most accurate?

scrutiny. And, if attention is what matters for memory—or, more broadly, if we remember what we pay attention to and think about—then memory for the coin should be quite poor.

In one study, participants were asked whether Lincoln's profile, shown on the heads side of the penny, is facing to the right or the left. Only half of the participants got this question right—exactly what we'd expect if they were just guessing. Other participants were shown drawings of the penny, and had to choose the "right one" (Figure 8.5). Their performance was quite poor. These results—participants' remarkably poor memory for this coin despite countless opportunities to view it, provides striking confirmation that memory does require attention—it requires mental engagement with a target, not mere exposure (Nickerson & Adams, 1979; Rinck, 1999; for some complications, see Martin & Jones, 2006; in Figure 8.5, the top left drawing shows the correct layout).

But we need to be more precise about what *paying attention* means, and what it accomplishes. To make the issue clear, imagine you want to order a pizza. You look up the pizza restaurant's phone number on the Web or in a phone book, and then you walk across the room to pick up your phone and make the call. In this setting, you need to retain the number long enough to complete the dialing—and so, presumably, you're paying attention to the number for that span of time. But you have no need to memorize the number for later use, and so you're likely to think about the number in a limited way. Specifically, you're likely to employ what's called **maintenance rehearsal**—a mechanical process of repeating the memory items over and over, giving little thought to what the items are or whether they form any pattern.

This maintenance is easy and effective: It keeps the digits in your thoughts, and so you remember them long enough to place your call. But what happens if the line is busy when you call, and so you need to try again a moment later? In this setting, it's quite likely that you'll have forgotten the number and will need to look it up again! Apparently, maintenance rehearsal kept the number in working memory long enough for you to dial it the first time but utterly failed to establish it in long-term memory. As a result, you forget the number after just a few seconds.

THE LINK BETWEEN LONG-TERM MEMORY AND UNDERSTANDING

Apparently, establishing information in long-term storage is not an automatic process that is triggered merely by having the stimulus in front of your eyes or ears, or by having an idea mechanically maintained in working memory for a few seconds. Instead,

maintenance rehearsal Mechanical repetition of material without thinking about its meaning or patterns.

some sort of work is involved so that, to put the matter simply, whether you'll remember something or not depends on how—and how fully—you thought about that information when you first met it.

As we've seen, we can confirm these claims by documenting how poor memory is for material that you've encountered but not paid much attention to. Further confirmation comes from studies that examine people's brain activity during learning. In brief, these studies show that during the learning process, some sort of effort is crucial for establishing long-term memories. Specifically, the studies show that greater levels of activity during the initial memory acquisition are reliably associated with greater probabilities of recall later on. This is especially true for brain activity in the hippocampus and regions of the prefrontal cortex (Brewer, Zhao, Desmond, Glover, & Gabrieli, 1998; A. Wagner, Koutstaal, & Schacter, 1999; A. Wagner et al., 1998), but it may also include brain activity in the parietal cortex (A. Wagner, Shannon, Kahn, & Buckner, 2005).

But what exactly is this brain activity accomplishing? Crucial information comes from studies that compare the memory effects of different types of engagement at the time of learning. In one study, participants were shown 48 words. As each word was presented, the participants were asked a question about it. For some words, they were asked about the word's physical appearance ("Is it printed in capital letters?"); this kind of question should produce **shallow processing**—an approach emphasizing the superficial characteristics of the stimulus. For other words, the participants were asked about the word's sound ("Does it rhyme with *train*?"); this should encourage an intermediate level of processing. For the remainder, they were asked about the word's meaning ("Would it fit into the sentence: The girl placed the _____ on the table?"); this presumably would lead to **deep processing**—an approach to the material that emphasizes what the stimulus means.

After the participants had gone through the entire list of words, they were given an unexpected task: They were asked to write down as many of the words as they could remember. The results were clear-cut: Participants recalled very few of the words that called for shallow processing (capitalization). Words that required an intermediary level (sound) were recalled a bit better; and words that demanded the deepest level (meaning), were recalled best of all (Craik & Tulving, 1975).

Attention to a word's sound, therefore, is better for establishing memories than thoughtless and mechanical rehearsal; but attention to a word's *meaning* is better still and, across many studies, attention to meaning is reliably associated with high levels of subsequent recall. And it's not just the *search* for meaning that helps long-term memory. Instead, memory is promoted by *finding* the meaning—that is, by gaining an understanding of the to-be-remembered materials. In some studies, for example, experimenters have given participants material to read that was difficult to understand; then, immediately afterward, they probed the participants to see whether (or how well) they understood the material. Some time later, the experimenters tested the participants' memory for this material. The result was straightforward: the better the understanding at the time the material was presented, the better the memory later on (e.g., Bransford, 1979).

Other studies have manipulated the to-be-remembered material itself. For example, in one experiment, investigators presented this (tape-recorded) passage:

> The procedure is actually quite simple. First you arrange things into different groups depending on their makeup. Of course, one pile may be sufficient depending on how much there is to do. If you have to go somewhere else due to lack of facilities that is the next step; otherwise you are pretty well set. It is important not to overdo any particular endeavor. That is, it is better to do too few things at once than too many. In the

shallow processing An approach to memorization that involves focusing on the superficial characteristics of the stimulus, such as the sound of a word or the typeface in which it's printed.

deep processing An approach to memorization that involves focusing on the meaning of the stimulus.

short run this may not seem important, but complications from doing too many can easily arise. A mistake can be expensive as well. The manipulation of the appropriate mechanisms should be self-explanatory, and we need not dwell on it here. At first, the whole procedure will seem complicated. Soon, however, it will become just another facet of life. It is difficult to foresee any end to the necessity for this task in the immediate future, but then one never can tell. (Bransford & Johnson, 1972, p. 722)

Half of the people heard this passage without any further information as to what it was about, and, when tested later, their memory for the passage was poor. The other participants, though, were given a clue that helped them to understand the passage—they were told, "The paragraph you will hear will be about washing clothes." This clue allowed that group to make sense of the material and dramatically improved their later recall (Bransford & Johnson, 1972; for a related example with a nonverbal stimulus, see Figure 8.6).

There's a powerful message here for anyone hoping to remember some body of material—for example, a student trying to learn material for the next quiz. Study techniques that emphasize efforts toward *understanding* the material are likely to pay off with good memory later on. Memory strategies that don't emphasize meaning will provide much more limited effects. Mechanical memory strategies—such as repeating the items over and over without much thought—may produce no benefits at all!

THE KEY ROLE FOR MEMORY CONNECTIONS

Attention to meaning is an effective way to establish long-term memories. Still, it's not the only way to establish memories, and we'll need to accommodate this point in our theorizing. What other memory acquisition procedures are effective? We can draw our answer from the study of **mnemonics**—deliberate techniques that people use to help them memorize new materials. Mnemonics come in many varieties, but all build on the same base: To remember well, it pays to establish memory connections. In some cases, the connections link the new material to ideas already in memory. In other cases, the connections link the various elements of the new material *to each other,* so that the mnemonic helps organize complex information into a small number of memory chunks.

The role of connections is clear, for example, in the various mnemonics that rely on *verse* in which a fixed rhythm or rhyme scheme links each element being memorized to the other elements within the poem. Thus, young children find it easier to memorize the calendar's layout if they cast the target information as a rhyme: "Thirty days hath September, April, June, and November," and high-school students have an easier time memorizing the fates of Henry VIII's wives by summarizing the history in a little verse: "divorced, beheaded, died; divorced, beheaded, survived."

Connections are also the key in other mnemonics, including ones that organize material by linking the first letters of the words in the sequence that's being memorized. Thus, students rely on ROY G. BIV to memorize the sequence of colors in the rainbow (*red, orange, yellow . . .*), and learn the lines in music's treble clef via "Every Good Boy Deserves Fudge" (the lines indicate the musical notes *E, G, B, D,* and *F*). Various first-letter mnemonics are also available for memorizing the taxonomic categories ("King Philip Crossed the Ocean to Find Gold and Silver," to memorize *kingdom,*

mnemonics Deliberate techniques people use to memorize new materials.

8.6 Nonverbal stimulus In general, we easily remember things that are meaningful but don't remember things that seem to have no meaning. This picture can be used to demonstrate this point with a nonverbal stimulus. At first the picture looks like a collection of meaningless blotches, and it's very hard to remember. But if viewers discover the pattern, the picture becomes meaningful and is then effortlessly remembered.

phylum, class, order, family, genus, and *species*). And so on for other memory tasks (Figure 8.7).

Still other mnemonics involve the use of mental imagery. One such technique, developed by the ancient Greeks, is the *method of loci,* which requires the learner to visualize each of the items she wants to remember in a different spatial location ("locus"). In recall, the learner mentally inspects each location and retrieves the item that she placed there in imagination. Does this work? In one study, college students had to learn lists of 40 unrelated nouns. Each list was presented once for about 10 minutes, during which the students tried to visualize each of the 40 objects in a specific location on their college campus. When tested immediately afterward, the students recalled an average of 38 of the 40 items; when tested one day later, they still managed to recall 34 (Bower, 1970; also see Bower, 1972; Higbee, 1977; Roediger, 1980; J. Ross & Lawrence, 1968). In other studies, participants using the method of loci were able to retain seven times more than their counterparts who learned by rote.

It's also worth mentioning that visualization is, on its own, an effective memorization tool. If you're trying to remember a list of words, for example, it's helpful to form a mental picture of each item on the list (a mental picture of a hammer, for example, and then a mental picture of a puppy, and so on.) Visualization is far more effective, though, if it serves to link the to-be-remembered words to each other—and so here, once again, we see the importance of memory connections. To make this idea concrete, consider a student trying to memorize a list of word pairs. He might decide just to visualize the items side by side—and so (for example), after hearing the pair *eagle-train,* he might visualize an eagle and then, separately, he might visualize a train. Alternatively, he might try to form mental pictures that bring the items into some kind of relationship—so he might, for example, imagine the eagle winging to its nest with a locomotive in its beak. Evidence indicates that images of the second (interacting) sort produce much better recall than nonunifying images do (Wollen, Weber, & Lowry, 1972; also Figure 8.8).

Whether mnemonics are based on imagery or some other system, though, there's no question that they are enormously useful in memorizing, say, a list of foreign vocabulary words or the names of various parts of the brain. But before we move on, we should note that there's also a downside to using mnemonics: During learning, someone trying to memorize via a mnemonic is likely to focus all their attention on just a narrow set of connections—the fact that the locomotive is in the eagle's beak, or that *September*

You simply associate each number with a word, such as "table" and 3,476,029.

8.7 Memory school Some mnemonics are more successful than others.

(A) Interactive depiction

(B) Noninteractive depiction

8.8 Interacting and noninteracting depictions Research participants shown related elements, such as a doll sitting on a chair and holding a flag (A), are more likely to recall the trio of words *doll, flag,* and *chair* than are participants shown the three objects next to each other but not interacting (B).

rhymes with *November*. This strategy guarantees that these connections will be well established; and that's great if, later on, those connections are just the ones you need. But at the same time, if you focus on just these few connections, you're putting little effort into developing other possible connections—so you're not doing much to promote your *understanding* of the material you're memorizing. On this basis, mnemonics—as effective as they are for memorization—are an unwise strategy if understanding is your goal.

STORAGE

We've been focusing on the first step involved in memory—namely memory acquisition. Once a memory is acquired, though, it must be held in storage—i.e., held in long-term memory until it's needed. The mental representation of this new information is referred to as the **memory trace**—and, surprisingly, we know relatively little about exactly how traces are lodged in the brain. At a microscopic level, it seems certain that traces are created through the three forms of neural plasticity described in Chapter 7: Presynaptic neurons can become more effective in sending signals; postsynaptic neurons can become more sensitive to the signals they receive; and new synapses can be created.

On a larger scale, evidence suggests that the trace for a particular past experience is not recorded in a single location within the brain. Instead, different aspects of an event are likely to be stored in distinct brain regions—one region containing the visual elements of the episode, another containing a record of our emotional reaction, a third area containing a record of our conceptual understanding of the event, and so on (e.g., A. Damasio & H. Damasio, 1994). But, within these broad outlines, we know very little about how the information content of a memory is translated into a pattern of neural connections. Thus, to be blunt, we are many decades away from the science-fiction notion of being able to inspect the wiring of someone's brain in order to discover what he remembers, or being able to "inject" a memory into someone by a suitable rearrangement of her neurons. (For a recent hint about exactly how a specific memory might be encoded in the neurons, see Han et al., 2009.)

One fact about memory storage, however, is well established: Memory traces aren't created instantly. Instead, a period of time is needed, after each new experience, for the record of that experience to become established in memory. During that time, **memory consolidation** is taking place; this is a process, spread over several hours, in which memories are transformed from a transient and fragile status to a more permanent and robust state (Hasselmo, 1999; McGaugh, 2000, 2003; Meeter & Murre, 2004; Wixted, 2004).

What exactly does consolidation accomplish? Evidence suggests that this time period allows adjustments in neural connections, so that a new pattern of communication among neurons can be created to represent the newly acquired memory. This process seems to require the creation of new proteins, so it is disrupted by chemical manipulations that block protein synthesis (H. Davis & Squire, 1984; Santini, Ge, Ren, deOrtiz, & Quirk, 2004; Schafe, Nader, Blair, & LeDoux, 2001).

The importance of consolidation is evident in the memory loss sometimes produced by head injuries. Specifically, people who have experienced blows to the head can develop **retrograde amnesia** (*retrograde* means "in a backward direction"), in which they suffer a loss of memory for events that occurred before the brain injury (Figure 8.9). This form of amnesia can also be caused by brain tumors, diseases, or

memory trace The physical record in the nervous system that preserves a memory.

memory consolidation The biological process through which memories are transformed from a transient and fragile status to a more permanent and robust state; according to most researchers, consolidation occurs over the course of several hours.

retrograde amnesia A memory deficit, often suffered after a head injury, in which the patient loses memory for events that occurred *before* the injury.

strokes (Cipolotti, 2001; M. Conway & Fthenaki, 1999; Kapur, 1999; Mayes, 1988; Nadel & Moscovitch, 2001).

Retrograde amnesia usually involves *recent* memories. In fact, the older the memory, the less likely it is to be affected by the amnesia—a pattern referred to as Ribot's law, in honor of the 19th-century scholar who first discussed it (Ribot, 1882). What produces this pattern? Older memories have presumably had enough time to consolidate, so they are less vulnerable to disruption. Newer memories are not yet consolidated, so they're more liable to disruption (A. Brown, 2002; Weingartner & Parker, 1984).

There is, however, a complication here: Retrograde amnesia sometimes disrupts a person's memory for events that took place months or even years before the brain injury. In these cases, interrupted consolidation couldn't explain the deficit unless one assumes—as some authors do—that consolidation is an exceedingly long, drawn-out process. (For discussion of when consolidation takes place, and how long it takes, see Hupbach et al., 2008; McGaugh, 2000.) However, this issue remains a point of debate, making it clear that we haven't heard the last word on how consolidation proceeds.

8.9 Retrograde and anterograde amnesia Retrograde amnesia disrupts memory for experiences *before* the injury, accident, or disease that triggered the amnesia. Anterograde amnesia disrupts memory for experiences *after* the injury or disease.

RETRIEVAL

When we learn, we transfer new information into our long-term store of knowledge, and then we consolidate this newly acquired information. But we still need one more step in this sequence, because memories provide no benefit for us if we can't retrieve them when we need them. Hence **retrieval**—the step of locating and activating information in memory—is crucial. Moreover, the success of retrieval is far from guaranteed, and many cases of apparent "forgetting" can be understood as *retrieval failures*—cases in which the information is in your memory, but you fail to locate it.

retrieval The process of searching for a memory and finding it.

tip-of-the-tongue (TOT) effect The condition in which one remains on the verge of retrieving a word or name but continues to be unsuccessful.

Partial Retrieval

Retrieval failure can be documented in many ways—including the fact that sometimes we remember *part* of the information we're seeking, but we can't recall the rest. This pattern can arise in many circumstances, but it's most clearly evident in the phenomenon psychologists call the **tip-of-the-tongue (TOT) effect.**

Try to think of the word that means "to formally renounce the throne." Try to think of the name of the Russian sled drawn by three horses. Try to think of the word that describes someone who, in general, does not like other people. Chances are that, in at least one of these cases, you found yourself in a frustrated state: certain you know the word but unable to come up with it. The word was, as people say, right on the "tip of your tongue."

People who are in the so-called TOT state can often remember roughly what the word sounds like—and so, when they're struggling to recall *abdicate*, they might remember *abrogate* or *annotate* instead. Likewise, they can often recall what letter the word begins with, and how many syllables it has, even though they can't recall the word itself (A. Brown, 1991; R. Brown & McNeill, 1966; Harley & Bown, 1998; L. James & Burke, 2000; B. Schwartz, 1999).

Similar results have been obtained when people try to recall specific names—for example, what is the capital of Nicaragua? Who was the main character in the movie *The*

Matrix? In response to these questions, people can often recall the number of syllables in the target name and the name's initial letter, but not the name itself (Brennen, Baguley, Bright, & Bruce, 1990; Yarmey, 1973). They also can often recall related material, even if they can't remember the target information. (Thus, they might remember Morpheus, but not the main character, from *The Matrix;* the main character, of course, was *Neo.* And the Russian sled is a *troika;* it's a *misanthrope* who doesn't like other people; Nicaragua's capital is *Managua.*)

People in the TOT state cannot recall the target word, but the word is certainly in their memory. If it weren't, they wouldn't be able to remember the word's sound, or its starting letter and syllable count. What's more, people often *recognize* the word when it's offered to them ("Yes! That's it!"). This is, therefore, unmistakably a case of retrieval failure—the information is preserved in storage, but for various reasons it is inaccessible.

Effective Retrieval Cues

Retrieval failure is also clearly the problem whenever you seem to have forgotten something, but then recall it once you're given an adequate **retrieval cue.** A clear illustration of this pattern often arises when someone returns to his hometown after a long absence. This return can unleash a flood of recollection, including the recall of many details the person thought he'd forgotten long ago. Since these memories do surface, triggered by the sights and sounds of the hometown, there's no doubt about whether the memories were established in the first place (obviously, they were) or lost from storage (obviously, they weren't). Only one explanation is possible, therefore, for why the memories had been unavailable for so many years prior to the person's return to his hometown. They were in memory, but not findable—exactly the pattern we call retrieval failure.

Why do some retrieval cues (but not others) allow us to locate seemingly long-lost memories? One important factor is whether the cue re-creates the context in which the original learning occurred. This is obviously the case in returning to your hometown— you're back in the context in which you had the experiences you're now remembering. But the same broad point can be documented in the lab; and so, for example, if an individual focused on the sounds of words while learning them, then she would be well served by reminders that focus on sound ("Was there a word on the list that rhymes with *log?*"); if she focused on meaning while learning, then the best reminder would be one that again draws her attention toward meaning ("Was one of the words a type of fruit?"; R. Fisher & Craik, 1977).

The explanation for this pattern lies in our earlier discussion of memory connections. Learning, we suggested, is essentially a process of creating (or strengthening) connections that link the to-be-remembered material to other things you already know. But what function do these connections serve? When the time comes to recall something, the connections serve as **retrieval paths**—routes that lead you back to the desired information. Thus, if you noticed in a movie that Jane's smile caused Tarzan to howl, this will create a link between your memory of the smile and your memory of the howl. Later on, thinking about the smile will bring Tarzan's howl into your thoughts—and so your retrieval is being guided by the connection you established earlier.

On this basis, let's think through what would happen if a person studied a list of words and focused, say, on the sound of the words. This focus would establish certain connections—perhaps one between *dog* and *log,* and one between *paper* and *caper.* These connections will be useful if, later, this person is asked questions about rhymes.

retrieval cue A hint or signal that helps one to recall a memory.

retrieval paths The mental connections linking one idea to the next that people use to locate a bit of information in memory.

If she's asked, "Was there a word on the list that rhymes with *log?*" the connection now in place will guide her thoughts to the target word *dog.* But the same connection will play little role in other situations. If she's asked, "Did any of the words on the list name animals with sharp teeth?" the path that was established during learning—from *log* to *dog*—is much less helpful; what she needs with this cue is a retrieval path leading from *sharp teeth* to the target.

The impact of these same retrieval cues would be different, though, if the person had thought about meaning during learning. This focus would have created a different set of connections—perhaps one between *dog* and *wolf.* In this case, the "rhymes with *log?*" cue would likely be ineffective, because the person has established no connection with *log.* A cue that focused on meaning, however, might trigger the target word.

Overall, then, an effective retrieval cue is generally one that takes advantage of an already established connection in memory. We've worked through this issue by pointing to the difference between meaning-based connections and sound-based connections, but the same point can be made in other ways. In one experiment, the researchers asked deep-sea divers to learn various materials. Some of the divers learned the material while sitting on land by the edge of the water. Others learned the material while 20 feet underwater, hearing the material via a special communication set. Within each of these two groups, half of the divers were then tested while above water, and half were tested below (Godden & Baddeley, 1975).

Imagine that you're a diver in the group that learned while underwater. In this setting, the world has a different look and feel than it does above water: The sound of your breathing is quite prominent; so is the temperature. As a result, you might end up thinking about your breathing (say) during learning, and this will likely create memory connections between these breathing thoughts and the materials you're learning. If you are then back underwater at the time of the memory test, the sound of your breathing will again be prominent, and this may lead you back into the same thoughts. Once thinking these thoughts, you will benefit from the memory connection linking the thoughts to the target materials—and so you'll remember the materials. In contrast, if you're on land during the memory test, then the sound of breathing is absent, and so these thoughts won't be triggered and the connections you established earlier will have no influence.

We might therefore expect the divers who learned underwater to remember best if tested underwater; this setting increases their chances of benefiting from the memory connections they established during learning. Likewise, the divers who learned on land should do best if tested on land. And that's exactly what the data show (Figure 8.10).

Related examples are easy to find. Participants in one study were asked to read an article similar to those they routinely read in their college classes; half read the article in a quiet setting, and half read it in a noisy environment. When tested later, those who read the article in quiet did best if they were tested in quiet; those who read it in a noisy environment did best if tested in a noisy setting (Grant et al., 1998). In both cases, participants showed the benefit of being able to use, at time of retrieval, the specific connections established during learning.

In case after case, then, it's helpful, at the time of memory retrieval, to return to the context of learning. Doing this will encourage some of the same thoughts that were in place during learning, and so will allow you to take advantage of the connections linking those thoughts to the target material. This broad pattern is referred to as a benefit of **context reinstatement**—a benefit of re-creating the state of mind you were in during learning.

Let's also note that, in these experiments, the physical setting (noisy or not; underwater or above) seems to have a powerful influence on memory. However,

context reinstatement A way of improving retrieval by re-creating the state of mind that accompanied the initial learning.

Method

1. One group of divers learned a word list on land. Another group of divers learned a word list underwater.

2. Each group was tested in both environments for recall of the list items.

Results

Divers who learned underwater recalled more words underwater, and those who studied on land tested better on land.

CONCLUSION: Information is best recalled in the environment where it is learned.

SOURCE STUDY: Godden & Baddeley, 1975

8.11 Context reinstatement for students These students are probably forming connections between the material they're learning and library-related cues. To help themselves recall this material later on, they'll want to think about what the library looked like and how they felt in that environment.

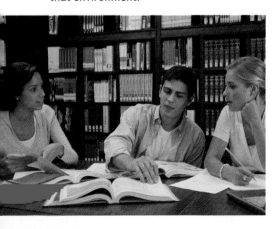

evidence suggests that the physical setting matters only indirectly: A return to the physical circumstances of learning does improve recollection, but only because this return helps re-create the mental context of learning—and it's the mental context that matters. This was evident, for example, in a study in which participants were presented with a long list of words. One day later, the experimenter brought the participants back for an unexpected recall test that took place in either the same room or a different one (one that differed in size, furnishings, and so on, from the context of learning). Not surprisingly, recall was better for those who were tested in the same physical environment—documenting, once again, the benefit of context reinstatement. Crucially, though, the investigator found a straightforward way of eliminating the difficulty caused by an environmental change: A different group of participants were brought to the new room; but just before the test, they were asked to think about the room in which they had learned the lists—what it looked like, how it made them feel. By doing so, they mentally re-created the old environment for themselves; on the subsequent recall test, these participants performed just as well as those who were tested in their original room (S. Smith, 1979; S. Smith & Vela, 2001; Figure 8.11). Apparently, then, what matters for retrieval is your mental perspective, not the room you're sitting in. If you change the physical context without changing your mental perspective, the physical relocation has no effect.

Encoding Specificity

The effectiveness of context reinstatement also tells us something important about how materials are recorded in memory in the first place. When people encounter some stimulus or event, they *think about* this experience in one way or another; and as we've described, this intellectual engagement serves to connect the new experience to other thoughts and knowledge. We've been discussing how these connections serve as retrieval paths, helping people to recall the target information, but let's now add that this is possible only because those connections are themselves part of the memory record. Thus, continuing an earlier example, if people see the word *dog* and think about what it rhymes with, what ends up being stored in memory is not just the word. What's stored must be the word plus some record of the connections made to rhyming words—otherwise, how could these connections influence retrieval? Likewise, if people see a picture and think about what it means, what's stored in memory is not just the picture, but a memory of the picture together with some record of the connections to other, related ideas.

In short, what's placed in memory is not some neutral transcription of an event. Instead, what's in memory is a record of the event *as understood from a particular perspective* or perceived within a particular context. Psychologists refer to this broad pattern as **encoding specificity**—based on the idea that what's recorded in memory is not just a "copy" of the original, but is instead *encoded from* the original (in other words, it's translated into some other form) and is also quite *specific* (and so represents the material *plus* your thoughts and understanding of the material; Tulving & Osler, 1968; Tulving & Thomson, 1973; also Hintzman, 1990).

This specificity, in turn, has powerful effects on retrieval—that is, on how (or whether) the past is remembered. For example, participants in one study read target words (e.g., *piano*) in either of two contexts: "The man lifted the piano" or "The man tuned the piano." These sentences led the participants to think about the target word in a particular way, and it was then this line of thinking that was encoded into each person's memory. Thus, continuing the example, what was recorded in memory was the idea of "piano as something heavy" or "piano as a musical instrument." This difference in memory content became clear when participants were later asked to recall the target words. If they had earlier seen the "lifted" sentence, then they were quite likely to recall the target word if given the hint "something heavy." The hint "something with a nice sound" was much less effective. But if participants had seen the "tuned" sentence, the result reversed: Now the "nice sound" hint was effective, but the "heavy" hint was not (Barcklay, Bransford, Franks, McCarrell, & Nitsch, 1974). In both cases, the memory hint was effective only if it was congruent with what was stored in memory—just as the encoding specificity proposal predicts.

This notion of encoding specificity is crucial in many contexts. For example, imagine two friends who have an argument. Each person is likely to interpret the argument in a way that's guided by his own position—and so he'll probably perceive his own remarks to be clear and persuasive, and his friend's comments to be muddy and evasive. Later on, how will each friend remember the event? Thanks to encoding specificity, what each person places in memory is the argument *as he understood it*. As a result, we really can't hope for a fully objective, impartial memory, one that might allow either of the friends to think back on the argument and perhaps reevaluate his position. Instead, each will, inevitably, recall the argument in a way that's heavily colored by his initial leaning.

encoding specificity The hypothesis that when information is stored in memory, it is not recorded in its original form but translated ("encoded") into a form that includes the thoughts and understanding of the learner.

MEMORY GAPS, MEMORY ERRORS

The processes we've been discussing—acquisition, storage, and retrieval—function extremely well in a huge range of circumstances. As a result, each of us can learn an enormous quantity of information, store that information for a long time, and then swiftly retrieve the information when we need it. But of course there are times when remembering is less successful. Sometimes we try to remember an episode but simply draw a blank. Sometimes we recall something, but with no conviction that we're correct: "I think it happened on Tuesday, but I'm not sure." And sometimes our memories fail us in another way: We recall a past episode, but it turns out that our memory is mistaken. Perhaps details of the event were different from the way we recall them; perhaps our memory is altogether wrong, misrepresenting large elements of the original episode. Why, and how often, do these memory failures occur?

Forgetting

There are many reasons why we sometimes cannot recall past events. In many cases, as we've noted, the problem arises because we didn't learn the relevant information in the first place! In other cases, though, we learn something—a friend's name, the lyrics to a song, the content of the Intro Bio course—and can remember the information for a while; but then, sometime later, we're unable to recall the information we once knew. What produces this pattern?

One clue comes from the fact that it's almost always easier to recall recent events (e.g., yesterday's lecture or this morning's breakfast) than it is to recall more distant events (a lecture or a breakfast 6 months ago). In technical terms, recall decreases, and forgetting increases, as the **retention interval** (the time that elapses between learning and retrieval) grows longer and longer.

This simple fact has been documented in many studies; indeed, the passage of time seems to work against our memory for things as diverse as past hospital stays, our eating or smoking habits in past years, car accidents we experienced, our consumer purchases, and so on (Jobe, Tourangeau, & Smith, 1993). The classic demonstration of this pattern, though, was offered more than a century ago by Hermann Ebbinghaus (1850–1909). Ebbinghaus systematically studied his own memory in a series of careful experiments, examining his ability to retain lists of nonsense syllables, such as *zup* and *rif*. (Ebbinghaus relied on these odd stimuli as a way of making sure he came to the memory materials with no prior associations or links; that way, he could study how learning proceeded when there was no chance of influence from prior knowledge.) Ebbinghaus plotted a **forgetting curve** by testing himself at various intervals after learning (using different lists for each interval). As expected, he found that memory did decline with the passage of time. However, the decline was uneven; it was sharpest soon after the learning and then became more gradual (Ebbinghaus, 1885; Figure 8.12).

There are two broad ways to think about the effect of retention interval. One perspective emphasizes the passage of time itself—based on the idea that memories *decay* as time passes, perhaps because normal metabolic processes wear down the memory traces until they fade and finally disintegrate. A different perspective suggests that time itself isn't the culprit. What matters instead is *new learning*—based on the idea that new information getting added to long-term memory somehow disrupts the old information that was already in storage. We'll need to sort through why this disruption might happen; but notice that this perspective, too, predicts that longer retention intervals will lead to more forgetting—because longer intervals provide more opportunity for new learning and thus more disruption from the new learning.

Which perspective is correct? Is forgetting ultimately a product of the passage of time, or a product of new learning? The answer is *both*. The passage of time, by itself, does seem to erode memories (e.g., E. Altmann & Gray, 2002; C. Bailey & Chen, 1989; Wixted, 2004); but the effect of new learning seems larger. For example, Baddeley and Hitch (1977) asked

retention interval The time that elapses between learning and retrieval.

forgetting curve The graphic pattern representing the relationship between measures of learning and the length of the retention interval: As the retention interval gets longer, memory decreases.

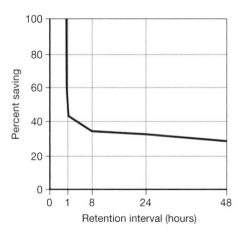

8.12 Forgetting curve The figure shows retention after various intervals since learning. Retention is here measured in percent saving—that is, the percentage decrease in the number of trials required to relearn the list after an interval of no practice. If the saving is 100%, then retention is perfect; no trials to relearn are necessary. If the saving is 0%, there's no retention at all; it takes just as many trials to relearn the list as it took to learn it initially.

rugby players to recall the names of the other teams they had played against over the course of a season; the researchers then systematically compared the effect of *time* with the effects of *new learning*. To examine the effects of time, Baddeley and Hitch capitalized on the fact that not all players made it to all games (because of illness, injuries, or schedule conflicts). These differences allowed them to compare players for whom "two games back" means 2 weeks ago, to players for whom "two games back" means 4 weeks ago. Thus, they were able to look at the effects of time (2 weeks vs. 4) with the number of more recent games held constant. Likewise, to examine the effects of new learning, these researchers compared (say) players for whom the game a month ago was "three games back" to players for whom a month ago means "one game back." Now we have the retention interval held constant, and we can look at the effects of intervening events. In this setting, Baddeley and Hitch report that the mere passage of time accounts for very little; what really matters is the number of intervening events—just as we'd expect if intervening learning, and not decay, is the major contributor to forgetting (Figure 8.13). (For other—classic—data on this issue, see Jenkins & Dallenbach, 1924; for a more recent review, see Wixted, 2004.)

An effect of new learning undoing old learning can also be demonstrated in the laboratory. In a typical study, a control group learns the items on a list (A) and then is tested after a specified interval. The experimental group learns the same list (A), but they must also learn the items on a second list (B) during the same retention interval. The result is a marked inferiority in the performance of the experimental group. List B seems to interfere with the recall of list A (Crowder, 1976; McGeoch & Irion, 1952).

Of course, not all new learning produces this disruption. No interference is observed, for example, between dissimilar sorts of material—and so learning to skate doesn't undo your memory for irregular French verbs. In addition, if the new learning is *consistent* with the old, then it certainly doesn't cause disruption; instead, the new learning actually *helps* memory. Thus, learning more algebra helps you remember the algebra you mastered last year; learning more psychology helps you remember the psychology you've already covered.

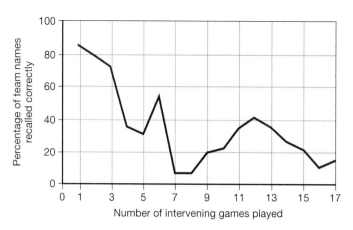

8.13 Forgetting from interfering events Members of a rugby team were asked to recall the names of teams they had played against. Their performance was heavily influenced by the number of games that intervened between the game to be recalled and the attempt to remember.

Memory Intrusions

We still need to ask *why* new learning seems sometimes to disrupt old. Why can't the newly acquired information peacefully coexist with older memories? In fact, there are several reasons. In some cases, the new information simply sits side by side with old memories, creating a danger that you'll get mixed up about which is which—recalling the newer information when you're trying to come up with the older. In other cases, the new information may literally *replace* the old memory, much as you delete an old version of a paper from your computer's hard drive once you've created a newer, updated version.

In most experiments, it's difficult to distinguish these two possibilities—that is, to tell whether the new information is merely competing with the old information, or whether it has literally replaced the old information. In either case, though, the new material will lead to **intrusion errors**—mistakes about the past in which other information is mixed into (*intrudes into*) your recall. These intrusions are often small (so that you recall having a cheese sandwich when you really had a salad) but can sometimes be quite large: People may confidently, vividly recall a past event that never took place at all.

intrusion errors Memory mistakes in which elements that were not part of the original information get mixed into ("intrude" into) someone's recall.

8.14 Eyewitness memory Considerable research has been done on the question of how accurately and how completely witnesses (or victims) to crimes will remember what they've experienced.

misinformation effect The result of a procedure in which, after an experience, people are exposed to questions or suggestions that misrepresent what happened. The term refers to people's tendency to include the misinformation as part of their recall of the original experience.

THE MISINFORMATION EFFECT

Intrusion errors can arise in many ways. Often, though, the intrusion involves information about an event that you learned *only after the event was over.* For example, imagine that you witness a crime and see the thief flee in a blue car. The next day, you read a newspaper account of the same crime and learn that another witness has reported that the thief fled in a *green* car (Figure 8.14). How will this experience influence your memory? A number of experiments have examined this issue by exposing participants to an event and then giving them some misinformation about the event. In some studies, the misinformation comes from another person's report ("Here's the way another witness described the event . . ."). In other studies, the misinformation is contained within a leading question: Participants might be asked, for example, "Did you see the children getting on the school bus?" after seeing a video that showed no bus. In all cases, though, the effect is the same: This misinformation is often incorporated into the participants' memory, so that they end up misremembering the original event, mistakenly including the bits suggested after the fact by the experimenter.

The errors produced by the **misinformation effect** can actually be quite large. Participants have in fact been led to remember buses that weren't actually present in an event as well as whole buildings that didn't exist (Loftus, 2003). Indeed, with slight variations of this technique, participants have been led to recall entire events that never occurred. In one study, participants were asked to recall a time they had been at an outdoor wedding and had accidentally knocked over the punchbowl, spilling it onto the bride's parents. With suggestive questioning, the researcher led 25% of the participants to "remember" this nonexistent episode (I. Hyman, Husband, & Billings, 1995). In similar experiments, participants have been led to recall a nonexistent episode in which they were hospitalized, or a hot-air balloon ride that really never happened (Figure 8.15), or a (fictitious) event in which they were the victim of a vicious animal attack (Loftus, 2003, 2004; also Chrobak & Zaragoza, 2008; Geraerts et al., 2006; Geraerts et al., 2009; Geraerts et al., 2007; Laney et al., 2008; and many more).

Errors like these are easily documented in the laboratory, but can also be observed in real-life settings. We are, after all, often exposed to alternate versions of events we've experienced—for example, whenever we discuss a shared experience with a friend, and the friend recalls things differently from the way we do. Moreover, the leading questions examined in much of this research are modeled directly on the questions sometimes asked in law enforcement investigations involving adults ("Did you see the gun?") as well as children ("When did Uncle Seth touch you?"; cf. Bruck & Ceci, 1999; Ceci &

8.15 The balloon ride that never was In this study, participants were shown a faked photo (as in B) created from a real childhood snapshot (as in A). With this prompt, many participants were led to a vivid, detailed recollection of the balloon ride—even though it never occurred!

(A)

(B)

Bruck, 1995; Melnyk, Crossman, & Scullin, 2007; Westcott, Davies, & Bull, 2002). As a consequence, we can readily find examples in which the memory errors made in the laboratory are mirrored by errors outside of the lab—including settings (like law enforcement) in which the memory mistakes are deeply troubling and potentially very costly.

INTRUSIONS FROM SCHEMATIC KNOWLEDGE

Intrusion errors, interfering with our memory of the past, can also come from another source—because sometimes we blur together our recollection of an episode with our broader knowledge about the world. Classic data on this topic come from studies performed by the British psychologist Frederic Bartlett more than 75 years ago. Bartlett presented British research participants with stories drawn from Native American folklore; and for these participants, many elements of these stories seemed strange. In the participants' recollection of these stories, though, the tales became less strange. Parts of the tales that had made no sense to them (such as the supernatural elements) either were left out of their recall or were reinterpreted along more familiar lines. Similarly, participants often added elements so that plot events that had initially seemed inexplicable now made sense to them (Bartlett, 1932).

What happened here? Bartlett's participants quite naturally tried to understand these stories by relating them to other things they knew and understood. In the process, they ended up creating connections in their memories, weaving together the story elements with various aspects of their own knowledge about the world. This weaving together helped the participants comprehend the materials they were hearing by linking the unfamiliar materials to a more familiar framework. But, at the same time, this weaving caused problems later on, because it made it difficult for participants to keep track of which elements were actually in the stories and which were merely associated with the story via their understanding of it. This is what produced the memory errors.

Other studies have replicated Bartlett's findings, showing in many contexts that memory is strongly affected by an individual's conceptual framework. For example, participants in one study were told about a person's visit to the dentist and then later asked to recall what they had heard. Many participants remembered being told about the patient checking in with the receptionist and looking at a magazine in the waiting room, even though these details were not mentioned in the original account (G. Bower, Black, & Turner, 1979). In a different experiment (which we first met in the Prologue), participants waited briefly in a professor's office and, seconds later, were asked to recall the contents of the office. One-third of the individuals "remembered" seeing books in the office, even though none were present (Brewer & Treyens, 1981). In this case the error is a substantial one (bookshelves are large; the participants were actually in the office; the recollection took place just moments after leaving the office); but, again, it is entirely in line with participants' expectations of what "should" be in a professor's office.

In all these examples, memory is strongly affected by the research participants' broad knowledge of the world and by the conceptual framework they bring to the situation. Following Bartlett, many psychologists describe these frameworks as **schemas**—mental representations that summarize what we know about a certain type of event or situation. Schemas reflect the simple fact that many aspects of our experience are redundant—professors' offices do tend to contain many books, patients visiting the dentist do generally check in with a receptionist—and schemas provide a convenient summary of this redundancy.

Let's also be clear that a reliance on schematic knowledge is generally a good thing. When we encounter an event—whether it's a trip to the dentist or a story from another culture—we seek to understand it by relating it to a schematic frame. This

schema An individual's mental representation that summarizes her knowledge about a certain type of event or situation.

helps us find meaning in our experience, and it also fills in the "gaps" that result from our failing to notice this or that detail. Then, when we try to remember the event, we rely on the same schema. And here, too, this strategy can help us by allowing us to make reasonable assumptions about what probably occurred, thus filling any gaps in what we recall. Even so, this reliance on schematic knowledge can lead to substantial memory errors. In particular, it can lead us to remember the past as being more regular and more orderly than it actually was.

INTRUSIONS FROM SEMANTIC ASSOCIATIONS

Intrusion errors can be documented in many settings, including settings that seem designed to encourage memory accuracy. For example, intrusion errors can be observed even with simple stimuli, short retention intervals, and instructions that warn participants about the kinds of memory errors they're likely to make. Even in these settings, participants make a surprising number of memory mistakes.

Evidence for these points comes from many studies that draw on the so-called **DRM paradigm**—named in honor of Deese, Roediger, and McDermott, the researchers who developed it (Deese, 1957; Roediger & McDermott, 1995, 2000; also Blair, Lenton, & Hastie, 2002; Brainerd, Yang, Reyna, Howe, & Mills, 2008; Sugrue & Hayne, 2006; etc.). In this procedure, participants hear a list of words, such as *bed, rest, awake, tired, dream, wake, snooze, blanket, doze, slumber, snore, nap, peace, yawn, drowsy*. Then, immediately after hearing the list, participants are asked to recall as many of the words as they can.

All of the words in this list are semantically associated with the word *sleep*, and the presence of this theme helps memory and makes the words on the list easy to recall. But as it turns out, *sleep*—the root of the list—isn't included in the presentation. Still, participants spontaneously make the connection between the list words and this associated word—and this almost invariably leads to a memory error. When the time comes for recall, participants are extremely likely to remember that they heard *sleep*. In fact, they're just as likely to recall this word as they are to recall the actual words on the list (Figure 8.16)!

Notice once again that participants' background knowledge both helps and hurts them. In the DRM task, the participants' knowledge helps them link together the list words according to a theme, and this strongly aids recall of the words. But the same knowledge leads to a remarkably high level of false recall—by powerfully encouraging recall for words that were never presented.

MISPLACED FAMILIARITY

One more mechanism plays a key role in producing intrusion errors in memory, and, with that, in encouraging misremembering of the past. To understand this mechanism, let's start with the fact that the memory processes that make a stimulus seem *familiar* are different from those that help us figure out *why* the stimulus feels familiar. As a result, sometimes the first process succeeds, so we correctly realize that a stimulus is familiar, but the second process fails, so we make a mistake about the source of that familiarity.

Familiarity (a general sense that a stimulus has been encountered before) and **recollection** (recall of the context in which a stimulus was encountered) can be distinguished in many ways. For a start, there's an obvious subjective difference—in other words, these two types of memory *feel* different from each other—and people can reliably tell whether they "remember" a prior event (and so have some recollection) or whether they don't remember the event, but just "know" that it happened (and so,

DRM paradigm A common procedure for studying memory, in which participants read and then immediately recall a list of related words, but the word providing the "theme" for the list is not included.

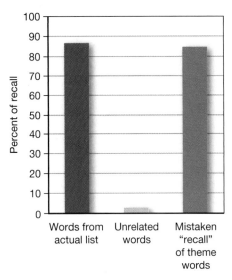

8.16 The effects of the DRM paradigm Because of the theme uniting the list, participants can remember almost 90% of the words they encountered. However, they're just as likely to "recall" the list's theme word—even though it was not presented.

familiarity A general sense that a certain stimulus has been encountered before.

recollection Recall of the context in which a certain stimulus was encountered.

apparently, are relying on familiarity—Rajaram, 1993; Tulving, 1985; also Aggleton & Brown, 2006). These two types of memory are also promoted by different types of strategies—so that some approaches to a stimulus or event are especially helpful for establishing a sense of familiarity; different strategies are needed for establishing the sort of memory that will later on lead to recollection.

Familiarity and recollection can also be distinguished biologically. During learning, activity in the rhinal cortex seems crucial for establishing a sense of familiarity; and so higher levels of activity in this brain area, during the initial encounter with a stimulus, are associated with greater likelihood of familiarity later on. In contrast, areas in and around the hippocampus seem essential for establishing a basis for recollection; higher levels of activity in these regions, during learning, are associated with greater likelihood of subsequent recollection (e.g., Davachi, Mitchell, & Wagner, 2003; Davachi & Dobbins, 2008; Ranganath et al., 2003; Figure 8.17).

Then, during retrieval, familiarity and recollection both rely on the prefrontal cortex; but they depend on clearly different areas within this cortex (e.g., Diana, Yonelinas, & Ranganath, 2007; Dobbins, Foley, Schacter, & Wagner, 2002; Kahn, Davachi, & Wagner, 2004; Rugg & Curran, 2007; A. Wagner et al., 2005). Therefore, the brain state of someone who remembers seeing a stimulus earlier is distinct from the brain state of someone who doesn't remember the earlier encounter but still feels that the stimulus is familiar.

This distinction between familiarity and recollection has many consequences, including the possibility of one process *succeeding* while the other *fails*. In fact, this pattern is easily detectable in everyday experience—when, for example, people have the frustrating experience of seeing someone, immediately knowing that the person is familiar, but not being able to figure out *why* the person is familiar. In that situation, you ask yourself: "Where do I know that guy from? Does he maybe work at the grocery store? At the shoe store? Where?" Here the familiarity process has succeeded—and so

(A) Subsequent familiarity effects

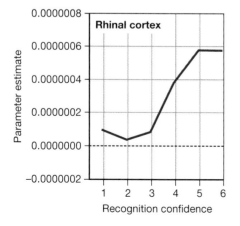

If the rhinal cortex was especially activated during encoding, then the stimulus was likely to seem familiar when viewed later on.

(B) Subsequent recollection effects

If the hippocampus was especially activated during encoding, then later on the participant was likely to recollect having seen that stimulus.

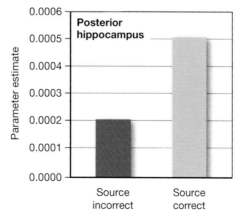

8.17 **Familiarity vs. source memory** In this study, researchers tracked participants' brain activity during encoding and then analyzed the data according to what happened later, when the time came for retrieval.

1_____ 2_____ 3_____

4_____ 5_____ 6_____

FOR OFFICIAL USE ONLY

8.18 A photo lineup On TV, crime victims view a live lineup, but it's far more common in the United States for the victim (or witness) to see a "photo lineup" like this one. The victim (or witness) is told that the perpetrator may or may not be present and is asked to pick out the perpetrator if he's there. Unfortunately, victims sometimes pick the wrong fellow, and this error is more likely if the suspect is familiar to the victim for some reason other than the crime.

you're sure the person is indeed familiar—but the recollection process, allowing you to attribute the familiarity to a specific source, has let you down.

A different problem can also arise, and brings us back to our main agenda—the ways in which new learning can intrude on (and thus disrupt) older learning. Here's the situation: You notice that a stimulus (perhaps a face, or a place) seems familiar, and you think you know why—but you're simply mistaken, and you attribute the familiarity to the wrong source. This phenomenon can arise in a variety of circumstances outside the lab, and researchers have re-created one of those circumstances in their studies: In the experimental procedure, participants witness a staged crime. Two days later, they're shown "mug shots" of individuals who supposedly had participated in the crime. But, as it turns out, the people in these photos are different from the people who were actually involved in the crime; no mug shots are shown for the truly "guilty" individuals. Finally, after a few more days, the participants are shown a lineup like the one in Figure 8.18 and asked to select from this lineup the individuals seen in step one—namely, the original staged crime.

In this procedure, participants correctly realize that one of the people in the lineup looks familiar, but they're often confused about the source of the familiarity. They falsely believe they had seen his face in the original "crime," when in truth they'd seen it only in a subsequent photograph. In fact, the likelihood of this error is quite high in some experiments, and sometimes more than a quarter of the participants (falsely) select from the lineup an individual they'd seen only in the mug shots (E. Brown, Deffenbacher, & Sturgill, 1977; also D. Davis, Loftus, Vanous, & Cucciare, 2008).

TRYING TO AVOID MEMORY ERRORS

We've now discussed many experiments in which participants made substantial memory errors. Similar errors, as we've frequently mentioned, can also be documented outside the lab—including errors in highly consequential settings. In fact, evidence suggests that eyewitness errors in the American court system may account for more false convictions than all other causes combined (Connors, Lundregan, Miller, & McEwan, 1996).

These points invite two questions: First, is there anything we can do to avoid the errors—and thus to improve memory accuracy? Second, what do these errors imply for our overall assessment of memory? Should we perhaps put less trust in our memories than we generally do? Let's tackle these questions in turn.

Some steps do seem helpful in avoiding (or at least diminishing) memory error. For example, we noted earlier in the chapter that some memory problems involve retrieval failures, and so we can improve memory by means of instructions or strategies that promote retrieval—such as trying, at the time of recall, to reinstate the psychological context of learning (for a real-world use of this procedure, see Fisher & Schreiber, 2007). Likewise, since attention to meaning seems an effective way to memorize, we can improve memory by encouraging people to think more deeply about the materials they're encountering; this will promote both understanding and memory.

People have also suggested more exotic means of improving memory—but these seem less helpful. For example, some people have proposed the use of *hypnosis* as an aid to memory, based on the idea that someone—for example, an eyewitness to a crime—

can be hypnotized, given the suggestion that she's back at a certain time and place, and asked to tell what she sees. On the surface, the results of this procedure—in a police station or in laboratory studies—are quite impressive. A hypnotized witness mentally returns to the scene of the crime and seems able to recall exactly what the various participants said; a hypnotized college student mentally returns to childhood and appears to relive his sixth birthday party with childlike glee.

Careful studies reveal, however, that hypnosis doesn't improve memory. Descriptions of crimes or childhood reports elicited under hypnosis often turn out to be false when checked against available records (Lynn, Lock, Myers, & Payne, 1997; Spanos, C. Burgess, M. Burgess, Samuels, & Blois, 1999; also Figure 8.19; for more on hypnosis, see Chapter 6).

(A) Drawings done at age 6

(B) Drawings done by hypnotized adult told that he was 6 years old

8.19 Hypnotic age regression In one study, participants were asked to draw a picture while mentally "regressed" to age 6. At first glance, their drawings (an example is shown in A) looked remarkably childlike. But when compared to the participants' own drawings made at that age (an example is shown in B), it's clear that the hypnotized adults' drawings were much more sophisticated. They represent an adult's conception of what a childish drawing is rather than being the real thing.

Likewise, certain drugs are sometimes proposed as improving memory—but here too the actual benefits are small. Some of the drugs used to promote memory (e.g., sodium amytal) are sedatives, so they put an individual in a less guarded, less cautious state of mind. This state does allow the person to report more about the past—but not because she remembers more. Instead, in the relaxed state, the person is just more willing to talk and less likely to discriminate between genuine memories and fantasy. As a result, the person who has taken the drug will spin out a mix of recollection and fiction that robs their "recall" of any value. What's more, this less guarded state leaves an individual more vulnerable to the effects of leading or misleading questions, which can further undermine memory accuracy.

This evidence is more encouraging for a different drug—ginkgo biloba—sometimes advertised as improving memory (and other aspects of intellectual functioning). Ginkgo has an entirely different effect from the sedatives just mentioned, and it does improve memory for certain groups of people. Specifically, ginkgo can help with some types of blood-circulation problems and can also reduce certain forms of inflammation. It can therefore help people whose mental functioning has been compromised by specific physical maladies; this includes patients suffering from Huntington's disease or Alzheimer's disease. There's little evidence, however, that ginkgo improves the memory of healthy individuals; that is, there's no reliable effect for people with no circulatory problems or inflammation (Gold, Cahill, & Wenk, 2002; McDaniel, Maier, & Einstein, 2002).

Finally, there's one more—less exotic—step that people have tried to improve their memories: They have tried simply *being careful* in their recollection. This effort begins with the fact that we feel sure about some of our memories ("I'm certain that he's the guy who robbed me!") but more tentative about others ("I think she said it was size 6, but I'm not sure"). The obvious strategy, therefore, is to rely only on the memories we feel sure about and to be more cautious otherwise.

Surprisingly, though, this commonsense strategy offers little benefit. Many studies have compared the accuracy of memories people are certain about with the accuracy of memories they're not sure of. These studies often find a relationship in which confident memories are slightly more likely to be correct than unconfident ones. But the relationship is weak, and some studies have found no relationship at all (e.g., Bernstein & E. Loftus, 2009; Douglas & Steblay, 2006; Reisberg, 2010; Semmler & Brewer, 2006; Wells, Olson, & Charman, 2002). As a result, if we rely on our confidence in deciding which memories to trust, we'll regularly accept false memories and reject true ones.

Memory: An Overall Assessment

It seems, therefore, that false memories are essentially undetectable and unavoidable. In addition, we've seen that the errors in our recollection can be large and consequential. Does all of this mean that we should lament the poor quality of human memory? The answer to this question is an emphatic *no*. It's certainly true that we sometimes remember less than we'd like (a common experience for students taking an exam). It's also true that our recollection is sometimes mistaken—so the past as it actually unfolded is rather different from the past we remember. Even so, there's reason to believe our memories function in just the way we want them to.

How could this be? One point to bear in mind here is that, even with the memory errors we've discussed, our memories are *correct* far more often than not—so we usually remember the past accurately, in detail, and for a very long time. It's also important to highlight a point that has come up already—namely, that the mechanisms leading to memory error are mechanisms that *help us* most of the time; and so, in a sense, the errors are just the price we pay to gain other advantages. For example, errors in the misinformation paradigm arise (in part) because our memories are densely interconnected with each other; this is what allows elements to be transplanted from one remembered episode to another. But the connections from one memory to the next are, of course, there for a purpose: They're the retrieval paths that make memory search possible. Thus, to avoid the errors, we would need to restrict the connections—but if we did that, we'd lose the ability to locate our own memories within long-term storage!

The memory connections that lead to error also help us in other ways. Our environment, after all, is in many ways predictable—and it's enormously useful for us to exploit that predictability. There's little point in scrutinizing a kitchen to make sure there's a stove in the room, because in the vast majority of cases there is. So why take the time to confirm the obvious? Likewise, there's little point in taking special note that, yes, this restaurant does have menus and that, yes, people in the restaurant are eating and not having their cars repaired. These too are obvious points, and it would be a waste of time to give them special notice.

On these grounds, a reliance on schematic knowledge is a good thing. Schemas guide our attention to what's informative in a situation, rather than what's self-evident (e.g., Gordon, 2006); they also guide our inferences at the time of recall. If this use of schemas sometimes leads us astray, this may be a small price to pay for the gain in efficiency that schemas allow.

Finally, what about forgetting? This too may be a blessing in disguise, because sometimes it's to our advantage to remember less and forget more. For example, think about all the times in your life when you've been with a particular friend. These episodes are related to each other in an obvious way, so they're likely to become interconnected in your memory. This will cause difficulties if you want to remember which episode is which, and whether you had a particular conversation last Tuesday or the day before. But rather than lamenting this as an example of forgetting, we may want to celebrate what's going on here. Because of the "interference," all of the episodes will merge in your thoughts, so that what resides in memory is one integrated package containing all of your knowledge about your friend. This is, in fact, the way that much of your general knowledge is created! In other words, the same blurring together that makes it difficult to remember episodes also makes it possible to think in a general way, with a focus on what diverse experiences have in common rather than on what makes each experience unique. Without this blurring together, our capacity for thinking in general terms might be dramatically impaired.

It seems, then, that our overall assessment of memory can be rather upbeat. We've discussed a wide range of memory errors, but these errors are the exception rather than the rule. In addition, we've now seen that in most cases the errors are a by-product of mechanisms that otherwise help us—to locate our memories within storage, to be efficient in our contact with the world, and to form general knowledge. Thus, even with the errors, even with forgetting, it seems that human memory functions in a fashion that serves us well.

VARIETIES OF MEMORY

So far in this chapter, we've been discussing how memory functions and have given little attention to *what* was being remembered—and, to a large extent, this approach works well: The principles we've described apply equally to memory for word lists in the laboratory, for movies you've seen or songs you've heard, and for complex events in your everyday life. At the same time, it's also possible to distinguish different types of memory—each with its own operating principles and its own neural basis. Let's look at some of the crucial distinctions.

A Hierarchy of Memory Types

Many psychologists distinguish memory types in terms of a hierarchy like the one in Figure 8.20. On the left side of the hierarchy are the various forms of **explicit memory**. These are conscious memories—memories that you can describe if you choose—and they can usually be triggered by a direct question, such as "Do you know whether...?" or "Do you recall the time when...?" In contrast, **implicit memories** are remnants of the past that we may not recall at all, but they are (unconsciously) still with us, and we can detect these memories by the influence they still have on us. We'll consider some examples of implicit memories in a moment—but, in general, these memories cannot be revealed by direct questions; instead, they're usually revealed by some sort of indirect test.

explicit memory Conscious memories that can be described at will and can be triggered by a direct question.

implicit memory Memories that we may not recall consciously, but that are still demonstrable through an indirect test.

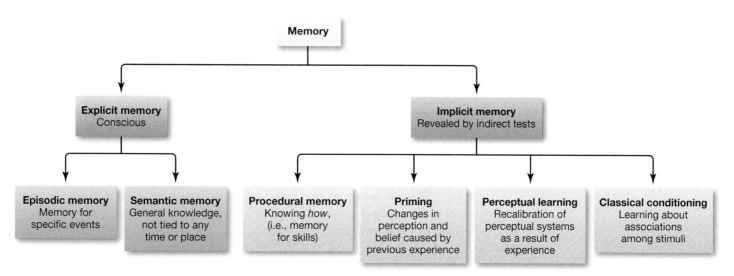

8.20 **Hierarchy of memory types**

Episodic and Semantic Memory

episodic memory Memory for specific events and experiences.

semantic memory Memory for facts (including word meanings); these memories are not tied to any specific time or place.

Both explicit and implicit memories can be subdivided further. Most of this chapter, in fact, has focused on just one type of explicit memory: **episodic memory.** This term refers to memory for specific events, including events outside the laboratory (e.g., the event of your 10th birthday) or inside (e.g., the event of memorizing a particular story). Just as important, though, is **semantic memory.** This is the memory that contains knowledge not tied to any time or place—your knowledge that London is the capital of England, that water is wet, that people become annoyed if you insult them. (Note that some information in semantic memory is concerned with semantics—including your memory for what the word *special* means, or what the opposite of *hot* is. Much of the information in this memory, however, is not specifically tied to semantics, and so some authors prefer to call it *generic memory,* or *generic knowledge.*)

Episodic and semantic memory can be distinguished on many grounds—including the specific brain areas that support each type of memory. This distinction is reflected in the fact that some forms of brain damage disrupt episodic memory but not semantic, and other forms do the reverse. For example, a patient known as Gene sustained a serious head injury in a motorcycle accident; the damage affected large areas of his frontal and temporal lobes, including his left hippocampus. As a result, he can recall no events at all from any time in his life. "Even when detailed descriptions of dramatic events in his life are given to him—such as the derailment, near his house, of a train carrying lethal chemicals that required 240,000 people to evacuate their homes for a week," Gene remembers nothing of this or any other event (D. Schacter, 1996, p. 150; Tulving, Schacter, McLachlan, & Moscovitch, 1988). But he does remember some things. He remembers that he owned two motorcycles and a car, he knows that his family has a summer cottage where he spent many weekends, and he recalls the names of classmates in a school photograph (D. Schacter, 1996). In short, Gene's episodic memory is massively disrupted, but his memory for generic information is largely intact.

Other patients show the reverse pattern. One woman, for example, suffered damage to the front portion of her temporal lobes as a result of encephalitis. As a consequence, she has lost her memory of many common words, important historical events, famous people, and even the fundamental traits of animate and inanimate objects. "However, when asked about her wedding and honeymoon, her father's illness and death, or other specific past episodes, she readily produced detailed and accurate recollections" (D. Schacter, 1996, p. 152).

Data like these make it clear that we need to distinguish between semantic and episodic memory. But these categories can themselves be subdivided. For example, people who have suffered brain damage sometimes lose the ability to name certain objects, or to answer simple questions about these objects (e.g., "Does a whale have legs?"). Often the problem is quite specific—and so some patients lose the ability to name living things but not nonliving things; other patients show the reverse pattern (Mahon & Caramazza, 2009). Indeed, sometimes the symptoms caused by brain damage are even more fine-grained: Some patients lose the ability to answer questions about fruits and vegetables, but they're still able to answer questions about other objects (living or nonliving). These data suggest that separate brain systems are responsible for different types of knowledge—and so damage to a particular brain area disrupts one type of knowledge but not others.

Possible Subdivisions of Episodic Memory

Plainly, then, we need to distinguish semantic memory from episodic, and we need to distinguish different types of semantic memory. Do we also need subdivisions within episodic memory? Some theorists believe we do, granting special status, for example, to *autobiographical memory*—the memory that defines, for each of us, who we are (e.g., Baddeley, Aggleton, & Conway, 2002; Cabeza & St. Jacques, 2007). Other theorists propose that *certain types of events* are stored in specialized memory systems—so that some authors argue for special status for *flashbulb memories*, and others suggest special status for memories for *traumatic events.*

FLASHBULB MEMORIES

Each one of us encounters a wide diversity of events in our lives. Many of these events are emotionally neutral (shopping for groceries, or buying a new Psychology textbook), while others trigger strong feelings (an especially romantic evening, or a death in the family). In general, emotional episodes tend to be better remembered—more vividly, more completely, and more accurately (e.g., Reisberg & Heuer, 2004)—and many mechanisms contribute to this effect. Among other points, emotional events are likely to be interesting to us, guaranteeing that we pay close attention to them; and we've already seen that attention promotes memory. Emotional events are also likely to involve issues or people we care about; this makes it likely that we'll readily connect the event to other knowledge (about the issues or the people)—and these connections, of course, also promote memory. In addition, the various biological changes that accompany emotion play a role—facilitating the process of memory consolidation (e.g., Buchanan & Adolphs, 2004; Dudai, 2004; Hamann, 2001; LaBar & Cabeza, 2006; LaBar, 2007).

Within the broad set of emotional memories, however, our memory for some events seems truly extraordinary for its longevity: People claim to remember these events, even decades later, "as if they happened yesterday." These especially vivid memories, called **flashbulb memories,** typically concern events that were highly distinctive and unexpected as well as strongly emotional. The most common examples involve emotionally *negative* events that triggered fear, or grief, or horror—such as the memory of an early morning phone call reporting a parent's death, or the memory of hearing about the attack on the World Trade Center in 2001 (Figure 8.21).

flashbulb memories Vivid, detailed memories said to be produced by unexpected and emotionally important events.

The clarity and longevity of flashbulb memories led psychologists R. Brown and Kulik (1977) many years ago to propose that we must have some special "flashbulb mechanism" distinct from the mechanisms that create other, more mundane memories.

8.21 Flashbulb memories (A) The classic example of a flashbulb memory is the assassination of John F. Kennedy in November 1963. Virtually all Americans (and most Europeans) who were at least 9 or 10 years old on that date still remember the day vividly. (B) The World Trade Center attack on September 11, 2001, is the sort of shocking and highly consequential event that seems very likely to create a flashbulb memory. Decades from now, people are likely to remember this day clearly.

The full pattern of evidence, however, suggests that there is no such special mechanism. As one concern, people usually talk with their friends about these remarkable events (i.e., you tell me your story, and I tell you mine), and it's probably this rehearsal, not some specialized mechanism, that makes these memories so long lasting. What's more, flashbulb memories—like other memories—are not immune to error: In fact, some flashbulb memories are filled with inaccuracies and represent the event in a fashion far from the truth (see, for example, M. Conway et al., 2009; Greenberg, 2004; Hirst et al., 2009; Luminet & Curci, 2009; Neisser, 1982a, 1986).

Moreover, the longevity of flashbulb memories may be less extraordinary than it seems, because other, more mundane, memories may also be extremely long lasting. One study tested people's memory for faces, asking in particular whether people could still identify photos of people they'd gone to high school with many years earlier (Bahrick et al., 1975; also see M. Conway, Cohen, & Stanhope, 1991; also see Bahrick & Hall, 1991; Bahrick, Hall, Goggin, Bahrick, & Berger, 1994). People who had graduated from high school 14 years earlier were still able to name roughly 90% of the faces; the success rate was roughly 75% for people who graduated 34 years earlier. A half-century after leaving high school, people could still name 60% of the faces (and it's unclear whether this small drop-off in accuracy reflects an erosion of memory or a more general decline in cognitive performance caused by normal aging). Clearly, therefore, even "non-flashbulb memories" can last for a very long time.

Flashbulb memories do seem remarkable—in their clarity, their durability, and (in some cases) their accuracy. But these attributes are likely to be the result of rehearsal plus the ordinary mechanisms associated with emotional remembering, and not a basis for claiming that flashbulb memories are somehow in a class by themselves.

MEMORY FOR TRAUMATIC EVENTS

There has been considerable controversy over a different proposal—the notion that memory for *traumatic events* might follow its own rules, different from the principles governing other types of episodic memory. Certainly, many of the principles we've discussed apply to traumatic memory, just as they apply to memories of other sorts. Thus, traumatic memories become harder to recall as time goes by; and they sometimes contain errors, just like all memories do. Traumatic memories are also better retained if they're rehearsed (thought about) once in a while. In these regards, traumatic memories seem quite similar to other sorts of episodic memory. The debate, however, is focused on a further issue—whether trauma memories are governed by a separate set of principles tied to how people might *protect themselves* from the painful recollection of horrific events.

Overall, how well are traumatic events remembered? If someone has witnessed wartime atrocities or has been the victim of a brutal crime, how fully will he remember these horrific events (Figure 8.22)? If someone suffers through the horrors of a sexual assault, will she be left with a vivid memory as a terrible remnant of the experience? The evidence suggests that traumatic events tend to be remembered accurately, completely, and for many years. Indeed, the victims of some atrocities seem plagued by a cruel enhancement of memory, leaving them with extra-vivid recollections of the awful event (see, for example, K. Alexander et al., 2005; Brewin, 1998; Goodman et al., 2003; McNally, 2003b; Pope, Hudson, Bodkin, & Oliva, 1998; S. Porter & Peace, 2007; Thomsen & Berntsen, 2009). In fact, in many cases these recollections can become part of the

8.22 Memory for traumatic events
There has been considerable debate over whether people have special mechanisms that protect them from recalling traumatic events.

package of difficulties that lead to a diagnosis of *post-traumatic stress disorder,* and so they may be horribly disruptive for the afflicted individual (see Chapter 16).

There are, however, some striking exceptions to this broad pattern. Researchers have documented many cases in which people have suffered through truly extreme events but seem to have little or no recall of the horrors (see, for example, Arrigo & Pezdek, 1997). Thus, someone might be in a terrible car crash but have absolutely no recollection of the accident. Someone might witness a brutal crime but be unable to recall it just a few hours later.

How should we think about this mixed pattern? Let's start with the outcome that's by far more common—the person whose trauma is remembered all too well. This outcome is probably best understood in terms of the biological process of consolidation, using the hypothesis that this process is promoted by the conditions that accompany bodily arousal (Buchanan & Adolphs, 2004; Hamann, 2001). But what about the cases of the other sort—the person with no memory of the trauma at all? In many of these cases, the traumatic events were accompanied by physical duress, such as sleep deprivation, head injuries, or alcohol abuse, each of which can disrupt memory (McNally, 2003b). In still other cases, the extreme stress associated with the event is likely to have disrupted the biological processes (the protein synthesis) needed for establishing the memory in the first place; as a result, no memory is ever established (Hasselmo, 1999; McGaugh, 2000; Payne, Nadel, Britton, & Jacobs, 2004).

Plainly, therefore, several factors are relevant to trauma memory. But the heated debate over these memories centers on a further claim: Some authors argue that highly painful memories will be *repressed*—that is, hidden from view by defense mechanisms designed to shield a person from psychological harm. In a related claim, some authors suggest that painful events will trigger the defense of *dissociation,* in which the person tries to create a sense of "psychological distance" between themselves and the horror. In either case, the proposal is that these memories are blocked by a specialized mechanism that's simply irrelevant to other, less painful, memories. According to this view, trauma memory is indeed a special subset within the broader domain of episodic memory.

Advocates for this special status point to several forms of evidence, including cases in which a memory seems to have been pushed out of consciousness and kept hidden for many years but is then "recovered" (brought back into consciousness) at some later point. This pattern is sometimes alleged in cases of child sexual abuse: The victim represses the memory (or dissociates) and so has no recollection of the abuse for years. Later in life, however, the victim recovers the memory, revealing at last the long-hidden crime.

Do these cases provide evidence for repression or dissociation, followed by a process of memory recovery? In answering, we need to start by acknowledging that incest and childhood sexual abuse are surely far more prevalent than many people suppose (Pipe, Lamb, Orbach, & Cederbork, 2007). It's also clear that some events—particularly emotionally significant events—can be held in memory for a very long time—years or even decades. We also know that it's possible for memories to be "lost" for years and then recovered (e.g., Geraerts et al., 2006; Geraerts et al., 2009; Geraerts et al., 2007). On all these grounds, then, it seems plausible that these memories of childhood abuse, hidden for decades, may be entirely accurate—and, indeed, provide evidence for horrid wrongdoing and criminal prosecution.

But there are some complications here. For one thing, the pattern just described—with memories lost from view and then recovered—may not involve repression or dissociation at all. As an alternative, these memories might just indicate a long-lasting retrieval failure that was eventually reversed, once the appropriate memory cue came

8.23 Recovered memories (A) Eileen Franklin (center) believed that she had repressed and then recovered memories of her father, George Franklin Sr., molesting and murdering her childhood friend 20 years earlier. (B) Based on his daughter's testimony about her recovered memories, George Franklin was found guilty and imprisoned until new evidence emerged showing that he could not have committed the crime.

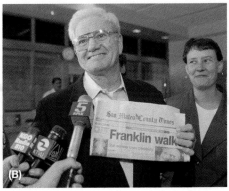

along. This would take none of the importance away from these memories: They still would reveal serious crimes, worthy of substantial punishment. But, from this perspective, our explanation of these memories involves no mechanism beyond the memory processes we've already been discussing—and so, on this basis, the *content* of these memories would be distinctive in a tragic way; but the *processes* that create and maintain these memories would be the same as those operating in other cases.

In addition, and far more troubling, at least some of the "recovered memories" may in fact be false—created through mechanisms we discussed earlier in this chapter. After all, many of these recovered memories involve events that took place years ago, and we know that the risk of error is greater in remembering the distant past than it is in remembering recent events. Likewise, the evidence is clear that people can have detailed (false) recollection of entire episodes—including highly emotional episodes—that never happened at all. And we know that these false memories are even more likely if the person, from her current perspective, regards the "remembered" event as plausible (see, for example, Bernstein & Loftus, 2009; Chrobak & Zaragoza, 2008; Loftus, 2005; Ofshe, 1992; Pezdek, Blandon-Gitlin, & Gabbay, 2006; Principe, Kanaya, Ceci, & Singh, 2006). We also know that false memories, when they occur, can be recalled just as vividly, just as confidently, and with just as much distress as when recalling actual memories (Figure 8.23). All of these points remind us that we cannot take the veracity of the recovered memories for granted. Some recovered memories are very likely to be accurate, but some are likely to be false. And, sadly, we have no means of telling which memories are which—which provide a factually correct record of terrible misdeeds and which provide a vivid and compelling *fiction*, portraying events that never happened. (For discussion of this difficult issue, see Freyd, 1996, 1998; Geraerts et al., 2006; Geraerts et al., 2009; Geraerts et al., 2007; Ghetti et al., 2006; Giesbrecht et al., 2008; Kihlstrom & Schacter, 2000; Loftus & Guyer, 2002; McNally & Geraerts, 2009; Schooler, 2001.)

The debate over recovered memories is ongoing and has many implications—including implications for the legal system, because these memories are sometimes offered as evidence for criminal wrongdoing. But in the meantime, what about our initial question? Are traumatic memories in a special category, involving mechanisms irrelevant to other categories of episodic memory? In light of the continuing debate, the answer remains a matter of substantial disagreement.

Explicit and Implicit Memory

We've now considered several ways that explicit memory might be subdivided—into episodic memory and semantic, and then with each of those categories potentially divided further. But what about *implicit memory?* As we'll see, this memory provides an entirely different means through which we're influenced by past experience, and it is distinct from explicit memory in its functioning and in its biological basis.

DISTINGUISHING IMPLICIT FROM EXPLICIT MEMORY

Implicit memories are distinguishable from explicit memories in many ways. Perhaps the clearest evidence, however, comes from the study of the memory disruption caused by brain damage. In general, this disruption is referred to as *amnesia*. Earlier in the chapter, we mentioned one type of amnesia: *retrograde amnesia*—a loss of memories for events that took place before the brain injury that caused the amnesia. In other cases, though, brain damage produces **anterograde amnesia**—an apparent inability to form new memories (see Figure 8.9).

In general, anterograde amnesia is caused by damage to certain sites in the temporal cortex—specifically, in the hippocampus and nearby subcortical regions. In some cases, this damage is the result of illness—especially if the illness causes *encephalitis*, an inflammation in the brain tissue. In other cases, the damage is caused by stroke or physical trauma. One of the most common causes, though, is a type of malnutrition associated with chronic alcoholism; in this case, the amnesia is a central symptom of the illness called *Korsakoff's syndrome*.

One of the most carefully studied cases of anterograde amnesia, however, had an entirely different cause: A patient known as H.M. suffered from severe epilepsy. When all other treatments failed, the physicians tried (in the late 1950s) to treat H.M.'s disease with a neurosurgical procedure that deliberately removed most of his hippocampus, amygdala, and a considerable amount of nearby tissue (Figure 8.24). The procedure was, in a very narrow sense, a success: It did control his epilepsy. But the surgery also had a tragic and unanticipated side effect. Across the 55 years he lived after his surgery, H.M. seemed incapable of adding new information to his long-term memory. As his obituary put it: "each time he met a friend, each time he ate a meal, each time he walked in the woods, it was as if for the first time" (Carey, 2008). He remembered none of the episodes in his life after the surgery; he was entirely unable to recognize people he'd first met after the surgery—even if he saw them day after day (Milner, 1966, 1970; also see O'Kane, Kensinger, & Corkin, 2004; Skotko et al., 2004).

Amnesia had devastating effects on H.M.'s life—including some effects that we might not think of as involving memory. For example, H.M. had an uncle he liked very much. When first told that his uncle had died, he was deeply distressed, but then he forgot all about this sad news. Some time later, he asked again when his uncle would come to visit, and he was told again of his uncle's death. His grief was as intense as before; indeed, each time he heard this sad news, he was hearing it for the first time—with all the shock and pain (Corkin, 1984; Hilts, 1995; Marslen-Wilson & Teuber, 1975; Milner, 1966; Milner, Corkin, & Teuber, 1968).

Crucially, and despite these remarkable problems, patients with anterograde amnesia—including H.M.—can acquire certain types of new memories which can be revealed with specialized testing. In some studies, for example, patients with anterograde amnesia have been given practice, day after day, in finding the correct path through a maze. Each time they're shown the maze, the patients insist they've never seen it before; this is simply a confirmation of their amnesia. Even so, they get faster and faster in solving the maze—and so apparently they do retain some information from each practice session.

Likewise, in another study, patients with Korsakoff's syndrome heard a series of brief melodies (Johnson, Kim, & Risse, 1985). A short time later, they listened to a new series

anterograde amnesia A memory deficit suffered after some kinds of brain damage, in which the patient seems unable to form new explicit memories; however, memories acquired before the injury are spared.

8.24 The brain of Henry Gustav Molaison Throughout his lifetime, Henry Molaison was identified in research papers only through his initials—H.M. His full name was released only after his death (in December 2008). Even after death, though, H.M. will contribute to our understanding of memory, because close analyses of his brain are underway. In these scans of his brain, we can see the space left by the surgical removal of tissue (marked with an asterisk). Note, though, that not all of H.M.'s hippocampus was destroyed; the remaining bit is marked with a small arrow.

and were told that some of the tunes in the second batch were repeats from the earlier presentation. As expected, these amnesic patients were completely unable to tell which tunes were the repeats and which were new; indeed, their memory responses were close to random. Remarkably, though, when asked which melodies they *preferred,* the patients uniformly preferred the familiar ones. The patients had no (explicit) memory for these tunes, but a memory did emerge with indirect testing—and emerged, in this case, as a preference.

In important ways, therefore, these patients can't remember their experiences. If we ask them directly about the past, they recall nothing. If we ask them which mazes they have solved before and which are novel, they can only guess. Thus it seems clear that these patients have no conscious recollection, no *explicit* memory, for the events in their lives. Still, we can find ways in which the patients' current skills and behaviors are shaped by their experiences—and so, apparently, the experiences have left some record, some residual imprint, in these patients. This lasting imprint, a demonstrable impact of the past, is what psychologists call *implicit memory*—an unnoticed "leftover" from life events that changes how someone now acts and thinks (Donaldson, Peterson, & Buckner, 2001; Fazio & Olson, 2003; Humphreys et al., 2003; Kinoshita, 2001; Yonelinas, 2002).

PROCEDURAL MEMORY

What exactly is implicit memory? In what circumstances does it influence us? And can implicit memory be demonstrated in people without amnesia, people whose brains are healthy and intact? To answer these questions, we need to distinguish different types of implicit memory, because each type influences us in its own way.

Some cases of implicit memory involve **procedural knowledge** rather than **declarative knowledge**. Procedural knowledge is knowing *how*—knowing how to ride a bicycle, for example, or how to use chopsticks. Declarative knowledge, in contrast, is represented in explicit memory, not implicit, and it's knowing *that*: knowing that there are three outs in an inning, that automobiles run on gasoline, or that you woke up late this morning.

The earlier example we mentioned in our discussion of amnesia—that of patients learning how to get through a maze—involves procedural memory, and other examples are easy to find. In some procedures, patients have been shown a complex shape and asked to trace the outline of the shape with a stylus. What made this task difficult was that the patients couldn't see the shape directly; they could see it (and the stylus) only by looking into a mirror (Figure 8.25). This task is moderately difficult—but the patients got better with practice, all the while insisting that each try at the task was their very first time.

What about people who don't have amnesia—people with normal brains? In some studies, research participants are given four buttons and told to press button 1 if light 1 comes on, button 2 for light 2, and so on (Figure 8.26). The lights are then turned on in rapid succession, and participants do their best to keep up. As it turns out, the lights are turned on in a repetitive sequence—perhaps always 1-3-4-2-1-4-1-3-4-2-1-4-1-3-4-2-1-4. Participants seem to learn this sequence; and so, with a bit of practice, can respond more quickly if the lights follow this sequence than they can if the sequence is random. But when asked whether the sequence was random or not, participants are clueless. Thus, they seem to have procedural knowledge that allows them to respond more quickly to the patterned lights, but they don't have declarative knowledge—the same distinction we observe in patients with amnesia (Gazzaniga et al., 2009).

procedural knowledge Knowledge of how to do something, such as riding a bike; expressed in behaviors rather than in words.

declarative knowledge Knowledge of information that can be expressed in words.

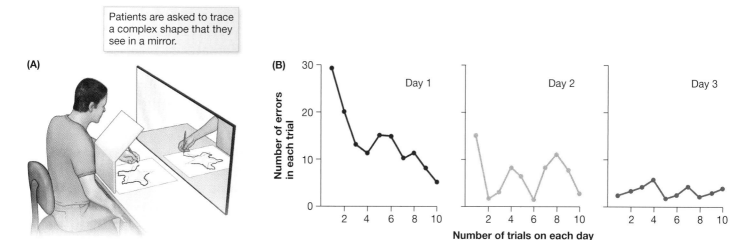

8.25 **Mirror drawing** (A) In mirror drawing, the research participant has to trace an outline of a figure while looking at his hand in a mirror. At first this task is very difficult, but after some practice the individual gets quite good at it. The same is true for amnesiacs. (B) The graphs show H.M.'s improvement on this task over a period of three days.

PRIMING EFFECTS

Procedural memories are typically concerned with behaviors—our actions and our skills. Other types of implicit memory, in contrast, influence our perceptions and our thoughts. Consider, for example, demonstrations of *priming*. Participants in one study were shown a number of words. Later, they were given a second task in which they simply had to identify words flashed briefly on a computer screen. Participants had no idea that many of the words in this second task were taken from the earlier list, but they still showed a pattern known as *repetition priming*: Words that had been on the original list were identified more readily than words that had not. This priming was observed even for words that the participants failed to recognize as familiar in a standard recognition task. Thus, the participants had no explicit memory for having seen these words, but they did have an implicit memory that showed up as priming. In other words, they were being influenced by a memory they didn't realize they had (Jacoby, 1983; Jacoby & Witherspoon, 1982).

Other procedures, with different tasks, show a similar pattern. In *fragment-completion tasks,* for example, participants are shown partial words (such as C__O__O__I__E) and asked to complete them to form actual words (CROCODILE). Success in this task is much more likely if the target word was encountered recently; this advantage is observed even when participants have no conscious recollection of the previous encounter (Graf & Mandler, 1984; Jacoby & Dallas, 1981; Tulving, Schacter, & Stark, 1982).

In another experiment, participants were asked to read sentences that were presented to them upside down. A *year* later, participants returned to the lab; there, they were shown a series of sentences and asked which ones they'd seen in their first visit to the lab and which ones were novel. Not surprisingly, after this long delay, participants couldn't tell which sentences they'd seen before. Still, when they were asked once again to read sentences presented upside down, they were faster with the sentences they'd seen before than they were with novel sentences—a case of priming that lasted across a full 12 months (Kolers & Roediger, 1984).

In each of these cases, it seems that an encounter with a stimulus leaves us better prepared for that stimulus the next time we meet it. This preparation can then influence

8.26 **Procedural learning** Participants have to press the appropriate key each time one of the numbered lights comes on. If there's a repeated sequence in the lights, participants seem to learn this and so get faster and faster in their task. However, participants have no declarative knowledge about the sequence—and may not even realize there was a repeated sequence.

us in many ways, quite independently of whether we can recall the earlier encounter with that stimulus. To illustrate how far this pattern can reach, consider the so-called illusion of truth. In the relevant studies, participants hear a series of statements like "The average person in Switzerland eats about 25 pounds of cheese each year," or "Henry Ford forgot to put a reverse gear in his first automobile."* Participants' task is to say how *interesting* each of these statements is. Later on, the same participants are presented with some more sentences but now have to rate the credibility of each one on a scale from "certainly true" to "certainly false." Needless to say, some of the sentences in this "truth test" are repeats from the earlier presentation; the question for us is how the judgments of sentence credibility are influenced by the earlier exposure.

The result of these studies is a propagandist's (or advertiser's) dream: Sentences heard before are more likely to be accepted as true, so that in essence familiarity increases credibility (Begg, Anas, & Farinacci, 1992). To make matters worse, the effect emerges even when participants are warned not to believe the sentences in the first list. That is, sentences plainly identified as false when they're first heard still create the illusion of truth, so that these sentences are subsequently judged to be more credible than sentences never heard before.

How could this be? Bear in mind that the participants in these procedures are shown a lot of sentences and that there's a delay between the first task (judging how interesting the sentences are) and the second (judging credibility). These steps make it difficult for participants to keep track of the sentences they hear; in other words, these steps work against explicit memory. As a result, participants have a hard time recalling which of the sentences in the truth test they encountered on the first list; so it doesn't help them to know that the sentences on that first list were all false. Thus, with no conscious memory of the earlier encounter, participants have no way to protect themselves from the illusion.

OTHER FORMS OF IMPLICIT MEMORY

We've now mentioned two forms of implicit memory—priming effects and procedural memory—but there are other forms as well. One plausible addition to this list is *perceptual learning*—the learning that you need to do whenever you "recalibrate" your perceptual systems. As an example, think of what happens when someone gets new eyeglasses, perhaps with a stronger prescription than they've had before. Across the next few days, he needs to "adjust" to the glasses—changing (among other things) how he interprets the degree of tension in his eye muscles as a cue to distance. This is surely a form of learning—and so places new information, or perhaps new skills, in memory. But it's learning that happens completely outside of awareness—and so involves implicit memory, not explicit.

A different example involves cases we considered in Chapter 7—including the learning called *classical conditioning*. This learning, too, creates new knowledge—knowledge about what follows what in the world—but can be done without conscious awareness. Indeed, classical conditioning can take place even if an organism is fully anesthetized during the learning (e.g., Cahoon, 2008).

These and other examples demonstrate the enormous breadth of implicit memory. We rely on *explicit* memory in many circumstances, and we're guided to an enormous extent by our conscious recollection of the past. But the reach of implicit memory may be even larger—so that in many situations, we're shaped in ways we do not notice by past experiences that we cannot recall.

---

*The first statement, by the way, is false; the average is closer to 18 pounds. The second statement is true.

SOME FINAL THOUGHTS: DIFFERENT TYPES, BUT COMMON PRINCIPLES

In the last few sections, we've seen that the term *memory* can be applied to a diverse set of phenomena. The term applies to the (episodic) memories that you draw on when you get together with friends and talk about what you did last summer. It also applies to your (semantic) memories that grass is green, "up" is the opposite of "down," and Beijing is the capital of China. The term also applies to your (procedural) memory of how to ride a bicycle, and your (classical conditioning) memory that makes you gag whenever you smell gin—a response rooted in the fact that you got horribly ill the day after you drank all those martinis.

Without question, these different types of memories obey different principles: Explicit memory, as we've seen, depends on active engagement with the materials at the time of learning. In contrast, many forms of implicit learning seem relatively passive and can perhaps be created by exposure alone. There has been debate over whether some forms of memory (episodic memory in particular) might be found only in a few species—perhaps those that are self-aware and capable of conscious reflection on the past. Other forms of memory (e.g., the memory that supports classical conditioning) can be found in a wide range of species—snails or worms, for example, as well as chimpanzees or humans.

We might worry that this broad usage of the term *memory* stretches things too far and might even be misleading in some cases. After all, if we say "the rat remembers that the tone was followed by food," this might imply that the rat is aware of this fact about the world, and can reflect on it and draw inferences from it. But this would be a mistake—misrepresenting the (unconscious, largely automatic) qualities of implicit memory in general and certainly misrepresenting rat capacities in particular.

How can we find a balance—so that we bring together the various memory achievements discussed in this chapter and the previous one, but so that we don't lose distinctions among the various types of memory? The answer may lie in careful emphasis on the distinction between implicit memory and explicit, keeping separate the types of memory that are conscious and allow reflection and the types of memory—crucial as they are for many purposes—that do not. This distinction, in turn, points us toward some new questions. For example, we know that humans have explicit memories; we see this in the simple fact that we can, if asked, report on our memories and describe the past as we recall it. Which other species also have explicit memories—and thus are aware of themselves and their own past? This question opens a window through which we might explore the intriguing issue of conscious experience and awareness in other creatures.

This distinction also highlights the key role that explicit memory plays for human experience—and, indeed, this is why we've devoted most of this chapter to this type of remembering. Explicit memories are—by definition—memories that we're aware of. We can therefore reflect on past experiences and discuss them with others—sometimes to instruct them, sometimes to foster social bonds. We can also report on our memories when someone else needs to learn what happened in a prior episode—whether it's a journalist trying to understand what happened in yesterday's storm or a police officer investigating how things unfolded in last night's robbery. And, finally, we can draw conclusions from these memories—and we often do so, because many of the decisions we reach, or judgments we make, are based on considerations drawn from memory. Plainly, then, explicit memories play important roles in many human functions, and we're obviously able to *think about* our explicit memories in ways that really matter for us. But what does this "thinking" involve? That will be the focus of our next chapter.

ACQUISITION, STORAGE, RETRIEVAL

- Any act of remembering begins with *acquisition*, the process of gathering information and placing it into memory. The next aspect of memory is *storage*, the holding of information in some enduring form in the mind for later use. The final phase is *retrieval*, the point at which we draw information from storage and use it in some fashion.

ACQUISITION

- Memory *acquisition* includes cases of *intentional learning* and *incidental learning*. In either case, the person must pay attention to the material to be remembered, and it is the product of this intellectual engagement that is stored in memory.

- According to the stage theory of memory, information is held in *working memory* while one is thinking about it, but it's lodged in *long-term memory* for storage for longer intervals. This theory is supported by studies of free recall. In these studies, *primacy effects* reflect the fact that early items in a presentation receive more rehearsal and are more likely to be transferred to long-term storage. *Recency effects* reflect the fact that just-heard items can be retrieved directly from working memory.

- *Chunking* is the process through which items are recoded into a smaller number of larger units. The active nature of memory is also evident in the fact that mere *maintenance rehearsal* does little to promote long-term storage.

- According to many studies, how well someone remembers will depend on the depth at which he or she processed the incoming information; *shallow processing* refers to encoding that emphasizes the superficial characteristics of a stimulus, and *deep processing* refers to encoding that emphasizes the meaning of the material. Consistent with this perspective, we remember best the material that we've understood, thanks to the memory connections linking one memory to the next. At the time of recall, these connections serve as retrieval paths.

- *Mnemonics* help a person form memory connections, and these connections can dramatically improve memory. Many mnemonics utilize imagery, and imagery is most helpful if the visualized items are imagined in some interaction—linking the items to each other, as one would expect if imagery is a means of promoting memory connections.

STORAGE

- More research is needed to explore how the *memory trace* is actually represented in the brain. However, evidence suggests that different elements of a single memory (what things looked like, how one felt) may be stored in different brain sites.

- The establishment of a long-term memory depends on a *memory consolidation* process, during which new connections are formed among neurons. The need for consolidation is reflected in cases in which this process has been disrupted, resulting in *retrograde amnesia*.

RETRIEVAL

- The *retrieval* of memories is often easy, but it sometimes fails. The failure can be complete or can be partial, as in the *tip-of-the-tongue effect*. The retrieval of memories is often promoted by our having an appropriate *retrieval cue*. Whether a cue is useful depends on whether the cue re-creates the context in which the original learning occurred. This *context reinstatement* allows the person to use the connections they formed earlier as *retrieval paths*.

- What's stored in memory reflects how the person thought about or reacted to the object or event being remembered. This *encoding specificity* is reflected in the fact that remembering is more likely if one thinks about the target information during retrieval in the same way that one did during encoding.

MEMORY GAPS, MEMORY ERRORS

- Many cases of forgetting can be understood as the result of inadequate encoding. This is reflected in the fact that fMRI data, collected during encoding, show different patterns for later-remembered material and later-forgotten material.

- Forgetting generally increases as the *retention interval* gets longer, but the causes of forgetting are still being debated. One theory holds that traces gradually decay. Another view argues that the cause of forgetting is interference produced by other memories. In some cases, this is because the other memories promote retrieval failure—an inability to find information that's nonetheless still in storage. Retrieval failure is evident whenever some new cue allows us to recall previously forgotten materials.

- Interference can also result from the mixing together of memories. These *intrusion errors* are evident in the *misinformation effect*, in which specific episodes are blurred together. In other cases, intrusion errors are the result of schematic knowledge intruding into someone's memory of a particular event. This reflects a broader pattern of evidence indicating that events are usually understood (and remembered) with reference to knowledge structures called *schemas*.

- Intrusion errors can also be produced by semantic associations with the material being recalled. This is the source of the errors often observed in the *DRM paradigm*.

- Another category of memory errors involves cases in which someone correctly realizes that an idea (or face or stimulus) is *familiar*, but makes an error about why the idea is familiar. This pattern reflects the fact that separate memory systems are the bases for familiarity and *recollection*.

- Psychologists have searched unsuccessfully for ways of distinguishing correct memories from mistaken ones. The *confidence* expressed by the person remembering turns out to be of little value for this discrimination. Hypnosis also does nothing to improve memory and can actually increase the risk of memory error.

VARIETIES OF MEMORY

- Researchers find it useful to distinguish several types of memory. *Episodic memories* concern specific episodes; *semantic memories* concern broader knowledge, not tied to a particular episode. *Explicit memories* are consciously recalled; *implicit memories* are revealed when there is an effect of some past experience without the person being aware that she's remembering at all—or even that there was a relevant past experience.

- Some theorists subdivide episodic memory, distinguishing autobiographical memories from memories for other episodes, and placing *flashbulb memories* or *traumatic* memories into their own category. However, current evidence suggests that flashbulb memories are governed by the same principles as other memories, and the same is true for traumatic memories—although debate continues over the possible role of "repression" or "dissociation" in memory for traumatic events.

- Certain injuries to the brain produce *anterograde amnesia*, in which the patient's ability to fix material in long-term memory is reduced. However, someone with amnesia may still have intact implicit memories. Implicit memories, in turn, can be divided into several types: procedural memories, involving changes in behavior, priming, changing our perceptions and thoughts, and perceptual learning.

 ONLINE STUDY TOOLS

Go to StudySpace, **wwnorton.com/studyspace**, to access additional review and enrichment materials, including the following resources for each chapter:

Organize
- Study Plan
- Chapter Outline
- Quiz+ Assessment

Learn
- Ebook
- Chapter Review
- Vocabulary Flashcards
- Drag-and-Drop Labeling Exercises
- Audio Podcast Chapter Overview

Connect
- Critical Thinking Activity
- Studying the Mind Video Podcasts
- Video Exercises
- Animations
- **ZAPS** Psychology Labs

Thinking

Phoebe Ellsworth was facing a difficult decision. As a young professor at Yale University, she had received a tempting job offer from the University of Michigan. Should she stay or should she go?

Following the advice of many experts in decision making, she took two large sheets of paper—one for each university—and listed their positives and negatives, assigned numbers to each item according to how important it was to her, and then added up those numbers. But, with the numbers neatly summed, Ellsworth discovered she wasn't content with the result. "It's not coming out right!" she exclaimed to fellow psychologist Robert Zajonc.

In the end, she went with her gut and made her decision based primarily on her feelings about the choice and not on her calculations. The decision has worked out well for her, and, three decades later, she's a distinguished professor of law and psychology at Michigan—where she studies, among many things, how emotions sway people's decisions about such crucial matters as murder trials. Meanwhile, Zajonc continued to research the interplay between feeling and thinking, and ended up arguing that cases like Ellsworth's are relatively common, so that, ironically, people rarely use only their minds to "make up their minds."

Zajonc's claim suggests that people are less "rational" than we believe we are—even when we're trying to be thoughtful and careful, and even when we're thinking about highly consequential issues. And, in fact, many other lines of evidence—and many other psychologists—raise their own questions about human rationality. For example, studies suggest that we tend to pay special attention to information that confirms our hunches and hopes and ignore (or overrule) evidence that might challenge our beliefs. We flip-flop in our preferences—even when making important decisions—influenced by trivial changes in how our options are described. We rely on reasoning "shortcuts," even when drawing life-altering conclusions, apparently making our conclusions using strategies that are efficient but prone to error. And we're easily persuaded by "man who" stories—"What do you mean cigarettes cause lung cancer? I know a man who smokes two packs a day, and he's perfectly healthy"—even though, with a moment's reflection, we see the illogic in this.

What should we make of these findings? Is it possible that humans—even smart, well-educated humans, doing their best to think carefully and well—are, in truth, often irrational? And if so, what does this imply about us? Are our heads filled with false beliefs—about ourselves, our friends, and our world? Will we make decisions that fail to bring us happiness? We'll tackle all these questions in this chapter, asking *how* people think, and also *how well*. We'll focus first on the *content* of thought and the ways that different types of ideas are represented in the mind. We'll then turn to the *processes* of thought, with our main focus on what psychologists call *directed thinking*—the mental activities we use to achieve goals. Specifically, we'll look at the processes used in interpreting information, judging the truth of an assertion, solving problems, and weighing the costs and benefits of a decision.

MENTAL REPRESENTATIONS

Common sense tells us that we're able to think about objects or events not currently in view. Thus, you can decide whether you want the chocolate ice cream or the strawberry before either is delivered. Likewise, you can draw conclusions about George by remembering how he acted at the party, even though the party was two weeks ago and a hundred miles away. In these (and many other cases), our thoughts must involve **mental representations**—contents in the mind that stand for some object or event or state of affairs, allowing us to think about those objects or events even in their absence.

Mental representations can also stand for objects or events that exist *only* in our minds—including fantasy objects, like *unicorns* or *Hogwarts School*, or impossible objects, like *the precise value of pi*. And even when we're thinking about objects in plain view, mental representations still have a role to play. If you're thinking about this page, for example, you might represent it for yourself in many ways: "a page from the Thinking chapter," or "a piece of paper," or "something colored white," and so on. These different ideas all refer to the same physical object—but it's the ideas (the mental representations), not the physical object, that matter for thought. (Imagine, for example, that you were hunting for something to start a fire with; for that, it might be helpful to think of this page as a piece of paper rather than a carrier of information.)

Mental representations of all sorts provide the content for our thoughts. Said differently, what we call "thinking" is just the set of operations we apply to our mental representations—analyzing them, contemplating them, and comparing them in order to draw conclusions, solve problems, and more. However, the nature of the operations applied to our mental operations varies—in part because mental representations come in different forms, and each form requires its own type of operations.

mental representations Contents in the mind that stand for some object, event, or state of affairs.

Distinguishing Images and Symbols

Some of our mental representations are **analogical**—they capture some of the actual characteristics of (and so are analogous to) what they represent. Analogical representations usually take the form of **mental images.** In contrast, other representations are **symbolic** and don't in any way resemble the item they stand for.

To illustrate the difference between images and symbols, consider a drawing of a cat (Figure 9.1). The picture consists of marks on paper, but the actual cat is flesh and blood. Clearly, therefore, the picture is not equivalent to a cat; it's merely a representation of one. Even so, the picture has many similarities to the creature it represents, so that, in general, the picture looks in some ways like a cat: The cat's eyes are side by side in reality, and they're side by side in the picture; the cat's ears and tail are at opposite ends of the creature, and they're at opposite ends in the picture. It's properties like these that make the picture a type of analogical representation.

In contrast, consider the word *cat.* Unlike a picture, the word in no way resembles the cat. The letter *c* doesn't represent the left-hand edge of the cat, nor does the overall shape of the word in any way indicate the shape of this feline. The word, therefore, is an entirely abstract representation, and the relation between the three letters *c-a-t* and the animal they represent is essentially arbitrary.

For some thoughts, mental images seem crucial. (Try thinking about a particular shade of blue, or try to recall whether a horse's ears are rounded at the top or slightly pointed. The odds are good that these thoughts will call mental images to mind.) For other thoughts, you probably need a symbolic representation. (Think about the causes of global warming; this thought may call images to mind—perhaps smoke pouring out of a car's exhaust pipes—but it's likely that your thought specifies relationships and issues not captured in the images at all.)

For still other thoughts, it's largely up to you how to represent the thought, and the form of representation is often consequential. If you form a mental image of a cat, for example, you may be reminded of other animals that look like the cat—and so you may find yourself thinking about lions or tigers. If you think about cats without a mental image, this may call a different set of ideas to mind—perhaps thoughts about other types of pet. In this way, the type of representation can shape the flow of your thoughts—and thus can influence your judgments, your decisions, and more.

Mental Images

People often refer to their mental images as "mental pictures" and comment that they inspect these "pictures" with the "mind's eye." In fact, references to a mind's eye have been part of our language at least since the days of Shakespeare, who used the phrase in Act 1 of *Hamlet.* But, of course, there is no (literal) mind's eye—no tiny eye somewhere inside the brain. Likewise, mental pictures cannot be actual pictures: With no eye deep inside the brain, who or what would inspect such pictures?

Why, then, do people describe their images as mental pictures? This usage presumably reflects the fact that images resemble pictures in some ways, but that simply invites the next question: What is this resemblance? A key part of the answer involves spatial layout. In a classic study, research participants were first shown the map of a fictitious island containing various objects: a hut, a well, a tree, and so on (Kosslyn, Ball, & Reisser, 1978; Figure 9.2). After memorizing this map, the participants were asked to

analogical representation An idea that shares some of the actual characteristics of the object it represents.

mental images Mental representations that resemble the objects they represent by directly reflecting the perceptual qualities of the thing represented.

symbolic representation A mental representation that stands for some content without sharing any characteristics with the thing it represents.

(A) Analogical representation

(B) Symbolic representation

cat

9.1 Analogical vs. symbolic representations (A) Analogical representations have certain things in common with the thing they represent. Thus, the left side of the drawing shows the left side of the cat; the right side of the drawing shows the cat's right side. (B) There's no such correspondence for a symbolic representation: The letter *c* doesn't indicate the left side of the cat!

Method

1. Participants were shown a map of a fictitious island containing various landmarks.

2. After memorizing this map the participants were asked to form a mental image of the island.

3. Participants were timed while they imagined a black speck zipping from one landmark on the island to another. When the speck "reached" the target, the participant pressed a button, stopping a clock.

Results

The time needed for the speck to "travel" between two points on the mental image was proportional to the distance between those points on the map.

CONCLUSION: Mental images accurately represent the spatial relationships inside a scene.

SOURCE STUDY: Kosslyn, Ball, & Reisser, 1978

form a mental image of the island. The experimenters then named two objects on the map (e.g., the hut and the tree), and participants had to imagine a black speck zipping from the first location to the second; when the speck "reached" the target, the participant pressed a button, stopping a clock. Then the experimenters did the same for another pair of objects—say the tree and the well—and so on for all the various pairs of objects on the island.

The results showed that the time needed for the speck to "travel" across the image was directly proportional to the distance between the two points on the original map. Thus, participants needed little time to scan from the pond to the tree; scanning from the pond to the hut (roughly four times the distance) took roughly four times as long; scanning from the hut to the patch of grass took even longer. Apparently, then, the image accurately depicted the map's geometric arrangement: Points close together on the map were somehow close to each other in the image; points farther apart on the map were more distant in the image. In this way, the image is unmistakably picture-like, even if it's not literally a picture.

Related evidence indicates enormous overlap between the brain areas crucial for creating and examining mental images and the brain areas crucial for visual perception. Specifically, neuroimaging studies show that many of the same brain structures (primarily in the occipital lobe) are active during both visual perception and visual imagery (Figure 9.3). In fact, the parallels between these two activities are quite precise: When people imagine movement patterns, high levels of activation are observed in brain areas that are sensitive to motion in ordinary perception. Likewise, for very detailed images, the brain areas that are especially activated tend to be those crucial for perceiving fine detail in a stimulus (Behrmann, 2000; Thompson & Kosslyn, 2000).

(A) Brain activity while viewing simple pictures

(B) Brain activity while thinking of mental pictures

9.3 Brain activity during mental imagery These fMRI images show different "slices" through the living brain, revealing levels of activity in different brain sites. More active regions are shown in yellow, orange, and red. (A) The first row shows brain activity while a person is making judgments about simple pictures. (B) The second row shows brain activity while the person is making the same sorts of judgments about "mental pictures," visualized before the "mind's eye."

Further evidence comes from studies using transcranial magnetic stimulation (TMS; see Chapter 3). Using this technique, researchers have produced temporary disruptions in the visual cortex of healthy volunteers—and, as expected, this causes problems in seeing. What's important here is that this procedure also causes parallel problems in visual imagery—consistent with the idea that this brain region is crucial both for the processing of visual inputs and for the creation and inspection of images (Kosslyn, Pascual-Leone, Felician, Camposano, Keenan et al., 1999).

All of these results powerfully confirm that visual images are indeed picture-like; and they lend credence to the often-heard report that people can "think in pictures." Be aware, though, that visual images are *picture-like*, but not pictures. In one study, participants were shown the drawing in Figure 9.4 and asked to memorize it (Chambers & Reisberg, 1985; also Reisberg & Heuer, 2005). The figure was then removed, and participants were asked to form a mental image of this now absent figure and to describe their image. Some participants reported that they could vividly see a duck facing to the left; others reported seeing a rabbit facing to the right. The participants were then told there was another way to perceive the figure and asked if they could reinterpret the image, just as they had reinterpreted a series of practice figures a few moments earlier. Given this task, not one of the participants was able to reinterpret the form. Even with hints and considerable coaxing, none were able to find a duck in a "rabbit image" or a rabbit in a "duck image." The participants were then given a piece of paper and asked to draw the figure they had just been imagining; every participant was now able to come up with the perceptual alternative.

These findings make it clear that a visual image is different from a picture. The *picture* of the duck/rabbit is easily reinterpreted; the corresponding *image* is not. This is because the image is already organized and interpreted to some extent (e.g., facing "to the left" or "to the right"), and this interpretation shapes what the imaged form seems to resemble and what the imaged form will call to mind.

9.4 Images are not pictures The duck/rabbit figure, first used in 1900 by Joseph Jastrow. The *picture* of this form is easily reinterpreted; the corresponding *mental image*, however, is not.

proposition A statement relating a subject and a claim about that subject.

node In network-based models of mental representation, a "meeting place" for the various connections associated with a particular topic.

associative links In network-based models of mental representation, connections between the symbols (or nodes) in the network.

spreading activation The process through which activity in one node in a network flows outward to other nodes through associative links.

9.5 Associative connections Many investigators propose that our knowledge is represented through a network of associated ideas, so that the idea of "Abe Lincoln" is linked to "Civil War" and "President."

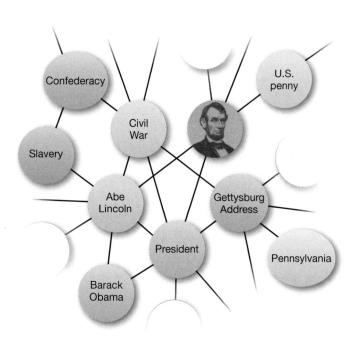

Propositions

As we've seen, mental images—and analogical representations in general—are essential for representing some types of information. Other information, in contrast, requires a symbolic representation. This type of mental representation is more flexible because symbols can represent any content we choose, thanks to the fact that it's entirely up to us what each symbol stands for. Thus, we can use the word *mole* to stand for an animal that digs in the ground, or we could use the word (as Spanish speakers do) to refer to a type of sauce used in cooking. Likewise, we can use the word *cat* to refer to your pet, Snowflake; but, if we wished, we could instead use the Romanian word *pisică* as the symbol representing your pet, or we could use the arbitrary designation X2ϕ. (Of course, for communicating with others, it's important that we use the same terms they do. This is not an issue, however, when we're representing thoughts in our own minds.)

Crucially, symbols can also be combined with each other to represent more complex contents—such as "San Diego is in California," or "cigarette smoking is bad for your health." There is debate about the exact nature of these combinations, but many scholars propose that symbols can be assembled into **propositions**—statements that relate a subject (the item about which the statement is being made) and a predicate (what's being asserted about the subject). For example, "Solomon loves to blow glass," "Jacob lived in Poland," and "Squirrels eat burritos" are all propositions (although the first two are true, and the last is false). But just the word *Susan* or the phrase "is squeamish" aren't propositions—the first is a subject without a predicate; the second is a predicate without a subject. (For more on how propositions are structured and the role they play in our thoughts, see J. Anderson, 1993, 1996.)

It's easy to express propositions as sentences, but this is just a convenience; many other formats are possible. In the mind, propositions are probably expressed via network structures, related to the network models we discussed for perception in Chapter 5. Individual symbols serve as **nodes** within the network—meeting places for various links—so if we were to draw a picture of the network, the nodes would look like knots in a fisherman's net, and this is the origin of the term *node* (derived from the Latin *nodus*, meaning "knot"). The individual nodes are connected to each other by **associative links** (Figure 9.5). Thus, in this system there might be a node representing *Abe Lincoln* and another node representing *President*, and the link between them represents part of our knowledge about Lincoln—namely, that he was a president. Other links have labels on them, as shown in Figure 9.6; these labels allow us to specify other relationships among nodes, and in this way we can use the network to express any proposition at all (after J. Anderson, 1993, 1996).

The various nodes representing a proposition are activated whenever a person is thinking about that proposition. This activation then spreads to neighboring nodes, through the associative links, much as electric current spreads through a network of wires. However, this spread of activation will be weaker (and will occur more slowly) between nodes that are only weakly associated. The **spreading activation** will also dissipate as it spreads outward, so that little or no activation will reach the nodes more distant from the activation's source.

In fact, we can follow the spread of activation directly. In a classic study, participants were presented with two strings of letters, like

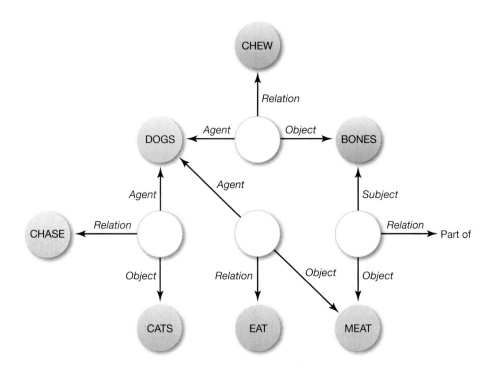

9.6 Propositions One proposal is that your understanding of dogs—what they are, what they're likely to do—is represented by an interconnected network of propositions. In this figure, each proposition is represented by a white circle, which serves as the meeting place for the elements included in the proposition. Thus, this bit of memory network contains the propositions "dogs chew bones," "dogs chase cats," and so on. A complete representation about your knowledge of dogs would include many other propositions as well.

NARDE–DOCTOR, or GARDEN–DOCTOR, or NURSE–DOCTOR (Meyer & Schvaneveldt, 1971). The participants' job was to press a "yes" button if both sequences were real words (as in the second and third examples here), and a "no" button if either was not a word (the first example). Our interest here is only in the two pairs that required a yes response. (In these tasks, the no items serve only as *catch trials*, ensuring that participants really are doing the task as they were instructed.)

Let's consider a trial in which participants see a related pair, like NURSE–DOCTOR. In choosing a response, they first need to confirm that, yes, NURSE is a real word in English. To do this, they presumably need to locate the word NURSE in their mental dictionary; once they find it, they can be sure that these letters do form a legitimate word. What this means, though, is that they will have searched for, and activated, the node in memory that represents this word—and this, we have hypothesized, will trigger a spread of activation outward from the node, bringing activation to other, nearby nodes. These nearby nodes will surely include the node for DOCTOR, since there's a strong association between "nurse" and "doctor." Therefore, once the node for NURSE is activated, some activation should also spread to the node for DOCTOR.

Once they've dealt with NURSE, the participants can turn their attention to the second word in the pair. To make a decision about DOCTOR (is this string a word or not?), the participants must locate the node for this word in memory. If they find the relevant node, then they know that this string, too, is a word and can hit the "yes" button. But of course the process of activating the node for DOCTOR has already begun, thanks to the activation this node just received from the node for NURSE. This should accelerate the process of bringing the DOCTOR node to threshold (since it's already partway there), and so it will take less time to activate. Hence, we expect quicker responses to DOCTOR in this context, compared to a context in which it was preceded by some unrelated word and therefore not primed. This prediction is correct. Participants' lexical decision responses are faster by almost 100 milliseconds if the stimulus words are related, so that the first word can prime the second in the way we just described.

We've described this sequence of events within a relatively uninteresting task—participants merely deciding whether letter strings are words in English or not. But the same dynamic—with one node priming other, nearby nodes—plays a role in, and can shape, the flow of our thoughts. For example, we mentioned in Chapter 6 that the sequence of ideas in a dream is shaped by which nodes are primed. Likewise, in problem solving, we sometimes have to hunt through memory, looking for ideas about how to tackle the problem we're confronting. In this process, we're plainly guided by the pattern of which nodes are activated (and so more available) and which nodes aren't. This pattern of activation in turn depends on how the nodes are connected to each other—and so the arrangement of our knowledge within long-term memory can have a powerful impact on whether we'll locate a problem's solution.

JUDGMENT: DRAWING CONCLUSIONS FROM EXPERIENCE

So far we've been discussing the content of thought, with an emphasis on how thoughts are represented in the mind. Just as important, though, are the processes of thought—what psychologists call **directed thinking**—the ways people draw conclusions or make decisions. What's more, these two broad topics—the contents of thought and the processes—are linked in important ways. As we've discussed, representing ideas with images will highlight visual appearance in our thoughts and thus may call to mind objects with similar appearance. Likewise, representing ideas as propositions will cause activation to spread to other, associated, nodes; and this too can guide our thoughts in one direction rather than another.

But, of course, the flow of our thoughts also depends on what we're trying to accomplish in our thinking. So it will be useful to divide our discussion of thought processes into four sections, each corresponding to a type of goal in our thinking: We will, therefore, consider *judgment, reasoning, decision making,* and *problem solving.* Let's begin with judgment.

The term **judgment** refers to the various steps we use when trying to reach beyond the evidence we've encountered so far, and to draw conclusions from that evidence. Judgment, by its nature, involves some degree of extrapolation because we're going beyond the evidence; and as such, this always involves some risk that the extrapolation will be mistaken. If, for example, we know that Jane has enjoyed many trips to the beach, we might draw the conclusion that she will always enjoy such trips. But there's no guarantee here, and it's surely possible that her view of the beach might change. Likewise, if you have, in the past, preferred spending time with quiet people, you might draw a conclusion about how much you'd enjoy an evening with Sid, who's quite loud. But here, too, there's no guarantee—and perhaps you'll have a great time with Sid.

Even with these risks, we routinely rely on judgment to reach beyond the evidence we've gathered so far—and so we do make forecasts about the next beach trip, whether the evening with Sid would be fun, and more. But how do we proceed in making these judgments? Research suggests that we often rely on a small set of shortcuts called *judgment heuristics.* The word **heuristics,** borrowed from computer science, refers to a strategy that's relatively efficient but occasionally leads to error. Heuristics, in other words, offer a trade-off between efficiency and accuracy, helping us to make judgments more quickly—but at the price of occasional mistakes.

Let's start our discussion with two of these shortcuts—the *availability* and *representativeness heuristics,* first described by Amos Tversky and Daniel Kahneman (Figure 9.7); their research in this domain is

directed thinking Thinking aimed at a particular goal.

judgment The process of extrapolating from evidence to draw conclusions.

heuristics A strategy for making judgments quickly, at the price of occasional mistakes.

9.7 Daniel Kahneman and Amos Tversky Much of what we know about judgment and decision making comes from pioneering work by Daniel Kahneman (A) and Amos Tversky (B); their work led to Kahneman receiving the Nobel Prize in 2002.

(A) (B)

part of the scholarship that led to Kahneman's winning the Nobel Prize in 2002.* As we'll see, these heuristics are effective but often do lead to errors, and so we'll turn next to the question of whether—and in what circumstances—people can rise above the shortcuts, and use more accurate judgment strategies.

The Availability Heuristic

In almost all cases, we want our conclusions to rest not just on one observation, but on *patterns* of observations. Is last-minute cramming an effective way to prepare for exams? Does your car start more easily if you pump the gas while turning the key? Do you get sick less often if you take vitamin tablets? In each case, you could reach a conclusion based on just one experience (one exam, or one flu season), but that's a risky strategy because that experience might have been a fluke of some sort, or in some way atypical. Thus, what you really want is a summary of *multiple* experiences, so that you can draw conclusions only if there's a consistent pattern in the evidence.

Generally, this summary of multiple experiences will require a comparison among *frequency estimates*—assessments of how often you've encountered a particular event or object. How often have you crammed for an exam and done well? How often have you crammed and done poorly? How many people do you know who take vitamins and still get sick? How many stay healthy?

In this way, frequency estimates are central for judgment, but there's an obvious problem here: Most people don't keep ledgers recording the events of their lives, and so they have no objective record of what happened each time they started their car or how many of their friends take vitamins. What do people do, then, when they need frequency estimates? They rely on a simple strategy: They try to think of specific cases relevant to their judgment—exams that went well after cramming, or frustrating mornings when the car just wouldn't start. If these examples come easily to mind, people conclude that the circumstance is a common one; if the examples come to mind slowly or only with great effort, people conclude that the circumstance is rare.

This strategy is referred to as the **availability heuristic,** because the judgment uses *availability* (i.e., how easily the cases come to mind) as the basis for assessing *frequency* (how common the cases actually are in the world). For many frequency estimates this strategy works well, because objects or events that are broadly frequent in the world are likely to be frequent in our personal experience and are therefore well represented in our memories. On this basis, "easily available from memory" is often a good indicator of "frequent in the world."

> **availability heuristic** A strategy for judging how frequently something happens—or how common it is—based on how easily examples of it come to mind.

But there are surely circumstances in which this strategy is misleading. In one study, participants were asked this question: "Considering all the words in the language, does *R* occur more frequently in the first position of the word (*rose, robot, rocket*) or in the third position (*care, strive, tarp*)?" Over two-thirds of the participants said that *R* is more common the first position—but actually the reverse is true, by a wide margin.

What caused this error? Participants made this judgment by trying to think of words in which *R* is the first letter, and these came easily to mind. They next tried to think of words in which it's the third letter, and these came to mind only with some effort. They then interpreted this difference in ease of retrieval (i.e., the difference in availability) as

---

*Amos Tversky died in 1996 and so could not participate in the Nobel Prize, which is never awarded posthumously.

if it reflected a difference in frequency—and so drew the wrong conclusion. As it turns out, the difference in retrieval merely shows that our mental dictionary, roughly like a printed one, is organized according to the starting sound of each word. This arrangement makes it easy to search memory using a word's "starting letter" as the cue; a search based on a word's third letter is more difficult. In this fashion, the organization of memory creates a bias in what's easily available; this bias, in turn, leads to an error in frequency judgment (Tversky & Kahneman, 1973).

In this task, it seems sensible for people to use a shortcut (the heuristic) rather than some more laborious strategy, such as counting through the pages in a dictionary. The latter strategy would guarantee the right answer but would surely be far more work than the problem is worth. In addition, the error in this case is harmless—nothing hinges on these assessments of spelling patterns. The problem, though, is that people rely on the same shortcut—using availability to assess frequency—in cases that are more consequential. For example, many friendships break up because of concerns over fairness: "Why am I always the one who does the dishes?" Or "Why is it that you're usually the one who starts our fights, but I'm always the one who reaches out afterward?" These questions hinge on frequency estimates—and use of the availability heuristic routinely leads to errors in these estimates (M. Ross & Siccoly, 1979). As a result, this judgment heuristic may leave us with a distorted perception of some social relations—in a way that can undermine some friendships!

As a different example, what are the chances that the stock market will go up tomorrow or that a certain psychiatric patient will commit suicide? The stockbrokers and psychiatrists who make these judgments regularly base their decisions on an estimate of probabilities. In the past, has the market generally gone up after a performance like today's? In the past, have patients with these symptoms generally been dangerous to themselves? These estimates, too, are likely to be based on the availability heuristic. Thus, for example, the psychiatrist's judgment may be poor if he vividly remembers a particular patient who repeatedly threatened suicide but never harmed himself. This easily available recollection may bias the psychiatrist's frequency judgment, leading to inadequate precautions in the present case.

The Representativeness Heuristic

When our judgments hinge on frequency estimates, we rely on the availability heuristic. Sometimes, though, our judgments hinge on *categorization*, and then we turn to a different heuristic (Figure 9.8). For example, think about Marie, who you met at lunch yesterday. Is she likely to be a psychology major? If she is, you can rely on your broader knowledge about psych majors to make some forecasts about her—what sorts of conversations she's likely to enjoy, what sorts of books she's likely to read, and so on.

If during lunch you asked Marie what her major is, then you're all set—able to apply your knowledge about the category to this particular individual. But what if you didn't ask her about her major? You might still try to guess her major, relying on the **representativeness heuristic**. This is a strategy of assuming that each member of a category is "representative" of the category—or, said differently, a strategy of assuming that each category is relatively homogeneous, so that every member of the category resembles every other member. Thus, if Marie resembled other psych majors you know (in her style of conversation, or the things she wanted to talk about), you're likely to conclude that she is in fact a psych major—so you can use your knowledge about the major to guide your expectations for her.

This strategy—like the availability heuristic—serves us well in many settings, because many of the categories we encounter in our lives are homogeneous in important ways.

representativeness heuristic A strategy for judging whether an individual, object, or event belongs in a certain category based on how typical of the category it seems to be.

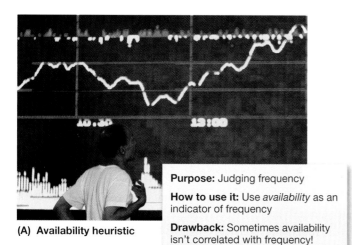

Purpose: Judging frequency

How to use it: Use *availability* as an indicator of frequency

Drawback: Sometimes availability isn't correlated with frequency!

(A) Availability heuristic

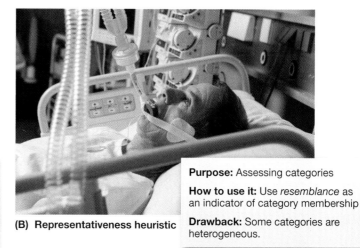

Purpose: Assessing categories

How to use it: Use *resemblance* as an indicator of category membership

Drawback: Some categories are heterogeneous.

(B) Representativeness heuristic

9.8 Heuristics In the availability heuristic, we use *availability* to judge *frequency.* This may be a problem, though, if examples that are in truth relatively rare are nonetheless available to us. Thus, a stockbroker might be misled by an easily accessible memory of an atypical stock! In the representativeness heuristic, we use resemblance to the category ideal as a basis for judging whether a case is in the category or not. But the problem is that some categories are internally diverse and pose the risk that we may be misled by an atypical case—as in the case of a "man who" story ("I know a man who smoked cigarettes and never developed health problems.")

People don't vary much in the number of fingers or ears we have. Birds uniformly share the property of having wings and beaks, and hotel rooms share the property of having beds and bathrooms. This uniformity may seem trivial, but it plays an enormously important role: It allows us to extrapolate from our experiences, so that we know what to expect the next time we see a bird or enter a hotel room.

Even so, evidence suggests that we *overuse* the representativeness strategy, extrapolating from our experiences even when it's clear we should not. This pattern is evident, for example, whenever someone offers a "man who" or "woman who" argument: "What do you mean, cigarettes cause cancer? I have an aunt who smokes cigarettes, and she's perfectly healthy at age 82!" Such arguments are often presented in conversations as well as in more formal settings (political debates, or newspaper editorial pages), presumably relying on the listener's willingness to generalize from a single case. What's more, these arguments seem to be persuasive: The listener (to continue the example) seems to assume that the category of all cigarette smokers is uniform, so that any one member of the category (including the speaker's aunt) can be thought of as representative of the entire group. As a result, the listener draws conclusions about the group based on this single case—even though a moment's reflection might remind us that the case may be atypical, making the conclusions unjustified.

In fact, people are willing to extrapolate from a single case even when they're explicitly warned that the case is an unusual one. In one study, participants watched a videotaped interview with a prison guard. Some participants were told in advance that the guard was quite atypical, explicitly chosen for the interview because he held such extreme views. Others weren't given this warning. Then, at the end of the videotape, participants were asked their own views about the prison system, and their responses showed a clear influence from the interview they had just seen. If the interview had shown a harsh, unsympathetic guard, participants were inclined to believe that, in general, prison guards are severe and inhumane. If the interview showed a compassionate, caring guard, participants reported more positive views of the prison system. Remarkably, though, participants who had been told clearly that the guard was atypical were just as willing to draw conclusions from the video as the participants given no warning. Essentially, participants' reliance on the representativeness heuristic made the warning irrelevant (Hamill, Wilson, & Nisbett, 1980; Kahneman & Tversky, 1972, 1973; Nisbett & Ross, 1980).

Dual-Process Theories

The two shortcuts we've discussed—availability and representativeness—generally work well. Things that are common in the world are likely also to be common in our memory, and so readily available for us; availability in memory is therefore often a good indicator of frequency in the world. Likewise, many of the categories we encounter are relatively homogeneous; a reliance on representativeness, then, often leads us to the correct conclusions.

At the same time, these shortcuts can (and sometimes do) lead to errors. What's worse, we can easily document the errors in consequential domains—medical professionals drawing conclusions about someone's health, politicians making judgments about international relations, business leaders making judgments about large sums of money. This demands that we ask: Is the use of the shortcuts inevitable? Are we simply stuck with this risk of error in human judgment?

The answer to these questions is plainly no, because people often rise above these shortcuts and rely on other, more laborious—but often more accurate—judgment strategies. For example, how many U.S. presidents have been Jewish? Here, you're unlikely to draw on the availability heuristic (trying to think of relevant cases and basing your answer on how easily these cases come to mind). Instead you'll swiftly answer, "zero"—based probably on a bit of reasoning. (Your reasoning might be: "If there had been a Jewish president, this would have been notable and often discussed, and so I'd probably remember it. I don't remember it. Therefore . . .")

Likewise, we don't always use the representativeness heuristic—and so we're often *not* persuaded by a man-who story. Imagine, for example, that a friend says, "What do you mean there's no system for winning the lottery? I know a man who tried out his system last week, and he won!" Surely you'd respond by saying this guy just got lucky—relying on your knowledge about games of chance to overrule the evidence seemingly provided by this single case.

Examples like these (and more formal demonstrations of the same points—e.g., Nisbett et al., 1983) make it clear that sometimes we rely on judgment heuristics and sometimes we don't. Apparently, therefore, we need a **dual-process theory** of judgment—one that describes two different types of thinking. The heuristics are, of course, one type of thinking; they allow us to make fast, efficient judgments in a wide range of circumstances. The other type of thinking is usually slower and takes more effort—but it's also less risky and often avoids the errors encouraged by heuristic use. A number of different terms have been proposed for these two types of thinking—intuition versus reasoning (Kahneman, 2003; Kahneman & Tversky, 1996); association-driven thought versus rule-driven thought (Sloman, 1996); a peripheral route to conclusions versus a central route (Petty & Cacioppo, 1985); intuition versus deliberation (Kuo et al., 2009), and so on. Each of these terms carries its own suggestion about how these two types of thought should be conceptualized, and theorists still disagree about this conceptualization. Therefore, many prefer the more neutral (but less transparent!) terms proposed by Stanovich and West (2000), who use **System 1** as the label for the fast, automatic type of thinking and **System 2** as the label for the slower, more effortful type (Figure 9.9).

dual-process theory The proposal that judgment involves two types of thinking: a fast, efficient, but sometimes faulty set of strategies, and a slower, more laborious, but less risky set of strategies.

System 1 In dual-process models of judgment, the fast, efficient, but sometimes faulty type of thinking.

System 2 In dual-process models of judgment, the slower, more effortful, and more accurate type of reasoning.

We might hope that people use System 1 for unimportant judgments and shift to System 2 when the stakes are higher. This would be a desirable state of affairs; but it doesn't seem to be the case because, as we've mentioned, it's easy to find situations in which people rely on System 1's shortcuts even when making consequential judgments.

What does govern the choice between these two types of thinking? The answer has several parts. First, people are—not surprisingly—more likely to rely on the fast and easy strategies of System 1 if they're tired or pressed for time (e.g., Finucane, Alhakami, Slovic, & Johnson, 2000; D. Gilbert, 1989; Stanovich & West, 1998). Second, they're much more likely to use System 2's better quality of thinking if the problem contains certain "triggers." For example, people are more likely to rely on System 1 if asked to think about *probabilities* ("If you have this surgery, there's a .2 chance of side effects"), but they're more likely to rely on System 2 when thinking about *frequencies* ("Two out of 10 people who have this surgery experience side effects"). There's some controversy about why this shift in data format has this effect, but it's clear that we can improve human judgment simply by presenting the facts in the "right way"—that is, in a format more likely to prompt System 2 thinking (Gigerenzer & Hoffrage, 1995, 1999; C. Lewis & Keren, 1999; Mellers et al., 2001; Mellers & McGraw, 1999).

The use of System 2 also depends on the type of evidence being considered. If, for example, the evidence is easily quantified in some way, this encourages System 2 thinking and makes errors less likely. As one illustration, people tend to be relatively sophisticated in how they think about sporting events. In such cases, each player's performance is easily assessed via the game's score or a race's outcome, and each contest is immediately understood as a "sample" that may or may not be a good indicator of a player's (or team's) overall quality. In contrast, people are less sophisticated in how they think about a job candidate's performance in an interview. Here it's less obvious how to evaluate the candidate's performance: How should we measure the candidate's friendliness, or her motivation? People also seem not to realize that the 10 minutes of interview can be thought of as just a "sample" of evidence, and that other impressions might come from other samples (e.g., reinterviewing the person on a different day or seeing the person in a different setting; after J. Holland, Holyoak, Nisbett, & Thagard, 1986; Kunda & Nisbett, 1986).

Finally, some forms of education make System 2 thinking more likely. For example, training in the elementary principles of statistics seems to make students more alert to the problems of drawing a conclusion from a small sample and also more alert to the possibility of bias within a sample. This is, of course, a powerful argument for educational programs that will ensure some basic numeracy—that is, competence in thinking about numbers. But it's not just courses in mathematics that are useful, because the benefits of training can also be derived from courses—such as those in psychology—that provide numerous examples of how sample size and sample bias affect any attempt to draw conclusions from evidence (Fong & Nisbett, 1991; Gigerenzer, Gaissmaier, Kurz-Milcke, Schwartz, & Woloshin, 2007; Lehman, Lempert, & Nisbett, 1988; Lehman & Nisbett, 1990; also see Perkins & Grotzer, 1997).

In short, then, our theorizing about judgment will need several parts. We rely on System 1 shortcuts, and these often serve us well—but can lead to error. We also can rise

(A) Brain areas activated by careful deliberation

(B) Brain areas activated by more intuitive thinking

9.9 Dual-process systems In this study, participants were asked to play either a game that required careful deliberation (System 2), or one that required only rough intuitions (System 1). The thought processes involved in these two games involved clearly different patterns of brain activation.

above the shortcuts and use System 2 thinking instead, and multiple factors govern whether (and when) this happens. Even so, the overall pattern of evidence points toward a relatively optimistic view—that our judgment is often accurate, and that it's possible to make it more so.

REASONING: DRAWING IMPLICATIONS FROM OUR BELIEFS

The processes involved in *judgment* are crucial for us because they allow us to draw new information from our prior experiences. No less important are the processes of **reasoning**, in which we start with certain beliefs and try to draw out the implications of these beliefs: "If I believe X, what other claims follow from this?" The processes in place here resemble the processes that philosophers call *deduction*—when someone seeks to derive new assertions from assertions already in place.

Why is reasoning (or deduction) so important? One reason is that this process allows you to use your knowledge in new ways. For example, you might know that engineers need to be comfortable with math, and you might know that Debby is an engineer. With a trivial bit of reasoning, you now know something about Debby— namely, that she's comfortable with math. Likewise, you might know that if it's raining, then today's picnic will be canceled. If you also know that it's now raining, some quick reasoning tells you that the picnic is off.

These are, of course, simple examples; even so, without the capacity for reasoning, these examples would be incomprehensible for you—making it clear just how important reasoning is. In addition, reasoning serves another function: It provides a means of *testing* your beliefs. Let's say, as an illustration, that you suspect that Alex likes you, but you're not sure. To check on your suspicion, you might try the following deduction: If he does like you, then he'll enthusiastically say yes when you ask him out. This provides an obvious way to confirm (or disconfirm) your suspicion.

In several ways, then, the skill of reasoning is quite important. We need to ask, therefore, how well humans do in reasoning. Do we reach sensible, justified conclusions? The answers parallel our comments about judgment: Examples of high-quality reasoning are easy to find, and so are examples of reasoning errors. We'll therefore need to explain both of these observations.

Confirmation Bias

One line of research on reasoning concerns a pattern known as **confirmation bias**. This term applies to several different phenomena but, in general, describes a tendency to take evidence that's consistent with our beliefs more seriously than evidence inconsistent with our beliefs. Thus, when they're trying to test a belief, people often tend to seek out information that would *confirm* the belief rather than information that might challenge the belief. Likewise, if we give people evidence that's consistent with their beliefs, they tend to take this evidence at face value and count it as persuasive— and so they strengthen their commitment to their beliefs. But if we give people evidence that's contrary to their beliefs, they often greet it with skepticism, look for flaws, or ignore it altogether (Figure 9.10).

This pattern is evident in many procedures. In one classic study, participants were presented with a *balanced* package of evidence concerned with whether capital punish-

reasoning The process of figuring out the implications of particular beliefs.

confirmation bias The tendency to take evidence that's consistent with your beliefs more seriously than evidence inconsistent with your beliefs.

syllogism A logic problem containing two premises and a conclusion; the syllogism is *valid* if the conclusion follows logically from the premises.

ment acts as a deterrent to crime. Half of the evidence favored the participant's view, and half challenged that view (C. Lord, Ross, & Lepper, 1979). We might hope that this balanced presentation would remind people that there's evidence on both sides of this issue, and thus reason to take the opposing viewpoint seriously. This reminder in turn should pull people away from extreme positions and toward a more moderate stance. Thanks to confirmation bias, however, the actual outcome was different. The participants found the evidence consistent with their view to be persuasive and the opposing evidence to be flimsy. Of course, this disparity in the evidence was created by the participants' (biased) interpretation of the facts, and participants with a different starting position perceived the opposite disparity! Even so, participants were impressed by what they perceived as the uneven quality of the evidence, and this led them to shift to views even more extreme than those they'd had at the start.

Notice the circularity here. Because of their initial bias, participants perceived an asymmetry in the evidence—the evidence offered on one side seemed persuasive; the evidence on the other side seemed weak. The participants then used that asymmetry, *created* by their bias, to reinforce and strengthen that same bias.

Confirmation bias can also be documented outside the laboratory. Many compulsive gamblers, for example, believe they have a "winning strategy" that will bring them great wealth. Their empty wallets provide powerful evidence against this belief, but they stick with it anyway. How is this possible? In this case, confirmation bias takes the form of influencing how the gamblers think about their past wagers. Of course, they focus on their wins, using those instances to bolster the belief that they have a surefire strategy. What about their past losses? They also consider these, but usually not as losses. Instead, they regard their failed bets as "near wins" ("The team I bet on would have won if not for the ref's bad call!") or as chance events ("It was just bad luck that I got a deuce of clubs instead of an ace."). In this way, confirming evidence is taken at face value, but disconfirming evidence is reinterpreted, leaving the gamblers' erroneous beliefs intact (Gilovich, 1991; for other examples of confirmation bias, see Schulz-Hardt, Frey, Lüthgens, & Moscovici, 2000; Tweney, Doherty, & Mynatt, 1981; Wason, 1960, 1968).

9.10 Confirmation bias In the Salem witch trials, the investigators believed the evidence that fit with their accusations and discounted (or reinterpreted) the evidence that challenged the accusation. Here we see Daniel Day-Lewis as John Proctor in a 1996 film version of *The Crucible*, Arthur Miller's play about the witch trials.

Faulty Logic

When people fall prey to confirmation bias, their thinking seems illogical: "If I know how to pick winners, then I should win my bets. In fact, though, I lose my bets. Therefore, I know how to pick winners." But could this be? Are people really this illogical in their reasoning? One way to find out is by asking people to solve simple problems in logic—for example, problems involving **syllogisms.**

A syllogism contains two premises and a conclusion, and the question is whether the conclusion follows logically from the premises; if it does follow, we say that the conclusion is *valid.* Figure 9.11 offers several examples; and let's be clear that in these (or any) syllogisms, the validity of the conclusion depends only on the premises. It doesn't matter if the conclusion is plausible or not, in light of other things you know about the world. It also doesn't matter if the premises happen to be true or not. All that matters is the relationship between the premises and the conclusion—and, in particular, whether the conclusion must be true if the premises are true.

Syllogisms seem straightforward, and so it's disheartening that people make an enormous number of errors in evaluating them. To be sure, some syllogisms are easier than others—and so participants are more accurate, for example, if a syllogism is set in

> All artwork is made of wood.
> All wooden things can be turned into clocks.
>
> Therefore all artwork can be turned into clocks.

> All artwork is valuable.
> All valuable things should be cherished.
>
> Therefore all artwork should be cherished.

> All A's are not B's.
> All A's are G's.
>
> Therefore some G's are not B's.

9.11 Categorical syllogisms All of the syllogisms shown here are valid—that is, if the two premises are true, then the conclusion must be true.

9.12 Deductive reasoning?

concrete terms rather than abstract symbols. Still, across all the syllogisms, mistakes are frequent, and error rates are sometimes as high as 70 or 80% (Gilhooly, 1988).

What produces this high error rate? Despite careful instructions and considerable coaching, many participants seem not to understand what syllogistic reasoning requires. Specifically, they seem not to get the fact that they're supposed to focus only on the relationship between the premises and conclusion. They focus instead on whether the conclusion seems plausible on its own—and if it is, they judge the syllogism to be valid (Klauer, Musch, & Naumer, 2000). Thus, they're more likely to endorse the conclusion "Therefore all artwork should be cherished" in Figure 9.11 than they are to endorse the conclusion "Therefore all artwork can be turned into clocks." Both of these conclusions are warranted by their premises, but the first is plausible and so more likely to be accepted as valid.

In some ways, this reliance on plausibility is a sensible strategy. Participants are doing their best to assess the syllogisms' conclusions based on all they know (cf. Evans & Feeney, 2004). At the same time, this strategy implies a profound misunderstanding of the rules of logic (Figure 9.12). With this strategy, people are willing to endorse a bad argument if it happens to lead to conclusions they already believe are true, and they're willing to reject a good argument if it leads to conclusions they already believe are false.

Triggers for Good Reasoning

We are moving toward an unflattering portrait of human reasoning. In logic, one starts with the premises and asks whether a conclusion follows from these premises. In studies of confirmation bias or syllogistic reasoning, however, people seem to do the opposite: They start with the conclusion, and use that as a basis for evaluating the argument. Thus, they accept syllogisms as valid if the conclusion seems believable on its own, and they count evidence as persuasive if it leads to a view they held in the first place.

We also know, however, that humans are capable of high-quality reasoning. After all, we do seem able to manage the pragmatic and social demands of our world, and we're able to make good use of our knowledge. None of this would be possible if we were utterly inept in reasoning; reasoning errors, if they occurred all the time, would trip us up in many ways and lead to a succession of beliefs completely out of line with reality.

In addition, impressive skill in reasoning is visible in some formal settings. Humans do, after all, sometimes lay out carefully argued positions on political matters and academic questions. Scientists trace through the implications of their theories as they develop new cancer-fighting drugs. And for that matter, mathematicians and logicians rely on deduction as a way of proving their theorems.

How should we think about this mixed pattern? Why is our reasoning sometimes accurate and sometimes filled with errors? Important insights into these questions come from studies of the *selection task*. In the standard version of this task, participants are shown four cards, like those in Figure 9.13. They're told that these cards may or may not follow a simple rule: "If there is a vowel on one side of the card, there must be an even number on the other side." Their task is to figure out which cards to turn over to determine whether the cards do, in fact, follow this rule; they can turn over however many cards they think are necessary—just one, perhaps; or two, three, or all four.

In this task, roughly half the participants make the mistake of turning over the "A" and the "6" cards. Another 33% make the mistake of turning over just the "A" card.

Which card(s) must be turned over to check this rule?

"If a card has a vowel on one side, it must have an even number on the other side."

9.13 The selection task The correct answer, offered by very few participants, is to turn over the A and the 7. If the A (a vowel) has an odd number on the reverse side, this would break the rule. If the 7 has a vowel on the reverse side, this too would break the rule. No matter what's on the other side of the 6, a vowel or consonant, this would be consistent with the rule. (After all, the rule didn't say that only vowels have even numbers on the reverse side.) Likewise, no matter what's on the reverse side of the J, this would be consistent with the rule.

Only 4% of the participants correctly select the "A" and the "7" cards; said differently, fully 96% of the participants get this problem wrong (Wason, 1966, 1968).

Performance is much better, though, in other versions of the selection task. In one study, participants were shown the four cards pictured in Figure 9.14 and were told that each card identified the age of a customer at a bar and what that customer was drinking. Their task was to evaluate this rule: "If a person is drinking beer, then the person must be over 19 years of age." This problem is logically identical to the original selection task, but performance was vastly better—three-fourths of the participants correctly chose the cards "drinking a beer" and "16 years old" (Griggs & Cox, 1982).

The contrast between this task and the standard version of the selection task makes it clear that the content of the problem matters—and so *how well* we reason depends on *what we are reasoning about.* But why is this? One proposal comes from an evolutionary perspective on psychology and begins with the suggestion that our ancient ancestors didn't have to reason about abstract matters like *A*s and *7*s, or vowels and even numbers. Instead, our ancestors had to worry about issues involving social interactions, including issues of betrayal and cheating: "I asked you to gather firewood; have you done it, or have you betrayed me?" "None of our clan is supposed to eat more than one share of meat; is that guy perhaps cheating and eating too much?"

Leda Cosmides and John Tooby have argued that if our ancestors needed to reason about these issues, then individuals who were particularly skilled in this reasoning would have had a survival advantage; and so, little by little, they would have become more numerous within the population, while those without the skill would have died off. In the end, only those skillful at social reasoning would have been left—and we, as their descendants, inherited their skills. This is why, according to Cosmides and Tooby, we perform badly with problems like the "classic" selection task (for which we're evolutionarily unprepared) but perform well with the drinking-beer problem, since it involves a specific content—cheating—for which we are well prepared (Cosmides, 1989; Cosmides & Tooby, 1992, 2005; Cummins & Allen, 1998; Gigerenzer & Hug, 1992).

A different approach emphasizes learning across the life span of the individual, rather than learning across the history of our species. Specifically, Patricia Cheng and Keith Holyoak have argued that, in our everyday lives, we often need to reason about down-to-earth issues that can be cast as "if-then" relationships. One example involves *permission,* in which we must act according to this rule: "If I want to do X, then I better get permission." Other examples include *obligation* and *cause-effect* relationships: "If I buy him lunch, then he'll probably lend me his iPod." Because of this experience, we've developed reasoning strategies that apply specifically to these pragmatic issues. In the laboratory, therefore, we'll reason well if an experimenter gives us a task that triggers one of these strategies—but not otherwise. Thus, for example, the drinking-beer problem involves permission, so it calls up our well-practiced skills in thinking about permission. The same logic problem cast in terms of vowels and even numbers has no obvious connection to everyday reasoning, so it calls up no strategy and leads to poor performance (Cheng & Holyoak, 1986; Cheng, Holyoak, Nisbett, & Oliver, 1985; for a different perspective on the selection task, see Ahn & Graham, 1999).

The available evidence doesn't favor one of these accounts over the other, mostly because the two proposals have a great deal in common. Both proposals, one cast in the light of evolution, one in the light of everyday experience, emphasize that the *content* of a problem influences our reasoning—and so, as we said earlier, how we reason depends

Which card(s) must be turned over to check this rule?

*"If the person is drinking beer,
then the person must be over 19 years of age"*

9.14 Variant of the selection task This task is formally identical to the standard selection task, but turns out to be much easier.

on the mental representations we're reasoning about. Likewise, both proposals emphasize pragmatic considerations—the need to reason well about cheaters and betrayal, in one view, or the need to reason about permission or obligation, in the other. Above all, both proposals emphasize the uneven quality of human reasoning. If we encounter a problem of the "right sort," our reasoning is usually accurate. (We note, though, that even with the drinking-beer problem, some people do make errors!) If, however, we encounter a problem that doesn't trigger one of our specialized reasoning strategies, then performance is—as we've seen—often poor.

Judgment and Reasoning: An Overview

There are both parallels and contrasts between judgment and reasoning. In both domains, we find uneven performance—sometimes people are capable of wonderfully high-quality thinking, and sometimes they make outrageous errors in their judging or reasoning. We also find, in both judgment and reasoning, that various factors or cues within a problem can trigger better quality thinking (System 2)—so that the way someone thinks depends heavily on what they're thinking about. Thus, when thinking about a Sunday football game, people are alert to the role of chance and wary of drawing conclusions from a single game. The same people, in thinking about a job interview, might not realize the sample of information is small and so might overinterpret the evidence. Likewise, people's performance in the selection task is fine if the problem contains cues suggesting a possibility of cheating or a need for permission; the same people perform miserably without these cues.

Judgment and reasoning differ, though, in how they proceed in the absence of these triggers. In making judgments, we often rely on System 1 thinking—a set of strategies that generally lead us to sensible conclusions and that are quick and efficient. But there's no obvious parallel to these strategies in many reasoning tasks—for example, when we're trying to evaluate an if-then sentence (like the one in the selection task). This situation is reflected in the fact that people don't make *occasional* errors with logic problems—instead, we've mentioned error rates of 80 and 90%! It's fortunate, therefore, that our daily experience unfolds in a context in which the triggers we need, leading us into better quality reasoning, are often in place.

One last parallel between judgment and reasoning is important and quite encouraging: In both domains, training helps. We've mentioned that courses in statistics, and training in the interpretation of data, seem to improve people's judgment—perhaps by making them more sensitive to the need to gather an adequate sample of evidence and by making them more cautious about samples that may be biased. Education also improves people's ability to reason well—and, again, the education seems to help by making people more alert to cues that might trigger decent reasoning—cues that help people to think about issues (for example) of permission or obligation (Lehman & Nisbett, 1990). Thus, we can offer the optimistic conclusion that, with the appropriate training, people can learn to think more carefully and accurately than they ordinarily do.

DECISION MAKING: CHOOSING AMONG OPTIONS

Judgment and reasoning allow us to expand our knowledge in important ways—when, for example, we draw some new conclusion from our experiences, or when we deduce a novel claim from our other beliefs. A third type of thinking, in contrast, is more closely tied to our *actions*. This is the thinking involved in *decision making*.

We make decisions all the time—some trivial (which brand of toilet paper should you buy?) and some deeply important (should you get that surgery, or not?). Some decisions get made over and over (should you go back to that Mexican restaurant one more time?) and some are made just once (should you get a job when you finish school, or seek out some further education?). Researchers have proposed, however, that all of these decisions get made in same way, with the same sort of processes, and so we obviously need to take a close look at what those processes involve.

Framing Effects

Two factors are obviously crucial for any decision, and these factors are central to *utility theory*, a conception of decision making endorsed by many economists. According to this theory, you should, first, always consider the possible outcomes of a decision and choose the most desirable one. Would you rather have $10 or $100? Would you rather work for 2 weeks to earn a paycheck or work for 1 week to earn the same paycheck? In each case, it seems obvious that you should choose the option with the greatest benefit ($100) or the lowest cost (working for just 1 week).

Second, you should consider the risks. Would you rather buy a lottery ticket with 1 chance in 100 of winning, or a lottery ticket—offered at the same price and with the same prize—with just 1 chance in 1,000 of winning? If one of your friends liked a movie and another didn't, would you want to go see it? If five of your friends had seen the movie and all liked it, would you want to see it then? In these cases, you should (and probably would) choose the options that give the greatest likelihood of achieving the things you value (increasing your odds of winning the lottery or seeing a movie you'll enjoy).

It's no surprise, therefore, that our decisions are influenced by both of these factors—the attractiveness of the outcome and the likelihood of achieving that outcome. But our decisions are also influenced by something else that seems trivial and irrelevant—namely, how a question is phrased or how our options are described. In many cases, these changes in the **framing** of a decision can reverse our decisions, turning a strong preference in one direction into an equally strong preference in the opposite direction. Take, for example, the following problem:

> Imagine that the United States is preparing for the outbreak of an unusual disease, which is expected to kill 600 people. Two alternative programs to combat the disease have been proposed. Assume that the exact scientific estimate of the consequences of the two programs is as follows:
>
> - If Program A is adopted, 400 people will die.
> - If Program B is adopted, there's a one-third probability that nobody will die and a two-thirds probability that 600 people will die.
>
> Which of the two programs would you favor?

framing The way a decision is phrased or the way options are described. Seemingly peripheral aspects of the framing can influence decisions by changing the point of reference.

With these alternatives, a clear majority of participants (78%) opted for Program B—presumably in the hope that, in this way, they could avoid any deaths. But now consider what happens when participants are given exactly the same problem but with the options framed differently. In this case, participants were again told that if no action is taken, the disease will kill 600 people. They were then asked to choose between the following options:

- If Program A is adopted, 200 of these people will be saved.
- If Program B is adopted, there's a one-third probability that 600 people will be saved and a two-thirds probability that no people will be saved.

> 1. Assume yourself richer by $300 than you are today. You have to choose between:
>
> A. A sure gain of $100, and
> B. A 50% chance to gain $200 and a 50% chance to gain nothing.

> 2. Assume yourself richer by $500 than you are today. You have to choose between:
>
> A. A sure loss of $100, and
> B. A 50% chance to lose nothing and a 50% chance to lose $200.

9.15 Framing effects The outcomes of these two choices are identical. In both cases, option A leaves you with $400, while option B leaves you with a 50–50 chance of getting either $300 or $500. Even so, 72% of research participants selected option A in choice 1, and 64% selected option B in choice 2. Once again, the way the outcomes were framed reversed the choices the participants made.

loss aversion The strong tendency to regard losses as considerably more important than gains of comparable magnitude—and, with this, a tendency to take steps (including risky steps) to avoid possible loss.

Given this formulation, a clear majority of participants (72%) opted for Program A. To them, the certainty of saving 200 people was clearly preferable to a one-third probability of saving everybody (Tversky & Kahneman, 1981). But of course the options here are identical to the options in the first version of this program—400 dead, out of 600, is equivalent to 200 saved out of 600. The only difference between the problems lies in how the alternatives are phrased, but this shift in framing has an enormous impact (Kahneman & Tversky, 1984). Indeed, with one framing, the vote is almost 4 to 1 in favor of A; with the other framing, the vote is almost 3 to 1 in the opposite direction!

It's important to realize that neither of these framings is "better" than the other—since, after all, the frames both present the same information. Nor is the selection of one of these options the "correct choice," and one can defend either the choice of Program A or the choice of B. What's troubling, though, is the inconsistency in people's choices—their preferences are flip-flopping based on the framing of the problem. It's also troubling that people's choices are so easily manipulated—by a factor that seems irrelevant to the options being considered.

Framing effects are quite widespread and can easily be observed in settings both inside and outside of the laboratory. For example, consider the fact that physicians are more willing to endorse a program of treatment that has a 50% success rate than they are to endorse a program with a 50% failure rate—because they're put off by a frame that emphasizes the negative outcome. Likewise, research participants make one choice in the problem shown in the top half of Figure 9.15 and the opposite choice in the problem shown in the bottom half of the figure—even though the *outcomes* are the same in the two versions of this problem; the only thing that's changed is the framing (Levin & Gaeth, 1988; Mellers, Chang, Birnbaum, & Ordóñez, 1992; also Schwarz, 1999).

In all cases, though, framing effects follow a simple pattern: In general, people try to make choices that will minimize or avoid losses—that is, they show a tendency called **loss aversion.** Thus—returning to our earlier example—if the "disease problem" is framed in terms of losses (people dying), participants are put off by this, and so they reject Program A, the option that makes the loss seem certain. They instead choose the gamble inherent in Program B, presumably in the hope that the gamble will pay off and the loss will be avoided. Loss aversion also leads people to cling tightly to what they already have, to make sure they won't lose it. If, therefore, the disease problem is framed in terms of gains (lives saved), people want to take no chances with this gain and so reject the gamble and choose the sure bet (Program A).

Loss aversion thus explains both halves of the data in the disease problem—a tendency to take risks when considering a potential loss, but an equally strong tendency to *avoid* risk when considering a potential gain. And, again, let's be clear that both of these tendencies are sensible; surely it's a good idea to hold tight to sure gains and avoid sure losses. The problem, though, is that what counts as a loss or gain depends on one's reference point. (Compared to the best possible outcome, everything looks like a loss; compared to the worst outcome, everything looks like a gain.) This is the key to framing effects. By recasting our options, the shift in framing changes our reference point—and the consequence is that people are left open to manipulation by whoever chooses the frame.

Affective Forecasting

Framing effects seem to represent a flaw in human decision making: People can be powerfully influenced by a factor that seems to be irrelevant to their choices. A second possible flaw lies in the fact that we don't know ourselves as well as we need to in order to make good decisions. To explore this issue, let's start with the fact that our decisions almost always involve a prediction about the future. You choose the chocolate ice cream while standing in the grocery store, but this selection rests on the expectation that you'll enjoy the ice cream that evening, or maybe the next day, when you actually eat it. This may be an easy forecast to make; but let's be clear that if you mis-predict tomorrow's preference, your choice today will not serve you well. Likewise, imagine that you're hoping to find a new roommate. You really like Andy's sense of humor, and you also know he'll lend you his car. But you're concerned about the loud, awful music he listens to. Should you take him on as a roommate? Here you'll need to make a prediction about whether the loud music will continue to annoy you in the months to come. If so, then you should choose someone else as your roommate. But if, in contrast, you'll soon grow used to the music and barely notice it, then Andy would be a good choice. And, of course, if your prediction about these points is wrong, you may end up creating real headaches for yourself.

In other cases, your prediction is different because it focuses on your future feelings about your own decision. For example, should you take the job offer from the company in Chicago? It's hard to know how the job will work out, and you don't know much about Chicago. Therefore, predicting your reaction to the job, and a new city, is difficult. Even so, your decision might be shaped by the worry that if you don't take the job, you would regret the idea of never having explored the opportunity. To avoid that regret, off to Chicago you go—a decision guided by your prediction of (and your wish to avoid) a feeling of regret.

In all of these examples, the quality of your decisions depends on the quality of your predictions, and this leads us to ask: How good are people at **affective forecasting**—predicting their own emotional response to upcoming events? In fact, evidence suggests that these forecasts are often inaccurate (e.g., D. Gilbert & Wilson, 2007). In one study, for example, people were asked how sad they would be if their current romance came to an end or how upset they'd be if their favorite sports team lost a big game. In these cases, people were usually accurate about whether their future feelings would be positive or negative—but they quite consistently overestimated how strongly, and for how long, they'd react to these events (D. Gilbert, Pinel, Wilson, Blumberg, & Wheatley, 2002; T. Wilson, Wheatley, Meyers, Gilbert, & Axsom, 2000). In yet other studies, people have been asked to predict how much they would regret a decision if it led to a less positive outcome than they'd hoped. Here, too, people were inaccurate and typically predicted more regret than they actually felt when the disappointment actually arrived (D. Gilbert, Morewedge, Risen, & Wilson, 2004).

affective forecasting Predicting one's own emotional response to upcoming events.

9.16 **Too many options** Modern grocery shops offer us a huge range of options (here dozens of types of canned meat). Consumers prefer having all of these options—but this may be unwise because having too many options makes it more difficult to choose. Worse, with too many options, consumers are actually less likely to be satisfied with whatever choice they make.

Too Many Options

Framing effects and poor affective forecasting are both obstacles to consistent, high-quality decision making. Yet another obstacle comes from a surprising source, because our decisions are sometimes undermined by our simply having too many options to choose from (Figure 9.16).

People like to be in control of their lives. Indeed, evidence suggests that people are healthier and happier when they can make their own choices rather than letting someone else make decisions for them (see Chapter 15). But in order to make choices, we need to have options—otherwise, there are no choices to make! And presumably, if having a few options is a good thing, then having more options is better still—because then we have enormous freedom to choose exactly the option that suits us best.

As a number of studies have made clear, though, this is a setting in which it's possible to have "too much of a good thing." In particular, if people are given too many choices, they're likely to make no selection at all. In one study, visitors to a grocery store encountered a table offering free samples of high-quality jams (Iyengar & Lepper, 2000). In one condition of the experiment, the table offered 6 varieties, and shoppers could taste as many of these as they wished. In another condition, the table offered 24 varieties, and again shoppers could choose the ones they wanted to try. The shoppers plainly showed a preference for having more options to choose from—of the shoppers who passed the 6-varieties table, 40% stopped to examine the display; of the shoppers who passed the 24-varieties table, 60% stopped to look.

Unmistakably, then, people like having lots of choices. However, once they have those choices, they seem put off by the sheer variety of options. Of the (many) shoppers who visited the 24-varieties table, only 3% actually purchased a jar of jam. In sharp contrast, of the shoppers who approached the 6-varieties table, nearly 30% purchased a jar—a 10-to-1 differential!

In addition, when we have too many options or too much flexibility we often end up less satisfied with our selection. In one study, participants were asked to select a photograph that they would keep at the end of the experiment (D. Gilbert & Ebert, 2002). Half of the participants were told that they had to make their final choice right away; the other participants were told that they had to make a selection but could revise this choice later if they wished to. Participants liked having this flexibility, but in fact they didn't benefit from it at all: Participants who had to stick with their initial choice actually ended up, in the long run, more content with their selection than did the participants who had the option of revising their choice.

Several factors contribute to these results, but part of the explanation lies in the impact of making comparisons. We noted earlier (in our discussion of loss aversion) that people are keenly sensitive to losses and do all they can to avoid them. In the same way, people are also very sensitive to an option's *disadvantages,* and so they give these more weight than the advantages (the gains) associated with the same option. Thus, in concrete terms, when people compare one photograph to another, or one jam to another, they pay special attention to the things they don't like about each option (its limitations and drawbacks) and attend less to the aspects they do like. As a result, the comparison ends up highlighting the negative features of each choice—with the result that all the options generally look worse after the comparison (i.e., their drawbacks are now salient) than they did before.

Let's now add the fact that, when you have more options to consider, you'll end up doing more comparisons among the options. Likewise, if you have the flexibility to revise your choice, this too encourages more comparison—because you make your selection, but continue mulling over your options, to make sure you picked the best one. In either case, more comparison translates into even greater salience for each option's disadvantages. Thus, in the jam experiment, the greater variety (leading to more comparisons) makes all the choices look worse—and so you choose none of them. In the photography experiment, the extended comparison makes your selected option look worse—and so the option to revise your choices leaves you less content with the decision's outcome.

In fact, this negative effect of making comparisons can be documented directly. In a study that we first met in the prologue, people in one condition were invited to evaluate options one by one—they were asked, for example, the highest price they would be willing to pay for a 1-year subscription to *People* magazine (Brenner, Rottenstreich, & Sood, 1999). In a different condition, people were asked about four different magazines (Figure 9.17). They were first asked to rank the magazines from

9.17 Choices, choices When we have lots of choices, this encourages more *comparisons*, and comparisons end up highlighting the *disadvantages* associated with each option. As a result, having more choices will leave us less satisfied with any of our options!

most favorite to least favorite and then asked the price they would pay for each one. The latter condition was designed to encourage comparisons, and this had a powerful impact: When the participants rated *People* magazine on its own, they were willing (on average) to pay more than $21 per year for a subscription. But when they evaluated *People* relative to other magazines, the comparison made *People* less attractive; and now people were willing to pay (on average) only $16 per year—almost a 25% decrease.

Reason-Based Choice

How should we think about the data we've reviewed? On the one side, our everyday experience suggests that we often make good decisions—and so people are generally quite pleased with the cell-phone model they selected, content with the car they bought, and happy with the friends they spend time with. At the same time, we've considered several obstacles to high-quality decision making: People can easily be tugged one way or another by framing; they're often inaccurate in predicting their own likes and dislikes; and they seek out lots of choice and flexibility but end up, as a result, less content with their own selections. How should we reconcile all of these observations?

The answer may hinge on how we *evaluate* our decisions. If we're generally happy with our choices, this may in many cases reflect our contentment with *how we made the choice* rather than *what option we ended up with*. In fact, people seem to care a lot about having a good decision-making process and seem in many cases to insist on making a choice only if they can easily and persuasively *justify* that choice.

Why should this be? Let's start with the fact that, for many of our decisions, our environment offers us a huge number of options—different things we could eat, different activities we could engage in. If we wanted to find the best possible food, or the best possible activity, we'd need to sift through all of these options and evaluate the merits of each one. This would require an enormous amount of time—so we'd spend too much of our lives making decisions, and we'd have no time left to enjoy the fruits of those decisions. Perhaps, therefore, we shouldn't aim our decisions at the *best possible* outcome. Instead, we can abbreviate the decision-making process if we simply aim at an option that's *good enough* for us, even if it's not the ideal. Said differently, it would take us too much time to *optimize* (seeking the optimum choice); doing so would involve examining too many choices, and we've seen the downside of that. Perhaps, therefore, we're better advised to **satisfice**—by seeking a satisfactory choice, even if it's not the ideal, and ending our quest for a good option as soon as we locate that satisfactory choice (Simon, 1983).

But how should we seek outcomes that are "satisfactory"? One possibility is to make sure our decisions are always justified by good reasons, so that we could defend each decision if we ever needed to. A process like this will often fail to bring us the best possible outcome, but at least it will lead us to decisions that are reasonable— likely to be adequate to our needs.

To see how this plays out, consider a study in which half of the participants were asked to consider Scenario A in Figure 9.18 (after Shafir, Simonson, & Tversky, 1993). In this scenario, 66% of the participants said they would buy the Sony CD player; only 34% said

satisfice In decision making, seeking a satisfactory option rather than spending more time and effort to locate and select the ideal option.

9.18 Reason-based choice

Scenario A

Suppose you are considering buying a compact disc player and have not yet decided which model to buy. You pass a store that is having a 1-day clearance sale. It offers a popular Sony player for just $99, well below the list price. Do you

A. buy the Sony player?
B. wait until you learn more about the various models?

Scenario B

Suppose you are considering buying a compact disc player and have not yet decided which model to buy. You pass a store that is having a 1-day clearance sale. It offers a popular Sony player for just $99 and a top-of-the-line Aiwa player for just $169, both well below the list price. Do you

A. buy the Sony player?
B. buy the Aiwa player?
C. wait until you learn more about the various models?

they would instead wait until they had learned about other models. Other participants, though, were presented with Scenario B. In this situation, 27% chose the Aiwa, 27% chose the Sony, and a much larger number—46%—chose to wait until they'd learned about other models.

In some ways, this pattern is peculiar. The results from Scenario A tell us that the participants perceived buying the Sony to be a better choice than continuing to shop; this is clear in the fact that, by a margin of 2 to 1, people choose to buy. But in Scenario B, participants show the reverse preference—choosing more shopping over buying the Sony, again by almost 2 to 1. It seems, then, that participants are flip-flopping; they preferred the Sony to more shopping in one case and indicated the reverse preference in the other.

This result makes sense, though, when we consider that people usually seek a *justification* for their decisions and make a choice only when they find persuasive reasons. When just the Sony is available, there are good arguments for buying it. (It's a popular model, available at a good price for just one day.) But when both the Sony and the Aiwa are available, it's harder to find compelling arguments for buying one rather than the other. Both options are attractive and, as a result, it's hard to justify why you would choose one of these models and reject the alternative. Thus, with no easy justification for a choice, people end up buying neither. (Also see Redelmeier & Shafir, 1995, for a parallel result involving medical doctors choosing treatments for their patients.)

Decision Making: An Overview

To a large extent, our lives are defined by the choices we make—where (or whether) to go to school, what jobs to pursue, whether to pursue that crush on Aisha, and more. It's disheartening, therefore, that we can easily find flaws in human decisions. Thanks to framing effects, people sometimes flip-flop in their preferences. Because of poor affective forecasting, people often choose options that ultimately will not bring them pleasure. People also desire lots of flexibility in their choices—and so they shop in stores that have a better selection, and they hesitate to make purchases that are nonrefundable. It seems, though, that people would be better advised to *satisfice*: With fewer choices, they'd have an easier time choosing and end up happier with the outcome!

In light of these points, some authors have suggested that our decision making is often irrational—guided by the wrong factors (such as the decision frame, or the presence of other choices that don't really interest us but that nonetheless distract us from more desirable options; e.g., Ariely, 2008). Another researcher has argued that the pattern of our decision making actually makes it difficult for us to achieve happy outcomes. If we want to do more than just "stumble" toward happiness, he claims, we need some other sort of decision-making process—one that gives considerable control over our decisions to outsiders, much like trusting your choice of a new car to *Consumer Reports* (D. Gilbert, 2006).

A different perspective, however, is to put less emphasis on the outcome of our decisions and more weight on the process. Perhaps the goal of human decision making is for each of us to feel comfortable with our choices and to feel that our choices have been reasonable. On this basis, our decisions may sometimes not move us toward the best possible outcome, but in most cases our choices will at least be satisfactory—and, above all, we will each feel that our choices have been sensible and justified.

PROBLEM SOLVING: FINDING A PATH TOWARD A GOAL

We've now considered three types of directed thinking—judgment, reasoning, and decision making. But there's a fourth form of thinking that we also need to consider: *problem solving*. Psychologists use this term to describe the thinking we do when we know what our goal is, but we need to find a sequence of steps that will move us toward that goal. Sometimes the problems we confront are practical: How can you fix that leaky faucet? Sometimes the problems are social: How can you persuade your friends to stop teasing you? Sometimes the problems are small, and the solution is obvious: How can you repair that torn fingernail? Sometimes the problems are huge, and the solution unclear: How can we avoid the many problems associated with global warming? In all cases, though, we want to ask: How does problem solving proceed?

The Role of the Goal State

Imagine that you're trying to locate a job, so that you'll be able to pay the rent in the coming months. One option is just to let your thoughts run: "Job" might remind you of "money," which would remind you of "bank," which would make you think about "bank tellers" and perhaps lead you to think that's the job you want. This sort of problem solving, which relies on a process of free association, surely does occur. But far more often, you rely on a more efficient strategy—guided not just by your starting point (technically: your *initial state*) but also by your understanding of the *goal state*. Said differently, your thoughts in solving a problem are guided both by where you are and where you hope to be.

The importance of the goal state shows up in many aspects of problem solving, including the different ways people approach well-defined problems and ill-defined problems. A *well-defined problem* is one in which you have a clear idea of the goal right at the start, and you also know what options are available to you in reaching that goal. One example is an anagram problem: What English word can be produced by rearranging the letters *subufoal*? Here you know immediately that the goal will involve just these eight letters and will be a word in the English language; you know that you'll reach that goal by changing the sequence of the letters (and not, for example, by turning letters upside down).

With a problem like this one, your understanding of the goal guides you in important ways. Thus, you won't waste time adding extra letters or turning some of the letters into numerals; those steps, you already know, are incompatible with your goal. You also won't try rewriting the word in a different font or in a different color of ink. Those steps are simply irrelevant for your goal. (The solution to this anagram, by the way, is *fabulous*; other examples of well-defined problems are shown in Figure 9.19.)

For an *ill-defined problem,* in contrast, you start the problem with only a hazy sense of the goal. For example, imagine you're trying to find something fun to do next summer, or you're trying to think of ways we might achieve world peace. For problems like these, you know some of the properties of the goal state (e.g., "fun," and "no war") but there are many things you don't know: Will you find your summer fun at home, or traveling? Will we achieve peace through diplomacy? Through increased economic interdependence? How?

If a problem is ill defined, the goal itself provides only loose guidance for your problem solving. It's no surprise, therefore, that people usually try to solve ill-defined

9.19 Examples of well-defined problems
For the solutions to all three problems, see
Figure 9.24.

NAGMARA
BOLMPER
SLEVO
STIGNIH
TOLUSONI

(A) Anagrams

*Rearrange the
letters on each
line to form a word.*

(B) Nine-dots problem

*Nine dots are arranged
in a square. Connect them
by drawing four continuous
straight lines without lifting
your pencil from the paper.*

(C) Matchstick problem

*Assemble all six matches
to form four equilateral
triangles, each side of
which equals the length
of one match.*

problems by first making them well defined—that is, by seeking ways to clarify and specify the goal state. In many cases, this effort involves adding extra constraints or extra assumptions ("Let me assume that my summer of fun will involve spending time near the ocean," or "Let me assume that my summer travel can't cost more than $500"). This narrows the set of options—and conceivably may hide the best options from view—but for many problems, defining the problem more clearly helps enormously in the search for a solution (Schraw, Dunkle, & Bendixen, 1995).

Hierarchical Organization

Problem solving is also guided by your broader understanding of the problem and its context. To see this, consider an often effective problem-solving strategy called **means-end analysis.** In using this strategy, one asks, "What is the difference between my current state and my goal?" Then, with that difference defined, one asks, "What means do I have available for reducing this difference?" Thus, for example: "I want to get to the store. What's the difference between my current state and my goal? One of distance. How can I reduce the distance? My car. My car won't work. What's needed to make it work? A new battery. Where do I get a battery?" And so on (after Newell & Simon, 1972).

A means-end analysis can replace the initial problem (e.g., getting to the store) with a series of subproblems (e.g., getting the car to work, obtaining a new battery); in that way, the initial goal is replaced by a series of subgoals. If this process is repeated (so subproblems are broken down into still smaller subproblems), it can create a hierarchical structure like the one shown in Figure 9.20.

Understanding a problem in terms of this sort of structure has several advantages. First, the subproblems are by definition less complex than the initial problem, so they're likely to be easier to solve than the original problem. Second, the subproblems are often quite straightforward. For example, a driver seeking to reach the store might realize that her best path is the freeway, so the larger problem ("get to the store") can be replaced with a simpler and more familiar routine ("get on the freeway"). This routine in turn is composed of still simpler **subroutines**—specific procedures for solving often-encountered, well-defined problems. Subroutines required for taking the freeway, for example, might include "go south on 18th Street," "accelerate when the light turns green," and so on. In this way, a series of modular units can be assembled into the larger-scale solution to the initial problem.

means-end analysis A problem-solving strategy in which you continually evaluate the difference between your current state and your goal, and consider how to use your resources to reduce the difference.

subroutines In problem solving, specific procedures for solving familiar, well-defined problems.

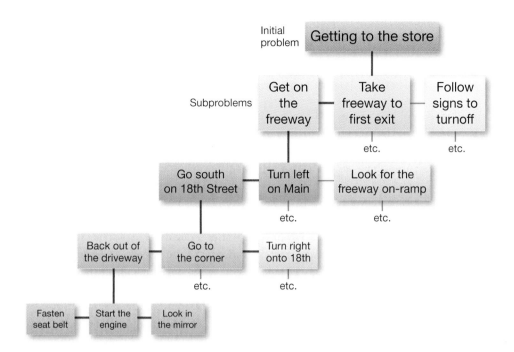

9.20 **Problems and subproblems** It's helpful to replace an initial problem with a series of subproblems. In solving these, the initial problem is also solved. Subproblems can be broken down into even smaller subproblems, creating a hierarchical structure.

Automaticity

Relying on subroutines also has another advantage: The modular units are generally well practiced, and this allows the problem solver to focus attention on the larger-scale plan rather than worry about the details of carrying out the plan. In fact, this is one reason why problems that seem impossible for the novice are absurdly easy for the expert: Even when the expert is facing a novel problem, she's likely to rely on several familiar subroutines that are already available as "chunks" in memory. Thus, the expert taxi driver gives little thought to maneuvering through traffic and so can focus his thoughts on the more general task of navigation. The novice driver must focus on the maneuvering—and while preoccupied with this task, he may miss his exit.

It's plainly helpful, then, that subroutines can be executed without much thought; this frees up your attention for other aspects of the task. Still, in some circumstances this **automaticity** (the ability to do a task without paying attention to it) can create problems of its own, because automatic actions, once set in motion, are often difficult to turn off or modify.

A striking example is known as the *Stroop effect,* named after its discoverer (Stroop, 1935). This effect hinges on the fact that many of the steps involved in ordinary reading have become quite automatic—which is a good thing, because it means that when you're reading a text, you can focus on the ideas being expressed rather than the mechanics of reading itself. Even so, this automaticity can cause troubles of its own.

To demonstrate the Stroop effect, people are asked to name the colors in which groups of letters are printed (Figure 9.21). If the letters are random sequences (*fwis, sgbr*) or irrelevant words (*chair, tape*), this task is rather easy. But if the letters form color names (*yellow, red*), the task becomes much harder. Thus, a participant might see *red* printed in green ink, *blue* in brown ink, and so on. Her task is simply to name the ink color, so she should say "green, brown" in this example. But in this setting, the participant cannot help but read the words, and this produces a strong competing response: She's likely to respond very slowly, because while trying to name the ink colors, she is fighting the tendency to read the words themselves aloud. (For more on

automaticity The ability to do a task without paying attention to it.

From top to bottom, as fast as you can, name out loud the colors in which these strings are printed.

(A)	**(B)**
ZYP	RED
QLEKF	**BLACK**
SUWRG	YELLOW
XCIDB	BLUE
WOPR	**RED**
ZYP	**GREEN**
QLEKF	**YELLOW**
XCIDB	BLACK

9.21 **The Stroop effect** The two lists, A and B, are printed in five colors—black, red, green, blue, and yellow. If you try this task, you'll probably have an easier time with list A than with list B—a demonstration of the Stroop effect.

automaticity, see Bargh & Ferguson, 2000; Pashler, Johnston, & Ruthruff, 2000; Stolz & Besner, 1999.)

Obstacles to Problem Solving

Broad strategies like means-end analysis, or a reliance on subroutines, help us to solve many problems. The fact remains, though, that some problems—whether an infuriating crossword puzzle or a demoralizing job dispute—seem downright intractable. Why is this? And above all, what can we do to help people solve the problems they encounter?

Problem solvers inevitably bring certain assumptions and habits with them whenever they approach a problem, and many of these assumptions are sensible and productive. For instance, a taxi driver—even a beginner—doesn't waste time wondering whether a magic carpet might be the fastest transport to the airport, and even a novice cook realizes that pickles are an unpalatable topping for the morning's pancakes. Likewise (and more plausibly), in solving the anagram *subufoal*, you relied on the background knowledge that some letter combinations are extremely rare in English, and so you didn't waste time searching memory for a solution to this anagram that began with the letters *bfl–* or *uua–*; that helped you to narrow the options enormously and arrive more quickly at the actual solution.

The same sorts of assumptions, however, can sometimes lead us astray—if, for example, the assumptions are simply wrong or just inappropriate to the present situation. In that case, the would-be problem solver can end up misled by a powerful **mental set**—the specific perspective that the person takes (including the assumptions the person makes) in approaching the problem.

A classic study illustrates this point and shows how people can become fixated on one approach to a task. Participants were told that they had three jars, A, B, and C. Jar A held exactly 21 quarts; jar B held exactly 127 quarts; jar C held exactly 3 quarts. The participants' job was to use these three jars to obtain exactly 100 quarts from a well.

Participants required a few minutes to solve this problem, but they generally did solve it. The solution is to fill B (127 quarts) completely and then pour out enough water from B to fill A. Now 106 quarts remain in B (127 − 21). Next, pour enough water out of B to fill up C (3 quarts), leaving 103 quarts in B. Finally, dump out C and fill it again from B, leaving the desired amount—100 quarts—in B (Figure 9.22).

mental set The perspective that a person takes and the assumptions he makes in approaching a problem.

Use these three jars to obtain exactly 100 quarts from a well.

First fill jar B completely and pour out enough water to fill jar A.

Then fill up jar C from jar B. Dump out C and fill it again from B, leaving the desired amount—100 quarts—in B.

127

21

3

A　　　*B*　　　*C*

9.22 The standard method for solving the water-jar problem

Participants then did several more problems, all of the same type. The numerical values differed in each problem, but in each case the solution could be obtained by the same sequence of steps: Fill B, pour from it into A, then pour from B into C, empty out C, and pour again from B into C. In each case, in other words, the desired amount could be reached by the arithmetical sequence of $B - A - 2C$.

After five such problems, the participants were given two critical tests. The first was a problem that required them to obtain 20 quarts, given jars whose volumes were 23, 49, and 3 quarts. The participants cheerfully solved this problem using the same sequence: $49 - 23 - (2 \times 3)$. Most of them failed to notice a simpler method that requires only a single step (just $B - C$).

The participants were next asked to obtain 25 quarts, given jars of 28, 76, and 3 quarts. Note that here the only method that works is the direct one; that is, $28 - 3 = 25$. But the mental set was so powerful that many subjects failed to solve the problem altogether. They tried the old procedure, but it didn't lead them to the goal ($76 - 28 - [2 \times 3] \neq 25$), and they couldn't find the alternative path! The mental set had made them so rigid that they became mentally blind (Luchins, 1942; for related examples, see Figure 9.19B and c).

Let's be clear that the participants in this study weren't being foolish. Once they found a way to solve a problem, it's entirely sensible that they did not go looking for an alternate path. As an analogy, if you know how to scramble an egg, isn't it reasonable to use the same tried-and-true technique each time rather than complicating your life by seeking a new procedure for each breakfast? The worry, though, is that this pattern—sensible as it generally is—can cause difficulties like those in the water-jar problem, often slowing (and sometimes even preventing) successful problem solving. (For more recent research on mental set, see, for example, Bilalic, 2008; Chrysikou & Weisberg, 2005; German & Barrett, 2005.)

Overcoming Obstacles to Solutions

If problem-solving sets can sometimes cause difficulties, then we want to ask: How can these sets be overcome? Similarly, we've emphasized the importance of subgoals and familiar routines, but what can we do if we fail to perceive the subgoals or are unfamiliar with the relevant routine?

A number of strategies are helpful when people are stuck on a difficult problem, but one of the most useful is to rely on an *analogy*. In other words, you can often solve a problem by recalling some previous, similar problem and applying its solution (or a minor variation on it) to your current problem. Thus, a business manager might solve today's crisis by remembering how she dealt with a similar crisis just a few months back. A psychotherapist might realize how to help one patient by recalling his approach to a similar patient a year ago.

Analogies turn out to be enormously helpful in many settings. They're useful as a form of *instruction*, and so students gain understanding of how gas molecules function by thinking about how the balls bump into each other on a pool table; they learn about memory by comparing it to a vast library. Analogies are also a powerful source of *discoveries*, and so (for example) scientists expanded their understanding of the heart, years ago, by comparing it to a pump (Gentner & Jeziorski, 1989). And, of course, analogies are also helpful in solving problems. In one study (Gick & Holyoak, 1980), for example, participants were given this problem:

> Suppose a patient has an inoperable stomach tumor. There are certain rays that can
> destroy this tumor if their intensity is great enough. At this intensity, however, the rays

will also destroy the healthy tissue that surrounds the tumor (e.g., the stomach walls, the abdominal muscles, and so on). How can the tumor be destroyed without damaging the healthy tissue through which the rays must travel on their way?

The problem is difficult; and in this experiment, 90% of the participants failed to solve it. A second group, however, did much better. Before tackling the tumor problem, they read a story about a general who hoped to capture a fortress. He needed a large force of soldiers for this, but all of the roads leading to the fortress were planted with mines. Small groups of soldiers could travel the roads safely, but the mines would be detonated by a larger group. How, therefore, could the general move all the soldiers he would need toward the fortress? He could do this by dividing his army into small groups and sending each group via a different road. When he gave the signal, all the groups marched toward the fortress, where they converged and attacked successfully.

The structure of the fortress story is similar to that of the tumor problem. In both cases, the solution is to divide the "conquering" force so that it enters from several different directions. Thus, to destroy the tumor, several weak rays can be sent through the body, each from a different angle. The rays converge at the tumor, inflicting their combined effects just as desired (Figure 9.23).

With no hints or analogies to draw on, only 10% of the participants were able to solve the tumor problem. However, if they were given the fortress story and told that it would help them, most (about 80%) did solve it. Obviously, the analogy was quite helpful. But just knowing the fortress story wasn't enough; participants also had to realize that the story was pertinent to the task at hand—and, surprisingly, they often failed to make this connection. In another condition, participants read the fortress story but were given no indication that this story was relevant to their task. In that case, only 30% solved the tumor problem (Gick & Holyoak, 1980, 1983).

Clearly, analogies are helpful. Even so, people often fail to use them, even if the plausible analogue is available in their memory. Is there anything we can do, therefore, to encourage the use of analogies? It turns out that there is. Evidence suggests, for example, that people are more likely to use analogies if they're encouraged to focus on the underlying dynamic of the problem (e.g., the fortress problem involves converging forces) rather than its superficial features (e.g., the problem involves mines). This focus on the underlying dynamic calls attention to the features shared by the problems, helping people to see the relevance of the analogies and enabling them to map one problem onto another (Blanchette & Dunbar, 2000; Catrambone, 1998; Cummins, 1992; Dunbar & Blanchette, 2001; Needham & Begg, 1991).

9.23 Solution to the tumor problem Like soldiers closing in on a fortress from several directions, several weak rays are sent from various points outside so that they meet at the tumor site. There the radiation of the rays will be intense, for all the effects will combine at this point. But since they're individually weak, the rays won't damage the healthy tissue surrounding the tumor.

Radiation source

Site of tumor in stomach wall

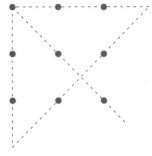

ANAGRAM

PROBLEM

SOLVE

INSIGHT

SOLUTION

(A) Anagrams   (B) Nine-dots problem   (C) Matchstick problem

9.24 Answers to problems in Figure 9.19 Problem B is solved by going outside of the grid formed by the dots. Most participants fail to hit on this solution because of a perceptual set imposed by the grid arrangement. To arrange 6 matches into 4 equilateral triangles in Problem C, the matches have to be assembled into a three-dimensional pyramid. Most participants implicitly assume the matches must lie flat.

Restructuring

These comments about analogies remind us that much depends on how a problem solver thinks about, or interprets, a problem. If she focuses on the problem's underlying dynamic and not its surface form, she's more likely to use an analogy. If she breaks the problem into subproblems, she's more likely to find a relevant subroutine. If she approaches the problem with an appropriate mental set, this too can be helpful.

These points suggest that when problem solving *fails*, a person's best bet may be to change her understanding of the problem—to one that highlights the problem's subgoals or one that suggests an analogy. This point certainly seems in line with common experience: Sometimes we're utterly baffled by a problem; but then, later, we find an alternative way to approach the issue and quickly come up with the answer. Sometimes this **restructuring** of the problem is gradual, as we change our ideas about the problem one by one; but sometimes it's quite abrupt, experienced as a flash of insight with an accompanying exclamation of "Aha!"

It should be said that these flashes of insight, when they occur, aren't uniformly beneficial. Sometimes the (apparent) insights turn out to be false alarms, because the new understanding simply leads to yet another dead end (Metcalfe, 1986; Metcalfe & Weibe, 1987). Thus, it seems that the "Aha!" experience should not be understood as "I see the solution!" Instead, the experience merely implies, "I've discovered a new approach!" Whether this approach will turn out to be productive can only be decided after the fact. One way or another, though, and whether the changes are sudden or slow, these changes in the way a problem is defined are often essential for breaking out of an unproductive mental set and moving toward one that will lead to a solution. (The problems in Figure 9.19 may also involve insight. See Figure 9.24 for their solutions.)

restructuring A reorganization of a problem that can facilitate its solution; a characteristic of creative thought.

Creative Thinking

If restructuring is crucial, how can a problem solver go about seeking some new perspective, some new mental set, when working on a difficult problem? One way to tackle these issues is by examining cases of problem solving in which someone finds an entirely new and wonderfully productive way to solve a problem. In these cases, we count the problem solution as *creative*—one that's both new and valuable—and this leads us to ask: How do creative problem solutions arise?

We can approach this issue by examining individuals who have undeniably been creative—great artists like Picasso or Bach, or innovative scientists like Charles Darwin or Marie Curie. Studies suggest that these creative individuals do tend to have certain things in common, so perhaps we can think of these shared elements as "prerequisites" for great creativity. These individuals, first of all, have an enormous storehouse of knowledge and skills in their domain of achievement. Second, they all tend to be intelligent and to have certain personality traits—a willingness to take risks, a willingness to ignore criticism, and an ability to tolerate ambiguous findings or situations. Third, these highly creative people seem to be motivated by the pleasure of their work rather than the promise of external rewards. Finally, there's an important sense in which these highly creative people seem to have been "in the right place at the right time"—that is, in environments that allowed them freedom, provided the appropriate support, and offered them problems that were "ripe" for solution with the resources available. (For discussion of these "prerequisites" for creativity, see Amabile, 2001; Nakamura & Csikszentmihalyi, 2001; Sawyer, 2006; Sternberg & Dess, 2001.)

But these various factors merely set the stage for creativity; we still need to ask what goes on inside the mind of the creative person. One proposal was offered many years ago by Graham Wallas (1926), who argued that creative thought proceeds through four stages: In the first stage, *preparation*, the problem solver gathers information about the problem. This stage is typically characterized by periods of hard and often frustrating work on the problem, generally with little progress. In the second stage, *incubation*, the problem solver sets the problem aside and seems not to be working on it. Wallas argued, though, that the problem solver was continuing to work on the problem during this stage, albeit unconsciously. Thus, the problem solution is continuing to develop, unseen—just like a baby bird develops, unseen, inside the egg. This period of incubation leads to the third stage, *illumination*, in which some key insight or new idea emerges; this stage paves the way for the fourth stage, *verification*, in which the problem solver confirms that the new idea really does lead to a solution and works out the details.

Modern scholars are, however, quite skeptical about Wallas's proposal; let's focus in particular on his notion of incubation. Wallas based this idea on the many historical accounts in which creative insights arose rather abruptly, when the thinker seemed not be working on the problem at all. Thus, Beethoven and Darwin both reported that their great ideas came to them not while sitting at the piano or a desk, but while riding in a carriage. The great mathematician Poincaré claimed his discoveries arose while he was stepping onto a bus. In the most celebrated case of all, Archimedes allegedly was sitting in a bathtub when he realized how to measure the volume of a complex shape (Figure 9.25).

The more systematic evidence on this point is, however, mixed. Several studies have shown that time away from a problem does help in finding the problem's solution, but many other studies find no such effect (Dodds, Ward, & Smith, 2003; Vul & Pashler, 2007; Zhong, Dijksterhuis, & Galinsky, 2008; but also see Sio & Ormerod, 2009). And even when time away from a problem is beneficial, incubation may not be the reason. Time away from a problem may simply allow fatigue and frustration to dissipate, which by itself may be helpful. The time away also may allow problem solvers to shake off unproductive mental sets, so that they can approach the problem unburdened by their earlier, unhelpful perspective and assumptions (S. Smith & Blankenship, 1989; Vul & Pashler, 2007).

If we set aside Wallas's ambitious notions, then, where do creative discoveries come from? The answer probably involves relatively straightforward mechanisms. For example, earlier in this chapter we discussed the notion of *spreading activation*, in which retrieval of one memory causes activation to spread out to the nearby nodes representing related memories. This sort of unguided memory search, letting the activation spread where the connections take it, is inefficient for

9.25 Archimedes in his bathtub This 16th-century engraving celebrates a great example of creative restructuring. The Greek scientist Archimedes (287–212 B.C.) tried to determine whether the king's crown was made of solid gold or had been adulterated with silver. Archimedes knew the weight of gold and silver per unit volume but didn't know how to measure the volume of a complicated object like a crown. One day, in his bath, he saw that the water level rose as he immersed his body. Here was the solution: The crown's volume can be determined by the water it displaces. Carried away by his sudden insight, he jumped from his bath and ran naked through the streets, shouting "Eureka! I have found it!"

most problem solving—and as we said at the start, problem solving is usually much more orderly than this. It's guided by your current thoughts, your sense of the goal, and your understanding of the problem's structure. Even so, an unguided memory search, relying on spreading activation, may be the best bet when the problem solver is otherwise uncertain how to proceed (Schooler, Ohlsson, & Brooks, 1993; Yaniv & Meyer, 1987). And, of course, this spreading activation is more likely to be productive if the problem solver has a lot of knowledge about the domain (and so many ideas that could be activated) and if that knowledge is richly interconnected (so that the activation is more likely to reach the target). Both of these points are typically in place for the individuals we call creative, and this may be a large part of what contributes to creative solutions.

Experts

Our discussion of creativity draws attention to another crucial point: People plainly differ in their ability to solve problems. Some people seem to be good problem solvers; others are not. Some people often seem able to find new ways to approach a problem; others invariably seem to rely on the procedures they've used in the past. What should we make of these differences?

Different authors have suggested a variety of perspectives on these points. Some writers emphasize innate factors in explaining why some individuals are creative and others not, or why some individuals seem especially successful in solving problems while others seem less so. Other writers, in contrast, seek to explain the same points in terms of the social or cultural context. (For a review of these diverse views, see Sawyer, 2006.) There's no question, though, that one factor is crucial: experience working in a particular domain. Thus, the quality of a physician's problem solving (e.g., her ability to find accurate diagnoses) is improved after many years of medical practice; the quality of an electrician's problem solving (the ability to troubleshoot a problem or lay out a complex wiring pattern) is likewise enhanced by on-the-job experience. The same is true for painters or professors or police officers—they all become better problem solvers with experience.

But why exactly does experience improve problem solving? Why does *experience* turn someone into an *expert*? The answer has several parts; but one crucial element lies in the fact that, over their years of work, experts gather a wealth of information about their domain of expertise—a database they can turn to in solving new problems. Indeed, this is why several theorists have suggested that someone usually needs a full decade to acquire expert status, whether the proficiency is in music, software design, chess, or any other arena. Ten years is the time needed to acquire a large enough knowledge base so that the expert has the necessary facts near at hand and well cross-referenced, so that he can access them when needed (Bédard & Chi, 1992; Ericsson, 1996; Hayes, 1985).

It's important to be aware, though, that experts don't just have *more* knowledge than novices do; they also have a different *type* of knowledge that is focused on higher-order patterns. This knowledge enables experts to think in larger units, tackling problems in big steps rather than small ones. This ability is evident, for example, in studies of chess players (Chase & Simon, 1973a, 1973b; de Groot, 1965). Novice chess players think about a game in terms of the position of individual pieces; experts, in contrast, think about the board in terms of pieces organized into broad strategic groupings (e.g., a king-side attack with pawns). This sort of thinking is made possible by the fact that chess masters have a "chess vocabulary" in which these complex concepts are stored as single memory chunks, each with an associated set of subroutines for how one should

(A) Actual position **(B) Typical master player's performance** **(C) Typical average player's performance**

9.26 Memory for chess positions in masters and average players (A) An actual chess position that was presented for 5 seconds, after which the player had to reconstruct the positions of the pieces. Typical performances by masters and average players are shown in (B) and (C) respectively. Errors are shown in red.

respond to that pattern. Some investigators estimate, in fact, that the masters may have as many as 50,000 of these chunks in their memories, each representing a strategic pattern (Chase & Simon, 1973b).

These memory chunks can be detected in many ways, including the way players recall a game. In one study, players of different ranks were shown chess positions for 5 seconds each and then asked to reproduce the positions a few minutes later. Grandmasters and masters did so with hardly an error; lesser players, however, made many errors (Figure 9.26). This difference in performance wasn't because chess masters had better visual memory. When presented with bizarre positions that were unlikely ever to arise in the course of a game, the chess masters recalled them no better than novices did—and in some cases, they remembered the bizarre patterns *less* accurately than did novices (Gobet & Simon, 1996a, 1996b; but also see Gobet & Simon, 2000; Lassiter, 2000). The superiority of the masters, therefore, was in their conceptual organization of chess, not in their memory for patterns as such.

Experts' sensitivity to a problem's organization can also be demonstrated in other ways. For example, intro-level physics students tend to group problems in terms of their surface characteristics, so they might group together all the problems involving springs or all the problems involving inclined planes. Experts, in contrast, instantly perceive the deeper structure of each problem; so they group problems not according to surface features, but according to the physical principles relevant to each problem's solution. Clearly, then, the experts are more sensitive to the higher-order patterns, and this calls their attention to the strategies needed for solving the problem (Chi, Feltovich, & Glaser, 1981; also Cummins, 1992; Reeves & Weisberg, 1994).

Finally, this knowledge of higher-order patterns also helps experts in another way. We've already said that analogies are a powerful aid to problem solving, but that people often fail to detect, or make use, of analogies. Experts, in contrast, routinely draw on analogies; and this gives them a huge advantage in their work. In fact, the experts' use of analogies is almost inevitable. We've already noted that analogy use is promoted by attention to a problem's underlying structure, rather than its surface characteristics. We've also said that an expert's knowledge is generally cast in terms of higher-order patterns that are typically defined in terms of the cause-and-effect structure within a problem. If we put these pieces together, it seems that experts have exactly the right perspective to make analogy use highly probable—and so it's entirely sensible that they frequently benefit from this problem-solving tool.

SOME FINAL THOUGHTS: BETTER THINKING

We have now considered four types of directed thinking, and across the four types, we've seen many examples of limitations or flaws in our thinking—example after example of bad conclusions, unsolved problems, and apparently foolish decisions. But it seems that we need different sorts of theory to explain these various findings. In the domain of judgment, the errors may simply be the price we pay for using strategies that are fast, efficient, and serve us well in many settings. In the domain of reasoning, it appears that humans are simply ill prepared for abstract deductions, and so we reason much more effectively if we can translate the deduction into more familiar terms. In decision making, it seems plausible that we rely on processes aimed at decisions that are easily defended—even if this means the choices we make don't move us toward the best possible outcome. And in problem solving, we're routinely victims of our own assumptions—although, without those assumptions, all problems would essentially be ill defined and therefore more difficult.

This is a mixed bag of theory, but perhaps we shouldn't be surprised. After all, the term *thinking* spans many different mental activities, thus making it plausible that we would need somewhat different types of explanation for different types of thinking. Even so, there's one question that cuts across all the types of thinking—namely, whether it's possible to lead people toward *better* thinking that involves more accurate conclusions, more compelling deductions, better decisions, and more successful problem solving. On this broad question, we've seen grounds for optimism—strategies that can help people, and methods of education that can be useful. Indeed, one often hears a call for educational programs that promote *critical thinking*, and some of the evidence we've reviewed suggests that such programs are indeed possible. Thus, in the domain of judgment, we've seen that training of the right sort makes System 2 thinking more likely. In reasoning, people are helped by an effort toward translating problems into the familiar terms of *permission* or *social obligation*. For decision making, the mere step of alerting people to the danger of seeking too many options may be helpful, perhaps leading people to change their decision-making strategies. And in problem solving, we've considered some of the ways one might approach a problem, and the ways one might study analogous cases, to increase the probability of finding a solution. These are all encouraging prospects suggesting that research in this domain can be both informative and genuinely useful.

Above all, though, we must not lose track of the fact that humans are already capable of excellent thinking. Of course, we do make errors; but it's not because we lack skill in judgment, reasoning, and problem solving. Instead, our thinking is thrown off course by certain obstacles, and by identifying these obstacles we can improve our performance. Indeed, some of the research discussed in this chapter suggests that in some settings an improvement in human thinking may be relatively easy—an enormously heartening conclusion from research on this complex topic.

MENTAL REPRESENTATIONS

- The components of knowledge can be regarded as *mental representations*. *Analogical representations* capture some of the actual characteristics of what they represent; *symbolic representations* bear no such relationship to what they represent.

- *Mental images* have many picture-like properties, as shown by studies of image scanning. However, other evidence indicates that visual images—like our visual perceptions—are not a simple re-embodiment of some stimulus but are already organized and interpreted in ways that the corresponding picture is not.

- Many of the same brain regions are active during visual perception and visual imagery. Related findings come from work on brain damage: Damage that disrupts vision also seems to disrupt visual imagery and vice versa, adding to the argument that imagery and perception rely on many of the same brain areas.

- Much of our knowledge is represented via *propositions*, which in turn are likely to be expressed in the mind in terms of *associative links* among *nodes*. When you think about a particular topic, *activation* spreads from the nodes representing this topic to other, related, nodes.

JUDGMENT: DRAWING CONCLUSIONS FROM EXPERIENCE

- In *judgment* we seek to reach beyond the evidence we've encountered, to draw new claims based on this evidence. In many cases, judgment relies on shortcuts called *heuristics*. The *availability heuristic* is used for making frequency estimates, relying on the availability of instances as an indicator of frequency in the world. This strategy is often effective but sometimes leads to error, including errors in consequential domains.

- The *representativeness heuristic* is used for making judgments about categories and amounts to an assumption that the category is homogeneous (so that each instance in the category is representative of the category overall). This strategy, too, is often successful but is overused—as, for example, in "man who" arguments.

- People sometimes rise above the use of heuristics, inviting *dual-process theories*. According to many authors, we use *System 1* thinking in many situations; but we sometimes use the slower, more effortful, and more accurate *System 2*. The use of *System 2* is more likely if appropriate triggers are in place, or if the person has been trained in how to think about quantitative evidence.

REASONING: DRAWING IMPLICATIONS FROM OUR BELIEFS

- In reasoning, we try to draw implications from our beliefs; this process is crucial for the use of knowledge and provides a means of testing our beliefs. However, people often show a pattern of confirmation bias—taking evidence more seriously if it confirms their beliefs than if it challenges them.

- In showing *confirmation bias*, people often seem illogical—and consistent with this notion, people often perform badly on simple tests of logical reasoning. In studies involving *syllogisms*, for example, participants are more likely to judge a conclusion valid if it strikes them as plausible—independent of whether the conclusion follows logically from the stated premises. More generally, the quality of reasoning is influenced by the content of a reasoning task, and performance is much better if logical problems are framed in ways that trigger pragmatic thinking. This is plainly evident in the selection task. People do poorly with the original version of this task, but they reason well with some variants of the task.

DECISION MAKING: CHOOSING AMONG OPTIONS

- In making choices, people are appropriately sensitive to the outcomes of a decision and to the degree of risk associated with each option. However, people are also heavily influenced by how the decision is framed. If the problem is cast in terms of gains, people tend to avoid any risk. If exactly the same problem is cast in terms of possible losses, people seek out risk, presumably in hopes of avoiding the risk.

- People are surprisingly inaccurate in *affective forecasting*—predicting their own future emotions. People often overestimate how strongly and for how much time they will react to upcoming events. People also overestimate how much regret they will feel if a decision turns out badly.

- People also seem to seek out options, but decision making is often *worse* when people have too many options. This may be because having options encourages comparisons, and comparisons tend to draw attention to each option's disadvantages rather than its advantages.

- The factors reviewed here suggest that people often make decisions that do not move them toward the things they value. However, it may be more sensible to evaluate decision making by focusing on the *process* rather than the *outcome,* because people often prefer decisions that they can justify or explain. This may not lead people to the best possible outcome, but will allow people to *satisfice*—i.e., to find satisfactory outcomes.

PROBLEM SOLVING: FINDING A PATH TOWARD A GOAL

- Problem solving is a process that moves us from an initial state to a goal state and depends heavily on how we understand the problem. Often this understanding involves a hierarchical organization—the problem is broken up into subproblems that can be solved via *subroutines,* some of which are well practiced enough to be automatic.

- Experts rely heavily on subroutines, but they also know more of—and pay attention to—a problem's higher-order patterns. These attributes are evident in how experts remember problems and in how they categorize them.

- Problem solving is sometimes blocked by an inappropriate *mental set.* A set can sometimes be overcome by working backward from the goal or by finding an analogy. Sometimes the solution to a problem requires a radical *restructuring* to overcome a misleading mental set, and restructurings may be an important feature of creative thinking. Some accounts suggest that restructuring often occurs after a period of incubation, although the nature of incubation—if it exists at all—has been a subject of dispute.

 ONLINE STUDY TOOLS

Go to StudySpace, **wwnorton.com/studyspace**, to access additional review and enrichment materials, including the following resources for each chapter:

Organize
- Study Plan
- Chapter Outline
- Quiz+ Assessment

Learn
- Ebook
- Chapter Review
- Vocabulary Flashcards
- Drag-and-Drop Labeling Exercises
- Audio Podcast Chapter Overview

Connect
- Critical Thinking Activity
- Studying the Mind Video Podcasts
- Video Exercises
- Animations
- **ZAPS** Psychology Labs

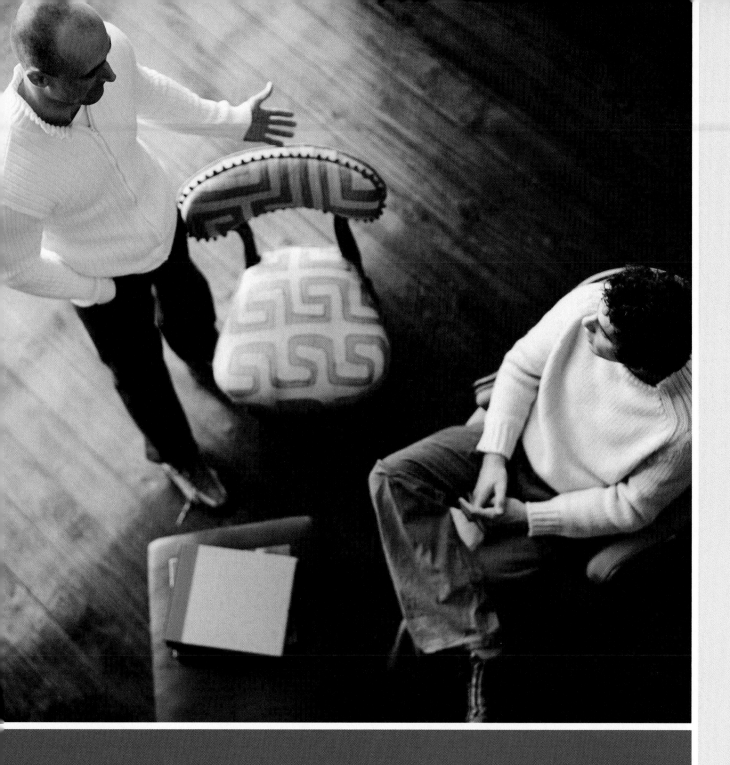

10 Language

By Lila Gleitman and Daniel Reisberg

It's a pretty good bet that if Martian psychologists came down (or is it "up"?) to Earth to investigate its creatures, they wouldn't immediately pick out the humans as being an especially remarkable example. After all, we don't have the lion's magnificent mane, the soaring flight of the eagle, the peacock's extravagant feathers, the elephant's impressive bulk or the shark's rapacious bite. In fact, ours seems a rather unspectacular species—dull of tooth and short of claw, awkwardly bobbing along on two legs with our patchy coats and pointy noses. We don't even have whiskers or tails.

But we humans have one unique glory that apes can't ape, crows can't crow about, and parrots can only parrot. We have the gift of language, and we have always understood the power it conveys, allowing us to leapfrog beyond the other creatures. As the Bible puts it, "The man gave names to all the cattle, and to the birds of the sky, and to every beast of the field" while even the most linguistically gifted animals can muster little more language than "Give me bananas," "D'oh! Snake!" and "Hey there, pal!" Echoing the Bible's words, the 17th-century philosopher René Descartes wrote that language is the mental function that sets us apart from all other beasts and is "the sole sign and only certain mark of thought hidden and wrapped up in the body" (Figure 10.1).

Today, scientific opinion continues to give the same prominence to language that our forebears did, recognizing it as a crucial cornerstone of human mental life.

10.1 Adam gives names to the animals
The belief that knowledge of word meanings sets humans above animals goes back to antiquity. An example is the biblical tale, illustrated in this painting by William Blake, in which Adam assigns names to the animals. According to some ancient legends, this act established Adam's intellectual superiority over all creation, including even the angels.

Armed with language, we not only can name all the things and creatures around us. We can transcend the here-and-now that surrounds and confines the mentality of all other animals. We can build bridges between the actual and the impossible; the concrete and the abstract; the physical and the mental; the past, present, and future; the ordinary and the sublime and, last but not least, with words and sentences we fashion a mental bridge between your brain and mine. Going on to recraft our language into squiggles and scratches on clay or stone or paper, we can store our thoughts forever, sending them down through time to generations of humankind as yet unborn.

In these ways and more, language obviously serves the crucial purpose of conveying information and ideas from person to person and from generation to generation. Yet the role of language in human life lies yet deeper than this. Conversation is embedded in the fundamental social fabric of our species' existence, starting to show itself even in infants a few months old and thus too young to sit up unaided or feed themselves, no less to understand any meaningful word. All the same, these smallest members of the human race have the rudimentary rhythms and tones of language stored in their genes, and so they happily babble and coo away their days. And their adult caretakers babble quite meaninglessly in return as the family and community forge social bonds using the sounds of language as a central medium. As Charles Darwin writes, language is "the sweet music of our species," the lifelong vehicle of our sociality as well as the transmission medium for our deepest thoughts, beliefs, and ideas. Humans have often been defined as "the creatures who think." One might as justly define them as "the creatures who gossip" (or who text, or who tweet).

In this chapter, we describe how languages are organized mentally and how they are learned. We begin with an overview of language structure, for our species has developed a rich computational system to serve its communicative needs.

THE BUILDING BLOCKS OF LANGUAGE

Languages consist of a hierarchy of unit types, which combine and recombine to form higher and higher level categories so that, with a relatively small number of basic units, each person can express and understand innumerable new thoughts. At the bottom are the units of sound such as *c*, *t*, and *a*, which combine into such words as *cat*, *act*, and *tact*. These words combine in turn into such phrases as *a fat cat*, and the phrases then combine into such sentences as *A fat cat acts with tact* and *That's the act of a tacky cat*. (Figure 10.2 illustrates this hierarchy of linguistic categories.) We now take up each of these levels of organization in turn.

The Sound Units

To speak, we force a column of air up from the lungs and out through the mouth, while simultaneously moving the various parts of the vocal apparatus from one position to another (Figure 10.3). Each of these movements shapes the column of moving air and thus changes the sound produced. The human speech apparatus can emit hundreds of different speech sounds clearly and reliably, but each language makes systematic use of

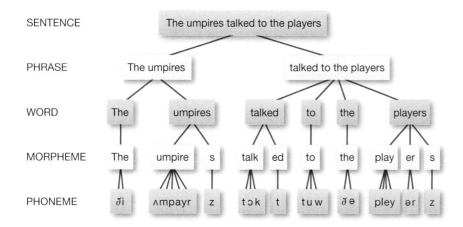

SENTENCE	The umpires talked to the players					
PHRASE	The umpires		talked to the players			
WORD	The	umpires	talked	to	the	players
MORPHEME	The	umpire s	talk ed	to	the	play er s
PHONEME	ð_i	ʌmpayr z	tɔk t	tuw	ð ə	pley ər z

10.2 The hierarchy of linguistic units
Language is hierarchical, with sentences at the top. Sentences are composed of phrases, which in turn are composed of words. Words are made up of morphemes, the smallest units of language that carry meaning. The units of sound that compose morphemes are called phonemes. Equivalent gestural units exist for signed languages.

phoneme The smallest significant unit of sound in a language. Alphabetic characters roughly correspond to phonemes (e.g., *apt*, *tap*, and *pat* are all made up of the same phonemes).

only a small number of these physical possibilities. For example, consider the English word *bus*, which can be pronounced with more or less of a hiss in the *s*. This sound difference, though audible, is irrelevant to the English-language listener, who interprets what was heard to mean "a large vehicle" in either case. But some sound distinctions do matter, for they signal differences in meaning. Thus, neither *butt* nor *fuss* will be taken to mean "a large vehicle." This suggests that the distinctions among *s*, *f*, and *t* sounds are relevant to the perception of English, while the difference in hiss duration is not. The sound categories that matter in a language are called its **phonemes**. English uses about 40 different phonemes.* Other languages select their own sets. For instance, German uses certain guttural sounds that are never heard in English, and French uses some vowels that are different from the English ones, making trouble for Americans who are trying to order *le veau* or *le boeuf* in Parisian restaurants (Ladefoged & Maddieson, 1996; Poeppel & Hackl, 2007).

Not every phoneme sequence occurs in every language. Sometimes these gaps are accidental. For instance, it just so happens that there is no English word *pilk*. But other gaps are systematic effects of the language design. As an illustration, could a new breakfast food be called *Pritos*? How about *Glitos* or *Tlitos*? Each of these would be a new word in English, and all can be pronounced, but one seems wrong: *Tlitos*. English speakers sense that English words never start with *tl*, even though this phoneme sequence is perfectly acceptable in the middle of a word (as in *motley* or *battling*). So the new breakfast food will be marketed as tasty, crunchy *Pritos* or *Glitos*. Either of these two names will do, but *Tlitos* is out of the question. The restriction against *tl* beginnings is not a restriction on what human tongues and ears can do. For instance, one Northwest Indian language is named Tlingit, obviously by people who are perfectly willing to have words begin with *tl*. This shows that the restriction is a fact about English specifically. Few of us are conscious of this pattern, but we have learned it and similar patterns exceedingly well, and we honor them in our actual language use.

Languages differ from one another in several other ways at the level of sound. There are marked differences in the rhythm in which the successive syllables occur, and

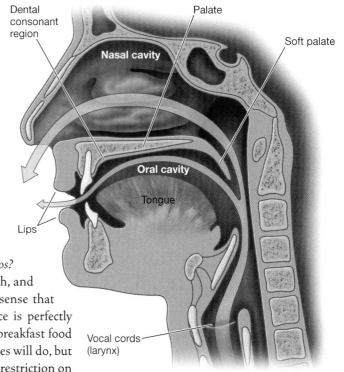

Dental consonant region

Palate

Soft palate

Nasal cavity

Oral cavity

Tongue

Lips

Vocal cords (larynx)

10.3 The human vocal tract Speech is produced by air flow from the lungs that passes through the larynx (popularly called the voice box) containing the vocal cords and from there through the oral and nasal cavities, which together make up the vocal tract. Different vowels are created by movements of the lips and tongue, which change the size and shape of the vocal cavity. Consonants are produced by various articulatory movements that temporarily obstruct the air flow through the vocal tract.

---

*The English alphabet provides only 26 symbols (letters) to write these 40 phonemes, and so often the same symbol is used for more than one phoneme. Thus, for example, the letter *O* stands for two different phonemes in *hot* and *cold*, an "ah" sound and an "oh" sound. This fact—that the written and spoken symbols do not quite match—contributes to the difficulty of learning how to read English.

10.4 The actual sound pattern of speech This figure shows the moment-by-moment sound amplitudes produced by a speaker uttering the sentence *There are no silences between words*. Listeners must figure out where one word ends and the next begins, a process known as segmentation. This problem is even harder for those just learning the language, including infants (see p. 399) and adult second-language learners as well: Because they cannot easily segment the speech stream into its component words, they get the subjective impression that the foreign speech is being pronounced "too fast."

| ThereAre | NoS | ilen | ces | Bet | weenWord | s |

10.5 Phoneme streams can create ambiguity

"Boy, he must think we're pretty stupid to fall for that again."

morpheme The smallest significant unit of meaning in a word (e.g., the word *boys* has two morphemes, *boy* and *-s*).

differences as well in the use and patterning of stress (or accent) and tone (or pitch). For instance, in languages such as Mandarin Chinese or Igbo, two words that consist of the same phoneme sequence, but that differ in tone, can mean entirely different things. Languages also differ in how the phonemes can occur together within syllables. Some languages, such as Hawaiian and Japanese, regularly alternate a single consonant with a single vowel. Thus, we can recognize words like *Toyota* and *origami* as "sounding Japanese" when they come into common English usage. In contrast, syllables with two or three consonants at their beginning and end are common in English; for example, *flasks* or *strengths*.

Speech can be understood at rates of up to about 250 words per minute. The normal rate is closer to 180 words per minute, which converts to about 15 phonemes per second. These phonemes are usually fired off in a continuous stream, without gaps or silences in between the words (Figure 10.4). This is true for phonemes within a single word and also for words within a phrase, so that sometimes it is hard to know whether one is hearing "that great abbey" versus "that gray tabby" or "The sky is falling" versus "This guy is falling" (Levelt, 1989; Liberman, Cooper, Shankweiler, & Studdert-Kennedy, 1967; see Figure 10.5).

Morphemes and Words

At the next level of the linguistic hierarchy (see Figure 10.2), fixed sequences of phonemes and syllables are joined together into morphemes. The **morphemes** are the smallest language units that carry bits of meaning. Examples of morphemes are *talk*, *tree*, and the *-ed* morpheme that marks the past tense. Some words consist of a single morpheme, such as *and*, *man*, and *bake*, while others contain more than one, for example, *waterfall*, *talked*, and *downstairs*.

CONTENT MORPHEMES AND FUNCTION MORPHEMES

Morphemes such as *bake* and *man* that carry the main burden of meaning are called **content morphemes**. The morphemes that not only add details to the meaning (such as plurality or tense) but also serve various grammatical purposes (such as the suffixes *-ed* and *-ness* and the connecting words *and* and *which*) are called **function morphemes**. This distinction of morpheme type, existing in all languages, is reflected in the sound characteristics of the language, so that content and function morphemes are pronounced somewhat differently, with the function words more likely to be shorter and unstressed (Shi, Morgan, & Allopenna, 1998). The intermixing of function and content morphemes in sentences is an important factor giving speech its rhythmic cadence of strong and weak beats (Nespor, Peña, & Mehler, 2003). Some function morphemes cannot stand alone and must be joined with others to make up a complex word. We mentioned *-ed*; other examples are *-er* (meaning "one who") and *-s* (meaning "more than one"). When these are joined with the morpheme *bake* (meaning "to cook by slow heating") into the complex word *bakers* (bake + *er* + *s*), the meaning becomes correspondingly complex ("ones who cook by slow heating"). And once again (just as with phonemes) there are constraints on where in the sequence each morpheme occurs. We could not, intelligibly, say *erbakes* or *bakeser* instead of *bakers*.

Recordings of activity in the brain reveal that content and function morphemes are processed in different ways during normal language activities (C. M. Brown, Hagoort, & ter Keurs, 1999). Relatedly, in brain injury a person's ability to utter or process function morphemes may be compromised while the content words remain intact (the reverse condition also occurs, though more rarely), confirming the fact that these two types of words rely on partly different brain circuits and are sited differently in the brain (see Chapter 3 for a discussion of aphasia).

Phrases and Sentences

Words and phrases now combine to form sentences. Once again, at this new level of complexity, there are constraints on the permitted sequences. *House the is red* and *Where put you the pepper?* are ungrammatical—not in keeping with the regularities of form that characterize a particular language. One might at first glance think that the grammaticality of a sentence is just a matter of meaningfulness—whether the sequence of words has yielded a coherent idea or thought. But this is not so. Some word sequences are easily interpretable, but still seem badly constructed (*That infant seems sleeping*). Other sequences are not interpretable, but seem well constructed even so (*Colorless green ideas sleep peacefully*). This latter sequence makes no sense (ideas neither sleep nor are colorful; green things are not colorless), and yet is well formed in a way that *Sleep green peacefully ideas colorless* is not. Thus grammaticality depends not directly on meaning, but on conformance with some rule-like system—patterns of sentence formation that are akin to those of the rules of arithmetic or of chess. Much as you cannot (as a competent calculator) add 2 and 2 to yield 5 or (as a competent chess player) move a King two squares in any direction, you cannot put the noun before the article (as in *House the is red*) to yield a sentence in English. So, by analogy to chess, and so on, the patterns describing how words and phrases can combine into sentences are called the "**rules of grammar**" or "**syntax**."

We should emphasize that we have not been speaking here about the "rules of proper English" imposed on groaning children by school teachers and literary critics—rules forbidding the use of "ain't," or of ending a sentence with a preposition. These latter rules are some people's prescriptions for *how language should be* (rather than *how it really is*), a matter that usually is based on which dialect of the language has the most prestige or social cachet (see Labov, 2007). In contrast, the rules of syntax that we are discussing are the implicitly known psychological principles that organize language use and understanding in all humans, including very young children as well as adults, and members of unschooled societies as well as professors of literature and CEOs of major corporations.

The study of syntax has been one of the chief concerns of linguists and psycholinguists, with much of the discussion building from the theories of Noam Chomsky (Chomsky, 1965, 1995; Figure 10.6). As Chomsky emphasized, this interest in the rules governing word combination is not surprising if one wants to understand the fact that we can say and understand a virtually unlimited number of new things, all of them "in English." We put our words together in ever new sentences to mean ever new things, but we have to do so systematically or our listeners won't be able to decipher the new combinations.

content morpheme A morpheme that carries the main semantic and referential content of a sentence. In English content morphemes are usually nouns, verbs, adjectives, or adverbs.

function morpheme A morpheme that, while adding such content as time, mode, individuation, and evidentiality, also serves a grammatical purpose (e.g., the suffixes -*s* and -*er*, or the connecting words *and* or *if*).

rules of syntax (or grammar) The regular principles governing how words can be assembled into sentences.

10.6 **Noam Chomsky (1928–)** Noam Chomsky is an American linguist who has pioneered modern approaches to the study of language. His theoretical and empirical contributions over several decades have underpinned the synthesis of linguistics, computer science, and psychology that today is known as cognitive science. Chomsky also is widely known for commentary on social and political issues.

THE BASICS OF SYNTACTIC ORGANIZATION

Consider the simple sentence *The zebra bit the giraffe*. It consists of two major subparts or phrases, a noun phrase (*the zebra*) and a verb phrase (*bit the giraffe*). Linguists depict this partitioning of the sentence by means of a **tree diagram**, so called because of its branching appearance:

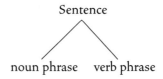

This notation is a useful way of showing that individual sentences comprise a hierarchy of structures (as in Figure 10.2). Each sentence can be broken down into phrases, and these phrases into smaller phrases. Thus, our verb phrase redivides as a verb (*bit*) and a noun phrase (*the giraffe*).

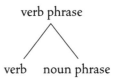

These subphrases in turn break down into the component words and morphemes. The descending branches of the tree correspond to the smaller and smaller units of sentence structure. The whole tree structure is called a **phrase structure description** (shown as Figure 10.7).

The phrase structure description is a compact way of describing our implicit knowledge of how sentences are organized. Notice that recurrent labels in these trees reflect the fact that phrases are organized in the same way regardless of where they occur. For example, there are two instances of the label "noun phrase" in Figure 10.7. Each English noun phrase (except for pronouns and proper names) follows the same pattern whether it is at the start, middle, or end of a sentence: Articles such as *a* and *the* come first; any adjectives come next; then the noun. This patterning accounts for why anyone who rejects a sentence like *The shirt green fit him well* as a grammatical sentence of English is guaranteed also to reject *Albert is wearing the shirt green* and *They bought the shirt green at Walmart on Thursday*. In essence, then, phrase structure rules define groups of words as modules that can be plugged in anywhere that the sentence calls for a phrase of the specified type. Other languages choose wholly or partly different

tree diagram A geometric representation of the structure of a sentence. Its nodes are labeled with phrase- (e.g., noun phrase) and word-class (e.g., adjective) category names, and the descending branches indicate relationships among these categories.

phrase structure description A tree diagram or labeled bracketing that shows the hierarchical structure of a sentence.

10.7 The structure of the sentence *The zebra bit the giraffe* This tree diagram is called a phrase structure description because it shows how the sentence can be analyzed into phrase units. Notice particularly that there are two noun phrases in this sentence. The first one (*the zebra*) is the subject of this sentence. The second one (*the giraffe*) is inside the verb phrase (*bit the giraffe*). A description of this kind also shows the word class types (e.g., article, noun, verb) of which each phrase consists. Finally, the tree shows the words of the sentence (the bottom row in the tree).

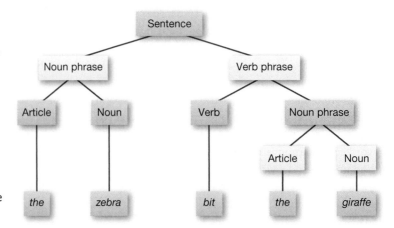

orderings of words inside the phrase (e.g., French *la chemise verte*) and of phrases within the sentence, but they make their phrase structure choices just as regularly and systematically as does English.

Because the phrase structure of a sentence is its fundamental organizing principle, anything that conforms to or reveals this structure will aid the listener during the rapid process of understanding a sentence, and anything that obscures or complicates the phrase structure will make comprehension that much more difficult. To illustrate, one investigator asked listeners to memorize strings of nonsense words that they heard spoken. Some of the strings had no discernible structure at all, for example, *yig wur vum rix hom im jag miv*. Other strings also included various function morphemes, for example, *the yigs wur vumly rixing hom im jagest miv*. One might think that sequences of the second type would be harder than the first to memorize, for they are longer. But the opposite is true. The function morphemes allowed the listeners to organize the sequence as a phrase structure, and these structured sequences were appreciably easier to remember and repeat (W. Epstein, 1961). Figure 10.8 shows that phrase structure organization facilitates reading much as it does listening.

HOW LANGUAGE CONVEYS MEANING

So far, our survey of language has concentrated attention on the forms of language. Now we turn to the topic of meaning. As we shall see, structure and meaning crucially link together in the linguistic organization of thought.

The Meanings of Words

Word meanings are of many different kinds. Some words such as *Madonna* and *Batman* describe individuals in the real and imaginary worlds; others such as *dog* and *unicorn* are more general and describe categories of things. Yet other words describe substances (*water*, *Kryptonite*), properties (*green*, *imaginary*), relations (*similar*, *uncle*), quantities (*some*, *zillions*), actions (*run*, *transform*), states of mind (*knowing*, *hoping*) or being (*am*, *seem*), and manners of doing (*carefully*, *musically*). A moment's thought reveals that the type of meaning is correlated with the so-called parts of speech, with things and stuff generally labeled by nouns, acts and states by verbs, properties by adjectives, and manners by adverbs. As can be expected with any informally evolving and changing system like a human language, these form-to-meaning correlations are not perfect and sometimes the exceptions can be striking. For instance, it is just an arbitrary fact, without semantic explanation, that in present-day English the word *thunder* can appear as either a noun or a verb (*Thunder frightens my dog*; *The king thunders out his commands to the peasants*) whereas *lightning* is a noun only (*Lightning frightens my dog* sounds fine, but *The king lightnings down his commands to the peasants* sounds ungrammatical).

Despite the fact that the form-meanings correlations are imperfect, they are nevertheless strong enough so that both children and adults successfully use form class (noun, verb, etc.) as a clue to the meanings of new words (R. Brown, 1957). Distinctions among word types accord with the representation of language in the brain: For example, words naming things (usually nouns) are retrieved from different neural systems than words naming actions (usually verbs), probably as a result of the different function morphemes that occur with these two word types (e.g., the plural *-s* occurs with

The large tomato	The
made	large tomato made
a satisfying splat	a satisfying
when	splat when it
it hit	hit the
the floor.	floor.

10.8 Phrase structure organization aids the reader The panel on the left (blue) shows a sentence written so that its phrases and major words mostly appear on their own lines of print. This makes reading easier because the sentence has been pre-organized so that the eye can move phrase by phrase down the page. In the panel on the right (green), the sentence has been rewritten so that bits of more than one phrase often appear on a single line. Reading is now slower and may contain more errors because the phrasal organization has been visually disrupted.

Tho' a particular colour, taste, and smell are qualities all united together in this apple, it is easy to perceive they are not the same, but are at least distinguishable from each other.

10.9 The definitional theory of meaning applied to the delicious complexity of apples David Hume (1711–1776), the great British Empiricist philosopher, was among the first to claim that most of our concepts (in this example, [apple]) are complex, constructed by putting together simpler concepts such as [red], [round], and [sweet].

definitional theory of word meaning The theory that mental representations of word meanings consist of a necessary and sufficient set of semantic features. The representation of *apple*, for example, might be [round], [edible], [sweet], [red], [juicy].

semantic feature A basic semantic category or concept that cannot be decomposed into smaller or less inclusive categories. According to several strict theories (e.g., Hume, 1739), the basic features are all sensory-perceptual.

10.10 Can a white rose be red? The Queen had ordered the gardeners to plant a red rose bush, but they planted a white one by mistake. They are now trying to repair their error by painting the white roses red. On the definitional theory of meaning, this seems reasonable enough. For the expressions *red rose bush* and *white rose bush* differ by only a single feature— [red] versus [white]. But if so, why are the gardeners so terrified that the Queen will discover what they did? (From Lewis Carroll's *Alice in Wonderland*)

nouns but the past-tense -*ed* occurs with verbs; Tyler, Bright, Fletcher, & Stamatakis, 2004). These distinct neural systems can be independently compromised in brain injury, so that the person loses the use of one type of word but still maintains the other type (Bates, Chen, Tzeng, Li, & Opie, 1991; Caramazza & Hillis, 1991).

THE DEFINITIONAL THEORY OF WORD MEANING

At first glance, the words of a language seem to be like little atoms of meaning, each distinct from all the others. But several theories of word meaning assert that only a handful of words in a language describe elementary, "simple" ideas or concepts. The rest are more like molecules: They are composites of more elementary atoms of meaning. Thus, words like *yellow* and *round* might indeed name simple ideas or concepts, but other words seem more complex: For example, the words *canary* and *banana* involve not only *yellowness* but other elements as well (in these cases, *animal* and *fruit*, respectively) (Hume, 1739; Jackendoff, 2002; Katz & Fodor, 1963; Figure 10.9).

These observations are central to a **definitional theory of word meaning,** which states that words are represented in our minds much as they are in ordinary dictionaries (Figure 10.10). According to this theory, each word can be understood as a bundle of meaning atoms, or **semantic features.** In a dictionary, for example, a *bachelor* would be defined as "an adult human male who has never married." The psychological representation of *bachelor* in our brains according to the definitional theory of meaning is much the same: The full meaning of each word is a set of semantic atoms that are essential for membership in the category named by the word. Thus, to continue with the same example, *bachelor* is composed of the set of semantic features [single], [human], [adult], and [male]. These features are individually necessary for bachelorhood and so, if some creature is missing any one of them (e.g., if the creature is married, or is an adult male duck), it could not correctly be called "a bachelor." And this set of features is

also jointly sufficient for bachelorhood, regardless of other traits: Some man may be tall or short, flirtatious or shy, but still can correctly be called *a bachelor*. The theory thus describes the boundary conditions for bachelorhood, and in so doing would account for how we identify and label those who are (and are not) bachelors when we encounter them.

The definitional theory of meaning also describes many other important facts about how words seem to be related to each other: Words that share features are to that extent predicted to be similar in meaning (*wicked-evil*); words with single opposed features are antonyms (*wicked-good*); words that share no features (*wicked-turqoise*) are unrelated in meaning. The feature similarities also allow us to identify clusters of words—for example, *bachelor, uncle, brother, gander,* and *stallion*—by all being items that share the feature of [maleness].*

Summarizing, then, the proposal is that we carry a semantic-feature definition in our heads for each word in our vocabulary. These features allow us to recognize new instances of each category, to understand how words are meaningfully related to each other, and to understand the sentences of which the words are the component parts.

THE PROTOTYPE THEORY OF MEANING

The definitional theory faces several problems. For one thing, it is surprisingly hard to come up with definitions that cover all the uses of words. Consider for example the (proposed) definition of *bird* in Figure 10.11. This definition seems promising, but, in fact, not all birds are feathered (neither baby birds nor plucked birds have feathers, but still they are birds). The author of the dictionary definition in the figure acknowledges this problem by hedging on the feathers issue, writing "more or less completely covered with feathers." And the picture helps in some ways, filling in what the words miss, but notice that the picture is far too particular to describe the range of real birds; it hardly seems appropriate for the emus or the albatrosses (Fodor, 1983; G. L. Murphy, 2002).

A related problem is that some members of a meaning category appear to exemplify that category better than others do. Thus, a German Shepherd strikes us as a more typical dog than a Pekinese, and an armchair is somehow a better example of furniture than is a reading lamp. This typicality difference is at odds with the analysis we have described thus far, whose aim was to specify the necessary and sufficient attributes that define a concept. A dictionary-type definition is meant to locate the boundaries of a category, so that each case is either inside the boundary (and thus a member of the category) or outside (and thus not a member). But this simple in-or-out division seems not to capture the intuition that some category members are "better" than others.

In general, the definitional theory fails even to pick out all and only the category members as it was designed to do. Returning to the example with which we began: Are there really semantic features that characterize all birds and that characterize birds only? One might think that being able to fly is a feature of all birds, but it is not. (Ostriches can't fly.) And not everything that lays eggs (turtles), or flies (airplanes, helicopters), or has feathers (hats, quilts, quill pens) is a bird. Besides, more than half the birds don't lay eggs at all (the babies and the males). With all these exceptions in mind, perhaps it is wrong to suppose that we can ever find a set of necessary and sufficient features for the concept of *bird* (Figure 10.12). But if not, then the definitional theory is not correct.

Objections like these have led many investigators to reject definitional theory and to argue for an alternative approach to the mental representation of concepts, called **prototype theory** (Medin, Goldstone, & Gentner, 1993; Rosch, 1973b; E. E. Smith &

---

*It is important to distinguish between the word and its semantic features. Thus, [male] may be a semantic feature or atom that constitutes part of the meaning of such words as *stallion* and *brother*. But there is also a word *male*. It is the kind of word that consists of only the single semantic feature [male]. At a lower level of language, a related phenomenon exists. The English indefinite article *a* is a word (the one that appears in the phrase *a cat*), but it is also a phoneme. That is, *a* is the rare case of a word that, at the level of sound, contains only one phoneme rather than a sequence of phonemes. In the same sense, *male* is the relatively rare case, according to definitional theory, of a word that contains only a single semantic feature, [male].

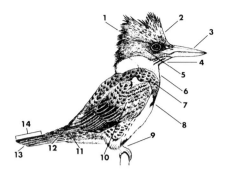

10.11 Is this the entry for *bird* in your mental dictionary? "bird . . . n. . . . [ME brid, bird, fr. OE bridd] . . . 2: Any of a class (Aves) of warm-blooded vertebrates distinguished by having the body more or less completely covered with feathers and the forelimbs modified as wings. . . . "bird 2 (kingfisher): 1 crest, 2 crown, 3 bill, 4 throat, 5 auricular region, 6 breast, 7 scapulars, 8 abdomen, 9 tarsus, 10 upper wing coverts, 11 primaries, 12 secondaries, 13 rectrix, 14 tail" (*Merriam-Webster's Collegiate Dictionary*, 11th ed.).

10.12 Diversity within categories These creatures differ in many regards, but both are instances of the category *bird*. The enormous diversity of instances within categories is one reason why categories are difficult to define. The robin (A) is a prototypical bird for temperate-zone dwellers. The ostrich (B) is a nonprototypical bird even in its native habitats because it is way bigger than any average-sized bird and it can't even fly.

prototype theory A theory in which concepts or word meanings are formed around average or typical values.

family resemblance structure An overlapping set of semantic features shared by members of a category, such that no members of the category need to have all of the features but all members have at least one of them.

prototype The typical or most familiar example of a category (e.g., a robin is a prototypical bird for many Americans but an auk might be the prototype for Laplanders).

Courtesy Sharon Armstrong

10.13 The Smith brothers and their family resemblance The Smith brothers are related through family resemblance, though no two brothers share all features. The one who has the greatest number of the family attributes is the most prototypical. In the example, it is Brother 9 who has all the family features: brown hair, large ears, large nose, moustache, and eyeglasses.

Medin, 1981; E. E. Smith, Osherson, Rips, & Keane, 1988). According to prototype theory, the meaning of many words is still described as a set of component features, but not a necessary and sufficient set of them. Instead, the concept is held together in a **family resemblance structure** (Wittgenstein, 1953). Consider the ways that members of a family resemble each other. Joe may look like his father to the extent that he has his eyes; he may look like his mother by virtue of his prominent chin. His sister Sue may look like her father because she has his nose, and she may smile just like her mother. But Joe and Sue may have no feature in common (he has his grandfather's nose and she has Aunt Fanny's eyes), so the two of them do not look alike at all. Even so, they are both easily recognized as members of the family, for they each bear some resemblance to their parents (Figure 10.13). Some members of the family may have more of these features than others do and thus are more "prototypical" or central for the category. Informally, such central members are often called "typical Smiths," or "perfect Schwartzes."

According to some psychologists, we carry in memory such mental **prototypes** for each of our concepts—a prototypical bird, a prototypical chair, and so on (Barselou, 1985; Gentner, 1983; Goldstone, Lippa, & Shiffrin, 2001). Each prototype provides something like a mental average of all the examples of the concept that we have encountered. In the case of birds, people in the mainland United States have seen far more robins than penguins. As a result, something that resembles a robin will be stored in their memory system and will then be associated with the word *bird*. When the person later sees a new object, she will judge it to be a bird to the extent that it resembles the prototype in some way. A sparrow resembles it in many ways and so is judged to be a "good" bird; a penguin resembles it just a little and hence is a "marginal" bird; a rowboat resembles it not at all and hence is judged to be no bird.

Support for the prototype view comes from numerous studies. When people are asked to come up with examples of some category, they generally first produce instances that are close to the prototype (e.g., robins rather than ostriches). People also respond "yes" more quickly when asked about the truth of the sentence *A robin is a bird* than of *An ostrich is a bird*. This is perfectly sensible. A robin resembles the bird prototype and so the similarity is readily discerned, allowing a fast response. For an ostrich, one must spend a moment searching for its relatively few birdy features, so verification is slower (Rosch, 1978; Tversky, 1977).

COMBINING DEFINITIONAL AND PROTOTYPE THEORIES

The prototype view helps us understand why a spindle-shaped trout seems fishier than a long, skinny seahorse, but the definitional theory seems important if we are to explain why a whale, which looks suspiciously like a fish, isn't one at all while a seahorse is a fish despite its shape (Connolly, Fodor, Gleitman, & Gleitman, 2007; Fodor & Lepore, 1996). Perhaps we can combine both views of meaning rather than choosing between them (Armstrong, Gleitman, & Gleitman, 1983).

Consider the word *grandmother*. For this term, there are necessary and sufficient features, so here the definitional theory seems just right: A grandmother is necessarily a female parent of a parent. But there may also be a prototype: A really grandmotherly grandmother is a woman who is old and gray, has a kindly twinkle in her eye, and bakes delicious cookies. When we say that someone is *grandmotherly*, we are surely referring to the prototypical attributes of grandmothers, not to genealogy. And, in many circumstances we use this prototype rather than the definition. For example, we are likely to rely on our grandmother prototype for picking a grandmother out of a crowd of people and for predicting what someone's grandmother will be like, even though such predictions are fallible (see Figure 10.14). We may also metaphorically call an individual "grandmotherly" if she is childless but has the prototypical gray-and-twinkly attributes of most—though not all—definitional grandmothers (Gleitman, Armstrong, & Connolly, in press; Landau, 1982).

It appears, therefore, that people have two partly independent mental representations of most if not all words. Though there are strict (necessary and sufficient) criteria for being a bachelor, we all know what is intended when someone meeting these criteria is ironically described as "not your typical bachelor" or metaphorically called "a married bachelor."

10.14 **Prototypes and definitions** Tyler Perry playing the role of Madea might resemble the typical grandmother, but as a male, he is surely not a real grandmother. In contrast, Goldie Hawn is far from the prototype but is, in reality, a grandmother.

WORD MEANINGS IN "FOLK THEORIES" OF THE WORLD

Our understanding of words is embedded in a web of beliefs that is broader than either the theory of definitions or the theory of prototypes can describe (Medin, Atran, Cox, Coley, & Proffitt, 2006). We seem to have well-developed ideas (sometimes called "folk theories") of why objects or properties are the way they are, and therefore how they could and could not change without becoming something altogether different (Keil, 1989; Locke, 1690). For instance, lawnmowers that are now made out of steel and plastics might one day be constructed from the kinds of exotic metals that today are only used in spacecraft. But some materials such as shaving cream or ice could never be considered for lawnmowers because they could not support the essential function of such a device. We therefore confidently say, *A lawnmower could be made out of wood or titanium, but cannot be made of ice.* This statement does not flow from a definition (which presumably would mention neither wood nor ice), and also cannot be easily derived from the prototype (since wood and ice lawnmowers would both be very distant from the prototype). No more does the statement derive from our experience, because we have never seen a (failed) lawnmower made of ice. Rather, this statement (and many other thoughts about this concept) reflects the fact that we hold a nonconscious mental "theory" of what makes a lawnmower a lawnmower, and this theory guides us in many aspects of our thinking about lawnmowers.

The Meanings of Sentences

Sentences have meanings too, over and above the meanings of the words they contain. This is obvious from the fact that two sentences can be composed of all and only the same words and yet be meaningfully distinct. For example, *The giraffe bit the zebra* and *The zebra bit the giraffe* describe different events, a meaning difference of some importance, at least to the zebra and the giraffe.

The typical sentence introduces some topic (the **subject** of the sentence) and then makes some comment, or offers some information, about that topic (the **predicate**). Thus, when we say, *The giraffe bit the zebra*, we introduce the giraffe as the topic, and then we *propose* or *predicate* of the giraffe that it bit the zebra. Accordingly, sentence meanings are often called **propositions**. In effect, a simple sentence describes a miniature drama in which the verb is the action and the nouns are the performers, each playing a different **semantic role.** In *The zebra bit the giraffe*, the zebra plays the role of doer or agent who causes or instigates the action, the giraffe is the done-to—the thing affected by the action, and biting is the action itself. The job of a listener who wants to

subject noun phrase The noun phrase immediately descending from the root of the sentence tree. In simple English sentences, this noun phrase usually plays the semantic role of actor or agent of the action.

predicate verb phrase The verb phrase immediately descending from the root of the sentence tree. In simple English sentences, this verb phrase usually expresses the action or state of the agent or actor.

proposition A predicate-argument structure. In a sentence, the verb is the predicated act or state and the noun phrases are its arguments, playing various semantic roles.

semantic role The part that each phrase plays in the "who did what to whom" drama described by a sentence. One word takes the role of being the cause of the action, another, its effect, and so on.

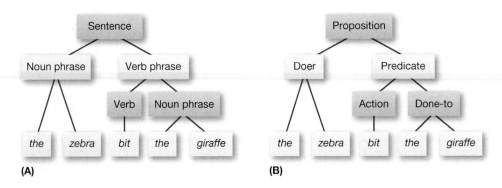

10.15 From structure to meaning (A) The structure of the sentence *The zebra bit the giraffe* (simplified); (B) The drama of who-did-what-to-whom as reconstructed by the listener from the structure in (A).

understand a sentence, then, is to determine which actors are portraying the various roles and what the plot (the action) is; that is, to decide on the basis of sentence structure who did what to whom.

For the very simplest sentences of a language, their grammatical structure links up rather directly to the semantics of who-did-what-to-whom (M. C. Baker, 2001; Grimshaw, 1990; Jackendoff, 2002). To get a feel for how this system works, see Figure 10.15A, which shows the phrase structure of the *zebra* sentence. We can "read" the semantic roles off of this syntactic tree by attending to its geometry, as shown in Figure 10.15B. The doer of the action is the noun phrase that branches directly from the root of the tree (a position known as "the sentence subject," namely, *the zebra*). The "done-to" is the noun phrase that branches off of the verb phrase (a position known as "the direct object," namely, *the giraffe*). So different noun phrases in the syntactic structure have different semantic roles. More complex sentences of the language will encode yet further semantic roles and relations, for example, *The* nanny (do-er) *feeds* (act) *some soup* (done-to, or thing affected) *to the baby* (recipient) *with a spoon* (instrument).

Summarizing, the position of the words and phrases in this simple sentence of English is providing the semantic role information to the listener. Serialization is of central importance in this regard in English and many other languages. However, there is another type of information, used in the English pronoun system, that can signal the semantic roles without regard to serial position. For instance, the sentences *He had always admired her intelligence* and *Her intelligence is what he had always admired* mean the same thing. It is the particular form of a pronoun (*he* versus *him*, *she* versus *her*) that assigns the semantic roles in this case. Many languages use something analogous to our pronoun system as the primary means for signaling semantic roles, for nouns as well as pronouns. They do this with **case markers**, which usually occur as function morphemes. When case markers occur regularly in a language, the word order itself can be much more flexible than it is in English. In Finnish, for example, the words meaning *zebra* and *giraffe* change their serial order in *Seepra puri kirahvia* and *Kirahvia puri seepra*, but in either order it is the giraffe (*kirahvia*) who needs the medical attention. It is the suffix *-a* (rather than *-ia*) that in both sentences identifies the zebra as the aggressor in this battle.

case marker A word or affix that indicates the semantic role played by some noun phrase in a sentence.

COMPLEX SENTENCE MEANINGS

In very simple sentences, as we have seen, the phrase structure straightforwardly reflects the propositional meaning of who-did-what-to-whom. But the sentences we encounter in everyday conversation are usually much more complicated than these first examples. Many factors contribute to complexity. Sometimes we reorder the phrases so as to emphasize aspects of the scene other than the doer (*It was the giraffe who got bitten by the zebra*). Sometimes we wish to question (*Who bit the giraffe?*) or command (*Bite that giraffe!*) rather than merely comment on the passing scene. And often we wish to express our attitudes (beliefs, hopes, and so forth) toward certain events (*I was delighted to hear that the zebra bit the giraffe*), or to relate one proposition to another, and so will utter two or more of them in the same sentence (*The zebra* **that arrived from Kenya** *bit the giraffe*). All this added complexity of meaning is mirrored by corresponding complexities in the sentence structures themselves.

Most ordinary language users fluently utter, write, and understand many sentences 50, 100, or more morphemes in length. The example below is from a blogger writing about ordering beauty supplies on line—so we can hardly protest that it was the unusual creation of some linguistic Einstein or literary giant:

> *However, I didn't know how to order it and came across your site where you found free trial supplies which is great because i dont want to pay for something i didnt know worked*

This author has managed to cram nine verbs in four different tenses into an informal but intricate grammatical narrative. How did he or she manage to do it? Surely not by memorizing superficial recipes like "an English sentence can end with two verbs in a row" but rather by nonconsciously appreciating combinatorial regularities of enormous generality and power that build up sentence units like acrobats' pyramids. The complex sentences are constructed by reusing the same smallish set of syntax rules that formed the simple sentences, but tying them all together using function morphemes for the nails and glue (Chomsky, 1959, 1981a; Z. Harris, 1951; Joshi, 2002).

AMBIGUITY IN WORDS AND SENTENCES

Not only do sentences often become complex. Very often a sentence can be interpreted more than one way: It is ambiguous. Sometimes, the ambiguity depends only on one word having two or more meanings (that is, having more than one "entry" in our mental dictionaries); examples can be seen in such newspaper headlines as *Children's Stools Useful for Garden Work; Red Tape Holds up Bridge; Prostitutes Appeal to Pope*. In many cases, though, the ambiguity depends on structure: in particular, on alternate ways that words are grouped together in the syntactic tree (*Police Are Ordered to Stop Drinking on Campus; Oil Given Free to Customers in Glass Bottles*). There is a big difference, after all, between police who [stop drinking] [on campus] and those who [stop] [drinking on campus].*

Such structural ambiguity is pervasive in everyday speech and writing, even with short and apparently simple sentences. For instance, *Smoking cigarettes can be dangerous* could be a warning that to inhale smoke could harm your health, or a warning that if you leave your butt smoldering in an ashtray, your house might burn down.

How We Understand

How do listeners decipher the drama of who-did-what-to-whom from the myriad complex and ambiguous sentence forms in which this drama can be expressed? A major portion of the answer lies in a complex, rapid, nonconscious processing system churning away to recover the structure—and hence the semantic roles—as the speaker's utterance arrives word by word at the listener's ear (Marcus, 2001; Savova et al., 2007; Tanenhaus & Trueswell, 2006). To get a hint of how this system operates, notice first that the various function morphemes in speech help mark the boundaries between phrases and propositions (for instance, *but* or *and*) and reveal the roles of various content words even when their order changes. For instance, when we reorder the phrases in a so-called

---

*Notice that the verbs *cease* or *prevent* could have been used instead of *stop* in this headline, with each of these two choices removing the ambiguity in a different way.

10.16 Phrase structure influences meaning The Queen suggests a visit to the Mock Turtle. Upon being asked what a Mock Turtle is, the Queen tells Alice, "It's the thing Mock Turtle Soup is made from." Lewis Carroll's joke here is that the Queen has grouped the words wrongly, as people of his time and place would easily recognize. In Victorian England [mock] [turtle soup] was turtle soup made from veal (thus "mock" or "ersatz" turtle soup). But if the words are whimsically regrouped as [mock turtle] [soup] the implication would be that there are creatures called Mock Turtles, and one could make soup from them. (From Lewis Carroll's *Alice in Wonderland*).

garden path A premature, false syntactic analysis of a sentence as it is being heard or read, which must be mentally revised when later information within the sentence falsifies the initial interpretation, as in, e.g., *Put the ball on the floor into the box.*

passive-voice sentence, we say, *The cheese was eaten by the mouse* instead of *The mouse ate the cheese*. The telltale morphemes *-en* and *by* cue the fact that the done-to rather than the do-er has become the subject (Bever, 1970). Sometimes the rhythmic structure of speech (or the hyphen punctuation in written English) helps to disambiguate the utterance, as in the distinction between *a black bird-house* and a *black-bird house* (L. R. Gleitman & H. Gleitman, 1970; Snedeker & Trueswell, 2003; see Figure 10.16). Listeners also are sensitive to many clues from background knowledge and plausibility that go beyond syntax to discern the real communicative intents of speakers. We next discuss some examples of how these kinds of clues work together to account for the remarkable speed and accuracy of human language comprehension despite the apparent complexity and ambiguity of the task that the listener faces.

THE FREQUENCY WITH WHICH THINGS HAPPEN

Often a listener's interpretation of a sentence is guided by background knowledge, knowledge that indicates the wild implausibility of one interpretation of an otherwise ambiguous sentence (G. Altmann & Steedman, 1988; Sedivy, Tanenhaus, Chambers, & Carlson, 1999). For example, no sane reader is in doubt over the punishment meted out to the perpetrator after seeing the headline *Drunk Gets Six Months in Violin Case* (Pinker, 1994). But in less extreme cases, the correct interpretation is not immediately obvious. Most of us have had the experience of being partway through hearing or reading a sentence and realizing that somewhere we went wrong. For example, we may make a word-grouping error, as in reading a sentence that begins *The fat people eat . . .* The natural inclination is to take *the fat people* as the subject noun phrase and *eat* as the beginning of the verb phrase (Bever, 1970). But suppose the sentence continues:

The fat people eat accumulates on their hips and thighs.

Now one must go back and reread. (Notice that this sentence would have been much easier if, as is certainly allowed in English, the author had placed the function word *that* before the word *people*: *The fat that people eat accumulates on their hips and thighs*.) The partial misreading (or "mishearing" in the case of spoken language) is termed a **garden path** (in honor of the cliché phrase "led down the garden path," in which someone can be deceived without noticing it). Because of the misleading content or structure at the beginning of the sentence, the reader is enticed toward one interpretation, but he must then retrace his mental footsteps to find a grammatical and understandable alternative.

Psycholinguists have various ways of detecting when people are experiencing a garden path during reading. One is to use a device that records the motion of the reader's eyes as they move across a page of print. Slowdowns and visible regressions of these eye movements tell us where and when the reader has gone wrong and is rereading the passage (MacDonald, Pearlmutter, & Seidenberg, 1994; Rayner, Carlson, & Frazier, 1983; Trueswell, Tanenhaus, & Garnsey, 1994). Using this technique, one group of investigators looked at the effects of plausibility on readers' expectations of the structure they were encountering (see Figure 10.17). Suppose that the first three words of a test sentence are

The detectives examined . . .

Participants who read these words typically assume that *The detectives* is the subject of the sentence and that *examined* is the main verb. They therefore expect the sentence to end with some noun phrase—for example: *the evidence*. As a result, they are thrown off track when they dart their eyes forward and instead read that the sentence continues

. . . by the reporter . . .

10.17 Interpreting two complex sentences (A) Here, the reporter is examining (interviewing) the detectives to find out about the crime. (B) Here, the reporter himself examines the tell-tale evidence (ladder, footsteps, drops of blood) to find out about the crime.

(A) The detectives examined by the reporter revealed the truth about the robbery.

(B) The evidence examined by the reporter revealed the truth about the robbery.

The readers' puzzlement is evident in their eye movements: They pause and look back at the previous words, obviously realizing that they need to revise their notion that *examined* was the main verb. After this recalculation, they continue on, putting all of the pieces together in a new way, and so grasp the entire sentence:

> *The detectives examined by the reporter revealed the truth about the robbery.*

The initial pause at *by the reporter* showed that readers had been led down the garden path and now had to rethink what they were reading. But what was it exactly that led the participants off course with this sentence? Was the difficulty just that passive-voice sentences are less frequent than active-voice sentences? To find out, the experimenters also presented sentences that began

> *The evidence examined by the reporter . . .*

Now the participants experienced little or no difficulty, and read blithely on as the sentence ended as it had before (. . . *revealed the truth about the robbery*). Why? After all, this sentence has exactly the same structure as the one starting *The detectives . . .* and so, apparently, the structure itself was not what caused the garden path in this case. Instead, the difficulty seems to depend on the plausible semantic relations among the words. The noun *detectives* is a "good subject" of verbs like *examined* because detectives often do examine things—such as footprints in the garden, spots of blood on the snow, and so on. Therefore, plausibility helps the reader to believe that the detectives in the test sentence did the examining—thus leading the reader to the wrong interpretation. Things go differently, though, when the sentence begins *The evidence*, because evidence, of course, is not capable of examining anything. Instead, evidence is a likely *object* of someone's examination, and so a participant who has read *The evidence examined . . .* is not a bit surprised that the next word that comes up is *by*. This is the function morpheme that signals that a passive-voice verb form is on its way—just what the reader expected given the meanings of the first three words of the sentence (Trueswell & Tanenhaus, 1992).

It seems, then, that the process of understanding makes use of word meanings and sentence structuring as mutual guides. We use the meaning of each word (*detectives* versus *evidence*) to guide us toward the intended structure, and we use the expected structure (active versus passive) to guess at the intended meanings of the words.

WHAT IS HAPPENING RIGHT NOW?

Humans often talk about the future, the past, and the altogether imaginary. We devour books on antebellum societies that are now gone with the wind, and tales that speak of a Voldemort universe that we hope never to experience. But much of our conversation is focused on more immediate concerns, and in these cases the listener can often see what is being referred to and can witness the actions being described in words. This sets up a two-way influence—with the language we hear guiding how we perceive our surroundings, and the surroundings in turn shaping how we interpret the heard speech.

For example, in one experiment, on viewing an array of four objects (a ball, a cake, a toy truck, and a toy train), participants listening to the sentence *Now I want you to eat some cake* turned their eyes toward the cake as soon as they heard the verb *eat* (Altmann & Kamide, 1999) and before hearing *cake*. After all, it was unlikely that the experimenter would be requesting the participants to ingest the toy train. In this case, the meaning of the verb *eat* focused listeners' attention on only certain aspects of the world in view—the edible aspects!

Just as powerful are the reverse phenomena: effects of the visually observed world on how we interpret a sentence (consider the array of toy objects in Figure 10.18A). These include a beanie-bag frog sitting on a napkin and another napkin that has no toy on it. When study participants look at such scenes and hear the instruction *Put the frog on the napkin into the box*, most of them experience a garden path, thinking (when they hear the first six words) that *on the napkin* is the destination where a frog should next be placed. After all, the empty napkin seems a plausible destination for the frog. But three words later (upon hearing *into the box*) they are forced to realize that the intended destination is really the box and not the empty napkin after all. This double-take reaction is evident in the participants' eye movements: On hearing *napkin*, they look first to the empty napkin, and then look around the scene in confusion when they hear *into the box*. Of course, adult participants rapidly recover from this momentary boggle, and go on to execute the instruction correctly, picking up the frog and putting it in the box. But the tell-tale movement of the eyes has identified the temporary misinterpretation, a garden path.*

But now consider the array of objects in Figure 10.18B. It differs from the array in Figure 10.18A, for now there are two frogs, only one of which is on a napkin. This has a noticeable effect on participants' eye movements. Now, on hearing the same instruction, most of the participants immediately look to the frog that's already on a napkin when they hear *napkin*, and they show no subsequent confusion on hearing *into the box*.

10.18 The observed world influences the interpretation of an ambiguous sentence Study participants are asked to follow the instruction to *Put the frog on the napkin in the box*, but the start of this sentence can be understood in two ways. Those who see the array containing a frog sitting on a napkin and a horse (panel A) initially interpret *on the napkin* as the required destination of the frog and so first peek at the other (empty) napkin. Those who see the array containing two frogs (panel B) interpret *on the napkin* as specifying a particular frog (the frog that is on a napkin). They immediately look at and pick up this particular frog without a garden-path peek at the empty napkin.

Put the frog *on the napkin* in the box.

(A)   (B)

---

*We say "adult" here because children are very poor at recovering from these garden path situations. Once they have hit on a particular interpretation of the sentence they are hearing, they stick to that interpretation and do not mentally consider alternatives. This rigidity is a linguistic example of young children's lack of "cognitive control," a matter we will discuss when we turn to the topic of child bilingualism (Novick, Trueswell, & Thompson-Schill, 2005; Trueswell, Sekerina, Hill, & Logrip, 1999).

What caused the difference in reaction? In the array of Figure 10.18A, with only one frog, a listener does not expect the speaker to identify it further by saying *the green frog* or *the frog to the left* or *the frog on the napkin*, for there would be no point in doing so. Though such descriptions are true of that particular frog, there is no need to say so—it is obvious which frog is being discussed, because only one is in view. When the listener hears *on the napkin*, therefore, she assumes (falsely) that this is a destination, not a further specification of the frog.

Things are different, though, with the array shown in Figure 10.18B. Now there is a risk of confusion about which frog to move, and so listeners expect more information. In this two-frog situation, therefore, the listener correctly assumes that *on the napkin* is the needed cue to the uniquely intended frog, and so he does not wander down the mental garden path (Crain & Steedman, 1985; Tanenhaus, Spivey-Knowlton, Eberhard, & Sedivy, 1995; Trueswell, Sekerina, Hill, & Logrip, 1999).

CONVERSATIONAL INFERENCE: FILLING IN THE BLANKS

The actual words that pass back and forth between people are merely hints about the thoughts that are being conveyed. In fact, talking would take just about forever if speakers literally had to say all, only, and exactly what they meant. It is crucial, therefore, that the communicating pair take the utterance and its context as the basis for making a series of complicated inferences about the meaning and intent of the conversation (P. Brown & Dell, 1987; Grice, 1975; Noveck & Sperber, 2005; Papafragou, Massey, & Gleitman, 2006). For example, consider this exchange:

A: Do you own a Cadillac?
B: I wouldn't own *any* American car.

Interpreted literally, Speaker B is refusing to answer Speaker A's yes/no question. But Speaker A will probably understand the response more naturally, supplying a series of plausible inferences that would explain how her query might have prompted B's retort. Speaker A's interpretation might go something like this: "Speaker B knows that I know that a Cadillac is an American car. He's therefore telling me that he does not own a Cadillac in a way that both responds to my question with a *no* and also tells me something else: that he dislikes all American cars."

Such leaps from a speaker's utterance to a listener's interpretation are commonplace. Listeners do not usually wait for everything to be said explicitly. On the contrary, they often supply a chain of inferred causes and effects that were not actually contained in what the speaker said, but that nonetheless capture what was intended (H. H. Clark, 1992).

LANGUAGE COMPREHENSION

We have seen that the process of language comprehension is marvelously complex, influenced by syntax, semantics, the extralinguistic context, and inferential activity, all guided by a spirit of communicative cooperation. These many factors are unconsciously processed and integrated "on line" as the speaker fires 14 or so phonemes (about 3 words, on average) a second toward the listener's ear. Indeed this immediate use of all possible cues is what sometimes sends us down the garden path with false and often hilarious temporary misunderstandings (Grodner & Gibson, 2005). But in the usual case, the process of understanding would be too slow and cumbersome to sustain conversation if the mind reacted to each sentence only at its very end, after all possible information had been delivered, word by word, to the ear. The mind thus makes a trade-off between rate and accuracy of comprehension—the small risk of error is compensated for by the great gain in speed of everyday understanding. When we hear *These missionaries are ready to eat* or *Will you join me in a bowl of soup*, our common sense and language skill combine in most cases to save us from drowning in confusion (Gibson, 2006). Most of the time we don't even consciously register the various zany interpretations that the language "theoretically" makes available for many sentences (Altmann & Steedman, 1988; Carpenter, Miyake, & Just, 1995; Dahan & Tanenhaus, 2004; MacDonald, Pearlmutter, & Seidenberg, 1994; Marslen-Wilson, 1975; Tanenhaus & Trueswell, 2006).

HOW WE LEARN A LANGUAGE

Our survey of language has revealed it to be so complex that one might wonder how mere children could acquire it. But as we will see now, not only can infants learn language: They are vastly better at doing so than even the wisest adults. They recognize many words before they can even walk. The rate of word learning rapidly accelerates to about 3 a day in toddlers, to 5 or 8 or so a day in the preschool years, and to 10 to 15 words a day throughout childhood and early adolescence (P. Bloom, 2000; S. Carey, 1978). The upshot is a vocabulary of about 10,000 words by age 5 and 65,000 or so by adulthood. Late in the second year of life, toddlers start to put the words together into little sentences—"Throw ball!" "No mommy eat!"—making us poignantly aware that another human mind is among us. How is this remarkable achievement to be explained?

The Social Origins of Language Learning

Courtesy Charles Yang Family

10.19 First communicative contact

Prelinguistic infants show an intense responsiveness to speech (Figure 10.19). Neonates' heart rate quickens or slows according to whether they hear a human speaking in a tone that is excited or soothing, or disapproving versus approving. Babies do not have to learn these emotive qualities of language any more than a puppy has to learn by experience which barks or growls from other dogs are playful and which are threatening. This was shown by recording German mothers talking to their infants and then replaying the audiotape to babies who had heard only English or French up until then. The recording was presented while the baby was playing with a novel toy. When infants hear an approving German sentence uttered with its high notes and mellow cadences, they go right on playing; but on hearing the sharp and low-toned sounds of disapproval, though in a totally unfamiliar language, they drop the toy like a hot potato (Fernald, 1992). Relatedly, infants prefer to look at and accept toys from strangers who are speaking the language they have been hearing in their own (so far very brief) lives. Remarkably, they even detect something strange if they hear strangers speaking the native language *but with a foreign accent* (Kinzler, Dupoux, & Spelke, 2007; Figure 10.20). Kindergartners, too, say they'd rather be friends with newcomers who have familiar dialects than with other children who have foreign accents, even if the latter look more familiar by being of the same race as the child subjects (Kinzler, Shutts, DeJesus, & Spelke, 2009). Thus, language appears to be social and interpersonal in its very origins (E. Bates, 1976; Mandler, 2000; Tomasello, 2008) with dialect differences serving as fundamental markers for who is closest to oneself. In adulthood these same linguistic properties continue to lead to strong emotional judgments about "us" versus "them" which may be decisive for social grouping (M. C. Baker, 2001; Labov, 1972; Figure 10.21).

Method

1. Infants 10 months of age (who do not yet speak) watch a smiling young woman speaking a language and dialect just like that of the infants' parents, or speaking an unfamiliar language or dialect.

English speaker   *French speaker*

2. Subsequently, the two young women silently offer a toy to the watching baby.

Silent toy offering

Results: Infants more often and more quickly reach out to grasp the toy held by the woman who had previously spoken in the language or dialect familiar to the baby.

CONCLUSION: Language serves as an important marker of one's own trusted social group even in the pre-speech period. Some commentators have speculated that language and dialect differences evolved in our species for this same purpose: so that we could distinguish members of our own tribe or extended family from that of strangers even when all are living in close proximity (Baker, 2002).

SOURCE STUDY: Kinzler, Dupoux, & Spelke, 2007

Discovering the Building Blocks of Language

Neuroscientific findings show that infants are ready for language learning at birth or almost immediately thereafter. One group of investigators recorded changes in the blood flow in 2-day-old babies' brains in the presence of linguistic stimulation. Half of the time the babies were hearing recordings of normal human speech, and the other half of the time they were hearing that speech played backward. Blood flow in the

10.21 The power of an "H" A scene from the stage production of *My Fair Lady* in which the cockney flower girl, Eliza (Julie Andrews) is taught by the linguist Henry Higgins (Rex Harrison) how to pronounce an "H" as the British upper classes do. She thus becomes "a lady." This spoofs on the idea that language and dialect determine social group.

10.22 Detecting phonetic distinctions
This baby's head is covered with a geodesic sensor net, which picks up signals from the brain. The baby, seated in a carrier on the mother's lap, faces a loudspeaker emitting meaningless syllables, and watches a video of moving colored objects. When repeated spoken syllables were changed to new, different ones, there were significant changes in the event-related potential signals (ERPs), showing that the baby had noticed the change.

babies' left hemisphere increased for the normal speech but not for the backward speech (Gervain, Macagno, Cogoi, Peña, & Mehler, 2008). Because the left hemisphere of the brain is the major site for linguistic activity in humans, this evidence suggests that the special responsiveness to language-like signals is already happening close to the moment of birth (Figure 10.22).

THE RHYTHMIC FOUNDATIONS OF LANGUAGE LEARNING

Recall that languages vary in their significant sounds (phonemes and syllables), tones, rhythms, and melodies, enough so that most of us can guess whether a speaker is uttering Japanese or German or French speech even if we do not understand a word of any of these languages. The amazing fact is that newborn infants can do almost as well. Babies' responsiveness can be measured by an ingenious method that takes advantage of the fact that, while newborns can do very few things voluntarily, one of their earliest talents—and pleasures—is sucking at a nipple. In one study, a nonnutritive nipple (or "pacifier") was connected to a recording device such that every time the baby sucked, a bit of French speech was heard coming from a nearby loudspeaker. The 4-day-old French babies rapidly discovered that they had the power to elicit this speech just by sucking, and they sucked faster and faster to hear more of it. After a few minutes, however, they apparently got bored (or habituated to the stimulus—see Chapter 6), and therefore the sucking rate decreased. Now the experimenter switched the speech coming from the microphone from French to English. Did these neonates notice? The answer is yes. When the switch was made, their interest was reawakened, and they began sucking faster and faster again (they *dis*habituated). To perfect the experimental proof, the same recordings were flown to the United States, and the experiment was repeated with 4-day-old American babies, with the same result. American newborns also can and do discriminate between English and French speech. Indeed, by 2 months of age, not only do infants make these discriminations, but now they become linguistically patriotic and listen longer when their own native language is being spoken (Nazzi, Bertoncini, & Mehler, 1998; see also Figure 10.23).

What is it about the native language that is attracting these infants' attention at these earliest ages? It cannot be the meanings of words, because they as yet do not know any. Evidently the first feature that babies are picking up about their native tongue has to do

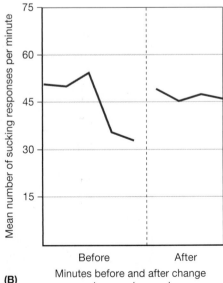

10.23 Sucking rate and speech perception in the infant (A) An infant sucks to hear "ba" or "ga." (B) The graph shows the sucking rate of 4-month-olds to "ba" or "ga." The infants soon become habituated, and the sucking rate drops. When a new stimulus is substituted ("ga" for "ba" and "ba" for "ga"), the infant dishabituates and sucks quickly once again. Similar results have been obtained for 1-month-olds. The point of the shift is indicated by the arrow.

with the characteristic rhythms of speech in that language (Darwin, 1877; Endress, Nespor, & Mehler, 2009; J. L. Morgan, 1996).

By the age of 1 or 2 months, before they can even sit up unaided, infants also become sensitive to distinctions between phonemes (Eimas, Siqueland, Jusczyk, and Vigorito, 1971). At first, infants respond to just about all sound distinctions made in any language, and so Japanese babies can detect the distinction between *la* versus *ra* as easily as American babies, despite the fact that this contrast is not readily discerned by adult Japanese speakers. However, these perceptual abilities erode if they are not exercised, and so infants lose the ability to make distinctions that are not used in their language community. Thus, Japanese infants gradually stop distinguishing between *la* and *ra*. In the same way, American infants stop distinguishing between two different *k* sounds that are perceptually distinct to Arabic speakers. By the age of 12 months, just as true speech begins, sensitivity to foreign contrasts has diminished significantly, as the baby recalibrates to listen specifically for the particulars of the language to which she is being exposed (Werker, 1995; Figure 10.24).

BUILDING THE MORPHEME AND WORD UNITS FROM THE SEPARATE SOUNDS AND SYLLABLES

Infants must also find the boundaries between words. Often it is a challenge to do so, as we see from errors that children sometimes make along the way. English-speaking toddlers often reach their arms up to their mothers and fathers, plaintively crying out, "Ca-ree-oo." This is, apparently, an infant pronunciation of *carry you*, but we know from other evidence that the children are not mixed up as to the words *you* and *me*, nor do they have an urge to lift and transport their parent. Where, then, does this odd usage come from? The children have repeatedly heard their caregivers ask them, "Do you want me to carry you?" and they apparently perceived this utterance to end in a single three-syllable word that is pronounced *carreeoo*—and means *Carry me!*

These kinds of errors often persist unnoticed for years. For instance, one 7-year-old, carefully writing her first story about a teacher, spelled out *Class be smissed!*—showing that she had falsely thought there was a word boundary within the word *dismissed* (L Gleitman, H. Gleitman, & Shipley, 1972). These word-segmentation problems come about because, as we noted earlier, spoken morphemes are not uttered with silent gaps between them, unlike the case for writing, where gaps (white spaces) demarcate the words. The right question, then, is not, How come learners make some mistakes in finding word boundaries? but rather, How come they get these right most of the time? The answer appears to be that infants mentally register which syllables occur right next to each other with unusual frequency. For instance, the syllables *rab* and *it* often occur next to each other; this is because together they form the frequent word *rabbit*. But *stub* followed by *it* is much rarer, because there does not happen to be a word in English pronounced *stubbit*. Beginning well before infants understand any meaningful words at all, they are sensitive to these frequencies of co-occurrence. This process has been demonstrated experimentally with artificial syllable sequences. Infants heard a 2-minute tape recording in which syllables were spoken in a monotonous tone, with no pauses in between the syllables. But there was a pattern. The experimenters had decided in advance to designate the sequence "pabiku" as a word. Therefore, they arranged the sequences so that if the infant heard "pabi," then "ku" was sure to follow (just as, in ordinary circumstances, hearing "rab" is a good predictor that one is about to hear "it"). For other syllables and syllable pairs, there was no invariant sequencing. Astonishingly, the babies

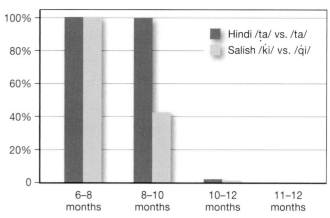

10.24 **Diminishing sensitivity to foreign language contrasts as true speech begins** The graph shows English babies' diminishing sensitivity in a dishabituation paradigm to two foreign language contrasts not made in English, as the babies move from the pre-speech period (6–8 months) to the time when they begin to speak English (11–12) months. One of these contrasts is between two *t*-like sounds that English treats as the same but the Indian language Hindi treats as significantly different—just as English treats *t* and *d* as significantly different. The other contrast is between two *k*-like sounds that English treats as the same but which the American Indian language Salish contrasts. When a sound track shifts from one of these contrasts (either /ṭa/ vs̩ /ta/ or /ki/ vs̩ /qi/, the 6-month-olds notice (and dishabituate) almost 100% of the time, but the 12-month-olds do not notice. The one-year-olds have become budding English speakers who couldn't care less about contrasts between foreign *t*'s and *k*'s.

detected these patterns and their frequencies. In a subsequent test, they showed no evidence of surprise if they heard the string "pabikupabikupabiku." From the babies' point of view, this simply repeated a pattern they already knew. However, the babies did show surprise if they were presented with the string "tudarotudarotudaro." This was not a pattern they had heard before, although they had heard each of its syllables many times. Thus, the babies had learned the vocabulary of this made-up language. They had detected the statistical pattern of which syllables followed which, despite their rather brief, entirely passive exposure to these sounds and despite the absence of any supporting cues such as pauses or meanings that go with the sounds (Aslin, Saffran, & Newport, 1998; G. F. Marcus, Vijayan, Bandi Rao, & Vishton, 1999; Saffran, 2003; Xu & Garcia, 2008).

The Growth of Word Meaning

We have just seen something of how the child discovers the basic word-like units of language. Children begin to understand a few of these words late in the first year of life, and start to talk themselves shortly thereafter, uttering such simple words as *duck* and *spoon* and *bye-bye* in appropriate contexts. How did they learn these meanings? The obvious answer appears to be that, once they have noticed a recurrent sound pattern—for example, the pattern r-a-b-i-t—they now look around the world to see which object or event is characteristically in view when that pattern of sound is heard. Aha! Rabbit! (Locke, 1690; Quine, 1960; Markman, 1994). But is such a procedure of matching up words to their extralinguistic circumstances really as easy as that? There are many reasons to suppose that the child's path to word learning is strewn with problems (Figure 10.25). One major problem is that the child's environment is complex and cluttered, so how can the baby decide what the caregiver's utterance really refers to? Even if the baby correctly identifies, say, a rabbit in view when the adult is saying "rabbit," what aspect of rabbit does the adult really have in mind? After all, whenever one sees a *rabbit*, one sees its *ear*, one sees something *furry*, and one necessarily sees an *animal* too. To which of these ideas is the adult's word really referring (Chomsky, 1959; L. R. Gleitman, 1990; Quine, 1960)? By repeated observations of words in different situations one would expect children to get much of this confusion of words and things all sorted out (Locke, 1690; Smith & Yu, 2008; Xu & Tenenbaum, 2007). For instance, if the child is lucky, she may one day hear her father say "rabbit" while she is viewing an earless rabbit or a rabbit whose ears are hidden among the cabbages. This might get the word *rabbit* sorted out from the word *ear*. But disentangling all these things, parts, properties, actions, and so forth within the visible world certainly seems to pose a formidable problem. Yet in actual fact children are impressively accurate in their discovery of word meaning and the errors that do occur are short-lived. By the time the child has a 100-word vocabulary, he is almost always correct in using words to refer to things and events in much the way that adults do. A number of factors intersect to solve this task.

Courtesy Tamara Nicol Medina

10.25 Can you guess what new word this child's mother was uttering? Maybe the rich clutter of things in infants' visible world should make them as happy as kings, but this same rich environment should make trouble for their attempts to figure out which of these objects an adult may be speaking of at any one moment, and thus to learn a new word meaning. Can you guess which word the mother was saying to the child as this photo was snapped? (See the caption accompanying Figure 10.27 for the right answer.) What clues did you use?

SOCIAL ORIGINS OF WORD LEARNING

Understanding the young learner's success in acquiring the word goes back to issues of sociality, the infant's focus on the adult's attentional state and communicative intent. We can see these effects in experiments where toddlers are taught new words (Figure 10.26; Baldwin, 1991). The child is shown a fascinating new toy and allowed to explore and play with it, whereupon the mother says excitedly, *That's a blicket! Wow, a blicket!* Will the child by a process of automatic association now think that the name for this new toy is *blicket*? In fact, rather than jumping to this conclusion right away, most children appear to seek evidence that the mother was attending to the toy too. Upon hearing the mother's voice, they immediately glance into her eyes (just as an adult would) to see if the mother herself was looking at the toy in the child's hands (and thus, probably, referring to it and not to something else when she said *blicket*). If the mother was indeed looking at this toy, then, when tested later on, the children showed that they had learned the *blicket* label for the new toy. But if the mother had been looking elsewhere—say, into a bucket whose contents were not visible to the child—the children did not assign this new word as the toy's name. Rather they thought it was the name for something, so far unseen, inside the bucket. In short, even children under 2 years of age use social context, in this case the caregiver's attentional stance toward an event, as a critical guide in language learning (Figure 10.27). They do not form word-to-meaning associations if the social context of language use does not guide them to do so (Baldwin, 1991; see also P. Bloom, 2002; Frank, Goodman, & Tenenbaum, 2009; Medina, Trueswell, Snedeker, & Gleitman, 2008; Nappa, Wessel, McEldoon, Gleitman, & Trueswell, 2009).

Look! A Dax!

(A) If the parent is looking at the toy when saying a new name, the child will assign the name "dax" to the toy.

(B) If the parent is looking at something else when saying a new name, the child will not assign the name "dax" to the toy.

10.26 Infants are mind readers! The mother says "Look! a dax!" but in (A) and (B) she is looking at two different things when she says this new word. When subsequently tested (asked to "find a dax"), the baby guesses that the mother meant "dax" to refer to the toy she (the baby) is holding only under condition (A). Under condition (B), the baby guesses that "dax" is the name for whatever the mother later pulls out of the bucket.

WHOLE OBJECTS AT THE BASIC LEVEL

Word learning is heavily influenced by the ways children think about and categorize objects and events in the world (Gordon, 2004; Rosch, 1978). This is reflected, for example, in the fact that young children acquire the **basic-level words** for whole

basic-level word A concept at some accessible, middling degree of abstractness or inclusiveness (e.g., *dog, spoon*).

10.27 If "the shoe" fits: Three contexts for learning the word *shoe* (A) The baby often can pick out the adult's intent by noticing where the adult and/or the learner himself is looking (see again Figures 10.25 and 10.26), even though there are many objects plainly in view. (B) Sometimes a lucky child will see several simplified pictures when hearing the word "shoe" (L. B. Smith & Yu, 2008). In this case the child is saved from (falsely) supposing that "shoe" means sandal, sneaker, or high heel just because the single general term applies to all three instances (Xu & Tenenbaum, 2007). (C) A particularly useful context for learning is when adult and child are socializing together on a matter relating to shoes (Medina, Trueswell, Snedeker, & Gleitman, 2008).

Courtesy Tamara Nicol Medina

(A)

(B)

(C)

superordinates Concepts that are more abstract or inclusive than basic-level concepts (e.g., *animal*, *utensil*).

subordinates Concepts that are less abstract or more particular than basic-level concepts (e.g., *poodle*, *soup spoon*).

objects (*dog*) before learning their parts (*ear*), **superordinates** (*animal*), or **subordinates** (*Chihuahua*). One might think this happens just because the basic-level words are used most frequently to children. But differential frequency does not seem to be the whole explanation. In some homes, the word *Spot* or *Rex* (specific names) is used much more often than *dog* (a basic-level term) for obvious reasons. And it is true that in this case the young learner will often come to use the word *Spot* before he learns to utter *dog*. But he first learns it as a basic-level term all the same. This is shown by the fact that he will utter *Spot* to refer to the neighbor's dog as well as his own. Similarly—and sometimes embarrassingly—the father is by far the most frequent man that many a toddler has seen and so she may point and say *Daddy*! in response to any man she sees in the street or the supermarket. Such overgeneralizations convert the interpretation from a specific name to the basic level of categorization, evidently, the most natural level for carving up experience (Mervis & Crisafi, 1978; Shipley, Kuhn, & Madden, 1983).

Children also have other biases in how they think about and use new words. In some studies, for example, experimenters have taught children nonsense words—pointing to some novel object and saying, "That is a biff." To what new objects will the child apply this new label? She generally will not use *biff* to describe other objects that happen to be made of the same material, size, or color. Instead, she uses *biff* to describe objects having the same shape as the entire original (Landau, Smith, & Jones, 1988; Soja, Carey, & Spelke, 1991). Apparently, then, learners naturally understand this new term as a label for the entire object (Markman & Hutchinson, 1984). And indeed investigation of infants' early vocabularies show that they learn many words for whole objects (such as *table*) before they acquire words for these objects' sizes (*big*), parts (*leg*), or material composition (*wood*) even though bigness, woodenness and table-leg are in principle just as visible as the whole table when the word *table* is uttered.

PERCEPTUAL AND CONCEPTUAL PROPERTIES OF CHILD LANGUAGE

The very first examples of language use (at roughly the age of 10 months) seem to involve direct labeling of objects that the child is looking at, without the inclination or ability to talk about absent things and events. But even at the tender age of 12 to 16 months, infants begin to search for an absent object whose name is mentioned (Huttenlocher, 1974). The ability to use words in the absence of their referents is firmly in place at about 18 months (Tomasello, Strosberg, & Akhtar, 1996). One demonstration is from investigators who followed 24-month-old children's gaze when they heard questions such as, "Where's the doggie?" In one condition of the experiment, the child was actually looking at a picture of a dog on a screen when she heard the question. In the second condition, the child was looking at another picture (say, of a car) to her right, but (because there were opportunities to look from side to side in advance) the child knew that the dog picture could be viewed if she shifted her eyes leftward. In the third condition, there was no dog picture—rather, a picture of a car to the right and, say, one of a shoe to the left. If the child was already looking at the picture of a dog (the first condition), naturally enough, her eyes did not shift in response to this question. In the second condition, she rapidly shifted her gaze toward the dog picture. But the big question is what the child would do in the total absence of dogs or dog pictures. If she really can think about absent objects, she ought to go right on searching to make sense of the utterance "Where is the doggie?" when a dog is not anywhere in sight. And this is precisely what happened. Apparently even the smallest toddlers can understand language "decontextualized"—that is, divorced from the immediate evidence of the senses (Swingley & Fernald, 2002).

USING KNOWN WORDS AND SENTENCES TO LEARN MORE WORDS

By the second year of life children acquire a remarkably complex new trick: They come to use the structure of the language they are learning as further information guiding their word learning (R. Brown, 1957; Fisher & Gleitman, 2002; L. R. Gleitman, 1990; D. G. Hall et al., 2000; Landau & Gleitman, 1985; Landau & Stecker, 1990; Lidz, Gleitman, & Gleitman, 2003; Fernandes, Marcus, DiNubila, & Vouloumanos, 2006; Papafragou, Cassidy, & Gleitman, 2007). In one study, 3- and 4-year-olds were shown a picture in which a pair of hands was performing a kneading sort of motion with a mass of red confetti-like material that was overflowing a low, striped container (Figure 10.28; R. Brown, 1957). Some of the children were asked, "In this picture, can you show me sebbing?" The children responded by making the same kneading motions with their hands. Other children were asked, "In this picture, can you show me a seb?" In response, the children pointed to the container. Still other children were asked, "Can you show me some seb?" These children pointed to the confetti. The evidence of grammatical word class (for example, *seb* + *ing* indicates that *seb* is a verb) for word meaning (verbs usually describe actions) influenced their understanding of what the new word referred to in the picture.

It seems, then, that children's learning proceeds in two directions at once. On the one hand, they use their growing knowledge of word classes within the language to guide their discovery of what a particular new word means. It is almost as if the child were saying to himself, "Because this new word was just used as a noun, it probably describes a thing." And similarly, they use their knowledge of individual words to predict how those words can be used: "Because this *Woodstock* toy is now an instrument for hitting me on the head, I can use it as a verb and tell my friend to 'Stop Woodstocking me or go home!'" (E. V. Clark, Gelman, & Lane, 1985; Pinker, 1984). Using both kinds of evidence, children efficiently find their way into knowledge of tens of thousands of words and the ways these words can be used in sentences (Bowerman, 1982; L. R. Gleitman, Cassidy, Papafragou, Nappa, & Trueswell, 2005; Golinkoff, Hirsh-Pasek, Cauley, & Gordon, 1987; Lidz, Gleitman, & Gleitman, 2003; Naigles, 1990; Snedeker & Gleitman, 2004).

10.28 Grammatical word classes give clues to word meaning When asked *In this picture, can you show me a seb?* (count noun), children pointed to the bowl, but when asked *In this picture, can you show me sebbing?* (verb), they pointed to the hands and made kneading or scooping motions with their own hands. And when asked *In this picture, can you show me some seb?* (mass noun), they pointed to the confetti-like contents of the bowl.

The Progression to Adult Language

Typically, children's speech progresses very rapidly by the beginning of the third year of life. Utterances now become longer and the children can say short sentences. Function words begin to appear. By 5 years the average child sounds much like an adult in the forms of her speech. How do children reach this level of sophistication? It is certainly not by memorizing all the sentences that are said to them. For one thing, we know that people, even little children, can understand sentences that are quite novel and even bizarre, such as *There is a unicorn hiding behind your left ear,* the very first time they hear them. More generally, a good estimate of the number of English sentences less than 20 words in length is 2^{30} (a bit more than a billion). A child memorizing a new sentence every 5 seconds, starting at birth, working at this 24 hours a day, would have mastered only 3% of this set by his fifth birthday, making the learning-by-memorizing strategy hopelessly implausible. But what is the alternative? We can get some hints by looking at the relatively simple case of word building. As so often, "errors" that the youngsters make along the way reveal something of the procedures involved in acquiring the adult system.

An example is the learning of the past tense. When children start using past tense verbs, often they say them correctly at first. They use the suffix *-ed* as an adult would, applying it to regular verbs, but not to irregular ones. Thus, the child says "walked" and "talked" and also (correctly) uses irregular forms such as *ran, came,* and *ate.* By the age of 4 or 5, however, the same children sometimes say "runned," "bringed," and "holded" (G. F. Marcus et al., 1992; Prasada & Pinker, 1993a) as in the following conversation:

CHILD: My teacher holded the baby rabbits and we patted them.
MOTHER: Did you say your teacher *held* the baby rabbits?
CHILD: Yes.
MOTHER: What did you say she did?
CHILD: She holded the baby rabbits and we patted them.
MOTHER: Did you say she *held* them tightly?
CHILD: No, she holded them loosely. (Bellugi, 1971)

This kind of error offers evidence that children do not learn language solely, or even mostly, by imitation. Few adults would say "holded" or "eated," and the mother in the quoted exchange repeatedly offers the correct form of the verb for imitation. In fact, parents are often aghast at these errors. A half-year earlier, their child was speaking correctly but now is making errors. Apparently, he is regressing! So parents often try to correct these errors, but to no avail: The child stands firm, despite the correction.

But if not the result of imitation, then what is it that leads children to produce "errors" even though there was conformity to the adult model's speech at an earlier developmental moment? Many investigators argue that the young child starts out by memorizing the past tense of each new verb, learning that the past tense of *want* is *wanted,* the past tense of *climb* is *climbed,* and so on. But this is a highly inefficient strategy. It is far more efficient to detect the pattern: Simply add the *-ed* suffix to a verb every time you are speaking of the past. But once the child detects this pattern, it is apparently quite easy to get carried away—to believe that what is very often true must be true in every single case—and so overregularization errors are produced. These errors will drop out later, when the child takes the further step of realizing that, while there is a pattern, there are also exceptions.

LANGUAGE LEARNING IN CHANGED ENVIRONMENTS

Under normal conditions, language seems to emerge in much the same way in virtually all children all over the world. They progress from babbling to one-word speech, advance to two-word sentences, and eventually graduate to complex sentence forms and meanings. But is this pattern truly universal? What happens when children grow up in environments radically different from those in which language growth usually proceeds? Examining these cases helps us to understand the biological roots of human language and which aspects of the early environment are essential.

Wild Children

In 1920, Indian villagers discovered a wolf mother in her den together with four cubs. Two were baby wolves, but the other two were human children, subsequently named Kamala and Amala. No one knows how they got there or why the wolf adopted them. Roger Brown (1958) tells us what these children were like:

> Kamala was about eight years old and Amala was only one and one-half. They were thoroughly wolfish in appearance and behavior: Hard callus had developed on their knees and palms from going on all fours. Their teeth were sharp edged. They moved their nostrils sniffing food. Eating and drinking were accomplished by lowering their mouths to the plate. They ate raw meat. . . . At night they prowled and sometimes howled. They shunned other children but followed the dog and cat. They slept rolled up together on the floor. . . . Amala died within a year but Kamala lived to be eighteen. . . . In time, Kamala learned to walk erect, to wear clothing, and even to speak a few words. (p. 100)

The outcome was much the same for the 30 or so other wild children about whom we have reports (Figure 10.29). When found, they were all shockingly animal-like. None of them could be rehabilitated to use language normally, though some, including Kamala, learned to speak a few words.

Isolated Children

The data from these wild children are difficult to interpret, in part because we do not know why or how the children were abandoned. Clearer data come from the (unfortunately many) cases of children raised by humans but under conditions that were hideously inhumane, for their parents were either vicious or deranged. Sometimes such parents will deprive a baby of all human contact. For example, "Isabelle" (a code name used to protect the child's privacy) was hidden away, apparently from early infancy, and given only the minimal attention necessary to sustain her life. No one spoke to her (the mother was deaf and also emotionally indifferent).

At the age of 6, Isabelle was discovered by other adults and brought into a normal environment. Of course, she had no language, and her cognitive development was below that of a normal 2-year-old. But within a year she learned to speak, her tested intelligence was normal, and she took her place in an ordinary school (R. Brown, 1958; K. Davis, 1947). Thus, Isabelle at 7 years, with 1 year of language practice, spoke about as well as her peers in the second grade, all of whom had had 7 years of practice.

But rehabilitation from isolation is not always so successful. "Genie," discovered in California about 40 years ago, was 14 years old when she was found. Since about the age of 20 months she had lived tied to a chair; she was frequently beaten and never spoken to but sometimes was barked at, because her father said she was no more than a dog. Once discovered, Genie was brought into foster care and taught by psychologists and linguists (Fromkin, Krashen, Curtiss, Rigler, & Rigler, 1974). But Genie did not become a normal language user. She says many words and puts them together into meaningful propositions as young children do, such as "No more take wax" and "Another house have dog." Thus, she has learned certain basics of language. Indeed, her semantic sophistication—what she means by what she says—is far beyond that of young children. Yet even after years of instruction, Genie has not learned the function words that appear in mature English sentences, nor does she combine propositions together in elaborate sentences (Curtiss, 1977).

10.29 A modern wild boy Ramu, a young boy discovered in India in 1976, appears to have been reared by wolves. He was deformed, apparently from lying in cramped positions, as in a den. He could not walk, and drank by lapping with his tongue. His favorite food was raw meat, which he seemed to be able to smell at a distance. After he was found, he lived at the home for destitute children run by Mother Theresa in Lucknow, Utter Pradesh. He learned to bathe and dress himself but never learned to speak. He continued to prefer raw meat and would often sneak out to prey upon fowl in the neighbor's chicken coop. Ramu died at the age of about 10 in February 1985.

Why did Genie not progress to full language learning? The best guess is that the crucial factor is the age at which language learning began. Genie was discovered after she had reached puberty, while Isabelle was only six years old when her rehabilitation began. As we shall see later, there is some reason to believe that there is a sensitive developmental period for language learning during which it is most easily acquired.

Language without Sound

American Sign Language (ASL) The manual-visual language used by most of deaf persons in the United States.

Deaf people obviously cannot perceive the spoken word. Yet they do learn a language, one that involves a complex system of gestures. In the United States, the deaf usually learn **American Sign Language** (**ASL**), but many other sign languages also exist. Plainly, then, language can exist in the absence of sound. Are these gestural systems genuine languages? One indication that they are is that these systems are not derived by translation from the spoken languages around them but are independently created within and by communities of deaf individuals (Klima et al., 1979; Senghas, 1995). Further evidence comes from comparing the structure and development of ASL to that of spoken languages. ASL has hand shapes and positions of which each word is composed, much like the tongue and lip shapes that allow us to fashion the phonemes of spoken language (Stokoe, 1960). It has morphemes and grammatical principles for combining words into sentences that are similar to those of spoken language (Supalla & Newport, 1978). Finally, babies born to deaf users of ASL (whether or not the babies themselves are deaf) pick up the system from these caregivers through informal interaction rather than by explicit instruction, just as we learn our spoken language (Newport & Ashbrook, 1977). And they go through the same steps on the way to adult knowledge as do hearing children learning English. Thus, language does not depend on the auditory-vocal channel. When the auditory modes of communication are denied to humans of normal mentality, they come up with an alternative that reproduces the same contents and structures as other language systems. It appears that language is an irrepressible human trait: Deny it to the mouth, and it will dart out through the fingers.

Language without a Model

What if children of normal mentality were raised in a loving and supportive environment but not exposed to either speech or signed language? Researchers found six children who were in exactly this sort of situation (Feldman, Goldin-Meadow, & Gleitman, 1978; Goldin-Meadow, 2000; Goldin-Meadow & Feldman, 1977). These children were deaf, so they were unable to learn spoken language. Their parents were hearing and did not know ASL. They had decided not to allow their children to learn a gestural language, because they shared the belief (held by some educators) that deaf children should focus their efforts on learning spoken language through special training in lip-reading and vocalization. This training often proceeds slowly and has limited success, so for some time these children did not have any usable access to spoken English. Not yet able to read lips, unable to hear, and without exposure to a gestural language, these children were essentially without any linguistic stimulation.

These language-isolated children soon did something remarkable: They invented a language of their own. For a start, the children invented a sizable number of gestures that were easily understood by others. For example, they would flutter their fingers in a downward motion to express snow, twist their fingers to express a twist-top bottle, and so on (Figure 10.30; Goldin-Meadow, 2003). This spontaneously developing communication system showed many parallels to ordinary language learning. The children began to gesture one sign at a time at approximately the same age that hearing children begin to speak one word at a time, and they progressed to more complex sentences in the next year or so. In these basic sentences, the deaf children placed the individual gestures in a fixed serial order, according to semantic role—again, just as hearing children do.

More recent evidence has shown just how far deaf children can go in inventing a language if they are placed into a social environment that favors their communicating with each other. In Nicaragua until the early 1980s, deaf children from rural areas were widely scattered and usually knew no others who were deaf. Based on the findings just mentioned, it was not surprising to discover that all these deaf individuals developed homemade gestural systems ("home signs") to communicate with the hearing people around them, each system varying from the others in an idiosyncratic way. But then a school was created just for such deaf children in Nicaragua, and since then they have been bused daily from all over the countryside to attend it. Just as in the American and many European cases, the school authorities have tried to teach these children to lip-read and vocalize. But on the bus and in the lunchroom, and literally behind the teachers' backs, these children (age 4 to 14 in the initial group) began to gesture to each other. Bit by bit their idiosyncratic home signs converged on conventions that they all used, and the system grew more and more elaborate (Figure 10.31; Senghas, Román, & Mavillapalli, 2006). The emerging gestural language of this school has now been observed over three generations of youngsters, as new 4-year-olds arrive at the school every year. These new members not only learn the system but also elaborate and improve on it, with the effect that in the space of 30 years a language system of considerable complexity and semantic sophistication has been invented and put to communicative use by these children (Kegl, Senghas, & Coppola, 1999; Senghas, Kita, and Özyürek, 2004). Perhaps it is true that Rome was not built in a day, but for all we know, maybe Latin was! In sum, if children are denied access to a human language, they go to the trouble to invent one for themselves.

Children Deprived of Access to Some of the Meanings

The extraordinarily robust nature of language development is also apparent when we consider language learning in the absence of vision. Imagine a child who hears, *Look! There's a big dog!* or *Do you see that man playing the guitar?* Surely, the child will find it easier to grasp the meaning of these phrases if she can observe the dog or the guitar player, using the perceptual experience to help decode the linguistic input. This would seem to suggest that language learning would proceed slowly or be distorted in a blind child cut off from many of the learning opportunities available to the sighted child. Remarkably, though, the evidence shows that blind children learn language as rapidly and as well as sighted children. One particularly striking example is vision-related words like *look* and *see*, which blind children use as early (2 years old) and as systematically as sighted children. Of course, there are differences in how blind and sighted children understand these words. A young sighted listener asked to *look up!* will tilt her face upward (even if her vision is blocked by a blindfold). For this child, *look* clearly refers to vision (Figure 10.32A). A congenitally blind child, when given the same command produces a different—but entirely sensible—response. Keeping her head immobile, she

(A) **(B)**

10.30 Self-made signs of a deaf boy never exposed to sign language A two-sign sequence. (A) The first sign means "eat" or "food." Immediately before, the boy had pointed to a grape. (B) The second sign means "give." The total sequence means "give me the food."

10.31 A new language is invented Deaf children in Nicaragua have invented a sign language, with younger children newly arriving at their school improving and elaborating on it with every passing year.

Look up!

(A)   (B)

10.32 **The meaning of** *look* (A) A blind-folded, sighted 3-year-old tilts her head upward in response to "Look up!" for to her the word *look* means "perceive by eye." (B) A congenitally blind 3-year-old raises her arms upward in response to "Look up!" for to her the word *look* means "perceive by hand."

reaches upward and searches the space above her body with her hands (Figure 10.32B; Landau & Gleitman, 1985). Thus, each of these children understands *look* to be an instruction to search a bit of the world by use of the sense organs.

Not only do these input-deprived youngsters come to understand terms that refer to sight for those of us with normal vision, but they also know much about the application of color terms. Perhaps it is not so surprising that a blind 5-year-old can respond to the query *Can a cow be green?* by saying *I think they are usually brown or white* for he might on some occasion have heard the phrase *a brown cow* uttered by sighted adults, and never *a green cow.* But to the query *Can an idea be green?* the blind child does not wildly guess at some color, but can sensibly answer *No, that's silly; ideas are not any color; they are only in your head.* All this knowledge without any personal experience of colors at all!

Once again, we see that language and even apparently sight-dependent concepts emerge in considerable complexity and on schedule despite a dramatic shift away from the standard circumstances of learning. This provides further support for the claim that language is a truly basic factor in human nature. Prepared as the human child is to acquire a language, its learning can proceed despite significant sensory deprivation.

Children Exposed to More Than One Language: The Case of Bilingualism

So far we have looked at learning in less than ideal environments, particularly where the input to the learners is diminished because of isolation or disability. What happens in a case that seems to be the opposite: when infants are exposed from earliest infancy to more than one language at a time, in the bilingual home? Notice that (unless bilingually reared babies sleep less!) they will hear each of the two languages only for half as much time as a monolingually reared baby hears the single language of the home. Yet remarkably enough, the budding bilinguals learn both languages as fast and as well as the monolinguals learn one language. A 3-year-old who hears, say, Italian and Slovenian spoken about equally often at home will speak and understand both these languages like a 3-year-old rather than being like an 18-month-old for each of them (Kovelman, Shalinsky, Berens, & Petitto, 2008). From one perspective, this is just what we would predict because these babies are in "the sensitive period" during which, as we have seen, they soak up language information like little cognitive sponges. But from another perspective, the outcome is surprising because babies and young preschoolers are known to be especially prone to confusion—to suffer interference—when trying to learn or perform two different tasks. Why don't they fail to differentiate the two languages they are hearing, or at least mix up the words and rules from the two of them with detrimental effects on language learning?

The answer seems to be that bilingual exposure in early infancy (termed **crib bilingualism**) enhances the ability to monitor and switch between competing tasks in a way that not only supports learning the two languages, but extends to flexible switching among other tasks as well. One group of investigators demonstrated this by testing monolingual and bilingual young children in the Dimensional Change Card Sorting Task (DCCS; Zelazo, 2006). The set of cards for this task differ both by color (say, red cards and green cards) and by shape (say, square cards and oval cards). The child exper-

crib bilingual A prelinguistic infant who is exposed to two or more languages in the home environment.

imental participant is first asked to sort the full deck of cards on one dimension, for example, color, and later asked to re-sort them, this time by shape. Children under 4 years of age, though they easily perform either of these sorts with no difficulty, tend to slow down and to err when trying to switch in the re-sorting phase of the experiment, when they have to drop the previously valid criterion of color and sort in terms of shape, or the reverse. In the present context, it is of great interest that young children who were crib bilinguals, while no better than the monolinguals in the sorting phase of the experiment, are reliably better in the re-sorting phase. Apparently the bilingual experience—in which one must constantly inhibit everything one knows about language B when one is hearing or speaking language A—has had a general effect on developing cognition. The bilingual achieves cognitive flexibility and "executive control" at an earlier than expected age (Bialystok, 1999; see also Diamond, Kirkham, & Anso, 2002). Indeed these positive effects of bilingual environments are observable even in 7-month-olds who can efficiently acquire and process incompatible linguistic patterns that their monolingual peers cannot (Kovács & Mehler, 2009; see Figure 10.33).

Early bilingualism also shows its positive linguistic-cognitive effects when we consider how young children comprehend sentences. Here again, we see failures of monitoring and flexible switching by children as old as 8 or 9 years. For instance, when a young child hears an ambiguous sentence of the kind we discussed earlier (see Figure 10.18), she is likely to skip confidently down one garden path, in most cases never to return. This is in contrast to the adult who rapidly notices and repairs wrong or questionable initial interpretations (Trueswell, Sekerina, Hill, & Logrip, 1999). For this very reason, children under 6 or 7 years of age do not "get" puns and verbal tricks like *Will you join me in a bowl of soup*, for they cannot switch from one to the other structural interpretation (Hirsh-Pasek, Gleitman, & Gleitman, 1978). The bilingual child again has the advantage over his monolingual age-mates, a kind of cognitive control that

10.33 SCIENTIFIC METHOD: Will a baby raised in a bilingual home ("crib bilingual") be more open to new patterns of language-like stimulation?

Method

1. The infant sits on mother's lap and hears different instances of the syllable pattern ABB (mo-la-la, bi-du-du, etc.).

2. Two seconds after any such ABB pattern is heard, a cute clown appears in Box 1, to the infant's left.

3. After 9 such trials, the syllable pattern AAB begins instead (e.g., mo-mo-la, bi-bi-du).

4. Two seconds after any such AAB pattern is heard, a clown appears in Box 2, to the infant's right. This latter pattern of sound and its visual reward continues for 9 more trials.

Results: Both 7-month-old monolinguals and crib bilinguals learn the initial ABB pattern as shown by the fact that they begin to turn their eyes quickly to Box 1 when they hear an instance of ABB, before the clown appears. But when the syllable pattern changes to AAB, only the crib bilinguals switch to anticipating that the visual reward will now appear to their right.

CONCLUSION: Hearing two languages in the home has evidently readied the crib bilinguals for new kinds of stimulation.

SOURCE STUDY: Kovács & Mehler, 2009

enables them to monitor, repair, and reinterpret sentences on the fly from an early age (Novick, Thompson-Schill, & Trueswell, 2008; Slobin, 1978).

We see then that the facts *about* early bilingualism are educational arguments *for* early bilingualism. There is every reason to suppose that exposing very young children to more than one language would be beneficial to cognitive growth and development. This is even leaving aside the social and economic benefits that accrue to competent multilinguals in the rapidly globalizing societies of the 21st century.

LANGUAGE LEARNING WITH CHANGED ENDOWMENTS

As we just saw, language learning can proceed in the face of severe environmental deprivations so long as the learner has a normal human brain. But what happens if the nature of the learners themselves is changed? Since language learning and use are determined by brain function, changes in the brain should have strong effects (Fowler, Gelman, & Gleitman, 1994; Lenneberg, 1967; G. F. Marcus, 2004; Newport, 1990).

There are many indications that the nature and state of the brain do have massive consequences for language functioning. In Chapter 3 we discussed the evidence of **aphasia,** in which damage in the brain's left hemisphere can have devastating and highly specific impacts on speech and comprehension. Further evidence comes from individuals with an apparently inherited syndrome known as **Specific Language Impairment** (**SLI**). Individuals with this syndrome are generally slow to learn language and throughout their lives have difficulty in understanding and producing many sentences. Yet these individuals perform normally on most other measures, including measurements of intelligence (Gopnik & Crago, 1990; Pinker, 1994; van Der Lely & Christian, 2000).

We can also find cases with the reverse pattern: preservation of language along with disruption of other mental capacities. Individuals with this pattern (called Williams syndrome) have mild to moderate retardation (with average IQ scores of 65) and severe disruption of spatial capacites, but they are still capable of quite fluent and articulate language (Figure 10.34; Bellugi, Marks, Bihrle, & Sabo, 1991; Landau & Zukowski, 2002; Musolino, Chunyo, & Landau, in press; Pinker, 1995).

Overall, we see from these unusual cases of brain organization (or injury) that language and general intelligence are partly distinct. Some of these conditions target language particularly, leaving much of the rest of cognition largely intact. Under other conditions, language knowledge and use function very well indeed, but in the presence of diminished cognitive capacities.

The Sensitive Period Hypothesis

The human brain continues to grow and develop in the years after birth, reaching its mature state more or less at the age of puberty, with some further brain development—especially in the prefrontal cortex—continuing well into adolescence. If language is indeed rooted in brain function, then we might expect language learning to be influenced by these maturational changes. Is it? According to the **sensitive period** hypothesis, the brain of the young child is particularly well suited to the task of language learning. As the brain matures, learning (both of a first language and of later languages) becomes more difficult (Lenneberg, 1967; Newport, 1990).

Sensitive periods for the uptake and consolidation of new information seem to govern some aspects of learning in many species. One example is the attachment of the

aphasia Any of a number of linguistic disorders caused by injury to or malformation of the brain.

Specific Language Impairment (SLI) A syndrome of unknown etiology in which the course of development of a first language is unusually protracted despite otherwise normally developing cognitive functions.

sensitive period An early period during the development of an organism when it is particularly responsive to environmental stimulation. Outside of this period, the same environmental events have less impact.

(A) The model figures the children were asked to copy

(B) Attempts from 11-year-old child with Williams syndrome

(C) Attempts from a normally developing 6-year-old

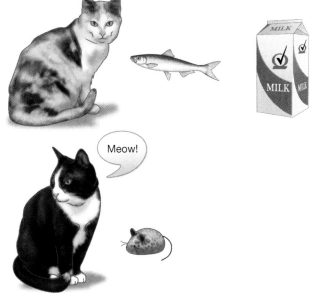

Meow!

The cat who meows will not be given a fish or milk.

(D) Complex-sentence picture match that both normally developing and Williams syndrome children understand

10.34 Children with Williams syndrome show severe spatial deficits but understand complex sentences and their meanings (A) Geometrical figures that children were asked to copy. (B) A sample copy from an 11-year-old child with Williams syndrome, in which this child shows severe spatial impairment. (C) A sample copy from a normally developing 6-year-old child. (D) illustrates that people with WS can understand sentences that are grammatically complex. For example, if they see the picture shown in (D), they know that one can truthfully say "The cat who meows will not be given a fish or milk." The stark contrast between their failures in spatial organization and their success in language tasks shows that these two capacities are independent.

young of various animals to their mothers, which generally can be formed only in early childhood (see Chapter 11). Another example is bird song. Male birds of many species have a song that is characteristic of their own kind. They learn this song by listening to adult males of their species. But this exposure will be effective primarily when it occurs at a certain period in the bird's life. To take a concrete case, baby white-crowned sparrows will learn their species song in all its glory, complete with trills and grace notes, only if they hear this music (sung, of course, by an adult white-crowned sparrow) sometime between the 7th and 60th day of their life. If they do not hear the song during this period, but instead hear it sometime during the next month, they acquire only the rudiments of the song, without the full elaborations heard in normal adults (Figure 10.35).

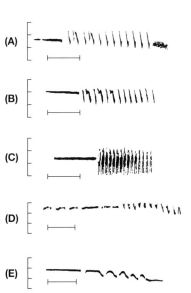

(A)

(B)

(C)

(D)

(E)

10.35 Sensitive period in the development of bird song (A) A graphic presentation of the song of an adult, male white-crowned sparrow. The figure, a sound spectrogram, shows that the normal song begins with a whistle or two, continues with a series of trills, and ends with a vibrato. (B) The song of a bird exposed to normal song only between the ages of 35 and 56 days. His adult song was almost normal. (C) The song of an isolated bird exposed to normal song between days 50 and 71. The adult song of this bird has some crude similarities to normal white-crowned sparrow song. (D) and (E) show the songs of birds whose exposure to normal song occurred very early in life (days 3 to 7) or very late (after 300 days of age), respectively. Training at either of these times had no effect (after Marler, 1970).

If the exposure comes still later, it has almost no effect. The bird will never sing normally (Marler, 1970).

Do human languages work in the same way? Are adults less able to learn language because they have passed beyond some sensitive learning period? Much of the evidence has traditionally come from studies of second-language learning.

SECOND-LANGUAGE LEARNING

In the initial stages of learning a second language, adults appear to be much more efficient than children (Snow & Hoefnagel-Hohle, 1978). The adult will venture halting but comprehensible sentences soon after arrival in the new language community while the 2-year-old may at first lapse into silence. But in the long run the outcome is just the reverse. After a few years, very small children speak the new language fluently and soon sound just like natives. This is much less common in adults. This point has been documented in many studies. In one investigation, the participants in the experiments were native Chinese and Korean speakers who came to the United States (and became immersed in the English-language community) at varying ages. These individuals were tested only after they had been in the United States for at least 5 years, so they had had ample exposure to English. And all of them were students and faculty members at a large midwestern university, so they shared some social background (and presumably were motivated to learn the new language so as to succeed in their university roles).

In the test procedure, half of the sentences the participants heard were grossly ungrammatical (e.g., *The farmer bought two pig at the market; The little boy is speak to a policeman*). The other half were the grammatical counterparts of these same sentences. The participants' task was to indicate which sentences were grammatical in English and which were not. The results are shown in Figure 10.36. Those who had been exposed to English before age seven performed just like native speakers of English. Thereafter there was an increasing decrement in performance as a function of age at first exposure. The older the subjects when they first came to the United States, the less well they acquired English (J. Johnson & Newport, 1989).

Recent experimentation confirms that very young children acquire second languages at native levels, and adds important detail about this process. Snedeker, Geren, and Shafto (2007) followed the language learning progress of Chinese children adopted (at ages 2 to 6 years) by Americans. After adoption, these children were immersed in monolingual English-language environments. Their English-language learning was compared with that of American-born infants. Would the older Chinese-born children learn differently (because they were more cognitively mature)? Or would they learn in the same way as the infants (because all of them were learning English from scratch)? The results show both effects: Just like infant first-language learners, the adoptees learned nouns before verbs, and content words before function words, suggesting that such words are easiest to learn regardless of cognitive status of the learner. But the adoptees acquired vocabulary at a faster rate, and so caught up to native-born agemates after 18 months or so of being in the new language community

Finally, we can ask how the native and later-learned languages are distributed in the brain. It could be, for example, that the usual brain locus for language gets set up precisely in the course of acquiring a first language and thereafter loses plasticity; as a result, the later-learned language must be shunted into new areas that are not specialized for, or are secondary for, language. This would be another way of explaining why knowledge of the first language is generally so much better than knowledge of the second or third or fourth language learned. There is in fact accumulating evidence that the brain loci of late-learned languages usually are different from those of the first-learned

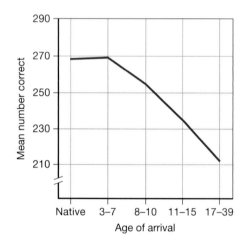

10.36 Ask your parents buy your tickets to Paris soon! The earlier in life one moves into a new linguistic community, the more "native-like" one's attainment of the new language will probably become. Results shown are scores (out of 276 items) on a test of grammaticality judgments by 46 Korean and Chinese individuals who came to the United States at different ages.

language, a finding consistent with this suggestion. However, there are other possible interpretations of the same finding. Possibly the real cause of different loci for the two languages is the individual's differential proficiency rather than the fact that one was learned before the other. One group of investigators supported this view by studying rare examples of people who learn a language in adulthood and become whizzes at it. Not surprisingly, many of these high-proficiency subjects were college instructors in modern language departments. The finding was that brain activity for both their languages occurred in the same brain sites (Perani et al., 1998).

LATE EXPOSURE TO A FIRST LANGUAGE

These second-language learning results lend some credence to the sensitive period hypothesis which, as earlier noted, is also consistent with the differential language recovery of isolated children (the cases of "Isabel" and "Genie"). However, there is an alternative explanation. Possibly, second languages are rarely as well learned as first languages because language habits ingrained with the first language interfere with learning the second one (Seidenberg & Zevin, 2006). To distinguish between the sensitive period hypothesis and such interference accounts, it would be helpful to find individuals who acquired their *first* language at different ages. The best line of evidence in this regard comes from American Sign Language (ASL). As we discussed earlier, many congenitally deaf children have hearing parents who choose not to allow their offspring access to ASL. Such children's first exposure to ASL, therefore, may be quite late in life when they first establish contact with the deaf community. Because their hearing deficit did not permit them to learn the spoken language of their caretakers either, such individuals are learning a first (signed) language at an unusually late point in maturational time.

How does this late start influence language learning? In one study, all of the participants had used ASL as their sole means of communication for at least 25 years, guaranteeing that they were as expert in the language as they would ever become. Some of them had been exposed to ASL from birth (because their parents were deaf signers). Others had learned ASL between the ages of 4 and 6 years. A third group had first come into contact with ASL after the age of 12.

Not surprisingly, all of these signers were quite fluent in ASL, thanks to 25-plus years of use. But even so, the age at first exposure had a strong effect (Figure 10.37). Those who had learned ASL from birth used and understood all of its elaborations. Those whose first exposure had come after the age of 4 years showed subtle deficits. Those whose exposure began in adolescence or adulthood had much greater deficits, and their use of function items was sporadic, irregular, and often incorrect (Newport, 1990, 1999).

Language in Nonhumans

We have seen that language learning is deeply rooted in the nature and development of human brains. Does this imply that creatures with different sorts of brains will be unable to learn language? As we will see, the evidence indicates that our nearest animal relatives cannot come close to attaining human language, even with the best of good will and the most strenuous educational procedures. At the same time, though, there is considerable overlap between our biological endowments and those of other primates. For this reason, we should not be too surprised if some rudiments of language can be made to grow in them. If so, they may offer insight into the origins of our own communicative organization.

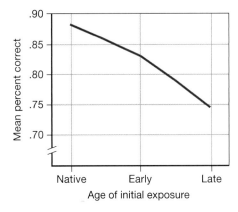

10.37 Evidence for a sensitive period for first-language learning These are scores on a test of ASL by congenitally deaf individuals who had not learned a spoken language because of their deafness. The test was performed between 25 and 30 years after these individuals had first been exposed to a sign language, and still, all those years later, one can still see big effects of the age at which they began.

Recent studies do reveal interesting commonalities between human and animal communication. For example, vervet monkeys have separate calls of alarm, depending on the predator—leopard, eagle, or snake, which are responded to differentially by other vervets (Cheney & Seyfarth, 1990; also see Ghazanfar & Hauser, 1999; S. Green, 1975). Related communicative uses have been demonstrated for dolphin whistles as well (Reiss, McCowan, & Marino, 1997; Tyack, 2000). However, animals' production of sounds is very restricted, with a vocabulary size of only a few dozen different signals, compared to the tens of thousands of words in an adult human's repertoire. And crucially for the comparison with humans, the animal signals do not combine together to enlarge the number of messages that can be conveyed. Humans link their words in ever new and structured ways so as to express new thoughts that listeners easily comprehend. This creative kind of communication appears to be closed even to our closest primate cousins. For instance, monkeys have no way to utter differentially *"Beware! Monkeys-eating-snakes"* versus *"Beware! Snakes-eating-monkeys."*

On the other hand, animals' perception of sounds (and comprehension of the meaning associated with the sounds) is much more impressive than their restricted speaking (or signing). Wild monkeys and apes live in groups that number into the hundreds, recognize all of these individuals' calls, and learn the alarm calls of birds, impala, and other animals. In captivity they learn to recognize the meaning of all sorts of sounds, like the voices of different caretakers or the beep of a card swipe that signals feeding time. And while monkeys and apes rarely produce combinations of calls to convey new messages, they hear and interpret call combinations all of the time, whenever two of their groupmates are interacting with each other. For instance, in one experiment, baboons were played a threatening grunt from Hannah, a low-ranking female in their group, paired with a submissive scream from Sylvia, a high-ranking female. This seemed to violate the existing dominance hierarchy and the listeners responded strongly as if startled by the oddity. On the other hand, they showed little or no response when they heard the threatening grunt from Sylvia and the submissive scream from Hannah (Bergman, Beehner, Cheney, & Seyfarth, 2003). Thus, the baboons seem insensitive to the *syntax* of other baboon utterances, and this limits their communicative prowess. But, even so, they do seem sensitive to the *context* of the utterances, and, in particular, who is saying what to whom. This context-sensitivity enormously enlarges the number of socially relevant messages that can be conveyed, making baboon communication richly informative despite its limits of form and structure (Cheney & Seyfarth, 2007).

Is it possible that with just the right training this limited repertoire of production can be overcome and animals can master communication skills that truly deserve the term *language*? Many researchers have pursued these possibilities, trying to teach language-like systems to animals in the laboratory, using a variety of communication media in which hand gestures, bits of colored plastic, or symbols on a computer screen stand for words. Researchers have also tried to train a range of species, including chimpanzees, dolphins, gorillas, dogs, parrots, and pygmy chimps (bonobos). These animals have made impressive progress—increasing their gesture "vocabulary" (to roughly 500 "words" in the case of the bonobo Kanzi and close to 300 for the border collie Rico; Figure 10.38; Kaminski, Call, & Fischer, 2004).

However, the results of these training efforts have all been rather limited and so utterly fail to support the extravagant descriptions of these "linguistic creatures" in the popular media. Even after extensive training, their utterances are rarely more than two words long; when longer, they tend to involve disorganized repetitions (*Give*

10.38 Rico the comprehending (but not talking) dog Rico, a border collie, knows the names for his 200 or so toys and balls, and will fetch any one of them upon verbal command. But alas, though Rico comprehends so well, his own speech is limited to the usual border-collie barks, yelps, and growls.

orange me give eat orange me eat orange give me orange give me you). Their utterances are typically imitations or expansions of the utterance they just heard from their human trainers, and their mastery of syntax is sharply limited. For example, no nonhuman has mastered the distinction between plural and singular nouns, or verb tense, or any means of marking words for their grammatical class, while every human child of normal mentality does so by the age of 3 or 4, without explicit training. (For reviews, see Kako, 1999; Petitto, 1988; Pinker, 1994; Tomasello, 1994, 2003; for contrary views see also Herman & Uyeyama, 1999; Pepperberg, 1999; Savage-Rumbaugh & Fields, 2000.)

The conclusion, then, is that animals do indeed have rich communicative systems of their own, but these systems are strikingly, qualitatively, different from human language. Nonetheless, we can learn from animals in the wild—particularly monkeys and apes—something about the ancestral communicative system from which language may have emerged. If modern primates are any guide, our prelinguistic ancestors had some calls that functioned like words (alarm calls, for example), and were exceptionally skilled at recognizing others' voices, distinguishing different call types (screams, threats, and others) and extracting a huge number of different messages from a limited vocabulary combined with their interpretation of the situation at hand. Before language, there was a rich set of meanings and concepts, all embedded in the animals' socially grounded knowledge of each other.

LANGUAGE AND THOUGHT

We have seen that the forms and contents of language are very much bound up with the organization of the human brain and with the ways that humans think and perceive the world. Languages are alike insofar as they are the central means for transmitting beliefs, desires, and ideas from one human to another. To accomplish these human communicative goals, each language must have phonemes, morphemes, phrases, and sentences, and tens of thousands of different meaningful words. But within these bounds, languages also differ from one another in various ways. And these differences are not only with the sounds of the words—that the word meaning "dog" is pronounced *dog, chien, perro,* and so on in different communities. Some languages will simply lack a word that another language has, or refer to the same thing in quite different ways. As one example, we speak of a certain tool as a *screwdriver,* literally alluding to the fact that it is used to push screws in; German uses the term *Schraubenzieher,* which translates as "a screw puller"; and French uses the word *tournevis* ("screw turner") for the same tool, thus referring to both the tool's pushing and pulling functions (Kay, 1996). As we have also mentioned, sometimes the structures differ across languages too, as with fixed word-order languages like English and Mandarin Chinese versus those with a quite free word order such as Finnish and Russian. Further differences are at the social level. For example, such languages as Italian and French have different pronouns for use when referring to relative strangers (e.g., French *vous,* or to intimates *tu*). Finally, languages differ in the idioms and metaphors with which they characteristically refer to the world. Witness English, where your new car can be a *lemon* even though it is inedible, your former friend can be a *snake in the grass,* and your future visit to an underground cave can be *up in the air* until its date is settled.

Do these differences matter? Certainly we would not think that Germans and Americans use different tools for inserting and extracting screws and that only the French have a single tool for both jobs. At the other extreme, having a linguistically built-in way to refer differentially to dear friends and total strangers just might reflect—or even cause—deep distinctions in the social organization of a culture. So here we consider the possibility that the particulars of one's language might influence thought (for an overview, see Gleitman & Papafragou, 2004).

How Language Connects to Thought

In one sense it is totally obvious that language influences thought. Otherwise we would not use it at all. When one person yells "FIRE!" in a crowded room, all of those who hear him rapidly walk, run, or otherwise proceed to the nearest exit. In this case, language influenced the listeners to think, *There's a fire; fire is dangerous; I'd better get out of here FAST.* Language use also influences our thought in other ways. It is a convenient way of coding, or chunking, information, with important consequences for memory. The way information is framed when we talk or write can also influence our decisions, so that a patient is more likely to choose a medical treatment if she is told it has a 50% chance of success than if she is told it has a 50% chance of failure (see Chapter 8). Finally, language can influence our attitudes (see Chapter 12), a fact well known to advertisers and propagandists: *Eat crunchy Pritos! Remember Pearl Harbor!*

In all these examples, the choice of words and sentences affects our thinking. Of course, language is not the only way to influence thought and action. Observing the flames is at least as powerful a motivator to flee as is hearing the cry *FIRE!* Still, language is an enormously effective conveyer of information, emotions, and attitudes. This much ought to be obvious. Why would we ever listen to a lecture or read a poem or a newspaper if we did not believe that language was a means of getting useful or aesthetically pleasing information? But when we speak of language differences influencing thought, it is in quite a different sense from this. In this latter case, we are asking whether the very forms and contents that a language can express change the nature of perception and cognition for its speakers.

Do People Who Talk Differently Come to Understand the World Differently?

The idea that "we dissect nature along lines laid down by our native languages" was forcefully presented by a linguistic anthropologist, Benjamin Whorf, who studied several native languages of the Americas. Whorf noticed many distinctions of language and culture between native American and European societies, and he argued that often the language differences themselves led to the cultural differences. In his words, "language is not merely a reproducing instrument for voicing ideas but rather is itself the shaper of ideas, the program and guide for the individual's mental activity" (Whorf, 1956, pp. 212–213). So influential have Whorf's ideas become that the general position that language affects thought has come to be identified with his name, as the **Whorfian hypothesis.**

One frequently mentioned example that Whorf discussed concerns the number of terms for snow in Inuit or Aleut (sometimes called "Eskimo" languages) compared to English. This number in Inuit is sometimes claimed to be as large as 300, with different terms for naming types of snow such as *powder, slush, ice, falling snow* versus *fallen snow,* and so forth. Whorf claimed that speakers of such languages are influenced by this richness and variety of vocabulary and so end up able to make much finer distinctions among snow types than are speakers of other languages.

But this example is flawed in several ways. The initial claim about vocabulary size is actually false; English turns out to have more snow-related terms than does Inuit (L. Martin, 1986; Pullum, 1991). And even if it were true that Inuit had more words for

Whorfian hypothesis The proposal that the language one speaks determines or heavily influences the thoughts one can think or the saliency of different categories of thought.

snow than English, would that explain why its speakers are more sensitive to snow distinctions (if they are) than, say, English-speaking residents of South Carolina or Hawaii? A plausible alternative is that the Inuits' day-to-day activities create a functional need for these discriminations, and this leads both to the larger vocabulary and to the greater skill in picking out different types of snow. On this view, language does not shape perception. On the contrary, language and perception are both shaped by environment and culture.

How Can We Study Language and Thought?

Although, as we have just seen, the Inuit snow case does not really hold water (perhaps we should say it does not hold ice), there are many other aspects in which language distinctions can be and have been more profitably studied.

COLOR TERMS AND COLOR PERCEPTION

Some languages have a rich and subtle vocabulary of color words (e.g., English *puce, mauve, tea, crimson*), while other languages have only a few color terms (Berlin & Kay, 1969). As an extreme case, the Dani people of New Guinea have only two terms for color, one meaning (roughly) *dark/cool* and the other meaning light/warm (see Chapter 5, for these distinctions in the perception of hue). Still, there are strong similarities in how speakers of English and speakers of Dani perceive color, with the named color categories in both cultures based on "favored percepts selected from restricted regions of color space," and with striking agreement, across the cultures, in which are "best examples" of each color (Heider, 1972; Regier, Kay, & Cook, 2005). Within these limits, however, recent evidence suggests that the different color labeling practices adopted in different languages can influence the ways that nonlinguistic categorization is carried out by the brain, with left-hemisphere advantages observed primarily in tasks that require the participant to discriminate between categories that are differently labeled in his or her language. Particularly interesting is recent evidence that these left-hemisphere advantages develop in childhood, in conjunction with the acquisition of the language's particular color terminology (Kay & Regier, 2006).

THE LANGUAGE OF SPATIAL POSITION AND DIRECTION

Another area in which we can examine the interaction of language and thought is in descriptions of space, because there are considerable differences in how various languages describe spatial position. For instance, English speakers would say that *the fruit is in the bowl* and also that *the DVD is in the laptop*, using the same preposition (*in*) in both cases. Korean speakers would use two different words in these cases, with one word conveying the idea of fitting loosely (as *the fruit is in the bowl*) and the other describing things that fit tightly (*the DVD is in the laptop*) (Figure 10.39; Choi & Bowerman, 1991). As another example, English distinguishes in the word most often used for vertical contact (*on*) and vertical noncontact (*above*), while both Japanese and Korean favor a single word to convey both *on* and *above*.

Despite these linguistic differences, Japanese, Korean, and English speakers all seem to think about spatial position in very similar ways. In one study, participants were shown pictures of objects located at various positions with respect to a reference object. A short time later, they were shown another picture and asked if it depicted the same scene or a slightly different one. In some cases, this new picture was altered slightly, but it preserved the relationship (of *on* or *above*) shown in the original picture. (The first

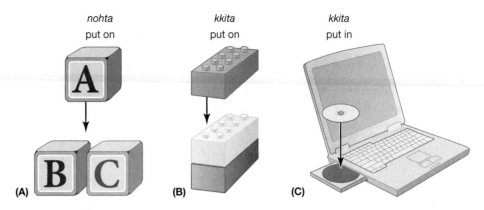

nohta
put on

kkita
put on

kkita
put in

(A)   (B)   (C)

10.39 Spatial words in English and Korean The three panels show items being put into spatial positions relative to each other. Panel A shows a block being put on other blocks. Panel B shows a Lego being put on other Legos. Panel C shows a disc being put into a computer. In English we use the same phrase (put on) to express the action in (A) and (B), and a different phrase (put in) for action (C). In contrast, Korean uses one term (*nohta*) to describe the act in (A), because it consists of putting something on something else loosely, and uses a different term (*kkita*) to describe the acts in (B) and (C), because both involve bringing the objects into a tight fit.

picture, for example, might have shown a cup on a table; the second, a cup still on a table but shifted slightly to the right.) In other cases, the new picture depicted a change in this relationship (with the original picture showing the cup on the table and the test picture showing the cup above the table). If English sensitizes us to the contrast between *on* and *above*, then English speakers should detect alterations that change these relationships more easily than Koreans or Japanese do. But the data show no such effect, and the memory performance of all groups was the same (Munnich, Landau, & Dosher, 2001; also see Hayward & Tarr, 1995; Xu, 2002).

Summarizing here, differences in the language of location and space are large and clear cut. Indeed speakers of one language express puzzlement at how other linguistic users express some of these ideas, and have trouble learning the differentiating aspects of the two languages (Figure 10.40). Yet we know that language itself cannot be what is creating these categories, because infants are sensitive to these distinctions in the prelinguistic period. For instance, 5-month-olds in habituation experiments show that they already distinguish between tightly fitting and loosely fitting (Hespos & Spelke,

10.40 These American birds are sitting in a tree (but these Korean birds are sitting on a tree) In many languages, including English, it sounds perfectly natural to hear that these birds are "in the tree." But to Korean listeners, it sounds very odd. They would only say "in" to describe these birds' position if the birds were inside a hole in the tree.

2004). Nor can it be said that speakers become less sensitive over time to these distinctions. If, for instance, a diminished sensitivity to "on" versus "above" were a result of learning Japanese rather than English, we should all be terrified of flying with Japan Airlines (Norbury, Waxman, & Song, 2008).

As another example, speakers of Tzeltal (a Mayan language) who live in Tenejapa, a rural region of Chiapas, Mexico, have no terms for "to the left of" or "to the right of," expressions that are obviously available (and often used) in, for example, English, Dutch, Japanese, and even the Spanish-speaking areas of Chiapas (Figure 10.41). Rather, these Tenejapans speak of things being roughly to the *east, to the south,* and so on. Of course, English speakers too can sensibly use terms like *east,* but in fact we rarely use these terms to refer to very nearby things. For instance, *Hand me the spoon that's to the* east *of your teacup* sounds quite unnatural.

This terminological distinction could be crucial, because words like *east* and *left* function differently: If you turn 180 degrees, what was previously to your east will still be to your east, but what was previously to your left will now be to your right. This is because *east* and *west* have to do with position relative to an outside landmark (where the sun rises), whereas *left* and *right* have to do with position relative to one's own body. This suggests the possibility that spatial reasoning might be different in languages that favor the *left-right* distinction versus those that favor the *east-west* distinction.

Do speakers of Tzeltal actually think about space differently than English or Dutch speakers do? In one study, speakers of these different languages were asked to memorize the positions of toy animals lined up on a table (Figure 10.42A). Then the animals were removed, and the participants were rotated 180degrees to a new table (Figure 10.42B). The participants were handed the animals and asked to set them up on this new table so that it is the same as before. Notice that there are two ways to do so (Figure 10.42C and D): The animals can be set up so that they are still going to the right or still going to the west. And, in fact, the terminology used by the subjects in their native tongue predicted the way they solved this problem (Levinson, 2003; Pederson et al., 1998).

This experiment makes a strong initial case that ways of thinking (here, thinking about space) may be directly influenced by the words in use in a specific language. But other investigators argue that these results reflect only the specific conditions of testing. To evaluate this suggestion, these later investigators created test conditions for English speakers like those under which the Tzeltal group had been studied, for

10.42 What is "the same" after rotation? (A) Subjects memorize the order and facing direction (west; right) of three toy animals while they are seated at the stimulus table. (B) After a brief delay, the subject is turned around to face a different, blank table (the recall table) and handed the animals to set up again so that the array is "the same as before." (C) The "absolute" response: The subject sets up the animals so they are still facing west (but now face the subject's left rather than her right). (D) The "relative" response: The subject sets up the animals so they are still facing her right (but now are pointing to the east). (Adapted from S. C. Levinson, 2003)

example, providing strong landmarks visible to the east and west of the testing area. Under these conditions, American college students behaved much as the Tzeltal speakers (who had been tested outdoors in their own community) had behaved in this same task (Li & Gleitman, 2002).

More recent evidence shows that the differences among speakers of different languages on rotation tasks are mainly in their understanding of what they think the experimenter wants them to do. It is no surprise that when the task is presented ambiguously ("make it the same") that Tzeltal speakers guess that you are referring to east-west-the-same and English speakers guess that you are referring to left-right-the-same. After all, that is the way their cultures most frequently talk about locations and directions. As we saw in our earlier discussion of language comprehension the frequency of words and constructions has a strong effect on our immediate interpretations of language that we hear (or read), especially under ambiguous circumstances. We are led down particular garden paths because these are the most probable ones, in our prior experience. But a further question—sometimes called the "strong form" of the Whorfian hypothesis—is whether our thought has become rigidified so that it is hard or impossible to think in any other way. To find out, investigators now asked what happens when the task requirements in the rotation experiments are made unambiguous. The answer is that the differences between Tzeltal and English performance vanish: In sum, if Tzeltal speakers know you want them to do a rotation task, or solve a maze, taking left-right perspective rather than east-west perspective, it turns out that they are as competent as English speakers in doing so (Li, Abarbinell, Gleitman, & Papafragou, in press). Several recent experiments have shown, similarly, that linguistic effects on how one thinks are "of the moment" and are easily reversible by momentary situational context, rather than being lifelong effects of language particulars on how one can think at all (Boroditsky, 2001; January & Kako, 2007).

SOME FINAL THOUGHTS: LANGUAGE AND COGNITION

Overall, then, there is no compelling evidence in favor of the strongest forms of Whorf's theory. When these claims are put to a direct test, there seem to be only limited relationships between specifics of our language and how we perceive or conceive of the world. These relationships are often not caused by the language; instead they frequently derive from aspects of the culture or environment in which people and societies exist, or they are general context effects that apply in much the same way inside and outside of language ("I just feel like a different person when I'm speaking French or wearing my Parisian beret").

In fact, there is little reason to have expected that the words and structures of our language would change or restrict our thought patterns in rigid and immutable ways. If they did, it would be very hard to account for how a second—and sometimes third, fourth, and fifth—language could possibly be learned. In addition, there is no doubt that forms of thought are often independent of language. For instance, infants who know no language seem able to think relatively complex thoughts, and some of our adult thought takes the form of nonlinguistic mental images. Moreover, creatures such as digger wasps and migrating birds are able to find their way from place to place across great distances without the benefit of words like *north* and *left* (Gallistel, 1990). Finally, throughout this chapter, we have emphasized the rather impressive sameness of languages in their units and hierarchical structure; in many aspects of their syntax and semantics; and in the processes involved in their processing and their acquisition. This linguistic sameness, in turn, is the reflection of sameness of mentality across the human species. The use of language influences us and guides us, and surely this is no surprise: This is one of the essential functions of communication. But this is quite different from Whorf's suggestion that language acts as a kind of mental straitjacket limiting *how* we can think or *what* we can think. The bulk of the evidence seems to point the other way: Language is a bright, transparent medium through which thoughts flow, relatively undistorted, from one mind to another.

- Language is the biologically given communication system of our species, and appears in all cultures. Not only does our language express thought and convey information, it also expresses and solidifies social and cultural bonding.

THE BUILDING BLOCKS OF LANGUAGE

- Languages consist of a hierarchy of units that combine and recombine to form higher-level categories. At the bottom are units of *sound*, which combine into *morphemes* and *words*.

- The sound categories that matter in a language are called its *phonemes*. English uses about 40 different phonemes. Other languages have their own sets.

- The smallest language units that carry meaning are *morphemes*. *Content morphemes* carry the main burden of meaning. *Function morphemes* add details to the meaning and also serve various grammatical purposes.

- A phrase is an organized grouping of words, and a sentence is an organized grouping of phrases. Some sequences of words in a language are allowed, but others are not, in accord with the *rules of syntax*. These rules describe the *phrase structure* of a sentence, which can be depicted by means of a *tree diagram*.

HOW LANGUAGE CONVEYS MEANING

- According to the *definitional theory of word meaning*, bundles of *semantic features* constitute the meaning of each word. Various observations have led to a second theory, that the meaning of words is represented by an ideal (or *prototype*) case, and membership in the category depends on resemblance to this prototype. A combination of these two theories best handles the psychological data on word meaning.

- Sentences express *propositions*, in which some comment, or *predicate*, is made about a topic (the *subject* of the sentence). A proposition can be regarded as a miniature drama in which the verb is the action and the nouns are the performers, each of which plays a different *semantic role*.

- Sentence interpretation is very rapid, beginning before whole sentences are heard. This often causes listeners to jump to temporary false interpretations, called *garden paths*. To recover from these momentary misunderstandings, lis-

teners and readers consider not only the structure they are hearing but also plausible *semantic relations* among the words. This includes integrating the sentence with what they can see in the visually observed world. In conversation, a further source of information comes from the fact that speakers and listeners continually fill in the blanks in what is uttered, using inference to help them interpret the full meaning of what is said.

HOW WE LEARN A LANGUAGE

- Language is part of our human endowment. However, human languages differ in myriad details from each other and thus have to be learned by children rather than being almost wholly innate as in many other animal species.

- From the very first moments after birth, infants' ears and minds are open to detect the sounds of language, and also to organize these sounds into words. Initially, infants respond to just about all sound distinctions made in any language, but by 12 months of age they are more sensitive to sound contrasts in their own language than to those in other languages.

- Infants rapidly learn to identify the boundaries between morphemes and words. One important cue that helps them do this is a keen sensitivity to the frequencies with which specific syllables occur right next to each other.

- Word learning is heavily influenced by the ways the child is disposed to categorize objects and events, as reflected in the fact that young children acquire the *basic-level words* for whole objects (*dog*) before learning the *superordinates* (*animal*) or *subordinates* (*Chihuahua*).

- Children also use the *structure* of the language as a way of guiding their word learning. Remarkably, some understanding of syntax, and the way it links up with meaning, is found in children under two years of age, even though these children themselves often speak only in single-word utterances.

- Children's speech progresses very rapidly by the beginning of the third year of life, with the start of little sentences and the use of function words. *Overregularization errors* (e.g., *holded* for *held*) are clear evidence that children do not learn language by imitation; they suggest instead that young children learn rules that govern how the language is structured.

LANGUAGE LEARNING IN CHANGED ENVIRONMENTS

- Under normal conditions, language emerges in much the same way in virtually all children. They progress from babbling to one-word speech, advance to two-word sentences, and eventually graduate to complex sentence forms and meanings. This progression is consistent with the claim that language development is rooted in our shared biological heritage. But what happens when children grow up in radically different environments? Data from *isolated children*, those deprived of ordinary human contact for many years, suggest that normal language development may take place as long as language learning begins during some *sensitive period* for the acquisition of linguistic information, which may end roughly at the age of puberty.

- Many persons born deaf learn *sign language*. This gestural system has hand shapes and positions that combine to form individual words (analogous to the phonemes of spoken language), and it has morphemes and grammatical principles for combining words into sentences that are closely similar to those of spoken language. Babies born to deaf users of sign language go through the same steps on the way to adult knowledge as do hearing children learning English. Thus, language does not depend on the auditory-vocal channel.

- Blind children learn language as rapidly and as well as sighted children do. Here too, language emerges in all of its complexity and on schedule despite a dramatic shift away from the standard circumstances of language learning.

LANGUAGE LEARNING WITH CHANGED ENDOWMENTS

- Since language learning and use are determined by brain function, changing the brain should have strong effects. This is confirmed by several sorts of evidence, including cases of *aphasia*, as well as cases of persons with apparently inherited syndromes such as *specific language impairment*. In addition, as the brain matures, a *sensitive period* for language learning draws to a close, so that later learning (both of a first language and of later languages) becomes more difficult.

- It appears that even our nearest animal relative, the chimpanzee, cannot come close to attaining human language. For now, the evidence suggests that animals including baboons, dogs, dolphins, and even parrots can learn words, and that they show evidence of rudimentary propositional thought. But there is little evidence that they can create (or understand) the sorts of syntactic structures that humans use routinely.

LANGUAGE AND THOUGHT

- According to the *Whorfian hypothesis*, the language one speaks determines the way one thinks. Language obviously conveys information, and this influences thought; language can also be used to draw our attention to some content, and, again, this influences thought. However, the ways that language governs how we can think generally, or what we can think at all, are probably quite limited. Special language features can dramatically influence interpretations of ambiguous speech in momentary ways because the language processing system is highly responsive to frequency information which differs cross-linguistically.

 ONLINE STUDY TOOLS

Go to StudySpace, **wwnorton.com/studyspace**, to access additional review and enrichment materials, including the following resources for each chapter:

Organize
- Study Plan
- Chapter Outline
- Quiz+ Assessment

Learn
- Ebook
- Chapter Review
- Vocabulary Flashcards
- Drag-and-Drop Labeling Exercises
- Audio Podcast Chapter Overview

Connect
- Critical Thinking Activity
- Studying the Mind Video Podcasts
- Video Exercises
- Animations
- **ZAPS** Psychology Labs

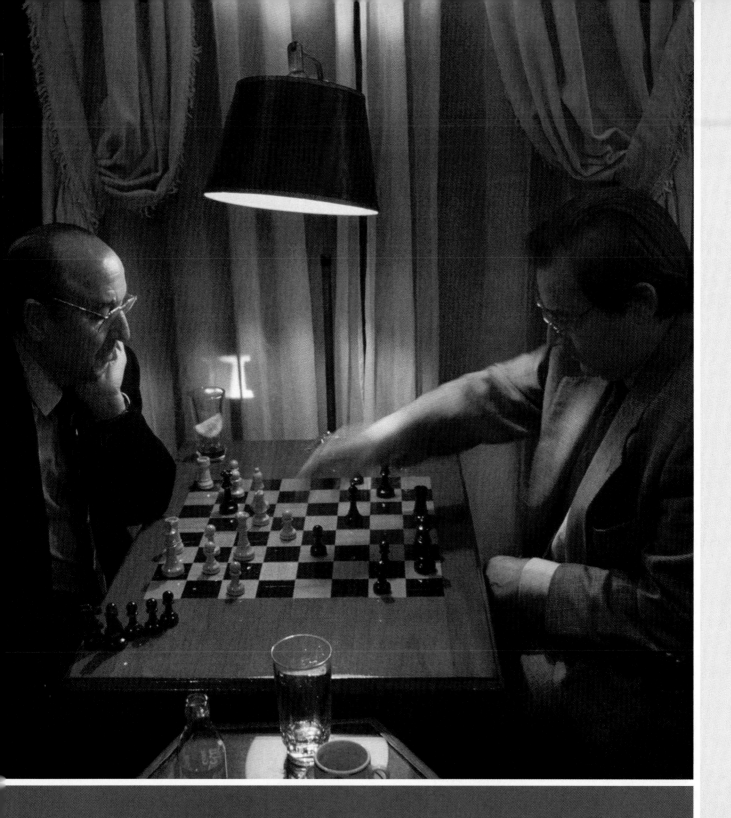

11 Intelligence

Intelligence tests used to make Bob Sternberg a little sick. "The school psychologist would come into the room and give us these group IQ tests. And I would freeze up, especially when I heard other kids turning the page and I was still on the first or second problem." As a result, Sternberg routinely bombed his IQ tests. But his fourth-grade teacher didn't believe the numbers, and she convinced Sternberg not to believe them either.

His teacher was right. Sternberg grew up to be an insightful, influential researcher and—ironically—a world-renowned expert on intelligence, first as a psychology professor at Yale University and now as the dean of arts and sciences at Tufts University. Throughout his career, he has explored the question of what intelligence is, where it comes from, and how people can get more of it. But Sternberg's own trajectory reminds us that the correlation between IQ scores and life success is far from 1.00.

IQ tests are designed to measure intelligence, but do they? For that matter, what *is* intelligence? More than a decade ago, 52 experts offered a multifaceted definition of this term: "the ability to reason, plan, solve problems, think abstractly, comprehend complex ideas, learn quickly and learn from experience" (Gottfredson, 1997a, p. 13). This is a complex definition, but we may need further complications, because, in this chapter, we'll consider proposals that would expand this definition by taking into account important talents excluded from the experts' conceptualization. We'll also look at proposals that would *subdivide* the definition, so that we end up speaking about different types, and different aspects, of intelligence.

These points should make it clear that, after a century of research in this domain, there's still room for debate about what intelligence is and how it should be defined. Despite these complications, we'll see that in the last century, researchers have made enormous progress in identifying the intellectual and motivational components that contribute to IQ scores, and also have learned an enormous amount about the roots of these components. To understand this progress, we need some historical context: Researchers first set out to measure intelligence 100 years ago, and much of what we've learned—and many of the questions that remain—can be traced directly to these early efforts. Let's begin our story, therefore, at the beginning, in France in the opening years of the 20th century.

INTELLIGENCE TESTING

In 1904, the French minister of public instruction appointed a committee with the specific task of identifying children who were performing badly in school and would benefit from remedial education. One member of this committee, Alfred Binet (1857–1911; Figure 11.1), played a pivotal role and had an extremely optimistic view of the project. As Binet saw things, the committee's goal was both to identify the weaker students and then—crucially—to improve the students' performance through training.

Measuring Intelligence

For their task, Binet and the other committee members needed an objective way to assess each child's abilities, and in designing their test, they were guided by the belief that intelligence is a capacity that matters for many aspects of cognitive functioning. This view led them to construct a test that included a broad range of tasks varying in content and difficulty: copying a drawing, repeating a string of digits, understanding a story, arithmetic reasoning, and so on. They realized that someone might do well on one or two of these tasks just by luck or due to some specific experience (perhaps the person had encountered that story before), but they were convinced that only a truly intelligent person would do well on all the tasks in the test. Therefore, intelligence could be measured by a composite score that took all the tasks into account. Moreover, they believed that the diversity of the tasks ensured that the test was not measuring some specialized talent but was instead a measure of ability in general. Indeed, Binet put a heavy emphasis on this diversity, and even claimed that, "It matters very little what the tests are so long as they are numerous" (1911, p. 329).

In its original form, the intelligence test was intended only for children. The test score was computed as a ratio between the child's "mental age" (the level of development reflected in the test performance) and his chronological age; the ratio was then multiplied by 100 to get the final score (Figure 11.2). This ratio (or *quotient*) was the source of the test's name: The test evaluated the child's "intelligence quotient," or IQ.

Other, more recent forms of the test no longer calculate a ratio between mental and chronological age, but they're still called IQ tests. One commonly used test for assessing children is the Wechsler Intelligence Scale for Children (WISC), released in its fourth revision

11.1 Alfred Binet (1857–1911) Binet sought to measure intelligence and to improve it. As his work developed, he prescribed courses in "mental orthopedics" for students who were performing poorly: In one book, his chapter on the "training of intelligence" began with the ambitious phrase: "After the illness, the remedy."

11.2 Calculating IQ

IQ = (mental age ÷ chronological age) × 100

This calculation of IQ scores, first proposed by German psychologist William Stern, was adopted as the routine procedure for many years.

Imagine little Johnny, born 10 years ago; his chronological age, therefore, is 10.

Johnny is able to do mental tasks that, on average, most 11-year-olds can't do, but most 12-year-olds can do. Mentally, Johnny seems quite advanced, and he therefore seems to resemble a normal 12-year-old.

His IQ = (12 ÷ 10) × 100 = 120

in 2003 (Wechsler, 2003). Adult intelligence is often evaluated with the Wechsler Adult Intelligence Scale (WAIS); its fourth edition was released in 2008. Like Binet's original test, these modern tests rely on numerous subtests. In the WAIS-IV, for example, there are verbal tests to assess general knowledge, vocabulary, and comprehension; a perceptual-reasoning scale includes visual puzzles like the one shown in Figure 11.3. Separate subtests assess working memory and speed of intellectual processing.

Other intelligence tests have different formats. For example, the Raven's Progressive Matrices test (Figure 11.4) contains no subtests and hinges entirely on someone's ability to analyze figures and detect patterns. Specifically, this test presents the test taker with a series of grids (these are the matrices), and she must select an option that sensibly completes the pattern in each grid. This test is designed to minimize any influence from verbal skills or background knowledge.

Reliability and Validity

Did Binet (and all who came after him) succeed in his aim of creating a test that truly measures *intelligence*? To find out, we need to evaluate the tests' reliability and validity—key notions that we introduced in Chapter 1. As we described there, *reliability* refers to how consistent a measure is in its results and is often evaluated by assessing *test-retest reliability*. This assessment boils down to a simple question: If we give the test, wait a while, and then give it again, do we get essentially the same outcome?

Intelligence tests actually have high test-retest reliability—even if the two test occasions are widely separated. For example, there is a high correlation between measurements of someone's IQ at, say, age 6 and measurements when she's 18. Likewise, if we know someone's IQ at age 11, we can predict with reasonable accuracy what his IQ will be at age 27 (see, for example, Deary, 2001a, 2001b; Deary, Whiteman, Starr, Whalley, & Fox, 2004; Plomin & Spinath, 2004). As it turns out, though, there are some departures from this apparent stability. For example, a substantial change in someone's environment can cause a corresponding change in his IQ score. We'll return to this point later in the chapter, when we consider the effects of poverty (which can drive IQ downward) or schooling (which can increase IQ). Even so, if someone stays in a relatively stable and healthy environment, IQ tests are quite reliable.

What about validity? This is the crucial evaluation of whether the tests really measure what we intend them to measure, and one way to approach this issue is to assess its **predictive validity:** If the tests truly measure intelligence, then someone's score on the test should allow us to predict how well that person will do in settings that require intelligence. And here, too, the results are promising. For example, there's roughly a +.50 correlation between someone's IQ and subsequent measures of academic performance (e.g., grade-point average; e.g., Kuncel, Hezlett, & Ones, 2004; P. Sackett, Borneman, & Connelly, 2008). This is obviously not a perfect correlation, because we can easily find lower-IQ students who do well in school, and higher-IQ students who do poorly. Still, this correlation is strong enough to indicate that IQ scores do allow us to make predictions about academic success—as they should, if the scores are valid.

IQ scores are also good predictors of performance outside the academic world. In fact, IQ scores are among the strongest predictors of success in the workplace, whether we measure success subjectively (for example, via supervisors' evaluations) or objectively (for example, in productivity or measures of product quality; Schmidt &

Which three of these pieces go together to make this puzzle?

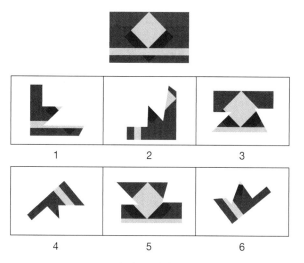

11.3 Wechsler Adult Intelligence Scale visual puzzle This sort of problem is included in the WAIS as part of the measure of perceptual reasoning.

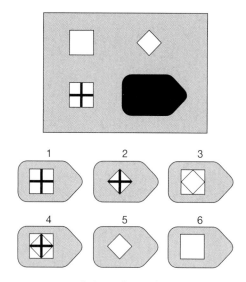

11.4 A sample item from the Raven's Progressive Matrices The task is to select the alternative that fits into the empty slot above. The item shown here is relatively easy; they get harder as the test progresses.

predictive validity An assessment of whether a test measures what it's intended to measure, based on whether the test score correlates with another relevant criterion measured later.

TABLE 11.1	The Relation between IQ and Highway Deaths	
	IQ	Death rate per 10,000 drivers
	115	51.3
	100–115	51.5
	85–99	92.2
	80–84	146.7

Source: Holden, 2003a.

Hunter, 1998, 2004; P. Sackett et al., 2008). Sensibly, though, IQ matters more for some jobs than for others. Jobs of low complexity require relatively little intelligence; so, not surprisingly, the correlation between IQ and job performance is small (although still positive) for such jobs. Thus, for example, there's a correlation of roughly .20 between IQ and someone's performance on an assembly line. As jobs become more complex, intelligence matters more, so the correlation between IQ and performance gets stronger (Gottfredson, 1997b). Thus we find correlations between .5 and .6 when we look at IQ scores and people's success as accountants or shop managers.

Still other results also confirm the importance of IQ scores and make it clear that, if we measure someone's IQ at a relatively early age, we can use that measure to predict many aspects of her life to come. For example, people with higher IQ scores tend, overall, to earn more money during their lifetime, to end up in higher-prestige careers, and even to live longer. Likewise, higher-IQ individuals are less likely to die in automobile accidents (Table 11.1) and less likely to have difficulty following a doctor's instructions. (For a glimpse of this broad data pattern, see Deary & Derr, 2005; Gottfredson, 2004; Kuncel et al., 2004; Lubinski, 2004; C. Murray, 1998.)

We should emphasize that, as with the correlation between IQ and grades, all of these correlations between IQ and life outcomes are appreciably lower than +1.00. This reflects the simple fact that there are exceptions to the pattern we're describing—and so some low-IQ people end up in high-prestige jobs, and some high-IQ people end up unsuccessful in life (with lousy jobs, low salaries, and a short life expectancy). These exceptions remind us that (of course) intelligence is just one of the factors influencing life outcomes—and so, inevitably, the correlation between IQ and life success isn't perfect. Nonetheless, there's still a strong statistical linkage between IQ scores and important life outcomes, making it clear that IQ tests do measure something interesting and consequential.

WHAT IS INTELLIGENCE? THE PSYCHOMETRIC APPROACH

Apparently, then, IQ tests are measuring something that helps people do better in both academic and work settings, something that helps them lead healthier, wealthier, and more productive lives. But can we be more precise about what this "something" is? Put differently, if the IQ test is in fact measuring intelligence, what exactly is intelligence?

For more than a century, these questions have been framed in terms of two broad options. One proposal comes from Binet himself: He and his collaborators assumed that the test measured a singular ability that can apply to virtually any content. In their view, someone's score on the IQ test revealed their general intelligence, a capacity that would provide an advantage on any mental task—whether it's solving a puzzle, writing a paper, or learning a new mathematical technique.

Many authors have offered an alternative view—namely, that there's really no such thing as being intelligent in a general way. Instead, each person's score on the IQ test represents a level of achievement produced by that person's collection of more specific talents, and each talent is relevant to some portions of the test but not others. In this view, if we look closely at the test scores, we're unlikely to find people who are successful in every aspect of the test or people who are inept in every mental task. Instead, each person will be strong on the tasks for which he has the relevant talents and somewhat weaker on the tasks that rely on talents he lacks. As a result, each person would have an individualized profile of strengths and weaknesses. If we then represent that profile with a single number—an IQ score—this is actually just a crude summary of the person's abilities because it averages together the things a person is good at and the things they're not.

Which of these proposals is correct? Is the IQ score a reflection of intelligence in general, so that it measures a capacity useful for all tasks? Or is the score just an average created by summing together diverse components?

The Logic of Psychometrics

We have before us two hypotheses concerned with the nature of intelligence, and the way we've described the hypotheses points toward the means of deciding which hypothesis is correct. What we need to do is take a closer look at the IQ tests themselves and try to find patterns within the test scores. This kind of scrutiny reflects the **psychometric approach to intelligence**—an approach that, at the start, deliberately holds theory and definitions to the side. Instead, it begins with the actual test results and proceeds on the belief that patterns within these results may be our best guide in deciding what the tests measure—and therefore what intelligence is. To see how this works, let's begin with a hypothetical example.

Imagine that we give a group of individuals three tests that seem at least initially different from each other; let's call the tests X, Y, and Z. One hypothesis is that all three tests measure the same underlying ability—and so, if a person has a lot of this ability, she has what she needs for all three tests and will do well on all of them. (This is, of course, the idea that there's a *general* ability used for many different tasks.) Based on this hypothesis, a person's score on one of these tests should be similar to her score on the other tests because, whatever the level of ability happens to be, it's the *same* ability that matters for all three tests. This hypothesis therefore leads to a prediction that there will be a strong correlation between each person's score on test X and his or her score on test Y, and the same goes for X and Z or for Y and Z.

A different hypothesis is that each of tests X, Y, and Z measures a different ability. This is, of course, the idea that there's no such thing as ability in general; instead, each person has their own collection of more specialized capacities. Based on this view, it's possible for a person to have the ability needed for X but not the abilities needed for Y or Z. It's also possible for a person to have the abilities needed for both Y and Z but not those needed for X. It's possible for a person to have all of these abilities or none of them. In short, *all* combinations are possible because we're talking about three separate abilities; thus, there is no reason to expect a correlation between someone's X score and his Y score, or between his Y score and his Z score, just as there's no reason to expect a correlation between, say, someone's ability to knit well and the size of his vocabulary. Knitting and knowing a lot of words are simply independent capacities—so you can be good at one, or the other, or both, or neither.

We could also imagine intermediary hypotheses: Perhaps X and Y tap into the same, somewhat general ability, but Z taps into some other, more specialized ability. Perhaps Y and Z overlap in the abilities relevant for each, but the overlap is only partial. Throughout, however, the logic is the same: If two tests overlap in the abilities they

psychometric approach to intelligence An attempt to understand the nature of intelligence by studying the pattern of results obtained on intelligence tests.

11.5 The logic of psychometrics The analytic procedures used in psychometrics are complex and mathematical, but the basic idea is simple. Imagine someone who observes these serpentine parts moving across a lake. Is there one serpent here, or two? In other words, are the visible pieces linked to each other (under the water)? This question is similar to asking how different tests are linked to each other—the test scores themselves are visible, but the (potential) links—the overlap in the capacities needed for each test—aren't. To ask about the serpents, we'd want to know whether the visible bits rise and fall together. If the rising and falling of, say, loop X are independent of the movements of loop Y, this suggests that the loops aren't linked, as shown in the observer's first hypothesis. But if loop Y always rises when loop X does, and vice versa, this suggests a link, as in the second hypothesis. We use roughly the same logic when we ask about test scores—using correspondence in the visible parts (the scores) to infer linkage in the unseen parts (the underlying capacities).

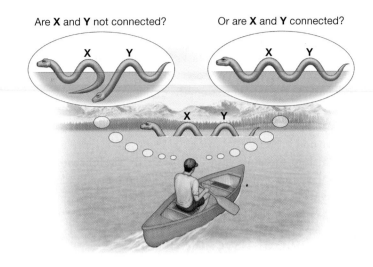

require, then they are to some extent measuring the same thing; so there should be a correlation between the scores on the two tests. If the overlap is slight, the correlation will be weak; if the overlap is greater, the correlation will be correspondingly stronger. (For a slightly different—and somewhat whimsical—view of these points, see Figure 11.5.)

Factor Analysis and the Idea of General Intelligence

What do we find when we apply this logic to real test data? Both the WAIS and the WISC (the adult and child tests, respectively) rely, as we've said, on numerous subtests. This arrangement allows us to compare each person's scores on one of the subtests to their scores on all the other subtests. When we make these comparisons, we find an impressive level of consistency from one subtest to the next. People who do well on one portion of the test tend to do well across the board; people who do poorly on one subtest tend to do poorly on the other subtests as well. In other words, we find substantial correlations among all the subtests' scores. The correlations aren't perfect—and so we know, by the logic we've developed, that the subtests don't overlap completely in what they measure. Even so, the correlations are telling us that the subtests are far from independent of each other; instead, they all overlap in what they're measuring.

To document and measure this overlap, psychologists rely on a statistical technique known as **factor analysis,** developed by Charles Spearman (1863–1945). This technique distills from the pattern of correlations a broad summary of how all the scores are related to each other. Specifically, factor analysis (as its name implies) looks for common factors—"ingredients" that are shared by several scores. The analysis detects these shared factors by using the logic we've already developed: If the scores on two separate tasks are correlated with each other, this suggests the tasks are influenced by the same factor. If scores on *three* tasks are all correlated with each other, then all the tasks, it seems, are influenced by the same factor. And so on.

Factor analyses confirm that there's a common element shared by *all* the components of the IQ test; indeed, in children's data, this single common element seems to account for roughly half of the overall data pattern (Watkins, Wilson, Kotz, Carbone, & Babula, 2006); a single common factor seems just as important in data drawn from testing of adults (e.g., Arnau & Thompson, 2000). The various subtests differ in how strongly they rely on this common element, and so some subtests (e.g., someone's comprehension of a simple story) depend heavily on this general factor; other tests (e.g., someone's ability to recall a string of digits) depend less on the factor. Nonetheless, this

factor analysis A statistical method for studying the interrelations among various tests. The goal is to discover whether the tests are all influenced by the same factors, or by distinct factors.

general factor seems to matter across the board, and that's why all the subtests end up correlated with each other.

But what is this common element? If the subtests overlap in some way, what is the nature of the overlap? More than 50 years ago, Charles Spearman offered the obvious hypothesis—namely, that the common element is **general intelligence**, usually abbreviated with the single letter g. Spearman proposed that g is a mental attribute called on for virtually any intellectual task. It follows, therefore, that any individuals with a lot of g have an advantage in every intellectual endeavor; if g is in short supply, the individual will do poorly on a wide range of tasks.

general intelligence (g) A mental attribute that is hypothesized as contributing to the performance of virtually any intellectual task.

A Hierarchical Model of Intelligence

Spearman realized, however, that g is not the sole determinant of test performance (e.g., Spearman, 1927). Instead, he argued, each subtest depends both on g and on some other abilities that are specific to that particular subtest. Thus, performance on an arithmetic subtest depends on how much g a person has and also on the strength of that person's (more specialized) numerical skills; performance on vocabulary tests depends on the combination of g and the person's verbal skill; and so on. This pattern would explain both why the scores on all the subtests are correlated (because all the subtests rely on g, and so all reflect whether the person has a lot of g or a little) and why the correlations aren't perfect (because performance on each subtest also depends on specialized abilities).

More recent studies have supported Spearman's claim and have also illuminated what the more specialized abilities might be. One specialized ability involves verbal and linguistic skill, and so someone who has a lot of this ability will do well on almost any task that hinges on language skills. A second specialized ability involves quantitative or numerical ability; a third involves spatial or mechanical ability. On this basis, we can think of intellectual performance as having a hierarchical structure as shown in Figure 11.6. Researchers disagree about the details of this hierarchy; but by most accounts, g is at the top of the hierarchy and contributes to virtually all tasks. At the next level down are the abilities we just described—language, quantitative, and spatial—and, according to some authors, several more besides (including a specialized ability for fast-paced mental tasks, a specialized ability to learn new materials, and so on). Then at the next level are a large number of even more specific capacities—at least 80 have been identified—each useful for a narrow and specialized set of tasks (J. Carroll, 1993; W. Johnson, Nijenhuis, & Bouchard, 2007; McGrew, 2009; R. Snow, 1994, 1996).

This hierarchical conception leads to a number of predictions that have been confirmed by psychometric research. Specifically, if we choose tasks from two different categories—say, a verbal task and a task requiring arithmetic—we should expect to find a correlation in performance because, no matter how different these tasks seem, they do have something in common: They both draw on g. If we choose tasks from the *same* category, though—say, two verbal tasks, or two quantitative tasks—we should expect to find a *higher* correlation because these tasks have two things in common: They both draw on g, and they both draw on the more specialized capacity needed for that category. The data confirm both of these predictions—moderately strong correlations among all of the IQ test's subtests, and even stronger correlations among subtests in the same category.

So where does this leave us regarding the two hypotheses we introduced earlier? One hypothesis, initially offered by Binet, is that intelligence is a general skill, useful for all endeavors. The other proposal is that

11.6 Hierarchical conception of intelligence According to many modern theories, intelligence has many components. At the highest level is g, a form of intelligence that applies to virtually any mental task. Each person also has a number of more specialized talents—so that performance on a verbal task depends both on g and on linguistic ability; performance on a mathematical task depends both on g and on numerical ability. Finally, each person also has a much larger number of even more specialized abilities—and so performance on a particular verbal task is also influenced by skills directly applicable to just that task; performance on a particular mechanical task is also influenced by skills applicable to just that sort of task, and so on.

there are multiple forms of intelligence, each useful for a particular type of task. We now see that both suggestions are correct. Each person has some amount of *g*, and he draws on that capacity in virtually everything he does. As a result, there is consistency in someone's performance—an overall level of achievement shaped by the person's *g*. But the consistency isn't perfect, because mental tasks also require more specialized abilities—and each person has each of these to some extent. This is why, in addition to the overall level of consistency, each person has his own profile of strengths and weaknesses, things he does relatively well and things he does less well.

Fluid and Crystallized **G**

Psychometric analyses of intelligence also draw our attention to another distinction. Alongside of verbal, quantitative, and spatial skills, we can also distinguish two more forms of intelligence: *fluid intelligence* and *crystallized intelligence*, often abbreviated *Gf* and *Gc*. These forms of intelligence therefore take their place at the middle level of the hierarchy shown in Figure 11.6 (J. Carroll, 2005; Horn, 1985; Horn & Blankson, 2005).

Fluid intelligence refers to the ability to deal with new and unusual problems. It involves the deliberate and controlled use of mental operations and is the form of intelligence you need when you have no well-practiced routines you can bring to bear on a problem. **Crystallized intelligence,** on the other hand, refers to your acquired knowledge. This includes your verbal knowledge and your broad repertoire of skills—skills useful for dealing with problems similar to those already encountered.

Fluid and crystallized intelligence are linked in an obvious way: Someone with a high level of fluid intelligence is likely to be a fast learner and so will easily acquire the skills and knowledge that crystallized intelligence comprises. As a result, someone with a lot of fluid intelligence will end up with a lot of crystallized intelligence. Even so, there are several reasons to distinguish these types of intelligence. For example, crystallized intelligence seems to increase with age—as long as the individual remains in an intellectually stimulating environment (see Chapter 14). Fluid intelligence, on the other hand, generally reaches its height in early adulthood and then, for most people, declines steadily with age (Horn, 1985; Horn & Noll, 1994; Salthouse, 2004). Similarly, many factors—including alcohol consumption, fatigue, depression, and some forms of brain damage—cause more impairment in tasks requiring fluid intelligence than in those dependent on crystallized intelligence (J. Duncan, 1994; E. Hunt, 1995). Thus, to put this concretely, someone who is tired (or drunk, or depressed) will probably perform adequately on tests involving familiar routines and familiar facts because these tests draw heavily on crystallized intelligence. That same individual, however, may be markedly impaired if the test requires quick thinking or a novel approach—both earmarks of fluid intelligence.

THE BUILDING BLOCKS OF INTELLIGENCE

Let's pause to take stock. We've now seen that IQ scores are reliable predictors of many important life outcomes; critically, the outcomes most closely linked to IQ—success in school, for example, or success in complex jobs—are exactly the sorts of things that *should* be correlated with IQ *if* the IQ test is measuring what it's intended to measure: intelligence.

fluid intelligence The ability to deal with new and unusual problems.

crystallized intelligence Acquired knowledge, including the person's repertoire of verbal knowledge and cognitive skills.

These points prompted us to take a closer look at the IQ scores, and that's what led us to separate general intelligence (*g*) from more specialized forms of mental ability. But can we take our analysis further? What is it, inside a person, that gives them more *g*, or less? Do smart people have certain skills that the rest of us don't have? Do smart people have bigger brains, or brains with a different structure? Let's look at the evidence relevant to these points.

Mental Speed

Intelligence tests require complex mental processes: The test taker has to detect complicated patterns, work her way through multiple-step plans, and so on. Each of these processes takes some time, and this invites the proposal that the people we consider intelligent may just be those who are especially fast in these processes. This speed would allow them to perform intellectual tasks more quickly; it also would give them time for *more steps* in comparison with those of us who aren't so quick.

One version of this hypothesis proposes that high-IQ people are faster in all mental steps, no matter what the steps involve (Eysenck, 1986; Nettelbeck, 2003; Vernon, 1987). A related hypothesis proposes that high-IQ people are faster not in all mental processes, but in just those needed for key mental operations such as memory retrieval (E. Hunt, 1976, 1985b). In either case, what could be the basis for this speed? One possibility is a greater degree of myelination of the neurons in the brains of high-IQ people (E. Miller, 1994; bear in mind that it's the myelin wrappers around axons that allow fast transmission of the neural impulse; axons without these wrappers transmit the action potential much more slowly; for details, see Chapter 3). Alternatively, high-IQ people may have a greater availability of metabolic "fuel" for the neurons (Rae, Digney, McEwan, & Bates, 2003). But, no matter what the neural mechanism might be, what is the evidence linking intelligence scores to measures of speed?

A number of studies have measured **simple reaction time**, in which the participant merely responds as quickly as he can when a stimulus appears. Others have measured **choice reaction time**, in which the participant must again respond as quickly as possible but now has to choose among several responses, depending on the stimulus presented. In such tasks, reaction times are in fact correlated with intelligence scores (note, though, that the correlation is negative, and that *lower* times—indicating greater speed—are correlated with *higher* IQ; see, for example, Jensen, 1987).

Other studies have focused on measures of **inspection time**—the time someone needs to make a simple discrimination between two stimuli (which of two lines is longer, or which of two tones is higher). These measures correlate around −.50 with intelligence scores (see, for example, T. Bates & Shieles, 2003; Dantiir, Roberts, Schulze, & Wilhelm, 2005; Deary & Derr, 2005; Grudnik & Kranzler, 2001; Lohman, 2000; Petrill, Luo, Thompson, & Detterman, 2001; again, the correlation is negative because lower response times go with higher scores on intelligence tests).

The suggestion, then, is that intelligent people may literally have brains that operate more swiftly and more efficiently than the brains of less intelligent people. This idea finds further support in a classic study that examined the relationship between brain activity and someone's ability to perform well on the Raven's Matrices, often used as a measure of *g* (see Figure 11.4). PET scans showed robust *negative* correlations between scores on the Raven's test and glucose metabolism in many areas distributed around the cortex (Haier et al., 1988). In other words, the data showed *less* energy consumption by the brains of people with higher IQs. This is certainly consistent with the idea that high *g* is somehow the product of more efficient brain function—as if smarter people were simultaneously getting more "horsepower" as well as better "fuel economy" out of their mental engine!

simple reaction time A measurement of how quickly someone can respond to a stimulus.

choice reaction time A measure of the speed of mental processing that takes place when someone must choose between several responses, depending on which stimulus is presented.

inspection time The time someone needs to make a simple discrimination between two stimuli.

Working Memory and Attention

Mental speed is likely to be one contributor to intelligence, but there are other elements as well—including a central role for *working memory capacity*. To understand the point here, bear in mind that many mental tasks involve multiple bits of information, and you need to keep track of them as you proceed. In addition, many tasks involve multiple steps, and they demand that you shift your focus from one moment to the next—thinking about your overall goal for a second, to figure out what to do next; then focusing on that next step, to deal with its specific demands; then focusing once again on your goal, to choose the *next* step; and so on .

On this basis, perhaps the people we call "intelligent" are those who have particularly good working memories, so that they can hold onto the information they need for complex tasks. They may also have especially good control of their attention—so they're able to coordinate their goals and priorities in an appropriate way, first by focusing *here* and then *there*, without getting lured off track by distraction.

To test this broad proposal, researchers have relied on measures that assess someone's **working memory capacity** (**WMC**; e.g., Engle, Tuholski, Laughlin, & Conway, 1999; also see Chapter 8). There are several varieties of these measures; but in one common procedure, the participant is asked to read aloud a brief series of sentences, such as

> *Due to his gross inadequacies, his position as director was terminated abruptly.*
> *It is possible, of course, that life did not arise on the Earth at all.*

Immediately after reading the sentences, the participant is asked to recall the final word in each one—in this case, *abruptly* and *all*. Participants are tested in this way with pairs of sentences (as in our example) and also with larger groups of sentences—as many as 6 or 7. The aim, of course, is to find each participant's limit: What's the largest group of sentences for which the participant can do this read-and-recall task?

This seemingly peculiar task provides a good measure of WMC because it involves storing some material (the final words of sentences) for later use in the recall test, while the person is simultaneously thinking about other material (the full sentences, which have to be read out loud). This juggling of processes, as we move from one part of the task to the next, is exactly how we use working memory and attention in everyday life. Thus, performance on this test is likely to reflect how efficiently a person's working memory will operate in more natural settings. And if, as hypothesized, this efficiency is essential for intelligent performance, then these measurements of WMC should be correlated with intelligence.

The data confirm this prediction. People with a larger WMC, measured as we've described, do have an advantage on many other tests. For example, people with a larger WMC do better on the verbal SAT, on tests of reasoning, on measures of reading comprehension, and on tests specifically designed to measure *g* (A. Conway et al., 2005; Gathercole & Pickering, 2000a, 2000b; Daneman & Carpenter, 1980; Kane, Poole, Tuholski, & Engle, 2006; Lépine, Barrouillet, & Camos, 2005; Salthouse & Pink, 2008).

Executive Control

How exactly does a larger WMC improve intellectual performance? A number of interrelated proposals have been offered; one proposal focuses on the construction and maintenance of the *task model* needed to perform a task. This model provides the

---

working memory capacity (WMC)
A measure of how efficiently a person can manage multiple mental processes at once.

"mental agenda" that a person needs to carry out the task; the model is based on the person's understanding of the task's goals, rules, and requirements as well as their knowledge of the relevant facts. Once constructed, the model governs the person's mental steps as he works his way through the task.

Tasks differ in the complexity of the model they require. The model will have to be more complicated (for example) if task performance involves either multiple goals or a sharp change in goals as certain cues come into view. Evidence suggests that the ability to handle this complexity is strongly linked to measures of *g*—so that higher-*g* individuals are able to maintain more complex task models, allowing them to out-perform lower-*g* people whenever such models are required (J. Duncan et al., 2008).

A different (but related) proposal is that measures of WMC are actually measures of each person's *executive control* over her own thoughts. This term—which we first met in Chapter 3—refers to the processes people use to launch mental actions, redirect their attention, or shift their strategies. From this perspective, the link between intelligence and WMC implies that smart people are literally in better control of their own thoughts than less intelligent people are.

What does executive control involve? Part of the answer lies in processes needed for **goal maintenance**—the mental activities that help us keep our goals in view, so that we consistently direct our behavior toward that goal. As we discussed in Chapter 3, these activities seem to depend on the frontmost part of the brain's frontal lobe—the prefrontal area (Figure 11.7). Damage to this brain site produces many problems, including *goal neglect* (in which the person fails to keep track of the goal) and *perseveration* (in which the person cannot make the necessary adjustment in behavior when a goal changes).

Executive control also requires other steps, rooted in other brain areas. For example, the anterior cingulate cortex seems to play a key role in detecting *conflict* between different mental processes—including the conflict that will arise if one process is pulling toward one goal while another process pulls toward a different goal (e.g., Botvinick, Cohen, & Carter, 2004; also Banich, 2009; Buckley, Mansouri, Hoda, Mahboubi, Browning et al., 2009; Egner, 2008). Once these conflicts are detected, this information feeds back to other mechanisms (probably in the prefrontal area) that actually control the flow of thoughts so that the conflict can be addressed. (For more on the frontal lobe, see Koechlin & Hyafil, 2007; for more on executive control, see J. Duncan, 1995; Gilbert & Shallice, 2002; Kane & Engle, 2003; Kimberg, D'Esposito, & Farah, 1998; Stuss & Levine, 2002.)

Notice that both of these proposals—one emphasizing task models, one emphasizing executive control—rely on claims about working memory (so that you can keep your task model or your goals in mind). They also rely on claims about *attention*,

goal maintenance The mental process of keeping one's goal in mind to guide the selection of the next actions.

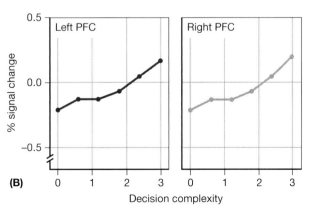

(A)   (B)

11.7 Executive control in brain areas The prefrontal cortex (PFC) is crucial for tasks involving intelligence, including tasks that require choices among options. In fact, the more options there are to choose among, the greater the PFC activation.

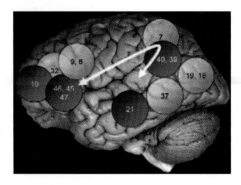

11.8 P-FIT model The white arrows indicate brain areas and connections crucial for intelligence. The numbers correspond to so-called Brodmann areas; this is a system for describing brain anatomy. Black circles indicate areas especially important in the left hemisphere; light-colored circles indicate areas important in both hemispheres.

so that you can focus on your task's steps or on the relationship between those steps and your current goal. Both proposals are thus fully compatible with the so-called parieto-frontal integration theory (P-FIT) of intelligence suggested by R. Jung & Haier (2007; Figure 11.8). This theory grows out of neuroimaging studies that have compared the brains of individuals at differing levels of intelligence; the theory identifies a network of brain sites that seem crucial for intellectual performance. As the theory's name implies, some of these brain sites are in the parietal lobe—sites crucial for the control of attention; other sites are in the frontal lobe and are essential for working memory. Still other important sites seem to play an important role in language processing. The P-FIT conception emphasizes, though, that what really matters for intelligence is the *integration* of information from all of these sites, and thus the coordinated functioning of many cognitive components. This is, of course, a biologically based proposal that fits well with the functionally defined proposals emphasizing task models and executive control.

Other Contributions to Intellectual Functioning

It seems, therefore, that one part of what makes someone "intelligent" is simply mental speed. This speed may make individual mental steps faster; it may also allow better communication among distinct brain areas. What's more, someone's working memory capacity and their ability to stay focused on a goal even in the face of interference or distraction also matters for intelligence. Related, intelligence also may depend on the ability to construct and employ complex task models; this ability is linked in turn to a higher degree of executive control.

Beyond these points, though, other factors also matter for intellectual performance. For example, even if someone is slow, or has poor executive control, he can benefit from the knowledge and skills he has gained from life experience. This is, of course, the contribution from *crystallized intelligence,* which helps people solve problems, draw sensible conclusions, and make good decisions (also Ackerman & Beier, 2005; Hambrick, 2005).

The performance of intellectual tasks is also powerfully shaped by attributes that we might not think of as "intellectual" capacities. These include someone's motivation, her attitude toward intellectual challenges, and her willingness to persevere when a problem becomes frustratingly difficult. (Indeed, these factors will be crucial for us later in the chapter, when we turn to differences among various *groups* in their average level of performance on these tests.)

Plainly, therefore, being intelligent requires a large and diverse set of attributes. If we choose, in light of these points, to represent someone's intelligence with a single number—an IQ score—this seems both useful and potentially misleading. This score does summarize someone's performance, so it can be useful in predicting how that person will perform in a wide range of other settings. At the same time, this single number blurs diverse constituents together; and so, if we wish to understand intelligence—and more important, if we want to find ways to *improve* someone's intelligence—then we need to look past this single measurement and examine the many components contributing to that score.

INTELLIGENCE BEYOND THE IQ TEST

We've now made good progress in filling in our portrait of intelligence. We know that we can speak of intelligence in general; the psychometric data tell us that. We also know how to distinguish some more specific forms of intelligence (linguistic, quantitative, spatial;

fluid, crystallized). And, finally, we know some of the elements that give someone a higher or lower *g*—namely, mental speed, working memory capacity, and executive control.

We might still ask, though, whether there are aspects of intelligence not included in this portrait—aspects that are somehow separate from the capacities we measure with our conventional intelligence tests. For example, you probably know people who are "street-smart" or "savvy," but not "school-smart." Such people may lack the sort of analytic skill required for strong performance in the classroom, but they're sophisticated and astute in dealing with the practical world. Likewise, what about social competence—the ability to persuade others and to judge their moods and desires? Shrewd salespeople have this ability, as do successful politicians, quite independent of whether they have high or low IQ scores.

A number of studies have explored these other nonacademic forms of intelligence. For example, one study focused on gamblers who had enormous experience in betting on horse races and asked them to predict the outcomes and payoffs in several upcoming races. This is a tricky mental task that involves highly complex reasoning. Factors like track records, jockeys, and track conditions all have to be remembered and weighed against one another. On the face of it, the ability to perform such mental calculations seems to be part of what intelligence tests should measure. But the results proved otherwise; the gamblers' success turned out to be completely unrelated to their IQs (Ceci & Liker, 1986). These findings and others have persuaded researchers that we need to broaden our conception of intelligence and consider forms of intelligence that aren't measured by the IQ test.

Practical Intelligence

One prominent investigator, Robert Sternberg, has argued that we need to distinguish several types of intelligence. One type, **analytic intelligence,** is measured by standard intelligence tests. A different type is **practical intelligence,** needed for skilled reasoning in the day-to-day world (Sternberg, 1985; also see Henry, Sternberg, & Grigorenko, 2005; Sternberg & Kaufman, 1998; Sternberg, R. Wagner, Williams, & Horvath, 1995; R. Wagner, 2000; Figure 11.9).

In one of Sternberg's studies, business executives read descriptions of scenarios involving problems similar to those they faced in their professional work. The

analytic intelligence The ability typically measured by intelligence tests and crucial for academic success.

practical intelligence The ability to solve everyday problems through skilled reasoning that relies on tacit knowledge.

11.9 **Practical intelligence** Bettors at a racetrack rely on sophisticated and complex strategies in deciding which horses will win, but these strategies seem to depend on a form of intelligence separate from that which is assessed by the IQ test. Likewise, business executives may depend more on "practical" intelligence than on "analytic" intelligence.

tacit knowledge Practical "how-to" knowledge accumulated from everyday experience.

emotional intelligence The ability to understand your own and others' emotions and to control your emotions appropriately.

executives also considered various solutions for each problem and rated them on a scale from 1 (poor solution) to 7 (excellent solution). These ratings were then used to assess how much **tacit knowledge** each of the executives had—that is, practical know-how gleaned from their everyday experience. The data showed that this measure of tacit knowledge was predictive of job performance (and so was correlated with on-the-job performance ratings as well as salary). Crucially, though, measures of tacit knowledge weren't correlated with IQ—and so are plainly assessing something separate from the sorts of "intelligence" relevant to the IQ test (Sternberg & Wagner, 1993; R. Wagner, 1987; R. Wagner & Sternberg, 1987).

Other research, however, has challenged the claim that practical intelligence is independent of analytic intelligence. In one study, for example, measures of practical intelligence were correlated with measures of *g* (Cianciolo et al., 2006; also see N. Brody, 2003; Gottfredson, 2003a, 2003b; Sternberg, 2003). Even so, many researchers believe that practical intelligence is different enough from analytic intelligence to justify separating them in our overall theorizing about people's different levels *and types* of intellectual ability.

Emotional Intelligence

A different effort toward broadening the concept of intelligence involves claims about **emotional intelligence**—the ability to understand one's own emotions and others', and also the ability to control one's emotions when appropriate. The term *emotional intelligence* might seem an oxymoron, based on the widely held view that emotions often *undermine* our ability to think clearly and so work against our ability to reason intelligently. Many psychologists, however, reject this claim. They argue that emotion plays an important role in guiding our problem solving and decision making (see, for example, Bechara, H. Damasio, & A. Damasio, 2000; A. Damasio, 1994); emotion also plays a role in guiding our attention and shaping what we remember (Reisberg & Hertel, 2004). In these ways, emotion and cognition interact and enrich each other in important ways. (For more on emotion, see Chapter 12.)

One theory suggests that emotional intelligence actually has four parts. First, there's an ability to perceive emotions accurately—so that, for example, you can tell when a friend is tense or when someone is becoming angry. Second, there's an ability to use emotions to facilitate thinking and reasoning, including a capacity to rely on your "gut feelings" in guiding your own decisions. Third, there's an ability to understand emotions, including the use of language to describe emotions, so that you're alert to how a friend will act when she's sad or to how fear can alter someone's perspective; also included here is the ability to talk about emotions—to convey to others how you're feeling and to understand what they tell you about their feelings. Finally, there's an ability to manage emotions in oneself and others; this includes the ability to abide by your culture's rules for "displaying" emotions as well as the ability to regulate your own emotions (Mayer, Roberts, & Barsade, 2008a; Mayer, Salovey, & Caruso, 2008b; Salovey & Mayer, 1990; also Brackett, Rivers, Shiffman, Lerner, & Salovey, 2006; for more on "emotion management," see Chapter 12).

Researchers have developed various measures of emotional intelligence, including the Mayer-Salovey-Caruso Emotional Intelligence Test (MSCEIT; Bracket & Mayer, 2003; Mayer, Salovey, Caruso, & Sitarenios, 2003; Figure 11.10). This measure appears to have predictive validity so that, for example, people who score higher on the MSCEIT seem to be more successful in social settings. They have fewer conflicts with their peers, are judged to create a more positive atmosphere in the workplace, are more tolerant of stress, and are judged to have more leadership potential (Lopes, Salovey, Côté, & Beers, 2005; Grewal & Salovey, 2005). Likewise, college students with higher

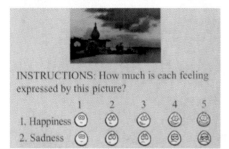

11.10 The Mayer-Salovey-Caruso Emotional Intelligence Test Shown here are two items similar to those used on the MSCEIT.

MSCEIT scores are rated by their friends as more caring and more supportive. They are also less likely to experience conflict with their peers (Brackett & Mayer, 2003; Mayer et al., 2008a).

The idea of emotional intelligence has received much attention in the media and popular literature; as a result, various claims have been offered in the media that are not supported by evidence. (For a glimpse of the relationship between the science and the mythology here, and some concerns about the idea of emotional intelligence, see Matthews, Zeidner, & Roberts, 2003, 2005.) Still, emotional intelligence does seem to matter for many aspects of everyday functioning, it can be measured, and it is one more way that people differ from one another in their broad intellectual competence.

The Theory of Multiple Intelligences

It seems that our measures of *g*—so-called general intelligence—may not provide as complete a measurement as we thought. The capacities measured by *g* are surely important, but so are other aspects of intelligence—including practical intelligence, emotional intelligence, and, according to some authors, *social intelligence* (see, for example, Kihlstrom & Cantor, 2000). Other authors would make this list even longer: In his theory of **multiple intelligences,** Howard Gardner argued for several further types of intelligence (Gardner, 1983, 1998): Three of these are incorporated in most standard intelligence tests: *linguistic intelligence, logical-mathematical intelligence,* and *spatial intelligence.* But Gardner also argued that we should acknowledge *musical intelligence, bodily-kinesthetic intelligence* (the ability to learn and create complex patterns of movement), *interpersonal intelligence* (the ability to understand other people), *intrapersonal intelligence* (the ability to understand ourselves), and *naturalistic intelligence* (the ability to understand patterns in nature).

Gardner based his argument on several lines of evidence, including studies of patients with brain lesions that devastate some abilities while sparing others. Thus, certain lesions will make a person unable to recognize drawings (a disruption of spatial intelligence), while others will make him unable to perform a sequence of movements (bodily-kinesthetic intelligence) or will devastate musical ability (musical intelligence). Gardner concluded from these cases that each of these capacities is served by a separate part of the brain (and so is disrupted when that part of the brain is damaged), and therefore each is distinct from the others.

Another argument for Gardner's theory comes from the study of people with so-called **savant syndrome.** These individuals have a single extraordinary talent, even though they're otherwise developmentally disabled (either autistic or mentally retarded) to a profound degree. Some display unusual artistic talent. Others are "calendar calculators," able to answer immediately (and correctly!) when asked questions such as "What day of the week was March 17 in the year 1682?". Still others have unusual mechanical talents or remarkable musical skills—for example, they can effortlessly memorize lengthy and complex musical works (A. Hill, 1978; L. K. Miller, 1999).

Gardner's claims have been controversial, partly because some of the data he cites are open to other interpretations (see, for example, Cowan & Carney, 2006; L. K. Miller, 1999; Nettelbeck & Young, 1996; Thioux, Stark, Klaiman, & Schultz, 2006). In addition, evidence indicates that several of the forms of "intelligence" Gardner describes are intercorrelated—and so if someone has what Gardner calls linguistic intelligence, they're also likely to have logical-mathematical, spatial, interpersonal, and naturalistic intelligence. This obviously challenges Gardner's assertion that these are separate and independent capacities (Visser, Ashton & Vernon, 2006).

multiple intelligences In Howard Gardner's theory, the six essential, independent mental capacities (linguistic, logical-mathematical, spatial, musical, bodily-kinesthetic, and personal intelligence).

savant syndrome A syndrome in a developmentally disabled person who has some remarkable talent that contrasts with his low level of general intelligence.

11.11 The original "Rain Man" Kim Peek (1951–2009) was a remarkable man with remarkable talents. He could read an entire book in an hour (scanning two pages at a time) and remembered everything he'd read; by one estimate, he memorized over 12,000 books. But, with an IQ of 73, he was retarded; Peek's story was told (in fictionalized form) in the 1988 film *Rain Man*.

"You can't build a hut, you don't know how to find edible roots and you know nothing about predicting the weather. In other words, you do terribly on our I.Q. test."

11.12 Intelligence in context

There's also room for disagreement about Gardner's basic conceptualization. Without question, some individuals—whether savants or otherwise—have special talents; and these talents are impressive (Figure 11.11). But is it appropriate to think of these talents as forms of intelligence? Or might we be better served by a distinction between *intelligence* and *talent*? It does seem peculiar to use the same term, *intelligence,* to describe both the capacity that Albert Einstein displayed in developing his theories and the capacity that Peyton Manning displays on the football field. Similarly, we might celebrate the vocal talent of Beyoncé Knowles; but is hers the same type of talent—and therefore sensibly described by the same term, *intelligence*—that a skilled debater relies on in rapidly thinking through the implications of an argument?

Whatever the ultimate verdict on Gardner's theory, he has undoubtedly done us a valuable service by drawing our attention to a set of abilities that are often ignored and undervalued. Gardner is surely correct in noting that we tend to focus too much on the skills and capacities that help people succeed in school, and do too little to celebrate the talents displayed by an artist at her canvas, a skilled dancer in the ballet, or an empathetic clergyman in a hospital room. Whether these other abilities should be counted as forms of intelligence or not, they're surely talents to be highly esteemed and, as much as possible, nurtured and developed.

The Cultural Context of Intelligence

Yet another—and perhaps deeper—challenge to our intelligence tests, and a powerful reason to think beyond the IQ scores, comes from a different source: the question of whether our tests truly measure intelligence, or whether they merely measure what's *called* intelligence in our culture.

Different cultures certainly have different ideas about what intelligence is. For example, some parts of the intelligence test put a premium on quick and decisive responses, but not all cultures share our Western preoccupation with speed. Indians (of southern Asia) and Native Americans, for example, place a higher value on being deliberate; in effect, they'd rather be right than quick. They also prefer to qualify, or to say "I don't know" or "I'm not sure," unless they're absolutely certain of their answer. Such deliberation and hedging would hurt their test scores on many intelligence tests because it's often a good idea to guess whenever you're not sure about the answer (Sinha, 1983; Triandis, 1989). Similarly, Taiwanese Chinese place a high priority on how they relate to others; this will, in some circumstances, lead them not to show their intelligence, thus undermining our standardized assessment (Yang & Sternberg, 1997; also Nisbett, 2003; for other cultural differences in how intelligence is defined, see Serpell, 2000; Sternberg, 2004).

These cultural differences guarantee that an intelligence test that seems appropriate in one cultural setting may be inappropriate in other cultural settings (Figure 11.12). Moreover, the specific procedure we need for measuring intelligence also depends on the cultural setting. This is because people in many countries fail to solve problems that are presented abstractly or that lack a familiar context, but they do perfectly well with identical problems presented in more meaningful ways. For example, consider the response of an unschooled Russian peasant who was asked, "From Shakhimardan to Vuadil it takes three hours on foot, while to Fergana it is six hours. How much time does it take to go on foot from Vuadil to Fergana?" The reply was "No, it's six hours from Vuadil to Shakhimardan. You're wrong. . . . It's far and you wouldn't get there in three hours" (Luria, 1976, p. 229). If this had been a question on a standard intelligence test, the peasant would have scored poorly—not because he was unintelligent, but because he did not regard the question as a test of arithmetical reasoning. It turned out that he was quite able to perform the relevant calculation but could not accept the form in which the question was presented.

In light of these concerns, we might well ask whether it's possible to measure intelligence in a way that's fair to all cultures and biased against none. The Raven's Progressive Matrices (Figure 11.4) are often claimed to be fair to all groups because the test is nonverbal and doesn't rely on any sort of specific prior knowledge. But the very idea of organizing items in rows and columns—an idea that's essential for this test—is unfamiliar in some settings, and this puts test takers in those settings at a disadvantage with this form of testing.

To put this worry somewhat differently, we could (if we wished) use a standard intelligence test to assess people living in, say, rural Zambia, and the test results probably would allow us to predict whether the Zambians will do well in Western schools or in a Western-style workplace. But this form of testing would tell us nothing about whether these Zambians have the intellectual skills they need to flourish in their own cultural setting. Just as bad, our test would probably give us an absurd understatement of the Zambians' intellectual competence because our test is simply in the wrong form to reveal that competence.

Against this backdrop, it's important to emphasize that some mental capacities can be found in all cultures—including (as just one example) the core knowledge needed to understand some aspects of mathematics (see, for example, Dehaene, Izard, Pica, & Spelke, 2006). But it's also clear that cultures differ not only in the skills they need and value but also in how they respond to our Westernized test procedures. As a result, we need to be extremely careful in how we interpret or use our measures of intelligence. Intelligence tests do capture important aspects of intellectual functioning, but they don't capture all aspects or all abilities, and the meaning and utility of the tests has to be understood in the appropriate cultural context. (For further discussion, see Greenfield, 1997; Serpell, 2000; Sternberg, 2004.)

THE ROOTS OF INTELLIGENCE

We are, it seems, moving toward a mixed assessment of intelligence tests. On the one side, these tests do measure something important; but on the other side, there are important talents and skills *not* tapped by these tests. Even so, the fact remains that these tests are widely used—by educators deciding which students to admit to a program and by employers deciding which applicants to hire. These are important matters, because these decisions obviously can have large-scale, long-term consequences for all involved. It's not surprising, therefore, that the test scores have been the focus of fierce debate regarding whether the tests are valid and fair. A large part of this debate has focused on *why* someone scores the way they do—and more specifically, the role of *genetics* in shaping intelligence.

The Politics of IQ Testing

Intelligence testing has been mired in political controversy from the very beginning. Recall that Binet intended his test as a means of identifying schoolchildren who would benefit from extra training. In the early years of the 20th century, however, some people—scientists and politicians—put the test to a different use. They noted the fact (still true today) that there was a correlation between IQ and socioeconomic status (SES): People with lower IQ scores usually end up with lower-paid, lower-status jobs; they're also more likely to end up as criminals than are people with higher IQs. The politicians therefore asked, why should we try to educate these low-IQ individuals? If we know from the start that those with low intelligence scores are unlikely ever to get far in life, then why waste educational resources on them?

In sharp contrast, advocates for the disadvantaged took a different view. To begin with, they often disparaged the tests themselves, arguing that bias built into the tests favored some groups over others. In addition, they argued that the connection between IQ and SES was far from inevitable. Good education, they suggested, can lift the status of almost anyone—and perhaps lift their IQ scores as well. Therefore, spending educational resources on the poor was an important priority, especially since it might be the poor who need and benefit from these resources the most. (For reviews of this history, see S. J. Gould, 1981; Kamin, 1974.)

These contrasting views obviously lead to different prescriptions for social policy, and for many years, those who viewed low scorers as a waste of resources dominated the debate. An example is the rationale behind the U.S. immigration policy between the two World Wars. The immigration act of 1924 (the National Origins Act) set rigid quotas to minimize the influx of what were thought to be biologically "weaker stocks"—specifically, immigrants from southern and eastern Europe, Asia, and Africa. To "prove" the genetic intellectual inferiority of these immigrants, a congressional committee pointed to the scores by members of these groups on the U.S. Army's intelligence test; the scores were indeed substantially below those attained by Americans of northern European ancestry (Figure 11.13).

As it turns out, we now know that these differences among groups, observed in the early 20th century, were due to the simple fact that the immigrants had been in the United States for only a short time. Because of their recent arrival, the immigrants lacked fluency in English and had little knowledge of certain cultural facts important for doing well on the tests. It's no surprise, then, that their test scores were low. After living in the United States for a while, the immigrants' U.S. cultural knowledge and English skills improved—and their scores became indistinguishable from those of native-born Americans. This observation plainly undermined the hypothesis of a hereditary difference in intelligence between, say, northern and eastern Europeans, but the proponents of immigration quotas didn't analyze the results so closely. They had their own reasons for restricting immigration, such as fears of competition from cheap labor. The theory that the excluded groups were innately inferior provided a convenient justification for their policies (Bronfenbrenner, McClelland, Wethington, Moen, & Ceci, 1996; Kamin, 1974; W. Williams & Ceci, 1997).

A more recent example of how intelligence testing can become intertwined with political and social debate grew out of a highly controversial book—*The Bell Curve*, by Richard J. Herrnstein and Charles Murray (1994). This book, and the debate it set off, showcased the differences among racial groups in their test scores: Whites in the United States (i.e., Americans of European ancestry) had scores that averaged roughly 10 points higher than the average score for blacks (Americans of African ancestry). Herrnstein and Murray argued that these differences had important policy implications, and urged (among other things) reevaluation of programs that in their view encouraged low-IQ people to have more babies.

Herrnstein and Murray's claims were criticized on many counts (e.g., Devlin et al., 1997; S. Fraser, 1995; R. Jacoby & Glauberman, 1995; R. Lynn, 1999; Montagu, 1999; Neisser et al., 1996; and many more). There has been considerable debate, for example, about their interpretation of the test scores as well as about whether "race," a key concept in their argument, is a meaningful biological category. We'll return to these points later in the chapter; for now, it's enough to note that these questions have profound political importance, so it's imperative that we ensure policy debates are informed by good science.

11.13 Anti-immigration sentiment in the United States "Immigration Restriction. Prop Wanted." This cartoon, which appeared in the January 23, 1903, issue of the *Philadelphia Inquirer*, called for more restrictive immigration laws.

The Problems with "Nature vs. Nurture"

Plainly, people differ from one another in their intelligence and their talents. But what causes these differences? This question is often framed in terms of two alternatives— the notion that what matters is genetics and heredity, or the notion that what matters is environment (and so learning and experience). The options, in other words, are boiled down to the dichotomy of "nature vs. nurture."

As we discussed in Chapter 2, however, this framing of the issue makes no sense, because the influences of genes and environment are inevitably intertwined. Specifically, someone's genetic heritage merely establishes his *genotype;* the traits he ends up with (his *phenotype*) depend on how the process of development, guided by that genotype, unfolds. That developmental process is, of course, heavily shaped by genetic factors. But it is also powerfully influenced by the person's environment—what nutrients he's exposed to, or what toxins; and, crucially, what experiences he has. In short: There's no such thing as genetic influences independent of environment.

Likewise, how someone benefits from experience depends on her capacity to perceive, to understand, and to form memories. And these capacities depend on the biological equipment that each person has—her eyes, for example, and her brain. This biological equipment, in turn, is heavily shaped by the person's genotype. As a result, there's no way for experience to influence us independent of genetics.

Even with these points acknowledged, it's clear that some traits are more directly shaped by genetic influences than others. For example, the color of someone's eyes (assuming he's not wearing tinted contact lenses) depends almost entirely on the genetic pattern he has inherited. Conversely, the language that someone speaks (French or Italian, Walbiri or Bantu) depends on where (and with whom) she grows up. As it turns out, to the fact that someone can learn language at all *is* heavily guided by genetics (see Chapter 10). But the *choice* of language depends on the environment, not on genes.

Where does intelligence fall in this range from heavily influenced by genes (like eye color is) to less influenced (like choice of language)? We took some steps toward answering this question in Chapter 2—and, as we saw there, the answer is complicated: In some circumstances, genetic factors play a large role; in others, genes count for less. And, as we'll see, the role for genetic influences depends on whether we're asking why various *individuals* perform differently on intelligence tests, or whether we're asking why various *groups* (racial groups in particular) perform differently on these tests. Let's start by asking why various individuals seem to have different levels of intelligence.

Genetics and Individual IQ

As we first saw in Chapter 2, there are several ways to evaluate how strongly a given trait (eye color, height, career choice) is influenced by genetics. One of our main methods, though, begins with an examination of relatives, asking in particular whether people who resemble each other genetically also resemble each other in terms of the target trait. For measures of intelligence, it turns out that the correlation between the IQs of children and the IQs of their biological parents is about $+.40$; the correlation between the IQs of biological siblings is roughly the same. These correlations indicate a relatively strong resemblance, but these correlations, on their own, are ambiguous. On the one side, biologically related family members resemble each other genetically, and this might be the source of the resemblance in IQ scores. But on the other side, the members of a family usually also resemble each other in their experiences: They live in similar social and financial circumstances; they all receive similar levels of health care and are likely to receive similar levels of education. It's plausible, then, that the resemblance in their IQs might be due to this shared environment rather than their overlapping sets of genes.

Clearly, then, we need better evidence to help us untangle the hereditary and environmental contributions to intelligence—and some of that evidence comes from the study of twins. As we've mentioned in other chapters, there are two types of twins: *Identical*, or monozygotic (MZ), *twins* originate from a single fertilized egg. Early in development, that egg splits into two exact replicas which develop into two genetically identical individuals. In contrast, *fraternal*, or dizygotic (DZ), *twins* arise from two different eggs, each fertilized by a different sperm cell. As a result, fraternal twins share only 50% of their genetic material, just as ordinary (nontwin) siblings do.

Identical twins, therefore, resemble each other genetically more than fraternal twins do; and this fact makes it striking that identical twins resemble each other in their IQs more than fraternal twins do. In an early summary of the data, the correlation for identical twins was .86; the correlation for fraternal twins was strongly positive but considerably lower, around .60 (Bouchard & McGue, 1981). Other, more recent data confirm this pattern (Figure 11.14). This certainly suggests a strong genetic component in the determination of IQ, with greater genetic similarity (in identical twins) leading to greater IQ similarity.

The impact of genetic factors is even clearer when we consider results obtained for identical twins who were separated soon after birth, adopted by different families, and reared in different households. The data show a correlation for these twins of about .75, which is not substantially less than the .86 correlation for identical twins reared together (Bouchard, Lykken, McGue, Segal, & Tellegen, 1990; McGue, Bouchard,

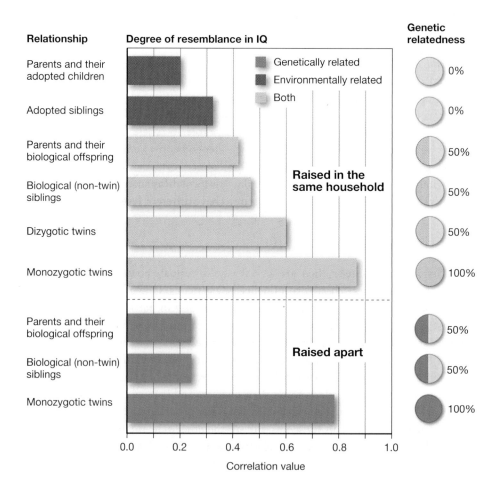

11.14 Genetics and intelligence Evidence powerfully suggests a strong genetic influence on intelligence scores. Monozygotic twins share 100% of their genetic material and tend to resemble each other closely in their intelligence. This is true whether the twins were raised in the same household or (because of adoption) raised apart. In contrast, there's only a low level of resemblance between the intelligence scores of children and their adopted siblings (second bar) or children who have been adopted and their (adoptive) parents (first bar).

Iacono, & Lykken, 1993; Plomin & Spinath, 2004). It appears, then, that identical genotypes lead to highly similar IQs even when the individuals grow up in different environments.

Similar conclusions derive from a study that drew its data from the Colorado Adoption Project (CAP). The CAP has been tracking 245 adopted children for roughly 20 years, testing them periodically on several different measures (Plomin, Fulker, Corley, & DeFries, 1997). Thus, we have intelligence scores for the children themselves at various ages; we also have scores for the children's biological parents, who each share 50% of their genetic material with the children but who are not the adults who raised the children. Third, we have scores for the adoptive parents—the adults who did raise the children and shared (and largely created) the environment in which the children grew up.

These scores allow us to compute the resemblance between the children and their biological parents, as an indicator of how much *shared genes* matter. The scores also allow us to compute the resemblance between the children and their adoptive parents, as an indicator of how much a *shared environment* matters. The data indicate a much greater resemblance in the first comparison—children and their biological parents—even though we're comparing individuals who (though biologically related) have never even met. This indicates a powerful role for genetic factors in shaping intellectual ability (Figure 11.15).

What's especially striking about the CAP data, though, is that the resemblance between children and their biological parents *increases* as the years go by. When the children are 4 years old, for example, there's roughly a .10 correlation between the children's intelligence scores and their biological parents' scores. By the time the children are 12, this correlation is almost .20. By the time the children are 16 years old, this correlation is almost .40—despite the fact that, by that point, it has been more than a dozen years since the children and their biological parents have seen each other!

How should we think about this result? One possibility is that what's inherited via the genes is a *learning capacity*—and so, in early childhood, a child's *potential* might resemble that of her biological parents, but the potential hasn't yet grown into skills we can measure. To detect the resemblance, we must wait until the child has had some experience in the world—and thus opportunity to *use* her learning capacity and to gain from the potential she inherited. Only then, when the potential has borne fruit, can we detect the full resemblance between parents and their biological offspring (cf. Plomin & DeFries, 1985; Plomin & Spinath, 2004; Figure 11.16).

Environment and Individual IQ

Undeniably, genetic influences play a powerful role in shaping someone's intellectual capacities. Indeed, researchers have begun to explore exactly how these genetic influences unfold—including an effort to specify which genes, on which chromosomes, are the ones that shape intelligence. (For glimpses of the modest progress so far, see Posthuma & deGeus, 2006; Zimmer, 2008.)

As we've repeatedly noted, though, genetic effects always unfold within an environmental context. So—inevitably—environmental factors also shape the development of our intellect. Evidence for this point comes from many sources; and thus, as we'll see, the IQ score someone ends up with depends on *both* her genes and the surroundings in which she grew up.

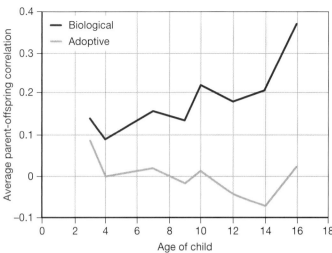

11.15 Colorado Adoption Project The intelligence scores for children in this study resembled those of their biological parents, and *not* those of their adopted parents. Notice that the correlation between children and their biological parents *increased* as the child grew, even though the children had no contact with their biological parents.

11.16 Genetic pattern potential Thanks to genetic influences, there will eventually be a close resemblance between the mother and her offspring. However, that resemblance will be visible only after the puppy has had a chance to develop her potential. As a result, the genetically based resemblance between biological kin will grow stronger and stronger as the young dog develops.

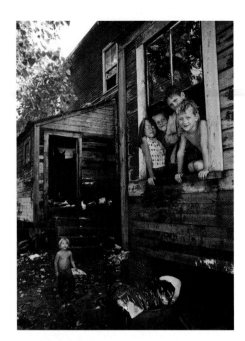

11.17 IQ and poverty IQ is clearly influenced by both genes and environment. The longer a child lives under conditions of poverty, the lower her IQ generally tends to be.

EFFECTS OF CHANGING THE ENVIRONMENT

The effect of the environment on IQ scores is evident in many facts. For example, one Norwegian study examined a huge data set that included intelligence scores for 334,000 pairs of brothers. The researchers found that the correlation between the brothers' intelligence scores was *smaller* for brothers who were more widely separated in age (Sundet, Eriksen, & Tambs, 2008). This result is difficult to explain genetically, because the genetic resemblance is the same for two brothers born, say, one year apart as it is for two brothers born five years apart. In both cases, the brothers share 50% of their genetic material. However, this result makes sense on environmental grounds. The greater the age difference between the brothers, the more likely it is that the family circumstances have changed between the years of one brother's childhood and the years of the other's. Thus, a greater age difference would increase the probability that the brothers grew up in different environments, and to the degree that these environments shape intelligence, we would expect the more widely spaced brothers to resemble each other less than the closely spaced siblings.

We've also known for many years that impoverished environments can impede intellectual development. For example, researchers studied children who worked on canal boats in England during the 1920s and rarely attended school; they also studied children who lived in rural mountainous Kentucky, where little or no schooling was available. These certainly seem like poor conditions for the development of intellectual skills, and it seems likely that exposure to these conditions would have a cumulative effect: The longer the child remains in such an environment, the lower his IQ should be (Figure 11.17). This is precisely what the data show—a negative correlation between IQ and age. That is, the older the child (the longer she had been in the impoverished environment), the lower her IQ (Asher, 1935; H. Gordon, 1923; also see Heckman, 2006). Related results come from communities where schools have closed. These closings typically lead to a decline in intelligence-test scores—in one study, a drop of about 6 points for every year of school missed (R. L. Green, Hoffman, Morse, Hayes, & Morgan, 1964; see also Ceci & Williams, 1997; Neisser et al., 1996).

More optimistically, we also know that *improving* the environment can to some extent *increase* IQ. For example, in a study in France, researchers focused on cases in which the government had removed children from their biological parents because of abuse or neglect (Duyme, Dumaret, & Tomkiewicz, 1999) The researchers were thus able to compare the children's "pre-adoption IQ" (i.e., when the children were still living in a high-risk environment) with their IQ in adolescence—after years of living with their adoptive families. The data (Figure 11.18) showed substantial improvements in the children's scores, thanks to this environmental change.

A similar conclusion flows from the effects of explicit training. The Venezuelan "Project Intelligence," for example, gave underprivileged adolescents in Venezuela extensive training in various thinking skills (Herrnstein, Nickerson, de Sanchez, & Swets, 1986). Assessments after training showed substantial benefits on a wide range of tests. A similar benefit was observed for American preschool children in the Carolina Abecedarian Project (F. A. Campbell & Ramey, 1994). These programs leave no doubt that suitable enrichment and education can provide substantial improvement in intelligence-test scores. (For still other evidence that schooling lifts intelligence scores, see Ceci & Williams, 1997; Grotzer & Perkins, 2000; M. Martinez, 2000; Perkins & Grotzer, 1997.)

We should note in passing that there's no conflict between these results and the results we mentioned earlier in the chapter when docu-

11.18 IQ improvement due to environmental change Researchers examined the IQ scores of children who were adopted out of horrible environments in which the children had been abused or neglected. After the adoption (when the children were in better environments), the children's IQ scores were markedly higher—and all the more so if the children were adopted into a family with higher socioeconomic status (SES).

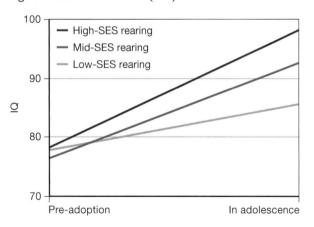

menting the *reliability* of the IQ test. There we noted that IQ scores are usually quite stable across the life span, so that (for example) if we know someone's IQ at, say, age 10, we can accurately predict what her IQ will be a decade or more later. This stability in scores is easily observed *if a person lives in a consistent environment*. As we now see, though, *changes* in the environment can produce substantial shifts in IQ—by a dozen or more points. Thus the IQ test is reliable, but this doesn't mean that IQ scores can't change.

WORLDWIDE IMPROVEMENT IN IQ SCORES

The impact of environmental factors on IQ scores is also undeniable in another fact. Around the globe, scores on intelligence tests have been gradually increasing over the last few decades, at a rate of approximately 3 points per decade. This pattern is known as the **Flynn effect**, after James R. Flynn (1984, 1987, 1999, 2009; see also Daley, Whaley, Sigman, Espinosa, & Neumann, 2003; Kanaya, Scullin, & Ceci, 2003), one of the first researchers to document this effect systematically. This improvement has been documented in many countries, including many developed (and relatively affluent) nations and also relatively impoverished third world nations (Figure 11.19). (There's also some suggestion that the improvement has now leveled off in some countries—Britain, for example—and may even be reversing; but it's too soon to make a judgment on this point; Flynn, 2009.)

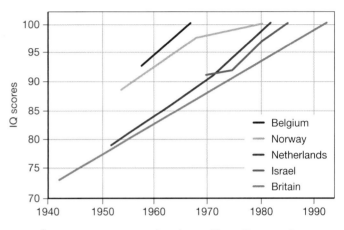

11.19 **The Flynn effect** IQ scores have been increasing across the last few decades, and this pattern has been documented in many different countries.

Could it be that people in the modern world are simply accumulating more and more information? If so, then the Flynn effect would be most visible in measures of crystallized intelligence. However, that's not what the evidence shows. Instead, the effect is stronger in measures of fluid intelligence—such as the Raven's Matrices—so it seems to be a genuine change in how quickly and flexibly people can think.

Some scholars suggest that this broad increase in scores is attributable to widespread improvement in nutrition and health care, and these factors surely do contribute to the Flynn effect in some parts of the world (for a study in Kenya, for example, see Daley et al., 2003). But we need some other explanation for why the effect is also evident in middle-class populations in relatively wealthy countries (Flynn, 2009). One proposal is that this worldwide improvement is the result of the increasing complexity and sophistication of our shared culture: Each of us is exposed to more information and a wider set of perspectives than were our grandparents, and this exposure may lead to a sharpening of skills that show up in our data as an improvement in IQ (for a broad discussion, see Dickens & Flynn, 2001; Greenfield, 2009; Neisser, 1997, 1998).

Whatever the explanation, though, one point is clear: The Flynn effect cannot be explained genetically. While the human genome does change (a prerequisite, of course, for human evolution), it doesn't change at a pace commensurate with this effect. Therefore, this worldwide improvement becomes part of the larger package of evidence documenting that intelligence can indeed be improved by suitable environmental conditions.

Flynn effect A worldwide increase in IQ scores over the last several decades, at a rate of about 3 points per decade.

THE INTERACTION AMONG GENETIC FACTORS, SES, AND IQ

Let's return, though, to the effects of *poverty* on IQ, because these effects are informative in two ways. First, these effects help us understand exactly how the environment shapes intelligence. Second, these effects also illuminate the *interaction* between environmental and genetic factors in shaping IQ.

The overall effects of poverty on IQ are easily documented, and in fact there's a correlation of .40 between a child's intelligence scores and the socioeconomic status of the family in which the child is raised (Lubinski, 2004). Looking beyond these broad effects, though, we can ask *what aspects* of intelligence are especially affected as well as *how* poverty shapes intelligence. We know, for example, that the impact of poverty is especially salient in tests of language skills and also in tasks hinging on executive control (Hackman & Farah, 2009). In addition, children who live in poverty in their preschool years seem more at risk than children who live in poverty in middle or late childhood (G. Duncan, Yeung, Brooks-Gunn, & Smith, 1998; Farah et al., 2006). Apparently, then, many of the harmful effects of poverty aren't due to inferior education. Instead, the effects derive from a mix of other factors, including exposure to various toxins found in lower-quality housing, lack of stimulation, poor nutrition, and inferior health care—and probably also the chronic stress that goes with poverty. All of these factors can interfere with the normal development of the brain, and they have important (and deeply unfortunate) consequences for intellectual functioning. (For more on the neurocognitive effects of poverty, see Hackman & Farah, 2009.)

These various problems, all associated with poverty, have a direct effect on brain development and also interact with genetic influences on development (Turkheimer, Haley, Waldron, D'Onofrio, & Gottesman, 2003). Specifically, when researchers focus on *higher*-SES families, they find the pattern we've already described—an appreciably stronger resemblance between identical twins' IQ scores than there is between fraternal twins' scores. This tells us (as we've discussed) that genetic factors are playing an important role here, so that people who resemble each other genetically are likely to resemble each other in their test scores. Among *lower*-SES families, though, the pattern is different. In this group, the degree of IQ resemblance is the *same* for identical and fraternal twins—which tells us that in this setting, genetic factors seem to matter much less for shaping a person's intelligence.

What's going on here? We suggested one explanation in Chapter 2 and echoed that proposal earlier in this chapter. Specifically, it may be best to think about our genes as providing our *potential*—a capacity to grow and develop if we're suitably nurtured. If, therefore, a child receives good schooling, health care, and adequate nutrition, he'll be able to develop this potential; and as the years go by, he'll be able to make the most of the genetically defined predisposition he was born with. But if a child grows up in an impoverished environment with poor schooling, minimal health care, and inadequate nutrition, it matters much less whether he has a fine potential—because the environment doesn't allow the potential to emerge. Hence, in impoverished environments, genetic factors—the source of the potential—count for relatively little.

Heritability Ratios

Clearly, then, the role of genetic factors in shaping intelligence depends on the circumstances. In some settings, genes play a large role; in other settings, they do not. This invites a new question: Is there some way to *measure* the contribution of genetics so that we can ask, in a particular setting, how much of the data pattern can be understood in genetic terms?

To address this question, investigators often rely on a measure we first met in Chapter 2: the **heritability ratio** (*H*). For any trait, this measure involves a comparison of two numbers. First, what is the total *phenotypic variability*—that is, how much do individuals differ from each other in their actual characteristics? Second, how much of this variability can be understood in genetic terms? Heritability is then calculated as the ratio between these two numbers—and so tells us, roughly, what percentage of the total variation can be attributed to genetics.

heritability ratio (*H*) A measure that describes, for a given population in a given environment, what proportion of the variance of a trait is due to genetic factors.

Let's be clear, though, that heritability is a measure that describes a *group*, because to calculate heritability, we need to ask how much variation occurs within that group, from one individual to the next. Thus, it makes no sense to apply measures of heritability to single individuals, and it would be a mistake (for example) to read a heritability estimate as implying that a certain percentage of a person's IQ (say) came from her genes, and the remainder from her environment. Instead, as we've emphasized throughout, the influence of genes and environment is, for any individual, fully intertwined—with both factors shaping all aspects of whatever the person becomes.

Overall, researchers estimate that the heritability for IQ is, in most environments, between .40 and .70; often, a figure of .50 or .60 is quoted (Neisser et al., 1996). This can be understood as the assertion that, of the variability we observe in IQ, half or a little more is attributable to variations in genetic material. (And, since the other 50% is attributable to factors other than genetics, this means that genes and environment have roughly equal weight in determining IQ.)

Let's be very clear, though, that these estimates are always calculated with reference to a particular group—and, in fact, we've already seen an example of how this matters: If we draw our data from low-SES groups, we find that the heritability of IQ is much lower—and may even be zero (Turkheimer et al., 2003). Likewise, we mentioned earlier that the genetic influence on IQ becomes more visible as people move from childhood into adulthood; this, too, is reflected in heritability estimates: Overall, the heritability for IQ in middle-class children is estimated as around .50; the heritability of middle-class adults, in contrast, may be as high as .80 (Plomin & Spinath, 2004).

The linkage between heritability and a particular set of circumstances was also evident in Chapter 2 when we discussed the medical condition known *phenylketonuria,* or *PKU* (Widaman, 2009). This condition is caused by a problem with a single gene that ordinarily governs the production of an enzyme needed to digest phenylalanine, an amino acid that's commonly part of our diet. A defect in this gene derails production of the required enzyme, with the result that phenylalanine is instead converted into a toxic agent. If an infant is born with PKU, the toxin accumulates in her bloodstream and damages her developing nervous system, leading to profound mental retardation.

PKU is unmistakably of genetic origin; and for many years, we had no way to remedy this condition. As a result, the heritability was extremely high. The phenotypic variation (whether someone did or did not have this type of retardation) was almost entirely attributable to whether or not he had the relevant genetic pattern. But we now know that a simple environmental manipulation can minimize the impact of PKU: All we need to do is ensure that the infant (and, later, the child) gets a special diet that contains very little phenylalanine (Figure 11.20). If this diet is introduced at an early enough age, retardation can be minimized or—far better—avoided altogether. As a result, the heritability estimate for PKU is, in most countries, currently quite low. Whether retardation is observed depends largely on the individual's diet, and so most of the phenotypic variation we observe is due to this environmental factor, not to genes.

Notice that the case of PKU offers us many lessons. First, the case reminds us once again that genetic effects don't unfold in a vacuum; instead, genetic effects interact with environmental influences—sometimes with good effect, sometimes with bad. Second (and related), the example of PKU makes it clear that patterns that are powerfully shaped by genes can still be dramatically altered. Indeed, PKU is a case in which having a particular genotype can (with a carefully controlled diet) end up having no impact at all on the phenotype! Be aware, therefore, that genetic factors are important but do not set someone's destiny (Figure 11.21).

11.20 Phenylalanine Many diet sodas contain the warning shown here. The warning is irrelevant to most of the population, but it's crucial for anyone suffering from phenylketonuria.

11.21 Heritability of hair color and height (A) The heritability of hair color regularly rises and falls as a function of changes in fashion. The *genetic* contribution to hair color doesn't change, of course; but the *relative importance* of the genes—and so the heritability—drops whenever dying one's hair is in style (because then the phenotype may bear little resemblance to the color specified in the genotype). (B) Our best estimate for the heritability of *height* is about .80. Still, the average height in most nations has increased markedly in the last century—probably because of improvements in nutrition and health care (see Rutter, 2006). This is one more reminder that high levels of heritability in no way imply that a trait cannot be modified.

(A) (B)

Third, keeping the case of PKU in mind will be helpful when you think about heritability ratios. These ratios are a powerful—and often useful—data summary that allows us to capture complex patterns in a single number. But the case of PKU reminds us that this number reflects only a particular set of circumstances for a particular group of individuals, and the heritability ratio can change if the circumstances change. In addition, heritability ratios tell us nothing about the future. Even if a trait's heritability ratio is near 1.00 (as it used to be, for PKU), we may be able to alter the trait enormously once a suitable intervention is found.

Group Differences in IQ

So far, we've focused on the intelligence scores of specific individuals—for example, we've compared the IQ scores of particular twins and compared a specific child's IQ with the IQs of her biological parents. But these person-by-person comparisons aren't the focus of the controversy over the roots of intelligence. The real fury is over another issue: the differences in average IQ, and the differences in academic achievement, that are found between *groups*. In particular, debate has focused on two comparisons: the possible difference between *men* and *women* in their intellectual skills, and the difference between *American whites* and *American blacks*.

Before examining these comparisons, we need to emphasize that what's at stake here are the differences between *averages*—the average test score (for example) for men and the average for women. This point is crucial, because—of course—men differ from each other in their intellectual prowess, and so do women. Likewise, the scores of European American test takers vary enormously, as do the scores of African American test takers. Indeed, this variation *within* each group (within each sex, or within a racially defined group) is much, much larger than any between-group variations researchers have detected. We therefore learn little about any individual's abilities simply by knowing his or her group membership, and so it would be wrong (and in most settings, illegal) to use group membership as a basis for making decisions about that individual. Nonetheless, the differences between the *averages* remain, so let's take a closer look at the research scrutinizing these differences.

BETWEEN-GROUP AND WITHIN-GROUP DIFFERENCES

The differences in intellectual performance between men and women, and also between whites and blacks, are relatively small. But the debate over these differences has been large and heated, and often framed in terms of heritability. To what extent is it helpful to think about these differences in terms of genetics? To what extent should we focus on the cultural surround, including differences in education or opportunity?

Before addressing these issues, we need to deal with a methodological point. We've discussed considerable evidence that genetic patterns matter a lot for intelligence; indeed, heritability estimates are as high as .80 for some groups. But we've also emphasized that these estimates apply only to a particular group: How much variation is there *within that group*? How much *of that group's* variation can be understood in genetic terms? As we first discussed in Chapter 2, and as we've reiterated here, the estimates—by definition—come from a group's data and cannot be applied to other groups. By the same logic, these same estimates certainly can't be used in comparing one group to another.

To make this point concrete, many scholars rely on a straightforward example: Imagine you've just bought a bag of grass seed at the garden store. The bag is likely to contain just one variety of seed—perennial rye grass, for example—but even so, it's unlikely that the seeds are all clones of each other, and so there will be some genetic variation from one seed to the next. Let's now imagine that you plant a handful of this seed in barren soil and give the plants poor-quality care. You don't water them enough, and they have minimal exposure to sunlight. In this setting the plants are likely to grow poorly, but some will do better than others—will be a bit healthier perhaps, or grow a bit taller. These differences from one plant to the next can't be attributed to environmental factors because, in this scenario, all of the seeds are in exactly the same environment: They all get the same low levels of nutrition; they all get the same bad care. If, therefore, some plants do better than others, their success must be attributed to genetic factors—some seeds are biologically better prepared for these poor conditions.

Now imagine another handful of seeds drawn from the same bag. These seeds are planted in rich soil and given excellent care. These plants will grow well—but again, some will grow taller than others. As before, these variations from one plant to the next can't be explained in terms of environmental factors, because all of these seeds are growing in exactly the same environment. Hence, we can't say that some plants grew taller because they got more water, or more light, because all plants got the same amount of water and light. Instead, the observed variation must be attributed entirely to genetic sources—some seeds are better prepared to flourish in this rich environment.

Notice where all of this leaves us. In the first environment, the within-group differences (comparisons among the various seeds growing in barren soil) are all produced by genetics. The same is true in the second environment; here, too, the within-group differences are produced by genetics. Thus, if we were to calculate the heritability of plant height (or any other measure of the plants' status) for either group, we get a value of 1.0—*all* of the variation within each group is due to genetic factors.

What about the comparison between the two groups? This difference is obviously attributable to the differences between their respective environments, in which one group gets high-quality care and the other does not (after Lewontin, 1976; Figure 11.22). Therefore it's the environment, and not genetics, that accounts for the between-group comparison—and so the heritability for this comparison is zero.

In this case, then, the between-group difference comes from a very different source than do the within-group differences. And that's the point: Even if we know a lot about within-group variation (specifically, if we know that this variation depends on the genes), we can draw no conclusions about what produces between-group variation. Sometimes between-group variations come from the same source as within-group variations, but sometimes they don't. Knowing a lot about one type of variation tells us nothing about the other.

11.22 Between-group and within-group differences Between-group differences and within-group differences may be due to very different factors. Here, the between-group difference reflects an environmental factor (soil, and water, and light), while the within-group difference reflects genetic variation (seed).

Within-group differences

Between-group differences

Within-group differences

Poor soil

Good soil

11.23 Mental rotation In the mental rotation task, participants have to judge whether two stimuli are different shapes, or the same but merely viewed from different perspectives. Men tend to have an advantage on this visuospatial task—and so they're faster and more accurate in their judgments.

With these preliminary points now established, we're ready for the data—starting with the difference between men and women. Of course, men and women do differ in some ways. For example, men tend to be more physically aggressive than women; women, in contrast, rely on social aggression (gossiping, or ostracizing) more than men do (Chapters 1 and 14). But men and women are also alike in many ways—and so, as just one illustration, evidence makes it clear that there's virtually no difference between men and women in their effectiveness as leaders or their competitiveness as negotiators (J. Hyde & Linn, 2006).

What about intellectual abilities? Overall, neither sex is more intelligent than the other; and there's no reliable difference between men and women in their IQ scores (e.g., Held, Alderton, Foley, & Segall, 1993; R. Lynn, 1994; although see N. Brody, 1992). We do detect differences, though, when we consider more specialized abilities. On average, men do better on certain tests designed to measure visuospatial abilities, such as tests requiring mental rotation (Figure 11.23). Men also do better on tasks that require them to navigate through a virtual (computerized) three-dimensional environment (like the fictional worlds one must "travel through" in many computer games; Halpern, Benbow, Geary, Gur, Hyde et al., 2007). Women, for their part, on average do better on certain verbal tasks—especially tasks that require clear and fluent writing (Halpern, 1992, 2000; Halpern et al., 2007; L. Levine et al., 1999).

These differences are easily documented in the laboratory; but men and women also differ in their intellectual achievement outside of the lab, and the interpretation of this point has been a matter of controversy. To understand the debate, let's start with the fact that many studies have documented differences between men and women in educational achievement—a so-called gender gap. One study examined the test scores for 15-year-olds in 41 different countries (Machin & Pekkarinen, 2008). In every country, girls outscored boys in tests of reading; in most countries, boys outscored girls in tests of mathematics. The data also showed that in both reading and mathematics, scores for boys were more *variable* than scores for girls; more boys than girls were likely to achieve scores rather distant from (above or below) the average for their sex (W. Johnson, Carothers, & Deary, 2008).

Another study compared the SAT scores of 40,000 American high-school students. The study showed that men (on average) did better than women on the math portion of the test, even when the investigators limited their comparison to men and women who had taken exactly the same high-school math courses and had expressed the same degree of interest in mathematics (Benbow, 1988; Benbow, Lubinski, Shea, & Eftekhari-Sanjani, 2000; for related data, see Halpern et al., 2007).

Other considerations, however, complicate the comparison between the sexes. As one concern, we probably shouldn't be comparing men and women in terms of math performance overall, because the gender comparison may depend on what type of math we're considering. For example, the advantage for men seems clearer for tests that showcase spatial relations or geometry (Crawford & Chaffin, 1997; Halpern et al., 2007; J. Hyde, 2005); for tests emphasizing computation, the advantage goes to women (J. Hyde & Linn, 2006).

In addition, some measures don't show women falling behind in mathematics. For example, National Science Foundation data indicate that men and women are equally likely to take calculus in high school, and it's the women who get better grades (A. Gallagher & Kaufman, 2005). Similarly, America's No Child Left Behind (NCLB) legislation requires states to assess student progress annually. A 2008 report on these assessments finds no difference between male and female high-school students in their average level of math achievement, although the scores for males continue to be somewhat more variable than the scores for females—so that males are more likely than females to obtain scores well below or well above the mean (J. Hyde, Lindberg, Linn, Ellis, & Williams, 2008; W. Johnson et al., 2008).

What about performance beyond high school? In college, men and women get equal math grades (Bridgeman & Lewis, 1996), even when we match their math classes for difficulty. Assessments of understanding of mathematical concepts in college courses likewise show no difference between the sexes (J. Hyde & Linn, 2006).

What lies behind all of these findings? For those studies that do detect sex differences in educational performance, what's the cause? And why is it that, in the laboratory, men consistently have an advantage in visuospatial reasoning? Some authors have suggested biological explanations for these facts, often pointing to a possible link between spatial abilities and the male sex hormone testosterone. In one study, for example, males who produced abnormally low levels of testosterone showed impairments in spatial reasoning (Hier & Crowley, 1982); in another study, older males (aged 60–75) showed dramatic improvements in spatial reasoning after receiving testosterone supplements (Cherrier et al., 2001; Janowsky, Oviatt, & Orwoll, 1994; also see Van Goozen, Cohen-Kettenis, Gooren, Frijda, & Can de Poll, 1995). But on the other hand, several studies have failed to confirm these hormonal effects on visuospatial performance, so any conclusions about this point must be tentative (e.g., Halari et al., 2005; Hines et al., 2003; Moffat & Hampson, 1996; also see Halpern, 2000; N. Newcombe, 2007; Spelke, 2005).

A different hypothesis focuses on cultural influences—including the important observation that in most Western cultures, young boys receive much more support and encouragement than young girls do for work in mathematics (Figure 11.24). Indeed, many people (including parents and teachers) seem to believe that women are ill suited for math and expect women not to do well in this domain (Halpern, 1992). Thus, parents expect their sons to do better in math courses than their daughters do (Frome & Eccles, 1998) and often attribute their sons' success in math to ability while attributing their daughter's success in math to hard work (Parsons, Adler, & Kaczala, 1982). Even young children endorse these stereotypes (C. Steele, 2003) and, by middle adolescence, girls seem to receive less support from their peers for science- and math-related activities than boys do (Stake & Nickens, 2005).

Do these social factors influence how children behave and what they achieve? Studies show that women perform less well on some math tests if they're asked, at the start of the test, simply to record their gender on the test form. Presumably, this serves to prime the relevant stereotype, and this undermines performance (Ambady, Shih, Kim, & Pittinsky, 2001; we'll go into greater detail about "stereotype threat" shortly). Similarly, sex differences in test scores are powerfully influenced by factors in the context that shape the test takers' expectations. In one study, male and female college students all took a math test. Half of the students were told that this test had shown sex differences in the past; in this group, male students outperformed the females. The other half of the students were told that the test had been shown in the past to be gender fair; in this group, there was no sex difference in performance (R. Brown & Josephs, 1999; Crawford & Chaffin, 1997; Halpern et al., 2007).

Hypotheses emphasizing the role of experience and encouragement find further support in the fact that visuospatial skills can be markedly improved through practice—a point that has been documented in a wide range of studies (Halpern et al., 2007). In one experiment, male and female college students practiced playing an action video game (*Medal of Honor: Pacific Assault*) for a total of 10 hours. This

11.24 Gender stereotypes In a wide range of cultures (including Tibet, where photo A was taken), boys are encouraged to be tough and strong—and they're often expected to be good in math. In contrast, girls (including this young girl in Japan) are expected to be soft and feminine—and poor in math.

(A) (B)

practice improved the spatial skills of all participants, but the improvement was greater in women and led to a clear reduction in the difference between the sexes (Feng, Spence, & Pratt, 2007).

Indeed, in light of the studies showing the positive influence of instruction, experience, and encouragement, we may want to put less emphasis on the ultimate causes of the apparent sex differences in achievement. We might instead put our emphasis on efforts toward eradicating these differences, to make sure that all of us—male and female—reach our full potential. Otherwise, as one author put it, we may "waste a most valuable resource: the abilities and efforts of more than half the world's population" (Shaffer, 2004, p. 237).

COMPARISONS BETWEEN AMERICAN WHITES AND AMERICAN BLACKS

Controversy has also swirled around another comparison—that between the IQ scores of American (and European) whites and those of African Americans. Many studies have indicated a difference between these scores, with the average score of the American white population higher by 10 to 15 IQ points (Jencks & Phillips, 1998; Jensen, 1985; Loehlin, Lindzey, & Spuhler, 1975; Reynolds, Chastain, Kaufman, & McLean, 1987). There has been energetic debate over whether this gap between the racial groups has been shrinking in recent years (e.g., Dickens & Flynn, 2006a, 2006b; Rushton & Jensen, 2006), and also debate over whether it's "important or proper" to study these racial differences at all (e.g., E. Hunt & Carlson, 2007a, 2007b; then N. Brody, 2007; Gottfredson, 2007; Sternberg & Grigorenko, 2007). Still, the difference in average scores between blacks and whites is well documented—making it important for us to ask what the difference is, and what it might or might not tell us about race differences and about intelligence itself.

Let's start with the hypothesis that has been most controversial, one that highlights genetic factors. Could it be that genes of African ancestry somehow lead to lower IQ scores than do genes of European ancestry? This hypothesis is actually problematic from the very start, because it assumes the groups we're comparing (modern American whites and modern African Americans) really are distinct genetically. This assumption is questionable, because the genetic overlap between these two groups is enormous (e.g., Cavalli-Sforza, Menozzi, & Piazza, 1994). More powerfully, though, researchers have used various methods to determine what proportion of someone's ancestors were black Africans and what proportion were Europeans. (In early studies, this determination was done by carefully collecting family histories; in later studies, this was done by means of biochemical markers in the blood.) If genetic factors are the cause of racial differences in IQ, then higher proportions of black African ancestry should be associated with lower IQ. They are not, and the evidence indicates no link between IQ scores and ancestry (Scarr & Carter-Saltzman, 1983).

How, therefore, should we explain the race difference in test scores? One hypothesis focuses on the intelligence tests themselves and proposes that the race difference is artificial—a result of bias built into the tests. This would surely be a problem if the test relied on vocabulary that was more familiar to the community of white test takers than to the community of black test takers. Likewise, the test might be biased if it were always administered by someone white—someone who might be warmer and more encouraging to white test takers than to blacks. These are real concerns that must be controlled if the racial comparison is to have any meaning at all. As it turns out, though, we can easily deal with these concerns—for example, by using nonverbal forms of testing (such as the Ravens' Matrices), having whites tested by someone white, and having blacks tested by someone black. With these precautions in place, the difference between blacks' and whites' scores (on average) remains. (For more on this point, see P. Sackett et al., 2008.)

A more promising hypothesis begins with the fact that—as we've noted—IQ scores are undeniably influenced by poverty and poor schooling. Let's now add that, sadly, blacks in the United States tend (on average) to have lower incomes than whites do, and blacks are also more likely to live in poverty. As a result, a higher proportion of blacks than whites are exposed to poor nutrition, lower-quality educational resources, and poorer health care (Neisser et al., 1996). Could these socioeconomic factors be the source of the race difference in IQ scores?

To address this question, let's focus our comparison just on blacks and whites with similar backgrounds. For example, we'll compare working-class blacks with working-class whites, or educated black professionals with educated white professionals. In this way, we can ask if race matters when we remove socioeconomic differences from the picture. And, in fact, studies using this logic find a reduced racial difference (see, for example, Jencks & Phillips, 1998). Clearly, then, factors associated with poverty do play a role here, and they make a substantial contribution to the observed race difference.

A different line of evidence makes a similar point: Rather than trying to match test takers based on their environments, we can ask what happens to test scores when the environment is changed. A widely cited example is a study of black children who were adopted at an early age by white middle-class parents, most of whom were college educated (Scarr & Weinberg, 1976). After adoption, these children had a mean IQ of 110—a value exceeding the national average for black children by about 25 points. (For further discussion, see Scarr & Carter-Saltzman, 1982; Scarr & Weinberg, 1983.)

We need to emphasize, though, that equalizing the socioeconomic variables diminishes the black-white difference, but doesn't erase it. Thus, it's clear that the many hardships associated with poverty are *part* of the explanation for the difference, but not the whole story. So we still need to ask what other factors contribute to the contrast between the races.

STEREOTYPE THREAT

In the previous section, we asked whether blacks' and whites' IQ scores would be the same if we could match their environments. If the answer is yes, then this obviously points toward an environmental explanation of the race difference. But to tackle this question in a thorough way, it may not be enough to match factors like parental education, income, and occupational level. Even if we succeed in matching for these aspects of life, black and white children still grow up in different environments. This is because, after all, black children grow up knowing they are black and knowing a lot about what life paths are easily open to them and what life paths are likely. White children correspondingly grow up knowing they are white, and they too have a sense of what life paths are open or likely. Moreover, each group, because of the color of their skin, is treated differently by the people in their social environment. In these ways, their environments and experiences are not matched—even if the parents have similar jobs and similar income levels, and even if the children have similar educational experiences.

Do these social experiences matter for intelligence scores? As one indication that they do, consider studies of **stereotype threat**, a term used to describe the negative impact that social stereotypes, once activated, can have on task performance. Here's an example: Imagine an African American is taking an intelligence test. She might well become anxious because she believes this is a test on which she is expected to do

stereotype threat A mechanism through which a person's performance is influenced by her perception that her score may confirm stereotypes about her group.

poorly. This anxiety might then be compounded by the thought that her poor performance will only serve to confirm others' prejudices. These feelings, of course, could then easily erode performance by making it more difficult for her to pay attention and do her best work. Moreover, given the discouraging thought that poor performance is inevitable, she might well decide not to expend enormous effort—if she's likely to do poorly, why struggle against the tide?

Evidence for these effects comes from various studies, including some in which two groups of African Americans are given exactly the same test. One group is told, at the start, that the test is designed to assess their intelligence; the other group is led to believe that the test is simply composed of challenges and is not designed to assess them in any way. The first group, for which the instructions trigger stereotype threat, does markedly worse (C. Steele, 1998; C. Steele & Aronson, 1995).

Related results have been shown in many other circumstances and have been demonstrated with children as well as adults. Similar data have also been reported for groups other than African Americans, and in fact stereotype threat is plainly relevant to our previous discussion of comparisons between men and women (Blascovich, Spencer, Quinn, & Steele, 2001; Cheryan & Bodenhausen, 2000). For example (and as we mentioned earlier), merely reminding test takers of their gender just before they take a math test seems to encourage women to think about the stereotype that women cannot do math, and this seems to undermine their test performance. This is because thoughts about the stereotype increase the women's anxiety about the test, cut into the likelihood that they'll work as hard as they can, and make it less likely that they'll persevere if the test grows frustrating (Ambady, Shih, Kim, & Pittinsky, 2001, Figure 11.25). A different study had students read an essay that argued that gender differences in math performance have genetic causes; women who read this essay then performed more poorly on a math test than did women who read essays on other topics (Dar-Nimrod & Heine, 2006). Presumably, the essay on genetic causes was demoralizing to the women and made them more vulnerable to stereotype threat—and therefore undermined their test performance.

Conversely, some interventions can improve performance, presumably by diminishing the anxiety and low self-expectations associated with stereotype threat. In one study, middle-school students were asked to write brief essays—just a few sentences—about things they valued. The participants were given a list of possible values to choose from: "athletic ability, being good at art, being smart, creativity" and so on (G. Cohen, Garcia, Apfel, & Master, 2006; Cohen, Garcia, Purdie-Vaughns, Apfel, & Brzustoski, 2009). This brief exercise was then repeated periodically during the school year; and this was enough to shift the students' perspective, getting them to focus on things they valued rather than school-based anxieties. In fact, the brief intervention improved the school grades of African American seventh-graders by a striking 40%, markedly reducing the difference between white students' and black students' grades. Remarkably, effects of the intervention were still detectable in a follow-up study with the same students, two years later.

These results draw our attention back to our earlier comments about what intelligence is—or, more broadly, what it is that "intellectual tasks" require. One requirement, of course, is a set of cognitive skills and capacities (e.g., mental speed, or working memory). A different requirement is the proper attitude toward testing—and the wrong attitude (anxiety about failing, fear of confirming other's negative expectations) can plainly undermine performance. This is why performance levels can be changed merely by priming people to think of themselves as members of a certain group—whether that group is women, Asians, or African Americans. In this way, social pressures and prejudice can powerfully shape each person's performance—and can, in particular, contribute to the differences between IQ scores for whites and blacks.

11.25 SCIENTIFIC METHOD: How do stereotypes influence test performance?

Method

1. One third of a group of Asian American girls were primed to remind them they were Asian Americans. One third of the children were primed to remind them of their gender. One third were not primed.

2. They all took a standardized math test.

3. For each age group, researchers analyzed how priming affected test scores.

Results

The youngest and oldest children were influenced by the prime. If reminded of their identity as Asian Americans (a group often expected to do well in math), the children performed better. If reminded of their identity as females (a group expected to do less well), the children scored lower. (It's not clear why this effect was not observed in the upper elementary school age group.)

CONCLUSION: Stereotypes relevant to test performance can significantly affect test scores.

SOURCE STUDY: Ambady, Shih, Kim, & Pittinsky, 2001

SOME FINAL THOUGHTS: SCIENTIFIC EVIDENCE AND DEMOCRATIC VALUES

Undeniably, individuals differ in their intellectual capacities, and in many circumstances genetic factors play a large role in shaping these capacities. But, as we've repeatedly noted, these genetic influences don't mean that intelligence is immutable, fixed for each of us by our genetic heritage. The example of PKU serves as a powerful reminder that patterns that are unambiguously rooted in the genome can be changed entirely by suitable environmental intervention. And in the case of intelligence itself, we have ample evidence that environmental changes (most prominently, schooling) can increase IQ scores and thus markedly improve life circumstances.

Perhaps, therefore, it does not matter what the origins are for the differences in IQ scores—whether we're comparing one individual to the next, or one group to another. In either case, whether the differences are produced primarily by genetic or environmental factors, the data tell us that training and enriched, supportive environments can improve IQ—and the implications for our policy goals seem clear.

Notice the irony here: More than a century ago, Binet designed the intelligence test in order to identify weaker students who would benefit from special training. Binet's conception, in other words, was that each individual's level of intelligence was pliable and certainly could be lifted through education. On this point, it seems, Binet was exactly right.

As scientists, though, we still seek to explain how people differ from each other; and here the data provide a relatively clear message: The differences in IQ from one individual to the next seem influenced both by genetic and environmental factors. For the difference between men and women, in contrast—or the difference between whites and blacks—the main source of group differences does appear to be environmental. Thus, women's performance (especially in mathematics) is surely shaped by widespread expectations that "girls can't do math." Academic performance by African Americans is undercut by various societal and individual-level factors, ranging from the availability of role models to expectations that are manifest in stereotype threat.

These group differences make Binet's optimistic goals all the more important. Low IQ scores are, as we've seen, statistically linked to a number of undesirable outcomes—ranging from poor school performance to lower levels of success in the workplace. Indeed, we mentioned earlier that low IQ scores are associated with shorter life expectancy. Points like these obviously motivate us to seek ways to close the "achievement gaps" between various groups, although this will require efforts on many fronts—including moves toward improving nutrition, health care, and education as well as combating the destructive effects of stereotypes.

Finally, what about the IQ tests themselves? These tests surely have their limits; even so, many researchers consider the enterprise of intelligence testing to be one of psychology's great success stories. As we've seen in this chapter, there's reason to believe our intelligence measurements are valid. We understand many of the mental processes that help make someone intelligent. And we understand some of the neural bases for these processes. It might seem overenthusiastic to declare this research—as one investigator did—"one of the most successful undertakings" of modern psychology (K. Lamb, 1994, p. 386). Still, the broad enterprise launched by Binet has clearly flourished.

SUMMARY CHAPTER 11

INTELLIGENCE TESTING

- Alfred Binet, the originator of intelligence tests, sought to identify children who would benefit from remedial education. Binet understood intelligence to be a general attribute, applicable to a very wide range of mental tasks. He measured intelligence by means of a comparison between a child's mental age and her chronological age.

- Intelligence tests have been developed for various uses, including the WAIS. This test has high test-retest reliability, even with gaps of many decades between the first test and subsequent tests. The test also seems valid, as indicated by correlations between IQ and academic performance, job performance, and other measurements.

WHAT IS INTELLIGENCE? THE PSYCHOMETRIC APPROACH

- The *psychometric approach to intelligence* seeks to understand intelligence by scrutinizing patterns among the test scores. One aspect of this approach is an examination of how different elements within the test are intercorrelated. These intercorrelations are readily observed, suggesting that all of the diverse subtests within the IQ test overlap in the abilities they are assessing. This finding is confirmed by *factor analysis*, which isolates the common element in all the subtests. That element is often referred to as *general intelligence*, or *g*.

- A hierarchical notion of intelligence places *g* at the top of the hierarchy; at the next level are verbal ability, quantitative ability, and spatial ability. Correlations between these abilities provide evidence for g. The stronger correlations *within* these more specific categories tell us there are also more specialized forms of intelligence.

- *Fluid g* is the ability to deal with new and unusual problems; *crystallized g* refers to someone's accumulated knowledge and skills. These two forms of intelligence are correlated, but they're also distinguishable in several ways. Fatigue and aging, for example, have a much greater impact on fluid intelligence than on crystallized intelligence.

THE BUILDING BLOCKS OF INTELLIGENCE

- One mechanism that contributes to intelligence is simply mental speed: Higher-IQ individuals show faster response times in many tasks, including tasks measuring *inspection time.*

- Another contribution to intelligence is *working memory capacity*—an ability to keep multiple goals in mind, and also an ability to control one's own attention. This capacity may allow the construction of more complex task models; it may also allow greater executive control over one's own thoughts. These points fit well with the P-FIT theory of intelligence, which suggests that intelligence depends on the integrated functioning of many brain sites including those in the parietal and frontal lobes.

INTELLIGENCE BEYOND THE IQ TEST

- Some investigators have concerned themselves with certain aspects of the term *intelligence* that go beyond IQ, such as *practical intelligence.* A related approach has led to measures of *emotional intelligence;* people with this sort of intelligence have fewer conflicts with their peers and are more tolerant of stress.

- A different proposal rests on the notion of *multiple intelligences,* which is buttressed by evidence from studies of brain lesions and people with *savant syndrome.*

- Our understanding of intelligence may also need to take into account the cultural context. People in different cultures have different abilities as well as a different understanding of the test-taking situation.

THE ROOTS OF INTELLIGENCE

- Intelligence-test performance is determined by both environmental and genetic factors. Evidence for the role of genetic factors includes the fact that the correlation between the IQs of identical (monozygotic) twins is higher than that for fraternal twins, and also the observation that the correlation between their IQ scores is remarkably high even when identical twins are reared apart. Further evidence for a hereditary contribution comes from adopted children, whose IQs correlate more highly with the IQs of their biological parents than with the IQs of their adoptive parents. At the same time, however, evidence for environmental effects is provided by increases and decreases in the mean IQ of populations whose cultural or educational level has risen or fallen. Environmental effects are also clearly implicated by the worldwide improvement in IQ scores observed over the last few decades.

- The relative weight of genetic and environmental factors in determining the variation of a given characteristic is given by the *heritability ratio,* or *H.* The value of *H* depends in part on the given population, for *H* describes only the degree to which the variability within that particular population can be attributed to genetic variance.

- In recent years, much interest (and debate) has focused on IQ differences among different groups of individuals—including a comparison between men and women, and a comparison between American whites and American blacks. Men and women do not differ in overall IQ, but men on average seem to have a small advantage in some tasks requiring visuospatial reasoning; women on average have a small advantage in some verbal tasks. These differences are certainly fostered by a cultural environment in which boys and girls have different types of experiences and receive types of encouragement.

- Several studies have documented a 10- to 15-point difference between average scores of American whites and blacks. This difference does not seem attributable to genetic factors. Part of the difference derives from the poverty and disadvantaged circumstances in which many American blacks live; part can be attributed to the effects of *stereotype threat.*

 ONLINE STUDY TOOLS

Go to StudySpace, **wwnorton.com/studyspace**, to access additional review and enrichment materials, including the following resources for each chapter:

Organize
- Study Plan
- Chapter Outline
- Quiz+ Assessment

Learn
- Ebook
- Chapter Review
- Vocabulary Flashcards
- Drag-and-Drop Labeling Exercises
- Audio Podcast Chapter Overview

Connect
- Critical Thinking Activity
- Studying the Mind Video Podcasts
- Video Exercises
- Animations
- **ZAPS** Psychology Labs

12 Motivation and Emotion

"Northerners definitely took some getting used to," laughs Clint McCabe, a native of Mobile, Alabama, who recently graduated from a university in the northeastern United States. Before winning a baseball scholarship that took him 1,000 miles away from his home, Clint had sojourned north of the Mason-Dixon Line only three times. "My family warned me that Yankees would be, well, different. And they were right."

The most obvious difference, he says, is that people in the North were simply less polite. "I know it sounds like a stereotype, but it's true. You go into the city, and cars are honkin' at each other. Kids are mouthin' off at their mothers. Grown men are hollerin' and cursin'. If someone acted like that in Mobile, I'd be obliged to jerk a knot in his head."

Indeed, for his first two years of college, McCabe often found his hands curling into fists and the back of his neck beading with cold sweat. After a while, though, he realized that he was alone in his readiness to tussle. "My friends didn't understand," he says. "They'd say, 'Hey, they don't mean anything by it. They're just blowing off some steam.'"

As you will discover in this chapter, McCabe was caught in a centuries-old culture clash. Back home in Alabama, Southern culture encouraged him to protect his honor and to be careful of insulting anyone else's. As a result, McCabe and his fellow Southerners tend to be chivalrous and respectful. Once offended or provoked, however, Southerners may explode—hence the saying, "Southerners will be polite until they are angry enough to kill you."

Northerners, on the other hand, are more likely to express anger early and often. That way, their thinking goes, the anger doesn't build up and lead to a blowout. In fact, the North has long enjoyed lower rates of murder and other violent crimes than has the South. Meanwhile, reflecting their willingness to use violence to protect people's honor, Southerners execute more felons, mete out more corporal punishment in their schools, and pass more lenient laws regarding gun ownership, child abuse, and spousal abuse.

After a few years up North, McCabe became more or less bicultural. While at school, he lost his tendencies to greet strangers with whom he made eye contact and to couch pointed remarks in euphemism. He came to ignore low-level incivilities. But once he stepped off the plane back home, "I was all 'Yes ma'am,' 'No sir,' and 'Thank you kindly.'"

People everywhere feel anger and other emotions such as fear and happiness, shame and disgust—psychological experiences that affect our actions, our feelings, and our bodies. People everywhere also have deep-seated biological urges such as feeding, fighting, fleeing, affiliating, and mating—as well as more recently evolved needs like achievement and self-actualization. Many of these *motives* reveal our basic mammalian core; like any other animal, we humans spend large portions of our lives finding food, seeking shelter, fending off rivals, tending to our allies, and seeking sex—in short, pursuing pleasure and avoiding pain.

Yet as McCabe's experiences in the North and South show, how we express these impulses is strongly shaped by the people and cultures around us. And our emotional responses are far from the only impulses that are jointly determined by our biological heritage and our cultural context. Take eating. All people eat. But cultures vary vastly in what, how, where, when, and with whom their members repast. Compared to French people, for example, Americans have more conflicting feelings about food and focus less on its taste and more on its contents—alternately worrying about fats, carbohydrates, protein, and cholesterol. French people, in contrast, largely view food as a path to pleasure, and so indulge in a wider variety of fare—chocolates and cheeses, tripe and truffles, champagnes and champignons. By amusing their mouths with smaller amounts of more foods, French people wind up eating a healthier diet—and have the slimmer figures to show it, argues psychologist Paul Rozin.

In this chapter, we will consider some of the major motivational states that shape our behavior, as well as emotional states such as anger, happiness, fear, and sadness. For each, we will see how physiological, cultural, and cognitive factors interact to shape the ways the motive or emotion is expressed.

MOTIVATIONAL STATES

Questions about why we act in a certain way, or why we feel as we do, can be answered in various ways. Some answers emphasize what we referred to in Chapter 2 as ultimate causes, including the powerful influence, over thousands and thousands of years, of natural selection. This reflects the key fact that, as we saw in that earlier chapter, evolutionary forces have shaped not only our physical features but also our psychological features.

Other answers about why we act or feel as we do focus on causes that are specific to the individual, but are nonetheless fairly remote from the present situation. For example, why do some people prefer to take psychology courses, while others prefer astrophysics? Here, the cause may be rooted in the person's childhood. Perhaps the person happened to experience unusual events, and this triggered a lifelong interest in human behavior and mental processes. Or perhaps the person is seeking to distance herself from her parents, and her parents have always been skeptical about psychology. In either case, these decades-past circumstances are now shaping the person's behavior.

Important as these remote causes are, they do not tell us everything we need to know. After all, we do not eat because we think, "Natural selection requires that I eat." Likewise, we usually do not choose courses by reasoning through "Will this selection help me to be different from my mother?" We need to ask, therefore, what the bridge is between remote causes, on the one side, and actual behaviors, on the other. What are the more immediate causes of our behavior?

The answer to this question can take many forms, because, quite simply, we are motivated by different forces in different circumstances. Early theorists emphasized the biological roots of our motivation, describing our diverse motivational states as all arising from genetically endowed *instincts*. Early theorists such as William James (1890) thought humans were impelled by innate motives that were activated by features of the environment, much as spiders spin webs and birds build nests (Figure 12.1). Following James's lead, early psychologists drew up lists of instincts that they believed governed human behavior. Thus, for example, William McDougal (1923) asserted that humans have 13 instincts, including parenting, food seeking, repulsion, curiosity, and gregariousness (i.e., a tendency to seek out social contact).

Unfortunately, different theorists came up with quite different lists of instincts, and in 1924, sociologist Luther Bernard counted over 5,000 instincts that had been proposed by one scholar or another. This meant that instinct theory was—at best—inelegant, but, worse, commentators increasingly wondered what work the theory was actually doing. What did it mean to "explain" the impulse to parent one's children by postulating a "parenting instinct"? We could, on this model, "explain" why people vote by asserting that there is a "self-governance instinct," and explain why they go shopping by asserting a "shopping instinct." In each case, our "explanation" merely provides a new bit of jargon that offers us no new information.

A different conception of motivation turns out to be more productive. More than a century ago, the French physiologist Claude Bernard (1813–1878) noted that every organism has both an external environment and an internal one. The external

12.1 **Instinctual actions** Early theorists suggested that humans' motivations arise from instincts like those that lead (A) spiders to spin webs or (B) birds to build nests.

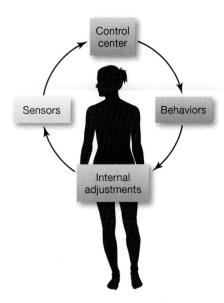

12.2 Homeostasis The control centers that maintain homeostasis continually monitor bodily conditions via sensors. When some aspect of bodily functioning deviates from an expected range, behaviors and internal adjustments help restore homeostasis.

homeostasis The body's tendency to maintain the conditions of its internal environment by various forms of self-regulation.

drive A term referring to a state of internal bodily tension, such as hunger or thirst or the need for sleep.

thermoregulation The process by which organisms maintain a constant body temperature.

environment includes the other creatures that the organism interacts with, and also the organism's physical surrounding—the temperature, the topography, the availability of shelter and water, and so on. But the organism's *internal* environment is just as important, and includes the concentrations of various salts in the body's fluids, the dissolved oxygen levels and pH, and the quantities of nutrients like glucose, the sugar that most organisms use as their body's main fuel.

Moreover, Bernard noted that even with large-scale fluctuations in the outside environment, there is a striking constancy in the organism's internal state. All of the internal conditions we just listed fluctuate only within narrow limits, and, indeed, they must stay within these limits, because otherwise the organism is at severe risk. Apparently, therefore, the organism is capable of making substantial changes in order to compensate for the variations it encounters in the world.

The maintenance of this internal equilibrium involves a process known as **homeostasis** (Figure 12.2). Homeostasis involves many mechanisms, including internal adjustments (e.g., mechanisms in the kidneys that control the concentration of sodium in the bloodstream), and also a diverse set of behaviors (e.g., eating when you are low on calories, seeking shelter when you are cold), and this returns us to our discussion of motives. Deviations from homeostasis can create an internal state of biological and psychological tension called a **drive**—a drive to eat, a drive to sleep, and so on. The resulting behavior then reduces the drive and thus returns us to equilibrium.

Drive-reduction allows us to explain many of our motivated behaviors—including behaviors essential for our survival. As we will see later in the chapter, though, some behaviors cannot be explained in this fashion, and so we will need a broader conception of motivation before we are through. Even so, drive-reduction plays a central role in governing the behavior of humans and many other species.

THERMOREGULATION

One of our basic biological motivations centers on **thermoregulation**, which refers to maintaining our body temperature so that we are neither too cold nor too hot. This powerful motive merits discussion on its own, but, in addition, our exploration of thermoregulation will lay the groundwork for considering other, more complex motives.

All mammals and birds are *endotherms*, organisms that maintain stable body temperatures. (Fish, reptiles, and many other organisms, in contrast, are *ectotherms*; they have a far more variable internal temperature.) Endotherms use many mechanisms to hold their temperatures more or less constant, including large-scale bodily changes such as gaining weight and growing fur in preparation for cold months, and losing both during warm months. They also change their behavior, such as moving into an insulated nest when the weather gets cold.

In addition, endotherms rely on a number of more immediate changes to control their temperatures, with these changes directly controlled by the two branches of the autonomic nervous system (*ANS*), which we discussed in Chapter 3. As noted there, the ANS has two parts: the sympathetic branch, which tends to "rev up" bodily activities in preparation for vigorous action, and the parasympathetic branch, which tends to restore the body's internal activities to normal after the action has been completed. These divisions of the ANS act reciprocally, and so excitation of the sympathetic branch leads to an increased heart rate, while excitation of the parasympathetic branch leads to cardiac slowing. Sympathetic activation slows down peristalsis (rhythmic contractions

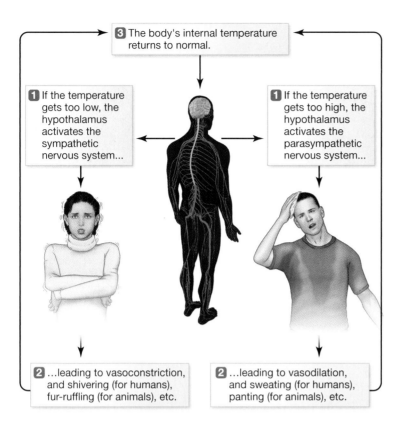

3 The body's internal temperature returns to normal.

1 If the temperature gets too low, the hypothalamus activates the sympathetic nervous system...

1 If the temperature gets too high, the hypothalamus activates the parasympathetic nervous system...

2 ...leading to vasoconstriction, and shivering (for humans), fur-ruffling (for animals), etc.

2 ...leading to vasodilation, and sweating (for humans), panting (for animals), etc.

12.3 Reflexive temperature regulation When body temperature is too high, the parasympathetic nervous system is activated, leading to vasodilation and sweating. When body temperature is too low, the sympathetic nervous system is activated, leading to vasoconstriction and shivering.

of the intestines) so that we're not using energy for digesting when we're on the run; parasympathetic activation does the opposite—it speeds up peristalsis.

How does the ANS help control temperature (Figure 12.3)? When the body's internal temperature gets too high, this activates the parasympathetic branch of the nervous system, which triggers a series of changes, including sweating (in humans) and panting (in dogs), both of which produce heat loss by evaporation, and vasodilation, a widening of the skin's capillaries. Vasodilation sends warm blood to the body's surface so that heat can be released. As the body cools, the triggers for these actions are no longer present, so sweating and vasodilation cease.

The opposite pattern comes into play when the animal's internal temperature drops too low. Here the sympathetic branch acts to conserve heat. Sweating and panting stop, and vasoconstriction occurs—a contraction of the capillaries that squeezes blood away from the body's cold periphery and keeps it instead in the warmer core.

What governs the ANS itself? Said differently, where is the body's (version of a) thermostat? A crucial brain region is the hypothalamus, located at the base of the forebrain (Figure 12.4). This brain structure is only about the size of a pea, but it contains over 20 clusters of neurons that regulate many of the body's internal systems. Among its other functions, the hypothalamus appears to contain a control mechanism that detects when the body is too cold or too hot. This was shown many years ago in an experiment in which researchers implanted an electrode in the anterior hypothalamus of cats. When the electrode was heated gently, the cats panted and vasodilated as though they were too hot and needed to cool themselves, even though their body temperature was well below normal (Magoun, Harrison, Brobeck, & Ranson, 1938).

Temperature regulation provides a clear example of homeostatic control, and also illustrates the ways homeostasis is often controlled by *anticipation*, rather than just immediate cues. Of course, all organisms do respond to current circumstances, and so

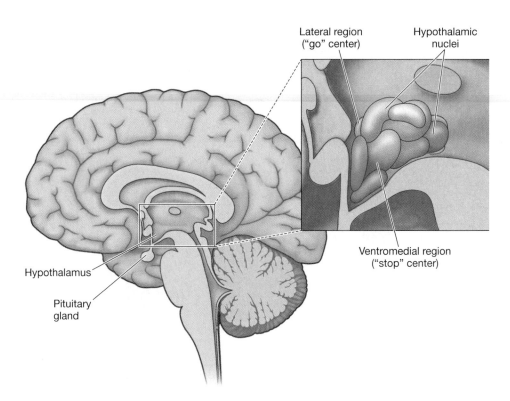

12.4 The hypothalamus The hypothalamus is a brain structure located at the base of the forebrain. It plays a crucial role in motivational states such as thermoregulation and eating. Although the hypothalamus is only the size of a pea, the detailed blowout shows that it contains over 20 clusters of neurons (nuclei) including the ventromedial and lateral nuclei, implicated in the control of eating. (Turn to page 469 for more information on the "go" and "stop" centers.)

Lateral region ("go" center)

Hypothalamic nuclei

Ventromedial region ("stop" center)

Hypothalamus

Pituitary gland

they sweat (or pant) and vasodilate when they are hot, and move into the shade. They shiver and vasoconstrict when cold, and seek out heat sources or shelter. In addition, many animals respond to temperature changes that haven't happened yet. Bears start growing their heavy winter coats weeks before the cold arrives. Many animals start building their nests, or digging their winter burrows, well before the seasons change. Desert foxes hunt during the cooler parts of the day so that they'll be ready to retire into the shade when the temperature rises. In all cases, the behaviors prevent (or diminish) a change in body temperature, rather than coping with the change when it occurs.

Humans do the same—although in richer and more sophisticated ways. We buy sweaters before the autumn begins. We pack bathing suits into our suitcase when we are headed for a warm-weather vacation. We stock up on cold drinks when tomorrow's forecast is sunny, and extra firewood when the forecast indicates that snow is coming. Plainly, therefore, thermoregulation relies on diverse mechanisms—at least some of which reflect a complexity that is rooted in our learning and culture.

HUNGER, EATING, AND OBESITY

It is often said that the surest path to the heart is via the stomach, and for many people, eating is indeed one of the great pleasures in life (Figure 12.5). This pairing of food and pleasure is no accident—the survival of every animal requires an adequate supply of energy and nutrients. These are provided via the process of digestion, through which nutrients from food are converted into energy that supplies body heat, enables the muscles to contract, and supports all our other life functions. An organism insensitive to these needs would have a short life span, and so it is no surprise that all animals have sophisticated internal mechanisms to monitor the availability of various nutrients within the body. Of course, when the need arises, these mechanisms can cause the animal to seek food.

12.5 The pleasures of eating *Peasant Wedding Feast* by Peter Brueghel the Elder, 1568.

How does the organism manage this feat of self-regulation? Is there an "appestat" that controls appetite and the behaviors that govern the intake of nutrients, the same way a thermostat controls the body's temperature? The answer turns out to be yes, but only within the context of a complicated, multipart control system. To understand this control system, we must consider its physiological, cultural, and cognitive aspects.

Physiological Aspects of Hunger and Eating

If animals are temporarily deprived of food, they usually eat more later, to return their bodies to the original weight. If they are force-fed extra food, they later eat *less*. These observations suggest that the animals have a caloric or body-weight **set point** that they seek to maintain. In other words, animals do act as if they have an internal "appestat," maintaining a relatively steady weight, just as the hypothalamus, acting as the body's thermostat, maintains a relatively constant inner temperature.

Evidence for some sort of internal set point also comes from the fact that when food is freely available, animals usually eat just about the right amount to satisfy their needs, while keeping their weight roughly constant. The "right amount" here refers not to the volume of food, but to the number of calories in the food—and hence, the metabolic energy it can provide. This was demonstrated in a study many years ago in which researchers decreased the caloric levels of rats' food by adding nonnutritive cellulose. The more diluted the food, the more the rats ate, in a quantity that kept their total caloric intake roughly constant (Adolph, 1947). Similar claims apply to humans, with the data indicating that each of us seems to have a target weight that our bodies work homeostatically to maintain. However, this set point is to some extent adjustable, and gradual changes in one's weight appear to alter the weight that is defended (Levitsky, 2002; Pinel, Assanand, & Lehman, 2000; Ruderman, 1986).

Evidence for set points in humans comes from many sources, including the fact that crash dieters usually return to their starting weight soon after they go off their diets. Moreover, dieters do not lose nearly as much weight as we might expect based on their reduced caloric intake. This is probably because the body compensates for the caloric loss by reducing its metabolic rate (Guesbeck et al., 2001). In other words, when the body gets less food, it responds by burning fewer calories, defending the set point weight. The consequence, of course, is that eating less does not lead to weight loss.

THE ROLE OF THE LIVER

What mechanisms maintain someone's body weight at its set point? The answer involves a number of internal signals, including signals that reflect the availability of glucose (the sugar that serves as the body's main fuel) in the blood.

Immediately after a meal, glucose is plentiful. Some is used right away, but much is converted to glycogen and various fatty acids, which are stored for later use. When this stored energy is needed, the process is reversed, and the glycogen and fatty acids are turned back into usable glucose. This conversion process is managed by the liver, and the liver keeps other organs informed about the direction in which the metabolic transaction is going, from glucose to glycogen or vice versa. If the supply of glucose exceeds the body's demand, so that the excess can be converted into glycogen and stored, the liver sends a satiety signal and the animal stops eating. If the body's demand for glucose exceeds the supply, so that energy reserves are being used, the liver sends a hunger signal and the animal eats (M. I. Friedman & Stricker, 1976; Russek, 1971).

set point A general term for the level at which negative feedback tries to maintain stability.

Notice, though, that this regulatory system must—like the thermoregulatory system—anticipate the animal's needs. Imagine that the liver only signaled the animal to eat when glucose supplies were already low. Since it often takes time to locate food, eat it, and then digest it, hours might elapse between the moment at which the liver sends a "Need glucose!" signal and the time that the glucose finally arrives. Nutrient supplies would be exhausted, and the animal could die. It's not surprising, therefore, that organisms have a well-defined mechanism for avoiding this catastrophe. When an organism has not eaten for a while, the level of glucose in the blood begins to drop. Before the level drops too far, the liver takes action, drawing some glycogen out of storage and converting it to glucose. As a result, the blood glucose level bounces back to normal. The result of this sequence of events is an easily identifiable pattern—a gradual drop in blood glucose, usually lasting many minutes, followed by a quick rise, resulting from the liver's compensatory action.

This slow-drop/quick-rise pattern means that the organism is drawing on its reserves, which signals the need for more glucose. When this blood glucose pattern occurs in rats, the animals start to eat (Campfield & Smith, 1990a, b). When it occurs in humans, they say they are hungry (Campfield & Rosenbaum, 1992).

OTHER CONTROL SIGNALS FOR FEEDING

The liver is only one part of the body's system for regulating food intake. The hypothalamus also contains cells that are sensitive to glucose levels in the blood, and if these **glucoreceptors** are damaged or disrupted, the result is ravenous eating (Miselis & Epstein, 1970).

Other signals come from other parts of the body. The stomach walls, for example, contain receptors sensitive to the nutrients dissolved in the digestive juices. When these receptors signal to the brain that nutrient supplies are on the way, the organism stops eating (Deutsch, Puerto, & Wang, 1978). Still other signals come from the fatty tissues themselves. To understand the importance of these signals, bear in mind that animals don't eat just for the moment. After all, they can't be sure that food will be available the next time they need energy, and so they must eat enough both to satisfy their current needs and to store nutrients for later. This long-term store is provided by the fat, or adipose cells, distributed throughout their body. These cells absorb the fatty acids created by the liver and swell in the process. The longer-term reserves then stand ready in case the animal's glycogen supplies are exhausted. If this happens, fatty acids drain from the adipose cells into the bloodstream and are converted into glucose.

Adipose tissue used to be regarded only as a kind of inert storage, but we now know that it plays a major role in governing hunger. Fat cells, when full, secrete the chemical **leptin** into the bloodstream, where it is sensed by receptors in several places in the brain, including the hypothalamus (Bouret, Draper, & Simerly, 2004; Maffei et al., 1995; McGregor et al., 1996; Pinto et al., 2004). Leptin seems to signal that there is plenty of fat in storage and no need to add more, and it may be one of the most important factors in governing an organism's food intake over the long term (Figure 12.6). Leptin appears to work by inhibiting the actions of several other neurochemicals, such as **neuropeptide Y (NPY)**, manufactured in the hypothalamus and the gut. NPY itself turns out to be a powerful appetite stimulant (Gibbs, 1996; B. G. Stanley, Magdalin, &

glucoreceptors Receptors in the brain (in the area of the hypothalamus) that detect the amount of glucose in the bloodstream.

leptin A chemical produced by the adipose cells that seems to signal that plenty of fat is stored and that no more fat is needed. This signal may diminish eating.

neuropeptide Y (NPY) A chemical found widely in the brain and periphery. In the brain, it acts as a neurotransmitter; when administered at sites in and near the hypothalamus, it is a potent elicitor of eating.

12.6 Leptin deficiency The chemical leptin plays an important role in eating. A boy with total leptin deficiency (A) before receiving regular leptin injections, and (B) after receiving regular leptin injections.

Leibowitz, 1989), so leptin secretion from fat cells seems to provide the negative feedback that holds NPY levels in check.

HYPOTHALAMIC CONTROL CENTERS

We have now talked about many cues that signal an organism's nutritional needs, but what mechanism detects, and responds to, these cues? For years, the best candidate was the hypothalamus. We have already mentioned that the hypothalamus monitors blood sugar levels, but in addition, the hypothalamus has been proposed as the receiving station for the body's other eating-related cues, so that the hypothalamus becomes, in effect, the main control center for feeding. The **dual-center theory** proposed that one part of the hypothalamus—the lateral region—served as the "go" center for eating, while a different part—the ventromedial region—served as the "stop" center (Figure 12.4 on page 466).

Consistent with this claim, damage to the lateral region of the hypothalamus seems to disrupt the *initiation* of feeding. If this region is lesioned, animals do not eat and will starve to death unless force-fed. Conversely, damage to the ventromedial region disrupts circuits that would ordinarily tell the animal when to *stop* feeding. Surgically induced lesions here cause rats to eat voraciously, until they finally reach a weight three times as great as before surgery (Figure 12.7). In humans, tumors in this hypothalamic region have the same effect—leading to extreme obesity (Hoebel & Teitelbaum, 1976; N. E. Miller, Bailey, & Stevenson, 1950; Teitelbaum & Epstein, 1962).

Subsequent research has shown, however, that the mechanisms described in this theory are only part of the story of how feeding is controlled. For example, lesions of the ventromedial hypothalamus (the supposed "stop" center) have been found not just to increase appetite (because the "stop" center is no longer functioning), but also to increase the rate of fat storage (Stricker & Zigmond, 1976). In addition, the lateral hypothalamus appears to be only one of the "go" centers for feeding. This is indicated by the fact that the appetite stimulant NPY exerts its strongest effects *outside* the lateral hypothalamus (Leibowitz, 1991). These and other results indicate that even though the hypothalamus is critical for the control of eating, other mechanisms are also crucial, some specialized for short-term energy needs, others for long-term storage.

WHY SO MANY SIGNALS?

We have acknowledged a broad set of signals controlling when an organism starts eating and when it stops, signals from the liver and from glucoreceptors in the brain, signals from the stomach and from the adipose tissue. In truth, other signals should be added to this list, including, of course, the sensory qualities of the food itself. Thus, when we see a delicious-looking pastry or smell hot, fresh popcorn, these sensory cues can make us feel hungry and cause us to eat even if we are experiencing no caloric need.

Why do we need so many cues? Part of the answer lies in the safety provided by backup systems—so that if one system fails, the organism can still self-regulate. And part of the answer is that different signals monitor different aspects of our nutritional needs—some (such as leptin) keeping tabs on our longer-term needs, and others (like cues from the stomach) signaling our more immediate status and allowing us to deal with hour-by-hour variations in our energy requirements.

The various cues also play different roles within the overall control of feeding. Some cues, like the sensory information from the food itself, directly signal the availability of food in the environment. Other, less direct cues play their main role in

dual-center theory The hypothesis that one area in the lateral hypothalamus is the "on" center, the initiator of eating, while another area in the ventromedial hypothalamus is the "off" center, the terminator of eating. Current evidence indicates that although these brain regions are crucial for eating, the regulation of eating also involves other circuits.

12.7 Rat with ventromedial hypothalamus lesion

creating a motivational state for the organism so that, broadly put, these cues lead the organism to feel hungry so it is motivated to seek food. Finally, some cues potentiate other cues—that is, they make the other cues more salient and more persuasive. In one study, for example, researchers recorded activity levels in cells in a waking monkey's hypothalamus (Mora, Rolls, & Burton, 1976; also Rolls, 1978). Those cells were activated when the animal was shown a peanut or banana, but only when the animal was hungry. In this fashion, the cues reflecting the animal's internal state did not directly influence its behavior. Instead, these cues potentiated the sensory cues, so that the animal would be more likely to detect (and respond to) the immediate availability of food when it needed nutrients.

Cultural and Cognitive Aspects of Hunger and Eating

The hypothalamus and other biological structures play a crucial role in deciding when and how much we eat. But other factors are also critical, including the culture in which we live.

CULTURE AND EATING

Why do many Europeans feel hungry for their main meal of the day in the early afternoon, while others on the continent—the French, for example—hunger for their main meal only in the evening? Why is it that most Americans grow hungry for dinner at 6:00 p.m. or so, while the British are likely to seek food a couple of hours earlier, at teatime? These questions surely cannot be answered in terms of differences among French, American, or British livers, or geographical variation in how the hypothalamus is wired. Instead these points remind us that our feeding patterns are shaped by our cultural environment.

Culture also governs *how much* we eat. Many of us put considerable effort into controlling our food intake, usually with the aim of achieving a particular appearance. But what defines the ideal toward which people are striving? The answer lies in the cultural setting, and cultures set quite different standards. The women painted by Rubens, Matisse, and Renoir, for example, were considered the feminine ideal in their day, and all three artists (two of them living just a century ago) would probably judge today's supermodels to be undernourished and quite unappealing (Figure 12.8).

Cultural factors provide a constant backdrop for our thinking, expectations, and perceptions. But we are also influenced by specific situations. As one example, let's note that there are direct social influences on feeding, so that we are more likely to eat when we are surrounded by others who are eating. The classic demonstration of this comes from an experiment done years ago; it showed that a hen who has had her fill of grain will eagerly resume her meal if joined by other hens that are still hungry (Bayer, 1929). Similar effects can easily be observed with humans.

Social influences are also tied to people's aspirations (and sometimes unhealthy aspirations) toward thinness. In ways we will discuss in Chapter 13, each of us is powerfully influenced by the people around us, so that how we act and, indeed, what we think about ourselves are shaped by how they perceive us and what they expect from us. The simple fact is that how people perceive us, and what they expect, are shaped by our bodily form—in particular, how heavy or thin we are.

12.8 Changing feminine ideals Cultural ideals regarding body shape change over time, as reflected by (A) Rubens's *Venus before a Mirror* (1614–1615) and (B) modern media portrayals.

One more factor influences our eating, and it is perhaps a surprising one. It turns out that whether we eat or not is influenced by what we remember—in particular, our memory for what else we have eaten recently. This was evident, as we saw in the Prologue, when patients suffering from clinical amnesia were presented with several lunches in a row, with just enough time between lunches so that the patients completely forgot they had eaten. Without that memory, patients proceeded to eat one lunch right after another. This suggests that our subjective experience of hunger, as well as our eating behavior, is powerfully shaped by our memory for how long it has been since our last meal.

Obesity

The physiological and cognitive mechanisms regulating an organism's food intake work remarkably well—but not perfectly. We see this in the fact that organisms (humans in particular!) can end up either weighing far more than is healthy for them or weighing too little. In some cases, the person is underweight because—tragically—poverty and malnutrition are common problems in many parts of the world (including nations that we would otherwise consider relatively wealthy). Even when food is available, though, people can end up underweight, and we will consider one version of this problem in our discussion of eating disorders in Chapter 16. Here, we deal with the more common problem in the Western world: obesity, a problem so widespread that the World Health Organization has classified obesity as a global epidemic (Ravussin & Bouchard, 2000).

Obesity is sometimes defined as a body weight that exceeds the average for a given height by 20%. More commonly, though, researchers use a definition cast in terms of the **Body Mass Index** (**BMI**), defined as someone's weight in kilograms divided by the square of his height in meters (Figure 12.9). A BMI between 18.5 and 24.9 is considered normal. A BMI between 25 and 30 counts as overweight, and a BMI of 30 or more is considered obese. A BMI over 40 defines **morbid obesity**—the level of obesity at which someone's health is genuinely at risk. For most people, morbid obesity means a weight roughly 100 pounds (45.3 kg) beyond their ideal.

Body Mass Index (BMI) The commonly-used measure of whether someone is at a healthy weight or not; BMI is calculated as weight in kilograms divided by the square of height in meters.

morbid obesity The level of obesity at which someone's health is genuinely at risk, usually defined as a BMI over 40.

12.9 Converting height and weight to Body Mass Index

Why do people become obese? The simplest hypothesis is that some people eat too much. In this view, obesity might be understood as the end result of self-indulgence, or perhaps the consequence of an inability to resist temptation. This hypothesis makes it seem like people could be blamed for their obesity, like the condition is, in essence, their own fault. Such a view of obesity, however, is almost certainly a mistake, because it ignores the powerful forces that can put someone on the path toward obesity in the first place. Although people do have considerable control over what and how much they eat, the evidence suggests that some people are strongly genetically predisposed toward obesity.

One long-term study examined 12 pairs of male identical twins. Each of these men ate about 1,000 calories per day above the amount required to maintain his initial weight. The activities of each participant were kept as close to equivalent as possible, and there was very little exercise. This regimen continued for 100 days. Needless to say, all 24 men gained weight, but the amounts they gained varied substantially, from about 10 to 30 pounds. The men also differed in terms of where on their bodies the weight was deposited. For some participants, it was the abdomen; for others, it was the thighs and buttocks. Crucially, though, the amount each person gained was statistically related to the weight gain of his twin (Figure 12.10). The twins also tended to deposit the weight in the same place. If one developed a prominent paunch, so did his twin; if another deposited the fat in his thighs, his twin did, too (Bouchard, Lykken, McGue, Segal, & Tellegen, 1990; also see Herbert et al., 2006).

It seems, therefore, that the tendency to turn extra calories into fat has a genetic basis. In fact, several mechanisms may be involved in this pattern, so that, in the end, obesity can arise from a variety of causes. For example, some people seem to be less sensitive to the appetite-reducing signals from leptin and thus are more vulnerable to the effects of appetite stimulants such as NPY (J. Friedman, 2003). For these people, a

(A)

(B)

(C)

12.10 **Similarity of weight gains in identical twins** Weight gains for 12 pairs of identical twins after 100 days of the same degree of overfeeding. Each point represents one twin pair, with the weight gain of twin A plotted on the vertical axis and the weight gain of twin B plotted on the horizontal axis. Weight gains are plotted in kilograms (1 kg = 2.2 lbs). The closer the points are to the diagonal line, the more similar the weight gains of the twins are to each other. The key finding from this study is that pairs of identical twins—such as those shown in (B) and (C)—tended to gain similar amounts of weight.

tendency to overeat may be genetically rooted. In addition, people differ in the efficiency of their digestive apparatus, with some people simply extracting more calories from any given food. People also differ in their overall metabolic level; if, as a result, less nutrient fuel is burned up, then more is stored as fat (Astrup, 2000; also M. I. Friedman, 1990a, b; Sims, 1986).

Given these various mechanisms, should we perhaps think about obesity as some sort of genetic *defect*, a biologically rooted condition that leads to substantial health risk? Proponents of the "thrifty gene" hypothesis emphatically reject this suggestion. They note that our ancestors lived in times when food supplies were unpredictable and food shortages were common, so natural selection may have favored individuals who had especially inefficient metabolisms and, as a result, stored more fat. These individuals would have been better prepared for lean times and thus may have had a survival advantage. As a result, the genes leading to this fat storage might have been assets, not defects (J. Friedman, 2003; Fujimoto et al., 1995; Groop & Tuomi, 1997; Ravussin, 1994).

ENVIRONMENTAL FACTORS AND OBESITY

Clearly, then, "thrifty genes" might have helped our ancestors to maintain a healthy body weight, but our ancestors lived in a time in which food was scarce. The same genes will have a different outcome in modern times—especially for people living in an affluent culture in which a quick trip to the supermarket provides all the calories one wishes. In this modern context, the "thrifty genes" can lead to levels of obesity that create serious health problems.

Whether for genetic reasons, though, or otherwise, the evidence is clear that obesity rates are climbing across the globe. In the United States, roughly 23% of the population in 1991 was obese; more recent estimates of the rate—30%—are appreciably higher (J. Friedman, 2003). Similar patterns are evident in other countries. Over the last 10 years, for example, the obesity rates in most European countries have increased by at least 10%, and, in some countries, by as much as 40%. These shifts cannot reflect changes in the human genome; genetic changes proceed at a much slower pace. Instead, the increase has to be understood in terms of changes in diet and activity level—with people consuming more calorically dense, high-fat foods and living a lifestyle that causes them to expend relatively few calories in their daily routines.

This increase in obesity rates is associated with increased rates of many health problems, including heart attack, stroke, Type 2 diabetes, and some types of cancer. The debate continues over the severity of these risks for people with moderate levels of obesity—e.g., a BMI between 30 and 40 (Couzin, 2005; Yan et al., 2006). There is no debate, however, about the health risks of so-called morbid obesity (a BMI of 40 or higher), and this makes the worldwide statistics on obesity a serious concern for health professionals.

THREAT AND AGGRESSION

Thermoregulation and hunger are primarily regulated by mechanisms that monitor and maintain the organism's internal environment (although, as we have seen, external cues are also important). Other motives, in contrast, depend primarily on external triggers, and an example is our reaction to intense threat. In this case, the instigation is the lion about to pounce, or the bully about to strike us down. Even so, our discussion of threat will bring us to the same themes that arose in our discussion of hunger. Our bodies make numerous internal adjustments in response to the threat; these adjustments are tightly controlled by complex regulatory mechanisms that seem to function similarly in humans and in other species. Genetic mechanisms are crucial, and—once again—these genetic mechanisms interact constantly with environment and our experiences.

Physiological Aspects of Threat and Aggression

What physiological mechanisms underlie our reactions to threat? One crucial mechanism is the sympathetic branch of the autonomic nervous system. This branch summons the body's resources in times of crisis and gets the organism ready for vigorous action. We have mentioned some of the effects of sympathetic excitation, but in addition, this excitation stimulates the inner core of the adrenal gland, the adrenal medulla, to pour epinephrine (adrenaline) and norepinephrine into the bloodstream. These chemicals have effects similar to activation of the sympathetic nervous system—they accelerate the heart rate, speed up metabolism, and so on. As a result, they amplify sympathetic effects even further.

THE "FIGHT OR FLIGHT" RESPONSE

The physiologist Walter Cannon argued that intense sympathetic arousal serves as an emergency reaction that mobilizes the organism for a crisis—for "fight or flight," as he described it. Consider a grazing zebra, placidly maintaining homeostasis by nibbling at the grass and vasodilating in the hot African sun. Suddenly it sees a lion closing in for the kill. Escape will require pronounced muscular exertion, with the support of the entire bodily machinery, and this is exactly what intense sympathetic activation provides. Because of this activation, more nutrient fuel is available to the muscles and can be delivered rapidly through wide-open blood vessels. At the same time, waste products are jettisoned and all less-essential bodily activities are brought to a halt.

Cannon produced considerable evidence suggesting that a similar autonomic reaction occurs when an organism prepares to attack rather than flee. A cat about to tangle with a dog shows accelerated heartbeat, piloerection (its hair standing on end, normally a heat-conserving device), and pupillary dilation—all signs of sympathetic arousal that show the body is girding itself for violent muscular effort (Figure 12.11).

It turns out, however, that Cannon's "fight or flight" formulation is overly simple, because organisms respond to threat in many different ways. While it is true that in some contexts, animals do indeed fight or flee, in other contexts, animals may stand immobile when threatened, so that predators are less likely to notice them. Other animals have more exotic means of self-protection. For example, some species of fish pale when threatened, which makes them harder to spot against the sandy ocean bottom. This effect results from the direct action of adrenal epinephrine on various pigments in the animal's skin (Odiorne, 1957).

A further complication for Cannon's formulation comes from variations *within a species*. For example, Taylor and colleagues noted that most studies of the stress response had been conducted using male rats or humans (S. E. Taylor et al., 2000; S. E. Taylor, 2006). When researchers examined females' responses, they found that their responses did not fit the "fight or flight" pattern of response. For example, women seemed to respond to stressful situations by "tending" (i.e., taking care of children) and "befriending" (i.e., using social support) (Figure 12.12).

12.11 Sympathetic emergency reaction A cat's response to a threatening encounter.

12.12 Tending and befriending Women may respond to stressful situations by "tending" (taking care of others) or "befriending" (using social support).

These limitations notwithstanding, the mechanism Cannon highlighted—an emergency system rooted in the sympathetic nervous system—is essential for many individuals in many species. At the same time, however, arousal of the sympathetic branch of the ANS can be disruptive and even damaging. This is especially clear in humans. In our day-to-day lives, we rarely encounter emergencies that call for violent physical effort, but our biological nature has not completely changed just because the modern world contains no threats from saber-toothed tigers. We are plagued instead by chronic stressors like traffic jams, ornery bosses, pressing deadlines, and agonizing world crises. Although we often feel impelled to defend ourselves against these threats of the modern world, physical action is frequently inappropriate, ineffective, or illegal. Nonetheless, we are stuck with the same emergency reactions that our ancestors had, and so we keep ourselves armed physiologically against situations we cannot really control. The resulting bodily wear and tear can take a serious toll (e.g., Sapolsky, 1998).

AGGRESSION AND PREDATION

It seems, then, that our biological reaction to threat may not always serve us well in our modern environment. Nonetheless, this reaction is well rooted in our biology, and it is certainly similar to the reaction pattern easily observed in many other species. It is a reaction pattern that has been shaped by natural selection and that has, over each species' history, contributed to survival by preparing the organism for whatever energetic activities it needs to escape the threat.

But what does the animal do once the emergency reaction is under way? Are the subsequent steps also shared across species? To answer this question, it is helpful to draw on the **comparative method**, studying nonhumans as well as humans to see what kinds of commonalities in our behavior reflect shared biological heritage.

As a first and crucial point, though, we need to distinguish two forms of violence that organisms engage in—*aggression* and *predation*. Predators hunt and kill for food, but they do so quite dispassionately. A predator about to pounce on its prey shows none of the signs of anger, and so a dog on the verge of catching a rabbit never growls, nor does it have its ears laid back (K. Z. Lorenz, 1966). Predatory attack is instead motivated by hunger, and it is controlled by the same brain sites as eating (Hutchinson & Renfrew, 1966). In contrast, aggressive or self-defense behaviors are controlled by distinct brain areas, are triggered by different situations, and certainly show different behavioral profiles. In our discussion of aggression, therefore, it will be best to hold predatory attack to the side—as part of an animal's food-gathering repertoire, and not part of its response to threat.

MALE AGGRESSION AND HORMONES

Genuine combat is, in fact, widespread among animals, and there is probably no species that has forsworn aggression altogether (Figure 12.13). Fish chase and nip each other; lizards lunge and push; birds attack with wing, beak, and claw; and on and on. In most cases, the individuals we identify as aggressive are male, because, among vertebrates, the male is by far the more physically aggressive sex. In some mammals, this sex difference in combativeness is apparent even in childhood play. Young male rhesus monkeys, for instance, engage in much more vigorous rough-and-tumble play than their sisters (Harlow, 1962). Among humans, boys worldwide are more physically aggressive than girls (Geary & Bjorklund, 2000), and as adults, male murderers outnumber females by a ratio of 10:1 (C. A. Anderson & Bushman, 2002).

comparative method A research method in which one makes systematic comparisons among different species in order to gain insights into the function of a particular structure or behavior, or the evolutionary origins of that structure or behavior.

12.13 **Animal combat** Animals in many species often engage in ferocious combat, usually over some resource (such as food, territory, or a potential mate).

testosterone The principal male sex hormone in mammals.

12.14 Social aggression In males, aggression is often physical (pushing or punching). In females, aggression usually takes a different form. They may attack each other, for example, by spreading gossip or rumors; they take steps to isolate someone from friends and allies.

However, this gender difference holds only for *physical* aggression. Human females are also aggressive, but their aggression tends to rely on verbal or social assaults, not physical violence. Thus, females attack by means of insults or the spreading of rumors; they take steps to isolate someone from friends and allies (Figure 12.14). If we focus on these sorts of aggression, then it is women, not men, who are the aggressive sex (Oesterman et al., 1998).

Why is physical aggression so much more prevalent in men? Biological factors are clearly relevant, because aggression is partially influenced by hormones, particularly the sex hormone **testosterone.** High testosterone levels in the bloodstream are associated with increased physical aggressiveness in many different species, including fish, lizards, turtles, birds, rats, mice, and monkeys (D. E. Davis, 1964; A. Siegel & Demetrikopoulos, 1993). However, the relationship between testosterone and physical aggression is complex. As one complication, at least some human aggression bears no relationship to testosterone levels, so it must be shaped by other factors (e.g., Book, Starzyk, & Qunisey, 2001). In addition, high testosterone levels can be both a cause and an effect of aggressive behavior. Thus, testosterone administered externally can increase subsequent aggressiveness, but successful aggressive encounters can also cause increased secretion of testosterone (Dabbs, 1992; Rosenzweig, Leiman, & Breedlove, 1996; Sapolsky, 1998).

Cultural and Cognitive Aspects of Threat and Aggression

In many cases, humans (just like other animals) become aggressive in an effort to secure or defend resources. This is evident in the wars that have grown out of national disagreements about who owns a particular expanse of territory; on a smaller scale, it is evident when two drivers come to blows over a parking space. Humans also become aggressive for reasons that hinge on symbolic concerns, such as insults to honor or objections to another person's beliefs or behavior. The latter type of aggression is clear in many of the hateful acts associated with stereotyping. It is also a powerful contributor to the conflict among ethnic groups or people of different religions.

12.15 Variation in human aggression Humans vary enormously in how aggressive they are. (A) Some (like His Holiness the Dalai Lama) develop a capacity for loving compassion that makes aggression almost unthinkable. (B) Others (like these gang members) participate in violent aggression in almost every day of their lives.

INDIVIDUAL DIFFERENCES IN AGGRESSION

Whatever the source of the aggression, it is obvious that people vary enormously in how aggressive they are (Figure 12.15). Some of us respond to provocation with violence. Some turn the other cheek. Some find nonviolent means of asserting themselves. What determines how someone responds?

For many years, investigators believed that aggression was more likely in people with relatively low self-esteem, on the argument that such individuals were particularly vulnerable to insult and also likely to have few other means of responding. More recent work, however, suggests that the opposite is the case, that social provocations are more likely to inspire aggression if the person provoked has unrealistically high self-esteem (Baumeister, 2001; Bushman & Baumeister, 2002). Such a person is particularly likely to perceive the provocation as a grievous assault, challenging his inflated self-image; in many cases, violence will be the result.

Other personality traits are also relevant to aggression, including a factor called sensation seeking, a tendency to seek out varied and novel experiences in their daily lives. High levels of sensation seeking are associated with aggressiveness, and so are high scores on tests that measure the trait of impulsivity, a tendency to act without reflecting on one's actions (Anderson & Bushman, 2002; Joireman, Anderson, & Strathman, 2003).

In addition, whether someone turns to aggression or not is influenced heavily by the culture in which he was raised. Some cultures explicitly eschew violence; this is true, for example, in communities of Quakers. But other cultures prescribe violence, often via rules of chivalry and honor that demand certain responses to certain insults. Gang violence in many U.S. cities can be understood partly in this way, as can some of the fighting among the warlords of Somalia. Cultural differences are also evident when we compare different regions within the United States; for example, the homicide rate in the South is reliably higher than in the North, and statistical evidence suggests that this contrast is best attributed to social differences and not to factors like population density, economic conditions, or climate (Nisbett & Cohen, 1996).

How exactly does culture encourage or discourage aggression? The answer in some cases involves explicit teaching—when, for example, our parents tell us not to be aggressive, or they punish us for some aggressive act. In other cases, the learning involves picking up subtle cues that tell us, for example, whether our friends think that aggression is acceptable, or repugnant, or cool. In still other cases, the learning is of a different sort and involves what we called *observational learning* in Chapter 7. This is learning in which the people around us model through their own actions how one should handle situations that might provoke aggression.

We noted in Chapter 7, though, that observational learning can also proceed on a much larger scale, thanks to the societal influences that we are all exposed to. Consider the violence portrayed on television and in movies. On some accounts, prime-time television programs contain an average of five violent acts per hour, as characters punch, shoot, and sometimes murder each other (Figure 12.16). Overall, investigators estimate that the average American child observes more than 10,000 acts of TV violence every year (e.g., Anderson & Bushman, 2001).

Evidence that this media violence promotes violence in the viewer comes from studies of violence levels within a community before and after television was introduced, or before and after the broadcast of particularly gruesome footage of murders or assassinations. These studies consistently show that assault and homicide rates increase after such exposures (Centerwall, 1989; Joy, Kimball, & Zabrack, 1986). Other studies indicate that children who are not particularly aggressive become more so after viewing TV violence (e.g., Huesmann, Lagerspetz, & Eron, 1984; Huesmann & Miller, 1994; for related data showing the effects of playing violent video games, see Carnagey & Anderson, 2005).

These studies leave little doubt that there is a strong correlation, such that those who view violence are more likely than other people to be violent themselves. But does this correlation reveal a cause-and-effect relationship, in which the viewing can actually cause someone to be more violent? Many investigators believe it can (Anderson & Bushman, 2001, 2002; Bushman & Anderson, 2009; Carnagey, Anderson, & Bartholow, 2007; Cassel & Bernstein, 2007). Indeed, the evidence persuaded six major professional societies (including the American Psychological Association, the American Medical Association, and the American Psychiatric Association) to issue a joint statement noting that studies "point overwhelmingly to a causal connection between media violence and aggressive behavior in some children" (Joint Statement, 2000, p. 1).

12.16 Television violence Prime-time television, on some estimates, displays an average of five violent acts per hour. Saturday-morning children's programming is far worse, as characters constantly punch and shoot at and sometimes kill each other.

LIMITING AGGRESSION

Whether motivated by a wish to defend a territory or a desire to repay an insult, aggression is costly. If we focus just on the biological costs to the combatants, aggression is

12.17 Threatening and conciliatory displays (A) Some species threaten by shouting at the top of their lungs, like howler monkeys, who scream at each other for hours on end. (B) In most species, animal combat ends before either animal suffers a mortal wound. As soon as one of the combatants determines that its defeat is likely, it surrenders and explicitly signals the surrender through a submissive display—such as exposing the belly or the throat.

(A)

(B)

dangerous and can lead to injury or death. For some species, and for some forms of violence, these costs are simply the price of certain advantages—for survival or for reproduction (e.g., Pennisi, 2005). Even so, natural selection has consistently favored ways of limiting the damage done by aggression.

One way that natural selection seems to have done this is by ensuring that animals are keenly sensitive to the strength of their enemies. If the enemy seems much stronger (or more agile or better armed or armored) than oneself, the best bet is to concede defeat quickly, or better yet, never to start the battle at all. Animals therefore use a variety of strategies to proclaim their strength, with a goal of winning the battle before it starts. They roar, they puff themselves up, and they offer all sorts of threats, all with the aim of appearing as powerful as they possibly can (Figure 12.17A). Conversely, once an animal determines that it is the weaker one and likely to lose a battle, it uses a variety of strategies for avoiding a bloody defeat, usually involving specific conciliatory signals, such as crouching or exposing one's belly (Figure 12.17B).

Similar mechanisms are evident in humans. For example, the participants in a bar fight or a schoolyard tussle try to puff themselves up to intimidate their opponents, just as a moose or a mouse would. Likewise, we humans have a range of conciliatory gestures we use to avoid combat—body postures and words of appeasement.

All of these mechanisms, however, apply largely to face-to-face combat; sad to say, these biologically based controls have little effect on the long-distance, large-scale aggression that our species often engages in. As a result, battles between nations will probably not be avoided by political leaders roaring or thumping their chests; soldiers operating a missile-launcher cannot see (much less respond to) their targets' conciliatory body posture. Our best hope for reducing human aggression, therefore, is that the human capacity for moral and intellectual reflection will pull us away from combat, and that considering the cruelty and destruction of violence will lead us to reconcile our differences by other means.

SEXUAL BEHAVIOR

We have now considered three powerful motives: thermoregulation, hunger, and responses to threat. In each case, we have discussed mechanisms that we share with other creatures (e.g., the autonomic responses associated with body temperature regulation, homeostatic regulation of blood sugar, the biological response to threat), and in each case, the adaptive function roots of these mechanisms are easy to discern. In addition, we have seen that these genetically rooted mechanisms are powerfully influenced by learning and culture (e.g., the fashions that dictate the clothes we wear, the implicit rules that determine what we eat, and the cultural practices that govern how we respond to provocation).

These motives are all very well and good, but you wouldn't even exist without another crucial motive, namely, sex. This motive is unmistakably rooted in our physiology just as thermoregulation, hunger, and the response to threat are. In some ways, however, sex is different. Unlike the other biological motives, sex is inherently social, and in humans its pursuit is intertwined with all manner of cultural patterns and attitudes.

Let us start our discussion with the aspects of sexual behavior that are most obviously biological—mating itself and the role of hormones in controlling an organism's behavior. We will then turn to aspects of sexual behavior for which the influence of biology, and of evolution in particular, is still hotly debated, touching on some of the topics that we first met in Chapter 2, in our broader discussion of evolution. (We will consider love and romance in Chapter 13, when we focus on the ways people relate to each other.)

Physiological Aspects of Sexuality

Sexual behavior in animals is ultimately about arranging for the union of sperm and ova, but this can proceed only after male and female have met, courted, and determined each other to be a suitable mate. At that point, at least for terrestrial mammals and birds, the male generally introduces his sperm cells into the genital tract of the female. The sperm then has to encounter a ready ovum, and finally, the fertilized egg can develop if it is provided with the appropriate conditions. (In Chapter 14, we will consider how a fertilized egg grows into a child.) For now, we note that the sequence of events requires a complex hormonal control system that links the brain, reproductive organs, and behavior.

HORMONAL CYCLES

In sex, timing is everything. Most animals are sexually receptive, and both biologically and behaviorally prepared to mate, only at certain points in the year. In mammals, this period of sexual receptivity is known as **estrus,** and how often it occurs depends on the species. Female rats, for example, go through a 15-hour estrus period every four days. At all other times, they will resolutely reject any male's advances. If a male nuzzles a female who is not in estrus or tries to mount, she will kick and bite him. But during estrus, the female responds quite differently to the male's approach. She first retreats in small hops, then stops to look back and wiggles her ears (McClintock & Adler, 1978). Eventually, she stands still, her back arched, her tail held to the side—a willing sexual partner.

The mechanism that causes this change in the female's behavior is an interlocking system of hormonal and neurological controls that involves the pituitary gland, the hypothalamus, and the ovaries. There are three phases (Figure 12.18). During the first phase, follicles (ova-containing sacs) in the ovary mature under the influence of pituitary secretions. The follicles produce the sex hormone **estrogen.** As the concentration of estrogen in the bloodstream rises, the hypothalamus responds by directing the pituitary to change its secretions. In consequence, follicle growth is accelerated until the follicle ruptures and releases the mature ovum.

Release of the ovum triggers the second phase, during which the animal is in estrus. Estrogen production peaks and stimulates certain structures in the hypothalamus, which make the animal sexually receptive.

estrus In mammals, the period in the cycle when the female is sexually receptive (in heat).

estrogen A female sex hormone that dominates the first half of the female cycle through ovulation.

12.18 The main stages of the human menstrual cycle Estrogen and progesterone levels and thickness of the uterine lining during the human menstrual cycle. The cycle begins with the growth of a follicle, continues through ovulation and a maximum estrogen level, is followed by a phase during which the uterus becomes prepared to receive the embryo, and ends with a flow phase during which the thickened uterine lining is sloughed off.

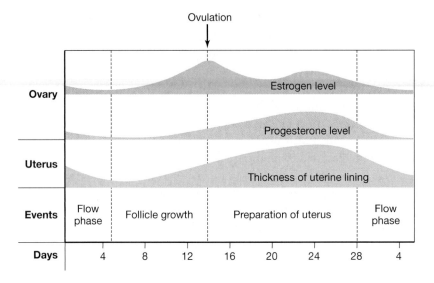

progesterone A female sex hormone that dominates the latter phase of the female cycle during which the uterine walls thicken to receive the embryo.

The ruptured follicle secretes another sex hormone, **progesterone**, which dominates the action of the third phase. Progesterone secretion leads to a thickening of the uterine lining, the first step in preparing the uterus to receive the embryo. If the ovum is fertilized, there are further steps in preparing the uterus. If it is not, the thickened uterine walls are reabsorbed, and another cycle begins. In humans and some primates, this thickening of the uterine wall involves too much extra tissue to be easily reabsorbed; the thickened uterine lining is therefore sloughed off as menstrual flow.

HORMONAL CHANGES AND BEHAVIOR

These hormonal changes affect behavior dramatically. When female rats' ovaries are removed, they soon lose all sexual interest and capacity, as do male rats when castrated. But sexual behavior is quickly restored in the male by appropriate injections of testosterone and in the female mainly by estrogen (the female also needs, and secretes, a small amount of testosterone).

Many investigators believe that the behavioral effects of these hormones are mediated by receptors in the hypothalamus. This hypothesis has been tested by injecting tiny quantities of various hormones into different regions of the hypothalamus. Such studies reveal, for example, that a spayed female cat will go into estrus when estrogen is implanted (G. W. Harris & Michael, 1964) and that castrated males will resume sexual behavior after receiving doses of the appropriate male hormones (J. M. Davidson, 1969; Feder, 1984; McEwen et al., 1982).

Hormones affect behavior, but the effect can also work in the opposite direction. What an animal experiences and what it does can substantially affect it hormonally. In some animals, the female's courtship behavior can trigger the release of testosterone in courting males. Conversely, the male's behavior also influences female hormones. In many rodents, the female's sexual receptivity is triggered by chemicals contained in the male's urine. In other cases, copulation itself produces reproductive readiness for the female. For example, the female rat secretes some progesterone during the normal cycle but not enough to permit the implantation of the fertilized ovum in the uterus. The critical dose is secreted only as a reflex response to sexual stimulation. This leaves the sexually aroused male rat with two reproductive functions: supplying sperm and providing the mechanical stimulation necessary for the female's hormonal secretion. Should he ejaculate too quickly and thus leave the female inadequately stimulated, all is lost, for no pregnancy results (Adler, 1979; Rosenzweig, Leiman, & Breedlove, 1996).

HORMONES AND HUMAN SEXUALITY

Compared to other animals, humans are less automatic in their sexual activities, more varied, and more affected by prior experience. This difference is especially marked when we consider the effects of sex hormones. In rats and cats, sexual behavior is highly dependent upon hormone levels; castrated males and spayed females stop copulating a few months after the removal of their gonads. In humans, on the other hand, sexual activity may persist for years, even decades, after castration or ovariectomy, provided that the operation was performed after puberty (Bermant & Davidson, 1974).

The liberation from hormonal control is especially clear in human females. The estrus cycle of the female rat or cat makes her receptive during only one period, but human females can respond sexually at virtually all points of their menstrual cycle. This does not mean, however, that human sexual desire is completely independent of hormonal influence. If a man or woman has abnormally low hormone levels, injections of hormones will generally increase his or her sex drive (J. M. Davidson, 1986; Rosenzweig et al., 1996), and men, with their higher levels of testosterone than those of women, tend to have a stronger sexual drive than women have (Baumeister, Cantanese, & Vohs, 2001).

Hormonal influences are also evident in the fact that women's preferences and behavior change as they move through their menstrual cycle. For example, women seem to prefer more "masculine" faces (with a slightly stronger chin and more prominent brows) if their preferences are assessed during the fertile phase of their cycle (Frost, 1994; Johnston, Hagel, Franklin, Fink, & Grammer, 2001; Penton-Voak & Perrett, 2000). In addition, some evidence suggests that women's sexual desire increases during the middle of the cycle, when ovulation occurs. This effect is not very pronounced, however, and has not been observed in all studies, and thus it seems to be only the vestige of an estrus cycle, left behind by waves of evolutionary change (Adams, Gold, & Burt, 1978; Bancroft, 1986; Hamburg, Moos, & Yalom, 1968; Spitz, Gold, & Adams, 1975).

THE HUMAN SEXUAL RESPONSE CYCLE

Our understanding of the **human sexual response cycle** has its foundation in the study of hundreds of men and women as they masturbated or had sexual intercourse in the laboratory (Masters & Johnson, 1966). Findings from these studies showed that people differed in many aspects of their sexual responses, but that four general stages seem to characterize both men's and women's sexual responses (Figure 12.19).

The first phase is the *excitement phase*. In this phase, heart rate and blood pressure increase, breathing quickens, and there is increased muscle tension and blood flow to the sexual organs. For men, the penis becomes erect; for women, the clitoris becomes swollen and the vagina becomes lubricated. In the second or *plateau phase*, heart rate, blood pressure, and muscle tension continue to rise, but more slowly, while muscles tighten at the base of the penis for men, and in the vagina for women. The third phase is the *orgasm phase*. This phase is characterized by heightened arousal and a series of rhythmic muscle contractions that lead to ejaculation of sperm in men, and to vaginal contractions in women that help to guide the sperm up the vagina. This orgasm phase is often experienced as intensely pleasurable. The fourth and final phase is the *resolution phase*, during which time heart rate and blood pressure drop and muscles relax. For men, there is typically a refractory period during which another orgasm is not possible; the length of this refractory period varies from minutes to hours, and increases with age.

human sexual response cycle
A sequence of four stages that characterizes the sexual response in both men and women: excitement, plateau, orgasm, and resolution.

12.19 Human sexual response Men and women have quite similar sexual response cycles.

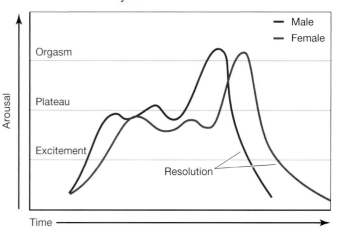

Cultural and Cognitive Aspects of Sexuality

As we have seen, our sexual behavior clearly has powerful physiological bases. At the same time, it also has substantial cultural and cognitive components. In this section, we consider proximal situational determinants of sexual behavior as well as more remote evolutionary determinants of mate choice.

SITUATIONAL DETERMINANTS OF SEXUAL BEHAVIOR

Sex is everywhere—in billboard advertisements, on television, in movies, and in supermarket tabloids (Figure 12.20). Do these sexually charged images encourage sexual feelings and behaviors? Or do they give vent to our sexual desires and thereby decrease our sexual behavior?

Laboratory studies find that men typically report greater sexual arousal in response to sexually explicit materials than women do (Gardos & Mosher, 1999). However, this finding may in part reflect the fact that most sexually explicit materials are developed to appeal to men rather than to women. When researchers presented sexually explicit films that were chosen by women, there were no gender differences in response to the films (Janssen, Carpenter, & Graham, 2003).

Does this arousal actually encourage sexual behavior? Findings on this point have been mixed, but it appears that exposure to such material does, for at least a few hours, increase the likelihood of engaging in sexual behavior (Both, Spiering, Everaerd, & Laan, 2004). Much more concerning, however, have been findings from studies of the effects of sexually explicit material on sexual attitudes. In one study, Zillmann and Bryant (1988) found that viewing sexually explicit films made participants less satisfied with their partner's appearance and sexual performance. Far more troubling, films of women being sexually coerced increased male participants' willingness to harm women (Zillman, 1989). In short, then, pornography may have a small effect in encouraging sexual behavior, but it may have a larger effect on perceptions, and, worst of all, *violent* pornography has a more powerful effect in encouraging sexual aggression.

12.20 Sex in the media Many different media use sexually laden images, often in order to sell products.

MATE CHOICE

In most cultures in the modern world, both men and women are selective in choosing their sexual partners, and mating usually happens only when both partners consent. However, as we mentioned in Chapter 2, the sexes differ in the criteria they use in making their choices (Figure 12.21). According to a number of surveys, the physical attractiveness of the partner seems more important to men than to women, while the social and financial status of the partner matters more to women than it does to men. It also appears that men generally prefer younger women, whereas women prefer older men. The data also indicate that all of these male-female differences are found in many countries, including the United States, China, India, France, Nigeria, and Iran (D. M. Buss, 1989, 1992; D. M. Buss & Barnes, 1986).

How should we think about all of these points? In Chapter 2, we looked closely at the evolutionary account: An attractive woman is likely to be healthy and fertile, so a male selecting an attractive partner would increase his chances of reproductive success. Likewise, a younger woman will have more reproductive years ahead of her, so a male choosing a younger partner could plausibly look forward to more offspring. Any male selecting his mates based on their youth and beauty would be more likely than other males to have many healthy offspring to pass along his genes. Thus, through the

12.21 Mating tendencies Rather consistently, women prefer mates somewhat older than they are; men prefer mates who are younger. For men, mate selection is often influenced by the woman's appearance; for women, mate selection is often influenced by the status and resources of a potential partner.

process of natural selection these preferences eventually would become widespread among the males of our species.

The female's preferences are also sensible from an evolutionary perspective. Because of her high investment in each child (at the least, 9 months of carrying the baby in her womb, and then months of nursing), she can maximize the chance of passing along her genes to future generations by having just a few offspring and doing all she can to ensure the survival of each. A wealthy, high-status mate would help her reach this goal, because he would be able to provide the food and other resources their children need. Thus, there would be a reproductive advantage associated with a preference for such a male, and so a gradual evolution toward all females in the species having this preference (Bjorklund & Shackelford, 1999; Buss, 1992; Schmitt, 2005).

We also noted in Chapter 2 that cultural factors play an important role. For example, in many cultures human females only come to prefer wealthy, high-status males because the females have learned, across their lifetimes, the social and economic advantages they will gain from such a mate. In these cultures, women soon learn that their professional and educational opportunities are limited, and so "marrying wealth" is their best strategy for gathering resources for themselves and their young.

The importance of culture becomes clear when we consider cultures that provide more opportunities for women. In these cultures, "marrying wealth" is not a woman's only chance for economic and social security, so a potential husband's resources become correspondingly less important in mate selection. Various studies confirm this prediction and show that in cultures that afford women more opportunities, women attach less priority to a male's social and economic status (Kasser & Sharma, 1999; also see Baumeister & Vohs, 2004; Buller, 2005; Eagly & Wood, 1999; W. Wood & Eagly, 2002).

In short, there seems to be considerable consistency in mating preferences and a contrast between the criteria males and females typically use. This consistency has been documented in many cultures and across several generations. But there are also variations in mate-selection preferences that are clearly attributable to the cultural context. These data clearly illustrate the interplay of biological and cultural factors that governs our motivational and emotional states.

Sexual Orientation

So far in this chapter, we have touched upon many different physiological and social aspects of sexual behavior. However, up to this point, we have neglected one very important question: What determines our sexual orientation?

The roots of someone's sexuality are established well before adolescence. As early as age 3 or 4, children start to have feelings of attraction (Bell, Weinberg, & Hammersmith, 1981). The first real sexual attraction, however, usually begins by age 10 or so (Herdt & McClintock, 2000), and children of this age often imagine starstruck romances (R. Green, 1979; Zuger, 1984). These feelings soon crystallize, and, by early adolescence, with the onset of puberty and an increased emphasis on social relations outside the family, sexual orientation becomes explicit, and actions based on the orientation become common (Figure 12.22).

How common is each of the sexual orientations—heterosexual, homosexual, or bisexual? Years ago, Alfred Kinsey and his associates reported that more than 80% of American men describe themselves as exclusively heterosexual and 4% as exclusively homosexual

12.22 **Sexual orientation** Differences in sexual orientation are usually established early on, often well before adolescence.

(Kinsey, Pomeroy, & Martin, 1948). The prevalence of exclusive homosexuality reported by women was lower—about 2% (Kinsey, Pomeroy, Martin, & Gebhard, 1953). A substantially larger group (13% of American men and 7% of women) described themselves as predominantly homosexual but had also had some heterosexual experience. More recent surveys confirm Kinsey's estimates, both in the United States and in other Western cultures (see, for example, ACSF Investigators, 1992; A. M. Johnson, Wadsworth, Wellings, Bradshaw, & Field, 1992; for some complications, though, see Savin-Williams, 2006).

What makes a particular individual homosexual, heterosexual, or bisexual? There is clearly a genetic influence, because it turns out that if a man's identical twin is gay, then the chances that he will also be gay are 52%; if the gay twin is fraternal, the chances drop to 22% (Bailey & Pillard, 1991). Likewise, a woman's chance of having a homosexual orientation is 48% if she has a lesbian identical twin. If her gay twin is fraternal, the chances drop to 16% (Bailey, Pillard, Neale, & Agyei, 1993). Clearly, then, the greater the similarity in genetic makeup, the greater the likelihood of having the same sexual orientation, powerfully suggesting that one's genotype carries a predisposition toward heterosexuality or homosexuality.

But how do genes influence sexual orientation? The mechanism probably involves the levels of prenatal hormones, especially the male hormone androgen. Part of the evidence on this point comes from androgenized females—those who were exposed in the uterus to high androgen levels—who are far more likely than others to describe themselves as homosexual or bisexual (37%). In these women, the high androgen levels are produced by a specific genetic pattern, but the same hormonal patterns can be produced by many other factors. In all cases, these shifts in hormone levels during prenatal development seem to influence sexual orientation (Dittman, Kappes, & Kappes, 1992; Ellis & Ames, 1987; Hines, 2004; Zucker, 2001).

If genes were the whole story, though, then identical twins (with 100% of the same genes) would show 100% resemblance in their sexual orientation; instead, the concordance rate is just 52%. Obviously, therefore, factors other than the genes matter, but no one is yet sure what these other factors are. Many hypotheses have been offered, but most of these are plainly wrong. For example, there is no evidence that especially strong fathers, or especially weak fathers, are more likely to have homosexual offspring. There is also no evidence that homosexuality derives from some sort of imitation; children who grow up with gay or lesbian parents are no more likely to be homosexual themselves (M. Bailey & Zucker, 1995; Golombok & Tasker, 1996).

What we do know is that the main predictor of adult homosexuality is the way people felt about sexuality when they were younger. As we mentioned earlier, sexual orientation can be detected in middle childhood—and certainly before the individual experiences any sexual encounters, homosexual or heterosexual. Indeed, people of any sexual orientation might well identify with the sentiment voiced by many homosexuals when they report simply that "I've been that way all my life" (Saghir & Robins, 1973).

Overall, then, we still have much to learn about what makes someone homosexual, heterosexual, or bisexual. Genes are certainly relevant, but we are still figuring out what the rest of the story involves. Whatever the origins of sexual orientation, though, it bears emphasizing that a homosexual (or bisexual) orientation is not a psychological disorder or defect. These orientations are "abnormal" only in the limited sense of being different from the majority. Many other traits are "abnormal" in exactly the same sense—being left-handed, for example. Gays, lesbians, and bisexuals are neither better nor worse than heterosexuals, and the factors that matter for their relationship quality and stability seem to be exactly the same as those that matter for heterosexual couples

(Kurdek, 2005). Their number includes great painters (Leonardo da Vinci), athletes (Martina Navratilova), musicians (Aaron Copland), writers (Oscar Wilde, Gertrude Stein), mathematicians and scientists (Alan Turing, Alfred Kinsey himself), philosophers (Wittgenstein), and warriors (Alexander the Great), but the great majority are ordinary people with ordinary lives. The same no doubt holds for left-handers—and for heterosexuals.

MOTIVES BEYOND DRIVES

We can understand the motives we have considered so far principally in terms of drive-reduction. In each case, the motive involves some internal tension—feeling cold or hot, feeling hungry, feeling threatened, or feeling sexual needs—and the motivated behaviors help us reduce (or escape) the tension. But surely we are motivated not only to avoid *negative* experiences, but also to seek *positive* experiences. Consider the satisfaction of solving a difficult problem, the exhilaration of riding a roller coaster or dancing, or the ecstasy of fulfilled love. Plainly we value these kinds of experiences for their own sake. Likewise, people will get out of bed and walk out into the cold simply to enjoy a beautiful sunrise. People will also spend money to see a play or attend a rock concert. All of these activities are difficult to understand in terms of drive-reduction.

In this section, we broaden our consideration of motivational states, and consider motives that go beyond tension-reduction, and are about more than survival. Theorists have described many, many such motives (including motives that lead people to seek affiliation, achievement, autonomy, control, competence, power, self-esteem, and differentiation, among others), and here we will consider two major motives that govern our daily activities, namely, our motive to belong to groups and our motive to achieve.

The Motive to Belong

We all want to belong, to have friends, and to fit in (Leary & Cox, 2008). Indeed, we go to great lengths to seek out and maintain friendships, and we are upset when our relationships are severed. As we will see in Chapter 13, much of our mental lives are spent considering others' thoughts and feelings toward us.

Abraham Maslow (1968, 1996) was one of the early theorists who insisted that to understand what is truly human, psychologists must consider all our motives, and he recognized in particular the motive to belong as a powerful force in human behavior (Figure 12.23). Most psychologists agree. For example, Baumeister and Leary (1995) put it clearly when they said: "The need to belong is a powerful, fundamental, and extremely pervasive motivation" (p. 497). Thus, people may go without food to make themselves more attractive to others, and they may risk life and limb to impress others around them.

At least part of the need to belong can be understood as yet another form of drive-reduction: We do not want to be alone, or rejected, and so we take steps to avoid these experiences (Schultheiss, 2008). But it is crucial that the motive to belong also has a positive "approach-orientation," as we seek out the many benefits of being with others. This latter, more positive aspect of affiliation is evident, for example, in the fact that social interaction is a powerful predictor of positive emotion (Watson & Clark, 1994). In addition, a lack of meaningful

12.23 **Motive to belong** Other people are an important source of both pleasure and support, and the motive to belong powerfully shapes our interactions with others.

tangible support Social support focused on practical or material needs.

emotional support Social support focused on emotional needs.

social interaction predicts a range of negative psychological and physical health outcomes.

Indeed, social contact provides many benefits. For example, other people can provide **tangible support**, and, in fact, few of us would get by without practical help from many different people—whether it's borrowing money to do laundry or getting help proofreading an assignment. Others also provide **emotional support.** Sometimes this support is direct, as when a friend consoles us when we are sad or distracts us when we are angry; sometimes it is indirect, taking the form of the many emotional connections to others that give our lives texture and meaning. A third reason we seek out others is that how we feel about ourselves is powerfully shaped by how others view us. Indeed, some researchers have argued that self-esteem is an internal readout of how one is faring socially (Leary, Tambor, Terdal, & Downs, 1995).

The Motive to Achieve

Imagine that all of your social needs and all of your drive-based needs mentioned in this chapter were satisfied, and that you were warm, comfortable, safe, well-fed, and surrounded by people who love you. That probably sounds pretty wonderful indeed—but not perfect. What's missing? For most of us, even this peaceful state of affairs wouldn't be entirely fulfilling, because it wouldn't satisfy the motive to create, accomplish, and achieve.

Like the motive to belong, the motive to achieve has a dual aspect—part avoidance, part approach. Half a century ago, McClelland and colleagues suggested that achievement-related behavior can arise either from a fear of failure (avoidance) or from a desire for success (approach) (D. C. McClelland, Atkinson, Clark, & Lowell, 1953). One might think that these two aspects of the achievement motive would be tightly correlated, but they are in fact independent, and they operate differently. It is individuals with a desire for success—rather than a fear of failure—who seek out challenges and excel when the going gets difficult (D. C. McClelland, 1989).

Achievement motivation matters, and in studies of high-school and college students, Duckworth and Seligman (2005) found that achievement motivation was a powerful predictor of school performance. A similar picture emerges from studies of scholars, artists, and athletes who were at the top of their respective fields (B. S. Bloom, 1995). Talent matters, but achievement motivation also matters a great deal (Figure 12.24).

What factors give rise to a fear of failure or a desire for success (Koestner & McClelland, 1990)? Early researchers focused on parenting style, and found some evidence that caregivers who punish failure but take success for granted can instill a fear of failure. By contrast, caregivers can promote a more positive desire for success by rewarding achievement but not punishing failure. More recent research has focused on cognitive factors, such as whether a child adopts a **mastery orientation**, which is characterized by a focus on learning and improving, or a **performance orientation**, characterized by a focus on performing well in front of others in order to look smart, or on avoiding failure to keep from looking stupid (Dweck, 1999; 2006). Two decades of research suggest that a mastery orientation is associated with high levels of interest and a deep engagement with the material. When individuals with a mastery orientation encounter adversity (such as a bad grade), they are likely to increase their effort and seek out ways of benefiting from the experience. By contrast, when individuals with a performance orientation get negative feedback, they are more likely to withdraw effort and shift their focus elsewhere (Senko, Durik, & Harackiewicz, 2008).

12.24 Motive to achieve The motive to create, accomplish, and achieve affects both the challenges we undertake, and the degree to which we persist when difficulties arise.

mastery orientation A learning orientation characterized by a focus on gaining new knowledge or abilities and improving.

performance orientation A learning orientation characterized by a focus on presenting oneself well and appearing intelligent to others.

THE DIVERSITY OF MOTIVES

Some of the wide range of motives we have discussed are well described in drive terms. Other motives seem to have both a prominent avoidance (drive-reduction) component and an approach component. As this list of motives grows, however, one pressing question is how to organize the many motives that energize and direct our behavior.

Maslow and the Hierarchy of Needs

One approach was suggested by Maslow, who described a **hierarchy of needs** in which the lower-order physiological needs are at the bottom of the hierarchy, safety needs are further up, the need for belonging is still higher, and the desire for esteem is higher yet. Higher still, toward the top of the hierarchy, is the striving for **self-actualization**—the desire to realize oneself to the fullest (Figure 12.25).

Maslow believed that people will strive for higher-order needs (e.g., self-esteem or artistic achievement) only when lower-order needs (e.g., hunger) are satisfied. By and large this is plausible enough; the urge to write poetry generally takes a back seat if one has not eaten for days. But as Maslow pointed out, there are exceptions. Some artists starve rather than give up their poetry or their painting, and some martyrs proclaim their faith regardless of pain or suffering. But to the extent that Maslow's assumption holds, a motive toward the top of his hierarchy—such as the drive toward self-actualization—will become primary only when all other needs beneath it are satisfied.

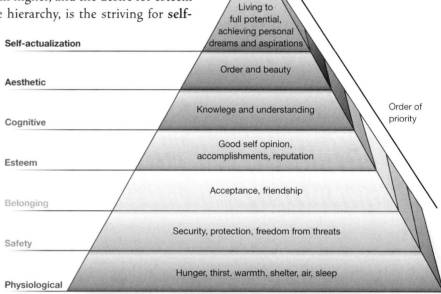

12.25 Maslow's hierarchy

The Twin Masters: Pain and Pleasure

A second approach to organizing our many motives, rather than listing them hierarchically as Maslow did, is to dig deeper and look for a few common principles that underlie our diverse motives. This approach leads us to consider the twin masters of pain and pleasure which may be said to govern much of our behavior.

THE AVOIDANCE OF PAIN

What do being too hot (or cold), being famished, being frightened, and being sexually frustrated have in common? We sometimes speak of each as involving its own type of *pain*, although this usage of the word might seem metaphorical. After all, we introduced the topic of pain in Chapter 4, in discussing a specific sensation typically associated with tissue injury or irritation. It turns out, though, that there is no metaphor here, and various states of discomfort do involve mechanisms overlapping with those associated with, say, stepping on a nail or bumping your head.

hierarchy of needs The theory that people will strive to meet their higher-order needs, such as love, self-esteem, and self-actualization, only when their lower, more basic needs like food and safety have been met.

self-actualization According to Abraham Maslow and some other adherents of the humanistic approach to personality, the full realization of one's potential.

12.26 Pain matrix Brain activations associated with (A) thermal stimulation (Farrell, Laird, & Egan, 2005) and (B) social exclusion (Eisenberger, Lieberman, & Williams, 2003). Although the source of the pain is quite different in these two situations, regions of the pain matrix are activated in each case.

■ Painful stimulation of left arm

■ Painful stimulation of right arm

■ Overlap (left and right)

pain matrix A distributed network of brain regions, including the thalamus and anterior cingulate cortex, thought to respond to many types of pain.

As we saw in Chapter 4, pain is a "general purpose" signal that all is not well. There are multiple pain pathways, including a fast pain pathway that detects localized pain and relays this information quickly via the thalamus to the cortex using thick, myelinated fibers, as well as a slow pain pathway that carries less localized sensations of burning or aching via the thalamus to subcortical brain structures such as the amygdala using thinner unmyelinated fibers. These pathways differ in important ways, but they both carry information that allows us to distinguish different types of painful stimulation, and an awareness of these differences is important, because this is what allows us to know what steps to take to decrease the pain we are feeling.

At the same time, researchers are beginning to appreciate that many different types of stimulation activate a common brain network, referred to as the **pain matrix.** The pain matrix consists of a distributed set of regions including the thalamus and the anterior cingulate cortex. The physical pain of accidentally touching a hot stove activates this matrix, but so does the psychological pain that comes with being socially snubbed, and this is what tells us that these various forms of discomfort really do have elements in common—both functionally and neurally. Figure 12.26 shows the similar brain activations associated with thermal stimulation (Panel A) as well as social exclusion (Panel B).

What's important here is to appreciate that pain in all of its forms has both a specific and a general motivational role. Some pain signals provide specific information about what is happening (there's a burning sensation in my right hand) and motivate a specific response (I need to move my hand away from the stove). Other pain signals alert us to different, broader kinds of problems, and suggest different types of responses, such as a departure from a socially awkward situation.

This overlap among very different types of "pain" is important for another reason. It provides a "common currency" in which to express a wide range of undesirable states. The function of this common currency becomes clear when we realize that many motives typically operate at a time, ranging from tight shoes to thirst to fatigue. In such settings, the generic aspect of pain allows us to decide which of these quite different states to attend to now and which can be handled later.

THE PURSUIT OF PLEASURE

Efforts to avoid or reduce painful states of tension govern many of our behaviors. However, as Maslow pointed out, reducing these states is not our only motive. We also have positive goals, and seek out pleasurable states.

Such states involve incentives, or positive goals that we seek to obtain. We therefore do not just feel "pushed" by an internal state of tension. Instead, the incentive seems to "pull" us in a certain direction. As we have seen in Chapter 7, though, these incentives come in different types. Some are an inherent part of the activity or object to which we are drawn (e.g., playing the guitar because the experience itself is *fun*). In such cases, the activity or object is said to be **intrinsically rewarding.** Other incentives, by contrast, are not an integral part of the activity or object to which we are drawn, but are instead artificially associated with it (e.g., getting paid for painting a picture). In this case, we say that the activity or object is **extrinsically rewarding.**

Historically, research on incentives has focused on external determinants of behavior—the specific rewards available to us and their influence on our behavior. It is becoming clear, however, that internal states of pleasure have a role in supporting incentives that parallels the role of the internal states of pain in supporting drives. This realization has directed researchers' attention to examining two different aspects of our responses to rewarding stimuli, namely, wanting and liking.

Wanting refers to the organism's motivation to obtain a reward and is measured by the amount of effort the organism will exert to obtain it. Because wanting is defined behaviorally, it can be assessed in any organism whose behavior we can measure. With rats, we can ask how many times they will press the bar to dispense a food pellet. In a similar fashion, we can see how hard people will work to obtain a reward: If you want brownies, do you want them badly enough to go through the trouble of making them? And if you don't have the ingredients, do you want brownies badly enough to first go shopping and then make them?

In contrast to wanting, **liking** refers to the pleasure that follows receiving the reward, like the pleasure deriving from the luscious taste of the warm brownies. We all know the sensation of liking, but unlike wanting, liking is difficult to define behaviorally. However, we can explore the neural basis of this experience. Research on this point dates back more than half a century to work by Olds and Milner, who electrically stimulated rats' brains in different regions. They found that stimulation in some regions led rats to engage in behaviors such as returning repeatedly to the location at which they were initially stimulated, seemingly in an attempt to repeat the stimulation. To understand this phenomenon, Olds and Milner made the brain stimulation contingent upon bar presses, and found that rats would bar press at very high rates for long periods of time, and to the exclusion of other activities, in order to obtain this stimulation (Figure 12.27). One particularly important spot for this effect—in rats and humans—appears to be the medial forebrain bundle, a nerve tract consisting of neurons with cell bodies in the midbrain which synapse in the **nucleus accumbens** (in the striatum).

Apparently, stimulation in this brain area is strongly rewarding—but *why?* Is this area involved in *wanting* or in *liking?* Modern neuroimaging research suggests an answer, and indicates that different brain regions are engaged by reward anticipation (wanting) and reward delivery (liking) (Schultz, Tremblay, & Hollerman, 2000). In particular, regions in the frontal cortex are activated by liking, whereas the nucleus accumbens is especially sensitive to wanting. In one of the first studies to demonstrate this dissociation in humans, Knutson and colleagues used fMRI during a task in which participants were shown various types of cues and were asked to respond to a target (Knutson, Fong, Adams, Varner, & Hommer, 2001). If participants responded quickly enough, they were able to win one dollar, and target presentation was adjusted for each individual so that each participant succeeded approximately two-thirds of the time. As shown in Figure 12.28, the period of anticipation and wanting was associated with greater activation in the nucleus accumbens, whereas the period of liking the reward was associated with activation in the frontal cortex. These activation patterns suggest that the processes of *wanting* and *liking* have separate bases in the brain.

Additional evidence that wanting and liking depend on separable brain systems comes from studies of the neurotransmitters that underlie reward processing. When

intrinsically rewarding An activity or object that is pursued for its own sake.

extrinsically rewarding An activity or object that is pursued because of rewards that are not an inherent part of the activity or object.

wanting An organism's motivation to obtain a reward.

liking The pleasure that follows receipt of a reward.

nucleus accumbens A dopamine-rich area in the forebrain that is critical in the physiology of reward.

12.27 Bar pressing for pleasure When rats receive brain stimulation for bar pressing, they press at high rates for long periods of time.

Method

1. On each trial, participants were shown one of three colored squares. Yellow signaled a reward was possible and blue signaled no reward was possible. Red indicated no response was required on that trial.

2. They then fixated on a cross-hair for various amounts of time (the reward anticipation period) until the target (a white square) appeared. On response trials, they were supposed to press a button as fast as possible when they saw the target.

Reward possible   No reward possible   No response needed

3. Participants who responded quickly after seeing a square were awarded $1 (the reward delivery period).

4. Target presentation was adjusted so that each participant won the reward two-thirds of the time.

5. At the same time, researchers monitored their responses with fMRI.

Results

The reward anticipation period (wanting) was associated with greater activation in the nucleus accumbens, whereas the reward delivery period was associated with greater activation in the frontal cortex.

Anticipation period   *Reward period*

CONCLUSION: The nucleus accumbens is sensitive to anticipating a reward (wanting), whereas areas in the frontal cortex are activated by getting a reward (liking).

SOURCE STUDY: Knutson et al., 2001

animals are trained to bar press for a reward, their neurons release dopamine into the nucleus accumbens neurons during anticipation but not during receipt of reward (Phillips et al., 2003). When dopamine antagonists are introduced, which interfere with the effects of dopamine, the animals will continue to engage in incentive-driven behavior for a time, but they will not work to receive rewards that are not present (Berridge & Robinson, 2003). These and other findings suggest that dopamine release plays a central role in wanting. Complementary studies have examined the neurotransmitters that are responsible for liking. These studies suggest that endorphins are released into the nucleus accumbens when rewards are delivered. When endorphin antagonists are administered (in humans), these appear to diminish the subjective pleasure associated with consuming the rewards (Yeomans & Gray, 1996).

EMOTION AND EMOTION REGULATION

So far, we've explored a number of different motives. However, we have left to the side one of the most important forces that energizes and directs our behavior, namely, our emotions. After all, when an event makes us happy, we are likely to seek out similar events in the future. When an event makes us afraid, we are motivated to leave the event and avoid it in the future. Before concluding our tour of the wellsprings of human behavior, therefore, we must consider what emotions are and how they influence us.

The Many Facets of Emotion

emotions Affective responses (such as joy, sadness, pride, and anger), which are characterized by loosely linked changes in behavior (how we act), subjective experience (how we feel), and physiology (how our bodies respond).

We experience **emotions** such as happiness, fear, sadness, pride, and anger when we consider our situation (either real or imagined) to be relevant to our active personal goals (Scherer, Schorr, & Johnstone, 2001). Some goals that make a situation meaningful are of long-term concern, such as wanting to be liked. Other goals may be more fleeting, such as hoping to get the last slice of cake, or rooting for the underdog in a football match.

Whatever the goal may be, once we've evaluated a situation as being personally relevant, three types of changes are evident that, taken together, characterize emotion. These changes affect our behavior (how we act), our subjective experience (how we feel), and our physiology (how various systems in the body are functioning) (Mauss, Levenson, McCarter, Wilhelm, & Gross, 2005). We can identify similar changes in the states we call **moods,** but psychologists distinguish emotions from moods in several ways. For one, emotions typically have a clear object or target (e.g., we are happy about something, or mad at someone); moods do not. Emotions are also usually briefer than moods, lasting seconds or minutes rather than hours or days.

moods Affective responses that are typically longer-lasting than emotions, and less likely to have a specific object.

BEHAVIORAL ASPECTS OF EMOTION

Some of our bodily responses to emotion are quite general, such as a broad pattern of approaching with interest in response to emotionally positive stimuli, or a general withdrawal in response to emotionally negative stimuli. Perhaps the most prominent behaviors associated with emotion, however, are our facial behaviors—our smiles, frowns, laughs, gapes, grimaces, and snarls.

Charles Darwin hypothesized that our facial expressions of emotion are actually vestiges of our ancestors' basic adaptive patterns (1872b). He argued, for example, that our "anger" face, often expressed by lowered brows, widened eyes, and open mouth with exposed teeth, reflects the facial movements our ancestors would have made when biting an opponent. Similarly, our "disgust" face, often manifested as a wrinkled nose and protruded lower lip and tongue, reflects the way our ancestors responded to foul odors or spit out foods. (For elaborations, see Ekman, 1980, 1984; Izard, 1977; Tomkins, 1963.)

In support of this position, Darwin noted that our facial expressions resemble many of the displays made by monkeys and apes, as we discussed in Chapter 2. Darwin also believed that the expressions would be identical among humans worldwide, even "those who have associated but little with Europeans" (Darwin, 1872b, p. 15). This point, too, can be confirmed—for example, in observations (also mentioned in Chapter 2) of children born blind, who nonetheless express emotions using the typical, recognizable set of facial expressions despite the fact that they could not have learned these expressions through imitation (see, for example, Eibl-Eibesfeldt, 1970; Galati, Scherer, & Ricci-Bitti, 1997; Goodenough, 1932).

A different test of this universality claim involves comparisons between cultures (Russell, 1994; Tracy & Robins, 2008), but only a tiny number of studies have used the participants most crucial for this test: members of relatively isolated non-Western cultures (Ekman, 1973; Ekman & Oster, 1979; Fridlund, Ekman, & Oster, 1983; Izard, 1971). Why is this group crucial? If research participants, no matter where they live, have been exposed to Western movies or television, their responses might indicate only the impact of these media and thus provide no proof of the universality claim. Therefore, we need participants who have not seen reruns of Western soap operas, or Hollywood movies, or a slew of Western advertising.

In one of the few studies of this critical group, American actors were photographed showing expressions that conveyed emotions such as happiness, sadness, anger, and fear. These photographs were then shown to members of various modern literate cultures (Swedes, Japanese, Kenyans) and to members of an isolated nonliterate New Guinea tribe. All participants who saw the photos were asked to pick the emotion label that

Method

1. American actors were photographed showing expressions of happiness, sadness, suprise, disgust, anger, and fear.

2. These photographs were then shown to members of various modern cultures and members of an isolated nonliterate New Guinea tribe.

3. All participants were asked to pick the emotion label that matched each photograph.

4. The procedure was reversed. New Guinea tribesmen were photographed portraying facial expressions associated with the same six emotions, and American college students were asked to pick the emotion label for each photograph.

Happiness   *Disgust*

Results

All participants, including those in relatively isolated cultures, identified the expressions reasonably well, but they accurately recognized some emotions (e.g., happiness) more consistently than others (e.g., fear).

CONCLUSION: The meaning of these basic emotional expressions transcends cultural and geographic boundaries.

SOURCE STUDY: Ekman & Friesen, 1975

12.30 Display rules Researchers found that when American and Japanese participants watched surgical film clips privately, they displayed similar facial expressions. When they watched the clips in the presence of the researcher, however, the Japanese participants displayed more positive emotion than the Americans.

display rules Cultural rules that govern the expression of emotion.

matched each photograph. In other cases, the procedure was reversed. For example, the New Guinea tribesmen were photographed portraying the facial expressions that they considered appropriate to various situations, such as happiness at the return of a friend, grief at the death of a child, and anger at the start of a fight (Figure 12.29). American college students then looked at the photographs and judged which situation the tribesmen in each photo had been asked to convey (Ekman & Friesen, 1975).

In these studies, all the participants, including those in relatively isolated cultures, did reasonably well. They were able to supply the appropriate emotion label for the photographs, or to describe a situation that might have elicited the expression shown in the photograph. But they were more successful at recognizing some expressions than at recognizing others. In Chapter 2, we highlighted the biological roots of smiling, and, in fact, these were, in this study, generally matched with "happy" terms and situations, with remarkable levels of consistency (Ekman, 1994; Izard, 1994; see also Russell, 1994). Other emotions, such as disgust, were less well recognized, but still identified at levels well above chance, suggesting that the meaning of emotional expressions transcends cultural and geographic boundaries.

Let us note, though, that even though the *perception* of emotions may be similar in all cultures, the *display* of emotions is surely not. A widely cited example comes from research in which American and Japanese participants were presented with harrowing surgical films (Figure 12.30). Participants first watched the films privately (i.e., with no one in the room with them), but their facial expressions were recorded by a hidden camera. The facial reactions of Americans and Japanese were virtually identical. But when the participants then watched one of the films again while being interviewed by an experimenter, the results were quite different. In this context, the Japanese showed more positive emotion than the Americans showed (Ekman, 1972; Friesen, 1972). Thus, when in public, participants' facial expressions were governed by the **display rules** set by their culture—deeply ingrained conventions, often obeyed without awareness, that govern the facial expressions considered appropriate in particular contexts (Ekman & Friesen, 1969; Ekman, Friesen, & O'Sullivan, 1988).

Of course, display rules are not limited to a person's reactions to a gruesome film. Other studies have extended the analysis of display rules in contexts as diverse as participating in sports (H. S. Friedman & Miller-Herringer, 1991) and receiving presents one does not like (P. M. Cole, 1985). Research has also explored the way in which individuals differ in their knowledge of display rules (Matsumoto, Yoo, & Nakagawa, 2008). These differences include variation not only from one person to the next, but also between the genders. For example, women in Western cultures are more likely to express their emotions than men are, particularly emotions such as sadness (Brody & Hall, 2000; Kring & Gordon, 1998).

EXPERIENTIAL ASPECTS OF EMOTION

Along with changes in our behavior, emotion also involves changes in how we feel. Indeed, emotional experience has long been the essence of poetry, literature, and other forms of artistic expression that are all replete with expressions of undying love, mortal hatred, and unquenchable sadness. How can we study these fleeting and complex feelings hidden inside the mind (Barrett, Mesquita, Ochsner, & Gross, 2007)?

Here, as elsewhere, scientists begin by seeking a proper *classification scheme,* and one proposal has focused on defining specific categories of emotions (see, for example, R. S. Lazarus, 1991). One problem with this approach, though, lies in defining exactly what the categories are. Common language gives few clues. There are over 550 emotion words in English (Averill, 1975), and many more in other languages that cannot be translated readily into English. However, as Phillip Shaver and his colleagues have shown, people typically use emotion words in ways that reveal a relatively small number of "clusters," which are defined by words with similar meanings (Shaver, Schwartz, Kirson, & O'Connor, 1987). As in Figure 12.31, one cluster involves words associated with love, another involves words associated with joy, and other clusters describe anger, sadness, and fear.

An alternative approach describes emotions in terms of *dimensions* rather than categories: "more this" or "less that" rather than "this type" versus "that type." There are various ways in which we might define these dimensions, but one relies simply on how pleasant or unpleasant the emotion feels, and then how activated the person feels when in the midst of the emotion (Barrett, 1998; Larsen & Diener, 1992; Russell, 1980, 1983); these two axes can be used to create a circle within which all the various intermixtures of the dimensions can be described, as in Figure 12.32.

Either of these categorization schemes can help us figure out how emotions relate to one another—which are similar, which are sharply distinct. But neither scheme really tells us what the emotions really *feel like,* and so neither scheme answers questions about individual or cultural differences in emotional experience. Does your happiness feel the same as mine? When someone in Paris feels *triste,* is that person's feeling the same as the feeling of someone in London who feels sad, or someone in Germany who feels *traurig*?

For that matter, how should we think about cultures that have markedly different terms for describing their emotions? The people who live on the Pacific Island of Ifalik lack a word for "surprise," and the Tahitians lack a word for "sadness." Likewise, other cultures have words that describe common emotions for which we have no special

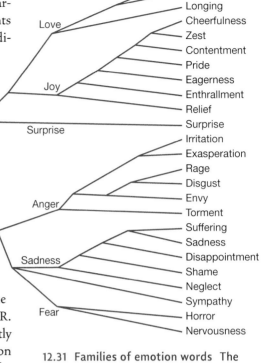

12.31 Families of emotion words The words people use to describe their emotional experiences cluster into small groups of similar words.

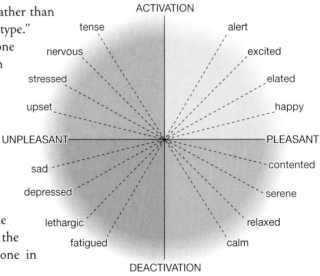

12.32 Dimensions of emotional experience The two major dimensions of emotional experience are pleasantness and activation.

12.33 Culturally defined emotions
(A) The Japanese word *amae* refers to a desire to be dependent and cared for.
(B) The German word *Schadenfreude* refers to the pleasure derived from another person's misfortune.

James-Lange theory of emotion
The theory that the subjective experience of emotion is the awareness of one's own bodily reactions in the presence of certain arousing stimuli.

Cannon-Bard theory of emotion
The theory that a stimulus elicits an emotion by triggering a particular response in the brain (in the thalamus) which then causes both the physiological changes associated with the emotion and the emotional experience itself.

terms. The Ifaluk sometimes feel an emotion they call *fago*, which involves a complex mixture of compassion, love, and sadness experienced in relationships in which one person is dependent on the other (Lutz, 1986, 1988). And the Japanese report a common emotion called *amae*, which is a desire to be dependent and cared for (Doi, 1973; Morsbach & Tyler, 1986). The German language reserves the word *Schadenfreude* for the special pleasure derived from another's misfortune. Do people in these cultures experience emotions that we do not (Figure 12.33)? Or are emotional experiences common across cultures, despite the variations in cultures' labels for emotional experiences? On these difficult questions, the jury is still out.

PHYSIOLOGICAL ASPECTS OF EMOTION

When we respond emotionally, it is often a whole body affair, and the bodily reactions associated with different emotions certainly *feel* different from one another (Levenson, 1994). That is, not only do the emotions differ in how they feel inside our "head," but they also seem to differ in how they feel in the rest of the body. The sick stomach and wrinkled nose of disgust, for example, feel decidedly different from the squared shoulders and puffed chest of pride. And anger's hot head and coiled muscles seem opposite fear's cold feet and faint heart.

From a common-sense perspective, it seems that emotions arise when we encounter a significant stimulus, and this encounter leads to bodily changes that differ by emotion (Figure 12.34A). Interestingly, this sequence of events was turned on its head by one of the first emotion theories in the field, namely, William James's theory that different emotions provoke different patterns of physiological response (James, 1884). According to the **James-Lange theory of emotion** (Carl Lange was a European contemporary of James's who offered a similar account), the reason emotions feel different from one another subjectively is that we sense the different physiological patterns produced by each emotion. Specifically, this view holds that emotion begins when we perceive a situation of an appropriate sort—we see the bear or hear the insult. But our perception of these events is, as James put it, "purely cognitive in form, pale, colorless, destitute of emotional warmth" (1890, vol. 2, p. 450). What turns this perception into genuine emotion is our awareness of the bodily changes produced by the arousing stimuli. These changes might consist of skeletal movements (running) or visceral reactions (pounding heartbeat), but only when we detect the biological changes do we move from cold appraisal to emotional feeling, from mere assessment to genuine affect (Figure 12.34B). Moreover, the claim is that the *specific character* of the biological changes is crucial—so that we feel fear because we are experiencing the pattern of bodily changes associated with fear; we feel happiness because of its pattern of changes in the body, and so on.

Subsequent theories, however, made quite different predictions about the degree of physiological patterning we should expect in emotion. For example, Walter Cannon, whom we met earlier in the chapter as a pioneer in the study of the "fight or flight" response, believed that our physiological responses are quite general (W. B. Cannon, 1927). According to the **Cannon-Bard theory of emotion** (Philip Bard was a contemporary of Cannon's who espoused a similar view), it's not easy to distinguish the bodily changes associated with different emotions, so that the bodily changes associated with anger are actually rather similar to the changes associated with happy excitement (Figure 12.34C).

(A) Commonsense

"I tremble because I feel afraid"

Stimulus → FEAR Experience → Arousal

(B) James-Lange

"I feel afraid because I tremble"

Stimulus → Arousal → FEAR Experience

(C) Cannon-Bard

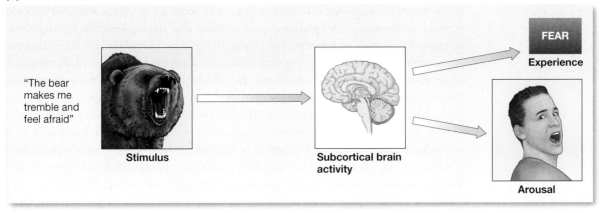

"The bear makes me tremble and feel afraid"

Stimulus → Subcortical brain activity → FEAR Experience / Arousal

(D) Schachter-Singer

"I label my trembling as fear because I appraise the situation as dangerous"

Stimulus → Arousal → "That is one scary bear! I'm afraid of it!" Appraisal → FEAR Experience

12.34 Emotion models

Cannon's view gained support from early studies in which participants received injections of epinephrine, which triggered broad sympathetic activation with all its consequences—nervousness, palpitations, flushing, tremors, and sweaty palms. These biological effects are similar to those that accompany fear and rage, and so, according to the James-Lange theory, people detecting these effects in their bodies

Schachter-Singer theory of emotion
The theory that emotional experience results from the interpretation of bodily responses in the context of situational cues.

confederate Someone who appears to be a research participant but actually is part of the research team.

affective neuroscience A field that uses cognitive neuroscience research methods to study emotion and related processes.

should experience these emotions. But that was not the case. Some of the participants who received the injections simply reported the physical symptoms. Others said they felt "as if" they were angry or afraid, a kind of "cold emotion," not the real thing (Landis & Hunt, 1932; Marañon, 1924). Apparently, the visceral reactions induced by the stimulant were by themselves not sufficient to produce emotional experience.

Even so, there is an obvious challenge to the Cannon-Bard theory. If different emotions produce comparable physiological responses, then why do we have the subjective impression that our bodies are doing quite different things in different emotional states? This question was addressed by the **Schachter-Singer theory of emotion** (Figure 12.34D). According to this theory, behavior and physiology are (as James proposed) crucial for emotional experience. James was wrong, though, in claiming that the mere perception of these bodily changes is sufficient to produce emotional experience. That is because, in addition, emotion depends on a person's judgments about *why* her body and physiology have changed (Schachter & Singer, 1962).

In a classic study supporting this theory, participants were injected with a drug that they believed was a vitamin supplement but really was the stimulant epinephrine. After the drug was administered, participants sat in the waiting room for what they thought was to be a test of their vision. In the waiting room with them was a **confederate** of the experimenter (someone who appeared to be another research participant but was actually part of the research team). In one condition the confederate acted irritable, made angry remarks, and eventually stormed out of the room. In another condition he acted exuberant, throwing paper planes out the window and playing basketball with balled-up paper. Of course, his behavior was all part of the experiment; the vision test that the participants were expecting never took place (Schachter & Singer, 1962). Participants exposed to the euphoric confederate reported feeling happy, and, to a lesser degree, participants exposed to the angry confederate reported that they felt angry. Although this study has come under criticism (G. D. Marshall & Zimbardo, 1979; Mezzacappa, Katkin, & Palmer, 1999; Reisenzein, 1983), it remains influential because it is a reminder that bodily arousal only partially determines the emotion that is experienced.

Over the past 50 years, researchers have tried to clarify how the body responds during emotional experiences. One of the most interesting conclusions from this research is that our perceptions of bodily differences among the emotions may in some cases be illusions, compelling experiences that are not well grounded in reality (Cacioppo, Berntson, & Klein, 1992). It seems, therefore, that the various emotions are surprisingly similar if we examine the body's response "from the neck down."

Even so, the emotions are distinguishable biologically—in the pattern of *brain activation* associated with each emotion. Evidence on this point comes from studies in the field of **affective neuroscience** (R. J. Davidson & Sutton, 1995; Panksepp, 1991, 1998), whose proponents argue that emotions arise not in one, but in multiple neural circuits. Some brain regions are activated in virtually all emotions (Murphy, Nimmo-Smith, & Lawrence, 2003; Phan, Wager, Taylor, & Liberzon, 2002)—for example, the medial prefrontal cortex. One likely possibility is that this section of the brain plays a general role in attention and meaning analysis related to emotion. Other brain regions, however, seem to be related to specific emotions. For example, fear is often associated with activation of the amygdala, and sadness is often associated with activation of the cingulate cortex just below the corpus callosum (although activation in these brain regions is not specific to these emotions; see Barrett & Wager, 2006). Many researchers are convinced that brain data like these will eventually allow us to determine the extent to which different emotions have different physiological profiles.

The Functions of Emotion

As we have seen, emotions consist of coordinated changes in behavior, experience, and physiology. Why is this? Is it possible that these interwoven effects were somehow useful to our ancestors, and so favored by evolution (Tooby & Cosmides, 1990)? One way to pursue this issue is to look at the consequences of emotion and to ask whether they benefit us.

Some aspects of our emotions plainly do help us—or, perhaps, helped our ancient ancestors. Fear, for example, is associated with sympathetic nervous system activity that prepares large muscles for fighting or fleeing (Frijda, 1986); these are exactly the bodily adjustments we would want for fending off (or escaping) a fearful encounter. Likewise, consider joy. In one study, participants had to prepare a speech that they believed would be videotaped and evaluated by judges (Fredrickson et al., 2000). Following this stressful task, the participants were randomly assigned to view a film clip that elicited joy, a neutral film clip, or a film clip that elicited sadness. The data showed that participants who had viewed the joy clip showed substantially greater cardiovascular recovery from their speech than did participants who had watched either the neutral or the sad clip. This finding seems to suggest that joy (and other positive emotions) can help us recover from stress.

In addition to these physiological effects, emotions also involve a variety of changes in how we perceive and think about the environment around us. Perceptual effects of fear include an increased intake of sensory information including widening of the eyes and greater nasal volume, while disgust involves a decreased sensory intake, including narrowing of the eyes and decreased nasal volume (Susskind et al., 2008; Figure 12.35). Emotions affect later information processing, too. Positive emotions like joy seem to lead us to greater cognitive flexibility and a broader focus, relying less on the details of a situation and more on top-down, schematic processing (Fredrickson, 1998). Negative emotions, in contrast, seem to focus our attention more narrowly—on specific aspects of a situation. Why should this be? Anger, for example, may focus our attention on the obstacle preventing us from reaching our goal; this may be exactly the right focus if we want to remove that obstacle in some way. Fear, in contrast, may focus our attention on the likely outcomes of a situation; again, this may be the right focus if we want to maximize our motivation to avoid this outcome (L. J. Levine & Pizarro, 2004; Phelps, 2006).

Emotions also have a powerful effect on memory, as we mentioned in the Prologue, and this brings its own benefits. Emotional events are likely to be consequential ones, involving great opportunities, for example, or powerful threats. We would be well served, therefore, by remembering these events well, and emotion

(A) **(B)**

12.35 **Perceptual effects of emotion** (A) Fear involves an increased intake of sensory information, whereas (B) disgust involves a decreased intake of sensory information (Susskind et al., 2008).

seems to promote this recollection. Several mechanisms probably contribute to this point, including the changes in our body chemistry that accompany emotion and activation of the amygdala, a common feature of several emotions. These mechanisms may together promote the process of memory *consolidation*, the biological process through which memories are established in permanent storage (T. W. Buchanan & Adolphs, 2004; Dolcos, LaBar, & Cabeza, 2006; Kilpatrick & Cahill, 2003; McGaugh, 2003; Reisberg & Hertel, 2004).

Emotions also serve interpersonal functions. One example is the way expressions of emotion indicate social intent (Fridlund, 1994). When we smile, for example, we signal that we are open to interacting with other people. When we scowl, we communicate "Back off!" When we burst into tears, we indicate that we need help (J. J. Gross, Fredrickson, & Levenson, 1994). Another example is the way emotion expressions facilitate group functioning. When we show embarrassment, we indicate to others that we know we have done something inappropriate (Keltner & Buswell, 1997). This signal has the effect of making amends for the gaffe. At the same time, embarrassment is a highly aversive state, and feels in the moment like a real calamity. The function of embarrassment may therefore be not only to repair social damage, but also to motivate us to avoid the same behavior in the future. Even expressions of pride—at least when they are appropriate to one's performance—are associated with leadership in group problem-solving (L. A. Williams & DeSteno, 2008).

Emotion Regulation

Plainly, then, emotions have many functions—preparing the body for action, directing our attention, facilitating social interactions, and more (Levenson, 1999). But emotions can hurt us, too, if they happen at the wrong time or at the wrong intensity level. Indeed, inappropriate emotional responses are involved in many forms of psychopathology (Gross & Levenson, 1997; see also Chapter 16) and even many forms of physical illness (Baum & Posluszny, 1999).

For all these reasons, humans need to experience their emotions, but they also sometimes need to regulate their emotions. **Emotion regulation** means influencing which emotions we have, when we have them, and how we experience or express them (J. J. Gross, 1998b, 2007). Emotion regulation may involve decreasing, increasing, or simply maintaining experiential, behavioral, or physiological aspects of emotion, depending on our goals. The most common forms of emotion regulation, though, involve efforts at decreasing the experience or behavior associated with anxiety, sadness, and anger (J. J. Gross, Richards, & John, 2006).

emotion regulation The ability to influence one's emotions.

cognitive reappraisal A form of emotion regulation in which an individual changes her emotional response to a situation by altering her interpretation of that situation.

suppression A form of emotion regulation that involves inhibiting emotion-expressive behavior.

TWO FORMS OF EMOTION REGULATION

Two forms of emotion regulation have received the most attention (J. J. Gross, 2001). The first is called **cognitive reappraisal,** which occurs when someone tries to decrease her emotional response by changing the meaning a situation has. For example, instead of thinking of a job interview as a matter of life or death, a person might think about the interview as a chance to learn more about the company, to see whether it would be fun to work there. The second kind of emotion regulation is called **suppression,** which occurs when someone tries to decrease the emotion he shows on his face or in his behavior. For example, instead of bursting into tears upon receiving disappointing news, a person might bite his lip and put on a brave face.

While both strategies can decrease emotional behavior, reappraisal seems to be a more effective way to regulate emotions. In part, this is because someone who suppresses an emotional reaction might block the display of emotion but does not make the feelings go away (J. J. Gross & Levenson, 1997). In fact, physiologically, suppression leads to even greater sympathetic nervous system activation, presumably because the individual must exert herself to keep her emotions from showing (J. J. Gross, 1998a). There is also a cognitive cost to suppression. When participants in an experiment were asked about material that had been presented while they were trying to suppress their emotions, they made more errors than they did when they had not been suppressing their emotions (Richards & Gross, 2000). Indeed, when asked to suppress their emotions, participants performed as badly on later memory tasks as participants who had been encouraged not to pay attention at all to the material that was being presented (Richards & Gross, 2006).

In contrast, reappraisal can make one feel better, and it does not have cognitive or physiological costs (J. J. Gross, 1998a). In one study, researchers showed participants neutral or negative emotion-eliciting slides during an fMRI study (Ochsner et al., 2004; Figure 12.36). In the critical conditions, participants were asked either to view the negative emotion-eliciting slides or to reappraise them by altering their meaning. For example, a participant might see a picture of women crying in front of a church. Instead of thinking of a funeral scene, the participant might try to think of it as a wedding scene that brought the woman to tears of joy. The reappraisal had many effects. Participants reported feeling less negative emotion when reappraising than they did when just watching the negative slides. Reappraisal also activated the prefrontal regions in the brain, which are associated with other kinds of self-regulation, and decreased activation in the amygdala and other brain regions associated with negative emotion.

The key message from these studies is that different forms of emotion regulation have quite different consequences. This is not to say one should always reappraise or never suppress. Both processes have their place. But it is becoming clear that compared with keeping a stiff upper lip by means of suppression, reappraisal is generally more adaptive.

12.36 The neural bases of reappraisal Results from a functional magnetic resonance imaging study in which participants were asked to use reappraisal to change their emotional responses to negative emotion-eliciting slides. Findings indicated that reappraisal was associated with increased activation in the (A) dorsolateral and (B) ventrolateral prefrontal cortex as well as the (C) dorsomedial prefrontal cortex.

THE DEVELOPMENT OF EMOTION REGULATION

How do the emotion regulation skills that are so necessary in adulthood develop? We know that children respond emotionally from an early age. From birth, babies cry when they are distressed and cease crying when they are comforted. Newborns and young infants also display facial responses when they are interested, distressed, disgusted, or contented (Izard et al., 1995; Figure 12.37). Smiles appear—to parents' delight—a bit

12.37 Facial displays of emotion Starting at an early age, infants produce facial expressions that resemble adult expressions.

later. Fleeting smiles are visible in 1-month-old infants; smiles directed toward other people appear when most infants are 2 or 3 months old. Fear arrives later still. The first clear signs of fear typically emerge only when the child is 6 or 7 months old (Witherington, Campos, & Hertenstein, 2001).

Of course, very young infants show little ability to control their emotions, and so it is up to the caregiver to soothe, distract, or reassure them. Soon, though, infants start showing the rudiments of regulation, so that 6-month-olds, for example, are likely to turn their bodies away from unpleasant stimuli (Mangelsdorf, Shapiro, & Marzolf, 1995). By their first birthday, infants regulate their feelings by rocking themselves, or chewing on objects, or clinging tightly to some beloved toy or blanket.

Children also begin to use display rules—and so begin expressing their emotions in a socially acceptable way—at an early age, so that, for example, 11-month-old American infants are more expressive of their feelings than Chinese babies (Freedman & Freedman, 1969). However, their self-control is limited at this early age, and clear adherence to display rules is usually not evident until the child is age 3 or so (Lewis, Stanger, & Sullivan, 1989)—and even then, children's attempts at disguising their emotions are often unsuccessful. It is clear, though, that children learn relatively early the value of managing one's expressions—sometimes to gain the response one wants from others, sometimes to protect others, and sometimes to deceive them (Vrij, 2002).

The real progress in emotion regulation, however, comes later, when the child is age 4 or 5. By that age, children seem to understand, for example, that they can diminish their fear by fleeing from, or removing, the scary object; they learn that they can diminish their sadness by seeking out an adult's aid or by reassuring self-talk (Harris, Guz, Lipian, & Man-Shu, 1985; Lagattuta, Wellman, & Flavell, 1997). These early skills are limited, but gradually grow and strengthen. Where do these skills come from?

Part of the answer lies in the child's conversational experience, because children's efforts in emotion regulation are influenced by the examples they have observed and the instructions they have received (R. A. Thompson, 1994, 1998). In fact, these conversations convey a range of strategies to children, including distraction ("Try thinking of something happy"), compensation ("Why don't we get ice cream after the appointment with the doctor?"), and reappraisal ("Dumbledore didn't really die; it's just pretend"). Conversations with children about emotion also convey when emotions should or should not be expressed, and the consequences of expressing or not expressing them (Eisenberg, Cumberland, & Spinrad, 1998).

SOME FINAL THOUGHTS: THE "WHY" OF BEHAVIOR

In this chapter, we have considered a number of crucial motives. However, there are countless others besides these. For example, we sometimes feel an urge to drink a cup of coffee. Or feel like reading a book, texting a friend, meditating, or taking a nap. Over the decades, researchers have tried to categorize motives in different ways. Some have arranged them hierarchically. Others have sought to identify the biological bases of the pain and pleasure responses that form part of many different motives. Each approach has its merits, and in this chapter, we have drawn several broad distinctions among motivational states. For one, we have distinguished the drive-based motives, such as thermoregulation, hunger, aggression, and sex, from the non-drive-based motives, such as the motive to belong and the motive to achieve.

Whereas drives can be described in terms of restoring homeostasis and avoiding painful states of tension, such concepts are less satisfactory descriptions of non-drive-based motives.

Emotions, though distinct from motives, share some of their important characteristics. Like other motivational states, emotions are biologically based responses that have been shaped by a long evolutionary history, and given particular form both by an organism's learning history and by its present circumstances. Motives and emotions also both involve a change in the organism's readiness to respond in particular ways, and this change in readiness often is felt as motives and emotions play themselves out. One way that motives and emotions differ, however, is that motivational states are often tied more specifically to particular classes of stimuli than are emotions. Thus, one is typically hungry for food, and perhaps even food of a specific type. By contrast, one can feel anger about almost anything—the weather, the fact that one doesn't have a date this weekend, economic disparities among nations, or a roommate's goofy taste in music.

Whether we're considering drive-based motives, non-drive-based motives, or emotions, what is important is that these motivational states are at play continually, and arise both because of external stimuli and by virtue of our thoughts. It is rare that only one motive is active. Instead, many motives cooperate to shape our thoughts, feelings, and behaviors. We must consider physiological, cultural, and cognitive factors to understand how even the most basic motives energize and direct our behavior. Even so, motives do not dictate our behavior. Instead, they make "suggestions" that carry varying degrees of weight. This means that we can regulate the motivational states that coordinate our responses to many kinds of situations. This regulation may take place in many different ways, and as we have seen—at least for the emotions—different approaches to self-regulation can have very different consequences.

SUMMARY CHAPTER 12

MOTIVATIONAL STATES

- When explaining why people and other animals do what they do, early theorists emphasized genetically endowed instincts. Other theorists have emphasized homeostatic mechanisms that monitor the organism's internal environment and work to maintain stability in that environment. Deviations from *homeostasis* create an internal state of biological and psychological tension called a *drive*.

THERMOREGULATION

- Homeostatic control is evident in many settings, including *thermoregulation*. When an endothermic organism is cold, thermoregulation activates the sympathetic branch of the autonomic nervous system, which leads to increased heart rate, vasodilation, a slowing down of digestion, and other

effects. When the organism is overheated, thermoregulation triggers the parasympathetic branch of the autonomic nervous system, which has the opposite effects.

HUNGER, EATING, AND OBESITY

- Homeostatic mechanisms also play a crucial role in the control of eating. Each person seems to have a biologically determined *set point* for his or her weight, and several mechanisms work to maintain that set point. Some of these mechanisms are in the liver; others depend on *glucoreceptors* in the hypothalamus; still others rely on signals from the adipose cells. When full of fat, these cells release *leptin*, a chemical that causes the organism to stop eating.

- This multiplicity of signals provides safety for the organism, because each signal provides a "backup" system in case the other signals fail. In addition, the various signals play different roles, with some monitoring long-term needs, some providing an index of immediate status, and some serving to potentiate other signals. Social signals also play an important role in governing eating.

- Some cases of obesity are produced by genetically rooted differences in a person's set point; other cases involve changes in metabolic efficiency. Obesity in some people may represent the operation of "thrifty genes" that code for slower metabolism. These genes were helpful in ancient times when food was scarce, but the same genes now promote unhealthy weights, thanks to the fact that we live in a world in which food is usually always available.

THREAT AND AGGRESSION

- Our response to threat is controlled by biological mechanisms centered on the operations of the autonomic nervous system. When we are threatened, the sympathetic branch activates the body by (among other steps) increasing the available metabolic fuel and accelerating the fuel's utilization by increasing heart rate and respiration. This emergency reaction was once understood as preparing us for "fight or flight," but actually it gets us ready for a number of different responses.

- Virtually every species shows some sort of aggression, and in most species, physical aggression is more prevalent in males, perhaps because of the influence of the hormone *testosterone*. Human aggression is commonly triggered by complex beliefs and symbol systems, and, in this regard, it seems different from aggression in other species. Humans vary in how aggressive they are, with some of the variation due to an individual's personality, and some due to the social and cultural setting.

SEXUAL BEHAVIOR

- Like all motivated behavior, sexual behavior is shaped by a mix of biological factors and cultural influences. The timing of sexual behavior, for example, is heavily influenced in most species by the estrus cycle, but the influence of this cycle is much less for humans than for other animals.

- The *human sexual response cycle* has four phases: excitement, plateau, orgasm, and resolution.

- A wide range of factors influence sexual behavior, and there appear to be widespread differences between the genders in the factors that govern mate preference. Men typically place greater emphasis on youth and physical attractiveness, whereas women place greater emphasis on social and financial status.

- Sexual preferences are rooted in childhood. One important determinant of sexual preference is genetic makeup. While it is clear that other factors shape sexual preferences, it is not clear what these nongenetic factors are or how they operate.

MOTIVES BEYOND DRIVES

- Whereas drives motivate us to reduce unpleasant tension states, other motives lead us to achieve positive goals.

- One nondrive motive is the motive to belong. Benefits of social support include *tangible* and *emotional* support. Another important nondrive motive is the *motive to achieve*.

THE DIVERSITY OF MOTIVES

- According to Abraham Maslow's *hierarchy of needs*, people strive for higher-order needs only when lower-order needs are satisfied.

- Many different types of aversive stimulation activate a common brain network called the *pain matrix*. Positive goals that we seek to obtain are called *incentives*. Two important incentive states are *wanting* and *liking*.

EMOTION AND EMOTION REGULATION

- Emotions involve changes in our behavior, including our facial behavior. The expression of emotion in the face may be universal (i.e., the same across cultures), although cultures certainly differ in their *display rules*.

- Emotions also involve changes in how we feel, and theorists have offered various schemes for classifying these feelings. People in different cultures certainly describe emotions in different ways. Whether people in difficult cultures all feel the same emotions, however, remains a matter for debate.

- Our bodily state changes when we are emotional. According to the *James-Lange theory*, emotions arise from our bodily reactions. The *Cannon-Bard theory* proposes that both emotion *and* the bodily reaction are caused by brain activity triggered by a suitable stimulus. According to the *Schachter-Singer theory*, emotion arises from the way we interpret our bodily reactions. Current evidence suggests there may be fewer distinctions than we might expect among emotions in the bodily changes produced. There are, however, changes in the brain that distinguish the various emotions, and this is a topic scrutinized by *affective neuroscience*.

- Emotions serve many purposes. For example, joy can help us recover from stress and can broaden our attentional focus. Negative emotions, in contrast, seem to focus attention. Emotion also promotes memory, perhaps because the bodily arousal promotes memory consolidation. Emotions also serve a social function, helping to convey our feelings to other people.

- It is often important to regulate our emotions—either by means of *cognitive reappraisal* or by means of *suppression*. Both decrease the emotional expression, but reappraisal seems to dampen emotion without exacting a cognitive or physiological cost. The ability to regulate emotions develops over the course of childhood.

 ONLINE STUDY TOOLS

Go to StudySpace, **wwnorton.com/studyspace**, to access additional review and enrichment materials, including the following resources for each chapter:

Organize
- Study Plan
- Chapter Outline
- Quiz+ Assessment

Learn
- Ebook
- Chapter Review
- Vocabulary Flashcards
- Drag-and-Drop Labeling Exercises
- Audio Podcast Chapter Overview

Connect
- Critical Thinking Activity
- Studying the Mind Video Podcasts
- Video Exercises
- Animations
- **ZAPS** Psychology Labs

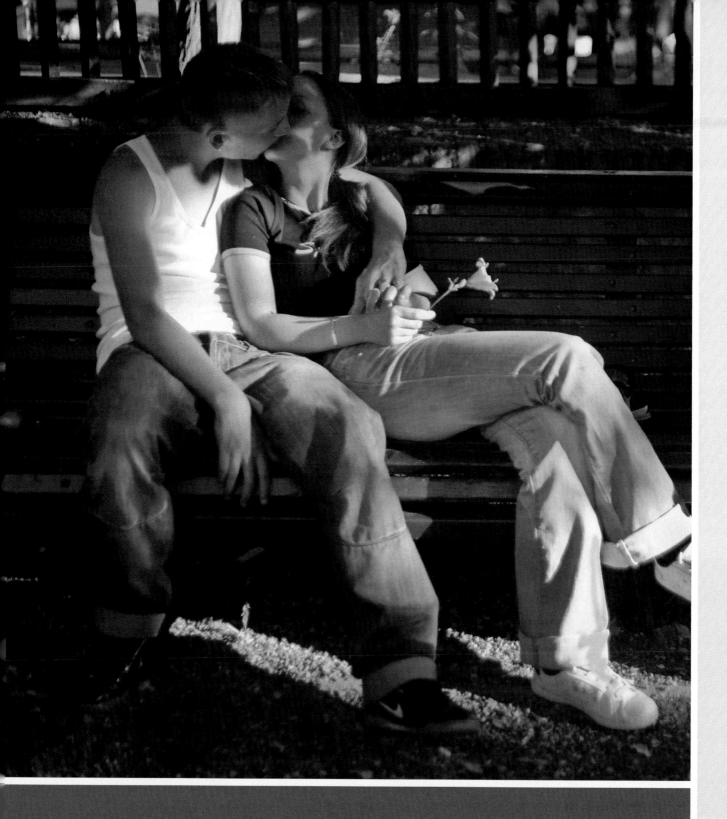

13

Social Psychology

Leaning over the corpse of Manadel al-Jamadi, U.S. Army specialist Sabrina Harman flashes a thumbs-up and a smile. Were it not for the dead body in the photograph, you might focus on how pretty she looks. But blood dribbles from beneath Jamadi's bandages, his bluish jaw is locked, and ice surrounds his torso. Something very wrong has happened here.

A few months after this picture was taken at Iraq's Abu Ghraib prison, the world learned that indeed many wrongs had happened here. U.S. military police and CIA interrogators killed Jamadi in November 2003 while interrogating him at the prison. Other photographs revealed that U.S. soldiers and personnel routinely tortured, humiliated, and sexually abused dozens of other prisoners—many of whom were not guilty of any crime.

Following investigations, 12 soldiers, including Harman, were tried, convicted, sentenced to federal prison, and dishonorably discharged from the military. Several years have passed since the Abu Ghraib atrocities were revealed, but people are still asking, Why did these seemingly normal soldiers behave so cruelly?

The easy answer is that these soldiers were just evil, or "bad apples," as some American leaders suggested. But despite their photographed smiles, many soldiers were bewildered by their own behavior. "I can't handle what's going on. . . . What if it was me in their shoes?" wrote Harman in a letter home, which was later excerpted in an article in the *New Yorker*. Moreover, all the soldiers had passed the Army's psychiatric evaluation, suggesting that at least when they enlisted, they were psychologically "normal."

And so we look to the situation: Working in a wartime prison, with substandard food and water, they were members of a large group of similarly trained, young soldiers surrounded by enemies. Many were part-time reservists who joined the military to earn money for college. In their hasty training, many had not learned about the international laws protecting prisoners of war. In the ambiguous and often frightening situation of Abu Ghraib, they looked to their leaders to show them the way. And like good soldiers, they did what they were told. "I was just following orders" was their common defense, echoing so many soldiers judged war criminals in the past. As the *New Yorker* article points out, by taking pictures of the prisoners the Abu Ghraib guards "demonstrated two things: that they never fully accepted what was happening as normal, and that they assumed they had nothing to hide."

In this chapter, you will learn about the many subtle reasons that ordinary people perform acts of extraordinary evil—as well as extraordinary good. As it turns out, the common thread that connects these explanations is that most human behavior is triggered in part by other people.

As you will also see, much of our everyday cognition resembles the work of social psychologists. We all try to figure out why people behave as they do—an activity called attribution. Like so much of our psychology, attribution is strongly shaped by culture. Just as America's leaders gave internal explanations for the Abu Ghraib guards' actions, Americans and Western Europeans generally explain behavior in terms of internal, individual factors like personality, moral goodness, psychiatric status, and mental state. Meanwhile, much of the rest of the world tends to look outside the individual—to situations, environments, relationships, and histories—for clues to account for people's actions.

Perhaps because of our cultural tendency to look inside people to explain their actions, Americans and Western Europeans are often wary of social influences. Yet there is no such thing as an isolated individual, free of context and immune to others' influences. Humans are hardy, long-lived, and widespread precisely because we form social connections and cultural bonds that help us make sense of our environments. This social nature is not just a source of bias and wrongdoing, as it was at Abu Ghraib; it is also the root of our strength, as individuals and as a species. To understand both our social vulnerabilities and our social prowess, we must consider how people think about, influence, and relate to one another. These topics will be our focus in this chapter.

SOCIAL COGNITION

As members of a social species, we humans are exquisitely attuned to each other. Many of our everyday behaviors—what we eat, how we dress, what kind of music we like, and how we think about current events—are shaped by the people around us. Even when we are not directly mingling with other people, we are often thinking about them, making plans involving them, and maybe even fantasizing about them—not to mention obeying (or breaking) their laws, using their products, reading their books, watching their television shows, and speaking their languages. In other words, most of our thoughts, feelings, and behaviors are shaped by the social world—often without us even noticing.

We don't respond to all these influences in a mechanical or reflexive fashion, however. Instead, our responses to the social world depend to an enormous extent on how we *interpret* others' behaviors and how others interpret ours. This is evident in the fact that if Mary smiles at you, your reaction will be quite different if you think she was flirting as opposed to merely being polite. If the salesman recommends the Macintosh rather than the Dell, your purchase may depend on whether you believe the salesman is sincere or, for that matter, knowledgeable. In these cases and most others, how we respond to other people depends on how we think about and interpret their actions. This crucial process of interpreting and thinking about the social world is referred to as *social cognition.*

Attribution

People everywhere spend a lot of time and energy observing the people around them and asking, "Why did she (or he) do that?" Social psychologists call the process of answering this question **causal attribution,** and the study of how people form attributions is one of social psychology's central concerns (see, for example, F. Heider, 1958; E. E. Jones, & Nisbett, 1972; H. H. Kelley, 1967; H. H. Kelley & Michela, 1980). As we saw in Chapters 4, 5, 8, and 9, thinking about the world often requires us to go beyond the information we are actually given. We interpret the visual images on our retinas, for example, by using top-down knowledge to supplement what we see. We draw inferences from the observations we make, to reach broader conclusions about the world. As we will see, similar intellectual activity is essential in the social domain.

> **causal attribution** An inference about what caused a person's behavior.
>
> **situational attributions** Attributions that explain someone's behavior in terms of the circumstances rather than aspects of the person.
>
> **dispositional attributions** Attributions that explain someone's behavior in terms of factors internal to the person, such as traits or preferences.

ATTRIBUTION AS LAY SCIENCE

People make attributions in roughly the same way that scientists track down the causes of physical events (H. H. Kelley, 1967). For a scientist, an effect (such as an increase in gas pressure) is attributed to a particular condition (such as a rise in temperature) if the effect occurs when the condition is present but does not occur when the condition is absent. In other words, the scientist needs to know whether the cause and the effect covary. According to social psychologist Harold Kelley, when people try to explain the behavior of others, they use a similar covariation principle.

This means that, to answer the question "Why did Mary smile at me?" we have to consider when Mary smiles. Does she smile consistently whenever you walk into the room? Does she refrain from smiling when others arrive? If the answer to both of these questions is yes, then her smile does covary with your arrival, and so is probably best understood as a result of her feelings about you. If it turns out, though, that Mary smiles just as broadly when greeting others, then we have to come up with a different explanation (F. Heider, 1958; H. H. Kelley, 1967).

Causal attributions can be divided into two broad types—those that focus on factors external to the person (e.g., Mary smiled because the situation demanded that she be polite) and those that focus on the person herself (e.g., Mary smiled because she is friendly). Explanations of the first type are called **situational attributions** and involve factors such as other people's expectations, the presence of rewards or punishments, or even the weather. Explanations of the second type, **dispositional attributions,** focus on factors that are internal to the person, such as traits, preferences, and other personal qualities (Figure 13.1).

13.1 Challenges to attribution In deciding why someone is behaving as he is, we need to decide whether his behavior is shaped primarily by the circumstances or primarily by who he is. Did Al Franken play an outrageous character on *Saturday Night Live* because that is what he is really like or because that is the sort of behavior appropriate for (and elicited by) a late-night comedy show? Does his behavior in this context tell us anything about how he will act as an elected official?

individualistic cultures Cultures in which people are considered fundamentally independent and which value standing out by achieving private goals.

collectivistic cultures Cultures in which people are considered fundamentally interdependent and which emphasize obligations within one's family and immediate community.

CULTURE AND ATTRIBUTION

How do people choose attributions for the behaviors they observe? Kelley's proposal was that people are sensitive to the evidence they encounter, just as a scientist would be, and draw their conclusions according to this evidence. It turns out, however, that this is not quite right, because people have strong biases in the way they interpret the behavior of others, biases that can sometimes lead them to overrule the evidence. These biases come from many sources, including the culture in which someone lives.

Every person is a part of many cultures—those defined by race, nationality, and ethnicity, and also those defined by gender, socioeconomic status, sexual preference, urbanicity (e.g., city dwelling or rural dwelling), economy (e.g., agricultural or industrial), and historical cohort (e.g., baby boomer or gen Xer). This diversity means that cultures differ on many dimensions, but there is reason to believe that one dimension is especially important—whether a culture is more individualistic or more collectivistic (Triandis, 1989, 1994).

As the name suggests, **individualistic cultures** cater to the rights, needs, and preferences of the individual. The majority cultures (e.g., middle-class, of European heritage) of the United States, western Europe, Canada, and Australia are individualistic (Figure 13.2). In these cultures, people tend to view themselves and others as independent entities—that is, as fundamentally separate from others and their environment. They also generally think that people behave according to their internal thoughts, feelings, needs, and preferences (A. P. Fiske, Kitayama, Markus, & Nisbett, 1998; Markus & Kitayama, 1991), and not according to outside influences, such as other people's expectations or the demands of a situation. To emphasize their independence and distinctiveness, people in individualistic cultures often strive to stand out by achieving personal goals. They still feel obligated to their families and communities, but regularly override these social obligations in order to pursue their own paths.

Collectivistic cultures, on the other hand, stress the importance of maintaining the norms, standards, and traditions of families and other social groups. Most of the world's cultures are collectivistic, including many of those of Latin America, Asia, and Africa. In collectivistic cultures, people tend to view themselves and others as interdependent—that is, as fundamentally connected to the people in their immediate community and to their environment. They usually think that people behave according to the demands of a situation or the expectations of others, and not according to their personal preferences or proclivities. People still have their own dreams, desires, and life plans, of course, but they are more likely to create those plans according to the wishes and expectations of others, and to change them when the situation demands.

13.2 **Individualistic and collectivistic cultures** Members of individualistic cultures (A) tend to view themselves and others as independent and seek to stand out by achieving personal goals. Members of collectivistic cultures (B) tend to view themselves and others as interdependent and seek to behave in accordance with situational demands and the expectations of others.

It bears emphasizing that not everyone in collectivistic cultures has an interdependent notion of the person, just as not everyone in individualistic cultures has an independent notion. Instead, these terms describe what is typical, as well as what each culture's traditions, laws, religions, schools, and media encourage.

THE FUNDAMENTAL ATTRIBUTION ERROR

These differences among cultures influence us in many ways—including the ways we think about other people's behavior. In particular, people from individualistic cultures routinely ascribe others' behavior to dispositions and not to situations—even when there is ample reason to believe that situations are playing a crucial role (Figure 13.3). Thus North Americans of European heritage tend to see people on public assistance as lazy (a dispositional attribution), for example, rather than struggling in an economy with high unemployment and few entry-level positions (a situational attribution). Likewise, members of these cultures tend to view poor performance on a test as a sign of low intelligence (disposition) rather than as a result of an overly difficult exam (situation). This bias is so pervasive that it is called the **fundamental attribution error** (D. T. Gilbert & Malone, 1995; L. Ross, 1977; Sabini, Siepmann, & Stein, 2001).

To dramatize this error, one early study had American college students participate in a simulated TV quiz show. Students were run in pairs and drew cards to decide who would be the "quizmaster" and who the "contestant." The quizmaster had to make up questions, drawn from any area in which she had some expertise; the contestant had to try to answer these questions. The game then proceeded, and, inevitably, some of the quizmasters' questions were extremely difficult (e.g., "What do the initials *W. H.* stand for in the poet W. H. Auden's name?").* A student audience watched and subsequently rated how knowledgeable the two participants were.

The situation plainly favored the quizmasters, who could choose any question or topic they wished. Hence, if a quizmaster had knowledge of just one obscure topic, he could focus all his questions on that topic, without revealing that he had little knowledge in other domains. The contestants, on the other hand, were at the mercy of whatever questions their quizmaster posed. Any interpretation of the quizmasters' "superiority" should take this obvious situational advantage into account. But the

"Otis, shout at that man to pull himself together."

13.3 **Fundamental attribution error**

> **fundamental attribution error** The tendency to attribute behaviors to a person's internal qualities while underestimating situational influences.

---

*The answer, by the way, is Wystan Hugh.

observers consistently failed to do this. They knew that the roles in the setting—who was quizmaster, who was contestant—had been determined by chance, for they had witnessed the entire procedure. Even so, they could not help regarding the quizmasters as more knowledgeable than the contestants—a tribute to the power of the fundamental attribution error (L. Ross, Amabile, & Steinmetz, 1977).

The pattern of attributions is quite different, though, in collectivistic cultures. In one study, Hindu Indians and European Americans were asked to discuss vignettes about other people's actions. Consistent with other research, the European Americans' comments included twice as many dispositional explanations as situational explanations. The Hindu Indians showed the opposite pattern. They gave twice as many situational explanations as dispositional explanations. As an illustration, one of the vignettes used in the study described an accident in which the back wheel of a motorcycle burst, throwing the passenger off the motorcycle, and the driver had done little to help the hurt passenger. Overall, the Americans typically described the driver as "obviously irresponsible" or "in a state of shock," whereas the Indians typically explained that it was the driver's duty to be at work or that the other person's injury must not have looked serious (J. G. Miller, 1984; see also A. P. Fiske et al., 1998; Maass, Karasawa, Politi, & Suga, 2006; P. B. Smith & Bond, 1993).

Person Perception

When we make causal attributions, we go beyond the information available to our senses in order to make sense of a particular action—why someone smiled, or did well on a test, or didn't help more after an accident. The role of social cognition—and our tendency to supplement what we perceive—is just as important when we try to make sense of another person—that is, whenever we ask ourselves, "What kind of person is she?"

IMPLICIT THEORIES OF PERSONALITY

Imagine that a friend says her sister Marie is especially outgoing. Or say that you see Marie at several parties, and each time she's the center of attention. In either case, you're likely to draw some inferences from what you hear about Marie or how you see her behaving—but in the process, you may lose track of which bits of information are based directly on what you've heard or seen and which bits are merely your interpretation. Thus, if you hear that Marie is outgoing, you may also remember (falsely) that your friend said she loves crowds, even though that was never mentioned (N. Cantor & Mischel, 1979; Dweck, Chiu, & Hong, 1995).

In this way, social cognition works much like other kinds of cognition. Our knowledge of the world is a blend of our own observations and the inferences we have made using our *schematic knowledge*—knowledge about the world in general. In the social domain, these schemas are called **implicit theories of personality** (Bruner & Tagiuri, 1954; D. J. Schneider, 1973), and we use them to make inferences about what a person is really like and how she is likely to behave in the future. We all hold these informal theories, and they bring together a cluster of beliefs, linking one trait (such as extraversion) to others (such as loving crowds) but also linking these traits to specific behaviors—so that we have expectations for what sort of husband the extravert will be, what sorts of sports he is likely to enjoy, and more.

These implicit theories are another point on which cultures differ (Church et al., 2006). People in individualistic cultures tend to understand the self as being stable

implicit theories of personality Beliefs about what kinds of behaviors are associated with particular traits and which traits usually go together; used to develop expectations about people's behavior.

across time and situations and so are more likely to go beyond the information given and make global judgments about others' personalities. People in collectivistic cultures, where the self is understood as changing according to relationships and situations, tend to view personality as malleable. They therefore tend to make more cautious and more limited generalizations about other people's personalities (Hong, Chiu, & Dweck, 1997).

STEREOTYPES

Implicit theories of personality—like schemas in any other domain—are enormously helpful. Thanks to these schemas, we do not have to scrutinize every aspect of every situation we encounter, because we can fill in any information we are missing by drawing on our schematic knowledge. Likewise, if our current information about a person is limited (perhaps because we only met her briefly), we can still make reasonable assumptions about her based on what we know about people in general. Though these steps make our social perception quick and efficient and generally lead us to valid inferences, they do leave us vulnerable to error, so that our perception (or recollection) of another person sometimes ends up more in line with our preconceptions than with the facts. In many cases this is a small price to pay for the benefits of using schemas, and for that matter, the errors produced are often easily corrected. But schemas can also lead to more serious errors.

The hazard of schematic thinking is particularly clear in the case of social **stereotypes,** schemas about the characteristics of whole groups that lead us to talk about Greeks, Jews, or African Americans (or women, the elderly, or liberals and conservatives) as if we know all of them and they are all the same (Figure 13.4). These stereotypes are, on their own, worrisome enough, because they can lead us to make serious errors of judgment about the different people we meet. Worse, stereotypes can lead to deeper problems, including (at the extreme) wars, genocides, and "ethnic cleansings." These larger calamities, however, are not fueled by stereotypes alone. They arise from **prejudice,** which can be defined as a negative attitude toward another person based on his group membership. Prejudice consists of three factors sometimes referred to as the ABCs of prejudice: an *affective* (emotional) component, which leads us to view the other group as "bad"; a *behavioral* component, which includes our tendencies to discriminate against other groups; and a *cognitive* component (the stereotype itself). Prejudice can lead to extreme cruelties and injustices, making the study of intergroup bias in general, and stereotypes and prejudice in particular, a topic of some urgency.

ORIGINS AND MEASUREMENT OF STEREOTYPES

Whether stereotypes are negative or positive, they often have deep historical roots and are transmitted to each new generation both explicitly ("Never trust a…") and implicitly (via jokes, caricatures, portrayals in movies, and the like). Thus, in Western cultures, we hear over and over about athletic blacks, academic Asians, moody women, and lazy Latinos, and, like it or not, these associations eventually sink in and are likely to affect our behavior—regardless of whether we believe that the association has any factual basis.

Other factors also foster the creation and maintenance of stereotypes. Consider, for example, the fact that most of us have a lot of exposure to people in our own group, and as a result, we have ample opportunity to see that the group is diverse and made up of unique individuals. We generally have less exposure to other groups, and so, with little

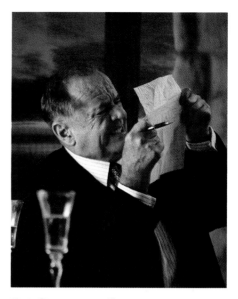

13.4 Stereotypes Stereotypes are schemas about the characteristics of whole groups. One example is the stereotype about older people, which holds that they can't read fine print as easily as younger adults.

stereotypes Schemas that are often negative and are used to categorize complex groups of people.

prejudice A negative attitude toward another person based on that person's group membership.

out-group homogeneity effect
The tendency for a member of a group (the in-group) to view members of another group (the out-group) as "all alike" or less varied than members of his or her own group.

opportunity for learning, we are likely to perceive the group as merely a mass of more or less similar people. This so-called **out-group homogeneity effect** is reflected in such statements as "All Asians are alike" or "All Germans are alike." The first statement is almost invariably made by a non-Asian; the second, by a non-German.

Just a few decades ago, many people did not hesitate to make derogatory comments in public settings about blacks, or women, or Jews. This made studying stereotypes relatively straightforward, in that researchers could use *explicit measures*, which involve some form of self-report, to assess negative stereotypes about groups of individuals.

The times have changed, however, and stereotyping has become much less socially acceptable in most quarters of life. As a result, people are now much less likely to endorse explicitly racist or sexist statements than they were in the recent past. Does this mean stereotypes no longer matter? Unfortunately not. Stereotypes still influence people's behavior, but the effects are quite subtle, often happening automatically, outside our awareness (Bargh, Chen, & Burrows, 1996; but see also Cesario, Plaks, & Higgins, 2006).

To assess these less overt stereotypes, researchers have begun to use *implicit measures*. For example, some researchers have measured brain responses to stereotype-relevant stimuli (Ito, Willadsen-Jensen, & Correll, 2007) or response times to stereotype-related questions (Fazio, 1995). These implicit measures allow us to detect biases that people might prefer to keep hidden. They also allow us to observe biases that people don't even realize they have—biases that, in fact, conflict with the person's explicit (conscious) beliefs. Thus, people who explicitly hold egalitarian views may still have assumptions about various outgroup members, unconsciously believing, for example, that African Americans are more likely than whites to be criminals, or that Hispanics are more hot-tempered than non-Hispanics (Blair & Banaji, 1996; Chen & Bargh, 1997; Kawakami, Dion, & Dovidio, 1998; Wittenbrink, Judd, & Park, 1997). In fact, this conflict between conscious beliefs and unconscious assumptions and associations seems to occur relatively often, thanks to the fact that our implicit and explicit views are shaped by different influences, and so can sometimes contradict each other (e.g., Nosek, 2007; Rydell, McConnell, Mackie, & Strain, 2006).

Another commonly used means of detecting implicit assumptions and associations is the Implicit Association Test (IAT; Greenwald et al., 2002; Greenwald, McGhee, & Schwartz, 1998; Grenwald, Nosek, & Banaji, 2003).* In the classic version of the IAT, people are asked to make two types of judgments: whether a face they see on the computer screen is that of a black person or a white person, and whether a word they see on the screen is a "good" word (e.g., *love, joy, honest, truth*) or a "bad" word (e.g., *poison, agony, detest, terrible*). This seems simple enough, but the trick here is that the trials with faces (black or white) are intermixed with the trials with words (good or bad), and participants must use the same two keys on the computer for both judgments. Thus, in one condition, participants must use one key to indicate "black" if a black face is shown and the same key to indicate "good" if a good word is shown; a different key is used for "white" (for face trials) and "bad" (for word trials). In another condition, things are arranged differently: Now participants use one key to indicate "black" and "bad" (for faces and words, respectively) and the other key to indicate "white" and "good."

This experiment assesses how easily the participants can manage each of these links. Do they have an easier time putting "white" and "good" together (and so using the same key to indicate both) than putting "white" and "bad" together? It turns out that the first combination is easier for white research participants—and for many African American participants as well (Figure 13.5). This seems to suggest that the participants arrive at the experiment already primed to associate each race with a certain evaluation

---

*To try the IAT yourself, see: https://implict.harvard.edu/implicit.

Method

1. On each trial, non-black participants were briefly shown a picture of one of two kinds of faces (white or black) followed by a picture of one of two kinds of objects (tools or weapons).

2. Participants were instructed to ignore the face stimuli and to press one button if the stimulus was a weapon, and a different button if the stimulus was a tool.

Trial 1   Trial 2   Trial 3

Results

Participants identified guns quickly after seeing a black face, and they identified tools faster after seeing a white face.

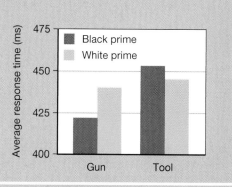

CONCLUSION: Non-black participants have different implicit associations with blacks than with whites.

SOURCE STUDY: Payne, 2001

and respond more slowly when the experiment requires them to break that association (see, for example, W. A. Cunningham, Preacher, & Banaji, 2001; Greenwald et al., 2002; Greenwald et al., 1998; B. K. Payne, 2001).

THE EFFECTS OF STEREOTYPES

Whether implicit or explicit, stereotypes have multiple effects. They influence what we believe about other people and how we act toward them. Perhaps worst of all, stereotypes influence how the targets of our stereotypes act—so that, specifically, the stereotype leads members of the targeted group to behave in a way that confirms the stereotype. In this way, stereotypes create **self-fulfilling prophecies.**

In a classic demonstration, Rosenthal and Jacobson (1968) told a group of elementary-school teachers that some of their students were "bloomers" and could be expected to show substantial increases in IQ in the year ahead. Although these "bloomers" were randomly chosen, they in fact showed substantial increases in their test scores over the course of the next year, an effect apparently produced by the teachers' expectations. Several factors probably contributed to this effect, including the greater warmth and encouragement the teachers offered, the individualized feedback they provided, and the increased number of opportunities they gave the children they expected would do well (M. J. Harris & Rosenthal, 1985; for a cautionary note about the reliability of these effects, see Jussim & Harber, 2005; R. Rosenthal, 1991, 2002; H. H. Spitz, 1999).

How does this finding apply to stereotypes? Here, too, it turns out that people are heavily influenced by others' expectations—even when we are considering expectations for a *group,* rather than expectations for an individual. As we saw in Chapter 11, this influence is plainly visible in the way that *stereotype threat* influences performance on tests designed to measure intellectual ability. In one study, for example, experimenters gave intelligence tests to African American students. Before taking the test, half of the students were led to think briefly about their race; the other half were not. The result showed—remarkably—that the students who thought about their race did less well on

self-fulfilling prophecies Beliefs about how a person will behave that actually make the expected behavior more likely.

the test (Steele, 1998). In other studies, women have been given math tests, and just before the test, half have been led to think briefly about their gender. This reminder leads the women to do more poorly on the test (Shih, Pittinsky, & Ambady, 1999).

What's going on in these studies? These reminders about group membership lead the test takers to think about the stereotypes for their group—that African Americans are unintelligent, or that women can't do math—and this makes the test takers anxious. They know that others expect them to do poorly, and they know that if they do not perform well, they will just confirm the stereotype. These fears distract the test takers, consume cognitive resources, and undermine their performance—so that the stereotype ends up confirming itself (Johns, Inzlicht, & Schmader, 2008). In addition, the test takers may fear that the stereotype is to some extent correct, and this fear may lead the test takers to lower their expectations and not try as hard. This, too, would undermine performance, which in turn would confirm the ugly stereotype.

Attitudes

attitude A fairly stable evaluation of something as good or bad that makes a person think, feel, or behave positively or negatively about some person, group, or social issue.

As we have now seen, our relations with the people who surround us depend to a large extent on our *beliefs*. These beliefs include our assumptions about how others' behavior should be interpreted, and our beliefs about how the various attributes in someone's personality fit together, and also our beliefs about Jews, or African Americans, or the Irish. Moreover, these beliefs are not just "cold" cognitions—dispassionate assertions about the world. Instead, they are often "hot," in the sense that they have motivational components and can trigger (and be triggered by) various emotions. Psychologists refer to these beliefs as **attitudes**.

People have attitudes about topics as diverse as the death penalty, abortion, bilingual education, the importance of environmental protection, and need for civility in everyday social interaction (Eagly & Chaiken, 1993). The belief that defines each attitude is almost inevitably associated with emotional feelings and a predisposition to act in accordance with the belief and feelings. Thus, people who differ in their attitudes on abortion are certain to have different beliefs about the moral status of this procedure, but also will have different feelings about the family planning clinic they pass every day, and different levels of commitment to showing up at a rally protesting their state's abortion laws (Figure 13.6).

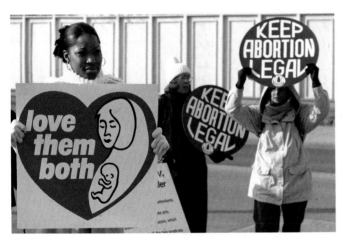

13.6 Attitudes Attitudes are beliefs that are often highly emotionally charged.

ATTITUDE FORMATION

How do attitudes arise? Some of our attitudes are based on our consideration of the facts. We carefully weigh the pros and cons of an argument and make up our minds about whether we should endorse the argument's conclusion or not. In many other cases, however, the sources of our attitudes are not quite so rational.

Sometimes we acquire our attitudes through one of the forms of learning we considered in Chapter 7. In some cases, the learning is akin to *classical conditioning*. For example, we might repeatedly see a brand of cigarettes paired with an appealing person or a cool cartoon character and wind up associating the two, leaving us with a positive attitude toward that brand of cigarettes (Figure 13.7; Cacioppo, Marshall-Goodell, Tassinary, & Petty, 1992). In other cases, attitudes can be formed via a process akin to *operant conditioning*, when, for example, parents reward behavior they would like to encourage, such as hard work at school and good table manners. The end result of this training, in many cases, is a favorable attitude toward certain work habits and certain forms of etiquette. In still other cases, attitudes emerge from a sort of *observational learning*. We see a respected peer endorse a particular attitude, or we observe someone benefit from an attitude. In either case, we may then to endorse the attitude ourselves.

ATTITUDE CHANGE: BEING PERSUADED BY OTHERS

What happens once we form an attitude? In many cases, we are bombarded by messages exhorting us to change the attitude; sometimes these messages are effective and sometimes not. Sometimes a TV commercial persuades us to switch our brand of toothpaste, but other times we remain loyal to our usual brand. Sometimes a politician persuades us to change our vote, but other times we hold our ground. Examples like these lead us to ask, When do attitudes change, and when do they stay the same?

To answer this question, we need to make a crucial distinction between two types of persuasion, each based on a different mode of processing information (Petty & Briñol, 2008). In the **central route to persuasion,** we carefully track the information we receive and elaborate its arguments with considerations of our own. We take this route if the issue matters to us and if we are not diverted by other concerns. In this case, we are keenly sensitive to the credibility and trustworthiness of the message's source (Aronson, Turner, & Carlsmith, 1963; Hovland and Weiss, 1952; Walster, Aronson, & Abrahams, 1966). We also pay close attention to the content of the persuasive message, and so—sensibly—strong arguments will be more effective in changing our mind than weak ones.

The situation is different, though, if a message comes by way of the **peripheral route to persuasion.** Here, we devote far fewer cognitive resources to processing incoming information. We use this mode of information processing if we do not care much about an issue or if we are distracted. In such circumstances, content and arguments matter little. What counts instead is how and by whom the message is presented (Petty & Briñol, 2008; Petty & Cacioppo, 1986; Petty, Wegener, & Fabrigar, 1997; for a closely related view, see Chaiken, Liberman, & Eagly, 1989). Thus, we are likely to be persuaded by an attractive and charismatic spokesperson offering familiar catchphrases—even if she makes poor arguments (Figure 13.8).

ATTITUDE CHANGE: THE ROLE OF EXPERIENCE

Another path to attitude change is direct experience with the target of one's attitude. This path has been particularly relevant in attempts to change prejudice toward the members of a particular group. In one early study of this issue, twenty-two 11- and 12-year-old boys took part in an outdoor program at Robbers Cave State Park in Oklahoma (so named because Jesse James was said to have hidden out there). The boys were divided into two groups, each of which had its own activities, such as baseball and swimming. Within a few days the two groups—the Eagles and the Rattlers—had their own identities, norms, and leaders. The researchers then began to encourage intergroup rivalry through a competitive tournament in which valuable prizes were promised to the winning side. Relations between the two groups became increasingly hostile and even violent, with food fights, taunts, and fist fights (Sherif, 1966; Sherif, Harvey, White, Hood, & Sherif, 1961).

At this point, the researchers intervened and established goals for the boys that could be achieved only through cooperation between the two groups. In one instance,

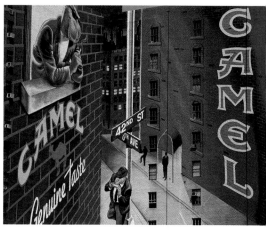

13.7 Advertisements and attitude change Advertisers try hard to shape our attitudes toward particular brands.

central route to persuasion The process involved in attitude change when someone carefully evaluates the evidence and the arguments.

peripheral route to persuasion The process involved in attitude change when someone relies on superficial factors, such as the appearance or charisma of the person presenting the argument.

13.8 Peripheral route to persuasion Attractive spokespersons who pitch perfumes and cosmetics often influence behavior via the peripheral route.

the researchers disrupted the camp's water supply, and the boys had to pool their resources in order to fix it. In another instance, the camp truck stalled, and the boys had to team up to get it moving. By working together on goals they all cared about—but could achieve only through collective effort—the boys broke down the divisions that had previously dominated camp life and ended their stay on good terms.

More recent studies have confirmed the implication of this study—namely, that intergroup contact can have a powerful effect on attitudes about the other group, especially if the contact is sustained over a period of time, involves active cooperation in pursuit of a shared goal, and provides equal status for all participants (see, for example, Aronson & Patnoe, 1997; Henry & Hardin, 2006; Pettigrew, 1998; Pettigrew & Tropp, 2006; Tropp & Pettigrew, 2005). We can also take steps to increase outgroup empathy (T. A. Cohen & Insko, 2008) and to encourage the prejudiced person to develop an individualized perception of the other group and so lose the "they're all alike" attitude (Dovidio & Gaertner, 1999).

ATTITUDE CHANGE: PERSUADING OURSELVES

Yet another route to attitude change is through our own behavior. At first, this may seem odd, because common sense argues that attitudes cause behavior, and not the other way around. But sometimes our own behaviors can cause us to change our views of the world.

In his classic work on this problem, Leon Festinger argued that people put a high value on being consistent, so that any perceived inconsistency among their beliefs, feelings, and behavior creates a very uncomfortable state of **cognitive dissonance** (Figure 13.9; J. Cooper, 2007; Festinger, 1957, 1962; Harmon-Jones & Mills, 1999). How do people escape this aversive state? In one study, Festinger and Carlsmith (1959) asked participants to perform several extremely boring tasks, such as packing spools into a tray and then unpacking them, or turning one knob after another for a quarter turn. When they were finished, the participants were induced to tell the next participant that the tasks were very interesting. Half the participants were paid reasonably well for this lie (they were given $20); the others were given just $1. Later, when asked

> **cognitive dissonance** An uncomfortable inconsistency among one's actions, beliefs, attitudes, or feelings. People attempt to reduce it by making their actions, beliefs, attitudes or feelings more consistent with one another.

13.9 Cognitive dissonance

how much they enjoyed the tasks, the well-paid participants said that the tasks were boring and that they understood that they had lied to the other participants. In contrast, the poorly paid participants claimed that the monotonous tasks were fairly interesting, and that what they told the other participants was the truth.

What produces this odd pattern? According to Festinger, the well-paid liars knew why they had mouthed sentiments they did not endorse: $20 was reason enough. The poorly paid liars, however, had experienced cognitive dissonance, thanks to the fact that they had misled other people without good reason for doing so. They had, in other words, received *insufficient justification* for their action. Taken at face value, this made them look like casual and unprincipled liars, a view that conflicted with how they wanted to see themselves. How could they reconcile their behavior with their self-concept? One solution was to reevaluate the boring tasks. If they could change their mind about the tasks and decide they were not so awful, then there was no lie and hence no dissonance. Judging from the data, this is apparently the solution that the participants selected—bringing their attitudes into line with their behavior.

These findings help make sense of why many organizations have difficult or aversive entrance requirements (Figure 13.10). For example, many American college fraternities have hazing rituals that are unpleasant and in some cases humiliating or worse. Although these rituals may be objectionable, they do serve a function. They lead new fraternity members to place a higher value on their membership than they otherwise would. They know what they have suffered to achieve membership, and it would create dissonance for them to believe that they have suffered for no purpose. They can avoid this dissonance though, if they are convinced that their membership is really valuable. In that case, their suffering was "worth it."

There is no question about the data patterns associated with cognitive dissonance, but many researchers have disagreed with Festinger over why the pattern emerges. The most important challenge to Festinger's account is Daryl Bem's **self-perception theory** (1967, 1972). According to this conception, there is no need to postulate the emotional distress that allegedly accompanies cognitive dissonance and, according to Festinger, propels attitude change. Instead, we can understand the data in terms of the information available to the participants in these experiments. Specifically, the research participants are simply trying to make sense of their own behavior in much the same way that an outside observer might. Thus, in the knob-turning study, self-perception theory would hold that a participant in the $1 condition would have known that $1 was insufficient justification for lying and so would have concluded that he did not lie. On this basis, if he said the task was fun and if he was not lying, then the task apparently was fun.

This line of interpretation makes sense of many other results as well. Consider studies of the so-called foot-in-the-door technique originally devised by door-to-door salesmen. In one study, an experimenter asked suburban homeowners to comply with an innocuous request, to put a 3-inch-square sign advocating auto safety in a window of their home. Two weeks later, a different experimenter came to visit the same homeowners and asked them to grant a much bigger request, to place on their front lawn an enormous billboard that proclaimed "Drive Carefully" in huge letters. The results showed that whether people granted the larger request was heavily influenced by whether they had earlier agreed to the smaller request. The homeowners who had complied with the small request were much more likely to give in to the greater one (Freedman & Fraser, 1966; although, for limits on this technique, see Burger & Guadagno, 2003; Chartrand, Pinckert, & Burger, 1999).

According to self-perception theory, the homeowners, having agreed to put up the small sign, now thought of themselves as active citizens involved in a public issue. "Why did I put up the sign? No one forced me to do it. I guess, therefore, that this is

13.10 Justification of effort Newly accepted members of a group tend to value their group membership even more if their initiation was especially harsh, as in the case of soldiers who have gone through boot camp.

self-perception theory The theory that we know our own attitudes and feelings only by observing our own behaviors and deciding what probably caused them, just as we do when trying to understand others.

an issue that I care about." Thus, they interpreted their actions as revealing a conviction that previously they did not know they had, and given that they now thought of themselves as active, convinced, and involved, they were ready to play the part on a larger scale. Fortunately for the neighbors, the billboards were never installed—after all, this was an experiment. But in real life we may not be so easily let off the hook, and the foot-in-the-door approach is a common device for persuading the initially uncommitted.

ATTITUDE STABILITY

We've now seen that attitudes can be changed in many ways—by certain forms of persuasion (if the source is credible and trustworthy and if the message is appropriate), by intergroup contact (in the case of prejudice), and by tendencies toward cognitive consistency (especially with regard to acts we have already performed). Given these points, and given all the many powerful forces aimed at changing our attitudes, it might seem that our attitudes would be in continual flux, changing from moment to moment and day to day. But on balance, the overall picture is one of attitude stability rather than attitude change. Attitudes can be altered, but it takes some doing. By and large, we seem to have a tendency to hold on to the attitudes we already have (Figure 13.11).

Why should this be so? One reason for attitude stability is that people rarely make changes in their social or economic environments. Their families, their friends and fellow workers, their social and economic situations—all tend to remain much the same over the years. All of this means that people will be exposed to many of the same influences year in and year out, and this sameness will obviously promote stability—in people's beliefs, values, and inclinations. Moreover, most of us tend to be surrounded by people with attitudes not so different from our own. After all, top-level executives know other top executives, college students know other college students, and trade union members know other union members. As a result, we are likely, day by day, to encounter few challenges to our attitudes, few contrary opinions, and this, too, promotes stability.

Of course, some events may transform attitudes completely—not just our own, but those of everyone around us. One example is the sneak attack on Pearl Harbor on December 7, 1941. Without a doubt, this led to an instant and radical change in Americans' attitudes toward Japan. A more recent example is the terrorist attacks of September 11,

13.11 Attitude stability One reason for attitude stability is that people often seek out others who have similar backgrounds and interests.

2001. These attacks dramatically increased Americans' fear of terrorism and raised public support for a number of actions (including two wars that would never have unfolded if Americans had been less concerned about the country's security). But by their very nature, such events—and the extreme changes in attitudes they produce—are rare.

SOCIAL INFLUENCE

So far in this chapter, we have emphasized the perceptions and beliefs of the social actor—how she interprets others' behaviors; what she infers about people, in light of their behaviors; how she forms (and perhaps changes) her attitudes. These points are crucial if we are going to understand how people act in groups, because—as we noted early on—our actions in a social setting depend on how we understand what is going on around us.

Let's note, though, that all of this makes it sound like our behavior in social settings is driven entirely "from within"—that is, shaped solely by our beliefs and perceptions. But, of course, our behavior is also powerfully shaped "from without"—that is, by various influences from our social world. How do those influences guide us? In pursuing this broad question, we need to distinguish three types of influence.

Conformity

People often do what they see others do. Sometimes this is a good thing, such as when people cross at the crosswalk, throw their trash in garbage cans, or drive on the side of the road they are supposed to. However, people's propensity to do as others do can also be a bad thing, as when people litter or even steal when they see that others are failing to behave appropriately (Keizer, Lindenberg, & Steg, 2008). **Confirmity** occurs whenever people change their behavior because of social pressure (either explicit or implicit).

One early demonstration of conformity comes from a classic study by Sherif (1937). In this study, participants seated in a dark room saw a point of light appear, move, and then disappear. This happened a number of times, and the participants' task was simply to judge how far the light had moved on each trial. In reality, however, the light never moved, and the appearance of movement was the result of a perceptual illusion known as the autokinetic effect.

When participants made their judgments alone, their responses differed substantially from one person to the next, ranging from an inch to more than a foot. Participants' responses also varied considerably from trial to trial. When participants viewed the light with one or two other people, however, their responses quickly began to converge with those of the other members of their group. Different groups converged upon different answers, but in each case the participants rarely strayed from the norm that had developed in their particular group.

Most telling, perhaps, was what Sherif found when he placed a confederate into the situation, someone who appeared to be a participant, but who in reality was an accomplice of the experimenters. When the confederate made responses that were much lower than those typically made by solitary participants, the other (real) participants quickly followed suit, and a group norm emerged that was much lower than normal. Similarly, when the confederate made responses that were much higher than typical, the others again followed this lead, and the resulting group norm was much higher than usual.

Sherif's findings are provocative because they suggest that others can influence even our basic perceptions of the world. Note, though, that Sherif had concocted a highly

conformity A change in behavior due to explicit or implicit social pressure.

13.12 The stimulus cards in Asch's social pressure experiment The cards are drawn to scale.

13.13 The participant in a social pressure experiment On hearing the unanimous verdict of the others, the true participant leans forward to look at the cards more carefully.

> **informational influence** A reason for conformity based on people's desire to be correct.

ambiguous situation in which participants were literally groping in the dark for an answer. Do people conform even when the correct answer is obvious?

Solomon Asch developed a procedure in which there could be no doubt as to the correct response (Asch, 1951, 1952, 1955, 1956). In his experiments, Asch brought groups of people into the laboratory and showed them pairs of cards, placed a few feet away (Figure 13.12). On one card was a black line, say, 8 inches long. On the other card were three lines of varying lengths, say, 6, 8, and 7 inches. The participants were asked simply to pick which of the three lines on the one card was equal in length to the single line on the other card.

The three lines were clearly different, and one of them exactly matched the original line, so the task was absurdly simple. But there was a catch. There was actually only one real participant. All of the others were confederates, with their seats arranged so that most of them would call out their judgments before the real participant had his turn.

In the first few trials, the confederates each called out the correct response and the real participant did the same. After the initial trials, however, the confederates began to unanimously render false judgments on most of the trials—declaring, for example, that a 6-inch line equaled an 8-inch line, and so on (Figure 13.13). In this situation, the clear evidence of the participant's senses was contradicted by everyone around him, so what should he do? Asch found that most participants wavered—sometimes offering the correct response but on many other trials yielding to the obviously mistaken suggestion offered by the group. Indeed, the chances were less than one in four that the participant would be fully independent and would stick to his guns on all trials on which the group disagreed with him (for an analysis that highlights the striking independence of some participants, see Friend, Rafferty, & Bramel, 1990).

THE CAUSES OF CONFORMITY

Why do people conform—in Asch's studies, and in many other settings (Figure 13.14)? Two influences appear to be crucial (M. Deutsch & Gerard, 1955).

The first—known as **informational influence**—involves people's desire to be right (Cialdini & Goldstein, 2004). Researchers have demonstrated the role of this sort of influence by altering the Asch-type experiment to make discriminating among the line segments very difficult. In this setting, we might expect people to be confused about the correct answer, and therefore more likely to seek out other cues for how they should respond. Plausibly, they might listen more to what others say—leading to the prediction that with more difficult discriminations, more social conformity will occur. This prediction is correct (Crutchfield, 1955). Conversely, we can alter the situation so that participants have *less* reason to listen to others (e.g., by convincing participants they are more competent or knowledgeable than others in some domain). In this case, we would expect the participants to rely less on the others' views, and so we would predict less conformity. This prediction also is correct (Campbell, Tesser, & Fairey, 1986; Wiesenthal, Endler, Coward, & Edwards, 1976).

This line of reasoning helps to explain why, in general, people seek the opinion of others when they encounter a situation that they do not fully understand. To evaluate the situation, they need more information. If they cannot get it firsthand, they will ask others, and if that is not an option, then they can try to gain information by comparing their own reactions to those of others (Festinger, 1954; Suls & Miller, 1977). This pattern of relying on others in the face of uncertainty can also be observed in young children, and even in infants. Infants who confront a scary situation and do not know whether to advance or retreat will glance toward their caretaker's face. If she smiles, the infant will tend to advance; if she frowns, he will tend to withdraw and return to her (we will come back to this point in Chapter 14). This early phenomenon of *social referencing* may be the prototype for what happens all our lives, a general process of validating our reactions by checking on how others are behaving.

Another aspect of informational influence is that the decisions of other people can shape the information we receive, and this, too, can lead to conformity. Suppose you're trying to decide what type of car to buy. If two of your neighbors have purchased Toyotas, you'll have a chance to observe these cars closely and learn about their attributes. In this way, your neighbors' selection will bias the information available and may lead you to follow their lead when you choose your own car (Denrell, 2008).

A second reason for going along with the crowd—known as **normative influence**—revolves around people's desire to be liked, or at least not to appear foolish (B. Hodges & Geyer, 2006). Consider the original Asch study in which a unanimous majority made an obviously incorrect judgment. In this context, the participant likely saw the world much as it is, but he had every reason to believe that the others saw it differently. If he now said what he believed, he could not help but be embarrassed; the others would probably think that he was a fool and might laugh at him. Under the circumstances, the participant would prefer to disguise what he really believed and go along, preferring to be "normal" rather than correct.

Direct evidence for the role of embarrassment as a normative influence comes from a variant of the Asch experiment in which the participant entered the room while the experiment was already in progress. The experimenter told her that since she arrived late, it would be simpler for her to write down her answers rather than to announce them out loud. Under these circumstances, there was little conformity. The lines being judged were of the original unambiguous sort (e.g., 8 inches vs. 6 inches in height), so that there was no informational pressure toward conformity. Since the judgments were made in private (no one else knew what she had written down), there was no (or little) motivational pressure either. As a result, participants showed a great deal of independence (Asch, 1952).

normative influence A reason for conformity based on people's desire to be liked (or not appear foolish).

MINORITY INFLUENCE

Asch's studies tell us that a unanimous majority exerts a powerful effect that makes it difficult for any individual to stray from the majority's position. What happens, though, when the individual is no longer alone? In one variation of his experiment, Asch had one of the confederates act as the participant's ally; all of the other confederates gave wrong answers, while the ally's judgments were correct. Under these conditions, the pressure to conform largely evaporated, and the participant yielded rarely and was not particularly upset by the odd judgment offered by (the majority of) the confederates.

Was the pressure to conform reduced because the ally shared the participant's views? Or was it merely because the consensus was broken, so that the participant was no longer alone in questioning the majority view? To find out, Asch conducted a variation of the study in which a confederate again deviated from the other confederates, but did not do so by giving the correct answer. On the contrary, she gave an answer even farther from the truth than the group's. Thus, on a trial in which the correct answer was 6 ¼ inches and the majority answer was 6 ¾ inches, the confederate's answer might be 8 inches. This response did not support the participant's perception (or reflect the truth!), but it helped to liberate him even so. The participant now yielded much less than when he was confronted by a unanimous majority. What evidently mattered was the group's unanimity; once this was broken, the participant felt that he could speak up without fear of embarrassment (Asch, 1952). Similar studies have been performed in other laboratories with similar results (V. L. Allen, 1975; V. L. Allen & Levine, 1971; Nemeth & Chiles, 1988). The power of even a lone dissident suggests that totalitarian systems have good reason to stifle dissent of any kind. The moment one dissident voice is raised, unanimity is broken, and then others may (and often do) find the courage to express their own dissent (Figure 13.15).

13.15 The effect of a consistent minority A steadfast minority can gradually create genuine changes in what people think and feel, as in the case of the American civil rights movement. Martin Luther King Jr. and Coretta Scott King lead the 1965 march from Selma to Montgomery.

CULTURE AND CONFORMITY

Asch's studies of conformity and most others like it were conducted on participants from an individualistic society, the United States. Many of these participants did conform but experienced enormous discomfort as a result, plainly suffering from the contrast between their own perceptions and the perceptions of others. The pattern is different in collectivistic cultures. Here individuals are less distressed about conforming even when it means being wrong. Over two dozen Asch-type conformity studies have now been conducted in collectivistic cultures, and they support such a conclusion (Bond & Smith, 1996).

Members of collectivistic and individualistic societies tend to differ in other ways too. Consider the group pressure that presumably led to conformity in Asch's experiments. On the face of it, one might expect collectivists to be more sensitive to this pressure, and so to endorse the group's judgments more often than do individualists. But it turns out that for collectivists, the likelihood of conformity depends on the nature of the group. Collectivists are more likely to conform with members of a group to which they are tied by traditional bonds—their family (including extended family), classmates, close friends, and fellow workers. In contrast, they are less affected than are individualists by people with whom they do not share close interpersonal bonds (Moghaddam, 1998).

Obedience

Conformity is one way that other people influence us. Another way is **obedience,** when people change their behavior because someone tells them to. A certain degree of obedience is a necessary ingredient of social life. After all, in any society some individuals need to have authority over others, at least within a limited sphere. Someone needs to direct traffic; someone needs to tell people when they should put their garbage out at the curb for collection; someone needs to instruct children and get them to do their homework (Figure 13.16). But obedience can also lead people to violate their own principles and do things they previously felt they should not do. The atrocities of the last 100 years—the Nazi death camps, the Soviet "purges," the Cambodian massacres, the Rwandan and Sudanese genocides—give terrible proof that the disposition to obedience can become a corrosive poison.

Why were people so obedient in these situations? Psychologists trying to answer this question have adopted two different approaches. One is based on the intuitively appealing notion that some individuals who are more obedient than others are the primary culprits. The other emphasizes the social situation in which the obedient person finds herself.

PERSONALITY AND OBEDIENCE

A half century ago, investigators proposed that it was people with *authoritarian personalities* who were most likely to be highly obedient and to show a cluster of traits related to their obedience. They are prejudiced against various minority groups and hold certain sentiments about authority, including a general belief that the world is best governed by a system of power and dominance in which each of us must submit to those above us and show harshness to those below. These authoritarian attitudes can be revealed (and measured) by a test in which people express how much they agree with statements such as "Obedience and respect for authority are the most important virtues children should learn" and "People can be divided into two distinct classes: the weak and the strong" (Adorno et al., 1950).

Contemporary researchers have broadened the conception of the authoritarian personality by analyzing the motivational basis for conservative ideology (Jost, Nosek, & Gosling, 2008), building on the supposition that this ideology—like any belief system—serves the psychological needs of the people who hold these beliefs. In particular, the **motivated social cognition** perspective maintains that people respond to threat and uncertainty by expressing beliefs that help them to manage their concerns. Evidence supporting this perspective has come from studies showing that political conservatism is positively related to a concern with societal instability and death, a need for order and structure, and an intolerance of ambiguity (e.g., Jost et al., 2003).

SITUATIONS AND OBEDIENCE

A very different approach to obedience is suggested by an often-quoted account of the trial of Adolf Eichmann, the man who oversaw the execution of 6 million Jews and other minorities in the Nazi gas chambers. In describing Eichmann, historian Hannah Arendt noted a certain "banality of evil": "The trouble with Eichmann was precisely that so many were like him, and that the many were neither perverted nor sadistic, that they were, and still are, terribly and terrifyingly normal" (Arendt, 1965, p. 276; Figure 13.17).

13.16 Obedience A certain degree of obedience is necessary for society to function smoothly. Think of the chaos that would ensue if no one obeyed police officers directing traffic.

obedience A change in behavior in response to an instruction or command from another person.

motivated social cognition Thinking about the social world in ways that serve an emotional need, such as when people hold beliefs that help them feel less anxious.

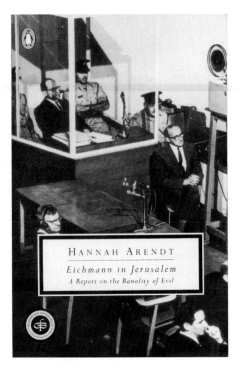

13.17 **The banality of evil** Hannah Arendt found Nazi war criminal Adolf Eichmann "terrifyingly normal."

What could have led a "normal" man like Eichmann to commit such atrocities? The answer probably lies in the situation in which Eichmann found himself, one that encouraged horrible deeds and powerfully discouraged more humane courses of action. But this simply demands a set of new questions: What makes a situation influential? And how coercive does a situation have to be in order to elicit monstrous acts? Stanley Milgram explored these questions in a series of experiments that are perhaps the best-known studies in all of social psychology (Milgram, 1963). In these studies, Milgram recruited his participants from the local population surrounding Yale University in Connecticut via a newspaper advertisement offering $4.50 per hour to people willing to participate in a study of how punishment affected human learning.

Participants in this experiment were asked to serve as "teachers," and their job was to read out the cue word for each trial, to record the "learner's" spoken answer, and—most important—to administer punishment—in the form of an electric shock—whenever a learner answered incorrectly (Figure 13.18). The first shock was slight. Each time the learner made a mistake, though, the teacher was required to increase the voltage by one step—proceeding through a series of switches on a "shock generator" with labels ranging from "Slight Shock" through "Danger: Severe Shock" to a final, undefined "XXX."

In truth, there was no "learner." Instead, a middle-aged actor who was a confederate of the experimenter pretended, at the experiment's start, to be the learner and then retreated into a separate room, with all subsequent communication between teacher and learner conducted over an intercom. And, in fact, the "shock generator" didn't deliver punishment. The point of the experiment was not to study punishment and learning at all; that was just a cover story. It was actually to determine how far the participants would go in obeying the experimenter's instructions.

13.18   SCIENTIFIC METHOD: To what extent will people obey harmful instructions?

Method

1. The participant's job was to be a "teacher" and administer shocks when the "learner" (a confederate) made mistakes on a purported memory test.

2. When the learner made a mistake, the experimenter (also a confederate) told the participant to increase the shock level by 15 volts, up to a maximum of 450 volts. (The learner was not actually shocked.)

3. As the voltage increased, so did the learner's distress. At 150 volts, he demanded that the experiment end; at 300 volts, he refused to answer more questions.

4. If the participant expressed reservations, the experimenter responded "The experiment requires that you continue," "It is absolutely essential that you continue," "You have no other choice, you must go on."

The learner, strapped into his chair.

Milgram's "shock box."

Results

About 65% of Milgram's subjects obeyed the experimenter in administering the highest level of voltage.

CONCLUSION: In certain situations, most people will obey harmful instructions, despite their misgivings.

SOURCE STUDY: Milgram, 1963

Within the procedure, the learner made a fair number of (scripted) errors, and so the shocks that the participant delivered kept getting stronger and stronger. By the time 120 volts was reached, the learner shouted that the shocks were becoming too painful. At 150 volts, he demanded that he be let out of the experiment. At 180 volts, he cried out that he could no longer stand the pain, sometimes yelling, "My heart, my heart!" At 300 volts, he screamed, "Get me out of here!" and said he would not answer anymore. At the next few shocks, there were agonized screams. After 330 volts, there was silence.

The learner's responses were all predetermined, but the participants—the teachers—did not know that, so they had to decide what to do. When the learner cried out in pain or refused to go on, the participants usually turned to the experimenter for instructions, a form of social referencing. In response, the experimenter told the participants that the experiment had to go on, indicated that he took full responsibility, and pointed out that "the shocks may be painful but there is no permanent tissue damage."

How far did subjects go in obeying the experimenter? The results were astounding: About 65% of Milgram's subjects—both males and females—obeyed the experimenter to the bitter end. Of course, many of the participants showed signs of being enormously upset by the procedure—they bit their lips, twisted their hands, sweated profusely, and in some cases, laughed nervously. Nonetheless, they did obey—and, in the process, apparently delivered lethal shocks to another human being. (See Burger, 2009, for a contemporary replication that showed obedience rates comparable to those in the initial Milgram reports. For similar data when the study was repeated in countries such as Australia, Germany, and Jordan, see Kilham & Mann, 1974; Mantell & Panzarella, 1976; Shanab & Yahya, 1977.)

These are striking data—suggesting that it takes remarkably little within a situation to produce truly monstrous acts. But we should also note the profound ethical questions raised by this study. Milgram's participants were of course fully debriefed at the study's end, and so they knew they had done no damage to the "learner" and had inflicted no pain. But the participants also knew that they had obeyed the researcher and had (apparently) been willing to hurt someone—perhaps quite seriously. We therefore need to ask whether the scientific gain from this study is worth the cost—including the horrible self-knowledge the study brought to the participants, or the stress they experienced. This question has been hotly debated, but this doesn't take away from the main message of the data—namely, it takes very little to get people to obey extreme and inhuman commands.

Why were Milgram's participants so obedient? Part of the answer may lie in how each of us thinks about commands and authority. In essence, when we are following other people's orders, we feel that it is they, and not we, who are in control; they, and not we, who are responsible. The soldier following a general's order and the employee following the boss's command may see themselves merely as the agents who execute another's will: the hammer that strikes the nail, not the carpenter who wields it. As such, they feel absolved of responsibility—and, if the consequences are bad, absolved of guilt.

This feeling of being another person's instrument, with little or no sense of personal responsibility, can be promoted in various ways. One way is by increasing the *psychological distance* between a person's actions and their end result. To explore this possibility, Milgram ran a variation of his procedure in which two "teachers" were involved: one a confederate who administered the shocks, and the other—actually, the real participant—who had to perform subsidiary tasks such as reading the words over a microphone and recording the learner's responses. In this new role, the participant was still an essential part of the experiment, because if he stopped, the learner would receive no further shocks. In this variation, though, the participant was more removed from the impact of his actions, like a minor cog in a bureaucratic machine. After all, he did not do the actual shocking! Under these conditions, over 90% of the participants went to the limit, continuing with the procedure even at the highest level of shock (Milgram, 1963, 1965; see also Kilham & Mann, 1974).

The obedient person also may reinterpret the situation to diminish any sense of culpability. One common approach is to try to ignore the fact that the recipient of one's actions is a fellow human being. According to one of Milgram's participants, "You really begin to forget that there's a guy out there, even though you can hear him. For a long time I just concentrated on pressing the switches and reading the words" (Milgram, 1974, p. 38). This **dehumanization of the victim** allows the obedient person to think of the recipient of his actions as an object, not a person, reducing (and perhaps eliminating) any sense of guilt at harming another individual (Bernard, Ottenberg, & Redl, 1965; Goff, Eberhardt, Williams, & Jackson, 2008).

The dehumanization of the victim in Milgram's study has a clear parallel outside the laboratory. Enemies in war and victims of atrocities are rarely described as people, but instead are referred to as bodies, objects, pests, and numbers (Figure 13.19). This dehumanization is propped up by euphemistic jargon. The Nazis used terms such as *final solution* (for the mass murder of 6 million people) and *special treatment* (for death by gassing); the nuclear age contributed *fallout problem* and *preemptive attack*; the Vietnam War gave us *free-fire zone* and *body count*; other wars gave *ethnic cleansing* and *collateral damage*—all dry, official phrases that keep the thoughts of blood and human suffering at a psychologically safe distance.

Thus, people obeying morally questionable orders can rely on two different strategies to let themselves off the moral hook—a cognitive reorientation aimed at holding another person responsible for one's own actions, or a shift toward perceiving the victim as an object, not a person. It is important to realize that neither of these intellectual adjustments happens in an instant. Instead, inculcation is gradual, making it important that the initial act of obedience be relatively mild and not seriously clash with the person's own moral outlook. But after that first step, each successive step can be slightly more extreme. In Milgram's study, this pattern created a slippery slope that participants slid down unawares. A similar program of progressive escalation was used in the indoctrination of death-camp guards in Nazi Germany and prison-camp guards in Somalia. The same is true for the training of soldiers everywhere. Draftees go through "basic training," in part to learn various military skills but much more importantly to acquire the habit of instant obedience. Raw recruits are rarely asked to point their guns at another person and shoot. It's not only that they don't know how; it's that most of them probably wouldn't do it.

Compliance

When we conform or obey, we change our behaviors because of pressure from a group or commands from authority. But we also alter our actions for a more mundane reason: Someone asks us to do so. **Compliance** is a third type of social influence. It occurs when people change their behavior because someone merely asks them to.

According to Cialdini, we feel most compelled to comply with a request when the requester has done something for us in the past (Cialdini, 1993; Cialdini & Goldstein, 2004). This is because of the **norm of reciprocity**—the notion that accepting a favor leads to a sense of indebtedness. Thus we feel that we must repay a donor, even if we did not want his gift in the first place.

One example involves the Disabled American Veterans organization, which uses mail appeals for donations. For a regular appeal, the response rate is 18%. But when the

---

dehumanization of the victim
Thinking about a potential victim in ways that make him seem inhuman (as vermin, for example, or as a mere number); this view makes aggression toward the victim more likely and less troubling to the aggressor.

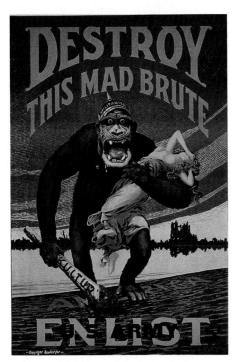

13.19 Dehumanizing the opponent In wartime, propaganda posters routinely dehumanize the opponent, as in this World War I poster that turns the German enemy into a gorilla savaging an innocent maiden. This dehumanization helps motivate the populace in support of the war effort and diminishes any sense of guilt about acts of aggression conducted against the enemy.

compliance A change in behavior in response to a request.

norm of reciprocity The social standard that suggests that a favor must be repaid.

appeal letter comes with a "gift" (address labels), the response rate doubles. Even people who have no use for the labels feel obligated to reciprocate and do so by donating. Another context in which the reciprocity rule operates is bargaining. The seller states her price. The potential buyer says no. Now the seller makes a concession by offering the item at a lower price. This exerts pressure on the buyer to increase his offer; since the seller offered a concession, he feels that he ought to give a little too.

This pattern can be demonstrated experimentally. In one study, an experimenter approached people walking on a university campus and first made a very large request—asking them to work as volunteer counselors in a juvenile detention center for 2 hours a week over a 2-year period. Not a single person agreed. The experimenter then made a much smaller request, that they accompany a group of boys or girls from the juvenile detention center on a single 2-hour trip to the zoo. When this smaller request came on the heels of the large request that had been refused, 50% of the people consented. In contrast, only 17% of the people acceded to the smaller request when it was not preceded by the larger demand. Apparently, the experimenter's concession (abandoning her large request and moving to the smaller one) made the people feel that they should make a concession of their own, saying yes even though they were initially inclined to say no (Cialdini et al., 1975).

A variant of this technique is the **that's-not-all technique.** This method produces compliance by starting with a modest offer and then improving on it—with this improvement likely to be perceived as a concession, pulling for reciprocation. This technique is well known from late-night commercials promising, say, a dozen steak knives for $19.99—and that's not all—this offer includes a free knife sharpener! One study demonstrated the power of this technique during a bake sale in which some customers were told that for 75 cents they could buy a cupcake and then—after a pause—were told that for this price the seller would also include a small bag of cookies. Compared to customers who were presented with the cupcake and cookies at the same time, those exposed to the that's-not-all technique were nearly twice as likely to purchase cupcakes (Burger, 1986; see also Burger, Reed, DeCesare, Rauner, & Rozolis, 1999).

that's-not-all technique A sales method that starts with a modest offer, then improves on it. The improvement seems to require reciprocation, which often takes the form of purchasing the item.

mere presence effect Changes in a person's behavior due to another person's presence.

Group Dynamics

So far, we have described social influence as though it were a "one-way street." The group presses you toward conformity. A salesperson leads you toward a concession. But, of course, social interactions often involve mutual influence—with each person in the group having an impact on every other person in the group. The study of this sort of interaction is the study of *group dynamics*.

MERE PRESENCE EFFECTS

More than a century ago, Triplett noticed that cyclists performed better when they competed against others than when they competed against the clock (Triplett, 1898; Figure 13.20). This observation inspired him to conduct one of social psychology's first experiments, in which he told children to turn a fishing reel as quickly as they could, either alone or with another child. Triplett found that children turned the reel more quickly when they were with others than when they were alone.

This finding was subsequently replicated many times, and initial results suggested that this **mere presence effect** was uniformly beneficial. For example, when working alongside others who are engaged in the same task, people learn simple mazes more

13.20 Mere presence effects
Performance is often better in a group.

social facilitation The tendency to perform simple or well-practiced tasks better in the presence of others than alone.

social inhibition The tendency to perform complex or difficult tasks more poorly in the presence of others.

social loafing A pattern in which people working together on a task generate less total effort than they would have if they had each worked alone.

quickly and perform more multiplication problems in the same period of time—illustrations of a pattern known as **social facilitation** (F. H. Allport, 1920). Other studies, however, show that the presence of others can sometimes hinder rather than help—an effect called **social inhibition**. While college students solve simple mazes more quickly when working with others, they are considerably slower at solving more complex mazes when others are around (Hunt & Hillery, 1973; Zajonc, 1965, 1980). How can we reconcile such divergent results?

Zajonc (1965) argued that the presence of other people increases our level of bodily arousal, which strengthens the tendency to perform highly dominant responses—the ones that seem to come automatically. When the dominant response is also the correct one, as in performing simple motor skills or learning simple mazes, social presence should help. But when the task gets harder, as in the case of complex mazes, then the dominant response is often incorrect. As a result, performance gets worse when others watch, for in that case the dominant response (enhanced by increased arousal) inhibits the less dominant but correct reaction.

Evidence supporting this view comes from a wide array of studies. In one study, researchers observed pool players in a college union building. When good players competed in front of an audience of four others, their accuracy rose from 71 to 80%. But when poor players were observed, their accuracy dropped from 35 to 25% (Michaels, Bloomel, Brocato, Linkous, & Rowe, 1982). Similar effects can be observed even in organisms very different from humans. In one study, cockroaches learned to escape from a bright light by running down a simple alley or by learning a maze. Some performed alone; others ran in pairs. When in the alley, the cockroaches performed better in pairs than alone—for this simple task, the dominant response was appropriate. In the maze, however, they performed better alone; for this more complex task, the dominant response was incorrect and inappropriate (Zajonc, Heingartner, & Herman, 1969).

SOCIAL LOAFING

The studies just described are concerned with people working independently of each other or people working in the presence of an audience. But what about people working together—such as a committee working on an administrative project, or a group of students working on a class project? In cases like these, everyone is a performer and an audience member, because every member of the group is contributing to the overall product. Likewise, everyone is able to see and perhaps evaluate others' contributions. How do group members influence each other in this setting?

In this situation, we are likely to observe a phenomenon known as **social loafing** (Latané, 1981), a pattern in which individuals working together in a group generate less total effort than they would if each worked alone. In one study, individual men were asked to pull on a rope; the average force for these pulls was 139 pounds. When groups of eight pulled together, the average was 546 pounds—only about 68 pounds per person. In another study, students were asked to clap and cheer as loudly as they could, sometimes alone, sometimes in groups of two, four, or six. Here, too, the results showed social loafing. Each person cheered and clapped less vigorously the greater the number of others she was with (Latané, Williams, & Harkins, 1979). This general finding that individuals work less hard in groups has now been replicated many times in the United States, India, and China (Karau & Williams, 1993).

Why do individuals work less hard in groups? One reason is that they may feel less accountable and therefore are less motivated to try as hard as they can. Another reason is that they may think that their contribution is not crucial to group success (Harkins

& Szymanski, 1989). There is an old adage: "Many hands make light work." The trouble is that they do not always make it as light as they could.

DEINDIVIDUATION

Apparently, then, the presence of others can influence us in multiple ways—in some circumstances facilitating our behavior, and in other circumstances inhibiting us. But the presence of others can also dramatically change how we act. In a riot or lynch mob, for example, people express aggression with a viciousness that would be inconceivable if they acted in isolation. A crowd that gathers to watch a disturbed person on a ledge atop a tall building often taunts the would-be suicide, urging him to jump. What does being in a crowd do to people to make them act so differently from their everyday selves?

One perspective on these questions describes crowd behavior as a kind of mass madness. This view was first offered by Le Bon (1841–1931), a French social psychologist who contended that people in crowds become wild, stupid, and irrational and give vent to primitive impulses. He believed their emotion spreads by a sort of contagion, rising to an ever-higher pitch as more and more crowd members become affected. Thus, fear becomes terror, hostility turns into murderous rage, and each crowd member becomes a barbarian—"a grain of sand among other grains of sand, which the wind stirs up at will" (Le Bon, 1895).

Many modern psychologists believe that although Le Bon may have overstated his case, his claims contain an important truth. To them, the key to crowd behavior is **deindividuation,** a state in which an individual in a group loses awareness of herself as a separate individual (Figure 13.21). This state is more likely to occur when there is a high level of arousal and anonymity—just as would be the case in a large and angry crowd or a large and fearful gathering. Deindividuation tends to release impulsive actions that are normally under restraint, and what the impulses are depends on the group and the situation. In a carnival, the (masked) revelers may join in wild orgies; in a lynch mob, the group members may torture or kill (Diener, 1979; Festinger, Pepitone, & Newcomb, 1952; Zimbardo, 1969).

To study deindividuation, one investigation had college students wear identical robes and hoods that made it impossible to identify them. Once in these hoods—which, not coincidentally, looked just like Ku Klux Klan robes—the students were asked to deliver an electric shock to another person; they delivered twice as much shock as those not wearing the robes (Zimbardo, 1970). In the robes, it seemed, the students felt free to "play the part"—and in this case the result was ugly. Other studies, though, reveal the good that can be produced by deindividuation. In a different experiment, students were asked to wear nurses' uniforms rather than KKK costumes; dressed in this way, students delivered less shock than a group without costumes (R. D. Johnson & Downing, 1979). Thus, deindividuation by itself is not bad—it simply makes it easy for us to give in to the impulses cued by the situation, and the nature of those impulses depends on the circumstances.

Notice also that deindividuation can happen in several different ways. Being in a large crowd produces deindividuation; this is part of why mobs act as they do. Wearing a mask can also produce deindividuation, largely because of the anonymity it provides. But deindividuation can also result merely from someone's wearing a uniform and having an assigned role—in essence, he "becomes" the

deindividuation A state in which an individual in a group experiences a weakened sense of personal identity and diminished self-awareness.

13.21 **Deindividuation** (A) Some deindividuation effects are harmless. (B) Others represent a menace to a humane, democratic society.

13.22 Stanford Prison Experiment In Zimbardo's classic study, students were randomly assigned to act as either guards or prisoners. The study had to be terminated early because of the inhumane behavior shown by the guards.

Stanford Prison Experiment Philip Zimbardo's study of the effect of roles on behavior. Participants were randomly assigned to play either prisoners or guards in a mock prison. The study was ended early because of the "guards'" role-induced cruelty.

group polarization A pattern in group discussions in which each member's attitudes become more extreme, even though the discussion draws attention to arguments that could have moderated their views.

risky shift A pattern in which a group appears more willing to take chances or to take an extreme stance than any individual members would have been on their own.

role. This third factor was plainly revealed in a classic study known as the **Stanford Prison Experiment**, in which Philip Zimbardo transformed the basement of Stanford University's psychology department into a mock prison and randomly assigned male undergraduate participants to the role of either guards or prisoners (Figure 13.22; Haney, Banks, & Zimbardo, 1973; Zimbardo, 1973; see also Haney & Zimbardo, 1998). Guards and prisoners wore uniforms appropriate to their roles, and prisoners were called by assigned numbers instead of their names. The experimenter gave the participants few instructions, and placed few constraints on their behavior. What rapidly evolved was a set of behaviors remarkably similar to those sometimes observed in actual prisons—with cruelty, inhumane treatment, and massive disrespect evident in all the participants. The behaviors observed were sufficiently awful that Zimbardo ended his study after only 6 days, before things got really out of hand, rather than letting it run for 2 weeks, as was originally planned.

Sadly, the powerful effects of deindividuation and stepping into a role extend well beyond the confines of the laboratory setting. As we saw at the outset of this chapter, one now-infamous real-world example is the abusive behavior exhibited by military personnel at Abu Ghraib prison. In the face of worldwide condemnation, Americans of all stripes struggled to understand how their own countrymen and countrywomen could behave in such an unconscionable fashion. Mindful of the lessons of the Stanford Prison Experiment, though, Zimbardo and other social psychologists have argued that powerful social forces were at work here that included—among others—the power of deindividuation through reducing people to their roles (Zimbardo, 2007). As a result, the situation itself may have done far more to create these abuses than the personal qualities of any of the soldiers involved.

GROUP POLARIZATION

Being in a group doesn't just influence our behavior; it also influences our thoughts—and often for the worse. For example, consider the phenomenon of **group polarization**, a tendency for group decisions to be more extreme than the decisions that would have been made by any of the members on their own. This pattern arises in many different group contexts, such as when juries decide how much money to award a plaintiff at the end of a lawsuit.

Often the polarization takes the form of a so-called **risky shift,** in which groups appear more willing to take risks, or more willing to take an extreme stance, than the group members would be individually (Bennett, Lindskold, & Bennett, 1973; C. P. Morgan & Aram, 1975; Schroeder, 1973). However, group polarization can also take the opposite form. If the group members are slightly cautious to begin with or slightly conservative in their choices, then these tendencies are magnified, and the group's decision will end up appreciably more cautious than the decisions that would have been made by the individuals alone (Levine & Moreland, 1998; Moscovici & Zavalloni, 1969).

What produces group polarization? One factor is the simple point that, during a discussion, individuals often state, restate, and restate again what their views are, which helps to strengthen their commitment to these views (Brauer, Judd, & Gliner, 1995). Another factor involves the sort of confirmation bias that we discussed in Chapter 9—the fact that people tend to pay more attention to, and more readily accept, information that confirms their views, in comparison to their (relatively hostile) scrutiny of information that challenges their views. How does this shape a group discussion? In the discussion, people are likely to hear sentiments on both sides of an issue. Owing to confirmation bias, the arguments that support their view are likely to seem clear, persuasive, and well informed. Opposing arguments, however, will seem weak and ambiguous. This allows people to conclude that the arguments favoring their view are strong, while the counterarguments are weak, which simply strengthens their commitment to their own prior opinion (for the classic example of this pattern, see C. G. Lord, Ross, & Lepper, 1979; also Kovera, 2002).

Another factor leading to group polarization hinges on two topics we have already mentioned. On the one hand, people generally try to conform with the other members of the group, both in their behavior and in the attitudes they express. But, in addition, people in individualistic cultures want to stand out from the crowd and be judged "better than average." How can they achieve both of these goals—conforming and excelling? They can take a position at the group's "leading edge"—similar enough to the group's position so that they have honored the demands of conformity, but "out in front" of the group in a way that makes them seem distinctive. Of course, the same logic applies to everyone in the group, so everyone will seek to take positions and express sentiments at the group's leading edge. As a result, this edge will become the majority view! In this way, right at the start the group's sentiments will be sharpened and made a step or two more extreme—exactly the pattern of group polarization.

GROUPTHINK

Group decision making also reveals a pattern dubbed **groupthink** (Janis, 1982). This pattern is particularly likely when the group is highly cohesive—such as a group of friends or people who have worked together for many years—and when the group is facing some external threat and is closed to outside information or opinions. In this setting, there is a strong tendency for group members to do what they can to promote the sense of group cohesion. As a result, they downplay doubts or disagreements, celebrate the "moral" or "superior" status of the group's arguments, stereotype enemies ("our opponents are stupid" or "evil"), markedly overestimate the likelihood of success, and discount or ignore risks or challenges to the group (Figure 13.23).

Arguably, groupthink caused a number of disastrous decisions, including the U.S. government's decision to invade Cuba in the early 1960s (Janis, 1971) and the National Aeronautics and Space Administration's decision to launch the *Challenger* on a cold day in 1986 despite the knowledge that one part of the space shuttle did not perform well at very cold temperatures (Moorhead, Ference, & Neck, 1991). Social psychologists are still working to understand exactly when the groupthink pattern emerges and what steps can be taken to limit the negative effects of groupthink on decision making (Kruglanski, Pierro, Mannetti, & De Grada, 2006; Packer, 2009).

groupthink A pattern of thinking that occurs when a cohesive group minimizes or ignores members' differences of opinion.

"All those in favor say 'Aye.'"
"Aye."   "Aye."   "Aye."
"Aye."   "Aye."

13.23 Groupthink

SOCIAL RELATIONS

More than 2,000 years ago, the Greek philosopher Aristotle described humans as "social animals," and, as we have seen, there are many facets to our social existence. We perceive others' actions, interpret those actions, and draw conclusions about what other people are like. We are shaped by the people around us—conforming with them, obeying them, complying with their requests.

Perhaps the most significant aspect of our social existence, though, concerns our social relationships—the way we interact with and feel about others and the way that they interact with and feel about us. These behaviors are social by definition, necessarily involving other individuals, and include the aggressive ways that we hurt others, which we considered in Chapter 12, as well as the positive things we do to help them, which we consider below. We also need to consider a central aspect of our social existence—the fact that we sometimes find ourselves attracted to others and even—at times—in love.

Helping and Altruism

One of our great sources of pride as a species is our ability to exhibit *prosocial* behaviors, behaviors that help others—assisting them in their various activities, supporting and aiding them in their time of need. But, of course, we don't always help. Sometimes we ignore the homeless man as we walk by him; sometimes we throw away a charity's fundraising plea; sometimes we scurry past the person who has just dropped his groceries. The question we need to ask, then, is why we sometimes help and sometimes don't. The answer, once again, involves a mix of factors—including our personalities (whether we tend to be helpful overall) and our social environment.

THE BYSTANDER EFFECT

Consider the case of Kitty Genovese, who was attacked and murdered one early morning in 1964 on a street in Queens, New York (Figure 13.24). While the details of the case are disputed (Manning, Levine, & Collins, 2007), it is clear that the assault lasted over half an hour, during which time Genovese screamed and struggled while her assailant stabbed her repeatedly. Many of her neighbors could see or hear her struggle but did not come to her aid. Why not? Why, in general, do we often fail to help those who are obviously in need—perhaps even in extreme danger?

According to Latané and Darley, the failure to help is often produced by the way people understand the situation. It's not that people don't care. It's that they don't understand what should be done because the situation is ambiguous. In the Genovese case, witnesses later reported that they were not sure what was happening. Perhaps it was a joke, a drunken argument, a lovers' quarrel. If it were any of these, intervention might have been very embarrassing.

The situation is further complicated by the fact that the various witnesses to the Genovese murder realized that others were seeing or hearing what they did. This circumstance created **pluralistic ignorance.** Each of the witnesses was uncertain whether there really was an emergency, and each looked to the others, trying to decide. Their reasoning was simple: "If my neighbors don't react, then apparently they've decided there's no emergency, and, if there's no emergency, there's no reason for me to react." The tragedy, of course, is that the neighbors were thinking roughly the same thoughts—with the consequence that each took the inactivity of the others as a cue to do nothing.

Even when people *are* convinced that they are viewing an emergency, the presence of multiple bystanders still has an effect. It creates a *diffusion of responsibility*, with each bystander persuaded that someone else will respond to the emergency, someone else will take the responsibility. This effect is illustrated by a study in which participants were asked to join in what they thought was a group discussion about college life with either one, three, or five other people. Participants sat in individual cubicles and took turns talking to each other over an intercom system. In actuality, though, there was only one participant; all the other speakers were voices on a previously recorded tape. The discussion began as one of these other speakers described some of his personal prob-

13.24 Kitty Genovese

pluralistic ignorance A type of misunderstanding that occurs when members of a group don't realize that the other members share their perception (often, their uncertainty about how to react to a situation). As a result, each member wrongly interprets the others' inaction as reflecting their better understanding of the situation.

lems, which included a tendency toward epileptic seizures in times of stress. When he began to speak again during the second round of talking, he seemed to have a seizure and gasped for help. At issue was what would happen next. Would the actual participant take action to help this other person apparently in distress?

The answer was powerfully influenced by the "crowd size." If the participant believed that she had been having just a two-way discussion (so that there was no one else around to help the person in distress), she was likely to leave her own cubicle to help. But if the participant thought it was a group discussion, a diffusion of responsibility occurred, and the larger the group the participant thought she was in, the less likely she was to come to the victim's assistance (Darley & Latané, 1968).

This **bystander effect** has been demonstrated in numerous other situations. In some, an actor posing as a fellow participant seems to have an asthma attack; in others, someone appears to faint in an adjacent room; in still others, the laboratory fills with smoke. Whatever the emergency, the result is always the same. The larger the group the participant is in (or thinks he is in), the smaller the chance that he will take any action (Latané & Nida, 1981; Latané, Nida, & Wilson, 1981; Figure 13.25).

One important qualification, however, is that larger (perceived) groups seem to breed less helping only when the group members are strangers. When group members are familiar others, larger group size can actually encourage helping behavior (M. Levine & Crowther, 2008). But this, too, makes sense if we consider the *costs* of not helping and the *benefits* of helping. First, your not taking action shifts the burden to someone else in the crowd—and if that other person is someone you're familiar with, you may feel uncomfortable imposing on them in this way. Second, there's likely to be some embarrassment at not helping in an emergency situation, and that embarrassment grows if you are with people you will be seeing again. Finally, taking action among friends has the benefit of enhancing social cohesion and increasing a sense of pride in group membership. Whether among strangers or friends, then, it appears that the social setting guides your actions.

THE COST OF HELPING

Our last example highlighted some of the costs of *not* helping, but there is also often a cost of helping—and both of these costs shape our behavior. In some cases, the cost of helping lies in physical danger—if, for example, you need to leap into an icy river to help someone who is drowning. In others, the cost is measured simply in time and effort. In all cases, though, the pattern is simple. The greater the cost of helping and the smaller the cost of not helping, the smaller the chance that a bystander will offer help to someone in need.

In one study, for example, students had to go one at a time from one campus building to another to give a talk. They were told to hurry, since they were already late. As students rushed to their appointments, they passed a shabbily dressed man lying in a doorway groaning. Only 10% of the students stopped to help this disguised confederate. Ironically, the students were attending a theological seminary, and the topic of their talk was the parable of the Good Samaritan who came to the aid of a man lying injured on a roadside (Figure 13.26). It appears that if the cost—here in time—is high enough, even theological students may not behave altruistically (Darley & Batson, 1973).

What is costly to one potential helper may not be equally so to another, however. Take physical danger. It is probably not surprising that bystanders who intervene in assault cases are generally much taller, stronger, and better trained to intervene than bystanders who do not intervene, and they are almost invariably men (Eagly & Crowley, 1986; Huston, Ruggiero, Conner, & Geis, 1981).

bystander effect One reason people fail to help strangers in distress: The larger the group a person is in, the less likely he is to help, partly because no one in the group thinks it is up to him to act.

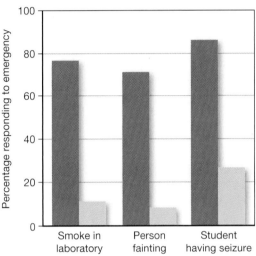

13.25 Group inhibition of bystander intervention in emergencies When people are alone (in blue), they are more likely to respond in an emergency than when they are—or think they are—with others (in yellow), in part because of diffusion of felt responsibility.

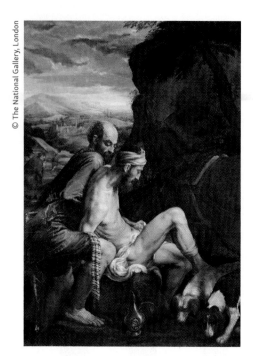

© The National Gallery, London

13.26 *The Good Samaritan* Painting by Jacopo Bassano, 1517/18–1592.

altruism Helping behavior that does not benefit the helper.

13.27 Helping The text describes many of the reasons why people often fail to help each other, but, happily, the fact remains that there are circumstances in which we do help one another. One powerful example comes from the outpouring of assistance that emerged following the attack on the World Trade Center. Many police officers and fire fighters performed heroically in immediately helping the victims of the attack; in the days following, many people made generous donations to help the victims.

In addition, the costs of providing help are sometimes weighed against the *benefits* of helping. Some of the benefits are various signs of social approval, as with a donor to charity who is sure to make a lavish contribution so long as everyone knows. A different benefit is one we alluded to earlier—namely, the avoidance of shame or embarrassment. Many city dwellers give 50 or 75 cents to a homeless person, for example, not because they want to help but because it would be embarrassing just to say no. Occasionally, the benefits of giving involve sexual attraction. In one study, the investigators posed as motorists in distress trying to flag passing cars to provide help with a flat tire. The passing cars were much more likely to stop for a woman than for a man, and the cars that stopped were generally driven by young men alone. The best guess is that the young men's altruism was not entirely unalloyed by sexual interest (West, Whitney, & Schnedler, 1975).

One additional factor that shapes whether people help each other is their cultural context. Compared to Hindu Indians, for example, European Americans are less likely to see that they have a moral imperative to help someone if they do not like that person (J. G. Miller & Bersoff, 1998). European Americans also see less of a moral imperative to help someone who has helped them in the past (J. G. Miller, Bersoff, & Harwood, 1990). And because of the cultural emphasis on taking care of "number one," Americans will say that they are acting out of self-interest, even when they are not (D. T. Miller, 1999). Overall, these findings suggest that cultural emphasis on self-reliance and self-interest may cause Americans and other members of individualistic societies to think twice before helping, while the cultural emphasis on relationships and connection may cause members of collectivistic societies to offer aid more readily.

ALTRUISM AND SELF-INTEREST

The preceding discussion suggests a somewhat unflattering portrait of human nature, especially for those of us in individualistic cultures. It seems that we often fail to help strangers in need, and when we do, our help is rather grudging and calculated, based on some expectation of later reciprocation. But that picture may be too one-sided. For while people can be callous and indifferent, they are also capable of true generosity and even, at times, of **altruism,** or helping behavior that does not benefit the helper (Figure 13.27). People share food, give blood, contribute to charities, volunteer at AIDS hospices, and resuscitate accident victims. Even more impressive are the unselfish deeds of living, genetically unrelated donors who give one of their kidneys to a stranger who would otherwise die (Sadler, Davison, Carroll, & Kounts, 1971). Consider too those commemorated by Jerusalem's Avenue of the Righteous—the European Christians who sheltered Jews during the Holocaust, risking (and often sacrificing) their own lives to save those to whom they gave refuge (London, 1970).

Why do people engage in these activities? When asked, most report that such altruistic actions make them better people (Piliavin & Callero, 1991; M. Snyder & Omoto, 1992), and the major texts of all major religions support this idea (Norenzayan & Shariff, 2008). Such acts of altruism suggest that human behavior is not always selfish. To be sure, acts of altruism in which the giver gets no benefits at all—no gratitude, no public acclaim—are fairly rare. The true miracle is that they occur at all.

Attraction

Acts of aggression or acts of helping often involve isolated incidents. Someone cuts you off in traffic, and you angrily honk your horn; a stranger on a street corner asks you for a few coins, and you do (or perhaps don't) give some. Other forms of social relationship are more enduring—and can color your life for many years. These long-lasting relationships include *friendship* and the exciting, comforting, and sometimes vexing relation that we call *love*.

What initially draws people together as friends or lovers? How do we win someone's affections? How do close relationships change over the long term? We first addressed these questions in Chapter 2, when considering the biological roots of mate selection. We will now flesh out the story by considering these issues from the vantage point of social psychology.

ATTRACTIVENESS

Common sense tells us that physical appearance is an important determinant of attraction, and formal evidence confirms that point. In one study, freshmen were randomly paired at a dance and later asked how much they liked their partner and whether he or she was someone they might want to date. After this brief encounter, what mainly determined each person's desirability as a future date was his or her physical attractiveness (Walster, Aronson, Abrahams, & Rottman, 1966). Similar results were found among clients of a commercial dating service who selected partners based on files that included a photograph, background information, and details about interests, hobbies, and personal ideals. When it came down to the actual choice, the primary determinant was the photograph (S. K. Green, Buchanan, & Heuer, 1984).

Physically attractive individuals also benefit from the common tendency to associate physical attractiveness with a variety of other positive traits, including intelligence, happiness, and good mental health (e.g., Bessenoff & Sherman, 2000; Dion, Berscheid, & Walster, 1972; Eagly, Ashmore, Makhijani, & Longo, 1991; Feingold, 1992; Jackson, Hunter, & Hodge, 1995; Langlois et al., 2000). This is, in fact, part of a larger pattern sometimes referred to as the **halo effect,** a term that refers to our tendency to assume that people who have one good trait are likely to have others (and, conversely, that people with one bad trait are likely to be bad in other regards as well). In some cases, there may be a kernel of truth in this pattern of beliefs, but unmistakably the "halo" extends farther than it should (Anderson, Adams, & Plaut, 2008). For example, people seem to make judgments about how *competent* someone is based only on facial appearance, and so, remarkably, judgments about appearance turn out to be powerful predictors of whom people will vote for in U.S. congressional elections (Todorov, Mandisodza, Goren, & Hall, 2005).

PROXIMITY

A second important factor in determining attraction is sheer proximity (Figure 13.28). By now, dozens of studies have shown that if you want to predict who will make friends with whom, the first thing to ask is who is nearby. Students who live next to each other in a dormitory or sit next to each other in classes develop stronger relations than those who live or sit only a bit farther away (Back, Schmukle, & Egloff, 2008). Similarly, members of a bomber crew became much friendlier with fellow crew members who worked right next to them than with others who worked only a few feet away (Berscheid, 1985).

In this case, what holds for friendship also holds for mate selection. The statistics are rather impressive. For example, one classic study considered all the couples who took out marriage licenses in Columbus, Ohio, during the summer of 1949. Among these couples, more than half were people who lived within 16 blocks of each other when they went out on their first date (Clarke, 1952). Much the same holds for the

halo effect The tendency to assume that people who have one good trait also have other good traits.

"Do you really love me, Anthony, or is it just because I live on the thirty-eighth floor?"

13.28 Proximity

13.29 **Familiarity and liking** The figure shows two versions of a rather well-known lady. Which do you like better?

probability that an engagement will ultimately lead to marriage; the farther apart the two live, the greater the chance that the engagement will be broken off (Berscheid & Walster, 1978).

Why is proximity so important? Part of the answer simply involves logistics rather than psychology. You cannot like someone you have never met, and the chances of meeting that someone are much greater if he is nearby. In addition, even if you have met someone and begun a relationship, distance can strain it. Indeed, the prospect of commuting and of communicating only by email and phone calls corrodes many marriages and ends many high school romances.

Beyond these obvious points, though, it also turns out that getting to know someone makes him more *familiar* to you, and familiarity in turn is itself a source of attraction. Indeed, whether we are evaluating a word in a foreign language, a melody, or the name of a commercial product, studies indicate that the more often something is seen or heard, the better it will be liked (Coates, Butler, & Berry, 2006; Moreland & Zajonc, 1982; Zajonc, 1968; also see Norton, Frost, & Ariely, 2007). Familiarity probably plays an important role in determining what we feel about other people as well. For example, people judge photographs of strangers' faces to be more likable the more often they have seen them (Jorgensen & Cervone, 1978). Likewise, which is preferred—a photo of a familiar face, or a mirror-image of that photo? If familiarity is the critical variable, our friends should prefer a photograph of our face to one of its mirror image, since they have seen the first much more often than the second. But we ourselves should prefer the mirror image, which for us is far more familiar. These predictions turn out to be correct (Mita, Dermer, & Knight, 1977; Figure 13.29).

SIMILARITY

Another important factor that influences attraction is *similarity*, but in which direction does the effect run? Do "birds of a feather flock together" or—perhaps in analogy with magnets—do "opposites attract"? Birds have more to teach us in this matter than do magnets—the evidence suggests that, in general, people tend to like others who are similar to themselves (Figure 13.30). For example, elementary school students prefer other children who perform about as well as they do in academics, sports, and music (Tesser, Campbell, & Smith, 1984), and best friends in high school tend to resemble each other in age, race, year in school, and grades (D. B. Kandel, 1978).

Often people who attract each other do differ in important personality characteristics, so that an unaggressive person might be attracted to someone relatively aggressive. On other dimensions, though, similarity is crucial. For example, attributes such as race, ethnic origin, social and educational level, family background, income, and religion do affect attraction in general and marital choice in particular. Also relevant are behavioral patterns such as the degree of gregariousness and drinking and smoking habits. One

13.30 **Similarity and attraction** People tend to be attracted to others who are similar to them, as illustrated by the pairing of soccer star Mia Hamm and baseball player Nomar Garciaparra.

widely cited study showed that engaged couples in the United States tend to be similar along all of these dimensions (Burgess & Wallin, 1943), a pattern that provides evidence for **homogamy**—a powerful tendency for like to select like.

homogamy The tendency of like to mate with like.

What produces the homogamy pattern? One possibility is that similarity really does lead to mutual liking, so that homogamy can be taken at face value. A different possibility, though, is that similarity does not matter on its own; instead, the apparent effects of similarity may be a by-product of proximity, of the fact that "few of us have an opportunity to meet, interact with, become attracted to, and marry a person markedly dissimilar from ourselves" (Berscheid & Walster, 1978, p. 87). The answer is uncertain, but in either case, the end result is the same. Like pairs with like, and heiresses rarely marry the butler except in the movies. We are not really surprised when a princess kisses a frog and he turns into a prince. But we would be surprised to see the frog turn into a peasant and then see the princess marry him anyway.

Love

Attraction tends to bring people closer together. If they are close enough, their relationship may be more than friendship and become something we celebrate with the term *love*. In fact, love involves many elements: a feeling, a physiological upheaval, a desire for sexual union, a set of living and parenting arrangements, a sharing of resources (from bank accounts to friends), a mutual defense and caretaking pact, a merging of extended families, and more. So complex is human love that, according to some authorities, psychologists might have been "wise to have abdicated responsibility for analysis of this term and left it to poets" (Reber, 1985, p. 409). Wise or not, psychologists have tried to say some things about this strange state of mind that has puzzled both sages and poets throughout the ages.

Psychologists distinguish among different kinds of love, and some of the resulting classification systems are rather complex. One scheme tries to analyze love relationships according to the presence or absence of three main components: *intimacy* (feelings of being close), *passion* (sexual attraction), and *commitment* (a decision to stay with one's partner) (Sternberg, 1986, 1988). Other psychologists propose that there are two broad categories of love. One is romantic—or passionate—love, the kind of love that one "falls into," that one is "in." The other is companionate love, a less turbulent state that emphasizes companionship, mutual trust, and care (Hatfield, 1988).

ROMANTIC LOVE

Romantic love has been described as essentially passionate: "a wildly emotional state [in which] tender and sexual feelings, elation and pain, anxiety and relief, altruism and jealousy coexist in a confusion of feelings" (Berscheid & Walster, 1978, p. 2). Lovers feel that they are in the grip of an emotion they cannot control, which comes across in the very language they use to describe their love. They "fall in love," "are swept off their feet," and "can't stop themselves." Perhaps surprisingly, men tend to fall in love more often and more quickly than women do, and women tend to fall out of love more easily than men do (Hill, Rubin, & Peplau, 1976).

romantic love An emotional state characterized by idealization of the beloved, obsessive thoughts of this person, and turbulent feelings.

According to some authors, romantic love involves two distinguishable elements: a state of physiological arousal, and a set of beliefs and attitudes that leads the person to interpret this arousal as passion. What leads to the arousal itself? One obvious source is erotic excitement, but other forms of stimulation may have the same effect. Fear, pain, and anxiety can all heighten general arousal and so can, in fact, lend fuel to romantic passion. One demonstration comes from a widely cited experiment in which

13.31 Arousal and romantic love Men who interacted with an attractive female experimenter on this bridge were more likely to show interest in her later than men who interacted with the same experimenter on solid ground.

men were approached by an attractive young woman who asked them to fill out a questionnaire (allegedly to help her with a class project); she then gave them her telephone number so they could call her later if they wanted to know more about the project. The study was conducted in Capilano Park, just north of Vancouver, British Columbia. The park is famous for its narrow, wobbly suspension bridge, precariously suspended over a shallow rapids 230 feet below (Figure 13.31). Some of the men in the study were approached while they were on the bridge itself. Others were approached after they had already crossed the bridge and were back on solid ground.

Did the men actually call the young woman later—ostensibly to discuss the experiment, but really to ask her for a date? The likelihood of their making this call depended on whether they were approached while they were on the bridge or later, after they had crossed it. If they filled out the questionnaire while crossing the bridge—at which point they might well have felt some fear and excitement—the chances were almost one in three that the men would call. If they met the young woman when they were back on safe ground, the chances of their doing so were very much lower (Dutton & Aron, 1974; but see also Kenrick & Cialdini, 1977; Kenrick, Cialdini, & Linder, 1979).

What is going on here? One way to think about it is to call to mind the Schachter-Singer theory of emotion (Chapter 12). Being on the bridge would make almost anyone feel a little jittery—it would, in other words, cause a state of arousal. The men who were approached while on the bridge detected this arousal, but they seem to have misinterpreted their own feelings, attributing their elevated heart rate and sweaty palms not to fear, but to their interest in the woman. Then, having misread their own state, they followed through in a sensible way, telephoning a woman whom they believed had excited them.

This sequence of events may help us understand why romantic love seems to thrive on obstacles. Shakespeare tells us that the "course of true love never did run smooth," but if it had, the resulting love probably would have been lacking in ardor. The fervor of a wartime romance or an illicit affair is probably fed in part by danger and frustration, and many a lover's passion becomes all the more intense for being unrequited. All of these cases involve increased arousal, whether through fear, frustration, or anxiety. We interpret this arousal as love, a cognitive appraisal that fits in perfectly with our romantic ideals, which include both the rapture of love and the agony.

13.32 The Romeo and Juliet effect Parental opposition tends to intensify rather than diminish a couple's romantic passion.

An interesting demonstration of this phenomenon is the so-called **Romeo-and-Juliet effect** (named after Shakespeare's doomed couple, whose parents violently opposed their love; Figure 13.32). This term describes the fact that parental opposition tends to intensify a couple's romantic passion rather than to diminish it. In one study, couples were asked whether their parents interfered with their relationship. The greater this interference, the more deeply the couples fell in love (Driscoll, Davis, & Lipetz, 1972). The moral is that if parents want to break up a romance, their best bet is to ignore it. If the feuding Montagues and Capulets had simply looked the other way, Romeo and Juliet might well have become bored with each other by the end of the second act.

COMPANIONATE LOVE

Romantic love tends to be a short-lived bloom. That wild and tumultuous state, with its intense emotional ups and downs, with its obsessions, fantasies, and idealizations, rarely, if ever, lasts forever. Eventually the adventure is over, and romantic love ebbs. Sometimes it turns into indifference or active dislike. Other times (and hopefully more often) it transforms into a related but gentler state of affairs—**companionate love** (Figure 13.33). This type of love is sometimes defined as the "affection we feel for those with whom our lives are deeply intertwined" (Berscheid & Hatfield, 1978, p. 176). In companionate love, the similarity of outlook, mutual caring, and trust that develop through day-to-day living become more important than the fantasies and idealization of romantic love, as the two partners try to live as happily ever after as it is possible to do in the real world. This is not to say that the earlier passion does not flare up occasionally. But it no longer has the obsessive quality that it once had, in which the lover is unable to think of anything but the beloved (Caspi & Herbener, 1990; Hatfield, 1988; Neimeyer, 1984).

CULTURE AND LOVE

It will come as no surprise that conceptions of love are—like the many other aspects of our interactions with others—a cultural product. Western cultural notions of what love is and what falling in love feels like have been fashioned by a historical heritage that goes back to Greek and Roman times (with tales of lovers hit by Cupid's arrows), was revived during the Middle Ages (with knights in armor slaying dragons to win a lady's favor), and was finally mass-produced by Hollywood (with a final fade-out in which the couple embraces and lives happily ever after). This complex set of ideas about what love is, and who is an appropriate potential love object, constitutes the context that may lead us to interpret physiological arousal as love.

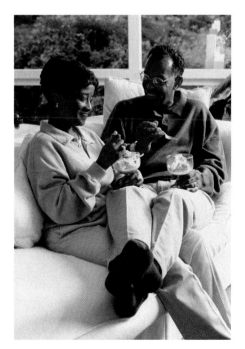

13.33 Companionate love This type of love is based upon the affection we feel for those with whom our lives are intertwined.

Romeo-and-Juliet effect The intensification of romantic love that can occur when the couple's parents oppose relationship.

companionate love An emotional state characterized by affection for those whose lives are deeply intertwined with one's own.

13.34 Culture and love Similar ideas about romantic love are found in many different cultural contexts.

Similar ideas about romantic love are found in many other cultures (Figure 13.34). Hindu myths and Chinese love songs, for example, celebrate this form of love, and, indeed, a review of the anthropological research revealed that romantic love was present in 147 of 166 cultures (Jankowiak & Fischer, 1992). Even so, it seems unlikely that any other culture has emphasized romantic love over companionate love to the extent that Western culture does (e.g., De Rougemont, 1940; V. W. Grant, 1976). This is reflected in many ways, including the fact that popular American love songs are only half as likely as popular Chinese love songs to refer to loyalty, commitment, and enduring friendship, all features of companionate love (Rothbaum & Tsang, 1998).

Why do cultures differ in these ways? One proposal derives, again, from the contrast between individualistic and collectivistic cultures. Collectivistic cultures emphasize connection to one's group, and this makes it unsurprising that (collectivistic) China would prefer songs emphasizing loyalty—a focus on the relationship, rather than on each individual's feelings. To put this point differently, romantic love often places a high premium on pursuing personal fulfillment, even, and perhaps especially, when it conflicts with other duties. On this basis, members of individualistic cultures are more likely than those in collectivistic cultures to consider romantic love important for marriage. (Dion & Dion, 1996).

SOME FINAL THOUGHTS: THE SOCIAL ANIMAL?

To what extent are we "social animals," as Aristotle claimed? As we have seen, many aspects of our thoughts, feelings, and behaviors are shaped by social forces. When we look out upon the world around us, the features of the landscape that register most deeply, and are most consequential for us, are often social features. We worry about what people think of us, whether they like us, and what intentions they harbor. We try to make sense of what they want us to do (or not do) and decide whether or not to comply with their wishes. Indeed, much of what we think about—and the source of many of our most intense emotions—is other people: strangers, friends, family, and romantic partners.

One of the principal lessons of social psychology is that we are not the autonomous individuals we might conceive ourselves to be. As we have seen, simply having another person pay attention to us changes our behavior. Far more substantial changes in our behavior arise as we conform to others' expectations, or when we are directly instructed or asked by others to act a certain way. We are intertwined within a complex web of social and cultural influences that shapes how we perceive the world and how we feel, behave, and think.

But if our analysis were to stop here, we would have missed our mark. This is because each of us is far from a passive and helpless player on the social stage. Instead, we actively try to make sense of the world, and so we work hard to understand what others are doing and thinking, and through our interpretations we create the realities with which we contend. At the same time, we make frequent efforts to act directly on our social worlds. Sometimes these efforts have small effects, but at other times their impact can be breathtaking.

A final lesson is that the social forces we have discussed can vary across time, place, and culture. Yet there is much commonality, too. Such diverse political theorists as Aristotle, Hobbes, and Confucius are still read despite the fact that they lived many centuries ago and under very different political systems than our own. They wrote about human social behavior that we can recognize even today. History provides many other examples of enduring social reactions. There are records of panics in Roman amphitheaters when the stands collapsed and of riots during sporting events in Byzantium. The Great Wall of China, the pyramids of South and Central America, and the cathedrals of Europe all testify to the ability of large groups of people to work together and to take direction from a leader. Some of the ancients even used familiar types of propaganda. When the ancient Roman city of Pompeii was destroyed by a volcano in 79 C.E., the city was evidently in the midst of a municipal election. Modern archeologists have found some of the election slogans on the excavated walls: "Vote for Vatius, all the whoremasters vote for him" and "Vote for Vatius, all the wife-beaters vote for him." While the techniques of the anti-Vatius faction may be a bit crude for our modern taste, they certainly prove that the psychology of the smear campaign has a venerable history (Raven & Rubin, 1976). Phenomena of this sort suggest that people's social nature can produce similar practices, understandings, and products in different times and places.

SUMMARY CHAPTER 13

SOCIAL COGNITION

- How we understand someone's behavior depends on the attribution we choose for the behavior. *Situational attributions* involve factors external to the person we are observing; *dispositional attributions* focus on factors internal to the person.

- People in *collectivistic cultures* emphasize the ways in which people are interdependent and tend to make situational attributions. People in *individualistic cultures* view themselves and others as independent and tend to make dispositional attributions; this tendency is so powerful that it is referred to as the *fundamental attribution error*.

- We rely on *implicit theories of personality* when we think about or remember other individuals. These theories help us understand the situations we encounter but also leave us vulnerable to error. These errors are obvious when we rely on social *stereotypes*, which are transmitted to each generation both explicitly and implicitly.

- Stereotypes can influence people's behavior implicitly. By priming a person's stereotype, the person's behavior can be influenced in an unconscious and automatic fashion. Stereotypes can also create *self-fulfilling prophecies*, leading the person we are interacting with to behave in a fashion consistent with the stereotype. A related case involves *stereotype threat*, in which anxiety about confirming the stereotype undermines someone's performance and in that fashion actually confirms the stereotype.

- *Attitudes* are a combination of beliefs, feelings about the target object or event, and some predisposition to act in accord with those beliefs and feelings. Attitudes are learned, and they can be changed in several ways. The *central route* involves cases in which we care about the issue; what matters here are arguments and evidence. If we do not care much about the issue or are distracted, we rely on the *peripheral route*, in which we are influenced by how or by whom a persuasive message is presented. Other paths to changing attitudes include intergroup contact (in the case of prejudice) and *cognitive dissonance*, which involves a person's changing her attitudes to bring them into line with her behavior.

SOCIAL INFLUENCE

- *Conformity*, *obedience*, and *compliance* are often denigrated, but these three forms of social influence are necessary for the smooth functioning of any social group.

- In studies by Sherif and by Asch, people's perceptions of the world were shaped by the way others reported what they perceived. One reason for this conformity was *informational influence*—people's desire to be right. Another reason was *normative influence*—people's desire not to appear foolish. The informational influence is increased when the situation is genuinely ambiguous; this leads to increased *social referencing*.

- Conformity is much reduced if there is any break in the group's unanimity. In collectivistic cultures, people appear to be less distressed about conforming than people in individualistic cultures appear to be.

- Some researchers propose that people with authoritarian personalities are more inclined to obedience. While there is some support for this claim, there is more powerful evidence for the influence of situations in producing obedience, as reflected in Milgram's famous studies of obedience, in which participants obeyed instructions even if these seemed to lead to injury to another person.

- Obedience is more likely if the individual believes he is not ultimately responsible for the actions, and it is increased either by a sense of psychological distance between one's actions and the result of those actions or by *dehumanizing the victim*. These adjustments, however, are usually achieved gradually, as the person slides down a slippery slope toward total obedience.

- Compliance with requests is often compelled by the *norm of reciprocity*. This is evident in the success of the *that's-not-all* technique.

- In *mere presence effects*, how people behave is influenced by the presence of an audience, although the audience can produce either *social facilitation* or *social inhibition*. This mixed data pattern is often explained by claiming that the audience increases an actor's arousal, and this strengthens the tendency to perform highly dominant responses.

- When people work as a team, often the contribution produced by each team member is less than the work she would have done if she were on her own—an effect known as *social loafing*.

- The presence of other people can cause *deindividuation*, a state in which the individual gives in to the impulses suggested by the situation. Deindividuation can lead to riotous behavior in large groups of people, but it can also lead to increased good behavior if the situation happens to produce impulses promoting those behaviors. Deindividuation can be produced by anonymity or by just having an assigned role, as was shown in the *Stanford Prison Experiment*.

- *Group polarization* refers to a tendency for decisions made by groups to be more extreme than the decisions that would have been made by any of the group members working on his own. This effect arises from several influences, including confirmation bias operating during group discussion and from each member of the group trying to take a position at the group's leading edge.

- Group decision making sometimes reveals *groupthink*, in which the group members do all they can to promote group cohesion; as a result, they downplay any doubts or disagreements, and they overestimate the likelihood of success.

SOCIAL RELATIONS

- People in groups of strangers are less likely to help others than are people who are alone or with friends, and several mechanisms contribute to this *bystander effect*. One factor is ambiguity in the situation, with many individuals convincing themselves that help is not needed. Another factor is *pluralistic ignorance*, with each individual turning to the others to find out if help is needed; but, with all doing this, each is convinced by the others' inaction that no help is needed. Yet another factor is *diffusion of responsibility*, with each group member able to think that others are the ones who should help.

- People often choose not to help because they are concerned about the time needed or the risks involved. The fact remains, however, that people sometimes do engage in altruistic acts of helping—even if doing so puts them in considerable danger.

- Many factors govern the ways people are drawn to one another, including physical attractiveness, proximity, and similarity. One reason physical attractiveness is emphasized is because of the *halo effect*, which leads us to suppose that people who have one good trait are likely to have others.

- The relationship of *love* involves many elements, including intimacy, passion, and commitment. In addition, psychologists often distinguish two types of love—romantic love and companionate love. *Romantic love* is often tumultuous, and it involves a state of physiological arousal and a set of beliefs that leads the person to interpret this arousal as passion. *Companionate love* involves a similarity of outlook, mutual caring, and trust that develop through day-to-day living together.

- Ideas about romantic love are found in many cultures, but romantic love plays a larger role in individualistic cultures than in collectivistic cultures, plausibly because collectivist cultures emphasize connection and loyalty to one's group, rather than the personal fulfillment often associated with romantic love.

 ## ONLINE STUDY TOOLS

Go to StudySpace, **wwnorton.com/studyspace**, to access additional review and enrichment materials, including the following resources for each chapter:

Organize
- Study Plan
- Chapter Outline
- Quiz+ Assessment

Learn
- Ebook
- Chapter Review
- Vocabulary Flashcards
- Drag-and-Drop Labeling Exercises
- Audio Podcast Chapter Overview

Connect
- Critical Thinking Activity
- Studying the Mind Video Podcasts
- Video Exercises
- Animations
- **ZAPS** Psychology Labs

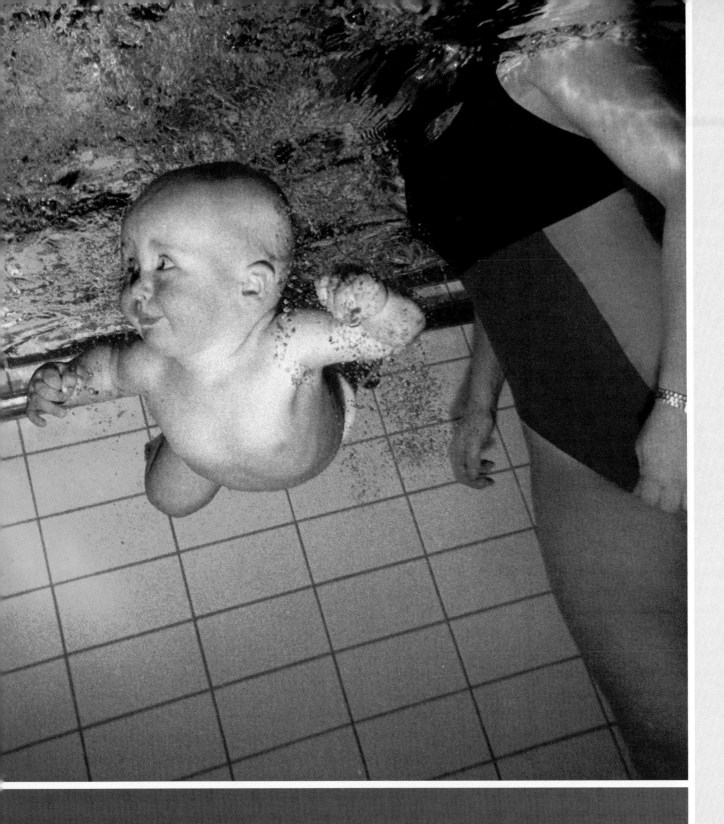

14 Development

For their first few months, chimpanzee babies are much better company than human infants. Chimps cry less, fuss less, and drool less. They're strong enough to support their heads and to ride, unassisted, on their mothers' bodies. When so inspired, they can even climb trees and swing from high branches. Human infants, in contrast, can't even hold up their heads, let alone cling to mom. They usually need a whole year to master the art of walking, and even then their gait resembles that of a slightly drunk person.

But as the weeks pass, we begin to see that lurking inside that chubby body is a sophisticated physicist, a subtle psychologist, and a versatile linguist. As the infant carefully watches the world, the world, in turn, is working on her psyche, teaching her how things fit together and how they fall apart; whom to trust and whom to avoid; what she can do with her building blocks and what to call the thing that barks. She is not only beginning to master the functions of her mind and body and the features of her environment, but also starting to understand the psyches of others—a skill known as having a *theory of mind*. This skill will enable her to work with fellow humans to imagine, plan, create, build, and do all the other things of which her species is capable. And the rest, as they say, is history—the history of the development of a single human being.

In this chapter, we'll consider what developmental psychologists have learned by studying all of these forms of development—physical and sensorimotor (changes in the body and the ability to sense and move), cognitive (growth in knowledge and intellectual skills), and socioemotional (growth in the skills needed to perceive, understand, and get along with others). And we'll see how changes in each one of these domains affect all the others, as when physical changes in the brain enable new modes of thinking and self control, which in turn support new ways of interacting with others.

At the same time, people are not just empty vessels into which the world pours its wisdom. To the contrary, a new generation of psychologists is showing that the mind comes wired with many ideas about the physical, social, and psychological worlds. As this chapter shows, those ideas continue to mature and change as development unfolds—through the social and cognitive flowering of childhood; to the risk-taking, back-talking tumult of adolescence; to the application of our knowledge throughout adulthood into old age.

Of course, nature cannot unfold without nurture, genes require environments to be expressed, and the individual needs other people to be fully realized. Accordingly, each of us provides part of the context in which others develop. As anyone who has fetched a child's thrown toy a dozen times can attest, children aren't just hanging out and growing up—they actively shape their environments. At the other end of the life span, our grandparents aren't just biding time in their rocking chairs. Rather, through the stories they tell, the examples they enact, and the things they create, they actively transmit the cultures of which they have been a part.

In William Shakespeare's *As You Like It*, the melancholy Jacques famously says, "All the world's a stage / And all the men and women merely players; / They have their exits and their entrances, / And one man in his time plays many parts / His acts being seven ages." Developmental psychologists might disagree about the stages of human development, but all agree that a person "plays many parts" across the lifespan. This chapter will help you understand the parts you have played, the parts you are playing, and the parts you will play as you move through life.

zygote The fertilized egg, formed by the union of sperm and egg.

embryonic stage The third through eighth week of prenatal development.

PRENATAL DEVELOPMENT

The story of how we grow and change across the life span is one of the most interesting in all of psychology. But as with any story, we must begin at the beginning, with a consideration of how genetic and environmental factors interact to shape us before we are even born.

From Conception to Birth

The voyage toward becoming a human being begins at conception, when a sperm and egg cell unite to form the fertilized egg or **zygote** (Figure 14.1). Within hours of this union of sperm and egg, the nuclei of the two cells merge, creating a novel combination of 23 pairs of chromosomes, half from the mother and half from the father. The zygote begins a process of dividing and redividing, producing a *blastocyst*, a mass of identical cells.

About 10 to 14 days after fertilization, the blastocyst attaches itself to the wall of the uterus. Then, the **embryonic stage** begins (Figure 14.2). During this phase, critical genes turn on and produce chemical signals that induce a process of differentiation among the proliferating cells. The mass of cells (now called an *embryo*) soon has three distinct cell types—those that will become the nervous system and the outer skin; those that will form the skeletal system and voluntary muscles; and those that will form the gut and digestive organs.

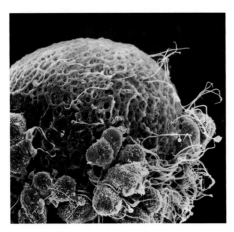

14.1 Egg and sperm cells The voyage toward becoming human begins at conception, with the union of the egg and sperm.

One month after conception, the placenta and umbilical cord have developed, and the embryo begins to develop the major organ systems of the body (including the heart and lungs), as well as arms, legs, and facial features. At about this same time, we can detect the beginnings of a nervous system: a structure called a **neural tube** with three identifiable subparts, one that will develop into the brain stem and spinal cord, and two others that will develop into the midbrain and forebrain (Figure 14.3).

neural tube The tubular structure formed early in the embryonic stage from which the central nervous system (brain and spinal cord) develops.

25 days 40 days 100 days 7 months

Forebrain
Midbrain
Brain stem and cerebellum
Spinal cord

9 months Adult (cross section)

14.3 Embryonic-fetal development of the human brain

fetal stage The prenatal period from the ninth week until birth.

Two months after conception, the **fetal stage** begins. By this point, the mass of cells (now called a *fetus*) has grown to 1 inch in length and the heart has begun to beat. The nervous system continues to grow at a remarkable pace. New nerve cells are generated at a rate that can approach 250,000 new cells per minute (Kolb & Whishaw, 2009; Mueller, 1996), and these cells start to form themselves into a network. Several mechanisms contribute to this networking, including specific genes that produce chemical signals that serve as "beacons," attracting connections that sprout from other nerve cells.

Even at this early stage, the fetus is capable of simple behaviors, and so will show a sucking reflex if its lips are touched. It's not long before other—more sophisticated—capacities come into view, including the capacity for learning. For example, in one now-classic study, DeCasper and Spence (1986) asked pregnant mothers to read aloud to their unborn infants twice a day for the last 6 weeks of their pregnancy from one of two Dr. Seuss books. Once the children were born, researchers set up an apparatus that was controlled by the way the newborns sucked on a special pacifier; if they sucked in one way, the apparatus played the story their mothers had read before they were born; if they sucked in another way, the apparatus played an unfamiliar story. The researchers found that infants adjusted their sucking pattern so that they could listen to the story to which they had been exposed in utero, indicating that the infants had "learned" one story and preferred it to the story they did not know.

The Prenatal Environment

A great deal of prenatal development is powerfully guided by the genome. Environmental factors are just as important, however, as we have seen in the capacity of the fetus to learn from its experiences. But what in general does "environment" mean in this early stage of development?

Consider the earliest stages of embryonic growth. Some of the cells in the embryo will eventually become the brain; others will become the gall bladder or the bones of the foot. But every cell in the embryo has the same genes, and so presumably all receive the same genetic instructions. How does each cell manage to develop appropriately?

The answer seems to be that the fate of each cell is determined in part by its cellular neighbors—the cells that form its physical environment. Evidence comes from studies of salamander embryos. Early in their development, salamanders have an outer layer of tissue that gradually differentiates, and cells in this layer will become teeth only if they make contact with certain other cells in the embryo's mouth region. Without this contact, cells in this layer become skin.

In humans, the cells that will become the brain initially show no distinction between neurons and glia. As the cells reproduce and differentiate, though, these two types become distinct, and the newly created neurons actually migrate toward their appropriate positions. This migration process is guided by glia that act as guidewires. Various chemicals also guide the process by attracting some types of nerve cells and repelling other types (Hatten, 2002). In all cases, the migrating neurons approach the surface of the developing cortex, but the first-arriving neurons stop short of the surface. Later-arriving neurons pass these now-stationary cells, and these late arrivals in turn are passed by even later arrivals. As a result, the cortex literally develops from the inside out, with layers closer to the surface established later than deeper layers.

Of course, it's not enough that the nerve cells end up in the right places; they also need to end up connected in the right way, so that each nerve cell sends its messages to the right target. How does each developing nerve cell come to know its eventual target? The answer, of course, begins with the genes. Early in development, genetic specifications lead neurons to form *protomaps*, providing a rough "wiring diagram" for the brain's circuits. The areas mapped in this way seem to attract connections from the appropriate inputs, so that, for example, the protomap in the projection area for vision attracts afferent fibers from the thalamus, with the result that the visual cortex comes to receive the right input signals (e.g., Rakic, 1995; for some complexities, though, see Sur & Rubenstein, 2005).

Inevitably, there are some wiring errors, but there is a safeguard in place to deal with these. Many more neurons are created than are needed, and each neuron tries to form far more connections than are required. If a neuron's connections prove either wrong or redundant, that neuron can withdraw its connections and find better targets, or it can be given a message to die (Kuan, Roth, Flavell, & Rakic, 2000; Rubenstein & Rakic, 1999). In fact, it is normal for between 20 and 80% of neurons to die as the brain develops, depending upon the region of the brain. This decimation primarily occurs early in development—in humans, about 4 to 6 months after conception (Rosenzweig, Leiman, & Breedlove, 1996)—but according to some investigators, it continues at a slower rate for much longer, perhaps even a decade.

So far, we have focused on how the local environment surrounding each neuron guides its differentiation and migration. More global features of the environment also play a major role, namely, the organism's own bodily fluids, especially its blood. Thus, for example, hormones circulating in the fetus's blood have a powerful influence on the development of the child's external anatomy, the development of the nervous system, and even later sex-typical play (Auyeung et al., 2009). Moreover, the bloodstream of mammalian embryos is intimately connected to the mother's blood supply, and so her blood, too, becomes part of the embryo's environment.

The maternal blood supplies oxygen and nutrition to the developing fetus, and this is one of the reasons why normal development depends on the nutritional state of the mother. But the mother's blood supply also plays another role—it provides a conduit through which factors in the external environment can influence the fetus. Unfortunately, many of these external factors are **teratogens**—factors that can disrupt development. The long list of teratogens includes environmental toxins such as lead and mercury, as well as alcohol, cigarette smoke, X-rays, and diseases such as rubella (German measles). Teratogens can have a number of negative effects, depending on the type, timing, and amount of exposure. For example, when a pregnant woman drinks alcohol, the alcohol enters both her bloodstream and that of her fetus. Even light drinking can affect the brain of the developing fetus (Ikonomidou et al., 2000), and heavy drinking can lead to **fetal alcohol syndrome,** which is characterized by both psychological problems (learning disorders and behavior difficulties) and physical abnormalities (smaller stature and a characteristic pattern of facial abnormalities; Figure 14.4).

teratogens Environmental factors that can disrupt healthy neural development. These include lead, alcohol, and cigarette smoke.

fetal alcohol syndrome A developmental disorder that affects children whose mothers consumed alcohol during pregnancy. Its effects include a range of psychological problems and physical abnormalities.

14.4 **Fetal alcohol syndrome** (A) Two children with fetal alcohol syndrome. (B) Clear differences are evident between the brain of a normally developing child (left) and one with an extreme case of fetal alcohol syndrome (right).

INFANCY AND CHILDHOOD

Nine months after conception, the human fetus is ready to leave the uterus to enter the outer world. *Ready*, however, is a relative term. Most other animals can walk shortly after birth, and many can take care of themselves almost immediately. Humans, in contrast, are extraordinarily helpless at birth and remain utterly dependent on others for many years.

Why is human development so slow? Lions (as just one example) chase their male cubs away from the pride by age 2 or 3. Human parents, in contrast, care for their offspring for the better part of 2 decades (or more!). One might think that this would be a great disadvantage for our species. It turns out, though, that this long period of dependency is ideal for a creature whose major specialization is its capacity for learning and whose basic invention is culture—the ways of coping with the world that each generation hands on to the next. Human infants, in other words, have a huge capacity for learning and a great deal to learn. Under these circumstances, there is much to be gained by two decades or so of living at home—even if this arrangement is at times inconvenient for child and parent alike.

In the following sections, we will consider three major aspects of development, including the infant's sensorimotor development, her cognitive development, and her socioemotional development. We should be clear at the outset that the distinctions among these aspects of development are, to some extent, just a convenience for researchers (and textbook writers), because the various aspects of development plainly interact with each other. The child's intellectual development, for example, is shaped by what she perceives and how she interacts with the world. Similarly, the child's socioemotional development depends on her cognitive development, and vice-versa.

A similar point must be made regarding the interplay of genetic and environmental factors. These, too, constantly interact to codetermine a child's developmental trajectory. For example, we mentioned in Chapters 2 and 11 that genetic factors are crucial for shaping a child's intellectual functioning, but as we discussed in those chapters, the environment also plays a huge role. Some environmental factors are biochemical (nutrients, toxins), and one tragic reminder of this comes from studies of mental retardation. For years, many types of paint contained lead-based pigments, and as the paint deteriorated, leaded dust would fall into the environment where it could be ingested or inhaled by children. Once inside the body, the lead interfered with the development of the nervous system, at large doses causing coma or even death, or at lower doses producing a litany of intellectual problems that often led to a diagnosis of mental retardation. This is why lead paint was banned for use in U.S. residences in 1978; other countries have similar (and older) bans in place.

Environmental influences also have other—and more positive—effects on the developing nervous system. Stimulus information—including objects to explore or manipulate, other organisms to interact with, and so on—seems by itself a spur to neural growth. In addition, the specifics of the stimulation help to refine the nervous system's functioning—so that the visual system, for example, becomes especially sensitive to the specific shapes in the infant's environment; circuits involved in language use are likewise adjusted so that the neural apparatus for understanding and producing language is precisely tuned to the language being spoken in the child's surroundings (Chapter 10).

Physical and Sensorimotor Development in Infancy and Childhood

The immaturity of the human infant is apparent if we examine the brain itself. Figure 14.5 shows sections of the human cortex in a newborn, a 3-month-old, and a 15-month-old child (Conel, 1939, 1947, 1955). Notice that the number of neural interconnections

(A)   **(B)**   **(C)**

14.5 Growth of neural interconnections
Sections of the human cortex in (A) a newborn, (B) a 3-month-old, and (C) a 15-month-old.

grows tremendously during this period. Indeed, by one estimate, new neural connections are formed in the infant's brain, and old ones removed, at an astonishing rate of 100,000 per second (Rakic, 1995).

This growth in brain size and complexity, and, indeed, growth in all aspects of the child's body, continues for many years, coming in spurts that each last a few months. This pattern is obvious for growth of the body (Hermanussen, 1998) but is also true for the child's brain, with the spurts typically beginning around ages 2, 6, 10, and 14 (H. T. Epstein, 1978). Each of these spurts leaves the brain up to 10% heavier than it was when the spurt began (Kolb & Whishaw, 2009).

Even at birth, the infant's immature brain is ready to support many activities. For example, infants' senses function quite well from the start. Infants can discriminate between tones of different pitch and loudness, and they show an early preference for their mother's voice over that of a strange female (Aslin, 1987; DeCasper & Fifer, 1980). Newborns' vision is not yet fully developed. Though quite near-sighted, newborns can see objects a foot or so away (the distance to a nursing mother's face) and readily discriminate brightness and color, and they can track a moving stimulus with their eyes (Aslin, 1987; Bornstein, 1985).

In contrast to newborns' relatively advanced sensory capacities, infants initially have little ability to control their body movements. They thrash around awkwardly and cannot hold up their heads. But they do have a number of important reflexes (Figure 14.6), including the **grasp reflex**—when an object touches an infant's palm, she closes her fist tightly around it. If the object is lifted up, the infant hangs on and is lifted along with it, supporting her whole weight for a minute or more.

Other infantile reflexes pertain to feeding. For example, the **rooting reflex** refers to the fact that when a baby's cheek is lightly touched, the baby's head turns toward the source of stimulation, his mouth opens, and his head continues to turn until the stimulus (usually a finger or nipple) is in his mouth. A related reflex, called the **sucking reflex**, then takes over and leads the child to suck automatically on whatever is placed in his mouth.

By her first birthday, the child will have gained vastly better control over her own actions, and this increase in skill continues over the next decade. These skills emerge in an orderly progression, as shown in Figure 14.7 (see p. 552). Infants first learn to roll over (typically by 3 months), then to sit (usually by 6 months), then to creep and then to walk (usually by 12 months). However, the ages associated with these various achievements must be understood as rough approximations, because there is variation from one infant to another and from one culture to another. For example, the Kipsigis of Kenya begin training their infants to stand and walk early on (Super, 1976), whereas the Ache of Paraguay carry their children nearly everywhere, leading to delayed onset of walking (Kaplan & Dove, 1987).

grasp reflex An infantile reflex in which an infant closes her hand into a fist when her palm is touched.

rooting reflex In an infant, the sucking elicited by stroking applied on or around the lips; the reflex aids breastfeeding.

sucking reflex An infantile reflex in which an infant sucks on whatever is placed in his mouth.

14.6 Infant reflexes Infants have a number of important reflexes, including (A) the grasp reflex, (B) the rooting reflex, and (C) the sucking reflex.

14.7 Developmental milestones

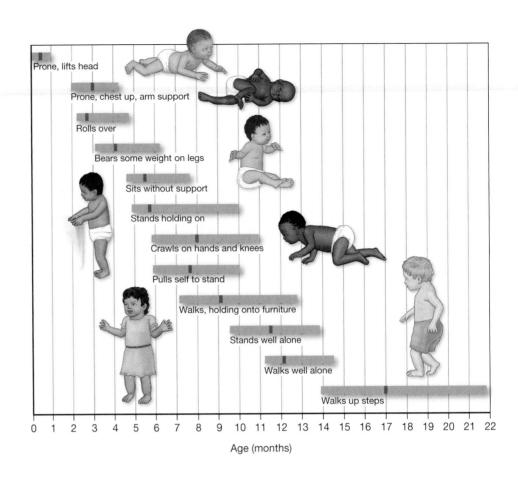

Prone, lifts head

Prone, chest up, arm support

Rolls over

Bears some weight on legs

Sits without support

Stands holding on

Crawls on hands and knees

Pulls self to stand

Walks, holding onto furniture

Stands well alone

Walks well alone

Walks up steps

0 1 2 3 4 5 6 7 8 9 10 11 12 13 14 15 16 17 18 19 20 21 22

Age (months)

Cognitive Development in Infancy and Childhood

Infants need to gain perceptual and motor skills—so that they can perceive the world and move around in it. But they also need to gain an understanding of the world in which they reside. This understanding includes simple facts about the physical world (for example, objects will fall if not adequately supported) and facts about events (for example, pouring liquid from one glass to another does not change the quantity of liquid). They also need to learn a great deal about other people—that others have different preferences and different knowledge, and that each person tends to act in accord with his own preferences, and more.

Researchers who focus on *cognitive development* study the growth of the child's understanding; for many decades, their exploration focused on claims developed by the Swiss psychologist Jean Piaget (1896–1980). Though many of Piaget's claims have been disputed, we cannot begin the study of cognitive development without considering Piaget's views, since the data he amassed and the way he framed the issues have helped shape the work of subsequent investigators.

PIAGET'S STAGE THEORY

According to Piaget, the child relies on a different *type* of thinking than an adult does. In Piaget's view, adult thinking emerges only after the child has moved through a series of stages of intellectual growth (Figure 14.8). They are the *sensorimotor period* (from birth to about 2 years), the *preoperational period* (roughly 2 to 7 years), the *concrete operational period* (7 to 12 years), and the *formal operational period* (approximately 12 years and up).

Stage	Characterization	Stage	Characterization
Sensorimotor (birth–2 years)	• Differentiates self from objects • Achieves object permanence: realizes that objects continue to exist even when no longer present to the senses	**Concrete operational** (7–12 years)	• Can think logically about concrete objects • Achieves conservation of number, mass, and weight
Preoperational (2–7 years)	• Learns to use language and to represent objects with images and words • Classifies objects by a single feature; for example, groups blocks by color (rather than shape or size)	**Formal operational** (12 years and up)	• Can think logically about abstract propositions • Becomes concerned with the possible as well as the real

14.8 Piaget's stages of intellectual growth

During the **sensorimotor period,** Piaget argued, the infant's world consists of his own sensations. Therefore, when an infant looks at a rattle, he is aware of looking at the rattle but has no conception of the rattle itself existing as a permanent, independent object. If the infant looks away from the rattle (and thus stops seeing it), then the rattle ceases to exist. It is not just "out of sight, out of mind"—it is "out of sight, out of existence." In this way, Piaget claimed, infants lack a sense of **object permanence**—the understanding that objects exist independent of our momentary sensory or motoric interactions with them.

Piaget developed this view based on his observation that infants typically look at a new toy with delight, but if the toy disappears from view, they show little concern (Figure 14.9). At a slightly later age, infants might show signs of distress when the toy disappears, but they still make no effort to retrieve it. This is true even if it seems perfectly obvious where the toy is located. For example, an experimenter might drape a light cloth over the toy while an infant is watching. In this situation, the toy is still easily within reach and its shape is still (roughly) visible through the folds of the cloth. The child watched it being covered just moments earlier. But still the infant makes no effort to retrieve it.

At about 8 months, infants do start to search for toys that have been hidden, but even then, their searching shows a peculiar limitation. Suppose, that a 9-month-old sees an experimenter hide a toy monkey under a cover located, say, to the child's right. The child

sensorimotor period In Piaget's theory, the period of cognitive development from birth to about 2 years, in which the child has not yet achieved object permanence.

object permanence The conviction that an object exists even when it is out of sight. Piaget believed infants didn't develop this level of understanding until the age of at least eight months.

14.9 Object permanence (A) A 6-month-old looks intently at a toy. (B) But when the toy is hidden from view, the infant does not search for it. According to Piaget, this is because the infant does not yet have the concept of object permanence.

14.10 The A-not-B effect (A) A 7-month-old looks at a toy that has just been placed in B, one of the two wells. (B) He continues to look at well B after both wells are covered. (C) When finally allowed to reach for the toy, he uncovers well A, in which he found the toy on a previous trial, rather than well B, in which he saw the toy being placed. In this particular sequence, he still looks at B while uncovering A, suggesting a dissociation between what the infant knows and what he does.

will happily push the cover off and snatch up the monkey. The experimenter now repeats the process a few times, always hiding the monkey under the same cover to the child's right. Again and again the child pulls the cover off and retrieves the monkey. But now the experimenter changes the procedure slightly. Very slowly and in full view of the child, she hides the toy in a different place, say, under a cover to the child's left. The child closely watches her every movement—and then does exactly what he did before. He searches under the cover on the right, even though he saw the experimenter hide the toy in another place just a moment earlier.

This phenomenon is often called the **A-not-B effect,** where *A* designates the place where the object was first hidden and *B* the place where it was hidden last (Figure 14.10). Why does this peculiar error occur? Piaget (1952) argued that the 9-month-old still has not grasped the fact that an object's existence is independent of his own actions. Thus, the child believes that his reaching toward place A (where he found the toy previously) is as much a part of the monkey as the monkey's tail is. In effect, then, the child is not really searching for a monkey; he is searching for the-monkey-that-I-find-on-the-right. No wonder, therefore, that the child continues searching in the same place (Flavell, 1985; P. L. Harris, 1987).

According to Piaget, a major accomplishment of the sensorimotor period is coming to understand that objects exist on their own—even when they are not reached for, seen, heard, or felt. Piaget held that what makes this accomplishment possible is the infant's increasingly sophisticated *schemas*—ways of interacting with the world and (at a later stage of development) ways of interacting with *ideas* about the world.

Piaget believed that newborns start life with very few schemas, and these tend to involve the infant's built-in reactions, such as sucking or grasping. In Piaget's view, these action patterns provide the infant's only means of responding to the world, and thus they provide the first mental categories through which infants organize their world. Infants understand the world, in other words, as consisting of the suckables, the graspables, and so on.

Across the first few months of life, though, the child refines and extends these schemas and learns how to integrate them into more complex ways of dealing with the world. This evolution, according to Piaget, depends on two processes that he claimed were responsible for all cognitive development: assimilation and accommodation. In the process of **assimilation,** children use the mental schemas they have already formed to interpret (and act on) the environment; in other words, they assimilate objects in the environment into their existing schemas. In the process of **accommodation,** the child's schemas change as a result of his experiences interacting with the world; that is, the schemas accommodate to the environment (Figure 14.11).

A-not-B effect The tendency of infants to reach for a hidden object where it was previously hidden (place A), rather than where it was hidden most recently while the child watched (place B).

assimilation In Piaget's theory, the developing child's process of interpreting the environment in terms of the schemas he already has.

accommodation In Piaget's theory, the developing child's process of changing his schemas based on his interactions with the environment.

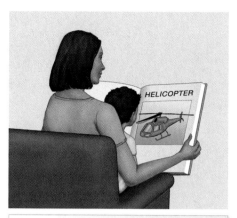

Two-year-old Josh has learned the schema for "helicopter" from his picture books.

Josh sees a plane and calls it a "helicopter." He is trying to assimilate this new flying machine into an existing schema. His mother tells him, "No, it's a plane."

Josh accommodates his schema for flying machines and continues to modify that schema to include "passenger plane," "fighter jet," and so forth.

14.11 Assimilation and accommodation

Through the processes of assimilation and accommodation, the child refines and differentiates her schemas, which gradually leads her to create a range of new schemas that enhance her ability to interact with the world. In addition, as the child becomes increasingly skilled at using schemas, she eventually becomes able to use more than one schema at a time—reaching while looking, grasping while sucking. Coordinating these individual actions into one unified exploratory schema helps to break the connection between an object and a specific way of acting on or experiencing that object. This liberation of the object from a specific action, in turn, helps propel the child toward understanding the object's independent existence—that is, it helps propel her toward object permanence and a mature understanding of what an object is.

Piaget believed that the sensorimotor period ends when children achieve object permanence (and, thus, the capacity for representational thought) at roughly 2 years of age. But, even so, the mental world of 2-year-olds is, in Piaget's view, a far cry from the world of adults. This is because 2-year-olds have not yet learned how to *interrelate* their mental representations in a coherent way. Piaget referred to the manipulation of mental representations as *operations*, and thus dubbed the period from age 2 to 7, before these mental operations are evident, as the **preoperational period.**

A revealing example of preoperational thought is the young child's apparent failure to conserve quantity. One procedure demonstrating this failure uses two identical glasses, A and B, which stand side by side and are filled with the same amount of liquid. The experimenter then asks the child whether there is more liquid in one glass or the other, then obligingly adds a drop here, a drop there until the child is completely satisfied that there is "the same to drink in this glass as in that."

The next step involves a new glass, C, which is taller but narrower than A and B (Figure 14.12). While the child is watching, the experimenter pours the entire contents of glass A into glass C. She then points to B and C and asks, "Is there more in this glass or in that, or are they the same?" To an adult, the amounts are obviously identical, since A was completely emptied into C, and A and B were made equal at the outset. But 4- or 5-year-olds insist that there is more liquid in C. When asked for their reason, they explain that the liquid comes to a much higher level in C. They seem to think that the amount has increased as it was transferred from one glass to another. They are too impressed by the visible changes in liquid level to realize that the amount nonetheless remains constant.

preoperational period In Piaget's theory, the period from about ages 2 to 7, in which a child can think representationally, but can't yet relate these representations to each other or take a point of view other than her own.

This child understands that two short glasses (A and B) contain the same amount of water.

She pours the water from one of the short glasses (A) into a tall glass (C).

When asked which glass has more water, she points to glass C, even though she poured the water from the equivalent shorter glass A.

14.12 Piaget's conservation task

In the preoperational period, children also fail tests that depend on the conservation of number. In one such test, the experimenter first shows the child two rows of pennies, and the child agrees that both rows contain the same number of coins. The experimenter then rearranges one row by spacing the pennies farther apart. Prior to age 5 or 6, children generally assert that there are now more coins in this row because "they're more spread out." But from about age 6 on, the child has no doubt that there are just as many coins in the tightly spaced row as there are in the spread-out line.

Why do preschool children fail to conserve? According to Piaget, part of the problem is their inability to interrelate the different dimensions of a situation. To conserve liquid quantity, for example, the children must first comprehend that there are two relevant factors: the height of the liquid column, and the width of the glass. They must then appreciate that a decrease in the column's height is accompanied by an increase in its width. Thus, the children must be able to attend to both dimensions simultaneously and relate the dimensions to each other. They lack this capacity, since it requires using a higher-order schema to combine initially discrete aspects of a perceptual experience into one conceptual unit.

By age 7 or so, once children have learned how to interrelate their mental representations, they enter the **concrete operational period.** They now grasp the fact that changes in one aspect of a situation can be compensated for by changes in some other aspect. They are also able to transform their own mental representations in a variety of ways and thus understand, for example, what would happen if the liquid were poured back into its original glass. But according to Piaget, children's intellectual capacities are still limited in an important way: They can apply their mental operations only to concrete objects or events (hence the term *concrete operations*). It is not until age 11 or 12 that formal operations are possible, and we will consider this stage in the following section on adolescence.

BEYOND PIAGET

Piaget's theories have shaped the ways in which psychologists, educators, and even parents conceptualize children's intellectual growth. The striking phenomena Piaget discovered seem to provide key insights into children's intellectual capacities and limitations. At the same time, though, Piaget's claims have not gone unchallenged. In particular, recent evidence has shown that Piaget underestimated the intellectual capacities of infants. Their minds, it turns out, are not a mere jumble of sensory impressions and motor reactions. Instead, infants seem to have rudimentary con-

concrete operational period In Piaget's theory, the period from about age 7 to about 12, in which the child is beginning to understand abstract ideas such as number and substance, but only as they apply to real, concrete events.

cepts of objects, numbers, and even other minds, and they use these concepts to organize their experience. In this way, the infant's world may resemble an adult's far more than Piaget realized.

EARLY CONCEPTIONS OF THE PHYSICAL WORLD

Consider Figure 14.13A, which shows an object partially occluding (hiding from view) another object behind it. Adults viewing this scene will surely perceive it as a child behind a gate. They are completely certain that when the gate is opened, they will see a whole child (Figure 14.13B) and would be astounded if the opened gate revealed a child with gaps in her body (Figure 14.13C).

Do infants perceive partially occluded objects in the same way? Or are infants' perceptual experiences fragmented, as Piaget proposed? To pursue these questions, many experiments employ **habituation procedures,** in which a stimulus is presented to the infant repeatedly. In one such study, infants were shown a rod that moved back and forth behind a solid block that occluded the rod's central portion (Figure 14.14). This display was kept in view, and the rod continued to move back and forth until the infants became bored with it (i.e., habituated) and stopped looking at the display. The investigators then presented the infants with either of two test displays. One was an unbroken rod that moved back and forth (Figure 14.14A). The other consisted of two aligned rod pieces that moved back and forth in unison (Figure 14.14B).

If these infants had perceived the original stimulus as a single complete rod, then Figure 14.14A would show them nothing new, but Figure 14.14B would seem novel. If the infants had perceived only the pieces of the original stimulus, however, Figure 14.14B would show them nothing new and Figure 14.14A would be the novel display.

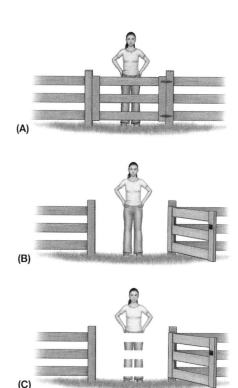

14.13 The perceptual effect of occlusion (A) A child occluded by a gate is perceived as a whole person behind a gate, so that she will look like (B) when the gate is opened, rather than being perceived as (C), a child with gaps in her body.

habituation procedure A method for studying infant perception. After some exposure to a stimulus, an infant becomes habituated and stops paying attention to it. If the infant shows renewed interest when a new stimulus is presented, this reveals that the infant regards the new stimulus as different from the old one.

Four-month-olds were shown a rod that moved back and forth behind an occluding block. After they became habituated to this display and stopped looking at it, they were shown the displays in A and B.

(A)

In this display the rod that moved back and forth was unbroken.

(B)

This display was made of two aligned rod pieces that moved back and forth together.

The infants spent much more time looking at B than at A.

14.14 The perceptual effect of occlusion in early infancy

Since these infants had already habituated to the original stimulus, a novel stimulus should attract their attention and hold it longer. Thus, by measuring how long the infants looked at each test display, we can find out which of these displays the infants considered novel—which reveals how they perceived the original display.

The evidence in this study is clear. The 4-month-old infants spent more time looking at the broken rod than at the complete rod. Apparently, they found the broken rod more novel, which suggests that they had not perceived the original stimulus as broken. Instead, they had perceived the parts of the rod in the original stimulus as connected to each other, just as an adult would (Kellman & Spelke, 1983; Kellman, Spelke, & Short, 1986; also Johnson, 2004).

Researchers have extended this finding in many ways—using habituation procedures to ask what kinds of stimuli infants find novel, and therefore learning how infants perceive the world in the first place. These studies make it clear that Piaget underestimated the perceptual sophistication of the infant, and that infants do perceive objects as having certain properties (shapes, sizes, positions) independent of the infants' momentary view of the objects. Put simply, Piaget seems to have been wrong in asserting that infants lack (what he called) object permanence. But how, therefore, can we explain Piaget's findings, which led him to conclude that infants lack object permanence? Why does an 8- or 9-month-old consistently fail in retrieving objects that are out of sight?

Most modern investigators suggest that—contrary to Piaget—infants do understand that objects continue to exist even when hidden from view, but they lack a full understanding of how to deal with those objects. To illustrate this, let's reconsider the A-not-B effect (Figure 14.10). If the infant has just reached toward A several times, then the reaching-toward-A response is well primed. To reach toward B, therefore, the infant must override this newly acquired habit. The infant knows where the toy is, but she is unable to inhibit the momentarily potent reach-toward-A response.

Consistent with this idea, many infants look at B at the same time that they reach for A, as if they know where the object is but cannot tell their arms what they have learned with their eyes (Baillargeon & Graber, 1987). Some investigators believe that the ability to override a dominant action depends on the maturation of certain areas in the prefrontal cortex, a region just in front of the motor projection area. Evidence comes from studies on monkeys with lesions in this area; they show a pattern very similar to the A-not-B error shown by human infants (A. Diamond, 1988, 1989; A. Diamond & Goldman-Rakic, 1989; also see Zelazo & Frye, 1998).

NUMBER AND MATHEMATICAL REASONING

Related points emerge when we scrutinize Piaget's other claims, such as the idea that children younger than 6 years do not conserve number, and so might say, for example, that a row of four buttons, all spread out, has more buttons in it than a row of four bunched closely together. This certainly sounds like they have failed to grasp the concept of numbers, but experiments have shown that even very young children do have some numerical ability. In one study, 6-month-olds were shown a series of slides that displayed different sets of objects. The items shown varied from one slide to the next, but each slide contained exactly three objects. One slide, for example, might show a comb, a fork, and a sponge; another might show a bottle, a brush, and a toy drum; and so on. Each slide also differed in the spatial arrangement of the items. They might be set up with two on top and one below, or in a vertical column, or with one above and two below.

With all these variables, would the infants be able to detect the one property that the slides shared—the fact that all contained three items? To find out, the experimenters used the habituation technique. They presented these sets of three until the infants became bored and stopped looking. Then they presented a series of new slides in which some of the slides showed two items, while others continued to show three. The infants spent more time looking at the slides that displayed two items rather than three. Evidently, the infants were able to step back from all the particulars of the various slides and detect the one property that all the slides had in common. In this regard, at least, the infants appear to have grasped the concept of "threeness" (Starkey, Spelke, & Gelman, 1983, 1990).

Toddlers, too, have more mathematical skill than Piaget realized and, even at this early age, grasp some aspects of what *counting* is all about. Thus, when asked to count, one 2-year-old counted "1, 2, 6," and another said "1, 13, 19." But what is important is that they used these series consistently and realized that each of these number tags has to be applied to just one object in the set to be counted. They also realized that the tags must always be used in the same order and that the last number applied is the number of items in the set. Thus, the child who counted "1, 13, 19" confidently asserted that there were 13 items when she counted a two-item set, and 19 items when she counted a three-item set. This child is obviously not using the adult's terms but does seem to have mastered some of the key ideas on which counting rests. (For more on the young child's grasp of mathematics, see Barth, Kanwisher, & Spelke, 2003; Brannon, 2003; Cordes & Brannon, 2008; Gallistel & Gelman, 2000; Gelman, 2006; Lipton & Spelke, 2006; McCrink & Wynn, 2004; N. S. Newcombe, 2002.)

Once again, though, we need to ask: If preschool children have a basic grasp of counting skills, why do they fail Piaget's tests—for example, his test for conservation of number? In part, the problem may lie in how the children were questioned in Piaget's studies. In these procedures, the child is typically questioned twice. First, the two rows of items are presented in an evenly spaced manner, so that both rows are the same length. When asked, "Which row has more, or do they both have the same?" the child quickly answers, "The same!" Now the experimenter changes the length of one of the rows—perhaps spreading the items out a bit more or pushing them more closely together—and asks again, "Which row has more, or do they both have the same?"

Why is the same question being asked again? From the point of view of the child, this may imply that the experimenter did not like his first answer and so, as adults often do, is providing him the opportunity to try again. This would obviously suggest to the child that his first answer must have been wrong, and so he changes it.

Of course, this misinterpretation is possible only because the child is not totally sure of his answer, and so he is easily swayed by what seems to be a hint from the experimenter. In other words, Piaget was correct in noting the limits of the preschool child's knowledge: The child's grasp of numerical concepts is tentative enough so that even a slight miscue can draw him off track. But this does not mean the child has no understanding of numbers or counting, and, in fact, if we question the child carefully, provide no misleading hints, and simplify the task just a little (by using smaller numbers of items), preschool children reliably succeed in the conservation task (Siegal, 1997).

SOCIAL COGNITION AND THEORY OF MIND

The social world provides yet another domain in which young children are surprisingly competent (Striano & Reid, 2006). For example, infants seem to have some understanding of other people's *intentions*. Specifically, they understand the world they observe in terms of others' goals, and not just their movements. In one study, 6-month-old infants saw an actor reach for a ball that was sitting just to the right of a teddy bear. (The left–right position of the toys was reversed for half of the infants tested.) The infant watched this event over and over, until he became bored with it. At that point, the position of the toys was switched, so now the teddy bear was on the right. Then the infant was shown one of two test events. In one, the actor again reached for the ball (although, given the switch in position, this was the first time the infant had seen a reach toward the left). In the other condition, the actor again reached for the object on the right (although, given the switch, this was the first time the infant had seen a reach toward the teddy bear).

If, in the initial observation, the infant was focusing on behavior ("reach right"), then the reach-for-ball test event involves a change, and so will be a surprise. If, however, the infant was focusing on the goal ("reach for ball"), then it is the reach for the teddy bear that involves a change, and will be a surprise. And, in fact, the latter is what the data show: Six-month-olds are more surprised by the change in goal than by the change in behavior (A. L. Woodward, 1998; Figure 14.15). Apparently, and contrary to Piaget, they understand that the object reached for is separate from the reach itself, and they are sophisticated enough in their perceptions that they understand others' actions in terms of intended goals (see also Brandone & Wellman, 2009; Luo & Baillargeon, 2005; Surian, Caldi, & Sperber, 2007; Woodward, 2009).

This emerging understanding of others' intentions is important, because it allows the young child to make sense of, and in many cases predict, how others will behave. However, understanding intentions is just one aspect of the young child's developing **theory of mind**—the set of beliefs that someone employs whenever she tries to make sense of her own behavior or that of others (Leslie, 1992; D. Premack & Woodruff, 1978;

theory of mind The set of interrelated concepts we use to make sense of our own thoughts, feelings, and behaviors, as well as those of others.

14.15 SCIENTIFIC METHOD: Can infants understand others' intentions?

Method

1. During training, 6-month-olds watched as an actor reached toward a ball on the right rather than a teddy bear on the left. The same action was repeated until the infants habituated to it.

3. The researchers measured how long the infants looked at each reach. (Longer looking would show that the infants perceived the event as new and different from the training.

 Repetition   or

Same goal   Same reach

2. During the test, the toys' positions were switched. In one condition, the actor again reached for the ball (same goal). In the other condition, the actor reached for the object in the same right-side position (same reach).

Results
Infants looked longer at a reach toward a bear on the right (a new goal, but the same behavior); they looked only briefly at a reach toward the ball on the left (same goal, but a new behavior).

CONCLUSION: Infants appear able to understand actions in terms of the actor's goal.

SOURCE STUDY: A. L. Woodward, 1998

H. M. Wellman, 1990). The theory of mind also involves *preferences*—and the young child must come to understand that people vary in their preferences and that people tend to make choices in accord with their preferences. Here, too, we see early competence: In one study, 18-month-olds watched as experimenters made "yuck" faces after tasting one food and smiled broadly after tasting another. The experimenters then made a general request to these toddlers for food, and the children responded appropriately—offering the food that the experimenter preferred, even if the children themselves preferred the other food (Repacholi & Gopnik, 1997; Rieffe, Terwogt, Koops, Stegge, & Oomen, 2001; for more on the child's theory of mind, see A. Gopnik & Meltzoff, 1997).

Yet another aspect of the theory of mind involves *beliefs*. Suppose you tell 3-year-old Susie that Johnny wants to play with his puppy. You also tell her that Johnny thinks the puppy is under the piano. If Susie is now asked where Johnny will look, she will sensibly say that he will look under the piano (H. M. Wellman & Bartsch, 1988). Like an adult, a 3-year-old understands that a person's actions depend not just on what he sees and desires, but also on what he believes.

Let's be careful, though, not to overstate young children's competence. If asked, for example, what color an object is, 3-year-olds claim that they can find out just as easily by touching an object as they can by looking at it (O'Neill, Astington, & Flavell, 1992). Likewise, 4-year-olds will confidently assert that they have always known something even if they first learned it from the experimenter just moments earlier (M. Taylor, Esbensen, & Bennett, 1994).

Another limitation concerns the child's understanding of false beliefs. According to many authors, a 3-year-old does not understand that beliefs can be true or false and that different people can have different beliefs. Evidence comes from studies using false-belief tests (Wimmer & Perner, 1983; also Lang & Perner, 2002). In a typical study of this kind, a child and a teddy bear sit in front of two boxes, one red and the other green. The experimenter opens the red box and puts a ball in it. He then opens the green box and shows the child—and the bear—that this box is empty. The teddy bear is now taken out of the room (to play for a while), and the experimenter and the child move the ball from the red box into the green one. Next comes the crucial step. The teddy bear is brought back into the room, and the child is asked, "Where will the teddy look for the ball?" Virtually all 3-year-olds and some 4-year-olds will answer, "In the green box." If you ask them why, they will answer, "Because that's where it is." It would appear, then, that these children do not really understand the nature of belief. They seem to assume that their beliefs are inevitably shared by others, and likewise, they seem not to understand that others might have beliefs that are false (Figure 14.16).

The child watches as the experimenter makes the teddy bear "hide" the ball in the red box.

(A)

While the teddy bear is gone, the experimenter and the child move the ball to the green box.

(B)

When the child is now asked, "Where does the teddy bear think the ball is?" she points to the green box.

(C)

14.16 The false-belief test

However, by age 4-1/2 or so, children get the idea that not all knowledge is shared. If they are asked, "Where will the teddy look for the candy?" they will answer, "He'll look in the red box because that's where he thinks the candy is" (H. Wellman & Lagattuta, 2000; H. Wellman, Cross, & Watson, 2001). The children now seem to have learned that different individuals have different beliefs, and that one's beliefs depend on access to the relevant information.

Socioemotional Development in Infancy and Childhood

So far, we have considered two major aspects of development—the child's sensorimotor development and her cognitive development. We now turn to a third major aspect of development: the child's emerging capacity to function as a social and emotional being.

Here, the growth from infancy to early childhood is immense. The newborn is keenly sensitive to (and quite vocal in expressing) her own needs but largely oblivious to the needs of others. Likewise, the newborn has no clue what it means to be a "friend" or how to behave differently at a birthday party than when sitting in church. Young children master these points—and many others—in a few short years.

As we turn to this third major aspect of development, recall that there are close connections among the various aspects of development. Thus the child's ability to function as a social being depends on her cognition and on her emerging theory of mind. Likewise, cognitive development is often spurred by learning from others—and so social interactions, which depend on newly developing social skills, can foster intellectual growth. With this important idea in mind, we take up the story of a child's socioemotional development.

THE EARLIEST INTERACTIONS

From the earliest days of life, infants seem predisposed to look at human faces, and even newborns just a few minutes old look longer at schematic faces than at a scrambled face (Figure 14.17; Fantz, 1963; Goren, Sarty, & Wu, 1975; M. H. Johnson, 1993; but also see Turati, 2004). Infants also tend to imitate faces. In one study, investigators sat face to face with infants less than 21 days old and made faces at them. The investigators stuck out their tongues at the infants or opened their mouths as wide as possible. Careful scrutiny of the infants' faces showed that when the investigators stuck out their tongues, the infants did too. When the investigators' mouths gaped wide open, so did the babies' (Meltzoff, 2002; Figure 14.18).

As infants attend to—and respond to—the faces they see, they are gaining an understanding of their social partners. For example, between 3 and 4 months of age, infants begin to appreciate some rudimentary facts about emotional expression and so respond more positively when their mother's facial expression (happy or sad) matches the emotional tone of the mother's voice (Kahana-Kalman & Walker-Andrews, 2001; Montague & Walker-Andrews, 2002). Infants also learn early on that their caretakers are a source of relief in times of distress. By 6 months or so, they start to calm down, apparently anticipating an adult's aid, as soon as they hear the sound of the adult's approaching footsteps. If the adult approaches and then does not pick up the distressed child, the infant is likely to protest loudly (Gekoski, Rovee-Collier, & Carulli-Rabinowitz, 1983; Lamb & Malkin, 1986).

14.17 Rudimentary face recognition in newborns Newborn babies look longer at a pattern showing a schematic face than at a scrambled or a blank pattern.

Face   Scrambled   Blank

14.18 Imitation in neonates In a remarkable study, investigators sat face-to-face with infants just a few days old. When the investigators stuck out their tongues, the infants did the same. When the investigators opened their mouths wide, or pursed their lips, the infants did too. The capacity for imitation, it seems, is in place even for very young babies!

In these ways, even the very young child begins learning about social interactions—and, in particular, starts to develop expectations for others' behavior. The opportunity for social learning broadens considerably when infants begin to crawl. This is because they soon end up in inappropriate or even dangerous situations: The infant wants to crawl toward the steep staircase, or the mud puddle, or the broken glass, and the caretaker needs to thwart these desires. Conflict is inevitable in these situations so it's no wonder that parental prohibitions, including use of the word *no*, become much more common when the child begins to move about (Zumbahlen & Crawley, 1997).

Locomotion also allows the infant to wander into strange or ambiguous situations, and this is why infants at this age begin to rely on social partners for guidance about how they should respond to unfamiliar events (Campos et al., 2000). Specifically, infants engage in **social referencing**—relying on the facial expression of their caregiver or some other adult as a source of information (Carver & Vaccaro, 2007). Is the cat dangerous? If Mom is looking at the cat and seems happy and unconcerned, then the infant relaxes. If Mom is looking at the cat and seems anxious, then the infant grows wary (Figure 14.19; Rosen, Adamson, & Bakeman, 1992; Striano & Rochat, 2000).

ATTACHMENT

As children start learning about the social world—developing expectations for how others will behave and learning to "read" the signals that others provide—they are also forming their first social relationship, with their primary caregiver, usually the mother. This is evident in the fact that, when they are between 6 and 8 months old, infants begin to show a pattern known as *separation anxiety*, in which they become visibly (and sometimes loudly) upset when their caregiver leaves the room. This is a powerful indication that the infant has formed an **attachment** to the caregiver—a strong, enduring, emotional bond.

This bond seems to grow out of the psychological comfort the mother provides the infant. Evidence for this claim comes from many sources, including a series of classic studies by Harry Harlow (1905–1981). Harlow (e.g., 1958) raised rhesus monkeys without their mothers; each rhesus infant lived alone in a cage that contained two stationary figures, one built of wire and the other of soft terry cloth. The wire figure was equipped with a nipple that yielded milk, but the terry-cloth model had none. Which figure would the monkey infants prefer—the one that provided nutrition, or the one that provided (what Harlow called) "contact comfort"? In fact, the infants spent much

14.19 Social referencing At an early age, children begin to rely on their social partners for guidance about how they should respond to unfamiliar events. They do this by examining an adult's facial expression, and they use the expression as a signal for whether a situation is dangerous or not.

social referencing A process of using others' facial expressions as a cue about the situation.

attachment The strong, enduring, emotional bond between a child and its caregivers that some psychologists consider the basis for relationships later in life.

14.20 SCIENTIFIC METHOD: Is contact comfort or food more important for infant rhesus monkeys' attachment?

Method

1. Harlow and his team raised rhesus monkeys in sterile cages without their mothers.

2. Each cage contained two stationary "mothers." One was built of wire, and the other was wrapped in soft terry-cloth.

3. In one condition, the wire mother had a nipple that provided milk, and the cloth mother did not. In the other condition, only the cloth mother provided milk.

4. Harlow measured the amount of time the infant monkeys spent with each mother.

Results: In both conditions, infants spent much more time on the terry-cloth mother than on the wire mother.

CONCLUSION: Contact comfort, not the provision of food, seems to be a key feature of attachment for rhesus monkeys.

SOURCE STUDY: Harlow, 1958

14.21 Mother as "secure base"

secure base According to John Bowlby, the relationship in which the child feels safe and protected.

imprinting In many species, the learned attachment that is formed at a particular early period.

more time on the terry-cloth "mother" than on the wire figure—especially when they were frightened. When approached by a clanking mechanical toy, they invariably rushed to the terry-cloth mother and clung tightly (Figure 14.20).

Is comfort (and not nutrition) also the key for human attachment? British psychiatrist John Bowlby argued forcefully that it is. In Bowlby's view, children become attached to a caregiver because this adult provides a **secure base** for the child, a relationship (and, for the young infant, a *place*) in which the child feels safe and protected (Figure 14.21). The child uses the secure base as a haven in times of threat, and, according to Bowlby, this provides the child with the sense of safety that allows her to explore the environment. The child is able to venture into the unknown, and explore, and learn, because she knows that, if the going gets rough, she can always return to the secure base (Waters & Cummings, 2000).

Bowlby argued that this tendency to form attachments, and to rely on the psychological comfort of a secure base, is rooted in our evolutionary past, and this is why we can easily find parallels to human attachment in other species. For example, consider the process of **imprinting**, a kind of learning that, in many species, provides the basis for an infant's attachment to its mother (e.g., Lorenz, 1935). To take a specific case, as soon as a duckling can walk (about 12 hours after hatching), it will approach and follow virtually any moving stimulus. If the duckling follows this moving object for about 10 minutes, an attachment is formed, and the bird has now imprinted on this object. From this point forward, the duckling will continue to follow the attachment object, show distress if separated from it, and run to it in circumstances involving threat.

This simple kind of learning is usually quite effective, since the first moving stimulus a duckling sees is usually its mother. But imprinting can occur to other objects, by accident or through an experimenter's manipulations. In some studies, ducklings have been exposed to a moving toy duck on wheels, or to a rectangle sliding back and forth behind a glass window, or even to the researcher's booted legs (Figure 14.22). In each case, the ducklings follow these objects as if following their mother, uttering plaintive distress calls whenever the attachment object is not nearby (E. H. Hess, 1959, 1973).

Do human infants show a similar pattern of imprinting? Some studies have compared the attachment of infants who had after-birth contact with their mothers to those who did not (usually due to medical complications in either mother or baby); the studies found little difference between the groups, and hence provided no evidence for a specific period during which human newborns form attachments (Eyer, 1992). Similarly, infants who must spend their initial days with a nurse or in an incubator do not form a lasting attachment to either. Clearly, then, the pattern of imprint-to-object-of-first-exposure, common in many species, is not found in humans.

Even with these differences between humans and other animals, the fact remains that human infants form a strong attachment to a caregiver, usually the mother—presumably because young children in most cultures spend the vast majority of their time with their mothers (M. E. Lamb, 1987, 1997). What role does this leave for the father? Infants do develop strong attachments to both parental figures (Pipp, Easterbrooks, & Brown, 1993), but mothers and fathers typically behave differently with their infant children, and there are corresponding differences in attachment. Fathers tend to be more physical and vigorous in their play, bouncing their children or tossing them in the air. In contrast, mothers generally play more quietly with their children, telling them stories or reciting nursery rhymes and providing hugs and caresses rather than tumbles and bounces. The children act accordingly, tending to run to the mother for care and comfort but to the father for active play (Figure 14.23; Clarke-Stewart, 1978; M. E. Lamb, 1997; Parke, 1981).

DIFFERENCES IN ATTACHMENT

Many aspects of the attachment process are similar for all children. But we also need to acknowledge that children differ in their patterns of attachment. To study these differences, Mary Ainsworth and her colleagues developed a procedure for assessing attachment—the so-called **strange situation** (Figure 14.24; Ainsworth & Bell, 1970; Ainsworth, Blehar, Waters, & Wall, 1978). In this procedure, the 12-month-old child is brought into an unfamiliar room that contains many toys and is allowed to explore and play with the mother present. After a while, an unfamiliar woman enters, talks to the mother, and then approaches the child. The next step is a brief separation—the mother leaves the child alone with the stranger. After a few minutes, the mother returns and the stranger leaves.

This setting is mildly stressful for most children, and by observing how the child handles the stress, Ainsworth argued that we can determine the nature of the child's attachment. Specifically, Ainsworth and subsequent researchers argued that children's behavior in this setting will fall into one of four categories. First, children who are *securely attached* will explore, play with the toys, and even make wary overtures to the stranger, so long as the mother is present. When the mother leaves, these infants will show minor distress. When she returns, they greet her with great enthusiasm.

Other children show patterns that Ainsworth regarded as signs of insecure attachment. Some of these children are described as *anxious/resistant*. They do not explore, even in the mother's presence, and become quite upset when she leaves. Upon reunion, they act ambivalent, crying and running to her to be picked up, but then kicking or slapping her and struggling to get down. Still other children show the third pattern, called *anxious/avoidant*. They are distant and aloof while the mother is present,

14.22 **Imprinted ducklings** follow Konrad Lorenz.

14.23 **Paternal bonding** Mothers play a major caregiving role across cultures. However, fathers also play an important role in caregiving.

strange situation An experimental procedure for assessing attachment, in which the child is allowed to explore an unfamiliar room with the mother present before the mother leaves for a few minutes, and then returns.

A mother and child enter an unfamiliar room with many interesting toys. The infant explores the room and plays with the toys. In the meantime, a stranger enters the room and the mother leaves.

When the mother returns to the room, she picks up the infant and comforts him if he was upset that she had left the room.

The mother then puts down the infant, who is free to return to playing with the toys.

14.24 The strange situation

internal working model A set of beliefs and expectations about how people behave in social relationships, and also guidelines for interpreting others' actions, and habitual responses to make in social settings.

and, although they sometimes search for her in her absence, they typically ignore her when she returns.

Children in the fourth category show an attachment pattern called *disorganized* (Main & Solomon, 1990). Children in this group seem to lack any organized way for dealing with the stress they experience. In the strange situation, they sometimes look dazed or confused. They show inconsistent behaviors—for example, crying loudly while trying to climb into their mothers' laps. They seem distressed by their mothers' absence, but sometimes move away from her when she returns.

In healthy, middle-class families, roughly 60% of the infants tested are categorized as "secure," 10% as "anxious/resistant," 15% as "anxious/avoidant," and 15% as "disorganized" (van Ijzendoorn, Schuengel, & Bakermans-Kranenburg, 1999). The proportion of children showing "secure" attachment is lower in lower-income families and families in which there are psychological or medical problems affecting either the parents or the children. One study, for example, assessed children who were chronically undernourished; only 7% of these were "securely attached" (Valenzuela, 1990, 1997). Likewise, mothers who are depressed, neurotic, or anxious are less likely to have securely attached infants (NICHD Early Child Care Research Network, 1997).

Many theorists argue that a child's attachment status shapes his social world in important ways. In part, this claim derives from the notion of a *secure base*: A securely attached child feels safe, confident, and willing to take initiative in a wide range of circumstances, and these traits will open a path to new experiences and new learning opportunities. Moreover, securely attached children usually have a more harmonious relationship with their caregivers and are therefore better able to learn from them; this, too, can lead to numerous advantages in months and years to come (cf. Bretherton, 1990).

In addition, Bowlby argued that the attachment relationship provides the child with an **internal working model** of the social world. This model includes a set of beliefs about how people behave in social relationships, guidelines for interpreting others' actions, and habitual responses to make in social settings. This model grows out of the child's relationship with a caregiver, and according to Bowlby, it provides a template that sets the pattern for other relationships, including friendships and even romances. Thus, for example, if the child's attachment figure is available and responsive, the child expects future relationships to be similarly gratifying. If the child's attachment figure is unavailable and insensitive, then the child develops low expectations for future relationships.

A number of studies have demonstrated that these working models of attachment do seem to have important consequences. For example, children who are securely attached at 1 year of age are more attractive to other toddlers as playmates in comparison to children who were insecurely attached (B. Fagot, 1997; Vondra, Shaw, Swearingen, Cohen, & Owens, 2001; also B. Schneider, Atkinson, & Tardif, 2001; R. A. Thompson, 1998, 1999). Likewise, children who were securely attached show more helping and concern for peers (van IJzendoorn, 1997; also see DeMulder, Denham, Schmidt, & Mitchell, 2000). Even more impressive, children who were securely attached as infants are more likely, as teenagers, to have close friends (Englund, Levy, Hyson, & Sroufe, 2000; Feeney & Collins, 2001; Shulman, Elicker, & Sroufe, 1994) and are less likely to suffer from anxiety disorders in childhood and adolescence (Warren, Huston, Egeland, & Sroufe, 1997).

Unmistakably, then, a child's attachment pattern when he is 1 year old is a powerful predictor of things to come in that child's life. But what is the mechanism behind this linkage? Bowlby argued that secure attachment leads to an internal working model that helps the child in subsequent relationships. If this is right, then secure attachment is associated with later positive outcomes because the attachment is what *produces* these outcomes, as depicted in Figure 14.25A. However, other interpretations of the data are possible. Imagine, for example, that a child has a sensitive and supportive caregiver. This could lead both to secure attachment *and* to better adjustment later on. In this case, too, we would expect secure attachment to be associated with good adjustment later in life—but not because the attachment caused the later adjustment; instead, they could be two different effects of a single cause (Figure 14.25B).

The cause-and-effect story is further complicated by the fact that someone's attachment pattern can change. Overall, attachment patterns tend to be consistent from infancy all the way to adulthood (Fraley, 2002)—and so, for example, a child who seems securely attached when first tested is likely to be classified the same way when assessed months (or even years) later. Even so, they may change, especially if there is an important change in the child's circumstances, like a parent losing a job or becoming ill. Thus, even if the 1-year-old's attachment pattern does create a trajectory likely to shape the child's life, there is nothing inevitable about that trajectory, and this, too, must be acknowledged when we try to think through how (or whether) a young child's attachment will shape life events in years to come (R. A. Thompson, 2000, 2006).

THE ROLE OF TEMPERAMENT

The differences in children's attachment styles can have important implications for later development. But *why* do children differ in this way? And in what other ways do children differ? The answers begin before birth.

Even in the uterus, some babies kick and move around more than others, and these differences in activity level continue after the child is born. Likewise, some babies are easily upset; others seem far calmer. Some babies are fearful when they encounter a novel stimulus; others show little fear and seem to constantly seek out new stimulation. Some babies seem to adjust easily to new circumstances; others seem upset by even small changes in their routine or surroundings (Figure 14.26).

Scholars refer to these variations as differences in *temperament*, defined as the characteristic pattern of emotion and behavior that is evident from an early age and determined to a considerable extent by genetic patterns (Chess & Thomas, 1982; Rothbart & Bates, 1998; Thomas & Chess, 1984). According to some theories, the child's temperament provides the core of his developing personality, and so we will have more to say about temperament in Chapter 15.

There has been debate, however, over how to describe an infant's temperament. One categorization scheme distinguishes "easy babies," who are playful and adapt quickly to new circumstances; "difficult babies," who are irritable and try to withdraw from new situations; and "slow to warm up babies," who are low in their activity level and moderate in most of their responses (Chess & Thomas, 1982). A different scheme categorizes babies in terms of three dimensions—roughly how active the baby is, whether the baby is generally cheerful or not, and whether the baby seems to have good control over itself (Rothbart & Bates, 1998). No matter how temperament is categorized, though, it seems to be heavily influenced by genetics. We know this because identical twins (who have the same genome) tend to have very similar temperaments; fraternal twins (who share only half their genes) tend to be less similar in temperament (A. Buss & Plomin, 1984).

Secure attachment → Good outcome

(A)

Secure mother → Secure attachment

Secure mother → Good outcome

(B)

14.25 Secure attachment In the first panel (A), the secure attachment and the good outcome are cause and effect. In the second panel (B), the secure attachment and the good outcome are both the effects of a third factor (the sensitive mother).

14.26 Temperament Babies differ in their characteristic patterns of emotion and behavior, including how easily they are upset.

14.27 The role of culture in training children The Oksapmin used a 27-body-part count system. Historically, the count begins with the thumb on one hand and enumerates 27 places around the upper contour of the body, ending on the little finger of the opposite hand. To count past 27, reverse up through the wrist, forearm, and around the body.

zone of proximal development The range of accomplishments that are beyond what the child can do on her own, but that she can achieve with help or guidance.

Another source of differences among children comes from the cultural context within which the child develops. Some cultural influences on development are obvious. In ancient Rome, for example, educated children learned to represent numbers with Roman numerals; modern children in the West, in contrast, learn to represent numbers with Arabic numerals. Modern children in the Oksapmin culture (in New Guinea) learn yet a different system, counting using parts of the body rather than numbers (Figure 14.27; Saxe, 1981). In each case, this culturally provided tool guides (and in some cases, limits) how the children think about and work with numerical quantities.

In addition, some social and cultural settings involve formal schooling, but others do not, and schooling is a powerful influence on the child's development (Christian, Bachman, & Morrison, 2000; Rogoff et al., 2003). Cultures also differ in what activities children are exposed to, how frequently these activities occur, and what the children's role is in the activity. These factors play an important part in determining what skills—intellectual and motor—the children will gain and the level of skill they will attain (M. Cole & Cole, 2001; Laboratory of Comparative Human Cognition, 1983; Rogoff, 1998, 2000).

In understanding these various cultural influences, though, it is crucial to bear in mind that the child is not a passive recipient of social and cultural input. Instead, the child plays a key role in selecting and shaping her social interactions in ways that, in turn, have a powerful effect on how and what she learns.

Part of the child's role in selecting and shaping her social interactions is defined by what Lev Vygotsky (1978) called the **zone of proximal development**. This term refers to the range of accomplishments that are beyond what the child could do on her own, but that are possible if the child is given help or guidance. Attentive caregivers or teachers structure their input to keep the child's performance within this zone—so that the child is challenged, but not overwhelmed, by the task's demands. Importantly, the child herself provides feedback to those around her that helps maintain this level of guidance. Thus, caregivers are able to monitor the child's progress and, in some cases, the child's frustration level, as a project proceeds, and they can then adjust accordingly how much help they offer.

The child also plays an active role whenever the processes of learning or problem solving involve the shared efforts of two or more people (after Rogoff, 1998). In such cases, it is clear that we cannot understand development if we focus either on the child or on the social context; instead, we must understand the interaction of the two and how each shapes the other.

One example of this interplay is seen in the child's capacity for remembering life events. This capacity might seem to depend entirely on processes and resources inside the individual, with little room for social influence. Evidence suggests, however, that the capacity for remembering events grows in part out of conversations in which adults help children to report on experiences. When the child is quite young, these conversations tend to be one-sided. The parent does most of the work of describing the remembered event and gets little input from the child. ("Remember when we went to see Grandma, and she gave you a teddy bear?") As the child's capacities grow, the parent retreats to a narrower role, first asking specific questions to guide the child's report ("Did you see any elephants at the zoo?"), then, at a later age, asking only broader questions ("What happened in school today?"), and eventually listening as the child reports on some earlier episode. Over the course of this process, the parent's specific questions, the sequence of questions, and their level of detail all guide the child as he figures out what is worth reporting in an event and, for that matter, what is worth paying attention to while the event is unfolding (Fivush, 1998; Fivush & Nelson, 2004; K. Nelson & Fivush, 2000; Peterson & McCabe, 1994).

Of course, parents talk to their children in different ways. Some parents tend to elaborate on what their children have said; some simply repeat the child's comments (Reese & Fivush, 1993). For example, Mexican Americans and Anglo-Americans differ in how they converse with their children and in what they converse about, with Mexican Americans' emotion talk tending to be less explanatory than Anglo-Americans'. There are also differences in adult-child conversations if we compare working-class and middle-class parents (see, for example, A. R. Eisenberg, 1999).

In each case, these differences in conversational pattern have an impact on how the child structures his or her memory. As one example, evidence suggests that American mothers talk with their children about past events much more than Asian mothers do (Mullen & Yi, 1995). These conversations may help American children to start organizing their autobiographical recall at an earlier age than Asian children. Consistent with this suggestion, when Caucasian adults are asked to report their earliest childhood memories, they tend to remember events earlier in life than do Asian adults (Fivush & Haden, 2003; Mullen, 1994). The same logic may help explain why women tend to remember events from earlier in their lives than men do. This difference in memory may result from differences in the way parents converse with their sons and daughters (Fivush & Haden, 2003; Fivush & Nelson, 2004).

THE ROLE OF PARENTING STYLES

Other kinds of differences between parents also powerfully shape the developing child. Some parents are strict, others less so; some are anxious and others not; some explain their instructions ("Go to bed so that you will feel better tomorrow") and others just assert their authority ("Go to bed!"). Across this diversity, though, researchers propose that parenting styles can be largely described in terms of just two dimensions (Maccoby & Martin, 1983). First, parents differ in how accepting they are of their children, and, with that, how responsive they are to the child's actions or needs. Second, parents differ in how demanding or controlling they are of their children's behavior. Putting these two dimensions together, we can think about parenting styles as being divided into four broad types.

Diana Baumrind (1967, 1971) described these four styles in detail. *Authoritarian parents* (high on demandingness but low on responsiveness) adhere to strict standards about how children should and should not speak and act, and attempt to mold their children's behavior accordingly. Such parents set down firm rules and meet any infractions with stern and sometimes severe punishment. Authoritarian parents do not believe it is necessary to explain the rules to their children, but expect their children to submit to them by virtue of parental authority: "It's because I say so; that's why."

At the opposite extreme, *permissive parents* (low on demandingness but high on responsiveness) set few explicit rules. These parents try not to assert their authority, impose few restrictions and controls, tend not to have set schedules (for, say, bedtime or watching TV), and rarely use punishment. They also make few demands on their children—such as putting toys away, doing schoolwork, or helping with chores.

Authoritarian parents brandish parental power; permissive parents abdicate it. A third approach lies between these extremes: *Authoritative parents* (high on both responsiveness and demandingness) exercise their power but also accept the reciprocal obligation to respond to their children's opinions and reasonable requests. These parents set down rules of conduct and enforce them, assign chores, and expect mature behavior. But they also spend time teaching their children how to act appropriately, encourage independence, and allow a good deal of verbal give and take.

Finally, a fourth pattern is that of *disengaged parents* (low on both responsiveness and demandingness). These parents exhibit a lax and undemanding approach, possibly because they are so overwhelmed by their own concerns that they have little time for child rearing. They provide few rules and demands and are relatively insensitive to their children's needs.

Why do parents adopt one parenting style over another? One factor is socioeconomic—poverty is associated with lower levels of involvement (Costello, Compton, Keeler, & Angold, 2003). A second factor is the characteristics of the child. Children who are disobedient and aggressive, for example, make it difficult for parents to use an authoritative style (Brody & Ge, 2001). Likewise, stubborn or impulsive children tend to elicit more demanding forms of parenting (Stoolmiller, 2001). In addition, children mature at different speeds, and a child who learns to crawl, walk, speak, or read precociously will be treated differently from a child who does not. Likewise, a child who understands and respects a logical reason ("Don't touch that because you'll get burned") will be more likely to elicit responsive parenting than a child who does not.

THE IMPACT OF CHILD CARE

Families differ not only in their parenting but also in their childcare arrangements. In the United States, most children grow up in households in which both parents work outside the home (National Research Council and Institute of Medicine, 2000); the situation is the same in many other countries. As a result, children often stay long hours each day with babysitters or professional childcare providers; in most of these cases, the child receives less one-on-one adult time and spends more time with other children. How does this influence children's development?

Reassuringly, research indicates that childcare centers do not harm children in any way (NICHD Early Child Research Network, 2001, 2003, 2006); in fact, high-quality childcare seems in some cases to promote the child's social competence (Figure 14.28). This optimistic assessment, however, must be tempered with concerns about variation in the *quality* of the childcare. In high-quality settings, the caregivers have had some training in child development and are usually warm, expressive, and responsive to the children's needs. In these settings, there are usually no more than a half-dozen toddlers per adult caregiver. In lower-quality settings, none of these conditions are met, and the forecast is correspondingly less positive (Love et al., 2003; N. L. Marshall, 2004; NICHD Early Child Care Research Network, 2006). One study indicated that infants enrolled in poor-quality daycare centers end up inattentive and unsociable in preschool, compared to children who spent the same amount of time in good daycare centers (Howes, 1990). In a similar study, 4-year-olds who attended higher-quality daycare centers showed better social and emotional development at age 8 than did children who attended poorer-quality centers, even when factors such as social class and income were equated (Vandell, Henderson, & Wilson, 1988).

Even with lower-quality care, though, we may not need to sound the alarm. Whatever the quality of the childcare, the main predictor of the child's status seems to be the quality of home life, including the parents' sensitivity to the child, the parents' health, and so on. As one recent report put it: "The primary conclusion is that parenting matters

14.28 Attachment and child care While some contend that any early separation from the primary caregiver may adversely affect the child, others contend that it is not the fact of child care that is important so much as it is the quality of child care.

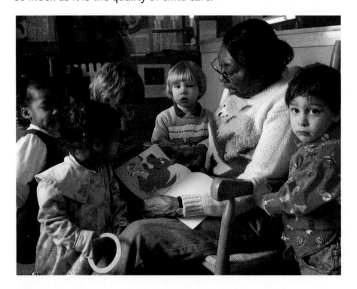

much more than does child care" (NICHD Early Child Care Research Network, 2006, p. 113). Thus, poor-quality childcare can cause problems, but these problems are much less likely if the parents are responsive to the child's needs. Even if the parents are relatively unresponsive, the magnitude of the childcare effects is small.

THE EFFECTS OF DOMESTIC CONFLICT AND DIVORCE

Another way that families differ is in the degree to which parents fight and, in some cases, whether they eventually divorce. There is no question that divorce can have negative effects on a child—but, happily, in many cases it does not. Thus, one study estimated that 20 to 25% of children of divorced families will experience significant problems (Hetherington, Bridges, & Insabella, 1998). This statistic is troubling—and is double the risk for children from intact families. Nonetheless, these same numbers tell us that 75 to 80% of children from divorced families do *not* experience significant problems.

What sorts of problems are associated with divorce? The list is long. Children whose parents have divorced are at greater risk for depression, have lower self-esteem, and tend to be less competent socially (Amato, 2001; Amato & Keith, 1991). Adolescents whose parents divorce are more likely to drop out of school and more likely to have unwanted early pregnancies (Hetherington, Bridges, & Insabella, 1998).

Can we predict which children will suffer from their parents' divorce, and which will not? The outcome tends to be worse if the children are younger at the time of the divorce. The outcome also tends to be worse if the children experienced significant conflict between their parents in the months (or years) leading up to the divorce (Cummings & Davies, 1994), although in such cases, it may be those pre-divorce tensions, and not the divorce itself, that are the source of the children's later troubles. Finally, this is another place where attachment matters. Children with secure attachments seem to cope more easily with parental conflict than children with insecure attachments (P. Davies & Forman, 2002).

WHAT HAPPENS WHEN THERE IS NO ATTACHMENT?

The data we have considered remind us that we are a resilient species. After all, most children cope perfectly well in childcare, even if it means they have less contact with their parents. Most children suffer no significant problems from divorce. But what about more severe disruption of early experience? What if there is no attachment at all? Here the effects are dramatic and remind us that the young of many species do not need just food and shelter, they also need social contact.

One source of evidence is a troubling series of experiments in which monkey infants were reared without any social interaction. They were kept warm and safe and had all the food and water they needed, but never saw another living creature (Harlow, 1962; Harlow & Novak, 1973). The results were devastating. After 3 months of isolation, these animals huddled in a corner of the cage, clasped themselves, and rocked back and forth. When they were brought together with normally reared age-mates, rather than engaging in the playful romping that is characteristic of monkeys at that age, the monkeys reared in isolation simply withdrew, huddled, rocked, and bit themselves (Figure 14.29).

Modern standards of animal care prohibit raising animals in this fashion. Sadly, though, human children do not have the same protections—a fact documented, for example, in the recent history of Romania. In the 1960s, dictator Nicolae Ceausescu launched a drive to double the population of his country in one generation. Romanian

14.29 Motherless monkeys (A) A monkey reared in isolation, huddling in terror in a corner of its cage. (B) An isolated monkey biting itself at the approach of a stranger.

14.30 Romanian orphans Many Romanian orphanages in the 1960s through the 1980s provided inadequate care and minimal social contact. Psychologists have studied children from these orphanages in order to better understand the effects of severe deprivation.

women were ordered to have five children each, and families too poor to rear all these children had to relinquish them to state-run orphanages. By 1989 (when Ceausescu was deposed and executed), the orphanages contained 150,000 children. The orphans had received inadequate nourishment and health care and had minimal social contact. For reasons that were unclear, the staff workers were instructed not to interact with the children even when bringing them their bottles (Figure 14.30).

Children who were adopted out of this setting in the first two years of life seem to have suffered no lasting effects of their experience. But children adopted later showed numerous effects. For example, years later and now living with adoptive parents, these orphans seem not to differentiate between their (adoptive) parents and other adults and do not look to their parents for reassurance in times of stress. The orphans also seem unable to form good relations with their peers (Castle et al., 1999; Croft et al., 2001; O'Connor et al., 2000; Rutter & O'Connor, 2004) and show multiple signs of impaired cognitive development (C. A. Nelson et al., 2007; Nelson, Furtado, Fox, & Zeanah, 2009).

PEER RELATIONSHIPS

So far, we have emphasized the relationship between a child and her caregivers, and for the first few years of life, this relationship is of paramount importance in the child's social world. As the child grows, however, her social world broadens—to include other children in the home, playmates, and classmates.

According to some researchers, relationships with peers exert more influence on a child's development than does the child's relationship with his parents (J. R. Harris, 1995, 1998, 2000; for contrary views, see Collins et al., 2000; Vandell, 2000). On any account, though, peer relations shape each child in crucial ways. Let's examine these relations, focusing on *friendship*.

From an early age, children prefer some of their peers over others, and by the time they are 2 years old, they show the beginnings of friendship. They seek out interactions with certain peers but avoid others. They display more positive emotions with these peers than they do with other children. They are more likely to imitate these peers and to cooperate with them than they are with others (Howes, 1996; H. S. Ross & Lollis, 1989; Werebe & Baudonniere, 1991).

Of course, as children grow, friendships change and develop. At age 6 or 7, children tend to focus on what they gain from their friends: "He has great toys"; "We can play together." This perspective gradually changes, though, to emphasize mutual liking, closeness, and loyalty (Berndt, 1996; Hartrup, 1996; Newcomb & Bagwell, 1995), and by age 9 or so, children define friendship in terms of taking care of one another, helping each other, and sharing feelings.

Friendships are important for the child for many reasons. They provide the positive experiences of shared play and shared activity. They also provide support in times of stress, information in times of uncertainty, and a training ground in which children can try out, and master, a variety of social skills. For example, children need to learn to handle conflict, and much of this learning takes place with friends. Friends quarrel, maybe even just as much as nonfriends (Fabes, Eisenberg, Smith, & Murphy, 1996). But they find ways to handle the conflict—through negotiation or cooperation—and are appreciably more likely than nonfriends to continue their interactions after the conflict is over. Having friends—and resolving conflicts with them—helps the child gain skills for solving social problems (Rubin, Bukowski, & Parker, 1998).

Children also learn valuable lessons from the candor and intimacy that friendship allows. All kinds of social interactions require interpreting others' thoughts and emotional states, and one way for children to gain that skill is via friendship. Friends discuss their thoughts and feelings in ways that nonfriends do not, and these conversations provide children with important insights into the minds of others (C. Hughes & Dunn, 1998; Maguire & Dunn, 1997).

Given all these benefits, having friends is likely to help children both immediately and in the long term. In fact, having close friends as a child is associated with many positive outcomes, including social success later in life and greater feelings of self-worth (Bagwell, Newcomb, & Bukowski, 1998; Hodges, Malone, & Perry, 1997; D. Schwartz, Dodge, Pettit, Bates, & the Conduct Problems Prevention Research Group, 2000). Children who enter kindergarten along with friends seem to like school better and have fewer adjustment problems, in comparison with children who enter kindergarten without their friends' company (Ladd, Kochenderfer, & Coleman, 1996; Ladd & Price, 1987). Children with friends are also less likely to become depressed (Bagwell, Newcomb, & Bukowski, 1998).

The effects of friendship can also be documented in another way—by looking at children who are *rejected* by their peers. Investigators have explored this point by first gathering **sociometric data**—data that describe group interactions—to determine which children are popular (liked by many), which are rejected (disliked by many), and which are neglected by peers (neither liked nor disliked). Often this determination is made simply by asking a group of children whom they like and whom they do not; a similar determination can be reached by asking teachers which of their students are accepted and which are not (Cillessen & Bukowski, 2000; Terry & Coie, 1991; Wu, Hart, Draper, & Olsen, 2001). No matter how this classification is carried out, the picture is not bright for the rejected children. When interviewed, rejected children report that they are lonely and, indeed, lonelier than the neglected children (Cassidy & Asher, 1992; N. R. Crick & Ladd, 1993). The rejected children are also the ones who are at greater risk for developing antisocial behaviors or adjustment difficulties later in life (Coie & Dodge, 1983; Dodge & Pettit, 2003; Laird, Jordan, Dodge, Pettit, & Bates, 2001).

Why does a specific child end up being popular or neglected or rejected (Figure 14.31)? Many factors contribute, including the child's attachment status (secure children tend to be popular) and the parenting style in the child's home (children with authoritative parents are more likely to be popular). Temperament matters, as inhibited or slow-to-warm-up children are more likely to be rejected (C. Hart, Newell, & Olsen, 2003). Appearances also matter, making rejection less likely for children who have attractive faces (Langlois et al., 2000) and attractive bodies (Sigelman, Miller, & Whitworth, 1986). For boys, maturing early tends to promote popularity (Duke et al.,

sociometric data Data that describe how individuals in a group interact.

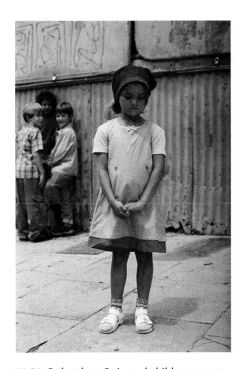

14.31 Rejection Rejected children are at elevated risk for developing antisocial behaviors and adjustment difficulties later in life.

1982; Livson & Peskin, 1980); for girls, the opposite may be the case (Aro & Taipale, 1987; Clausen, 1975).

Whatever the causes of acceptance or rejection, this dimension of social status surely does matter. We can debate which is the cause here and which is the effect, but the data indicate that so-called **aggressive-rejected** children are more aggressive (Crick, 1996), less cooperative (Newcomb, Bukowski, & Pattee, 1993), and more likely to become chronically hostile in adolescence and adulthood (J. Parker, Rubin, Price, & DeRosier, 1995; Rubin et al., 1998). **Withdrawn-rejected** children are likely to be anxious (Downey, Lebolt, Rincon, & Freitas, 1998; Zakriski & Coie, 1996) and are at increased risk for depression (Hymel, Bowker, & Woody, 1993).

All of these results speak to the importance and benefits of friendship and to the difficulties associated with being rejected. But we should also note that friends can influence each other negatively. Aggressive and disruptive friends can teach this kind of behavior (Berndt, 1999; Brendgen, Vitaro, & Bukowski, 2000). Likewise, as we will see in the next section, adolescents are often led into bad habits by their friends—including alcohol and substance abuse (Mounts & Steinberg, 1995; Urberg, Degirmenciogl & Pilgrim, 1997). Friendships are thus a double-edged sword, capable of conferring both great benefit and lasting harm.

THE DEVELOPMENT OF MORAL THINKING

One last issue draws us back to the interplay between the child's intellectual, social, and emotional development. This is the issue of morality—and the child's growing sense of right and wrong. For many years, researchers framed these issues in terms of claims offered by Lawrence Kohlberg. Kohlberg began with data gathered with a simple method. He presented boys with stories that posed moral dilemmas and questioned them about the issues these stories raised. One often-quoted example is a story about a man whose wife would die unless treated with a drug that cost far more money than the man had. The husband scraped together all the money he could, but it was not enough, so he promised the pharmacist that he would pay the balance later. The pharmacist still refused to give him the drug. In desperation, the husband broke into the pharmacy and stole the drug, and this led to the question for the research participants: They were asked whether the husband's actions were right or wrong and why.

Kohlberg posed this question and similar ones to boys of various ages. Based on their answers, he concluded that moral reasoning develops through a series of three broad levels; each level, in turn, is divided into an early stage and a late stage, so that the entire conception contains six distinct stages. The first pair of stages (and so the first level) relies on what Kohlberg calls **preconventional reasoning**—moral judgments focused on getting rewards and avoiding punishment. A child at this level might say, "If you let your wife die, you'll get in trouble." The second pair of stages relies on **conventional reasoning** and is centered on social relationships, conventions, and duties. A response such as "Your family will think you're bad if you don't help your wife" would be indicative of this type of reasoning. The final pair of stages involves **postconventional reasoning** and is concerned with ideals and broad moral principles: "It's wrong to let somebody die" (Figure 14.32).

Kohlberg intended his conception to describe all people, no matter who they are or where they live, but a number of scholars have challenged this claim. One set of concerns was raised by Carol Gilligan (1982), who argued that Kohlberg's test did a better job of reflecting males' moral reasoning than females'. In her view, men tend to see morality as a matter of justice, ultimately based on abstract, rational principles by which

aggressive-rejected The social status of children who are not respected or liked by peers and become aggressive as a result.

withdrawn-rejected The social status of children who are not respected or liked by peers and become anxious as a result.

preconventional reasoning According to Kohlberg, the first and second stages of moral reasoning, which are focused on getting rewards and avoiding punishments.

conventional reasoning According to Kohlberg, the third and fourth stages of moral reasoning, which are focused on social relationships, conventions, and duties.

postconventional reasoning According to Kohlberg, the fifth and sixth stages of moral reasoning, which are focused on ideals and broad moral principles.

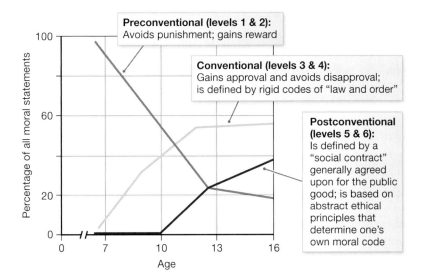

14.32 **Level of moral reasoning as a function of age** With increasing age, the level of moral reasoning changes. At age 7, virtually all moral judgments are in terms of avoiding punishment or gaining reward. At age 10, about half the judgments are based on criteria of social approval and disapproval or of a rigid code of laws. From age 13 on, children more often refer to abstract rules or ethical principles.

all individuals will end up being treated fairly. Women, in contrast, see morality more in terms of compassion, human relationships, and special responsibilities to those with whom one is intimately connected.

Gilligan's view certainly does not imply that one gender is less moral than the other. In fact, studies of moral reasoning reveal no reliable sex differences on Kohlberg's test (Brabeck, 1983; L. J. Walker, 1984, 1995; but see Baumrind, 1986; L. J. Walker, 1989). Even with these demonstrations of gender equality, though, the possibility remains that men and women do emphasize different values in their moral reasoning—a claim that raises questions about the universality of Kohlberg's proposal.

A similar critique focuses on cultural differences. A number of studies have shown that when members of less technological societies are asked to reason about moral dilemmas, they generally attain low scores on Kohlberg's scale. They justify acts on the basis of concrete issues, such as what neighbors will say, or concern over one's wife, rather than on more abstract conceptions of justice and morality (Kohlberg, 1969; Tietjen & Walker, 1985; Walker & Moran, 1991; also see Rozin, 1999). This does not mean that the inhabitants of, say, a small Turkish village are less moral than the residents of Paris or New York City. A more plausible interpretation is that Turkish villagers spend their lives in frequent face-to-face encounters with their community's members. Under the circumstances, they are likely to develop a more concrete morality that gives the greatest weight to care, responsibility, and loyalty (Kaminsky, 1984; Simpson, 1974). Given their circumstances, it is not clear that their concrete morality should be considered—as Kohlberg did—a "lower" level of morality.

Even acknowledging these points, there is clearly value in Kohlberg's account. Children do seem to progress through the stages he describes, so that there is a strong correlation between a child's age and the maturity of her moral reasoning as assessed by Kohlberg's procedure (Colby & Kohlberg, 1987). Children also seem to move through these six stages in a sequence, just as Kohlberg proposed (Colby & Kohlberg, 1987; Rest, Narvaez, Bebeau, & Thomas, 1999). There also seems to be a link between a person's moral maturity (as assessed by Kohlberg) and the likelihood that he will actually behave morally. In one study, college students were given an opportunity to cheat on a test. Only 15% of the students who reasoned at a "postconventional" level took this opportunity, compared to 55% of the "conventional" students and 70% of the "preconventional" students (Judy & Nelson, 2000; Kohlberg, Levine, & Hewer, 1984).

Even so, the relationship between someone's capacity for moral reasoning and the likelihood that he will behave morally is, at best, only moderate (Bruggeman & Hart, 1996). This makes it clear that a number of other factors also influence moral behavior in everyday life (Krebs & Denton, 2005).

CONSCIENCE AND MORAL FEELING

One way to describe what's missing from Kohlberg's theory is any discussion of conscience—the desire to act in a moral manner, and a feeling of guilt when one does not act morally. A conscience can lead someone away from bad actions (Kochanska, 1993, 2002) and toward good actions (Eisenberg, 1986, 2000), but how does a conscience emerge? One proposal is that the child learns to feel guilty about bad acts by being rewarded for good deeds and punished for bad ones.

This emphasis on reward and punishment would make sense according to the law of effect (Chapter 7). It would also make sense on other grounds. Freud argued, for example, that the threat of punishment creates anxiety in the child, and the anxiety then becomes a powerful source of "self-punishment" whenever the child approaches—or even thinks about—a forbidden action (Chapter 15).

However, the data on the effects of physical punishment challenge these ideas. If punishment leads a child to avoid bad actions, one might think that stronger, harsher punishments would lead to more avoidance. This prediction turns out to be not only false but exactly backward. Evidence suggests that, in fact, a sense of conscience is less likely to emerge in children whose parents rely on severe or harsh discipline. For example, the children of power-asserting (authoritarian) parents are more likely to cheat for a prize when they think no one is looking, and less likely to feel guilt about their misdeeds or to confess them when confronted (M. L. Hoffman, 1970).

Likewise, spanking (and other forms of physical punishment) seems to lead to decreased internalization of a moral code (Gershoff, 2002; Kazdin & Benjet, 2003), the opposite of what we would expect if physical punishments facilitate moral development. If severe physical punishment is not the key to developing a moral sense, what is? The answer lies in the child's relationship with her parents. As we have seen, young infants are intensely interested in social contact and interaction, and soon become very sensitive to an adult's signs of approval or disapproval. For some children, the disapproval itself serves as a punishment, and hence a source of anxiety.

For most children, though, the disapproval is upsetting because it undermines a social relationship, and so the child tries to avoid the disapproval in order to preserve the relationship. To gain approval, the child also does what he can to imitate the parent's behavior and motivations and to adopt the parent's beliefs. Consistent with this perspective, the better the quality of the parent-child relationship, the faster the child's progress in developing a conscience (Kochanska, 1997; Laible & Thompson, 2000). More specifically, conscience development seems to be fostered by a relationship in which the child and adult are each responsive to the other's status and needs. By the same logic, secure attachment is associated with conscience development (Kochanska, 1995; Kochanska, Aksan, Knaack, & Rhines, 2004).

ADOLESCENCE

Adolescence is a time of transition during which children become adults. The boundaries of this period are not precisely specified, but in Western society today, adolescence typically is thought to span the period from puberty through the early twenties. It is important to note that the boundaries of adolescence have varied considerably across cultures and over time (Larson & Wilson, 2004). Indeed, even in our own culture, there has been an expansion of adolescence over the past century or so.

By any measure, adolescence is a time of change. Adolescence involves physical changes, including a growth spurt, the attainment of sexual maturity, and important changes in the brain. There are also cognitive changes, including a developing capacity for abstract thought, as well as socioemotional changes, including a growing sense of self, romantic attachments, and increased independence from parents and other caregivers. Let's look at each of these types of change in turn.

Physical Development in Adolescence

One of the harbingers of adolescence is **puberty,** a several-year period of physical and sexual maturation during which time the body of a child morphs into its adult shape (Figure 14.33). In boys, puberty usually begins at about age 12. It is accompanied by a growth spurt that includes both **primary sexual characteristics** (bodily structures directly related to reproduction, such as penis, testes, and related internal organs) and **secondary sexual characteristics** (bodily structures that change with sexual maturity but are not themselves directly related to reproduction, such as facial, pubic, and underarm hair, muscle growth in the upper torso, and a deepening of the voice). One milestone in early puberty is a boy's first ejaculation, or *spermarche,* which typically occurs by about age 14.

In girls, puberty usually begins about age 10 and is accompanied by a growth spurt that involves changes in both primary sexual characteristics (genitalia and reproductive organs) and secondary sexual characteristics (growth of breasts and hips, pubic and underarm hair). One milestone in early puberty for girls is *menarche,* or the first menstrual period, which usually occurs about age 12.

As with all developmental phases, there are substantial individual differences in the timing of the various steps in puberty—and these differences matter. For boys, early

puberty The period of physical and sexual maturation in which the child's body begins to develop into its adult form.

primary sexual characteristics Bodily structures directly related to reproduction.

secondary sexual characteristics Bodily structures that change with sexual maturity but are not directly related to reproduction.

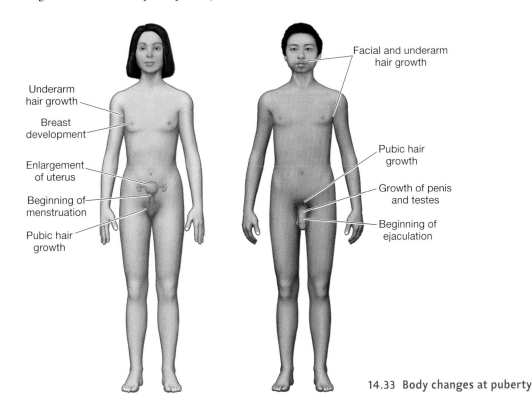

Underarm hair growth

Breast development

Enlargement of uterus

Beginning of menstruation

Pubic hair growth

Facial and underarm hair growth

Pubic hair growth

Growth of penis and testes

Beginning of ejaculation

14.33 Body changes at puberty

14.34 Temptation Brain regions sensitive to immediate rewards include (A) the posterior cingulate cortex (PCC) and medial prefrontal cortex (MPFC); (B) ventral striatum (VStr); and (C) the medial orbitofrontal cortex (MOFC).

maturation is generally beneficial, because it means that they are bigger and stronger than peers who have not yet entered puberty. Early-maturing boys are (as we mentioned earlier) more likely to be popular and often more successful athletes and more confident socially (Susman, Dorn, & Schiefelbein, 2003). It is also true, however, that early maturation can be associated with greater impulsivity, delinquency, and alcohol use (Steinberg & Morris, 2001).

In contrast, girls who develop earlier than their peers may feel more stressed than their peers, due to a mismatch between their physical and emotional levels of development, as well as the attention their changing bodies attract from older adolescents. Early-maturing girls are also more likely to have earlier sexual experiences and unwanted pregnancies and are at elevated risk for a number of psychological disorders (Archibald, Graber, & Brooks-Gunn, 2003).

For both boys and girls, adolescence also includes important changes in the nervous system. One aspect of this neurological development is the gradual myelination of the frontal lobes—a portion of the brain essential for self-regulation (Chapter 3). Myelination is a slow process and is incomplete for most (and perhaps all) of the time span of adolescence. This means that at a time when adolescents are negotiating new demands and relationships, and feeling new levels of sexual and aggressive drives, they do not have fully functional self-regulatory capacities. This mismatch between newly strengthened drives and still immature self-regulation is thought to underlie adolescents' greater levels of impulsiveness and risk taking (Figure 14.34; McClure, Laibson, Loewenstein, & Cohen, 2004; Steinberg, 2007).

Cognitive Development in Adolescence

As we have seen, infants and children make astonishing intellectual strides between birth and preadolescence, so that 10- and 11-year-olds are quite sophisticated in their cognitive capacities. Even so, preadolescents' cognitive abilities are limited in an important way. They have gained skill in a variety of mental operations, but they seem to apply these operations only to relations between concrete events; this is why Piaget referred to this stage of thinking as relying on *concrete operations*.

What did Piaget mean by "concrete" thinking? Typical 8- and 9-year-olds can easily see that 4 is an even number and 4 + 1 is odd. Similarly, they understand that 6 is even, while 6 + 1 is odd, and likewise for 8 and 8 + 1. But the same children fail to see the inevitability of this pattern; they fail to see that the addition of 1 to any even number must always produce a number that is odd. According to Piaget, children are not able to comprehend this abstract and formal relationship until about age 11 or 12, when they enter the **formal operational period.**

Piaget argued that when children enter this final stage, their ability to reason and solve problems takes a large step forward. They are now able to think about the pos-

formal operational period In Piaget's theory, the period from about age twelve on, in which a child can think abstractly and consider hypothetical possibilities.

sible as well as the real. This change is evident in an early study by Ward and Overton (1990), who asked children of various ages to perform tasks that required simple steps of logical reasoning. Roughly 15% of the 4th graders they tested were able to master the tasks, in contrast to 25% of the 6th graders and roughly 50% of the 8th graders. By the 12th grade, approximately 80% of the children showed evidence of logical reasoning.

Children apply these new capacities in their schoolwork by thinking about scientific hypothesis testing or mathematical proofs in a way they could not before. They also apply these capacities to their own lives. They imagine new possibilities in their social relations, in politics, or in religion and may start to challenge beliefs and conventions that had seemed beyond question just a few years earlier.

There is room for debate, however, about whether we should think of these changes in the terms Piaget described. Some theorists believe that adolescent cognition is not fundamentally different from the thinking of middle childhood (e.g., Siegler, 1998). What, then, produces the advances in reasoning just described? The answer may lie in the fact that older children have acquired a set of more efficient strategies, and also have markedly greater memory capacity, compared to younger children. This memory capacity (among its other benefits) allows adolescents to relate different aspects of a task to one another in ways they could not at an earlier age, and this is why their intellectual performance takes a large step forward.

No matter how we conceptualize these changes, though, one other point is crucial. Adolescents' thinking is highly variable, using sophisticated logic in some cases, but relying on much more concrete strategies in other settings. This is evident in the laboratory, and also in adolescents' day-to-day thinking (when, for example, they are exquisitely thoughtful in their challenges to political institutions but then remarkably short-sighted when thinking about the consequences of drinking and driving).

Similar variability is crucial when we compare adolescents (or adults) in different cultures. Adults in many parts of the world fail Piaget's tests of formal operations, inviting the notion that only a minority of the world's people achieve formal thinking. Other studies, however, paint a different portrait—and suggest that cultural differences tell us more about when and where people use logical thinking than about whether people *can* use logical thinking.

Socioemotional Development in Adolescence

The physical changes in adolescence are easily visible as young teens undergo a wholesale remodeling of their bodies. Even more obvious are the changes in the adolescent's social and emotional world as the adolescent asserts a new independence, his focus shifts from family to friends, and he copes with a wide range of new social, romantic, and sexual experiences.

The psychoanalyst Erik Erikson provided one influential framework for thinking about these and other major life changes in his "eight ages of man" (Figure 14.35). According to Erikson (1963), all human beings endure a series of crises as they go through the life cycle. At each stage, there is a critical confrontation between the self the individual has achieved thus far and the various social and personal demands relevant to that phase of life (Erikson & Coles, 2000). The first few of these "crises" occur in early childhood. However, a major new crisis arises in adolescence and lasts into early adulthood. This crisis concerns self-identity, and Erikson referred to this crisis as **identity versus role confusion.**

identity versus role confusion
According to Erikson, the major developmental task of adolescence is developing a stable ego identity, or sense of who one is. Failure results in developing a negative identity or in role confusion.

Stage	Developmental Task	Psychosocial Crisis	Stage	Developmental Task	Psychosocial Crisis
Infancy (0–1½ years)	Attachment to mother, which lays foundation for later trust in others	Trust versus mistrust	**Adolescence**	Making transition from childhood to adulthood; developing a sense of identity	Identity versus role confusion
Early childhood (1½–3 years)	Gaining some basic control of self and environment (e.g., toilet training, exploration)	Autonomy versus shame and doubt	**Early adulthood**	Establishing intimate bonds of love and friendship	Intimacy versus isolation
Preschool (3–6 years)	Becoming purposeful and directive	Initiative versus guilt	**Middle age**	Fulfilling life goals that involve family, career, and society; developing concerns that embrace future generations	Productivity versus stagnation
School age (6 years–puberty)	Developing social, physical, and school skills	Competence versus inferiority	**Later years**	Looking back over one's life and accepting its meaning	Integrity versus despair

14.35 Erikson's eight ages of man

THE DEVELOPMENT OF SELF-IDENTITY

One of the major tasks of adolescence is determining who one is. As part of this effort toward discovery, adolescents try on many different roles to see which ones fit best—which vocation, which ideology, which ethnic group membership. In many cases, this means trying on roles that will allow the adolescents to mark the clear distinctions between them and their parents. If their parents prefer safe behaviors, this will tempt the adolescents toward dangerous activities. If their parents prefer slow-paced recreation, the adolescents will seek excitement (J. R. Harris, 1995, 1998).

The crucial life task at this stage, in Erikson's view, is integrating changes in one's body, one's intellectual capacities, and one's role in a way that leads to a stable sense of *ego identity,* which Erikson defined as "a feeling of being at home in one's body, a sense of 'knowing where one is going,' and an inner assuredness of anticipated recognition from those who count" (Erikson, 1968, p. 165). Developing an ego identity is difficult—and success is not guaranteed. Less satisfactory outcomes include *identity confusion,* in which no stable identity emerges, or the emergence of a *negative identity,* based on undesirable roles in society, such as the identity of a delinquent.

RELATIONS WITH PARENTS AND PEERS

Traditionally, adolescence has been considered a period of great emotional stress. In adolescent years, children break away from parental control and seek to make their own choices about their activities, diet, schedule, and more. At the same time, adolescents are shifting the focus of their social worlds, so that they spend more time with, and gain much more emotional support from, peers rather than family members (Figure 14.36). These shifts allow adolescents to explore a variety of newfound freedoms, including participating in activities away from adult supervision—a prospect that is simultaneously exciting and emotionally stressful.

With all of these changes, the stage seems to be set for tension between adolescents and their parents, so it is no surprise that, across the centuries, literature (and, more recently, film) has featured youths in desperate conflict with the adult world. Perhaps surprisingly, a number of studies suggest that emotional turbulence is by no means universal among adolescents. There are conflicts, of course, and the nature of the conflict changes over the course of adolescence (Laursen, Coy, & Collins, 1998). But many investigators find that even though "storm and stress" is more likely during adolescence than at other points (Arnett, 1999), for most adolescents "development . . . is slow, gradual, and unremarkable" (Josselson, 1980, p. 189).

What determines whether adolescence will be turbulent or not? Despite the growing importance of peers during this period, parenting styles continue to make a clear difference. Evidence suggests that the adolescent children of authoritative parents (who exercise their power, but respond to their children's opinions and reasonable requests) tend to be more cheerful, more responsible, and more cooperative—both with adults and peers (Baumrind, 1967). Teenagers raised by authoritative parents also seem more confident and socially skilled (Baumrind, 1991). This parental pattern is also associated with better grades and better SAT scores as well as better social adjustment (Dornbusch, Ritter, Liederman, Roberts, & Fraleigh, 1987; Steinberg, Elkman, & Mounts, 1989; L. H. Weiss & Schwarz, 1996). These are striking findings and—impressively—are not limited to Western (individualistic) cultures. Authoritative parenting is also associated with better adolescent outcomes in collectivistic cultures (Sorkhabi, 2005; Steinberg, 2001).

No matter what the parents' style, adolescence poses serious challenges as young adults prepare to become autonomous individuals. Sometimes the process does not go well. Some adolescents engage in highly risky forms of recreation. Some end up with unplanned (and undesired) pregnancies. Some commit crimes. Some become drug users. Indeed, statistics show that all of these behaviors (including theft, murder, reckless driving, unprotected sex, and use of illegal drugs) are more likely during adolescence than at any other time of life (Arnett, 1995, 1999), although it bears emphasizing that only a minority of adolescents experience serious negative outcomes.

Why are risky and unhealthy behaviors more common among adolescents than among other age groups? Several factors seem to contribute (Reyna & Farley, 2006). We have already mentioned one—the absence of a fully mature forebrain may make it more difficult for adolescents to rein in their impulses. As a further element, it seems in many settings that adolescents simply do not think about, or take seriously, the dangers and potential consequences of their behaviors, acting instead as if they are somehow invulnerable to harm or disease (Elkind, 1978). Moreover, other evidence suggests that adolescents are especially motivated to seek out new and exciting experiences, and this *sensation seeking* regularly exposes them to risk (Arnett, 1995; Keating, 2004; Kuhn, 2006).

Hand in hand with this relative willingness to take risks, adolescents seek more and more to identify with their own generation. As a result, their actions are increasingly influenced by their friends—especially since, in adolescence, people care more and

14.36 The shifting focus of adolescent social worlds Although family members remain important to many adolescents, there is an increased focus on peer relationships.

more about being *accepted* by their friends (Bigelow & LaGaipa, 1975). They are also influenced by other peers, including the circle of individuals they interact with every day and the "crowd" they identify with—the "brains" or the "jocks" or the "druggies" (B. Brown, Moray, & Kinney, 1994). And, of course, if their friends engage in risky activities, it is more likely that they will, too (Berndt & Keefe, 1995; Reed & Roundtree, 1997).

We need to be careful, though, not to overstate the problems caused by peer influence. In fact, most teenagers report that their friends are more likely to discourage bad behaviors than to encourage them (B. Brown, Clasen, & Eicher, 1986). More generally, most peer influence is aimed at neither good behaviors nor bad ones, but behaviors that are simply *different* from those of the previous generation, like styles of clothing, hair styles, and slang that adolescents adopt (B. B. Brown, 1990; Dunphy, 1963). Of course, these styles change quickly. As they diffuse rapidly into the broader social world and in some cases become adult fashions, new trends spring up to maintain the differentiation.

ADULTHOOD AND OLDER AGE

The start of adolescence is typically defined by the onset of puberty. The end of adolescence, in contrast, and the entry into adulthood are not well marked. This is evident, for example, in the wide variety of ages that different countries (and different states) use for deciding when someone is eligible for "adult privileges" such as buying tobacco products or alcohol, voting, marrying, or serving in a nation's armed forces. Many of these privileges arrive at different ages, highlighting the uncertainty about when adulthood begins.

Even when young adults have cleared all these hurdles, though, development continues. Young adults need to develop a capacity for closeness and intimacy through love. In many cases, they prepare for the commitments of marriage and then the joys and burdens of parenting. They learn how to manage the social and financial obligations of adulthood and settle into their careers. They may have to cope with responsibilities both for their children and for their aging parents. Eventually, as they age, they must come to terms with their own lives, accepting them with a sense of integrity rather than despair. Erikson (1963) eloquently sums up this final reckoning: "It is the acceptance of one's own and only life cycle as something that had to be and that, by necessity, permitted of no substitutes" (p. 268).

Physical and Sensorimotor Changes in Adulthood

Unlike all prior developmental periods, which were characterized by increases in strength and agility, changes in physical and sensorimotor abilities throughout adulthood are largely a story of decline. Many of our physical and sensory abilities peak in our early to mid-twenties and then gradually deteriorate from this point forward. There are of course professional athletes who manage to compete at the highest levels into their forties, and healthier lifestyles have made it possible for adults to run marathons and water ski into their eighties, but these individuals are the exceptions rather than the rule (Figure 14.37). The passing decades still bring undeniable losses in physical and sensorimotor functioning.

Both sexes experience physical changes in middle age, including weight gain, loss of muscle mass, and hair thinning and graying. The age-related declines in physical and sensory capabilities accelerate in older age, and so, as people age, they become markedly weaker and slower. There are also significant declines in sight, smell, and hearing (see Figure 14.38). These various changes in turn cause other problems. For example, the risk of a fatal accident while driving (per mile driven) increases in later adulthood and jumps markedly after age 70 (Coughlin, Mohyde, D'Ambrosio, & Gilbert, 2004).

14.37 Physical abilities in older age Physical abilities peak in the early-to-mid-20s and decline from this point forward. There are, however, many people who continue to remain physically fit and active well into older age.

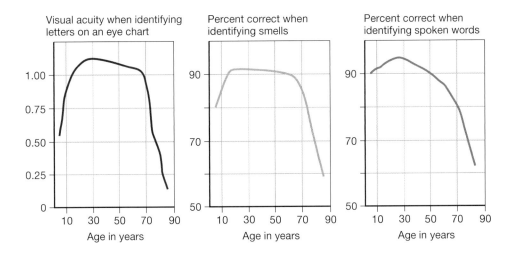

14.38 Sensory decline Older age brings declines in (A) sight, (B) smell, and (C) hearing.

Cognitive Changes in Adulthood

Life expectancies have increased dramatically. In the years of the Roman Empire, people lived only two or three decades; early in the twentieth century, death by age 40 was common. By 1955, worldwide life expectancy had reached 48 years; the world average was 68 in 1998 and is far beyond that today in many countries (WHO, 1998). These demographic changes mean that a larger proportion of the world's population is old than ever before, and this has encouraged a growing interest in the nature of age-related changes in cognitive functioning, as well as the steps that can be taken to halt or even reverse the decline associated with aging. A number of encouraging early studies have suggested predictors of "successful aging" and other studies have offered mental training programs or strategies that can help people retain and improve their cognitive abilities (Baltes, Staudinger, & Lindenberger, 1999; Freund & Baltes, 1998; Hertzog, Kramer, Wilson, & Lindenberger, 2009). To appreciate this work, we need to consider how cognitive performance changes with age.

CHANGES IN INTELLECTUAL PERFORMANCE

Failing memory has long been considered an unavoidable part of aging. However, some aspects of memory—including implicit memory and some measures of semantic memory—show little or no decline with aging. Age-related declines are evident, however, in measures of working memory and episodic memory (see, for example, Earles, Connor, Smith, & Park, 1998). The elderly also have trouble in *accessing* their memories; in fact, one of the most common complaints associated with aging is the difficulty in recalling names or specific words (G. Cohen & Burke, 1993).

The broader decline in intellectual functioning is similarly uneven—the key difference is between fluid and crystallized intelligence. As noted in Chapter 11, *fluid intelligence* refers to a person's ability to deal with new and unusual problems, whereas *crystallized intelligence* refers to a person's accumulated knowledge, including his vocabulary, the facts he knows, and the strategies he has learned.

Crystallized intelligence remains relatively stable across the life span and, in some studies, seems to grow as the individual gains life experience. Fluid intelligence shows a very different pattern. The decline starts when the person is in his twenties and continues as the years go by (Figure 14.39). However, the decline is gradual, and many individuals maintain much of their intellectual capacity into their sixties and seventies (Craik & Salthouse, 2000; Salthouse, 2000, 2004; Schaie, 1996; Verhaeghen & Salthouse, 1997).

14.39 Aging and intellectual performance As they age, people gradually decline in their intellectual performance; the decline can be documented in a range of different tests. However, the opposite pattern—an improvement with age—emerges when we consider vocabulary size, which is a reflection of crystallized, not fluid, intelligence. This figure casts these trends in terms of z-scores, which measure performance relative to the average. (Performance at the average yields a z-score of zero.)

Alzheimer's disease A degenerative brain disorder characterized by memory loss followed by increasing disorientation and culminating in physical and mental helplessness.

Figure 14.39 suggests that the decline in mental capacities proceeds steadily across much of the life span. Why, therefore, do we notice the decline primarily in the elderly? Why do people often lament the loss of cognitive capacities between ages 60 and 80, but not comment on the similar drop-off between ages 20 and 40? One reason is that as one matures, gains in crystallized intelligence often compensate for declines in fluid intelligence. Thus, as the years pass, people master more and more strategies that help them in their daily functioning, and this balances out the fact that their thinking is not as nimble as it used to be. In addition, 30- or 40-year-olds might be less able than 20-year-olds, but we do not detect the decline because the 30- or 40-year-olds still have more than adequate capacity to manage their daily routines. We detect cognitive decline only later, when the gradual drop-off in mental skills eventually leaves people with insufficient capacity to handle their daily chores (Salthouse, 2004).

Common sense also suggests that people differ markedly in how they age—some show a dramatic drop in mental capacities but others experience very little loss. This may be an instance in which common sense doesn't match the facts. If we focus on individuals who are still reasonably active and who describe themselves as being in "good to excellent health," then we find impressive consistency from one individual to the next in how they are affected by the passing years (Salthouse, 2004). Put differently, the drop-off we see in Figure 14.39 is not the result of a few unfortunate individuals who rapidly lose their abilities and pull down the average. Instead, the decline seems to affect most people, to roughly the same degree.

CAUSES OF AGE-RELATED DECLINES IN COGNITIVE FUNCTIONING

What factors are responsible for age-related cognitive declines? Some investigators propose biological explanations, cast in terms of age-related changes in blood flow or neuroanatomy, or the gradual death of neurons across the life span (Figure 14.40; Resnick et al., 2003). Still others have suggested that the cause of many of these cognitive changes is an age-related decline in working memory or the capacity for paying attention (Craik & Bialystok, 2006). In fact, all of these hypotheses may be correct, and each may describe one of the factors that governs how individuals age.

The way each individual ages is also shaped by other factors. One factor is the degree of stimulation in the individual's life (Schaie & Willis, 1996); those who are less stimulated are more vulnerable to the effects of aging. Also relevant are a wide variety of medical factors. This reflects the fact that the cells making up the central nervous system can function only if they receive an ample supply of oxygen and glucose. (In fact, the brain consumes almost 20% of the body's metabolic energy, even though it accounts for only about 2 or 3% of the overall body weight.) As a result, a wide range of bodily changes that diminish the availability of these resources can also impair brain functioning. For example, a decline in kidney function will have an impact throughout the body, but because of the brain's metabolic needs, the kidney problem may lead to a loss in mental functioning well before other symptoms appear. Likewise, circulatory problems (including problems with the heart itself or hardening of the arteries) will obviously diminish the quantity and quality of the brain's blood supply, and so can contribute to a cognitive decline (see, for example, Albert et al., 1995).

Finally, cognitive functioning in the elderly is also affected by a number of age-related diseases, including **Alzheimer's disease,** a disorder characterized by a progressive and widespread loss of nerve cells, leading to memory problems, disorientation, and, eventually, total helplessness. Evidence has made it clear that genetic factors can increase someone's risk of Alzheimer's disease (Goedert & Spillantini, 2006), but its exact causes remain uncertain.

These declines may sound downright discouraging, because they highlight the many fronts on which we are all vulnerable to aging, but there are ways to slow the process. For example, physical exercise has been shown to be good for not only the body (maintaining muscle strength and tone, as well as cardiovascular fitness) but also the mind. Although fitness programs are not a cure-all for the effects of aging, physical exercise can, in many cases, help preserve mental functioning in the elderly (Colcombe & Kramer, 2003; Cotman & Neeper, 1996; A. F. Kramer & Willis, 2002). There is also a growing literature on the efficacy of *mental* exercise, although the jury is still out on the extent and breadth of gains associated with mental exercise (Salthouse, 2006, 2007; Schooler, 2007).

Socioemotional Development in Adulthood

When we are told that Will is 2 and Sarah is 10, we can make pretty good guesses about each of their socioemotional concerns. Will is likely to be newly mobile, upset when separated from his mother, and good at saying no. Sarah is likely focused on peer acceptance and school performance and may be facing the onset of puberty. However, when we are told that Eduardo is 42 and Leticia is 50, we are much less certain what their socioemotional concerns will be. Are Eduardo and Leticia single, or married? Does either of them have children? If so, are the children still living at home? In school? Working? If Eduardo and Leticia work, do they have low-level positions, or are they CEOs of companies they have founded? If they don't work, have they already retired, or are they still in school? As these questions suggest, socioemotional concerns are linked with age much less in adulthood than in any prior stage. Nonetheless, some broad patterns are evident in adults' socioemotional goals and challenges.

THE STAGES OF ADULTHOOD

As we saw earlier, Erikson provided an 8-stage model of life-span development. Four of these stages relate to infancy and childhood, one stage relates to adolescence, and the remaining three stages relate to adulthood. These adulthood stages are concerned with *intimacy versus isolation* (20s through early 40s), *generativity versus stagnation* (40s to 60s), and *integrity versus despair* (60s to death).

The major concern during the **intimacy versus isolation** stage is developing an intimate relationship. Whether an individual's romantic relationship is heterosexual or homosexual, the key accomplishment of this stage is building a partnership (Figure 14.41; Peplau & Fingerhut, 2007). Often, these close relationships lead to marriage, and as discussed in Chapter 13, the passionate love that characterizes early romance grows into companionate love. Sometimes, close relationships lead to having or adopting children and to building a family. Many find that this is the biggest life transition of all. Becoming a parent requires large changes in work, hobbies, and perhaps most of all, one's primary relationship. Researchers have found that couples' marital satisfaction typically drops with the birth of their first child but rebounds once the children reach school age (Cowan & Cowan, 2000).

14.40 Age-related changes in the brain Aging is associated with decreases in brain tissue, as shown in these depictions of tissue loss over four years in a sample of healthy older adults (Resnick, Pham, Kraut, Zonderman, & Davatzikos, 2003). Red regions denote areas of greatest tissue loss.

intimacy versus isolation According to Erikson, a major developmental task of early adulthood is developing an intimate relationship. Failure to do so may lead to isolation.

generativity versus stagnation
According to Erikson, a major developmental task of later adulthood is finding meaning in one's work, which produces a sense of generativity. Failure leads to a sense of stagnation.

In contrast to the *relationship* goal of the intimacy versus isolation stage, the goal of the **generativity versus stagnation** stage concerns work, broadly defined. For some, the work that they do is merely a job—a means of earning a paycheck. For others, their career forms an important part of their self-identity. When asked who they are, they respond by saying what they do ("I am a doctor" or "I am a lawyer"). For others still, the work that they do is a calling—something they feel compelled to do and would do even if they weren't paid (Wrzesniewski, McCauley, Rozin, & Schwartz, 1997).

No matter what form their work takes, though, people are generative, in Erikson's view, to the extent that they contribute to the next generation and, more generally, to causes that will outlive them. Generativity can include teaching students, or training a new generation of executives. It may take the form of raising children, or of volunteer activities, such as working in a soup kitchen, coaching a soccer team, or volunteering as a docent in a museum.

AGE-RELATED CHANGES IN WELL-BEING

Before we turn to the last of the crises Erikson describes, we need to deal with a separate issue, often mentioned in discussing the adult years. This is the so-called *midlife transition* (or, sometimes, the *midlife crisis*), the point (according to conventional wisdom) at which adults reappraise what they have done with their lives thus far and may reevaluate their marriage and career (Wethington, 2000; Willis & Reid, 1999). It is a period when individuals begin to see physical changes that show that the summer of life is over and its autumn has begun, a recognition that may occur earlier in women than in men (in part because of the psychological and physiological impact of menopause). There is a shift in the way one thinks about time, from "How long have I lived?" to "How much time do I have left?" This is thought to prompt some people (especially men) to get hot new cars and seek younger playmates to reassure themselves (and the world) of their virility and power (Figure 14.42).

14.41 Intimacy versus isolation Building a partnership is a key accomplishment during early adulthood.

What do the data tell us about this period of apparent turmoil? Contrary to conventional accounts, depression, anxiety, and emotional instability do not appear to change throughout the 40s (McCrae & Costa, 2003; Mroczek & Kolarz, 1998). People do, of course, have emotional crises at various points, including their 40s. However, such emotional crises do not appear to be particularly more likely in the 40s than at other points in the life span.

It seems, then, that a midlife crisis is far from inevitable. One further crisis—and the third in the series Erikson associated with adulthood—is, however, inevitable, because it is linked to the fact of eventual death. Erikson described this stage as revolving around the polarity of **integrity versus despair.** In this stage, the individual looks back on his or her life and considers what it has all meant. If she is able to find meaning in the life she has lived, she is said to have achieved integrity and may come to some sense of peace with her life. By contrast, if a person looks back on life with feelings of regret and disappointment about missed opportunities, he is said to have fallen into despair.

integrity versus despair According to Erikson, the major developmental task of older age is finding meaning in the life that one has led. Success gives rise to a sense of integrity, whereas failure leads to despair.

A century ago in the United States, various support systems within the family, or within one's neighborhood, made this transition appreciably easier. Different generations often lived close together as an extended family, and there was much less segregation by age. Nursing homes and retirement communities were unheard of. Older people contributed to the family even when they were too old to work outside the home. They cared for the children, helped with the housekeeping, and so on. Older people were also sought out for advice on matters of child rearing and housekeeping. But today, it is less common for the elderly to have such a recognized family role. They usually live apart from their family, are effectively segregated from the rest of society, are excluded from the workforce, and have lost their role as esteemed advisers. Given these changes, it follows that the transition into senescence is quite different in the United States from what it was 100 years ago—the elderly now seem less esteemed and are certainly more isolated.

These points seem to suggest that old age would be a sorrowful time. Surprisingly, though, this hypothesis is wrong, and, in fact, positive feelings seem to be greater in older age than in earlier periods (Mroczek, 2001). What produces this pattern? According to Laura Carstensen's *socioemotional-selectivity theory* (2006), because of their shrinking time horizon, older adults increasingly value emotional goals (feeling good rather than bad) over informational goals (learning new things), and this leads to maintained or even increased levels of positive emotion. Older adults also report being able to better control their emotions than younger adults (Gross et al., 1998). These reports are borne out by the finding that older adults attend to negative aspects of their environments to a lesser degree than younger adults (Mather & Carstensen, 2003). Thus, despite the losses that older adults face, these data tell us that they enjoy comparable—or even enhanced—levels of well-being, which is good news indeed for all of us who aspire to live to a ripe old age.

"Happy fortieth. I'll take the muscle tone in your upper arms, the girlish timbre of your voice, your amazing tolerance for caffeine, and your ability to digest French fries. The rest of you can stay."

14.42 Midlife transition

SOME FINAL THOUGHTS: AVOIDING DICHOTOMIES

In many domains, theorists are fond of *dichotomies*—either-or proposals, typically cast in fairly stark terms. Over and over, though, we have seen that these dichotomies can mislead us. One prevalent dichotomy in the study of development is evident when we ask, Does development proceed through distinct stages, or is it continuous? Theorists such as Piaget used the term *stage* in the same way that the term is used in embryology, to indicate distinct phases of an animal's life with sharp discontinuities between them. As an example, the difference between a tadpole and a frog is not just a matter of "more this" or "less that." Instead, there is a qualitative difference between the two, with different anatomy (absence of tail, presence of legs), different breathing mechanisms (lungs vs. gills), different food needs, and more. To be sure, the change from one to the other takes a while, but by the time the creature is a frog, its tadpole days are emphatically over. Is this stage conception a valid description of a child's developmental trajectory, say, in the domain of cognitive development? The answer turns out to be yes and no, because young children and older ones are plainly different but also have much in common.

The status of a stage theory is similarly unclear if we ask whether the intellectual abilities of older adults differ from those of younger adults. Sensory acuity and processing speed clearly change with age but crystallized intelligence remains largely intact throughout adulthood. Even within a single domain—memory, for example—we find elements of change (e.g., a decline in working memory) and elements of stability (e.g., in implicit memory). Over and over, we see that development involves *change*, but there is much more continuity in development than a view emphasizing distinct stages would suggest. In the end, the dichotomy between "stages" and "continuity" is unproductive, because each notion captures important aspects of the truth.

A second misleading dichotomy is evident when we ask, Should we understand development in terms of biological influences or experience? The "nature/nurture" distinction is just as misleading here as it is in other domains, such as what determines a person's personality or IQ. Throughout development, we see a constant interplay between biological influences and experience, with the biologically rooted maturational tendencies interacting with (and sometimes dependent on) environmental factors that range from exposure to toxins, to educational opportunities, to patterns of physical and mental activity.

Finally, we also need to avoid either-or frameworks that imply clear distinctions among physical, cognitive, and socioemotional aspects of development. To take just one example, a child's intellectual development depends on the physical maturation of his brain, as well as his social interactions with others. Intellectual development also includes a growing ability to think about and understand others—the child's theory of mind. This interpenetration of physical, cognitive, and socioemotional aspects of functioning is also evident throughout adulthood: people seek to build on physical assets, and compensate for physical challenges, by using cognitive and emotional resources to their fullest. Hence, just as the influences of nature and nurture are evident only through their interaction, so physical, cognitive, and socioemotional development are interwoven to constitute the whole person.

SUMMARY CHAPTER 14

PRENATAL DEVELOPMENT

- Organisms grow as they change from a fertilized egg to an embryo, and then to a fetus. Prenatal development is guided by the genome, but environmental factors are also crucial.

- Some environmental factors are local, such as those that shape cell differentiation in the brain. Other environmental factors are global, such as the presence of *teratogens*, factors that disrupt development.

INFANCY AND CHILDHOOD

- In humans, growth and brain maturation continue long after birth, but this lengthy period of development is advantageous for a species whose major specialization is its capacity for learning and whose basic invention is culture.

- Infants have a number of reflexes that help them through their initial period of helplessness. Examples are the *grasp reflex,* the *rooting reflex,* and the *sucking reflex.* Newborns also have reasonably mature sensory capacities.

- According to Jean Piaget, the first stage of cognitive development is the *sensorimotor period* (birth to to age 2). During this period, the infant develops the concept of *object permanence.* In the *preoperational period* (age 2 to 7), children are capable of representational thought but lack the ability to organize that thought. This is evident in their inability to conserve number and quantity. Piaget believed that at about age 7, children begin to manipulate mental representations. In his view, they remain in the *concrete operational period,* which lacks an element of abstractness, until they are about age 12.

- Studies of visual perception using *habituation procedures* suggest that—despite Piaget's claims—infants come equipped with some built-in understanding of the physical world. Infants show appropriate reactions to perceptual occlusion and have some concept of object permanence, although they are rather inept in searching for hidden objects. One reason is that the infant has difficulty in overriding the tendency to reach for an object at a place she had previously seen it, as shown by the *A-not-B effect.*

- Further studies show that infants can perceive numerical equivalence if the number of objects in the set is small enough and that they have some rudiments of numerical reasoning.

- Piaget also underestimated infants' capacity for social cognition. Infants seem to understand others' actions in terms of their goals, and not in terms of the specific movements themselves. It also turns out that preschoolers have the rudiments of a *theory of mind,* although their emerging competence sits side by side with limitations, as can be seen in children's poor performance with false belief tasks.

- In the domain of socioemotional development, from a very early age, infants are keenly interested in face-to-face interaction. Between 7 and 9 months, infants begin to crawl, creating the first conflicts between infants and caregivers (if the infant crawls into a dangerous or inappropriate situation), and creating the need for *social referencing.*

- Infants begin to feel *separation anxiety* between 6 and 8 months of age and have a need for contact comfort, which, according to Bowlby, provides the infant with a *secure base.*

- Infants differ in their beliefs about the social world—or *internal working models*—and this is evident in different patterns of *attachment.* Attachment is usually assessed by observing the behavior of children in the *Strange Situation.* In this situation, some children are classified as *securely attached,* others show *anxious/resistant* or *anxious/avoidant* attachment, and others show a *disorganized* pattern of attachment. Styles of attachment are relatively stable, but they can change if the child's circumstances change. The style of attachment is predictive of many subsequent events in the child's social and emotional development, but there is debate over the mechanisms behind these correlational findings.

- Differences in attachment are in part due to differences in *temperament*, and in part due to differences in caregiver responsiveness.

- Parents differ in their parenting styles, whether *authoritarian, permissive, authoritative,* or *disengaged*. Which style parents adopt depends partly on the parents and partly on the child's own characteristics. Evidence to date suggests that authoritative parenting is often preferable.

- Infants' attachment does not seem to be disrupted by childcare, especially if the childcare is of high quality. However, social development may be disrupted by divorce or separation of the parents. Development is more severely disrupted if there is no attachment at all, as reflected in the tragic evidence from Romanian orphanages.

- Friendships are important for many reasons, including the support they provide for a child and the various skills and knowledge a child can gain from friendships. For example, children learn how to handle conflict by quarreling—and then making up—with their friends.

- Children with friends seem better able to handle many stresses. Conversely, *rejected* children tend to be more aggressive and, in some cases, more anxious.

- The study of moral development has been strongly affected by Kohlberg's analysis of progressive stages in *moral reasoning*. There may, however, also be sex differences in moral orientation and differences among cultural groups.

- A person's moral reasoning is clearly tied to his moral behavior, but other factors also matter, including the person's sense of *conscience*. The development of a conscience seems to depend on the child's relationship with his parents and his wish to preserve that relationship.

ADOLESCENCE

- Puberty is associated with the development of *primary* and *secondary sexual characteristics*. For boys, early maturation is generally beneficial. For girls, early maturation appears to be less beneficial.

- Cognitive development in adolescence is characterized by the shift from *concrete operations* to *formal operations* around age 12.

- Erik Erikson charted socioemotional development during adolescence. For Erikson, the key developmental focus during adolescences is *identity versus role confusion*. A successful outcome of this stage is a stable sense of *ego identity*. Less satisfactory outcomes include *identity confusion* or the emergence of a *negative identity*.

- While adolescence is sometimes turbulent, it is not usually so. Adolescence is also often characterized by risk-taking behaviors; these are in turn the result of adolescents' failing to take

dangers seriously and immaturity in the adolescents' prefrontal cortex. During this period, peer relationships assume an even greater importance than they have previously.

ADULTHOOD AND OLDER AGE

- Physical changes in adulthood include a general decline in physical and sensory abilities.

- Cognitive changes are also evident during adulthood and older age. *Fluid intelligence* refers to the efficiency and speed of intellectual functioning, usually in areas that are new to the person, and this aspect of intelligence declines across the life span. *Crystallized intelligence* refers to an individual's accumulated knowledge, including his or her vocabulary, known facts, and learned strategies. This form of intelligence remains relatively stable over the life span and may even grow as the person gains more and more experience. Many hypotheses have been offered for what lies behind this decline. Some emphasize the individual's biological and/or medical status (including Alzheimer's disease). Others emphasize the individual's mental life, so that people who are mentally more active preserve their memory more fully as they age.

- According to Erikson, socioemotional development during adulthood can be described using three stages: *intimacy versus isolation, generativity versus stagnation,* and *integrity versus despair*.

- One surprising finding concerning older age is that older adults have relatively high levels of well-being. One explanation for these unexpectedly high levels of well-being is provided by *socioemotional-selectivity theory*, which holds that older adults increasingly prioritize emotion regulation goals, which leads them to feel less negative emotion and more positive emotion.

 ONLINE STUDY TOOLS

Go to StudySpace, **wwnorton.com/studyspace**, to access additional review and enrichment materials, including the following resources for each chapter:

Organize
- Study Plan
- Chapter Outline
- Quiz+ Assessment

Learn
- Ebook
- Chapter Review
- Vocabulary Flashcards
- Drag-and-Drop Labeling Exercises
- Audio Podcast Chapter Overview

Connect
- Critical Thinking Activity
- Studying the Mind Video Podcasts
- Video Exercises
- Animations
- ZAPS Psychology Labs

15 Personality

When Amanda Turner joined an Internet dating service several years ago, she knew exactly what she wanted, and why.

"I was looking for someone who was somewhat extraverted and quite open to new experiences, yet also very emotionally stable," says Amanda. A researcher with a marketing firm in New York City, Amanda studied personality psychology in graduate school. As a result, she knew the lingo of the Big Five theory of personality, which compresses the astounding range of human traits into five dimensions: openness to experience, conscientiousness, extraversion, agreeableness, and neuroticism.

"I'm quite outgoing and adventurous myself, and so I wanted someone who shares those qualities. He didn't have to be super conscientious," she continues, "because I can run a tight ship all by myself. But he did need to be high in agreeableness. Trust, after all, is the foundation of a good relationship."

Amanda chose a Web site that offered personality tests with dimensions similar to those of the Big Five. She then sorted through bachelors' profiles until she found a few who met her criteria. Within 3 years, she had met and married John Chu, a New York stage actor.

John likewise consulted the site's personality test results. "I was shy when I was a kid—partly because my family had just immigrated, and so we were all a little cautious. But I always liked the loud girls," he laughs, "and so I knew I wanted to be with an extravert." Otherwise, though, John didn't have strong preferences about the personality traits of his partner. "I was more interested in people's values and activities," he says. "After all, how people act so often depends on the situations they find themselves in, and how they view those situations."

From choosing life partners, to describing our friends and enemies, to understanding ourselves, we appeal to the notion of *personality*. But are we really the same person across situations, or do we act differently at different times? Amanda, for example, chats with strangers on the subway, but finds herself subdued in museums and places of worship. Likewise, John is often soft-spoken with his grandparents, but loud and commanding with his two younger brothers. "Those roughnecks need to know who's in charge," he jokes.

But can we change our personalities entirely? Can others change us? John says that marriage has made him more conscientious, although he admits to carrying an electronic calendar to compensate for his dispositional lateness. Amanda points out, though, that John *believes* he can change more than she believes she can change. "I usually just try to accept my personality quirks," she says. "He tries to be a better person every day."

Where do personalities come from, anyway—our genes, our experiences, or both? Amanda's mother says that Amanda "was born early, and has been early to everything ever since." Amanda notes, however, that her mother wouldn't have tolerated anything else: "She's done with her Christmas shopping by September, and expects her children to be, also." And so Amanda's experiences with her family enhanced her seemingly inborn inclination to be conscientious. Meanwhile, John notes that he was an introverted child, but acting brought out his extraverted side.

People differ in many ways, including their desires, feelings, and behavior, their views of themselves and others, and their outlooks on the world. Some people are a delight; others are obnoxious. Some like to be with a crowd; others prefer to be alone. These distinctions and many others fall under the heading of personality, an area of psychology that describes how people differ and explores how the many aspects of each person come together. As it turns out, this is an undertaking so ambitious that no one approach provides a completely satisfying account of all of personality. In this chapter, therefore, we describe four different approaches to personality and show how each focuses on a different part of the puzzle of who we are.

THE TRAIT APPROACH: DEFINING OUR DIFFERENCES

traits Relatively stable patterns of thought, feeling, or behavior that characterize an individual.

states Temporary patterns of thought, feeling, or behavior.

The trait approach to the study of personality assumes that the differences among people can be captured by talking about what **traits** a person has—whether he is friendly or not, helpful or not, formal or not. Unlike **states**, which are temporary (e.g., being angry at this moment), traits are relatively enduring (e.g., being generally hot-headed), and, as a result, trait labels allow us to summarize what someone is like, often in a single word, and serve as a basis for making predictions about what she is likely to do in the future. The trick, however, is to figure out which traits to use in forming a description of a person that succinctly captures who he is but also is precise enough to predict his actions.

Think about one of your close friends. How would you describe this person to others? Shy? Confident? Bashful? Fun-loving? Upbeat? Notice how many words come to mind. Indeed, if we want to describe how people differ from one another, we seem to have a nearly endless supply of terms to work with. But do we really need all of these terms? Or can we reduce the list, perhaps by eliminating redundant or rarely used terms, to reveal a (much smaller) set of basic personality traits?

The Big Five

An unabridged English dictionary contains almost 18,000 personality-relevant terms (Allport & Odbert, 1936). To reduce this list to manageable size, early trait theorists put many of these words to the side simply because they were synonyms, slang, or just uncommon words. Raymond Cattell, one of the pioneers in this arena, gave this kind of shortened list of words to a panel of judges, asking them to use these words to rate a group of people they knew well (Cattell, 1957). Their ratings were compared to find out which terms were redundant. This process allowed Cattell (1966) to eliminate the redundant terms, yielding what he thought were the 16 primary personality dimensions.

Subsequent investigators presented evidence from further analyses that several of Cattell's dimensions still overlapped, so they reduced the set still further. A few investigators, such as Hans Eysenck (1967), argued that just two dimensions were needed to describe all the variations in personality, although he later added a third. Others argued that this was too severe a reduction, and, over time a consensus has emerged around five major personality dimensions as the basis for describing all personalities; this has led to a personality system appropriately named the **Big Five** (D. W. Fiske, 1949; Norman, 1963; Tupes & Christal, 1961).

The Big Five dimensions are *extraversion* (sometimes called extroversion), *neuroticism* (sometimes labeled with its positive pole, emotional stability), *agreeableness*, *conscientiousness*, and *openness to experience* (L. R. Goldberg, 2001; John & Srivastava, 1999; McCrae & Costa, 2003).* These dimensions seem useful for describing people from childhood through old age (Allik, Laidra, Realo, & Pullman, 2004; McCrae & Costa, 2003; Soto, John, Gosling, & Potter, 2008) in many different cultural settings (John & Srivastava, 1999; McCrae & Costa, 1997; McCrae & Terracciano, 2005; Yamagata et al., 2006). The Big Five traits even seem useful in describing the personalities of other species, including chimpanzees, dogs, cats, fish, and octopi (Gosling, 2008; Gosling & John, 1999; Weiss, King, & Figueredo, 2000).

What do these dimension labels mean? *Extraversion* means having an energetic approach toward the social and physical world. Extraverted people often feel positive emotion and tend to agree with statements like "I see myself as someone who is outgoing, sociable," while people who are introverted (low in extraversion) tend to disagree with these statements. (This and the following items are from the Big Five Inventory: John, Donahue, & Kentle, 1991). *Neuroticism* means being prone to negative emotion, and its opposite is emotional stability. This dimension is assessed by finding out whether people agree with statements like "I see myself as someone who is depressed, blue." *Agreeableness* is a trusting and easygoing approach to others, as indicated by agreement with statements like "I see myself as someone who is generally trusting." *Conscientiousness* means having an organized, efficient, and disciplined approach to life, as measured via agreement with statements like "I see myself as someone who does things efficiently." Finally, *openness to experience* refers to unconventionality, intellectual curiosity, and interest in new ideas, foods, and activities. Openness is indicated by agreement with statements like "I see myself as someone who is curious about many different things."

Big Five Five crucial dimensions of personality determined through factor analyses of trait terms: extroversion, neuroticism (or emotional instability), agreeableness, conscientiousness, and openness to experience.

---

*To remember the Big Five, Oliver John (1990) suggests the mnemonic OCEAN.

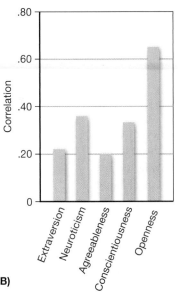

15.1 Reading personality from a bedroom Researchers have found that reliable personality ratings can be based on quite limited information. For example, Sam Gosling and colleagues have demonstrated that Big Five personality ratings may be made reliably on the basis of (A) a person's bedroom as shown by (B) correlations between observers' ratings and combined self- and peer-ratings of the rooms' occupants (Gosling, Ko, Mannarelli, & Morris, 2002).

self-report data Data supplied by the research participant describing herself (usually, ratings of attitudes or moods, or tallies of behavior), rather than that collected by the experimenter.

informant data Data about a person derived from others who know the person well.

Notice that the Big Five—like Cattell's initial set of 16 dimensions—is cast in terms of personality dimensions, and we identify someone's personality by specifying where he falls on each dimension. This allows us to describe an infinite number of combinations, or, to put it differently, an infinite number of personality profiles created by different mixtures of the five basic dimensions.

MEASUREMENT AND MEANING

As we will see throughout this chapter, personality theorists rely on many different types of data. To measure where a person stands on each of the Big Five dimensions, researchers typically use **self-report data**, employing measures such as Costa and McCrae's NEO-PI-R (1992)—asking people in essence to describe themselves, or to indicate how much they agree with proposed statements that might describe them. Self-report measures assume, though, that each of us knows a great deal about our own beliefs, emotions, and past actions, and so can describe ourselves. But is this assumption correct? What if people lack either the self-knowledge or the honesty required for an accurate self-report (Dunning, Heath, & Suls, 2004)?

To find out, one option is to collect data not just from the people we are interested in, but also from others who know these people well. These **informant data** can come from parents, teachers, coaches, camp counselors, fellow parishioners, and so on (Figure 15.1). Though informants' perspectives are not perfect, they provide another important window onto the person, and across studies researchers have found that self-report and informant data generally agree well in the case of ratings of the Big Five (McCrae & Costa, 1987). It seems, then, that most people do know themselves reasonably well—a point that is interesting for its own sake, and also makes our assessment of traits relatively straightforward.

No matter how they're measured, the Big Five dimensions are probably best conceptualized in hierarchical terms, as shown in Figure 15.2. This figure presents just one of the Big Five dimensions, extraversion, and shows that this dimension is really a broad summary of many more specific facets of personality. Each of these facets in turn is made up of even more specific behavioral tendencies, which are themselves made up of specific behaviors. If we choose terms higher in the hierarchy (e.g., the Big Five themselves), we gain a more economical description with fewer, broader terms.

At the same time, though, if we choose terms lower in the hierarchy, we gain accuracy, with the traits providing a more direct and precise description of each person's behavior (John & Srivastava, 1999). Thus, for example, if we want to predict how a new

15.2 The hierarchical organization of personality One of the Big Five personality traits, extraversion, encompasses a broad summary of many more specific facets of personality, each of which is defined by particular behavioral tendencies and still more specific behaviors.

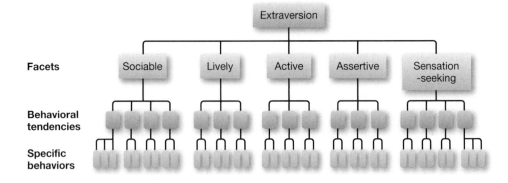

employee will perform on the job, or predict how well a nurse will perform under stress, we might want more than the overarching description provided by the Big Five itself; we might want to zoom in for a closer look at the way the Big Five traits can manifest themselves in a particular individual. One way to do this is to use the Q-Sort, a set of 100 brief descriptions that a rater sorts into a predetermined number of piles, corresponding to the degree to which they describe a person (Block, 2008). There are also hundreds of more-specific measures available, each seeking to describe a particular aspect of who someone is and how he or she behaves.

CULTURAL DIFFERENCES

Cattell and the Big Five theorists developed their personality factors in English, and they used mostly middle-class English-speaking subjects to validate their theories. As discussed in Chapter 13, though, cultures differ in how they view human nature. Are the Big Five dimensions equally useful as we move from one culture to the next?

We have already alluded to the fact that the Big Five dimensions do seem to describe personalities in a wide range of cultures. More precisely, as we move from one culture to the next, we still find that the trait labels people use to describe each other can be "boiled down" to the same five dimensions (McCrae & Costa, 1997; McCrae & Terracciano, 2005). There are, however, reasons to be cautious about these findings. As one concern, instead of allowing natives of a culture to generate and organize personality terms themselves (Marsella, Dubanoski, Hamada, & Morse, 2000), most researchers simply administer a test that was already developed using English-speaking subjects. This approach may not allow people's natural or routine understandings to emerge (Greenfield, 1997), and so, even if these studies confirm the existence of the Big Five dimensions in a population, they do not show us whether these are the most frequently used categories in that culture, or whether they are useful in predicting the same behaviors from one culture to the next.

In fact, when participants have been allowed to generate personality terms on their own, support for the cross-cultural generality of the Big Five has been mixed. For example, when researchers explored the personality traits used by Hong Kong and mainland Chinese samples, they found four factors that could be related to the Big Five, but one factor that seemed to be uniquely Chinese, which reflected interpersonal relatedness and harmony (Cheung, 2004; Cheung & Leung, 1998; see Figure 15.3). In Spanish samples, seven factors seem best to describe personality (Benet-Martinez, 1999), five of which map reasonably well onto the Big Five. Other researchers have found three factors in Italian samples (Di Blas, Forzi, & Peabody, 2000), and nine factors bearing little resemblance to the Big Five were used by students in Mexico (La Rosa & Diaz-Loving, 1991). Thus, although the Big Five seem to be well established among many cultures, there is room for debate about whether these dimensions are truly universal.

15.3 Culture and personality Interpersonal relatedness and harmony are particularly important in China.

The Consistency Controversy

Whether they endorse the Big Five dimensions or not, trait theorists agree that individuals' personalities can be described in terms of stable and enduring traits. After all, when we say that someone is friendly and warm, we are doing more than describing how he acted on a particular occasion. Instead, we are describing the person and, with that, providing some expectations about how he will act on other occasions, in other settings. But is this right? Is someone's behavior stable in this way?

HOW CONSISTENT ARE PEOPLE?

In one classic study, researchers examined the behavior of schoolchildren—and, in particular, the likelihood that each child would be dishonest in one setting or another (Hartshorne & May, 1928). Quite remarkably, the researchers found little consistency in children's behavior: Children who were inclined to cheat on a school test were often quite honest in other settings (e.g., an athletic contest), and vice versa. Based on these findings, it would be misleading to describe these children with trait labels like "honest" or "dishonest"—sometimes they were one, and sometimes the other.

Some 40 years ago, Walter Mischel reviewed this and related studies, and concluded that people behave much less consistently than a trait conception would predict, a state of affairs which has been referred to as the **personality paradox** (Mischel, 1968). Thus, for example, the correlation between honesty measured in one setting and honesty measured in another situation was .30, which Mischel argued was quite low. Mischel noted that behaviors were similarly inconsistent for many other traits, such as aggression, dependency, rigidity, and reactions to authority. Measures for any of these, taken in one situation, typically do not correlate more than .30 with measures of the same traits taken in another situation. Indeed, in some studies, there is no detectable correlation at all (Mischel, 1968; Nisbett, 1980). These findings led Mischel to conclude that trait conceptions of personality dramatically overstate the real consistency of a person's behavior.

WHY AREN'T PEOPLE MORE CONSISTENT?

How should we think about these results? One option is to argue that our personalities are, in fact, relatively stable just as the trait approach suggests, but acknowledge that situations often do shape our behavior. Given a red light, most drivers stop; given a green light, most go—regardless of whether they are friendly or unfriendly, stingy or generous, dominant or submissive. Social roles likewise often define what people do independent of their personalities. To predict how someone will act in a courtroom, for example, there is little point in asking whether he is sociable, careless with money, or good to his mother. What we really want to know is the role that he will play—judge, prosecutor, defense attorney, or defendant.

In Chapter 13 we reviewed studies indicating that the influence of a situation can be incredibly powerful—leading ordinary college students to take on roles in which they are vicious and hurtful to their peers. It's no wonder, then, that there is sometimes little correspondence between our traits and our behavior and less consistency in our behavior than the trait perspective might imply. The reason, in brief, lies in what's called *the power of the situation*. Because of that power, our behavior often depends more on the setting we are in than on who we are.

Sometimes, though, our behavior *does* depend on who we are. Particularly in weak situations—ones in which the environment provides few guides for our behavior—our personalities shape our actions (Figure 15.4). Even in strong situations—ones in which the environment provides clear guides for our behavior—different people react to the situation in somewhat different ways, so that their behavior in the end reflects the *interaction* of the situation with their personality (Fleeson, 2004; Magnusson & Endler, 1977). Moreover, it's not a matter of chance how a particular person reacts to this situation or that one; instead, people seem to be relatively consistent in how they act in certain *types* of situations. Thus, for example, someone might be punctual in professional settings, but regularly late for social occasions; they might be shy in larger groups, but quite outgoing when they are with just a few friends.

personality paradox The idea that people seem to behave much less consistently than a trait conception would predict.

(A) A weak situation

(B) A strong situation

15.4 Weak and strong situations (A) An example of a weak situation is a casual party where different people behave quite differently. (B) An example of a strong situation is an examination, where very similar behavior is seen across individuals.

Evidence for these points comes from many sources, including a study in which children in a summer camp were observed in a variety of situations—settings, for example, in which they were teased or provoked by a peer, or settings in which they were approached in a friendly way by a peer, or settings in which they were scolded by an adult (Cervone & Shoda, 1999; Mischel, Shoda, & Mendoza-Denton, 2002). In this study, the researchers relied on **behavioral data**—data based on observations of specific actions—and these data showed that each child's behavior varied from one situation to the next. For example, one child was not at all aggressive when provoked by a friend, but responded aggressively when scolded by an adult. Another child showed the reverse pattern. Thus, the trait label *aggressive* would not consistently fit either child—sometimes they were aggressive and sometimes they were not.

There was, however, a clear pattern to the children's behavior, but the pattern emerges only when we consider both the person and the situation. As the investigators described it, the data suggested that each of the children had a reliable "if … then …" profile: "If in this setting, then act in this fashion; if in that setting, then act in that fashion" (Mischel et al., 2002). Because of these "if … then …" patterns, the children were, in fact, reasonably consistent in how they acted, but their behaviors were "tuned" to the situations they found themselves in. Thus, we need to be careful when we describe any of these children as being "friendly" or "aggressive" or "helpful," relying only on global trait labels. To give an accurate description, we need to be more specific, saying things like "tends to be friendly in this sort of setting," "tends to be helpful in that sort of setting," and so on.

ARE SOME PEOPLE MORE INFLUENCED BY THE SITUATION THAN OTHERS?

There is one more complexity we must keep in mind as we consider how personality and situations interact to shape behavior. Some individuals are more consistent than others across situations, or, turning this around, some individuals are more flexible than others. This difference among people is assessed by the **Self-Monitoring Scale**, developed by Mark Snyder and designed to assess the degree to which people are sensitive to their surroundings and likely to adjust their behaviors to fit in. The scale includes items such as "In different situations and with different people, I often act like very different persons."

High self-monitors care a great deal about how they appear to others, and so, at a cocktail party, they are charming and sophisticated; in a street basketball game, they "trash talk." In contrast, low self-monitors are less interested in how they appear to

behavioral data Data about a person based on direct observation of that person's actions or behavior.

Self-Monitoring Scale A personality measure that seeks to determine the degree to which a person alters or adjusts their behavior in order to act appropriately in new circumstances.

15.5 The extremes of the self-monitoring scale (A) Matt Damon as Tom Ripley in *The Talented Mr. Ripley*: the high self-monitor, who can fit in with anybody, anywhere, anytime. (B) Heath Ledger as the Joker in *The Dark Knight*: the ultimate low self-monitor, who stays true to himself regardless of the situation.

others. They are who they are regardless of the momentary situation, making their behavior much more consistent across situations (Figure 15.5; Gangestad & Snyder, 2000; M. Snyder, 1987, 1995). This suggests that the extent to which situations determine an individual's behavior varies by person, with situations being more important determinants of high self-monitors' behavior than of low self-monitors' behavior.

How consistent individuals are also varies at the cultural level of analysis. Americans, for example, are relatively consistent in how they describe themselves, no matter whether they happen at the time to be sitting alone, next to an authority figure, or in a large group (Kanagawa, Cross, & Markus, 2001). By contrast, Japanese participants' self-descriptions varied considerably across contexts, and they were far more self-critical when sitting next to an authority figure than when they were by themselves. There also cultural differences in how consistent individuals *want* to be. In one study, researchers asked American and Polish participants how they would respond to a request to take a survey about beverage preferences. When asked to imagine they had previously agreed to such requests, American participants said they would again agree to the request—apparently putting a high value on self-consistency. Polish participants, by contrast, were much less concerned with self-consistency, and so were less influenced by imagining that they had agreed to similar requests in the past (Cialdini, Wosinka, Barrett, Butner, & Gornik-Durose, 1999).

Traits and Biology

Where does all of this leave us? Plainly, situations do matter in shaping how we act, and, as a result, we can easily document inconsistencies in how someone behaves: She might be honest in one setting but treacherous in another, friendly in one situation but hostile otherwise, with her behavior in each case governed as much by where she is as by who she is. At the same time, we can also document ways in which each of us is consistent in who we are. We shouldn't be surprised, therefore, that personality traits have been shown to predict important life outcomes (Ozer & Benet-Martinez, 2006; Roberts, Kuncel, Shiner, Caspi, & Goldberg, 2007). For example, the Big Five personality dimensions are related to outcomes ranging from career success (Barrick, Mount, & Gupta, 2003) to criminal activities (Wiebe, 2004) to health and mortality (Roberts, Walton, & Bogg, 2005).

Personality consistency thus seems to be alive and well, especially if we understand trait labels to be descriptions of how a person tends to act in a certain sort of situation, rather than a description of what he is like at all times and in all places. However, this simply leads to a new question: Given that people do differ in their personalities, how do these differences arise?

GENES AND PERSONALITY

Mounting evidence suggests that personality traits grow out of the individual's **temperament**, a characteristic pattern of emotion, attention, and behavior that is evident from an early age and is determined to a considerable degree by genetic patterns (Kagan, 1994; Rothbart & Bates, 2006; Thomas & Chess, 1977). Evidence for this genetic influence—both on temperament and on personality in general—comes from the same methods used to study heritability in other contexts, including studies of twins (monozygous or not, raised separately or apart) and studies of adoptees (Figure 15.6). Data from these studies tell us that in just about all cases, identical twins turn out to be more alike than fraternal twins on various personality attributes (see A. H. Buss & Plomin, 1984; Zuckerman, 1987a). For example, one study compared the personalities of 123 pairs of identical twins and 127 pairs of fraternal twins and found that heritability for the Big Five personality dimensions ranged from 40 to 60% (Borkenau, Riemann, Angleitner, & Spinath, 2001; Jang, Livesley, & Vernon, 1996; Loehlin, 1992).

Peculiarly, though, genetic influences have also been identified for much more specific traits such as television watching, traditionalism, and the willingness to divorce (Bouchard, Lykken, McGue, Segel, & Tellegen, 1990; McGue & Lykken, 1992; Plomin, Corley, DeFries, & Fulker, 1990). In each case, there is a greater resemblance between identical twins with regard to these traits than between fraternal twins. Of course, natural selection unfolds at a slow pace, but television has existed for less than a century. Therefore, the genetic influence on these kinds of tendencies may reflect the operation of other, more general personality dimensions—such as those named in the Big Five. For example, television watching may be associated with extraversion, and traditionalism with conscientiousness. Likewise, in a study of adult twins, those twins who divorced had higher average scores on measures related to extraversion and neuroticism, and lower scores on measures of impulse control (Jockin, McGue, & Lykken, 1996). This is certainly consistent with the idea that the specific trait (tendency to divorce) is derived from the more general biologically based tendencies such as extraversion or neuroticism, and it is the latter that are influenced by the genes.

temperament A person's characteristic level of reactivity and energy; often thought to be constitutional.

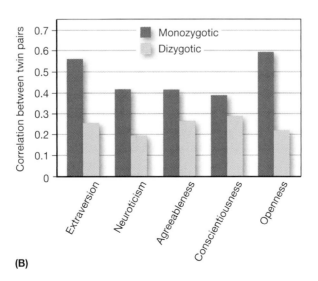

15.6 The similarity of twins (A) Identical twins Fred and Don Lamb are both astrophysicists (although with different specialties), and both have been enormously successful in their careers. (B) The greater similarity between identical twins than between fraternal twins suggests to many that personality, ability, and interests are all shaped by inheritance (since, after all, identical twins have the same genetic pattern).

PHYSIOLOGY AND PERSONALITY

physiological data Data about a person derived from measurement of biological structures and processes.

sensation seeking A predisposition to seek novel experiences, look for thrills and adventure, and be highly susceptible to boredom.

If our personalities have a basis in our genes, what exactly do the genes code for? Using **physiological data**, psychologists are beginning to explore how people with different personality traits differ in their biological functioning, with the hope that these data will offer a glimpse into how our genes shape who we are.

One example of this work is inspired by Hans Eysenck's theory of extraversion/introversion. Eysenck proposed that the observable difference in personality derives from the fact that introverts react more strongly than extraverts to external stimuli (M. W. Eysenck, 1987). As a result, he argued, introverts often guard against stimulation from the outside, which to them feels like overstimulation. This is why, for example, introverts shy away from social settings—the stimulation in that setting would be more than they are comfortable with. It also turns out that introverts have a lower tolerance for pain (Bartol & Costello, 1976), and, when they are studying, they prefer less noise and fewer opportunities for socializing (J. B. Campbell & Hawley, 1982).

Can we confirm this proposal through studies of the brain? In one study, investigators measured how people's brain stems reacted when the people heard clicking noises. In line with Eysenck's theory, introverts showed a quicker response than extraverts, indicating more reactive brain stems (Bullock & Gilliland, 1993; also see Kumari, Ffytche, Williams, & Gray, 2004).

Similar arguments may help us to understand a more specific trait, **sensation seeking**, which refers to the tendency to seek varied and novel experiences, to look for thrills and adventure, and to be highly susceptible to boredom (Zuckerman, 1979, 1994; Figure 15.7). People high in sensation-seeking are more likely to participate in risky sports; to get more restless in monotonous, confined situations; and to drive faster than people with low sensation-seeking scores (Zuckerman, 1979, 1983).

What leads to this pattern of behavior? One suggestion is that sensation seekers are people whose neurotransmitter systems (especially those relying on norepinephrine and dopamine) are underreactive. As a result, these people are chronically underaroused, and this makes them seek thrills and take risks to jog their sluggish neurotransmitter systems into greater activity (Zuckerman, 1987b, 1990, 1994). Consistent with this hypothesis, sensation seekers seem to be at greater risk for abusing drugs that influence dopamine levels. Researchers explain this finding by suggesting that in this case, the sensation seekers are using drugs, rather than activities such as sky diving or snake handling, to activate their underactive brain systems (Bardo, Donohew, & Harrington, 1996). These findings are buttressed by those of researchers who have developed a "rat model" of drug use.

15.7 Sensation seeking Some people actively seek thrills and arousal; others seek quiet activities. This difference in personality may derive from the responsiveness of the person's nervous system.

Using this model, researchers have shown that high levels of sensation seeking (measured by animals' activity levels in a novel environment) predict the animals' propensity to give themselves cocaine (Belin, Mar, Dalley, Robbins, & Everitt, 2008).

Sensation seeking is common among extraverts; a very different pattern—called **inhibited temperament**—is associated with introversion and neuroticism (Fox, Henderson, Marshall, Nichols, & Ghera, 2005; Kagan, 1994, 2003; Kagan & Snidman, 1991; Putnam & Stifter, 2005). As infants, people with inhibited temperaments tend to react strongly when they are distressed, crying vigorously and showing high levels of motor activity. As young children, inhibited individuals are unwilling to approach novel stimuli or people, become anxious in new situations, and frequently seek reassurance from their caregivers. Adolescents and adults who were categorized as inhibited at an early age are much less likely than others to be outgoing and socially spontaneous.

The explanation for inhibited temperament may mirror the account of sensation seeking, and in particular may be associated with an overreactive brain (and attempts to compensate for this) just as sensation seeking is associated with an underreactive brain. Specifically, Kagan and colleagues hypothesize that inhibited children have a low threshold for activity in the amygdala, a subcortical brain structure crucial for detecting important stimuli in the environment. This hypothesis was tested using an fMRI study of young adults who had been classified when they were infants as either inhibited or uninhibited (Schwartz, Wright, Shin, Kagan, & Rauch, 2003; Figure 15.8). These participants viewed a series of familiar and unfamiliar faces. As predicted, when the inhibited participants viewed unfamiliar faces, their amygdalae showed higher levels of activation than did the amygdalae of uninhibited participants. The two groups did not differ, however, when they were viewing familiar faces, suggesting that it was the newness of the faces that led the inhibited individuals' amygdalae to respond more strongly.

inhibited temperament A personality style associated with introversion and neuroticism, and characterized by a fear of novelty that is evident early in life.

15.8 SCIENTIFIC METHOD: Do inhibited individuals have lower thresholds for activation in the amygdala?

Method

1. Adult participants had been classified either as inhibited or uninhibited at age two.

2. Participants first saw six different faces presented repeatedly in random order so that these faces became familiar.

3. During the test phase, fMRIs were taken as the participants viewed a series of faces that mixed familiar ones with novel ones.

Results

When viewing novel faces, adults previously classified as inhibited showed greater activations in their amygdalae than those classified as uninhibited. This difference was markedly reduced with familiar faces.

The most significant differences in inhibited participants' brain responses centered in the amygdala.

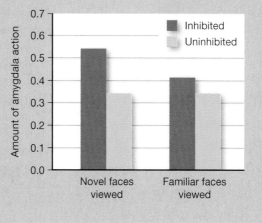

CONCLUSION: Inhibited people show stronger amygdalar responses to unfamiliar faces than uninhibited people do. These findings suggest that some patterns of brain activity relating to temperament are preserved from infancy into early adulthood.

SOURCE STUDY: Schwartz, Wright, Shin, Kagan, & Rauch, 2003

Traits and the Environment

It seems plausible, then, that genes influence personality in a variety of ways—by determining the reactivity of neurotransmitter systems, the threshold for activation in the amygdala, and more. But, as we have repeatedly noted, genetic influence will emerge only if certain environmental supports are in place. In addition, virtually any characteristic shaped by the genes is also likely to be shaped by environmental factors. What are the environmental factors relevant to the development of someone's personality? Three sources of influence have been widely discussed: cultures, families, and differences among members within the same family.

CULTURAL EFFECTS

As we have seen, the evidence is mixed on whether the Big Five dimensions are as useful for describing personalities in Korea as they are in Kansas, as useful in Niger as they are in Newport. But no matter what we make of this point, we need to remember that the Big Five is simply a framework for describing how people differ; if the framework is in fact universal, this simply tells us that we can describe personalities in different cultures using the same (universal) measuring system, just as we can measure objects of different sizes using the same ruler. This still leaves open, however, what the personalities are in any given culture—that is, what we will learn when we use our measuring system.

Scholars have long suggested that people in different cultures have different personalities—so that we can speak of a "German personality," or a "typical Italian," and so on. One might fear that these suggestions amount to little beyond stereotyping, and indeed, some scholars have argued that these perceptions may be entirely illusory (McCrae & Terracciano, 2006). Mounting evidence suggests, however, that there is a kernel of truth in some of these claims about **national character**. For example, one study has shown that there are differences from one country to the next in how conscientious people seem to be. These differences are manifest in such diverse measures as pedestrians' walking speed, postal workers' efficiency, accuracy of public clocks, and even longevity in each of these countries (Heine, Buchtel, & Norenzayan, 2008)!

Where might these cultural differences in personality come from? One long-standing hypothesis is that the key lies in how a group of people sustains itself, whether through farming or hunting or trade (Barry, Child, & Bacon, 1959; Hofstede, 2001; Maccoby, 2000). More recent models, in contrast, take a more complex view, and suggest that cultural differences in personality—whether between nations or across regions within a single nation—arise via a combination of forces (Jokela, Elovainio, Kivimaki, & Keltikangas-Jarvinen, 2008; Rentfrow, Gosling, & Potter, 2008). These forces include historical migration patterns, social influence, and environmental factors that dynamically reinforce one another over time. To make this concrete, let's consider immigrants who first make their way to a new geographical region (whether fleeing persecution or seeking prosperity). It seems unlikely that these trailblazers will be a random sample of the larger population. Instead, the mere fact that they decided to relocate suggests that they may be willing to take risks and more open to new experiences in comparison to others who were not willing to emigrate. This initial difference might then be magnified via social influence—perhaps because the especially extraverted or open individuals engaged in practices that shaped the thoughts, feelings, and behaviors of those around them.

Arguments like these may help us understand why different regions within the United States often seem characterized by distinct personality types, with neuroticism especially common in some of the mid-Atlantic states and openness to new experience

national character The idea that people in different cultures have different personalities.

common in the Pacific Northwest. Indeed, one recent book (Florida, 2008) urges people to seek out regions that have personalities compatible with their own—providing yet another factor shaping regional or national personality: People may move to an area because they believe (or hope) certain traits are common there, and this selective migration can itself create or magnify regional differences (Figure 15.9).

FAMILY EFFECTS

It seems likely that another factor shaping personality is one's family. If the family environment does influence personality, we would expect a resemblance between the personalities of adopted children and those of their adoptive siblings, because, after all, they grow up in the same environment. However, the data show no such resemblance. In one series of studies, in which researchers collected various personality measures for adopted children and for their adoptive siblings, the average correlation for these various measures was .04; that between the adopted children and their adoptive parents was .05 (Plomin & Daniels, 1987; also see Loehlin, 1992).

A similar message emerges from a study that compared the personality traits of pairs of adult twins. Some of the twins had been reared within the same family; others had been reared apart and had been separated for an average of over 30 years. Among the twins reared together the personality scores for identical twins were, as usual, more highly correlated than the scores of fraternal twins, with correlations of .51 and .23, respectively. Thus, greater genetic resemblance (identical twins, remember, share all of their genes; fraternal twins share only half of their genes) led to greater personality resemblance. Amazingly, though, the twins who were reared apart and had been separated for many years showed nearly the same pattern of results as twins who grew up together. The correlations were .50 and .21 for identical and fraternal twins, respectively. (Moloney, Bouchard, & Segal, 1991).

One might have expected the correlations to be considerably lower for the traits of the twins who had been raised apart, since they were reared in different family environments. That the results were nearly the same whether the twins were raised together or apart speaks against granting much importance to the various environmental factors that make one family different from the next (Bouchard, 1984; Bouchard et al., 1990; Tellegen et al., 1988; also see Turkheimer & Waldron, 2000).

Some authors have drawn strong conclusions from these data—namely, that the family plays little role in shaping personality (J. R. Harris, 1998). We would urge caution, though, in making this sweeping claim. Most of the available evidence comes from families whose socioeconomic status was working class or above, and this range is rather limited. It does not include the environments provided by parents who are unemployed or those of parents who abuse or neglect their children. If the range had been broadened to include more obviously different environments, between-family environmental differences would surely have been demonstrated to be more important (Scarr, 1987, 1992).

WITHIN-FAMILY EFFECTS

If—within the range of environments studied—between-family environmental differences are less important than one might expect, what environmental factors do matter? According to Plomin and Daniels (1987), the key lies in how the environments vary for different children within the same family. To be sure, children within a family

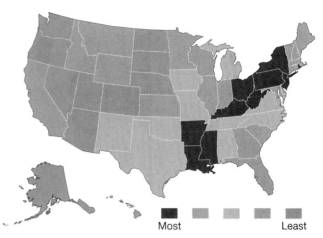

15.9 Map of neuroticism in the United States According to these data, the eastern side of the country is a more "neurotic" place to live than the western side (Rentfrow, Gosling, & Potter, 2008).

15.10 Birth order Like other later-born individuals, (A) Voltaire was more rebellious and more open to new experiences than many first-borns. (B) Alec and Billy Baldwin are a good example of the types of personalities associated with first-born and later-born siblings.

share many aspects of their objective environment. They have the same parents, they live in the same neighborhood, they have the same religion, and so on. But the environments of children within a family also differ in crucial ways. They have different friends, teachers, and peer groups, and these can play an important role in shaping how they behave. Moreover, various accidents and illnesses can befall one child but not another, with potentially large effects on their subsequent personalities. Another difference concerns the birth order of each child, since the family dynamic is different for the first-born than it is for later-born children (Figure 15.10). Some authors have suggested that birth order may have a powerful influence on personality, with later-borns being more rebellious and more open to new experiences than first-borns (Sulloway, 1996).

Factors like these suggest that the family environment may matter in shaping personality, but they indicate that we need to focus on within-family differences rather than between-family factors, like the fact that one family is strict and another lenient, or the fact that some parents value education while others value financial achievement. Indeed, within-family factors may be especially important since parents often do what they can to encourage differences among their children; some authors have suggested that this is a useful strategy for diminishing sibling rivalry (Schachter, 1982).

The gender of the child also plays a role. A brother and sister grow up in the same household, but are likely to be treated differently by their parents (not to mention other relatives, teachers, and friends). This, too, will provide a family influence shaping personality (although obviously these gender effects reach well beyond the family), but will once again produce within-family contrasts. In any case, this sort of differential treatment for men and women may—especially when combined with the biological differences between the sexes—help us understand why women score higher on the "agreeableness" dimension of the Big Five (Figure 15.11; Srivastava, John, Gosling, & Potter, 2003), and why women are less likely to be sensation-seekers (Zuckerman, 1994). In this context, though, we should also note that many of the popular conceptions about gender differences in personality—which are surprisingly robust across cultures (Heine, 2008)—are probably overstated; in fact, women and men appear remarkably similar, on average, on many aspects of personality (Feingold, 1994; J. S. Hyde, 2005).

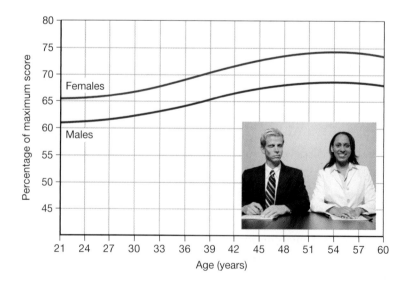

15.11 Gender differences regarding agreeableness At every age, women score higher on agreeableness than men.

Contributions of the Trait Approach

People differ from one another in a huge number of ways, and one of the major contributions of the trait approach lies in its systematic description of these differences and its success in reducing the apparently large number of these differences to manageable size. Moreover, the trait approach provides a set of continuous personality dimensions on which people can vary in almost infinite ways. This has certainly increased the precision of our personality descriptions. The trait approach offers us a rich notion of how personality and situations jointly shape behavior—leaving us with a more sophisticated theory and appreciably better predictions about how people of various personalities will behave in various settings.

The emergence of the broad Big Five framework has also enabled researchers working within very different traditions to use agreed-upon measures and to share the data they collect. As a result, progress on determining the genetic bases and brain correlates of personality differences has accelerated dramatically. Still, we must draw on other perspectives as well if we are to understand what a "personality" is, and how it comes to be.

THE PSYCHODYNAMIC APPROACH: PROBING THE DEPTHS

The comic theater of the classical and Renaissance ages presented personality types as stable and well-defined. Once a character entered, the audience knew what to expect of him. If the actor wore the mask of the cowardly soldier, he would brag and run away; if he wore the mask of the miserly old man, he would jealously guard his money.

As we have seen, the trait approach has amended this view in important ways but has still left one crucial claim: We are who we seem to be, and our various traits and motivations are in plain view for all to see. Indeed, the trait approach often relies on self-report data—a reflection of the assumption that we can perceive ourselves with relative accuracy.

According to the *psychodynamic approach*, however, we need to revise this understanding both of personality and of self-knowledge—and shift to an understanding that parallels a more modern approach to drama, in which nothing is quite what it seems. In this approach, actors playing a character must pay attention to the subtext, the unspoken thoughts that go through the character's head while she speaks her lines. And many actors are interested in a still deeper subtext, the thoughts and wishes of which the character is unaware. According to the psychodynamic approach, this deeper subtext is the wellspring of all human personality.

Adherents of the psychodynamic approach do not deny that some people are more sociable than others, or that some are more impulsive or emotionally unstable. But they contend that it is superficial to explain such tendencies as either the expression of a personality trait or the product of situational factors. In their view, what people do and say—and even what they consciously think—is only the tip of the iceberg. As they see it, human acts and thoughts are just the outer expression of a whole host of motives and desires that are often derived from early childhood experiences, and that are for the most part unknown to the person himself. They believe that to understand a person is to understand these hidden psychological forces or *dynamics*.

15.12 Sigmund Freud (1856–1939) The founder of psychoanalysis.

hysteria An older term for a group of presumably psychogenic disorders that included a wide variety of physical and mental symptoms.

psychogenic symptoms Symptoms believed to result from some psychological cause rather than from tissue damage.

(A)   **(B)**

15.13 Glove anesthesia (A) Areas of the arm's skin that send sensory information to the brain by way of different nerves. (B) A typical region of anesthesia in a patient with hysteria. If there were a nerve injury (in the spinal cord), the anesthesia would extend over the length of the arm, following the nerve distribution shown in (A).

Psychoanalysis: Theory and Practice

The founder of psychoanalysis, Sigmund Freud (1856–1939; Figure 15.12), was a physician by training. After a stint as a medical researcher, though, financial pressures led Freud to open a neurology practice in which he found that many of his patients were suffering from a disorder then called **hysteria** (now called *conversion disorder*). The symptoms of hysteria presented a helter-skelter catalog of physical and mental complaints—total or partial blindness or deafness, paralysis or anesthesia of various parts of the body, uncontrollable trembling or convulsive attacks, and gaps in memory. Was there any underlying cause that could make sense of this confusing array of symptoms?

FROM HYPNOSIS TO THE TALKING CURE

Freud suspected that the hysterical symptoms were **psychogenic symptoms**—the results of some unknown psychological cause—rather than the product of organic damage to the nervous system. His hypothesis grew out of the work of Jean Charcot (1825–1893), a French neurologist who noticed that many of the bodily symptoms of hysteria made no anatomical sense. For example, some patients who suffered from anesthesia (i.e., lack of feeling) of the hand still had feeling above the wrist. This *glove anesthesia* (so called because of the shape of the affected region) could not possibly be caused by any nerve injury, since an injury to any of the relevant nerve trunks would also affect a portion of the arm above the wrist (Figure 15.13). This ruled out a simple physical cause and suggested that glove anesthesia had some psychological basis.

In collaboration with another physician, Josef Breuer (1842–1925), Freud came to believe that these hysterical symptoms were a disguised way to keep certain emotionally charged memories under mental lock and key (S. Freud & Breuer, 1895). The idea, in brief, was that the patients carried some very troubling memory that they needed to express (because it held such a grip on their thoughts) but also to hide (because thinking about it was so painful). The patients' "compromise," in Freud's view, was to express the memory in a veiled form, and this was the source of their physical symptoms.

To support this hypothesis, Freud needed to find out both what a patient's painful memory was and why she (almost all of Freud's patients were women) found directly expressing her memory to be unacceptable. At first, Freud and Breuer tried to uncover these memories while the patients were in a hypnotic trance. Eventually, though, Freud abandoned this method, and came to the view that crucial memories could instead be recovered in the normal, waking state through the method of **free association**. In this method, his patients were told to say anything that entered their mind, no matter how trivial it seemed, or how embarrassing or disagreeable. Since Freud assumed that all ideas were linked by association, he believed that the emotionally charged "forgotten" memories would be mentioned sooner or later.

But a difficulty arose: Patients did not readily comply with Freud's request. Instead, they avoided certain topics and carefully tuned what they said about others, showing resistance that the patients themselves were often unaware of. In Freud's view, this resistance arose because target memories (and related acts, impulses, or thoughts) were especially painful or anxiety-provoking. Years before, as an act of self-protection, the patients had pushed these experiences out of consciousness, or, in Freud's term, they had **repressed** the memories. The same self-protection was operating in free association, keeping the memories from the patients' (or Freud's) view. On this basis, Freud concluded that his patients would not, and perhaps could not, reveal their painful memories directly. He therefore set himself the task of developing *indirect* methods of analysis—as he called it, **psychoanalysis**—that he thought would uncover these ideas and memories and the conflicts that gave rise to them.

ID, EGO, AND SUPEREGO

Much of Freud's work, therefore, was aimed at uncovering his patients' unconscious conflicts. He was convinced that these conflicts were at the root of their various symptoms, and that, by revealing the conflicts, he could diminish the symptoms. But Freud also believed that the same conflicts and mechanisms for dealing with them arise in normal persons, so he viewed his proposals as contributions not only to psychopathology but also to a general theory of personality.

But what sorts of conflict are we considering here? What are the warring factions, supposedly hidden deep inside each individual? According to Freud, the conflicts hampering each of us involve incompatible wishes and motives, such as a patient's desire to go out with friends versus her guilt over leaving a sick father at home. Freud devised a conception of personality that encapsulated these conflicting forces within three distinct subsystems: the *id*, the *ego*, and the *superego* (Figure 15.14). In some of his writings, Freud treated these three mental systems as if they were separate persons inhabiting the mind. But this is only a metaphor that must not be taken literally; id, ego, and superego are just the names he gave to three sets of very different reaction patterns, and not persons in their own right (S. Freud, 1923).

The **id** is the most primitive portion of the personality, the portion from which the other two emerge. It consists of all of the basic biological urges, and seeks constantly to reduce the tensions generated by these biological urges. The id abides entirely by the *pleasure principle*—satisfaction now and not later, regardless of the circumstances and whatever the cost.

At birth, the infant's mind is all id. But the id's heated striving is soon met by cold reality, because some gratifications take time. Food and drink, for example, are not always present; the infant or young child has to cry to get them. Over the course of early childhood, these confrontations between desire and reality lead to a whole set of new reactions that are meant to reconcile the two. Sometimes the result is appropriate

free association Method used in psychoanalytic therapy in which the patient is to say anything that comes to her mind, no matter how apparently trivial, unrelated, or embarrassing.

repression In psychoanalytic theory, a mechanism of defense by means of which thoughts, impulses, or memories that give rise to anxiety are pushed out of consciousness.

psychoanalysis A theory of human personality development formulated by Freud, based on assertions about unconscious conflict and early psychosexual development; also the method of therapy that draws heavily on this theory.

id In Freud's theory, a term for the most primitive reactions of human personality, consisting of blind striving for immediate biological satisfaction regardless of cost.

15.14 Models of mind Freud distinguished among three mental systems: the id, ego, and superego. He held that the id was unconscious, whereas the ego and superego were partly unconscious, partly preconscious (easily brought to consciousness), and partly conscious.

ego In Freud's theory, a set of reactions that try to reconcile the id's blind pleasure strivings with the demands of reality.

superego In Freud's theory, reaction patterns that emerge from within the ego, represent the internalized rules of society, and come to control the ego by punishment with guilt.

action (e.g., saying "please"), and sometimes the result is suppressing a forbidden impulse (e.g., not eating food from someone else's plate). In all cases, though, these efforts at reconciling desire and reality become organized into a new subsystem of the personality—the **ego**. The ego obeys a new principle, the *reality principle*. It tries to satisfy the id (i.e., to gain pleasure), but it does so pragmatically, finding strategies that work but also accord with the demands of the real world.

If, for a very young child, the ego inhibits some id-inspired action, it is for an immediate reason. Early in the child's life, the reason is likely to be some physical obstacle (perhaps the food is present, but out of reach). For a slightly older child, the reason may be social. Grabbing the food from your brother will result in punishment by a nearby parent. As the child gets older still, though, a new factor enters the scene. Imagine that the child sees a piece of candy within reach but knows that eating the candy is forbidden. By age 5 or so, the child may overrule the desire to eat the candy even when there is no one around and so no chance of being caught and punished. This inhibition of the desired action occurs because the child has now internalized the rules and admonitions of the parents and so administers praise or scolding to himself, in a fashion appropriate to his actions. At this point, the child has developed a third aspect to his personality: a **superego**, an internalized code of conduct. If the ego lives up to the superego's dictates, the child is rewarded with feelings of pride. But if one of the superego's rules is broken, the superego metes out punishment—feelings of guilt or shame.

Psychological Defenses and Development

Freud's threefold division of the personality was just a way of saying that our thoughts and actions are determined by the interplay of three major factors: our biological drives (the id), the commands and prohibitions of society (the superego), and the various ways we have learned to satisfy the former while respecting the latter (the ego).

Obviously, though, these three forces will sometimes pull us in different directions—for example, when we want to do something but know we cannot or should not—and this guarantees conflict among the competing forces. Imagine that a child performs some forbidden act and is then scolded or disciplined by his parents. The child feels threatened with the loss of his parents' love and becomes anxious about this. This anxiety leaves its mark, and the next time the child is about to perform the same act—say, touch his penis or pinch his baby brother—he will feel a twinge of anxiety, an internal reminder that his parents may castigate him and the worry that he will be abandoned and alone.

PSYCHOLOGICAL DEFENSES

Since anxiety is unpleasant, the child will do everything he can to ward it off. If the cause of the anxiety is a real-world event or object, the child can simply run away and remove himself from it. But how can he cope with a danger lurking within—a threatening fantasy, a forbidden wish? To quell this anxiety, the child must suppress the thoughts that triggered it, pushing the thoughts from conscious view. In short, the thought must be repressed.

According to Freud, repression serves as the primary **defense mechanism** that protects the individual from anxiety. But repression is often incomplete. The thoughts and urges that were pushed underground may resurface along with the associated anxiety. As a result, various further mechanisms of defense are brought into play to reinforce the original dam against the forbidden impulses.

defense mechanism A collective term for a number of reactions that try to ward off or lessen anxiety by various unconscious means.

One such mechanism is **displacement**—a process in which repressed urges find new and often disguised outlets, outlets that are more acceptable to the ego and super-ego. An example is a child who is disciplined by her parents and who then vents her anger by punching or kicking her doll. A different defense is **reaction formation**, in which she guards against the repressed wish by turning to thoughts and behaviors which provide the diametrical opposite of the forbidden ideas. A young boy who hates his sister and is punished for calling her names may protect himself by bombarding her with exaggerated love and tenderness, a desperate bulwark against aggressive wishes that he cannot accept.

In still other defense mechanisms, the repressed thoughts break through but are reinterpreted or unacknowledged. One example of this is **rationalization**, in which the person interprets her own feelings or actions in more acceptable terms. The cruel father beats his child mercilessly but is sure that he does so "for the child's own good." A related mechanism is **projection**. Here the forbidden urges well up and are recognized as such. But the person does not realize that these wishes are his own; instead, he attributes them to others. "I desire you" becomes "You desire me," and "I hate you" becomes "You hate me"—desperate defenses against repressed sexual or hostile wishes that can no longer be banished from consciousness (S. Freud, 1911; Schul & Vinokur, 2000).

STAGES OF PSYCHOSEXUAL DEVELOPMENT

Why does one person develop one pattern of defenses, while the next develops another pattern? The answer for Freud lies in the events of early childhood, events that, in Freud's view, were remarkably similar from person to person, and that give rise to a general set of stages through which we all pass (S. Freud, 1905). Freud called these the **stages of psychosexual development**, and, although he believed the stages were universal, the way the conflicts at each stage were handled differed from person to person. It is these differences, Freud believed, that give rise both to observable variations in personality and to psychopathology.

According to Freud, the child starts life as a bundle of instincts to seek pleasure, with the pleasure readily found in the stimulation of certain sensitive zones of the body. For the youngest child, most of the pleasure seeking is through the mouth, a period of life that Freud termed the *oral stage*. As the infant attains bowel control, the emphasis shifts to pleasures associated with the anus (the *anal stage*). Still later, the child shows increased interest in pleasure from genital stimulation (the *phallic stage*). The culmination of psychosexual development is attained in adult sexuality when pleasure involves not just one's own gratification but also the social and bodily satisfaction brought to another person (the *genital stage*).

Within this sequence, Freud held that the pivotal point in the child's psychosexual development is the *Oedipus complex*, named after the Theban king of classical Greek literature who unwittingly committed two awful crimes—killing his father and marrying his mother (Figure 15.15). Because Freud came to believe that the sequence of steps is somewhat different in the two sexes (S. Freud, 1905), we will take them up separately.

At about the age of 3 or 4 years, the phallic stage begins for the young boy. At this time, he becomes increasingly interested in his penis, and he seeks an external object for his sexual urges. The inevitable choice, in Freud's view, is the most important woman in the boy's young life—his mother. But there is an obstacle—the boy's father. The little boy wants to have his mother all to himself, as a comforter as well as an erotic partner, but this sexual utopia is out of the question. His father is a rival, and he is bigger. The little boy therefore wants his father to go away and not come back—in short, to die.

displacement A redirection of an impulse from a channel that is blocked into another, more available outlet.

reaction formation A mechanism of defense in which a forbidden impulse is turned into its opposite.

rationalization A mechanism of defense by means of which unacceptable thoughts or impulses are reinterpreted in more acceptable and, thus, less anxiety-arousing terms.

projection A mechanism of defense in which various forbidden thoughts and impulses are attributed to another person rather than the self.

stages of psychosexual development The sequence of four developmental stages from infancy through the attainment of adult sexuality that is considered universal in psychoanalytic theory: the oral stage, the anal stage, the phallic stage, and the genital stage.

"Why can't you be more like Oedipus?"

15.15 Oedipus complex

At this point, a new element enters into the family drama. The little boy begins to fear the father he is jealous of. According to Freud, this is because the boy is certain that the father knows of his son's hostility and will surely answer hate with hate. With childish logic, the little boy becomes convinced the punishment his father will mete out will be catastrophic. This leads to intolerable anxiety, and the anxiety escalates still further until the father is unconsciously viewed as an overwhelming ogre who threatens to annihilate his little son. As the little boy grows, so does his rivalry with his father and its accompanying terror. Eventually, though, he hits on a solution. He throws in the towel, relinquishes his mother as an erotic object, identifies with his father, and renounces genital pleasure until he is older.

What about girls? In Freud's view, females go through essentially identical oral and anal phases as do males. In many ways, the development of the young girl's phallic interests (Freud used the same term for both sexes) corresponds to the boy's. As he focuses his erotic interests on the mother, so she focuses hers on the father. As he resents and eventually fears his father, so does she her mother. In short, there is a female version of the Oedipus complex, sometimes called the *Electra complex*, after the Greek tragic heroine who goaded her brother into slaying their mother.

Of course, like young boys, young girls' first attachment is to their mother. It is the mother, after all, who nurses the infant (and so provides pleasure during the oral phase). It is likewise the mother who, for most infants, is the primary caregiver. So why, according to Freud, does a girl switch love objects and come to desire her father? To answer this question, Freud proposed that the shift of attachment begins as the little girl discovers that she does not have a penis. According to Freud, she regards this lack as a catastrophe, considers herself unworthy, and develops **penis envy**. One consequence is that she withdraws her love from the mother, whom she regards as equally unworthy. Freud argued that, painfully, she turns to her father, who has the desirable organ and who she believes can help her obtain a penis substitute—a child. From here on, the rest of the process unfolds more or less like its counterpart in the boy: love of father, jealousy of mother, increasing fear of mother, eventual repression of the entire complex, and identification with the mother (S. Freud, 1925, 1933; LaFarge, 1993).

penis envy In psychoanalytic theory, the wish for a penis that is assumed to ensue normally in females as part of the Electra complex.

The Empirical Basis of Freud's Claims

Many people regard Freud's claims—especially his account of the Electra complex—as incredibly far-fetched, but Freud believed firmly that his conception was demanded by the evidence he collected. In the next section, we first consider why Freud believed his claims were justified. Then, in the following section, we consider contemporary criticisms of Freud's methods and inferences.

THE NATURE OF FREUD'S EVIDENCE

As we have seen, Freud believed that painful beliefs and ideas were repressed, but that the repression was never complete. Therefore, these anxiety-producing ideas would still come to the surface—but (thanks to other defense mechanisms) only in disguised form. The evidence for Freud's theory therefore had to come from a process of interpretation that allowed Freud to penetrate the disguise and thus to reveal the crucial underlying psychological dynamics.

As one category of evidence, Freud continually drew attention to what he called the "psychopathology of everyday life." For example, we might forget a name or suffer a slip of the tongue, and, for Freud, these incidents were important clues to the person's hidden thoughts: Perhaps the name reminded us of an embarrassing moment, and perhaps the slip of the tongue allowed us to say something that we wanted to say, but knew we shouldn't (Figure 15.16). Freud argued that in some cases these slips were revealing, and, if properly interpreted in the context of other evidence, they could provide important insights into an individual's unconscious thoughts and fears.

Freud also believed that we could learn much about an individual through the interpretation of dreams (S. Freud, 1900), because, in Freud's view, all dreams are attempts at wish fulfillment. While one is awake, a wish is usually not acted on right away, for there are considerations of both reality (the ego) and morality (the superego) that must be taken into account: Is it possible? Is it allowed? But during sleep these restraining forces are drastically weakened, and the wish then leads to immediate thoughts and images of gratification. In some cases the wish fulfillment is simple and direct. Starving explorers dream of sumptuous meals; people stranded in the desert dream of cool mountain streams. According to a Hungarian proverb quoted by Freud, "Pigs dream of acorns, and geese dream of maize."

What about our more fantastic dreams, the ones with illogical plots, bizarre characters, and opaque symbolism? These are also attempts at wish fulfillment, Freud believed, but with a key difference. They touch on forbidden, anxiety-laden ideas that cannot be entertained directly. As a result, various mechanisms of defense prohibit the literal expression of the idea but allow it to slip through in disguised, symbolic form (e.g., a penis may be symbolized as a sword, a vagina as a cave). Because of this disguise, the dreamer may never experience the underlying *latent content* of the dream—the actual wishes and concerns that the dream is constructed to express. What he experiences instead is the carefully laundered version that emerges after the defense mechanisms have done their work—the dream's *manifest content*. This self-protection takes mental effort, but, according to Freud, the alternative—facing our impulses unadulterated—would let very few of us sleep for long.

Yet another form of evidence that Freud pointed to are the myths, legends, and fairy tales shared within a culture. He contended that just as dreams are a window into the individual's unconscious, these (often unwritten) forms of literature allow us a glimpse into the hidden concerns shared by whole cultural groups, if not all of humanity. Indeed, one of Freud's earliest colleagues, the Swiss psychiatrist Carl Jung (1875–1961), argued for a **collective unconscious** consisting of primordial stories and images—he called these **archetypes**—that shape our perceptions and desires just as much as Freud's psychodynamics (Jung, 1964; Figure 15.17). Psychoanalysts

"Good morning, beheaded—uh, I mean beloved."

15.16 Freudian slip If this king were Henry VIII, famous for executing several wives, this would be a good example of a Freudian slip.

collective unconscious A set of primordial stories and images, hypothesized by Carl Jung to be shared by all of humanity, and which he proposed underlie and shape our perceptions and desires.

archetypes According to Carl Jung, the stories and images that constitute our collective unconscious.

(A)

(B)

15.17 Jungian archetype and the collective unconscious Jung believed that humans have a collective or shared unconscious, whose images are expressed in universal archetypes such as this (A) Tibetan mandala and (B) Hebrew manuscript illustration.

15.18 Freud and mythology Many myths, legends, and stories can be interpreted in psychoanalytic terms. According to psychoanalytic authors, this fairy tale is a veiled allegory of the Oedipal sequence (Bettelheim, 1975). The wicked queen is the mother on whom the child projects her own hate and sexual jealousy. The Electra complex is temporarily resolved as the child's erotic urges go underground and remain dormant for the seven years of the latency period, symbolized both by the seven dwarfs and Snow White's long sleep. At the end of this period, her sexuality is reawakened in adult form by the young prince. (The meaning of the sword is left as an exercise for the reader.)

who have delved into such tales have found, for example, an ample supply of Oedipal themes. There are numerous ogres, dragons, and monsters to be slain before the prize can be won. The villain is often a cruel stepparent—a fairly transparent symbol, in their view, of Oedipal hostilities (see Figure 15.18).

CONCERNS ABOUT PSYCHODYNAMIC EVIDENCE

As we have just seen, Freud's evidence generally involved his patients' symptoms, actions, slips of the tongue, dreams, and so on. Freud was convinced, however, that these observations should not be taken at face value; instead, they needed to be *interpreted,* in order to unmask the underlying dynamic that was being expressed. The difficulty, though, is that Freud allowed himself many options for this interpretation—and so, if someone said "I hate my father," that might mean (via the defense of projection) that the person is convinced her father hates her or it might mean (via displacement) that the person hates her mother, or it might mean something else altogether. With this much flexibility, one might fear, there is no way to discover the correct interpretation of this utterance, and so no way to be certain our overall account is accurate. Indeed, it is telling that some of Freud's followers were able to draw very different conclusions from the same clinical cases that Freud himself studied—a powerful indicator that the interpretations Freud offered were in no sense demanded by the evidence.

When we turn to more objective forms of evidence we often find facts that do not fit well with Freudian theory. For example, one of the cornerstones of psychoanalytic thought is repression. Yet results of empirical studies of repression have been mixed. Some results point in the same direction as Freud's claims about repression (M. C. Anderson et al., 2004; M. C. Anderson & Levy, 2006; Joslyn & Oakes, 2005), but other research yields no evidence for the mechanisms Freud proposed (Holmes, 1990), and at least some of the studies that allegedly show repression have been roundly criticized by other researchers (Kihlstrom, 2002).

Psychodynamic Formulations after Freud

Plainly, therefore, we need to be very careful about interpreting Freud's claims—with powerful challenges raised to both his central methods and his key concepts. Even so, many scholars are convinced that Freud's body of work contains a number of important (some would say brilliant) insights, and so we might ask how we can preserve these insights without endorsing the entire Freudian conception. As it turns out, many scholars have tried to do this, producing a welter of schools and camps, each offering its own extensions and elaborations of Freud's thinking.

EGO PSYCHOLOGY AND MECHANISMS OF DEFENSE

One major theme among those who carried forward the torch of psychoanalytic theory was that Freud had not sufficiently emphasized the skills and adaptive capacities of the ego. Writers of this persuasion, loosely grouped under the heading of **ego psychology**, sought to extend and complete Freud's theorizing.

The various ego psychologists each have their own theoretical emphases, but all agree with Freud's contention that unconscious conflict is found in the well adjusted as

ego psychology A school of psychodynamic thought that emphasizes the skills and adaptive capacities of the ego.

well as in people with disabling mental disorders. What is essential for these more modern theorists, though, is how those conflicts can be resolved in a fashion that is appropriate, pragmatic, and, ultimately, healthy. Adherents of this position stress the positive aspects of the self as it tries to cope with the world—to deal with reality as it is rather than to distort it or hide from it. Seen in this light, the ego is not just an arbiter between id and superego, but a clever strategist with intrinsic competencies (A. Freud, 1946; Hartmann, 1964).

Building on this perspective, investigators have explored how coping patterns evolve over the course of the life span, and some of the data derive from longitudinal studies covering a span of 20 to 30 years (J. Block & J. H. Block, 2006). An example is George Vaillant's analysis of the case reports of 94 male Harvard College graduates studied at different points in their life span. They were extensively interviewed at age 19, then again at 31, and yet again at 47. Vaillant studied the predominant patterns of defense—that is, ways of coping—each man used at these three ages. He classified the coping patterns according to their level of psychological maturity. At the bottom of the hierarchy were mechanisms that are often found in early childhood and during serious mental disorder, such as denial or gross distortions of external reality. Further up the ladder were patterns often seen in adolescence and in disturbed adults, such as projection, hypochondria, and irrational, emotional outbursts. Still higher were the mechanisms studied by Freud and

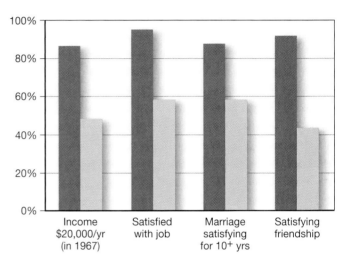

15.19 **Maturity of defense mechanisms and life adjustment** Adult success at work and love, as shown by men with predominantly mature (blue) and immature (yellow) adaptive styles.

seen in many adults—repression, reaction formation, and the like. At the top of the hierarchy were coping patterns that Vaillant considered healthy—such as humor, suppression (a conscious effort to push anxiety-provoking thoughts out of mind, at least for the time being, as opposed to repression, which is an unconscious process), and altruism (in which one tries to give to others what one might wish to receive oneself).

Vaillant's findings indicated considerable continuity. Men with more adaptive coping patterns at age 19 were more likely to have mature patterns in their forties, and these patterns in turn predicted the results on various objective indices that personality psychologists refer to as **life data**, such as satisfaction in marriage, rewarding friendships, gratifying jobs, and good physical health (Figure 15.19). As is often the case, it is unclear whether the mature coping defenses produced success in marriage and career or vice versa, but it is worth knowing that the two tend to be correlated (Vaillant, 1974, 1976, 1977, 1994). This correlation was also observed in a study of 131 inner-city males interviewed in junior high school and then surveyed 30 years later (G. E. Vaillant, Bond, & Vaillant, 1986).

life data Data about a person concerning concrete, real-world outcomes.

object relations A school of psychodynamic thought that emphasizes the real (as opposed to fantasized) relations an individual has with others.

OBJECT RELATIONS AND ATTACHMENT THEORY

Yet another development of Freud's thinking comes from scholars who broadly supported Freud's theorizing, but felt he had insufficiently emphasized the real (as opposed to fantasized) relations an individual had with others. Despite their many differences, these **object relations** theorists held that relationships with important others, whom they rather oddly referred to as "objects," constitute a crucial and relatively neglected motive underlying human behavior. Arguably, though, the object relations theorist with the broadest and most enduring impact was John Bowlby (1907–1990).

As described in Chapter 14, Bowlby was a British psychiatrist who believed people were motivated by the desire for connection and closeness with others. In particular, Bowlby believed that a child was powerfully shaped by her experiences with her *primary attachment figure* (typically, but not always, her mother) and emerged from childhood

(A) Secure attachment   **(B)** Insecure attachment

15.20 Attachment styles (A) Securely attached and (B) insecurely attached partners.

with a set of foundational beliefs about both herself (as essentially good and lovable or not) and others (as essentially good and loving or not). These mental representations of self and other are referred to as *internal working models*.

Bowlby emphasized that different children develop different working models, but it was Mary Ainsworth (1913–1999) who created an experimental procedure designed to probe these differences, and, specifically, to assess what type of attachment a child had formed with his caregiver (Ainsworth, Blehar, Waters, & Wall, 1978). As we discussed in Chapter 14, this Strange Situation test can be used to categorize children as *securely attached, anxious/avoidant* in their attachment, *anxious/resistant*, or *disorganized* in their attachment. These attachment patterns, in turn, can then be used as predictors for a number of subsequent measures—including the child's personality in the next years, and the quality of the child's social relations.

Atttachment theory has been a significant source of inspiration for researchers in personality, who have found that the attachment patterns established in early childhood seem to have considerable staying power (Bartholomew & Horowitz, 1991; Brennan, Clark, & Shaver, 1998; Mikulincer & Shaver, 2007). For example, Shaver and Clark (1994) found that compared to secure adults, anxious/avoidant adults are less interested in romantic relationships and seem less upset when the relationships end. In contrast, anxious/resistant adults are highly focused on their relationships, and they fret and fume about them to a much greater extent than secure individuals (Figure 15.20).

Does all of this mean that one is simply out of luck if one has not developed the "right" working model in childhood? Happily, the answer appears to be no. Working models of self and other seem to be at least somewhat malleable and context dependent, and new experiences (whether with friends, dating partners, or a therapist) seem to have the power to refashion a person's early ideas about self and other. Even so, the ability to predict adult outcomes, based on childhood patterns, does support at least one part of Freud's perspective—namely, the claim that the early years play a critical role in shaping adult behaviors, expectations, and personality.

Contributions of the Psychodynamic Approach

In the early part of the twentieth century, the public—especially in the United States—was fascinated by the bearded Viennese doctor who spoke so frankly about sex. Scholars in the social sciences, literature, and the arts flocked to read his writings because they were so far-reaching in scope, so profound in their implications.

Since then, a number of criticisms have—as we have seen—been leveled against the psychodynamic approach. Even with these criticisms, though, Freud's contribution to psychology—and to Western thinking—is enormous (Figure 15.21). His work draws our attention to a set of ideas whose relevance today belies the hundred plus years that have passed since he started articulating his views (Westen, 1998). These ideas include the notion that many important psychological processes—especially affective and motivational processes—operate outside awareness, and the idea that our motives and impulses are often at odds with one another. Contemporary psychologists would still endorse Freud's claim that people's thoughts, feelings, and behaviors are strongly influenced by their mental representations of important people in their lives, as well as his claim that among other things, development revolves around finding socially acceptable ways of managing sexual and aggressive impulses. Admittedly, many of these ideas have their origins in theories predating Freud. It is also true that the modern conce-

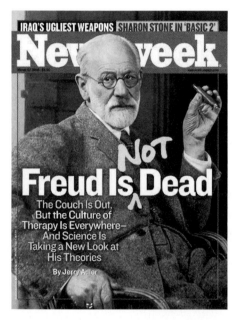

15.21 Reflecting on Freud Freud's legacy continues today.

ption of these ideas is, in important ways, different from Freud's specific proposals, and that these ideas, in the modern era, have a less central position than they had in Freud's theorizing. Nonetheless, Freud undeniably deserves credit for making these essential ideas prominent for many modern theories of personality.

THE HUMANISTIC APPROACH: APPRECIATING OUR POTENTIAL

Half a century or so ago, a new approach to human motivation and personality—the *humanistic approach*—gained prominence. According to its adherents, both trait theorists and psychodynamic theorists have lost sight of what is truly human about human beings. Healthy individuals, the humanists argue, want to feel free to choose and determine their own lives rather than to exist as mere pawns pushed around by stimuli from without or driven by demons from within. They seek more than food and sex, and strive for more than mere adjustment—they want to grow and develop their potential.

Phenomenology and Self-actualization

At the heart of the humanistic approach is a commitment to **phenomenology**, or understanding a person's own unique first-person perspective on his life. Rather than describing how a person typically behaves (as in the trait perspective), or how a person's unconscious dynamics operate (as in the psychodynamic perspective), a proponent of the humanistic perspective seeks to step into another person's shoes and experience the world as he does. The goal is to understand a person's conscious experience by understanding his **construal**, or interpretation, of the world around him.

phenomenology The study of individuals' own unique, first-person, conscious experience.

construal The way an individual makes sense of the world around him.

A second defining feature of the humanistic approach is its conception of human motivation. As we have seen in Chapter 12, drive theories commonly view humans as being engaged in a never-ending struggle to remove some internal tension or make up for some deficit. However, a release from anxiety and tension does not account for everything we strive for. We sometimes seek things for their own sake, as positive goals in themselves, and Maslow (1968, 1996) insisted that psychologists consider the full range of motives, not just those that arise from physical requirements such as food, water, and the like.

These concerns led Maslow to propose his *hierarchy of needs* (see Chapter 12), in which the lower-order physiological needs are at the bottom and the striving for *self-actualization*—realizing one's potential to the fullest—is at the top. But what exactly does self-actualization mean?

Maslow answered this question largely by presenting case histories of people he and his collaborators regarded as self-actualized (Figure 15.22). Some of them were individuals he had personally interviewed (the healthiest 1% of college students); others were historical figures (e.g., Thomas Jefferson and Eleanor Roosevelt) whose lives he studied by means of historical documents. As Maslow (1968, 1970, 1996) saw it, these self-actualizers were all realistically oriented, accepted themselves and others, were spontaneous, cared more about the problems they were working on than about themselves, had intimate relationships with a few people rather than superficial relationships with many, and had democratic values—all in all, an admirable list of human qualities.

15.22 Self-actualizers According to Maslow, Thomas Jefferson and Eleanor Roosevelt are clear examples of people who self-actualized.

These traits, and Maslow's roll call of self-actualized individuals, might make self-actualization sound as though it were possible only for the few and the powerful. Not so. Even though self-actualization is rare, one of the major themes of humanistic psychology is that we each have within us the impulse to self-actualize. Indeed, one of the other major humanists—Carl Rogers (1902–1987)—regarded this as our one basic motive, and he argued that we often manage to self-actualize against extraordinary odds, much as a plant improbably pushes through a crack in concrete. (C. R. Rogers, 1951, 1961).

The Self

This discussion of self-actualization raises an important question: What exactly is the self that the humanists talked about, and where does it come from? More than a century ago—well before the humanists such as Maslow and Rogers came onto the scene—William James (1890; Figure 15.23) distinguished two aspects of the self, which he called the "I" and the "me." (This is the same William James whose emotion theory we considered in Chapter 12.) The "I" is the self that thinks, acts, feels, and believes. The "me," by contrast, is the set of physical and psychological attributes and features that define who you are as a person. These include the kind of music you like, what you look like, and the activities that currently give your life meaning.

Half a century after James first made this distinction, the humanist Carl Rogers used similar language to talk about how the self-concept develops in early childhood and eventually comes to include one's sense of oneself—the "I"—as an agent who takes actions and makes decisions. It also includes one's sense of oneself as a kind of object—the "me"—that is seen and thought about, liked or disliked (C. R. Rogers, 1959, 1961). Indeed, the self-concept was such an important aspect of Rogers' approach that he referred to his theory as **self theory**, an approach that continues to inspire contemporary researchers who seek to explain the motives that activate and support human behavior (Deci & Ryan, 2000).

SELF-SCHEMA

For each of us, our sense of self is a key aspect of our personality, and each of us has a set of beliefs about who we are and who we should be, and a body of knowledge about our values and our past behaviors. This knowledge about ourselves constitutes, for each person, a

15.23 William James (1842–1910) James was an important influence on the early field of psychology—but no less of an influence on philosophy and religious studies!

self theory Carl Rogers's theory of personality, which emphasizes the individual's active attempts to satisfy his needs in a manner that is consistent with his self-concept.

self-schema An organized body of knowledge about the self and that shapes one's behaviors, perceptions, and emotions.

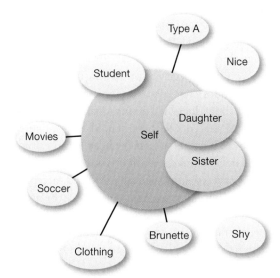

15.24 Self-schema diagram The self-schema consists of interrelated descriptions of the self. Some descriptions are central to self (e.g., daughter); other descriptions are relevant but less central (e.g., brunette); while others still are not relevant to the self-schema (e.g., shy).

self-schema (Markus, 1977; Figure 15.24). This schema is not just a passive record of our prior experiences; instead, the schema actively shapes our behaviors, perceptions, and emotions. For example, a person might have a schema of himself as a smart person who does well at school. This self-schema will make certain situations, such as academic tests, seem more important and consequential. The self-schema will also guide many of his choices, such as opting to attend a more rigorous college rather than a "party school" or spending the extra hour polishing a term paper rather than heading off to get coffee with friends.

The self-schema is not just a random list of characteristics. Instead, it is a highly organized (although not always entirely consistent) narrative about who one is. McAdams and colleagues (McAdams, 1993, 2001; McAdams & Pals, 2006) refer to such personal narratives as **personal myths**—in essence, "stories" that provide a sense of direction and meaning for our lives. Moreover, given this important role for these narratives, it cannot be surprising that these narratives are resistant to change, and, in fact, studies have shown that even people with negative self-concepts tenaciously cling to these views, and seek out others who will verify these views (Swann, Rentfrow, & Guinn, 2002).

Information relevant to our self-schema is also given a high priority. For example, in several studies, people have been shown a series of trait words and asked to make simple judgments regarding these words (e.g., Is the word in capital letters? Is it a positive word? Does it describe me?). When asked later to remember the traits that they previously saw, participants were more likely to recall words presented in the "Does it describe me?" condition than in the other conditions, suggesting that material encoded in relationship to the self is better remembered (T. B. Rogers, Kuiper, & Kirker, 1977). These findings are buttressed by neuroimaging studies that show the portions of the medial prefrontal cortex are particularly active when people are engaged in self-referential processes (as compared to when they are making judgments about how the words are written, whether the words are good or bad, or even whether they are characteristic of a friend; Heatherton et al., 2006).

Interestingly, people seem to have schemas not only for who they are now, their **actual selves**, but also for who they may be in the future—mental representations of **possible selves** (Markus & Nurius, 1986; Figure 15.25). These include a sense of the *ideal self* that one would ideally like to be (e.g., someone who saves others' lives), and the *ought self* that one thinks one should be (e.g., someone who never lies or deceives others) (E. T. Higgins, 1997). According to E. Tory Higgins, when we compare our actual self to our ideal self, we become motivated to narrow the distance between the two, and we develop what he calls a **promotion focus**. When we have this sort of focus, we actively pursue valued goals—a pursuit that results in pleasure. In contrast, when we compare our actual self to our ought self, we become motivated to avoid doing harm, and we develop what Higgins calls a **prevention focus**. This kind of focus is associated with feelings of relief.

Notice, therefore, that schemas are not just dispassionate observations about ourselves; instead, they often have powerful emotions attached to them and can be a compelling source of motivation. This is why the schemas are typically thought of as an aspect of *"hot" cognition* (emotional and motivational) rather than *"cold" cognition* (dispassionate and analytical).

SELF-ESTEEM AND SELF-ENHANCEMENT

The "hot" nature of self-schemas is also evident in the fact that these schemas play a powerful role in shaping a person's **self-esteem**—a broad assessment that reflects the relative balance of positive and negative judgments about oneself (Figure 15.26). Not surprisingly, self-esteem is not always based on objective self-appraisals. Indeed, people in Western

personal myths The personal narratives or stories that provide a person with a sense of direction and meaning.

actual selves Self-schema for whom one is at the moment.

possible selves Self-schemas for whom one may be in the future; these include the ideal self and the ought self.

promotion focus An orientation to actively pursue valued goals thought to arise when we compare our actual self to our ideal self.

prevention focus An orientation to avoid doing harm thought to arise when we compare our actual self to our ought self.

self-esteem The relative balance of positive and negative judgments about oneself.

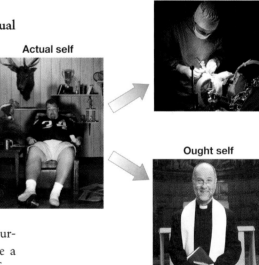

Ideal self

Actual self

Ought self

15.25 Possible selves People not only have mental representations of their actual selves, or who they are now, but also possible selves, including their ideal self and ought self.

IT'S ALWAYS 'GOOD DOG'— NEVER 'GREAT DOG.'

GREGORY

15.26 Canine self-esteem?

cultures seem highly motivated to view themselves as different from and superior to other people—even in the face of evidence to the contrary (Sedikides & Gregg, 2008). This is manifest, for example, in the fact that most Americans judge themselves to be above average on a broad range of characteristics (see Harter, 1990). Thus, in 1976–1977 the College Board asked 1 million high-school students to rate themselves against their peers on leadership ability. In response, 70% said they were above average, and only 2% thought they were below. Similar findings have been obtained in people's judgments of talents ranging from managerial skills to driving ability (see Dunning, Meyerowitz, & Holzberg, 1989). And it is not just high-school students who show these effects. One study of university professors found that 94% believed they were better than their colleagues at their jobs (Gilovich, 1991).

What is going on here? Part of the cause lies in the way we search our memories in order to decide whether we have been good leaders or bad, good drivers or poor ones. Evidence suggests that this memory search is often selective, showcasing the occasions in the past on which we have behaved well and neglecting the occasions on which we have done badly—leading, of course, to a self-flattering summary of this biased set of events (Kunda, 1990; Kunda, Fong, Sanitioso, & Reber, 1993).

In addition, people seem to capitalize on the fact that the meanings of these traits—effective leader, good at getting along with others—are often ambiguous. This ambiguity allows each of us to interpret a trait, and thus to interpret the evidence, in a fashion that puts us in the best possible light. Take driving ability. Suppose Henry is a slow, careful driver. He will tend to think that he's better than average precisely because he's slow and careful. But suppose Jane, on the other hand, is a fast driver who prides herself on her ability to whiz through traffic and hang tight on hairpin turns. She will also think that she's better than average because of the way she's defined driving skill. As a result, both Henry and Jane (and, indeed, most drivers) end up considering themselves above average. By redefining success or excellence, we can each conclude that we are successful (Dunning & Cohen, 1992; Dunning et al., 1989).

CULTURE AND THE SELF

Although the self-schema is important for all of us, the *content* of the schema varies from individual to individual and, it seems, from one culture to the next. When they think about themselves, Americans tend to think about their broad, stable traits, traits that apply in all settings, such as athletic, disorganized, and creative. Things are different for people living in interdependent, collectivist cultures. They also view themselves as having certain traits, but only in specific situations, and so their self-descriptions tend to emphasize the role of the situation, such as quiet at parties, or gentle with their parents (Ellemers, Spears, & Dossje, 2002; D. Hart, Lucca-Irizarry, & Damon, 1986; Heine, 2008). Similarly, people in interdependent cultures tend to have self-concepts that emphasize their social roles, and so, when asked to complete the statement "I am . . . ," Japanese students are more likely to say things like "a sister" or "a student," whereas American students are more likely to mention traits like "smart" or "athletic" (Cousins, 1989). Similar differences can show up within a single culture. Thus, as shown in Figure 15.27, Kenyans who were least westernized overwhelmingly described themselves in terms of roles and memberships and mentioned personal characteristics such as traits only 2% of the time. By contrast, Kenyans who were most westernized used trait terms nearly 40% of the time, and only slightly less than American undergraduates (Ma & Schoeneman, 1997).

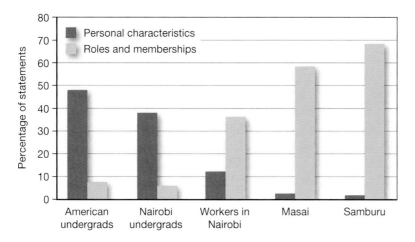

15.27 **Self-descriptions** The proportion of self-descriptions that are personal characteristics versus roles and memberships varies according to degree of westernization.

There is also variation from one culture to the next in how people evaluate themselves. In individualistic cultures, people seek to distinguish themselves through personal achievement and other forms of self-promotion, with the result of increased self-esteem. In collectivistic cultures, on the other hand, any form of self-promotion threatens the relational and situational bonds that glue the society together. Indeed, to be a "good" person in these cultures, one should seek to be quite ordinary—a strategy that results in social harmony and meeting collective goals, not increased self-esteem (Kitayama, Markus, Matsumoto, & Norasakkunkit, 1997; Pyszczynski, Greenberg, Solomon, Arndt, & Schimel, 2004). For them, self-aggrandizement brings disharmony, which is too great a price to pay. Evidence for this conclusion comes from a study in which American and Japanese college students were asked to rank their abilities in areas ranging from math and memory to warmheartedness and athletic skill. The American students showed the usual result: Across all the questions, 70% rated themselves above average on each trait. But among the Japanese students, only 50% rated themselves above average, indicating no self-serving bias, and perhaps pointing instead to a self-harmonizing one (Markus and Kitayama, 1991; Takata, 1987; also Dhawan, Roseman, Naidu, & Rettek, 1995).

Positive Psychology

Modern researchers have taken heed of another insight offered by Maslow, Rogers, and other humanists, who enjoined psychologists not to focus so much on deficiency and pathology. Instead, these early humanists emphasized that humans also have positive needs—to be healthy and happy, and to develop their potential. These points underlie a relatively new movement called **positive psychology**.

In the last decade or so, there has been a tremendous burst of research activity that has sought scientifically to examine optimal human functioning (C. Peterson, 2006). The focus of this research has been on *positive subjective experiences*, such as happiness, fulfillment, and flow; *positive individual traits*, including character strengths, values, and interests; and *positive social institutions*, such as families, schools, universities, and societies. In the next sections, we consider what positive psychology has found concerning positive states and positive traits.

positive psychology A research movement that emphasizes factors that make people psychologically healthy, happy, or able to cope well with their life circumstances.

POSITIVE STATES

Novelists, philosophers, and social critics have all voiced their views about what happiness is and what makes it possible. Recently, academic psychologists have also entered this discussion (e.g., Ariely, 2008; Gilbert, 2006; Haidt, 2006; Lyubomirsky, 2008; B. Schwartz, 2004). What has research taught us about happiness?

One intriguing finding concerns the notion of a happiness *set point*, a level that appears to be heavily influenced by genetics (Lykken & Tellegen, 1996) and is remarkably stable across the lifetime—and thus relatively independent of life circumstances. What produces this stability? The key may be *adaptation*, the process through which we grow accustomed to (and cease paying attention to) any stimulus or state to which we are continually exposed. One early demonstration of this point comes from a study that compared the sense of well-being in people in two rather different groups. One group included individuals who had recently won the lottery; the other was a group of paraplegics (Brickman, Coates, & Janoff-Bullman, 1978). Not surprisingly, the two groups were quite different in their level of happiness soon after winning the lottery or losing the use of their limbs. When surveyed a few months after these events, however, the two groups were similar in their sense of contentment with their lives—an extraordinary testimony to the power of adaptation and to the human capacity for adjusting to extreme circumstances.

Adaptation is a powerful force, but we must not overstate its role. Evidence suggests that everyone tends to return to their happiness set point after a change (positive or negative) in circumstances, but there are large individual differences in how rapid and complete this return is. Thus, some people show much more of a long-term effect of changes in marital status (Lucas, Clark, Georgellis, & Diener, 2003) or long-term disability (Lucas, 2007). Clearly, set points are not the whole story; circumstances matter as well—more for some people than for others.

So far, we have focused on what positive psychologists have been learning about happiness, but they are also concerned with other positive states, such as the energy and focus that are evident when the individual is fully engaged by what she is doing. Csikszentmihalyi (1990) has examined such states by studying the experiences of highly creative artists. He found that the painters he studied became so immersed in their painting that they lost themselves in their work, becoming temporarily unaware of hunger, thirst, or even the passage of time. Csikszentmihalyi called the positive state that accompanied the artists' painting "flow," and he documented that far from being unique to artists, the same sort of highly immersed and intrinsically rewarding state is evident in rock climbers, dancers, and chess players (Figure 15.28). By systematically studying people as they work and play,

15.28 Flow states Flow states are energized, positive psychological states that occur when there is an optimal balance between the challenge presented by an activity and one's skills to meet that challenge, as shown in (A) the upper right quadrant of this figure, and in (B) the artist Jackson Pollock and (C) chess grandmaster Bobby Fischer.

Csikszentmihalyi has found that flow is most likely to be experienced when there is an optimal balance between the challenge presented by an activity and one's skills to meet that challenge. If the level of challenge is too low for one's ability, one feels bored. If the level of challenge is too high for one's ability, one feels anxiety. But if the challenge is just right—and one feels that the activity is voluntarily chosen—one may experience flow.

POSITIVE TRAITS

Positive psychologists have been concerned not just with positive states, like feeling happy; they have also been concerned with positive traits—what we might think of broadly as being a good person (Peterson & Seligman, 2004). This interest has aligned them to some degree with the trait approach, which we considered at the beginning of this chapter. However, positive psychologists emphasize delineating a set of narrower and more specific traits, namely, the "positive" or "desirable" traits.

Defining and understanding these traits has been a central concern since the earliest days of psychology (James, 1890), but the topic was set aside as too philosophical and value-laden for many years. Only in the past decade has the systematic exposition of positive traits again come to the fore. One notable effort, led by Christopher Peterson and Martin Seligman, has focused on developing a classification of **character strengths** (Peterson and Seligman, 2004)—personal characteristics that (1) contribute to a person's happiness without diminishing the happiness of others, (2) are valued in their own right, rather than as a means to an end, (3) are trait-like and show variation across people, (4) are measurable using reliable instruments, and (5) are evident across cultures, rather than specific to one or a few cultures (C. Peterson, 2006).

Peterson and Seligman have identified 24 character strengths with these attributes, organized into six clusters, as shown in Table 15.1. The first cluster of character strengths centers around wisdom and knowledge; the second cluster centers around courage; the third cluster centers around humanitarian concerns; the fourth cluster centers around justice; the fifth cluster centers around temperance, defined by an absence of excess; and the final cluster centers around transcendence.

This is a broad list—but may not be broad enough. For example, other researchers have emphasized a role for *optimism*—a generalized expectation of desirable rather than undesirable outcomes (Scheier & Carver, 1985). Another important character strength is *resilience*, which refers to surviving and even thriving in the face of adversity—including such extreme circumstances as serious illness, hostile divorce, bereavement, and even rape

character strengths Personal characteristics that contribute to a person's happiness without diminishing the happiness of others.

TABLE 15.1	Peterson and Seligman's 24 Character Strengths					
	CLUSTER 1 Wisdom and Knowledge	CLUSTER 2 Courage	CLUSTER 3 Humanitarian Concerns	CLUSTER 4 Justice	CLUSTER 5 Temperance	CLUSTER 6 Transcendence
	Creativity, curiosity, love of learning, open-mindedness, and having perspective	Authenticity, bravery, persistence, and zest (approaching life as an adventure)	Kindness, love, and social intelligence	Fairness, leadership, and team-orientation	Mercy, modesty, prudence (not taking unreasonable risks), and self-regulation	Appreciation of beauty or excellence, gratitude, hope, humor, and spirituality

and the ravages of war. These positive tendencies appear to be associated with a number of important life outcomes, such as greater success at work, with friends, and in marriage (Lyubomirsky, King, & Diener, 2005). The strengths also matter for one's physiological functioning and health (Ryff et al., 2006; Salovey, Rothman, Detweiler, & Steward, 2000). For example, people who are generally optimistic also have a better-functioning immune system and so are more resistant to problems that range from the common cold to serious illness (Pressman & Cohen, 2005; Segerstrom, 2000).

Contributions of the Humanistic Approach

How should we evaluate the humanistic approach to personality? We certainly need to be cautious about the claims offered by Maslow, Rogers, and their contemporaries. After all, their key terms, like *self-actualization* or *being yourself*, are only vaguely defined, making it difficult to evaluate the humanists' claims. In light of these (and related) concerns, some critics contend that the humanists' concepts are too vague and their assertions too unproven (and maybe unprovable) to count as serious scientific accomplishments.

At the same time, the humanists have reminded us of several important points that more modern researchers have since developed in detail. These points include a crucial role for each person's sense of self—a sense that colors their perceptions, shapes their behavior, and in many ways defines their experience. The humanists also highlighted the fact that people strive for more than food and sex and prestige; they read poetry, listen to music, fall in love, and try to better themselves. Psychologists in the positive psychology movement are exploring these desires and tendencies using the tools of science to ask what makes us content with our lives and our relationships. Thus, among other specific issues, researchers are beginning to answer questions about how to stimulate creativity, acquire wisdom, and nourish the intellect. Positive psychology is leading researchers in new directions, and it certainly carries on Maslow's vision of a psychology concerned not only with what is basic about human nature, but also with what is good and admirable about us.

THE SOCIAL-COGNITIVE APPROACH: THE POWER OF BELIEFS

Each of the perspectives we have considered has drawn our attention to a different aspect of the personality puzzle. Trait theorists remind us that people do have stable, internal predispositions—that is, traits—and an emphasis on these traits allowed us to explore a number of crucial issues, such as the biological underpinnings of personality. Psychodynamic theorists remind us of the importance of unconscious motivations and conflicts, and the need to dig beneath the surface in our understanding of who each of us is. Humanistic theorists, in turn, remind us that humans have positive motivations as well as negative ones—goals we hope to achieve, and not just hardships or tensions we want to avoid or reduce.

The social-cognitive approach to personality endorses all of these claims, but notes that we have still paid insufficient attention to one essential part of the puzzle— namely, the power of people's beliefs in shaping their responses to others and to the world around them. We saw the first inklings of this emphasis on beliefs in our discussion of the self, and the ways in which the self-schema influences our emotions and actions. However, in the *social-cognitive approach,* our beliefs about ourselves and our world take center stage.

Origins of the Social-Cognitive Approach

Social-cognitive theories vary in their specifics, but all derive from two long-standing traditions. The first is the behavioral tradition, set in the vocabulary of reward, punishment, instrumental responses, and observational learning (see Chapter 6). The second is the cognitive view, which emphasizes the individual as a thinking being.

BEHAVIORAL ROOTS OF SOCIAL-COGNITIVE THEORIES

Central to the behavioral tradition is a worldview that, in its extreme form, asserts that virtually anyone can become anything given proper training. This American "can-do" view was distilled in a well-known pronouncement by the founder of American behaviorism, John B. Watson (Figure 15.29):

> Give me a dozen healthy infants, well-formed, and my own specified world to bring them up in and I'll guarantee to take any one at random and train him to become any type of specialist I might select—doctor, lawyer, artist, merchant-chief, and, yes, even beggarman and thief, regardless of his talents, penchants, tendencies, abilities, vocations, and race of his ancestors. (1925, p. 82)

Watson's version of behaviorism was relatively primitive, but elements of his view are still visible in subsequent theorizing within the social-cognitive perspective. For example, Albert Bandura (like Watson) places a heavy emphasis on the role of experience and learning, and the potential each of us has for developing in a variety of ways. But Bandura's view of personality goes considerably beyond Watson's in its emphasis on the role we play as agents in fashioning our own lives. According to Bandura (2001), we observe relationships between certain actions (whether ours or others') and their real-world consequences (rewards or punishments), and from this we develop a set of internalized **outcome expectations**, which then come to govern our actions.

In addition, we gradually become aware of ourselves as agents able to produce certain outcomes, marking the emergence of a sense of **self-efficacy**, or a belief that one can perform the behaviors that will lead to particular outcomes (Bandura, 2001, 2006). When a person's sense of self-efficacy is high, she believes that she can behave in ways that will lead to rewarding outcomes. By contrast, when a person's sense of self-efficacy is low, she believes herself incapable, and she may not even try. Researchers have found high self-efficacy beliefs to be associated with better social relationships, work, and health outcomes (Bandura, 1997; 2001; Maddux, 1995; Schwarzer, 1992). Likewise, self-efficacy beliefs about a particular task ("I'm sure I can do this!") are associated with success in that task. This attitude leads to more persistence and a greater tolerance of frustration, both of which contribute to better performance (Schunk, 1984, 1985).

Once outcome expectations and beliefs about self-efficacy are in place, our actions depend less on the immediate environment, and more on an internalized system of self-rewards and self-punishments—our values and moral sensibilities. This reliance on internal standards makes our behavior more consistent than if we were guided simply by the exigencies of the moment, and this consistency is what we know as personality. As seen from this view, personality is not just a reflection of who the individual is, with a substantial contribution from biology. Instead, in Bandura's perspective, personality is a reflection of the situations the person has been exposed to in the past, and the expectations and beliefs that have been gleaned from those situations.

15.29 John B. Watson (1878–1958) The founder of American behaviorism.

outcome expectations A set of beliefs, drawn from experience, about what the consequences (rewards or punishments) of certain actions are likely to be.

self-efficacy The sense a person has about what things he can plausibly accomplish.

COGNITIVE ROOTS OF SOCIAL-COGNITIVE THEORIES

personal constructs The dimensions used by a person to organize his or her experience.

A related tradition underlying social-cognitive theories of personality is the cognitive view, first detailed by George Kelly (1955). Like many other psychologists, Kelly acknowledged that people's behavior depends heavily on the situation. Crucially, though, he emphasized that much depends on their *interpretations* of the situation, which Kelly called their **personal constructs**, or the dimensions they use to organize their experience.

From Kelly's perspective, each person seeks to make sense of the world and find meaning in it. To explain how people do this, Kelly used the metaphor of a scientist who obtains data about the world and then develops theories to explain what he has observed. These theories concern specific situations, but, when taken together, constitute each individual's personal construct system. To assess these personal constructs, Kelly used the Role Construct Repertory Test. This test asks people to list three key individuals in their life, and then to say how two of these three were different from a third. By repeating this process with different groups of three ideas, traits, or objects, Kelly was able to elicit the dimensions each person used (such as intelligence, strength, or goodness) to make sense of the world.

Kelly's work is important in its own right, but his influence is especially visible in the work of his former student, Walter Mischel. For Mischel (whom we met earlier), the study of personality must consider neither fixed traits nor static situations, but should focus instead on how people dynamically process various aspects of their ever-changing world. Like Kelly, Mischel contends that the qualities that form personality are essentially cognitive: different ways of seeing the world, thinking about it, and interacting with it, all acquired over the course of an individual's life. But how should we conceptualize this cognition, and, with it, the interaction between the individual and the setting?

Mischel's answer to this broad question is framed in terms of each individual's cognitive-affective personality system (CAPS), which consists of five key qualities on which people can differ. The first is the individual's *encodings*, the set of construals by which the person interprets inner and outer experiences. Second, individuals develop *expectancies and beliefs* about the world, which include the outcome expectations and sense of self-efficacy stressed by Bandura. Third, people differ in their *affects*—that is, their emotional responses to situations. Fourth, they differ in their *goals and values*, the set of outcomes that are considered desirable. Finally, CAPS includes the individual's *competencies and self-regulatory plans*, the way an individual regulates her own behavior by various self-imposed goals and strategies (Mischel, 1973, 1984, 2004; Mischel & Shoda, 1995, 1998, 2000).

Other researchers have filled in many details about what these various beliefs involve. For example, as we saw in Chapter 12, Carol Dweck and her colleagues have argued that people differ in their fundamental assumptions about their own abilities (Dweck, 1999, 2006; Dweck & Leggett, 1988; Molden & Dweck, 2006). Some people assume their abilities are relatively fixed and unlikely to change in the future. In contrast to this *entity view*, others hold an *incremental view*—assuming their abilities can change and grow in response to new experience or learning (Figure 15.30). These assumptions turn out to be rather important, because people with the incremental view are more willing to confront challenges and better able to bounce back from frustration (Dweck, 2009). Evidence comes from many sources, including studies that have tried to shift people's thinking from the entity view to the incremental view. In one study, Blackwell, Trzesniewski, and Dweck (2007) randomly assigned junior high school students either to a regular study skills group or to an experimental condition that taught students that the brain is like a muscle and can get stronger with use. Compared to

(A) Children with incremental views regarding intelligence believe their intelligence can grow, and respond positively to challenging feedback. (B) Children with entity views regarding intelligence believe their intelligence is fixed, and respond negatively to challenging feedback.

those in the study skills group, those in the experimental group showed increased motivation and better grades.

These differences in belief are another point in which cultures differ. Evidence suggests, for example, that Americans tend toward the entity view, while the Japanese tend toward an incremental view. This is reflected in the belief among many students in the United States that the major influence on intelligence is genetics; Japanese students, in contrast, estimate that the majority of intelligence is due to one's efforts (Heine et al., 2001). This result is likely related to another finding we mentioned earlier in the chapter: Americans tend to perceive themselves as consistent in their behaviors as they move from one situation to the next, a view similar to the entity view of intelligence, which emphasizes the stability of one's abilities. Some other cultures put less emphasis on personal consistency, leaving them ready to embrace the potential for growth and change at the heart of the incremental view.

Key Social-Cognitive Concepts

Social-cognitive theorists differ in focus and emphasis, but across theorists, three concepts play a crucial role. These are *control*, *attributional style* (which refers to how we typically explain the things that happen in our lives), and *self-control*. We take up each of these in turn.

CONTROL

There is a great deal of evidence that people desire control over the circumstances of their life and benefit from feeling that they have such control (C. Peterson, 1999; Rodin, 1990; also see Chapter 6).

A widely cited illustration involves elderly people in a nursing home. Patients on one floor of the nursing home were given small houseplants to care for, and they were also asked to choose the time at which they wanted to participate in some of the nursing-home activities (e.g., visiting friends, watching television, planning social events). Patients on another floor were also given plants but with the understanding that the plants would be tended by the staff. They participated in the same activities as the first group of patients, but at times chosen by the staff. The results were clear-cut. According to both nurses' and the patients' own reports, the patients who tended their own houseplants and scheduled their own activities were more active and felt better than the patients who lacked this control, a difference that was still apparent a year later (Langer & Rodin, 1976; Rodin & Langer, 1977; Figure 15.31).

15.31 **Control** A person's well-being as she ages may be strongly influenced by whether she has (A) a high degree or (B) a low degree of control over her routine and her environment.

(A) Too little control?   **(B) Just the right amount of control?**

Having control means being able to make choices, and so, if having control is a good thing, then having choices would seem to be a good thing too, and the more the better. This line of reasoning is certainly consistent with the way various goods and services are marketed—with both retail stores and large corporations offering us dozens of options whenever we order a latte, buy a new cell phone, select an insurance plan, or go on a vacation. However, in a series of studies, Sheena Iyengar and Mark Lepper (2000) found that there is such a thing as too much choice. One of these studies was conducted in a gourmet food store, where the researchers created displays featuring fancy jams that customers could taste. Some displays had 6 kinds of jam to taste. Other displays had 24 kinds of jam to taste. Although people flocked to the larger display, it turned out that people were actually 10 times as likely to purchase a jam they had tasted if they had seen the smaller display as compared to the larger display. Reviewing this and related studies, Barry Schwartz (2004) concluded that although having some choice (and hence control) is extremely important, having too much choice leads to greater stress and anxiety rather than greater pleasure. These findings indicate there can be too much of an apparently good thing, and suggest that other considerations (such as managing the anxiety occasioned by having too many choices) may under some circumstances lead us to prefer lesser rather than greater control (see also Shah & Wolford, 2007).

ATTRIBUTIONAL STYLE

Control beliefs are usually forward looking: Which jam will I buy? When will I visit my friends? A different category of beliefs, in contrast, is oriented toward the past and—more specifically—concerns people's explanations for the events they have experienced.

In general, people tend to offer dispositional attributions for their own successes ("I did well on the test because I'm smart"), but situational attributions for their failures ("My company is losing money because of the downturn in the economy"; "I lost the match because the sun was in my eyes"). This pattern is obviously self-serving, and has been documented in many Western cultures (Bradley, 1978). In most studies, participants perform various tasks—ranging from alleged measures of motor skills to tests of social sensitivity—and then receive fake feedback on whether they had achieved some criterion of success (see, for example, Luginbuhl, Crowe, & Kahan, 1975; D. T. Miller, 1976; Sicoly & Ross, 1977; M. L. Snyder, Stephan, & Rosenfield, 1976; Stevens & Jones, 1976). The overall pattern of results is always the same: By and large, the participants attribute their successes to internal factors (they were pretty good at such tasks, and they worked hard) and their failures to external factors (the task was too difficult, and they were unlucky).

The same pattern is evident outside the laboratory. One study analyzed the comments of football and baseball players following important games, as published in newspapers. Of the statements made by the winners, 80% were internal attributions: "Our team was great," "Our star player did it all," and so on. In contrast, only 53% of the losers gave internal attributions, and they often explained the outcomes by referring to external, situational factors: "I think we hit the ball all right. But I think we're unlucky" (Lau & Russell, 1980, p. 32).

These attributions are offered, of course, after an event—after the team has won or lost, or after the business has succeeded or failed. But a related pattern arises *before* an event, allowing people to protect themselves against failure and disappointment. One such strategy is known as **self-handicapping**, in which one arranges an obstacle to one's own performance. This way, if failure occurs, it will be attributed to the obstacle and not to one's own limitations (Higgins, Snyder, & Berglas, 1990; Jones & Berglas, 1978). Thus, if Julie is afraid of failing next week's biology exam, she might spend more time than usual watching television. Then, if she fails the exam, the obvious interpretation will be that she did not study hard enough, rather than that she is stupid.

Not surprisingly, all these forms of self-protection are less likely in collectivistic cultures—that is, among people who are not motivated to view themselves as different from and better than others. But there is some subtlety to the cultural patterning. A recent analysis of the self-serving bias found that the Japanese and Pacific Islanders showed no self-serving biases, Indians displayed a moderate bias, and Chinese and Koreans showed large self-serving biases. It is not clear why these differences arose, and explaining this point is a fruitful area for future research. In the meantime, though, this analysis reminds us of the important point that there is a great deal of variation within collectivistic, interdependent cultures.

Even within a given culture, there are notable differences in **attributional style,** the way a person typically explains the things that happen in his or her life (Figure 15.32). This style can be measured by a specially constructed attributional-style questionnaire (ASQ) in which a participant is asked to imagine himself in a number of situations (e.g., failing a test) and to indicate what would have caused those events if they had happened to him (Dykema, Bergbower, Doctora, & Peterson, 1996; C. Peterson & Park, 1998; C. Peterson et al., 1982). His responses on the ASQ reveal how he explains his failure. He may think he did not study enough (an internal cause) or that the teacher

self-handicapping A self-protective strategy of arranges for an obstacle to one's own performance, so that failure can be attributed to the obstacle instead of one's own limitations.

attributional style The way a person typically explains the things that happen in his or her life.

(A) Negative attributional style

(B) Positive attributional style

15.32 **Attributional style** (A) A. A. Milne's Eeyore personifies a negative attributional style. (B) Cheerful SpongeBob SquarePants has a positive attributional style.

misled him about what to study (an external cause). He may think he is generally stupid (a global explanation) or is stupid on just that test material (a specific explanation). Finally, he may believe he is always bound to fail (a stable explanation) or that with a little extra studying he can recover nicely (an unstable explanation).

Differences in attributional style matter (Peterson & Park, 2007). More specifically, greater use of external, specific, and unstable attributions for failure predicts important outcomes ranging from performance in insurance sales (Seligman & Schulman, 1986) to success in competitive sports (Seligman, Nolen-Hoeksema, Thornton, & Thornton, 1990). Importantly, variation in attributional style has also been shown to predict the onset of some forms of psychopathology, such as whether a person is likely to suffer from depression (see Chapter 16). Specifically, being prone to depression is correlated with a particular attributional style—a tendency to attribute unfortunate events to causes that are internal, global, and stable. Thus, a person who is prone to depression is likely to attribute life events to causes related to something within her that applies tomany other situations and will continue indefinitely (G. M. Buchanan & Seligman, 1995; C. Peterson & Seligman, 1984; C. Peterson & Vaidya, 2001; Seligman & Gillham, 2000).

SELF-CONTROL

So far we have emphasized each person's control over his life circumstances, but just as important for the social-cognitive theorists is the degree of control each person has over himself and his own actions. Surely people differ in this regard, and these differences in **self-control** are visible in various ways (Figure 15.33). People differ in their ability to do what they know they should—whether the issue is being polite to an obnoxious supervisor at work, or keeping focused despite the distraction of a talkative roommate. They also differ in whether they can avoid doing what they want to do but should not—for example, not joining friends for a movie the night before an exam. People also differ from each other in their capacity to do things they dislike in order to get what they want eventually—for example, studying extra hard now in order to do well later in job or graduate school applications.

Examples of self-control (and lack thereof) abound in everyday life. Self-control is manifested whenever we get out of bed in the morning, because we know we should, even though we are still quite sleepy. It is also evident when we eat an extra helping of dessert when we're dieting (or don't), or quit smoking (or don't). In each case, the ability to control oneself is tied to what people often call *willpower*, and, according to popular wisdom, some people have more willpower than others. But do they really? That is, is "having a lot of willpower" a trait that is consistent over time and across situations?

Walter Mischel (1974, 1984) and his associates (Mischel, Shoda, & Rodriguez, 1992) studied this issue in children. The participants in his studies were between four and five years of age and were shown two snacks, one preferable to the other (e.g., two marshmallows or pretzels versus one). To obtain the snack they preferred, they had to wait about 15 minutes. If they did not want to wait, or grew tired of waiting, they immediately received the less desirable treat but had to forgo the more desirable one.

Whether the children could manage the wait was powerfully influenced by what the children did and thought about while they waited. If they looked at the marshmallow, or worse, thought about eating it, they usually succumbed and grabbed the lesser reward. But they were able to wait for the preferred snack if they found (or were shown) some way of distracting their attention from it, for example, by thinking of something fun, such as Mommy pushing them on a swing. They could also wait for the preferred snack if they thought about the snack in some way other than eating it, for example, by focusing on the pretzels' shape and color rather than on their

self-control The ability to pursue a goal while adequately managing internal conflicts about it, or to delay pursuing a goal because of other considerations or constraints.

W Miller

15.33 Self-control?

crunchiness and taste. By mentally transforming the desired object, the children managed to delay gratification and thereby obtain the larger reward (Mischel, 1984; Mischel & Baker, 1975; Mischel & Mischel, 1983; Mischel & Moore, 1980; Rodriguez, Mischel, & Shoda, 1989).

These various findings show that whether a child delays gratification depends in part on how she construes the situation. But it apparently also depends on some qualities of the child herself. The best evidence comes from follow-up studies that show remarkable correlations between children's ability to delay gratification at age 4 (e.g., the ability to wait for the two pretzels) and some of their personality characteristics a decade or more later (Figure 15.34). Being able to tolerate lengthy delays of gratification in early childhood predicts both academic and social competence in adolescence (as rated by the child's parents) and general coping ability. When compared to the children who could not delay gratification, those who could were judged (as young teenagers) to be more articulate, attentive, self-reliant, able to plan and think ahead, academically competent, and resilient under stress (Eigsti et al., 2006; Mischel, Shoda, & Peake, 1988; Shoda, Mischel, & Peake, 1990).

Why should a 4-year-old's ability to wait 15 minutes to get two pretzels rather than one predict such important qualities as academic and social competence 10 years later? The answer probably lies in the fact that the cognitive processes that underlie this deceptively simple task in childhood are the same ones needed for success in adolescence and adulthood. After all, success in school often requires that short-term goals (e.g., partying during the week) be subordinated to long-term purposes (e.g., getting good grades). The same holds for social relations, because someone who gives in to every momentary impulse will be hard-pressed to keep friends, sustain commitments, or participate in team sports. In both academic and social domains, reaching any long-term goal inevitably means renouncing lesser goals that beckon in the interim.

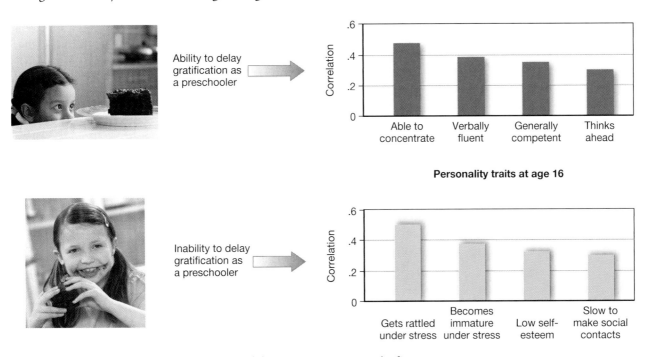

15.34 **Childhood delay of gratification and adolescent competence** The figure indicates the relation between the ability to delay gratification at age 4 or 5 and personality traits at about age 16; it depicts correlations between various personality traits of adolescents as rated by their parents and the length of time they delayed gratification as preschoolers.

If there is some general capacity for delaying gratification, useful for child and adult alike, where does it originate? As we saw in Chapter 11, intelligence has a heritable component, and the executive control processes that support delaying gratification also may have a heritable component. It seems likely, however, that there is also a large learned component. Children may acquire certain cognitive skills (e.g., self-distraction, reevaluating rewards, and sustaining attention to distant goals) that they continue to apply and improve upon as they get older. However they originate, though, these attention-diverting strategies appear to emerge in the first two years of life and can be seen in the child's attachment behavior with the mother. In one study, toddlers were observed during a brief separation from their mothers, using a variant of the Strange Situation task already discussed. Some of the toddlers showed immediate distress, while others distracted themselves with other activities. Those who engaged in self-distraction as toddlers were able to delay gratification longer when they reached the age of 5 (Sethi, Mischel, Aber, Shoda, & Rodriguez, 2000).

But what if one didn't develop these valuable self-regulatory capacities and skills by early childhood? Is one simply out of luck? Proponents of a social cognitive perspective would argue not, pointing to studies in which self-regulatory ability was enhanced by simple changes in how individuals construed the situation in which they found themselves. In one study, for example, Magen and Gross (2007) asked participants to solve simple math problems. What made this task difficult was that a hilarious comedy routine was playing loudly on a television just beside the monitor on which the math problems were being presented. Participants were instructed to do their best, and they understood that they could win a prize if they had a particularly good math score. Even though they were motivated to do well, participants peeked at the television show even though this hurt their performance on the test. Then, halfway through the math test, one group of test-takers was simply reminded to do as well as they could on the second half of the math test. The second group got the same reminder, but in addition, they were told that they might find it helpful to think of the math test as a test of their willpower. Because these participants highly valued their willpower, this provided an extra incentive for them to stay focused on their task. This simple reconstrual of the math test context as a test of their willpower led them to peek less often during the second half of the math test than did the participants in the other instructional group.

Contributions of the Social-Cognitive Approach

Like the trait approach theorists, social-cognitive theorists have taken a considerable interest in relatively stable personality traits, as revealed by studies of attributional style and delay of gratification. How, then, do social-cognitive theorists differ from trait theorists? There are two answers. One has to do with the role of the situation. By now, theorists from all perspectives agree that both traits and situations matter, but even so, social-cognitive theorists are more likely than trait theorists to stress the role of the situation and how the individual understands and deals with it. Thus, Mischel found that delay of gratification is an index of a surprisingly stable personal attribute, but he was quick to point out that this index is strongly affected by the way the situation was set up (was the reward visible?) and how it was construed (did the child think about eating the reward?). The second answer concerns the origins of personality. Unlike trait theorists, who tend to emphasize the genetic basis of personality, social-cognitive theorists typically place greater emphasis on the role played by learning in shaping personality.

Like the psychodynamic theorists, social-cognitive theorists want to dig deeper than the surface of personality in order to understand the psychological processes that support behavior and mental processes. In doing so, social-cognitive theorists are often addressing problems such as delay of gratification that come straight out of Freud's playbook, and the psychological processes that these two types of theorists are interested in overlap considerably, particularly if we include the ego psychologists, with their emphasis on an adaptive, active ego, and the object relations theorists with their emphasis on social reinforcement. Note, however, the differences. Theorists from the social-cognitive and psychodynamic approaches go about their work using starkly different languages and methods and holding up quite different views of the role of conscious processes. Social-cognitive theorists emphasize cognitive processes such as construal and beliefs, and prioritize tightly controlled experiments. In contrast, psychodynamic theorists emphasize unconscious impulses and defenses, and rely on insights drawn from clinical work with patients.

The parallels between the social-cognitive approach and the humanistic approach are similarly instructive. The positive outlook of the humanistic psychologist Carl Rogers resonates with social-cognitive theorists such as Bandura. Both are optimistic about the individual's capacity to overcome difficult circumstances and to show extraordinary resilience in the face of trying times. This optimism hinges for both schools of thought on the conviction that we are not just passively shaped by the swirl of life around us, but also actively seek to shape our world. Despite this shared optimism about the human capacity for growth and change, the traditions differ. The humanistic theorist describes the growth in terms of a self that is actualized to varying degrees, while the social-cognitive theorist draws attention to a malleable set of processes that guide how the individual acts and, ultimately, who he is.

SOME FINAL THOUGHTS: THE NEED FOR MULTIPLE APPROACHES

As our tour of the major approaches to studying personality draws to a close, we can see that each of these approaches focuses on a different part of the puzzle of who we are, and each privileges a somewhat different combination of the various types of data used by personality psychologists, including self-report data, informant data, behavioral data, physiological data, and life data.

Today, relatively few theorists would espouse any of these approaches in their most extreme form, or would claim that none of the other approaches has any merit in understanding personality. Most adherents of the trait perspective, for example, appreciate the power of situations that are construed in different ways by different people. Most psychodynamic theorists see unconscious defenses and conscious coping mechanisms as parts of a continuum, and they recognize the extent to which each individual is richly embedded in a social network. Most humanistically oriented theorists grant that what people do depends on both traits and situations, as well as the motive to self-actualize.

Even so, some important differences in approach clearly remain. Some aspects of personality have clear temperamental origins (trait theory); others are learned, and they derive from how we think about ourselves and the world (social-cognitive theory). Some reflect conflicts of which we are not aware (psychodynamic theory); still others reveal the need for self-actualization (the humanistic approach). We cannot envision what a complete theory of personality will ultimately look like, but it will surely have to describe all of these aspects of human functioning.

THE TRAIT APPROACH: DEFINING OUR DIFFERENCES

- *Traits* define a person's predominant thoughts, feelings, and behaviors. Five personality dimensions have been identified—extraversion, neuroticism, agreeableness, conscientiousness, and openness to experience—the so-called *Big Five*. There has been debate, however, about how useful the Big Five dimensions are for describing personalities across cultures.

- One challenge to trait theories is the *personality paradox:* people often behave less consistently than might be expected. Part of the explanation for this paradox is the power of the situation. Most theorists now believe that both personality and situations matter, usually in interaction, and some theorists describe personalities in terms of an *if . . . then . . .* pattern: "If in this setting, then act in this fashion; if in that setting, then act in that fashion." Some people are more consistent in their behaviors than others; this complexity is assessed by the *Self-Monitoring Scale.*

- Traits grow to some extent out of the individual's *temperament*, or characteristic emotional or behavioral pattern. Twin studies of the Big Five dimensions confirm a high heritability. In the case of extraversion, genetic influences may depend on each individual's level of central nervous system reactivity, with introverts more reactive than extraverts. A similar logic has been used to explain *sensation seeking* and *inhibited temperament*.

- Studies of *national character* underline the importance of cultural differences in personality. Family effects are also important, but they reflect differences within families (e.g., contrasts between first-borns and second-borns) rather than differences between families. The correlation between the personality traits of adopted children and their adoptive siblings is essentially zero, and the correlations between the traits of identical twins reared together are comparable to those of identical twins reared apart.

THE PSYCHODYNAMIC APPROACH: PROBING THE DEPTHS

- The psychodynamic approach to personality is derived from Sigmund Freud's theory of *psychoanalysis*. Freud distinguished three subsystems of personality: the *id*, a blind striving toward biological satisfaction that follows the pleasure principle; the *ego*, a system that tries to reconcile id-derived needs with the actualities of the world; and the *superego*, which represents the internalized rules of the parents and punishes deviations through feelings of guilt.

- According to Freud, internal conflict gives rise to anxiety, which leads a child to push the forbidden thoughts out of consciousness. *Repression* is the primary vehicle for this, but the repressed materials may surface again, demanding the use of other *defense mechanisms*, including *displacement, reaction formation, rationalization*, and *projection*.

- According to Freud, the child passes through specific *stages of psychosexual development*, with each stage characterized by the erogenous zones through which gratification is obtained. Freud proposed that during the phallic stage, the boys develop the Oedipus complex and girls develop the Electra complex.

- Freud drew evidence from several sources, including the errors that people make in everyday life. He also felt that dreams hold important clues about the unconscious mind, although it was crucial to understand a dream's latent content and not just its manifest content. Another source of information about the unconscious comes from the study of myths and legends, which may give insights into our *collective unconscious*.

- After Freud, psychodynamic theorists, called *ego psychologists*, focused on the skills and adaptive capacities of the ego. They emphasized coping patterns, which show considerable consistency over an individual's lifetime. Other psychodynamic theorists, called *object relations* theorists, focused on the relations an individual has with others.

THE HUMANISTIC APPROACH: APPRECIATING OUR POTENTIAL

- The humanistic approach maintains that what is most important about people is how they achieve their own selfhood and actualize their potential. This approach emphasizes *phenomenology*, or each person's own unique perspective based on that person's *construal*, or interpretation of the world around him.

- This perspective emphasizes positive human motives, such as self-actualization, rather than what it calls deficiency needs.

According to Carl Rogers' *self theory*, children only achieve a solid sense of personal self-worth if they have experienced a sense of unconditional positive regard.

- *Self-schemas* play a powerful role in determining a person's *self-esteem*. The content of self-schema vary by culture.

- Many themes stressed by humanistic psychologists underlie a more recent movement called *positive psychology*, which has led to a number of empirical investigations regarding positive subjective experiences, positive individual traits, and positive social institutions.

THE SOCIAL-COGNITIVE APPROACH: THE POWER OF BELIEFS

- Social-cognitive theorists focus on the various cognitive characteristics along which personalities may differ. Albert Bandura emphasizes the role of experience, through which individuals develop *outcome expectations* that govern their actions; individuals also develop a sense of *self-efficacy*. Walter Mischel has emphasized the way people interpret the world around them, and also their competencies and self-regulatory plans.

- Social-cognitive theorists emphasize the notion of control—a person's ability to do what he wants to do.

- They also emphasize *attributional style*, the way a person typically explains the things that happen in his or her life.

- A third crucial construct is self-control, which refers to an individual's ability to refrain from doing what he wants to do in order to get something he wants even more. The importance of self-control is reflected in evidence that 4-year-olds who are able to tolerate delay of gratification show more social and academic competence in adolescence.

 ONLINE STUDY TOOLS

Go to StudySpace, **wwnorton.com/studyspace**, to access additional review and enrichment materials, including the following resources for each chapter:

Organize
- Study Plan
- Chapter Outline
- Quiz+ Assessment

Learn
- Ebook
- Chapter Review
- Vocabulary Flashcards
- Drag-and-Drop Labeling Exercises
- Audio Podcast Chapter Overview

Connect
- Critical Thinking Activity
- Studying the Mind Video Podcasts
- Video Exercises
- Animations
- **ZAPS** Psychology Labs

16

Psychopathology

British singer/songwriter Amy Winehouse shot to the top of the charts in 2006 with such international hits as "Rehab," "Love Is a Losing Game," and "You Know I'm No Good." Awards quickly followed, including a record number of Grammys and several big prizes in Great Britain. Meanwhile, Winehouse's beehive hairdo, dramatic eye makeup, vintage dresses, and elaborate tattoos caught the imagination of the public and fashion designers alike.

But as her career took off, Winehouse's life spun out of control. Her hospitalizations for overdoses of heroin, ecstasy, cocaine, and alcohol; arrests for possessing drugs and assaulting fans; no-shows at concerts; and bizarre public behavior filled the tabloids. Her increasingly skimpy clothes revealed dramatic weight loss and self-inflicted wounds.

The media has focused on Winehouse's drug and alcohol problems, but is substance abuse her only woe? She has talked about struggling with depression, as well as eating disorders and self-harm. Some observers suggest that she may have bipolar disorder, an illness that causes people to cycle between deep depressions and extreme manias, often with intermittent stretches of relative calm. Many creative people throughout history—from composer Ludwig van Beethoven, to artist Vincent van Gogh, to writer Virginia Woolf, to scientist Isaac Newton, to politician Winston Churchill—have shown symptoms of bipolar disorder, and Winehouse's eccentric flair and haunting lyrics may bear the marks of this condition. Her substance abuse may be another sign, as nearly 60% of people with this illness abuse alcohol or drugs.

Winehouse's behaviors are also consistent with borderline personality disorder, a diagnosis that shares many symptoms with bipolar disorder, including mood swings and impulsivity. Unique to borderline personality disorder, however, is a profound fear of abandonment, which Winehouse has expressed in songs such as "Rehab." Cutting, which Winehouse admits to, is also a symptom of borderline personality disorder.

As we scan the list of possible explanations for Amy Winehouse's behavior—a list that could also include attention-deficit/hyperactivity disorder (ADHD), anorexia nervosa, an eccentric personality, or some combination of all these—you may wonder why it matters which disorders she (or anyone else) may have. One reason is that the correct diagnosis of mental illness can lead to correct treatment, while an incorrect diagnosis can exacerbate mental problems. The antidepressants that ease depression, for example, can fuel a manic phase in a person with bipolar disorder. Diagnosis also gives us clues about the origins of mental disorders. As you will learn in this chapter, most mental disorders arise from a complex interplay of nature and nurture, biologies and environments, diatheses (vulnerabilities) and stressors. Understanding these many interacting factors can help us not only to treat mental illnesses more effectively but also to try to prevent them.

But there is one other reason to care about Amy Winehouse's struggles. In her we sense the familiar: most of us know someone with psychiatric problems and perhaps have a few of our own. Almost half of Americans will have at least one mental disorder during their lifetimes. The information about psychopathology that you are about to encounter may hit close to home and may, we hope, instill a deep compassion for people living with mental disorders.

CONCEPTIONS OF MENTAL DISORDERS

We have seen over the past two chapters that people differ from one another in many ways, both in their desirable qualities, like being intelligent or helpful, and in their undesirable ones, like being selfish or aggressive. Even so, the attributes we have considered all fall within the range that most people consider acceptable or normal. In this chapter, we consider differences that are outside the normal range of variation—differences that carry us into the realm of mental disorders such as depression, anxiety, and schizophrenia. These are conditions that cause considerable suffering and profoundly disrupt people's lives—both the lives of the people afflicted with the disorders and, often, the lives of others around them.

The study of mental disorders is the province of **psychopathology**, or, as it is sometimes called, abnormal psychology. Like many corners of psychology, this domain has been studied scientifically only in the last century. Concerns about mental illness, however, have a much longer history. One of the earliest-known medical documents, the Ebers papyrus (written about 1550 C.E.), refers to the disorder we now know as depression (Okasha & Okasha, 2000). Other ancient cases include King Saul of Judaea, who alternated between bouts of homicidal frenzy and suicidal depression, and the Babylonian king Nebuchadnezzar, who walked on all fours in the belief that he was a wolf (Figure 16.1). Across the millennia, though, people have had very different conceptions of what causes these disorders.

16.1 An early example of mental disorder King Nebuchadnezzar as depicted by William Blake (1795).

Early Conceptions of Mental Disorders

The earliest theories held that a person afflicted by a mental disorder was possessed by evil spirits. As we will see in Chapter 17, people tried various extreme remedies to deal with this problem, such as flogging and starving, with the aim of driving the evil spirits away.

In recent centuries, a more sophisticated conception of mental disorders began to develop—namely, that they are a type of disease, to be understood in the same way as other illnesses. Proponents of this **somatogenic hypothesis** (from the Greek *soma*, meaning "body") argued that mental disorders, like other forms of illness, could be traced to an injury or infection. This position gained considerable credibility in the late nineteenth century, thanks to discoveries about *general paresis*.

General paresis is a disorder characterized by a broad decline in physical and psychological functions, culminating in marked personality aberrations that may include grandiose delusions ("I am the king of England") or profound hypochondriacal depressions ("My heart has stopped beating"). Without treatment, the deterioration progresses to the point of paralysis, and death occurs within a few years. The breakthrough in understanding paresis came in 1897, when the Viennese physician Richard von Krafft-Ebing (1840–1902) discovered that it was actually a consequence of infection with syphilis. This discovery paved the way for the development of antibiotics that could cure the infection, and, if the drugs were given early enough, the symptoms of paresis could be avoided altogether.

It seems, then, that general paresis can be understood and treated like any other medical problem. Should other forms of mental disorder be understood in the same fashion—as the result of an infection or perhaps an injury? This view gained many supporters in the late 1800s, including Emil Kraepelin (Figure 16.2), whose textbook, *Lehrbuch der Psychiatrie*, emphasized the importance of brain pathology in producing mental disorders.

However, a somatogenic approach cannot explain all mental disorders. For example, more than a hundred years ago, scholars realized that this approach was not appropriate for the disorder then known as hysteria, which we encountered in our discussion of psychoanalysis (see Chapter 15). Patients with hysteria typically showed odd symptoms that seemed to be neurological, but with other indications that made it plain there was no neurological damage. Some patients reported that their limbs were paralyzed, but under hypnosis they could move their arms and legs perfectly well, indicating that the nerves and muscles were fully functional. Their symptoms, therefore, were not the result of a bodily injury; instead, they had to be understood in terms of a **psychogenic hypothesis**, which holds that the symptoms arise via psychological processes.

Across much of the late 19th and early 20th centuries, the most prominent version of this hypothesis was Sigmund Freud's, which described mental illness as resulting from inner conflicts and defensive maneuvers aimed at dealing with those conflicts. Early in the 20th century, other theorists offered alternative conceptions of mental illness—but, like Freud, argued that the illness arose from psychological processes, and not from bodily injury. For example, the early behaviorists offered **learning models** of mental illness, building on the mechanisms we discussed in Chapter 7. In this view, many mental disorders result from maladaptive learning and are best corrected with remedial learning.

Modern Conceptions of Mental Disorders

Historically, the somatogenic and psychogenic approaches were offered as sharply distinct proposals, and scholars debated the merits of one over the other. We now know

psychopathology The study of mental disorders, or a term for the mental disorder itself.

somatogenic hypothesis The hypothesis that mental disorders result from organic (bodily) causes.

psychogenic hypothesis The hypothesis that mental disorders result from psychological causes.

learning model The hypothesis that mental disorders result from some form of faulty learning.

16.2 Emil Kraepelin (1856–1926) The major figure in psychiatric classification, Kraepelin distinguished two groups of severe mental disorders, schizophrenia and manic-depressive psychosis (now called bipolar disorder).

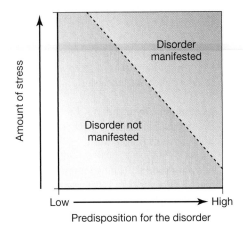

16.3 Diathesis-stress model According to this model, a disorder results when a person has both a predisposition for a disorder and a high level of stress.

diathesis-stress model A conception of psychopathology that distinguishes factors that create a risk of illness (the diathesis) from the factors that turn the risk into a problem (the stress).

multicausal model A conception of how mental disorders arise that emphasizes the roles played by many different factors.

that both approaches have considerable validity. Biomedical factors play a critical role in producing some forms of psychopathology; childhood experiences and maladaptive learning contribute as well. As a consequence, each of these approaches by itself is too narrow, and it would be a mistake to point to either somatogenic or psychogenic factors as "the sole cause" of any disorder. To understand why, let's look more closely at the idea of *cause* in this domain.

DIATHESIS-STRESS MODELS

Imagine someone who goes through a difficult experience—perhaps the breakup of a long-term relationship—and subsequently becomes depressed. We might be tempted to say that the breakup caused the depression, but the breakup was not the only force in play here. Many people experience breakups without becoming depressed; this tells us that a breakup will cause depression only if other factors are present.

What are those other factors? Part of the answer lies in a person's biology, because, as we will see, some people have a genetic tendency toward depression. This tendency remains unexpressed (and so the person suffers no depression) until the person experiences a particularly stressful event. Then, when that stressful event takes place, the combination of the event plus the biological tendency will likely lead to depression.

This example suggests that we need a two-part theory of depression, and the same is true for virtually every other form of psychopathology as well. This two-part conception is referred to as a **diathesis-stress model** (Bleuler, 1963; Meehl, 1962; Rosenthal, 1963), with one set of factors (the *diathesis*) creating a predisposition for the disorder, and a different set of factors (the *stress*) providing the trigger that turns the potential into the actual disorder (Figures 16.3). Notice that, by this model, neither the diathesis nor the stress by itself causes the disorder; instead, the disorder emerges only if both are present.

MULTICAUSAL MODELS

In many cases, the diathesis takes the form of a genetic tendency—one that makes a person vulnerable to depression if, during his lifetime, he encounters a significant source of stress. It's the combination of the vulnerability plus the stress that leads to the illness. In other cases, the diathesis can take a very different form. For example, a different factor may be how a person *thinks about* the events he experiences—in particular, whether he tends to see himself as somehow responsible for stressful, negative events (see Chapter 15). But, again, this style of thinking, by itself, does not cause depression. Instead, the style of thinking is only a diathesis: It creates a *risk* or a vulnerability to depression, and if someone has this problematic thinking style but leads a sheltered life—protected from the many losses and difficulties faced by others—then he may never develop depression.

Examples like these show the power of the diathesis-stress model, but they also reveal that the model may be too simple. Often there are *multiple* diatheses for a particular individual and a particular mental illness—including genetic factors, styles of thinking, and more. Likewise, multiple factors often create the stress, including combinations of harsh circumstances (for example, relationship difficulties or ongoing health concerns) and specific events (being the victim of a crime, perhaps, or witnessing a devastating accident).

For all these reasons, many investigators now adopt a **multicausal model** of depression, which acknowledges that many different factors contribute to the disorder's emergence. Other mental disorders also require a multicausal model. Indeed, to emphasize the diversity of factors contributing to each disorder, most investigators now urge that we take a **biopsychosocial perspective**, which considers biological factors (like genetics), psychological factors (like a style of thinking), and social factors (like the absence of social support; Figure 16.4).

biopsychosocial perspective A perspective on psychopathology that emphasizes the biological, psychological, and social factors that contribute to mental illness.

DEFINING, ASSESSING, AND DIAGNOSING MENTAL DISORDERS

What exactly are mental disorders? And how can a clinician learn whether someone has one?

Defining Mental Disorders

Phrases such as "mental disorder" and "abnormal psychology" suggest that when defining mental disorders, we should start with some conception of normalcy and then define disorders as variations that are not normal. Thus, taking depression as an example, we might acknowledge that everyone is occasionally sad, but we might worry about (and try to treat) someone whose sadness is deeper and lasts longer than normal sadness.

However, this perspective invites difficulties, because even something normal can be problematic. For example, almost everyone gets cavities, which makes them normal, but this does not change the fact that cavities are a problem. Likewise, many things are "abnormal" without necessarily being symptoms of disorders. Pink is not a normal hair color, but this does not mean that someone who dyes his hair pink is sick. It seems clear, therefore, that we cannot equate being "abnormal" with being "ill."

How, then, should we define mental disorders? The most commonly accepted definition is the one provided by the American Psychiatric Association (2000) in the *Diagnostic and Statistical Manual of Mental Disorders* (now in the text revision of its fourth edition, and hence known as the *DSM-IV-TR*; for the sake of simplicity, we'll refer to this work as *DSM* from this point forward). The *DSM* states that each of the mental disorders is a

16.4 Social support

Diagnostic and Statistical Manual for Mental Disorders (DSM) The manual that provides specific guidance on how to diagnose each of the nearly 200 psychological disorders; currently in its fourth edition, text revision (DSM-IV-TR).

> Behavioral or psychological syndrome or pattern that occurs in a person and that is associated with present distress (e.g., a painful symptom) or disability (i.e., impairment in one or more important areas of functioning) or with a significantly increased risk of suffering death, pain, disability, or an important loss of freedom. In addition, this syndrome or pattern must not be merely an expectable and culturally sanctioned response to a particular event, for example, the death of a loved one. Whatever its original cause, it must currently be considered a manifestation of a behavioral, psychological, or biological dysfunction in the individual. (p. xxxi)

Notice that this is a functional definition—it focuses on distress and disability—rather than one that specifies the causes or origins of the problem. Notice too the requirement that the behaviors in question be not "expectable and culturally sanctioned." This aspect of the definition is important, because what is expectable varies across cultures and over time, and so it's valuable to remind ourselves that we need to take social context into account when assessing an individual's thoughts, feelings, and behaviors.

TABLE 16.1	Lifetime Prevalence of Selected Categories of Psychiatric Disorders	
Disorder type	**Projected lifetime risk (%)**	
Anxiety disorders	29	
Mood disorders	21	
Impulse-control disorders	25	
Substance use disorders	16.3	
Two or more disorders	28	
Any disorder	46	

Source: Data from Kessler et al. 2005.

Using this definition, we can tackle a crucial question: Just how common is mental illness? Are we considering problems that are, in fact, relatively rare? Or is mental illness common? Table 16.1 shows the prevalence of different psychiatric disorders in the United States. The term *prevalence* refers to how widespread a disorder is, and researchers typically consider two types of prevalence. **Point prevalence** refers to how many people in a given population have a given disorder at a particular point in time. **Lifetime prevalence** refers to how many people in a certain population will have the disorder at any point in their lives. Reviewing this table, we can see that nearly half of the U.S. population (46%) will experience at least one mental disorder during their lifetimes, and more than a quarter (28%) will experience two or more disorders. Most common are anxiety disorders (lifetime prevalence rate of 29%) and impulse-control disorders (lifetime prevalence rate of 25%). These statistics make it clear that large numbers of people suffer mental disorders directly, and of course an even larger number of people (the friends, family members, co-workers, and neighbors of the mentally ill) suffer indirectly. We are, in short, talking about a problem that is severe and widespread.

Assessing Mental Disorders

In addition to this general definition of mental disorder, the *DSM* gives definitions of the specific mental disorders, definitions that we can use to decide which disorder—if any—a person has. These "definitions" consist of lists of specific criteria, a certain number of which must be met for a given disorder to be diagnosed. The diagnosis is important because it is the first step both in understanding why a person is suffering and (crucially!) in deciding how to help that person.

Mental health professionals use the term **assessment** to refer to the set of procedures for gathering information about an individual, and an assessment may or may not lead to a diagnosis—a claim that an individual has a specific mental disorder. Clinical assessment often includes clinical interviews, self-report measures, and projective tests. It may also include laboratory tests such as neuroimaging (see Chapter 1) or blood analyses that can inform the practitioner about the patient's physical well-being—for example, whether the patient has suffered a stroke or taken a mood-altering drug.

CLINICAL INTERVIEWS

Assessments usually begin with a clinical interview, in which the clinician asks the patient to describe her problems and concerns (Figure 16.5). Some aspects of the interview will be open-ended and flexible, as the clinician explores the patient's current state and history. In addition, the clinician may rely on a **semistructured interview**, in which specific questions are asked in a specific sequence, with attention to certain types of content. For example, the clinician might use the Structured Clinical Interview for DSM Disorders (SCID), which is designed to ask questions directly pertinent to certain diagnostic categories.

Throughout, the clinician will pay careful attention to the patient's set of complaints, or **symptoms**. Patients who say, "I hear voices," "I feel nervous all the time,"

point prevalence The percentage of people in a given population who have a given disorder at any particular point in time.

lifetime prevalence The percentage of people in a certain population who will have a given disorder at any point in their lives.

assessment The set of procedures for gathering information about an individual's psychological state, sometimes leading to a diagnosis.

semistructured interview An interview in which questions are posed in a standardized yet flexible way.

symptoms In psychopathology, what the patient reports about his physical or mental condition.

and "I feel hopeless" are reporting symptoms. The clinician also looks for any objective **signs** that might accompany these symptoms. If the same patients, respectively, turn toward a stapler as though it were speaking, shake visibly, and look teary-eyed, these would be signs that parallel the patients' symptoms. Sometimes, though, symptoms do not correspond to signs, and such discrepancies are also important. For example, a patient might state, "My head hurts so bad it's like there's a buzz saw running through my brain," even thought the patient seems to be calm and unconcerned, and this discrepancy, too, is informative.

The full pattern of the patient's symptoms and signs, taken together with their onset and course, will usually allow the clinician to form an opinion as to the specific disorder(s). This diagnosis is not set in stone, but serves as the practitioner's best judgment about the patient's current state. The diagnosis may well be revised as the clinician gains new information, including information about how the patient responds to a particular form of treatment.

SELF-REPORT MEASURES

In some clinical assessments, a clinician will also seek information about a patient by administering self-report measures. Some of these measures are relatively brief and target a certain set of symptoms. These include measures such as the Beck Depression Inventory (Beck, Steer, & Brown, 1996); sample items from this inventory are shown in Figure 16.6. Other self-report measures are much broader (and longer), such as the Minnesota Multiphasic Personality Inventory, or MMPI. This test was developed in 1940 and was redesigned in 1989; the current version, the MMPI-2, includes an imposing 567 items (Butcher, Dahlstrom, Graham, Tellegen, & Kaemmer, 2001; Butcher et al., 1992).

To construct the MMPI, its authors began with a large pool of test questions and administered them to patients known to have a variety of different mental disorders, as well as to a group of nonpatients. Next, they compared the patients' responses to those of the nonpatients. If all groups tended to respond to a particular question in the same way, that question was deemed uninformative and was removed from the test. A question was kept on the test only if one of the patient groups tended to answer it differently from how the nonpatient group answered it. The result was a test specifically

signs In psychopathology, what the clinician observes about a patient's physical or mental condition.

16.5 The clinical interview The clinical interview involves an open-ended and flexible exploration of a patient's current concerns. During the interview, the clinician observes the patient's grooming, mannerisms, style and content of speech, and overall mood, and may ask the patient to engage in brief tasks to assess attention, memory, and judgment.

1. Sadness

    0   I do not feel sad.
    1   I feel sad much of the time.
    2   I am sad all the time.
    3   I am so sad or unhappy that I can't
        stand it.

4. Loss of Pleasure

    0   I get as much pleasure as I ever did from
        the things I enjoy.
    1   I don't enjoy things as much as I used to.
    2   I get very little pleasure from the things I
        used to enjoy.
    3   I can't get any pleasure from the things I
        used to enjoy.

16.6 Sample items from the Beck Depression Inventory This inventory consists of 21 items such as these. For each item the patient picks one statement in each group that best describes the way he or she has been feeling during the past two weeks, including today.

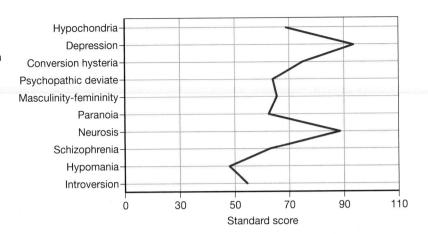

16.7 MMPI profile The profile is of an adult male seeking help in a community mental health center. This profile strongly suggests considerable depression and anxiety.

designed to differentiate among patients with different mental disorders. Figure 16.7 shows an MMPI score profile.

PROJECTIVE TESTS

Some clinicians supplement clinical interviews with what is called a projective test. Advocates of projective tests argue that when the patient is asked to respond to stimuli that are essentially unstructured or ambiguous, he cannot help but impose a structure of his own, and, in the process of describing (or relying on) this structure, he gives valuable information about unconscious wishes and conflicts that could not be revealed by direct testing.

One such test has the participant make up a story to describe what is going on in a picture (the Thematic Apperception Test, or TAT; C. D. Morgan & Murray, 1935). Responses to these pictures are seen as revealing implicit or otherwise hidden motives (Figure 16.8; McAdams, 1980; for variants on this procedure, see McClelland, Koestner, & Weinberger, 1989; Winter, 1999). Another projective test, the Rorschach Inkblot Test, has the patient describe what he sees in an inkblot (Figure 16.9; Rorschach, 1921).

16.8 Projective tests An examiner administers the Thematic Apperception Test. Responses to these ambiguous pictures are thought to provide information about the deeper layers of an individual's personality.

Projective tests such as these are extremely popular—with more than 8 in 10 clinicians reporting that they use them at least occasionally (Watkins, Campbell, Nieberding, & Hallmark, 1995). However, there is general agreement in the research community that these tests' popularity outstrips their demonstrated validity. One review of Rorschach findings reported only small correlations with mental health–related criteria (Garb, Florio, & Grove, 1998), and there is ongoing debate about the role projective tests should play in diagnosis (Garb, Wood, Nezworski, Grove, & Stejskal, 2001; Lilienfeld, Wood, & Garb, 2000; Rosenthal, Hiller, Bornstein, Berry, & Brunell-Neuleib, 2001; Westen & Weinberger, 2005).

Making Diagnoses Using the *DSM*

We have now described the information a clinician would gather in moving toward a diagnosis. But what form will the diagnosis take? In the last 50 years, the answer has typically come from either of two classification schemes: the *International Classification of Diseases* (*ICD*-10), published by the World Health Organization and used mainly in Europe, and the *DSM*, published by the American Psychiatric Association and used as the standard guide in the United States. We will focus here on the *DSM*, because research in psychopathology (research that examines the causes and treatments of mental disorders) is almost always guided by the definitions provided by the *DSM*.

The first edition of the *Diagnostic and Statistical Manual of Mental Disorders* (*DSM-I*) was published in 1952; since then, the manual has been reviewed and revised several times. In particular, the *DSM-III*, published in 1980, was heavily revamped to emphasize the specific signs and symptoms required for each diagnosis, holding theory to the side as much as possible. Subsequent revisions (including the most recent, *DSM-IV-TR*, published in 2000) have continued this trend, as will the next edition (*DSM-V*), which is due out in 2012. In addition, some terms ("neurosis") have been dropped as not meaningful, and some diagnostic labels ("hysteria") have been largely abandoned. Moreover, some disorders have been eliminated altogether—with the most prominent example being homosexuality. Until *DSM-III*, homosexuality was counted as a "disorder" to be "diagnosed." For the last 30 years, though, the successive editions of *DSM* have abandoned this position as indefensible, and modern psychologists no longer count homosexuality as a "disorder" in any sense.

Across all of its editions, the *DSM* has tackled a crucial clinical question—namely, how severe does a set of symptoms have to be before it merits a diagnosis? After all, every one of us sometimes feels sad; how long must the sadness last and what other symptoms must be present for this to count as depression? Every one of us sometimes feels fearful; under what circumstances should feelings of fear be counted as a phobia? As we will see in the following sections, the *DSM-IV-TR* addresses these issues by setting out specific criteria for each disorder—often in terms of a particular duration for the symptoms, or a certain frequency.

Using the *DSM*, a clinician evaluates an individual with reference to five *axes*, or dimensions of functioning. The first two axes are designed to describe an individual's current psychological condition: Axis I describes clinical syndromes such as depression, eating disorders, and drug dependence. Axis II describes two broad sets of difficulties: mental retardation and personality disorders (such as antisocial personality disorder). Axis III is concerned with general medical conditions that may contribute to a person's psychological functioning (such as constant pain from a continuing medical problem). Axis IV assesses social or environmental problems (including family or legal difficulties), and Axis V provides a global assessment of functioning—that is, how well a person is coping with her overall situation.

The current version of the *DSM* also includes, as an appendix, disorders that seem to appear in only some cultures. These culture-specific disorders include *dhat*, a term used in India to refer to severe anxiety about the discharge of semen; *shenjing shauiro*, a diagnosis in China characterized by fatigue, dizziness, and headaches; and *ghost sickness*, a powerful preoccupation with death found among some Native American tribes. Despite this nod toward cultural context, even some of the disorders listed in the main section of the *DSM* may be culture-bound—for example, bulimia nervosa, an eating disorder that we will consider later in this chapter, seems to appear only in Western cultures or in cultures that have been heavily exposed to the West (Smith, Spillane, & Annus, 2006). It may well be that all of the *DSM*'s diagnostic categories are best understood in terms of their cultural setting—a point that's certainly in line with the *DSM*'s broad definition of what a "mental disorder" actually is.

Our discussion in this chapter will focus largely on the Axis I classifications, although we will also say a little about Axis II. We will emphasize just a handful of the diagnostic categories. Nonetheless, the mental disorders we will discuss are persistent and prominent sources of human suffering. Studying how psychologists think about and try to explain them will help us to understand how they approach the other 200 or so disorders included in the *DSM*.

16.9 An inkblot of the type used in the Rorschach test The Rorschach Inkblot Test consists of 10 cards which are presented one at a time, with each card showing a symmetrical inkblot, some colored and some black and white. For each card, the examinee is asked what he sees. Responses are scored according to various categories, such as portion of the blot used in the response (e.g., the whole blot, a large detail, a small detail), attributes of the stimulus that are the basis of the response (e.g., form, shading, color), and content of the response (e.g., human figures, parts of human figures, animals or parts of animals, inanimate objects, blood).

The Costs and Benefits of Labeling

Before turning to specific mental disorders, we need to comment briefly on one important aspect of diagnoses, namely, the costs and benefits of *labeling* of mental disorders.

The diagnostic labels provided by the *DSM* have unquestionably been enormously useful. As one great benefit, the labels have improved the *treatment* of mental illness—by making sure that patients get the treatment (the therapy or medication) that is appropriate to their condition. A second benefit is providing a uniform framework for describing the difficulties a patient is having, so that different health-care providers, all working with the same patient, can coordinate their treatment efforts.

Diagnostic labels are also crucial in the search for the causes of mental disorders. Without accurate diagnoses, we'd have no way to know whether, for example, the patients with schizophrenia studied in one hospital actually had the same illness as the patients who received the same diagnosis in another hospital. With uncertainty on this fundamental point, we wouldn't know whether we could legitimately compare the results of different studies, whether we could pool results across studies, and so on. The development of an increasingly reliable and valid set of diagnostic categories has increased the possibility of integrating very different approaches to psychopathology—including bringing together neuroscientific findings with clinical and first-person accounts of mental disorders (Hyman, 2007).

At the same time, diagnostic labels can be problematic. It is easy to fall into the trap of thinking that once we have labeled a disorder, we have explained a person's problems. But diagnostic labels are just a first step on the path toward explanation and treatment.

In addition, mental disorders are, sadly, marked with considerable stigma, and both people with mental disorders and their family members are often viewed negatively (Hinshaw, 2007). Labels can therefore have an unfortunate effect on how we perceive someone and, indeed, on how people perceive themselves: "I'm depressed, and so there is no point in seeking treatment" or ". . . and so nothing else in my life matters" (Corrigan, 2005). Unfortunately, these self-defeating attitudes are in many cases reinforced by media portrayals of the mentally ill as losers, or hopeless, or violent criminals (Diefenbach, 1997).

It is important to combat these destructive and ill-conceived stereotypes—and to humanize the face of mental illness. Specifically, psychologists prefer not to speak of someone as "a depressive" or "a schizophrenic," as though the person had no identity beyond the disease. Instead, we speak of a patient as "someone suffering from depression" or "a person with schizophrenia," never losing track of the fact that people—no matter what their diagnosis—have an identity, value, and dignity.

ANXIETY DISORDERS

anxiety disorders A group of disorders distinguished by feelings of intense distress and worry, and in many cases, disruptive and unsuccessful attempts to deal with these feelings.

The main symptom of the **anxiety disorders** is, as the name implies, a feeling of intense anxiety, and in many cases people with an anxiety disorder will take steps (often disruptive to their lives, and usually unsuccessful) to deal with the anxiety. Anxiety disorders are the most common mental disorders; we mentioned earlier that the lifetime prevalence for these disorders is 29% (Kessler et al., 2005). These disorders are found in both sexes, although more commonly in women than in men (Breslau, Chilcoat, Kessler, & Davis, 1999; Graaf, Bijl, Smit, Vollebergh, & Spijker, 2002). There are many types of anxiety disorders, and in the following sections, we discuss each of the major types in turn before considering the roots of these disorders.

Phobias

A **phobia** is characterized by intense and irrational fear coupled with great efforts to avoid the feared object or situation (Figure 16.10). The word *irrational* is important here. Someone living in the middle of a swamp and constantly worried about snakes is not manifesting a phobia; her fear is perfectly reasonable. But someone living in a San Francisco apartment and incapacitated by the same fear probably does have a phobia. And it does not help that the person with the phobia knows that the fear is groundless; for someone with a phobia, this knowledge does not in any way diminish the fear.

SPECIFIC PHOBIAS

There are several types of phobias, including **specific phobias**, that are directed at a particular object, like snakes or blood (Figure 16.11). During the nineteenth century, many of these irrational fears were cataloged and assigned exotic-sounding Greek or Latin names. Examples are fear of high places (acrophobia), enclosed places (claustrophobia), crowds (ochlophobia), germs (mysophobia), cats (ailurophobia), and even the number 13 (triskaidekaphobia)—the list is long. However, these phobias are not equally common; some are quite frequent (fear of heights, fear of snakes); others are extremely rare (fear of specific numbers). Overall, though, the lifetime prevalence for any kind of specific phobia is estimated at 13% (Kessler et al., 2005), and women are about twice as likely as men to have specific phobias (Bourdon et al., 1988).

Some of these phobias seem relatively harmless, but others can be life changing, because the person suffering from a phobia almost always develops strategies (sometimes elaborate ones) for avoiding the phobic object. Thus, people with claustrophobia may climb many flights of stairs rather than step into an elevator. Likewise, an executive with a fear of heights may choose to quit his job rather than accept a promotion that gives him an office with a glorious view from a 20th-story window. These phobias will often expand in scope, so that a fear of spiders, say, can grow to become a fear of insects—and a fear of being outdoors where the spiders or insects might lurk, or a fear of anything brushing across the person's face, because it might be a spiderweb.

How do these fears feel to the person experiencing the phobia? One person describes the fear of flying this way:

> I used to start dreading a plane trip a month before I was due to leave. It was an awful feeling when that airplane door closed and I felt trapped. My heart would pound, and I would sweat bullets. When the airplane would start to ascend, it just reinforced the feeling that I couldn't get out. When I think about flying, I picture myself losing control, freaking out, and climbing the walls, but of course I never did that. I'm not afraid of crashing or hitting turbulence. It's just that feeling of being trapped.... These days I only go places where I can drive or take a train. My friends always point out that I couldn't get off a train traveling at high speeds either, so why don't trains bother me? I just tell them it isn't a rational fear. (NIMH, 2009, p. 11)

Similar accounts can be offered for most of the other specific phobias, but, even so, one of the phobias is unique: the blood-injection-injury phobia. This phobia often is experienced as a feeling of *disgust* rather than *fear*, and is also distinctive in how people

16.10 Phobias Fear of flying is one of the most widespread phobias.

phobia An anxiety disorder characterized by an intense and, at least on the surface, irrational fear.

specific phobias Any of the disorders characterized by extreme and irrational fear of a particular object or situation.

16.11 Specific phobias Phobias relating to spiders and snakes are very common, even though other objects in our world pose a much greater threat. Falls in bathtubs, for example, are more frequent than snakebites, but this fact seems not to give rise to bathtub phobias.

react to the feared object. For most phobias, an encounter with the phobic stimulus produces panic responses: quick pulse, elevated blood pressure, sweating, and tremor. These are all emergency reactions produced by the sympathetic branch of the autonomic nervous system (Lang, Davis, & Öhman, 2000; see Chapter 3). For the blood-injection-injury phobia, the reaction is essentially the opposite. The pulse slows, the blood pressure drops, the muscles go slack, and the person can fall to the ground in a faint. In addition, the treatment for blood-injection-injury phobia runs exactly opposite of that for other phobias. For most phobias, the treatment involves teaching the phobic person to relax. For the blood-injection-injury phobia, the sufferer must keep up her blood pressure, and so must learn, on cue, to become tense (Hellstrom, Fellenius, & Ost, 1996).

SOCIAL PHOBIA

Unlike the object-specific fears seen in specific phobias, individuals with social phobia (also referred to as social anxiety disorder) are intensely afraid of being watched and judged by others (Figure 16.12). Typically, these concerns center around negative evaluations ("He'll think I'm an idiot"), but there is increasing evidence that even positive evaluations can be threatening (Weeks, Heimberg, Rodebaugh, & Norton, 2008). The lifetime prevalence for social phobia is 13% (Kessler et al., 2005), and women and men are equally affected by this disorder.

Social phobia typically emerges in childhood or adolescence (Robins & Regier, 1991) and may be accompanied by other anxiety disorders or depression (Regier et al., 1998). Sometimes a person's fears are limited to one type of situation (e.g., speaking in front of others, writing in front of others, or eating in front of others). For others, many different situations trigger the anxiety; in this case, social phobia is described as being "generalized."

People with social phobia will desperately try to avoid situations in which they must expose themselves to public scrutiny. They will avoid public speaking or performing because they think others will think they are stupid, they will not eat in restaurants for fear that they will choke on their food, and they will not go to parties or meetings because they may stutter and stammer when trying to talk. As one person with social anxiety disorder put it, "In school I was always afraid of being called on, even when I knew the answers. When I got a job, I hated to meet with my boss. I couldn't eat lunch with my co-workers. I worried about being stared at or judged, and worried that I would make a fool of myself. My heart would pound, and I would start to sweat when I thought about meetings. The feelings got worse as the time of the event got closer. Sometimes I couldn't sleep or eat for days before a staff meeting" (NIMH, 2007a, p. 7). When forced into situations of this sort, they may try to "fortify" themselves with alcohol or drugs, making substance abuse or dependence a real risk (Pollack, 2001).

16.12 Social phobia Interacting with others can make people with social phobia intensely anxious.

panic disorder An anxiety disorder characterized by repeated or disabling panic attacks.

panic attack A sudden episode of terrifying bodily symptoms such as labored breathing, choking, dizziness, tingling hands and feet, sweating, trembling, heart palpitations, and chest pain.

Panic Disorder and Agoraphobia

A different type of anxiety disorder is **panic disorder**, characterized by the occurrence of unexpected **panic attacks**—sudden episodes of terrifying bodily symptoms, such as labored breathing, choking, dizziness, tingling hands and feet, sweating, trembling, heart palpitations, and chest pain. In many cases, the person becomes convinced that she is having a heart attack and is near death. It is no surprise that panic attacks usually include feelings of intense terror and a sense of impending doom (Figure 16.13).

Panic attacks occur in almost all anxiety disorders, so that, for example, a snake-phobia sufferer may have one at the sight of a snake. But the hallmark of panic disorder is that the panic attacks seem to come out of the blue. As a result, the patient often has an intense experience of unreality and fears that he is losing control or going insane. Panic disorder is diagnosed when there are recurrent unexpected attacks and when either behavioral or psychological troubles follow the attacks. Based on those criteria, panic disorder is found in about 5% of women and 2% of men (see, for example, Barlow, 2002).

One person with panic attacks describes her first attack this way:

> When I had my first panic attack I literally thought I was going crazy. I was 17 years old and I was the passenger in a car when suddenly I felt my heart racing. I was terrified but I did not really know why. I just had very strong feelings of dread and fear. Almost immediately I felt I needed to escape.... The problem was that ... we were on a winding narrow road leading up [a] mountain. It was very dark and lightly raining.
>
> I began to feel as though I could not breathe. I was trying my best to hide my anguish from my boyfriend. I did not want him to think I was crazy.... Although my symptoms were basic textbook panic attack symptoms, at the time this was happening I did not know what panic attacks were.... I asked my boyfriend if we could stop the car for a minute but of course he wanted to know why and ... explained that there really was not anyplace to stop. I truly was trapped in the vehicle.
>
> There was no way that I could explain to him how I was feeling.... I remember having flashes of opening my car door and jumping out. I was glad it was dark because I was sure that my fear was obviously showing on my face. My hands were shaking and I felt dizzy. I was not thinking straight; I only knew that I needed to get away from the situation as quickly as possible. (Allen, 2009)

Panic attacks are frightening enough, but even the mere anticipation of the attacks can be awful. Indeed, people with panic disorder sometimes develop a profound fear of having an attack, especially in public places, where an attack might be embarrassing, or in circumstances such as driving, where the attack could be dangerous. As a result, people with panic disorder often develop a powerful tendency not to venture outside their designated "safe" places—their houses or even just their bedrooms. This is why panic disorder is often accompanied by **agoraphobia**, a fear of being in situations in which help might not be available or escape might be difficult or embarrassing. Agoraphobia can be quite paralyzing, and someone with this disorder might refuse to leave her home for days or weeks at a time (Robins & Regier, 1991).

Generalized Anxiety Disorder

Both phobias and panic attacks are a source of enormous suffering and can be horribly disruptive to someone's life. But both are limited in an important sense: In the absence of the phobic stimulus, someone with phobias feels all right. Between attacks, someone with panic disorder can function more or less normally. These limits are not in place, however, for someone who suffers from **generalized anxiety disorder (GAD)**. For this person, the anxiety is not related to anything in particular; instead, it is continuous, pervasive, and very difficult to control.

GAD is relatively common, with a lifetime prevalence of 6% (Kessler et al., 2005), and it is seen twice as frequently in women as in men. Patients with this disorder are visibly worried almost all the time. One form this may take is worry about family members: as one patient put it, "I worry all the time about whether my husband is safe so I telephone him half a dozen times a day to see if he's okay" (White, 1999, p. 72). Another form it may take is worry about work: as another patient put it, "I'm so nervous about making a mistake at work I take all my reports home to rewrite them the night before

16.13 Panic attacks *The Scream* (1893) by Edvard Munch vividly illustrates the overwhelming anxiety associated with panic attacks. Munch himself is thought to have suffered from bipolar disorder.

agoraphobia A fear of being in situations in which help might not be available or escape might be difficult or embarrassing.

generalized anxiety disorder (GAD) A disorder characterized by pervasive, free-floating anxiety.

I'm supposed to hand them in" (White, 1999, p. 72). In fact, people with GAD worry about anything and everything. As still another patient put it, "I was worried all the time about everything. It didn't matter that there were no signs of problems, I just got upset. I was having trouble falling asleep at night, and I couldn't keep my mind focused at work. I felt angry at my family all the time" (NIMH, 2007b, p. 7).

People with GAD feel inadequate, are oversensitive, cannot concentrate, and may suffer from insomnia. They have enormous difficulty making decisions and worry afterward about whether each decision was a mistake. This state of affairs is often accompanied by bodily symptoms: rapid heart rate, irregular breathing, excessive sweating, and chronic diarrhea (Rickels & Rynn, 2001).

Obsessive-Compulsive Disorder

In **obsessive-compulsive disorder** (**OCD**), the main symptoms are, as the name implies, **obsessions** (recurrent unwanted and disturbing thoughts) and **compulsions** (ritualistic behaviors that serve in some way to deal with the obsessions). OCD afflicts about 2% of the population sometime in their lives (Kessler et al., 2005; March, Leonard, & Swedo, 1995). It affects both sexes equally and is quite serious: If untreated, most cases worsen over time and are accompanied by recurrent bouts of depression (Barlow, 1988).

One striking feature of OCD is how early it often starts. One-third of adults with OCD developed their symptoms in childhood, often before age 10. As one person with OCD describes it:

> When I was six years old I started picking up things with my elbows because I thought I would get my hands dirty if I picked things up with my hands. By the time I was seven I was washing my hands 35 times a day.... When I swallowed saliva I had to crouch down and touch the ground. I didn't want to lose any saliva—for a bit I had to sweep the ground with my hand—and later I had to blink my eyes if I swallowed. I was frustrated because I couldn't stop the compulsions. Each time I swallowed I had to do something. For a while I had to touch my shoulders to my chin. I don't know why. I had no reason. I was afraid. It was just so unpleasant if I didn't. (Rapoport, 1989, pp. 43–44)

The obsessions come in many varieties, but common ones involve concerns about dirt and contamination (Figure 16.14), fears of harming someone, and an extraordinary need for balance and symmetry. A salesperson, for example, might worry constantly about infection and so refuse to shake hands with his customers; an otherwise loving parent may have recurrent thoughts of strangling her children; and a seemingly normal businessman may spend hours each night straightening the paintings hanging in his apartment.

Obsessive thoughts can produce considerable anxiety, and many compulsions may be understood as attempts to counteract this anxiety. An obsession with dirt may lead to compulsions like ritualistic cleaning or continual hand washing; in severe cases, someone with OCD will wash her hands so often to ward off germs that she will end up with open and bleeding sores on her skin. An obsession with forgetting things might lead to checking and rechecking—to make sure that the alarm clock is really turned on, or that the door is really locked. Here, too, the compulsion can become crippling: Someone with OCD may check and recheck the stove so many times, making certain it is really turned off, that he needs hours to leave the house for even the simplest errand. And, in most cases, the sufferers know that their behavior is irrational and that they are washing or checking far more than they need to. However, they are unable to stop their thoughts and urges, and so are all the more tormented by them.

obsessive-compulsive disorder (OCD) A disorder whose symptoms are *obsessions* and *compulsions*, which seem to serve as defenses against anxiety.

obsessions Recurrent unwanted or disturbing thoughts.

compulsions Repetitive or ritualistic acts that, in OCD, serve in some way to deal with the obsessions.

16.14 Symptoms of OCD One common obsession involves a concern with dirt and contamination. This is typically accompanied by a compulsion to wash one's hands.

The Stress Disorders

One final category of anxiety disorders includes the two stress disorders, both of which are triggered abruptly by an identifiable and horrific event (Figure 16.15). For women, the most common such event is rape or physical assault; for men, it is military combat. Other calamities can also trigger the stress disorders—being in a serious automobile accident, witnessing a homicide, or encountering the devastation following a natural disaster or terrorist attack (Andreasen & Black, 1996; Wolf & Mosnaim, 1990).

Regardless of what the traumatic event is, the psychological effects are usually the same. Immediately after the trauma, there is generally a period of numbness, during which the sufferer feels wholly estranged, socially unresponsive, and oddly unaffected by the event, a reaction technically known as *dissociation*. With this **acute stress disorder**, there are often recurrent nightmares and waking flashbacks of the traumatic event. These can be so intense and intrusive that the sufferer may momentarily believe that she is back in the situation, reliving the battle, or being attacked once again by the rapist. For some people, the reactions to such traumas are enduring, and if they persist for 1 month after the stressor, the diagnosis becomes **post-traumatic stress disorder (PTSD)**.

The lifetime prevalence of PTSD is 7% (Kessler et al., 2005), and women are more likely to develop PTSD than men, even when controlling for differences in the number of potentially traumatic events to which women and men are exposed (Olff, Langeland, Draijer, & Gersons, 2007; Tolin & Foa, 2006; for some complications in diagnosing PTSD, and therefore some complexity in estimating the prevalence of PTSD, see Dobbs, 2009).

One patient describes her experience with PTSD as follows:

> I was raped when I was 25 years old. For a long time, I spoke about the rape as though it was something that happened to someone else. I was very aware that it had happened to me, but there was just no feeling. Then I started having flashbacks. They kind of came over me like a splash of water. I would be terrified. Suddenly I was reliving the rape. Every instant was startling. I wasn't aware of anything around me, I was in a bubble, just kind of floating. And it was scary. Having a flashback can wring you out. The rape happened the week before Thanksgiving, and I can't believe the anxiety and fear I feel every year around the anniversary date. It's as though I've seen a werewolf. I can't relax, can't sleep, don't want to be with anyone. I wonder whether I'll ever be free of this terrible problem. (NIMH, 2009, p. 7)

Symptoms of PTSD fall into three major clusters. *Re-experiencing symptoms* include nightmares about the event and recalling the traumatic event, often in the form of flashbacks that seize the person's thoughts. The flashbacks are often an accurate reflection of the event but may sometimes be a composite of different events or of different perspectives on the event. In other cases, the flashbacks may include images of what the person thought might happen as part of the trauma. *Arousal symptoms* include difficulties in concentration, problems falling asleep, and extreme responses to being startled. *Avoidance symptoms* include an active avoidance of people, places, or objects that are linked to the trauma (Friedman, Keane, & Resick, 2007). Other common symptoms include emotional numbness, a loss of interest in things that once were pleasurable, and outbursts of anger. Still another symptom may be "survivor guilt"—that is, the feeling that one has done something wrong by surviving a traumatic event when friends or relatives were harmed or killed (M. J. Friedman & Marsella, 1996).

16.15 **Stress disorders** Post-traumatic stress disorders are triggered by identifiable traumas such as those associated with military combat.

acute stress disorder A reaction sometimes observed in individuals who have experienced a trauma, characterized by flashbacks and recurrent nightmares.

post-traumatic stress disorder (PTSD) A chronic, sometimes lifelong disorder that may follow a traumatic experience. Symptoms include dissociation, recurrent nightmares, flashbacks, and sleep disturbances.

Roots of the Anxiety Disorders

comorbidity The tendency for different mental disorders to occur together in the same person.

concordance rate The probability that a person with a particular familial relationship to a patient (e.g., an identical twin) has the same disorder as the patient.

As we have now seen, the *DSM* distinguishes among a number of different anxiety disorders. However, there is considerable **comorbidity** among these disorders, meaning that having one of these anxiety disorders makes it more likely that one will have another anxiety disorder. Indeed, more than half the people with one anxiety disorder will at some point also have some other anxiety disorder (T. Brown et al., 2001). This suggests that there are risk factors shared by the various anxiety disorders (factors that make a person vulnerable to more than one of these disorders) as well as specific risk factors (factors that make someone vulnerable to one of the disorders but not the others).

GENETIC RISK FACTORS

One cluster of risk factors involves the person's genetic pattern, because twin studies clearly show a heritable basis for the anxiety disorders. Thus, the probability that one member of a twin pair will have an anxiety disorder if the other does (the **concordance rate**) is much higher for identical twins than for fraternal twins (or ordinary siblings) (Hettema, Neale, & Kendler, 2001).

A number of different genes are thought to contribute to the anxiety disorders (Binder et al., 2008; Kendler, Karkowski, & Prescott, 1999; Lesch et al., 1996; Noyes et al., 1992), and genetic factors may be particularly important in OCD (Black & Noyes, 1990; S. A. Rasmussen, 1993). In fact, different aspects of OCD seem to have separate inheritance paths so that, for example, someone may inherit a specific tendency toward hoarding, or a specific tendency toward excessive cleaning (Leckman, Zhang, Alsobrook, & Pauls, 2001; but see Holden, 2008b). However, here as elsewhere, it is important to emphasize that these genetic factors do not directly "cause" the anxiety disorders. Instead, the genetic factors provide part of the diathesis for these disorders, and the disorder itself will emerge only if the person with the genetic vulnerability is exposed to some sort of stressor (Binder et al., 2008; Stein, Schork, & Gelernter, 2008).

BRAIN BASES

Genetic factors clearly play a role in anxiety disorders, but what is this role? How does a person's biology contribute to the problems we have discussed? We still have much to learn about the biological underpinnings of these disorders, but some intriguing findings recently have begun to emerge.

For example, functional neuroimaging studies show that the anxiety disorders, despite all they have in common, are quite different from each other in their biological underpinnings. Thus, the brain regions implicated in fear learning (including the amygdala and insula) seem to be especially active in people suffering from the specific phobias and social phobia (Etkin & Wager, 2007; Goldin et al., 2009). The pattern is different, though, in PTSD; here studies show that people with this disorder have less brain activation in prefrontal regions associated with emotion regulation. Yet a different pattern of brain activity is associated with panic disorder—one that involves apparent instability in the autonomic nervous system (Andreasen & Black, 1996; Wilhelm, Trabert, & Roth, 2001). OCD in turn may be linked to overactivity in three other brain areas—the orbitofrontal cortex, the caudate nucleus, and the anterior cingulate—although it is unclear whether this activity is the cause of the disease or one of its consequences (Micallef & Blin, 2001).

PSYCHOLOGICAL RISK FACTORS

So far, we have focused on genetic and biological risk factors. Other risk factors are psychological. Some of these, such as psychological maltreatment in childhood, seem to confer a general risk for several different anxiety disorders (Scher & Stein, 2003). Other psychological risk factors play a role in specific anxiety disorders, especially specific phobias and PTSD.

Many have proposed that specific phobias are the result of experiences that created a mental association between the phobic stimulus and a fearful idea, and often this proposal is cast in the language of Pavlovian conditioning (Chapter 7). The broad notion is that, at some point in the past, the person who suffers from the phobia experienced a painful, frightening, or embarrassing event; this is the unconditioned stimulus, leading to the unconditioned response of fear. The conditioned stimulus, in turn, was an object or cue linked to the event. Perhaps, for example, the person was in a closed space when something frightening happened. As a result, he now associates the closed space with fear, in much the same way that the ringing of a bell that is followed by food delivery becomes a signal that the food will soon arrive. In this way, claustrophobia (fear of closed spaces) might be produced (Wolpe, 1958).

In fact, the onset of many phobias can be traced to a traumatic experience, just as the conditioning account requires (see, for example, Hackmann, Clark, & McManus, 2000). But we need more theory than this if we are to account for all the facts about phobias. For example, phobias sometimes emerge without a history of conditioning— so that, for example, someone can develop a snake phobia even if he has never had a frightening experience with a snake. In addition, a simple conditioning account does not explain why some phobias are rare while others are common. For example, cars, bathtubs, and hammers are all (statistically) dangerous; painful accidents involving them are not uncommon. In contrast, few people have been bitten by a snake or a spider. If associations with pain or trauma produce phobias, we would expect to see many hammer or bathtub phobias but relatively few snake or spider phobias. But the opposite is the case.

These puzzles are easily solved. A century ago, Ivan Pavlov argued that classical conditioning was necessarily rooted in an organism's own experiences, but more recent studies have demonstrated *vicarious conditioning*, in which a person (or, in some studies, a monkey) can acquire a conditioned response merely by observing someone else's fear (e.g., Mineka & Ben Hamida, 1998). In addition, in Chapter 7 we discussed the fact that organisms seem "prepared" for some associations (and so learn them quickly) but "unprepared" for other associations (and so learn them more slowly if at all), and, in each case, the degree of preparedness is usually understandable in evolutionary terms.

How does this apply to phobias? Snakes and spiders were common dangers for our primate ancestors; natural selection may therefore have favored animals that were innately predisposed (i.e., prepared) to learn to fear snakes and spiders very quickly, after just one or two experiences with them (Öhman & Mineka, 2001; Seligman, 1971). If this was the case, limited but painful experience with these stimuli might still be enough to create and sustain a substantial number of phobias. With these relatively small modifications, then, we can preserve the claim that, in many cases, phobias are the product of learning—and, in particular, the product of classical conditioning (Mineka & Zinbarg, 2006).

With PTSD, the stress that precipitated the disorder is often obvious—a rape, a terrorist attack, a battlefield experience. But even when the trauma is easily identified, we need to consider more than just this immediate stress as the "cause" of the disorder. Not everyone who experiences a trauma develops PTSD. Indeed, according to one estimate, more than 90% of the U.S. population have experienced a trauma at some point, but only 5 to 12% develop PTSD (Lee & Young, 2001). Among Vietnam War veterans, many of whom were exposed to horrific violence, only one in ten developed PTSD (Dohrenwend et al., 2006).

Why is this? Part of the answer lies in the severity of the trauma; more severe trauma is more likely to produce the disorder (McNally, 2006; Sutker, Allain, & Winstead, 1993; E. Jones & Wessely, 2001). The individual's level of social support is also relevant, with more and better support after a trauma associated with a decreased likelihood of later developing PTSD (Ozer & Weiss, 2004). Yet another factor is the diathesis inherent in the person's genetic pattern. The odds of developing PTSD increase fivefold if a parent has had it (Radant, Tsuang, Peskind, McFall, & Raskind, 2001); identical twins who served in Vietnam were found to be far more similar to one another than fraternal twins in the likelihood of developing PTSD, and, for those who did develop PTSD, in the type of symptoms they experienced (True et al., 1993).

MOOD DISORDERS

In the anxiety disorders, the primary symptoms involve heightened levels of anxiety. In the **mood disorders**, the predominant disturbances lie in positive and negative mood. Specifically, the *DSM* distinguishes *depression* (also called major depressive disorder or unipolar depression) and *bipolar disorder* (formerly called manic-depressive illness). These disorders (sometimes called affective disorders) are characterized by emotional and energetic extremes—the despair of depression, the maelstrom of mania, or both.

Depression

mood disorders A group of disorders distinguished primarily by changes in positive and negative affective state.

depression A mood disorder characterized by disabling sadness, hopelessness, and apathy; a loss of energy, pleasure, and motivation; and disturbances of sleep, diet, and other bodily functions.

Depression involves feelings of sadness, hopelessness, and broad apathy about life; the depressed person loses interest in eating, hobbies, sex, and, for that matter, almost everything else. Of course, everyone has these feelings at one point or another, especially after some difficult event, such as sickness or the death of a friend, the end of a relationship, a significant career failure, and so on. But diagnosable depression is different, distinguished by both its severity and duration. In fact, the *DSM* suggests a diagnosis of depression only if the feelings of sadness have lasted at least 2 weeks and are accompanied by other symptoms such as insomnia and feelings of worthlessness.

Depression is one of the most common mental disorders, with a lifetime prevalence of 7 to 12% in men and 20 to 25% in women (Kessler et al., 2005; Figure 16.16). It is not clear why women are more likely to become depressed than men, but one crucial factor seems to be women's greater use of maladaptive forms of rumination—which involve repetitively turning emotional difficulties over and over in their mind (Nolen-Hoeksema, Wisco, & Lyubomirsky, 2008; Treynor, Gonzalez, & Nolen-Hoeksema, 2003).

In his memoir *Darkness Visible* (1990), the novelist William Styron (1925–2006) provided a portrait of depression:

All sense of hope vanished, along with the idea of a futurity; my brain, in thrall to its outlaw hormones, had become less an organ of thought than an instrument registering, minute by minute, varying degrees of its own suffering. The mornings themselves were becoming bad now as I wandered about lethargic . . . but afternoons were still the worst, when I'd feel the horror, like some poisonous fogbank, roll in upon my mind, forcing me

16.16 Depression *Woman Sitting on a Quilt* (1993) by Helen J. Vaughn.

into bed. There I would lie for as long as six hours, stuporous and virtually paralyzed, gazing at the ceiling and waiting for that moment of evening when, mysteriously, the crucifixion would ease up just enough to allow me to force down some food and then, like an automaton, seek an hour or two of sleep again. (1990, pp. 58–59)

Many people with depression experience considerable anxiety, and about 20% suffer from psychotic delusions—unshakable false beliefs. Some are variations on the theme of worthlessness: "It would be better if I had not been born. . . . I am the most inferior person in the world" (Beck, 1967, p. 38). Other delusions concern guilt about an unspeakable, unpardonable sin, and some patients report hearing the devil tell them that they will burn in hell for eternity (Andreasen & Black, 1996). Whatever the manifestation, depressions with psychotic features are more severe, less responsive to treatment, and more likely to recur (Coryell, 1996).

Specific cognitive deficits, including disrupted attention and working memory, also accompany severe depression. Moreover, depressed patients often exhibit physical manifestations that can include a loss of appetite and weight, weakness, fatigue, poor bowel functioning, sleep disorders, and lack of interest in sex. It is as if both bodily and psychic batteries have run down completely.

Depression is not tied to any particular age or life stage. It is most common in adolescence through middle adulthood, but depression can also emerge in children and in the elderly (Garber & Horowitz, 2002; Kessler, Keller, & Wittchen, 2001). Depressed adolescents show most of the symptoms we have described, but some of their symptoms may come in distinctly teenage form. Their despair often leads them to substance abuse; their apathy about life shows up in the number of classes they miss; their irritability emerges as belligerence and defiance. To be sure, all these behaviors can occur without depression, but any or all of them, together with other symptoms of depression, can indicate profound emotional problems.

Bipolar Disorder

Unlike depression, which is characterized by depressed mood and/or a loss of pleasure, **bipolar disorder** is characterized by manic and depressive episodes (with normal periods interspersed) (Figure 16.17). These episodes may be as short as a few hours or as long as several months, and they need not alternate. Some patients with bipolar disorder rarely have manic episodes; others have a large number. Moreover, although depression and mania were once regarded as opposite and mutually exclusive, they are now known to co-occur. In such **mixed states**, patients exhibit signs of both (e.g., tearfulness and pessimism combined with grandiosity and racing thoughts).

In their milder form, manic states are often hard to distinguish from buoyant spirits. At this point the person is said to show **hypomania**. She seems to have shifted into high gear. She is infectiously happy, utterly self-confident, and indefatigable. It is hard to see that something is amiss unless one notices that she jumps from one plan to another, seems unable to sit still for a moment, and quickly shifts from unbounded elation to brittle irritation if she meets even the smallest frustration. Kay Redfield Jamison, an expert on bipolar disorder—and a sufferer of it as well—provided a lyrical and frank account of the ecstatic allure of hypomania:

When you're high it's tremendous. The ideas and feelings are fast and frequent like shooting stars, and you follow them until you

bipolar disorder A mood disorder in which the patient swings between emotional extremes, experiencing both manic and depressive episodes.

mixed states A pattern sometimes observed with bipolar disorder in which the person displays a combination of manic and depressive symptoms.

hypomania A mild manic state in which the individual seems infectiously merry, extremely talkative, charming, and tireless.

16.17 **Bipolar disorder** Actress and writer Carrie Fisher (at left, as Princess Leia in *Star Wars*) is frank about her struggles with bipolar disorder and chronicles her ups and downs in the autobiographical one-woman show *Wishful Drinking* (right).

find better and brighter ones. Shyness goes, the right words and gestures are suddenly there, the power to captivate others a felt certainty. There are interests found in uninteresting people. Sensuality is pervasive and the desire to seduce and be seduced irresistible. Feelings of ease, intensity, power, well-being, financial omnipotence, and euphoria pervade one's marrow. (1995, p. 67)

Hypomania feels good, but it may breed overconfidence and the relentless pursuit of overly ambitious goals (Johnson, 2005). Even more serious problems arise when hypomania develops into full-blown **mania**. Now the motor is racing and all brakes are off, and in her perceived invincibility the sufferer will likely stop taking her mood-stabilizing medication. She may begin to stay up all night or engage in an endless stream of talk that runs from one topic to another and knows no inhibitions of social or personal propriety.

These feelings of omnipotence are short-lived, however. They recede as acute or psychotic mania sets in, and feelings of invincibility are replaced by terror as the person loses her grip on reality. People in the acute manic state may burst into shouts of song, smash furniture, exercise endlessly, sleep only rarely, engage in reckless sexual escapades, spend all their money on gambling, conceive grandiose plans for redirecting the nation's foreign policy or making millions in the stock market, and go on drinking or drug binges (nearly 60% of people with bipolar disorder are alcohol or drug abusers; Feinman & Dunner, 1996). Jamison described this chaotic state:

> I kept on with my life at a frightening pace. I worked ridiculously long hours and slept next to not at all. When I went home at night it was a place of increasing chaos: Books, many of them newly purchased, were strewn everywhere. . . . There were hundreds of scraps of paper as well. . . . One scrap contained an incoherent and rambling poem; I found it weeks later, apparently triggered by my spice collection, which, needless to say, had grown by leaps and bounds during my mania. I had titled it, for reasons that I am sure made sense at the time, "God is an Herbivore." (1995, p. 79)

Bipolar disorder—which has a lifetime prevalence rate of 4% (Kessler et al., 2005)—is a recurrent disorder: nearly everyone with bipolar disorder has recurrences, and between episodes, most experience mild-to-moderate symptoms (Miklowitz & Johnson, 2006). Although we have focused only on adults, children can also have bipolar disorder. Indeed, there has been a 40-fold increase in the past decade or so in the number of people under 20 who have received a diagnosis of bipolar disorder (Moreno et al., 2007). It is not clear, however, whether this dramatic increase reflects a change in the way diagnostic labels are used or whether there is really an increase in the prevalence of childhood onset bipolar disorder (Holden, 2008a).

Both those with depression and those in a depressive phase of bipolar disorder can become suicidal. Some actually attempt suicide, and more than a few succeed. Here is Kay Jamison's description of an episode of depression:

> Each day I awoke deeply tired, a feeling as foreign to my natural self as being bored or indifferent to life. Those were next. Then a gray, bleak preoccupation with death, dying, decaying, that everything was born but to die, best to die now and save the pain while waiting. (1995, p. 38)

The risk of suicide is greater among those with bipolar disorder than among those with any other psychiatric disorder, even depression. In fact, up to 20% of individuals with bipolar disorder commit suicide. As might be expected, people with bipolar disor-

mania A state characterized by racing thoughts, pressured speech, irritability or euphoria, and impaired judgment.

der rarely commit suicide during manic episodes (Andreasen & Black, 1996), but surprisingly, suicide risk is also relatively low for those in the depths of depression. At that point, gloom is deepest, but so is inertia, and although the patient may have decided to kill herself, she will have neither the energy nor the tenacity to complete the act. She is more likely to follow through on her resolution as she begins to recover from depression and emerges from closely supervised care. Times of greatest risk, therefore, include weekend leaves from a hospital and the period immediately after discharge.

In general, women are three times as likely to attempt suicide as men, but when men make the attempt, they are much more likely to succeed; in fact, four times as many men as women kill themselves (Arias et al., 2003). One reason for the difference is the choice of methods. Women are more likely than men to cut their wrists or swallow a bottle of sleeping pills, methods for which there is some chance of rescue. Men tend to use methods that are irreversible, such as shooting themselves or jumping off a rooftop (Fremouw, Perczel, & Ellis, 1990).

The Roots of Mood Disorders

What produces the mood disorders? Depression and bipolar disorder are thought to result from multiple contributing factors, factors that include genetic, neurochemical, and psychological influences.

GENETIC FACTORS

The mood disorders have important genetic components. This is reflected in the fact that the concordance rate is roughly two times higher in identical twins than in fraternal twins (Sullivan, Neale, & Kendler, 2000). The pattern is even clearer for bipolar disorder: If someone's identical twin has the disorder, there is a 60% chance that he, too, will have the disorder; the concordance rate for fraternal twins is much lower, 12% (Kelsoe, 1997).

Adoption studies point to the same conclusion, and the biological relatives of adopted children with depression are themselves at high risk for depression (Wender, Kety, Rosenthal, Schulsinger, & Ortmann, 1986). Likewise, the risk of suicide is much higher among the biological relatives of depressed adoptees than it is in the biological kin of nondepressed adoptees (Wallace, Schneider, & McGuffin, 2002).

Importantly, though, the genetic evidence indicates a clear distinction between depression and bipolar disorder. The two disorders overlap in their symptoms (i.e., clinical depression resembles the depressed phase of bipolar disorder), but they probably arise from different sources. This is evident, for example, in the fact that people with one of these disorders tend to have relatives with the same condition but not the other. Apparently, then, there are separate inheritance pathways for each, making it likely that they are largely separate disorders (Gershon, Nurnberger, Berrettini, & Goldin 1985; Moffitt, Caspi, & Rutter, 2006; Torgersen, 1986; Wender et al., 1986).

BRAIN BASES

Drugs that influence the effects of various neurotransmitters can often relieve symptoms of mood disorders, and this suggests that these mood disorders arose in the first place because of a disorder in neurotransmission. Three neurotransmitters seem critical for mood disorders: norepinephrine, dopamine, and serotonin. Many of the antidepressant and mood-stabilizing medications work by altering the availability of these chemicals at the synapse (Miklowitz & Johnson, 2006; Schildkraut, 1965).

How these neurochemical abnormalities lead to mood disorders is uncertain, but it is clear that these disorders involve more than a simple neurotransmitter shortage or excess. In the case of depression, this is evident in the fact that antidepressant drugs work almost immediately to increase the availability of neurotransmitters, but their clinical effects usually do not appear until a few weeks later. Thus, neurotransmitter problems are involved in depression (otherwise the drugs would not work at all), but the exact nature of those problems remains unclear.

In the case of bipolar disorder, the mystery lies in the cycling between manic and depressive episodes, especially since, in some patients, this cycling is quite rapid and seemingly divorced from external circumstances. Some believe the cycling is related to dysfunction in neuronal membranes, with the consequence that the membranes mismanage fluctuations in the levels of various neurotransmitters (Hirschfeld & Goodwin, 1988; Meltzer, 1986).

To better understand the underlying brain bases of these mood disorders, researchers have used both structural and functional brain imaging. Studies using positron emission tomography (PET) show that severe depression is associated with heightened brain activation in a limbic system region known as the subgenual cingulate cortex (Drevets, 1998). This finding makes sense, given that inducing sadness in healthy participants leads to increased activation in this brain region (Mayberg et al., 1999), as well as the evidence that when depression is successfully treated, brain activity in this region returns to normal levels (Mayberg et al., 1997). (We will return to this point in Chapter 17.)

In the case of bipolar disorder, imaging studies suggest that adults with bipolar disorder have greater amygdala volumes than age-matched healthy controls (Brambrilla et al., 2003). Functional-imaging studies parallel these structural studies, showing greater brain activity in subcortical emotion-generative brain regions such as the amygdala (Phillips, Ladouceur, & Drevets, 2008).

PSYCHOLOGICAL RISK FACTORS

Our account of the mood disorders also needs to take account of life experiences. For example, depression and bipolar disorder are often precipitated by an identifiable life crisis, whether that crisis involves marital or professional difficulties, serious physical illness, or a death in the family (S. L. Johnson, 2005a; Monroe & Hadjiyannakis, 2002; Neria et al., 2008). Broader contextual factors, such as whether someone lives in a good or bad neighborhood, may also influence whether a person develops depression, even when controlling for risk factors associated with the person's age, ethnicity, income, education, and employment status (Cutrona, Wallace, & Wesner, 2006). The importance of psychological factors is also evident in the fact that individuals with mood disorders are at much greater risk for relapse if they return after hospitalization to families who show high levels of criticism and hostility (Hooley, Gruber, Scott, Hiller, & Yurgelin-Todd, 2005; Miklowitz, 2007; Segal, Pearson, & Thase, 2003).

As we mentioned earlier, though, personal and environmental stresses do not, by themselves, cause mood disorders. What we need to ask is why some people are unable to bounce back after a hard blow and why, instead of recovering, they spiral downward into depression.

Part of the explanation may be genetic, and some researchers are focusing on a gene that regulates how much serotonin is available at the synapse. As discussed in Chapter 2, the gene itself is not the source of depression; instead, the gene seems to create a vulnerability to depression. The illness itself will emerge only if the vulnerable person also experiences some significant life stress (Caspi et al., 2003). However, this finding has been controversial, and research in this area is ongoing (e.g., Munafo, Durrant, Lewis, & Flint, 2009; Risch et al., 2009).

Another part of the explanation for why stress puts some people at greater risk for depression than others turns out to be social: severe stress is less likely to lead to a mood disorder if a person has supportive family and friends (Brown & Harris, 1978; Johnson et al., 1999; Joiner, 1997). Still another crucial factor is how a person thinks about stressful events when they occur.

Many depressed individuals—whether they are experiencing unipolar depression or are in the depressive phase of bipolar disorder—believe that both they and the world are hopeless and wretched. It seems plausible that these beliefs are produced by the patient's mood, but, according to the psychiatrist Aaron Beck, the opposite is true, at least in the case of depression: The beliefs come first; they produce the depression (see, for example, Beck, 1967, 1976). Beck argues that depression stems from a set of intensely negative and irrational beliefs: the beliefs some people hold that they are worthless, that their future is bleak, and that whatever happens around them is sure to turn out for the worst. These beliefs form the core of a **negative cognitive schema** by which a person interprets whatever happens to her, leaving her mood nowhere to go but down.

A related account of depression also focuses on how people think about what happens to them. As we saw in Chapter 15, people differ in how they explain bad events. Do we think that a bad event happened because of something we did, so that, in some direct way, we caused the event? Do we believe that similar bad events will arise in other aspects of our lives? And do we think that bad events will continue to happen to us, perhaps for the rest of our lives? Peterson and Seligman propose that much depends on how we answer these questions, and, moreover, they suggest that each of us has a consistent style for how we tend to answer such questions—which they call an **explanatory style**. In their view, a person is vulnerable to depression if her explanatory style tends to be internal ("I, and not some external factor, caused the event"), global ("This sort of event will also happen in other areas of my life"), and stable ("This is going to keep happening"). This explanatory style is not by itself the source of depression; once again, we need to separate diathesis and stress. But if someone has this explanatory style and then experiences a bad event, that person is at considerably elevated risk for depression (Peterson & Seligman, 1984). In addition, it appears that the explanatory style usually predates the depression, with the clear implication that this way of interpreting the world is not caused by depression but is instead a factor predisposing an individual toward depression (Abramson et al., 2002; Alloy, Abramson, & Francis, 1999; Peterson & Park, 2007).

negative cognitive schema According to Aaron Beck, the core cognitive component of depression, consisting of an individual's automatic negative interpretations concerning himself, his future, and the world.

explanatory style A person's characteristic way of explaining his experiences. Consistently attributing bad experiences to internal, global, and stable causes may increase vulnerability to depression.

SOCIAL AND CULTURAL RISK FACTORS

Clearly, there are both biochemical and cognitive contributors to mood disorders. As we mentioned earlier, though, mood disorders are also influenced by social settings. This is evident, for example, in the fact that depression is less likely among people with a strong social netowork of friends or family. The importance of social surroundings is also visible in another way: the role of culture in shaping the likelihood that depression will emerge, or the form that the disorder takes.

Depression occurs in all cultures, and, in fact, the World Health Organization ranked depression fourth among all causes of disability worldwide (Miller, 2006b). However, its prevalence varies widely from one country to the next. For example, depression is—not surprisingly— more common in countries such as Afghanistan that

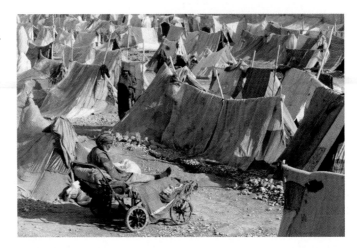

16.18 Depression around the world War has many horrid effects—including an increase in the rate of mental disease. Depression rates are, for example, high in countries like Afghanistan that have been torn apart by war, with many people displaced from their homes and living in poverty in refugee camps like this one.

have been torn apart by war (Bolton & Betancourt, 2004; Figure 16.18); the difficulties in such countries also lead to other disorders, including post-traumatic stress disorder. In contrast, depression is much less commonly diagnosed in China, Taiwan, and Japan than in the West. When the disorder is detected in these Asian countries, the symptoms are less often psychological (such as sadness or apathy) and more often bodily (such as sleep disturbance, weight loss, or, in China, heart pain; Kleinman, 1986; G. Miller, 2006a; Tsai & Chentsova-Dutton, 2002). Why is this? There are several possibilities, starting with the fact that cultures differ in their *display rules* for emotion (see Chapter 12), which will obviously influence the presentation and diagnosis of almost any mental disorder. In addition, people in these Asian countries may differ in how they understand and perhaps even experience their own symptoms, and this, too, can influence diagnosis.

Even within a single country, the risk of mood disorders varies. Depression, for example, is more common among lower socioeconomic groups (Dohrenwend, 2000; Monroe & Hadjiyannakis, 2002), perhaps because these groups are exposed to more stress. In contrast, bipolar disorder is more common among *higher* socioeconomic groups (Goodwin & Jamison, 1990), conceivably because the behaviors produced during a person's hypomanic phases may lead to increased accomplishment.

SCHIZOPHRENIA

schizophrenia A group of severe mental disorders characterized by at least some of the following: marked disturbance of thought, withdrawal, inappropriate or flat emotions, delusions, and hallucinations.

prognosis The forecast of how a situation (including an illness) will improve or fail to improve in the future.

psychosis Loss of contact with reality, most often evidenced as *delusions* or *hallucinations*.

So far, we have considered two of the most common types of mental disorders, the anxiety disorders and the mood disorders. We now turn to **schizophrenia**, whose name was coined by the Swiss psychiatrist Eugen Bleuler from the Greek *schizo*, "split," and *phren*, "mind," to designate what he regarded as an abnormal disintegration of mental functions (1911).*

The lifetime prevalence of schizophrenia is about 1% (roughly the same prevalence as epilepsy). This overall estimate may be misleading, however, because the rates of schizophrenia are especially high in some nations and in some regions—including, for example, Croatia and the western half of Ireland; conversely, the schizophrenia rate is quite low in Papua New Guinea. These geographic variations are not well understood.

---

*The Greek roots of this term are probably the source of the widespread confusion between schizophrenia and what used to be called a split personality (now called dissociative identity disorder). Schizophrenia does not involve "multiple personalities."

Schizophrenia is typically diagnosed in late adolescence or early adulthood and tends to begin earlier in men than in women (Jablensky & Cole, 1997). Men also seem to develop a more severe form of the disorder (Nopoulos, Flaum, & Andreasen, 1997).

Unfortunately, the **prognosis** (the prospect for recovery) for people with this disorder is discouraging. One study tracked down 200 people in the United States who had been diagnosed with schizophrenia some 30 years previously. Of these patients, 20% were doing well at the time of the follow-up, while 45% were incapacitated. Two-thirds had never married, and 58% had never worked (Andreasen & Black, 1996; Cutting, 1986).

Signs and Symptoms

People with schizophrenia experience many different types of symptoms (Hyman, 2007). *Positive symptoms* are behaviors that are not evident in healthy people. *Negative (deficit) symptoms* reflect an absence of behaviors that are usually evident in healthy people. *Cognitive symptoms* reflect impairments in executive functions such as working memory and attentional control and can include the state of **psychosis**, or loss of contact with reality, so that the beliefs and perceptions of someone with schizophrenia are often extremely bizarre (Figure 16.19). Here is one account of what it feels like to have schizophrenia:

> When my first episode of schizophrenia occurred, I was 21, a senior in college in Atlanta, Georgia. I was making good grades, assistant vice president of my chapter in my sorority, president of the Spanish club, and very popular. Everything in my life was just perfect. . . .
>
> All of a sudden things weren't going so well. I began to lose control of my life and, most of all, myself. I couldn't concentrate on my school-work, I couldn't sleep, and when I did sleep, I had dreams about dying. I was afraid to go to class, imagined that people were talking about me, and on top of that I heard voices. I called my mother in Pittsburgh and asked for her advice. She told me to move off campus into an apartment with my sister.
>
> After I moved in with my sister, things got worse. I was afraid to go outside and when I looked out of the window, it seemed that everyone outside was yelling "kill her, kill her." My sister forced me to go to school. I would go out of the house until I knew she had gone to work; then I would return home. Things continued to get worse. I imagined that I had a foul body odor and I sometimes took up to six showers a day. I recall going to the grocery store one day, and I imagined that the people in the store were saying "Get saved, Jesus is the answer." Things worsened—I couldn't remember a thing. I had a notebook full of reminders telling me what to do on that particular day. I couldn't remember my schoolwork, and I would study from 6:00 p.m. until 4:00 a.m., but never had the courage to go to class on the following day. I tried to tell my sister about it, but she didn't understand. She suggested that I see a psychiatrist, but I was afraid to go out of the house to see him. (O'Neal, 1984, pp. 109–110)

POSITIVE SYMPTOMS

Positive symptoms—behaviors that are not evident in healthy people—can take several forms. People with schizophrenia typically suffer from **delusions**—incorrect beliefs that are rigidly maintained despite the absence of any evidence for the belief, and, in many cases, despite contradictory evidence. By one estimate, 90% of all

16.19 Paintings by sufferers of schizophrenia Paintings by people with schizophrenia often have an odd, eerie quality. In many cases the usual artistic conventions are disregarded, and the pictures include written comments, digits, and other idiosyncratic material. (top) *Saint-Adolf-Grand-Grand-God-Father* (1915), a painting by Adolf W., who was institutionalized in early adulthood and elaborated a fantastic autobiography in which he featured himself as Saint Adolf II, a young god who travels through space and has many adventures. (bottom) *Guardian Angels* by Else B., an institutionalized woman with schizophrenia. In all her works the legs of angels are painted as though they had fused at the top, to make sure that "nothing happens there."

delusions Systematized false beliefs, often of grandeur or persecution.

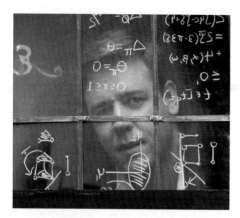

16.20 Delusions In *A Beautiful Mind*, Russell Crowe depicted John Nash's struggle with schizophrenia, including elaborate delusions.

hallucinations Perceived experiences that occur in the absence of actual sensory stimulation.

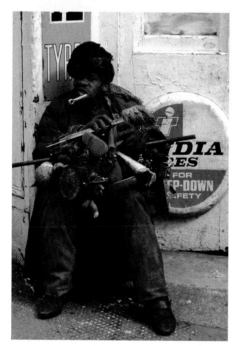

16.21 Odd attire Unusual dressing can be one positive symptom of schizophrenia.

patients with schizophrenia suffer from delusions (Cutting, 1995). Thus a patient with schizophrenia might be convinced he is Moses, or the king of England, or a special messenger from God. Likewise, people with schizophrenia often believe that their thoughts or actions are being controlled by someone else (by space aliens, for example, or by the CIA; Figure 16.20). Sometimes they believe their thoughts are being broadcast (and so are fully audible) to other people. *Delusions of reference* are also common, in which the patient is convinced that some neutral environmental event is somehow directed at her. For example, a patient might observe two strangers talking and be certain they are talking about him; she sees some people walk by and decides they are following her; he sees a television commercial and is sure it contains a secret message aimed only at him.

A second type of positive symptom is **hallucinations**—sensory experiences in the absence of any actual input. Most common in schizophrenia are auditory hallucinations, and, in particular, voices. Thus, the patient might "hear" the voice of God, or the devil, or a neighbor. If the patient can make out what the voices are saying, she will often report that they are talking about her, shouting obscenities at her, threatening her, or telling her what to do. Researchers have explored these hallucinations via functional brain imaging and have documented increased brain activation, during the hallucinations, in primary auditory regions in the temporal lobe (Lennox, Park, Medley, Morris, & Jones, 2000). This finding suggests that when people with schizophrenia have auditory hallucinations, they are hearing voices that sound every bit as vivid and real to them as actual voices.

Positive symptoms also may take the form of unusual behaviors. People with schizophrenia sometimes dress peculiarly (wearing layers of warm clothing on a hot day) and show *disorganized behavior*, becoming frenzied, running haphazardly, shouting nonsensically, and acting violently (Figure 16.21). In many ways, the disorganized behavior associated with schizophrenia is the closest match to the popular stereotype of madness: A person who has schizophrenia may have speech that is bizarre and babbling, and while he is talking, he may giggle, make silly smiles or odd grimaces, assume odd postures, and have sudden fits of laughing and crying.

NEGATIVE SYMPTOMS

In addition to positive symptoms, people with schizophrenia may show several types of negative symptoms. One negative symptom is a flattening or cessation of behavioral responses. For example, someone with schizophrenia may express little emotion, may say relatively little, and may be unable to persist in many activities. People who have been ill for a long time will often stare vacantly into space, their faces expressionless, and, if they answer questions at all, they do so in a monotone. At the extreme, individuals with schizophrenia may show *catatonic behavior*, standing or sitting "frozen" for hours on end, sometimes in unusual postures (Figure 16.22).

A second type of negative symptom is anhedonia, the loss of interest in activities that we would ordinarily expect to be pleasurable. People with schizophrenia also seem not to anticipate pleasure in the way that healthy people do, a finding that corresponds with lower levels of goal-oriented behavior (Gard et al., 2007).

A third negative symptom—which may be related to the failure to anticipate pleasure—is withdrawal from other people (Tarbox & Pogue-Geile, 2008). In some patients, this withdrawal begins quite early, with a history of few childhood friends and limited adolescent social contact. In others, the individual gradually develops an inner world that becomes more and more private and less and less involved with the social world. As a result, the thoughts of this person become ever more idiosyncratic, until she may have trouble communicating with others even if she wants to. This situation makes it even more likely that others will rebuff her because they cannot understand her and think she is "weird." The vicious cycle of rejections can lead to further withdrawal and idiosyncrasy.

COGNITIVE SYMPTOMS

People with schizophrenia often display marked cognitive difficulties. They seem unable to maintain a coherent train of thought, but rather skip from one idea to the next, and this typically shows up in their speech. An example is a fragment of a letter written by one of Bleuler's patients. The writing starts out normally enough, but then deteriorates:

> I am writing on paper. The pen I am using is from a factory called "Perry & Co." This factory is in England. I assume this. Behind the name of Perry Co., the city of London is inscribed; but not the city. The city of London is in England. I know this from my school-days. Then, I always liked geography. My last teacher in that subject was Professor August A. He was a man with black eyes. I also like black eyes. There are also blue and gray eyes and other sorts too. I have heard it said that snakes have green eyes. All people have eyes. There are some, too, who are blind. These blind people are led about by a boy. (1911, p. 17)

16.22 Catatonic schizophrenia This patient, who was diagnosed with catatonic schizophrenia, spent virtually all his waking hours in a crouched position.

It is also common for people with schizophrenia to have significant impairments starting with the earliest stages of sensory processing (Walker, Kestler, Bollini, & Hochman, 2004) and extending through episodic memory and cognitive control (Reichenberg & Harvey, 2007). Other perceptual and motor abnormalities are evident in people who have not been diagnosed with schizophrenia but who are at elevated risk for the disease; these abnormalities include deficits in two-point discrimination (distinguishing between 1 and 2 points touching the skin) and simple line drawing (Lenzenweger, 2006). These (and other) cognitive problems may all contribute to the broad pattern of symptoms that are typical of schizophrenia. An inability to inhibit thoughts and actions, for example, contributes to disrupted speech and behavior, while difficulties in executive function interfere with the ability to reason and so foster the delusions.

The Roots of Schizophrenia

What leads to these symptoms? Like the other causes of disorders we have discussed, the causes of schizophrenia are complex, involving genetic, prenatal, neural, social, and psychological factors.

GENETIC AND PRENATAL FACTORS

It has long been known that schizophrenia runs in families (Figure 16.23). For example, if a person has a sibling with schizophrenia, the likelihood that he has (or will get) the disease himself is four times greater than the likelihood of schizophrenia in the general population—8%, compared with 1 or 2% in the broad population (Andreasen & Black, 1996; D. Rosenthal, 1970). But this fact, by itself, does not prove a genetic contribution. (After all, the increased risk among siblings might reflect a factor in the home or family environment.) Better evidence comes from concordance rates between twins, which are between 41 and 65% if twins are identical, and between 0 and 28% if they are fraternal (Cardno & Gottesman, 2000).

Separate evidence comes from adoption studies. Consider a child who is born to a mother with schizophrenia and placed in a foster home (with foster parents who are

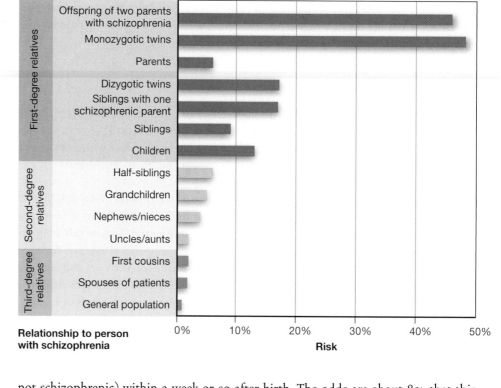

16.23 Genes and schizophrenia The risk of developing schizophrenia is much higher if one has a close relative with schizophrenia.

16.24 The Genain quadruplets All four of these identical quadruplets, born in 1930, suffer from schizophrenia. (The name Genain is fictitious, and used to preserve their anonymity.)

not schizophrenic) within a week or so after birth. The odds are about 8% that this child will develop schizophrenia, the same percentage as for children who remain with a biological parent who has the disease (Kendler & Gruenberg, 1984; Kety, 1988; Tsuang, Gilbertson, & Faraone, 1991).

All of these findings suggest that there is some genetic contribution to the development of schizophrenia (Sullivan, Kendler, & Neale, 2003), and, in fact, scientists may be closing in on the specific genes that are responsible. For example, two separate studies have found that people with two specific DNA deletions are substantially more likely than people without these deletions to develop schizophrenia (International Schizophrenia Consortium, 2008; Stefansson et al., 2008).

However, if genes were the whole story for schizophrenia, the concordance rate would be 100% for identical twins, and of course it is not. In addition, if genes were all that mattered, we would expect that genetically identical individuals who develop schizophrenia will have identical symptom profiles. This is not the case. For example, the genetically identical Genain quadruplets (see Figure 16.24) all have schizophrenia, but two of the sisters have a more serious symptom profile than the others. These observations lead us to ask what other (nongenetic) factors play a role. In recent years, attention has focused on factors associated with birth—both prenatal factors and factors during delivery.

One line of evidence suggests that the mother's exposure to an infectious agent during pregnancy may increase the likelihood that her child will develop schizophrenia. The influenza virus has attracted special attention based on the finding that when mothers are in the second trimester of pregnancy during an influenza epidemic, their children are more likely to develop schizophrenia (Brown, Cohen, Harkavy-Friedman, & Babulas, 2001; Mednick, Huttunen, & Macho'n, 1994; Sham et al., 1992). These findings are supported by epidemiological studies that show that children who develop schizophrenia are disproportionately likely to have been born during the winter (January to March in the Northern Hemisphere, July to September in the Southern Hemisphere), the season during which people stay inside more and thus share more

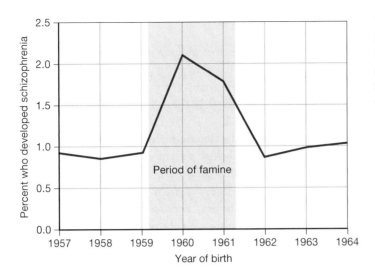

16.25 **Prenatal factors and schizophrenia** Severe maternal malnutrition during pregnancy increases the risk of schizophrenia. This is demonstrated by a study showing that children who were born during a period of severe famine in China had double the usual risk of developing schizophrenia (St. Clair et al., 2005).

viral infections. In geographic areas where there are no seasons—that is, in areas near the equator—there is no link between schizophrenia and birth month (Battle, Martin, Dorfman, & Miller, 1999; McGrath, Welham, & Pemberton, 1995; Parker, Mehendran, Koh, & Machin, 2000).

Infections, however, are likely not the whole story. Another line of evidence suggests that maternal malnutrition during pregnancy also increases the risk that the child will later develop schizophrenia (Figure 16.25). Thus, children born just after a major crop failure in China in the early 1960s were twice as likely as Chinese children born earlier or later to develop schizophrenia (St. Clair et al., 2005).

Evidence further suggests that a diverse set of birth complications is associated with schizophrenia, and what these complications have in common seems to be a period of diminished oxygen supply to the newborn. This oxygen deprivation by itself is not enough to produce the disease, but it may interfere with the newborn's brain development in a way that increases the likelihood that a genetic predisposition will eventually be expressed as schizophrenia (T. D. Cannon et al., 2000; Zorilla & Cannon, 1995).

We still need to ask, though, what these various factors do to produce the illness we call schizophrenia. What are the effects of the infection, or the oxygen deprivation, or the genetic pattern associated with this illness? According to many investigators, the answer lies in the fact that schizophrenia is, at its heart, a **neurodevelopmental disorder** (Sawa & Snyder, 2002; Waddington, Torrey, Crow, & Hirsch, 1991). In other words, the various factors we have mentioned cause the child's brain (in both its structure and its chemistry) not to develop as it should from a fairly early age. By this logic, though schizophrenia may not be diagnosed until adolescence, it reflects developmental problems that occurred years earlier.

Consistent with this notion, evidence suggests that many individuals who are eventually diagnosed with this illness are, in fact, unusual in early childhood. For example, close examination of home movies of children who, years later, were diagnosed with schizophrenia reveals that the "preschizophrenic children" showed less positive emotion in their facial expressions and more negative facial emotion, compared with siblings who did not later develop schizophrenia (Walker, Grimes, Davis, & Smith, 1993; Walker, Kestler, Bollini, & Hochman, 2004; Walker, Savoie, & Davis, 1994). The preschizophrenic children also showed unusual motor patterns, including odd hand movements. In some cases, these differences were visible at a very early age—as young as 2 years old—which strongly suggests that the disease starts influencing the person in early childhood, even if the full disruption it causes is not detected for years (Figure 16.26).

neurodevelopmental disorder A disorder that stems from early brain abnormalities.

16.26 **Precursors of illness** Individuals who will develop schizophrenia start showing precursors of the disease at an early age. This has been detected by examining the childhood videos of people who later developed schizophrenia.

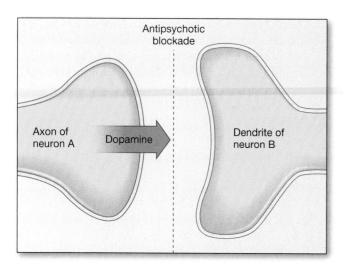

16.27 The dopamine-blockade hypothesis of classical antipsychotic action According to the dopamine hypothesis, people with schizophrenia suffer from overactivity in the brain circuits that rely on the neurotransmitter dopamine. Consistent with this view, symptoms diminish if dopamine's actions are blocked.

dopamine hypothesis Asserts that the brains of people with schizophrenia are oversensitive to the neurotransmitter dopamine.

classical antipsychotics Drugs (such as Thorazine and Haldol) that block dopamine receptors. These drugs seem to treat many positive symptoms of schizophrenia.

BRAIN BASES

Clearly, genetic factors and environmental factors before and during birth contribute to schizophrenia and seem to throw brain development somehow off-course. But off-course *how*? Can we pinpoint the biological changes that these various factors produce, which then lead to the illness?

According to the **dopamine hypothesis**, schizophrenia is associated with an abnormally high level of activity in the brain circuits sensitive to the neurotransmitter dopamine. The strongest line of evidence for this hypothesis comes from the effects of a number of medications known as **classical antipsychotics**, medications that include the drugs Thorazine and Haldol. These drugs block receptors for dopamine (Figure 16.27), and, as the dopamine hypothesis predicts, they relieve many of the symptoms associated with schizophrenia. In addition, some antipsychotics are more effective than others in blocking dopamine receptors, and the stronger the blockade, the more therapeutic the drug.

Other evidence comes from people who do not have schizophrenia but who have taken overdoses of amphetamines. Amphetamines are stimulants whose effects include the enhancement of dopamine activity and, when taken in large enough doses, produce a temporary psychosis similar to schizophrenia. (For more on amphetamine effects, see Chapter 6.) As the dopamine hypothesis would predict, medications that block dopamine activity at the synapse also reduce the psychotic symptoms that follow amphetamine abuse.

The dopamine hypothesis has much to recommend it, but in recent years investigators have realized that it is incomplete (Carlsson et al., 1995). One clue is that many of the newer antipsychotic medications—which are at least as effective as older antipsychotics but generally have fewer side effects—do not appear to be strong dopamine antagonists (Burris et al., 2002). Researchers now believe that people with schizophrenia may suffer both from excessive dopamine stimulation in some brain circuits (Laruelle, Kegeles, & Abi-Darham, 2003) and from insufficient dopamine stimulation elsewhere (e.g., in the prefontal cortex; Koh, Bergson, Undie, Goldman-Rakic, & Lidow, 2003).

Other neurotransmitter systems also seem to be implicated in schizophrenia. For example, people with schizophrenia may have a dysfunction in glutamate transmission in their brains, either because they have insufficient glutamate or because they are relatively insensitive to it. Several pieces of evidence point in this direction, including the fact that the illicit drug phencyclidine (more commonly known as PCP or angel dust) blocks glutamate receptors and induces symptoms similar to those seen in schizophrenia (Gorelick & Balster, 1995). In addition, drugs that increase glutamate activity alleviate both positive and negative symptoms of schizophrenia (Goff & Coyle, 2001).

We probably should not think of the dopamine and glutamate proposals as competitors; both might capture part of the truth. Indeed, this reflects one of the messages emerging from recent research on schizophrenia: Multiple neurotransmitters seem to be involved, affecting multiple brain areas, under the control of multiple genes (cf. Javitt & Coyle, 2004; Sawa & Snyder, 2002).

In addition to the neurochemical disruptions in schizophrenia, research indicates that patients with this disorder also suffer from structural abnormalities in their brains. MRI scans show that a certain proportion of people with schizophrenia—males, especially—have an enlargement of the ventricles, the fluid-filled cavities in the brain. Simply put, the ventricles become enlarged because there is not enough brain to fill the skull (Figure 16.28). This finding indicates that in many cases of schizophrenia, there is either a dramatic loss of brain tissue or a deficiency that existed from the start (Andreasen et al., 1986; Chua & McKenna, 1995; Lawrie & Abukmeil, 1998; Nopoulos, Flaum, & Andreasen, 1997).

Abnormalities associated with schizophrenia have also been reported in other areas of the brain (Heckers, 1997; L. K. Jacobsen et al., 1997), but the most persuasive findings involve the frontal and temporal lobes (Black & Andreasen, 1994; Martin & Albers, 1995). Studies of brain structure have documented a loss of gray matter in prefrontal regions that support working memory, and the degree of tissue loss seems to be correlated with symptom severity (Cannon et al., 2002). When these areas are examined during autopsy, individuals with schizophrenia also show various irregularities, including missing or abnormally sized neurons. These neuronal defects—not surprisingly—affect overall brain function: neuroimaging studies of patients with schizophrenia indicate atypical functioning in the areas where neuronal defects are common (Barch et al., 2001; Tan et al., 2006).

SOCIAL AND PSYCHOLOGICAL RISK FACTORS

Almost a century ago, epidemiological studies revealed a link between schizophrenia and socioeconomic status, or SES (Faris & Dunham, 1939). In fact, one study suggested that low-SES individuals are nine times more likely to develop schizophrenia than are high-SES individuals (Hollingshead & Redlich, 1958). The same point can be made geographically, since the prevalence of schizophrenia is highest in the poorest and most dilapidated areas of a city and diminishes as one moves toward higher-income regions (Figure 16.29; M. L. Kohn, 1968).

What produces this relationship? Part of the answer is, sadly, daily stress—poverty, inferior status, and low occupational rank are all stressful, and so can help trigger schizophrenia in someone who is (for biological reasons) already vulnerable (Goldberg & Morrison, 1963). But there is another reason why schizophrenia is associated with poverty: Someone who suffers from schizophrenia is less likely to do well in school and less likely to get or hold a good job. As a result, people with schizophrenia suffer from *downward drift*. Their disease produces problems that, in turn, put them into a lower social class (Dohrenwend et al., 1992; Jones et al., 1993). Notice, then, that cause and effect run in both directions here: Poverty is a risk factor for schizophrenia, making the disease more likely, but schizophrenia is itself a risk factor that makes poverty more likely.

What about someone's immediate environment—for example, her family? Some investigators have looked to the personality of a person's parents as a potential source of schizophrenia. Others have focused on communication patterns in the family (Bateson,

16.28 MRI scans of the brains of twins MRI scans of the brains of 28-year-old identical twins. One (right) is hospitalized for schizophrenia; the other (left) is well. The twin with schizophrenia has enlarged cerebral ventricles. The fact that just one twin has schizophrenia shows that heredity is not the only factor in producing this disorder; the slightly different prenatal environments of the twins, as well as birth complications, may be involved.

Schizophrenia rate per 10,000

- 100+
- 60–99
- 40–59
- 30–39
- 20–29
- 10–19

16.29 The prevalence of schizophrenia in different regions of a city A map of Chicago (1922–1934) is represented by a series of concentric zones. The center zone is the business and amusement area, which is without residents except for some transients and vagabonds. Surrounding this center is a slum region inhabited largely by unskilled laborers. Farther out are more stable regions: a zone largely populated by skilled workers, followed by zones of middle- and upper-middle-class apartment dwellers, and, farthest out, the upper-middle-class commuters. The map shows clearly that the incidence of schizophrenia increases the closer one gets to the city's center.

1959, 1960). There is little evidence, however, in favor of either of these claims. In families that include someone with schizophrenia disturbances may be common, but this is likely to be a consequence of the disease rather than its cause. After all, having a family member who suffers from schizophrenia can be tragic for the family. Parents often blame themselves for their child's illness and are likely to become frustrated and despondent in their attempts to reach their child (Mishler & Waxler, 1968; Torrey, 1983).

Children with schizophrenia may have difficult parents for another reason. Given the link between schizophrenia and genetics, a child with schizophrenia is likely to have at least one parent with the same pathological genes as the child's. Thus, the parents may have a muted (or perhaps just an undiagnosed) version of the disease, contributing to the family's problems (Holtzman et al., 1988; Reveley, Reveley, & Clifford, 1982; Tsuang et al., 1991).

In short, there is no reason to believe that poor familial relations cause the disorder. But the family context surely matters in other ways, including how well a person with schizophrenia copes with the disorder. This is reflected in the fact that patients, once treated and released from a hospital, are rehospitalized more often if their parents are hostile and critical toward them (Hooley, 2004). Such negative reactions from family members are likely to impede the patient's adjustment to his disorder and may create such distress that another hospital stay becomes necessary.

OTHER AXIS I AND AXIS II DISORDERS

So far in this chapter, we have examined three common and important families of disorders listed in the *DSM*. In this section, we expand our focus by considering—albeit in less detail—several other important Axis I and Axis II disorders.

Developmental Disorders

As we have noted in the preceding sections, many disorders emerge in children or adolescents. Both depression and anxiety disorders are often diagnosed at a young age, and precursors of schizophrenia can be detected in childhood, years before the disease is diagnosed. But, in all these cases, the child's development itself seems more or less normal: The child still acquires the knowledge and cognitive capacities that we described in Chapter 14, as well as most of the social skills and culturally encouraged behaviors. However, development is not normal in a different group of disorders—including mental retardation, various learning disorders, and communication disorders. Let us explore this category of developmental disorders by focusing on just two diagnoses within it: *autism* and *attention-deficit/hyperactivity disorder*.

AUTISM

Autism involves a wide range of developmental problems, including language and motor problems, and problems in the social sphere. Autism is not common (affecting less than 0.1% of the world's population), but it is far more frequent among boys than among girls (Volkmar, Szatmari, & Sparrow, 1993). The disorder is usually diagnosed at a very young age—before a child is three years old (Figure 16.30).

Children with autism show a range of symptoms. They tend to have little interest in other people—and so they are not cuddly as infants or interested in playmates later on.

16.30 Autism Children with autism often have little interest in others or can become completely attached to a single toy—although they usually do not play in the ordinary way with the toy.

autism A disorder usually diagnosed in young children, and characterized by a wide range of developmental problems, including language and motor problems.

When they do interact with others, they seem to have little understanding of the others' intentions, beliefs, or goals and show little or no empathy (Oberman & Ramachandran, 2007). It is not surprising, then, that children with autism often seem unable to join cooperative activities or form friendships. They also seem to lack emotional intelligence (Chapter 11), and so seem unable to understand others' expressions of emotions or how to use their own faces and gestures to convey emotion (Charman et al., 1998).

Children with autism also show marked deficits in language—often not speaking, and typically showing neither skill nor interest in communicating with others. In many cases, they produce high-pitched, birdlike noises instead of speech, or show a pattern of simply echoing speech they have heard—perhaps just a moment ago, or perhaps a few days earlier. Often, they have trouble with pronouns—reversing *I* and *you* and referring to themselves by name, rather than saying "I" (Lee, Hobson, & Chiat, 1994).

Autistic children also show peculiar repetitive movement patterns—spinning around for long periods of time, or rocking back and forth for hours. They also seem insistent on sameness, and so become deeply upset—and may throw severe tantrums—if the furniture in the house is rearranged, or their parents vary the household routine in some small way. They may become completely attached to one single toy, carrying it around constantly, but often not playing with it in the ordinary manner.

Finally, children with autism are often mentally retarded, but here there is an odd twist. In a minority of cases, they show islands of preserved (indeed, enhanced) skill, so that a child with autism might turn out to be an extraordinary musician or unbelievably fast in arithmetic calculations.

What produces this broad range of symptoms? There is compelling evidence that autism has a substantial genetic component (Sutcliffe, 2008), and most accounts of autism emphasize some form of biological dysfunction, but there are a variety of proposals about what we should count as the "core problem." One hypothesis is that individuals with autism have some problem in the functioning of their amygdala, a brain structure that plays an essential role in emotion and motivation (Waterhouse, Fein, & Modahl, 1996). A different hypothesis focuses on abnormalities in the cerebellum (Courchesne, Townsend, & Saitoh, 1994). Another hypothesis is that the problem lies in a brain structure that specifically helps the child learn about and understand other people's thoughts and intentions (Scott & Baron-Cohen, 1996).

Whatever the causes of autism, treatment typically focuses on modifying the behavior of the person with autism. Various medications for autism have been tried, but none seem particularly effective. Instead, therapists have had more success with behavior-modification techniques—building on the principles of shaping and reinforcement that we described in Chapter 7. These efforts seem to improve both social and intellectual functioning and can produce appreciable long-term benefits.

ATTENTION-DEFICIT/HYPERACTIVITY DISORDER

Children with **attention-deficit/hyperactivity disorder** (ADHD) are impulsive, doing or saying the first thing that occurs to them, often blurting out answers in class without raising their hands. They also fidget, getting out of their seats at school and tapping pencils, fingers, or feet (Figure 16.31). They have difficulty keeping their attention focused on a task and have trouble organizing or completing projects. Their school performance tends to be poor, and they usually are perceived by others as intrusive and immature.

ADHD is common: It is estimated 8% of children are diagnosed with ADHD, with a greater prevalence in boys than in girls (CDC, 2005). Symptoms are most common in young children (e.g., before age 8) and frequently persist into adulthood. ADHD is

attention-deficit/hyperactivity disorder (ADHD) A disorder usually diagnosed in young children, and characterized by impulsivity, difficulty staying focused on a task, and a range of behavioral problems.

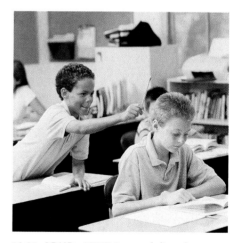

16.31 ADHD ADHD is a real disorder, but there is concern that it is being overdiagnosed and may be a label given to any child who is just particularly active.

often treated using the stimulant methylphenidate, which is sold under tradenames such as Ritalin and Concerta. There is no question that these medications can be effective, and global spending on ADHD medications rose threefold from 1993 through 2003 (Jensen et al., 2007; Scheffler, Hinshaw, Modrek, & Levine, 2007). Given the symptoms of ADHD, it may seem odd that a stimulant would be prescribed to treat it, but methylphenidate enhances the release of dopamine and norepinephrine, which in turn activates inhibitory circuits that guard against impulses that might be triggered by the person's environment.

The ADHD diagnosis has been a source of great controversy because many worry that this "diagnosis" is sometimes just a handy label for children who are particularly active or children who don't easily adjust to a school routine or a crowded classroom (Livingstone, 1997; Panksepp, 1998). Critics point out that the number of people diagnosed as having ADHD has dramatically increased over the past few decades. Even today, prevalence rates differ dramatically by country, as well as by region within the United States (LeFever, Arcona, & Antonuccio, 2003). The potential for overdiagnosis is troubling for many reasons, ranging from the stigma associated with receiving any diagnosis of a mental disorder to the fact that (especially in the United States) many children who are diagnosed with ADHD take stimulants for years (Diller, 1999), even though these drugs are known to have clear addictive potential.

Despite this controversy, most now agree that ADHD is a genuine mental disorder (Hinshaw, 2008; World Federation for Mental Health, 2005), and that genetic factors playing a large role in producing the symptoms (Burt, Krueger, McGue, & Iacono, 2001; Rutter, 2006; Tannock, 1998). One key biological feature of ADHD appears to be a deficiency in prefrontal brain circuits (Barkley, 1997). When these circuits are working normally, they protect us from distractions and momentary impulses; when these circuits are dysfunctional, the result is the pattern of scattered thoughts and actions that characterize ADHD.

Eating Disorders

Two different eating disorders are identified by the *DSM*. The first—*anorexia nervosa*—is defined by a refusal to maintain a minimally appropriate body weight. The second—*bulimia nervosa*—is defined by an alternating sequence of "binges" and "purges"—rapid food intake followed by maladaptive (and often extreme) attempts to keep from gaining weight.

ANOREXIA NERVOSA

Individuals with **anorexia nervosa** are preoccupied with food and eating and have an intense fear of gaining weight. This fear is nurtured by a disturbance in how these people perceive their own bodies—they genuinely believe themselves to be fat, despite the fact that in many cases they are extremely, even dangerously, thin (Figure 16.32). They spend enormous amounts of time measuring various parts of their bodies and critically examining themselves in the mirror. Any slight change in weight is momentous to them, with tiny decreases celebrated and minute gains lamented (Figure 16.33). It's not surprising, therefore, that individuals with anorexia nervosa relentlessly pursue thinness and usually achieve unhealthy reductions in body weight through a regimen of incredibly strict dieting. They may also exercise excessively or purge (self-induce vomiting or misuse laxatives or diuretics).

anorexia nervosa An eating disorder characterized by an extreme concern with being overweight and by compulsive dieting, sometimes to the point of self-starvation.

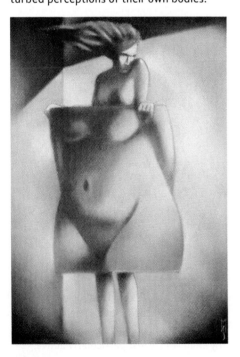

16.32 Eating disorders Women with anorexia nervosa often have severely disturbed perceptions of their own bodies.

The lifetime prevalence of anorexia nervosa among females is about 0.5%, and although men can also have anorexia nervosa, they are 10 times less likely than women to have this disorder. Still, the features associated with anorexia nervosa are similar for men and for women—including increased risk of depression and substance abuse. Anorexia nervosa can begin before puberty, but this is rare. Typically, it develops in adolescence, between the ages of 14 and 18. The prognosis varies considerably. In severe cases, anorexia nervosa can be life-threatening, as the extreme dieting can lead to dangerous fluid and electrolyte imbalances. Individuals with less extreme cases often recover fully, although some continue throughout their lives to show a fluctuating pattern of weight gain and loss.

Anorexia nervosa has a clear genetic component (Strober, Freeman, Lampert, Diamond, & Kaye, 2000), and a person is 10 times as likely to have anorexia nervosa if she has a close relative with the disorder than if she does not. Sociocultural factors also play a role. Anorexia nervosa is much more common in cultures that equate being thin with being attractive than in cultures that do not (Striegel-Moore et al., 2003).

BULIMIA NERVOSA

Like individuals with anorexia nervosa, individuals with **bulimia nervosa** are extremely concerned with their weight and appearance, and this concern fuels disordered eating behavior (Figure 16.34). Unlike those with anorexia nervosa, however, individuals with bulimia nervosa often have normal weight (Hsu, 1990). What marks this disorder is the combination of binge eating and compensatory behavior (Wilson & Pike, 2001). **Binge eating** refers to eating a large amount of food within a relatively brief time period (e.g., 2 hours), usually while feeling little or no control over what or how much one eats. **Compensatory behavior** refers to the actions taken to try to ensure that the binge eating does not translate into weight gain—including self-induced vomiting, misuse of laxatives or diuretics, or extreme levels of exercise.

Because people with bulimia nervosa feel shame about their binges, they often try to hide their behavior from others and may spend considerable time planning their secretive eating sessions. When they do binge, the targeted foods are typically high-calorie "junk" foods such as donuts, cake, or ice cream.

Many people binge at one point or another, and some occasionally purge. The *DSM* diagnosis for bulimia nervosa applies only if a person exhibits binge eating and inappropriate compensatory behaviors at least twice a week for at least 3 months. By this definition, the lifetime prevalence of bulimia nervosa among women is approximately 1 to 3% and—as with anorexia nervosa—it is approximately 10 times more common in women than in men. The onset of bulimia nervosa is usually late adolescence, and over the long term, the illness can lead to many health problems. For example, women whose compensatory behaviors include purging may develop fluid and electrolyte imbalances. The vomiting that is usually associated with bulimia nervosa leads to a significant erosion of dental enamel, giving teeth a worn and yellowed look.

16.33 Assessing body image Women with anorexia nervosa often believe that there is a large difference between their current body weight and their ideal body weight.

bulimia nervosa An eating disorder characterized by repeated binge-and-purge bouts.

binge eating Eating a large amount of food within a brief period.

compensatory behavior Actions taken to ensure that binge eating does not translate into weight gain (e.g., self-induced vomiting).

16.34 Bulimia Britain's Princess Diana suffered from bulimia, which involves binge eating and compensatory behavior.

Both genetic and sociocultural factors contribute to the onset and maintenance of bulimia nervosa. Women who have close relatives with bulimia nervosa are four times more likely to have this disorder than are women who do not (Strober et al., 2000). In addition, research suggests that bulimia nervosa may be confined to westernized cultural contexts (Keel & Klump, 2003); as cultures become more westernized, rates of bulimia nervosa increase (Nasser, 1997).

Dissociative Disorders

There is no question that many disorders—and, indeed, many life experiences—involve considerable pain or distress. To protect themselves against this discomfort, people engage in a variety of defensive strategies. One of these strategies, which we have mentioned in other contexts, is *dissociation*—a term that covers the various ways in which people try to distance themselves psychologically from ongoing events. They establish this distance by saying things like "This can't be happening" or "This is all a dream" or "This isn't happening to me." With these defenses in place, people may, during a calamity, even experience themselves as eerily calm, floating outside their own bodies as they watch themselves react.

These adjustments are often adaptive, a way of coping with horrific events. But such adjustments can go too far and, in their extreme form, are the defining feature of the dissociative disorders. In some cases, for example, a person develops **dissociative amnesia** and is suddenly unable to remember some period of his life, or even his entire past, including his own identity. Such episodes usually last less than 1 week (Kihlstrom & Schacter, 2000; Maldonado, Butler, & Spiegel, 2002). In other cases, the dissociation produces **dissociative fugue**, in which the person wanders away from home and then, days or even months later, suddenly realizes that she is in a strange place, does not know how she got there, and has total amnesia for the entire period.

Far more controversial is the diagnosis of **dissociative identity disorder** (**DID**), a condition formerly known as multiple personality disorder. Here the dissociation is said to be so massive that it results in two or more distinct personalities, each with its own style, habits, and beliefs. The personalities often differ in their interests, their age, their sexual orientation, and their morals.

In one case, a patient named Julie mentioned, during therapy, that she wanted to introduce someone to the therapist. She closed her eyes, frowned, and then opened her eyes slowly, asserting that she was Jerrie, not Julie. Roughly 1 hour later, in the same way, she introduced Jenny, a third personality in the same body. These three women were different in many ways: Julie and Jenny were heterosexuals; Jerrie was a lesbian. Jenny was frightened and insecure; Julie was a sophisticated and caring mother. Jerrie was accomplished and proficient in the business world and hated the fact that Julie was a heavy smoker (Davis & Osherson, 1977).

Until several decades ago, cases like this were rare, with fewer than 200 reported before 1975. Now cases number in the thousands; the large majority are women (Kluft, 1987; C. A. Ross, 1999). The number of personalities reported in each case has also increased dramatically: A review of the early cases indicated that most people with DID had only 2 or 3 separate identities (Taylor & Martin, 1944); a more recent survey indicates that the average number of identities reported by patients is 15, with some cases reporting far more than this (C. A. Ross, 1997).

These massive increases are one of the reasons this disorder has been a focus of so much debate, with some critics arguing that the flood of diagnoses may reflect a fad among therapists who inadvertently lead suggestible patients to develop the signs and

dissociative amnesia The inability of an individual to remember some period of her life, or even her entire past, including her identity; often understood as a way of coping with extremely painful events.

dissociative fugue A state in which someone leaves home, then, days or months later, suddenly realizes he is in a strange place and doesn't know how he got there; often understood as a means of coping with (and escaping from) extremely painful events.

dissociative identity disorder (DID) A disorder that results in a person developing two or more distinct personalities.

symptoms of the syndrome (Lalonde, Hudson, Gigante, & Pope, 2001; Lilienfeld et al., 1999; Spanos, 1996; for a very different view, see Lewis, Yeager, Swica, Pincus, & Lewis, 1997). Contributing to this trend, the critics claim, are the books and movies about DID, including *Sybil* and *The Three Faces of Eve* (Figure 16.35).

What should we make of this debate? It seems likely that at least some cases of DID are in fact faked or inadvertently created by therapists. But it also seems likely that many cases are genuine, and debate continues about the nature of this disorder, its causes, and the best way to treat it (Lilienfeld et al., 1999; C. A. Ross, 1999).

Stepping away from the controversy over DID, and returning to the broader category of dissociative disorders, we can ask: What factors or events lead to these disorders? Here, too, some investigators propose a genetic basis, but research has yielded mixed results (Jang, Paris, Zweig-Frank, & Livesley, 1998; Waller & Ross, 1997). One thing we do know is that people naturally seem to differ in how much, and under what circumstances, they dissociate. Some of the relevant evidence comes from a measure known as the Dissociative Experiences Scale, which asks people directly how often they have experienced various perceptions or behaviors characteristic of dissociation (Carlson & Putnam, 1993). Other evidence comes from work on hypnosis, which some investigators regard as a form of guided dissociation (Hilgard, 1986; for more on hypnosis, see Chapter 6). People differ enormously in how readily or how deeply they can be hypnotized (Ganaway, 1989), and this opens an interesting possibility: Perhaps some people were, as children, particularly adept at self-hypnosis and learned to use this skill as a defense—putting themselves into a self-induced hypnotic trance to escape from the stresses (or perhaps traumas) in their lives (Bliss, 1980). This skill may then create a readiness to dissociate in everyday life, perhaps predisposing these individuals to develop a dissociative disorder.

Thus, a skill in (or habit of) dissociation may create the diathesis for a dissociative disorder. To precipitate the full-fledged disorder, however, there also has to be some unusual stress, and, in fact, most cases of dissociative amnesia occur after the same kinds of cataclysmic events that lead to post-traumatic stress disorder. The same holds for dissociative fugues, which can also develop suddenly after personal misfortunes or financial pressures (Andreasen & Black, 1996). The same may be true as well for dissociative identity disorder: In a large percentage of DID case histories, there are terrifying stories of brutal physical or sexual abuse in childhood, often including incest (Putnam, Guroff, Silberman, Barban, & Post, 1986). However, these reports—like the diagnosis of DID itself—have been controversial, inasmuch as they often rely on the person's *recall* of the abuse, and, as we discussed in Chapter 8, there has been debate over how to interpret this recall.

16.35 Dissociative identity disorder According to some critics, the huge increase in DID diagnoses is the result of a diagnostic fad among therapists, or perhaps a result of people imitating famous cases of DID—including the case depicted in the 1958 movie *The Three Faces of Eve*.

Personality Disorders

All of the disorders we have considered so far are included on Axis I of the *DSM*. Each involves a specific syndrome with a well-defined set of signs and symptoms. *DSM*'s Axis II diagnoses, in contrast, are characterized by much broader patterns of behaviors and problems that are much more consistent across the lifespan (Clark, 2009). These diagnoses are concerned with traits or habits that characterize almost everything a person does, and so are disorders, in essence, in someone's personality.

Of course, people differ widely in their personalities (see Chapter 15), and, because of these variations, some people are easier to be with than others, and some have a smoother path through life than others. In some cases, though, a person's personality is so maladaptive that it creates considerable distress both for that person and for those around her and impairs the person's day-to-day functioning. Someone with these difficulties may well be diagnosed as having one or another of the **personality disorders**.

personality disorders Relatively stable, pervasive patterns of behavior and inner experience that are culturally discrepant and lead to distress or impairment; noted on Axis II of the DSM.

The *DSM* recognizes 10 personality disorders. These are *paranoid personality disorder* (in which a person shows widespread suspiciousness and mistrust of others); *schizoid personality disorder* (in which a person shows a striking detachment from others); *schizotypal personality disorder* (in which a person shows a discomfort with close relationships, cognitive or perceptual distortions, and odd behavior); *antisocial personality disorder* (in which a person shows consistent disregard for—and violation of—others' rights); *borderline personality disorder* (in which a person shows impulsive behavior and marked instability in relationships, self-concept, and affect); *histrionic personality disorder* (in which a person shows an unusual degree of attention seeking and emotionality); *narcissistic personality disorder* (in which a person is grandiose, lacks empathy, and needs the attention and admiration of others); *avoidant personality disorder* (in which a person shows social inhibition and social insecurity); *dependent personality disorder* (in which a person shows an excessive need to be taken care of by others); and *obsessive-compulsive personality disorder* (in which a person is preoccupied with orderliness, perfection, and control). Each of these disorders, and indeed all of the Axis II personality disorders, are difficult to diagnose, and disagreements about diagnosis are common (L. A. Clark & Harrison, 2001; Livesley, 2001).

Part of the difficulty is that the definitions of these disorders tell us what a clear-cut and "pure" case of the disorder might look like. In reality, though, an individual's traits are likely only to approximate this prototype, and many people have traits that leave them resembling more than one of the prototypes (Shea, 1995). This obviously makes diagnosis complicated. In addition, each of these disorders can be thought of as merely the extreme of some ordinary pattern (Livesley, 2001; Widiger & Sanderson, 1995). Many people, for example, are vain, and it is therefore a judgment call whether someone's vanity is so powerful that it signals a narcissistic personality disorder. Likewise, many people are shy, and it is sometimes difficult to decide whether someone's shyness is consistent with avoidant personality disorder. Clinicians often disagree in these judgments, increasing the uncertainty of the Axis II diagnoses.

These diagnostic problems have in turn been difficult for researchers, because it is obviously hard to study a group that cannot be accurately identified (Clark, 2007). Despite this limitation, investigators have made impressive progress in understanding several of the personality disorders. For example, the diagnosis of antisocial personality disorder (and the closely related diagnosis of psychopathy) is a powerful predictor of whether someone will slide into crime again after a period of imprisonment (Hare, Cooke, & Hart, 1999; Hemphill, Hare, & Wong, 1998) and so can be an important source of information in making parole decisions about a prisoner. Similarly, the diagnosis of borderline personality disorder predicts compromised social cognition, as evidenced in neuroimaging findings that show that people with borderline personality disorder fail to discriminate between situations in which another person signaled that they *trusted* the diagnosed individual and situations in which the other person signaled *no trust* (King-Casas, Sharp, Lomax-Bream, Lohrenz, Fonagy, & Montague, 2008; Meyer-Lindenberg, 2008).

SOME FINAL THOUGHTS: SYNDROMES WITHOUT STIGMA?

Throughout this chapter, we have described the diagnostic criteria for each mental illness—and, in particular, the diagnostic criteria identified by the *DSM*. These criteria have allowed clinicians to achieve impressive reliability and validity in their diagnoses, and, as we have mentioned, this has been a boon for both therapists and researchers.

At the same time, we should acknowledge that the boundaries associated with many diagnoses—the lines that separate "mentally ill" from "not ill"—are actually quite porous. Thus, someone who "has" a disorder may differ by only a single symptom from someone who "does not have" a disorder, and the mental disorders themselves often appear to be related as points on a continuum rather than as discrete and distinct categories (Krueger & Markon, 2006; Widiger & Trull, 2007).

The "fuzziness" in these diagnostic categories is not often a problem, because with many patients, the diagnosis is clear-cut. In these cases, there is no question that the person is experiencing both considerable disruption in his life and significant emotional distress—whether it is the paralyzing fears associated with the phobias, the sadness of depression, or the emotional flattening common in schizophrenia. In situations like these, it seems fully appropriate to offer a diagnosis and to seek treatment for the afflicted person, trying to bring him back to a normal life.

But what about people who have a *subsyndromal case* of a disorder—people who do show symptoms, but not at the level that would justify a formal diagnosis? This would include people who worry about whether they really did turn off the gas and so check and recheck the stove so often that it becomes an inconvenience—but not often enough to justify a diagnosis of OCD. It would also include people who are sad and not sleeping well but not quite at the level of severity or for the duration required for a diagnosis of depression. Should these people be diagnosed and treated?

If we do not offer a formal diagnosis for these cases, we risk ignoring people who do need help, even if their condition does not quite reach the level specified by our diagnostic manual. But if we diagnose them, we risk creating a situation in which more and more people with less and less extreme symptoms are defined as having mental disorders. In the end, the term *mental disorder* might be stretched so far that it loses meaning and is applied to virtually any form of human behavior that causes social harm or personal unhappiness. We need to broaden our diagnostic categories enough to include everyone who could benefit from help, without expanding them so far that they lose meaning. Where this balance point lies is a matter of debate. The one certainty is that our categories will continue to change as our knowledge grows.

One other issue that deserves attention is what attitude we should take toward mental disorders. Historically, mental disorders have been a source of severe stigma, both for the person with the disorder and for the person's family (Hinshaw, 2007). Today, the stigma associated with mental disorders may be easing. It's now been a decade since U.S. president Bill Clinton held the first White House conference on mental health and the surgeon general of the United States wrote the first report on mental disorders, in which he described stigma as the greatest obstacle to progress. Official attention to mental disorders continued with the President's New Freedom Commission on Mental Health (2003), and many celebrities have now come forth to describe their experiences with mental disorders, including depression (Mike Wallace, Sheryl Crow), anxiety (Kim Basinger, John Madden), bipolar disorder (Jane Pauley), and ADHD (Michael Phelps) (Figure 16.36).

At the same time, the stigma of having a mental disorder persists, delaying people from seeking treatment and multiplying the distress associated with these disorders. These issues are all the more troubling in light of the enormous number of people they affect: Statistics indicate that nearly half of us will develop a mental disorder in our lifetimes, and this means that virtually every one of us

16.36 Celebrities with mental disorders In recent years, many celebrities have courageously shared their struggles with mental disorders including Kim Basinger and Michael Phelps.

either has been or will be touched—at least indirectly—by mental disorder. In this chapter, we have avoided reducing people to their disorders, and we have provided many case vignettes both to humanize the face of mental disorders and to bring closer the time when all of us will respond with informed compassion to those with mental disorders.

CONCEPTIONS OF MENTAL DISORDERS

- Early views of mental disorders held to the *somatogenic hypothesis*, which perceives the disorders as the result of a specific injury or infection. Sigmund Freud, in contrast, argued for the *psychogenic hypothesis*, which considers mental disorders to be rooted in psychological processes.

- Modern theorists describe mental disorders using a *diathesis-stress model*, with the *diathesis* creating the predisposition toward mental disorder, and the *stress* providing a trigger that turns the risk into the actual disorder. However, the fact that multiple factors often give rise to both diathesis and stress has led theorists to propose a *multicausal model* guided by a *biopsychosocial viewpoint*.

DEFINING, ASSESSING, AND DIAGNOSING MENTAL DISORDERS

- A *diagnosis* is generally made with reference to the categories identified in the *Diagnostic and Statistical Manual for Mental Disorders (DSM)*. The *prevalence* of a disorder refers to how widespread it is. The Axis I classifications in the *DSM* include the more familiar categories of mental disorders; Axis II classifications describe various personality disorders.

- *Assessment* of any individual may include a *semi-structured interview*, which is one way in which a clinician evaluates the patient's *symptoms* and *signs*. The assessment may also include *self-report measures* (such as the Beck Depression Inventory) or *projective measures* (such as the Thematic Apperception Test).

- Diagnostic labels have evolved over time and psychiatric labeling has both costs and benefits.

ANXIETY DISORDERS

- *Anxiety disorders* are the most common mental disorder. The *phobias* are characterized by intense and irrational fear, as well as efforts to avoid the feared object or situation. *Panic disorder* is characterized by the occurrence of *panic attacks*. *Generalized anxiety disorder* is characterized by continuous and all-pervasive feelings of anxiety. *Obsessive-compulsive disorder* involves both *obsessions* (disturbing thoughts) and *compulsions* (ritualistic behaviors). The *stress disorders* result from identifiable and horrific events such as rape or military combat.

- A number of different genes are thought to contribute to the anxiety disorders, and neuroimaging studies reveal that different anxiety disorders have quite different biological bases. Conditioning accounts of the anxiety disorders emphasize the role played by learning.

MOOD DISORDERS

- *Mood disorders*—also known as *affective disorders*—involve disturbances of positive and negative mood. In *major depression*, patients suffer periods of sadness, apathy, and lack of energy. In *bipolar disorder*, patients endure manic episodes and episodes of deep depression. Both disorders are associated with a considerable suicide risk.

- Mood disorders have important hereditary components. A disruption of neurotransmission is also implicated, with norepinephrine, dopamine, and serotonin systems involved.

- Life crises often trigger depression, although the crises by themselves do not cause the disorder. According to Aaron Beck, depression is more likely to occur if a person interprets life events through a *negative cognitive schema* rather than a positive one. A related account focuses on *explanatory style*, or how people explain what happens to them. Individuals who explain bad things that happen to them as the result of internal, global, and stable factors are at elevated risk of depression.

SCHIZOPHRENIA

- Someone suffering from *schizophrenia* is likely to suffer from *positive symptoms* (e.g., delusions, hallucinations, disorganized behavior), *negative symptoms* (e.g., an absence of emotional expression), and *cognitive symptoms* (e.g., impairments in working memory and attentional control).

- Evidence suggests that genetic predisposition, a period of diminished oxygen supply to the newborn, and a variety of prenatal viral infections contribute to schizophrenia. These factors suggest that schizophrenia is a *neurodevelopmental disorder*, and, consistent with this view, precursors of schizophrenia may be detected in early childhood.

- Schizophrenia involves problems with neurotransmission, with evidence coming from the efficacy of the *classical antipsychotics*. There is debate about whether the problem lies in dopamine systems, glutamate systems, or both. People with schizophrenia also have defects in the structure of many areas of the brain.

- Stress also contributes to schizophrenia, and this factor is one reason schizophrenia is especially prevalent among people with a low socioeconomic status.

OTHER AXIS I AND AXIS II DISORDERS

- *Developmental disorders* include *autism* and *attention-deficit/hyperactivity disorder*. Children with *autism* show a range of symptoms, including little interest in other people, marked defects in language, and peculiar movement patterns; they are often mentally retarded. Children with *attention-deficit/hyperactivity disorder* are impulsive, fidget constantly, and have difficulty keeping their attention focused

- *Eating disorders* include *anorexia nervosa* and *bulimia nervosa*. Individuals with anorexia nervosa are preoccupied with food and eating, have an intense fear of gaining weight, and are often severely underweight. Individuals with bulimia nervosa are also very concerned with their weight and appearance, but typically have normal weight, and engage in *binge eating* followed by *compensatory behaviors* that include vomiting, laxative use, or extreme levels of exercise.

- *Dissociative disorders* involve extreme responses to horrific events. In *dissociative amnesia*, the person is unable to remember some period of her life; in *dissociative fugue*, the person wanders away from home, loses track of who he is, and then, months later, realizes that he is in a strange place and does not know how he got there. The diagnosis of *dissociative identity disorder*—in which a person develops more than one personality—remains highly controversial.

- *Personality disorders* involve traits or habits that characterize almost everything a person does. These disorders are difficult to diagnose, in part because the diagnostic manual describes "pure" cases and in part because the same behavior patterns often emerge in less extreme, less disruptive forms in ordinary personalities.

Ⓢ ONLINE STUDY TOOLS

Go to StudySpace, **wwnorton.com/studyspace**, to access additional review and enrichment materials, including the following resources for each chapter:

Organize
- Study Plan
- Chapter Outline
- Quiz+ Assessment

Learn
- Ebook
- Chapter Review
- Vocabulary Flashcards
- Drag-and-Drop Labeling Exercises
- Audio Podcast Chapter Overview

Connect
- Critical Thinking Activity
- Studying the Mind Video Podcasts
- Video Exercises
- Animations
- **ZAPS** Psychology Labs

17

Treatment of Mental Disorders

We figured out it wasn't depression after I had been taking Prozac for about three months," recalls Chris Clark, a restaurant owner living in Memphis, Tennessee. Clark was a junior in college when he was diagnosed with depression and prescribed the antidepressant Prozac. "I had spent a semester locked in my dorm room, thinking about killing myself and feeling horribly guilty about it." But after taking the Prozac: "Next thing I know, I'm in Mexico, trying to open a chain of drive-thru gourmet French restaurants with some woman I met at a club in New Orleans.

"It seemed like a great idea at the time," Clark muses, "despite the fact that turning gourmet French cuisine into fast food is pretty much impossible." After he charged about $20,000 worth of restaurant equipment to his father's credit card, Clark reports, "my dad flew down, scooped me up, and deposited me directly in the psych ward." There, the doctors changed his diagnosis to bipolar disorder—the mood disorder that makes people cycle between depression, mania, and normalcy—and prescribed lithium, a mood stabilizer.

Unlike antidepressants, which can trigger a manic episode in people with bipolar disorder, mood stabilizers regulate both the highs and the lows of the condition. "But man, I hated that lithium," Clark recalls. "I felt totally out of it." Nevertheless, he took lithium through college, eventually graduating with honors.

Once on his own, though, Clark stopped taking his meds and within a year his mood plummeted. He reached out to a psychologist but did not disclose his diagnosis of bipolar disorder. "I think I was in denial." he says. "Somehow, depression was more acceptable to me than bipolar." He also refused to take medications, opting instead to try just talk therapy and exercise.

Two marathons and one year of therapy later, Clark was feeling good—and then too good. He stopped seeing his therapist, explaining that he was "cured." He took over a friend's struggling restaurant and, suddenly needing only three hours of sleep per night, threw all his energy into rescuing the business. Just as the restaurant began to rebound, though, Clark took off for a month of partying in Greece.

When he followed the trip by splurging on a vintage Camaro, Clark's friends confronted him about his irresponsibility, but he didn't listen. The restaurant foundered. His girlfriend left him. He overdrew his bank account. Then came the crash. "One morning, I just couldn't get out of bed. After sleeping for 30 hours, and then hating myself for another 10, I had to confront the truth: I have bipolar disorder, and I have to treat it, all the time, with everything I've got."

Clark enlisted the help of a psychiatrist, who prescribed Lamictal, a medication that for many people has fewer side effects than lithium. He returned to his therapist, who helped him with his feelings of hopelessness. Through the Depression and Bipolar Support Alliance he met people who understood his problems. And he supplemented his running with adequate sleep, good nutrition, and meditation to reduce stress.

Although Clark has since opened a successful restaurant, he says, "My main job will always be managing my mind." The same is true for millions who struggle with psychological disorders. As this chapter shows, people now have more and better options for doing this job than ever before. Just as Clark relies on medication, talk therapy, social support, and a healthy lifestyle to manage his bipolar disorder, so do many people combine treatments to suit their individual needs. The mind, after all, is a biological, psychological, and social achievement, so mental health requires biological, psychological, and social balance.

The previous chapter described a number of mental disorders that can cause extreme suffering and disrupt people's lives, making it hard to hold a job, sustain a relationship, or, in some cases, manage the basics of day-to-day life. Because many factors give rise to these disorders, the different approaches to treatment each have a distinct focus. Practitioners who rely on psychological approaches employ various kinds of psychotherapy. Others favor biomedical interventions such as medications. Still others use an amalgam of psychological and biomedical treatments. Do these treatments help? Are some better than others? This chapter will examine the options for treatment and look at the evidence that the right treatments often can genuinely improve the lives of people with mental disorders.

TREATMENTS PAST AND PRESENT

Mental disorders have been with us since the dawn of recorded history. So too have efforts to alleviate the suffering—as well as the problematic behaviors—associated with these disorders. Early treatments stemmed from the view that mental disorders were caused by evil spirits, and these treatments were often harsh and rarely effective. As our understanding of mental disorders grew, other (often more humane) treatments developed. In this chapter, we will examine two major types of treatments—

psychological and biomedical—and assess whether these treatments work as intended. Before doing so, we first set the stage by considering historical trends as well as contemporary practices.

Early Treatments for Mental Disorders

The early idea that mental disorders were caused by evil spirits suggested a number of strategies for treatment. In some cases, large holes were cut in a person's skull, so that the demons could be driven out through this "exit." Other treatments sought to calm the demons with music, to chase them away with prayers, or to purge them with potions that induced vomiting. Another approach was to make the evil spirits so uncomfortable in the patient's body that they would be induced to flee. Accordingly, patients were starved, flogged, or immersed in boiling water. Not surprisingly, these treatments did not work and often made patients worse.

As we saw in Chapter 16, recent centuries have seen the rise of a very different conception of mental illness, one that treats mental disorders as physical diseases like any other. Unfortunately, this conception has not always lead to more humane treatment of the afflicted. In the Middle Ages, diseased "madmen" were given little sympathy, and the interests of society were deemed best served by "putting them away." Beginning in the 16th century, a number of special hospitals for the insane were established throughout Europe (Figure 17.1). But most of these institutions were hospitals in name only. Their real function was to confine all kinds of social "undesirables" and isolate them from the rest of humanity. Criminals, beggars, epileptics, and "incurables" of all sorts were institutionalized and treated along with the mentally disturbed. And the treatments were barbaric. One author described conditions in the major mental hospital for Parisian women at the end of the 1700s: "Madwomen seized by fits of violence are chained like dogs at their cell doors, and separated from keepers and visitors alike by a long corridor protected by an iron grille; through this grille is passed their food and the straw on which they sleep; by means of rakes, part of the filth that surrounds them is cleaned out" (Foucault, 1965, p. 72).

Gradually, reformers succeeded in eliminating the worst of these practices. The French physician Philippe Pinel (1745–1826), for example, was put in charge of the Parisian hospital system in 1793, at the height of the French Revolution. Pinel wanted to remove the inmates' shackles and chains and give them exercise and fresh air; the government permitted these changes—although only grudgingly. A half century later, in the United States, a retired schoolteacher named Dorothea Dix became a passionate

17.1 **Early mental institutions** The tarot card (left) shows a 16th-century depiction of a madhouse. The painting (right) shows London's Bethlehem Hospital (known as Bedlam, as it sounds when pronounced with a Cockney accent), where patients were exhibited as though they were zoo animals to anyone curious enough to pay the required penny per visit. In 1814, there were 96,000 such visits. (William Hogarth, *The Rake's Progress: The Rake in Bedlam* [1735])

advocate for appropriate treatment for the mentally ill. In her report to the Massachusetts legislature in 1843, Dix said: "I come as the advocate of helpless, forgotten, insane, and idiotic men and women; of beings, sunk to a condition from which the most unconcerned would start with a real horror. . . . I proceed, Gentlemen, briefly to call your attention to the *present* state of Insane Persons confined within this Commonwealth, in *cages, closets, cellars, stalls, pens! Chained, naked, beaten with rods,* and *lashed* into obedience" (Shannonhouse, 2000, pp. 8–11). Dix's report is, of course, a powerful indictment of the treatment of the mentally ill in 19th-century America, and fortunately the indictment had an effect. Dix's tireless work on behalf of the mentally ill was an important impetus to the dramatic growth of state-supported institutions for mental care during the latter part of the 19th century.

Amid calls for reform, other developments in the 19th century profoundly shaped how people thought about, and tried to treat, mental illness. One triumph was the treatment of paresis (see Chapter 16). This was important for its own sake, but it can also be understood as the leading edge of a much larger trend, and, across the next decades, it became more and more common to take a medical perspective on mental illness—in many cases, this meant treatment via medications of one sort or another. Another major development, also at the end of the 19th century, was the advent of Freud's "talking cure." This treatment proved to be the first in a long line of psychological therapies, which collectively drew attention to the environmental and social dimensions of mental illness and provided many powerful tools for treating mental disorders.

Current Treatments for Mental Disorders

As we saw in Chapter 16, mental disorders typically involve many factors, some biological and some rooted in a person's circumstances. Different treatments target different aspects of this network of interrelated causes. Psychological treatments aim to alter psychological and environmental processes via "talk therapy." Biomedical treatments seek to alter underlying biological processes directly, often through medication or neurosurgery.

For convenience, we will use this distinction between psychological and biomedical treatments in this chapter. However, this shorthand does risk introducing some confusion. If we focus narrowly on the overt steps in treatment, we can distinguish psychological approaches (talking to a patient, perhaps leading her to new insights or new beliefs) from biomedical approaches (perhaps prescribing a pill for the patient to take twice a day). However, if we broaden our focus, the distinction between the psychological and the biological becomes less clear-cut. After all, psychological processes are the products of functioning brains—and so changes in people's psychology necessarily involve changes in their brain. Hence psychological treatments have biological effects. Conversely, biomedical treatments may in many cases work by altering a person's thought processes or shifting a person's mood; for this reason, the biological treatments often need to be understood in "psychological" terms. In either direction, therefore, a distinction between "psychological" and "biological" treatments is somewhat artificial (Kumari, 2006). In addition, as we will see, contemporary treatments often combine talk therapy with medication, further blurring the line between psychological and biological treatment.

That said, it is still useful to distinguish between treatments that emphasize psychological approaches and those that emphasize biological approaches, and this leads us to ask: How does a practitioner decide which emphasis is best in a given case? The answer depends on the illness and our understanding of its causes. If the illness seems shaped primarily by environmental causes (such as a hostile family environment) or by the person's perceptions and beliefs, then a psychological intervention may be best—

helping the person to find ways to cope with (or change) the environment, or persuading the person to adopt new beliefs. If the illness seems shaped primarily by some biological dysfunction (perhaps an overreactive stress response, for example, or a shortage of some neurotransmitter), then a biomedical intervention may be preferable.

However, these points are at best rough rules of thumb. In many cases, there may be no direct correspondence between what triggers a disorder (a specific biological dysfunction or some life problem) and the nature of the treatment. Some problems arising from a difficult situation are best treated medically; some problems arising from a biological dysfunction are best treated with psychotherapy. In choosing a form of therapy, practitioners must focus on what works, rather than focusing exclusively on how the disorder arose.

TREATMENT PROVIDERS

We will have a great deal to say in this chapter about these two broad emphases in treatment—the psychological and the biological—and the specific ways that treatment unfolds. Before we turn to these details, let's consider the providers and recipients of these treatments.

An extraordinarily wide range of professionals and non-professionals provide treatments for mental disorders. Individuals licensed to provide psychological treatments include clinical psychologists; psychiatrists; psychiatric nurses; marriage, family, and child counselors; school and vocational counselors; mental health counselors; and clinical social workers. Psychological interventions are also administered by individuals with varying degrees of psychological training including pastoral counselors, religious leaders, and paraprofessionals. A description of each of these treatment providers is given in Table 17.1.

TABLE 17.1	Treatment Providers		
	Occupation	Duties	Setting
	Clinical psychologist	Assessment and psychological treatment	Private practice, medical centers, agencies, clinics, schools
	Psychiatrist	Assessment and psychological and biological treatment	Private practice, medical centers, clinics
	Neurologist	Assessment and treatment, with a focus on the brain and nerves	Private practice, medical centers, clinics
	Psychiatric nurse	Assessment and psychological and biological treatment	Medical centers, clinics
	Marriage, family, and child Counselor	Psychological treatment, with a focus on couples, families, and children	Private practice, clinics
	School and vocational counselor	Assessment and counseling, with a focus on vocation and adjustment	Schools
	Mental health counselor	Assessment and counseling	Private practice, medical centers, agencies, clinics
	Clinical social worker	Psychological treatment and assistance with housing, health care, and treatment	Private practice, medical centers, agencies, clinics
	Pastoral counselor	Counseling and support, with a focus on spiritual well-being	Religious institutions, medical centers

Surprisingly, more experienced providers are not always more effective than less experienced providers (McFall, 2006), and even professional credentials are not necessarily a good predictor of therapeutic success (Blatt, Sanislow, Zuroff, & Pilkonis, 1996). These findings suggest that who the therapist is, what he or she does, and how well this matches the patient's needs may be far more important than the therapist's level of experience or the degrees he has earned. Also crucial is the quality of the *rapport* the therapist establishes with the patient—whether the patient respects and trusts the therapist and feels comfortable in the therapeutic setting. This rapport, too, is often more important than the therapist's credentials or type and degree of training.

Psychological treatments can be administered either with or without a license (with the license usually given by the state in which the therapist is practicing). In clear contrast, the administration of biomedical treatments does require a license. Here too, however, there are many different providers, including psychiatrists, neurologists, and psychiatric nurses. In fact, this list has been growing, with some jurisdictions now permitting "prescription privileges" for clinical psychologists—that is, allowing people with Ph.D.s to write prescriptions, a privilege that used to be reserved for people with medical degrees.

TREATMENT RECIPIENTS

subsyndromal disorder An instance of a mental disorder in which someone does show symptoms, but not at a level of intensity, frequency, or duration that would justify a formal diagnosis.

People seek treatment for a wide variety of reasons. Some seek relief from the pain and dysfunction associated with a diagnosable mental disorder. Others suffer with **subsyndromal disorders**—versions of mental disorders that don't meet the criteria for diagnosis but that may nonetheless cause significant problems (Ratey & Johnson, 1997). Others have neither a full-fledged nor a sybsyndromal disorder but instead seek help with feelings of loss, grief, or anxiety, with relationship difficulties, or with confusion about a major life decision. Still others seek therapy in order to live happier and more fulfilled lives.

Just as important is a listing of people who might benefit from therapy but don't seek it. Surveys reveal that in the United States, only about 40% of those with clinically significant disorders (such as depression, anxiety, or substance use disorders) had received treatment in the past year (Wang, Bergulund, et al., 2005). Women are more likely than men to seek treatment (Addis & Mahalik, 2003; Wang, Berglund, et al., 2005), and European Americans are more likely to seek treatment than Asian Americans and Hispanic Americans (Sue & Lam, 2002; Wang, Berglund, et al., 2005).

There is yet another (and very large) group of people who might benefit from therapy but cannot get it. According to the World Health Organization, roughly 450 million people worldwide suffer from various mental disorders, and the clear majority live in developing countries—90% of these people have no access to treatment (Miller, 2006b). Access is also an issue in developed countries. Many forms of mental illness are more common among the poor, but the poor are less likely to have insurance coverage that will make the treatment possible (Wang, Lane, et al., 2005).

CULTURAL CONSIDERATIONS

Some of the problems just described could—in theory—easily be solved. We could train more therapists and open more clinics so that treatment would be available to more people. We could improve insurance coverage or arrange for alternative forms of financing. These steps, however, would not be sufficient, because there is still another factor that limits the number of people who can benefit from therapy: the limited availability of *culturally appropriate therapy* and *culturally competent* therapists.

A therapist shows **cultural competence** by understanding how a patient's beliefs, values, and expectations for therapy are shaped by his cultural background (Sue, 1998). A therapist with this understanding can modify the goals of therapy to conform to the patient's values (Hwang, 2006). For example, many Asian cultures emphasize formality in all their affairs. Social roles within these cultures are often clearly defined and tend to be structured largely by age and sex, such that a father's authority is rarely challenged within the family. Growing up in such a culture may play an important part in shaping the values a patient brings to therapy. A therapist insensitive to these values risks offending the patient and endangering the therapy. Similarly, a therapy that emphasizes individual autonomy over family loyalties might inadvertently violate the patient's cultural traditions and so be counterproductive.

Cultural sensitivity also includes other issues. For example, therapists who expect their patients to take responsibility for making changes in their lives may be ineffective with patients whose cultural worldview stipulates that important events are caused by factors such as fate, chance, or powerful others. Likewise, practitioners who consider psychotherapy a secular endeavor would do well to remember that in many cultures, any kind of healing must acknowledge the patient's spirituality.

Attention to such cultural differences may also be valuable for another reason: it's possible that the Western world can learn something about the treatment of mental disorders from the cultures in developing countries. For example, the long-term prognosis for schizophrenia is considerably better in developing countries than it is in the United States (Thara, 2004). Patients with schizophrenia in India, as one illustration, show far more remission of symptoms and fewer relapses than patients with schizophrenia in the United States and often recover enough to hold a full-time job, marry, and otherwise lead reasonably normal lives.

Why is this? Some suggest that physicians in the United States rely too much on medication in treating schizophrenia and too little on interventions that emphasize job training and a supportive social network. The opposite is the case in India, where medication is often not available and institutionalization is usually not an option. Indeed, it is estimated that roughly 99% of individuals with schizophrenia live with their families in India, compared with 15 to 25% in the United States (Thara, 2004). Of course, the style of treatment in the United States is encouraged by many factors, including families that may want to distance themselves from the patient and insurance companies that will reimburse patients for psychotropic drugs but hesitate to pay for social programs.

It seems, then, that cultural competence needs to be broadly understood. It includes the need for Western-style practitioners to be alert to the cultural background (and so to the assumptions, beliefs, and values) of their patients. But it also includes an openness to the possibility that the style of treating mental illness in other cultures may, for some disorders, be preferable to the methods used in the developed countries. We need to keep these points in mind as we turn to a consideration of what the various forms of treatment involve.

PSYCHOLOGICAL TREATMENTS

Psychological treatments involve systematic efforts to change a patient's thinking and behavior, usually by means of some form of discussion, instruction, or training. In the minds of many people, psychotherapy involves a patient lying on a couch, talking about his distant childhood, and a therapist quietly drawing conclusions about unconscious

cultural competence An understanding of how a patient's cultural background shapes his beliefs, values, and expectations for therapy.

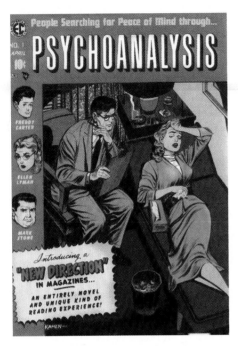

17.2 Psychologist as comic book hero? Popular portrayals of psychotherapy have a long history in the media; this comic book series appeared in 1955.

psychodynamic approaches Approaches to therapy that are derived from psychoanalytic theory, which asserts that clinical symptoms arise from unconscious conflicts rooted in childhood.

transference A patient's tendency to respond to the analyst or therapist in ways that re-create her responses to major figures in her life.

fears or desires (Figure 17.2). This image fails to do justice to the fact that psychotherapy comes in over 500 forms (Eisner, 2000). Indeed, the form of therapy implied by this common image is actually quite rare.

Some forms of psychotherapy are based on psychoanalysis; these are the closest to the popular image of therapy, emphasizing unconscious conflicts and encouraging introspection and insight. Other modes of therapy grow out of the humanistic tradition and focus on questions of growth and realizing one's potential. Still others rely on behavioral findings from human and nonhuman experimentation; these seek to identify maladaptive responses and then teach new responses. Others take a cognitive approach, focusing on the disabling role of faulty thinking while teaching more rational thought. In what follows, we will discuss some of the more common modes of psychotherapy that have grown out of each of these various approaches.

Psychodynamic Approaches

Psychodynamic approaches to therapy have their origins in the psychoanalytic method that Sigmund Freud developed at the beginning of the twentieth century. Freud's basic assumption was that a patient's ills (in Freud's terms, her neuroses) stemmed from unconscious conflicts that developed early in childhood (see Chapter 15). By adulthood, the patient had developed a range of defenses to deal with these conflicts, but these defenses also shielded her from seeing clearly both the outer world and her own inner world. This led to a range of problems that manifested as psychological symptoms.

Freud believed that for a patient to overcome her neuroses, she must gain insight into her own buried thoughts and wishes. Importantly, though, this insight cannot be just an intellectual matter. Freud argued that the person must "work through" the conflict, in order to gain control over her passions and not just intellectualize them. If this working through is successful, the person will integrate her thoughts and memories in a coherent way, and will at last overcome the maladaptive patterns that grew out of the unresolved conflicts.

What does it mean to "work through" a conflict? For Freud, the process involved many elements, but one crucial aspect is **transference**, the patient's tendency to respond to the analyst in ways that re-create her responses to the major figures in her own life. Thus, the patient ends up loving or hating the analyst just as she loved or hated her mother, father, siblings, and, more recently, her lovers or friends. All of these feelings are "transferred" to the analyst, as a kind of repetition of the unresolved problems of the patient's childhood.

Freud argued that the transference-charged relationship with the analyst could be a powerful therapeutic tool. It lets the analyst hold up a mirror to the patient to show her how she really feels and acts toward the important people in her life. For example, take a person who expresses violent anger toward his psychoanalyst and then is immediately anxious. How would his analyst interpret this? Perhaps the patient is reacting to the analyst much as he would respond to his tyrannical father, and having acted with disrespect, is now expecting some horrible retribution. Needless to say, the analyst will not act like Daddy, but instead might say something mildly reassuring, such as "That was hard to get out, wasn't it?" The analyst might then point out how the patient's traumatic memories of Daddy (and, more generally, the pattern of the patient's past relationships) are distorting his current relationships.

Through many such experiences, the patient's symptoms lessen. By maintaining her neutrality, the analyst allows herself temporarily to stand in for the significant characters in the patient's early family drama but does not let herself be drawn into the play.

She lets the patient say the same old lines and go through the same old motions, but she does not respond to them as the cast of characters from the patient's childhood did. Her job is to let the patient see what she is really doing and to help the patient see that old patterns need not be repeated. The result of all this emotional reeducation is the creation of a new life script with better lines and more acceptable outcomes.

Many present-day psychotherapists use techniques that bear Freud's imprint, but they have modified the treatment in various ways. Most have stepped away from the intensity of Freud's regimen (he insisted on at least three sessions per week) and abandoned the familiar icon of Freud's practice—the analyst's couch (which, in Freud's office, allowed the patient to relax while Freud sat in a position out of the patient's sight; Figure 17.3). These more modern practitioners endorse many of Freud's claims, they tend to emphasize current interpersonal and cultural factors rather than the psychological traumas of early childhood. If they discuss early development with their patients, it is strictly to identify how the patterns of interaction established in childhood influence current choices. In these more modern therapies, conscious thoughts receive as much scrutiny as unconscious conflicts, and therapist and patient work together to help the patient develop a coherent and complete sense of self, and to find ways of relating to others that are undistorted by past conflicts or maladaptive defense mechanisms.

In Chapter 15, we discussed the fact that many of the neo-Freudian traditions emphasize an individual's social relationships. These more modern approaches have led to several forms of therapy, including **interpersonal therapy (IPT)**, a brief (12- to 16-session) treatment that builds on the claim that mental disorders are often created by a social isolation that cuts a person off from the emotional sustenance provided by healthy relationships (Klerman & Weissman, 1993; Weissman & Markowitz, 1994).

IPT is often used as a treatment for depression, and so a course of IPT might start with an assessment of what factors changed in the person's life at the time the depression began. For example, one class of factors involves interpersonal role transitions, such as graduation from college, beginning a love affair, or getting married. The therapist can help a person having trouble with these transitions learn to act the new part and fill the expectations of the other people involved in the new social setting. (Thus, for example, a recently married man must learn what it means to be a husband.) The therapist will also help the patient understand the advantages and disadvantages of both the old and the new roles. In these ways, the therapy helps the patient gain an understanding of how he interacts with others and then helps him learn new and more beneficial ways of interacting and communicating.

Humanistic Approaches

We have seen that Freud played a pivotal role in launching the treatment that we now call psychotherapy; indeed, the idea of a "talking cure" that could help someone deal with mental distress through conversation or instruction was essentially unknown before Freud. Nonetheless, most modern psychotherapists employ methods very different from Freud's and base their therapies on conceptions that explicitly reject many of Freud's ideas.

As we discussed in Chapter 15, psychologists who take a **humanistic approach** have regarded psychoanalysis as being too concerned with basic urges (like sex and aggression) and not concerned enough with the search for meaning. This orientation led

17.3 **Extensions of psychotherapy** Even pets can benefit from a good therapist.

interpersonal therapy (IPT) A form of therapy focused on helping the patient understand how she interacts with others and then learn better ways of interacting and communicating.

humanistic approach An approach to therapy centered around the idea that people must take responsibility for their lives and actions.

17.4 Active listening Carl Rogers (right) empathizes with a client during this group therapy session.

them to propose several different types of therapy, which have in common the idea that people must take responsibility for their lives and their actions and live fully in the present.

Carl Rogers's **client-centered therapy** seeks to help a person accept himself as he is and to be himself with no pretense or self-imposed limits. In this therapy, the therapist listens attentively and acceptingly to the patient (Figure 17.4). The therapist is not there to question or to direct, but to create an atmosphere in which the patient feels valued and understood (Rogers, 1951, 1959). Based on his analysis of his own and others' therapeutic attempts, Rogers concluded that three factors were crucial to a therapist's success: *genuineness,* or sharing authentic reactions with the patient; *unconditional positive regard,* which refers to a nonjudgmental and accepting stance; and *empathic understanding,* which refers to sensing what it must be like to be in the patient's shoes (Rogers, 1980).

Rogers's therapeutic stance is evident in the following interaction with a patient:

PATIENT: I cannot be the kind of person I want to be. I guess maybe I haven't the guts or the strength to kill myself, and if someone else would relieve me of the responsibility or I would be in an accident, I—just don't want to live.

ROGERS: At the present time things look so black that you can't see much point in living.

PATIENT: Yes, I wish I'd never started this therapy. I was happy when I was living in my dream world. There I could be the kind of person I wanted to be. But now there is such a wide, wide gap between my idea and what I am . . .

ROGERS: It's really tough digging into this like you are, and at times the shelter of your dream world looks more attractive and comfortable.

PATIENT: My dream world or suicide . . . So I don't see why I should waste your time coming in twice a week—I'm not worth it—what do you think?

ROGERS: It's up to you. . . . It isn't wasting my time. I'd be glad to see you whenever you come, but it's how you feel about it.

PATIENT: You're not going to suggest that I come in oftener? You're not alarmed and think I ought to come in every day until I get out of this?

ROGERS: I believe you're able to make your own decision. I'll see you whenever you want to come.

PATIENT: I don't believe you are alarmed about—I see—I may be afraid of myself but you aren't afraid for me.

ROGERS: You say you may be afraid of yourself and are wondering why I don't seem to be afraid for you.

PATIENT: You have more confidence in me than I have. I'll see you next week, maybe.

[The patient did not attempt suicide.] (Rogers, 1951, p. 49)

client-centered therapy A form of humanistic therapy associated with Carl Rogers, in which the therapist's genuineness, unconditional positive regard, and empathic understanding are crucial to therapeutic success.

motivational-enhancement therapy A brief, nonconfrontational, client-centered therapy designed to change specific problematic behaviors such as alcohol or drug use.

Gestalt therapy A form of humanistic therapy associated with Fritz Perls that aims to help the patient integrate inconsistent aspects of herself into a coherent whole by increasing self-awareness and self-acceptance.

Rogers's client-centered therapy has, in turn, inspired a number of other forms of intervention, one of which is **motivational-enhancement therapy** (Miller & Rollnick, 2002). This is a brief, nonconfrontational, client-centered intervention designed to change problematic behavior (such as alcohol and other drug use) by reducing ambivalence and clarifying discrepancies between how individuals are actually living and how they say they would like to live (Ball et al., 2007).

A second humanistic therapy is Fritz Perls's **Gestalt therapy**. Perls was a highly charismatic and original clinician who was trained psychodynamically but drew inspiration from the gestalt theory of perception (Chapter 5). Perls believed that psychological difficulties stemmed from a failure to integrate mutually inconsistent aspects of self into an integrated whole or gestalt. His techniques were aimed at helping patients become aware of and then integrate disparate aspects of self by increasing self-awareness and self-acceptance (Perls, 1967, 1969).

For example, Perls was famous for asking his patients about what they were feeling in the moment, and for pointing out apparent discrepancies between what they said they felt and how they appeared to be feeling. Perls also used the *empty chair technique*, in which a patient imagines that he is seated across from another person, such as his parent or his partner, and tells him honestly what he feels. Using such strategies, Perls helped his patients acknowledge and confront their feelings.

In more modern versions of humanistic therapies—collectively referred to as the **experiential therapies**—these approaches are integrated, seeking to create a genuinely empathic and accepting atmosphere but also to challenge the patient in a more active fashion with the aim of deepening his experience (Elliott, Greenberg, & Lietaer, 2004; Follette & Greenberg, 2005). This approach views the patient and, indeed, all humans as oriented toward growth and full development of their potential, and the therapist uses a number of techniques to encourage these tendencies.

Although these challenges to live more actively and deeply can be disconcerting, experiential therapies involve genuine concern and respect for the person, with an emphasis on all her qualities, and not just those symptoms that led to a particular diagnosis. The person's subjective experience is also a primary focus, and the therapist tries to be as empathic as possible, in order to understand that experience. Moreover, experiential therapists reject Freud's notion of transference; in their view, the relationship between patient and therapist is a genuine connection between two people, one that provides the patient with an opportunity for a new, emotionally validating experience.

experiential therapies A family of therapies that seek to create an empathic and accepting therapeutic atmosphere, while challenging the patient to deepen his experience.

Behavioral Approaches

Like the humanistic therapies, behavior therapies emerged in part as a reaction to the Freudian tradition of psychoanalysis (Figure 17.5). But while the humanists regarded psychoanalysis as too mechanistic, the behavior theorists, ironically, offered exactly the opposite criticism; they regarded psychoanalysis as too loose and unscientific.

Behavior therapists focus on overt behavior rather than unconscious thoughts and wishes, which they regard as hard to define and impossible to observe. The patient's behaviors, in other words, are not regarded as "symptoms" through which one can identify and then cure an underlying illness. Instead, these therapists view the maladaptive behaviors themselves as the problem to be solved. These behaviors, in turn, are, from a behaviorist's perspective, simply the results of learning—albeit learning that led the person to undesired or undesirable behaviors.

The remedy, therefore, involves new learning, in order to replace old habits with more effective or adaptive ones. For this purpose, the therapeutic procedures draw on the principles of behavior change that have been well documented in the laboratory—classical conditioning, operant conditioning, and modeling, as discussed in Chapter 7.

17.5 Therapeutic approaches

CLASSICAL CONDITIONING TECHNIQUES

To see how behavior therapy proceeds, consider the treatment for specific phobias (Emmelkamp, 2004; Wolpe & Plaud, 1997). According to behavior therapists, the irrational fears that characterize these phobias are simply classically conditioned

| 1 String | 2 Worm | 3 Handling a worm | 4 Snake | 5 Handling a snake | 6 |

17.6 Exposure therapy Exposure therapy begins with the construction of an anxiety hierarchy, in which feared objects or situations are ranked from least to most anxiety-producing. While maintaining a state of relaxation, the patient then calls to mind each object or situation in turn, and process which often culminates in actually encountering the feared object or situation.

responses, evoked by stimuli that have become associated with a truly fearful stimulus (see Chapters 7 and 16). The way to treat these phobias, therefore, is to break the connection between the phobic stimuli and the associated fears, using a technique akin to the *extinction* procedures that are effective in diminishing conditioned responses in the laboratory.

One early version of this procedure is the technique originally known as systematic desensitization, now referred to as **exposure therapy**. Here, the therapist seeks not only to break the connection between the phobic stimulus and the fear response but also to create a new connection between this stimulus and a different response, one that is incompatible with fear and will therefore displace it (Figure 17.6). The new response is usually deep muscular relaxation, and the patient is taught a relaxation technique, typically through meditation-like exercises, before the formal therapy begins. Then, once the patient has learned to relax deeply on cue, the goal is to condition this relaxation response to the stimuli that have been evoking fear.

To begin the therapy, the patient constructs an anxiety hierarchy, in which feared situations are identified and then ranked from least to most anxiety provoking. This hierarchy is then used to set the sequence for therapy. The patient starts out by imagining the first scene in the hierarchy (e.g., being on the first floor of a tall building) while in a state of deep relaxation. He will stay with this scene—imagining and relaxing—until he no longer feels any anxieties. After this, he imagines the next scene (perhaps looking out a fourth-floor window in the building), and this scene, too, is thoroughly "counterconditioned," meaning that the old link between the scene and an anxiety response is broken, and a new link between the scene and a relaxation response is forged. The process continues, climbing up the anxiety hierarchy until the patient finally can imagine the most frightening scene of all (leaning over the railing of the building's observation tower, more than 100 floors above the ground) and still be able to relax.

Sometimes this imagined exposure is sufficient to treat the phobia, but often patients need to extend the graduated exposure to the real world—for example, actually visiting a tall building rather than merely thinking about one. This process, called **in vivo desensitization**, may take place with the therapist present or may use guided homework assignments (Figure 17.7; Craske, 1999; Goldfried & Davison, 1994). In addition, interactive computer graphics now provide yet another option: exposing the patient to a virtual-reality version of the frightening stimulus, which seems to be another way to extend and strengthen the desensitization procedure (Figure 17.8; see, for example, Emmelkamp et al., 2002). However the feared stimulus or situation is presented, exposure is a key ingredient in therapeutic success.

exposure therapy A behavior therapy that aims to remove the anxiety connected to a feared stimulus by gradually conditioning relaxed responses to the stimulus.

in vivo desensitization One key step in the behavioral treatment of a phobia in which the patient is gradually exposed to the phobic stimulus.

17.7 In vivo desensitization

17.8 **High-tech therapy** A common way to treat anxiety is to expose patients gradually to the anxiety-provoking stimulus. Psychologists sometimes use virtual-reality displays, like this combat scene, to make the exposures more and more realistic as the therapy progresses.

OPERANT CONDITIONING TECHNIQUES

A second set of behavioral techniques is based on the principles of instrumental or operant conditioning. These techniques aim to change behavior through reinforcement by emphasizing the relationship between acts and consequences.

An example of this approach is the use of **token economies** in hospital psychiatric wards. In these settings, patients earn the tokens through various helpful or healthy behaviors such as making the bed, being neatly dressed, or performing ward chores. They can then exchange tokens for desirable items, such as snacks or the chance to watch TV. In this fashion, the patient is systematically rewarded for producing desirable behaviors and is not rewarded for producing undesirable ones.

As in the learning laboratory, the reinforcement contingencies can then be gradually adjusted, using the process known as shaping. Early on, the patient might be reinforced merely for getting out of bed; later, tokens might be awarded only for getting out of bed and walking to the dining hall. In this fashion, the patient can be led, step-by-step, to a higher level of functioning. The overall effects of this technique are that the patients become less apathetic and the general ward atmosphere is much improved (Higgins, Williams, & McLaughlin, 2001).

Other reinforcement procedures can be useful in individual behavior therapy as part of **contingency management**. In this procedure, the person learns that certain behaviors will be followed by strict consequences (Craighead, Craighead, Kazdin, & Mahoney, 1994). For example, a child who is oppositional and defiant can be presented with a menu of "good behaviors" and "bad behaviors," with an associated reward and penalty for each. Being a "good listener" can earn the child the chance to watch a video, cleaning up her room every day can get her a dessert after dinner, and so forth, whereas talking back to Mom or making a mess may result in an early bedtime or a time-out in her room. The idea is not to bribe or coerce the child but to show her that her actions can change the way people react to her. Ideally, her changed behavior will result in a more positive social environment that will eventually make explicit rewards and punishments unnecessary.

These operant techniques have been applied to a number of mental disorders. In one study, parents spent 40 hours a week attempting to shape the behavior of their uncommunicative 3-year-olds who had autism (Lovaas, 1987). By first grade, more than half of the children were functioning successfully in school, and these treatment gains were still evident four years later (McEachin, Smith, & Lovaas, 1993). In a group of 40 comparable children who did not receive this intervention, only one child showed comparable improvement by first grade. Others have applied this technique to other serious mental disorders such as mental retardation, with positive results (Reid, Wilson, & Faw, 1991).

token economy A behavioral therapy technique based on operant conditioning in which patients' positive behaviors are reinforced with tokens that they can exchange for desirable items.

contingency management A form of behavior therapy in which certain behaviors are reliably followed by well-defined consequences.

17.9 Modeling By watching another person's behavior, a patient learns new skills and behavior patterns.

MODELING TECHNIQUES

One last (and powerful) technique for the behavior therapist is *modeling*, in which someone learns new skills or changes his behavior by imitating another person (Figure 17.9). Sometimes, the therapist serves as the model, but this need not be the case. Therapy with children, for example, may draw on young "assistants" (children roughly the same age as the child in therapy) who work with the therapist and model the desired behaviors or skills.

Modeling is not limited to overt behaviors; a therapist can also model a thought process or a decision-making strategy. In some forms of therapy, the therapist "thinks out loud" about commonplace decisions or situations, in this way providing a model for how the patient should consider similar settings (Kendall, 1990; Kendall & Braswell, 1985). Likewise, modeling can be used for emotional responses, so that, for example, the therapist can model fearlessness in the presence of some phobic stimulus and in this fashion diminish the phobia (Bandura, 1969, 2001).

Modeling can also be supported by vicarious reinforcement, a procedure in which the patient sees the model experience some good outcome after exhibiting the desired behavior or emotional reaction. Like other forms of reinforcement (Chapter 7), vicarious reinforcement seems to increase the likelihood that the person in therapy will later produce the desired behavior or reaction.

Cognitive-Behavioral Approaches

In its early versions, behavior therapy focused on overt behaviors and regarded a person's inner thoughts and feelings as unimportant, and, in any case, not something that could be studied or influenced directly. Several decades ago, however, behavior therapists started to broaden their view, realizing both that thoughts and perceptions do matter and that some of the techniques they had already developed could be applied to these mental events in much the same way they are applied to behaviors. This is obvious in the case of modeling, for example, in which the target for change is often how someone thinks or feels. However, the same is true for operant techniques, which also can be used to encourage more positive self-evaluations and various adaptive strategies.

In the 1950s, Albert Ellis began to focus on the role cognitions play in causing psychological difficulties (Ellis, 1962). He expounded an approach that is now known as **rational emotive behavioral therapy**. In Ellis's view, people typically believe that the things that happen to them (such as being ignored at a party by a roommate) directly lead them to feel or behave in certain ways (such as feeling angry). One way of putting this idea is that people believe that an activating event, which we can call A, leads to a consequence, which we can call C.

Ellis made the point that if this were true—that A directly caused C—then everyone should respond the same way to activating event A each time A occurs. It's obvious, however, that neither of these things is true. Why not? According to Ellis, what people fail to notice is the hidden element tucked between the A and the C, namely, a belief, or B. That is, Ellis argued that the A never has the power to cause us to feel or behave unless there's also a belief that translates A into C, leading to an A → B → C sequence. Different people can react to A in different ways because they have their own distinct beliefs. Individuals' beliefs can also change, leading to new consequences the next time they encounter the activating event.

Ellis claimed that these beliefs, linking activating events to consequences, are often the cause of the problems that lead people to seek therapy. In particular, Ellis suggested

rational emotive behavioral therapy A form of cognitive therapy associated with Albert Ellis, in which the therapist actively challenges the patient's irrational beliefs.

that some people have highly irrational beliefs, such as "Everything I do must be perfect" or "I must be in complete control at all times." Ellis viewed these beliefs as the source of a person's problems and targeted them with his clinical intervention.

To the A → B → C sequence Ellis added D (disputing the irrational beliefs) and E (substituting more effective beliefs). Ellis sought to effect change in a direct fashion—by means of argument and instruction. He would explicitly discuss and literally dispute (D) the patient's beliefs and would offer specific—and more effective (E)—substitutes. His manner was teacherlike, and he frequently lectured his patients and exhorted them to modify their irrational ideas about themselves and the world.

In a similar vein, Aaron Beck—who was initially trained as a psychoanalyst—developed **cognitive therapy** (Beck, 1976; Beck, Rush, Shaw, & Emery, 1979). Beck's core insight—like Ellis's—is that dysfunctional cognitions play a key role in the development of mental disorders. For example, Beck held that depressed people have negative beliefs about themselves ("I am unlovable"), the world ("It's a cruel world out there"), and the future ("Things are only going to get worse"). These beliefs are supported by distorted thought processes, such as all-or-nothing thinking ("Now that I've lost the election, I'm worthless"), overgeneralization ("I lost my car keys—that's just like me, I lose everything!"), disqualifying the positive ("My doing well on the test today was just a fluke"), and emotional reasoning ("I feel it, therefore I know it's true") (Burns, 1980).

To challenge these thought processes, Beck used **cognitive restructuring**, a set of techniques for changing a person's beliefs or habits of interpreting the world. These techniques include outright persuasion and, in some cases, confronting the patient with her maladaptive beliefs. In other cases, patients are taught strategies for keeping certain thoughts readily available, to be applied instead of more destructive or distressing interpretations of life's events. In short, there is no single list of techniques that are used in cognitive therapy, but the effort is always toward changing both a person's behaviors *and* how she thinks about the world.

To get a feel for how Beck interacts with his patients, consider the following interview with a 26-year-old graduate student who sought treatment for depression:

PATIENT: I agree with the descriptions of me, but I guess I don't agree that the way I think makes me depressed.

BECK: How do you understand it?

PATIENT: I get depressed when things go wrong. Like when I fail a test.

BECK: How can failing a test make you depressed?

PATIENT: Well, if I fail I'll never get into law school.

BECK: So failing the test means a lot to you. But if failing a test could drive people into clinical depression, wouldn't you expect everyone who failed the test to have a depression? . . . Did everyone who failed get depressed enough to require treatment?

PATIENT: No, but it depends on how important the test was to the person.

BECK: Right, and who decides the importance?

PATIENT: I do.

BECK: And so, what we have to examine is your way of viewing the test (or the way that you think about the test) and how it affects your chances of getting into law school. Do you agree?

PATIENT: Right.

BECK: Do you agree that the way you interpret the results of the test will affect you? You might feel depressed, you might have trouble sleeping, not feel like eating, and you might even wonder if you should drop out of the course.

PATIENT: I have been thinking that I wasn't going to make it. Yes, I agree.

cognitive therapy An approach to therapy that tries to change some of the patient's habitual modes of thinking about herself, her situation, and her future.

cognitive restructuring A set of cognitive therapy techniques for changing a person's maladaptive beliefs or interpretations through persuasion and confrontation.

BECK:	Now what did failing mean?
PATIENT:	(*tearful*) That I couldn't get into law school.
BECK:	And what does that mean to you?
PATIENT:	That I'm just not smart enough.
BECK:	Anything else?
PATIENT:	That I can never be happy.
BECK:	And how do these thoughts make you feel?
PATIENT:	Very unhappy.
BECK:	So it is the meaning of failing a test that makes you very unhappy. In fact, believing that you can never be happy is a powerful factor in producing unhappiness. So, you get yourself into a trap—by definition, failure to get into law school equals "I can never be happy." (Beck, Rush, Shaw, & Emery, 1979, 145–146)

Beck's therapy was initially developed to treat depression (Beck, Rush, Shaw, & Emery, 1979). This makes sense because—as discussed in Chapter 16—major depression seems to involve a set of cognitive problems linked to how a person perceives herself and her world: She believes that she is worthless, and her future is bleak. If bad things occur in her life, they are her fault, and they indicate widespread patterns of upcoming difficulties.

There is room for debate over whether these beliefs produced the depression in the first place, but there is no question that they foster and sustain the depression—and so, to help the patient, it is important to work toward changing the beliefs. However, Beck's cognitive therapy has also been successfully applied to disorders in which the role of maladaptive beliefs may be less prominent. These include bipolar disorder (Miklowitz & Johnson, 2006), a range of anxiety disorders (Hollon, Stewart, & Strunk, 2006), schizophrenia (Hogarty et al., 2004), obesity (Cooper & Fairburn, 2001), personality disorders (Beck, Freeman, Davis, & Associates, 2004), and chronic pain (Hollon & Beck, 2004).

Although Ellis and Beck both drew attention to the cognitive aspects of mental disorders, they and their followers skillfully blended together cognitive and behavioral techniques. This hybrid or **cognitive-behavioral approach** is now far more common than "pure" behavioral or "pure" cognitive therapy. There are many variants of cognitive-behavioral therapy, tailored to specific treatment contexts, but as a general rule cognitive-behavioral therapists are present-focused, and are concerned with identifying and solving problems the patient wishes to address. Therapy sessions are highly structured, and the patient is often expected to do homework, which may consist of practicing new skills or new ways of thinking learned during the therapy sessions.

Integrated Treatments and Eclecticism

The marriage of behavioral and cognitive therapies that yields the cognitive-behavioral approach is not the only blending of therapy types that has been going on. Indeed, the last few decades have seen a strong trend toward psychotherapists endorsing what is sometimes called multimodal therapy or **eclecticism**—a deliberate weaving together of the various traditions (Beitman, Goldfried, & Norcross, 1989; Lazarus, 2006; Norcross & Freedheim, 1992). This broad tendency is evident in the work of many clinicians; in fact, when U.S. psychologists are asked to describe their work, the therapeutic approach that most identify with is eclectic/integrative (Prochaska & Norcross, 2007; see Figure 17.10). As one example of this tendency, consider Marsha Linehan's dialectical behavior therapy (DBT) for borderline personality disorder. DBT grew out of the cognitive approach, but includes elements from cognitive, behavioral, humanistic,

cognitive-behavioral approach
A hybrid form of psychotherapy focused on changing the patient's habitual interpretations of the world and ways of behaving.

eclecticism An approach to treatment that deliberately weaves together multiple types and forms of therapy.

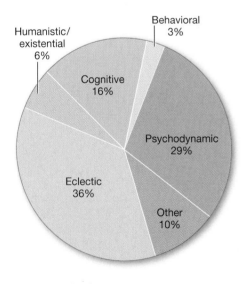

17.10 Psychotherapy orientations
Primary psychotherapy orientations of psychologists who are members of the American Psychological Association's Division of Psychotherapy.

and psychodynamic therapies to address the profound emotion dysregulation associated with borderline personality disorder (Linehan, Bohus, & Lynch, 2007).

This eclecticism obviously allows the therapist flexibility to tailor his approach to the specific needs and symptoms of each patient. And over the course of treatment, it allows the therapist to pursue lines of discussion or specific interventions that are working and to back off from interventions that are ineffective. In addition, multimodal therapy makes sense theoretically. In Chapter 16, we saw that mental disorders rarely have a single cause; instead, they emerge from a complex set of factors creating the diathesis as well as factors creating the more immediate stressors. It seems sensible, therefore, that treatment might need to work on multiple fronts, which is precisely what multimodal therapy is designed to do.

Beyond One-on-One Therapy

So far, we have considered various approaches to one-on-one therapy—that is, one therapist working with one patient. Over the past few decades, therapists have also been exploring various modes of group therapy that feature all conceivable permutations: one therapist and several patients, several therapists and several patients, several patients and no therapist, and so on. Treating patients in groups has an obvious advantage: more patients can be accommodated by a limited number of therapists. But group treatment is appealing for other reasons as well, including the fact that it allows therapists to observe and work with problems that emerge more readily in group settings.

SHARED PROBLEM GROUPS

One approach to group therapy is to gather people who have the same problem. They may all be alcoholics, or abuse victims, or ex-convicts. The members meet, share relevant advice and information, help newcomers along, and exhort and support one another in their resolve to overcome their difficulties (Figure 17.11). The classic example is Alcoholics Anonymous (AA), which gives the recovering alcoholic the knowledge that she is not alone, helps her weather crises without suffering a relapse, and assists her in getting back on her feet if relapses do occur. Another is Toastmasters, a social club for people with public-speaking phobias. In these "we are all in the same boat" groups, the primary aim is to manage the problem that all the members share. Relatively little attention is paid to any one individual's unique emotional problems.

THERAPY GROUPS

The rules of the game are very different in groups explicitly organized for group therapy. Here, a number of selected patients, usually around 8 to 10, are treated together under the guidance of a trained therapist. Within this format, the techniques used by the therapist vary considerably. In some groups, the therapist encourages psychodynamically oriented insights; in others, the therapist may use behavioral or cognitive procedures. No matter the technique, the treatment of each group member really begins as he realizes that he is not all that different from the others. He learns that there are other people who are painfully afraid of rejection, are desperately lonely, have hostile fantasies about their parents, and so on. Additional benefits come from a sense of group belongingness, support, and encouragement. Most importantly, the group provides a ready-made laboratory in interpersonal relations. The patient can

"When Jud accuses Zack, here, of hostility towards his daughter, like he seems to every session, why, it's plain to me he's only rationalizing his own lack of gumption in standing up to a stepson who's upsurping the loyalty of his second wife."

17.11 Group therapy

discover just what he does that rubs others the wrong way, how he can relate to certain kinds of people more effectively, and the like.

COUPLE THERAPY AND FAMILY THERAPY

In the therapy groups we have considered so far, the members are almost always strangers before the sessions begin. This contrasts markedly with couple and family therapy. Here, the people seeking help know one another very well (sometimes all too well) before they enter therapy.

Couple therapy (including marriage counseling) and family therapy have become major therapeutic movements (Figure 17.12; Kerr & Bowen, 1988; Minuchin, 1974; Satir, 1967; Snyder, Castellani, & Whisman, 2006). It is probably no coincidence that this growth has occurred during a time of turmoil in American families, evidenced by spiraling divorce rates and reports of child and spousal abuse and by the increasing number of single-parent households.

Family and couple therapists generally regard the family as an emotional system, with the feelings and functioning of each individual heavily influenced by interactions within the system. Thus, one person in the family may be depressed, or one member of a couple may be aggressive, but the difficulty does not lie in that person alone. Instead, she is merely the "identified patient" within the system, and her symptoms may reflect some broader problem within the family or the couple (Dadds, 1995). Likewise, when one person in the couple or family has a problem, its effects can ricochet through the family and affect all its members.

For example, let's imagine that one family member suffers from bipolar disorder. This will lead to behaviors that may be destructive to the whole family—disrupting their routines, causing them to worry, draining their finances. This may lead to hostility, or perhaps overprotection, toward the patient with the initial disorder, and this, in turn, can cause further problems for the patient, aggravating the disorder and producing new difficulties. As a result, the treatment may have to include medication for the bipolar disorder and steps to repair the dynamic within the family. In fact, there is now good evidence that patients with bipolar disorder are less likely to relapse if their treatment plan includes family-level interventions as well as medication (Miklowitz, 2007).

BIOMEDICAL TREATMENTS

The psychological treatments described so far are widely used and, as we will discuss later, are often quite effective. However, as we mentioned at the outset of this chapter, there is a second major class of treatments—the biomedical treatments—which are designed to alter the brain's functioning more directly.

Biomedical treatments for mental illness have a long history. As mentioned earlier, the first known biomedical treatment is a prehistoric surgical procedure called trephination, in which pieces of the skull were removed to provide an escape path for the spirits or demons thought to be causing the affliction (Figure 17.13). Other early procedures involved bloodlettings or purgatives, both intended somehow to restore mental equilibrium. Later developments were hardly milder. For example, Benjamin Rush (1745–1813), one of the signers of the Declaration of Independence and the acknowledged father of American psychiatry, submerged patients in hot or cold water until they were just short of drowning or twirled them on special devices at speeds that rendered

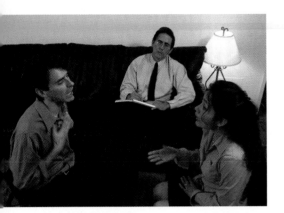

17.12 Couple therapy In couple therapy, a therapist works with both members of a couple, sometimes together and sometimes separately.

17.13 Trephination The ancient practice of trephination involved the cutting of holes in the skull, through which demons could be driven out. This photo shows a trephined prehistoric skull found in Peru. The patient apparently survived the operation for a while, for there is some evidence of bone healing.

them unconscious (Figure 17.14). Such methods were said to reestablish balance between bodily and mental functions. They almost certainly had no such positive effects, although hospital attendants probably welcomed them, since they undoubtedly terrified the inmates and so helped to "keep order" (Mora, 1975).

More recent biomedical treatments have been more humane, have had more secure empirical foundations, and have certainly been more effective than these early treatments. Some of these are pharmacological and consist of medications that alter information flow at the synapse, thereby influencing thoughts, feelings, and behaviors. Others are nonpharmacological and involve the direct manipulation of the nervous system via surgery or electrical or magnetic pulses.

Pharmacological Treatments

The past half century or so has seen the development of a number of **psychotropic drugs**, medications that control, or at least moderate, the manifestations of mental disorders. These medications have had an enormous impact on mental-health care and have allowed patients with many different disorders to be treated successfully, often without hospitalization. The development of psychotropic drugs has gone hand in hand with advances in our understanding of mental illness. As we have learned more about the causes of each disorder, better understanding has often pointed the way toward new drug treatments, and—conversely—new drug treatments have often allowed us to test claims about what the causes might be. At the same time, many of these treatments have important limitations, which we will also consider.

ANTIPSYCHOTIC MEDICATIONS

As we discussed in Chapter 16, schizophrenia involves many elements, including a specific chemical abnormality involving the neurotransmitter dopamine. A major source of evidence for this neurochemical abnormality was the effectiveness of certain drugs called antipsychotics. The classical antipsychotics, most of which were developed in the 1950s, reduce the major positive symptoms of schizophrenia, such as thought disorder and hallucination (see Chapter 16), apparently by blocking dopamine receptors in key

psychotropic drugs Medications that control, or at least moderate, the manifestations of some mental disorders.

brain pathways; the most common versions of these antipsychotics include Thorazine, Haldol, and Stelazine.

Unfortunately, these drugs are less effective in treating negative symptoms, such as flat affect and the inability to feel pleasure. This shortcoming has been addressed by a newer set of medications, the so-called atypical antipsychotics, such as Risperdal, Clozaril, and Seroquel (Glick, Murray, Vasudevan, Marder, & Hu, 2001). Like the classical antipsychotics, the atypical antipsychotics block the neurotransmission of dopamine, but their enhanced benefits, especially with negative symptoms, are probably caused by other mechanisms. These may include alterations in serotonin neurotransmission or a more selective effect on particular subsets of dopamine neurons (Bantick, Deakin, & Grasby, 2001; Kapur & Remington, 2001; Tandon & Kane, 1993; Wirshing, Marder, Van Putten, & Ames, 1995).

These medications have provided enormous advances in our treatment of schizophrenia; however, the benefits have not come without problems. In the United States, the development of the first antipsychotic medications in the 1950s spurred a movement called **deinstitutionalization**, intended to allow for better and less expensive care for patients in their own communities, at local community mental-health centers rather than at large, centralized hospitals. To some extent, this movement worked. In the 1950s, mental hospitals housed about 600,000 patients; the current figure is a mere 10% of that figure (Lamberg, 2004). Medications have also made it possible to discharge patients with schizophrenia more quickly than ever. Prior to the introduction of the antipsychotic medications, two out of three patients with schizophrenia spent most of their lives in mental hospitals. In the 1980s, the average stay was about two months (J. M. Davis, 1985a; Lamb, 1984; Lamb & Bachrach, 2001).

But deinstitutionalization was at best a partial success. Many individuals with serious mental illness have not found appropriate care in community settings, nor have they been integrated into the community, in terms of employment, or social relations, or support services. As a result, some 200,000 mentally ill individuals are homeless in the United States, and an equal number are in jail, often for minor crimes (Fleishman, 2004; Lamberg, 2004; Figure 17.15). Thousands more exist in marginal living situations, and although it is true that fewer patients with schizophrenia remain in psychiatric hospitals, the number of times they are readmitted for short stays has increased by 80% since the 1960s (Rosenstein, Milazzo-Sayre, & Manderscheid, 1989). The current inadequacy—and, in many cases, the complete lack—of appropriate community services for mental illness may be linked to the point, raised earlier, that the outlook for a patient with schizophrenia is appreciably worse in the United States than it is in countries where such support is more available.

ANTIDEPRESSANT AND MOOD-STABILIZING MEDICATIONS

Even with all their complications, the antipsychotic medications have provided enormous advances in the treatment of schizophrenia. Medications have been just as important in the treatment of other mental disorders. Shortly after the introduction of antipsychotics as a treatment for schizophrenia, drugs were found that seemed to act specifically on depression. These early **antidepressants** fell into two major classes, the monoamine oxidase (MAO) inhibitors, such as Nardil, and the tricyclic antidepressants (so called because of their chemical structure), such as Tofranil. Of these, the tricyclics became the more widely used, mostly because patients taking MAO inhibitors must conform to difficult dietary restrictions (Burke & Preskhorn, 1995).

17.15 Adverse effects of deinstitutionalization Some of the homeless in American cities are people who have been discharged from mental hospitals and are unable to adjust to the world outside.

deinstitutionalization A movement that began in the 1950s that aimed to provide better, less expensive care for chronically mentally ill patients in their own communities rather than at large, centralized hospitals.

antidepressants Medications designed to counteract depression.

17.16 Antidepressants and synaptic transmission (A) MAO inhibitors increase the amount of norepinephrine and serotonin available at the synapse by preventing MAO enzymes from breaking down these neurotransmitters. (B) Tricyclics increase the amount of norepinephrine and serotonin available at the synapse by blocking neurotransmitter reuptake.

Both the MAO inhibitors and the tricyclics appear to work in part by increasing the amount of norepinephrine and serotonin available for synaptic transmission (Blier & Abbott, 2001). These two classes of drugs accomplish this in different ways (for details, see Figure 17.16), but both are effective in alleviating depression, producing marked improvement in up to 65% of the patients who take them (Hollister & Csernansky, 1990). The drugs are not interchangeable, however, because some patients do far better with one than with another (Hollon, Thase, & Markowitz, 2002), presumably because different patients suffer from somewhat different neurochemical deficits.

These early drug treatments for depression were quite successful, but the use of medication for treating depression changed dramatically in 1988 with the introduction of the first "designer drug" for depression, Prozac (Kramer, 1993). Prozac was engineered to act minimally on norepinephrine and dopamine and maximally on serotonin, thus marking a new class of antidepressants, known as *selective serotonin reuptake inhibitors* (*SSRIs*). For most patients, Prozac and the other SSRIs (such as Zoloft, Paxil, Celexa, and Lexapro) ameliorate depression as effectively and as completely as their predecessors (Mulrow et al., 2000), but they have fewer side effects. SSRIs have become so popular—both for depression and for other disorders, such as eating disorders and anxiety disorders—that they are now prescribed not only by psychiatrists but also by primary-care physicians (Olfson & Klerman, 1993).

For patients who are bothered by side effects from SSRIs and cannot take the tricyclics or MAO inhibitors, a separate array of antidepressants is available. These *atypical antidepressants,* which work in various ways on serotonin, norepinephrine, and dopamine systems, include Wellbutrin, Effexor, and Serzone. Of these, Wellbutrin is of special interest. It seems to have little effect on serotonin and probably operates on the dopamine and norepinephrine systems instead. However it works, Wellbutrin has none of the negative sexual side effects associated with some of the other antidepressants; indeed, many patients actually report heightened sexual interest and response. It is also generally stimulating, and in addition to curbing nicotine cravings (for which it is sold as Zyban), it is widely used to treat adults with attention-deficit/hyperactivity disorder.

While some have touted these new antidepressants as panaceas, they—like all medications—have limitations. First, the beneficial effects of the drug fully emerge only after the medication is taken for a month or so. In addition, considerable uncertainty persists about why each of the antidepressants helps some people but not others. As a result, therapists often resort to a process of trial and error, prescribing a variety of drugs, one at a time, until they find one that helps the particular patient. This trial and error can take quite some time since, as we have said, the drugs often take effect only after a month or so.

In addition, all of these drugs do have side effects, which vary by drug and by person but which, overall, include weight gain, nausea, diarrhea, and—in upward of 30% of patients—insomnia, as well as a loss of sexual desire or response (Clayton, 2001; Ferguson, 2001; Gursky & Krahn, 2000; E. Hollander & McCarley, 1992; Jacobsen, 1992; Montgomery, 1995). There has also been some concern that these drugs may be addictive, although many regard the evidence supporting this claim as unpersuasive (Haddad, 1999).

Medications to treat bipolar disorder are called **mood stabilizers** (so called because they treat or prevent manic, mixed, or depressive states). The first medication used specifically for its mood stabilizing action was lithium carbonate. Patients who begin taking lithium can generally expect that their manic episodes will subside within 5 to 10 days. Because of this delay, antipsychotic medications are sometimes also prescribed to reduce agitation until the lithium takes effect. In addition, antidepressants are often prescribed along with lithium because lithium is more effective in reducing manic than in reducing depressive symptoms (Sachs & Thase, 2000).

Unfortunately, lithium works in only 60 to 70% of patients with bipolar disorder (Miklowitz & Johnson, 2007). Taking it also causes unpleasant side effects for many patients, such as weight gain, sedation, dry mouth, and tremors. Moreover, the fact that lithium is toxic at higher doses means that patients must have their blood tested frequently and makes it a risky treatment for patients who are potentially suicidal and might overdose. Nor can lithium be taken during pregnancy or when a patient has kidney disease. In addition, many patients with bipolar disorder choose not to take their medication because they do not want to give up either the pleasures or the productivity often associated with the manic state; they may decide that these elements outweigh the (sometimes enormous) disruption and distress that the disorder also produces.

ANTIANXIETY MEDICATIONS

Patients suffering from disabling anxiety are often treated with medications that are popularly called tranquilizers and technically known as **anxiolytics**. Most anxiolytics apparently work by increasing neurotransmission at synapses containing the neurotransmitter gamma-aminobutric acid (GABA; Brailowsky & Garcia, 1999; Shader & Greenblatt, 1995). Probably the most commonly used anxiolytic, though, is self-administered and not prescribed by a therapist: alcohol. Many people, patients or otherwise, medicate themselves for their anxiety as part of their lifestyle, inviting the risk of alcohol abuse.

Physicians also sometimes treat the anxiety disorders by prescribing a *beta-blocker*, a medication intended to control autonomic arousal. In addition, for the uncomfortable feelings associated with anxiety, they often prescribe one of the *benzodiazepines*. Some of these medications, such as Valium Xanax, or Klonopin are prescribed so often that their names have become household words. They are useful as short-term treatments (usually taking effect in 30 or 40 minutes) for generalized anxiety disorder, panic disorder, post-traumatic stress disorder, alcohol withdrawal, insomnia, muscle spasms, tension headaches, and various other stress-related disorders.

Benzodiazepines are rarely used for long-term treatment, however, because they are highly addictive, interact dangerously with alcohol, and like alcohol, can cause profound fetal damage if a patient is pregnant. There are also concerns that the benzo-

mood stabilizers Medications that treat bipolar disorder, such as lithium.

anxiolytics Drugs that alleviate the symptoms of anxiety.

diazepines can produce a "rebound" effect, so that a person who stops taking the medication may end up more anxious than she was prior to taking the drug (Chouinard, 2004). These are, of course, major concerns, and so researchers continue to seek new anxiolytics. Happily, some of the newer drugs, such as BuSpar, are not addictive and are becoming popular substitutes for the older medications, especially for patients who are prone to alcohol or drug abuse or have to take the medication over a long period of time (Lydiard, Brawman-Mintzer, & Ballenger, 1996; Schweitzer, Rickels, & Uhlenhuth, 1995). Anxiety is also commonly treated using tricyclic antidepressants and SSRIs.

COSTS AND BENEFITS OF MEDICATION

Overall, drug therapies effectively reduce symptoms for people with a wide range of mental disorders. Indeed, these drugs have lifted many people out of misery and distress and help them resume a reasonably normal life. These drugs have also allowed many patients to remain in a family or community setting when they would otherwise have been relegated to the hospital. These are, by any measure, enormous gains.

At the same time, drug therapy for mental disorders is not an unqualified success. Drugs do not cure the disorder; instead, they help to control it, and in many cases, if the person stops taking his pills, he quickly relapses into his full set of symptoms. It is also often tricky to get the *doses* correct for many of these drugs, because individuals differ both in their drug reactions and in how rapidly they metabolize the medication. There are also some group differences—for example, many African Americans metabolize antidepressant medications more slowly than whites (U.S. Department of Health and Human Services, 2001). This aggravates a concern that we have already raised—namely, that a clinician prescribing one of these medications often needs some amount of trial and error to find the right drug at the right dose.

We have also highlighted the fact that many of these drugs have unpleasant (or even dangerous) side effects. These include increases as well as decreases in sleepiness and agitation, decreased sexual performance, and facial tics. These side effects are bad enough on their own, but, in addition, they often lead people to stop taking their medication, in which case (obviously) the drugs can bring no benefit. Thus, a college student might refuse to take her antidepressant because she is concerned about the associated weight gain, even though, without the drug, her bulimia nervosa may cause long-term health problems. Likewise, someone might refuse to take medication because of a fear that it will disrupt sexual functioning, even though, without it, depression is disrupting his life to the point where a relationship is not possible.

"I medicate first and ask questions later."

17.17 Overprescribing

A more general concern about these psychoactive drugs is that they may be overprescribed (Figure 17.17). This worry is magnified by the fact that these drugs are increasingly used to treat a wide variety of conditions in children and adolescents, even though we know less about their side effects in children than in adults. Two flashpoints for this particular controversy are the use of SSRIs for depression and the use of stimulants for ADHD.

Some researchers have raised questions about whether the SSRIs may increase the risk of suicide in some young people. But others claim the opposite is the case, and that by alleviating depression, SSRIs *decrease* suicide risk (Bachtold, 2003; Couzin, 2004). In view of the potential for risks, however, the U.S. Food and Drug Administration (FDA) now requires "black box" warnings on SSRIs (literally, a black box around the label) regarding possible increased risk of suicide (Figure 17.18).

Suicidality and Antidepressant Drugs

Antidepressants increased the risk compared to placebo of suicidal thinking and behavior (suicidality) in children, adolescents, and young adults in short-term studies of major depressive disorder (MDD) and other psychiatric disorders. Anyone considering the use of [Insert established name] or any other antidepressant in a child, adolescent, or young adult must balance this risk with the clinical need. Short-term studies did not show an increase in the risk of suicidality with antidepressants compared to placebo in adults beyond age 24; there was a reduction in risk with antidepressants compared to placebo in adults aged 65 and older. Depression and certain other psychiatric disorders are themselves associated with increases in the risk of suicide. Patients of all ages who are started on antidepressant therapy should be monitored appropriately and observed closely for clinical worsening, suicidality, or unusual changes in behavior. Families and caregivers should be advised of the need for close observation and communication with the prescriber. [Insert Drug Name] is not approved for use in pediatric patients. [The previous sentence would be replaced with the sentence, below, for the following drugs: Prozac: Prozac is approved for use in pediatric patients with MDD and obsessive compulsive disorder (OCD). Zoloft: Zoloft is not approved for use in pediatric patients except for patients with obsessive compulsive disorder (OCD). Fluvoxamine: Fluvoxamine is not approved for use in pediatric patients except for patients with obsessive compulsive disorder (OCD).] (See Warnings: Clinical Worsening and Suicide Risk, Precautions: Information for Patients, and Precautions: Pediatric Use)

17.18 Antidepressant "black box" label The FDA requires warning labels on SSRIs that alert patients to a possible increase in the risk of suicide.

As we have seen, controversy also swirls around the number of prescriptions now being written for ADHD, which has increased fourfold since the early 1990s. Critics claim that active children are being medicated so that they will behave themselves in crowded and understimulating classrooms where they are expected to perform well on standardized tests. Others reply that medications are an important treatment tool as long as children are thoroughly assessed by appropriate professionals.

Nonpharmacological Treatments

Nonpharmacological treatments for mental illness include psychosurgery and electroconvulsive therapy as well as a number of promising newer treatments. These treatments conjure up disturbing images for many people, in part because of the portrayals of these techniques in the popular media (see Figure 17.19). However, as we will see below, there is a place for each of these treatments in contemporary practice.

PSYCHOSURGERY

Psychosurgery, or brain surgery, aims to alter thinking or behavior by removing brain areas or disconnecting them from each other. In a prefrontal lobotomy, for example, the surgeon severs the neurological connections between the thalamus and the frontal lobes, in whole or in part. This operation was originally meant to liberate a patient's thoughts from the pathological influence of her emotions, on the ill-informed assumption that thought and emotion were localized in the frontal lobes and the thalamus, respectively. In the 1940s and 1950s, tens of thousands of patients were subjected to lobotomies, and early reports on the procedure were quite enthusiastic. It soon became clear, however, that the surgery had powerful side effects, including a disruption of many higher cognitive functions such as memory and the ability to plan and self-regulate, and so the procedure is now rarely used (Tierney, 2000; Valenstein, 1986).

Recently, psychosurgery has reemerged as a useful technique, but it has been refined considerably, both in the procedures used and in the patients judged suitable for them (Hurley, Black, Stip, & Taber, 2000). Neurosurgeons still manipulate the nervous system directly, but they do so by creating very precise lesions in specific brain areas instead of disconnecting or destroying whole lobes or regions (see Figure 17.20). In these cases, the surgery is reserved for patients who are severely

17.19 Negative media portrayals of nonpharmacological treatments McMurphy's electroshock treatments in *One Flew Over the Cuckoo's Nest* (1975). Negative portrayals have given this type of treatment a bad name. However, electroconvulsive therapy as currently administered is an important tool for managing severe depression.

17.20 Neurosurgery Neurosurgeons can use a computer-controlled robot arm to locate and remove small brain tumors with minimal damage to surrounding areas. The computer screen shows virtual reality images of the device using CT and 3-D MRI.

disabled and show no improvement after all other treatment alternatives have been exhausted. This surgery-as-last-resort has been used in patients with intractable depression and epilepsy, severe obsessive-compulsive disorder, and chronic physical pain, and it is often beneficial. Clearly, it poses risks, but for some patients they may be acceptable compared with the severity of the ongoing disability (Baer et al., 1995; Bridges, 1987; Davies & Weeks, 1993; Hay et al., 1993; Jenike, 2001; Mahli & Bartlett, 2000).

ELECTROCONVULSIVE THERAPY

Another form of biomedical therapy is **electroconvulsive therapy (ECT)**, sometimes called shock treatment. When ECT first came into use, in the 1930s, 100 volts of electricity were administered to fully awake patients, some of whom had such violent convulsions that they suffered serious bruises or bone fractures. By contrast, modern ECT looks relatively tame (Figure 17.21). In modern ECT, a current of moderate intensity is passed for about half a second between two electrodes attached to the patient's head. The result is a 30- to 60-second convulsive seizure similar to that seen in epilepsy, with the usual course of ECT consisting of six to ten treatments over a period of 1 or 2 weeks. Patients are given short-acting anesthetics to render them temporarily unconscious and muscle relaxants to reduce the manifestations of the seizure to a few slight twitches (Andreasen & Black, 1996).

ECT was originally intended to treat schizophrenia but was soon established as particularly effective for depression. It works for as many as 70 to 90% of patients who have not responded to any antidepressant medication (Andreasen & Black, 1996; Janicak et al., 1985; Petrides et al., 2001) or who cannot take such medications because of overdose potential or other medical problems. In addition, ECT acts more quickly than antidepressant medications (Fink, 2008). ECT also seems quite effective in treating acute mania as well as various psychotic states associated with drug intoxication (Gitlin, 2001; Sackeim, Devanand, & Nobler, 1995). It is not clear what the mechanisms of action are, but ECT is clearly more than a high-tech placebo: The real ECT treatment consistently outperforms sham ECT (Carney & Geddes, 2003).

psychosurgery Neurosurgery performed to alleviate manifestations of mental disorders that cannot be alleviated using psychotherapy, medication, or other standard treatments.

electroconvulsive therapy (ECT) A somatic treatment, mostly used for cases of severe depression, in which a brief electric current is passed through the brain to produce a convulsive seizure.

ECT device

Stimulating electrode

Recording EEG

Ground

Recording

Blood pressure cuff monitor

ECG (heart rate)

Intravenous line (sedative, muscle relaxant)

To oximeter (blood-oxygen level)

17.21 Electroconvulsive therapy Although ECT is controversial, it is the preferred treatment for depression that does not respond to drug therapy.

Despite these advantages, ECT remains controversial, partly because in many cases it produces memory impairment (Rami-Gonzalez et al., 2001). These cognitive side effects are diminished if the ECT is delivered to just one side of the brain during therapy, as is now commonly done (Sackeim et al., 2000). In any case, ECT is generally used only after medication has failed or when there seems to be a serious chance of suicide. In such contexts, there is now a clear consensus that modern ECT represents one of the most effective treatments for depression (Glass, 2001).

EMERGING BIOMEDICAL TREATMENTS

A number of emerging biomedical treatments have also attracted attention. Here we'll highlight three treatments that are in varying stages of development and testing. The first—**vagal nerve stimulation**—involves implanting a battery-powered stimulator in the chest just underneath the skin. This stimulator delivers carefully calibrated electrical pulses to the vagus nerve. Although this treatment has FDA approval for use with treatment-resistant depression, information about its short- and long-term efficacy is still being gathered.

A second promising treatment is **deep brain stimulation (DBS)**. This treatment is based on the finding that severe forms of psychopathology are often associated with abnormalities in the activation levels of certain brain systems, as described in Chapter 16. For example, depression is associated with heightened brain activation in a limbic system region known as the subgenual cingulate cortex. On the basis of these findings, Mayberg and her colleagues implanted electrodes in these brain areas in patients whose severe depression had not responded to conventional interventions.

vagal nerve stimulation An emerging biomedical treatment for depression that involves electrically stimulating the vagus nerve with a small battery-powered implant.

deep brain stimulation (DBS) An emerging biomedical treatment for depression and OCD that involves stimulating specific parts of the brain with implanted electrodes.

17.22   SCIENTIFIC METHOD: Does deep brain stimulation relieve depressive symptoms?

Method

1. The six patients selected had severe depression that could not be treated by conventional methods.

2. Two holes were drilled in each patient's head and electrodes were implanted deep in the brain, underneath the anterior portion of the corpus callosum on both sides of the brain.

3. A battery pack and pulse generator were implanted in the chest wall, beneath the skin, to stimulate the electrodes implanted in the brain.

4. After surgery, the patient's medical team determined the magnitude and frequency of the electrical pulses that the patient received.

Electrode

Pulse generator

One patient who has received deep brain stimulation of the sort described by Mayberg is shown to the right. The X-ray shows her electrodes and the wires that connect her electrodes to the pulse generator in her chest.

Results

In an initial study, four of the six patients who received deep brain stimulation showed clear decreases in depressive symptoms.

CONCLUSION: Deep brain stimulation may provide some relief for some patients with otherwise intractable depression.

SOURCE STUDY: Mayberg et al., 2005

17.23 **Magnets for the mind** Repetitive transcranial magnetic stimulation (rTMS) sends a painless magnetic field through the skull to the cortical surface, where pulses can be used to stimulate or dampen activity in various areas.

They then used DBS to disrupt abnormal patterns of activity, thereby normalizing the activity of this portion of the brain (Mayberg et al., 2005; Figure 17.22). In initial findings, four of six patients showed clear benefits from this treatment, a finding that has provoked considerable interest and spurred research efforts to better understand the brain bases of depression (Lozano et al., 2008; Ressler & Mayberg, 2007; for more on DBS, see Miller, 2009). This treatment is currently being evaluated by other groups, both for depression and for other disorders, such as medication-resistant obsessive-compulsive disorder (Abelson et al., 2005; Mallet et al., 2008).

A third type of treatment is called **repetitive transcranial magnetic stimulation (rTMS)**. In this treatment, rapid pulses of magnetic stimulation from a hand-held coil placed close to the scalp are used to alter neuronal activity in fully awake participants (Figure 17.23). Treatments last 20 to 30 minutes for several weeks, and the procedure is painless and not associated with any cognitive side effects. When used to treat medication-resistant depression, rTMS has been shown to be as effective as ECT (Janicak et al., 2002). These are exciting findings because, unlike ECT, rTMS does not require anesthetic and doesn't appear to have cognitive side effects (Janicak, 2005).

repetitive transcranial magnetic stimulation (rTMS) An emerging biomedical treatment for depression that involves applying rapid pulses of magnetic stimulation to the brain from a coil held near the scalp.

COMMON FACTORS AND COMBINED TREATMENTS

We have now described the major modes of psychological and biomedical treatment, emphasizing how each of these forms of therapy is distinct from the others—both in its conceptual grounding and in its practice. With respect to the psychological treatments, some modes of therapy focus on behaviors; some focus on thoughts and patterns of interpretation that the patient can see within himself; others focus on unconscious beliefs or memories. In some modes of therapy, the therapist actively gives instructions or directions; in others, the therapist merely asks questions; in still others, the therapist is a quiet listener. With respect to the biomedical therapies, in pharmacological treatments, newer generations of drugs are constantly being developed with the aim of targeting increasingly specific neurotransmitter systems. At the same time, nonpharmacological treatments are focusing on increasingly specific regions in the nervous system.

Common Factors

Even within this diversity of treatments—particularly psychological treatments—the forms of therapy have elements in common. These include establishing a strong relationship with the patient, instilling hope, and offering new ways of thinking, feeling, and behaving (Frank & Frank, 1991; Miller, Duncan, & Hubbel, 2005). These shared elements must be considered when we ask how—or whether—therapy helps people with their problems.

RELATIONSHIP EFFECTS

Several benefits of therapy are not the direct result of any specific therapeutic techniques; instead, these benefits grow out of the relationship that the patient establishes with the therapist (Figure 17.24). One of these benefits is simply that the patient gains an ally against his problems; this **therapeutic alliance** helps most patients believe that they really can conquer their difficulties and achieve better lives (Barber, Connolly, Crits-Christoph, Gladis, & Siqueland, 2000). In fact, some researchers believe that the therapeutic alliance is the most important ingredient in effective psychotherapy and is indispensable even when medication is the primary treatment.

Why is the relationship so important? Among other considerations, it provides the patient with an intimate, confiding connection with another person, reassuring the patient that there is at least one other person in the world whom he can trust and who will help him. This connection also allows the patient to safely say things that otherwise might never be said, and in this fashion provides what some people think of as a kind of secular confessional.

17.24 Relationship effects Films such as *Good Will Hunting* (1997) portray a positive (if somewhat dramatic) relationship between therapist and client.

therapeutic alliance The relationship between therapist and patient that helps many patients feel hopeful and supported.

HOPE

People who seek help often feel discouraged and hopeless. They worry that their problems are weird or shameful and either too trivial to warrant therapy or so severe that no treatment will work. They may yearn for, yet dread, the chance to reveal things they have kept secret, often for years.

All psychotherapists, regardless of their approach, spend a great deal of time hearing these concerns and secrets and responding to them in an accepting and nonjudgmental manner. With some reassurance and a little education, patients often let go of their anxieties as they learn that their problems are understandable, rather common, not shameful, and quite treatable. As the therapist confidently describes the rationale for treatment, and what benefits might be expected, the patient begins to feel hope for recovery, often for the first time. This hope is a crucial common factor across therapies.

The fostering of hope is also a feature of the biomedical therapies. When a patient speaks with a medical professional about his problems and finally hears a name given to what previously seemed a mass of unconnected symptoms, the patient often feels great relief. Hearing that a medication may help him, the patient may feel that at last there's hope he may get better, which may amplify the drug's effects. Indeed, as we will shortly see, placebo effects—which may arise because of an expectation that symptoms will improve—are so powerful that they need to be controlled whenever we try to test the effectiveness of a biomedical therapy.

NEW WAYS OF THINKING, FEELING, AND BEHAVING

People who seek treatment often feel "stuck" and unsure how to proceed with one or more aspects of their lives. Psychological or biomedical treatments can address these feelings by exposing the patient to new ways of thinking about their problems. In psychodynamic therapies, a patient may for the first time understand her role in interpersonal conflicts that seem to repeat themselves. In humanistic-experiential therapies, a patient may begin to appreciate her conflicting goals and see a path toward reconciling them. In behavioral therapies, a patient may gain understanding of the triggers for his anxiety and develop confidence that he can interact with the feared object despite his anxiety. In cognitive-behavioral therapies, a new way of viewing the world may open up as the patient for the first time sees the powerful role of automatic thoughts that can make relatively innocuous events seem like life-or-death situations. Even in the biomedical therapies, a patient may gain an appreciation of the biological processes that underlie his mental disorder and come to view this disorder as just as treatable as other medical problems. In each case, new ways of thinking provide the basis for healthier and more adaptive ways of feeling and behaving.

Combined Treatments

In light of these common factors, it seems likely that the various forms of therapy all contain some of the same "active ingredients." Of course, the trend toward multimodal therapy, in which therapists from each tradition borrow ideas and techniques from other traditions, also leads to increasing overlap among their approaches.

Another development that makes the distinctions between therapy types less clearcut is that many therapists join a multimodal approach to psychotherapy with medication. Indeed, one survey indicates that more than half the patients being treated for mental disorders receive both drugs and psychotherapy (Pincus et al., 1999). Thus, for example, patients suffering from depression are often treated with antidepressants and cognitive-behavioral therapy, with the aim that the drugs will ease the patients' distress in the short term and the therapy will provide longer-lasting effects (DeRubeis, Siegle, & Hollon, 2008; Hollon & Fawcett, 1995). By a similar logic, patients suffering from anxiety disorders often receive medication as well as psychotherapy (Walkup et al., 2008).

EVALUATING TREATMENTS

Now that we have considered some important differences between therapy types, we need to ask: How do we know whether any of these therapies actually help people feel better and function better?

empirically supported treatments (EST) Clinical methods that research has shown to be effective for treating a given disorder.

The Importance of Empirically Supported Treatments

Practitioners of any form of therapy obviously want to be sure that they are providing benefits and doing no harm, and this has led many clinicians and researchers to seek ways of validating their therapy—making certain it works (Figure 17.25). In addition, validation has become more urgent in the last few years, fueled by a worldwide movement toward identifying **empirically supported treatments (EST)**—that is, treatments that are based on solid research. This movement was initially aimed at the broad practice of medicine (Sackett, Straus, Richardson, Rosenberg, & Haynes, 2000; Sox & Woolf, 1993) but has led to a similar movement within education, social work, and psychology (American Psychological Association Presidential Task Force on Evidence-Based Practice, 2006; Chambless & Ollendick, 2001; de los Reyes & Kazdin, 2008).

Many factors have contributed to this movement toward EST in psychology. One consideration lies in a number of prominent critiques of psychotherapy. An early attack launched by the British psychologist Hans Eysenck was particularly concerned with the efficacy of psychoanalysis and similar "insight" therapies (Eysenck, 1952). Although more recent studies have challenged Eysenck's conclusion that psychotherapy has no curative effects, his criticisms and concerns fed into the broader movement demanding that psychotherapy be validated empirically.

A second factor that has contributed to the EST movement has been the development of pharmacological treatments. These medications, as we have seen, can be extremely helpful, but they can also have unfortunate side effects, making it crucial that we use them only for the patients and the disorders for which they are clearly effective. In addition, the availability of these medications invites questions about the value of nonmedical treatment—namely, psychotherapy. Is it possible that hours of therapy might be replaced by simply taking a pill? This notion obviously demands a careful evaluation of whether psychotherapy works or not.

One last factor fueling the EST movement involves the *cost* of therapy. Psychotherapy requires hours with a trained professional, and many of the medications for mental disorders are quite expensive, too. In many cases, the expenses are covered by insurance, but as health expenses have risen, insurance companies have grown more concerned about making certain that the treatments they are paying for are worthwhile (Zarkin, Grabowski, Mauskopf, Bannerman, & Weisler, 1995).

The Logic of Outcome Research

How can we find out whether a psychological or biomedical treatment truly provides relief for someone with a particular mental disorder? As a way of tackling this issue, let us suppose that we want to find out whether a given drug—say, Wellbutrin—reduces the symptoms of depression. For a first step, we could administer Wellbutrin to a group of patients diagnosed with depression, and assess the patients' status before and after receiving the medication. This assessment would provide useful information, but a little reflection shows that relying only on this procedure would be a mistake.

One problem with the before-and-after assessment is that it ignores the possibility of spontaneous improvement. With some disorders, many patients get better on their own, whether they receive treatment or not. Therefore, if patients are indeed better off after taking Wellbutrin than they were before, their improvement might simply reflect spontaneous improvement and have nothing to do with the medication. In addition, even without spontaneous improvement, most disorders fluctuate in their severity, and it seems likely that patients will seek treatment when they are feeling particularly bad. If so, the odds are good that the normal ups and downs of the disorder will make the patients look better a few weeks (or months) later. If they have been taking medication during those weeks, we might be inclined to assume that the drugs had caused the improvement.

To control for these factors, we need to compare two groups of patients, with one group taking Wellbutrin for, say, 6 weeks, while the other group receives no treatment. We also need to make certain that these two groups are matched at the start of the study—with similar symptoms, similar backgrounds, and so on. As we discussed in Chapter 1, our best means of achieving this matching would be via *random assignment*—with a coin toss (or the equivalent) determining whether each participant in the study ends up in the treatment group or the no-treatment group. Then, if the participants in the two groups differ at the end of the procedure, we can be reasonably sure that the difference arose *during* the study—presumably as a result of the treatment.

In addition, we would want to ensure that the participants in our study are reasonably uniform in their disorder. Thus, we would want to make certain that all of the participants were truly depressed, and that their depression was not complicated by other problems that might mask the effects of the treatment. Likewise, we would probably want to make sure the participants were all similar to one another in the duration and severity of their depression. Otherwise, variations from one participant to the next might prevent us from detecting the therapy's effects.

Evaluating Psychological vs. Biomedical Treatments

The elements we have described characterize what is usually termed a **randomized clinical trial** (RCT), so called because of the random assignment of participants to groups. In most ways an RCT would be run in the same fashion for evaluating a new medication or for evaluating a specific type of therapy. There are, however, a few differences between RCTs for drugs and RCTs for therapy.

CONTROLLING FOR PLACEBO EFFECTS

In evaluating biomedical treatments, we need to be alert to the possibility of **placebo** effects—the influence of a patient's beliefs and expectations in bringing about a cure. We generally test for placebo effects by giving the patient a medically neutral substance (the placebo); the placebo often diminishes symptoms, but because it has no active ingredients, its effect has to be understood in terms of the patient's beliefs: The patient believes in the pill's powers, and it is his faith in the medication, not the medication itself, that brings the benefits.

In the broad practice of medicine, the evidence is mixed regarding how powerful placebos are. In some studies, placebos seem to produce real improvement (Benson & Friedman, 1996); in others, the placebo effect is weak or nonexistent (Hrobjartsson & Gotzsche, 2001). In the study of mental disorders, though, we need to take the placebo

randomized clinical trial (RCT) A procedure for evaluating the outcome of therapy, usually involving random assignment of participants to one or more treatment groups or a no-treatment control group.

placebo A chemically inert substance that produces real medical benefits because the patient believes it will help her.

effect seriously because it is surely plausible that a patient's distress might be alleviated by her belief in the cure rather than by the cure itself.

In studies of a medication, therefore, we give the medication we are interested in—Wellbutrin, in our example—to one group of patients, and a placebo to the other group. This second group will receive the same attention from the treatment staff as the Wellbutrin group, and they will be told exactly the same things about their treatment. They will also be given the same number of pills as the patients in the true-drug group, and on the same schedule. In this fashion, we ensure that the two groups have the same expectations and the same beliefs about the treatment. If we find, therefore, that the groups differ at the end of the study, the difference must be attributed to the one element that distinguished the two groups—the fact that the patients in one group actually took a medication, while those in the other took inert pills.

In principle, the same logic regarding a placebo control applies to the study of psychological treatments. In practice, however, it is not clear what the placebo would be in this case. Would we want the placebo group to work with a therapist who listens, but without warmth? A therapist who expresses warmth, but provides no counsel? A therapist who offers counsel irrelevant to the patient's problems? The choice between these (or other) options is not clear, making this one source of ambiguity in interpreting RCT data for psychotherapy (Nathan et al., 2000). For this reason, many RCTs for psychological treatments do not have special placebo control conditions. Instead, the treatment of interest is compared either to other standard treatments or to a **wait-list control**. The wait-list control is one in which participants are randomly assigned to receive either immediate or delayed treatment, and the immediate treatment participants' responses to treatment are evaluated by comparing them to the delayed treatment participants—who have not yet started therapy.

MANUALIZED THERAPY

There is one other important way in which RCT procedures differ for psychological and biomedical treatments. When we are testing a medicine, it is easy to ensure that each patient gets the same number of pills and that the chemical constituents of the pills are the same for everyone in the study. But how can we ensure, in a study of therapy, that each patient gets the same treatment and the same "dose"?

Investigators usually address this point by developing a treatment manual that tells the therapists exactly how to proceed during the study—what steps to take in therapy, what instructions to offer, and so on. This **manualized therapy** denies the therapist the option of improvising or adjusting procedures midstream, which may sometimes undermine the quality of the therapy (Addis & Krasnow, 2000). However, this standardization seems essential if we are to assess whether a particular therapy is effective.

Clearly, there are trade-offs associated with manualized therapy. On the positive side, this procedure seems our best hope for learning whether a particular type of treatment works. On the negative side, it may not accurately represent the way that treatment would be used outside the study, since most clinicians adopt an eclectic approach. Clinicians also often adjust their approach as the therapy proceeds and they learn which steps seem promising for a particular individual and which do not.

Efficacy vs. Utility

RCT data are extremely useful for allowing us to identify certain therapies as "empirically supported treatments." But some authors are skeptical about the reliance on RCT data (Nathan et al., 2000; Westen & Bradley, 2005; Westen, Novotny, & Thompson-

wait-list control In randomized clinical trials, a control condition in which patients receive delayed treatment rather than no treatment. Before being treated, they are compared to patients treated earlier.

manualized therapy A form of therapy, often used in research, in which a manual describes a set course of therapy, indicating what steps the therapist should take, what instructions to offer, and so on.

Brenner, 2004; Zimmerman, Mattia, & Posternack, 2002). Specifically, they argue that an RCT might inform us about a therapy's **efficacy** (whether it works in carefully designed tests) but might not tell us about its **clinical utility** (whether it works in more typical circumstances; APA Presidential Task Force on Evidence-Based Practice, 2006).

We have already considered one of the bases for this concern—the reliance on manualized therapy. A different concern hinges on the patient groups used in many RCT studies. We discussed earlier the need for reasonably uniform patient groups in an RCT—people whose disorders are relatively uncomplicated by other problems. This uniformity allows us to ask whether our therapy works for people in a well-defined group, but it undermines external validity. Many of the people who seek out therapy do not have a clear diagnosis, and, if they do, the diagnosis may be complex. That is because many forms of mental disorder have high rates of *comorbidity*—they occur together with some other disorder. Thus, for example, there is considerable comorbidity between anxiety and depression disorders—someone who has one often suffers from the other as well. As a result, the RCT data may tell us what happens in therapy with "pure" cases, but not what happens in the (much more common) mixed cases encountered in most clinics.

For these and other reasons, we must combine RCT data with other sorts of data, including studies of ordinary clinical practice, case studies, studies of the actual process of change within psychotherapy, and more (APA Presidential Task Force on Evidence-Based Practice, 2006; Shadish et al., 1997). This broader package of evidence will help us understand whether therapy as it is usually practiced, with more typical patients, has the desired effects; it will also tell us whether the worries about manualized therapy are justified.

Meta-Analyses of Therapy Outcome

It seems, then, that our efforts to evaluate therapies will need to draw on diverse lines of evidence from many different studies. This creates a new question for us: How should we put together the evidence? What is the best way to integrate and summarize the available data? For many investigators, the answer lies in a statistical technique called **meta-analysis**, which we first encountered in Chapter 1 by means of which the results of many different studies can be combined.

In one of the earliest analyses of this kind, 475 studies comprising 25,000 patients were reviewed (M. L. Smith et al., 1980; Figure 17.26). In each of these studies, patients who received some kind of psychotherapy were compared with a similar group of

efficacy Whether a therapeutic intervention works under carefully controlled conditions.

clinical utility Whether a therapeutic intervention works under real-world conditions.

meta-analysis A statistical technique for combining the results of many studies on a particular topic, even when the studies used different data collection methods.

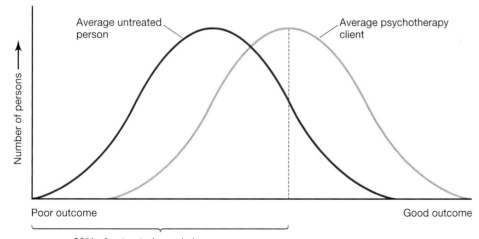

17.26 Psychotherapy versus no treatment These two normal distribution curves based on data from 475 studies show the improvement of untreated people and psychotherapy clients. The outcome for the average therapy client surpassed that for 80% of the untreated people.

patients who did not receive any. The studies included in this analysis differed in many respects. One was the kind of psychotherapy used—whether psychodynamic, humanistic, behavioral, or cognitive. Another factor that varied was the criterion of improvement. In some cases, it was the level of a symptom: the amount of avoidance that a person with snake phobias eventually showed toward snakes, the number of washing episodes shown by a patient who washed compulsively, and so on. In others, it was based on an improvement in functioning, such as a rise in the grade-point average (GPA) of a student who was disturbed. In still others, such as studies of patients with depression, it was an improvement in mood as rated by scales completed by the patient himself or by knowledgeable outsiders, such as his spouse and children.

Given all these differences among the studies, combining the results seems problematic, but meta-analysis provides a method. Consider two hypothetical studies, A and B. Let us say that Study A shows that, after treatment, the average patient with snake phobia can move closer to a snake than the average patient who received no treatment. Let us also assume that Study B found that students with depression who received psychotherapy show a greater increase in GPA than do equivalent students in an untreated control group. On the face of it, there is no way to average the results of the two studies because they use completely different units. In the first case, the average effect of therapy—that is, the difference between the group that received treatment and the one that did not—is measured in feet (how near the snake the patient will go); in the second, it is counted in GPA points. But here is the trick provided by meta-analysis. Let us suppose we find that in Study A, 85% of the treated patients are able to move closer to the snake than the average untreated patient. Let us further suppose that in Study B, 75% of the students who received psychotherapy earn a GPA higher than the average GPA of the untreated students. Now we can average the scores. To be sure, distance and GPA points are like apples and oranges and cannot be compared. But the percentage relationships—in our case, 85 and 75—are comparable. Since this is so, they can be averaged across different studies.

What, therefore, do we learn from meta-analyses? The conclusion drawn by averaging across the 475 studies was that the "average person who receives therapy is better off at the end of it than 80% of the persons who do not" (M. L. Smith et al., 1980, p. 87). Later meta-analyses have used different criteria in selecting studies for inclusion but yield similar results (see, for example, Wampold et al., 1997). Other studies found that even months or years after treatment, patients still show these improvements (Nicholson & Berman, 1983).

Does One Size Fit All?

At many junctures, we have emphasized the suffering and disruption caused by mental illness; we can now add the key fact that various forms of therapy can help with these profound problems. Meta-analyses indicate that both psychotherapy and drug therapy are effective treatments for many mental disorders. More focused studies provide a similarly encouraging message. Specific modes of therapy, and specific drugs, considered one by one, also provide help—so that people who receive treatment end up better off than those who do not.

However, many questions remain: Is everyone equally likely to benefit from these therapies? Or are some people more likely to benefit than others? And, crucially, how do the various forms of therapy compare with one another? Are some therapies faster, or more complete, or more successful than others? These are important questions to ask if we want our therapies to be effective, and also cost-efficient, in terms of time, emotional energy, and, of course, dollars.

Overall, therapy often improves the lives of adults who suffer from a range of psychological, addictive, and health problems (see, for example, Barlow, 2004; Nathan & Gorman, 2002; Roth & Fonagy, 2004; Wampold et al., 1997). Therapy also helps children at various ages (Kazdin & Weisz, 2003; Weisz, Hawley, & Doss, 2004; Weisz, Doss, & Hawley, 2006).

Even so, therapy does not work for every individual, and, in fact, a certain proportion of patients—between 5 and 10%—actually get *worse* as a result of therapy (Lambert & Bergin, 1994; Lilienfeld, 2007; M. L. Smith, Glass, & Miller, 1980). What produces this deterioration? In many cases, the problem seems to be a bad therapist-patient relationship; in other cases, the problem may be outright incompetence in the therapist (Hadley & Strupp, 1976; M. L. Smith, Glass, & Miller, 1980). Still other cases of deterioration may have a subtler cause. Psychotherapy sometimes disrupts what is stable in the patient's life yet provides no substitute (Hadley & Strupp, 1976; Lambert & Bergin, 1994). For example, the therapy may lead a patient to regard her marriage as unsatisfactory, but as she takes steps toward separation or divorce, she may become severely depressed at the prospect of being alone. Good psychotherapists are alert to such dangers and attempt to avert such deterioration whenever possible.

For many years, researchers thought that therapy was most likely to succeed with patients who were young, physically attractive, high in verbal ability, intelligent, and successful in other domains; however, these turn out *not* to be the key factors (Nathan, Stuart, & Dolan, 2000). Instead, therapy seems to have roughly equal benefits for people from a wide range of socioeconomic backgrounds (Petry, Tennen, & Afflect, 2000; Prochaska & Norcross, 2007). To put the point somewhat differently, what matters for the therapeutic benefit may not be who exactly the patient is, but (as we highlighted earlier) whether the patient feels a strong sense of alliance with the therapist (J. P. Barber et al., 2000; Martin, Garske, & Davis, 2000). Also crucial is whether the patient is, at the start, fully motivated to participate in the therapy and optimistic about the chances of recovery (Mussell et al., 2000). Improvement is also more likely with more therapy sessions rather than fewer (Hansen, Lambert, & Forman, 2002; Seligman, 1995). And some disorders—for example, phobias—are more responsive to psychotherapy than others, such as schizophrenia.

One point, however, is less clear and remains the focus of debate: Should people with subsyndromal conditions be treated? Some critics believe that they should and note that evidence suggests that these syndromes are a genuine concern. For example, one study surveyed over 2,000 individuals for the presence of major depression. Based on their signs and symptoms, these individuals were classified into three groups: normal, diagnosable for major depression, or having *subsyndromal* depression—that is, they had some of the signs and symptoms of major depression but not enough to be diagnosed as having the disorder. On most measures, the people with subsyndromal and major depression were equally impaired (Judd, Paulus, Wells, & Rapaport, 1996; also Rapaport & Judd, 1998).

Others argue that treating all these individuals (and so offering similar therapies to those diagnosed with depression and those who are not-quite-depressed) would be a first step down a dangerous path, one in which people take pills or seek therapy to adjust their personalities just as they now seek nose jobs, liposuction, and face-lifts to adjust their body shapes. Indeed, this view might lead to a world in which nearly any eccentricity is regarded as problematic and a candidate for treatment, with the term *normal* reserved for the relatively few who are sufficiently bland to avoid labeling. Moreover, such indiscriminate diagnosis might lead people to use their subsyndromal conditions to excuse bad social conduct or poor job performance (see W. K. Olson, 1997; J. Q. Wilson, 1997). There are obvious dangers here, but let us note as well that diagnostic criteria that are too stringent and rigid may raise barriers to treatment for people who might benefit from it.

ARE ALL INTERVENTIONS EQUALLY EFFECTIVE?

What about differences among therapies? Are some forms of therapy particularly successful? Remarkably, many studies indicate that the various interventions we have considered, when compared with one another, are all equally effective. This assessment has led some to offer the *dodo bird verdict*, after the dodo bird in *Alice in Wonderland*, who organized a race among various Wonderland creatures and concluded, "Everyone has won and all must have prizes" (Figure 17.27; Elkin et al., 1989; Luborsky, Singer, & Luborsky, 1975; Shear et al., 1994; Sloane, Staples, Cristol, Yorkston, & Whipple, 1975; M. L. Smith et al., 1980; Wampold et al., 1997).

Others have taken strong issue with this conclusion, pointing to studies of the effects of specific modes of therapy for different clinical disorders (Chambless & Ollendick, 2001). Thus, for example, behavior therapy seems especially effective in treating anxiety disorders, particularly the phobias (P. E. Nathan & Gorman, 2002) but is rarely used for, say, personality disorders. Cognitive therapy is effective in treating mood disorders (Hollon et al., 2002) and, indeed, may be just as effective as drug treatment (but with longer-lasting impact and without the side effects); it is also useful for other diagnoses, such as panic disorder (Hollon, Stewart, & Strunk, 2006; Shear, Pilkonis, Cloitre, & Leon, 1994) and bulimia nervosa (Wilson & Fairburn, 2002). Cognitive therapy may be less effective, however, with other sorts of problems—for example, phobias. Evidence likewise suggests that the experiential therapies can alleviate depression and anxiety disorders (Elliott et al., 2004), but these therapies, too, have their limits and are less effective for schizophrenia. The evidence is least compelling for the earliest form of therapy—Freud's psychoanalytic technique. The more modern psychodynamic therapies derived from Freud's procedure—especially interpersonal therapy—do seem to be effective, especially for depression (Frank & Spanier, 1995; Hollon et al., 2002).

Although the dodo bird verdict remains controversial (see, for example, Crits-Christoph, 1997; Howard, Krause, Saunders, & Kopta, 1997), this "verdict" contains a substantial kernel of truth, and the differences among treatments for a given disorder do seem smaller than some would have expected. Thus, for example, the data suggest that cognitive therapy, drug therapy, and some combination of the two with interpersonal therapy are each effective treatments for depression (although within this set, the benefits of some therapies last longer than others).

On the one hand, the similarity in outcomes is surprising, because the various forms of therapy differ enormously. At the same time, we have already mentioned a number of points that help explain why different therapies have similar outcomes. For one, the placebo effect creates the expectation of improvement, as well as hope. This point is shared across various forms of therapy, and so would contribute to the resemblance among the therapeutic outcomes.

In addition, the therapies have other key elements in common: gaining an ally, taking active steps to improve a condition, and so on. To the extent that these elements are beneficial and common to the various modes of therapy, we would again expect all the modes to be effective.

"Everyone has won and all must have prizes."

17.27 Dodo bird verdict In the context of psychotherapy outcome studies, the dodo bird verdict holds that all forms of psychological therapy are equally effective. Critics have vigorously challenged this idea.

Another factor that favors the dodo bird verdict is that mental disorders usually are produced by a mix of factors, some constituting the diathesis, and some the more immediate trigger. If all these factors are relevant, then removing *any* of them should be helpful in preventing or treating the disorder. Depression, for example, is more likely if a person has a particular style of thinking about the world, and so it might be alleviated by shifting this style of thought (as in cognitive therapy). But depression is also more likely if the person does not have an adequate social network, and so might be alleviated by taking steps toward getting more support (as in interpersonal therapy). This logic suggests that either form of therapy might be helpful—although for different reasons—and this, too, helps us understand why different forms of therapy can have similar outcomes.

SOME FINAL THOUGHTS: FAR, BUT NOT YET FAR ENOUGH

Where does all of this leave us? It has been more than 100 years since antibiotics were first used to treat general paresis and Freud developed his "talking cure." What can we say today about the treatment of mental disorders?

Without question, there has been enormous progress. Let us begin with the psychological interventions. There is no doubt that therapy produces benefits; we see this in both the RCT data and the meta-analyses. In some cases, these benefits may last longer than those of drug treatments, and, of course, psychotherapy does not raise concerns about medical side effects. But important questions remain, especially regarding how psychotherapy works. Some mechanisms appear to be specific to particular therapies, as demonstrated by the fact that some therapies are more effective in treating particular disorders than others. However, other factors seem to apply more broadly, such as the relationship that forms between therapist and patient.

With respect to biomedical therapies, the progress has been striking. Antipsychotic medications control some of the most disabling manifestations of schizophrenia. The antidepressants and mood-stabilizing medications (and, where appropriate, ECT) are remarkably effective in treating the extreme moods involved in depression and mania, and the anxiolytics do the same for disabling anxiety. Yet these advances are far from what one might wish. We have mentioned that the medicines do not cure; they just keep symptoms in check. We have also discussed the sometimes substantial side effects of various medications and our uncertainty about exactly how some of these effective biomedical interventions work. Nonetheless, the biomedical treatments for mental disorders are an extraordinarily powerful tool for diminishing many forms of human suffering.

Overall, then, we have come a great distance from where we started more than a century ago. This is especially clear when we compare current practices with those at the time of the American Revolution, when Benjamin Rush dunked his patients in ice cold water or whirled them around until they were unconscious. Good treatments are now available for a number of mental disorders, and they enable many people to rebound from disability and return to normal functioning. The future seems bright, too. There is growing interest in early detection and even prevention of mental disorders (Schmidt & Gösele, 2007); advances in neuroscience hold out the promise of refinements in both diagnosis and treatment (Hyman, 2007); and new findings from genetics may one day allow us to predict with far greater precision who will benefit from specific forms of therapy (Binder et al., 2004). We have much further to go, of course, but there is still a great deal to celebrate.

TREATMENTS PAST AND PRESENT

- Early treatments for mental disorders were frequently harsh and rarely effective. Over the centuries, reformers have succeeded in eliminating many of the worst practices.

- Contemporary treatments target different aspects of the network of interrelated biological and environmental factors that give rise to mental disorders. For convenience, researchers make a distinction between *psychological* and *biomedical* treatments. However, the boundaries between psychological and biological aspects of treatments are by no means clear-cut; many treatments emphasize both aspects.

- A wide range of professionals provide treatments for mental disorders, including clinical psychologists; psychiatrists; psychiatric nurses; marriage, family, and child counselors; school and vocational counselors; mental health counselors; and clinical social workers. *Cultural competence* refers to taking into account a patient's cultural beliefs, values, and expectations.

PSYCHOLOGICAL TREATMENTS

- Psychological treatments involve efforts to change the patient's thinking and behavior directly, usually by some form of discussion, instruction, or training.

- *Psychodynamic approaches* to therapy have their origins in the classical psychoanalytic method developed by Sigmund Freud. The goal of this therapy is to have the patient "work through" psychological conflicts. Transformative insights are not merely intellectual, and this working through depends crucially on the process of *transference*, which illuminates the ways in which a patient's pattern of interaction in childhood can influence (and distort) current social relationships.

- *Humanistic approaches* have in common the idea that people must take responsibility for their lives and their actions, and live fully in the present. Carl Rogers's *client-centered therapy* stresses genuineness, unconditional positive regard, and empathic understanding. Fritz Perls's *gestalt therapy* uses a variety of techniques to help his patients integrate previously disparate aspects of self.

- *Behavioral approaches* seek to change a patient's behavior directly, drawing on principles of classical and operant conditioning as well as observational learning. One classical conditioning technique is *exposure therapy*. One operant conditioning technique is the use of *token economies*. One observational learning technique is *modeling*.

- *Cognitive-behavioral approaches* seek to change a person's beliefs and mode of thinking. One example is Albert Ellis's *rational-emotive behavioral therapy*, which challenges irrational beliefs. A second example is Aaron Beck's *cognitive therapy*, which helps patients identify their automatic thoughts and reactions, and substitute more beneficial reactions.

- Therapists often practice *eclecticism*, which weaves together various approaches. The last few decades have also seen extensions beyond one-on-one therapy. These include shared problem groups, therapy groups, and couple and family therapy.

BIOMEDICAL TREATMENTS

- Biomedical treatments are designed to alleviate mental disorders by directly altering the brain's functioning.

- Pharmacological treatments involve the administration of *psychotropic drugs*. Classical *antipsychotics* are helpful in treating the major positive symptoms of schizophrenia; newer antipsychotics show promise in treating negative symptoms. *Antidepressants*, such as the selective serotonin reuptake inhibitors (SSRIs), influence one or more neurotransmitter systems and offer relief from the symptoms of depression and other mental disorders. *Anxiolytics* decrease feelings of anxiety associated with the anxiety disorders.

- Drug treatments provide substantial symptom relief for many people with mental disorders. Drug therapy has not been an unqualified success, however, because of the prevalence of side effects and because it is difficult to determine which drug an individual should take—and in what quantity—for a given mental disorder. For example, the widespread use of medications for developmental disorders such as attention-deficit/hyperactivity disorder continues to be controversial.

- Nonpharmacological treatments for mental disorders include *psychosurgery* and *electroconvulsive therapy*, as well as newer treatments such as *vagal nerve stimulation*, *deep brain stimulation*, and *repetitive transcranial magnetic stimulation* (*rTMS*).

COMMON FACTORS AND COMBINED TREATMENTS

- Although the various psychological and biomedical therapies differ in many regards, they all benefit from *relationship effects*, including the *therapeutic alliance*. Other shared benefits include hope and learning new ways of thinking, feeling, and behaving.

EVALUATING TREATMENTS

- The *empirically supported treatments* movement calls for identifying treatments that are based on solid research. Outcome research is more difficult than it appears. For example, if people are better off after therapy than before, this might be the result of spontaneous improvement. To address this concern, a group receiving therapy should be compared with a matched group that receives no therapy, and the two groups should be uniform in their disorder at the start of therapy.
- *Randomized clinical trials (RCTs)* are often used to assess the *efficacy* of therapy, but the conditions of these trials are often different from those in actual clinical practice. One difference lies in the use of *manualized therapy*; another lies in the focus on patients with a single diagnosis and no comorbidity. For these reasons, it is important to combine data from randomized clinical trials with other forms of data collection. When testing a new drug, it is also crucial to control for the *placebo effect*. It is not as clear, however, how to control for this effect when testing a form of psychotherapy.
- One tool for assessing therapies is *meta-analysis*, by means of which the results of many different studies can be combined. The results of such analyses indicate that many of the various psychological and biomedical treatments are effective. Surprisingly, meta-analyses suggest that very different forms of therapy can be equally effective, a result often referred to as the dodo bird verdict.

ONLINE STUDY TOOLS

Go to StudySpace, **wwnorton.com/studyspace**, to access additional review and enrichment materials, including the following resources for each chapter:

Organize
- Study Plan
- Chapter Outline
- Quiz+ Assessment

Learn
- Ebook
- Chapter Review
- Vocabulary Flashcards
- Drag-and-Drop Labeling Exercises
- Audio Podcast Chapter Overview

Connect
- Critical Thinking Activity
- Studying the Mind Video Podcasts
- Video Exercises
- Animations
- **ZAPS** Psychology Labs

Credits

TEXT

Ch. 16: Debbie Allen, "My First Panic Attack: A Memorable Experience!" http://www.streetdirectory.com/travel_guide/108953/anxiety/my_first_panic_attack_a_memorable_experience.html. Reprinted by permission of the author.

ILLUSTRATIONS

Prologue: **xxii** George Georgiou/Panos; **2** Mark Harmel/Photo Researchers, Inc.; **3** "How does moral judgment work?" J. Greene, J. Haidt, Trends in Cog Sciences Vol. 6 No.12 Dec. 2002, Fig. 1; **5** Rob Melnychuk/Corbis; **7** (*top left*) Kevin Muggleton/Corbis, (*top middle*) Blend Images/Alamy, (*top right*) Don Enger/Animals Animals/Earth Images; **7** (*bottom*) NBC/Universal/Will Hart/The Kobal Collection; **9** A. Todorov, Dept of Psychology, Princeton University & I. R. Olson, Dept. of Psychology, Temple University; **10** (*left*) New Line Cinema/Everett Collection, (*right*) Gallo Images/Getty Images; **11** Getty Images; **12** (*left*) Chris Collins/Corbis, (*right*) Win McNamee/Reuters/Landov; **13** © Jerry Cooke/Corbis; **15** AP/Wide World Photos; **17** (*right bottom*) NBC/Universal/Will Hart/The Kobal Collection, (*middle*) AP/Wide World Photos, (*top*) Getty Images, (*right top*) "How does moral judgment work?" J. Greene, J. Haidt, Trends in Cog Sciences Vol.6 No.12 Dec. 2002, Fig. 1, (*left bottom*) Gallo Images/Getty Images, (*left top*) Kevin Muggleton/Corbis

Chapter 1: **20** © Daniel Grizelj; **23** (*top*) Somos Images/Corbis, (*bottom*) Courtesy of American Media, Ltd; **24** (*top*) © 2002, The New Yorker Collection from Cartoonbank.com. All rights reserved, (*bottom*) AP/Wide World Photos; **25** Courtesy of Clarence Brown; **26** Archives Jean Piaget/Université de Genevé; **27** (*top*) Fancy/Veer/Corbis, (*bottom*) SW Productions/Getty Images; **28** Courtesy John Chase/Chasecartoons.com; **33** (*left*) Roy Botterell/zefa/Corbis, (*right*) Helen King/Corbis; **35** (*top*) Kevin Muggleton/Corbis; **37** Dimitri Lindt/TempSport/Corbis; **41** Courtesy of Sidney Harris, ScienceCartoonPlus.com; **43** Corbis; **45** David R. Frazier Photolibrary, Ltd./Alamy

Chapter 2: **50** Henrik Spohler/laif/Redux; **53** (*top left*) Andrew Syred/Photo Researchers, (*top right*) University of Edinburgh, Wellcome Image, (*top middle*) Visuals Unlimited/Corbis, (*top right*) Jim Zuckerman/Corbis, (*bottom*) Biophoto Associates; **54** (*top*) Science Photo Library, (*bottom*) Leonard Lessin, Photo Researchers, Inc.; **56** Bettmann/Corbis; **59** Wikimedia Commons; **62** Biophoto/Cordier Sylvain/Peter

Arnold; **63** Wikimedia Commons; **64** scienceblogs.com; **66** Heinrich Van Denberg/WWI/Still/Peter Arnold; **68** (*top*) Andersen Ross/cultura/Corbis, (*bottom*) Corbis; **70** (*top*) **74** Wikimedia Commons; **75** (*top left*) © Andersen Ross/cultura/Corbis, (*top right*) John-Francis Bourke/Corbis; **75** Carol Beckwith & Angela Fisher/HAGA/The Image Works; **77** (*top*) WILDLIFE/Peter Arnold Inc., (*bottom*) Biosphoto/Vernay Pierre/Peter Arnold, Inc.; **78** Stuart Freedman/Panos Pictures; **80** Michael Newman/Photo Edit

Chapter 3: **84** Cary Wolinsky/Aurora Photos; **86** Courtesy National Library of Medicine; **87** From Descartes, R. (1662), Trait de L'homme, Cambridge University Press; **88** David Becker/Science Photo Library/Photo Researchers, Inc.; **89** (*left*) Science Photo Library/Photo Researchers, Inc., (*middle*) CNRI/Science Photo Library/Photo Researchers, Inc., (*right*) Guigoz/Dr. a/Privat/Science Source/Photo Researchers, Inc.; **90** Nancy Kedersha/Science Photo Library/Photo Researchers, Inc.; **91** (*top*) Dennis Kunkel, Inc., (*bottom*) Biophoto Associates/Photo Researchers, Inc.; **96** Eccles, J.C., *The Understanding of the Brain*, Copyright © The McGraw-Hill Companies; **98** Lewis, Everhart, and Zeevi/Visuals Unlimited; **107** (*left*) Wikimedia.com, (*right*) Damasio, et al. (1994) The Return of Phineas Gage. Science, 264. Courtesy of Hanna Damasio; **108** Marcello Massimini/University of Wisconsin-Madison; **109** AJ Photo/Photo Researchers; **110** (*left*) Custom Medical Stock Photo, (*right*) Neil Borden/Photo Researchers; **111** Medical Body Scans/Photo Researchers, Inc.; **115** Corbis; **118** Courtesy of University of Wisconsin Madison, Brain Collection; **120** Courtesy of The Natural History Museum, London; **122** Physiological Psychology, 2e, by Rosenzweig and Leiman; **123** Nature Reviews Neuroscience 5, 812–819 (October 2004); **124** From Higher Cortical Functions in Man, 2e, by A. R. Luria. © 1979. Consultants Bureau Enterprises and Basic Books; **125** Dennis Kunkel, Inc.; **127** (*left*) Everett Collection, (*right*) Ziv Koren-Pool/Getty Images; **128** (*left*) Jason LaVeris/FilmMagic/Getty Images, (*right*) AP Photo/Eric Draper

Chapter 4: **132** Ian Teh/Panos; **134** Courtesy National Portrait Gallery, London; **136** (*top*) Pushkin Museum, Moscow. Photo: Bridgeman Art Library, (*bottom*) Culver Pictures, Inc., New York; **141** © Scott Camazine/Phototake—All rights reserved; **146** Hill Street Studios/Getty Images; **147** Scott Hortop/Alamy; **149** Atlantide Phototravel/Corbis; **150** © 1980 The New Yorker, Inc.; **151** Clouds Hill Imaging Ltd./Corbis; **152** (*left*) Michael Newman/Photo Edit, (*right*) Butch Martin/Alamy; **158** (*top*) Courtesy National Library of Medicine; **163** Omikron/Photo Researchers, Inc.; **166** (*right*) "Mach Bands," from Coren, Porac, and Ward, *Sensation and Perception*. Copyright © John Wiley & Sons, Inc. Reprinted by permission of John Wiley & Sons,

Inc.; **168** (*bottom*) Figure from L.M. Hurvich & D. Jameson, "An Opponent-Process Theory of Color Vision," *Psychological Review* 64 (1957): 384-404. Figure from L.M. Hurvich, *Color Vision* (Sinauer Associates, 1981). Reprinted by permission of the Estate of Leo M. Hurvich; **171** (*bottom*) Photographs by Fritz Goro. © Time Warner, Inc.; **175** Ira Wyman/Sygma/Corbis

Chapter 5: **180** Henry Georgi/Aurora; **183** (*top*) Russell Glenister/Corbis; **184** (*left*) Kanizsa, G. "Subjective Contours" from *Scientific American* 234. Copyright © 1976. Reprinted by permission of Jerome Kuhl; **185** (*top*) Photograph by Jeffrey Grosscup, (*bottom*) Jupiterimages/Getty Images; **187** (*bottom*) From Penrose & Penrose, "Impossible Objects: A special type of visual illusion," *British Journal of Psychology* 49.1 (1958): 31-33. Reproduced with permission of the British Journal of Psychology, © The British Psychological Society; **191** (*right*) Adapted from Biederman, I., "Recognition-by-components: A theory of human image understanding," *Psychological Review* 94 (1987): 115-147; **192** Milner & Goodale, 1995, p. 127; **196** W. W. Norton staff photo; **199** Shepard, R. N. (1990); **201** W. W. Norton staff photo; **202** (*top*) ScienceCartoonsPlus.com, (*middle*) Stephen J. Kraseman/Allstock, (*bottom*) Lee Snider/Corbis; **202** Gibson, James J. The Perspectives of the Visual World. (1950) Hougton Mifflin Co. Reprinted with permission; **205** Globus Studios/The Stock Market/Corbis; **209** Fig. 1, J. M. Henderson, "Regarding Scenes," Current Directions in Psychological Science, Vol. 16, No 4, p. 220; **213** Anton Vengo/Superstock; **215** (*top*) M.C. Escher's "Convex and Concave" © 2009 The M.C. Escher Company-Holland. All rights reserved, (*bottom*) Courtesy of the Metropolitan Museum of Art

Chapter 6: **218** Adrian Weinbrecht/Getty Images; **221** (*top*) Big Cheese Photo/IPN Stock; **226** Monika Bender/Getty Images; **229** Alamy; **234** Flying Colours Ltd/Getty images; **235** Bubbles Photolibrary/Alamy; **236** ScienceCartoonsPlus.com; **238** Science, vol. 324, p. 22, April 3, 2009; **239** (*top*) Scott Stulberg/Corbis, (*bottom*) Blend Images/SuperStock; **244** (*left*) Bettmann/Corbis, (*right*) Bubbles Space Photolibrary/Alamy; **246** Loomis Dean//Time Life Pictures/Getty Images; **247** Roger Cracknell/Alamy; **250** Chris Pearsall/Alamy; **251** (*bottom*) www.projects.olin.edu; **255** 2004, Sidney Harris

Chapter 7: **258** John And Lisa Merrill/Aurora Photos; **262** (*left*) Frank Lukasseck/Corbis, (*right*) Ed Kashi/Corbis; **263** Bettman/Corbis; **265** (*top*) Archives of the History of American Psychology/University of Akron, (*bottom*) Archives of the History of American Psychology/University of Akron; **271** Andy Newman/AP/Wide World Photos; **279** New York Public Library; **281** Nina Leen/Time Pix/Getty Images; **284** (*left*) Richard Vogel/AP Photo, (*right*) R. A. Homiski; **286** Julian Cotton/International Stock/Image State; **286** Brownie Harris/Corbis; **287** (*top left*) Marc Romanelli/Getty Images, (*top right*) Andrew Harrington/naturepl.com, (*bottom*) Courtesy Psychology Department, University of California, Berkeley; **292** Nathan Benn/Corbis; **294** (*top*) Hamburger Kunsthalle, Hamburg, Germany. Photo: Bildarchiv Preussischer Kulturbesitz/Art Resource, NY, (*bottom*) W. Perry Conway/Corbis

Chapter 8: **300** Stanley Greene/Noor/Aurora Photos; **303** (*left*) Geri Enberg Photography; **303** (*right*) Simon Jarratt/Corbis; **306** Talmi, D. et al. (2005). Neuroimaging the serial position curve. pg, 16, 716-723. **310** Photograph by Ronald James; **311** © Sidney Harris; **320** (*left*) Les Stone/Sygma/Corbis; **316** (*top left*) Bjorn Svensson/Alamy, (*top right*) Chris A. Crumley/Alamy, (*bottom*) Tetra Images/Alamy; **320** (*right*) Wade, Garry, Read & Lindsay, A picture is worth a thousand lies. Psychonomic Bulletin & Review 2002, 9 (3), 597-603, Fig. 1; **329** (*left*) AP Photos, (*right*) Chris Collins/Corbis; **330** Reuters/Paul Jarvis/MOD/Landov; **332** AP Photo/Peter DaSilva; **333** Suzanne Corkin, et al. H. M.'s Medial Temporal Lobe Lesion. *The Journal of Neuroscience*, May 15, 1997, 17(10):3964–3979

Chapter 9: **340** Max Ferguson/The Bridgeman Art Library/Getty Images; **345** Kosslyn, Ball & Reisser, 1978; **349** (*left*) Ed Souza/Stanford News Service, (*right*) Don Murray/Getty Images; **351** (*left*) AP/Wide World Photos, (*right*) Sebastian Pfuetze/Corbis; **353** Wen-Jui Kuo et al; Intuition and Deliberation, SCIENCE, VOL 324, April 24, 2009 Figures 2-3; **355** Kobal Collection/20th Century Fox; **356** 1998 © Sidney Harris; **361** Amanda Ahn/Alamy; **363** Chris Smith/Photo Edit; **372** Courtesy of the Granger Collection; **374** R. Bootzin, *Psychology Today: An Introduction*. Copyright © The McGraw-Hill Companies.

Chapter 10: **378** SuperStock; **380** William Blake, Adam Naming the Beasts, Sterling Maxwell Collection, Pollok House, Glasgow Nuseum & Art Galleries; **382** (*bottom*) © Courtney Leigh Rubin/Creators Syndicate, Inc.; **383** Dennis Van Tine/Retna Ltd./Corbis; **386** (*top*) The Granger Collection, New York, (*bottom*) Reprinted from Lewis Carroll's Alice in Wonderland; original illustration: John Tenniel. Color for this edition: Martina Selvay, Castle Books; **387** (*top*) Merriam-Webster's Collegiate Dictionary, 11th ed., (*left*) © Tim Wright, (*right*) Kevin Schafer/Corbis; **389** (*left*) Rune Hellestad/Corbis, (*right*) Alfeo Dixon/ZUMA/Corbis; **392** Reprinted from Lewis Carroll's Alice in Wonderland; original illustration: John Tenniel. Color for this edition: Martina Selvay, Castle Books; **396** Courtesy of Charles Yang; **397** Courtesy Everett Collection; **398** (*top*) Jack Liu, (*bottom*) Photograph by Philip Morse, University of Wisconsin, (*graph*) From Eimas, et al., "Speech Perception in Infants," *Science* 171 (1971): 303-306. Copyright © 1971, AAAS. Reprinted with permission from AAAS; **400** Courtesy Tamara Nicol Medina; **401** (*left*) Courtesy Tamara Nicol Medina, (*right*) iStockphoto; **405** (*left*) AP Photos, (*right*) AP Photos; **407** Courtesy Ann Senghas; **411** Musolino, J., Chunyo, G., & Landau, B. (in press). Uncovering knowledge of core syntactic and semantic principles in individuals with Williams Syndrome. To appear in Language Learning and Development. Drawings part A-C courtesy of B. Landau. Drawing part D courtesy of J. Musolino; **412** Reprinted from *Cognitive Psychology*, Vol. 21, Johnson & Newport, "Critical period effects in second language learning", pp. 60–99, Copyright © 1989, with permission from Elsevier; **413** Elissa L. Newport, Figure from "Maturational constraints on language learning," *Cognitive Science*, 14.1. Reprinted by permission of the author; **414** Manuela Hartling/Reuters/Landov; **418** Herbert Zettl/Corbis; **419** Courtesy Lila Gleitman

Chapter 11: **424** Joanna B. Pinneo/Aurora; **426** Courtesy National Library of Medicine; **427** (*top*) *Wechsler Adult Intelligence Scale, Fourth Edition (WAIS-IV)*. Copyright © 2008 NCS Pearson, Inc. Reproduced with permission. All rights reserved. "*Wechsler Adult Intelligence Scale*" and "WAIS" are trademarks, in the US and/or other countries, of Pearson Education, Inc. or its affiliates(s), (*bottom*) Sample item similar to those in the Raven's Progressive Matrices (Standard Parallel, Sets A-E). Copyright © 1998 NCS Pearson, Inc. Reproduced with permission. All rights reserved. "Raven's Progressive Matrices" is a registered trademark, in the US and/or other countries, of Pearson Education, Inc. or its affiliates(s); **435** Etienne Koechlin, et al. Human Decision-Making, SCIENCE VOL 318 26 OCT. 2007, Fig. 1; **436**, Fig. 8. Reprinted by permission of Tom Dunne; **437** (*left*) Joseph Katzmarak/AP Photos; **438** Emotional Intelligence Test, "Feeling Smart" American Scientist Vol. 93, pg; **440** (*top*) Richard Green/Salinas Valley Memorial Healthcare System, (*bottom*) © Sidney Harris; **442** Courtesy of The New York Public Library, Astor, Lenox and Tilden Foundations; **446** Nathan Benn/Alamy; **449** Junenoire Photography; **450** (*left*) Picture Partners/Alamy, (*right*) Asiaselects/Alamy; **453** (*left*) Robert Van Der Hilst/Getty Images, (*right*) Chris Rennie/Getty Images; **457** Charles Gupton/Corbis

Chapter 12: **460** Russell Monk/Getty Image; **463** (*left*) Wolfgang Kaehler/Corbis, (*right*) James Warwick/Photo Researchers; **466** Kunsthistorisches Museum/Erich Lessing/Art Resource; **468** (*left*) Sadaf Farooqi, et al. Vol. 110, Issue 8 (Oct. 15, 2002) 110(8): 1093–1103 doi:10.1172/JCI15693. © 2002, American Society for Clinical Investigation, (*right*) Sadaf Farooqi, et al. Vol. 110, Issue 8 (Oct. 15, 2002) 110(8): 1093–1103 doi:10.1172/JCI15693. © 2002, American Society for Clinical Investigation; **469** Yoav Levy/PhotoTake; **470** (*left*) Art Resource, NY, (*right*) Xinhua/XINHUA/Corbis; **472** (*right*) Ed Freeman/Getty Images; **474** (*top*) Photograph by Walter Chandoha; **475** Kenneth W. Fink/Photo Researchers; **476** (*left*) Mike Cassese/Corbis, (*right*) Jérome Sesini/Visu/Corbis; **477** Warner Bros/Photofest; **478** (*left*) Kevin Schafer/Corbis, (*right*) William Manning/Corbis; **482** (*top*) The Advertising Archives, (*bottom*) Phil McCarten/Reuters/Corbis; **483** (*left*) Templer/Corbis, (*right*) Hugh Sitton/Corbis; **485** Ariel Skelley/Corbis; **486** STR/AFP/Getty Images; **488** Courtesy Naomi Eisenberger. Does Rejection Hurt? Naomi I. Eisenberger, et al. Science 10 Oct. 2003: Vol. 302. no. 5643, pp. 290–292; **489** Olds, J., Pleasure Centers in the Brain; Scientific American, October, 1956, 112; **492** (*top*) Ekman, P. & Friesen, W.V. © 1975. Photographs courtesy of Paul Ekman, (*bottom*) Paul Ekman, from Unmasking the Face. © 1980. Reprinted with permission of the author; **494** (*left*) Christina Kennedy/Photo Edit, (*right*) ColorBlind Images/Getty Images; **497** Susskind et al, 2008, Nature Neuroscience, Fig 2B; **499** (*bottom left*) Jose Luis; Pelaez Inc/Getty Images/Blend Image, (*bottom right*) Eric Bean/Getty Images

Chapter 13: 504 Stuart Freedman/Panos Images; 508 (left) AP Photo/Craig Lassig, (right) Owen Franken/Corbis; 509 (left) Yvon-Lemanour/Photolibrary, (right) Alain Le Garsmeur/AgeFotostock, (bottom) The New Yorker Collection, 1980, J.B. Handelsman/cartoonbank.com; 511 Warner Bros./Photofest; 513 Courtesy of Keith Payne; 515 (bottom) Vivian Moos/Corbis, (top) The Advertising Archives; 516 DILBERT: © Scott Adams/United Features Syndicate; 517 Courtesy of the U.S. Army; 518 (left) Patrick Ward/Corbis, (right) Belousov Vitaly/ITAR-TASS/Corbis; 520 (top) Asch, S.E. "Studies of independence and conformity: A minority of one against a unanimous majority." *Psychological Monographs* 70 (9, Whole No. 416), 1956; 521 (left) Photograph by Frank Radway, (right) Peter Turnley/Corbis; 522 William Lovelace/Express/Getty Images; 523 Stephen Studd/Getty Images 524 (top) From Eichmann in Jerusalem by Hannah Arendt © 1963, 1964. Used by permission of Viking Press, a division of Penguin Group (USA) Inc., (middle) © Stanley Milgram. From the film Obedience, distributed by Penn State Audio-Visual Services, (bottom) © Stanley Milgram. From the film Obedience, distributed by Penn State Audio-Visual Services; 526 Hoover Institution Archives, Stanford University; 527 Reuters/Corbis; 529 (left) Michel Sheil/Black Star/Getty Images, (right) Detroit Free Press, 1988, Pauline Rubens/Black Star/Getty Images; 530 © Philip G. Zimbardo; 531 Henry Martin/Cartoonbank; 532 NY Public Library, Astor, Lenox, and Tilden Foundations; 534 (top) The National Gallery, London, (bottom) Stephanie Maze/Corbis; 535 The New Yorker Collection. Claude from Cartoonbank.com. 1959, 1987. All rights reserved; 536 (top) Mona Lisa, La Réunion des Musées Nationaux/Art Resource, NY, (bottom) AP Photo/Danny Moloshok; 538 (top) Rudy Sulgan/AgeFotostock, (bottom) 20th Century Fox/Photofest; 539 Rob Gage/Getty Images

Chapter 14: 544 Fredrik Naumann/Panos; 546 Lennart Nilsson/Albert Bonniers Publishing Company; 547 (left top) MedicalRF;, (left bottom) Nestle/Petit Format, (right) MedicalRF; 549 (left) David Young-Wolff/Photo Edit. (right) Courtesy of Dr. Sterling Clarren; 550 Postnatal Development of the Human Cortex, vols. 1, 3, 5. Harvard University Press, 1955; 551 (left) Alamy, (middle) Laura Dwight, (right) Jose Luis Pelaez, Inc./Blend Images/Corbis; 553 (top left) Alamy, (top right) Alamy, (middle left) Alamy, (middle right) Alamy; 554 Courtesy Adele Diamond; 556 Michael Newman/PhotoEdit; 562 Johnson & Morton, "Rudimentary face recognition in new-borns" from *Biology & Cognitive Development: The Case of Face Recognition*, Fig. 2.3, p. 31. Copyright © 1991 Blackwell Publishing Ltd. Reproduced with permission of Blackwell Publishing Ltd.; 563 (top) Meltzoff & Moore, "Imitation of facial and manual gestures" Science, 1977, 198, 75-78. 563 (bottom) Corbis; 564 (top) Harlow Primate Laboratory, University of Wisconsin, (bottom) Photograph by J. Blyenburg/Leo de Wys; 567 Larry Williams/Corbis; 568 Geoffrey Saxe, www.gse.berkeley.edu/faculty/gsaxe/Research.htm; 570 Stephen Shames/Matirx; 572 (top) Harlow Primate Laboratory, University of Wisconsin, (bottom) Mike Abrahams/Alamy; 573 Jupiter Images; 578 McClure, Laibson, Loewenstein & Cohen (2004); 581 (top) image100/Alamy, (bottom) Corbis RF/Alamy; 582 Stock Connection/Alamy; 585 Resnick, Pham, Kraut, Zonderman, & Davatzikos, 2003; 586 Queerstock, Inc./Alamy; 587 The New Yorker Collection, 1999. Tom Cheney from cartoonbank.com. All Rights Reserved

Chapter 15: 590 Stanley Greene/Noor/Aurora Photos; 594 Richard Hutchings/Corbis; 595 Kevin R. Morris/Bohemian Nomad Picturemakers/Corbis; 597 Yellow Dog Productions/Getty Images; 597 Bryn Colton/Assignments Photographers/Corbis; 598 (left) Paramount/Courtesy: Everett Collection, (right) Warner Bros./Courtesy Everett Collection; 599 Science Magazine courtesy of Champaign Studio One Photography; 600 (left) Warren Morgan/Corbis, (middle) Eric Perlman/Corbis, (right) David Bartruff/Corbis; 601 Schwartz, Wright, Shin, Kagan, & Rauch, 2003; 604 (left) The Granger Collection, (right) Paul Buck/epa/Corbis, (bottom) Image Source/Getty Images; 606 Courtesy National Library of Medicine; 609 © The New Yorker

Collection 1975 Chas. Addams from Cartoonbank. com. All rights reserved; 611 (top) The New Yorker Collection, copyright 1979 Dana Fradon from cartoonbank.com. All rights reserved, (bottom left) Rubin Museum of Art/Art Resource, NY, (bottom right) Wikimedia.com; 612 Photos21.com; 614 (top left) Erin Ryan/Corbis, (top right) Jason Horowitz/Corbis, (bottom) © 2006 Newsweek Inc., All rights reserved. Reprinted by permission. Max Halberstadt/Imagno/Getty Images; 615 (left) National Portrait Gallery, Smithsonian Institution/Art Resource, NY, (right) AP Photos, (right) AP Photos; 617 (top left) Radius Images/Alamy, (top right) PHANIE/Photo Researchers, (left) Radius Images/Alamy; 618 © Alex Gregory/Cartoonbank.com. All rights reserved; 620 (left) Martha Holmes/Time & Life Pictures/Getty Images, (right) AP/Wide World Photos; 623 Archives of the History of Psychology, University of Akron, Akron ,OH; 625 (left) Pixland/Corbis, (right) Con Tanasiuk/Design Pics/Corbis; 626 (left) AP Photo, 626 (right) INSADCO Photography/Alamy; 627 (right) Paramount/Photofest; 628 © The New Yorker Collection 1963 W. Miller from Cartoonbank.com. All rights reserved; 629 (top) JLP/Jose L. Pelaez/Corbis, (bottom) BananaStock/SuperStock

Chapter 16: 634 Olivia Arthur/Magnum Photos; 636 William Blake, King Nebuchandnezzar, 1795; courtesy the Tate Gallery, London.; 637 Courtesy Historical Pictures Service; 639 Park Street/Photo Edit; 641 Corbis; 642 Lewis J. Merrim/Photo Researchers, Inc.; 643 Photograph by Mimi Forsyth/Monkmeyer; 645 (top) Udo Kroener/Alamy, (bottom) Frank Lane Picture Agency/Corbis. 646 Tony Freeman/Photo Edit; 647 Edward Munch; The Scream, 1893; © The Munch Museum/The Munch-Ellingsen Group/ARS 1994; 648 Stockbyte/Photolibrary; 649 Scott Peterson/Getty Images; 652 Helen Vaughn/SuperStock; 653 (left) Photofest, (right) Tammie Arroyo/AP; 658 Reuters/Corbis; 659 Courtesy Galerie Rothe Heidelberg; 660 (top) Universal Pictures/Photofest, (bottom) David Hoffman Photo Library/Alamy; 661 Photograph by Bill Bridges/Globe Photos; 663 Terry Smith Images/Alamy; 666 John Birdsall/Phototake—All rights reserved; 667 Banana Stock/Alamy; 668 (left) Mary Ann Smith/The Image Bank; 669 David Levenson/Getty Images; 671 Twentieth Century Fox Film Corp./Photofest; 673 (left) Matthew Simmons/Getty Images, (right) Russell Price/Alamy

Chapter 17: 676 Tony Law/Redux; 679 (left) The Granger Collection, (right) Wikimedia Commons; 684 © Cathy Gaines; 685 © The New Yorker Collection 1989 Danny Shanahan from CartoonBank.com. All Rights Reserved; 686 Michael Rougier/Time & Life Pictures/Getty Images; 687 © 1994 by Sidney Harris; 688 Peter Dench/Corbis; 689 AP Photo/Peter Cosgrove; 690 Jeff Greenberg/Photo Edit; 693 The New Yorker Collection 1976 Whitney Darrow, Jr., from Cartoonbank.com. All rights reserved; 694 (top) Gary Conner/Phototake/Alamy, (bottom) Negative #31568. Courtesy Department of Library Services, The American Museum of Natural History. 695 (left) Courtesy Historical Pictures Service, (right) Courtesy National Library of Medicine. 696 Alex Segre/Alamy; 699 © The New Yorker Collection 1993 Tom Cheney from cartoonbank.com. All Rights Reserved; 700 (top left) Damien Lovegrove/Science Photo Library, (top right) webmd.com, (middle) Courtesy Everett Collection, (bottom) Science Photo Library; 704 Courtesy Everett Collection; 705 Culver Pictures; 706 DILBERT: © Scott Adams/Dist. by United Feature Syndicate, Inc.; 712 Reprinted from Lewis Carroll's *Alice in Wonderland*; original illustration: John Tenniel. Color for this edition: Martina Selvay, Castle Books

Every effort has been made to contact the copyright holder of each of the illustrations. Rights holders of any pieces not credited should contact Permissions Department, W. W. Norton & Company, Inc., 500 Fifth Avenue, New York, NY 10110, in order for a correction to be made in the next reprinting of our work.

References

ABELSON, J. L., CURTIS, G. C., SAGHER, O., ALBUCHER, R. C., HARRIGAN, M., TAYLOR, S. F., ET AL. (2005). Deep brain stimulation for refractory obsessive compulsive disorder. *Biological Psychiatry, 57,* 510–516.

ABRAHAM, K. (1927). The influence of oral eroticism on character formation. In K. Abraham, *Selected papers* (pp. 393–406). London: Hogarth Press.

ABRAMS, D. B. & WILSON, G. T. (1983). Alcohol, sexual arousal, and self-control. *Journal of Personality and Social Psychology 45* (1):188–198.

ABRAMSON, L. Y., ALLOY, L. B., HANKIN, B. L., HAEFFEL, G. J., MACCOON, D. G., & GIBB, B. E. (2002). Cognitive vulnerability—stress models of depression in a self-regulatory and psychobiological context. In I. H. Gotlib & C. L. Hammen (Eds.), *Handbook of depression* (pp. 268–294). New York: Guilford.

ABRAMSON, L. Y., SELIGMAN, M. E. P., & TEASDALE, J. D. (1978). Learned helplessness in humans: Critique and reformulation. *Journal of Abnormal Psychology, 87,* 49–74.

ACKERMAN, P. L., & BEIER, M. E. (2005). Knowledge and intelligence. In O. Wilhelm & R. Engle (Eds.), *Handbook of understanding and measuring intelligence* (pp. 125–139). Thousand Oaks, CA: Sage.

ACKERMAN, P. L., BEIER, M. E., & BOYLE, M. O. (2002). Individual differences in working memory within a nomological network of cognitive and perceptual speed abilities. *Journal of Experimental Psychology: General, 131,* 567–589.

ACKERMAN, P. L., BEIER, M. E., & BOYLE, M. O. (2005). Working memory and intelligence: The same or different constructs? *Psychological Bulletin, 131,* 30–60.

ACSF INVESTIGATORS. (1992). AIDS and sexual behaviour in France. *Nature, 360,* 407–409.

ADAMS, D. B., GOLD, A. R., & BURT, A. D. (1978). Rise in female initiated sexual activity at ovulation and its suppression by oral contraceptives. *New England Journal of Medicine, 299,* 1145–1150.

ADAMSON, L., & FRICK, J. (2003). The still face: A history of a shared experimental paradigm. *Infancy, 4,* 451–473.

ADDIS, M. E., & KRASNOW, A. D. (2000). A national survey of practicing psychologists' attitudes towards psychotherapy treatment manuals. *Journal of Consulting and Clinical Psychology, 68,* 331–339.

ADDIS, M. E., & MAHALIK, J. R. (2003). Men, masculinity, and the contexts of help seeking. *American Psychologist, 58,* 5–14.

ADELSON, E. H., & BERGEN, J. R. (1985). Spatiotemporal energy models for the perception of motion. *Journal of the Optical Society of America A, 2*(2), 284–299.

ADLER, N. T. (1979). On the physiological organization of social behavior: Sex and aggression. In P. Marler & J. G. Vandenbergh (Eds.), *Handbook of behavioral neurobiology: Vol. 3. Social behavior and communication* (pp. 29–71). New York: Plenum.

ADOLPH, E. F. (1947). Urges to eat and drink in rats. *American Journal of Physiology, 151,* 110–125.

ADORNO, T. W., ADORNO, E. F.-B., LEVINSON, D. J., SANFORD, R. N., IN COLLABORATION WITH ARON, B., LEVINSON, M. H., & MORROW, W. (1950). *The authoritarian personality.* New York: Harper.

AGGLETON, J. P., & BROWN, M. W. (2006). Interleaving brain systems for episodic and recognition memory. *Trends in Cognitive Sciences, 10,* 455–463.

AHN, W.-K, & GRAHAM, L. M. (1999). The impact of necessity and sufficiency in the Wason four-card task. *Psychological Science, 10,* 237–242.

AINSWORTH, M. D. S., & BELL, S. M. (1970). Attachment, exploration, and separation: Illustrated by the behavior of one-year-olds in a strange situation. *Child Development, 41,* 49–67.

AINSWORTH, M. D. S., BLEHAR, M. C., WATERS, E., & WALL, S. (1978). *Patterns of attachment.* Hillsdale, NJ: Erlbaum.

ALANKO L. O., LAITINEN, J. T., STENBERG, D., & PORKKA-HEISKANEN, T. (2004). Adenosine A1 receptor-dependent G-protein activity in the rat brain during prolonged wakefulness. *NeuroReport, 15,* 2133–2137.

ALBERT, M. S., JONES, K., SAVAGE, C. R., BERKMAN, L., SEEMAN, T., BLAZER, D., ET AL. (1995). Predictors of cognitive change in older persons: MacArthur studies of successful aging. *Psychology and Aging, 10,* 578–589.

ALDAG, R. J., & FULLER, S. R. (1993). Beyond fiasco: A reappraisal of the groupthink phenomenon and a new model of group decision processes. *Psychological Bulletin, 113*(3), 533–552.

ALEXANDER, F., & FRENCH, T. (1946). *Psychoanalytic theory.* New York: Ronald Press.

ALEXANDER, K. W., QUAS, J. A., GOODMAN, G. S., GHETTI, S., EDELSTEIN, R. S., REDLICH, A. D., ET AL. (2005). Traumatic impact predicts long-term memory for documented child sexual abuse. *Psychological Science, 16,* 33–40.

ALKIRE, M., HUDETZ, A., & TONONI, G. (2008). Consciousness and anesthesia. *Science, 322,* 876–880.

ALLDERIDGE, P. (1979). Hospitals, mad houses, and asylums: Cycles in the care of the insane. *British Journal of Psychiatry, 134,* 321–324.

ALLEN, D. (2009). My first panic attack: A memorable experience! Editorial. *Streetdirectory.com.* Retrieved Aug. 10, 2009, from http://www.streetdirectory.com/travel_guide/108953/anxiety/my_first_panic_attack_a_memorable_experience.html.

ALLEN, J., & SEIDENBERG, M. S. (1999). The emergence of grammaticality in connectionist networks. In B. MacWhinney (Ed.), *The emergence of language* (pp. 115–151). Hillsdale, NJ: Erlbaum.

ALLEN, L. S., HINES, Z. M., SHRYNE, J. E., & GORSKI, R. A. (1989). Two sexually dimorphic cell groups in the human brain. *Journal of Neuroscience, 9,* 497–506.

ALLEN, V. L. (1975). Social support for non-conformity. In L. Berkowitz (Ed.), *Advances in experimental social psychology: Vol. 8.* New York: Academic Press.

ALLEN, V. L., & LEVINE, J. M. (1971). Social support and conformity: The role of independent assessment. *Journal of Experimental Social Psychology, 7,* 48–58.

ALLIK, J., LAIDRA, K., REALO, A., & PULLMAN, H. (2004). Personality development from 12 to 18 years of age: Changes in mean levels and structure of traits. *European Journal of Personality, 18,* 445–462.

ALLOY, L. B., ABRAMSOM, L. Y., & FRANCIS, E. L. (1999). Do negative cognitive styles confer vulnerability to depression? *Current Directions in Psychological Science, 8,* 128–132.

ALLPORT, G. W. (1921). Personality and character. *Psychological Bulletin, 18,* 441–455.

ALLPORT, F. H. (1920). The influence of the group upon association and thought. Journal of *Experimental Psychology, 3,* 159–182.

ALLPORT, G. W. (1937). *Personality: A psychological interpretation.* New York: Henry Holt.

ALLPORT, G. W. (1968). The historical background of modern social psychology. In G. Lindzey & E. Aronson (Eds.), *The handbook of social psychology* (2nd ed., Vol. 1, pp. 1–80). Reading, MA: Addison-Wesley.

ALLPORT, G. W., & ODBERT, H. S. (1936). Trait-names: A psychological study. *Psychological Monographs, 47*(Whole No. 211).

ALTMANN, E. M., & GRAY, W. D. (2002). Forgetting to remember: The functional relationship of decay and interference. *Psychological Science, 13,* 27–33.

ALTMANN, G., & STEEDMAN, M. (1988). Interaction with context during human sentence processing. *Cognition, 30,* 191–238.

ALTMANN, G. T. M., & KAMIDE, Y. (1999). Incremental interpretation at verbs: Restricting the domain of subsequent reference. *Cognition, 73,* 247–264.

AMABILE, T. M. (2001). Beyond talent: John Irving and the passionate craft of creativity. *American Psychologist, 56,* 333–336.

AMATO, P. R. (2001). Children of divorce in the 1990s: An update of the Amato and Keith (1991) meta-analysis. *Journal of Family Psychology, 15*(3), 355–370.

AMATO, P. R., & KEITH, B. (1991). Parental divorce and the well-being of children: A meta-analysis. *Psychological Bulletin, 110,* 26–46.

AMBADY, N., SHIH, M., KIM, A., & PITTINSKY, T. L. (2001). Stereotype susceptibility in children: Effects of identity activation on quantitative performance. *Psychological Science, 12,* 385–390.

AMERICAN PSYCHIATRIC ASSOCIATION. (2000). *Diagnostic and statistical manual of mental disorders* (4th ed., text rev.). Washington, DC: Author.

AMERICAN PSYCHOLOGICAL ASSOCIATION. (1981). Ethical principles of psychologists. *American Psychologist, 36,* 633–638.

AMERICAN PSYCHOLOGICAL ASSOCIATION. (1982). *Ethical principles in the conduct of research with human participants.* Washington, DC: Author.

AMERICAN PSYCHOLOGICAL ASSOCIATION PRESIDENTIAL TASK FORCE ON EVIDENCE-BASED PRACTICE. (2006). Evidence-based practice in psychology. *American Psychologist, 61,* 271–285.

ANDERSEN, E., DUNLEA, A., & KEKELIS, L. (1993). The impact of input: Language acquisition in the visually impaired. *First Language, 13,* 23–49.

ANDERSON, C. A., & BUSHMAN, B. J. (2001). Effects of violent video games on aggressive behavior, aggressive cognition, aggressive affect, physiological arousal, and prosocial behavior: A meta-analytic review of the scientific literature. *Psychological Science, 12,* 353–360.

ANDERSON, C. A., & BUSHMAN, B. J. (2002). Human aggression. *Annual Review of Psychology, 53,* 27–51.

ANDERSON, J. R. (1990). *Cognitive psychology and its implications* (3rd ed.). San Francisco: Freeman.

ANDERSON, J. R. (1993). *Rules of the mind.* Hillsdale, NJ: Erlbaum.

ANDERSON, J. R. (1996). ACT: A simple theory of complex cognition. *American Psychologist, 51,* 355–365.

ANDERSON, M. C., & LEVY, B. J. (2006). Encouraging the nascent cognitive neuroscience of repression. *Behavioral and Brain Sciences, 29,* 511–513.

ANDERSON, M. C., OCHSNER, K. N., KUHL, B., COOPER, J., ROBERTSON, E., GABRIELI, J., ET AL. (2004). Neural systems underlying the suppression of unwanted memories. *Science, 303,* 232–235.

ANDERSON, S. L., ADAMS, G., & PLAUT, V. C. (2008). The cultural grounding of personal relationship: The importance of attractiveness in everyday life. *Journal of Personality and Social Psychology, 95*(2), 352–368.

ANDERSSON, M. (1982). Female choice selects for extreme tail length in a widowbird. *Nature, 299,* 818–820.

ANDREASEN, N. C., ARNDT, S., ALLIGER, R., MILLER, D., & FLAUM, M. (1995). Symptoms of schizophrenia. *Archives of General Psychiatry, 52,* 341–351.

ANDREASEN, N. C., & BLACK, D. W. (1996). *Introductory textbook of psychiatry* (2nd ed.). Washington, DC: American Psychiatric Press.

ANDREASEN, N. C., NASRALLAH, H. A., DUNN, V., OLSEN, S. C., GROVE, W. M., EHRHARDT, J., ET AL. (1986). Structural abnormalities in the frontal system in schizophrenia: A magnetic resonance imaging study. *Archives of General Psychiatry, 43,* 136–144.

ANDREWS, G., & HARVEY, R. (1981). Does psychotherapy benefit neurotic patients? A reanalysis of the Smith, Glass, and Miller data. *Archives of General Psychiatry, 38,* 1203–1208.

ANGRIST, B., SATHANANTHAN, G., WILK, S., & GERSHON, S. (1974). Amphetamine psychosis: Behavioral and biochemical aspects. *Journal of Psychiatric Research, 11,* 13–24.

ANTHONY, L. (2000). Naturalizing radical translation. In A. Orenstein & P. Kotatko (Eds.), *Knowledge, language, and logic* (pp. 141–150). Dordrecht: Kluwer.

ARCHIBALD, A. B., GRABER, J. A., & BROOKS-GUNN J. (2003). Pubertal processes and physiological growth in adolescence. In G. R. Adams & M. D. Berzonsky (Eds.), *Handbook on adolescence* (pp. 24–47). Malden, MA: Blackwell.

ARENDT, H. (1965). *Eichmann in Jerusalem: A report on the banality of evil.* New York: Viking Press.

ARIAS, E., ANDERSON, R. N., KUNG, H. C., MURPHY, S. L., & KOCHANEK, K. D. (2003). *Deaths: Final reports, 52.* Hyattsville, MD: National Center for Health Statistics. DHHS Publication No. 2003-1120.

ARIAS, B., CATALÁN, R., GASTÓ, C., GUTIÉRREZ, B., & FAÑANÁS, L. (2003). 5-HTTLPR polymorphism of the serotonin transporter gene predicts non-remission in major depression patients treated with citalopram in a 12-weeks follow up study. *Journal of Clinical Psychopharmacology, 23,* 563–576.

ARIELY, D. (2008). *Predictably irrational: The hidden forces that shape our decisions.* New York: HarperCollins.

ARIETI, S. (1959). Schizophrenia: The manifest symptomatology, the psychodynamic and formal mechanisms. In S. Arieti (Ed.), *American handbook of psychiatry: Vol. 1* (pp. 455–484). New York: Basic Books.

ARMITAGE, R., HOFFMANN, R., & MOFFITT, A. (1992). Interhemispheric EEG activity in sleep and wakefulness: Individual differences in the basic rest-activity cycle (BRAC). In J. S. Antrobus & M. Bertini (Eds.), *The neuropsychology of sleep and dreaming* (pp. 17–45). Hillsdale, NJ: Erlbaum.

ARMITAGE, C. J., & CONNER, M. (2001). Efficacy of the theory of planned behaviour: A meta-analytic review. *British Journal of Social Psychology, 40,* 471–499.

ARMSTRONG, S. L., GLEITMAN, L. R., & GLEITMAN, H. (1983). What some concepts might not be. *Cognition, 13,* 263–308.

ARNAU, R., & THOMPSON, B. (2000). Second order confirmatory factor analysis of the WAIS-III. *Assessment, 7,* 237–246.

ARNDT, S., ANDREASEN, N. C., FLAUM, M., MILLER, D., & NOPOULOS, P. (1995). A longitudinal study of symptom dimensions in schizophrenia. Prediction and patterns of change. *Archives of General Psychiatry, 52,* 352–360.

ARNETT, J. (1995). The young and the reckless: Adolescent reckless behavior. *Current Directions in Psychological Science, 4*(3), 67–71.

ARNETT, J. J. (1999). Adolescent storm and stress, reconsidered. *American Psychologist, 54,* 317–326.

ARNOLD, M. (1960). *Emotion and personality* (2 vols.). New York: Columbia University Press.

ARO, H., & TAIPALE, V. (1987). The impact of timing of puberty on psychosomatic symptoms among fourteen- to sixteen-year-old Finnish girls. *Child Development, 58*(1), 261–268.

ARONSON, E., & MILLS, J. (1959). The effect of severity of initiation on liking for a group. *Journal of Abnormal and Social Psychology, 59,* 177–181.

ARONSON, E., & PATNOE, S. (1997). *Cooperation in the classroom: The jig-saw method.* New York: Longman.

ARONSON, E., TURNER, J. A., & CARLSMITH, J. M. (1963). Communicator credibility and communication discrepancy as determinants of opinion change. *Journal of Abnormal and Social Psychology, 67,* 31–36.

ARONSON, E., WILSON, T. D., & AKERT, R. (2005). *Social psychology* (5th. ed.). New York: Prentice-Hall.

ARRIGO, J. M., & PEZDEK, K. (1997). Lessons from the study of psychogenic amnesia. *Current Directions in Psychological Science, 6*, 148–152.

ASCH, S. E. (1951). Effects of group pressure upon the modification and distortion of judgments. In H. Guetzkow (Ed.), *Groups, leadership and men* (pp. 177–190). Pittsburgh: Carnegie Press.

ASCH, S. E. (1952). *Social psychology.* New York: Prentice-Hall.

ASCH, S. E. (1955, November). Opinions and social pressure. *Scientific American, 193*, 31–35.

ASCH, S. E. (1956). Studies of independence and conformity: A minority of one against a unanimous majority. *Psychological Monographs, 70*(9, Whole No. 416).

ASHER, E. J. (1935). The inadequacy of current intelligence tests for testing Kentucky Mountain children. *Journal of Genetic Psychology, 46*, 480–486.

ASLIN, R. N. (1987). Visual and auditory development in infancy. In J. D. Osofksy (Ed.), *Handbook of infant development* (2nd ed., pp. 5–97). New York: Wiley.

ASLIN, R. N., SAFFRAN, J. R., & NEWPORT, E. L. (1998). Computation of conditional probability statistics by 8-month-old infants. *Psychological Science, 9*, 321–324.

ASTRUP, A. (2000). Thermogenic drugs as a strategy for treatment of obesity. *Endocrine, 13*, 207-212.

ATKINS, C. M., SELCHER, J. C., PETRAITIS, J. J., TRZASKOS, J. M., & SWEATT, J. D. (1998). The MAPK cascade is required for mammalian associative learning. *Nature Neuroscience, 1*, 602–609.

ATKINSON, R. C., & SHIFFRIN, R. M. (1968). Human memory: A proposed system and its control. In K. W. Spence & J. T. Spence (Eds.), *The psychology of learning and motivation: Vol. 2* (pp. 89–105). New York: Academic Press.

ATRAN, S. (1998). Folk biology and the anthropology of science: Cognitive universals and cultural particular. *Behavior and Brain Sciences, 21*, 541–611.

AUYEUNG, B., BARON-COHEN, S., ASHWIN, E. KNICKMEYER, R., TAYLOR, K., HACKETT, G., ET AL. (2009). Fetal testosterone predicts sexually differentiated childhood behaviors in girls and in boys. *Psychological Science, 20*, 144–148.

AVERILL, J. R. (1975). A semantic atlas of emotional concepts. *JSAS Catalog of Selected Documents in Psychology, 5*, 330.

AVERILL, J. R. (1985). The social construction of emotion: With special reference to love. In K. J. Gergen & K. E. Davis (Eds.), *The social construction of the person* (pp. 89–109). New York: Springer-Verlag.

AVIEZER, O., SAGI, A., JOELS, T., & ZIV, Y. (1999). Emotional availability and attachment representations in kibbutz infants and their mothers. *Developmental Psychology, 35*(3), 811–821.

AVIS, N. E. (2003). Depression during the menopausal transition. *Psychology of Women Quarterly, 27*, 91–100.

AWH, E., DHALIWAL, H., CHRISTENSEN, S., & MATSUKURA, M. (2001). Evidence for two components of object-based selection. *Psychological Science, 12*, 329–334.

AX, A. F. (1953). The physiological differentiation of fear and anger in humans. *Psychosomatic Medicine, 15*, 433–442.

AXEL, R. (1995, October). The molecular logic of smell. *Scientific American*, 154–159.

AYLLON, T., & AZRIN, N. H. (1968). *The token economy: A motivational system for therapy and rehabilitation.* New York: Appleton-Century-Crofts.

AZRIN, N. H., & HOLZ, W. C. (1966). Punishment. In W. K. Honig (Ed.), *Operant behavior: Areas of research and application.* New York: Appleton-Century-Crofts.

———

BAARS, B. J. (1988). Momentary forgetting as a "resetting" of a conscious global workspace due to competition between incompatible contexts. In M. J. Horowitz (Ed.), *Psychodynamics and cognition* (pp. 269–293). Chicago: University of Chicago Press.

BAARS, B. J. (2002). The conscious access hypothesis: Origins and recent evidence. *Trends in Cognitive Science, 6*, 47–52.

BAARS, B.J., & FRANKLIN, S. (2003). How conscious experience and working memory interact. *Trends in Cognitive Science, 7*, 166–172.

BACHTOLD, D. (2003). Drug safety: Conflict-of-interest allegations derail inquiry into antidepressant's "dark side." *Science, 300*, 33.

BACK, M. D., SCHMUKLE, S. C., & EGLOFF, B. (2008). Becoming friends by chance. *Psychological Science, 19*(5), 439–440.

BADDELEY, A. D., AGGLETON, J. P., & CONWAY, M.A. (EDS.). (2002). *Episodic memory.* New York: Oxford University Press.

BADDELEY, A. D., & HITCH, G. J. (1977). Recency re-examined. In S. Dornic (Ed.), *Attention and performance* (Vol. 6, pp. 646–667). Hillsdale, NJ: Erlbaum.

BAER, L., RAUCH, S. L., BALLANTINE, H. T., MARTUZA, R., COSGROVE, R., CASSEM, E., ET AL. (1995). Cingulotomy for intractable obsessive-compulsive disorder: Prospective long-term follow-up of 18 patients. *Archives of General Psychiatry, 52*, 384–392.

BAGWELL, C. L., NEWCOMB, A. F., & BUKOWSKI, W. M. (1998). Preadolescent friendship and peer rejection as predictors of adult adjustment. *Child Development, 69*(1), 140–153.

BAHRICK, H. P., BAHRICK, P. O., & WITTLINGER, R. P. (1975). Fifty years of memory for names and faces: A cross-sectional approach. *Journal of Experimental Psychology: General, 104*, 54–75.

BAHRICK, H. (1984). Semantic memory content in permastore: 50 years of memory for Spanish learned in school. *Journal of Experimental Psychology: General, 113*, 1–29.

BAHRICK, H., & HALL, L. (1991). Lifetime maintenance of high school mathematics content. *Journal of Experimental Psychology: General, 120*, 20–33.

BAHRICK, H., HALL, L., GOGGIN, J., BAHRICK, L., & BERGER, S. (1994). Fifty years of language maintenance and language dominance in bilingual Hispanic immigrants. *Journal of Experimental Psychology: General, 123*, 264–283.

BAILEY, C., & CHEN, M. (1989). Time course of structural changes at identified sensory neuron synapses during long-term sensitization in aplysia. *Journal of Neuroscience, 9*, 1774–1780.

BAILEY, J. M., & PILLARD, R. C. (1991). A genetic study of male sexual orientation. *Archives of General Psychiatry, 48*, 1089–1096.

BAILEY, J. M., PILLARD, R. C., NEALE, M. C., & AGYEI, Y. (1993). Heritable factors influence sexual orientation in women. *Archives of General Psychiatry, 50*, 217–223.

BAILEY, M., & ZUCKER, K. (1995). Childhood sex-typed behavior and sexual orientation: A conceptual analysis and quantitative review. *Developmental Psychology, 31*, 43–55.

BAILLARGEON, R. (1987). Object permanence in 31/2- and 41/2-month-old infants. *Developmental Psychology, 23*, 655–664.

BAILLARGEON, R. (1994). How do infants learn about the physical world? *Current Directions in Psychological Science, 3*(5), 133–140.

BAILLARGEON, R. (2004). Infants' physical world. *Current Directions in Psychological Science, 13*, 89–94.

BAILLARGEON, R., & GRABER, M. (1987). Where is the rabbit? 51/2-month-old infants' representation of the height of hidden objects. *Cognitive Development, 2*, 375–392.

BAILLARGEON, R., SPELKE, E. S., & WASSERMAN, S. (1985). Object permanence in five-month-old infants. *Cognition, 20*, 191–208.

BAILLARGEON, R., & WANG, S.-H. (2002). Event categorization in infancy. *Trends in Cognitive Science, 6*, 85–93.

BAKER, M. (2005). Mapping the terrain of language learning. *Language Learning and Development, 1*(1), 65–93.

BAKER, M. C. (2001). *The atoms of meaning: The mind's hidden rules of grammar.* New York: Basic Books.

BALDWIN, D. A. (1991). Infants' contribution to the achievement of joint reference. *Child Development, 62*, 875–890.

BALL, S. A., MARTINO, S., NICH, C., FRANKFORTER, T. L., VAN HORN, D., CRITS-CHRISTOPH, P., ET AL. (2007). Site matters: Multisite randomized trial of motivational enhancement therapy in community drug abuse clinics. *Journal of Consulting and Clinical Psychology, 75*(4), 556–567.

BALTES, P. B., & STAUDINGER, U. M. (2000). Wisdom: A metaheuristic (pragmatic) to orchestrate mind and virtue toward excellence. *American Psychologist, 55*(1), 122–136.

BALTES, P. B., STAUDINGER, U. M., & LINDENBERGER, U. (1999). Lifespan psychology: Theory and application to intellectual functioning. *Annual Review of Psychology, 50*, 471–507.

BANCROFT, J. (1986). The roles of hormones in female sexuality. In L. Dennerstein & I. Fraser (Eds.), *Hormones and behaviour* (pp. 551–560). Amsterdam: International Society of Psychosomatic Obstetrics and Gynecology, Elsevier.

BANDURA, A. (1969). *Principles of behavior modification.* New York: Holt, Rinehart & Winston.

BANDURA, A. (1977). *Social learning theory.* Englewood Cliffs, NJ: Prentice Hall.

BANDURA, A. (1986). *Social foundations of thought and action: A social cognitive theory.* Englewood Cliffs, NJ: Prentice Hall.

BANDURA, A. (1997). *Self-efficacy: The exercise of control.* New York: Freeman.

BANDURA, A. (2001). Social cognitive theory: An agentic perspective. *Annual Review of Psychology, 52,* 1–26.

BANDURA, A. (2006). Toward a psychology of human agency. *Perspectives on Psychological Science, 1,* 164–180.

BANICH, M. (2009). Executive function: The search for an integrated account. *Current Directions in Psychological Science, 10,* 89–94.

BANKS, W. P., & ISHAM, E. A. (2009). We infer rather than perceive the moment we decided to act. *Psychological Science, 20,* 17–21.

BANTICK, R. A., DEAKIN, J. F., & GRASBY, P. M. (2001). The 5–HT1A receptor in schizophrenia: A promising target for novel atypical neuroleptics? *Journal of Psychopharmacology, 15,* 37–46.

BARBER, J. P., CONNOLLY, M. B., CRITS-CHRISTOPH, P., GLADIS, L., & SIQUELAND, L. (2000). Alliance predicts patients' outcome beyond in-treatment change in symptoms. *Journal of Consulting and Clinical Psychology, 68,* 1027–1032.

BARCH, D. M. (2003). Cognition in schizophrenia: Does working memory work? *Current Directions in Psychological Science, 12,* 146–150.

BARCH, D. M., CARTER, C. S., BRAVER, T. S., SABB, F. W., MACDONALD, A., NOLL, D. C., ET AL. (2001). Selective deficits in prefrontal cortex function in medication-naive patients with schizophrenia. *Archives of General Psychiatry, 58,* 280–288.

BARCKLAY, J. R., BRANSFORD, J. D., FRANKS, J. J., MCCARRELL, N. S., & NITSCH, K. (1974). *Comprehension and semantic flexibility. Journal of Verbal Learning and Verbal Behavior, 13,* 471–481.

BARDO, M. T., DONOHEW, R. L., & HARRINGTON, N. G. (1996). Psychobiology of novelty seeking and drug seeking behavior. *Behavioural Brain Research, 77,* 23–43.

BARGH, J. (2005). Bypassing the will: Toward demystifying the nonconscious control of social behavior. In R. Hassin, J. Uleman, & J. Bargh (Eds.), *The new unconscious* (pp. 37–58). New York: Oxford University Press.

BARGH, J. A., CHEN, M., & BURROWS, L. (1996). Automaticity of social behavior: Direct effects of trait construct and stereotype activation on action. *Journal of Personality and Social Psychology, 71,* 230–244.

BARGH, J. A., & FERGUSON, M. J. (2000). Beyond behaviorism: On the automaticity of higher mental processes. *Psychological Bulletin, 126*(6), 925–945.

BARKLEY, R. A. (1997). *ADHD and the nature of self-control.* New York: Guilford.

BARLOW, D. H. (2002). *Anxiety and its disorders: The nature and treatment of anxiety and panic* (2nd ed.). New York: Guilford.

BARLOW, D. H. (2004). Psychological treatments. *American Psychologist, 59,* 869–879.

BARLOW, D. H., & HERSON, M. (1984). *Single case experimental designs: Strategies for studying behavior change* (2nd ed.). New York: Pergamon Press.

BARNES, V. A., TREIBER, F., & DAVIS, H. (2001). The impact of Transcendental Meditation on cardiovascular function at rest and during acute stress in adolescents with high normal blood pressure. *Journal of Psychosomatic Research, 51,* 597–605.

BARNIER, A. J., & MCCONKEY, K. M. (2004). Defining and identifying the highly hypnotizable person. In M. Heap, R. J. Brown, and R. J. Oakley (Eds.), *The highly hypnotizable person: Theoretical, experimental, and clinical issues* (pp. 30–60). New York: Brunner-Routledge.

BARRETT, L. F. (1998). Discrete emotions or dimensions? The role of valence focus and arousal focus. *Cognition and Emotion, 12,* 579–599.

BARRETT, L. F. (2004). Feelings or words? Understanding the content in self- report ratings of emotional experience. *Journal of Personality and Social Psychology, 87,* 266–281.

BARRETT, L. F., MESQUITA, B., OCHSNER, K. N., & GROSS J. J. (2007). The experience of emotion. *Annual Review of Psychology, 58,* 373–403.

BARRETT, L. F., & RUSSELL, J. A. (1999). The structure of current affect: Controversies and emerging consensus. *Current Directions in Psychological Science, 8*(1), 10–14.

BARRETT, L. F., & WAGER, T. D. (2006). The structure of emotion: Evidence from neuroimaging studies. *Current Directions in Psychological Science, 15,* 79–83.

BARRICK, M. R., MOUNT, M. K., & GUPTA, R. (2003). Meta-analysis of the relationship between the Five Factor model of personality and Holland's occupational types. *Personnel Psychology, 56,* 45–74.

BARRY, H., III, CHILD, I. L., & BACON, M. K. (1959). Relation of child training to subsistence economy. *American Anthropologist, 61,* 51–63.

BARSELOU, I. W. (1985). Ideals, central tendency and frequency of instantiation as determinants of graded structure in categories. *Journal of Experimental Psychology: Learning, Memory, and Cognition, 11,* 629–654.

BARTH, H., KANWISHER, N., & SPELKE, E. (2003). The construction of large number representations in adults. *Cognition, 86,* 201–221.

BARTHOLOMEW, K., & HOROWITZ, L. M. (1991). Attachment styles among young adults: A test of a four-category model. *Journal of Personality and Social Psychology, 61,* 226–244.

BARTLETT, F. C. (1932). *Remembering: A study in experimental and social psychology.* Cambridge: Cambridge University Press.

BARTOL, C. R., & COSTELLO, N. (1976). Extraversion as a function of temporal duration of electric shock: An exploratory study. *Perceptual and Motor Skills, 42,* 1174.

BARTOSHUK, L. M. (2000). Psychophysical advances aid the study of genetic variation in taste. *Appetite, 34*(1), 105.

BARTOSHUK, L. M., & BEAUCHAMP, G. (1994). Chemical senses. *Annual Review of Psychology, 45,* 419–449.

BARTOSHUK, L. M., DUFFY, V. B., & MILLER, I. J. (1994). PTC/PROP tasting: Anatomy, psychophysics, and sex effects. *Physiology & Behavior, 56*(6): 1165–1171.

BASS, B. M. (1981). From leaderless group discussions to the cross-national assessment of managers. *Journal of Management, 7,* 63–76.

BASS, E., & DAVIS, L. (1988). *The courage to heal.* New York: Harper & Row.

BASSILI, J. N. (1993). Response latency versus certainty as indexes of the strength of voting intentions in a CATI survey. *Public Opinion Quarterly, 57*(1), 54–61.

BASSILI, J. N. (1995). Response latency and the accessibility of voting intentions: What contributes to accessibility and how it affects vote choice. *Personality and Social Psychology Bulletin, 21*(7), 686–695.

BATES, E. (1976). *Language and context: The acquisition of pragmatics.* New York: Academic Press.

BATES, E., CHEN, S., TZENG, O., LI, P., & OPIE, M. (1991). The noun-verb problem in Chinese aphasia. *Brain and Language, 41,* 203–233.

BATES, T. C., & SHIELES, A. (2003). Crystallized intelligence as a product of speed and drive for experience: The relationship of inspection time and openness to *g* and *Gc. Intelligence, 31,* 275–287.

BATESON, G. (1959). Cultural problems posed by a study of schizophrenic process. In A. Auerbach (Ed.), *Schizophrenia: An integrated approach* (pp. 125–148). New York: Ronald Press.

BATESON, G. (1960). Minimal requirements for a theory of schizophrenia. *Archives of General Psychiatry, 2,* 477–491.

BATSON, C. D., KOBRYNOWICZ, D., DINNERSTEIN, J. L., KAMPF, H. C., & WILSON, A. D. (1997). In a very different voice: Unmasking moral hypocrisy. *Journal of Personality and Social Psychology, 72,* 1335–1348.

BATSON, C. D., & THOMPSON, E. R. (2001). Why don't moral people act morally? Motivational considerations. *Current Directions in Psychological Science, 10,* 54–57.

BATSON, C. D., THOMPSON, E. R., & CHEN, H. (2002). Moral hypocrisy: Addressing some alternatives. *Journal of Personality and Social Psychology, 83,* 330–339.

BATSON, C. D., THOMPSON, E. R., SEUFERLING, G., WHITNEY, H., & STRONGMAN, J. A. (1999). Moral hypocrisy: Appearing moral to oneself without being so. *Journal of Personality and Social Psychology, 77,* 525–537.

BATTLE, Y. L., MARTIN, B. C., DORFMAN, J. H., & MILLER, L. S. (1999). Seasonality and infectious disease in schizophrenia: The birth hypothesis revisited. *Journal of Psychiatric Research, 33,* 501 509.

BAUER, P. J. (2005). Developments in declarative memory: Decreasing susceptibility to storage failure over the second year of life. *Psychological Science, 16,* 41–47.

BAUER, P. J., WIEBE, S. A., CARVER, L. J., WATERS, J. M., & NELSON, C. A. (2003). Developments in long-term explicit memory late in the first year of life. *Psychological Science, 14,* 629–635.

BAUM, A., & POSLUSZNY, D. M. (1999). Health psychology: Mapping biobehavioral contributions to health and illness. *Annual Review of Psychology, 50,* 137–163.

BAUMANN, B., & BOGERTS, B. (2001). Neuroanatomical studies on bipolar disorder [Suppl.]. *British Journal of Psychiatry, 41,* 142–147.

BAUMEISTER, R. F. (2001). Violent pride. *Scientific American, 284,* 96–101.

BAUMEISTER, R. F., CAMPBELL, J. D., KRUEGER, J. I., & VOHS, K. D. (2003). Does high self-esteem cause better performance, interpersonal success, happiness, or healthier lifestyles? *Psychological Science in the Public Interest, 4*(1), 1–44.

BAUMEISTER, R. F., CATANESE, K. R., & VOHS, K. D. (2001). Is there a gender difference in strength of sex drive? Theoretical views, conceptual distinctions, and a review of relevant evidence. *Personality & Social Psychology Review, 5*, 242–273.

BAUMEISTER, R. F., & LEARY, M. R. (1995). The need to belong: Desire for interpersonal attachments as a fundamental human motivation. *Psychological Bulletin, 117*, 497–529.

BAUMEISTER, R. F., & VOHS, K. D. (2004). Sexual economics: Sex as female resource for social exchange in heterosexual interactions. *Personality & Social Psychology Review, 8*(4), 339–363.

BAUMRIND, D. (1964). Some thoughts on the ethics of research: After reading Milgram's behavioral study of obedience. *American Psychologist, 19*, 421–423.

BAUMRIND, D. (1967). Child care practices anteceding three patterns of preschool behavior. *Genetic Psychology Monographs, 75*, 43–88.

BAUMRIND, D. (1971). Current patterns of parental authority. *Genetic Psychology Monographs, 1*.

BAUMRIND, D. (1977). Socialization determinants of personal agency. Paper presented at the biennial meetings of the Society for Research in Child Development, New Orleans. Cited in Maccoby, E. E. (1980). *Social development*. New York: Harcourt Brace Jovanovich.

BAUMRIND, D. (1986). Sex differences in moral reasoning: Response to Walker's (1984) conclusion that there are none. *Child Development, 57*, 511–521.

BAUMRIND, D. (1991). The influence of parenting style on adolescent competence and substance use. *Journal of Early Adolescence, 11*(1), 56–95.

BAYER, E. (1929). Beitrage zur Zweikomponententheorie des Hungers. *Zeitschrift der Psychologie, 112*, 1–54.

BAZERMAN, M. H. (1998). *Judgment in managerial decision making* (4th ed.). New York: Wiley.

BEAR, M. F., CONNORS, B. W., & PARADISO, M. A. (1996). *Neuroscience: Exploring the brain*. Baltimore: Williams & Wilkins.

BECHARA, A., DAMASIO, H., & DAMASIO, A. R. (2000). Emotion, decision making, and the orbitofrontal cortex. *Cerebral Cortex, 10*, 295–307.

BECK, A. T. (1967). *Depression: Causes and treatment*. Philadelphia: University of Pennsylvania Press.

BECK, A. T. (1976). *Cognitive therapy and the emotional disorders*. New York: International Universities Press.

BECK, A. T. (1985). Cognitive therapy. In H. I. Kaplan & J. Sadock (Eds.), *Comprehensive textbook of psychiatry* (4th ed.). Baltimore: Williams & Wilkins.

BECK, A. T., FREEMAN, A., & DAVIS, D. D., & ASSOCIATES. (2004). *Cognitive therapy of personality disorders* (2nd ed.). New York: Guilford.

BECK, A. T., RUSH, A. J., SHAW, B. F., & EMERY, G. (1979). *Cognitive therapy of depression*. New York: Guilford.

BECK, A. T., STEER, R. A., & BROWN, G. K. (1996). *Manual for the Beck Depression Inventory-II*. San Antonio, TX: Psychological Corporation.

BECKERS, T., MILLER, R. R., DE HOUWER, J., & URUSHIHARA, K. (2006). Reasoning rats: Forward blocking in Pavlovian animal conditioning is sensitive to constraints of causal inference. *Journal of Experimental Psychology: General, 135*(1), 92–102.

BÉDARD, J., & CHI, M. (1992). Expertise. *Current Directions in Psychological Science, 1*, 135–139.

BEER, R. D. (2000). Dynamical approaches to cognitive science. *Trends in Cognitive Science, 4*, 91–99.

BEGG, I., ANAS, A., & FARINACCI, S. (1992). Dissociation of processes in belief: Source recollection, statement familiarity, and the illusion of truth. *Journal of Experimental Psychology: General, 121*, 446–458.

BEHRMANN, M. (2000). The mind's eye mapped onto the brain's matter. *Current Directions in Psychological Science, 9*, 50–54.

BEITMAN, B. D., GOLDFRIED, M. R., & NORCROSS, J. C. (1989). The movement toward integrating the psychotherapies: An overview. *American Journal of Psychiatry, 146*, 138–147.

BÉKÉSY, G. VON. (1957). The ear. *Scientific American, 197*, 66–78.

BELIN, D., MAR, A. C., DALLEY, J. W., ROBBINS, T. W., & EVERITT, B. J. (2008). High impulsivity predicts the switch to compulsive cocaine-taking. *Science, 320*(5881), 1352–1355.

BELL, A. P., WEINBERG, M. S., & HAMMERSMITH, S. K. (1981). *Sexual preference: Its development in men and women*. Bloomington: Indiana University Press.

BELLUGI, U. (1971). Simplification in children's language. In R. Huxley & E. Ingram (Eds.), *Language acquisition: Models and methods*. New York: Academic Press.

BELLUGI, U., MARKS, S., BIHRLE, A., & SABO, H. (1991). Dissociation between language and cognitive function in Williams syndrome. In D. Bishop & K. Mogford (Eds.), *Language development in exceptional circumstances*. Hillsdale, NJ: Erlbaum.

BELOFF, H. (1957). The structure and origin of the anal character. *Genetic Psychology Monographs, 55*, 141–172.

BEM, D. J. (1967). Self-perception: An alternative interpretation of cognitive dissonance phenomena. *Psychological Review, 74*, 183–200.

BEM, D. J. (1972). Self-perception theory. In L. Berkowitz (Ed.), *Advances in experimental social psychology: Vol. 6* (pp. 2–62). New York: Academic Press.

BENBOW, C. P. (1988). Sex differences in mathematical reasoning ability in intellectually talented preadolescents: Their nature, effects, and possible causes. *Behavior and Brain Sciences, 11*, 169–232.

BENBOW, C. P., LUBINSKI, D., SHEA, D. L., & EFTEKHARI-SANJANI, H. (2000). Sex differences in mathematical reasoning ability at age 13: Their status 20 years later. *Psychological Science, 11*, 474–480.

BENBOW, C. P., & STANLEY, J. C. (1983). Sex differences in mathematical reasoning: More facts. *Science, 222*, 1029–1031.

BENET-MARTÍNEZ, V. (1999). Exploring indigenous Spanish personality constructs with a combined emic-etic approach. In J. C. Lasry, J. G. Adair, & K. L. Dion (Eds.), *Latest contributions to cross-cultural psychology:*

Selected papers from the Thirteenth International Congress of the International Association for Cross-Cultural Psychology (pp. 151–175). Lisse, The Netherlands: Swets & Zeitliner.

BENNETT, C., LINDSKOLD, S., & BENNETT, R. (1973). The effects of group size and discussion time on the risky shift. *Journal of Social Psychology, 91*(1), 137–147.

BENSON, H., & FRIEDMAN, R. (1996). Harnessing the power of the placebo effect and renaming it "remembered wellness." *Annual Review of Medicine, 47*, 193–199.

BERENBAUM, S. (2002). Prenatal androgen and sexual differentiation of behavior. In E. Eugster & O. Pescovitz (Eds.), *Developmental endrocrinology: From research to clinical practice* (pp. 293–311). Totowa, NJ: Humana Press.

BERGEN, S. E., GARDNER, C. O., & KENDLER, K. S. (2007). Age-related changes in heritability of behavioral phenotypes over adolescence and young adulthood: a meta-analysis. *Twin Research & Human Genetics, 10*, 423–433.

BERGER, P. L., & LUCKMANN, T. (1966). *The social construction of reality: A treatise in the sociology of knowledge*. Garden City, NY: Doubleday.

BERGMAN, T., BEEHNER, J., CHENEY, D. L., & SEYFARTH, R. M. (2003). Hierarchical classification by rank and kinship in baboons. *Science, 302*, 1234–1236.

BERLIN, B., & KAY, P. (1969). *Basic color terms: Their universality and evolution*. Berkeley and Los Angeles: University of California Press.

BERMAN, D. E., & DUDAI, Y. (2001). Memory extinction, learning anew, and learning the new: Dissociations in the molecular machinery of learning in the cortex. *Science, 291*, 2417–2419.

BERMANT, G., & DAVIDSON, J. M. (1974). *Biological bases of sexual behavior*. New York: Harper & Row.

BERNARD, L. L. (1924). *Instinct: A study in social psychology*. New York: Henry Holt.

BERNARD, V. W., OTTENBERG, P., & REDL, F. (1965). Dehumanization: A composite psychological defense in relation to modern war. In M. Schwebel (Ed.), *Behavioral science and human survival* (pp. 64–82). Palo Alto, CA: Science and Behavior Books.

BERNDT, T. J. (1996). Friendship quality affects adolescents' self-esteem and social behavior. In W. Bukowski, A. Newcomb, & W. Hartup (Eds.), *The company they keep: Friendship during childhood and adolescence* (pp. 346–365). New York: Cambridge University Press.

BERNDT, T. J. (1999). Friends' influence on students' adjustment to school. *Educational Psychologist, 34*(1), 15–28.

BERNDT, T. J., & KEEFE, K. (1995). Friends' influence on adolescents' adjustment to school. *Child Development, 66*, 1312–1329.

BERNSTEIN, A. E., & LENHART, S. A. (1993). *The psychodynamic treatment of women*. Washington, DC: American Psychiatric Press.

BERNSTEIN, D., & LOFTUS, E. (2009). How to tell if a particular memory is true or false. *Perspectives on Psychological Science, 4*, 370–374.

BERRIDGE, K. C., & ROBINSON, T. E. (2003). Parsing reward. *Trends in Neurosciences, 26*(9), 507–513.

BERSCHEID, E. (1985). Interpersonal attraction. In G. Lindzey & E. Aronson (Eds.), *The handbook of social psychology* (Vol. 2, pp. 413–484). New York: Random House.

BERSCHEID, E., DION, K., WALSTER, E., & WALSTER, G. W. (1971). Physical attractiveness and dating choice: A test of the matching hypothesis. *Journal of Experimental Social Psychology, 7,* 173–189.

BERSCHEID, E., & HATFIELD, E. (1978). *Interpersonal attraction* (2nd ed.). Reading, MA: Addison-Wesley.

BERSCHEID, E., & WALSTER, E. (1974). Physical attractiveness. In L. Berkowitz (Ed.), *Advances in experimental social psychology: Vol. 7.* New York: Academic Press.

BERSCHEID, E., & WALSTER, E. H. (1978). *Interpersonal attraction* (2nd ed.). Reading, MA: Addison-Wesley.

BESSENOFF, G. R., & SHERMAN, J. W. (2000). Automatic and controlled components of prejudice toward fat people: Evaluation versus stereotype activation. *Social Cognition, 18*(4), 329–353.

BEST, D., WILLIAMS, J., CLOUD, J., DAVIS, S., ROBERTSON, L., EDWARDS, J., ET AL. (1977). Development of sex-trait stereotypes among young children in the United States, England, and Ireland. *Child Development, 48,* 1375–1384.

BETTELHEIM, B. (1975). *The uses of enchantment: The meaning and importance of fairy tales.* New York: Random House.

BETTENCOURT, B., TALLEY, A., BENJAMIN, A., & VALENTINE, J. (2006). Personality and aggressive behavior under provoking and neutral conditions: A meta-analytic review. *Psychological Bulletin, 132,* 751–777.

BEVER, T. G. (1970). The cognitive basis for linguistic structures. In J. R. Hayes (Ed.), *Cognition and the development of language* (pp. 279–362). New York: Wiley.

BHARDWAJ, R. D., CURTIS, M. A. SPALDING, K. L., BUCHHOLZ, B. A., FINK, D., BJÖRK-ERIKSSON, T., ET AL. 2006. Neocortical neurogenesis in humans is restricted to development. *Proceedings of the National Academy of Sciences, 103,* 12564–12568.

BIALYSTOK, E. (1999). Cognitive complexity and attentional control in the bilingual mind. *Child Development, 70*(3), 636–644.

BIEDERMAN, I. (1987). Recognition-by-components: A theory of human image understanding. *Psychological Review, 94,* 115–147.

BIEDERMAN, J., WILENS, T. E., MICK, E., MILBERGER, S., SPENCER, T. J., & FARAONE, S. V. (1995). Psychoactive substance use disorders in adults with attention deficit hyperactivity disorder (ADHD): Effects of ADHD and psychiatric comorbidity. *American Journal of Psychiatry, 152,* 1652–1658.

BIELLO, S. M., & DAFTERS, R. I. (2001). MDMA and fenfluramine alter the response of the circadian clock to a serotonin agonist in vitro. *Brain Research, 920,* 202–209.

BIGELOW, A. (1987). Early words of blind children. *Journal of Child Language, 14*(1), 1–22.

BIGELOW, B., & LAGAIPA, J. (1975). Children's written descriptions of friendship: A multi-dimensional analysis. *Developmental Psychology, 41,* 857–858.

BILALIC, M., MCLEOD, P., & GOBET, F. (2008). Why good thoughts block better ones: The mechanism of the pernicious Einstellung (set) effect. *Cognition, 108,* 652–661.

BINDER, E. B., BRADLEY, R. G., LIU, W., EPSTEIN, M. P., DEVEAU, T. C., MERCER, K. B., ET AL. (2008). Association of FKBP5 polymorphisms and childhood abuse with risk of posttraumatic stress disorder symptoms in adults. *Journal of the American Medical Association, 299*(11), 1291–1305.

BINDER, E. B., SALYAKINA, D., LICHTNER, P., WOCHNIK, G. M., ISING, M., PÜTZ, B., ET AL. (2004). Polymorphisms in FKBP5 are associated with increased recurrence of depressive episodes and rapid response to antidepressant treatment. *Nature Genetics, 36*(12), 1319–1325.

BINET, A. (1911). *Les idées modernes sur les enfants.* Paris: Flammarion. Republished by Flammarion in 1973 with a preface by Jean Piaget. (Published in English as *Modern Ideas about Children.* Menlo Park, CA: Suzanne Heisler, 1984.)

BIRMAHER, B., & BRENT, D. (1998). Practice parameters for the assessment and treatment of children and adolescents with depressive disorders. *Journal of the American Academy of Child and Adolescent Psychiatry, 37,* 63S–83S.

BJORKLUND, D. F., & SHACKELFORD, T. K. (1999). Differences in parental investment contribute to important differences between men and women. *Current Directions in Psychological Science, 8*(3), 86–89.

BLACK, D. W., & ANDREASEN, N. C. (1994). Schizophrenia, schizophreniform disorder, and delusional paranoid disorder. In J. A. Talbott, R. E. Hales, & S. C. Yudofsky (Eds.), *American Psychiatric Press textbook of psychiatry* (pp. 411–463). Washington, DC: American Psychiatric Press.

BLACK, D. W., & NOYES, R. (1990). Comorbidity in obsessive-compulsive disorder. In J. D. Maser & C. D. Cloninger (Eds.), *Comorbidity in anxiety and mood disorders* (pp. 305–316). Washington, DC: American Psychiatric Press.

BLACKWELL, L., TRZESNIEWSKI, K., & DWECK, C. S. (2007). Implicit theories of intelligence predict achievement across an adolescent transition: A longitudinal study and an intervention. *Child Development, 78,* 246–263.

BLAIR, I. V., & BANAJI, M. R. (1996). Automatic and controlled processes in stereotype priming. *Journal of Personality and Social Psychology, 70.*

BLAIR, I., LENTON, A., & HASTIE, R. (2002). The reliability of the DRM paradigm as a measure of individual differences in false memories. *Psychonomic Bulletin and Review, 9,* 590–596.

BLAKEMORE, J. E. O. (2003). Children's beliefs about violating gender norms: Boys shouldn't look like girls, and girls shouldn't act like boys. *Sex Roles, 48*(9–10), 411–419.

BLANCHETTE, I., & DUNBAR, K. (2000). How analogies are generated: The roles of structural and superficial similarity. *Memory and Cognition, 28*(1), 108–124.

BLASCOVICH, J., SPENCER, S. J., QUINN, D., & STEELE, C. (2001). African Americans and high blood pressure: The role of stereotype threat. *Psychological Science, 12,* 225–229.

BLASS, T. (ED.). (2000). *Obedience to authority: Current perspectives on the Milgram paradigm.* Mahwah, NJ: Erlbaum.

BLATT, S. J., SANISLOW, C. A., III, ZUROFF, D. C., & PILKONIS, P. A. (1996). Characteristics of effective therapists: Further analyses of data from the National Institute of Mental Health Treatment of Depression Collaborative Research Program. *Journal of Consulting and Clinical Psychology, 64*(6), 1276–1284.

BLEULER, E. (1911). *Dementia praecox, or the group of schizophrenias* (J. Zinkin & N. D. C. Lewis, Trans.). New York: International Universities Press, 1950.

BLEULER, M. (1963). Conception of schizophrenia within the last fifty years and today. *Proceedings of the Royal Society of Medicine, 56,* 945–952.

BLIER, P., & ABBOTT, F. V. (2001). Putative mechanisms of action of antidepressant drugs in affective and anxiety disorders and pain. *Journal of Psychiatry and Neuroscience, 26,* 37–43.

BLISS, E. L. (1980). Multiple personalities: Report of fourteen cases with implications for schizophrenia and hysteria. *Archives of General Psychiatry, 37,* 1388–1397.

BLISS, T., COLLINGRIDGE, C., & LAROCHE, S. (2006). ZAP and ZIP, a story to forget. *Science, 313,* 1058–1059.

BLISS, T. V. P., & LOMO, T. (1973). Long-term potentiation of synaptic transmission in the dentate area of the anesthetized rabbit following stimulation of the perforant path. *Journal of Physiology, 232,* 331–356.

BLOCK, J. (2008). *The Q-sort in character appraisal: Encoding subjective impressions of persons quantitatively.* Washington, DC: American Psychological Association.

BLOCK, J., & BLOCK, J. H. (2006). Venturing a 30-year longitudinal study. *American Psychologist, 61,* 315–327.

BLOCK, N. (1997). Biology vs. computation in the study of consciousness. *Behavioral and Brain Sciences, 20,* 1.

BLOCK, N. (2001). Paradox and cross purposes in recent work on consciousness. *Cognition, 79,* 197–219.

BLOCK, N. (2005). Two neural correlates of consciousness. *Trends in Cognitive Sciences, 9,* 46–52.

BLOOM, B. S. (Ed) (1985). *Developing talent in young people.* New York: Ballantine.

BLOOM, F. E. (1993). Advancing a neurodevelopmental origin for schizophrenia. *Archives of General Psychiatry, 50,* 224–227.

BLOOM, L. (1993). *The transition from infancy to language: Acquiring the power of expression.* New York: Cambridge University Press.

BLOOM, P. (1996). Intention, history, and artifact concepts. *Cognition, 60,* 1–29.

BLOOM, P. (2000). *How children learn the meanings of words.* Cambridge, MA: MIT Press.

BLOOM, P. (2002). Mindreading, communication, and the learning of the names for things. *Mind and Language, 17,* 37–54.

BLURTON-JONES, N., & KONNER, M. J. (1976). !Kung knowledge of animal behavior. In B. Lee & I. DeVore (Eds.), *Kalahari hunter-gatherers.* Cambridge, MA: Harvard University Press.

BODENHAUSEN, G. V. (1990). Stereotypes as judgmental heuristics: Evidence of circadian variations in discrimination. *Psychological Science, 1,* 319–322.

BOGEN, J. E., FISHER, E. D., & VOGEL, P. J. (1965). Cerebral commissurotomy: A second case report. *Journal of the American Medical Association, 194,* 1328–1329.

BOLLES, R. C. (1970). Species-specific defense reactions and avoidance learning. *Psychological Review, 77,* 32–48.

BOLLES, R. C., & BEECHER, M. D. (EDS.). (1988). *Evolution and learning.* Hillsdale, NJ: Erlbaum.

BOLTON, P., & BETANCOURT, T. S. (2004). Mental health in postwar Afghanistan. *Journal of the American Medical Association, 292,* 626–628.

BOND, R., & SMITH, P. B. (1996). Culture and conformity: A meta-analysis of studies using Asch's (1952, 1956) line judgment task. *Psychological Bulletin, 119*(1), 111–137.

BONNET, M. H. (2005). Acute sleep deprivation. In M. H. Kryger, T. Roth, & W. C. Dement (Eds.), *Principles and practice of sleep medicine.* Philadelphia: Elsevier Saunders.

BOOK, A. S., STARZYK, K. B., & QUNISEY, V. L (2001). The relationship between testosterone and aggression: A meta-analysis. *Aggression and Violent Behavior, 6,* 579–599.

BOOTH, A. E., & WAXMAN, S. R. (2002). Word learning is "smart": Evidence that conceptual information affects preschoolers' extension of novel words. *Cognition, 84,* B11–B22.

BORDEN, V. M. H., & LEVINGER, G. (1991). Interpersonal transformations in intimate relationships. In W. H. Jones & D. Perlman (Eds.), *Advances in personal relationships: Vol. 2* (pp. 35–56). London: Jessica Kingsley.

BORKENAU, P., RIEMANN, R., ANGLEITNER, A., & SPINATH, F. M. (2001). Genetic and environmental influences on observed personality: Evidence from the German Observational Study of Adult Twins. *Journal of Personality and Social Psychology, 80*(4), 655–668.

BORNSTEIN, M. H. (1973). Color vision and color naming: A psychophysiological hypothesis of cultural difference. *Psychological Bulletin, 80,* 257–285.

BORNSTEIN, M. H. (1985). Human infant color vision and color perception. *Infant Behavior and Development, 8*(1), 109–113.

BORODITSKY, L. (2001). Does language shape thought? Mandarin and English speakers' conceptions of time. *Cognitive Psychology, 43,* 1–22.

BOTH, S., SPIERING, M., EVERAERD, W., & LAAN, E. (2004). Sexual behavior and responsiveness to sexual stimuli following laboratory-induced sexual arousal. *Journal of Sex Research, 41,* 242–258.

BOTVINICK, M. M., COHEN, J. D., & CARTER, C. S. (2004). Conflict monitoring and anterior cingulate cortex: An update. *Trends in Cognitive Science, 8,* 539–546.

BOUCHARD, T. J., JR. (1984). Twins reared apart and together: What they tell us about human diversity. In S. Fox (Ed.), *The chemical and biological bases of individuality* (pp. 147–184). New York: Plenum.

BOUCHARD, T. J., JR., LYKKEN, D. T., MCGUE, M., SEGAL, N. L., & TELLEGEN, A. (1990). Sources of human psychological differences: The Minnesota study of twins reared apart. *Science, 250,* 223–250.

BOUCHARD, T. J., JR., & MCGUE, M. (1981). Familial studies of intelligence: A review. *Science, 212,* 1055–1059.

BOURDON, K. H., BOYD, J. H., RAE, D. S., BURNS, B. J., THOMPSON, J. W., & LOCKE, B. Z. (1988). Gender differences in phobias: Results of the ECA community survey. *Journal of Anxiety Disorders, 2,* 227–241.

BOURET, S. G., DRAPER, S. J., & SIMERLY, R. B. (2004). Trophic action of leptic on hypothalamic neurons that regulate feeding. *Science, 304,* 108–110.

BOWER, G. H. (1970). Analysis of a mnemonic device. *American Scientist, 58,* 496–510.

BOWER, G. H. (1972). Analysis of a mnemonic device. In M. Coltheart (Ed.), *Readings in cognitive psychology.* Toronto: Holt, Rinehart & Winston.

BOWER, G. H., BLACK, J. B., & TURNER, T. J. (1979). Scripts in memory for text. *Cognitive Psychology, 11,* 177–220.

BOWER, G. H., MCLEAN, J., & MEACHEM, J. (1966). Value of knowing when reinforcement is due. *Journal of Comparative and Physiological Psychology, 62,* 184–192.

BOWER, J. M., & PARSONS, L. M. (2003). Rethinking the "lesser brain." *Scientific American, 289,* 50–57.

BOWERMAN, M. (1982). Reorganizational processes in language development. In E. Wanner & L. R. Gleitman (Eds.), *Language development: State of the art.* New York: Cambridge University Press.

BOWLES, S. (2008). Policies designed for self-interested citizens may undermine "the moral sentiments": Evidence from economics experiments. *Science, 320,* 1605–1609.

BOWMAKER, J. K., & DARTNALL, H. J. A. (1980). Visual pigments and rods and cones in a human retina. *Journal of Physiology, 298,* 501–511.

BRABECK, M. (1983). Moral judgement: Theory and research on differences between males and females. *Developmental Review, 3,* 274–291.

BRACKETT, M. A., & MAYER, J. D. (2003). Convergent, discriminant, and incremental validity of competing measures of emotional intelligence. *Personality and Social Psychology Bulletin, 29,* 1147–1158.

BRACKETT, M. A., RIVERS, S. E., SHIFFMAN, S., LERNER, N., & SALOVEY, P. (2006). Relating emotional abilities to social functioning: A comparison of self-report and performance measures of emotional intelligence. *Journal of Personality and Social Psychology, 91,* 780–795.

BRADLEY, G. W. (1978). Self-serving biases in the attribution process: A reexamination of the fact or fiction question. *Journal of Personality and Social Psychology, 13,* 420–432.

BRADLEY, S. J., OLIVER, G. D., CHERNICK, A. B., & ZUCKER, K. J. (1998). Experiment of nurture: Ablatio penis at 2 months, sex reassignment at 7 months, and a psychosexual follow-up in young adulthood. *Pediatrics, 102,* e9 (electronic article available at http://www.pediatrics.org/cgi/content/full/102/1/e9).

BRADSHAW, J. L. (2001). *Developmental disorders of the frontostrial system: Neuropsychological, neuropsychiatric, and evolutionary perspectives.* Philadelphia: Psychology Press/Taylor & Francis.

BRAILOWSKY, S., & GARCIA, O. (1999). Ethanol, GABA and epilepsy. *Archives of Medical Research, 30,* 3–9.

BRAINERD, C., YANG, Y., REYNA, V., HOWE, M., & MILLS, B. (2008). Semantic processing in "associative" false memory. *Psychonomic Bulletin & Review, 15,* 1035–1053

BRAMBILLA, P., HARENSKI, K., NICOLETTI, M., SASSI, R. B., MALLINGER, A. G., FRANK, E., ET AL. (2003). MRI investigation of temporal lobe structures in bipolar patients. *Journal of Psychiatric Research, 37,* 287–295.

BRANDONE, A. C., & WELLMAN, H. M. (2009). You can't always get what you want: Infants understand failed goal-directed actions. *Psychological Science, 20*(1), 85–91.

BRANNON, E. (2003). Number knows no bounds. *Trends in Cognitive Science, 7,* 279–281.

BRANSFORD, J. D., & JOHNSON, M. K. (1972). Contextual prerequisites for understanding. *Journal of Verbal Learning and Verbal Behavior, 11,* 717–726.

BRANSFORD, J. (1979). *Human cognition: Learning, understanding and remembering.* Belmont, CA: Wadsworth.

BRAUER, M., JUDD, C. M., & GLINER, M. D. (1995). The effects of repeated expressions on attitude polarization during group discussions. *Journal of Personality and Social Psychology, 68*(6), 1014–1029.

BRECHBÜHL, J., KLAEY, M., & BROILLET, M.-C. (2008). Grueneberg ganglion cells mediate alarm pheromone detection in mice. *Science, 321,* 1092–1094.

BREMNER, J. D., SOUTHWICK, S. M., JOHNSON, D. R., YEHUDA, R., & CHARNEY, D. S. (1993). Childhood physical abuse and combat-related posttraumatic stress disorder in Vietnam veterans. *American Journal of Psychiatry, 150,* 235–239.

BRENDGEN, M., VITARO, F., & BUKOWSKI, W. (2000). Deviant friends and early adolescents' emotional and behavioral adjustment. *Journal of Research on Adolescence, 10,* 173–189.

BRENNAN, K. A., CLARK, C. L., & SHAVER, P. R. (1998). Self-report measurement of adult attachment: An integrative overview. In J. A. Simpson & W. S. Rholes (Eds.), *Attachment theory and close relationships* (pp. 46–76). New York: Guilford.

BRENNEN, T., BAGULEY, T., BRIGHT, J., & BRUCE, V. (1990). Resolving semantically induced tip-of-the-tongue states for proper nouns. *Memory & Cognition, 18,* 339–347.

BRENNER, C. (1982). *The mind in conflict.* New York: International Universities Press.

BRENNER, L., ROTTENSTREICH, Y., & SOOD, S. (1999). Comparison, grouping, and preference. *Psychological Science, 10,* 225–229.

BRESLAU, N., CHILCOAT, H. D., KESSLER, R. C., & DAVIS, G. C. (1999). Previous exposure to trauma and PTSD effects of subsequent trauma: Results from the Detroit Area Survey of Trauma. *American Journal of Psychiatry, 156,* 902–907.

BRETHERTON, I. (1990). Open communication and internal working models: Their role in the development of attachment relationships. In R. A. Thompson (Ed.), *Socioemotional development: Vol. 36. Nebraska Symposium on Motivation* (pp. 57–113). Lincoln: University of Nebraska Press.

BREWER, J., ZHAO, Z., DESMOND, J., GLOVER, G., & GABRIELI, J. (1998). Making memories: Brain activity that predicts how well visual experience will be remembered. *Science, 281,* 1185–1187.

BREWER, W. F., & TREYENS, J. C. (1981). Role of schemata in memory for places. *Cognitive Psychology, 13,* 207–230.

BREWIN, C. R. (1998). Intrusive autobiographical memories in depression and post-traumatic stress disorder. *Applied Cognitive Psychology, 12,* 359–370.

BRICKMAN, J. C., & D'AMATO, B. (1975). Exposure effects in a free-choice situation. *Journal of Personality and Social Psychology, 32,* 415–420.

BRICKMAN, P., COATES, D., & JANOFF-BULLMAN, R. (1978). Lottery winners and accident victims: Is happiness relative? *Journal of Personality and Social Psychology, 36,* 917–927.

BRIDGEMAN, B., & LEWIS, C. (1996). Gender differences in college mathematics grades and SAT-M scores: A reanalysis of Wainer & Steinberg. *Journal of Educational Measurement, 33,* 257–270.

BRIDGEMAN, B., & STARK, L. (1991). Ocular proprioception and efference copy in registering visual direction. *Vision Research, 31,* 1903–1913.

BRIDGES, P. (1987). Psychosurgery for resistant depression. In J. Zohar & R. H. Belmaker (Eds.), *Treating resistant depression* (pp. 397–411). New York: PMA Publishing.

BROADBENT, D. E. (1958). *Perception and communication.* London: Pergamon Press.

BRODY, G. H., & GE, X. (2001). Linking parenting processes and self-regulation to psychological functioning and alcohol use during early adolescence. *Journal of Family Psychology, 15*(1), 82–94.

BRODY, L., & HALL, J. (2000). Gender, emotion, and expression. In M. Lewis & J. Haviland-Jones (Eds.), *Handbook of emotions* (2nd ed., pp. 338–349). New York: Guilford.

BRODY, N. (1992). *Intelligence* (2nd ed.). New York: Academic Press.

BRODY, N. (2003). Construct validation of the Sternberg Triarchic Abilities Test: Comment and reanalysis. *Intelligence, 31,* 319–329.

BRODY, N. (2007). Barriers to understanding racial differences in intelligence: Commentary on Hunt and Carlson (2007). *Perspective on Psychological Science, 2,* 214–215.

BRONFENBRENNER, U., McCLELLAND, P., WETHINGTON, E., MOEN, P., & CECI, S. J. (1996). *The state of Americans: This generation and the next.* New York: Free Press.

BROWN, A. (1991). A review of the Tip-of-the-Tongue Experience. *Psychological Bulletin, 109,* 204–223.

BROWN, A. (2002). Consolidation theory and retrograde amnesia in humans. *Psychonomic Bulletin and Review, 9,* 403–425.

BROWN, A., & MITCHELL, D. (1994). A reevaluation of semantic versus nonsemantic processing in implicit memory. *Memory and Cognition, 22,* 533–541.

BROWN, A. S., COHEN, P., HARKAVY-FRIEDMAN, J., & BABULAS, V. (2001). Prenatal rubella, premorbid abnormalities, and adult schizophrenia. *Biological Psychiatry, 49,* 473–486.

BROWN, B., CLASEN, D., & EICHER, S. (1986). Perception of peer pressure, peer conformity dispositions and self reported behavior among adolescents. *Developmental Psychology, 22,* 521–530.

BROWN, B., MORAY, M., & KINNEY, D. (1994). Casting adolescent crowds in a relational perspective: Caricature, channel and context. In R. Montemayor, G. Adams, & T. Gullotta (Eds.), *Personal relationships in adolescence: Vol. 6. Advances in adolescent development.* Thousand Oaks, CA: Sage.

BROWN, B. B. (1990). Peer groups and peer cultures. In S. S. Feldman & G. R. Elliott (Eds.), *At the threshold: The developing adolescent.* Cambridge, MA: Harvard University Press.

BROWN, C. M., HAGOORT, P., & TER KEURS, M. (1999). Electrophysiological signatures of visual lexical processing of open- and closed-class words. *Journal of Cognitive Neuroscience, 11,* 261– 281.

BROWN, D. A., SALMON, K., PIPE, M.-E., RUTTER, M., CRAW, S., & TAYLOR, B. (1999). Children's recall of medical experiences. *Child Abuse & Neglect, 23,* 209–216.

BROWN, D. E. (1991). *Human universals.* New York: McGraw-Hill.

BROWN, E., DEFFENBACHER, K., & STURGILL, W. (1977). Memory for faces and the circumstances of encounter. *Journal of Applied Psychology, 62,* 311–318.

BROWN, G. W., & HARRIS, T. (1978). *Social origins of depression: A study of psychiatric disorder in women.* London: Tavistock.

BROWN, J., & DUNN, J. (1996). Continuities in emotion understanding from 3 to 6 years. *Child Development, 67,* 789–802.

BROWN, J. F. (1940). *The psychodynamics of abnormal behavior.* New York: McGraw-Hill.

BROWN, P., & DELL, G. L. (1987). Adapting production to comprehension: The explicit mention of instruments. *Cognitive Psychology, 19,* 441–472.

BROWN, R. (1957). Linguistic determinism and parts of speech. *Journal of Abnormal and Social Psychology, 55,* 1–5.

BROWN, R. (1958). *Words and things.* New York: Free Press, Macmillan.

BROWN, R. (1965). *Social psychology.* New York: Free Press, Macmillan.

BROWN, R., & BELLUGI, U. (1964). Three processes in the child's acquisition of syntax. *Harvard Educational Review, 34,* 133–151.

BROWN, R., & KULIK, J. (1977). Flashbulb memories. *Cognition, 5,* 73–99.

BROWN, R., & McNEILL, D. (1966). The tip of the tongue phenomenon. *Journal of Verbal Learning and Verbal Behavior, 5,* 325–327.

BROWN, R. P., & JOSEPHS, R. A. (1999). A burden of proof: Stereotype relevance and gender differences in math performance. *Journal of Personality and Social Psychology, 76,* 246–257.

BROWN, T. A., CAMPBELL, L. A., LEHMAN, C. L., GRISHAM, J. R., & MANCILL, R. B. (2001). Current and lifetime comorbidity of the *DSM-IV* anxiety and mood disorders in a large clinical sample. *Journal of Abnormal Psychology, 110*(4), 585–599.

BRUCH, H. (1973). *Eating disorders.* New York: Basic Books.

BRUCH, H. (1978). *The golden cage.* Cambridge, MA: Harvard University Press.

BRUCK, M., & CECI, S. J. (1999). The suggestibility of children's memory. *Annual Review of Psychology, 50.*

BRUGGEMAN, E., & HART, K. (1996). Cheating, lying, and moral reasoning by religious and secular high school students. *Journal of Educational Research, 89,* 340–344.

BRUNER, J. S., & TAGIURI, R. (1954). The perception of people. In G. Lindzey (Ed.), *Handbook of social psychology: Vol. 2.* Reading, MA: Addison-Wesley.

BUCHANAN, G. M., & SELIGMAN, M. E. P. (EDS.). (1995). *Explanatory style.* Hillsdale, NJ: Erlbaum.

BUCHANAN, T. W., & ADOLPHS, R. (2004). The neuroanatomy of emotional memory in humans. In D. Reisberg & P. Hertel (Eds.), *Memory and emotion* (pp. 42–75). New York: Oxford University Press.

BUCKLEY, M., MANSOURI, F., HODA, H., MAHBOUBI, M., BROWNING, P., KWOK, S., ET AL. (2009). Dissociable components of rule-guided behavior depend on distinct medial and prefrontal regions. *Science, 325,* 52–58.

BUGNYAR, T., & KOTRSCHAL, K. (2002). Observational learning and the raiding of food caches in ravens, *Corvus corax:* Is it "tactical" deception? *Animal Behavior, 64,* 185–195.

BULLER, D. J. (2005). Evolutionary psychology: The emperor's new paradigm. *Trends in Cognitive Science, 9,* 277–283.

BULLER, D. J., FODOR, J., & CRUME, T. L. (2005). The emperor is still under-dressed. *Trends in Cognitive Science, 9,* 508–510.

BULLOCK, T. H., BENNETT, M. V., JOHNSTON, D., JOSEPHSON, R., MARDER, E., & FIELDS, R. D. (2005). The Neuron Doctrine, redux. *Science, 310,* 791–793.

BULLOCK, W. A., & GILLILAND, K. (1993). Eysenck's arousal theory of introversion-extraversion: A covergent measures investigation. *Journal of Personality and Social Psychology, 64,* 113–123.

BURGER, J. M. (1986). Increasing compliance by improving the deal: The that's-not-all technique. *Journal of Personality and Social Psychology, 51*(2), 277–283.

BURGER, J. M. (2009). Replicating Milgram: Would people still obey today? *American Psychologist, 64,* 1–11.

BURGER, J. M., & GUADAGNO, R. E. (2003). Self-concept clarity and the foot-in-the-door procedure. *Basic and Applied Social Psychology, 25,* 79–86.

BURGER, J. M., REED, M., DeCESARE, K., RAUNER, S., & ROZOLIS, J. (1999). The effects of initial request size on compliance: More about the that's-not-all technique. *Basic and Applied Social Psychology, 21*(3), 243–249.

BURGESS, E. W., & WALLIN, P. (1943). Homogamy in social characteristics. *American Journal of Sociology, 49,* 109–124.

BURKE, M. J., & PRESKHORN, S. H. (1995). Short-term treatment of mood disorders with standard antidepressants. In F. E. Bloom & D. Kupfer (Eds.), *Psychopharmacology: The fourth generation of progress* (pp. 1053–1065). New York: Raven.

BURNETT, S. A., LANE, D. M., & DRATT, L. M. (1979). Spatial differences and sex differences in quantitative ability. *Intelligence, 3,* 345–354.

BURNS, D. D. (1980). *Feeling good: The new mood therapy.* New York: Penguin.

BURNS, J. M. (1978). *Leadership.* New York: Harper & Row.

BURRIS, K. D., MOLSKI, T. F., XU, C., RYAN, E., TOTTORI, K., KIKUCHI, T., ET AL. (2002). Aripiprzole, a novel antipsychotic, is a high-affinity partial agonist at human dopamine D2 receptors. *Journal of Pharmacology and Experimental Therapies, 302,* 381–389.

BURT, S. A., KRUEGER, R. F., MCGUE, M., & IACONO, W. G. (2001). Sources of covariation among attention-deficit/hyperactivity disorder, oppositional defiant disorder, and conduct disorder: The importance of shared environment. *Journal of Abnormal Psychology, 110,* 516–525.

BUSEY, T. A., TUNNICLIFF, J., LOFTUS, G. R., & LOFTUS, E. F. (2000). Accounts of the confidence-accuracy relation in recognition memory. *Memory & Cognition, 7,* 26–48.

BUSHMAN, B., & ANDERSON, C. (2009). Comfortably numb: Desensitizing effects of violent media on helping others. *Psychological Science, 20,* 273–277.

BUSHMAN, B. J., & BAUMEISTER, R. F. (2002). Does self-love or self-hate lead to violence? *Journal of Research in Personality, 36*(6), 543–545.

BUSS, A. H., & PLOMIN, R. (1984). *Temperament: Early developing personality traits.* Hillsdale, NJ: Erlbaum.

BUSS, D. M. (1989). Sex differences in human mate preferences: Evolutionary hypotheses tested in 37 cultures. *Behavioral and Brain Sciences, 12,* 1–50.

BUSS, D. M. (1992). Mate preference mechanisms: Consequences for partner choice and intrasexual competition. In J. H. Barkow, L. Cosmides, & J. Tooby (Eds.), *The adapted mind* (pp. 249–266). New York: Oxford University Press.

BUSS, D. M. (1999). Human nature and individual differences: The evolution of human personality. In L. A. Pervin & O. P. John (Eds.), *Handbook of personality: Theory and research* (pp. 31–56). New York: Guilford Press.

BUSS, D. M. (2004). *Evolutionary psychology: The new science of the mind.* Boston: Allyn & Bacon.

BUSS, D. M. (2009). The great struggles of life: Darwin and the emergence of evolutionary psychology. *American Psychologist, 64,* 140–148.

BUSS, D. M., & BARNES, M. F. (1986). Preferences in human mate selection. *Journal of Personality and Social Psychology, 50,* 559–570.

BUSS, D. M., & HASELTON, M. (2005). The evolution of jealousy. *Trends in Cognitive Science, 9,* 506–507.

BUSS, D. M., LARSEN, R. J., WESTEN, D., & SEMMELROTH, J. (2001). Sex differences in jealousy: Evolution, physiology, and psychology. In W. Parrott (Ed.), *Emotions in social psychology: Essential readings.* Philadelphia: Psychology Press.

BUSS, D. M., & SCHMITT, D. P. (1993). Sexual strategies theory: An evolutionary perspective on human mating. *Psychological Review, 100*(2), 204–232.

BUTCHER, J. N., DAHLSTROM, W. G., GRAHAM, J. R., TELLEGEN, A., & KAEMMER, B. (2001). *MMPI-2 (Minnesota Multiphasic Personality Inventory-2) manual for administration and scoring* (2nd ed.). Minneapolis: University of Minnesota Press.

BUTCHER, J. N., WILLIAMS, C. L., GRAHAM, J. R., ARCHER, R. P., TELLEGEN, A., BEN-PORATH, Y. S., ET AL. (1992). *MMPI-A (Minnesota Multiphasic Personality Inventory—Adolescent) manual for administration, scoring, and interpretation.* Minneapolis: University of Minnesota Press.

BUTLER, R. A. (1954). Incentive conditions which influence visual exploration. *Journal of Experimental Psychology, 48,* 19–23.

BUTTERWORTH, G., & COCHRAN, E. (1980). Towards a mechanism of joint visual attention in human infancy. *International Journal of Behavioral Development, 3,* 253–272.

BUTTERWORTH, G., & JARRETT, N. (1991). What minds have in common is space: Spatial mechanisms serving joint visual attention in infancy. Perspectives on the child's theory of mind [Special issue]. *British Journal of Developmental Psychology, 9,* 55–72.

BUZSÁKI, G., & DRAGUHN, A. (2004). Neuronal oscillations in cortical networks. *Science, 304,* 1926–1929.

BYRNE, R. W., & WHITEN, A. (EDS.). (1988). *Machiavellian intelligence: Social expertise and the evolution of intellect in monkeys, apes, and humans.* New York: Oxford University Press.

BYRNES, J. P. (2005). Gender differences in math: Cognitive processes in an expanded framework. In A. M. Gallagher & J. C. Kaufman (Eds.), *Gender differences in mathematics: An integrative psychological approach* (pp. 73–98). New York: Cambridge University Press.

———

CABEZA, R., & NYBERG, L. (2000). Imaging cognition II: An empirical review of 275 PET and fMRI studies. *Journal of Cognitive Neuroscience, 12,* 1–47.

CABEZA, R., & ST. JACQUES, P. (2007). Functional neuroimaging of autobiographical memory. *Trends in Cognitive Sciences, 11,* 219–227.

CABRERA, N. J., TAMIS-LEMONDA, C. S., BRADLEY, R. H., HOFFERTH, S., & LAMB, M. E. (2000). Fatherhood in the twenty-first century. *Child Development, 71,* 127–136.

CACIOPPO, J. T., BERNTSON, G. G., & KLEIN, D. J. (1992). What is emotion? The role of somatovisceral afference, with special emphasis on somatovisceral "illusions." *Review of Personality and Social Psychology, 14,* 63–98.

CACIOPPO, J. T., BERNTSON, G. G., LARSEN, J. T., POEHLMANN, K. M., & ITO, T. A. (2000). The psychophysiology of emotion. In M. Lewis & J. Haviland-Jones (Eds.), *Handbook of emotions* (2nd ed., pp. 173–191). New York: Guilford.

CACIOPPO, J. T., MARSHALL-GOODELL, B. S., TASSINARY, L. G., & PETTY, R. E. (1992). Rudimentary determinants of attitudes: Classical conditioning is more effective when prior knowledge about the attitude stimulus is low than high. *Journal of Experimental Social Psychology, 28,* 207–233.

CACIOPPO, J. T., & PETTY, R. E. (1981). Electromyograms as measures of extent and affectivity of information processing. *American Psychologist, 36,* 441–456.

CAHILL, L., BABINSKY, R., MARKOWITSCH, H. J., & MCGAUGH, J. L. (1996). The amygdala and emotional memory. *Nature, 377,* 295–296.

CAHOON, L. (2008). Learning under anesthesia. *Science, 321,* 1153.

CALABRESE, J. R., & WOYSHVILLE, M. J. (1995). Lithium therapy: Limitations and alternatives in the treatment of bipolar disorders. *Annals of Clinical Psychiatry, 7,* 103–112.

CALLAGHAN, T., ROCHAT, P., LILLARD, A., CLAUX, M. L., ODDEN, H., ITAKURA, S., ET AL. (2005). Synchrony in the onset of mental-state reasoning: Evidence from five cultures. *Psychological Science, 16,* 378–384.

CAMPBELL, F. A., & RAMEY, C. T. (1994). Effects of early intervention on intellectual and academic achievement: A follow-up study of children from low-income families. *Child Development, 65*(2), 684–698.

CAMPBELL, J. B., & HAWLEY, C. W. (1982). Study habits and Eysenck's theory of extraversion-introversion. *Journal of Research in Personality, 16,* 139–146.

CAMPBELL, J. D., TESSER, A., & FAIREY, P. J. (1986). Conformity and attention to the stimulus: Some temporal and contextual dynamics. *Journal of Personality and Social Psychology, 51,* 315–324.

CAMPFIELD, L. A., & ROSENBAUM, M. (1992). Human hunger: Is there a role for blood glucose dynamics? *Appetite, 18,* 244.

CAMPFIELD, L. A., & SMITH, F. J. (1990a). Systemic factors in the control of food intake. In E. M. Stricker (Ed.), *Handbook of behavioral neurobiology: Vol. 10. Neurobiology of food and fluid intake* (pp. 183–206). New York: Plenum.

CAMPFIELD, L. A., & SMITH, F. J. (1990b). Transient declines in blood glucose signal meal initiation. *International Journal of Obesity, 14,* 15–33.

CAMPOS, J., ANDERSON, D. BARBU-ROTH, M., HUBBARD, E., HERTENSTEIN, M., & WITHERINGTON, D. (2000). Travel broadens the mind. *Infancy, 1,* 149–219.

CANLI, T., ZHAO, Z., BREWER, J., GABRIELI, J. D. E., & CAHILL, L. (2000). Event-related activation in the human amygdala associates with later memory for individual emotional response. *Journal of Neuroscience, 20*(19).

CANNON, T. D., MEDNICK, S. A., & PARNAS, J. (1990). Antecedents of predominantly negative- and predominantly positive-symptom schizophrenia in a high-risk population. *Archives of General Psychiatry, 47,* 622–632.

CANNON, T. D., ROSSO, I. M., HOLLISTER, J. M., BEARDEN, C. E., SANCHEZ, L. E., & HADLEY, T. (2000). A prospective cohort study of genetic and perinatal influences in schizophrenia. *Schizophrenia Bulletin, 26,* 351–366.

CANNON, T. D., THOMPSON, P. M., VAN ERP, T.G.M., TOGA, A. W., PUTANEN, V-P, HUTTUNEN, M., ET AL. (2002). Cortex mapping reveals regionally specific patterns of genetic and disease-specific gray-matter deficits in twins discordant for schizophrenia. *Proceedings of the National Academy of Sciences, 99*(5), 3228–3233.

CANNON, W. B. (1927). The James-Lange theory of emotions: A critical examination and an alternative theory. *American Journal of Psychology, 39,* 106–124.

CANNON, W. B. (1929). *Bodily changes in pain, hunger, fear and rage* (rev. ed.). New York: Appleton-Century.

CANNON, W. B. (1932 and 1960). *The wisdom of the body* (revised and enlarged). New York: Norton.

CANTOR, J., & ENGLE, R. (1993). Working-memory capacity as long-term memory activation: An individual-differences approach. *Journal of Experimental Psychology: Learning, Memory and Cognition, 19,* 1101–1114.

CANTOR, N., & MISCHEL, W. (1979). Prototypes in person perception. In L. Berkowitz (Ed.), *Advances in experimental social psychology: Vol. 12.* New York: Academic Press.

CARAMAZZA, A., & HILLIS, A. (1991). Lexical organization of nouns and verbs in the brain. *Nature, 349,* 788–790.

CARDINO, A. G., & GOTTESMAN, I. I. (2000). Twin studies of schizophrenia: From bow-and-arrow concordances to Star Wars Mx and functional genomics. *American Journal of Medical Genetics, 97,* 12–17.

CAREY, B. (2008, December 5). H. M., an unforgettable amnesiac, dies at 82. *New York Times.* Retrieved July 8, 2009, from http://www.nytimes.com.

CAREY, D. B. (2001). Do action systems resist visual illusions? *Trends in Cognitive Science, 5,* 109–113.

CAREY, S. (1978). The child as word learner. In M. Halle, J. Bresnan, & G. A. Miller (Eds.), *Linguistic theory and psychological reality* (pp. 264–293). Cambridge, MA: MIT Press.

CAREY, S. (1985). *Conceptual change in childhood.* Cambridge, MA: MIT Press.

CARLSON, E. B., & PUTNAM, E. W. (1993). An update on the Dissociative Experiences Scale. *Dissociation, 6,* 16–27.

CARLSON, G., & TANENHAUS, M. (1988). Thematic roles and language comprehension. In W. Wilkins (Ed.), *Syntax and semantics: Vol. 21. Thematic relations.* San Diego, CA: Academic Press.

CARLSSON, A. (1995). The dopamine theory revisited. In S. R. Hirsch and D. R. Weinberger (Eds.), *Schizophrenia* (pp. 379–400). Oxford, England: Blackwell.

CARLYLE, T. (1841). *On heroes, hero-worship, and the heroic in history.* Berkeley: University of California Press, 1992.

CARNAGEY, N. L., & ANDERSON, C. A. (2005). The effects of reward and punishment in violent video games on aggressive affect, cognition and behavior. *Psychological Science, 16,* 883–889.

CARNAGEY, N. L., ANDERSON, C. A., & BARTHOLOW, B. B. (2007). Media violence and social neuroscience: New questions and new opportunities. *Current Directions in Psychological Science, 16,* 178–182.

CARNEY, S., & GEDDES, J. (2003). Electroconvulsive therapy. *British Medical Journal, 326,* 1343–1344.

CARPENTER, P. A., MIYAKE, A., & JUST, M. A. (1995). Language comprehension: Sentence and discourse processing. *Annual Review of Psychology, 46,* 91–120.

CARROLL, J. B. (1993). *Human cognitive abilities: A survey of factor-analytic studies.* New York: Cambridge University Press.

CARROLL, J. B. (2005). The three-stratum theory of cognitive abilities. In D. P. Flanagan & P. L. Harrison (Eds.), *Contemporary intellectual assessment: Theories, tests, and issues* (2nd ed., pp. 69-76). New York: Guilford.

CARROLL, L. (1969). *Alice in wonderland.* Abridged by J. Frank and illustrated by M. M. Torrey. New York: Random House (originally published 1865).

CARSKADON, M. A., ACEBO, C., & JENNI, O. G. (2004). Regulation of adolescent sleep: Implications for behavior. In R. Dahl & L. P. Spear (Eds.), *Annals of the New York Academy of Sciences, adolescent brain development: Vulnerabilities and opportunities* (Vol. 1021, pp. 276–291). New York: New York Academy of Sciences.

CARSTENSEN, L. L. (2006). The influence of a sense of time on human development. *Science, 312*(5782), 1913–1915.

CARTER, C. S., MINTUN, M., NICHOLS, T., & COHEN, J. D. (1997). Anterior cingulate gyrus dysfunction and selective attention deficits in schizophrenia: 15OH2O PET study during single-trial Stroop task performance. *American Journal of Psychiatry, 154,* 1670–1675.

CARTWRIGHT, R. D. (1977). *Night life: Explorations in dreaming.* Englewood Cliffs, NJ: Prentice-Hall.

CARTWRIGHT, R. D. (1994). Dreams and their meaning. In M. H. Kryger, T. Roth, & W. C. Dement (Eds.), *Principles and practice of sleep medicine* (2nd ed.). Philadelphia: Saunders.

CARVER, L. J., & VACCARO, B. G. (2007). 12-month-old infants allocate increased neural resources to stimuli associated with negative adult emotion. *Developmental Psychology, 43*(1), 54–69.

CASE, R., & OKAMOTO, Y. (1996). The role of central conceptual structures in the development of children's thought. *Monographs of the Society for Research in Child Development, 61*(1–2), v-265.

CASELLI, M.-C., BATES, E., CASADIO, P., & FENSON, J. (1995). A cross-linguistic study of early lexical development. *Cognitive Development, 10*(2), 159–199.

CASH, S., HALGREN, E., DEHGHANI, N., ROSSETTI, A., THESEN, T., WANG, C. M., ET AL. (2009). The human K-complex represents an isolated cortical down-state. *Science, 324,* 1084–1087.

CASPI, A., & HERBENER, E. (1990). Continuity and change: Assortative marriage and the consistency of personality in adulthood. *Journal of Personality and Social Psychology, 58,* 250–258.

CASPI, A., & MOFFITT, T. E. (1991). Individual differences are accentuated during periods of social change: The sample case of girls at puberty. *Journal of Personality and Social Psychology, 61*(1), 157–168.

CASPI, A., & MOFFITT, T. E. (1993). When do individual differences matter? A paradoxical theory of personality coherence. *Psychological Inquiry, 4*(4), 247–271.

CASPI, A., SUGDEN, K., MOFFITT, T. E., TAYLOR, A., CRAIG, I. W., HARRINGTON, H., ET AL. (2003). Influence of life stress on depression: Moderation in the 5–HTT gene. *Science, 301*(5631), 386–389.

CASSEL, E., & BERNSTEIN, D. A. (2007). *Criminal behavior* (2nd ed.). Mahwah, NJ: Erlbaum.

CASSIDY, J., & ASHER, S. R. (1992). Loneliness and peer relations in young children. *Child Development, 63*(2), 350–365.

CASTELLANOS, F. X., SONUGA-BARKE, E. J., MILHAM, M. P., & TANNOCK, R. (2006). Characterizing cognition in ADHD: Beyond executive dysfunction. *Trends in Cognitive Sciences, 10,* 117–123.

CASTLE, J., GROOTHUES, C., BREDENKAMP, D., BECKETT, C., O'CONNOR, T., RUTTER, M., ET AL. (1999). Effects of qualities of early institutional care on cognitive attainment. *American Journal of Orthopsychiatry, 69,* 424–437.

CASTONGUAY, L., REID, J., & HALPERIN, G. (2003). Reconciliation and integration in psychotherapy: A strategy to address the complexity of human change. In G.

Stricker, T. A. Widiger, & I. B. Weiner (Eds.), *Handbook of psychology: Vol. 8. Clinical psychology.* New York: Wiley.

CATE, R. M., LEVIN, L. A., & RICHMOND, L. S. (2002). Premarital relationship stability: A review of recent research. *Journal of Social and Personal Relationships, 19,* 261–284.

CATRAMBONE, R. (1998). The subgoal learning model: Creating better examples so that students can solve novel problems. *Journal of Experimental Psychology: General, 127*(4), 355–376.

CATTELL, R. B. (1957). *Personality and motivation structure and measurement.* New York: Harcourt, Brace and World.

CATTELL, R. B. (1963). Theory of fluid and crystallized intelligence: A critical experiment. *Journal of Educational Psychology, 54,* 1–22.

CATTELL, R. B. (1966). *The scientific analysis of personality.* Chicago: Aldine.

CATTELL, R. B. (1971). *Abilities: Their structure, growth, and action.* Boston: Houghton Mifflin.

CAVALLI-SFORZA, L., MENOZZI, P., & PIAZZA, A. (1994). *The history and geography of human genes.* Princeton, NJ: Princeton University Press.

CECI, S., & BRUCK, M. (1995). *Jeopardy in the courtroom: A scientific analysis of children's testimony.* Washington, DC: American Psychological Association.

CECI, S., HUFFMAN, M., & SMITH, E. (1994). Repeatedly thinking about a non-event: Source misattributions among preschoolers. *Consciousness and Cognition, 3,* 388–407.

CECI, S., & LIKER, J. (1986). Academic and nonacademic intelligence: An experimental separation. In R. J. Sternberg & R. K. Wagner (Eds.), *Practical intelligence: Nature and origins of competence in everyday life* (pp. 119–142). New York: Cambridge University Press.

CECI, S. J., & WILLIAMS, W. M. (1997). Schooling, intelligence, and income. *American Psychologist, 52,* 1051–1058.

CELIO, A. A., WINZELBERG, A. J., DEV, P., & TAYLOR, C. B. (2002). Improving compliance in on-line, structured self-help programs: Evaluation of an eating disorder prevention program. *Journal of Psychiatric Practice, 8,* 14–20.

CENTERS FOR DISEASE CONTROL AND PREVENTION (CDC). (2005). Mental health in the United States: Prevalence of diagnosis and medication treatment for attention-deficit/hyperactivity disorder—United States, 2003. *Morbidity and Mortality Weekly Report, 54*(34), 842–847.

CENTERWALL, B. S. (1989). Exposure to television as a risk factor for violence. *American Journal of Epidemiology, 129,* 643–652.

CERNOCH, J. M., & PORTER, R. H. (1985). Recognition of maternal axillary odors by infants. Child Development, 56, 1593–98.

CERVONE, D., & SHODA, Y. (1999). Beyond traits in the study of personality coherence. *Current Directions in Psychological Science, 8,* 27–32.

CESARIO, J., PLAKS, J., & HIGGINS, E. T. (2006). Automatic social behavior as motivated preparation to interact. *Journal of Personality and Social Psychology, 80,* 893–910.

CHAIKEN, S., LIBERMAN, A., & EAGLY, A. H. (1989). Heuristic and systematic information processing within and beyond the persuasion context. In J. S. Uleman & J. A. Bargh (Eds.), *Unintended thought* (pp. 212–252). New York: Guilford.

CHALMERS, D. (1995). Facing up to the problem of consciousness. *Journal of Consciousness Studies, 2,* 200–219.

CHAMBERS, D., & REISBERG, D. (1985). Can mental images be ambiguous? *Journal of Experimental Psychology: Human Perception and Performance, 11,* 317–328.

CHAMBLESS, D. L., BAKER, M. J., BAUCOM, D. H., BEUTLER, L. E., CALHOUN, K. S., CRITS-CHRISTOPH, P., ET AL. (1998). Update on empirically validated therapies, II. *Clinical Psychologist, 51,* 3–16.

CHAMBLESS, D. L., & OLLENDICK, T. H. (2001). Empirically supported psychological interventions: Controversies and evidence. *Annual Review of Psychology, 52,* 685–716.

CHANDLER, C. (1994). Studying related pictures can reduce accuracy, but increase confidence, in a modified recognition test. *Memory & Cognition, 22,* 273–280.

CHAPMAN, M., ZAHN-WAXLER, C., COOPERMAN, G., & IANNOTTI, R. (1987). Empathy and responsibility in the motivation of children's helping. *Developmental Psychology, 23,* 140–145.

CHARMAN, T., BARON-COHEN, S., SWETTENHAM, J., COX, A., BAIRD, G., & DREW, A. (1998). An experimental investigation of social-cognitive abilities in infants with autism: Clinical implications. *Infant Mental Health Journal, 19,* 260–275.

CHARTRAND, T., PINCKERT, S., & BURGER, J. M. (1999). When manipulation backfires: The effects of time delay and requester on the foot-in-the-door technique. *Journal of Applied Social Psychology, 29*(1), 211–221.

CHASE, W. G., & ERICSSON, K. A. (1978). *Acquisition of a mnemonic system for digit span.* Paper presented at the Annual meeting of the Psychonomic Society, San Antonio, Texas.

CHASE, W. G., & ERICSSON, K. A. (1979). *A mnemonic system for digit span: One year later.* Paper presented at the Annual meeting of the Psychonomic Society, Phoenix, Arizona.

CHASE, W. G., & ERICSSON, K. A. (1982). Skill and working memory. In G. H. Bower (Ed.), *The psychology of learning and motivation.* New York: Academic Press.

CHASE, W. G., & SIMON, H. A. (1973a). The mind's eye in chess. In W. G. Chase (Ed.), *Visual information processing.* New York: Academic Press.

CHASE, W. G., & SIMON, H. A. (1973b). Perception in chess. *Cognitive Psychology, 4,* 55–81.

CHEN, M., & BARGH, J. A. (1997). Nonconscious behavioral confirmation processes: The self-fulfilling consequences of automatic stereotype activation. *Journal of Experimental Social Psychology, 33*(5), 541–560.

CHENEY, D. L., & SEYFARTH, R. M. (1990). *How monkeys see the world.* Chicago: University of Chicago Press.

CHENEY, D. L., & SEYFARTH, R. M. (2007). *Baboon metaphysics.* Chicago: University of Chicago Press.

CHENG, P. W., & HOLYOAK, K. J. (1986). Pragmatic reasoning schemas. *Cognitive Psychology, 17,* 391–416.

CHENG, P. W., HOLYOAK, K. J., NISBETT, R. E., & OLIVER, L. M. (1985). Pragmatic versus syntactic approaches to training deductive reasoning. *Cognitive Psychology, 18,* 293–328.

CHERRIER, M. M., ASTHANA, S., PLYMATE, S., BAKER, L., MATSUMOTO, A. M., PESKIND, E., ET AL. (2001). Testosterone supplementation improves spatial and verbal memory in healthy older men. *Neurology, 57,* 80–88.

CHERRY, E. C. (1953). Some experiments upon the recognition of speech, with one and with two ears. *Journal of the Acoustical Society of America, 25,* 975–979.

CHERYAN, S., & BODENHAUSEN, G. V. (2000). When positive stereotypes threaten intellectual performance: The psychological hazards of "model minority" status. *Psychological Science, 11,* 399–402.

CHESS, S., & THOMAS, A. (1982). Infant bonding: Mystique and reality. *American Journal of Orthopsychiatry, 52,* 213–221.

CHEUNG, F. M. (2004). Use of Western and indigenously developed personality tests in Asia. *Applied Psychology: An International Review, 53,* 173–191.

CHEUNG, F. M., & LEUNG, K. (1998). Indigenous personality measures: Chinese examples. *Journal of Cross-Cultural Psychology, 29,* 233–248.

CHEVRIER, J., & DELORME, A. (1983). Depth perception in Pandora's box and size illusion: Evolution with age. *Perception, 12,* 177–185.

CHI, M. T., & KOESKE, R. D. (1983). Network representation of a child's dinosaur knowledge. *Developmental Psychology, 19*(1), 29–39.

CHI, M. T. H. (1978). Knowledge structures and memory development. In R. S. Siegler (Ed.), *Children's thinking: What develops?* (pp. 73–96). Hillsdale, NJ: Erlbaum.

CHI, M. T. H., FELTOVICH, P. J., & GLASER, R. (1981). Categorization and representation of physics problems by experts and novices. *Cognitive Science, 5,* 121–152.

CHOI, S., & BOWERMAN, M. (1991). Learning to express motion events in English and Korean: The influence of language-specific lexicalization patterns. *Cognition, 41,* 83–121.

CHOMSKY, N. (1959). Review of B. F. Skinner "Verbal Behavior." *Language, 35,* 26–58.

CHOMSKY, N. (1965). *Aspects of the theory of syntax.* Cambridge, MA: MIT Press.

CHOMSKY, N. (1981a). Knowledge of language: Its elements and origins. *Philosophical Transactions of the Royal Society of London, 295*(1077, Series B), 223–234.

CHOMSKY, N. (1981b). *Lectures on government and binding.* Dordrecht: Foris.

CHOMSKY, N. (1995). *The minimalist program.* Cambridge, MA: MIT Press.

CHOUINARD, C. (2004). Issues in the clinical use of benzodiazepines: Potency, withdrawal, and rebound. *Journal of Clinical Psychiatry, 65*(Suppl. 5), 7–12.

CHRISTIAN, K., BACHMAN, H. J., & MORRISON, F. J. (2000). Schooling and cognitive development. In R. J. Sternberg & R. L. Grigorenko (Eds.), *Environmental effects on cognitive abilities.* Mahwah, NJ: Erlbaum.

CHRISTIANSEN, M. H., & CHATER, N. (2001). Connectionist psycholinguistics: Capturing the empirical data. *Trends in Cognitive Science, 5*(2), 82–88.

CHRISTIANSEN, M. H., CHATER, N., & SEIDENBERG, M. S. (1999). Connectionist models of human language processing: Progress and prospects [Special issue]. *Cognitive Science, 23.*

CHROBAK, Q. M., & ZARAGOZA, M. S. (2008). Inventing stories: Forcing witnesses to fabricate entire fictitious events leads to freely reported false memories. *Psychonomic Bulletin & Review, 15,* 1190–1195.

CHRYSIKOU, E., & WEISBERG, R. W. (2005). Following the wrong footsteps: Fixation effects of pictorial examples in a design problem-solving task. *Journal of Experimental Psychology: Learning, Memory and Cognition, 31,* 1134–1148.

CHUA, S. E., & MCKENNA, P. J. (1995). Schizophrenia: A brain disease? *British Journal of Psychiatry, 166,* 563–582.

CHURCH, A. T., KATIGBAK, M. S., DEL PRADO, A. M., ORTIZ, F. A., MASTOR, K. A., HARUMI, Y., ET AL. (2006). Implicit theories and self-perceptions of traitedness across cultures: Toward integration of cultural and trait psychology perspectives. *Journal of Cross-Cultural Psychology, 37,* 694–716.

CHURCH, R. M. (1969). Response suppression. In B. A. Campbell & R. M. Church (Eds.), *Punishment and aversive behavior.* New York: Appleton-Century-Crofts.

CHURCHLAND, P. S., & SEJNOWSKI, T. J. (1992). *The computational brain.* Cambridge, MA: MIT Press.

CIALDINI, R. B. (1993). *Influence: Science and practice* (3rd ed.). New York: HarperCollins.

CIALDINI, R. B., & GOLDSTEIN, N. J. (2004). Social influence: Compliance and conformity. *Annual Review of Psychology, 55,* 591–621.

CIALDINI, R. B., PETTY, R. E., & CACIOPPO, J. T. (1981). Attitude and attitude change. In M. R. Rosenzweig & L. W. Porter (Eds.), *Annual Review of Psychology, 32,* 357–404.

CIALDINI, R. B., TROST, M. R., & NEWSOM, J. T. (1995). Preference for consistency: The development of a valid measure and the discovery of surprising behavioral implications. *Journal of Personality and Social Psychology, 69*(2), 318–328.

CIALDINI, R. B., VINCENT, J. E., LEWIS, S. K., CATALAN, J., WHEELER, D., & DARBY, B. L. (1975). Reciprocal concessions procedure for inducing compliance: The door-in-the-face technique. *Journal of Personality and Social Psychology, 31*(2), 206–215.

CIALDINI, R. B., WOSINKA, W., BARRETT, D. W., BUTNER, J., & GORNIK-DUROSE, M. (1999). Compliance with a request in two cultures: The differential influence of social proof and commitment/consistency on collectivists and individualists. *Personality and Social Psychology Bulletin, 25,* 1242–1253.

CIANCIOLO, A. T., GRIGORENKO, E. L., JARVIN, L., GUILLERMO, G., DREBOT, M. E., & STERNBERG, R. J. (2006). Practical intelligence and tacit knowledge: Advancements in the measurement of developing expertise. *Learning and Individual Differences, 16,* 235–253.

CILLESSEN, A. H. N., & BUKOWSKI, W. M. (2000). Conceptualizing and measuring peer acceptance and rejection. In A. H. N. Cillessen & W. M. Bukowski (Eds.), *Recent advances in the measurement of acceptance and rejection in the peer system* (pp. 3–10). San Francisco: Jossey-Bass.

CIPOLOTTI, L. (2001). Long-term retrograde amnesia . . . The crucial role of the hippocampus. *Neuropsychologia, 39,* 151–172.

CIZKOVA, D., KAKINOHANA, O., KUCHAROVA, K., MARSALA, S., JOHE, K., HAZEL, T., ET AL. (2007). Functional recovery in rates with ischemic paraplegia after spinal grafting of human spinal stem cells. *Neuroscience, 147,* 546–560.

CLARK, D. A., & BECK, A. T. (WITH ALFORD, B.). (1999). *Scientific foundations of cognitive theory and therapy of depression.* New York: Wiley.

CLARK, D. M. (1986). A cognitive approach to panic. *Behavior Research and Therapy, 24,* 461–470.

CLARK, E. V. (1987). The principle of contrast: A constraint on acquisition. In B. MacWhinney (Ed.), *Mechanisms of language acquisition.* Hillsdale, NJ: Erlbaum.

CLARK, E. V., GELMAN, S. A., & LANE, N. M. (1985). Compound nouns and category structure in young children. *Child Development, 56,* 84–94.

CLARK, H. H. (1992). *Arenas of language use.* Chicago: University of Chicago Press.

CLARK, L. A. (2007). Assessment and diagnosis of personality disorder: Perennial issues and an emerging reconceptualization. *Annual Review of Psychology, 58,* 227–257.

CLARK, L. A. (2009). Stability and change in personality disorder. *Current Directions in Psychological Science, 18,* 27–31.

CLARK, L. A., & HARRISON, J. A. (2001). Assessment instruments. In W. J. Livesley (Ed.), *Handbook of personality disorders* (pp. 277–306). New York: Guilford.

CLARK, M. S., & MILLS, J. (1979). Interpersonal attraction in exchange and communal relationships. *Journal of Personality and Social Psychology, 37,* 12–24.

CLARK, M. S., & MILLS, J. (1993). The difference between communal and exchange relationships: What it is and is not. *Personality and Social Psychology Bulletin, 19,* 684–691.

CLARK, M. S., MILLS, J., & POWELL, M. C. (1986). Keeping track of needs in communal and exchange relationships. *Journal of Personality and Social Psychology, 51*(2), 333–338.

CLARK, M. S., OUELLETTE, R., POWELL, M. C., & MILBERG, S. (1987). Recipient's mood, relationship type, and helping. *Journal of Personality and Social Psychology, 53*(1), 94–103.

CLARK, R. E., MANNS, J. R., & SQUIRE, L. R. (2003). Classical conditioning, awareness, and brain systems. *Trends in Cognitive Science, 6,* 524–531.

CLARKE, A. C. (1952). An examination of the operation of residual propinquity as a factor in mate selection. *American Sociological Review, 27,* 17–22.

CLARKE-STEWART, A. (1978). And daddy makes three: The father's impact on mother and young child. *Child Development, 49,* 466–478.

CLAUSEN, J. (1975). The social meaning of differential physical and sexual maturation. In S. Dragastin & J. Elder (Eds.), *Adolescence in the life cycle.* Washington, DC: Hemisphere Press.

CLAYTON, A. H. (2001). Recognition and assessment of sexual dysfunction associated with depression [Suppl.]. *Journal of Clinical Psychiatry, 62*(3), 5–9.

COATES, S., BUTLER, L., & BERRY, D. (2006). Implicit memory and consumer choice: The mediating role of familiarity. *Applied Cognitive Psychology, 20,* 1101–1116.

COBB, S. (1941). *Foundations of neuropsychiatry.* Baltimore: Williams & Wilkins.

COHEN, A., & RAFAL, R. D. (1991). Attention and feature integration: Illusory conjunctions in a patient with a parietal lobe lesion. *Psychological Science, 2,* 106–110.

COHEN, G., & BURKE, D. (EDS.). (1993). *Memory for proper names.* Hillsdale, NJ: Erlbaum.

COHEN, G., GARCIA, J., APFEL, N., & MASTER, A. (2006). Reducing the racial achievement gap: A social-psychological intervention. *Science, 313,* 1307–1310.

COHEN, G. L., GARCIA, J., PURDIE-VAUGHNS, V., APFEL, N., & BRZUSTOSKI, P. (2009). Recursive processes in self-affirmation: Intervening to close the minority achievement gap. *Science, 324,* 400–403.

COHEN, N. J., & SQUIRE, L. R. (1980). Preserved learning and retention of pattern-analyzing skill in amnesia: Dissociation of knowing how and knowing what. *Science, 210,* 207–210.

COHEN, T. A., & INSKO, C. A. (2008). War and peace: Possible approaches to reducing intergroup conflict. *Perspectives on Psychological Science, 3*(2), 87–147.

COHEN, Y. A. (1953). A study of interpersonal relations in a Jamaican community. Unpublished doctoral dissertation, Yale University.

COIE, J. D., & DODGE, K. A. (1983). Continuities and changes in children's social status: A five-year longitudinal study. *Merrill-Palmer Quarterly, 29*(3), 261–282.

COLAPINTO, J. (2000). *As nature made him: The boy who was raised as a girl.* New York: HarperCollins.

COLBY, A., & KOHLBERG, L. (1987). *The measurement of moral judgment, Vol. 1: Theoretical foundations and research validation; Vol. 2: Standard issue scoring manual.* New York: Cambridge University Press.

COLCOMBE, S., & KRAMER, A. F. (2003). Fitness effects on the cognitive function of older adults: A meta-analytic study. *Psychological Science, 14*(2), 125–130.

COLE, M., & COLE, S. R. (2001). *The development of children* (4th ed.). New York: Worth.

COLE, P. M. (1985). Display rules and the socialization of affective displays. In G. Zivin (Ed.), *The development of expressive behavior: Biology-environmental interactions* (pp. 269–290). New York: Academic Press.

COLE, S. (2009). Social regulation of human gene expression. *Current Directions in Psychological Science, 18,* 132–137. COLLAER, M., & HINES, M. (1995). Human behavioral sex differences: A role for gonadal hormones during early development? *Psychological Bulletin, 118,* 55–107.

COLLINS, A. M., & LOFTUS, E. F. (1975). A spreading activation theory of semantic processing. *Psychological Review, 82,* 407–428.

COLLINS, W. A., MACCOBY, E. E., STEINBERG, L., HETHERINGTON, E. M., & BORNSTEIN, M. H. (2000). Contemporary research on parenting: The case for nature and nurture. *American Psychologist, 55*(2), 218–232.

COLOMBO, J. (2001). The development of visual attention in infancy. *Annual Review of Psychology, 52,* 337–367.

COLWILL, R. M., & RESCORLA, R. A. (1985). Post-conditioning devaluation of a reinforcer affects instrumental responding. *Journal of Experimental Psychology: Animal Behavior Processes, 11,* 120–132.

COMAN, A., MANIER, D., & HIRST, W. (2009). Forgetting the unforgettable through conversation: Socially shared retrieval-induced forgetting of September 11 memories. *Psychological Science, 20,* 627–633.

CONEL, J. L. (1939). *The postnatal development of the human cortex: Vol. 1.* Cambridge, MA: Harvard University Press.

CONEL, J. L. (1947). *The postnatal development of the human cortex: Vol. 3.* Cambridge, MA: Harvard University Press.

CONEL, J. L. (1955). *The postnatal development of the human cortex: Vol. 5.* Cambridge, MA: Harvard University Press.

CONNOLLY, A., FODOR, J., GLEITMAN, H., GLEITMAN, L., DAHAN, D., & TANENHAUS, M. K. (2004). Continuous mapping from sound to meaning in spoken language comprehension. *Journal of Experimental Psychology: Learning, Memory & Cognition, 30,* 498–513.

CONNOLLY, A., FODOR, J. A., GLEITMAN, L. R., & GLEITMAN, H. (2007). Why stereotypes don't even make good defaults. *Cognition, 103*(1), 1–22.

CONNORS, E., LUNDREGAN, T., MILLER, N., & MCEWAN, T. (1996). *Convicted by juries, exonerated by science: Case studies in the use of DNA evidence to establish innocence after trial.* Alexandria, VA: National Institute of Justice.

CONWAY, A. R., KANE, M. J., BUNTING, M. F., HAMBRICK, D. Z., WILHELM, O., & ENGLE, R. (2005). Working memory span tasks: A methodological review and user's guide. *Psychonomics Bulletin and Review, 12,* 769–786.

CONWAY, A. R. A., COWAN, N., & BUNTING, M. (2001). The cocktail party phenomenon revisited: The importance of working memory capacity. *Psychonomics Bulletin & Review, 8,* 331–335.

CONWAY, M., ANDERSON, S., LARSEN, S., DONNELLY, C., MCDANIEL, M., MCCLELLAND, A. G. R., ET AL. (1994). The formation of flashbulb memories. *Memory and Cognition, 22,* 326–343.

CONWAY, M. A. (ED.). (1997). *Recovered memories and false memories.* New York: Oxford University Press.

CONWAY, M. A., COHEN, G., & STANHOPE, N. (1991). On the very long-term retention of knowledge acquired through formal education: Twelve years of cognitive psychology. *Journal of Experimental Psychology (General), 120,* 395–409.

CONWAY, M. A., & FTHENAKI, K. (1999). Disruption and loss of autobiographical memory. In L. S. Cermak (Ed.), *Handbook of neuropsychology: Memory.* Amsterdam: Elsevier.

COOK, M., & MINEKA, S. (1989). Observational conditioning of fear to fear-relevant versus fear-irrelevant stimuli in rhesus monkeys. *Journal of Abnormal Psychology, 98,* 448–459.

COOK, R. G., CAVOTO, K. K., & CAVOTO, B. R. (1995). Same-different texture discrimination and concept learning by pigeons. *Journal of Experimental Psychology: Animal Behavior Processes, 21*(3), 253–260.

COOLEY, C. H. (1902). *Human nature and the social order.* New York: Scribner's.

COONEY, J. W., & GAZZANIGA, M. S. (2003). Neurological disorders and the structure of human consciousness. *Trends in Cognitive Science, 7,* 161–165.

COOPER, J. (2007). *Cognitive dissonance: 50 years of a classic theory.* London: Sage.

COOPER, J., ZANNA, M. P., & GOETHALS, G. R. (1974). Mistreatment of an esteemed other as a consequence affecting dissonance reduction. *Journal of Experimental Social Psychology, 10,* 224–233.

COOPER, L. A., & SHEPARD, R. N. (1973). The time required to prepare for a rotated stimulus. *Memory and Cognition, 1,* 246–250.

COOPER, Z., & FAIRBURN, C. G. (2001). A new cognitive behavioural approach to the treatment of obesity. *Behavior Research and Therapy, 39,* 499–511.

CORDES, S., & BRANNON, E. M. (2008). Discrimination of continuous quantities in 6-month old infants: Using number is just easier. *Child Development, 79*(2), 476–489.

CORKIN, S. (1965). Tactually-guided maze-learning in man: Effects of unilateral cortical excisions and bilateral hippocampal lesions. *Neuropsychologia, 3,* 339–351.

CORKIN, S. (1984). Lasting consequences of bilateral medial temporal lobectomy: Clinical course and experimental findings in H.M. *Seminar in Neurology, 4,* 249–259.

CORRIGAN, P. W. (2005). *On the stigma of mental illness: Practical strategies for research and social change.* Washington, DC: American Psychological Association.

CORY, T. L., ORMISTON, D. W., SIMMEL, E., & DAINOFF, M. (1975). Predicting the frequency of dream recall. *Journal of Abnormal Psychology, 84,* 261–266.

CORYELL, W. (1996). Psychotic depression. *Journal of Clinical Psychiatry, 57*[Suppl.](3), 27–31.

COSMIDES, L. (1989). The logic of social exchange: Has natural selection shaped how humans reason? Studies with the Wason selection task. *Cognition, 31,* 187–276.

COSMIDES, L., & TOOBY, J. (1992). Cognitive adaptations for social exchange. In J. H. Barkow, L. Cosmides, & J. Tooby (Eds.), *The adapted mind: Evolutionary psychology and the generation of culture* (pp. 163–228). New York: Oxford University Press.

COSMIDES, L., & TOOBY, J. (2005). Neurocognitive adaptations designed for social exchange. In D. M. Buss (Ed.), *The handbook of evolutionary psychology* (pp. 583–627). Hoboken, NJ: Wiley.

COSMIDES, L., TOOBY, J., FIDDICK, L., & BRYANT, G. A. (2005). Detecting cheaters. *Trends in Cognitive Science, 9,* 505–506.

COSTA, P. T., & MCCRAE, R. R. (1992). *Revised NEO Personality Inventory (NEO-PI-R) and NEO Five-Factor Inventory professional manual.* Odessa, FL: Psychological Assessment Resources.

COSTELLO, E. J., COMPTON, F. N., KEELER, G., & ANGOLD, A. (2003). Relationships between poverty and psychopathology: A natural experiment. *Journal of the American Medical Association, 290,* 2023–2029.

COTMAN, C. W., & NEEPER, S. (1996). Activity-dependent plasticity and the aging brain. In E. L. Schneider & J. W. Rose (Eds.), *Handbook of the biology of aging* (4th ed.). San Diego, CA: Academic Press.

COUGHLIN, J. F., MOHYDE, M., D'AMBROSIO, L. A. & GILBERT, J. (2004). Who drives older driver decisions? Cambridge, MA: MIT AgeLab/The Hatford.

COURAGE, M., & HOWE, M. (2002). From infant to child: The dynamics of cognitive change in the second year of life. *Psychological Bulletin, 128,* 250–277.

COURCHESNE, E., TOWNSEND, J. P., & SAITOH, O. (1994). The brain in infantile autism: Posterior fossa structures are abnormal. *Neurology, 44,* 214–223.

COUSINS, S. D. (1989). Culture and self-perception in Japan and the United States. *Journal of Personality and Social Psychology, 56,* 124–131.

COUVILLON, P., & BITTERMAN, M. E. (1980). Some phenomena of associative conditioning in honeybees. *Journal of Comparative and Physiological Psychology, 94,* 878–885.

COUZIN, J. (2004). Volatile chemistry: Children and antidepressants. *Science, 305,* 468–470.

COUZIN, J. (2005). A heavyweight battle over CDC's obesity forecasts. *Science, 308,* 770–771.

COWAN, C. P., & COWAN, P. A. (2000). When partners become parents: The big life change for couples. Mahwah, NJ: Erlbaum.

COWAN, R., & CARNEY, D. (2006). Calendrical savants: Exceptionality and practice. *Cognition, 100,* B1–B9.

COWEY, A., & STOERIG, P. (1992). Reflections on blindsight. In A. D. Milner & M. D. Rugg (Eds.), *The neuropsychology of consciousness* (pp. 11–38). San Diego, CA: Academic Press.

CRABBE, J. C. (2002). Alcohol and genetics: New models. *American Journal of Medical Genetics Part B: Neuropsychiatric Genetics, 114,* 969–974.

CRAIGHEAD, L. W., CRAIGHEAD, W. E., KAZDIN, A. E., & MAHONEY, M. J. (EDS.). (1994). *Cognitive and behavioral interventions: An empirical approach to mental health problems.* Boston: Allyn & Bacon.

CRAIK, F., & JENNINGS, J. M. (1992). Human memory. In F. Craik & T. Salthouse (Eds.), *Handbook of aging and cognition* (pp. 51–110). Hillsdale, NJ: Erlbaum.

CRAIK, F. I. M., & BIALYSTOK, E. (2006). Cognition through the lifespan: Mechanisms of change. *Trends in Cognitive Science, 10,* 131–138.

CRAIK, F. I. M., & LOCKHART, R. S. (1972). Levels of processing. A framework for memory research. *Journal of Verbal Learning and Verbal Behavior, 11,* 671–684.

CRAIK, F. I. M., & SALTHOUSE, T. A. (EDS.). (2000). *The handbook of aging and cognition* (2nd ed.). Hillsdale, NJ: Erlbaum.

CRAIK, F. I. M., & TULVING, E. (1975). Depth of processing and the retention of words in episodic memory. *Journal of Experimental Psychology: General, 104,* 268–294.

CRAIK, F. I. M., & WATKINS, M. J. (1973). The role of rehearsal in short-term memory. *Journal of Verbal Learning and Verbal Behavior, 12,* 599–607.

CRAIN, S., & STEEDMAN, M. (1985). On not being led up the garden path: The use of context by the psychological syntax parser. In D. Dowty, L. Kartunnen, & A. Zwicky (Eds.), *Natural language parsing.* Cambridge: Cambridge University Press.

CRASKE, M. G. (1999). *Anxiety disorders: Psychological approaches to theory and treatment.* Boulder, CO: Westview Press.

CRAWFORD, M., & CHAFFIN, R. (1997). The meanings of difference: Cognition in social and cultural context. In P. J. Caplan, M. Crawford, J. S. Hyde, & J. T. E. Richardson (Eds.), *Gender differences in human cognition* (pp. 81–130). New York: Oxford University Press.

CRESPI, L. (1942). Quantitative variation in incentive and performance in the white rat. *American Journal of Psychology, 55,* 467–517.

CRICK, F., & KOCH, C. (2003). A framework for consciousness. *Nature Neuroscience, 6,* 119–126.

CRICK, N. R. (1996). The role of overt aggression, relational aggression, and prosocial behavior in the prediction of children's future social adjustment. *Child Development, 67*(5), 2317–2327.

CRICK, N. R., & LADD, G. W. (1993). Children's perceptions of their peer experiences: Attributions, loneliness, social anxiety, and social avoidance. *Developmental Psychology, 29*(2), 244–254.

CRICK, R., & KOCH, C. (1995). Are we aware of neural activity in primary visual cortex? *Nature, 375,* 121–123.

CRITS-CHRISTOPH, P. (1997). Limitations of the "dodo bird" verdict and the role of clinical trials in psychotherapy research: Comment on Wampold et al. (1997). *Psychological Bulletin, 122,* 216–220.

CROCKER, J., & LUHTANEN, R. (1990). Collective self-esteem and ingroup bias. *Journal of Personality and Social Psychology, 58,* 60–67.

CROFT, C., O'CONNOR, T. G., KEAVENEY, L., GROOTHUES, C., RUTTER, M., & ENGLISH AND ROMANIAN ADOPTION STUDY TEAM (2001). Longitudinal change in parenting associated with developmental delay and catch-up. *Journal of Child Psychology and Psychiatry and Allied Disciplines, 42,* 649–659.

CROOK, C. (1987). Taste and olfaction. In P. Salapatek & L. Cohen (Eds.), *Handbook of infant perception: From perception to cognition: Vol. 2* (pp. 237–264). Orlando, FL: Academic Press.

CROW, T. J. (1982). Two dimensions of pathology in schizophrenia: Dopaminergic and non-dopaminergic. *Psychopharmacology Bulletin, 18,* 22–29.

CROW, T. J. (1985). The two-syndrome concept: Origins and current status. *Schizophrenia Bulletin, 11,* 471–486.

CROWDER, R. G. (1976). *Principles of learning and memory.* Hillsdale, NJ: Erlbaum.

CROWLEY, K., CALLANAN, M. A., TENENBAUM, H. R., & ALLEN, E. (2001). Parents explain more often to boys than to girls during shared scientific thinking. *Psychological Science, 12,* 258–261.

CRUTCHFIELD, R. S. (1955). Conformity and character. *American Psychologist, 10,* 191–199.

CSIBRA, G., DAVIS, G., SPRATLING, M. W., & JOHNSON, M. H. (2000). Gamma oscillations and object processing in the infant brain. *Science, 290,* 1582–1585.

CSIBRA, G., & GERGELY, G. (2005). Social learning and social cognition: The case for pedagogy. In M. H. Johnson

& Y. Munakata (Eds.), *Processes of change in brain and cognitive development: Attention and performance XXI* (pp. 1–15). New York: Oxford University Press.

CSIBRA, G., & GERGELY, G. (2009). Natural pedagogy. *Trends in Cognitive Sciences, 13*, 148–153.

CULBERTSON, F. (1997). Depression and gender. *American Psychologist, 52*, 25–31.

CUMMINGS, E. M., & DAVIES, P. (1994). *Children and marital conflict: The impact of family dispute and resolution. Guilford series on social and emotional development.* New York: Guilford.

CUMMINS, D. (1992). Role of analogical reasoning in induction of problem categories. *Journal of Experimental Psychology: Learning, Memory and Cognition, 18*, 1103–1124.

CUMMINS, D. D., & ALLEN, C. (EDS.). (1998). *The evolution of mind.* New York: Oxford University Press.

CUNNINGHAM, M. R., ROBERTS, A. R., BARBEE, A. P., DRUEN, P. B., & WU, C.-H. (1998). "Their ideas of beauty are, on the whole, the same as ours": Consistency and variability in the cross-cultural perception of female physical attractiveness. *Journal of Personality and Social Psychology, 68*, 261–279.

CUNNINGHAM, W. A., PREACHER, K. J., & BANAJI, M. R. (2001). Implicit attitude measures: Consistency, stability, and convergent validity. *Psychological Science, 121*(2), 163–170.

CURTISS, S. (1977). *Genie: A linguistic study of a modern-day "wild child."* New York: Academic Press.

CUTLER, A. (1994). Segmentation problems, rhythmic solutions. In L. R. Gleitman & B. Landau (Eds.), Lexical acquisition [Special issue]. *Lingua, 92*, 81–104.

CUTLER, A., MEHLER, J., NORRIS, D., & SEGUI, J. (1986). The syllable's differing role in the segmentation of French and English. *Journal of Memory and Language, 25*.

CUTLER, A., & OTAKE, T. (1994). Mora or phoneme? Further evidence for language-specific listening. *Journal of Memory and Language, 33*, 824–844.

CUTRONA, C. E., WALLACE, G., & WESNER, K. (2006). Neighborhood characteristics and depression. *Current Directions in Psychology, 15*, 188–192.

CUTTING, J. (1986). Outcome in schizophrenia: Overview. In T. A. Kerr & R. P. Snaith (Eds.), *Contemporary issues in schizophrenia* (pp. 436–440). Washington, DC: American Psychiatric Press.

CUTTING, J. (1995). Descriptive psychopathology. In S. Hirsch & D. Weinberger (Eds.), *Schizophrenia* (pp. 15–27). London: Blackwell Science.

———

DABBS, J. M. (1992). Testosterone measurements in social and clinical psychology. *Journal of Social and Clinical Psychology, 11*, 302–321.

DADDS, M. R. (1995). *Families, children, and the development of dysfunction.* Thousand Oaks, CA: Sage.

DAHAN, D. & TANENHAUS, M. K. (2004). Continuous mapping from sound to meaning in spoken language comprehension. *Journal of Experimental Psychology: Learning, Memory & Cognition, 30*, 498–513.

DALE, A. J. D. (1975). Organic brain syndromes associated with infections. In A. M. Freedman, H. I. Kaplan, & B. J.

Sadock (Eds.), *Comprehensive textbook of psychiatry—II: Vol. 1* (pp. 1121–1130). Baltimore: Williams & Wilkins.

DALEY, T. C., WHALEY, S. E., SIGMAN, M. D., ESPINOSA, M. P., & NEUMANN, C. (2003). IQ on the rise: The Flynn effect in rural Kenyan children. *Psychological Science, 14*, 215–219.

DALY, M., & WILSON, M. (1988). *Homicide.* New York: Aldine de Gruyter.

DALY, M., & WILSON, M. (2001). An assessment of some proposed exceptions to the phenomenon of nepotistic discrimination against stepchildren. *Annales Zoologici Fennici, 38*, 287–296.

DALY, M., & WILSON, M. (2005). The "Cinderella effect" is no fairy tale. *Trends in Cognitive Science, 9*, 507–508.

DALY, M., & WILSON, M. (2007). Is the "Cinderella effect" controversial? A case study of evolution-minded research and critiques thereof. In C. Crawford & D. Krebs (Eds.), *Foundations of evolutionary psychology* (ch. 20). Mahwah, NJ: Erlbaum.

DAMASIO, A. R. (1994). *Descartes' error: Emotion, reason, and the human brain.* New York: G. P. Putnam.

DAMASIO, A. R., & DAMASIO, H. (1994). Cortical systems for retrieval of concrete knowledge: The convergence zone framework. In C. Koch & J. L. Davis (Eds.), *Large-scale neuronal theories of the brain* (pp. 61–74). Cambridge, MA: MIT Press.

DAMASIO, A. R. (1999). *The feeling of what happens: Body and emotion in the making of consciousness.* New York: Harcourt Brace.

DAMASIO, A. R., DAMASIO, H., & VAN HOESEN, G. W. (1982). Prosopagnosia: Anatomic basis and behavioral mechanisms. *Neurology, 32*, 331–341.

DAMASIO, A. R., TRANEL, D., & DAMASIO, H. (1989). Disorders of visual recognition. In H. Goodglass & A. R. Damasio (Eds.), *Handbook of neuropsychology: Vol. 2.* New York: Elsevier.

DANEMAN, M., & CARPENTER, P. (1980). Individual differences in working memory and reading. *Journal of Verbal Learning and Verbal Behavior, 19*, 450–466.

DANEMAN, M., & HANNON, B. (2001). Using working memory theory to investigate the construct validity of multiple-choice reading comprehension tests such as the SAT. *Journal of Experimental Psychology: General, 130*, 208–223.

DANTHIIR, V., ROBERTS, R. D., SCHULZE, R., & WILHELM, O. (2005). Mental speed: On frameworks, paradigms, and a platform for the future. In O. Wilhelm & R. W. Engle (Eds.), *Handbook of understanding and measuring intelligence* (pp. 27–46). Thousand Oaks, CA: Sage.

DARLEY, J., & LATANÉ, B. (1968). Bystander intervention in emergencies: Diffusion of responsibility. *Journal of Personality and Social Psychology, 10*, 202–214.

DARLEY, J. M., & BATSON, C. D. (1973). "From Jerusalem to Jericho": A study of situational and dispositional variables in helping behavior. *Journal of Personality and Social Psychology, 27*, 100–108.

DAR-NIMROD, I., & HEINE, S. (2006). Exposure to scientific theories affects women's math performance. *Science, 314*, 435.

DARNTON, R. (1984). The meaning of Mother Goose. *New York Review of Books, February 2*, 41–47.

DARWIN, C. (1871). *The descent of man, and selection in relation to sex.* London: Murray.

DARWIN, C. (1859). *On the origin of species.* New York: Macmillan, 6th ed., 1962.

DARWIN, C. (1872). *The expression of the emotions in man and animals.* London: Appleton.

DARWIN, C. (1877). A biographical sketch of a young child. *Kosmos, 1*, 367–376. As cited in Bornstein, M. H., Chromatic vision in infancy. In H. Reese & L. Lipsitt (Eds.), *Advances in child development and behavior* (Vol. 12). New York: Academic Press.

DARWIN, C. R. (1887). Autobiography. In F. Darwin (Ed.), *The life and letters of Charles Darwin, including an autobiographical chapter* (Vol. 1, ch. 2). London: John Murray.

DAVACHI, L., & DOBBINS, I. (2008). Declarative memory. *Current Directions in Cognitive Science, 17*, 112–118.

DAVACHI, L., MARIL, A., & WAGNER, A. (2001). When keeping in mind supports later bringing to mind: Neural markers of phonological rehearsal predict subsequent remembering. *Journal of Cognitive Neuroscience, 13*, 1059–1070.

DAVACHI, L., MITCHELL, J., & WAGNER, A. (2003). Multiple routes to memory: Distinct medial temporal lobe processes build item and source memories. *Proceedings of the National Academy of Science, 100*, 2157–2162.

DAVIDSON, A. R., & JACCARD, J. J. (1979). Variables that moderate the attitude-behavior relation: Results of a longitudinal survey. *Journal of Personality and Social Psychology, 37*, 1364–1376.

DAVIDSON, J. M. (1969). Hormonal control of sexual behavior in adult rats. In G. Rasp (Ed.), *Advances in bioscience: Vol. 1* (pp. 119–169). New York: Pergamon.

DAVIDSON, J. M. (1986). Androgen replacement therapy in a wider context: Clinical and basic aspects. In L. Dennerstein & I. Fraser (Eds.), *Hormones and behavior* (pp. 433–440). Amsterdam: International Society of Psychosomatic Obstetrics and Gynecology, Elsevier.

DAVIDSON, R. J., & SUTTON, S. K. (1995). Affective neuroscience: The emergence of a discipline [Special issue]. *Current Opinion in Neurobiology, 5*, 217–224.

DAVIDSON, R. J., PIZZAGALLI, D., NITSCHKE, J. B., & KALIN, N. H. (2003). Parsing the subcomponents of emotion and disorders of emotion: Perspectives from affective neuroscience. In R. J. Davidson, K. R. Scherer, & H. H. Goldsmith (Eds.), *Handbook of affective sciences.* Oxford: Oxford University Press.

DAVIES, K. G., & WEEKS, R. D. (1993). Temporal lobectomy for intractable epilepsy: Experience with 58 cases over 21 years. *British Journal of Neurosurgery, 7*, 23–33.

DAVIES, P., & FORMAN, E. (2002). Children's patterns of preserving emotional security in the interparental subsystem. *Child Development, 73*, 1880–1903.

DAVIS, D. E. (1964). The physiological analysis of aggressive behavior. In W. Etkin (Ed.), *Social behavior and organization among vertebrates.* Chicago: University of Chicago Press.

DAVIS, D., LOFTUS, E. F., VANOUS, S., & CUCCIARE, M. (2008). "Unconscious transference" can be an instance of "change blindness." *Applied Cognitive Psychology, 22,* 605–623.

DAVIS, H. P., & SQUIRE, L. R. (1984). Protein synthesis and memory: A review. *Psychological Bulletin, 96,* 518–559.

DAVIS, J. M. (1985a). Antipsychotic drugs. In H. I. Kaplan & J. Sadock (Eds.), *Comprehensive textbook of psychiatry* (4th ed., pp. 1481–1513). Baltimore: Williams & Wilkins.

DAVIS, J. O., & PHELPS, J. A. (1995). Twins with schizophrenia: Genes or germs? *Schizophrenia Bulletin, 21,* 13–18.

DAVIS, J. O., PHELPS, J. A., & BRACHA, H. S. (1995). Prenatal development of monozygotic twins and concordance for schizophrenia [erratum appears in *Schizophrenia Bulletin, 21*(4), 539]. *Schizophrenia Bulletin, 21,* 357–366.

DAVIS, K. (1947). Final note on a case of extreme social isolation. *American Journal of Sociology, 52,* 432–437.

DAVIS, P. H., & OSHERSON, A. (1977). The concurrent treatment of a multiple-personality woman and her son. *American Journal of Psychotherapy, 31,* 504–515.

DAWES, R. M. (1994). *House of cards: Psychology and psychotherapy built on myth.* New York: Free Press.

DECASPER, A. J., & SPENCE, M. J. (1986). Prenatal maternal speech influences newborns' perception of speech sounds. *Infant Behavior and Development, 9,* 133–150.

DE GROOT, A. D. (1965). *Thought and choice in chess.* The Hague: Mouton.

DE LOS REYES, A., & KAZDIN, A. E. (2008). When the evidence says, "yes, no, and maybe so": Attending to and interpreting inconsistent findings among evidence-based interventions. *Current Directions in Psychological Science, 17*(1), 47–51.

DENNETT, D. (2001). Are we explaining consciousness yet? *Cognition, 79,* 221–237.

DENRELL, J. (2008). Indirect social influence. *Science, 321*(5885), 47–48.

DE QUERVAIN, D. J., FISCHBACHER, U., TREYER, V., SCHELLHAMMER, M., SCHNYDER, U., BUCK, A., ET AL. (2004). The neural basis of altruistic punishment. *Science, 305,* 1254–1258.

DE RENZI, E. (2000). Prosopagnosia. In M. J. Farah & T. E. Feinberg (Eds.), *Patient-based approaches to cognitive neuroscience* (pp. 85–95). Cambridge, MA: MIT Press.

DE RIDDER, D., SCHREURS, K., & BENSING, J. (2000). The relative benefits of being optimistic: Optimism as a coping resource in multiple sclerosis and Parkinson's disease. *British Journal of Health Psychology, 5,* 141–155.

DE ROUGEMONT, D. (1940). *Love in the western world.* New York: Harcourt Brace Jovanovich.

DERUBEIS, R. J., SIEGLE, G. J., & HOLLON, S. D. (2008). Cognitive therapy versus medication for depression: Treatment outcomes and neural mechanisms. *Nature Reviews Neuroscience, 9,* 788–796.

DESMURGET, M., REILLY, K., RICHARD, N., SZATHMARI, A., MOTTOLESE, C., & SIRIGU, A. (2009). Movement intention after parietal cortex stimulation in humans. *Science, 324,* 811–813.

DE VALOIS, R. L. (1965). Behavioral and electrophysiological studies of primate vision. In W. D. Neff (Ed.), *Contributions of sensory physiology: Vol. 1.* New York: Academic Press.

DE WAAL, F. (1982). *Chimpanzee politics.* New York: Harper & Row.

DEARY, I. J. (2000). *Looking down on human intelligence: From psychometrics to the brain.* Oxford, England: Oxford University Press.

DEARY, I. J. (2001a). Human intelligence differences: A recent history. *Trends in Cognitive Science, 5,* 127–130.

DEARY, I. J. (2001b). Human intelligence differences: Toward a combined experimental-differential approach. *Trends in Cognitive Science, 5,* 164–170.

DEARY, I. J., & DERR, G. (2005). Reaction time explains IQ's association with death. *Psychological Science, 16,* 64–69.

DEARY, I. J., & STOUGH, C. (1996). Intelligence and inspection time: Achievements, prospects, and problems. *American Psychologist, 51,* 599–608.

DEARY, I. J., WHITEMAN, M. C., STARR, J. M., WHALLEY, L. J., & FOX, H. C. (2004). The impact of childhood intelligence on later life: Following up the Scottish Mental Surveys of 1932 and 1947. *Journal of Personality and Social Psychology, 86,* 130–147.

DECASPER, A. J., & FIFER, W. P. (1980). Of human bonding: Newborns prefer their mothers' voices. *Science, 208,* 1174–1176.

DECI, E. L., KOESTNER, R., & RYAN, R. M. (1999a). A meta-analytic review of experiments examining the effects of extrinsic reward. *Psychological Bulletin, 125,* 627–668.

DECI, E. L., KOESTNER, R., & RYAN, R. M. (1999b). The undermining effect is a reality after all—Extrinsic rewards, task interest, and self-determination: Reply to Eisenberger, Pierce, and Cameron (1999) and Lepper, Henderlong, and Gingras (1999). *Psychological Bulletin, 125,* 692–700.

DECI, E. L., & RYAN, R. M. (2000). The "what" and "why" of goal pursuits: Human needs and the self-determination of behavior. *Psychological Inquiry, 11,* 227–268.

DEECKE, L., SCHEID, P., & KORNHUBER, H. H. (1968). Distribution of readiness potential, pre-motion positivity, and motor potential of the human cerebral cortex preceding voluntary finger movements. *Experimental Brain Research, 7,* 158–168.

DEESE, J. (1957). Serial organization in the recall of disconnected items. *Psychological Reports, 3,* 577–582.

DEHAENE, S., & CHAGEUX, J.-P. (2004). Neural mechanisms for access consciousness. In M. Gazzaniga (Ed.), *The cognitive neurosciences III.* Cambridge, MA: MIT Press.

DEHAENE, S., IZARD, V., PICA, P., & SPELKE, E. (2006). Core knowledge of geometry in an Amazonian indigene group. *Science, 311,* 381–384.

DEHAENE, S., & NACCACHE, L. (2001). Toward a cognitive neuroscience of consciousness: Basic evidence and work-space framework. *Cognition, 79,* 1–37.

DEHAENE-LAMBERTZ, G., DEHAENE, S., & HERTZ-PANNIER, L. (2002). Functional neuroimaging of speech perception in infants. *Science, 298,* 2013–2015.

DELL, G. S., ET AL. (1999). Connectionist models of language production: Lexical access and grammatical encoding. *Cognitive Science, 23,* 517–542.

DELTON, A., ROBERTSON, T., & KENRICK, D. (2006). The mating game isn't over: A reply to Buller's critique of the evolutionary psychology of mating. *Evolutionary Psychology, 4,* 262–273.

DEMENT, W. C. (1978). *Some must watch while some must sleep.* New York: Norton.

DEMENT, W. C., & KLEITMAN, N. (1957). The relation of eye movements during sleep to dream activity: An objective method for the study of dreaming. *Journal of Experimental Psychology, 53,* 339–346.

DEMENT, W. C., & VAUGHAN, C. (1999). *The promise of sleep.* New York: Delacorte Press.

DEMENT, W. C., & WOLPERT, E. A. (1958). The relationship of eye-movements, body motility, and external stimuli to dream content. *Journal of Experimental Psychology, 55,* 543–553.

DEMONET, J. F., WISE, R., & FRACKOWIAK, R. S. J. (1993). Language functions explored in normal subjects by positron emission tomography: A critical review. *Human Brain Mapping, 1,* 39–47.

DEMULDER, E., DENHAM, S., SCHMIDT, M., & MITCHELL, J. (2000). Q-sort assessment of attachment security during the preschool years: Links from home to school. *Developmental Psychology, 36,* 274–282.

DESIMONE, R., ALBRIGHT, T. D., GROSS, C. G., & BRUCE, C. (1984). Stimulus-selective properties of inferior temporal neurons in the macaque. *Journal of Neuroscience, 4,* 2051–2062.

DESMOND, A., & MOORE, J. (1991). *Darwin.* New York: Viking Penguin.

DEPRINCE, A. P., & FREYD, J. J. (2007). Trauma-induced dissociation. In M. J. Freidman, T. M. Keane, & P. A. Resick (Eds.), *Handbook of PTSD: Science & practice* (pp. 135–150). New York: Guilford.

DESTENO, D., BARTLETT, M. Y., & SALOVEY, P. (2002). Sex differences in jealousy: Evolutionary mechanism or artifact of measurement. *Journal of Personality and Social Psychology, 83,* 1103–1116.

DEUTSCH, J. A., PUERTO, A., & WANG, M. L. (1978). The stomach signals satiety. *Science, 201,* 165–167.

DEUTSCH, M., & GERARD, H. B. (1955). A study of normative and informational social influence upon individual judgment. *Journal of Abnormal and Social Psychology, 51,* 629–636.

DEVANE, W. A., DYSARZ, F. A., JOHNSON, M. R., MELVIN, L. S., & HOWLETT, A. C. (1988). Determination and characterization of a cannabinoid receptor in rat brain. *Molecular Pharmacology, 34,* 605–613.

DEVANE, W. A., HANUS, L., BREUER, A., PERTWEE, R. G., STEVENSON, L. A., GRIFFIN, G., ET AL. (1992). Isolation and structure of a brain constituent that binds the cannabinoid receptor. *Science, 258,* 1946–1949.

DEVLIN, B., ET AL. (EDS.). (1997). *Intelligence, genes and success: Scientists respond to the Bell Curve.* New York: Springer.

DHAWAN, N., ROSEMAN, I. J., NAIDU, R., & RETTEK, S. (1995). Self-concepts across two cultures: India and the United States. *Journal of Cross-Cultural Psychology, 26,* 606–621.

DI BLAS, L., FORZI, M., & PEABODY, D. (2000). Evaluative and descriptive dimensions from Italian personality factors. *European Journal of Personality, 14,* 279–290.

DIAMOND, A. (1988). The abilities and neural mechanisms underlying A-not-B performance. *Child Development, 59*, 523–527.

DIAMOND, A. (1989, May). Developmental progression in human infants and infant monkeys, and the neural bases of A-not-B and delayed response performance. Paper presented at a meeting on "The development and neural bases of higher cognitive functions," Philadelphia, PA.

DIAMOND, A., & GOLDMAN-RAKIC, P. S. (1989). Comparative development of human infants and rhesus monkeys on Piaget's A-not-B task: Evidence for dependence on dorsolateral prefrontal cortex. *Experimental Brain Research, 74*, 24–40.

DIAMOND, A., KIRKHAM, N. Z., & AMSO, D. (2002). Conditions under which children can hold two roles in mind and inhibit a prepotent response. *Developmental Psychology, 38*, 352–362.

DIAMOND, M., & SIGMUNDSON, K. (1997). Sex reassignment at birth: A long-term review and clinical implications. *Archives of Pediatric and Adolescent Medicine, 151*, 298–304.

DIAMOND, R., & ROZIN, P. (1984). Activation of existing memories in the amnesic syndrome. *Journal of Abnormal Psychology, 93*, 98–105.

DIANA, R., YONELINAS, A., & RANGANATH, C. (2007). Imaging recollection and familiarity in the medial temporal lobe: A three-component model. *Trends in Cognitive Sciences, 11*, 379–386.

DICKENS, W. T., & FLYNN, J. R. (2001). Heritability estimates versus large environmental effects: The IQ paradox resolved. *Psychological Review, 108*(2), 346–369.

DICKENS, W. T., & FLYNN, J. R. (2006a). Black Americans reduce the racial IQ gap: Evidence from standardization samples. *Psychological Science, 17*, 913–920.

DICKENS, W. T., & FLYNN, J. R. (2006b). Common ground and differences. *Psychological Science, 17*, 923–924.

DICKINSON, A. (1987). Animal conditioning and learning theory. In H. J. Eysenck & I. Martin (Eds.), *Theoretical foundations of behavior theory.* New York: Plenum.

DICKS, H. V. (1972). *Licensed mass murder: A sociopsychological study of some S. S. killers.* New York: Basic Books.

DIEFENBACH, D. L. (1997). The portrayal of mental illness on prime-time television. *Journal of Community Psychology, 25*, 289–302.

DIENER, E. (1979). Deindividuation: The absence of self-awareness and self-regulation in group members. In P. Paulus (Ed.), *The psychology of group influence* (pp. 209–242). Hillsdale, NJ: Erlbaum.

DIENER, E., SHIGEHIRO, O., & LUCAS, R. E. (2003). Personality, culture, and subjective well-being: Emotional and cognitive evaluations of life. *Annual Review of Psychology, 54*, 403–425.

DIENER, E., SMITH, H., & FUJITA, F. (1995). The personality structure of affect. *Journal of Personality and Social Psychology, 69*, 130–141.

DILLER, L.H. (1999). Cultural factors in attention deficit-hyperactivity disorder. *New England Journal of Medicine, 340*(22), 1766.

DINGES, D. F., ROGERS, N. L., & BAYNARD, M. D. (2005). Chronic sleep deprivation. In M. H. Kryger, T. Roth, & W. C. Dement (Eds.), *Principles and practice of sleep medicine.* Philadelphia: Elsevier Saunders.

DION, K., BERSCHEID, E., & WALSTER, E. (1972). What is beautiful is good. *Journal of Personality and Social Psychology, 24*, 285–290.

DION, K. K., & DION, K. L. (1996). Cultural perspectives on romantic love. *Personal Relationships, 3*, 5–17.

DITTMAN, R. W., KAPPES, M. W. E., & KAPPES, M. H. (1992). Sexual behavior in adolescent and adult females with congenital adrenal hyperplasia. *Psychoneuroendocrinology, 17*, 153–170.

DOBBINS, I., FOLEY, H., SCHACTER, D., & WAGNER, A. (2002). Executive control during episodic retrieval: Multiple prefrontal processes subserve source memory. *Neuron, 35*, 989–996.

DOBBS, D. (2009). The post-traumatic stress trap. *Scientific American, 300*(4), 64–69.

DODGE, K. A., & PETTIT, G. S. (2003). A biopsychosocial model of the development of chronic conduct problems in adolescence. *Developmental Psychology, 39*(2), 349–371.

DODDS, R. A., WARD, T. B., & SMITH, S. M. (2003). A review of experimental literature on incubation in problem solving and creativity. In M. A. Runco (Ed.), *Creativity research handbook* (Vol. 3). Cresskill, NJ: Hampton Press.

DOHRENWEND, B. P. (2000). The role of adversity and stress in psychopathology: Some evidence and its implications for theory and research. *Journal of Health and Social Behavior, 41*, 1–19.

DOHRENWEND, B. P., LEVAV, I., SHROUT, P. E., SCHWARTZ, S., NAVEH, G., LINK, B. G., ET AL. (1992). Socioeconomic status and psychiatric disorders: The causation-selection issue. *Science, 255*, 946–952.

DOI, T. (1973). *The anatomy of dependence.* Tokyo: Kodansha.

DOHRENWEND, B. P., TURNER, J. B., TURSE, N. A., ADAMS, B. G., KOENEN, K. C., & MARSHALL, R. (2006). The psychological risks of Vietnam for U.S. veterans: A revisit with new data and methods. *Science, 313*(5789), 979–982.

DOLCOS, F., LABAR, K. S., & CABEZA, R. (2006). The memory-enhancing effect of emotion: Functional neuroimaging evidence. In B. Uttl, N. Ohta, & A. L. Siegenthaler (Eds.), *Memory and emotion: Interdisciplinary perspectives* (pp. 107–134). Malden, MA: Blackwell Publishing.

DOMHOFF, G. (1996). *Finding meaning in dreams: A quantitative approach.* New York: Plenum.

DOMHOFF, G. W. (2003). *The scientific study of dreams: Neural networks, cognitive development, and content analysis.* Washington, DC: American Psychological Association.

DOMJAN, M. (1983). Biological constraints on instrumental and classical conditioning: Implications for general process theory. In G. H. Bower (Ed.), *The psychology of learning and motivation: Vol. 17.* New York: Academic Press.

DOMJAN, M. (2005). Pavlovian conditioning: A functional perspective. *Annual Review of Psychology, 56*, 179–206.

DOMJAN, M., CUSATO, B., & KRAUSE, M. (2004). Learning with arbitrary versus ecological conditioned stimuli: Evidence from sexual conditioning. *Psychonomics Bulletin & Review, 11*, 232–246.

DONALDSON, D., PETERSEN, S., & BUCKNER, R. (2001). Dissociating memory retrieval processes using fMRI. *Neuron, 31*, 1047–1059.

DONLEA, J. M., RAMANAN, N., & SHAW, P. J. (2009). Use-dependent plasticity in clock neurons regulates sleep need in *Drosophila. Science, 324*, 105–108.

DORNBUSCH, S. M., RITTER, P. L., LIEDERMAN, P. H., ROBERTS, D. F., & FRALEIGH, M. J. (1987). The relation of parenting style to adolescent school performance: Schools and development [Special issue]. *Child Development, 58*, 1244–1257.

DOUGHERTY, D. D., RAUCH, S. L., & JENIKE, M. A. (2002). Pharmacological treatments for obsessive compulsive disorder. In P. E. Nathan, & J. M. Gorman (Eds.), *A guide to treatments that work* (2nd ed., pp. 387–410). New York: Oxford University Press.

DOUGLAS, A. B., & STEBLAY, N. (2006). Memory distortion in eyewitnesses: A meta-analysis of the post-identification feedback effect. *Applied Cognitive Psychology, 20*, 859–870.

DOUVAN, E., & ADELSON, J. (1958). The psychodynamics of social mobility in adolescent boys. *Journal of Abnormal and Social Psychology, 56*, 31–44.

DOVIDIO, J. F., & GAERTNER, S. L. (1999). Reducing prejudice: Combating intergroup biases. *Current Directions in Psychological Science, 8*(4), 101–105.

DOWNEY, G., LEBOLT, A., RINCON, C., & FREITAS, A. (1998). Rejection sensitivity and children's interpersonal difficulties. *Child Development, 69*, 1074–1091.

DRAGUNS, J. G., KRYLOVA, A. V., ORYOL, V. E., RUKAVISHNIKOV, A. A., & MARTIN, T. A. (2000). Personality characteristics of the Nentsy in the Russian Arctic: A comparison with ethnic Russians by means of NEO-PI-R and POI. *American Behavioral Scientist, 44*, 126–140.

DREVETS, W. C. (1998). Functional neuroimaging studies of depression: The anatomy of melancholia. *Annual Review of Medicine, 49*, 341–361.

DRISCOLL, R., DAVIS, K. E., & LIPETZ, M. E. (1972). Parental interference and romantic love: The Romeo and Juliet effect. *Journal of Personality and Social Psychology, 24*, 1–10.

DUCKWORTH, A. L., & SELIGMAN, M.E.P. (2005). Self-discipline outdoes IQ in predicting academic performance of adolescents. *Psychological Science, 16*(12), 939–944.

DUDAI, Y. (2004). The neurobiology of consolidations, or, how stable is the engram? *Annual Review of Psychology, 55*, 51–86.

DUFFY, J. F., RIMMER, D. W., & CZEISLER, C. A. (2001). Association of intrinsic circadian period with morningness-eveningness, usual wake time, and circadian phase. *Behavioral Neuroscience, 115*(4):895–899.

DUKE, P., CARLSMITH, J., JENNINGS, D., MARTIN, J., DORNBUSCH, S., GROSS, R., ET AL. (1982). Educational correlates of early and late sexual maturation in adolescence. *Journal of Pediatrics, 100*, 633–637.

DUKER, P. C., & SEYS, D. M. (1996). Long-term use of electrical aversion treatment with self-injurious behavior. *Research in Developmental Disabilities, 17*, 293–301.

DUMAY, N., & GASKELL, M. G. (2007). Sleep-associated changes in the mental representation of spoken words. *Psychological Science, 18*, 35–39.

DUNBAR, K., & BLANCHETTE, I. (2001). The in vivo/in vitro approach to cognition: The case of analogy. *Trends in Cognitive Science, 5*, 334–339.

DUNCAN, G. J., YEUNG, W. J., BROOKS-GUNN, J., & SMITH, J. R. (1998). How much does childhood poverty affect the life chances of children? *American Sociological Review, 63*, 406–423.

DUNCAN, J. (1994). Attention, intelligence, and the frontal lobes. In M. Gazzaniga (Ed.), *The cognitive neurosciences.* Cambridge, MA: MIT Press.

DUNCAN, J. (1995). Attention, intelligence, and the frontal lobes. In M. S. Gazzaniga (Ed.), *The cognitive neurosciences* (pp. 721–733). Cambridge, MA: MIT Press.

DUNCAN, J., BUNDESEN, C., OLSON, A., HYMPHREYS, G., CHAVDA, S., & SHIBUYA, H. (1999). Systematic analysis of deficits in visual attention. *Journal of Experimental Psychology: General, 128*, 450–478.

DUNCAN, J., PARR, A., WOOLGAR, A., THOMPSON, R., BRIGHT, P., COX, S., ET AL. (2008). Goal neglect and Spearman's g: Competing parts of a complex task. *Journal of Experimental Psychology: General, 137*, 131–148.

DUNCAN, J., RUDIGER, J. S., KOLODNY, J., BOR, D., HERZOG, H., AHMED, A., ET AL. (2000). A neural basis for general intelligence. *Science, 289*, 457–460.

DUNCKER, K. (1945). On problem solving. *Psychological Monographs* (Whole No. 270), 1–113.

DUNNING, D., & COHEN, G. L. (1992). Egocentric definitions of traits and abilities in social judgment. *Journal of Personality and Social Psychology, 63*, 341–355.

DUNNING, D., HEATH, C., & SULS, J. M. (2004). Flawed self-assessment: Implications for health, education, and the workplace. *Psychological Science in the Public Interest, 5*, 69–106.

DUNNING, D., MEYEROWITZ, J. A., & HOLZBERG, A. D. (1989). Ambiguity and self-evaluation: The role of idiosyncratic trait definitions in self-serving assessments of ability. *Journal of Personality and Social Psychology, 57*, 1082–1090.

DUNPHY, D. C. (1963). The social structure of urban adolescent peer groups. *Sociometry, 26*, 230–246.

DUPAUL, G. J., & BARKLEY, R. A. (1998). Medication therapy. In R. A. Barkley (Ed.), *Attention-deficit hyperactivity disorder: A handbook for diagnosis and treatment.* New York: Guilford.

DUPOUX, E., ET AL. (1997). A distressing "deafness" in French? *Journal of Memory and Language, 36*, 406–421.

DUTTON, D. G., & ARON, A. P. (1974). Some evidence for heightened sexual attraction under conditions of high anxiety. *Journal of Personality and Social Psychology, 30*, 510–517.

DUYME, M., DUMARET, A.-C., & TOMKIEWICZ, S. (1999). How can we boost IQs of "dull children"? A late adoption study. *Proceedings of the National Academy of Sciences, 96*, 8790–8794.

DWECK, C. S. (1999). *Self-theories: Their role in motivation, personality and development.* Philadelphia: Psychology Press.

DWECK, C. S. (2006). *Mindset: The new psychology of success.* New York: Random House.

DWECK, C. S. (2009). Can personality be changed? The role of beliefs in personality and change. *Current Directions in Psychological Science, 17*, 391–394.

DWECK, C. S., CHIU, C., & HONG, Y. (1995). Implicit theories and their role in judgments and reactions: A world from two perspectives. *Psychological Inquiry, 6*, 267–285.

DWECK, C. S., HONG, Y.-Y., & CHIU, C. Y. (1993). Implicit theories and individual differences in the likelihood and meaning of dispositional inference. *Personality and Social Psychology Bulletin, 19*, 644–656.

DWECK, C. S., & LEGGETT, E. L. (1988). A social-cognitive approach to motivation and personality. *Psychological Review, 95*, 256–273.

DYKEMA, J., BERGBOWER, K., DOCTORA, J. D., & PETERSON, C. (1996). An attributional style questionnaire for general use. *Journal of Psychoeducational Assessment, 14*, 100–108.

———

EAGLE, M. N., & WOLITSKY, D. L. (1992). Psychoanalytic theories of psychotherapy. In D. K. Freedheim (Ed.), *History of psychotherapy.* Washington, DC: American Psychological Association.

EAGLY, A. H., & CHAIKEN, S. (1993). *The psychology of attitudes.* Fort Worth, TX: Harcourt Brace Jovanovich.

EAGLY, A. H., & CROWLEY, M. (1986). Gender and helping behavior: A meta-analytic review of the social psychological literature. *Psychological Bulletin, 100*, 283–308.

EAGLY, A. H., & WOOD, W. (1999). The origins of sex differences in human behavior: Evolved dispositions versus social roles. *American Psychologist, 54*(6), 408–423.

EAGLY, A. H., ASHMORE, R. D., MAKHIJANI, M. G., & LONGO, L. C. (1991). What is beautiful is good, but . . . : A meta-analytic review of research on the physical attractiveness stereotype. Psychological Bulletin, 110, 109–128.

EARLES, J. L., CONNOR, L. T., SMITH, A. D., & PARK, D. C. (1998). Interrelations of age, self-reported health, speed, and memory. *Psychology and Aging, 12*, 675–683.

EATON, W. O., & YU, A. P. (1989). Are sex differences in child motor activity a function of sex differences in maturational status? *Child Development, 60*, 1005–1011.

EBBINGHAUS, H. (1885). *Memory.* New York: Teacher's College, Columbia University, 1913. Reprint edition, New York: Dover, 1964.

EDMONDS, J. M. (ED.). (1929). *The characters of Theophrastus.* Cambridge, MA: Harvard University Press.

EFRON, R. (1990). *The decline and fall of hemispheric specialization.* Hillsdale, NJ: Erlbaum.

EGETH, H., JONIDES, J., & WALL, S. (1972). Parallel processing of multielement displays. *Cognitive Psychology, 3*, 674–698.

EGLIN, M., ROBERTSON, L. C., & KNIGHT, R. T. (1989). Visual search performance in the neglect syndrome. *Journal of Cognitive Neuroscience, 1*, 372–385.

EGNER, T. (2008). Multiple conflict-driven control mechanisms in the human brain. *Trends in Cognitive Sciences, 12*, 374–380.

EHRHARDT, A., & BAKER, S. (1974). Fetal androgens, human central nervous system differentiation, and behavior sex differences. In R. C. Friedman, R. M. Richart, & R. L. van de Wiele (Eds.), *Sex differences in behavior* (pp. 33–52). New York: Wiley.

EHRHARDT, A., EPSTEIN, R., & MONEY, J. (1968). Fetal androgens and female gender identity in the early-treated adrenogenital syndrome. *Johns Hopkins Medical Journal, 122*, 165–167.

EIBL-EIBESFELDT, I. (1970). *Ethology: The biology of behavior.* New York: Holt, Rinehart & Winston.

EIGSTI, I. M., ZAYAS, V. MICHEL, W., SHODA, Y., AYDUK, O., DADLANI, M. B., DAVIDSON, M. C., & CASEY, B. J. (2006). Predicting cognitive control from preschool to late adolescence and young adulthood. *Psychological Science, 17*, 478–484.

EIMAS, P. D., SIQUELAND, E. R., JUSCZYK, P., & VIGORITO, J. (1971). Speech perception in infants. *Science, 171*, 303–306.

EISENBERG, A. R. (1999). Emotion talk among Mexican American and Anglo American mothers and children from two social classes. *Merrill-Palmer Quarterly, 45*(2), 267–284.

EISENBERG, N. (1986). *Altruistic emotion, cognition and behavior.* Hillsdale, NJ: Erlbaum.

EISENBERG, N. (2000). Emotion, regulation and moral development. In S. Fiske, D. Schacter, & C. Zahn-Waxler (Eds.), *Annual Review of Psychology, 51*, 665–697.

EISENBERG, N., CUMBERLAND, A., & SPINRAD, T. L. (1998). Parental socialization of emotion. *Psychological Inquiry, 9*(4), 241–273.

EISENBERG, N., & FABES, R. (1998). Prosocial development. In W. Damon (Ed.), *Handbook of child psychology* (5th Ed.): Vol. 3. *Social, emotional, and personality development* (N. Eisenberg, Vol. Ed.; pp. 701–778). New York: Wiley.

EISENBERG, N., FABES, R., GUTHRIE, I., & REISER, M. (2000). Dispositional emotionality and regulation: Their role in predicting quality of social functioning. *Journal of Personality and Social Psychology, 78*, 136–157.

EISENBERG, N., FABES, R. A., KARBON, M., MURPHY, B. C., ET AL. (1996). The relations of children's dispositional prosocial behavior to emotionality, regulation, and social functioning. *Child Development, 67*(3), 974–992.

EISENBERG, N., FABES, R. A., MILLER, P., SHELL, R., SHEA, C., & MAY-PLUMLESS, T. (1990). Preschoolers' vicarious motion responding and their situational and dispositional prosocial behavior. *Merrill-Palmer Quarterly, 36*, 507–529.

EISENBERG, N., FABES, R. A., SCHALLER, M., CARLO, G., ET AL. (1991). The relations of parental characteristics and practices to children's vicarious emotional responding. *Child Development, 62*(6), 1393–1408.

EISENBERG, N., FABES, R., SHEPARD, S., MURPHY, B., JONES, S., & GUTHRIE, I. (1998). Contemporaneous and longitudinal prediction of children's sympathy from dispositional regulation and emotionality. *Developmental Psychology, 34*, 910–924.

EISENBERG, N., GERSHOFF, E. T., FABES, R. A., SHEPARD, S. A., CUMBERLAND, A. J., LOSOYA, S. H., ET AL. (2001). Mother's emotional expressivity and children's behavior problems and social competence: Mediation through children's regulation. *Developmental Psychology, 37*(4), 475–490.

EISENBERG, N. I., LIEBERMAN, M. D., & WILLIAMS, K. D. (2003). Does rejection hurt? An fMRI study of social exclusion. *Science, 302*(5643), 290–292.

EISENBERGER, R., PIERCE, W. D., & CAMERON, J. (1999). Effects of reward on intrinsic motivation—negative, neutral, and positive: Comment on Deci, Koestner, and Ryan (1999). *Psychological Bulletin, 125,* 677–691.

EISNER, D. A. (2000). *The death of psychotherapy: From Freud to alien abductions.* Westport, CT: Praeger.

EKMAN, P. (1972). Universals and cultural differences in facial expressions of emotion. In J. Cole (Ed.), *Nebraska Symposium on Motivation, 1971: Vol. 19* (pp. 207–283). Lincoln: University of Nebraska Press.

EKMAN, P. (1973). Cross-cultural studies of facial expression. In P. Ekman (Ed.), *Darwin and facial expression* (pp. 169–222). New York: Academic Press.

EKMAN, P. (1980). *The face of man: Expression of universal emotions in a New Guinea village.* New York: Garland STPM Press.

EKMAN, P. (1984). Expression and the nature of emotion. In P. Ekman & K. Scherer (Eds.), *Approaches to emotion* (pp. 319–343). Hillsdale, NJ: Erlbaum.

EKMAN, P. (1994). Strong evidence for universals in facial expression: A reply to Russell's mistaken critique. *Psychological Bulletin, 115,* 268–287.

EKMAN, P., & FRIESEN, W. V. (1969). Nonverbal leakage and clues to deception. *Psychiatry, 32,* 88–106.

EKMAN, P., & FRIESEN, W. V. (1975). *Unmasking the face.* Englewood Cliffs, NJ: Prentice-Hall.

EKMAN, P., FRIESEN, W. V., & O'SULLIVAN, M. (1988). Smiles when lying. *Journal of Personality and Social Psychology, 54,* 414–420.

EKMAN, P., & OSTER, H. (1979). Facial expression of emotion. *Annual Review of Psychology, 30,* 527–554.

ELBERT, T., PANTEV, C., WIENBRUCH, C., ROCKSTROH, B., & TAUB, E. (1995). Increased cortical representation of the fingers of the left hand in string players. *Science, 270,* 305–307.

ELFENBEIN, H. A., & AMBADY, N. (2002). On the universality of cultural specificity of emotion recognition: A meta-analysis. *Psychological Bulletin, 128,* 203–235.

ELKIN, I., SHEA, M. T., WATKINS, J. T., IMBER, S. D., SOTSKY, S. M., COLLINS, J. S., ET AL. (1989). National Institute of Mental Health treatment of depression collaborative research program: General effectiveness of treatments. *Archives of General Psychiatry, 46,* 971–982.

ELKIN, R. A., & LEIPPE, M. R. (1986). Physiological arousal, dissonance, and attitude change: Evidence for a dissonance-arousal link and a "don't remind me" effect. *Journal of Personality and Social Psychology, 51,* 55–65.

ELKIND, D. (1978). *The child's reality: Three developmental themes.* Hillsdale, NJ: Erlbaum.

ELKINS, R. L. (1991). An appraisal of chemical aversion emetic therapy approaches to alcoholism treatment. *Behaviour Research and Therapy, 29,* 387–413.

ELLEMERS, N., SPEARS, R., & DOSSJE, B. (2002). Self and social identity. *Annual Review of Psychology, 53,* 161–186.

ELLENBERGER, H. F. (1970). *The discovery of the unconscious.* New York: Basic Books.

ELLIOT, M. A., & MÜLLER, H. J. (2000). Evidence for 40-Hz oscillatory short-term visual memory revealed by human reaction-time measurements. *Journal of Experimental Psychology: Learning, Memory, and Cognition, 26,* 7093–7718.

ELLIOTT, R., GREENBERG, L. S., & LIETAER, G. (2004). Research on experiential psychotherapies. In M. J. Lambert (Ed.), *Bergin and Garfield's handbook of psychotherapy and behavior change* (5th ed., pp. 493–540). New York: Wiley.

ELLIS, A. (1962). *Reason and emotion in psychotherapy.* Secaucus, NJ: Lyle Stuart.

ELLIS, L., & AMES, M. A. (1987). Neurohormonal functioning and sexual orientation: A theory of homosexuality-heterosexuality. *Psychological Bulletin, 101,* 233–258.

ELMAN, J. L. (1991). Distributed representation, simple recurrent networks, and grammatical structure. *Machine Learning, 7,* 195–225.

ELPHICK, M. R., & EGERTOVA, M. (2001). The neurobiology and evolution of cannabinoid signalling. *Philosophical Transactions: Biological Sciences, 356,* 381–408.

EMMELKAMP, P. M. G. (2004). Behavior therapy with adults. In M. J. Lambert (Ed.), *Bergin and Garfield's handbook of psychotherapy and behavior change* (5th ed., pp. 393–446). New York: Wiley.

EMMELKAMP, P. M. G., KRIJN, M., HULSBOSCH, A. M., DE VRIES, S., SCHUEMIE, M. J., & VAN DER MAST, C. A. P. G. (2002). Virtual reality treatment versus exposure in vivo: A comparative evaluation in acrophobia. *Behaviour Research and Therapy, 40,* 509–516.

EMMERICH, W. (1966). Continuity and stability in early social development, II. Teacher ratings. *Child Development, 37,* 17–27.

ENDRESS, A., NESPOR, M., & MEHLER, J. (2009). Perceptual and memory constraints on language acquisition. *Trends in Cognitive Sciences, 13*(8), 348–353.

ENGEL, A. K., & SINGER, W. (2000). Temporal binding and the neural correlates of sensory awareness. *Trends in Cognitive Science, 5,* 16–25.

ENGLE, R. W., TUHOLSKI, S. W., LAUGHLIN, J. E., & CONWAY, A. R. A. (1999). Working memory, short-term memory, and general fluid intelligence: A latent variable approach. *Journal of Experimental Psychology: General, 128,* 309–331.

ENGLUND, M., LEVY, A., HYSON, D., & SROUFE, L. (2000). Adolescent social competence: Effectiveness in a group setting. *Child Development, 71,* 1049–1060.

ENNS, J. T. (2004). *The thinking eye, the seeing brain.* New York: Norton.

ENQUIST, M., & LEIMAR, O. (1990). The evolution of fatal fighting. *Animal Behaviour, 39,* 1–9.

EPSTEIN, H. T. (1978). Growth spurts during brain development: Implications for educational policy and practice. In J. S. Chard & A. F. Mirsky (Eds.), *Education and the brain.* Chicago: University of Chicago Press.

EPSTEIN, S. (1979). The stability of behavior: I. On predicting most of the people much of the time. *Journal of Personality and Social Psychology, 37,* 1097–1126.

EPSTEIN, W. (1961). The influence of syntactical structure on learning. *American Journal of Psychology, 74,* 80–85.

ERDELYI, M. H. (1985). *Psychoanalysis: Freud's cognitive psychology.* New York: Freeman.

ERICSSON, K. (Ed.) (1996). *The road to excellence: The acquisition of expert performance in the arts and sciences, sports and games.* Mahwah, NJ: Erlbaum.

ERICSSON, K. A. (2003). Exceptional memorizers: made, not born. *Trends in Cognitive Sciences, 7,* 233–235.

ERIKSEN, C. W., & HOFFMAN, J. E. (1972). Temporal and spatial characteristics of selective encoding from multi-element displays. *Perception and Psychophysics, 12,* 201–204.

ERIKSON, E. H. (1963). *Childhood and society.* New York: Norton.

ERIKSON, E. H. (1968). *Identity, youth, and crisis.* New York: Norton.

ERIKSON, E. H., & COLES, R. (EDS.). (2000). *The Erik Erikson reader.* New York: Norton.

ERIKSSON, P. S., PERFILIEVA, E., BJÖRK-ERIKSSON, T., ALBORN, A., NORDBORG, C., PETERSON, D., ET AL. (1998). Neurogenesis in the adult human hippocampus. *Nature Medicine, 4,* 1313–1317.

ESSER, J. K. (1998). Alive and well after 25 years: A review of groupthink research. *Organizational Behavior and Human Decision Processes, 73*(2–3), 116–141.

ESSES, V. M., HADDOCK, G., & ZANNA, M. P. (1993). Values, stereotypes, and emotions as determinants of intergroup attitudes. In D. M. Mackie & D. L. Hamilton (Eds.), *Affect, cognition, and stereotyping: Interactive processes in group perception* (pp. 137–166). New York: Academic Press.

ESTES, W. K., & SKINNER, B. F. (1941). Some quantitative properties of anxiety. *Journal of Experimental Psychology, 29,* 390–400.

ETKIN, A., & WAGER, T. D. (2007). Functional neuroimaging of anxiety: A meta-analysis of emotional processing in PTSD, social anxiety disorder, and specific phobia. *American Journal of Psychiatry, 164,* 1476–1488.

EVANS, J. S. B. T., & FEENEY, A. (2004). The role of prior belief in reasoning. In J. P. Leighton & R. J. Sternberg (Eds.), *The nature of reasoning* (pp. 78–102). New York: Cambridge University Press.

EVANS, J. S. B. T., NEWSTEAD, S. E., & BYRNE, R. M. J. (1993). *Human reasoning: The psychology of deduction.* London: Erlbaum.

EVERSON, C. A. & TOTH, L. A. (2000). Systemic bacterial invasion induced by sleep deprivation. *American Journal of Physiology: Regulatory, Integrative and Comparative Physiology, 278,* R905–R916.

EXNER, J. E. (1974). *The Rorschach system.* New York: Grune and Stratton.

EXNER, J. E. (1978). *A comprehensive system: Current research and advanced interpretation: Vol. 2.* New York: Wiley Interscience.

EXNER, J. E., JR. (1993). *The Rorschach: A comprehensive system: Vol. 1. Basic foundations* (3rd ed). New York: Wiley.

EYER, D. E. (1992). *Mother-infant bonding: A scientific fiction.* New Haven, CT: Yale University Press.

EYSENCK, H. J. (1952). The effects of psychotherapy: An evaluation. *Journal of Consulting and Clinical Psychology, 16*, 319–324.

EYSENCK, H. J. (1961). The effects of psychotherapy. In H. J. Eysenck (Ed.), *Handbook of abnormal psychology* (pp. 697–725). New York: Basic Books.

EYSENCK, H. J. (1967). *The biological basis of personality.* Springfield, IL: Thomas.

EYSENCK, H. J. (1986). Toward a new model of intelligence. *Personality and Individual Differences, 7*(5), 731–736.

EYSENCK, H. J., VERSUS KAMIN, L. (1981). *The intelligence controversy.* New York: Wiley.

EYSENCK, M. W. (1987). Arousal and personality: The origins of a theory. In J. Strelau & H. J. Eysenck (Eds.), *Personality dimensions and arousal* (pp. 1–13). New York: Plenum.

———

FABES, R. A., EISENBERG, N., SMITH, M. C., & MURPHY, B. C. (1996). Getting angry at peers: Associations with liking of the provocateur. *Child Development, 67*(3), 942–956.

FAGOT, B. (1997). Attachment, parenting, and peer interactions of toddler children. *Developmental Psychology, 33*, 389–499.

FAGOT, B. I. (1995). Psychosocial and cognitive determinants of early gender-role development. *Annual Review of Sex Research, 6*, 1–31.

FAGOT, B. I., LEINBACH, M. D., & HAGEN, R. (1986). Gender labeling and adoption of same-sex behaviors. *Developmental Psychology, 22*, 440–443.

FAIRBURN, C. G., JONES, R., PEVELER, R., HOPE, R., & O'CONNOR, M. (1993). Psychotherapy and bulimia nervosa: Long-term effects of interpersonal psychotherapy, behavior therapy, and cognitive behavior therapy. *Archives of General Psychiatry, 50*, 419–428.

FALLON, A. E., & ROZIN, P. (1985). Sex differences in perceptions of desirable body shape. *Journal of Abnormal Psychology, 94*, 102–105.

FANSELOW, M. S., & POULOS, A. M. (2005). The neuroscience of mammalian associative learning. *Annual Review of Psychology, 56*, 207–234.

FANT, L. G. (1972). *Ameslan: An introduction to American Sign Language.* Silver Springs, MD: National Association of the Deaf.

FANTZ, R. (1963). Pattern vision in newborn infants. *Science, 140*, 296–297.

FARAH, M. (1988). Is visual imagery really visual? Overlooked evidence from neuropsychology. *Psychological Review, 95*, 307–317.

FARAH, M. J. (1990). *Visual agnosia.* Cambridge, MA: MIT Press.

FARAH, M. J. (2004). *Visual agnosia* (2nd ed.). Cambridge, MA: MIT Press/Bradford Books.

FARAH, M. J., & FEINBERG, T. E. (2000). Disorders of perception and awareness. In M. J. Farah & T. E. Feinberg (Eds.), *Patient-based approaches to cognitive neuroscience* (pp. 143–154). Cambridge, MA: MIT Press.

FARAH, M. J., SHERA, D. M., SAVAGE, J. H., BETANCOURT, L., GIANNETTA, J. M., BRODSKY, N. L., ET AL. (2006).

Childhood poverty: Specific associations with neurocognitive development. *Brain Research, 1110*, 166–174.

FARIS, R. E. L., & DUNHAM, H. W. (1939). *Mental disorders in urban areas.* Chicago: University of Chicago Press.

FARRELL, M. J., LAIRD, A. R., & EGAN, G. F. (2005). Brain activity associated with painfully hot stimuli applied to the upper limb: A meta-analysis. *Human Brain Mapping, 25*(1), 129–139.

FAZIO, R. H. (1995). Attitudes as object-evaluation associations: Determinants, consequences, and correlates of attitude accessibility. In R. E. Petty & J. A. Krosnick (Eds.), *Attitude strength: Antecedents and consequences* (pp. 247–282). Mahwah, NJ: Erlbaum.

FAZIO, R. H., ZANNA, M. P., & COOPER, J. (1977). Dissonance and self-perception: An integrative view of each theory's proper domain of application. *Journal of Experimental Social Psychology, 13*, 464–479.

FAZIO, R., & OLSON, M. (2003). Implicit measures in social cognition research: Their memory and use. *Annual Review of Psychology, 54*, 294–327.

FEDER, H. H. (1984). Hormones and sexual behavior. *Annual Review of Psychology, 35*, 165–200.

FEENEY, B. C., & COLLINS, N. L. (2001). Predictors of caregiving in adult intimate relationships: An attachment theoretical perspective. *Journal of Personality and Social Psychology, 80*(6), 972–994.

FEIN, S., & SPENCER, S. J. (1997). Prejudice as self-image maintenance: Affirming the self through derogating others. *Journal of Personality and Social Psychology, 73*, 31–44.

FEINGOLD, A. (1988). Matching for attractiveness in romantic partners and same-sex friends: A meta-analysis and theoretical critique. *Psychological Bulletin, 104*, 226–232.

FEINGOLD, A. (1992). Good-looking people are not what we think. *Psychological Bulletin, 111*, 304–341.

FEINGOLD, A. (1994). Gender differences in personality: A meta-analysis. *Psychological Bulletin, 116*, 429–456.

FEINMAN, J. A., & DUNNER, D. L. (1996). The effect of alcohol and substance abuse on the course of bipolar affective disorder. *Journal of Affective Disorders, 37*, 43–49.

FELDMAN, H., GOLDIN-MEADOW, S., & GLEITMAN, L. R. (1978). Beyond Herodotus: The creation of language by linguistically deprived deaf children. In A. Lock (Ed.), *Action, gesture, and symbol: The emergence of language* (pp. 351–414). New York: Academic Press.

FENG, J., SPENCE, I., & PRATT, J. (2007). Playing an action video game reduces gender differences in spatial cognition. *Psychological Science, 18*, 850–855.

FERGUSON, J. M. (2001). The effects of antidepressants on sexual functioning in depressed patients: A review [Suppl.]. *Journal of Clinical Psychiatry, 62*(3), 22–34.

FERNALD, A. (1985). Four-month-old infants prefer to listen to motherese. *Infant Behavior and Development, 8*, 181–195.

FERNALD, A. (1992). Human maternal vocalizations to infants as biologically relevant signals: An evolutionary perspective. In J. H. Barkow, L. Cosmides, & J. Tooby (Eds.), *The adapted mind* (pp. 391–428). New York: Oxford.

FERNANDES, K. J., MARCUS, G. F., DINUBILA, J. A., & VOULOUMANOS, A. (2006). From semantics to syntax and back again: Argument structure in the third year of life. *Cognition, 100*, B10–20.

FESHBACH, S., & TANGNEY, J. (2008). Television viewing and aggression. *Perspectives on Psychological Science, 3*, 387–389.

FESTINGER, L. (1954). A theory of social comparison processes. *Human Relations, 7*, 117–140.

FESTINGER, L. (1957). *A theory of cognitive dissonance.* Stanford, CA: Stanford University Press.

FESTINGER, L. (1962, October). Cognitive dissonance. *Scientific American, 207*, 93–107.

FESTINGER, L., & CARLSMITH, J. M. (1959). Cognitive consequences of forced compliance. *Journal of Abnormal and Social Psychology, 58*, 203–210.

FESTINGER, L., PEPITONE, A., & NEWCOMB, T. (1952). Some consequences of deindividuation in a group. *Journal of Abnormal and Social Psychology, 47*, 387–389.

FIEDLER, F. E. (1978). Recent developments in research on the contingency model. In L. Berkowitz (Ed.), *Group processes.* New York: Academic Press.

FIGLEY, C. R. (1978). Symptoms of delayed combat stress among a college sample of Vietnam veterans. *Military Medicine, 143*, 107–110.

FILLMORE, C. (1968). The case for case. In E. Bach & R. Harms (Eds.), *Universals in linguistic theory.* New York: Holt, Rinehart and Winston.

FINK, B., & PENTON-VOAK, I. (2002). Evolutionary psychology of facial attractiveness. *Current Directions in Psychological Science, 11*, 154–158.

FINK, M. (2008). *Electroconvulsive therapy: A guide for professionals and their patients.* New York: Oxford University Press.

FINKE, R. (1993). Mental imagery and creative discovery. In B. Roskos-Ewoldsen, M. J. Intons-Peterson, & R. Anderson (Eds.), *Imagery, creativity, and discovery* (pp. 255–285). New York: North-Holland.

FINKE, R., WARD, T., & SMITH, S. (1992). *Creative cognition: Theory, research and applications.* Cambridge, MA: MIT Press.

FINUCANE, M. L., ALHAKAMI, A., SLOVIC, P., & JOHNSON, S. M. (2000). The affect heuristic in judgments of risks and benefits. *Journal of Behavioral Decision Making, 13*, 1–17.

FISHER, C., & GLEITMAN, L. R. (2002). Breaking the linguistic code: Current issues in early language learning. In C. R. Gallistel (Vol. Ed.), *Stevens' handbook of experimental psychology: Vol. 3. Learning, motivation, and emotion* (pp. 1–54). New York: Wiley.

FISHER, C., GLEITMAN, L., & GLEITMAN, H. (1991). On the semantic content of subcategorization frames. *Cognitive Psychology, 23*, 331–392.

FISHER, C., HALL, G., RAKOWITZ, S., & GLEITMAN, L. (1994). When it is better to receive than to give: Structural and cognitive factors in acquiring a first vocabulary. *Lingua, 92*, 333–376.

FISHER, R. P., & CRAIK, F. I. M. (1977). The interaction between encoding and retrieval operations in cued recall. *Journal of Experimental Psychology: Human Learning and Memory, 3*, 701–711.

FISHER, R. P., & SCHREIBER, N. (2007). Interviewing protocols to improve eyewitness memory. In M. P. Toglia, J. D. Read, D. F. Ross, & R. C. L. Lindsay (Eds.), *Handbook of eyewitness psychology, Vol. 1: Memory for events* (pp. 401–427). Mahwah, NJ: Erlbaum.

FISHER, S., & GREENBERG, R. P. (1977). *The scientific credibility of Freud's theory and therapy.* New York: Basic Books.

FISHER, S., & GREENBERG, R. P. (1996). *Freud scientifically reappraised: Testing the theories and therapy.* New York: Wiley.

FISKE, A. P. (1992). The four elementary forms of sociality: Framework for a unified theory of social relations. *Psychological Review, 99,* 689–723.

FISKE, A. P. (2004). Relational models theory 2.0. In N. Haslam (Ed.), *Relational models theory: A contemporary overview* (pp. 3–25). Mahwah, NJ: Erlbaum.

FISKE, A. P., & HASLAM, N. (2005). The four basic social bonds: Structures for coordinating interactions. In M. W. Baldwin (Ed.), *Interpersonal cognition* (pp. 267–298). New York: Guilford.

FISKE, A. P., KITAYAMA, S., MARKUS, H. R., & NISBETT, R. E. (1998). The cultural matrix of social psychology. In D. T. Gilbert, S. T. Fiske, & G. Lindzey (Eds.), *The handbook of social psychology* (4th ed., pp. 915–981). New York: McGraw-Hill.

FISKE, D. W. (1949). Consistency of the factorial structures of personality ratings from different sources. *Journal of Abnormal Social Psychology, 44,* 329–344.

FISKE, S. T. (1998). Stereotyping, prejudice, and discrimination. In D. T. Gilbert, S. T. Fiske, & G. Lindzey (Eds.), *The handbook of social psychology* (4th ed., pp. 357–411). New York: McGraw-Hill.

FITZGERALD, P. B., FOUNTAIN, S., & DASKALAKIS, Z. J. (2006). A comprehensive review of the effects of rTMS on motor cortical excitability and inhibition. *Clinical Neurophysiology, 117*(12), 2584–2596.

FIVUSH, R. (1993). Emotional content of parent-child conversations about the past. In C. Nelson (Ed.), *Memory and affect in development. Minnesota Symposia on Child Psychology,* Vol. 23 (pp. 39–77). Hillsdale, NJ: Erlbaum.

FIVUSH, R. (1998). The stories we tell: How language shapes autobiography. *Applied Cognitive Psychology, 12*(5), 483–487.

FIVUSH, R., BROTMAN, M. A., BUCKNER, J. P., & GOODMAN, S. H. (2000). Gender differences in parent-child emotion narratives. *Sex Roles, 42*(3–4), 233–253.

FIVUSH, R., & HADEN, C. (EDS.). (2003). *Autobiographical memory and the construction of a narrative self: Developmental and cultural perspectives.* Hillsdale, NJ: Erlbaum.

FIVUSH, R., & NELSON, K. (2004). Culture and language in the emergence of autobiographical memory. *Psychological Science, 15,* 573–577.

FLAVELL, J. H. (1985). *Cognitive development* (2nd ed.). Englewood Cliffs, NJ: Prentice-Hall.

FLAVELL, J. H., FLAVELL, E. R., & GREEN, F. L. (1983). Development of the appearance-reality distinction. *Cognitive Psychology, 15,* 95–120.

FLEESON, W. (2004). Moving personality beyond the person-situation debate: The challenge and the opportunity of within-person variability. *Current Directions in Psychological Science, 13,* 83–87.

FLEISHMAN, M. (2004). The problem: How many patients live in residential care facilities? *Psychiatric Services, 55,* 620–622.

FLODERUS-MYRHED, B., PEDERSEN, N., & RASMUSON, L. (1980). Assessment of heritability for personality, based on a short form of the Eysenck Personality Inventory: A study of 12,898 twin pairs. *Behavior Genetics, 10,* 153–162.

FLORIDA, R. [0](2008). *Who's your city? How the creative economy is making where to live the most important decision of your life.* New York: Basic Books.

FLYNN, J. R. (1984). The mean IQ of Americans: Massive gains 1932 to 1978. *Psychological Bulletin, 95*(1), 29–51.

FLYNN, J. R. (1987). Massive IQ gains in 14 nations: What IQ tests really measure. *Psychological Bulletin, 101*(2), 171–191.

FLYNN, J. R. (1999). Searching for justice: The discovery of IQ gains over time. *American Psychologist, 54,* 5–20.

FLYNN, J. R. (2009). Requiem for nutrition as a cause of IQ gains: Raven's gains in Britain 1938–2008. *Economics & Human Biology,7,* 18–27.

FOA, E., DANCU, C., HEMBREE, E., JAYCOX, L., MEADOWS, E., & STREET, G. (1999). A comparison of exposure therapy, stress inoculation training, and their combination for reducing posttraumatic stress disorder in female assault victims. *Journal of Consulting and Clinical Psychology, 67,* 194–200.

FOCH, T. T., & McCLEARN, G. E. (1980). Genetics, body weight, and obesity. In A. J. Stunkard (Ed.), *Obesity* (pp. 48–71). Philadelphia: Saunders.

FODOR, J. (1997). Connectionism and the problem of systematicity (continued): Why Smolensky's solution still doesn't work. *Cognition, 62*(1), 109–119.

FODOR, J. A. (1983). *The modularity of mind.* Cambridge, MA: MIT Press, Bradford Books.

FODOR, J. A., & LEPORE, E. (1996). The red herring and the pet fish: Why concepts still can't be prototypes. *Cognition, 58,* 253–270.

FODOR, J. A., & PYLYSHYN, Z. W. (1988). Connectionism and cognitive architecture: A critical analysis. *Cognition, 28,* 3–71.

FOLLETTE, W., & GREENBERG, L. S. (2005). Technique factors in treating dysphoric disorders. In L. Castonguay & L. Beutler (Eds.), *Therapeutic principles of change that work* (pp. 83–110). New York: Oxford University Press.

FONG, G., & NISBETT, R. (1991). Immediate and delayed transfer of training effects in statistical reasoning. *Journal of Experimental Psychology: General, 120,* 34–45.

FONG, G., KRANTZ, D., & NISBETT, R. (1986). The effects of statistical training on thinking about everyday problems. *Cognitive Psychology, 18,* 253–292.

FORD, C. S., & BEACH, F. A. (1951). *Patterns of sexual behavior.* New York: Harper & Row.

FOSSHAGE, J. L. (1983). The psychological function of dreams: A revised psychoanalytic perspective. *Psychoanalysis and Contemporary Thought, 6,* 641–669.

FOUCAULT, M. (1965). *Madness and civilization.* New York: Random House.

FOULKES, D. (1985). *Dreaming: A cognitive-psychological analysis.* Hillsdale, NJ: Erlbaum.

FOWLER, A., GELMAN, R., & GLEITMAN, L. (1994). Language learning in children with Down Syndrome. In H. Flager-Flusberg (Ed.), *Constraints on language acquisition: Studies of atypical children.* Hillsdale, NJ: Erlbaum.

FOX, N. A., HENDERSON, H. A., MARSHALL, P. J., NICHOLS, K. E., & GHERA, M. M. (2005). Behavioral inhibition: Linking biology and behavior within a developmental framework. *Annual Review of Psychology, 56,* 235–262.

FRALEY, R. (2002). Attachment stability from infancy to adulthood: Meta-analysis and dynamic modeling of developmental mechanisms. *Personality and Social Psychology Review, 6,* 123–151.

FRANK, E., & SPANIER, C. (1995). Interpersonal psychotherapy for depression: Overview, clinical efficacy, and future directions. *Clinical Psychology Science and Practice, 2,* 349–369.

FRANK, J. D., & FRANK, J. B. (1991). *Persuasion and healing: A comparative study of psychotherapy* (3rd ed.). Baltimore: Johns Hopkins University Press.

FRANK, M. C., GOODMAN, N. D., & TENENBAUM, J. B. (2009). Using speakers' referential intentions to modelearly cross-situational word learning. *Psychological Science, 20*(5), 578–585.

FRANKEL, F. H. (1993). Adult reconstruction of childhood events in the multiple personality disorder literature. *American Journal of Psychiatry, 150,* 954–958.

FRANKLIN T., ACTON, P., MALDJIAN, J., GRAY, J., CROFT, J., DACKIS, C., O'BRIEN, C., & CHILDRESS, A. (2002). Decreased gray matter concentration in the insular, orbitofrontal, cingulate, and temporal cortices of cocaine patients. *Biological Psychiatry, 51,* 134–142.

FRASIER, L., & FODOR, J. D. (1978). The sausage machine: A new two-stage parsing model. *Cognition, 6,* 291–325.

FRASER, S. (1995). *The Bell Curve wars: Race intelligence, and the future of America.* New York: Basic Books.

FREDRICKSON, B. L. (1998). What good are positive emotions? *Review of General Psychology, 2,* 300–319.

FREDRICKSON, B. L., MAYNARD, K. E., HELMS, M. J., HANEY, T. L., SIEGLER, I. C., & BAREFOOT, J. C. (2000). Hostility predicts magnitude and duration of blood pressure response to anger. *Journal of Behavioral Medicine, 23,* 229–243.

FREEDMAN, D., & FREEDMAN, N. (1969). Behavioural differences between Chinese-American and European-American newborns. *Nature, 224,* 1227.

FREEDMAN, J. L., & FRASER, S. C. (1966). Compliance without pressure: The foot-in-the-door technique. *Journal of Personality and Social Psychology, 4,* 195–202.

FREEMAN, D. (1983). *Margaret Mead and Samoa: The making and unmaking of an anthropological myth.* Cambridge, MA: Harvard University Press.

FREESE, J., & MELAND, S. (2002). Seven tenths incorrect: Heterogeneity and change in the waist-to-hip ratios of *Playboy* centerfold models and Miss America pageant winners—Statistical data included. *Journal of Sex Research, 39,* 133–138.

FREMOUW, W. J., PERCZEL, M., & ELLIS, T. E. (1990). *Suicide risk: Assessment and response guidelines.* Elmsford, NY: Pergamon.

FREUD, A. (1937). *The ego and the mechanisms of defence.* Oxford, England: Hogarth.

FREUD, A. (1946). *The ego and the mechanisms of defense.* London: Hogarth Press.

FREUD, S. (1900). The interpretation of dreams. In J. Strachey (Trans. and Ed.), *The complete psychological works: Vols. 4–5.* New York: Norton, 1976.

FREUD, S. (1901). *The psychopathology of everyday life* (A. Tyson, Trans.). New York: Norton, 1971.

FREUD, S. (1905). Three essays on the theory of sexuality. In J. Strachey (Trans. and Ed.), *The complete psychological works: Vol. 7.* New York: Norton, 1976.

FREUD, S. (1908). Character and anal eroticism. In P. Rieff (Ed.), *Collected papers of Sigmund Freud: Character and culture.* New York: Collier Books, 1963.

FREUD, S. (1911). Psychoanalytic notes upon an autobiographical account of a case of paranoia (dementia paranoides). In J. Strachey (Trans. and Ed.), *The complete psychological works: Vol. 12.* New York: Norton, 1976.

FREUD, S. (1917). *A general introduction to psychoanalysis* (J. Riviere, Trans.). New York: Washington Square Press, 1952.

FREUD, S. (1923). *The ego and the id* (J. Riviere, Trans.). New York: Norton, 1962.

FREUD, S. (1925). Some psychical consequences of the anatomical distinction between the sexes. In J. Strachey (Trans. and Ed.), *The complete psychological works: Vol. 19.* New York: Norton, 1976.

FREUD, S. (1933). Femininity. In J. Strachey (Trans. and Ed.), *The complete psychological works: Vol. 22* (pp. 112–115). New York: Norton, 1976.

FREUD, S. (1933/1964). *New introductory lectures on psychoanalysis.* New York: Norton.

FREUD, S., & BREUER, J. (1895). Studies on hysteria. In J. Strachey (Trans. and Ed.), *The complete psychological works: Vol. 2.* New York: Norton, 1976.

FREUND, A. M., & BALTES, P. B. (1998). Selection, optimization, and compensation as strategies of life management: Correlations with subjective indicators of successful aging. *Psychology and Aging, 13,* 531–543.

FREYD, J. (1996). *Betrayal trauma: The logic of forgetting childhood abuse.* Cambridge, MA: Harvard University Press.

FREYD, J. J. (1998). Science in the memory debate. *Ethics & Behavior, 8,* 101–113.

FRIDLUND, A. J. (1994). *Human facial expression: An evolutionary view.* San Diego, CA: Academic Press.

FRIDLUND, A. J., EKMAN, P., & OSTER, H. (1983). Facial expression of emotion: Review of literature, 1970–1983. In A. Siegman (Ed.), *Nonverbal behavior and communication.* Hillsdale, NJ: Erlbaum.

FRIEDERICI, A. D., & WESSELS, J. M. I. (1993). Phonotactic knowledge of word boundaries and its use in infant speech perception. *Perception and Psychophysics, 54,* 287–295.

FRIEDMAN, H. S., & MILLER-HERRINGER, T. (1991). Nonverbal displays of emotion in public and private: Self-monitoring, personality, and expressive cues. *Journal of Personality and Social Psychology, 61,* 766–775.

FRIEDMAN, J. (2003). A war on obesity, not the obese. *Science, 299,* 856–858.

FRIEDMAN, M. I. (1990a). Body fat and the metabolic control of food intake. *International Journal of Obesity, 14,* 53–67.

FRIEDMAN, M. I. (1990b). Making sense out of calories. In E. M. Stricker (Ed.), *Handbook of behavioral neurobiology: Vol. 10. Neurobiology of food and fluid intake* (pp. 513–529). New York: Plenum.

FRIEDMAN, M. I., & STRICKER, E. M. (1976). The physiological psychology of hunger: A physiological perspective. *Psychological Review, 83,* 409–431.

FRIEDMAN, M. J., KEANE, T. M., & RESICK, P. A. (Eds.). (2007). *Handbook of PTSD: Science and practice.* New York: Guilford.

FRIEDMAN, M. J., & MARSELLA, A. J. (1996). Posttraumatic stress disorder: An overview of the concept. In A. J. Marsella, M. J. Friedman, E. T. Gerrity, & R. M. Scurfield (Eds.), *Ethnocultural aspects of posttraumatic stress disorder: Issues, research, and clinical applications* (pp. 11–32). Washington, DC: American Psychological Association.

FRIEDMAN, N., MIYAKE, A., CORLEY, R., YOUNG, S., DEFRIES, J., & HEWITT, J. (2006). Not all executive functions are related to intelligence. *Psychological Science, 17,* 172–179.

FRIEND, R., RAFFERTY, Y., & BRAMEL, D. (1990). A puzzling misinterpretation of the Asch "conformity" study. *European Journal of Social Psychology, 20,* 29–44.

FRIES, P., REYNOLDS, J. H., RORIE, A. E., & DESIMONE, R. (2001). Modulation of oscillatory neural synchronization by selective visual attention. *Science, 291,* 1560–1563.

FRIESEN, W. V. (1972). *Cultural differences in facial expressions in a social situation: An experimental test of the concept of display rules.* Unpublished doctoral dissertation, University of California, San Francisco.

FRIJDA, N. H. (1986). *The emotions.* New York, NY; Paris, France: Cambridge University Press; Editions de la Maison des Sciences de l'Homme.

FRITH, C. D., & FRITH, U. (1999). Interacting minds—a biological basis. *Science, 286,* 1692–1695.

FROME, P. M., & ECCLES, J. S. (1998). Parents' influence on children's achievement-related perceptions. *Journal of Personality and Social Psychology, 74*(2), 435–452.

FROMKIN, V., KRASHEN, S., CURTISS, S., RIGLER, D., & RIGLER, M. (1974). The development of language in Genie: A case of language acquisition beyond the "critical period." *Brain and Language, 1,* 81–107.

FROST, P. (1994). Preference for darker faces in photographs at different phases of the menstrual cycle: Preliminary assessment of evidence for a hormonal relationship. *Perceptual and Motor Skills, 79*(1, Pt. 2), 507–514.

FRYE, D., ZELAZO, P. D., & BURACK, J. A. (1998). Cognitive complexity and control: I. Theory of mind in typical and atypical development. *Current Directions in Psychological Science, 7,* 116–120.

FUJIMOTO, W. Y., BERGSTROM, R. W., BOYKO, E. J., LEONETTI, D. L., NEWELL-MORRIS, L. L., & WAHL, P. W. (1995). Susceptibility to development of central adiposity among populations. *Obesity Research, 3*(suppl. 2), 179S–186S.

FULLER, R. K., & HILLER-STURMHOFEL, S. (1999). Alcoholism treatment in the United States: An overview. *Alcohol Research and Health, 23,* 69–77.

FURNHAM, A., TAN, T., & MCMANUS, C. (1997). Waist-to-hip ratio preferences for body shape: A replication and extension. *Personality and Individual Differences, 22,* 539–549.

GABRIELI, J. D. E., FLEISCHMAN, D. A., KEANE, M. M., REMINGER, S. L., & MORRELL, F. (1995). Double dissociation between memory systems underlying explicit and implicit memory in the human brain. *Psychological Science, 6,* 76–82.

GALANTER, E. (1962). Direct measurement of utility and subjective probability. *American Journal of Psychology, 75,* 208–220.

GALATI, D., SCHERER, K. R., & RICCI-BITTI, P. E. (1997). Voluntary facial expression of emotion: Comparing congenitally blind with normally sighted encoders. *Journal of Personality and Social Psychology, 73,* 1363–1379.

GALEA, S. AHERN, J., RESNICK, H., KILPATRICK, D., BUCUVALAS, M., GOLD, J., & VLAHOV, D. (2002). Psychological sequelae of the September 11 terrorist attacks in New York City. *New England Journal of Medicine, 346* (13), 982–987.

GALLAGHER, A. M., & KAUFMAN, J. C. (2005). Gender differences in mathematics: What we know and what we need to know. In A. M. Gallagher & J. C. Kaufman (Eds.), *Gender differences in mathematics: An integrative psychological approach* (pp. 316–331). New York: Cambridge University Press.

GALLAGHER, H. L., & FRITH, C. D. (2003). Functional imaging of "theory of mind." *Trends in Cognitive Science, 7,* 77–83.

GALLISTEL, C. R. (1990). *The organization of learning.* Cambridge, MA: MIT Press (Bradford).

GALLISTEL, C. R. (1994). Space and time. In N. J. Mackintosh (Ed.), *Animal learning and cognition* (pp. 221–253). New York: Academic Press.

GALLISTEL, C. R., & GELMAN, R. (2000). Non-verbal numerical cognition: From reals to integers. *Trends in Cognitive Science, 4,* 59–65.

GALLO, V., & CHITAJALLU, R. (2001). Unwrapping glial cells from the synapse: What lies inside? *Science, 292,* 872–873.

GALTON, F. (1883). *Inquiries into human faculty and its development.* London: Macmillan.

GANAWAY, G. K. (1989). Historical versus narrative truth: Clarifying the role of exogenous trauma in the etiology of MPD and its variants. *Dissociation, 2,* 205–220.

GANEV, K., ONCHEV, G., & IVANOV, P. (1998). A 16–year follow-up study of schizophrenia and related disorders in Sofia, Bulgaria. *Acta Psychiatrica Scandinavica, 98,* 200–207.

GANGESTAD, S., & SNYDER, M. (2000). Self-monitoring: Appraisal and reappraisal. *Psychological Bulletin, 126,* 530–555.

GARB, H. N., FLORIO, C. M., & GROVE, W. M. (1998). The validity of the Rorschach and the Minnesota Multiphasic Personality Inventory: Results from meta-analyses. *Psychological Science, 9*(5), 402–404.

GARB, H. N., WOOD, J. M., LILIENFELD, S. O., & NEZWORSKI, M. T. (2002). Effective use of projective techniques in clinical practice: Let the data help with selection and interpretation. *Professional Psychology: Research & Practice, 33,* 454–463.

GARB, H. N., WOOD, J. M., NEZWORSKI, M. T., GROVE, W. M., & STEJSKAL, W. J. (2001). Toward a resolution of the Rorschach controversy. *Psychological Assessment, 13*(4), 433–448.

GARBER, J., & HOROWITZ, J. L. (2002). Depression in childhood. In I. H. Gotlib & C. L. Hammen (Eds.), *Handbook of depression* (pp. 510–540). New York: Guilford.

GARCIA, J., & KOELLING, R. A. (1966). The relation of cue to consequence in avoidance learning. *Psychonomic Science, 4,* 123–124.

GARD, D. E., KRING, A. M., GERMANS GARD, M., HORAN, W. P., & GREEN, M. F. (2007). Anhedonia in schizophrenia: Distinctions between anticipatory and consummatory pleasure. *Schizophrenia Research, 93,* 253–260.

GARDNER, H. (1983). *Frames of mind: The theory of multiple intelligences.* New York: Basic Books.

GARDNER, H. (1998). Are there additional intelligences? The case for naturalist, spiritual, and existential intelligences. In J. Kane (Ed.), *Education, information, and transformation* (pp. 111–131). Upper Saddle River, NJ: Merrill–Prentice Hall.

GARDOS, P. S., & MOSHER, D. L. (1999). Gender differences in reactions to viewing pornographic vignettes: Essential or interpretive? *Journal of Psychology and Human Sexuality, 11,* 65–83.

GATHERCOLE, S. E., & PICKERING, S. J. (2000a). Assessment of working memory in six- and seven-year-old children. *Journal of Educational Psychology, 92,* 377–390.

GATHERCOLE, S. E., & PICKERING, S. J. (2000b). Working memory deficits in children with low achievements in the national curriculum at seven years of age. *British Journal of Educational Psychology, 70,* 177–194.

GAUVAIN, M. (2001). Cultural tools, social interaction and the development of thinking. *Human Development, 44*(2–3), 126–143.

GAY, P. (1998). *Freud: A life for our time.* New York: Norton.

GAZZANIGA, M. S., IVRY, R. B., & MANGUN, G. R. (2009). *Cognitive neuroscience: The biology of the mind,* 3rd ed. New York: Norton.

GEARY, D. C. (1998). *Male, female: The evolution of human sex differences.* Washington, DC: American Psychological Association.

GEARY, D. C. (2000). Evolution and proximate expression of human paternal investment. *Psychological Bulletin, 126,* 55–77.

GEARY, D. C. (2005). Evolution of life-history trade-offs in mate attractiveness and health: Comment on Weeden & Sabini (2005). *Psychological Bulletin, 131,* 654–657.

GEARY, D. C., & BJORKLUND, D. F. (2000). Evolutionary developmental psychology. *Child Development, 71,* 57–65.

GEEN, R. G. (2001). *Human aggression* (2nd ed.). London: Taylor & Francis.

GEISLER, J. H., & J. M. THEODOR. (2009). Hippopotamus and whale phylogeny. *Nature, 458,* E1–E4.

GEKOSKI, M., ROVEE-COLLIER, C., & CARULLI-RABINOWITZ, V. (1983). A longitudinal analysis of inhibition of infant distress: The origins of social expectations? *Infant Behavior and Development, 6,* 339–351.

GELMAN, R. (1978). Cognitive development. *Annual Review of Psychology, 29,* 297–332.

GELMAN, R. (2006). Young natural-number arithmeticians. *Current Directions in Psychological Science, 15,* 193–197.

GELMAN, R., & BAILLARGEON, R. (1983). A review of some Piagetian concepts. In P. Mussen (Ed.), E. M. Markman, & J. H. Flavell (Vol. Eds.), *Carmichael's manual of child psychology: Vol 3. Cognitive development* (pp. 167–230). New York: Wiley.

GELMAN, R., & GALLISTEL, R. C. (1978). *The child's understanding of number.* Cambridge, MA: Harvard University Press.

GELMAN, S., & RAMAN, L. (2002). Folk biology as a window onto cognitive development. *Human Development, 45,* 61–68.

GENTNER, D. (1983). Structure-mapping: A theoretical framework for analogy. *Cognitive Science 7,* 155–170.

GENTNER, D., & BORODITSKY, L. (2001). Individuation, relativity and early word learning. In M. Bowerman & S. C. Levinson (Eds.), *Language acquisition and conceptual development* (pp. 215–256). New York: Cambridge University Press.

GENTNER, D., & JEZIORSKI, M. (1989). Historical shifts in the use of analogy in science. In B. Gholson, W. Shadish, R. Neimeyer, & A. Houts (Eds.), *Psychology of science: Contributions to metascience.* Cambridge: Cambridge University Press.

GERARD, H. B., & MATHEWSON, G. C. (1966). The effects of severity of initiation on liking for a group: A replication. *Journal of Experimental Social Psychology, 2,* 278–287.

GERAERTS, E., ARNOLD, M. M., LINDSAY, D. S., MERCKELBACH, H., JELICIC, M., & HAUER, B. (2006). Forgetting of prior remembering in people reporting recovered memories of childhood sexual abuse. *Psychological Science, 17,* 1002–1008.

GERAERTS, E., LINDSAY, D.S., MERCKELBACH, H., JELICIC, M., RAYMAEKERS, L., ARNOLD, M., ET AL. (2009). Cognitive mechanisms underlying recovered-memory experiences of childhood sexual abuse. *Psychological Science, 20,* 92–98.

GERAERTS, E., SCHOOLER, J. W., MERCKELBACH, H., JELICIC, M., HAUER, B., & AMBADAR, Z. (2007). The reality of recovered memories: Corroborating continuous and discontinuous memories of childhood sexual abuse. *Psychological Science, 18*(7), 564–568.

GERGELY, G., & WATSON, J. (1999). Early socio-emotional development: Contingency perception and the social-biofeedback model. In P. Rochat (Ed.), *Early social cognition* (pp. 101–136). Mahwah, NJ: Erlbaum.

GERHARDT, P. F., HOLMES, D. L., ALESSANDRI, M., & GOODMAN, M. (1991). Social policy on the use of aversive interventions: Empirical, ethical, and legal considerations. *Journal of Autism and Developmental Disorders, 21,* 265–277.

GERKEN, L. (1996). Prosody's role in language acquisition and adult parsing. *Journal of Psycholinguistic Research, 25*(2), 345–356.

GERKEN, L. (2006). Decisions, decisions: Infant language learning when multiple generalizations are possible. *Cognition,* B67–B74.

GERKEN, L., LANDAU, B., & REMEZ, R. (1990). Function morphemes in young children's speech perception and production. *Developmental Psychology, 26*(2), 204–216.

GERMAN, T. P., & BARRETT, H. C. (2005). Functional fixedness in a technologically sparse culture. *Psychological Science, 16,* 1–5.

GERSHOFF, E. (2002). Corporal punishment by parents and associated child behaviors and experiences: A meta-analysis. *Psychological Bulletin, 128,* 539–579.

GERSHON, A., DANNON, P., & GRUNHAUS, L. (2003). Transcranial magnetic stimulation in the treatment of depression. *American Journal of Psychiatry, 160,* 835–845.

GERSHON, E. S., NURNBERGER, J. I., JR., BERRETTINI, W. H., & GOLDIN, L. R. (1985). Affective disorders: Genetics. In H. I. Kaplan & J. Sadock (Eds.), *Modern synopsis of comprehensive textbook of psychiatry* (4th ed.). Baltimore: Williams & Wilkins.

GERSTNER, C., & DAY, D. V. (1994). Cross-cultural comparison of leadership prototypes. *Leadership Quarterly, 5,* 121–134.

GERVAIN, J., MACAGNO, F., COGOI, S., PEÑA, M., & MEHLER, J. (2008). The neonate brain detects speech structure. *Proceedings of the National Academy of Sciences, 105,* 14222–14227.

GESCHWIND, N. (1970). The organization of language and the brain. *Science, 170,* 940–944.

GEWIRTZ, J. C., & DAVIS, M. (2000). Using Pavlovian higher-order conditioning paradigms to investigate the neural substrates of emotional learning and memory. *Learning & Memory, 7,* 257–266.

GHAZANFAR, A. A., & HAUSER, M.D. (1999). The neuroethology of primate vocal communication: Substrates for the evolution of speech. *Trends in Cognitive Sciences, 3*(10), 377–381.

GHETTI, S., EDELSTEIN, R. S., GOODMAN, G. S., CORDON, I. M., QUAS, J. A., ALEXANDER, K. W., ET AL. (2006). What can subjective forgetting tell us about memory for childhood trauma? *Memory & Cognition, 34,* 1011–1025.

GIBBS, W. W. (1996). Gaining on fat. *Scientific American, 275,* 88–94.

GIBSON, E. (2006). The interaction of top-down and bottom-up statistics in the resolution of syntactic category ambiguity. *Journal of Memory and Language, 54,* 363–388.

GIBSON, J. J. (1950). *The perception of the visual world.* Boston: Houghton Mifflin.

GIBSON, J. J. (1966). *The senses considered as perceptual systems.* Boston: Houghton Mifflin.

GIBSON, J. J. (1979). *The ecological approach to visual perception*. Boston: Houghton Mifflin.

GICK, M. L., & HOLYOAK, K. J. (1980). Analogical problem solving. *Cognitive Psychology, 12*, 306–355.

GICK, M. L., & HOLYOAK, K. J. (1983). Schema induction and analogical transfer. *Cognitive Psychology, 15*, 1–38.

GIESBRECHT, T., LYNN, S. J., LILIENFELD, S., & MERCKELBACH, H. (2008). Cognitive processes in dissociation: An analysis of core theoretical assumptions. *Psychological Bulletin, 134*, 617–647.

GIGERENZER, G., GAISSMAIER, W., KURZ-MILCKE, E., SCHWARTZ, L., & WOLOSHIN, S. (2007). Helping doctors and patients make sense of health statistics. *Psychological Science in the Public Interest, 8*, 53–96.

GIGERENZER, G., & HOFFRAGE, U. (1995). How to improve Bayesian reasoning without instruction: Frequency formats. *Psychological Review, 102*, 684–704.

GIGERENZER, G., & HOFFRAGE, U. (1999). Overcoming difficulties in Bayesian reasoning: A reply to Lewis and Keren (1999) and Mellers and McGraw (1999). *Psychological Review, 106*, 425–430.

GIGERENZER, G., & HUG, K. (1992). Domain-specific reasoning: Social contracts, cheating and perspective change. *Cognition, 43*, 127–172.

GILBERT, A. (2008). *What the nose knows: The science of smell in everyday life*. New York: Crown Publishing.

GILBERT, D. T. (1989). Thinking lightly about others: Automatic components of the social inference process. In J. S. Uleman & J. A. Bargh (Eds.), *Unintended thought* (pp. 189–211). New York: Guilford.

GILBERT, D. T. (2006). *Stumbling on happiness*. New York: Random House.

GILBERT, D. T., & EBERT, J. E. J. (2002). Decisions and revisions: The affective forecasting of changeable outcomes. *Journal of Personality and Social Psychology, 82*, 503–514.

GILBERT, D. T., & MALONE, P. S. (1995). The correspondence bias. *Psychological Bulletin, 117*, 21–38.

GILBERT, D. T., MOREWEDGE, C. K., RISEN, J. L., & WILSON, T. D. (2004). Looking forward to looking backward: The misprediction of regret. *Psychological Science, 15*, 346–350.

GILBERT, D. T., PINEL, E. C., WILSON, T. D., BLUMBERG, S. J., & WHEATLEY, T. P. (2002). Durability bias in affective forecasting. In T. Gilovich, D. Griffin, & D. Kahneman (Eds.), *Heuristics and biases: The psychology of intuitive judgment* (pp. 292–312). Cambridge: Cambridge University Press.

GILBERT, D. T., & WILSON, T. D. (2007). Prospection: Experiencing the future. *Science, 317*, 1351–1354.

GILBERT, S. J., & SHALLICE, T. (2002). Task switching: A PDP model. *Cognitive Psychology, 44*(3), 297–337.

GILES, J. W., GOPNIK, A., & HEYMAN, G. D. (2002). Source monitoring reduces the suggestibility of preschool children. *Psychological Science, 13*, 288–291.

GILESTRO, G., TUNONI, G., & CIRELLI, C. (2009). Widespread changes in synaptic markers as a function of sleep and wakefulness in *Drosophila*. *Science, 324*, 109–112.

GILHOOLY, K. (1988). *Thinking: Direct, undirected and creative* (2nd ed.). New York: Academic Press.

GILLIGAN, C. (1982). *In a different voice: Psychological theory and women's development*. Cambridge, MA: Harvard University Press.

GILLIGAN, C. (1986). Profile of Carol Gilligan. In S. Scarr, R. A. Weinberg, & A. Levine, *Understanding development* (pp. 488–491). New York: Harcourt Brace Jovanovich.

GILOVICH, T. (1991). *How we know what isn't so*. New York: Free Press.

GILOVICH, T., KELTNER, D., & NISBETT, R. E. (2006). Social psychology. New York: Norton.

GINGERICH, P. D., UL-HAQ, M., VON KOENIGSWALD, W., SANDERS, W. J., SMITH, B. H., ET AL. (2009). New protocetid whale from the middle Eocene of Pakistan: Birth on land, precocial development, and sexual dimorphism. *PLoS ONE, 4*(2), e4366.

GITLIN, M. J. (2001). Treatment-resistant bipolar disorder. *Bulletin of the Menninger Clinic, 65*, 26–40.

GIURFA, M., ZHANG, S., JENETT, A., MENZEL, R., & SRINIVASAN, M. V. (2001). The concepts of "sameness" and "difference" in an insect. *Nature, 410*(6831), 930–933.

GLADUE, B. A., GREEN, R., & HELLMAN, R. E. (1984). Neuroendocrine responses to estrogen and sexual orientation. *Science, 225*, 1496–1498.

GLASER, J., & KIHLSTROM, J. F. (2005). Compensatory automaticity: Unconscious volition is not an oxymoron. In R. Hassin, J. Uleman, & J. Bargh (Eds.), *The new unconscious* (pp. 171–195). New York: Oxford University Press.

GLASS, R. M. (2001). Electroconvulsive therapy: Time to bring it out of the shadows. *Journal of the American Medical Association, 285*(10), 1346–1348.

GLEITMAN, H. (1963). Place-learning. *Scientific American, 209*, 116–122.

GLEITMAN, H. (1971). Forgetting of long-term memories in animals. In W. K. Honig & P. H. R. James (Eds.), *Animal memory* (pp. 2–46). New York: Academic Press.

GLEITMAN, H. (1985). Some trends in the study of cognition. In S. Koch, & D. E. Leary (Eds.), *A century of psychology as science* (pp. 420–436). New York: McGraw-Hill.

GLEITMAN, H. (1990). Some reflections on drama and the dramatic experience. In I. Rock (Ed.), *The legacy of Solomon Asch: Essays in cognition and social psychology*. Hillsdale, NJ: Erlbaum.

GLEITMAN, H., & JONIDES, J. (1976). The cost of categorization in visual search: Incomplete processing of targets and field items. *Perception and Psychophysics, 20*(4), 281–288.

GLEITMAN, L. R. (1986). Biological dispositions to learn language. In W. Demopolous & A. Marras (Eds.), *Language learning and concept acquisition*. Norwood, NJ: Ablex.

GLEITMAN, L. R. (1990). The structural sources of verb meanings. *Language Acquisition, 1*, 3–55.

GLEITMAN, L. R., ARMSTRONG, S. & CONNOLLY, A. (In press). Compositionality and prototype representations. In W. Hintzen & T. Machery (Eds.), *Compositionality*, Vol. III. Oxford, England: Oxford University Press.

GLEITMAN, L. R., CASSIDY, K., PAPAFRAGOU, A., NAPPA, R., & TRUESWELL, J. T. (2005). Hard words. *Journal of Language Learning and Development, 1*(1), 23–64.

GLEITMAN, L. R., & GLEITMAN, H. (1970). *Phrase and paraphrase*. New York: Norton.

GLEITMAN, L. R., & GLEITMAN, H. (1997), What is a language made out of? *Lingua, 100*, 29–55.

GLEITMAN, L. R., GLEITMAN, H., LANDAU, B., & WANNER, E. (1988). Where learning begins: Initial representations for language learning. In F. J. Newmeyer (Ed.), *Linguistics: The Cambridge survey: Vol. 3. Language: Psychological and biological aspects* (pp. 150–193). New York: Cambridge University Press.

GLEITMAN, L. R., GLEITMAN, H., & SHIPLEY, E. F. (1972). The emergence of the child as grammarian. *Cognition, 1*(2), 137–164.

GLEITMAN, L. R., LI, P., PAPAFRAGOU, A., GALLISTEL, C.R., & ABARBINELL, L. (2005). Spatial reasoning and cognition: cross-linguistic studies. Symposium conducted at annual meeting of the Cognitive Science Society, Stresa, Italy.

GLEITMAN, L. R., & PAPAFRAGOU, A. (2004). Language and thought. In R. Morrison & K. Holyoak (Eds.), *Cambridge handbook of thinking and reasoning*. New York: Cambridge University Press.

GLEITMAN, L. R., & WANNER, E. (1982). Language acquisition: The state of the state of the art. In E. Wanner & L. R. Gleitman (Eds.), *Language acquisition: State of the art* (pp. 3–48). New York: Cambridge University Press.

GLICK, I. D., MURRAY, S. R., VASUDEVAN, P., MARDER, S. R., & HU, R. J. (2001). Treatment with atypical antipsychotics: New indications and new populations. *Journal of Psychiatric Research, 35*, 187–191.

GLICK, J. (1975). Cognitive development in cross-cultural perspective. In F. G. Horowitz (Ed.), *Review of child development research: Vol. 4*. Chicago: University of Chicago Press.

GOBET, F., LANE, P. C. R., CROKER, S., CHENG, P. C.-H., JONES, G., OLIVER, I., ET AL. (2001). Chunking mechanisms in human learning. Trends in *Cognitive Science, 5*, 236–243.

GOBET, F., & SIMON, H. A. (1996a). Recall of random and distorted chess positions: Implications for the theory of expertise. *Memory and Cognition, 24*, 493–503.

GOBET, F., & SIMON, H. A. (1996b). The roles of recognition processes and look-ahead search in time-constrained expert problem solving: Evidence from grand-master-level chess. *Psychological Science, 7*, 52–55.

GOBET, F., & SIMON, H. A. (2000). The relative contributions of recognition and search-evaluation processes to high-level chess performance: Reply to Lassiter. *Psychological Science, 11*(2), 174.

GODDEN, D. R., & BADDELEY, A. D. (1975). Context-dependent memory in two natural environments: On land and underwater. *British Journal of Psychology, 66*, 325–332.

GOEBEL, R., KHORRAM-SEFAT, D., MUCKLIN, L., HACKER, H., & SINGER, W. (1998). The constructive nature of vision: Direct evidence from functional magnetic resonance imaging studies of apparent motion and motion imagery. *European Journal of Neuroscience, 10*(5), 1563–1573.

GOEDERT, M., & SPILLANTINI, M. G. (2006). A century of Alzheimer's disease. *Science, 314*(5800), 777–781.

GOFF, D. C., & COYLE, J. T. (2001). The emerging role of glutamate in the pathophysiology and treatment of schizophrenia. *American Journal of Psychiatry, 158,* 1367–1377.

GOFF, P. A., EBERHARDT, J. L., WILLIAMS, M. J., & JACKSON, M. C. (2008). Not yet human: Implicit knowledge, historical dehumanization, and contemporary consequences. *Journal of Personality and Social Psychology, 94,* 292–306.

GOLD, P., CAHILL, L., & WENK, G. (2002). Ginkgo biloba: A cognitive enhancer? *Psychological Science in the Public Interest, 3,* 2–11.

GOLDBERG, E. M., & MORRISON, S. L. (1963). Schizophrenia and social class. *British Journal of Psychiatry, 109,* 785–802.

GOLDBERG, L. R. (1982). From ace to zombie: Some explorations in the language of personality. In C. Spielberger & J. N. Butcher (Eds.), *Advances in personality assessment: Vol. 1.* Hillsdale, NJ: Erlbaum.

GOLDBERG, L. R. (2001). Analyses of Digman's child-personality data: Derivation of Big-Five factor scores from each of six samples. *Journal of Personality, 69,* 709–743.

GOLDEN, T. (1990, April 2). Ill, possibly violent, and no place to go. *New York Times,* pp. A1, B4.

GOLDENTHAL, P., JOHNSTON, R., & KRAUT, R. (1981). Smiling, appeasement and the silent bared-teeth display. *Ethology and Sociobiology, 2,* 127–133.

GOLDIN, P. R, MANBER, T., HAKIMI, S., CANLI, T., & GROSS, J. J. (2009). Neural bases of social anxiety disorder: Emotional reactivity and cognitive regulation during social and physical threat. *Archives of General Psychiatry, 66*(2), 170–180.

GOLDFRIED, M. R., & DAVISON, G. C. (EDS.). (1994). *Clinical behavior therapy.* New York: Wiley.

GOLDIN-MEADOW, S. (2000). Learning with and without a helping hand. In B. Landau, J. Sabini, J. Jonides, & E. L. Newport (Eds.), *Perception, cognition, and language: Essays in honor of Henry and Lila Gleitman* (pp. 121–138). Cambridge, MA: MIT Press.

GOLDIN-MEADOW, S. (2003). *The resilience of language: What gesture creation in deaf children can tell us about how all children learn language.* New York: Psychology Press.

GOLDIN-MEADOW, S., & FELDMAN, H. (1977). The development of language-like communication without a language model. *Science, 197,* 401–403.

GOLDMAN, M. S. BROWN, S. A. & CHRISTIANSEN, B. A. (1987). Expectancy theory: Thinking about drinking. In H. T. Blane, & K. E. Leonard (Eds.), *Psychological theories of drinking and alcoholism* (pp. 181–266). New York: Guilford Press.

GOLDMAN-RAKIC, P. (1987). Development of cortical circuitry and cognitive function. *Child Development, 58,* 601–622.

GOLDMAN-RAKIC, P. (1998). The prefrontal landscape: Implications of functional architecture for understanding human mentation and the central executive. In A. C. Roberts & T. W. Robbins (Eds.), *The prefrontal cortex: Executive and cognitive functions* (pp. 87–102). New York: Oxford University Press.

GOLDSTEIN, E. B. (1999). *Sensation and perception* (5th ed.). Pacific Grove, CA: Brooks-Cole.

GOLDSTONE, R. L., LIPPA, Y., & SHIFFRIN, R. M. (2001). Altering object representations through category learning. *Cognition, 78,* 27–43.

GOLINKOFF, R. M., HIRSH-PASEK, K., CAULEY, K. M., & GORDON, L. (1987). The eyes have it: lexical and syntactic comprehension in a new paradigm. *Journal of Child Language, 14*(1), 23–45.

GOLOMBOK, S., & TASKER, F. (1996). Do parents influence the sexual orientation of their children? Findings from a longitudinal study of lesbian families. *Developmental Psychology, 32*(1), 3–11.

GOMBRICH, E. H. (1961). *Art and illusion.* Princeton, NJ: Bollingen Series, Princeton University Press.

GOMEZ, R. L., BOOTZIN, R. R., & NADEL, L. (2006). Naps promote abstraction in language-learning infants. *Psychological Science, 17,* 670–674.

GOOD, G. E., & SHERROD, N. B. (2001). The psychology of men and masculinity: Research status and future directions. In R. K. Unger (Ed.), *Handbook of the psychology of women and gender* (pp. 201–214). New York: Wiley.

GOODALE, M. A. (1995). The cortical organization of visual perception and visuomotor control. In S. M. Kosslyn & D. Osherson (Eds.), *Visual cognition: An invitation to cognitive science* (2nd ed.). Cambridge, MA: MIT Press.

GOODALE, M. A., & MILNER, A. D. (2004). *Sight unseen.* New York: Oxford University Press.

GOODALE, M. A., MILNER, A. D., JACOBSON, L. S., & CAREY, D. P. (1991). A neurological dissociation between perceiving objects and grasping them. *Nature, 349,* 154–156.

GOODENOUGH, F. L. (1932). Expression of the emotions in a blind-deaf child. *Journal of Abnormal and Social Psychology, 27,* 328–333.

GOODMAN, G. S., GHETTI, S., QUAS, J. A., EDELSTEIN, R. S., ALEXANDER, K. W., REDLICH, A. D., ET AL. (2003). A prospective study of memory for child sexual abuse: New findings relevant to the repressed-memory controversy. *Psychological Science, 14,* 113–118.

GOODWIN, F. K., & JAMISON, K. R. (1990). *Manic depressive illness.* New York: Oxford University Press.

GOOLEY, J. J. & SAPER, C. B. (2005). Anatomy of the mammalian circadian system. In M. H. Kryger, T. Roth, & W. C. Dement (Eds.), *Principles and practice of sleep medicine.* Philadelphia: Elsevier Saunders.

GOPNIK, A. (1999). Theory of mind. In R. A. Wilson & F. C. Keil (Eds.), *The MIT encyclopedia of the cognitive sciences* (pp. 838–841). Cambridge, MA: MIT Press.

GOPNIK, A., & MELTZOFF A. N. (1997). *Words, thoughts and theories.* Cambridge, MA: MIT Press.

GOPNIK, M., & CRAGO, M. B. (1990). Familial aggregation of a developmental language disorder. *Cognition, 39,* 1–50.

GORDON, H. (1923). Mental and scholastic tests among retarded children. *Educational pamphlet,* no. 44. London: Board of Education.

GORDON, P. (2004). The origin of argument structure in infant event representations. In A. Brugos, L. Micciulla, & C. E. Smith (Eds.), *Proceedings of the 28th Annual Boston University Conference on Language Development,* Boston, MA: November 2004 (pp. 189–198). Somerville, MA: Cascadilla Press.

GORDON, R. D. (2006). Selective attention during scene perception: Evidence from negative priming. *Memory & Cognition, 34,* 1484–1494.

GORELICK, D. A., & BALSTER, R. L. (1995). Phencyclidine (PCP). In F. E. Bloom & D. J. Kupfer (Eds.), *Psychopharmacology: The fourth generation of progress* (pp. 1767–1776). New York: Raven Press.

GOREN, C. C., SARTY, M., & WU, P. Y. K. (1975). Visual following and pattern discrimination of face-like stimuli by newborn infants. *Pediatrics, 56,* 544–559.

GOSLING, S. D. (2008). Personality in non-human animals. *Social and Personality Psychology Compass, 2,* 985–1001.

GOSLING, S. D., KO, S. J., MANNARELLI, T., & MORRIS, M. E. (2002). A room with a cue: Personality judgments based on offices and bedrooms. *Journal of Personality and Social Psychology, 82,* 379–398.

GOSLING, S. D., & JOHN, O. P. (1999). Personality dimensions in nonhuman animals: A cross-species review. *Current Directions in Psychological Science, 8,* 69–75.

GOTTESMAN, I. I. (1991). *Schizophrenia genesis: The origins of madness.* New York: Freeman.

GOTTFREDSON, L. S. (1997a). Mainstream science on intelligence: An editorial with 52 signatories, history, and bibliography. *Intelligence, 24,* 13–23.

GOTTFREDSON, L. S. (1997b). Why g matters: The complexity of everyday life. *Intelligence, 24,* 79–132.

GOTTFREDSON, L. S. (2003a). Dissecting practical intelligence theory: Its claims and evidence. *Intelligence, 31,* 343–397.

GOTTFREDSON, L. S. (2003b). On Sternberg's "Reply to Gottfredson." *Intelligence, 31,* 415–424.

GOTTFREDSON, L. S. (2004). Intelligence: Is it the epidemiologists' elusive "fundamental cause" of social class inequalities in health? *Journal of Personality and Social Psychology, 86,* 174–199.

GOTTFREDSON, L. S. (2007). Applying double standards to "divisive" ideas: Commentary on Hunt and Carlson (2007). *Perspective on Psychological Science, 2,* 216–220.

GOULD, J. L. (1990). Honey bee cognition. *Cognition, 37,* 83–103.

GOULD, S. J. (1981). *The mismeasure of man.* New York: Norton.

GOULD, S. J. (1991). Exaptation: A crucial tool for evolutionary psychology. *Journal of Social Issues, 47,* 43–65.

GOULD, S. J., & LEWONTIN, R. C. (1979). The spandrels of San Marco and the Panglossian paradigm: A critique of the adaptationist programme. *Proceedings of the Royal Society of London, 205,* 581–598.

GOULDNER, A. W. (1960). The norm of reciprocity: A preliminary statement. *American Sociological Review, 25,* 161–179.

GOUREVITCH, M. N., & ARNSTEN, J. H. (2005). Medical complications of drug use. In J. H. Lowinson, P. Ruiz, R. B. Millman, & J.G. Langrod (Eds.), *Substance abuse: A comprehensive textbook.* Philadelphia: Lippincott/Williams & Wilkins.

GRAAF, R. DE, BIJL, R. V., SMIT, F., VOLLEBERGH, W. A. M., & SPIJKER, J. (2002). Risk factors for 12-month comorbidity of mood, anxiety, and substance use disorders: Findings from the Netherlands Mental Health Survey and Incidence Study. *American Journal of Psychiatry, 159*, 620–629.

GRAF, P., & MANDLER, G. (1984). Activation makes words more accessible, but not necessarily more retrievable. *Journal of Verbal Learning and Verbal Behavior, 23*, 553–568.

GRAF, P., MANDLER, G., & HADEN, P. (1982). Simulating amnesic symptoms in normal subjects. *Science, 218*, 1243–1244.

GRAF, P., MANDLER, G., & SQUIRE, L. R. (1984). The information that amnesic patients don't forget. *Journal of Experimental Psychology: Learning, Memory, and Cognition, 10*, 164–178.

GRAHAM, C. H., & HSIA, Y. (1954). Luminosity curves for normal and dichromatic subjects including a case of unilateral color blindness. *Science, 120*, 780.

GRAHAM, J.W., MARKS G., & HANSEN, W.B. (1991). Social influence processes affecting adolescent substance use. *Journal of Applied Psychology, 76*, 291–298.

GRAHAM, P. J. (ED.). (1998). *Cognitive-behaviour therapy for children and families.* New York: Cambridge University Press.

GRAINGER, J., REY, A., & DUFAU, S. (2008). Letter perception: From pixels to pandemonium. *Trends in Cognitive Sciences, 12*, 381–387.

GRAMMER, K., FINK, B., MOLLER, A. P., & MANNING, J. T. (2005). Physical attractiveness and health: Comment on Weeden & Sabini (2005). *Psychological Bulletin, 131*, 658–661.

GRAMMER, K., FINK, B., MOLLER, A., & THORNHILL, R. (2003). Darwinian aesthetics: Sexual selection and the biology of beauty. *Biological Reviews, 78*, 385–407.

GRANT, H. M., BREDAHL, L. C., CLAY, J., FERRIE, J., GROVES, J. E., McDORMAN, T.A., ET AL. (1998). Context-dependent memory for meaningful material: Information for students. *Applied Cognitive Psychology, 12*, 617–623.

GRANT, V. W. (1976). *Falling in love.* New York: Springer.

GRAY, C. M., KOENIG, P., ENGEL, A. K., & SINGER, W. (1989). Oscillatory responses in cat visual cortex exhibit inter-columnar synchronization which reflects global stimulus properties. *Nature, 338*(6213), 334–337.

GRAY, J. A. (1994). Three fundamental emotion systems. In P. Ekman & R. J. Davidson (Eds.), *The nature of emotion: Fundamental questions* (pp. 243–247). New York: Oxford University Press.

GRAY, J. R., CHABRIS, C. F., & BRAVER, T. S. (2003). Neural mechanisms of general fluid intelligence. *Nature Neuroscience, 6*, 316–322.

GREEN, D. M. (1976). *An introduction to hearing.* New York: Academic Press.

GREEN, G. D., & CLUNIS, D. M. (1988). Married lesbians. Lesbianism: Affirming nontraditional roles [Special issue]. *Women and Therapy, 8*, 41–49.

GREEN, M. F., KERN, R. S., BRAFF, D. L., & MINTZ, J. (2000). Neurocognitive deficits and functional outcome in schizophrenia: Are we measuring the "right stuff"? *Schizophrenia Bulletin, 26*, 119–136.

GREEN, R. (1979). Childhood cross-gender behavior and subsequent sexual preference. *American Journal of Psychiatry, 136*, 106–108.

GREEN, R. G. (1998). Aggression and antisocial behavior. In D. T. Gilbert, S. T. Fiske, & G. Lindzey, G. (Eds.), *The handbook of social psycology: Vol. 2* (4th ed., pp. 317–356). New York: McGraw Hill.

GREEN, R. L., HOFFMAN, L. T., MORSE, R., HAYES, M. E. B., & MORGAN, R. F. (1964). *The educational status of children in a district without public schools.* Cooperative Research Project No. 23211. Washington, DC: Office of Education. U.S. Department of Health, Education, and Welfare.

GREEN, S. (1975). Variation of vocal pattern with social situation in the Japanese monkey (Macaca fuscata): A field study. In L. A. Rosenblum (Ed.), *Primate behavior* (pp. 1 –102). New York: Academic Press.

GREEN, S. K., BUCHANAN, D. R., & HEUER, S. K. (1984). Winners, losers, and choosers: A field investigation of dating initiation. *Personality and Social Psychology Bulletin, 10*, 502–511.

GREENBERG, D. L. (2004). President Bush's false "flashbulb" memory of 9/11/01. *Applied Cognitive Psychology, 18*(3), 363–370.

GREENBERG, P., SISITSKY, T., KESSLER, R., FINKELSTEIN, S., BERNDT, E., DAVIDSON, J., ET AL. (1999). The economic burden of anxiety disorders in the 1990s. *Journal of Clinical Psychiatry, 60*, 427–435.

GREENE, J., & HAIDT, J. (2002). How (and where) does moral judgment work? *Trends in Cognitive Science, 6*, 517–523.

GREENE, J., SOMMERVILLE, R., NYSTROM, L. DARLEY, J., & COHEN, J. (2001). An fMRI investigation of emotional engagement in moral judgment. *Science, 293*, 2105–2108.

GREENFIELD, P. M. (1966). On culture and conservation. In J. R. Bruner, R. R. Olver, & P. M. Greenfield (Eds.), *Studies in cognitive growth.* New York: Wiley.

GREENFIELD, P. M. (1997). You can't take it with you: Why ability assessments don't cross cultures. *American Psychologist, 52*, 1115–1124.

GREENFIELD, P. M. (2009). Technology and informal education: What is taught, what is learned. *Science, 323*, 69–71.

GREENFIELD, P. M., KELLER, H., FULIGNI, A., & MAYNARD, A. (2003). Cultural pathways through universal development. *Annual Review of Psychology, 54*, 461–490.

GREENWALD, A., SPANGENBERG, E., PRATKANIS, A., & ESKENAZI, J. (1991). Double-blind tests of subliminal self-help audiotapes. *Psychological Science, 2*, 119–122.

GREENWALD, A. G., BANAJI, M. R., RUDMAN, L. A., FARNHAM, S. D., NOSEK, B. A., & MELLOTT, D. S. (2002). A unified theory of implicit attitudes, stereotypes, self-esteem, and self-concept. *Psychological Review, 109*(1), 3–25.

GREENWALD, A. G., McGHEE, D. E., & SCHWARTZ, J. L. K. (1998). Measuring individual differences in implicit cognition: The implicit association test. *Journal of Personality and Social Psychology, 74*(6), 1464–1480.

GREENWALD, A. G., & NOSEK, B. A. (2001). Health of the Implicit Association Test at age 3. *Zeitschrift Fuer Experimentelle Psychologie, 48*(2), 85–93.

GREENWALD, A. G., NOSEK, B. A., & BANAJI, M. R. (2003). Understanding and using the implicit association test: I. An improved scoring algorithm. *Journal of Personality and Social Psychology, 85*, 197–216.

GREGORIOU, G. G., GOTTS, S. J., ZHOU, H., & DESIMONE, R. (2009). High-frequency, long-range coupling between prefrontal and visual cortex during attention. *Science, 324*, 1207–1210.

GREWAL, D., & SALOVEY, P. (2005). Feeling smart: The science of emotional intelligence. *American Scientist, 93*, 330–339.

GRICE, H. P. (1975). Logic and conversation. In P. Cole & J. L. Morgan (Eds.), *Syntax and semantics 3: Speech acts.* New York: Academic Press.

GRIGGS, R. A., & COX, J. R. (1982). The elusive thematic-materials effect in Wason's selection task. *British Journal of Psychology, 73*, 407–420.

GRIMSHAW, J. (1990). *Argument structure.* Cambridge, MA: MIT Press.

GRINSPOON, L., BAKALAR, J. B., & RUSSO, E. (2005). Marihuana: Clinical aspects. In J. H. Lowinson, P. Ruiz, R. B. Millman, & J.G. Langrod (Eds.), *Substance abuse: A comprehensive textbook.* Philadelphia: Lippincott/Williams & Wilkins.

GRODNER, D., & GIBSON, E. (2005). Consequences of the serial nature of linguistic input. *Cognitive Science, 29*, 261–291.

GRODZINSKY, Y., & SANTI, A. (2008). The battle for Broca's region. *Trends in Cognitive Sciences, 12*, 474–480.

GROOP, L. C., & TUOMI, T. (1997). Non-insulin-dependent diabetes mellitus—a collision between thrifty genes and an affluent society. *Annals of Medicine, 29*, 37–53.

GROSS, A. L., & BALLIF, B. (1991). Children's understanding of emotion from facial expressions and situations: A review. *Developmental Review, 11*(4), 368–398.

GROSS, J. J. (1998a). Antecedent- and response-focused emotion regulation: Divergent consequences for experience, expression, and physiology. *Journal of Personality and Social Psychology, 74*, 224–237.

GROSS, J. J. (1998b). The emerging field of emotion regulation: An integrative review. *Review of General Psychology, 2*, 271–299.

GROSS, J. J. (2001). Emotion regulation in adulthood: Timing is everything. *Current Directions in Psychological Science, 10*, 214–219.

GROSS, J. J. (ED.). (2007). *Handbook of emotion regulation.* New York: Guilford.

GROSS, J. J., CARSTENSEN, L. C., PASUPATHI, M., TSAI, J., GOTTESTAM, K., & HSU, A.Y.C. (1997). Emotion and aging: Experience, expression, and control. *Psychology and Aging, 12*, 590–599.

GROSS, J. J., FREDRICKSON, B. F., & LEVENSON, R. W. (1994). The psychophysiology of crying. *Psychophysiology, 31*, 460–468.

GROSS, J. J., & LEVENSON, R. W. (1997). Hiding feelings: The acute effects of inhibiting negative and positive emotion. *Journal of Abnormal Psychology, 106*, 95–103.

GROSS, J. J., RICHARDS, J. M., & JOHN, O. P. (2006). Emotion regulation in everyday life. In D. K. Snyder, J. A. Simpson, & J. N. Hughes (Eds.), *Emotion regulation in families: Pathways to dysfunction and health* (pp. 13–35). Washington, DC: American Psychological Association.

GROTZER, T. A., & PERKINS, D. N. (2000). Teaching intelligence: A performance conception. In R. J. Sternberg (Ed.), *Handbook of intelligence* (pp. 492–515). Cambridge: Cambridge University Press.

GRUBER-BALDINI, A. L., SCHAIE, K. W., & WILLIS, S. L. (1995). Similarity in married couples: A longitudinal study of mental abilities and rigidity-flexibility. *Journal of Personality and Social Psychology, 69,* 191–203.

GRUDNIK, J. L., & KRANZLER, J. H. (2001). Meta-analysis of the relationship between intelligence and inspection time. *Intelligence, 29,* 523–535.

GRÜNBAUM, A. (1996). Is psychoanalysis viable? In W. O'Donohue & R. F. Kitchener (Eds.), *The philosophy of psychology* (pp. 281–290). London: Sage.

GUDYKUNST, W. B., YANG, S. M., & NISHIDA, T. (1987). Cultural differences in self-consciousness and self-monitoring. *Communication Research, 14,* 7–34.

GUESBECK, N. R., HICKEY, M. S., MACDONALD, K. G., PORIES, W. J., HARPER, I., RAVUSSIN, E., ET AL. (2001). Substrate utilization during exercise in formerly morbidly obese women. *Journal of Applied Physiology, 90,* 1007–1012.

GURSKY, J. T., & KRAHN, L. E. (2000). The effects of antidepressants on sleep: A review. *Harvard Review of Psychiatry, 8,* 298–306.

GUTH, W., SCHMITTBERGER, R., & SCHWARZE, B. (1982). An experimental analysis of ultimatum bargaining. *Journal of Economic Behavior and Organizations, 3,* 367–388.

GUTTMANN, N., & KALISH, H. I. (1956). Discriminability and stimulus generalization. *Journal of Experimental Psychology, 51,* 79–88.

HABIB, M., DEMONET, J. F., & FRACKOWIAK, R. (1996). Neuroanatomie cognitive du langage: contribution de l'imagerie fonctionnelle ceʹreʹbrale. *Revue Neurologique, 152,* 249–260.

HACKMAN, D., & FARAH, M. (2009). Socioeconomic status and the developing brain. *Trends in Cognitive Sciences, 13,* 65–73.

HACKMANN, A., CLARK, D. M., & MCMANUS, F. (2000). Recurrent images and early memories in social phobia. *Behaviour Research and Therapy, 38,* 601–610.

HADDAD, P. (1999). Do antidepressants have any potential to cause addiction? *Journal of Psychopharmacology, 13,* 300–307.

HADLEY, S. W., & STRUPP, H. H. (1976). Contemporary accounts of negative effects in psychotherapy: An integrated account. *Archives of General Psychiatry, 33,* 1291–1302.

HAGEN, D. W., & GILBERTSON, L. G. (1972). Geographic variation and environmental selection in *Gasterosteus aculeatus L.* in the Paci?c Northwest, America. *Evolution, 26,* 32–51.

HAGGARD, P. (2009). The sources of human volition. *Science, 324,* 731–733.

HAGGARD, P., & EIMER, M. (1999). On the relation between brain potentials and conscious awareness. *Experimental Brain Research, 126,* 128–133.

HAIDT, J. (2006). *The happiness hypothesis: Finding modern truth in ancient wisdom.* New York: Basic Books.

HAIER, R., SIEGEL, B., NUECHTERLEIN, K., HAZLETT, E., WU, J. PAEK, ET AL. (1988). Cortical glucose metabolic rate correlates of abstract reasoning and attention studid with positron emission tomography. *Intelligence, 12,* 199–217.

HALBERSTADT, J., & RHODES, G. (2000). The attractiveness of nonface averages: Implications for an evolutionary explanation of the attractiveness of average faces. *Psychological Science, 11,* 285–289.

HALARI, R., HINES, M., KUMARI, V., MEHROTRA, R., WHEELER, M., NG, V., ET AL. (2005). Sex differences and individual differences in cognitive performance and their relationship to endogenous gonadal hormones and gonadotrophins. *Behavioral Neuroscience, 119,* 104–117.

HALL, C. S., & VAN DE CASTLE, R. (1966). *The content analysis of dreams.* New York: Appleton-Century-Crofts.

HALL C. S., DOMHOFF, G. W., BLICK, K.A., WEESNER, K. E. (1982). The dreams of college men and women in 1950 and 1980: A comparison of dream contents and sex differences. *Sleep, 5,* 188–194.

HALL, C. S. (1966). *The meaning of dreams.* New York: McGraw-Hill.

HALL, D. G., QUANTZ, D. H., PERSONAGE, K. A., ET AL. (2000). Preschoolers' use of form class cues in word learning. *Developmental Psychology, 36*(4), 449–462.

HALPERN, D. (1992). *Sex differences in cognitive abilities* (2nd ed.). Hillsdale, NJ: Erlbaum.

HALPERN, D. (2000). *Sex differences in cognitive abilities* (3rd ed.). Mahwah, NJ: Erlbaum.

HALPERN, D., BENBOW, C., GEARY, D., GUR, R. C., HYDE, J., & GERNSBACHER, M. (2007). The science of sex differences in science and mathematics. *Psychological Science in the Public Interest, 8,* 1–51.

HAMANN, S. (2001). Cognitive and neural mechanisms of emotional memory. *Trends in Cognitive Sciences, 5,* 394–400.

HAMBRICK, D. Z. (2005). The role of domain knowledge in higher-level cognition. In O. Wilhelm & R. Engle (Eds.), *Handbook of understanding and measuring intelligence* (pp. 361–372). Thousand Oaks, CA: Sage.

HAMBURG, D. A., MOOS, R. H., & YALOM, I. D. (1968). Studies of distress in the menstrual cycle and the post-partum period. In R. P. Michael (Ed.), *Endocrinology and human behavior* (pp. 94–116). London: Oxford University Press.

HAMILL, R., WILSON, T. D., & NISBETT, R. E. (1980). Insensitivity to sample bias: Generalizing from atypical cases. *Journal of Personality and Social Psychology, 39,* 578–589.

HAMILTON, C. (2000). Continuity and discontinuity of attachment from infancy through adolescence. *Child Development, 71,* 690–694.

HAMILTON, D. L., & ROSE, T. L. (1980). Illusory correlation and the maintenance of stereotypic beliefs. *Journal of Personality and Social Psychology, 39,* 832–845.

HAN, J.-H., KUSHNER, S., YIU, A., HSIANG, H.-L., BUCH, T., WAISMAN, A., ET AL. (2009). Selective erasure of a fear memory. *Science, 323,* 1492–1496.

HANDELSMAN, J., CANTOR, N., CARNES, M., DENTON, D., FINE, E., GROSZ, B., ET AL. (2005). More women in science. *Science, 309,* 1190–1191.

HANEY, C., & ZIMBARDO, P. (1998). The past and future of U.S. prison policy: Twenty-five years after the Stanford Prison Experiment. *American Psychologist, 53*(7), 709–727.

HANEY, C., BANKS, C., & ZIMBARDO, P. (1973). Interpersonal dynamics in a simulated prison. *International Journal of Criminology and Penology, 1*(1), 69–97.

HANNON, B., & DANEMAN, M. (2001). A new tool for measuring and understanding individual differences in the component processes of reading comprehension. *Journal of Educational Psychology, 93,* 103–128.

HANSEN, N. B., LAMBERT, M. J., & FORMAN, E. M. (2002). The psychotherapy dose-response effect and its implications for treatment delivery services. *Clinical Psychology: Science & Practice, 9*(3), 329–343.

HAPPÉ, F., BROWNELL, H., & WINNER, E. (1999). Acquired "theory of mind" impairments following stroke. *Cognition, 70,* 211–240.

HARE, R. D., COOKE, D. J., & HART, S. D. (1999). Psychopathy and sadistic personality disorder. In T. B. P. Millon (Ed.), *Oxford textbook of psychopathology* (pp. 555–584). Oxford, England: Oxford University Press.

HAREVEN, T. K. (1978). The last stage: Historical adulthood and old age. In E. H. Erikson (Ed.), *Adulthood* (pp. 201–216). New York: Norton.

HARKINS, S. G., & SZYMANSKI, K. (1989). Social loafing and group evaluation. *Journal of Personality and Social Psychology, 56*(6), 934–941.

HARLEY, T. A., & BOWN, H. E. (1998). What causes a tip-of-the-tongue state? Evidence for lexical neighbourhood effects in speech production. *British Journal of Psychology, 89,* 151–174.

HARLOW, H. F. (1958). The nature of love. *American Psychologist, 13,* 673–685.

HARLOW, H. F. (1962). The heterosexual affectional system in monkeys. *American Psychologist, 17,* 1–9.

HARLOW, H. F., & HARLOW, M. K. (1972). The young monkeys. In *Readings in psychology today* (2nd ed.). Del Mar, CA: CRM Books.

HARLOW, H. F., & NOVAK, M. A. (1973). Psychopathological perspectives. *Perspectives in Biology and Medicine, 16,* 461–478.

HARMON-JONES, E., & MILLS, J. (1999). *Cognitive dissonance: Progress on a pivotal theory in social psychology.* Washington, DC: American Psychological Association.

HARRIS, C. R. (2002). Sexual and romantic jealousy in heterosexual and homosexual adults. *Psychological Science, 13,* 7–12.

HARRIS, G. W., & MICHAEL, R. P. (1964). The activation of sexual behavior by hypothalamic implants of estrogen. *Journal of Physiology, 171,* 275–301.

HARRIS, J. R. (1995). Where is the child's environment? A group socialization theory of development. *Psychological Review, 102,* 458–489.

HARRIS, J. R. (1998). *The nurture assumption: Why children turn out the way they do.* New York: Free Press.

HARRIS, J. R. (2000). Socialization, personality development and the child's environments: A comment on Vandell (2000). *Developmental Psychology, 36,* 711–723.

HARRIS, M. J., & ROSENTHAL, R. (1985). Mediation of interpersonal expectancy effects: 31 meta-analyses. *Psychological Bulletin, 97,* 363–386.

HARRIS, P. (1989). *Children and emotion.* Oxford, England: Blackwell.

HARRIS, P., GUZ, G., LIPIAN, M., & MAN-SHU, Z. (1985). Insight into the time course of emotion among Western and Chinese children. *Child Development, 56,* 972–988.

HARRIS, P. L. (1987). The development of search. In P. Salapatek & L. Cohen (Eds.), *Handbook of infant perception* (pp. 155–208). New York: Academic Press.

HARRIS, Z. (1951). *Methods in structural linguistics.* Chicago: Chicago University Press.

HART, C., KSIR, C., & RAY, O. (2009). *Drugs, society, and human behavior,* 13th ed. New York: McGraw-Hill.

HART, C., NEWELL, L., & OLSEN, S. (2003). Parenting skills and social-communicative competence in childhood. In J. Green & B. Burleson (Eds.), *Handbook of communication and social interaction skills* (pp. 753–800). Mahwah, NJ: Erlbaum.

HART, D., & CHMIEL, S. (1992). Influence of defense mechanisms on moral judgment development: A longitudinal study. *Developmental Psychology, 28*(4), 722–730.

HART, D., & FEGLEY, S. (1995). Prosocial behavior and caring in adolescence: Relations to self-understanding and social judgment. *Child Development, 66*(5), 1346–1359.

HART, D., LUCCA-IRIZARRY, N., & DAMON, W. (1986). The development of self-understanding in Puerto Rico and the United States. *Journal of Early Adolescence, 6,* 293–304.

HARTER, S. (1990). Causes, correlates and the functional role of global self-worth: A life span perspective. In R. J. Sternberg & J. Kolligan (Eds.), *Competence considered* (pp. 67–97). New Haven, CT: Yale University Press.

HARTMANN, H. (1964). *Essays on ego psychology: Selected problems in psychoanalytic theory.* New York: International Universities Press.

HARTRUP, W. (1996). The company they keep: Friendships and their developmental significance. *Child Development, 67,* 1–13.

HARTSHORNE, H., & MAY, M. A. (1928). *Studies in the nature of character: Vol. 1.* New York: Macmillan.

HARVEY, L. O., JR., & LEIBOWITZ, H. (1967). Effects of exposure duration, cue reduction, and temporary monocularity on size matching at short distances. *Journal of the Optical Society of America, 57,* 249–253.

HASSELMO, M. E. (1999). Neuromodulation: Acetylcholine and memory consolidation. *Trends in Cognitive Science, 6,* 351–359.

HATFIELD, E. (1988). Passionate and companionate love. In R. J. Sternberg & M. L. Barnes (Eds.), *The psychology of love.* New Haven, CT: Yale University Press.

HATTEN, M. E. (2002). New directions in neuronal migration. *Science, 297,* 1660–1663.

HAURI, P. (1977). *The sleep disorders.* Kalamazoo, MI: Upjohn Pharmaceuticals.

HAUSER, M. (1996). *The evolution of commmunication.* Cambridge, MA: MIT Press.

HAY, P., SACHDEV, P., CUMMING, S., SMITH, J. S., LEE, T., KITCHENER, P., ET AL. (1993). Treatment of obsessive-compulsive disorder by psychosurgery. *Acta Psychiatrica Scandinavica, 87,* 197–207.

HAYES, J. (1985). Three problems in teaching general skills. In S. Chipman, J. Segal, & R. Glaser (Eds.), *Thinking and learning skills* (pp. 391–406). Hillsdale, NJ: Erlbaum.

HAYNES, J.-D. (2009). Decoding visual consciousness from human brain signals. *Trends in Cognitive Sciences, 13,* 194–202.

HAYWARD, W. G., & TARR, M. J. (1995). Spatial language and spatial representation. *Cognition, 55,* 39–84.

HEALY, A. F., & MILLER, G. A. (1970). The verb as the main determinant of sentence meaning. *Psychonomic Science, 20,* 372.

HEATHERTON, T. F., WYLAND, C. L., MACRAE, C. N., DEMOS, K. E., DENNY, B. T., & KELLEY, M. W. (2006). Medial prefrontal activity differentiates self from close others. *Social Cognitive and Affective Neuroscience, 1,* 18–25.

HECKERS, S. (1997). Neuropathology of schizophrenia: Cortex, thalamus, basal ganglia, and neurotransmitter-specific projection systems. *Schizophrenia Bulletin, 23,* 403–421.

HECKMAN, J. J. (2006). Skill formation and the economics of investing in disadvantaged children. *Science, 312,* 1900–1902.

HEDGES, L. V., & NOWELL, A. (1995). Sex differences in mental test scores, variability, and numbers of high-scoring individuals. *Science, 269,* 41–45.

HEIDER, E. R. (1972). Universals in color naming and memory. *Journal of Experimental Psychology, 93,* 1–20.

HEIDER, F. (1958). *The psychology of interpersonal relationships.* New York: Wiley.

HEIM, C., OWENS, M. J., PLOTSKY, P. M., & NEMEROFF, C. B. (1997). Endocrine factors in the pathophysiology of mental disorders. *Psychopharmacology Bulletin, 33,* 185–192.

HEINE, S. J. (2005). Constructing good selves in Japan and North America. In R. M. Sorrentino, M. Richard, D. Cohen, J. M. Olson, & M. P. Zanna (Eds.), *Culture and social behavior: The Tenth Ontario Symposium* (pp. 115–143). Hillsdale, NJ: Erlbaum.

HEINE, S. J. (2008). *Cultural psychology.* New York: Norton.

HEINE, S. J., BUCHTEL, E., & NORENZAYAN, A. (2008). What do cross-national comparisons of self-reported personality traits tell us? The case of conscientiousness. *Psychological Science, 19,* 309–313.

HEINE, S. J., KITAYAMA, S., LEHMAN, D. R., TAKATA, T., IDE, E., LEUNG, C., ET AL. (2001). Divergent consequences of success and failure in Japan and North America: An investigation of self-improving motivations and malleable selves. *Journal of Personality and Social Psychology, 81,* 599–615.

HEINE, S. J., & LEHMAN, D. R. (1997). The cultural construction of self-enhancement: An examination of group-serving biases. *Journal of Personality and Social Psychology, 72,* 1268–1283.

HELD, J. D., ALDERTON, D. L., FOLEY, P. P., & SEGALL, D. O. (1993). Arithmetic reasoning gender differences: Explanations found in the Armed Services Vocational Aptitude Battery (ASVAB). *Learning and Individual Differences, 5,* 171–186.

HELLSTROM, K., FELLENIUS, J, & OST, L. G. (1996). One versus five sessions of applied tension in the treatment of blood phobia. *Behaviour Research and Therapy, 34,* 101–112.

HELMHOLTZ, H. (1909). *Wissenschaftliche Abhandlungen, II* (pp. 764–843). Leipzig: Barth.

HEMPHILL, J. F., HARE, R. D., & WONG, S. (1998). Psychopathy and recidivism: A review. *Legal and Criminological Psychology, 3,* 139–170.

HENDERLONG, J., & LEPPER, M. R. (2002). The effects of praise on children's intrinsic motivation: A review and synthesis. *Psychological Bulletin, 128*(5), 774–795.

HENDRY, D. P. (ED.). (1969). *Conditioned reinforcement.* Homeward, IL: Dorsey Press.

HENRY, P. J., & HARDIN, C. D. (2006). The contact hypothesis revisited: Status bias in the reduction of implicit prejudice in the United States and Lebanon. *Psychological Science, 17*(10), 862–868.

HENRY, P. J., STERNBERG, R. J., & GRIGORENKO, E. (2005). Capturing successful intelligence through measures of analytic, creative, and practical skills. In O. Wilhelm & R. Engle (Eds.), *Understanding and measuring intelligence* (pp. 295–311). Thousand Oaks, CA: Sage.

HENSS, R. (2000). Waist-to-hip ratio and female attractiveness. Evidence from photographic stimuli and methodological considerations. *Personality and Individual Differences, 28,* 501–513.

HERBERT, A., GERRY, N. P., MCQUEEN, M., HEID, I. M., PFEUFER, A., ILLIG, T., ET AL. (2006). A common genetic variant is associated with adult and childhood obesity. *Science 312,* 279–283.

HERDT, G., & MCCLINTOCK, M. (2000). The magical age of 10. *Archives of Sexual Behavior, 29*(6), 587–606.

HERMAN, L., & UYEYAMA, R. (1999). The dolphin's grammatical competency: Comments on Kako (1999). *Animal Learning & Behavior, 27,* 18–23.

HERMANN, D., & YODER, C. (1998). The potential effects of the implanted memory paradigm on child subjects. *Applied Cognitive Psychology, 12*(3), 198–206.

HERMANUSSEN, M. (1998). The analysis of short-term growth. *Hormone Research, 49,* 53–64.

HERNESS, M., & GILBERTSON, T. (1999). Cellular mechanisms of taste transduction. *Annual Review of Physiology, 61,* 837–900.

HERR, S. S. (1990). The law on aversive and nonaversive behavioral intervention. In S. L. Harris & J. S. Handleman (Eds.), *Aversive and nonaversive interventions: Controlling life-threatening behavior by the developmentally disabled* (pp. 80–118). New York: Springer.

HERRNSTEIN, R. J. (1979). Acquisition, generalization, and discrimination reversal of a natural concept. *Journal of*

Experimental Psychology: Animal Behavior Processes, 5, 118–129.

HERRNSTEIN, R. J., LOVELAND, D. H., & CABLE, C. (1976). Natural concepts in pigeons. *Journal of Experimental Psychology: Animal Behavior Processes, 2,* 285–311.

HERRNSTEIN, R. J., & MURRAY, C. A. (1994). *The bell curve: Intelligence and class structure in American life.* Cambridge, MA: Free Press.

HERRNSTEIN, R. J., NICKERSON, R. S., DE SANCHEZ, M., & SWETS, J. A. (1986). Teaching thinking skills. *American Psychologist, 41,* 1279–1289.

HERTZOG, C., KRAMER, A., WILSON, R., & LINDENBERGER, U. (2009). Enrichment effects on adult cognitive development: Can the functional capacity of older adults be preserved and enhanced? *Psychological Science in the Public Interest, 9,* 1–65.

HESPOS, S. J., & BAILLARGEON, R. (2001a). Infants' knowledge about occlusion and containment events: A surprising discrepancy. *Psychological Science, 12,* 141–147.

HESPOS, S. J., & BAILLARGEON, R. (2001b). Reasoning about containment events in very young infants. *Cognition, 78,* 207–245.

HESPOS, S. J., & SPELKE, E. S. (2004). Conceptual precursors to spatial language. *Nature, 430,* 453–456.

HESS, E. H. (1959). Imprinting. *Science, 130,* 133–141.

HESS, E. H. (1973). *Imprinting: Early experience and the developmental psychobiology of attachment.* New York: Van Nostrand.

HETHERINGTON, E. M., BRIDGES, M., & INSABELLA, G. M. (1998). What matters? What does not? Five perspectives on the association between marital transitions and children's adjustment. *American Psychologist, 53*(2), 167–184.

HETTEMA, J. M., NEALE, M. C., & KENDLER, K. S. (2001). A review and meta-analysis of the genetic epidemiology of anxiety disorders. *American Journal of Psychiatry, 158,* 1568–1578.

HEWSTONE, M., RUBIN, M., & WILLIS, H. (2002). Intergroup bias. *Annual Review of Psychology, 53,* 575–604.

HIER, D. B., & CROWLEY, W. F. (1982). Spatial ability in androgen-deficient men. *New England Journal of Medicine, 306,* 1202–1205.

HIGBEE, K. L. (1977). *Your memory: How it works and how to improve it.* Englewood Cliffs, NJ: Prentice-Hall.

HIGGINS, E. T. (1997). Beyond pleasure and pain. *American Psychologist, 52,* 1280–1300.

HIGGINS, J., WILLIAMS, R., & MCLAUGHLIN, T. (2001). The effects of a token economy employing instructional consequences for a third-grade student with learning disabilities: A data-based cast study. *Education and Treatment of Children, 24,* 99–106.

HIGGINS, R., SNYDER, C. R., & BERGLAS, S. (EDS.). (1990). *Self-handicapping: The paradox that isn't.* New York: Plenum Press.

HILGARD, E. R. (1986). *Divided consciousness: Multiple controls in human thought and action* (rev. ed.). New York: Wiley.

HILGARD, E. R. (1992). Dissociation and theories of hypnosis. In E. Fromm & M. R. Nash (Eds.), *Contemporary hypnosis research.* New York: Guilford.

HILGARD, E. R., & HILGARD, J. R. (1975). *Hypnosis in the relief of pain.* Los Altos, CA: Kaufmann.

HILL, A. L. (1978). Savants: Mentally retarded individuals with specific skills. In N. R. Ellis (Ed.), *International review of research in mental retardation: Vol. 9.* New York: Academic Press.

HILL, C. T., RUBIN, L., & PEPLAU, L. A. (1976). Breakups before marriage: The end of 103 affairs. *Journal of Social Issues, 32,* 147–168.

HILTS, P. J. (1995). *Memory's ghost: The strange tale of Mr. M and the nature of memory.* New York: Simon and Schuster.

HINELINE, P. N., & RACHLIN, H. (1969). Escape and avoidance of shock by pigeons pecking a key. *Journal of the Experimental Analysis of Behavior, 12,* 533–538.

HINES, M. (1990). Gonadal hormones and human cognitive development. In J. Balthazar (Ed.), *Hormones, brains, and behaviors in vertebrates 1. Sexual differentiation neuroanatomical aspects, neurotransmitters, and neuropeptides l.* Basel: Karger.

HINES, M. (2004). Androgen, estrogen, and gender: Contributions of the early hormone environment to gender-related behavior. In A. Eagly, A. Beall, & R. J. Sternberg (Eds.), *The psychology of gender* (2nd ed., pp. 9–37). New York: Guilford.

HINES, M., BROOK, C., & CONWAY, G. (2004). Psychosexual development: Core gender identity, sexual orientation and recalled childhood gender role behavior in women and men with congenital adrenal hyperplasia (CAH). *Journal of Sex Research, 1,* 75–81.

HINES, M., FANE, B., PASTERSKI, V., MATHEWS, G., CONWAY, G., & BROOKS, C. (2003). Spatial abilities following prenatal androgen abnormality: Targeting and mental rotations performance in individuals with congenital adrenal hyperplasia. *Psychoneuroendocrinology, 28,* 1010–1026.

HINSHAW, S. P. (2007). *The mark of shame: Stigma of mental illness and an agenda for change.* New York: Oxford University Press.

HINSHAW, S. P. (2008). Childhood ADHD: Biological reality or social construction, with policy implications. In J. D. Berrick & N. Gilbert (Eds.), *Raising children; emerging needs, modern risks, and social responses* (pp. 167–182). New York: Oxford University Press.

HINTZMAN, D. L. (1990). Human learning and memory: Connections and dissociations. *Annual Review of Psychology, 41,* 109–139.

HIRSCHFELD, R. M. A., & GOODWIN, F. K. (1988). Mood disorders. In J. A. Talbott, R. E. Hales, & S. C. Yudosfsky (Eds.), *The American Psychiatric Press textbook of psychiatry: Vol. 7.* Washington, DC: American Psychiatric Press.

HIRSH-PASEK, K., GLEITMAN, L., & GLEITMAN, H. (1978), What did the brain say to the mind? A study of the detection and report of ambiguity by young children. In A. Sicnlair, R. Jaravella, & W.J.M Levelt (Eds.), *The child's conception of language.* New York: Springer-Verlag.

HIRSH-PASEK, K., & GOLINKOFF, R. (1996). *The origins of grammar: Evidence from early language comprehension.* Cambridge, MA: MIT Press.

HIRSH-PASEK, K., GOLINKOFF, R., FLETCHER, A., DeGASPE-BEAUBIEN, F., & CAULEY, K. (1985, October). In the beginning: One-word speakers comprehend word order. Paper presented at Boston Child Language Conference, Boston, MA.

HIRST, W., PHELPS, E., BUCKNER, R., BUDSON, A., CUC, A., GABRIELI, J., ET AL. (2009). Long-term memory for the terrorist attack of September 11: Flashbulb memories, event memories, and the factors that influence their retention. *Journal of Experimental Psychology: General, 138,* 161–176.

HOBSON, J. A. (1995). *Sleep.* New York: Scientific American Library.

HOBSON, J. A. (2002). *Dreaming: An introduction to the science of sleep.* New York: Oxford University Press.

HODGES, B., & GEYER, A. L. (2006). A nonconformist account of the Asch experiments: Values, pragmatics, and moral dilemmas. *Personality and Social Psychology Review, 10,* 2–19.

HODGES, E. V. E., MALONE, M. J., & PERRY, D. G. (1997). Individual risk and social risk as interacting determinants of victimization in the peer group. *Developmental Psychology, 33*(6), 1032–1039.

HOEBEL, B. G., & TEITELBAUM, P. (1976). Weight regulation in normal and hyperphagic rats. *Journal of Physiological and Comparative Psychology, 61,* 189–193.

HOFF-GINSBERG, E., & TARDIF, T. (1995). Socioeconomic status and parenting. In M. H. Bornstein (Ed.), *Handbook of parenting: Vol. 2. Biology and ecology of parenting* (pp. 161–188). Hillsdale, NJ: Erlbaum.

HOFFMAN, M. (2000). *Empathy and moral development: Implications for caring and justice.* New York: Cambridge University Press.

HOFFMAN, M. L. (1970). Moral development. In P. H. Mussen (Ed.), *Carmichael's manual of child psychology* (3rd. ed., vol. 2, pp. 457–558). New York: Wiley.

HOFFMAN, M. L. (1977a). Empathy, its development and prosocial implications. In C. B. Keasey (Ed.), *Nebraska Symposium on Motivation, 25,* 169–217.

HOFFMAN, M. L. (1977b). Sex differences in empathy and related behaviors. *Psychological Bulletin, 84,* 712–722.

HOFFMAN, M. L. (1979). Development of moral thought, feeling, and behavior. *American Psychologist, 34,* 295–318.

HOFFMAN, M. L. (1984). Empathy, its limitations, and its role in a comprehensive moral theory. In W. M. Kurtines & L. Gewirtz (Eds.), *Morality, moral behavior, and moral development* (pp. 283–302). New York: Wiley.

HOFSTEDE, G. (2001). *Culture's consequences: Comparing values, behaviors, institutions, and organizations across nations* (2nd ed.). Thousand Oaks, CA: Sage.

HOFSTEDE, G., & MCCRAE, R. R. (2004). Personality and culture revisited: Linking traits and dimensions of culture. *Cross-Cultural Research: The Journal of Comparative Social Science, 38*(1), 52–88.

HOGARTY, G. E., FLESHER, S., ULRICH, R., CARTER, M., GREENWALD, D., POGUE-GEILE, M., ET AL. (2004). Cognitive enhancement therapy for schizophrenia: Effects of a 2-year randomized trial on cognition and behavior. *Archives of General Psychiatry, 61,* 866–876.

HOLDEN, C. (2003a) The practical benefits of general intelligence. *Science, 299,* 192–93.

HOLDEN, C. (2003b). Psychiatric drugs: Excited by glutamate. *Science, 300,* 1866–1868.

HOLDEN, C. (2008a). Bipolar disorder: Poles apart. *Science, 321*(5886), 193–195.

HOLDEN, C. (2008b). Parsing the genetics of behavior. *Science, 322*(5903), 892–895.

HOLLAND, J. H., HOLYOAK, K. F., NISBETT, R. E., & THAGARD, P. R. (1986). *Induction*. Cambridge, MA: MIT Press.

HOLLAND, P. (1984). Origins of behavior in Pavlovian conditioning. *Psychology of Learning and Motivation, 18,* 129–174.

HOLLANDER, E., & McCARLEY, A. (1992). Yohimbine treatment of sexual side effects induced by serotonin reuptake blockers. *Journal of Clinical Psychiatry, 53,* 197–199.

HOLLANDER, E. P. (1985). Leadership and power. In G. Lindzey & E. Aronson (Eds.), *Handbook of social psychology: Vol. 2* (3rd ed.). New York: Random House.

HOLLINGSHEAD, A. B., & REDLICH, F. C. (1958). *Social class and mental illness: A community study.* New York: Wiley.

HOLLIS, K. L. (1984). The biological function of Pavlovian conditioning: The best defense is a good offense. *Journal of Experimental Psychology: Animal Learning and Behavior, 10,* 413–425.

HOLLISTER, L. E., & CSERNANSKY, J. G. (1990). *Clinical pharmacology of psychotherapeutic drugs* (3rd. ed.). New York: Churchill-Livingstone.

HOLLON, S. D., & BECK, A. T. (2004). Cognitive and cognitive behavioral therapies. In M. J. Lambert (Ed.), *Garfield and Bergin's handbook of psychotherapy and behavior change: An empirical analysis* (5th ed., pp. 447–492). New York: Wiley.

HOLLON, S. D., & FAWCETT, J. (1995). Combined medication and psychotherapy. In G. O. Gabbard (Ed.), *Treatments of psychiatric disorders, Vol. 1* (2nd ed., pp. 1221–1236). Washington, DC: American Psychiatric Press.

HOLLON, S. D., STEWART, M. O., & STRUNK, D. (2006). Enduring effects for cognitive behavior therapy in the treatment of depression and anxiety. *Annual Review of Psychology, 57,* 285–315.

HOLLON, S. D., THASE, M. E., & MARKOWITZ, J. C. (2002). Treatment and prevention of depression. *Psychological Science in the Public Interest, 3,* 39–77.

HOLLOS, M., & RICHARDS, F. A. (1993). Gender-associated development of formal operations in Nigerian adolescents. *Ethos, 21*(1), 24–52.

HOLM, K. H., CICCHETTI, F., BJÖRKLUND, L., BOONMAN, Z., TANDON, P., COSTANTINI, L. C., ET AL. (2001). Enhanced axonal growth from fetal human bcl-2 transgenic mouse dopamine neurons transplanted to the adult rat striatum. *Neuroscience 104,* 397–405.

HOLMES, D. (1990). The evidence for repression: An examination of sixty years of research. In J. Singer (Ed.), *Repression and dissociation: Implications for personality theory, psychopathology, and health* (pp. 85–102). Chicago: University of Chicago Press.

HOLTZMAN, P. S., KRINGLEN, E., MALTHYSSE, S., FLANAGAN, S. D., LIPTON, R. B., CRAMER, G., ET AL. (1988). A single dominant gene can account for eye tracking dysfunctions and schizophrenia in offspring of discordant twins. *Archives of General Psychiatry, 45,* 641–647.

HOLWAY, A. F., & BORING, E. G. (1947). Determinants of apparent visual size with distance variant. *American Journal of Psychology, 54,* 21–37.

HÖNEKOPP, J. (2006). Once more: Is beauty in the eye of the beholder? Relative contributions of private and shared taste to judgments of facial attractiveness. *Journal of Experimental Psychology: Human Perception and Performance, 32,* 199–209.

HONG, Y.-y., CHIU, C. Y., & DWECK, C. S. (1997). Lay dispositionism and implicit theories of personality. *Journal of Personality and Social Psychology, 73,* 19–30.

HONG, Y.-y., CHIU, C. Y., DWECK, C. S., & SACKS, R. (1997). Implicit theories and evaluative processes in person cognition. *Journal of Experimental Social Psychology, 33,* 296–323.

HOOK, S. (1955). *The hero in history.* Boston: Beacon Press.

HOOLEY, J. (2004). Do psychiatric patients do better clinically if they live with certain kinds of families? *Current Directions in Psychological Science, 13,* 202–205.

HOOLEY, J. M. (1985). Expressed emotion: A review of the critical literature. *Clinical Psychology Review, 5,* 119–139.

HOOLEY, J. M., GRUBER, S. A., SCOTT, L. A., HILLER, J. B., & YURGELUN-TODD, D. A. (2005). Activation in dorsolateral prefrontal cortex in response to maternal criticism and praise in recovered depressed and healthy control participants. *Biological Psychiatry, 57,* 809–812.

HORN, J. L. (1985). Remodeling old models of intelligence. In B. B. Wolman (Ed.), *Handbook of intelligence: Theories, measurements, and applications* (pp. 267–300). New York: Wiley.

HORN, J. L., & BLANKSON, N. (2005). Foundations for better understanding of cognitive abilities. In D. Flanagan & P. Harrison (Eds.), *Contemporary intellectual assessment: Theories, tests, and issues* (2nd ed., pp. 41–68). New York: Guilford.

HORN, J. L., & NOLL, J. (1994). A system for understanding cognitive capabilities: A theory and the evidence on which it is based. In D. K. Detterman (Ed.), *Current topics in human intelligence: Vol. 4. Theories of intelligence.* Norwood, NJ: Ablex.

HORVATH, A. O., & LUBORSKY, L. (1993). The role of the therapeutic alliance in psychotherapy. *Journal of Consulting and Clinical Psychology, 61,* 561–573.

HOSHINO-BROWNE, E., ZANNA, A. S., SPENCER, S. J., & ZANNA, M. P. (2004). Investigating attitudes cross-culturally: A case of cognitive dissonance among East Asians and North Americans. In G. R. Maio & G. Haddock (Eds.), *Contemporary perspectives on the psychology of attitudes: The Cardiff Symposium.* East Sussex, England: Psychology Press.

HOSKEN, D. J. (2001). Size and fluctuating asymmetry in sexually selected traits. *Animal Behaviour, 62,* 603–605.

HOVLAND, C. I., & WEISS, W. (1952). The influence of source credibility on communication effectiveness. *Public Opinion Quarterly, 15,* 635–650.

HOWARD, K. I., KRAUSE, M. S., SAUNDERS, S. M., & KOPTA, S. M. (1997). Trials and tribulations in the meta-analysis of treatment differences: Comments on Wampold et al. (1997). *Psychological Bulletin, 122,* 221–225.

HOWES, C. (1990). Can the age of entry into child care and the quality of child care predict adjustment in kindergarten? *Developmental Psychology, 26,* 292–303.

HOWES, C. (1996). The earliest friendships. In W. Bukowski, A. Newcomb, & W. Hartrup (Eds.), *The company they keep: Friendships in childhood and adolescence* (pp. 66–86). New York: Cambridge University Press.

HRDY, S. B., & WILLIAMS, G. C. (1983). Behavioral biology and the double standard. In S. K. Wasser (Ed.), *The social behavior of female vertebrates* (pp. 3–17). New York: Academic Press.

HROBJARTSSON, A., & GOTZSCHE, P. C. (2001). Is the placebo powerless? An analysis of clinical trials comparing placebo with no treatment. *New England Journal of Medicine, 344,* 1594–1602.

HSU, L.K.G. (1990). *Eating disorders.* New York: Guilford.

HUANG, M. P., & ALESSI, N. E. (1996). The Internet and the future of psychiatry. *American Journal of Psychiatry, 153,* 861–869.

HUBEL, D. H., & WIESEL, T. N. (1959). Receptive fields of single neurons in the cat's visual cortex. *Journal of Physiology, 148,* 574–591.

HUBEL, D. H., & WIESEL, T. N. (1968). Receptive fields and functional architecture of monkey striate cortex. *Journal of Physiology, 195,* 215–243.

HUDSPETH, A. J. (1989). How the ear's works work. *Nature, 341,* 397–404.

HUESMANN, L. R., LAGERSPETZ, K., & ERON, L. D. (1984). Intervening variables in the TV violence-aggression relation: Evidence from two countries. *Developmental Psychobiology, 20,* 1120–1134.

HUESMANN, L. R., & MILLER, L. S. (1994). Long-term effects of repeated exposure to media violence in childhood. In L. R. Huesmann (Ed.), *Aggressive behavior: Current perspectives.* New York: Plenum.

HUGHES, C., & CUTTING, A. L. (1999). Nature, nurture, and individual differences in early understanding of mind. *Psychological Science, 10*(5), 429–432.

HUGHES, C., & DUNN, J. (1998). Understanding mind and emotion: Longitudinal associations with mental-state talk between young friends. *Developmental Psychology, 34,* 1026–1037.

HUGHES, J., SMITH, T. W., KOSTERLITZ, H., FOTHERGILL, L., MORGAN, B., & MORRIS, H. (1975). Identification of two related pentapeptides from the brain with potent opiate agonist activity. *Nature, 258,* 577–579.

HUGUET, P., GALVAING, M. P., MONTEIL, J. M., & DUMAS, F. (1999). Social presence effects in the Stroop task: Further evidence for an attentional view of social facilitation. *Personality and Social Psychology, 77*(5), 1011–1025.

HUME, D. (1739/1978). *A treatise on human nature.* Oxford, England: Clarendon.

HUMPHREYS, M. S., DENNIS, S., MAGUIRE, A. M., REYNOLDS, K., BOLLAND, S. W., & HUGHES, J. D. (2003). What you get out of memory depends on the question you ask. *Journal of Experimental Psychology: Learning, Memory & Cognition, 29,* 797–812.

HUNSLEY, J., & BAILEY, J. M. (1999). The clinical utility of the Rorschach: Unfulfilled promises and an uncertain future. *Psychological Assessment, 11,* 266–277.

HUNT, E. (1976). Varieties of cognitive power. In L. B. Resnick (Ed.), *The nature of intelligence*. Hillsdale, NJ: Erlbaum.

HUNT, E. (1985a). The correlates of intelligence. In D. K. Detterman (Ed.), *Current topics in human intelligence: Vol. 1*. Norwood, NJ: Ablex.

HUNT, E. (1985b). Verbal ability. In R. J. Sternberg (Ed.), *Human abilities: An information processing approach* (pp. 31–58). New York: Freeman.

HUNT, E. (1995). *Will we be smart enough? A cognitive analysis of the coming workforce*. New York: Russell Sage Foundation.

HUNT, E., & CARLSON, J. (2007a). Considerations relating to the study of group differences in intelligence. *Perspective on Psychological Science, 2*, 194–213.

HUNT, E., & CARLSON, J. (2007b). Reply to commentators. *Perspective on Psychological Science, 2*, 224–226.

HUNT, P. J., & HILLERY, J. M. (1973). Social facilitation in a coaction setting: An examination of the effects over learning trials. *Journal of Experimental Social Psychology, 9*, 563–571.

HUPBACH, A., GOMEZ, R., HARDT, O., & NADEL, L. (2008). Reconsolidation of episodic memories: A subtle reminder triggers integration of new information. *Learning & Memory, 14*, 47–53.

HURLEY, R. A., BLACK, D. N., STIP, E., & TABER, K. H. (2000). Surgical treatment of mental illness: Impact of imaging. *Journal of Neuropsychiatry and Clinical Neuroscience, 12*, 421–424.

HURVICH, L. M. (1981). *Color vision*. Sunderland, MA: Sinauer Assoc.

HURVICH, L. M., & JAMESON, D. (1957). An opponent-process theory of color vision. *Psychological Review, 64*, 384–404.

HUSTON, T. L., RUGGIERO, M., CONNER, R., & GEIS, G. (1981). Bystander intervention into crime: A study based on naturally occurring episodes. *Social Psychology Quarterly, 44*, 14–23.

HUTCHINSON, R. R., & RENFREW, J. W. (1966). Stalking attack and eating behaviors elicited from the same sites in the hypothalamus. *Journal of Comparative and Physiological Psychology, 61*, 360–367.

HUTTENLOCHER, J. (1974). The origins of language comprehension. In R. L. Solso (Ed.), *Theories in cognitive psychology: The Loyola symposium* (pp. 331–368). Potomac, MD: Erlbaum.

HUTTENLOCHER, J., SMILEY, P., & CHARNEY, R. (1983). Emergence of action categories in the child: Evidence from verb meanings. *Psychological Review, 90*, 72–93.

HUTTENLOCHER, P. R. (1979). Synaptic density in human frontal cortex—developmental changes and effects of aging. *Brain Research, 163*, 195–205.

HWANG, W. (2006). The Psychotherapy Adaptation and Modification Framework (PAMF): Application to Asian Americans. *American Psychologist, 61*(7), 702–715.

HYDE, D. M. (1959). An investigation of Piaget's theories of the development of the concept of number. Unpublished doctoral dissertation, University of London. Quoted in J. H. Flavell (Ed.), (1963). *The developmental psychology of Jean Piaget* (p. 383). New York: Van Nostrand Reinhold.

HYDE, J. S. (2005). The gender similarities hypothesis. *American Psychologist, 60*, 581–592.

HYDE, J., LINDBERG, S., LINN, M., ELLIS, A., & WILLIAMS, C. (2008). Gender similarities characterize math performance. *Science, 321*, 494–495.

HYDE, J., & LINN, M. (2006). Gender similarities in mathematics and science. *Science, 314*, 599–600.

HYMAN, I., & BILLINGS, F. J. (1998). Individual differences and the creation of false childhood memories. *Memory, 6*, 1–20.

HYMAN, I., HUSBAND, T., & BILLINGS, F. (1995). False memories of childhood experiences. *Applied Cognitive Psychology, 9*, 181–198.

HYMAN, S. E. (2007). Can neuroscience be integrated into the *DSM-V? Nature Reviews Neuroscience, 8*, 725–732.

HYMAN, S. E., & FENTON, W. S. (2003). What are the right targets for psychopharmacology? *Science, 299*, 350–351.

HYMEL, S., BOWKER, A., & WOODY, E. (1993). Aggressive versus withdrawn unpopular children: Variations in peer and self-perceptions in multiple domains. *Child Development, 64*(3), 879–896.

IGLOWSTEIN, I., JENNI, O. G., MOLINARI, L., & LARGO, R. H. (2003). Sleep duration from infancy to adolescence: Reference values and generational trends. *Pediatrics, 111*, 302–307.

IKONOMIDOU, C., BITTIGAU, P., ISHIMARU, M. J., WOZNIAK, D. F., KOCH, C., GENZ, K., ET AL. (2000). Ethanol-induced apoptotic neurodegeneration and fetal alcohol syndrome. *Science, 287*(5455), 1056–1060.

INFANTE, J. R., TORRES-AVISBAL, M., PINEL, P., VALLEJO, J. A., PERAN, F., GONZALEZ, F., CONTRERAS, P., PACHECO, C., ROLDAN, A., & LATRE, J. M. (2001). Catecholamine levels in practitioners of the transcendental meditation technique. *Physiology & Behavior, 72* (1–2), 141–146.

INAGAKI, K., & HATANO, G. (2004). Vitalistic causality in young children's naive biology. *Trends in Cognitive Science, 8*, 356–362.

INTERNATIONAL HUMAN GENOME SEQUENCING COSORTIUM (IHGSC). (2001). Initial sequencing and analysis of the human genome. *Nature, 409*, 860–921.

INTERNATIONAL SCHIZOPHRENIA CONSORTIUM. (2008). Rare chromosomal deletions and duplications increase risk of schizophrenia. *Nature, 455*, 237–241.

IRVINE, J. T. (1978). Wolof "magical thinking": Culture and conservation revisited. *Journal of Crosscultural Psychology, 9*, 300–310.

ISACSON, O. (1999). The neurobiology and neurogenetics of stem cells. *Brain Pathology, 9*, 495–498.

ISHA, A., & SAGI, D. (1995). Common mechanisms of visual imagery and perception. *Science, 268*, 1772–1774.

ITO, T. A., WILLADSEN-JENSEN, E. C., & CORRELL, J. (2007). Social neuroscience and social perception: New perspectives on categorization, prejudice, and stereotyping. In E. Harmon-Jones & P. Winkielman (Eds.), *Social neuroscience: Integrating biological and psychological explanations of social behavior* (pp. 401–421). New York: Guilford.

IYENGAR, S., & LEPPER, M. (2000). When choice is demotivating: Can one desire too much of a good thing? *Journal of Personality and Social Psychology, 79*, 995–1006.

IVY, G. O., MACLEOD, C. M., PETIT, T. L., & MARKUS, E. J. (1992). A physiological framework for perceptual and cognitive changes in aging. In F. I. M. Craik & T. A. Salthouse (Eds.), *The handbook of aging and cognition*. Hillsdale, NJ: Erlbaum.

IZARD, C. E. (1971). *The face of emotion*. New York: Appleton-Century-Crofts.

IZARD, C. E. (1977). *Human emotions*. New York: Plenum.

IZARD, C. E. (1994). Innate and universal facial expressions: Evidence from developmental cross-cultural research. *Psychological Bulletin, 115*, 288–299.

IZARD, C., FANTAUZZO, C., CASTLE, J., HAYNES, O., RAYIAS, M., & PUTNAM, P. (1995). The ontogeny and significance of infants' facial expressions in the first 9 months of life. *Developmental Psychology, 31*, 997–1013.

JABLENSKY, A., & COLE, S.W. (1997). Is the earlier age at onset of schizophrenia in males a confounded finding? *British Journal of Psychiatry, 170*, 234–240.

JACKENDOFF, R. (1987). *Consciousness and the computational mind*. Cambridge, MA: MIT Press.

JACKENDOFF, R. (2002). *Foundations of language: Brain, meaning, grammar, evolution*. Oxford, England: Oxford University Press.

JACKSON, L. A., HUNTER, J. E., & HODGE, C. N. (1995). Physical attractiveness and intellectual competence: A meta-analytic review. *Social Psychology Quarterly, 58*, 108–122.

JACOBS, A. (1955). Formation of new associations to words selected on the basis of reaction-time-GSR combinations. *Journal of Abnormal and Social Psychology, 51*, 371–377.

JACOBS, B. L. (2004). Depression: The brain finally gets into the act. *Current Directions in Psychological Science, 13*, 103–106.

JACOBSEN, F. M. (1992). Fluoxetine-induced sexual dysfunction and an open trial of yohimbine. *Journal of Clinical Psychiatry, 53*, 119–122.

JACOBSEN, L. K., GIEDD, J. N., BERQUIN, P. C., KRAIN, A. L., HAMBURGER, S. D., KUMRA, S., ET AL. (1997). Quantitative morphology of the cerebellum and fourth ventricle in childhood-onset schizophrenia. *American Journal of Psychiatry, 154*, 1663–1669.

JACOBY, L. L. (1983). Perceptual enhancement: Persistent effects of an experience. *Journal of Experimental Psychology: Learning, Memory and Cognition, 9*, 21–38.

JACOBY, L. L., & DALLAS, M. (1981). On the relationship between autobiographical memory and perceptual learning. *Journal of Experimental Psychology: General, 3*, 306–340.

JACOBY, L. L., & WITHERSPOON, D. (1982). Remembering without awareness. *Canadian Journal of Psychology, 36*, 300–324.

JACOBY, R., & GLAUBERMAN, N. (1995). *The Bell Curve Debate: History, Documents, Opinions*. New York: Random House.

JAMES, L. E., & BURKE, D. M. (2000). Phonological priming effects on word retrieval and tip-of-the-tongue experiences in young and older adults. *Journal of Experimental Psychology: Learning, Memory and Cognition, 26,* 1378–1391.

JAMES, W. (1884). What is an emotion? *Mind, 9,* 188–205.

JAMES, W. (1890/1980). *The principles of psychology.* New York: Henry Holt.

JAMISON, K. R. (1995). Manic-depressive illness and creativity. *Scientific American, 272,* 62–67.

JANG, K. L., LIVESLEY, W. J., & VERNON, P. A. (1996). Heritability of the big five personality dimensions and their facets: A twin study. *Journal of Personality, 64,* 577–591.

JANG, K. L., PARIS, J., ZWEIG-FRANK, H., & LIVESLEY, W. J. (1998). Twin study of dissociative experience. *Journal of Nervous and Mental Disease, 186,* 345–351.

JANICAK, P. G. (2005).Treating psychiatric disorders using transcranial magnetic stimulation. *Psychiatric Annals, 35*(2), 102+.

JANICAK, P. G., DAVIS, J. M., GIBBONS, R. D., ERICKSEN, S., CHANG, S., & GALLAGHER, P. (1985). Efficacy of ECT: A meta-analysis. *American Journal of Psychiatry, 142,* 297–302.

JANICAK, P. G., DOWD, S. M., MARTIS, B., ALAM, D., BEEDLE, D., KRASUSKI, J., ET AL. (2002). Repetitive transcranial magnetic stimulation versus electroconvulsive therapy for major depression: Preliminary results of a randomized trial. *Biological Psychiatry, 51*(8), 659–667.

JANIS, I. (1971). Groupthink. *Psychology Today, 5,* 43–76.

JANIS, I. (1982). *Groupthink: Psychological studies of policy decisions and fiascoes* (2nd ed.). Boston: Houghton Mifflin.

JANKE, A., ERPENBECK, D., NILSSON, M., & ARNASON, U. (2001). The mitochondrial genomes of the iguana (*Iguana iguana*) and the caiman (*Caiman crocodylus*): Implications for amniote phylogeny. *Proceedings of the Royal Society of London B, 268,* 623–631.

JANKOWIAK, W. R., & FISCHER, E. F. (1992). A cross-cultural perspective on romantic love. *Ethnology, 31,* 149–155.

JANOWSKY, J. S., OVIATT, S. K., & ORWOLL, E. S. (1994). Testosterone influences spatial cognition in older men. *Behavioral Neuroscience, 108,* 325–332.

JANSSEN, E., CARPENTER, D., & GRAHAM, C. A. (2003). Selecting films for sex research: Gender differences in erotic film preference. *Archives of Sexual Behavior, 32,* 243–251.

JANUARY, D., & KAKO, E. (2007). Re-evaluating evidence for the linguistic relativity hypothesis: Response to Boroditsky (2001). *Cognition, 104,* 417–426.

JAVITT, D. C., & COYLE, J. T. (2004, January). Decoding schizophrenia. *Scientific American, 290,* 48–55.

JENCKS, C., & PHILLIPS, M. (EDS.). (1998). *The Black-White test score gap.* Washington, DC: Brookings Institution.

JENIKE, M. A. (2001). An update on obsessive-compulsive disorder. *Bulletin of the Menninger Clinic, 65,* 4–25.

JENKINS, J. G., & DALLENBACH, K. M. (1924). Oblivescence during sleep and waking. *American Journal of Psychology, 35,* 605–612.

JENNINGS, E. E. (1972). *An anatomy of leadership: Princes, heroes, and supermen.* New York: McGraw-Hill.

JENSEN, A. R. (1985). The nature of the black-white difference on various psychometric tests: Spearman's hypothesis. *Behavioral and Brain Sciences, 8,* 193–263.

JENSEN, A. R. (1987). Individual differences in the Hick paradigm. In P. A. Vernon (Ed.), *Speed of information processing and intelligence.* Norwood, NJ: Ablex.

JENSEN, P. S., ARNOLD, L. E., SWANSON, J., VITIELLO, B., ABIKOFF, H. B., GREENHILL, L. L., ET AL. (2007). Follow-up of the NIMH MTA study at 36 months after randomization. *Journal of the American Academy of Child and Adolescent Psychiatry, 46,* 988–1001.

JETTEN, J., POSTMES, T., & MCAULIFFE, B. J. (2002). "We're all individuals": Group norms of individualism and collectivism, levels of identification and identity threat. *European Journal of Social Psychology, 32*(2), 189–207.

JOBE, J., TOURANGEAU, R., & SMITH, A. (1993). Contributions of survey research to the understanding of memory. *Applied Cognitive Psychology, 7,* 567–584.

JOCKIN, V., MCGUE, M., & LYKKEN, D. T. (1996). Personality and divorce: A genetic analysis. *Journal of Personality and Social Psychology, 71,* 288–299.

JOHN, O. P. (1990). The "Big Five" taxonomy: Dimensions of personality in the natural language and in questionnaires. In L. A. Pervin (Ed.), *Handbook of personality: Theory and research* (pp. 676–1000). New York: Guilford.

JOHN, O. P., DONAHUE, E. M., & KENTLE, R. L. (1991). *The Big Five Inventory—Versions 4a and 54.* Berkeley: University of California, Berkeley, Institute of Personality and Social Research.

JOHN, O. P., & SRIVASTAVA, S. (1999). The Big Five trait taxonomy: History, measurement, and theoretical perspectives. In L. A. Pervin & O. P. John (Eds.), *Handbook of personality: Theory and research* (2nd ed., pp. 139–153). New York: Guilford.

JOHNS, M., INZLICHT, M., & SCHMADER, T. (2008). Stereotype threat and executive resource depletion: Examining the influence of emotion regulation. *Journal of Experimental Psychology: General, 137,* 691–705.

JOHNS, M., SCHMADER, T., & MARTENS, A. (2005). Knowing is half the battle: Teaching stereotype threat as a means of improving women's math performance. *Psychological Science, 16,* 175–179.

JOHNSON, M. K., KIM, J. K., & RISSE, G. (1985). Do alcoholic Korsakoff's syndrome patients acquire affective reactions? *Journal of Experimental Psychology: Learning, Memory & Cognition, 11,* 27–36.

JOHNSON, A. M., WADSWORTH, J., WELLINGS, K., BRADSHAW, S., & FIELD, J. (1992). Sexual lifestyles and HIV risk. *Nature, 360,* 410–412.

JOHNSON, J., & NEWPORT, E. (1989). Critical period effects in second-language learning: The influence of maturational state on the acquisition of English as a second language. *Cognitive Psychology, 21,* 60–99.

JOHNSON, M. H. (1993). Cortical maturation and the development of visual attention in early infancy. In M. H. Johnson (Ed.), *Brain development and cognition.* Cambridge, MA: Blackwell.

JOHNSON, R. D., & DOWNING, L. L. (1979). Deindividuation and valence of cues: Effects on prosocial and antisocial behavior. *Journal of Personality and Social Psychology, 37*(9), 1532–1538.

JOHNSON, R. E. (1979). *Juvenile delinquency and its origins.* New York: Cambridge University Press.

JOHNSON, S. L. (2005a). Life events in bipolar disorder: Towards more specific models. *Clinical Psychology Review, 25,* 1008–1027.

JOHNSON, S. L. (2005b). Mania and dysregulation in goal pursuit: A review. *Clinical Psychology Review, 25,* 241–262.

JOHNSON, S.L., WINETT, C. A., MEYER, B., GREENHOUSE, W. J., & MILLER, I. (1999). Social support and the course of bipolar disorder. *Journal of Abnormal Psychology, 108,* 558–566.

JOHNSON, S. P. (2004). Development of perceptual completion in infancy. *Psychological Science, 15,* 769–775.

JOHNSON, W., CAROTHERS, A., & DEARY, I. J. (2008). Sex differences in variability in general intelligence. *Perspectives on Psychological Science, 3,* 518–531.

JOHNSON, W., NIJENHUIS, J., & BOUCHARD, T. (2007). Replication of the hierarchical visual-perceptual-image rotation model in de Wolff and Buiten's (1963) battery of 46 tests of mental ability. *Intelligence, 35,* 69–81.

JOHNSTON, V. S., HAGEL, R., FRANKLIN, M., FINK, B., & GRAMMER, K. (2001). Male facial attractiveness: Evidence for hormone mediated adaptive design. *Evolution and Human Behavior, 22,* 251–267.

JOINER, T. E., JR. (1997). Shyness and low social support as interactive diatheses, with loneliness as mediator: Testing an interpersonal-personality view of vulnerability to depressive symptoms. *Journal of Abnormal Psychology, 106,* 386–394.

JOINT STATEMENT ON THE IMPACT OF ENTERTAINMENT VIOLENCE ON CHILDREN: CONGRESSIONAL PUBLIC HEALTH SUMMIT. (2000, July 26). Retrieved July 1, 2009, from http://www.aap.org/advocacy/releases/jstmtevc.htm.

JOIREMAN, J., ANDERSON, J., & STRATHMAN, A. (2003). The aggression paradox: Understanding links among aggression, sensation seeking, and the consideration of future consequences. *Journal of Personality and Social Psychology, 84,* 1287–1302.

JOKELA, M., ELOVAINIO, M., KIVIMAKI, M., & KELTIKANGAS-JARVINEN, L. (2008). Temperament and migration patterns in Finland. *Psychological Science, 19,* 831–837.

JONES, E. E., & BERGLAS, S. (1978). Control of attributions about the self through self handicapping strategies: The appeal of alcohol and the role of underachievement. *Personality and Social Psychology Bulletin, 4*(2), 200–206.

JONES, E. E., & NISBETT, R. E. (1972). The actor and the observer: Divergent perceptions of the cause of behavior. In E. E. Jones, D. E. Karouse, H. H. Kelley, R. E. Nisbett, S. Valins, & B. Weiner (Eds.), *Attribution perceiving the causes of behavior.* Morristown, NJ: General Learning Press.

JONES, E., & WESSELY, S. (2001). Psychiatric battle casualties: An intra- and interwar comparison. *British Journal of Psychiatry, 178,* 242–247.

JONES, P. B., BEBBINGTON, P., FOERSTER, A., LEWIS, S. W., MURRAY, R. M., RUSSELL, A., ET AL. (1993). Premorbid social underachievement in schizophrenia: Results from the Camberwell Collaborative Psychosis Study. *British Journal of Psychiatry, 162*, 65–71.

JONES, R. E. (1983). Street people and psychiatry: An introduction. *Hospital Community Psychiatry, 34*, 807–811.

JONES, S. S. (1996). Imitation or exploration? Young infants' matching of adults' oral gestures. *Child Development, 67*, 1952–1969.

JONIDES, J. (1980). Toward a model of the mind's eye's movement. *Canadian Journal of Psychology, 34*, 103–112.

JONIDES, J. (1983). Further toward a model of the mind's eye's movement. *Bulletin of the Psychonomic Society, 21*, 247–250.

JONIDES, J. (2000). Mechanisms of verbal working memory revealed by neuroimaging studies. (2000). In B. Landau, J. Sabini, J. Jonides, and E. Newport (Eds.), *Perception, cognition, and language: Essays in honor of Henry and Lila Gleitman* (pp. 87–104). Cambridge, MA: MIT Press.

JORGENSEN, B. W., & CERVONE, J. C. (1978). Affect enhancement in the pseudo recognition task. *Personality and Social Psychology Bulletin, 4*, 285–288.

JOSHI, A. K. (2002). Tree adjoining grammar. In R. Mitkov (Ed.), *Handbook of computational linguistics* (pp. 483–498). New York: Oxford University Press.

JOSLYN, S. L., & OAKES, M. A. (2005). Directed forgetting of autobiographical events. *Memory & Cognition, 33*, 577–587.

JOSSELSON, R. (1980). Ego development in adolescence. In J. Adelson (Ed.), *Handbook of adolescent psychology* (pp. 188–211). New York: Wiley.

JOST, J. T., GLASER, J., KRUGLANSKI, A. W., & SULLOWAY, F. J. (2003). Political conservatism as motivated social cognition. *Psychological Bulletin, 129*(3), 339–375.

JOST, J. T., NOSEK, B. A., & GOSLING, S. D. (2008). Ideology: Its resurgence in social, personality, and political psychology. *Perspectives on Psychological Science, 3*, 126–136.

JOUVET, M. (1967). The stages of sleep. *Scientific American, 216*, 62–72.

JOY, L. A., KIMBALL, M. M., & ZABRACK, M. L. (1986). Television and aggressive behavior. In T. M. Williams (Ed.), *The impact of television: A natural experiment involving three towns.* New York: Academic Press.

JUDD, L. L., PAULUS, M. P., WELLS, K. B., & RAPAPORT, M. H. (1996). Socioeconomic burden of subsyndromal depressive symptoms and major depression in a sample of the general population. *American Journal of Psychiatry, 153*, 1411–1417.

JUDY, B., & NELSON, E. S. (2000). Relationship between parents, peers, morality, and theft in an adolescent sample. *High School Journal, 83*(3), 31–42.

JUNG, C. G. (1964). *Man and his symbols.* Garden City, NY: Doubleday.

JUNG, R., & HAIER, R. (2007). The parieto-frontal integration theory (P-FIT) of intelligence: Converging neuroimaging evidence. *Behavioral and Brain Sciences, 30*, 135–154.

JUSCZYK, P. W., CUTLER, A., & REDANZ, N. J. (1993). Infants' preference for the predominant stress patterns of English words. *Child Development, 64*, 675–687.

JUSCZYK, P. W., FRIEDERICI, A. D., WESSELS, J. M., SVENKERUD, V. Y., & JUSCZYK, A. M. (1993). Infants' sensitivity to the sound patterns of native language words. *Journal of Memory and Language, 32*, 402–420.

JUSSIM, L., & HARBER, K. D. (2005). Teacher expectations and self-fulfilling prophecies: Knowns and unknowns, resolved and unresolved controversies. *Personality and Social Psychology Review, 9*, 131–155.

JUST, M. A., & CARPENTER, P. A. (1992). A capacity theory of comprehension: Individual differences in working memory. *Psychological Review, 99*(1), 122–149.

JUSTER, H. R., & HEIMBERG, R. G. (1995). Social phobia. Longitudinal course and long-term outcome of cognitive-behavioral treatment. *Psychiatric Clinics of North America, 18*, 821–842.

KAGAN, J. (1994). *Galen's prophecy: Temperament in human nature.* New York: Basic Books.

KAGAN, J. (2003). Biology, context, and developmetnal inquiry. *Annual Review of Psychology, 54*, 1–23.

KAGAN, J., & SNIDMAN, N. (1991). Temperamental factors in human development. *American Psychologist, 46*, 856–862.

KAHANA-KALMAN, R., & WALKER-ANDREWS, A. (2001). The role of person familiarity in young infants' perception of emotional expressions. *Child Development, 72*, 352–369.

KAHN, I., DAVACHI, L., & WAGNER, A. (2004). Functional-neuroanatomic correlates of recollection: Implications for models of recognition memory. *Journal of Neuroscience, 24*, 4171–4180.

KAHNEMAN, D. (2003). A perspective on judgment and choice: Mapping bounded rationality. *American Psychologist, 58*, 697–720.

KAHNEMAN, D., DIENER, E., & SCHWARZ, N. (Eds.). (1999). *Well-being: The foundations of hedonic psychology.* New York: Russell Sage Foundation.

KAHNEMAN, D., & TVERSKY, A. (1972). Subjective probability: A judgment of representativeness. *Cognitive Psychology, 3*, 430–454.

KAHNEMAN, D., & TVERSKY, A. (1973). On the psychology of prediction. *Psychological Review, 80*, 237–251.

KAHNEMAN, D., & TVERSKY, A. (1984). Choices, values and frames. *American Psychologist, 39*, 341–350.

KAHNEMAN, D., & TVERSKY, A. (1996). On the reality of cognitive illusions. *Psychological Review, 103*, 582–591.

KAISER, E., & TRUESWELL, J. C. (2002, March). A new "look" in the processing of non-canonical word orders. Paper presented at the 15th Annual CUNY Conference on Human Sentence Processing, New York, NY.

KAKO, E. (1999). Elements of syntax in the systems of three language-trained animals. *Animal Learning & Behavior, 27*, 1–14.

KALICK, S. M., ZEBROWITZ, L. A., LANGLOIS, J. H., & JOHNSON, R. M. (1998). Does human facial attractiveness honestly advertise health? Longitudinal data on an evolutional question. *Psychological Science, 9*, 8–13.

KAMIN, L. J. (1965). Temporal and intensity characteristics of the conditioned stimulus. In W. F. Prokasy (Ed.), *Classical conditioning.* New York: Appleton-Century-Crofts.

KAMIN, L. J. (1968). "Attention-like" processes in classical conditioning. In M. R. Jones (Ed.), *Miami symposium on the prediction of behavior: Aversive stimuli.* Miami: University of Miami Press.

KAMIN, L. J. (1974). *The science and politics of IQ.* New York: Wiley.

KAMINSKI, J., CALL, J., & FISCHER, J. (2004). Word learning in a domestic dog: Evidence for "fast mapping." *Science, 304*, 1682–1683.

KAMINSKY, H. (1984). Moral development in historical perspective. In W. M. Kurtines & J. L. Gerwitz (Eds.), *Morality, moral behavior, and moral development.* New York: Wiley.

KAMPERT, J. B., BLAIR, S. N., BARLOW, C. E., & KOHL, H. W., III. (1996). Physical activity, physical fitness, and all-cause and cancer mortality: A prospective study of men and women. *Annals of Epidemiology, 6*, 452–457.

KAMPMAN, K. M., VOLPICELLI, J. R., MULVANEY, F., RUKSTALIS, M., ALTERMAN, A. I., PETTINATI, H., WEINRIEB, R. M., & O'BRIEN, C. P. (2002). Cocaine withdrawal severity and urine toxicology results from treatment entry predict outcome in medication trials for cocaine dependence. *Addictive Behaviors, 27*(2), 251–260.

KANAWAGA, C., CROSS, S. E., & MARKUS, H. R. (2001). "Who am I?": The cultural psychology of the conceptual self. *Personality and Social Psychology Bulletin, 27*, 90–103.

KANAYA, T., SCULLIN, M. H., & CECI, S. (2003). The Flynn effect and U.S. policies: The impact of rising IQ scores on American society via mental retardation diagnoses. *American Psychologist, 58*, 778–790.

KANDEL, D. B. (1978). Similarity in real-life adolescent friendship pairs. *Journal of Personality and Social Psychology, 36*, 306–312.

KANDEL, E. R. (2007). *In search of memory.* New York: Norton.

KANDEL, E. R., & HAWKINS, R. D. (1992). The biological basis of learning and individuality. *Scientific American, 267*, 78–87.

KANE, M. J., POOLE, B. J., TUHOLSKI, S. W., & ENGLE, R. W. (2006). Working memory capacity and the top-down control of visual search: Exploring the boundaries of "executive attention." *Journal of Experimental Psychology: Learning, Memory, and Cognition, 32*, 749–777.

KANE, M. J. (2005). Full frontal fluidity? Looking in on the neuroimaging of reasoning and intelligence. In O. Wilhelm & R. Engle (Eds.), *Handbook of understanding and measuring intelligence* (pp. 141–163). Thousand Oaks, CA: Sage.

KANE, M. J., & ENGLE, R. W. (2003). Working-memory capacity and the control of attention: The contributions of goal neglect, response competition, and task set to Stroop interference. *Journal of Experimental Psychology: General, 132*, 47–70.

KANE, M. J., HAMBRICK, D. Z., & CONWAY, A. R. (2005). Working memory capacity and fluid intelligence are strongly related constructs: Comment on Ackerman, Beier, and Boyle (2005). *Psychological Bulletin, 131*, 66–71.

KANE, M. J., POOLE, B. J., TUHOLSKI, S. W., & ENGLE, R. (2006). Working memory capacity and the top-down control of visual search: Exploring the boundaries of "executive attention." *Journal of Experimental Psychology: Learning, Memory & Cognition, 32,* 749–777.

KAPLAN, H., & DOVE, H. (1987). Infant development among the Ache of eastern Paraguay. *Developmental Psychology, 23,* 190–198.

KAPUR, N. (1999). Syndromes of retrograde amnesia. *Psychological Bulletin, 125,* 800–825.

KAPUR, S., & REMINGTON, G. (1996). Serotonin-dopamine interaction and its relevance to schizophrenia. *American Journal of Psychiatry, 153,* 466–476.

KAPUR, S., & REMINGTON, G. (2001). Dopamine D(2) receptors and their role in atypical antipsychotic action: still necessary and may even be sufficient. *Biological Psychiatry, 50*(11), 873–883.

KARAU, S. J., & WILLIAMS, K. D. (1993). Social loafing: A meta-analytic review and theoretical integration. *Journal of Personality and Social Psychology, 65*(4), 681–706.

KARCH, S. (Ed.). (2007). *Drug abuse handbook* (2nd ed.). New York: Taylor & Francis.

KASSER, T., & SHARMA, Y. S. (1999). Reproductive freedom, educational equality, and females' preference for resource-acquisition characteristics in mates. *Psychological Science, 10*(4), 374–377.

KASSIN, S. M., & GUDJONSSON, G. H. (2004). The psychology of confession evidence: A review of the literature and issues. *Psychological Science in the Public Interest, 5,* 35–69.

KATO, T., & KATO, N. (2000). Mitochondrial dysfunction in bipolar disorder. *Bipolar Disorders, 2*(3, Pt. 1), 180–190.

KATZ, J. J., & FODOR, J. A. (1963). The structure of a semantic theory. *Language, 39,* 170–210.

KAUFFMAN, T., THEORET, H., & PASCUAL-LEONE, A. (2002). Braille character discrimination in blindfolded human subjects. *Neuroreport, 13,* 571–574.

KAWAKAMI, K., DION, K. L., & DOVIDIO, J. F. (1998). Racial prejudice and stereotype activation. *Personality and Social Psychology Bulletin, 24*(4), 407–416.

KAY, P. (1996). Intra-speaker relativity. In J. J. Gumperz & S. C. Levinson (Eds.), *Rethinking linguistic relativity. Studies in the social and cultural foundations of language.* Cambridge: Cambridge University Press.

KAY, P., & REGIER, T. (2006). Language, thought, and color: Recent developments. *Trends in Cognitive Sciences, 10*(2), 51–54.

KAZDIN, A. E. (2003). Psychotherapy for children and adolescents. *Annual Review of Psychology, 54,* 253–276.

KAZDIN, A. E., & BENJET, C. (2003). Spanking children: Evidence and issues. *Current Directions in Psychological Science, 12*(3), 99–103.

KAZDIN, A. E., & WEISZ, J. R. (Eds.). (2003). *Evidence-based psychotherapies for children and adolescents.* New York: Guilford.

KEATING, D. (2004). Cognitive and brain development. In R. Lerner & L. Steinberg (Eds.), *Handbook of adolescent psychology* (pp. 45–84). New York: Wiley.

KECK, P. E., JR., & McELROY, S. L. (2002). Carbamazepine and valproate in the maintenance treatment of bipolar disorder. *Journal of Clinical Psychiatry, 63*(Suppl. 10), 13–17.

KEEL, P. K., & KLUMP, K. L. (2003). Are eating disorders culture-bound syndromes? Implications for conceptualizing their etiology. *Psychological Bulletin, 129*(5), 747–769.

KEGL, J., SENGHAS, A., & COPPOLA, M. (1999). Creation through contact: Sign language emergence and sign language change in Nicaragua. In M. Degraff (Ed.), *Language creation and language change: Creolization, diachrony, and development* (pp. 179–237). Cambridge, MA: MIT Press.

KEIL, F. L. (1989). *Concepts, kinds, and cognitive development.* Cambridge, MA: MIT Press.

KEIZER, K., LINDENBERG, S., & STEG, L. (2008). The spreading of disorder. *Science, 322,* 1681–1685.

KELLEY, H. H. (1967). Attribution theory in social psychology. In D. Levine (Ed.), *Nebraska Symposium on Motivation* (pp. 192–238). Lincoln: University of Nebraska Press.

KELLEY, H. H., & MICHELA, J. L. (1980). Attribution theory and research. *Annual Review of Psychology, 31,* 457–501.

KELLEY, S., & MIRER, T. W. (1974). The simple act of voting. *American Political Science Review, 68,* 572–591.

KELLMAN, P. J., GARRIGAN, P., & SHIPLEY, T. F. (2005). Object interpolation in three dimensions. *Psychological Review, 112,* 586–609.

KELLMAN, P. J., & SHIPLEY, T. F. (1991). A theory of visual interpolation in object perception. *Cognitive Psychology, 23,* 141–221.

KELLMAN, P. J., & SPELKE, E. S. (1983). Perception of partially occluded objects in infancy. *Cognitive Psychology, 15,* 483–524.

KELLMAN, P. J., SPELKE, E. S., & SHORT, K. R. (1986). Infant perception of object unity from translatory motion in depth and vertical translation. *Child Development, 57,* 72–86.

KELLY, G. A. (1955). *The psychology of personal constructs.* New York: Norton.

KELLY, M. H., & MARTIN, S. (1994). Domain-general abilities applied to domain-specific tasks: Sensitivity to probabilities in perception, cognition, and language. In L. R. Gleitman & B. Landau (Eds.), Lexical acquisition [Special issue]. *Lingua, 92,* 108–140.

KELSOE, J. R. (1997). The genetics of bipolar disorder. *Psychiatric Annals, 27,* 285–292.

KELTNER, D., & BUSWELL, B. N. (1997). Embarrassment: Its distinct form and appeasement functions. *Psychological Bulletin, 122,* 250–270.

KELTNER, D., GRUENFELD, D. H., & ANDERSON, C. (2003). Power, approach, and inhibition. *Psychological Review, 110,* 265–284.

KENDALL, P. C. (1990). Cognitive processes and procedures in behavior therapy. In C. M. Franks, G. T. Wilson, P. C. Kendall, & J. P. Foreyt (Eds.), *Review of behavior therapy: Theory and practice* (pp. 103–137). New York: Guilford.

KENDALL, P. C., & BRASWELL, L. (1985). *Cognitive-behavioral therapy for impulsive children.* New York: Guilford.

KENDALL-TACKETT, K. A., WILLIAMS, L. M., & FINKELHOR, D. (1993). Impact of sexual abuse on children: A review

and synthesis of recent empirical studies. *Psychological Bulletin, 113,* 164–180.

KENDLER, K. S., & BAKER, J. H. (2007). Genetic influences on measures of the environment: A systematic review. *Psychological Medicine, 37,* 615–626.

KENDLER, K. S., & GRUENBERG, A. M. (1984). An independent analysis of the Danish adoption study of schizophrenia: VI. The relationship between psychiatric disorders as defined by DSM-III in the relatives and adoptees. *Archives of General Psychiatry, 41,* 555–564.

KENDLER, K. S., KARKOWSKI, L. M., & PRESCOTT, C. A. (1999). Fears and phobias: Reliability and heritability. *Psychological Medicine, 29,* 539–553.

KENNY, D., & ZACCARO, S. J. (1983). An estimate of variance due to traits in leadership. *Journal of Applied Psychology, 68,* 678–685.

KENRICK, D. T., & CIALDINI, R. B. (1977). Romantic attraction: Misattribution versus reinforcement explanations. *Journal of Personality and Social Psychology, 35,* 381–391.

KENRICK, D. T., CIALDINI, R. B., & LINDER, D. E. (1979). Misattribution under fear-producing circumstances: Four failures to replicate. *Personality and Social Psychology Bulletin, 5,* 329–334.

KENSINGER, E. (2007). Negative emotion enhances memory accuracy. *Current Directions in Psychological Science, 16,* 213–218.

KEREN, G. (2007). Framing, intentions, and trust-choice incompatibility. *Organizational Behavior and Human Decision Processes, 103,* 238–255.

KERR, M. E., & BOWEN, M. (1988). *Family evaluation.* New York: Norton.

KERR, N., & BRAY, R. (2005). Simulation, realism, and the study of the jury. In N. Brewer & K. Williams (Eds.), *Psychology and law: An empirical perspective* (pp. 322–364). New York: Guilford.

KERR, N. L., & TINDALE, R. S. (2004). Group performance and decision making. *Annual Review of Psychology, 55,* 623–655.

KESSLER, R. C., AVENEVOLI, S., & RIES MERIKANGAS, K. (2001). Mood disorders in children and adolescents: An epidemiologic perspective. *Biological Psychiatry, 49,* 1002–1014.

KESSLER, R. C., BERGLUND, P., DEMLER, O., JIN, R., MERIKANGAS, K. R., & WALTERS, E. E. (2005). Lifetime prevalence and age-of-onset distributions of *DSM-IV* disorders in the National Comorbidity Survey Replication. *Archives of General Psychiatry, 62,* 593–602.

KESSLER, R. C., HEERINGA, S., LAKOMA, M. D., PETUKHOVA, M., RUPP, A. E., SCHOENBAUM, M., ET AL. (2008). Individual and societal effects of mental disorders on earnings in the United States: Results from the National Comorbidity Survey Replication. *American Journal of Psychiatry, 165,* 703–711.

KESSLER, R. C., KELLER, M. B., & WITTCHEN, H.-U. (2001). The epidemiology of generalized anxiety disorder. *Psychiatric Clinics of North America, 24,* 19–39.

KESSLER, R. C., McGONAGLE, K. A., ZHAO, S., NELSON, C. B., HUGHES, M., ESHLEMAN, S., ET AL. (1994). Lifetime and 12-month prevalence of *DSM-III-R* psychiatric disorders in the United States: Results from the National

Comorbidity Survey. *Archives of General Psychiatry, 51,* 8–19.

KETY, S. S. (1988). Schizophrenic illness in the families of schizophrenic adoptees: Findings from the Danish National Sample. *Schizophrenia Bulletin, 14,* 217–222.

KHAN, R., LUK, C.-H., FLINKER, A., AGGARWAL, A., LAPID, H., HADDAD, R., ET AL. (2007). Predicting odor pleasantness from odorant structure: Pleasantness as a reflection of the physical world. *Journal of Neurosicence, 27,* 10015–10023.

KHANNA, S. M., & LEONARD, D. G. B. (1982). Basilar membrane tuning in the cat cochlea. *Science, 215,* 305–306.

KIHLSTROM, J. F. (1993). The recovery of memory in the laboratory and the clinic. Paper presented at the 1993 conventions of the Rocky Mountain and the Western Psychological Associations, Phoenix, AZ.

KIHLSTROM, J. F. (1987). The cognitive unconscious. *Science, 238,* 1638.

KIHLSTROM, J. F. (1997). Suffering from reminiscences: Exhumed memory, implicit memory, and the return of the repressed. In M. Conway (Ed.), *Recovered memories and false memories* (pp. 100–117). New York: Oxford University Press.

KIHLSTROM, J. F. (2002). No need for repression. *Trends in Cognitive Sciences, 6*(12), 502.

KIHLSTROM, J. F., & CANTOR, N. (2000). Social intelligence. In R. J. Sternberg (Ed.), *Handbook of intelligence* (2nd ed., pp. 359–379). Cambridge, England: Cambridge University Press.

KIHLSTROM, J. F., & MCCONKEY, K. M. (1990). William James and hypnosis: A centennial reflection. *Psychological Science, 1* (3), 174–178.

KIHLSTROM, J. F., & SCHACTER, D. L. (2000). Functional amnesia. In F. Boller & J. Grafman (Eds.), *Handbook of neuropsychology* (2nd ed., Vol. 2, pp. 409–427). Amsterdam: Elsevier.

KILHAM, W., & MANN, L. (1974). Level of destructive obedience as a function of transmitter and executant roles in the Milgram obedience paradigm. *Journal of Personality and Social Psychology, 29,* 696–702.

KILLEEN, P. R., & NASH, M. R. (2003). The four causes of hypnosis. *International Journal of Clinical and Experimental Hypnosis, 51,* 195–231.

KILPATRICK, L., & CAHILL, L. (2003). Amygdala modulation of parahippocampal and frontal regions during emotionally influenced memory storage. *Neuroimage, 20,* 2091–2099.

KIM, C.-Y., & BLAKE, R. (2005). Psychophysical magic: Rendering the visible "invisible." *Trends in Cognitive Sciences, 9,* 381–388.

KIM, H., & MARKUS, H. R. (1999). Deviance or uniqueness, harmony or conformity? A cultural analysis. *Journal of Personality and Social Psychology, 77*(4), 785–800.

KIM, J. Y., & NAM, S. H. (1998). The concept and dynamics of face: Implications for organizational behavior in Asia. *Organization Science, 9*(4), 522–534.

KIM, W.-Y., & SNIDER, W. (2008). Overcoming inhibitions. *Science, 322,* 869–872.

KIMBERG, D. Y., D'ESPOSITO, M., & FARAH, M. J. (1998). Cognitive functions in the prefrontal cortex—working memory and executive control. *Current Directions in Psychological Science, 6,* 185–192.

KIMBLE, G. A. (1961). *Hilgard and Marquis' conditioning and learning.* New York: Appleton-Century-Crofts.

KIMURA, D., & WATSON, N. (1989). The relation between oral movement and speech. *Brain and Language, 37,* 565–590.

KING-CASAS, B., SHARP, C., LOMAX-BREAM, L., LOHRENZ, T., FONAGY, P., & MONTAGUE, P. (2008). The rupture and repair of cooperation in borderline personality disorder. *Science, 321*(5890), 806–810.

KINGSTONE, A., FRIESEN, C., & GAZZANIGA, M. (2000). Reflexive joint attention depends on lateralized cortical connections. *Psychological Science, 11,* 159–166.

KINOSHITA, S. (2001). The role of involuntary aware memory in the implicit stem and fragment completion tasks: A selective review. *Psychonomic Bulletin & Review, 8,* 58–69.

KINSBOURNE, M. (2000). How is consciousness expressed in the cerebral activation manifold? *Brain and Mind, 2,* 265–274.

KINSEY, A., POMEROY, W. B., & MARTIN, C. E. (1948). *Sexual behavior in the human male.* Philadelphia: Saunders.

KINSEY, A., POMEROY, W., MARTIN, C., & GEBHARD, P. (1953). *Sexual behavior in the human female.* Philadelphia: Saunders.

KINZLER, K. D., DUPOUX, E., & SPELKE, E. S. (2007). The native language of social cognition. *Proceedings of the National Academy of Sciences, 104,* 12577–12580.

KINZLER, K. D., SHUTTS, K., DEJESUS, J., & SPELKE, E. S. (in press). Accent trumps race in guiding children's social preferences. *Social Cognition.*

KIRSCH, I. (2001). The response set theory of hypnosis: Expectancy and physiology. American Journal of Clinical Hypnosis, 44, 69–73.

KIRSCH, I., & BRAFFMAN, W. (2001). Imaginative suggestibility and hypnotizability. Current Directions in Psychological Science, 10(2), 57–61.

KITANO, J., & BOLNICK, D. I. (2008). Reverse evolution of armor plates in the threespine stickleback. *Current Biology, 18,* 769–774.

KITAYAMA, S., MARKUS, H. R., MATSUMOTO, H., & NORASAKKUNKIT, V. (1997). Individual and collective processes in the construction of the self: Self-enhancement in the United States and self-criticism in Japan. *Journal of Personality and Social Psychology, 72,* 1245–1267.

KITAYAMA, S., SNIBBE, A. C., MARKUS, H. R., & SUZUKI, T. (2004). Is there any "free" choice? Self and dissonance in two cultures. *Psychological Science, 15,* 527–533.

KITZINGER, C. (2001). Sexualities. In R. K. Unger (Ed.), *Handbook of the psychology of women and gender* (pp. 272–285). New York: Wiley.

KLAHR, D., & SIMON, H. A. (2001). What have psychologists (and others) discovered about the process of scientific discovery? *Current Directions in Psychological Science, 10,* 75–79.

KLAUER, K. C., MUSCH, J., & NAUMER, B. (2000). On belief bias in syllogistic reasoning. *Psychological Review, 107,* 852–884.

KLAUS, M. H., & KENNELL, J. H. (1976). *Maternal-infant bonding: The impact of early separation or loss on family development.* St. Louis, MO: Mosby.

KLAUS, M. H., KENNELL, J. H., PLUMB, N., & ZUEHLKE, S. (1970). Human maternal behavior at the first contact with her young. *Pediatrics, 46,* 187.

KLEINMAN, A. (1986). *Social origins of distress and disease: Neurasthenia, depression, and pain in modern China.* New Haven, CT: Yale University Press.

KLERMAN, G., & WEISSMAN, M. (1993). Interpersonal psychotherapy for depression: Background and concepts. In *New applications of interpersonal therapy.* Washington, DC: American Psychological Association Press.

KLIMA, E., & BELLUGI, U., WITH BATTISON, R., BOYES-BRAEM, P., FISCHER, S., FRISHBERG, N., ET AL. (1979). *The signs of language.* Cambridge, MA: Harvard University Press.

KLINE, P. (1995). A critical review of the measurement of personality and intelligence. In D. H. Saklofske & M. Zeidner (Eds.), *International handbook of personality and intelligence* (pp. 505–524). New York: Plenum.

KLOPFER, B., AINSWORTH, M., KLOPFER, W. G., & HOLT, R. R. (1954). *Developments in the Rorschach technique.* Yonkers, NY: World Book.

KLUFT, R. P. (1987). An update on multiple-personality disorder. *Journal of Hospital and Community Psychiatry, 38,* 363–373.

KNUTSON, B. (2004). Sweet revenge? *Science, 305,* 1246–1247.

KNUTSON, B., FONG, G. W., ADAMS, C. M., VARNER, J. L., & HOMMER, D. (2001). Dissociation of reward anticipation and outcome with event-related fMRI. *Neuroreport, 12*(17), 3683–3687.

KOCH, C. (2008). The neuroscience of consciousness. In L. R. Squire, F. E. Bloom, N. C., Spitzer, S. du Lac, A. Ghosh & D. Berg (Eds.), *Fundamental Neuroscience,* 3rd Ed. (pp. 1223–1236). Burlington, MA: Academic Press.

KOCHANSKA, G. (1993). Toward a synthesis of parental socialization and child temperament in early development of conscience. *Child Development, 64,* 325–347.

KOCHANSKA, G. (1995). Children's temperament, mother's discipline, and security of attachment: Multiple pathways to emerging internalization. *Child Development, 66,* 597–615.

KOCHANSKA, G. (1997). Multiple pathways to conscience for children with different temperaments: From toddlerhood to age 5. *Developmental Psychology, 33,* 228–240.

KOCHANSKA, G. (2001). Emotional development in children with different attachment histories: The first three years. *Child Development, 72*(2), 474–490.

KOCHANSKA, G. (2002). Mutually responsive orientation between mothers and their young children: A context for the early development of conscience. *Current Directions in Psychological Science, 11*(6), 191–195.

KOCHANSKA, G., AKSAN, N., KNAACK, A., & RHINES, H. (2004). Maternal parenting and children's conscience: Early security as a moderator. *Child Development, 75,* 1229–1242.

KOECHLIN, E., & HYAFIL, A. (2007). Anterior prefrontal function and the limits of human decision-making. *Science, 318*, 594–598.

KOEKKOEK, S., HULSCHER, H., DORTLAND, B., HENBROEK, R., ELGERSMA, Y., RUIGROK, T., ET AL. (2003). Cerebellar LTD and learning-dependent timing of conditioned eyelink responses. *Science, 301*, 1736–1739.

KOESTNER, R., & MCCLELLAND, D. C. (1990). Perspectives on competence motivation. In L. A. Pervin (Ed.), *Handbook of personality theory and research* (pp. 527–548). New York: Guilford.

KOH, P. O., BERGSON, C., UNDIE, A. S., GOLDMAN-RAKIC, P. S., & LIDOW, M. S. (2003). Up-regulation of the D1 dopamine receptor-interacting protein, calcyon, in patients with schizophrenia. *Archives of General Psychiatry, 60*, 311–319.

KOHLBERG, L. (1969). Stage and sequence: The cognitive developmental approach to socialization. In D. A. Goslin (Ed.), *Handbook of socialization theory of research* (pp. 347–480). Chicago: Rand McNally.

KOHLBERG, L., LEVINE, C., & HEWER, A. (1984). Synopses and detailed replies to critics. In L. Kohlberg (Ed.), *The psychology of moral development: The nature and validity of moral stages* (pp. 320–386). San Francisco: Harper & Row.

KOHN, A. (1993). *Punished by rewards.* New York: Houghton Mifflin.

KOHN, M. L. (1968). Social class and schizophrenia: A critical review. In D. Rosenthal & S. S. Kety (Eds.), *The transmission of schizophrenia* (pp. 155–174). London: Pergamon.

KOLB, B., GIBB, R., & ROBINSON, T. E. (2003). Brain plasticity and behavior. *Current Directions in Psychological Science, 12*, 1–5.

KOLB, B., & WHISHAW, I. Q. (2009). *Fundamentals of human neuropsychology* (6th ed.). New York: Worth.

KOLB, I., & WHISHAW, I. Q. (2009). *An introduction to brain and behavior.* 6th ed. New York: Worth.

KOLERS, P., & ROEDIGER, H. (1984). Procedures of mind. *Journal of Verbal Learning and Verbal Behavior, 23*, 425–449.

KONDZIOLKA, D., WECHSLER, L., GOLDSTEIN, S., MELTZER, C., THULBORN, K. R., GEBEL, J., ET AL. (2000). Transplantation of cultured human neuronal cells for patients with stroke. *Neurology, 55*(4), 565–569.

KORN, J. H. (1997). *Illusions of reality: A history of deception in social psychology.* Albany: State University of New York Press.

KOSSLYN, S. M., BALL, T. M., & REISSER, B. J. (1978). Visual images preserve metric spatial information: Evidence from studies of image scanning. *Journal of Experimental Psychology: Human Perception and Performance, 4*, 1–20.

KOSSLYN, S. M., PASCUAL-LEONE, A., FELICIAN, O., CAMPOSANO, S., KEENAN, J. P., THOMPSON, W. L., ET AL. (1999). The role of area 17 in visual imagery: Convergent evidence from PET and rTMS. *Science, 284*, 167–170.

KOTTER, R., & MEYER, N. (1992). The limbic system: A review of its empirical foundation. *Behavioural Brain Research, 52*, 105–127.

KOVACS, A., & MEHLER, J. (2009). Cognitive gains in 7-month-old bilingual infants. *Proceedings of the National Academy of Sciences, 106*(16), 6556–6560.

KOVELMAN, I., SHALINSKY, M. H., BERENS, M. S., & PETITTO, L. (2008). Shining new light on the brain's "bilingual signature": A functional Near Infrared Spectroscopy investigation of semantic processing. *NeuroImage, 39*(3), 1457–1471.

KOVERA, M. B. (2002). The effects of general pretrial publicity on juror decisions: An examination of moderators and mediating mechanisms. *Law and Human Behavior, 26*(1), 43–72.

KRAMER, A. F., & WILLIS, S. L. (2002). Enhancing the cognitive vitality of older adults. *Current Directions in Psychological Science, 11*, 173–177.

KRAMER, P. D. (1993). *Listening to Prozac.* New York: Viking.

KRASNE, F. B., & GLANZMAN, D. L. (1995). What we can learn from invertebrate learning. *Annual Review of Psychology, 45*, 585–624.

KRAUS, S. J. (1995). Attitudes and the prediction of behavior: A meta analysis of the empirical literature. *Personality and Social Psychology Bulletin, 21*(1), 58–75.

KREBS, D. L., & DENTON, K. (2005). Toward a more pragmatic approach to morality: A critical evaluation of Kohlberg's model. *Psychological Review, 112*(3), 629–649.

KREBS, J. R. (1982). Territorial defence in the great tit (Parus Major L.). *Ecology, 52*, 2–22.

KRING, A. M., & GORDON, A. H. (1998). Sex differences in emotion: Expression, experience, and physiology. *Journal of Personality and Social Psychology, 74*, 686–703.

KRUEGER, R. F., & MARKON, K. E. (2006). Understanding psychopathology: Melding behavior genetics, personality, and quantitative psychology to develop an empirically based model. *Current Directions in Psychological Science, 15*, 113–117.

KRUGLANSKI, A. W., PIERRO, A., MANNETTI, L., & GRADA, E. D. (2006). Groups as epistemic providers: Need for closure and the unfolding of group-centrism. *Psychological Review, 113*(1), 84–100.

KRUPNICK, J. L., SOTSKY, S. M., SIMMENS, S., MOYER, J., ELKIN, I., WATKINS, J., ET AL. (1996). The role of the therapeutic alliance in psychotherapy and pharmacotherapy outcome: Findings in the National Institute of Mental Health Treatment of Depression Collaborative Research Program. *Journal of Consulting and Clinical Psychology, 64*, 532–539.

KRUSCHKE, J. K., & BLAIR, N. J. (2000). Blocking and backward blocking involve learned inattention. *Psychonomics Bulletin and Review, 7*, 636–645.

KUAN, D. Y., ROTH, K. A., FLAVELL, R. A., & RAKIC, P. (2000). Mechanisms of programmed cell death in the developing brain. *Trends in Neuroscience, 23*, 291–297.

KUHL, P., WILLIAMS, K., LACERDA, F., STEVENS, K., & LINDBLOM, B. (1992). Linguistic experience alters phonetic perception in infants by six months of age. *Science, 255*, 606–608.

KUHN, D. (2006). Do cognitive changes accompany developments in the adolescent brain? *Perspectives on Psychological Science, 1*, 59–67.

KUHN, D., NASH, S., & BRUCKEN, L. (1978). Sex-role concepts of two- and three-year-olds. *Child Development, 49*, 445–451.

KUMARI, V. (2006). Do psychotherapies produce neurobiological effects? *Acta Neuropsychiatrica, 18*, 61–70.

KUMARI, V., FFYTCHE, D. H., WILLIAMS, S. C., & GRAY, J. A. (2004). Personality predicts brain responses to cognitive demands. *Journal of Neuroscience, 24*, 10636–10641.

KUNCEL, N. R., HEZLETT, S. A., & ONES, D. S. (2004). Academic performance, career potential, creativity, and job performance: Can one construct predict them all? *Journal of Personality and Social Psychology, 86*, 148–161.

KUNDA, Z. (1990). The case for motivated reasoning. *Psychological Bulletin, 108*, 480–498.

KUNDA, Z., FONG, G. T., SANITIOSO, R., & REBER, E. (1993). Directional questions direct self conceptions. *Journal of Experimental Social Psychology, 29*(1), 63–86.

KUNDA, Z., & NISBETT, R. E. (1986). The psychometrics of everyday life. *Cognitive Psychology, 18*, 195–224.

KURDEK, L. A. (2005a). Gender and marital satisfaction early in marriage: A growth curve approach. *Journal of Marriage and Family, 67*(1), 68–84.

KURDEK, L. A. (2005b). What do we know about gay and lesbian couples? *Current Directions in Psychological Science, 14*, 251–254.

KURIHARA, K., & KASHIWAYANAGI, M. (1998). Introductory remarks on umami taste. *Annals of the New York Academy of Sciences, 855*, 393–397.

KURTZ, S. N. (1991). Polysexualization: A new approach to Oedipus in the Trobriands. *Ethos, 19*, 68–101.

KURZBAN, R., & LEARY, M. R. (2001). Evolutionary origins of stigmatization: The functions of social exclusion. *Psychological Bulletin, 127*, 187–208.

KYLLONEN, P. C., & CHRISTAL, R. E. (1990). Reasoning ability is (little more than) working memory capacity? *Intelligence, 14*(4), 389–433.

———

LABAR, K. (2007). Beyond fear: Emotional memory mechanisms in the human brain. *Current Directions in Psychological Science, 16*, 173–177.

LABAR, K. S., & CABEZA, R. (2006). Cognitive neuroscience of emotional memory. *Nature Reviews Neuroscience, 7*, 54–64.

LABORATORY OF COMPARATIVE HUMAN COGNITION. (1983). Culture and cognitive development. In P. Mussen (Ed.), *Handbook of child psychology: Vol. 1. History, theory and methods* (4th ed.). New York: Wiley.

LABOV, W. (1972). *Language in the inner city: Studies in the Black English vernacular.* Philadelphia: University of Pennsylvania Press.

LABOV, W. (2007). Transmission and diffusion. *Language, 83*(2), 344–387.

LADD, G., KOCHENDERFER, B., & COLEMAN, C. (1996). Friendship quality as a predictor of young children's early school adjustment. *Child Development, 67*, 1103–1118.

LADD, G., & PRICE, J. (1987). Predicting children's social and school adjustment following the transition from preschool to kindergarten. *Child Development, 58*, 1168–1189.

LADEFOGED, P. (1975). *A course in phonetics*. New York: Harcourt Brace Jovanovich.

LADEFOGED, P., & MADDIESON, I. (1996). *The sounds of the world's languages*. Cambridge, MA: Blackwell.

LAFARGE, L. (1993). The early determinants of penis envy. In R. A. Glick & S. P. Roose (Eds.), *Rage, power, and aggression. The role of affect in motivation, development, and adaptation: Vol. 2* (pp. 80–101). New Haven, CT: Yale University Press.

LAGATTUTA, K., WELLMAN, H., & FLAVELL, J. (1997). Preschoolers' understanding of the link between thinking and feeling: Cognitive cuing and emotional change. *Child Development, 68*, 1081–1104.

LAIBLE, D. (2004). Mother-child discourse surrounding a child's past behavior at 30 months: Links to emotional understanding and early conscience development at 36 months. *Merrill-Palmer Quarterly, 50*, 159–180.

LAIBLE, D., & THOMPSON, R. A. (1998). Attachment and emotional understanding in preschool children. *Developmental Psychology, 34*, 1038–1045.

LAIBLE, D., & THOMPSON, R. A. (2000). Mother-child discourse, attachment security, shared positive affect, and early conscience development. *Child Development, 71*, 1424–1440.

LAIBLE, D., & THOMPSON, R. A. (2002). Mother-child conflict in the toddler years: Lessons in emotion, morality, and relationships. *Child Development, 73*, 1187–1203.

LAIRD, R., JORDAN, K., DODGE, K., PETTIT, G., & BATES, J. (2001). Peer rejection in childhood, involvement with antisocial peers in early adolescence, and the development of externalizing problems. *Development and Psychopathology, 13*, 337–354.

LALONDE, J. K., HUDSON, J. I., GIGANTE, R. A., & POPE, H. G., JR. (2001). Canadian and American psychiatrists' attitudes toward dissociative disorders diagnoses. *Canadian Journal of Psychiatry, 46*, 407–412.

LALUMIERE, M., BLANCHARD, R., & ZUCKER, K. (2000). Sexual orientation and handedness in men and women: A meta-analysis. *Psychological Bulletin, 126*, 575–592.

LAMARINE, R. (1995). Child and adolescent depression. *Journal of School Health, 65*, 390–394.

LAMB, H. R. (1984). Deinstitutionalization and the homeless mentally ill. *Hospital Community Psychiatry, 35*, 899–907.

LAMB, H. R. (1998). Deinstitutionalization at the beginning of the new millennium. *Harvard Review of Psychiatry, 6*, 1–10.

LAMB, H. R., & BACHRACH, L. L. (2001). Some perspectives on deinstitutionalization. *Psychiatric Services, 52*, 1039–1045.

LAMB, K. (1994). Genetics and Spearman's "g" factor. *Mankind Quarterly, 34*, 379–391.

LAMB, M., & MALKIN, C. (1986). The development of social expectations in distress-relief sequences: A longitudinal study. *International Journal of Behavioral Development, 9*, 235–249.

LAMB, M. E. (Ed.). (1987). *The father's role: Cross-cultural perspectives*. Hillsdale, NJ: Erlbaum.

LAMB, M. E. (Ed.). (1997). *The role of the father in child development* (3rd ed.). New York: Wiley.

LAMBERG, L. (2004). Efforts to keep mentally ill out of jails. *Journal of the American Medical Association, 292*(5), 555–556.

LAMBERT, M. J., & BERGIN, A. E. (1994). The effectiveness of psychotherapy. In A. E. Bergin & S. L. Garfield (Eds.), *Handbook of psychotherapy and behavior change* (4th ed., pp. 143–189). New York: Wiley.

LANDAU, B. (1982). Will the real grandmother please stand up? The psychological reality of dual meaning representations. *Journal of Psycholinguistic Research, 11*, 47–62.

LANDAU, B., & GLEITMAN, L. R. (1985). *Language and experience: Evidence from the blind child*. Cambridge, MA: Harvard University Press.

LANDAU, B., & MUNNICH, E. (1998). The representation of space of spatial language: Challenges for cognitive science. In P. Olivier & K. Gapp (Eds.), *Representation and processing of spatial expressions* (pp. 263–272). Mahwah, NJ: Erlbaum.

LANDAU, B., SMITH, L., & JONES, S. (1988). The importance of shape in early lexical learning. *Cognitive Development, 3*, 299–321.

LANDAU, B., & STECKER, D. (1990). Objects and places: Geometric and syntactic representations in early lexical learning. *Cognitive Development, 5*, 287–312.

LANDAU, B., & ZUKOWSKI, A. (2002). Objects, motions, and paths: Spatial language of children with Williams Syndrome. *Developmental Neuropsychology* [Special issue, C. B. Mervis (Ed.)].

LANDIS, C., & HUNT, W. A. (1932). Adrenalin and emotion. *Psychological Review, 39*, 467–485.

LANE, S. D., CHEREK, D. R., TCHEREMISSINE, O. V., LIEVING, L. M., & PIETRAS, C. J. (2005). Acute Marijuana Effects on Human Risk Taking. *Neuropsychopharmacology, 30*, 800–809.

LANEY, C., MORRIS, E. K., BERNSTEIN, D. M., WAKEFIELD, B. M., & LOFTUS, E. F. (2008). Asparagus, a love story: Healthier eating could be just a false memory away. *Experimental Psychology, 55*, 291–300.

LANG, B., & PERNER, J. (2002). Understanding of intention and false belief and the development of self-control. *British Journal of Developmental Psychology, 20*(1), 67–76.

LANG, P. J., DAVIS, M., & OHMAN, A. (2000). Fear and anxiety: Animal models and human cognitive psychophysiology. *Journal of Affective Disorders, 61*, 137–159.

LANGER, E. J., & RODIN, J. (1976). The effects of choice and enhanced personal responsibility for the aged: A field experiment in an institutional setting. *Journal of Personality and Social Psychology, 34*, 191–198.

LANGLOIS, J. H., & DOWNS, A. C. (1980). Mothers, fathers, and peers as socialization agents of sex-typed play behaviors in young children. *Child Development, 51*, 1237–1347.

LANGLOIS, J. H., KALAKANIS, L., RUBENSTEIN, A. J., LARSON, A., HALLAM, M., & SMOOT, M. (2000). Maxims or myths of beauty? A meta-analytic and theoretical review. *Psychological Bulletin, 126*(3), 390–423.

LANGLOIS, J. H., ROGGMAN, L. A., CASEY, R. J., RITTER, J. M., RIESER-DANNER, L. A., & JENKINS, V. Y. (1987). Infant preferences for attractive faces: Rudiments of a stereotype. *Developmental Psychobiology, 23*, 363–369.

LANYON, R. I., & GOLDSTEIN, L. D. (1971). *Personality assessment*. New York: Wiley.

LAPIERE, R. (1934). Attitudes versus actions. *Social Forces, 13*, 230–237.

LARSEN, R. J., & DIENER, E. (1992). Promises and problems with the circumplex model of emotion. In M. S. Clark (Ed.), *Emotion: Review of personality and social psychology* (Vol. 13, pp. 25–59). Newbury Park, CA: Sage.

LARSON, R., & WILSON, S. (2004). Adolescence across place and time: Globalization and the changing pathways to adulthood. In R. M. Lerner & L. Steinberg (Eds.), *Handbook of adolescent psychology* (pp. 299–330). New York: Wiley.

LA ROSA, J., & DIAZ-LOVING, R. (1991). Evaluation of the self-concept: A multidimensional inventory/Evaluacion del autoconcepto: una escala multidimensional. *Revista Latinoamericana de Psicologia. Special Personality, 23*, 15–33.

LARSEN, R. J., KASIMATIS, M., & FREY, K. (1992). Facilitating the furrowed brow: An unobtrusive test of the facial feedback hypothesis applied to unpleasant affect. *Cognition and Emotion, 6*, 321–338.

LARUELLE, M., KEGELES, L. S., & ABI-DARHAM, A. (2003). Glutamate, dopamine, and schizophrenia: From pathophysiology to treatment. *Annals of the New York Academy of Sciences, 1003*, 138–158.

LASSITER, G. D. (2000). The relative contributions of recognition and search-evaluation processes to high-level chess performance: Comment on Gobet and Simon. *Psychological Science, 11*(2), 172–173.

LATANÉ, B. (1981). The psychology of social impact. *American Psychologist, 36*, 343–356.

LATANÉ, B., & NIDA, S. (1981). Group size and helping. *Psychological Bulletin, 89*, 308–324.

LATANÉ, B., NIDA, S. A., & WILSON, D. W. (1981). The effects of group size on helping behavior. In J. P. Rushton & R. M. Sorrentino (Eds.), *Altruism and helping behavior: Social, personality, and developmental perspectives*. Hillsdale, NJ: Erlbaum.

LATANÉ, B., WILLIAMS, K., & HARKINS, S. (1979). Many hands make light the work: The causes and consequences of social loafing. *Journal of Personality and Social Psychology, 37*, 822–832.

LATTAL, K. M., HONARVAR, S., & ABEL, T. (2004). Effects of post-session injections of anisomycin on the extinction of a spatial preference and on the acquisition of a spatial reversal preference. *Behavioural Brain Research, 153*, 327–339.

LAU, R. R., & RUSSELL, D. (1980). Attributions in the sports pages. *Journal of Personality and Social Psychology, 39*, 29–38.

LAU, H. C., ROGERS, R. D., HAGGARD, P., & PASSINGHAM, R. E. (2004). Attention to intention. *Science, 303* (5661), 1208–1210.

LAURSEN, B., COY, K., & COLLINS, W. (1998). Reconsidering changes in parent-child conflict across adolescence: A meta-analysis. *Child Development, 69*, 817–832.

LAUREYS, S. (2005). The neural correlate of (un)awareness: Lessons from the vegetative state. *Trends in Cognitive Sciences, 9* (12), 556–559.

LAWRIE, S. M., & ABUKMEIL, S. S. (1998). Brain abnormality in schizophrenia: A systematic and quantitative review of volumetric magnetic resonance imaging studies. *British Journal of Psychiatry, 172,* 110–120.

LAYZER, D. (1972). Science or superstition: A physical scientist looks at the I.Q. controversy. *Cognition, 1,* 265–300.

LAZAREVA, O. F., FREIBURGER, K. L., & WASSERMAN, E. A. (2004). Pigeons concurrently categorize photographs at both basic and superordinate levels. *Psychonomic Bulletin & Review, 11*(6), 1111–1117.

LAZARUS, A. A. (1971). *Behavior therapy and beyond.* New York: McGraw-Hill.

LAZARUS, A. A. (1981). *The practice of multi-modal therapy.* New York: McGraw-Hill.

LAZARUS, A. A. (2006). *Brief but comprehensive psychotherapy: The multimodal way.* New York: Springer.

LAZARUS. R. S. (1991). *Emotion and adaptation.* Oxford, England: Oxford University Press.

LE BON, G. (1895). *The crowd.* New York: Viking Press, 1960.

LEA, S. E. G., & RYAN, C. M. E. (1990). Unnatural concepts and the theory of concept discrimination in birds. In M. L. Commons, R. J. Herrnstein, S. Kosslyn, & D. Mumford (Eds.), *Quantitative analysis of behavior, Vol. 8: Behavioral approaches to pattern recognition and concept formation* (pp. 165–185). Hillsdale, NJ: Erlbaum.

LEAPER, C., ANDERSON, K. J., & SANDERS, P. (1998). Moderators of gender effects on parents' talk to their children: A meta-analysis. *Developmental Psychology, 34*(1), 3–27.

LEARY, M. R., & COX, C. B. (2008). Belongingness motivation: A mainspring of social action. In J. Y. Shah & W. L. Gardner (Eds.), *Handbook of motivation science* (pp. 27–40). New York: Guilford.

LEARY, M. R., TAMBOR, E. S., TERDAL, S. K., & DOWNS, D. L. (1995). Self-esteem as an interpersonal monitor: The sociometer hypothesis. *Journal of Personality and Social Psychology, 68,* 518–530.

LEBEDEV, M., & NICOLELIS, M. (2006). Brain-machine interfaces: Past, present and future. *Trends in Neurosciences, 29,* 536–546.

LECKMAN, J. F., ZHANG, H., ALSOBROOK, J. P., & PAULS, D. L. (2001). Symptom dimensions in obsessive-compulsive disorder: Toward quantitative phenotypes. *American Journal of Medical Genetics, 105,* 28–30.

LEDOUX, J. E. (1995). Emotion: Clues from the brain. *Annual Review of Psychology, 46,* 209–235.

LEDOUX, J. E. (1996). The emotional brain: The mysterious underpinnings of emotional life. New York: Simon & Schuster.

LEE, A., HOBSON, R. P., & CHIAT, S. (1994). I, you, me, and autism: An experimental study. *Journal of Autism and Developmental Disorders, 24,* 155–176.

LEE, D., & YOUNG, K. (2001). Post-traumatic stress disorder: Diagnostic issues and epidemiology in adult survivors of traumatic events. *International Review of Psychiatry, 13,* 150–158.

LEE, P., & BROWN, N. (2004). Delay related changes in personal memories for September 11, 2001. *Applied Cognitive Psychology, 14,* 1007–1015.

LEFEVER, G. B., ARCONA, A. P., & ANTONUCCIO, D. O. (2003). ADHD among American schoolchildren: Evidence of overdiagnosis and overuse of medication. *Scientific Review of Mental Health Practice, 2,* 49–60.

LEHMAN, D., LEMPERT, R. O., & NISBETT, R. E. (1988). The effects of graduate training on reasoning: Formal discipline and thinking about everyday-life events. *American Psychologist, 43,* 431–442.

LEHMAN, D., & NISBETT, R. (1990). A longitudinal study of the effects of undergraduate education on reasoning. *Developmental Psychology, 26,* 952–960.

LEIBOWITZ, S. F. (1991). Brain neuropeptide Y: An integrator of endocrine, metabolic and behavioral processes. *Brain Research Bulletin, 27,* 333–337.

LEICHSENRING, F., & RABUNG, S. (2008). Effectiveness of long-term psychodynamic psychotherapy: A meta-analysis. *Journal of the American Medical Association, 300,* 1551–1565.

LENNEBERG, E. H. (1967). *Biological foundations of language.* New York: Wiley.

LENNOX, B. R., PARK, B. G., MEDLEY, F., MORRIS, P. G., & JONES, P. B. (2000). The functional anatomy of auditory hallucinations in schizophrenia. *Psychiatry Research: Neuroimaging, 100,* 13–20.

LENZENWEGER, M. F. (2006). Schizotypy: An organizing framework for schizophrenia research. *Current Directions in Psychological Science, 15*(4), 162–166.

LÉPINE, R., BARROUILLET, P., & CAMOS, V. (2005). What makes working memory spans so predictive of high-level cognition? *Psychonomic Bulletin and Review, 12,* 165–170.

LEPPER, M. R., GREENE, D., & NISBETT, R. E. (1973). Undermining children's intrinsic interest with extrinsic rewards: A test of the "overjustification" hypothesis. *Journal of Personality and Social Psychology, 28,* 129–137.

LEROITH, D., SHILOACH, J., & ROTH, J. (1982). Is there an earlier phylogenetic precursor that is common to both the nervous and endocrine systems? *Peptides, 3,* 211–215.

LESCH, K. P., BENGEL, D., HEILS, A., SABOL, S. Z., GREENBERG, B. D., PETRI, S., ET AL. (1996). Association of anxiety-related traits with a polymorphism in the serotonin transporter gene regulatory region. *Science, 274*(5292), 1527–1531.

LESLIE, A. M. (1992). Pretense, autism, and the theory of mind module. *Current Directions in Psychological Science, 1,* 18–21.

LETTVIN, J. Y., MATURAN, H. R., McCULLOCH, W. S., & PITTS, W. H. (1959). What the frog's eye tells the frog's brain. *Proceedings of the Institute of Radio Engineers, 47,* 1940–1951.

LEVAY, S. (1991). A difference in hypothalamic sctructure between heterosexual and homosexual men. *Science, 253,* 1034–1037.

LEVELT, W. (1970). A scaling approach to the study of syntactic relations. In G. Flores d'Arcais & W. Levelt (Eds.), *Advances in psycholinguistics* (pp. 109–121). Amsterdam: North-Holland.

LEVELT, W. J. M. (1989). *Speaking: From intention to articulation.* Cambridge, MA: MIT Press.

LEVENSON, R. W. (1992). Autonomic nervous system differences among emotions. *Psychological Science, 3,* 23–27.

LEVENSON, R. W. (1994). The search for autonomic specificity. In P. Ekman & R. J. Davidson (Eds.), *Human emotions: A functional view* (pp. 252–257). New York: Oxford University Press.

LEVENSON, R. W. (1999). The intrapersonal functions of emotion. *Cognition and Emotion, 13,* 481–504.

LEVENSON, R. W. (2003). Autonomic specificity and emotion. In R. J. Davidson, K. R. Scherer, & H. H. Goldsmith (Eds.), *Handbook of affective sciences* (pp. 212–224). New York: Oxford University Press.

LEVENSON, R. W., EKMAN, P., HEIDER, K., & FRIESEN, W. V. (1992). Emotion and autonomic nervous system activity in the Minangkabau of West Sumatra. *Journal of Personality and Social Psychology, 62,* 972–988.

LEVEY, D. J., DUNCAN, R. S., & LEVINS, C. F. (2004). Animal behaviour: Use of dung as a tool by burrowing owls. *Nature, 431,* 39.

LEVIN, I., & GAETH, G. (1988). How consumers are affected by the framing of attribute information before and after consuming the product. *Journal of Consumer Research, 15,* 374–378.

LEVIN, I. P., GAETH, G. J., EVANGELISTA, F., ALBAUM, G., & SCHREIBER, J. (2001). How positive and negative frames influence the decisions of persons in America and Australia. *Asia-Pacific Journal of Marketing and Logistics, 13,* 64–71.

LEVINE, J. M., & MORELAND, R. L. (1998). Small groups. In D. Gilbert, S. Fiske, & G. Lindzey (Eds.), *The handbook of social psychology* (4th ed., pp. 415–469). Boston: McGraw-Hill.

LEVINE, L. J., & PIZARRO, D. A. (2004). Emotion and memory research: A grumpy overview. *Social Cognition, 22*(5), 530–554.

LEVINE, L. J., STEIN, N. L., & LIWAG, M. D. (1999). Remembering children's emotions: Sources of concordant and discordant accounts between parents and children. *Developmental Psychology, 35,* 790–801.

LEVINE, M., & CROWTHER, S. (2008). The responsive bystander: How social group membership and group size can encourage as well as inhibit bystander intervention. *Journal of Personality and Social Psychology, 95,* 1429–1439.

LEVINE, S. C., HUTTENLOCHER, J., TAYLOR, A., & LANGROCK, A. (1999). Early sex differences in spatial skill. *Developmental Psychology, 35,* 940–949.

LEVINSON, S. (2003). Space in language and cognition: Explorations in linguistic diversity. Cambridge: Cambridge University Press.

LEVITSKY, D. A. (2002). Putting behavior back into feeding behavior: A tribute to George Collier. *Appetite, 38,* 143–148.

LEVY, G. D., TAYLOR, M. G., & GELMAN, S. A. (1995). Traditional and evaluative aspects of flexibility in gender roles, social conventions, moral rules, and physical laws. *Child Development, 66*(2), 515–531.

LEVY, J. (1985). Right brain, left brain: Facts and fiction. *Psychology Today, 19,* 38–44.

LEVY, W. B., & STEWARD, O. (1979). Synapses as associative memory elements in the hippocampal formation. *Brain Research, 175*, 233–245.

LEWIN, K. (1939). Field theory and experiment in social psychology: Concepts and methods. *American Journal of Sociology, 44*, 868–897.

LEWINSOHN, P. M., JOINER, T., & ROHDE, P. (2001). Evaluation of cognitive diathesis-stress models in predicting major depressive disorder in adolescents. *Journal of Abnormal Psychology, 110*, 203–215.

LEWIS, C., & KEREN, G. (1999). On the difficulties underlying Bayesian reasoning: A comment on Gigerenzer and Hoffrage. *Psychological Review, 106*, 411–416.

LEWIS, D. O., YEAGER, C. A., SWICA, Y., PINCUS, J. H., & LEWIS, M. (1997). Objective documentation of child abuse and dissociation in 12 murderers with dissociative identity disorder. *American Journal of Psychiatry, 154*, 1703–1710.

LEWIS, J. R., BATES, B. C., & LAWRENCE, S. (1994). Empirical studies of projection: A critical review. *Human Relations, 47*(11), 1295–1319.

LEWIS, M., ALESSANDRI, S., & SULLIVAN, M. (1990). Violation of expectancy, loss of control, and anger expressions in young infants. *Developmental Psychology, 26*, 745–751.

LEWIS, M., STANGER, C., & SULLIVAN, M. W. (1989). Deception in 3-year-olds. *Developmental Psychology, 25*(3), 439–443.

LEWIS, M. D., & GRANIC, I. (2000). *Emotion, development, and self-organization: Dynamic systems approaches to emotional development.* New York: Cambridge University Press.

LEWONTIN, R. C. (1976). Race and intelligence. In N. J. Block & G. Dworkin (Eds.), *The IQ controversy* (pp. 78–92). New York: Pantheon.

LI, P., ABARBINELL, L., PAPAFRAGOU, A., & GLEITMAN, L. (In press). Spatial reasoning skills in Tenejapan Mayans. Ms., University of Pennsylvania (under review, *Cognition*).

LI, P., & GLEITMAN, L. R. (2002). Turning the tables: Language and spatial reasoning. *Cognition, 83*, 265–294.

LIBERMAN, A. M., COOPER, F. S., SHANKWEILER, D. P., & STUDDERT-KENNEDY, M. (1967). Perception of the speech code. *Psychological Review, 74*, 431–461.

LIBET, B., GLEASON, C. A., WRIGHT, E. W., & PEARL, D. K. (1983). Time of conscious intention to act in relation to onset of cerebral activity (readiness-potential). The unconscious initiation of a freely voluntary act. *Brain, 106*, 623–642.

LICHTER, D. G., & CUMMINGS, J. L. (Eds.). (2001). *Frontal-subcortical circuits in psychiatric and neurological disorders.* New York: Guilford.

LIDZ, J., GLEITMAN, H., & GLEITMAN, L. (2003). Understanding how input matters: Verb learning and the footprint of universal grammar. *Cognition, 87*(3), 151–178.

LIEBERMAN, J. A. (1995). Signs and symptoms. Commentary. *Archives of General Psychiatry, 52*, 361–363.

LIEBERMAN, M. D., OCHSNER, K. N., GILBERT, D. T., & SCHACTER, D. L. (2001). Attitude change in amnesia and under cognitive load. *Psychological Science, 12*, 135–140.

LIFF, Z. A. (1992). Psychoanalysis and dynamic techniques. In D. K. Freedheim (Ed.), *History of psychotherapy.* Washington, DC: American Psychological Association.

LILIENFELD, S. O. (2007). Psychological treatments that can cause harm. *Perspectives on Psychological Science, 2*, 53–70.

LILIENFELD, S. O., KIRSCH, I., SARBIN, T. R., LYNN, S. J., CHAVES, J. F., GANAWAY, G. K., ET AL. (1999). Dissociative identity disorder and the sociocognitive model: Recalling the lessons of the past. *Psychological Bulletin, 125*, 507–523.

LILIENFELD, S. O., LYNN, S. J., NAMY, L. L., & WOOLF, N. J. (2008). *Psychology: From inquiry to understanding.* Boston: Allyn & Bacon.

LILIENFELD, S. O., WOOD, J. M., & GARB, H. N. (2000). The scientific status of projective techniques. *Psychological Science in the Public Interest, 1*, 27–66.

LILLARD, A. (1998). Enthnopsychologies: Cultural variations in theories of mind. *Psychological Bulletin, 123*, 3–32.

LILLARD, A. S. (1997). Other folks' theories of mind and behavior. *Psychological Science, 8*, 268–274.

LINEHAN, M. M., BOHUS, M., & LYNCH, T. R. (2007). Dialectical behavior therapy for pervasive emotion dysregulation: Theoretical and practical underpinnings. In J. J. Gross (Ed.), *Handbook of emotion regulation* (pp. 581–605). New York: Guilford.

LINTON, M. (1978). Real world memory after six years: An in vivo study of very long term memory. In M. M. Gruneberg, P. E. Morris, & R. N. Sykes (Eds.), *Practical aspects of memory* (pp. 69–76). London: Academic Press.

LIPTON, J. S., & SPELKE, E. S. (2006). Preschool children master the logic of number word meanings. *Cognition, 98*, B57–B66.

LISMAN, J. (2003). Long-term potentiation: Outstanding questions and attempted synthesis. *Philosophical Transactions of the Royal Society London: B. Biological Science, 348*, 829–842.

LIVESLEY, W. J. (ED.). (2001). *Handbook of personality disorders: Theory, research, and treatment.* New York: Guilford.

LIVINGSTONE, K. (1997, Spring). Ritalin: Miracle drug or cop-out? *Public Interest, 127*, 3–18.

LIVSON, N., & PESKIN, H. (1980). Perspectives on adolescence from longitudinal research. In J. Adelsen (Ed.), *Handbook of adolescent psychology.* New York: Wiley.

LOCKE, J. (1690). *An essay concerning human understanding.* A. D. Woozley (Ed.). Cleveland: Meridian Books, 1964.

LOCKRIDGE, C., & BRENNAN, S. (2002). Addressees' needs influence speakers' early syntactic choices. *Psychonomic Bulletin and Review, 9*, 550–557.

LOEHLIN, J. C. (1992). *Genes and environment in personality development.* Newbury Park, CA: Sage.

LOEHLIN, J. C., LINDZEY, G., & SPUHLER, J. N. (1975). *Race difference in intelligence.* San Francisco: Freeman.

LOFTUS, E. F. (1993). The reality of repressed memories. *American Psychologist, 48*, 518–537.

LOFTUS, E. F. (1997). Creating false memories. *Scientific American, 277*(3), 70–75.

LOFTUS, E. F. (2003). Make-believe memories. *American Psychologist, 58*(11), 867–873.

LOFTUS, E. F. (2004). Memories of things unseen. *Current Directions in Psychological Science, 13*, 145–147.

LOFTUS, E. (2005). Planting misinformation in the human mind: A 30-year investigation of the malleability of memory. *Learning and Memory, 12*, 361–366.

LOFTUS, E. F., & GUYER, M. J. (2002). Who abused Jane Doe? The hazards of the single case history. *Skeptical Inquirer, 26*, 24–32.

LOGOTHETIS, N. K. (1998). Single units and conscious vision. *Philosophical Transactions of the Royal Society of London Series B-Biological Sciences, 353*, 1801–1818.

LOGUE, A. W. (1986). *The psychology of eating and drinking.* New York: Freeman.

LOHMAN, D. (2000). Complex information processing and intelligence. In R. J. Sternberg (Ed.), *Handbook of human intelligence* (2nd ed., pp. 285–340). Cambridge, MA: Cambridge University Press.

LONDON, P. (1970). The rescuers: Motivational hypotheses about Christians who saved Jews from the Nazis. In J. Macaulay & L. Berkowitz (Eds.), *Altruism and helping behavior* (pp. 241–250). New York: Academic Press.

LOPES, P. N., SALOVEY, P., CÔTÉ, S., & BEERS, M. (2005). Emotion regulation ability and the quality of social interaction. *Emotion, 5*, 113–118.

LORD, C. G., ROSS, L., & LEPPER, M. R. (1979). Biased assimilation and attitude polarization: The effects of prior theories on subsequently considered evidence. *Journal of Personality and Social Psychology, 37*(11), 2098–2109.

LORD, R. G., DEVADER, C. L., & ALLIGER, G. M. (1986). A meta-analysis of the relationship between personality traits and leadership perceptions: An application of validity generalization procedures. *Journal of Applied Psychology, 7*, 401–410.

LORENZ, K. (1935). Der Kumpan in der Umwelt des Vogels. Der Artgenosse als auslösendes Moment sozialer Verhaltensweisen. *Journal für Ornithologie, 83*, 137–215, 289–413.

LORENZ, K. Z. (1966). *On aggression.* London: Methuen.

LOVAAS, O. I. (1987). Behavioral treatment and normal educational and intellectual functioning in young autistic children. *Journal of Consulting and Clinical Psychology, 55*(1), 3–9.

LOVE, J., HARRISON, L., SAGI-SCHWARTZ, A., ET AL. (2003). Child care quality matters: How conclusions may vary with context. *Child Development, 74*, 1021–1033.

LOZANO, A. M., MAYBERG, H. S., GIACOBBE, P., HAMANI, C., CRADDOCK, R. C., & KENNEDY, S. H. (2008). Subcallosal cingulate gyrus deep brain stimulation for treatment-resistant depression. *Biological Psychiatry, 64*, 461–467.

LUBINSKI, D. (2004). Introduction to the special section on cognitive abilities: 100 years after Spearman's (1904) "'General intelligence,' objectively determined and measured." *Journal of Personality and Social Psychology, 86*, 96–111.

LUBINSKI, D., & BENBOW, C. P. (2000). States of excellence. *American Psychologist, 55*(1), 137–150.

LUBORSKY, L. I., SINGER, B., & LUBORSKY, L. (1975). Comparative studies of psychotherapies. *Archives of General Psychiatry, 20*, 84–88.

LUCAS, R. E. (2007). Long-term disability is associated with lasting changes in subjective well-being: Evidence from two nationally representative longitudinal studies. *Journal of Personality and Social Psychology, 92*, 717–730.

LUCAS, R. E., CLARK, A. E., GEORGELLIS, Y., & DIENER, E. (2003). Reexamining adaptation and the set point model of happiness: Reactions to changes in marital status. *Journal of Personality and Social Psychology, 84*, 527–539.

LUCHINS, A. S. (1942). Mechanization in problem-solving: The effect of Einstellung. *Psychological Monographs, 54*(entire no. 248).

LUGINBUHL, J. E. R., CROWE, D. H., & KAHAN, J. P. (1975). Causal attributions for success and failure. *Journal of Personality and Social Psychology, 31*, 86–93.

LUMINET, O., & CURCI, A. (EDS.). (2009). *Flashbulb memories: New issues and new perspectives.* New York: Psychology Press.

LUO, Y., & BAILLARGEON, R. (2005). Can a self-propelled box have a goal? Psychological reasoning in 5-month-old infants. *Psychological Science, 16*, 601–608.

LURIA, A. R. (1966). *Higher cortical functions in man.* New York: Basic Books.

LURIA, A. R. (1976). Cognitive development: Its cultural and social foundations. Cambridge, MA: Harvard University Press.

LUTZ, A., BREFCZYNSKI-LEWIS, J., JOHNSTONE, T., & DAVIDSON, R. J. (2008). Regulation of the neural circuitry of emotion by compassion meditation: Effects of meditative expertise. *PLoS ONE 3* (3).

LUTZ, A., GREISCHAR, L. L., RAWLINGS, N. B., RICARD, M., & DAVIDSON, R. J., (2004). Long-term meditators self-induce high-amplitude gamma synchrony during mental practice. *Proceedings of the National Academy of Sciences, 101* (46), 16369–16373.

LUTZ, C. (1986). The domain of emotion words on Ifaluk. In R. Harr (Ed.), *The social construction of emotions* (pp. 267–288). Oxford, England: Blackwell.

LUTZ, C. (1988). *Unnatural emotions.* Chicago: University of Chicago Press.

LUZZATTI, C., RAGGI, R., ZONCA, G., PISTARINI C., CONTARDI A., & PINNA G. (2001). Verb-noun double dissociation in aphasic lexical impairments: The role of word frequency and imageability. *Brain and Language*, 1–13.

LYDIARD, R. B., BRAWMAN-MINTZER, O., & BALLENGER, J. C. (1996). Recent developments in the psychopharmacology of anxiety disorders. *Journal of Consulting and Clinical Psychology, 64*, 660–668.

LYKKEN, D. T., & TELLEGEN, A. (1996). Happiness is a stochastic phenomenon. *Psychological Science, 7*, 186–189.

LYNN, R. (1994). Sex differences in intelligence and brain size: A paradox resolved. *Personality and Individual Differences, 17*(2), 257–271.

LYNN, R. (1999). The attack on The Bell Curve. *Personality and Individual Differences, 26*, 761–765.

LYNN, S. J., LOCK, T. G., MYERS, B., & PAYNE, D. G. (1997). Recalling the unrecallable: Should hypnosis be used to recover memories in psychotherapy? *Current Directions in Psychological Science, 6*, 79–83.

LYUBOMIRSKY, S. (2008). *The how of happiness: A scientific approach to getting the life you want.* New York: Penguin.

LYUBOMIRSKY, S., KING, L. A., & DIENER, G. (2008). The benefits of frequent positive affect: Does happiness lead to success? *Psychological Bulletin, 131*, 803–855.

———

MA, V., & SCHOENEMAN, T. J. (1997). Individualism versus collectivism: A comparison of Kenyan and American self-concepts. *Basic and Applied Social Psychology, 19*, 261–273.

MAASS, A., KARASAWA, M., POLITI, F., & SUGA, S. (2006). Do verbs and adjectives play different roles in different cultures? A cross-linguistic analysis of person representation. *Journal of Personality and Social Psychology, 90*, 734–750.

MACCOBY, E. E. (2000). Parenting and its effects on children: On reading and misreading behavior genetics. *Annual Review of Psychology, 51*, 1–27.

MACCOBY, E. E., & JACKLIN, C. N. (1974). *The psychology of sex differences.* Stanford, CA: Stanford University Press.

MACCOBY, E. E., & JACKLIN, C. N. (1980). Sex differences in aggression: A rejoinder and reprise. *Child Development, 51*, 964–980.

MACCOBY, E. E., & MARTIN, J. A. (1983). Socialization in the context of the family: Parent-child interaction. In P. H. Mussen (Ed.) & M. E. Hetherington (Vol. Ed.), *Carmichael's manual of child psychology: Vol. 4. Socialization, personality and social development* (pp. 1–102). New York: Wiley.

MACDONALD, A. W., III, COHEN, J. D., STENGER, V. A., & CARTER, C. S. (2000). Dissociating the role of dorso-lateral prefrontal cortex and anterior cingulated cortex in cognitive control. *Science, 288*, 1835–1837.

MACDONALD, M. C., PEARLMUTTER, N. J., & SEIDENBERG, M. S. (1994). The lexical nature of syntactic ambiguity resolution. *Psychological Review, 101*(4), 676–703.

MACDONALD, T. K., ZANNA, M. P, & FONG, G. T. (1996).Why common sense goes out the window: Effects of alcohol on intentions to use condoms. *Personality and Social Psychology Bulletin, 22*, 763–775.

MACFARLANE, A. (1975). Olfaction in the development of social preferences in the human neonate. *Parent-infant interaction.* Amsterdam: CIBA Foundation Symposium.

MACGUIRE, E. A., GADIAN, D. G., JOHNSRUDE, I. S., GOOD, C. D., ASHBURNER, J., FRACKOWIAK, R. S., & FRITH, C. D. (2000). Navigation-related structural change in the hippocampi of taxi drivers. *Proceedings of the National Academy of Sciences, 97*, 4398–4403.

MACHIN, S., & PEKKARINEN, T. (2008). Global sex differences in test score variability. *Science, 322*, 1331–1332.

MACK, A. (2003). Inattentional blindness: Looking without seeing. *Current Directions in Psychological Science, 12*, 180–184.

MACK, A., & ROCK, I. (1998). *Inattentional blindness.* Cambridge, MA: MIT Press.

MACLEAN, P. (1949). Psychosomatic disease and the "visceral" brain: Recent developments bearing on the Papez theory of emotion. *Psychosomatic Medicine, 11*, 338–353.

MACLEAN, P. (1952). Some psychiatric implications of physiological studies on frontotemporal portion of limbic system (visceral brain). *Electroencephalography & Clinical Neurophysiology, 4*, 407–418.

MACNAMARA, J. (1982). *Names for things.* Cambridge, MA: MIT Press.

MACNICHOL, E. F., JR. (1986). A unifying presentation of photopigment spectra. *Vision Research, 29*, 543–546.

MACPHAIL, E. M. (1996). Cognitive function in mammals: The evolutionary perspective. *Cognitive Brain Research, 3*, 279–290.

MADDUX, J. E. (1995). *Self-efficacy, adaptation, and adjustment: Theory, research, and application.* Englewood Cliffs, NJ: Prentice-Hall.

MAFFEI, M., HALAAS, J., RAVUSSIN, E., PRATLEY, R. E., LEE, G. H., ZHANG, Y., ET AL. (1995). Leptin levels in human and rodent: Measurement of plasma leptin and ob RNA in obese and weight-reduced subjects. *Nature Medicine, 1*, 1155–1161.

MAGEN, E., & GROSS, J. J. (2007). Harnessing the need for immediate gratification: Cognitive reconstrual modulates the reward value of temptations. *Emotion, 7*, 415–428.

MAGNUSSON, D., & ENDLER, N. S. (1977). Interactional psychology: Present status and future prospects. In D. Magnusson & N. S. Endler (Eds.), *Personality at the crossroads* (pp. 3–31). New York: Wiley.

MAGOUN, H. W., HARRISON, F., BROBECK, J. R., & RANSON, S. W. (1938). Activation of heat loss mechanisms by local heating of the brain. *Journal of Neurophysiology, 1*, 101–114.

MAGUIRE, M. C., & DUNN, J. (1997). Friendships in early childhood, and social understanding. *International Journal of Behavioral Development, 21*(4), 669–686.

MAGUIRE, E. A., GADIAN, D. G., JOHNSRUDE, I. S., GOOD, C. D., ASHBURNER, J., FRACKOWIAK, R. S. J., ET AL. (2000). Navigation-related structural change in the hippocampi of taxi drivers. *Proceedings of the National Academy of Sciences of the United States of America, 97*(8), 4398–4403.

MAHER, B. A. (1966). *Principles of psychopathology.* New York: McGraw-Hill.

MAHON, B. Z., & CARAMAZZA, A. (2009). Concepts and categories: A cognitive neuropsychological perspective. *Annual Review of Psychology, 60*, 27–51.

MAHEU, M. M., & GORDON, B. L. (2000). Counseling and therapy on the Internet. *Professional Psychology: Research and Practice, 31*, 484–489.

MAIA, T. V., & CLEEREMANS, A. (2005). Consciousness: Converging insights from connectionist modeling and neuroscience. *Trends in Cognitive Sciences, 9*, 397–404.

MAIN, M., & SOLOMON, J. (1990). Procedures for identifying infants as disorganized/disoriented during the Ainsworth Strange Situation. In M. T. Greenberg, D. Cicchetti, & E. M. Cummings (Eds.), *Attachment in the preschool years: Theory, research, and intervention* (pp. 121–160). Chicago: University of Chicago Press.

MALDONADO, J. R., BUTLER, L. D., & SPIEGEL, D. (2002). Treatments for dissociative disorders. In P. Nathan and J. M. Gorman (Eds.), *A guide to treatments that work* (2nd ed., pp. 463–496). New York: Oxford University Press.

MALHI, G. S., & BARTLETT, J. R. (2000). Depression: A role for neurosurgery? *British Journal of Neurosurgery, 14*, 415–422.

MALINOWSKI, B. (1926). *Crime and custom in savage society.* London: Paul, Trench, and Trubner.

MALINOWSKI, B. (1927). *Sex and repression in savage society.* New York: Meridian, 1955.

MALLET, L., POLOSAN, M., JAAFARI, N., BAUP, N., WELTER, M.-L., FONTAINE, D., ET AL. (2008). Subthalamic nucleus stimulation in severe obsessive-compulsive disorder. *New England Journal of Medicine, 359,* 2121–2134.

MANDLER, J. M. (2000). Perceptual and conceptual processes in infancy. *Journal of Cognition and Development, 1,* 3–36.

MANGELSDORF, S. C., SHAPIRO, J. R., & MARZOLF, D. (1995). Developmental and temperamental differences in emotional regulation in infancy. *Child Development, 66*(6), 1817–1828.

MANNING, R., LEVINE, M., & COLLINS, A. (2007). The Kitty Genovese murder and the social psychology of helping: The parable of the 38 witnesses. *American Psychologist, 62*(6), 555–562.

MANTELL, D. M., & PANZARELLA, R. (1976). Obedience and responsibility. *British Journal of Social and Child Psychology, 15,* 239–245.

MARAÑON, G. (1924). Review of Fr. *Endocrinology, 2,* 301.

MARCH, J. S., LEONARD, H. L., & SWEDO, S. E. (1995). Obsessive-compulsive disorder. In J. S. March (Ed.), *Anxiety disorders in children and adolescents* (pp. 251–275). New York: Guilford.

MARCUS, D. E., & OVERTON, W. F. (1978). The development of cognitive gender constancy and sex-role preferences. *Child Development, 49,* 434–444.

MARCUS, G. F. (2001). *The algebraic mind: Integrating connectionism and cognitive science.* Cambridge, MA: MIT Press.

MARCUS, G. F. (2004). *The birth of the mind: How a tiny number of genes creates the complexity of the human mind.* New York: Basic Books.

MARCUS, G. F., PINKER, S., ULLMAN, M., HOLLANDER, M., ROSEN, T. J., & XU, F. (1992). Overregularization in language acquisition. *Monographs of the Society for Research in Child Development, 57*(4, Serial No. 228).

MARCUS, G. F., VIJAYAN, S., BANDI RAO, S., & VISHTON, P. M. (1999). Rule learning by seven-month-old infants. *Science, 283,* 77–80.

MARCUS, J., HANS, S. L., AUERBACH, J. G., & AUERBACH, A. G. (1993). Children at risk for schizophrenia: The Jerusalem Infant Development Study. II. Neuro behavioral deficits at school age. *Archives of General Psychiatry, 50,* 797–809.

MARESCHAL, D. (2000). Object knowledge in infancy: Current controversies and approaches. *Trends in Cognitive Science, 4,* 408–416.

MARKMAN, E. (1989). *Categorization and naming in children: Problems of induction.* Cambridge, MA: MIT Press.

MARKMAN, E. M. (1994). Constraints children place on word meanings. In P. Bloom (Ed.), *Language acquisition: Core readings.* Cambridge, MA: MIT Press.

MARKMAN, E. M., & HUTCHINSON, J. E. (1984). Children's sensitivity to constraints on word meaning: Taxonomic vs. thematic relations. *Cognitive Psychology, 16,* 1–27.

MARKMAN, E. M., & WACHTEL, G. A. (1988). Children's use of mutual exclusivity to constrain the meaning of words. *Cognitive Psychology, 20,* 121–157.

MARKSON, I., & BLOOM, P. (1997). Evidence against a dedicated system for word learning in children. *Nature, 385,* 813–815.

MARKUS, H. R. (1977). Self-schemata and processing information about the self. *Journal of Personality and Social Psychology, 35,* 63–78.

MARKUS, H. R., & KITAYAMA, S. (1991). Culture and the self: Implications for cognition, emotion, and motivation. *Psychological Review, 98,* 224–253.

MARKUS, H. R., & NURIUS, P. (1986). Possible selves. *American Psychologist, 41,* 954–969.

MARLER, P. R. (1970). A comparative approach to vocal learning: Song development in white-crowned sparrows. *Journal of Comparative and Physiological Psychology Monographs, 71* (No. 2, Part 2), 1–25.

MARLOWE, F., & WETSMAN, A. (2001). Preferred waist-to-hip ratio and ecology. *Personality and Individual Differences, 30,* 481–489.

MARR, D. (1982). *Vision.* San Francisco: Freeman.

MARSELLA, A. J., DUBANOSKI, J., HAMADA, W. C., & MORSE, H. (2000). The measurement of personality across cultures: Historical conceptual, and methodological issues and considerations. *American Behavioral Scientist, 44,* 41–62.

MARSHALL, G. D., & ZIMBARDO, P. G. (1979). Affective consequences of inadequately explained physiological arousal. *Journal of Personality and Social Psychology, 37,* 970–988.

MARSHALL, N. L. (2004). The quality of early child care and children's development. *Current Directions in Psychological Science, 13,* 165–168.

MARSLEN-WILSON, W. (1975). Sentence perception as an interactive parallel process. *Science, 189,* 226–228.

MARSLEN-WILSON, W. D., & TEUBER, H. L. (1975). Memory for remote events in anterograde amnesia: Recognition of public figures from news photographs. *Neurobiologia, 13,* 353–364.

MARTIN, D. J., GARSKE, J. P., & DAVIS, M. K. (2000). Relation of the therapeutic alliance with outcome and other variables: A meta-analytic review. *Journal of Consulting and Clinical Psychology, 68,* 438–450.

MARTIN, M., & JONES, G. V. (2006). Visual sharpness contingency in recognition memory for orientation: Mnemonic illusion suppressed by sensory signature. *Journal of Experimental Psychology: General, 135,* 542–552.

MARTIN, J. A., KING, D. R., MACCOBY, E. E., & JACKLIN, C. N. (1984). Secular trends and individual differences in toilet-training progress. *Journal of Pediatric Psychology, 9,* 457–467.

MARTIN, L. (1986). "Eskimo words for snow": A case study in the genesis and decay of an anthropological example. *American Anthropologist, 88,* 418–423.

MARTIN, P., & ALBERS, P. (1995). Cerebellum and schizophrenia: A review. *Schizophrenia Bulletin, 21,* 241–251.

MARTINEZ, J. L., & DERRICK, B. E. (1996). Long-term potentiation and learning. *Annual Review of Psychology, 47,* 173–203.

MARTINEZ, M. E. (2000). *Education as the cultivation of intelligence.* Mahwah, NJ: Erlbaum.

MARX, J. (2003). Cellular warriors at the battle of the bulge. *Science, 299,* 846–849.

MASLACH, C. (1979). Negative emotional biasing of unexplained physiological arousal. *Journal of Personality and Social Psychology, 37,* 953–969.

MASLOW, A. H. (1968). *Toward a psychology of being* (2nd ed.). Princeton, NJ: Van Nostrand.

MASLOW, A. H. (1970). *Motivation and personality* (2nd ed.). New York: Harper.

MASLOW, A. H. (1996). *Future visions: The unpublished papers of Abraham Maslow* (E. Hoffman, Ed.). Thousand Oaks, CA: Sage.

MASSIMINI, M., FERRARELLI, F., HUBER, R., ESSER, S. K., SINGH, H., & TONONI, G. (2005). Breakdown of cortical effective connectivity during sleep. *Science, 309,* 2228–2232.

MASTERS, M. S., & SANDERS, B. (1993). Is the gender difference in mental rotation disappearing? *Behavior Genetics, 23,* 337–341.

MASTERS, W. H., & JOHNSON, V. E. (1966). *Human sexual responses.* Boston: Little, Brown.

MATARAZZO, J. D. (1983). The reliability of psychiatric and psychological diagnosis. *Clinical Psychology Review, 3,* 103–145.

MATHER, M., & CARSTENSEN, L. L. (2003). Aging and attentional biases for emotional faces. *Psychological Science, 14,* 409–415.

MATIN, L., PICOULT, E., STEVENS, J., EDWARDS, M., & MACARTHUR, R. (1982). Ocuparalytic illusion: Visual-field dependent spatial mislocations by humans partially paralyzed with curare. *Science, 216,* 198–180.

MATSON, J. L., & SEVIN, J. A. (1994). Issues in the use of aversives: Factors associated with behavior modification for autistic and other developmentally disabled people. In E. Schopler & G. B. Mesibov (Eds.), *Behavioral issues in autism* (pp. 211–225). New York: Plenum.

MATSUMOTO, D., & WILLINGHAM, B. (2009). Spontaneous facial expressions of emotion of congenitally and non-congenitally blind individuals. *Journal of Personality and Social Psychology, 96,* 1–10.

MATSUMOTO, D., YOO, S. H., HIRAYAMA, S., & PETROVA, G. (2005). Development and validation of a measure of display rule knowledge: The Display Rule Assessment Inventory. *Emotion, 5,* 23–40.

MATSUMOTO, D., YOO, S. H., & NAKAGAWA, S. (2008). Culture, emotion regulation, and adjustment. *Journal of Personality and Social Psychology, 94*(6), 925–937.

MATTHEWS, G., ZEIDNER, M., & ROBERTS, R. D. (2003). *Emotional intelligence: Science and Myth.* Cambridge, MA: MIT Press.

MATTHEWS, G., ZEIDNER, M., & ROBERTS, R. D. (2005). Emotional intelligence: An elusive ability? In O. Wilhelm & R. Engle (Eds.), *Handbook of understanding and measuring intelligence* (pp. 79–99). Thousand Oaks, CA: Sage.

MATTHEWS, K. A., BATSON, C. D., HORN, J., & ROSENMAN, R. H. (1981). "Principles in his nature which interest him in the fortune of others . . .": The heritability of empathic concern for others. *Journal of Personality, 49*(3), 237–247.

MATTISON, A., & MCWHIRTER, D. (1987). Male couples: The beginning years. Intimate Relationships: Some Social Work Perspectives on Love [Special issue]. *Journal of Social Work and Human Sexuality, 5*, 67–78.

MAUSS, I. B., LEVENSON, R. W., MCCARTER, L., WILHELM, F. H., & GROSS, J. J. (2005). The tie that binds? Coherence among emotional experience, behavior, and autonomic physiology. *Emotion, 5*, 175–190.

MAY, C. P., & HASHER, L. (1998). Synchrony effects in inhibitory control over thought and action. *Journal of Experimental Psychology: Human Perception and Performance, 24*, 363–379.

MAYBERG, H. S., BRANNAN. S. K., MAHURIN, R. K., JERABEK, P. A., BRICKMAN, J. S., TEKELL, J. L., ET AL. (1997). Cingulate function in depression: A potential predictor of treatment response. *Neuroreport, 8*, 1057–1061.

MAYBERG, H. S., LIOTTI, M., BRANNAN, S. K., MCGINNIS, S., MAHURIN, R. K., JERABEK, P. A., ET AL. (1999). Reciprocal limbic-cortical function and negative mood: Converging PET findings in depression and normal sadness. *American Journal of Psychiatry, 156*, 675–682.

MAYBERG, H. S., LOZANO, A. M., VOON, V., MCNEELY, H. E., SEMINOWICZ, D., HAMANI, C., ET AL. (2005). Deep brain stimulation for treatment-resistant depression. *Neuron, 45*(5), 651–660.

MAYER, J. D., ROBERTS, R. D., & BARSADE, S. G. (2008a). Human abilities: Emotional intelligence. *Annual Review of Psychology, 59*, 507–536.

MAYER, J. D., SALOVEY, P., & CARUSO, D. R. (2008b). Emotional intelligence: New ability or eclectic traits? *American Psychologist, 63*, 503–517.

MAYER, J. D., SALOVEY, P., CARUSO, D. R., & SITARENIOS, G. (2003). Measuring emotional intelligence with the MSCEIT V2.0. *Emotion, 3*, 97–105.

MAYES, A. R. (1988). *Human organic memory disorders.* New York: Cambridge University Press.

MAYHAN, W. G. (2001). Regulation of blood-brain barrier permeability. *Microcirculation, 8*, 89–104.

MCADAMS, D. P. (1980). A thematic coding system for the intimacy motive. *Journal of Research in Personality, 14*, 413–432.

MCADAMS, D. P. (1993). *The stories we live by: Personal myths and the making of the self.* New York: Morrow.

MCADAMS, D. P. (2001). The psychology of life stories. *Review of General Psychology, 5*, 100–122.

MCADAMS, D. P., & PALS, J. L. (2006). A new Big Five: Fundamental principles for an integrative science of personality. *American Psychologist, 61*, 204–217.

MCCLEARN, G. E., & DEFRIES, J. C. (1973). *Introduction to behavioral genetics.* San Francisco: Freeman.

MCCLEARN, G. E., JOHANSSON, B., GERG, S., PEDERSEN, N., AHEM, F., PETRILL, S., ET AL. (1997). Substantial genetic influence on cognitive abilities in twins 80 or more years old. *Science, 276*, 1560–1563.

MCCLELLAND, D. C. (1989). *Human motivation.* New York: Cambridge University Press.

MCCLELLAND, D. C., ATKINSON, J. W., CLARK, R. A., & LOWELL, E. L. (1953). *The achievement motive.* New York: Appleton-Century-Crofts.

MCCLELLAND, D. C., KOESTNER, R., & WEINBERGER, J. (1989). How do self-attributed and implicit motives differ? *Psychological Review, 96*, 690–702.

MCCLELLAND, J. L., & PATTERSON, K. (2002). Rules or connections in past-tense inflections: What does the evidence rule out? *Trends in Cognitive Science, 6*(11), 465–472.

MCCLELLAND, J. L., & RUMELHART, D. E. (EDS.). (1986). *Parallel distributed processing: Explorations in the microstructure of cognition: Vol. 2. Psychological and biological models.* Cambridge, MA: MIT Press.

MCCLELLAND, J. L., RUMELHART, D. E., & HINTON, G. E. (1986). The appeal of parallel distributed processing. In D. E. Rumelhart, J. L. McClelland, and the PDP Research Group (Eds.), *Parallel distributed processing: Vol. 1. Foundations* (pp. 3–44). Cambridge, MA: MIT Press.

MCCLELLAND, J. L., & SEIDENBERG, M. S. (2000). Why do kids say goed and brang? *Science, 287*, 47–48.

MCCLINTOCK, M. K. (1971). Menstrual synchrony and suppression. *Nature, 229*, 244–245.

MCCLINTOCK, M. K., & ADLER, N. T. (1978). The role of the female during copulation in wild and domestic Norway rats (*Rattus Norvegicus*). *Behaviour, 67*, 67–96.

MCCLOSKEY, M., WIBLE, C. G., & COHEN, N. J. (1988). Is there a special flashbulb-memory mechanism? *Journal of Experimental Psychology: General, 117*, 171–181.

MCCLURE, S. M., LAIBSON, D. I., LOEWENSTEIN, G., & COHEN, J. D. (2004). Separate neural systems value immediate and delayed monetary rewards. *Science, 306*, 503–507.

MCCONNELL, A. R., & LEIBOLD, J. M. (2001). Relations among the Implicit Association Test, discriminatory behavior, and explicit measures of racial attitudes. *Journal of Experimental Social Psychology, 37*(5), 435–442.

MCCRAE, R. R., & COSTA, P. T. (1987). Validation of the five-factor model of personality across instruments and observers. *Journal of Personality and Social Psychology, 52*, 81–90.

MCCRAE, R. R., & COSTA, P. T., JR. (1990). *Personality in adulthood.* New York: Guilford.

MCCRAE, R. R., & COSTA, P. T., JR. (2003). *Personality in adulthood: A five-factor theory perspective* (2nd ed.). New York: Guilford.

MCCRAE, R. R., & TERRACCIANO, A. (2005). Universal features of personality traits from the observer's perspective: Data from 50 cultures. *Journal of Personality and Social Psychology, 88*, 547–561.

MCCRAE, R. R., & TERRACCIANO, A. (2006). National character and personality. *Current Directions in Psychological Science, 15*, 156–161.

MCCRANIE, E. W., HYER, L. A., BOUDEWYNS, P. A., & WOODS, M. G. (1992). Negative parenting behavior, combat exposure and PTSD symptom severity. Test of a person-event interaction model. *Journal of Nervous and Mental Disease, 180*, 431–438.

MCCREARY, D. R. (1994). The male role and avoiding femininity. *Sex Roles, 31*, 517–531.

MCCRINK, K., & WYNN, K. (2004). Large-number addition and subtraction by 9-month-old infants. *Psychological Science, 15*, 776–781.

MCDANIEL, M. A., MAIER, S. F., & EINSTEIN, G. O. (2002). "Brain-specific" nutrients: A memory cure? *Psychological Science in the Public Interest, 3*, 12–38.

MCDOUGAL, W. (1923). *Outline of psychology.* New York: Scribner.

MCEACHIN, J. J., SMITH, T., & LOVAAS, O. I. (1993). Long-term outcome for children with autism who received early intensive behavioral treatment. *American Journal on Mental Retardation, 97*, 359–372.

MCEWEN, B. S., BIEGON, A., DAVIS, P. G., KREY, L. C., LUINE, V. N., MCGINNIS, M., ET AL. (1982). Steroid hormones: Humoral signals which alter brain cell properties and functions. *Recent Progress in Brain Research, 38*, 41–83.

MCFALL, R. M. (2006). Doctoral training in clinical psychology. *Annual Review of Clinical Psychology, 2*, 21–49.

MCFALL, R. M., & TREAT, T. A. (1999). Quantifying the information value of clinical assessments with signal detection theory. *Annual Review of Psychology, 50*, 215–242.

MCGAUGH, J. L. (2000). Memory—a century of consolidation. *Science, 287*, 248–251.

MCGAUGH, J. (2003). *Memory and emotion.* New York: Columbia University Press.

MCGEE, A. W., YANG, Y., FISCHER, Q. S., DAW, N. W., & STRITTMATTER, S. M. (2005). Experience-driven plasticity of visual cortex limited by myelin and Nogo receptor. *Science, 5744*, 2222–2226.

MCGEOCH, J. A., & IRION, A. L. (1952). *The psychology of human learning* (2nd ed.). New York: Longmans, Green.

MCGHIE, A., & CHAPMAN, J. (1961). Disorders of attention and perception in early schizophrenia. *British Journal of Medical Psychology, 34*, 103–116.

MCGRATH, J., WELHAM, J., & PEMBERTON, M. (1995). Month of birth, hemisphere of birth, and schizophrenia. *British Journal of Psychiatry, 167*, 783–785.

MCGREGOR, G. P., DESAGA, J. F., EHLENZ, K., FISCHER, A., HEESE, F., HEGELE, A., ET AL. (1996). Radiommunological measurement of leptin in plasma of obese and diabetic human subjects. *Endocrinology, 137*, 1501–1504.

MCGREW, K. (2009). CHC theory and the human cognitive abilities project: Standing on the shoulders of the giants of psychometric intelligence research. *Intelligence, 37*, 1–10.

MCGUE, M., BOUCHARD, T. J., JR., IACONO, W. G., & LYKKEN, D. T. (1993). Behavioral genetics of cognitive ability: A life span perspective. In R. Plomin & G. E. McClearn (Eds.), *Nature, nurture and psychology* (pp. 59–76). Washington, DC: American Psychological Association.

MCGUE, M., & LYKKEN, D. T. (1992). Genetic influence on risk of divorce. *Psychological Science, 3*, 368–372.

MCGUIRE, W. J. (1985). The nature of attitude and attitude change. In G. Lindzey & E. Aronson (Eds.), *Handbook of social psychology: Vol. 2* (3rd ed.). New York: Random House.

MCINTOSH, A. R., RAJAH, M. N., & LOBAUGH, N. J. (1999). Interactions of prefrontal cortex in relation to awareness in sensory learning. *Science, 284*, 1531–1533.

McNally, R. J. (2003a). Progress and controversy in the study of posttraumatic stress disorder. *Annual Review of Psychology, 54*, 229–252.

McNally, R. J. (2003b). *Remembering trauma.* Cambridge, MA: Harvard University Press.

McNally, R. J. (2006). Psychiatric casualties of war. *Science, 313*, 923–924.

McNally, R., & Geraerts, E. (2009). A new solution to the recovered memory debate. *Perspectives on Psychological Science, 4*, 126–134.

McNaughton, B. L., Douglas, R. M., & Goddard, G. V. (1978). Synaptic enhancement in fascia dentata: Cooperativity among coactive afferents. *Brain Research, 157*, 277–293.

Mead, G. H. (1934). *Mind, self, and society from the standpoint of a social behaviorist* (C. W. Morris, Ed.). Chicago: University of Chicago Press.

Mead, M. (1928). *Coming of age in Samoa.* New York: William Morrow.

Mealey, L., Bridgstock, R., & Townsend, G. C. (1999). Symmetry and perceived facial attractiveness: A monozygotic co-twin comparison. *Journal of Personality and Social Psychology, 76*, 151–158.

Medin, D. I., Atran, S., Cox, D., Coley, J., & Proffitt, J. S. (2006). Folkbiology of freshwater fish, *Cognition, 99*(3), 237–273.

Medin, D. L., & Bazerman, M. H. (1999). Broadening behavioral decision research: Multiple levels of cognitive processing. *Psychonomic Bulletin & Review, 6*, 533–546.

Medin, D. L., Goldstone, R. L., & Gentner, D. (1993). Respects for similarity. *Psychological Review, 100*(2), 254–278.

Medin, D. L., Schwartz, H., Blok, S. V., & Birnbaum, L. A. (1999). The semantic side of decision making. *Psychonomics Bulletin and Review, 6*, 562–569.

Medina, T. N., Trueswell, J., Snedeker, J., & Gleitman, L. (2008, November 2). *When the shoe fits: Cross-situational word learning in realistic learning environments.* Talk presented at the Boston University Conference on Language Development (BUCLD), Boston, MA.

Mednick, S. A., Huttunen, M. O., & Macho'n, R. A. (1994). Prenatal influenza infections and adult schizophrenia. *Schizophrenia Bulletin, 20*, 263–267.

Mednick, S., Nakayama, K, & Stickgold, R. (2003). Sleep-dependent learning: A nap is as good as a night. *Nature Neuroscience, 6*, 697–698.

Meehl, P. E. (1962). Schizotaxia, schizotypy, schizophrenia. *American Psychologist, 17*, 827–838.

Meeter, M., & Murre, J. M. J. (2004). Consolidation of long-term memory: Evidence and alternatives. *Psychological Bulletin, 130*, 843–857.

Mehler, J., et al. (1996). Coping with linguistic diversity: The infant's viewpoint. In J. L. Morgan & K. Demuth (Eds.), *Signal to syntax: Bootstrapping from speech to grammar in early acquisition* (pp. 101–116). Hillsdale, NJ: Erlbaum.

Mehler, J., Jusczyk, P., Lambertz, G., Halsted, N., Bertoncini, J., & Amiel-Tison, C. (1988). A precursor to language acquisition in young infants. *Cognition, 29*, 143–178.

Mehler, J., & Nespor, M. (2004). Linguistic rhythm and the development of language. In A. Belletti & L. Rizzi (Eds.), *Structures and beyond: The cartography of syntactic structures.* Oxford, England: Oxford University Press.

Meichenbaum, D. (1985). *Stress inoculation training.* New York: Pergamon.

Meichenbaum, D. (1993). Changing conceptions of cognitive behavior modification: Retrospect and prospect. *Journal of Consulting and Clinical Psychology, 61*, 202–204.

Meichenbaum, D. (1996). Stress inoculation training for coping with stressors. *Clinical Psychologist, 49*, 4–7.

Mellers, B., Chang, S.-J., Birnbaum, M., & Ordóñez, L. (1992). Preferences, prices, and ratings in risky decision making. *Journal of Experimental Psychology: Human Perception and Performance, 18*, 347–361.

Mellers, B., Hertwig, R., & Kahneman, D. (2001). Do frequency representations eliminate conjunction effects? An exercise in advance collaboration. *Psychological Science, 12*, 269–275.

Mellers, B. A., & McGraw, A. P. (1999). How to improve Bayesian reasoning: Comment on Gigerenzer and Hoffrage. *Psychological Review, 106*, 417–424.

Melnyk, L., Crossman, A. M., & Scullin, M. H. (2007). The suggestibility of children's memory. In M. P. Toglia, J. D. Read, D. F. Ross, & R. C. L. Lindsay (Eds.), *Handbook of eyewitness psychology, Vol. 1: Memory for events* (pp. 401–427). Mahwah, NJ: Erlbaum.

Meltzer, H. Y. (1986). Lithium mechanisms in bipolar illness and altered intracellular calcium functions. *Biological Psychiatry, 21*, 492–510.

Meltzer, H. Y. (1987). Biological studies in schizophrenia. *Schizophrenia Bulletin, 13*, 77–111.

Meltzoff, A. N. (1995). Understanding the intentions of others: Re-enactment of intended acts by 18-month-old children. *Developmental Psychology, 31*(5), 838–850.

Meltzoff, A. N. (2002). Elements of a developmental theory of imitations. In A. N. Meltzoff, N. Andrew, & W. Prinz (Eds.), *The imitative mind: Development, evolution, and brain bases* (pp. 19–41). Cambridge studies in cognitive perceptual development. New York: Cambridge University Press.

Meltzoff, A. N., Gopnik, A., & Repacholi, B. M. (1999). Toddlers' understanding of intentions, desires and emotions: Explorations of the dark ages. In P. D. Zelazo & J. W. Astington (Eds.), *Developing theories of intention: Social understanding and self-control* (pp. 17–41). Mahwah, NJ: Erlbaum.

Meltzoff, A. N., & Moore, M. K. (1977). Imitation of facial and manual gestures by human neonates. *Science, 198*, 75–78.

Meltzoff, A. N., & Moore, M. K. (1998). Infant intersubjectivity: Broadening the dialogue to include imitation, identity and intention. In S. Braten (Ed.), *Intersubjective communication and emotion in early ontogeny.* Cambridge: Cambridge University Press.

Melzack, R., & Casey, K. (1968). Sensory, motivational and central control determinants of pain. In D. Kenshalo, (Ed.), *The skin senses* (pp. 423–443). Springfield, IL: Thomas.

Melzack, R., & Wall, P. (1982). *The challenge of pain.* New York: Basic Books.

Mennella, J. A., Pepino, M. Y., & Reed, D. R. (2005). Genetic and environmental determinants of bitter perception and sweet preferences. *Pediatrics, 115*, 216–222.

Menyuk, P. (1977). *Language and maturation.* Cambridge, MA: MIT Press.

Menzel, E. W. (1973). Chimpanzee spatial memory organization. *Science, 182*, 943–945.

Menzel, E. W. (1978). Cognitive maps in chimpanzees. In S. H. Hulse, H. Fowler, & W. K. Honig (Eds.), *Cognitive processes in animal behavior* (pp. 375–422). Hillsdale, NJ: Erlbaum.

Mervis, C. B., & Crisafi, M. (1978). Order acquisition of subordinate, basic, and superordinate level categories. *Child Development, 49*, 988–998.

Metcalfe, J. (1986). Premonitions of insight predict impending error. *Journal of Experimental Psychology: Learning, Memory and Cognition, 12*, 623–634.

Metcalfe, J., & Weibe, D. (1987). Intuition in insight and noninsight problem solving. *Memory and Cognition, 15*, 238–246.

Meyer, D. E., & Schvaneveldt, R. W. (1971). Facilitation in recognizing pairs of words: Evidence of a dependence between retrieval operations. *Journal of Experimental Psychology, 90*, 227–234.

Meyer-Bahlburg, H. F. L., Gruen, R. S., New, M. I., Bell, J. J., Morishima, A., Shimshi, M., et al. (1996). Gender change from female to male in classical congenital adrenal hyperplasia. *Hormones and Behavior, 30*, 319–332.

Meyer-Lindenberg, A. (2008). Trust me on this. *Science, 321*, 778–780.

Mezzacappa, E. S., Katkin, E. S., & Palmer, S. N. (1999). Epinephrine, arousal, and emotion: A new look at two-factor theory. *Cognition and Emotion, 13*, 181–199.

Micallef, J., & Blin, O. (2001). Neurobiology and clinical pharmacology of obsessive-compulsive disorder. *Clinical Neuropharmacology, 24*, 191–207.

Michael, R. P., & Keverne, E. B. (1968). Pheromones in the communication of sexual status in primates. *Nature, 218*, 746–749.

Michaels, J. W., Bloomel, J. M., Brocato, R. M., Linkous, R. A., & Rowe, J. S. (1982). Social facilitation and inhibition in a natural setting. *Replications in Social Psychology, 2*, 21–24.

Miklowitz, D. J. (2007). The role of the family in the course and treatment of bipolar disorder. *Current Directions in Psychological Science, 16*(4), 192–196.

Miklowitz, D. J., & Johnson, S. L. (2006). The psychopathology and treatment of bipolar disorder. *Annual Review of Clinical Psychology, 2*, 199–235.

Mikulincer, M., & Shaver, P. R. (2005). Attachment theory and emotions in close relationships: Exploring the attachment-related dynamics of emotional reactions to relational events. *Personal Relationships, 12*, 149–168.

Mikulincer, M., & Shaver, P. R. (2007). *Attachment in adulthood: Structure, dynamics, and change.* New York: Guilford.

Milam, J. E., Richardson, J. L., Marks, G., Kemper, C. A., & McCutchan, A. J. (2004). The roles of dispositional optimism and pessimism in HIV disease progression. *Psychology & Health, 19*, 167–181.

MILGRAM, S. (1963). Behavioral study of obedience. *Journal of Abnormal and Social Psychology, 67,* 371–378.

MILGRAM, S. (1965). Some conditions of obedience and disobedience to authority. *Human Relations, 18,* 57–76.

MILGRAM, S. (1974). *Obedience to authority.* New York: Harper & Row.

MILGRAM, S., & MURRAY, T. H. (1992). Can deception in research be justified? In B. Slife & J. Rubenstein (Eds.), *Taking sides: Clashing views on controversial psychological issues* (7th ed.). Guilford, CT: Dushkin Publishing Group.

MILLER, (2007).

MILLER, A. G. (1986). *The obedience experiments: A case study of controversy in social science.* New York: Praeger.

MILLER, D. T. (1976). Ego involvement and attribution for success and failure. *Journal of Personality and Social Psychology, 34,* 901–906.

MILLER, D. T. (1999). The norm of self-interest. *American Psychologist, 54*(12), 1053–1060.

MILLER, E. M. (1994). Intelligence and brain myelination: A hypothesis. *Personality and Individual Differences, 17,* 803–832.

MILLER, G. (2005a). The dark side of glia. *Science, 308,* 778–781.

MILLER, G. (2005b). Mutant mice reveal secrets of the brain's impressionable youth. *Science, 309,* 2145.

MILLER, G. (2006a). China: Healing the metaphorical heart. *Science, 311,* 462–463.

MILLER, G. (2006b). The unseen: Mental illness's global toll. *Science, 311,* 458–460.

MILLER, G. (2007). Hunting for meaning after midnight. *Science, 315* (5817) 1360–1363.

MILLER, G. (2009). Rewiring faulty circuits in the brain. *Science, 323*(5921), 1554–1556.

MILLER, G. A. (1956). The magical number seven plus or minus two: Some limits in our capacity for processing information. *Psychological Review, 63,* 81–97.

MILLER, J., SCOTT, E., & OKAMOTO, S. (2006). Public acceptance of evolution. *Science, 313,* 765–766.

MILLER, J. G. (1984). Culture and the development of everyday social explanation. *Journal of Personality and Social Psychology, 46,* 961–978.

MILLER, J. G., & BERSOFF, D. M. (1998). The role of liking in perceptions of the moral responsibility to help: A cultural perspective. *Journal of Experimental Social Psychology, 34*(5), 443–469.

MILLER, J. G., BERSOFF, D. M., & HARWOOD, R. L. (1990). Perceptions of social responsibilities in India and in the United States: Moral imperatives or personal decisions? *Journal of Personality and Social Psychology, 58*(1), 33–47.

MILLER, L. C., PUTCHA-BHAGAVATULA, A. D., & PEDERSEN, W. C. (2002). Men's and women's mating preferences: Distinct evolutionary mechanisms? *Current Directions in Psychological Science, 11,* 88–93.

MILLER, L. K. (1999). The savant syndrome: Intellectual impairment and exceptional skill. *Psychological Bulletin, 125,* 31–46.

MILLER, N. E., BAILEY, C. J., & STEVENSON, J. A. F. (1950). Decreased "hunger" but increased food intake resulting from hypothalamic lesions. *Science, 112,* 256–259.

MILLER, P. A., EISENBERG, N., FABES, R. A., & SHELL, R. (1989). Mothers' emotional arousal as a moderator in the socialization of children's empathy. *New Directions for Child Development, 44.*

MILLER, R. R., BARNET, R. C., & GRAHAME, N. J. (1995). Assessment of the Rescorla-Wagner model. *Psychological Bulletin, 117,* 363–387.

MILLER, S. D., DUNCAN, B. L., & HUBBLE, M. A. (2005). Outcome-informed clinical work. In J. C. Norcross & M. R. Goldfried (Eds.), *Handbook of psychotherapy integration* (2nd ed., pp. 84–102). New York: Oxford University Press.

MILLER, W. R., & ROLLNICK, S. (2002). *Motivational interviewing: Preparing people to change.* New York: Guilford.

MILLS, J., & CLARK, M. S. (1994). Communal and exchange relationships: Controversies and research. In R. Erber & R. Gilmour (Eds.), *Theoretical frameworks for personal relationships* (pp. 29–42). Hillsdale, NJ: Erlbaum.

MILNER, B. (1966). Amnesia following operation on the temporal lobes. In C. W. M. Whitty & O. L. Zangwill (Eds.), *Amnesia* (pp. 109–133). London: Butterworth.

MILNER, B., CORKIN, S., & TEUBER, H.-L. (1968). Further analysis of the hippocampal syndrome: 14-year follow-up study of H. M. *Neuropsychologia, 6,* 215–234.

MILNER, B., & PETRIDES, M. (1984). Behavioural effects of frontal-lobe lesions in man. *Trends in Neurosciences, 7,* 403–407.

MINEKA, S., & BEN HAMIDA, S. (1998). Observational and nonconscious learning. In W. O'Donohue (Ed.), *Learning and behavior therapy* (pp. 421–439). Needham Heights, MA: Allyn & Bacon.

MINEKA, S., & ÖHMAN, A. (2002). Phobias and preparedness: The selective, automatic, and encapsulated nature of fear. *Biological Psychiatry, 52,* 927–937.

MINEKA, S., & ZINBARG, R. (2006). A contemporary learning theory perspective on the etiology of anxiety disorders: It's not what you thought it was. *American Psychologist, 61*(1), 10–26.

MINSKY, M. (1986). *The society of mind.* New York: Simon & Schuster.

MINUCHIN, S. (1974). *Families and family therapy.* Cambridge, MA: Harvard University Press.

MISCHEL, W. (1968). *Personality and assessment.* New York: Wiley.

MISCHEL, W. (1973). Towards a cognitive social learning reconceptualization of personality. *Psychological Review, 80,* 252–283.

MISCHEL, W. (1974). Processes in delay of gratification. In L. Berkowitz (Ed.), *Advances in experimental social psychology: Vol. 7.* New York: Academic Press.

MISCHEL, W. (1984). Convergences and challenges in the search for consistency. *American Psychologist, 39,* 351–364.

MISCHEL, W. (2004). Toward an integrative science of the person. *Annual Review of Psychology, 55,* 1–22.

MISCHEL, W., & BAKER, N. (1975). Cognitive appraisals and transformations in delay behavior. *Journal of Personality and Social Psychology, 31,* 254–261.

MISCHEL, W., & MISCHEL, H. N. (1983). Development of children's knowledge of self-control strategies. *Child Development, 54,* 603–619.

MISCHEL, W., & MOORE, B. (1980). The role of ideation in voluntary delay for symbolically presented awards. *Cognitive Therapy and Research, 4,* 211–221.

MISCHEL, W., & SHODA, Y. (1995). A cognitive-affective system theory of personality: Reconceptualizing situations, dispositions, dynamics, and invariance in personality structure. *Psychological Review, 102,* 246–268.

MISCHEL, W., & SHODA, Y. (1998). Reconciling processing dynamics and personality dispositions. *Annual Review of Psychology, 49,* 229–258.

MISCHEL, W., & SHODA, Y. (2000). A cognitive-affective system theory of personality: Reconceptualizing situations, dispositions, dynamics, and invariance in personality structure. In E. T. Higgins & A. W. Kruglanski (Eds.), *Motivational science: Social and personality perspectives* (pp. 150–176). Philadelphia: Psychology Press/Taylor & Francis.

MISCHEL, W., SHODA, Y., & MENDOZA-DENTON, R. (2002). Situation-behavior profiles as a locus of consistency in personality. *Current Directions in Psychological Science, 11,* 50–54.

MISCHEL, W., SHODA, Y., & PEAKE, P. K. (1988). The nature of adolescent competencies predicted by preschool delay of gratification. *Journal of Personality and Social Psychology, 54,* 687–696.

MISCHEL, W., SHODA, Y., & RODRIGUEZ, M. L. (1992). Delay of gratification in children. In G. Loewenstein & J. Elster (Eds.), *Choice over time* (pp. 147–164). New York: Russell Sage Foundation.

MISELIS, R. R., & EPSTEIN, A. N. (1970). Feeding induced by 2-deoxy-D-glucose injections into the lateral ventrical of the rat. *Physiologist, 13,* 262.

MISHLER, E. G., & WAXLER, N. E. (1968). Family interaction and schizophrenia: Alternative frameworks of interpretation. In D. Rosenthal & S. S. Kety (Eds.), *The transmission of schizophrenia* (pp. 213–222). New York: Pergamon.

MISTLBERGER, R. E. (2005). Circadian regulation of mammalian sleep: Role of the suprachiasmatic nucleus. *Brain Research Reviews, 49,* 429–454.

MITA, T. H., DERMER, M., & KNIGHT, J. (1977). Reversed facial images and the mere exposure hypothesis. *Journal of Personality and Social Psychology, 35,* 597–601.

MIYASHITA, Y. (1995). How the brain creates imagery: Projection to primary visual cortex. *Science, 268,* 1719–1720.

MOFFAT, S., & HAMPSON, E. (1996). A curvilinear relationship between testosterone and spatial cognition in humans: Possible influence of hand preference. *Psychoendocrinology, 21,* 323–337.

MOFFITT, T. E., CASPI, A., HARKNESS, A. R., & SILVA, P. A. (1993). The natural history of change in intellectual performance: Who changes? How much? Is it meaningful? *Journal of Child Psychology and Psychiatry and Allied Disciplines, 34*(4), 455–506.

MOFFITT, T. E., CASPI, A., & RUTTER, M. (2006). Measured gene-environment interactions in psychopathology: Concepts, research strategies, and implications for research, intervention, and public understanding of genetics. *Perspectives on Psychological Sciences, 1,* 5–27.

MOGHADDAM, F. (1998). *Social psychology: Exploring universals across cultures.* New York: Freeman.

MOLDEN, D. C., & DWECK, C. S. (2006). Finding "meaning" in psychology: A lay theories approach to self-regulation, social perception, and social development. *American Psychologist, 61,* 192–203.

MOLONEY, D. P., BOUCHARD, T. J., JR., & SEGAL, N. L. (1991). A genetic and environmental analysis of the vocational interests of monozygotic and dizygotic twins reared apart. *Journal of Vocational Behavior, 39,* 76–109.

MONEY, J. (1980). *Love and love sickness.* Baltimore: Johns Hopkins University Press.

MONEY, J., & EHRHARDT, A. A. (1972). *Man and woman, boy and girl.* Baltimore: Johns Hopkins University Press.

MONROE, S. M., & HADJIYANNAKIS, K. (2002). The social environment and depression: Focusing on severe life stress. In I. H. Gotlib and C. L. Hammen (Eds.), *Handbook of depression* (pp. 314–340). New York: Guilford.

MONTAGU, A. (ED.). (1999). *Race & IQ.* New York: Oxford University Press.

MONTAGUE, D., & WALKER-ANDREWS, A. (2002). Mothers, fathers, and infants: The role of person familiarity and parental involvement in infants' perception of emotional expressions. *Child Development, 73,* 1339–1352.

MONTE, C. F., & SOLLOD, R. N. (2003). *Beneath the mask: An introduction to theories of personality* (7th ed.). Danvers, MA: Wiley.

MONTGOMERY, S. A. (1995). Selective serotonin reuptake inhibitors in the acute treatment of depression. In F. E. Bloom & D. Kupfer (Eds.), *Psychopharmacology: The fourth generation of progress* (pp. 1043–1051). New York: Raven.

MOONEY, C. (2005). The Republican war on science. New York: Basic Books.

MOORE, C., & DUNHAM, P. (EDS.). (2004). *Joint attention: Its origin and role in development.* Hillsdale, NJ: Erlbaum.

MOORHEAD, G., FERENCE, R., & NECK, C. P. (1991). Group decision fiascoes continue: Space shuttle Challenger and a revised groupthink framework. *Human Relations, 44*(6), 539–550.

MORA, F., ROLLS, E. T., & BURTON, M. J. (1976). Modulation during learning of the responses of neurons in the lateral hypothalamus to the sight of food. *Experimental Neurology, 53,* 508–519.

MORA, G. (1975). Historical and theoretical trends in psychiatry. In A. M. Freedman, H. I. Kaplan, & B. J. Sadock (Eds.), *Comprehensive textbook of psychiatry: Vol. 1* (pp. 1–75). Baltimore: Williams & Wilkins.

MORAY, N. (1959). Attention in dichotic listening: Affective cues and the influence of instructions. *Quarterly Journal of Experimental Psychology, 11,* 56–60.

MORELAND, R. L., & ZAJONC, R. B. (1982). Exposure effects in person perception: Familiarity, similarity, and attraction. *Journal of Experimental Social Psychology, 18,* 395–415.

MORELLI, G., ROGOFF, B., OPPENHEIM, D., & GOLDSMITH, D. (1992). Cultural variation in infants sleeping arrangements: Questions of independence. *Developmental Psychology, 28,* 604–613.

MORENO, C., LAJE, G., BLANCO, C., JIANG, H., SCHMIDT, A. B., & OLFSON, M. (2007). National trends in the outpatient diagnosis and treatment of bipolar disorder in youth. *Archives of General Psychiatry, 64,* 1032–1039.

MOREWEDGE, C., & NORTON, M. I. (2005). When dreaming is believing: The (motivated) interpretation of dreams. *Journal of Personality and Social Psychology, 96,* 249–254.

MORGAN, M. J. (2000). Ecstasy (MDMA): A review of its possible persistent psychological effects. *Psychopharmacology, 152,* 230–248.

MORGAN, C. D., & MURRAY, H. A. (1935). A method for investigating fantasies: The Thematic Apperception Test. *Archives of Neurological Psychiatry, 34,* 289–306.

MORGAN, C. P., & ARAM, J. D. (1975). The preponderance of arguments in the risky shift phenomenon. *Journal of Experimental Social Psychology, 11*(1), 25–34.

MORGAN, J. L. (1996). A rhythmic bias in preverbal speech segmentation. *Journal of Memory and Language, 35,* 666–688.

MORRIS, M. W., & PENG, K. (1994). Culture and cause: American and Chinese attributions for social and physical events. *Journal of Personality and Social Psychology, 67,* 949–971.

MORSBACH, H., & TYLER, W. J. (1986). In R. Harr (Ed.), *The social construction of emotions* (pp. 289–307). Oxford, England: Blackwell.

MORSELLA, E. (2005). The function of phenomenal states: Supramodular interaction theory. *Psychological Review, 112,* 1000–1021.

MORSELLA, E., LEVINE, L. R., & BARGH, J. A. (2004). Nonconscious activation of action plans: A cascade model of automatic social behavior. Unpublished manuscript, Yale University.

MOSCOVICI, S., & ZAVALLONI, M. (1969). The group as a polarizer of attitudes. *Journal of Personality and Social Psychology, 12*(2), 125–135.

MOSER, M. B. (1999). Making more synapses: A way to store information? *Cellular and Molecular Life Sciences, 55,* 593–600.

MOTOHASHI, K., & UMINO, M. (2001). Heterotopic painful stimulation decreases the late component of somatosensory evoked potentials induced by electrical tooth stimulation. *Brain Research, 11,* 39–46.

MOUNTS, N. S., & STEINBERG, L. (1995). An ecological analysis of peer influence on adolescent grade point average and drug use. *Developmental Psychology, 31*(6), 915–922.

MOZEL, M., SMITH, B., SMITH, P., SULLIVAN, R., & SWENDER, P. (1969). Nasal chemoreception in flavor identification. *Archives of Otolaryngology, 90,* 131–137.

MROCZEK, D. K. (2001). Age and emotion in adulthood. *Current Directions in Psychological Science, 10,* 87–90.

MROCZEK, D. K., & KOLARZ, C. M. (1998). The effect of age on positive and negative affect: A developmental perspective on happiness. *Journal of Personality and Social Psychology, 75*(5), 1333–1349.

MUELLER, W. A. (1996). *Developmental biology.* New York: Springer-Verlag.

MULFORD, R. (1986). First words of the blind child. In M. Smith & J. Locke (Eds.), *The emergent lexicon: The child's development of a linguistic vocabulary.* New York: Academic Press.

MULICK, J. A. (1990). The ideology and science of punishment in mental retardation. *American Journal on Mental Retardation, 95,* 142–156.

MULLEN, M. K. (1994). Earliest recollections of childhood: A demographic analysis. *Cognition, 52*(1), 55–79.

MULLEN, M. K., & YI, S. (1995). The cultural context of talk about the past: Implications for the development of autobiographical memory. *Cognitive Development, 10*(3), 407–419.

MULROW, C. D., WILLIAMS, J. W., JR., CHIQUETTE, E., AGUILAR, C., HITCHCOCK-NOEL, P., LEE, S., ET AL. (2000). Efficacy of newer medications for treating depression in primary care patients. *American Journal of Medicine, 108,* 54–64.

MUNAFO, M. R., DURRANT, C., LEWIS, G., & FLINT, J. (2009). Gene X environment interactions at the serotonin transporter locus. *Biological Psychiatry, 65,* 211–219.

MUNNICH, E., LANDAU, B., & DOSHER, B. (2001) Spatial language and spatial representation: A cross-linguistic comparison. *Cognition, 81*(3), 171–208.

MURPHY, F. C., NIMMO-SMITH, I., & LAWRENCE, A. D. (2003). Functional neuroanatomy of emotion: A meta-analysis. *Cognitive, Affective, and Behavioral Neuroscience, 3,* 207–233.

MURPHY, G. L. (2002). *The big book of concepts.* Cambridge, MA: MIT Press.

MURRAY, C. (1998). *Income inequality and IQ.* Washington, DC: American Enterprise Institute.

MURRAY, L., & TREVARTHEN, C. (1985). *Social perception in infants.* New York: Ablex.

MUSOLINO, J., CHUNYO, G., & LANDAU, B. (In press). Uncovering knowledge of core syntactic and semantic principles in individuals with Williams syndrome. *Language Learning and Development.*

MUSSELL, M., MITCHELL, J., CROSBY, R., FULKERSON, J., HOBERMAN, H., & ROMANO, J. (2000). Commitment to treatment goals in prediction of group cognitive-behavioral therapy treatment outcome for women with bulimia nervosa. *Journal of Consulting and Clinical Psychology, 68,* 432–437.

NADEL, L., & JACOBS, W. J. (1998). Traumatic memory is special. *Current Directions in Psychological Science, 7,* 154–157.

NADEL, L., & MOSCOVITCH, M. (2001). The hippocampal complex and long-term memory revisited. *Trends in Cognitive Science, 5,* 228–230.

NAGEL, T. (1974). What is it like to be a bat? *Philosophical Review, 83,* 435–450.

NAIGLES, L. G. (1990). Children use syntax to learn verb meanings. *Journal of Child Language, 17,* 357–374.

NAKAMURA, J., & CSIKSZENTMIHALYI, M. (2001). Catalytic creativity: The case of Linus Pauling. *American Psychologist, 56*(4), 337–341.

NAPPA, R., WESSEL, A., MCELDOON, K. L., GLEITMAN, L. R., & TRUESWELL, J. C. (2009). Use of speaker's gaze and syntax in verb learning. *Language Learning and Development,* 5(4), 203–234.

NARROW, W. REGIER, D., RAE, D., MANDERSCHEID, R., & LOCKE, B. (1993). Use of services by persons with mental and addictive disorders: Findings from the National Institute of Mental Health Epidemiologic Catchment Area Program. *Archives of General Psychiatry, 50,* 95–107.

NASH, M. R. (2001). The truth and hype of hypnosis. *Scientific American, 285,* 36–43.

NASSER, M. (1997). *Culture and weight consciousness.* London: Routledge.

NATHAN, P. E., & GORMAN, J. M. (EDS.). (2002). *A guide to treatments that work* (2nd ed.). New York: Oxford University Press.

NATHAN, P. E., STUART, S. P., & DOLAN, S. L. (2000). Research on psychotherapy efficacy and effectiveness: Between Scylla and Charybdis? *Psychological Bulletin, 126,* 964–981.

NATIONAL INSTITUTE OF MENTAL HEALTH (NIMH). (2000). NIMH Research on Treatment for Attention Deficit Hyperactivity Disorder (ADHD): Questions and Answers about the Multimodal Treatment Study. Retrieved from http://www.nimh.nih.gov/health/trials/nimh-research-treatment-adhd-study.shtml

NATIONAL INSTITUTE OF MENTAL HEALTH (NIMH). (2007a). Always embarrassed: Social phobia (social anxiety disorder). NIH Publication No. 07-4678. Bethesda, MD: National Institutes of Health.

NATIONAL INSTITUTE OF MENTAL HEALTH (NIMH). (2007b). When worry gets out of control: Generalized anxiety disorder. NIH Publication No. 07-4677. Bethesda, MD: National Institutes of Health.

NATIONAL INSTITUTE OF MENTAL HEALTH (NIMH). (2009). Anxiety disorders. NIH Publication No. 09-3879. Bethesda, MD: National Institutes of Health.

NATIONAL RESEARCH COUNCIL AND INSTITUTE OF MEDICINE (2000). *From neurons to neighborhoods: The science of early childhood development.* Committee on Integrating the Science of Early Childhood Development. J. Shonkoff & D. Phillips (Eds.), Board on Children, Youth, and Families, Commission on Behavioral and Social Sciences and Education. Washington, DC: National Academy Press.

NAUTA, W. J. H., & FEIRTAG, M. (1986). *Fundamental neuroanatomy.* New York: Freeman.

NAVARRA, P., DELLO RUSSO, C., MANCUSO, C., PREZIOSI, P., & GROSSMAN, A. (2000). Gaseous neuromodulators in the control of neuroendocrine stress axis. *Annals of the New York Academy of Sciences, 917,* 638–646.

NAZZI, T., BERTONCINI, J., & MEHLER, J. (1998). Language discrimination by newborns: Toward an understanding of the role of rhythm. *Journal of Experimental Psychology: Human Perception and Performance, 24*(3), 756–766.

NEEDHAM, D., & BEGG, I. (1991). Problem-oriented training promotes spontaneous analogical transfer: Memory-oriented training promotes memory for training. *Memory and Cognition, 19,* 543–557.

NEIMEYER, G. J. (1984). Cognitive complexity and marital satisfaction. *Journal of Social and Clinical Psychology, 2,* 258–263.

NEISSER, U. (1982a). *Memory observed.* San Francisco: Freeman.

NEISSER, U. (1982b, January). On the trail of the tape-recorder fallacy. Paper presented at a symposium on "The influence of hypnosis and related states on memory: Forensic implications" at the meetings of the American Association for the Advancement of Science, Washington, DC.

NEISSER, U. (1986). Remembering Pearl Harbor: Reply to Thompson and Cowan. *Cognition, 23,* 285–286.

NEISSER, U. (1997). Rising scores on intelligence tests. *American Scientist, 85,* 440–447.

NEISSER, U. (ED.). (1998). *The rising curve: Long-term gains in IQ and related measures.* Washington, DC:American Psychological Association.

NEISSER, U., & BECKLEN, R. (1975). Selective looking: Attending to visually specified events. *Cognitive Psychology, 7*(4), 480–494.

NEISSER, U., BOODOO, G., BOUCHARD, T. J., JR., BOYKIN, A. W., BRODY, N., CECI, S. J., ET AL. (1996). Intelligence: Knowns and unknowns. *American Psychologist, 51*(2), 77–101.

NEISSER, U., & HARSCH, N. (1992). Phantom flashbulbs: False recollections of hearing the news about *Challenger.* In E. Winograd & U. Neisser (Eds.), *Affect and accuracy in recall: Studies of "flashbulb" memories* (pp. 9–31). Cambridge: Cambridge University Press.

NELSON, C. A., III, FURTADO, E., FOX, N., & ZEANAH, C. (2009). The deprived human brain. *American Scientist, 97,* 222–229.

NELSON, C. A., III, ZEANAH, C. H., FOX, N. A., MARSHALL, P. J., SMYKE, A. T., & GUTHRIE, D. (2007). Cognitive recovery in socially deprived young children: The Bucharest Early Intervention Project. *Science, 318,* 1937–1940.

NELSON, K., & FIVUSH, R. (2000). Socialization of memory. In E. Tulving & F. I. M. Craik (Eds.), *The Oxford handbook of memory* (pp. 283–295). London: Oxford University Press.

NEMETH, C., & CHILES, C. (1988). Modeling courage: The role of dissent in fostering independence. *European Journal of Social Psychology, 18,* 275–280.

NERIA, Y., OLFSON, M., GAMEROFF, M. J., WICKRAMARATNE, P., PILOWSKY, D., VERDELI, H., ET AL. (2008). Trauma exposure and posttraumatic stress disorder among primary care patients with bipolar spectrum disorder. *Bipolar Disorder, 10,* 503–510.

NESPOR, M., PEÑA, M., & MEHLER, J. (2003). On the different roles of vowels and consonants in speech processing and language acquisition. *Lingue e Linguaggio, 2,* 221–240.

NETTELBECK, T. (2003). Inspection time and *g.* In H. Nyborg (Ed.), *The scientific study of General intelligence: A tribute to Arthur Jensen* (pp. 77–92). New York: Elsevier.

NETTELBECK, T., & YOUNG, R. (1996). Intelligence and the savant syndrome: Is the whole greater than the sum of the fragments? *Intelligence, 22,* 49–68.

NEUGEBAUER, R. (1979). Medieval and early modern theories of mental illness. *Archives of General Psychiatry, 36,* 477–484.

NEWCOMB, A. F., & BAGWELL, C. L. (1995). Children's friendship relations: A meta-analytic review. *Psychological Bulletin, 117*(2), 306–347.

NEWCOMB, A. F., BUKOWSKI, W. M., & PATTEE, L. (1993). Children's peer relations: A meta-analytic review of popular, rejected, neglected, controversial, and average sociometric status. *Psychological Bulletin, 113*(1), 99–128.

NEWCOMBE, F., RATCLIFF, G., & DAMASIO, H. (1987). Dissociable visual and spatial impairments following right posterior cerebral lesions: Clinical, neuropsychological, and anatomical evidence. *Neuropsychologia, 25*(1 B), 149–161.

NEWCOMBE, N. S. (2002). The nativist-empiricst controversy in the context of recent research on spatial and quantitative development. *Psychological Science, 13,* 395–401.

NEWCOMBE, N. S. (2007). Taking science seriously: Straight thinking about spatial sex differences. In S. Ceci & W. Williams (Eds.), *Why aren't more women in science?* (pp. 69–77). Washington, DC: American Psychological Association.

NEWELL, A., & SIMON, H. A. (1972). *Human problem solving.* Englewood Cliffs, NJ: Prentice-Hall.

NEWMAN, E. A., & ZAHS, K. R. (1998). Modulation of neuronal activity by glial cells in the retina. *Journal of Neuroscience, 18,* 4022–4028.

NEWPORT, E. L. (1990). Maturational constraints on language learning. *Cognitive Science, 14,* 11–28.

NEWPORT, E. L. (1999). Reduced input in the acquisition of signed languages: Contributions to the study of creolization. In M. DeGraff (Ed.), *Language creation and language change: Creolization, diachrony, and development.* Cambridge, MA: MIT Press.

NEWPORT, E. L., & ASHBROOK, E. F. (1977). The emergence of semantic relations in American Sign Language. *Papers and Reports in Child Language Development, 13,* 16–21.

NICHD EARLY CHILD CARE RESEARCH NETWORK. (1997). The effects of infant child care on infant-mother attachment security: Results of the NICHD study of early child care. *Child Development, 68,* 860–879.

NICHD EARLY CHILD CARE RESEARCH NETWORK. (2001). Child-care and family predictors of preschool attachment and stability from infancy. *Developmental Psychology, 37,* 847–862.

NICHD EARLY CHILD CARE RESEARCH NETWORK. (2003).Does quality of child care affect child outcomes at age 4 1/2? *Developmental Psychology, 39,* 451–469.

NICHD EARLY CHILD CARE RESEARCH NETWORK. (2006). Child-care effect sizes for the NICHD Study of Early Child Care and Youth Development. *American Psychologist, 61,* 99–116.

NICHOLSON, R. A., & BERMAN, J. S. (1983). Is follow-up necessary in evaluating psychotherapy? *Psychological Bulletin, 93,* 261–278.

NICKERSON, R. A., & ADAMS, M. J. (1979). Long-term memory for a common object. *Cognitive Psychology, 11,* 287–307.

NISBETT, R. E. (1980). The trait construct in lay and professional psychology. In L. Festinger (Ed.), *Retrospections on social psychology* (pp. 109–130). New York: Oxford University Press.

NISBETT, R. E. (2003). *The geography of thought: Why we think the way we do.* New York: Free Press.

NISBETT, R. E., & COHEN, D. (1996). *Culture of honor: The psychology of violence in the South.* Boulder, CO: Westview Press.

NISBETT, R. E., KRANTZ, D. H., JEPSON, C., & KUNDA, Z. (1983). The use of statistical heuristics in everyday inductive reasoning. *Psychological Review, 90,* 339–363.

NISBETT, R. E., & MIYAMOTO, Y. (2005). The influence of culture: Holistic versus analytic perception. *Trends in Cognitive Science, 9,* 467–473.

NISBETT, R. E., PENG, K., CHOI, I., & NORENZAYAN, A. (2001). Culture and systems of thought: Holistic versus analytic cognition. *Psychological Review, 108*(2), 291–310.

NISBETT, R. E., & ROSS, L. (1980). *Human inference: Strategies and shortcomings of social judgment.* Englewood Cliffs, NJ: Prentice-Hall.

NISBETT, R. E., & SCHACHTER, S. (1966). Cognitive manipulation of pain. *Journal of Experimental Social Psychology, 2,* 277–236.

NISBETT, R. E., & WILSON, T. D. (1977). Telling more than we can know: Verbal reports on mental processes. *Psychological Review, 84,* 231–259.

NOLEN-HOEKSMA, S. (1987). Sex differences in unipolar depression: Evidence and theory. *Psychological Bulletin, 101,* 259–282.

NOLEN-HOEKSEMA, S., WISCO, B. E., & LYUBOMIRSKY, S. (2008). Rethinking rumination. *Perspectives on Psychological Science, 3,* 400–424.

NOPOULOS, P., FLAUM, M., & ANDREASEN, N. C. (1997). Sex differences and brain morphology in schizophrenia. *American Journal of Psychiatry, 154,* 1648–1654.

NORBURY, H. M., WAXMAN, S. R., & SONG, H. (2008). *Tight* and *loose* are not created equal: An asymmetry underlying the representation of fit in English- and Korean-speakers. *Cognition. 109*(3), 316–325.

NORCROSS, J. C., & FREEDHEIM, D. K. (1992). Into the future: Retrospect and prospect in psychotherapy. In D. K. Freedheim (Ed.), *History of psychotherapy.* Washington, DC: American Psychological Association.

NORENZAYAN, A., & SHARIFF, A. F. (2008). The origin and evolution of religious prosociality. *Science, 322*(5898), 58–62.

NORMAN, W. T. (1963). Toward an adequate taxonomy of personality attributes: Replicated factor structure in peer nomination personality ratings. *Journal of Abnormal and Social Psychology, 66,* 574–583.

NORTON, M. I., FROST, J. H., & ARIELY, D. (2007). Less is more: The lure of ambiguity, or why familiarity breeds contempt. *Journal of Personality and Social Psychology, 92,* 97–105.

NOSEK, B. A. (2007). Implicit-explicit relations. *Current Directions in Psychological Science, 16*(2), 65–69.

NOVECK, J., & SPERBER, D. (2005). *Experimental pragmatics.* Oxford: Oxford University Press.

NOVICK, J. M., THOMPSON-SCHILL, S., & TRUESWELL, J. C. (2008). Putting lexical constraints in context into thew visual-world paradigm. *Cognition, 107*(3), 850–903.

NOVICK, J. M., TRUESWELL, J. C., & THOMPSON-SCHILL, S. L. (2005). Cognitive control and parsing: Re-examining the role of Broca's area in sentence comprehension. *Journal of Cognitive, Affective, and Behavioral Neuroscience, 5*(3), 263–281.

NOYES, R., WOODMAN, C., GARVEY, M. J., COOK, B. L., SUELZER, M., CLANCY, J. ET AL. (1992). Generalized anxiety disorder vs. panic disorder: Distinguishing characteristics and patterns of comorbidity. *Journal of Nervous & Mental Disease, 180*(6), 369–379.

NUTT, D. J. (2001). Neurobiological mechanisms in generalized anxiety disorder [Suppl.]. *Journal of Clinical Psychiatry, 62*(11), 22–27.

NYITI, R. M. (1976). The development of conservation in the Meru children of Tanzania. *Child Development, 47*(4), 1122–1129.

OAKES, P. J., & TURNER, J. C. (1980). Social categorization and intergroup behavior: Does minimal intergroup discrimination make social identity more positive? *European Journal of Social Psychology, 10,* 295–301.

OBERMAN, L. M., & RAMACHANDRAN, V. S. (2007). The simulating social mind: The role of the mirror neuron system and simulation in the social and communicative deficits of autism spectrum disorders. *Psychological Bulletin, 133*(2), 310–327.

OBERAUER, K., SCHULZE, R., WILHELM, O., & SÜSS, H.-M. (2005). Working memory and intelligence: Their correlation and their relation: Comment on Ackerman, Beier, and Boyle (2005). *Psychological Bulletin, 131,* 61–65.

OBHI, S., PLANETTA, P., & SCANTLEBURY, J. (2009). On the signals underlying conscious awareness of action. *Cognition, 110,* 65–73.

OCHSNER, K. N., KNIERIM, K., LUDLOW, D. H., HANELIN, J., RAMACHANDRAN, T., GLOVER, G., ET AL. (2004). Reflecting upon feelings: An fMRI study of neural systems supporting the attribution of emotion to self and other. *Journal of Cognitive Neuroscience, 16,* 1746–1772.

O'CONNOR, T. G., RUTTER, M., BECKETT, C., KEAVENEY, L., KREPPNER, J. M., & ENGLISH AND ROMANIAN ADOPTION STUDY TEAM. (2000). The effects of global severe privation on cognitive competence: Extension and longitudinal follow-up. *Child Development, 71*(2), 376–390.

ODIORNE, J. M. (1957). Color changes. In M. E. Brown (Ed.), *The physiology of fishes: Vol. 2.* New York: Academic Press.

OESTERMAN, K., BJOERKQVIST, K., LAGERSPETZ, K. M. J., KAUKIAINEN, A., LANDAU, S. F., FRACZEK, A., ET AL. (1998). Cross-cultural evidence of female indirect aggression. *Aggressive Behavior, 24*(1), 1–8.

OFSHE, R. (1992). Inadvertent hypnosis during interrogation: False confession due to dissociative state; misidentified multiple personality and the Satanic Cult Hypothesis. *International Journal of Clinical and Experimental Hypnosis, 40,* 125–136.

OGDEN, J. A. (2005). *Fractured minds: A case-study approach to clinical neuropsychology.* New York: Oxford University Press.

ÖHMAN, A. (2005). The role of the amygdala in human fear: Automatic detection of threat. *Psychoneuroendocrinology, 30,* 953–958.

ÖHMAN, A., & MINEKA, S. (2001). Fears, phobias, and preparedness: Toward an evolved module of fear and fear learning. *Psychological Review, 108,* 483–522.

ÖHMAN, A., & MINEKA, S. (2003). The malicious serpent: Snakes as a prototypical stimulus for an evolved module of fear. *Current Directions in Psychological Science, 12,* 5–9.

ÖHMAN, A., & SOARES, J. J. (1993). On the automatic nature of phobic fear: Conditioned electrodermal responses to masked fear-relevant stimuli. *Journal of Abnormal Psychology, 102*(1), 121–132.

ÖHMAN, A., & SOARES, J. J. F. (1994). "Unconscious anxiety": Phobic responses to masked stimuli. *Journal of Abnormal Psychology, 103,* 231–240.

O'KANE, G., KENSINGER, E. A., & CORKIN, S. (2004). Evidence for semantic learning in profound amnesia: An investigation with patient H.M. *Hippocampus, 14*(4), 417–425.

OKASHA, A., & OKASHA, T. (2000). Mental health in Cairo (Al-Qahira). *International Journal of Mental Health, 28,* 62–68.

OLFF, M., LANGELAND, W., DRAIJER, N., & GERSONS, B.P.R. (2007). Gender differences in posttraumatic stress disorder. *Psychological Bulletin, 133*(2), 183–204.

OLFSON, M., & KLERMAN, G. L. (1993). Trends in the prescription of psychotropic medications. The role of physician specialty. *Medical Care, 31,* 559–564.

OLLENDICK, T., & KING, N. (EDS.). (1994). *International handbook of phobic and anxiety disorders in children and adolescents: Issues in clinical child psychology.* New York: Plenum.

OLSON, D. J. (1991). Species differences in spatial memory among Clark's nutcrackers, scrub jays, and pigeons. *Journal of Experimental Psychology: Animal Behavior Processes, 17*(4), 363–376.

OLSON, W. K. (1997). *The excuse factory: How employment law is paralyzing the American workplace.* New York: Free Press.

O'NEAL, J. (1984). First person account: Finding myself and loving it. *Schizophrenia Bulletin, 10,* 109–110.

O'NEILL, D. K., ASTINGTON, J. W., & FLAVELL, J. H. (1992). Young children's understanding of the role that sensory experiences play in knowledge acquisition. *Child Development, 63*(2), 474–490.

ONISHI, K., & BAILLARGEON, R. (2005). Do 15-month-old infants understand false belief? *Science, 308,* 255–258.

OPPENHEIM, D., SAGI, A., & LAMB, M. (1988). Infant-adult attachments on the kibbutz and their relation to socioemotional development 4 years later. *Developmental Psychology, 24,* 427–433.

ORLANSKY, H. (1949). Infant care and personality. *Psychological Bulletin, 46,* 1–48.

ORNE, M. T. (1951). The mechanisms of hypnotic age regression: An experimental study. *Journal of Abnormal and Social Psychology, 58,* 277–299.

ORNE, M. T., & EVANS, F. J. (1965). Social control in the psychological experiment: Antisocial behavior and hypnosis. *Journal of Personality and Social Psychology, 1,* 189–200.

ORNSTEIN, P. A., BAKER-WARD, L., MYERS, J., PRINCIPE, G. F., & GORDON, B. N. (1995). Young children's long-term retention of medical experiences: Implications for testimony. In F. E. Weinert & W. Schneider (Eds.), *Memory performance and competencies: Issues in growth and development* (pp. 347–371). Mahwah, NJ: Erlbaum.

ORTONY, A., CLORE, G. L., & COLLINS, A. (1988). *The cognitive structure of emotions.* New York: Cambridge University Press.

OZER, E. J., & WEISS, D. S. (2004). Who develops post-traumatic stress disorder? *Current Directions in Psychological Science, 13,* 169–172.

OZER, D. J., & BENET-MARTINEZ, V. (2006). Personality and the prediction of consequential outcomes. *Annual Review of Psychology, 57,* 401–421.

PACIFICI R., ZUCCAROA, P., FARRÉB, M., PICHINIA,S., DI CARLOA, S., ROSETB, P. N., ORTUÑOB, J., PUJADASB, M., BACOSIA, A., MENOYOB, E., SEGURAB, J., & DE LA TORREB, R. (2001). Effects of repeated doses of MDMA ("Ecstasy") on cell-mediated immune response in humans. *Life Sciences, 69,* 2931–2941.

PACKER, D. J. (2009). Avoiding groupthink: Whereas weakly identified members remain silent, strongly identified members dissent about collective problems. *Psychological Science, 20,* 546–548.

PALLIER, C., CHRISTOPHE, A., & MEHLER, J. (1997). Language-specific listening. *Trends in Cognitive Science, 1*(4).

PALMER, S. E. (2002). Perceptual grouping: It's later than you think. *Current Directions in Psychological Science, 11*(3), 101–106.

PANKSEPP, J. (1991). Affective neuroscience: A conceptual framework for the neurobiological study of emotions. *International Review of Studies on Emotion, 1,* 59–99.

PANKSEPP, J. (1998). *Affective neuroscience: The foundations of human and animal emotions.* Oxford, England: Oxford University Press.

PANKSEPP, J. (1998). Attention deficit/hyperactivity disorders, psychostimulants, and intolerance of childhood playfulness: A tragedy in the making? *Current Directions in Psychological Science, 7,* 91–98.

PAPAFRAGOU, A.; CASSIDY, K., & GLEITMAN, L. R. (2007). When we think about thinking: The acquisition of belief verbs. *Cognition, 105*(1), 125-165.

PAPAFRAGOU, A., MASSEY, C., & GLEITMAN, L. R. (2006). When English proposes what Greek presupposes. *Cognition, 98*(3), B75–B86.

PARKE, R. D. (1981). *Fathers.* Cambridge, MA: Harvard University Press.

PARKER, G., MAHENDRAN, R., KOH, E. S., & MACHIN, D. (2000). Season of birth in schizophrenia: No latitude at the equator. *British Journal of Psychiatry, 176,* 68–71.

PARKER, J., RUBIN, K., PRICE, J., & DEROSIER, M. (1995). Peer relationships, child development and adjustment: A developmental psychopathology. In D. Cicchetti & D. Cohen (Eds.), *Developmental Psychopathology.* New York: Wiley.

PARNAS, J., & JORGENSEN, A. (1989). Premorbid psychopathology in schizophrenia spectrum. *British Journal of Psychiatry, 155,* 623–627.

PARSONS, J. E., ADLER, T. F., & KACZALA, C. M. (1982). Socialization of achievement attitudes and beliefs: Parental influences. *Child Development, 53*(2), 310–321.

PASHLER, H., JOHNSTON, J. C., & RUTHRUFF, E. (2000). Attention and performance. *Annual Review of Psychology, 52,* 629–651.

PATTERSON, B. W. (2004). The "tyranny of the eyewitness." *Law & Psychology Review, 28,* 195–203.

PATTERSON, D., & JENSEN, M. (2003). Hypnosis and clinical pain. *Psychological Bulletin, 129* (4), 495–521.

PAVLOV, I. (1927). *Conditioned reflexes.* Oxford, England: Oxford University Press.

PAYNE, B. K. (2001). Prejudice and perception: The role of automatic and controlled processes in misperceiving a weapon. *Journal of Personality and Social Psychology, 81,* 181–192.

PAYNE, J. D., NADEL, L., BRITTON, W. B., & JACOBS, W. J. (2004). The biopsychology of trauma and memory. In D. Reisberg & P. Hertel (Eds.), *Memory and emotion* (pp. 76–128). New York: Oxford University Press.

PEARCE, J. M., & BOUTON, M. E. (2001). Theories of associative learning in animals. *Annual Review of Psychology, 52,* 111–139.

PEDERSEN, P. B., FUKUYAMA, M., & HEATH, A. (1989). Client, counselor, and contextual variables in multicultural counseling. In P. B. Pedersen, J. G. Draguns, W. J. Lonner, & J. E. Trimble (Eds.), *Counseling across cultures* (pp. 23–52). Honolulu: University of Hawaii.

PEDERSEN, W. C., MILLER, L. C., PUTCHA-BHAGAVATULA, A. D., & YANG, Y. (2002). Evolved sex differences in the number of partners desired? The long and the short of it. *Psychological Science, 13,* 157–161.

PEDERSON, E., DANZIGER, E., WILKINS, D., LEVINSON, S., KITA, S., & SENFT, G. (1998). Semantic typology and spatial conceptualization. *Language 74*(3), 557–589.

PEÑA, M., BONATTI, L., NESPOR, M., & MEHLER, J. (2002). Signal driven computations in speech processing. *Science, 298,* 604–607.

PEÑA, M., MAKI, A. , KOVA, D., DEHAENE-LAMBERTZ, G., KOIZUMI, H., BOUQUET, F., ET AL. (2003). Sounds and silence: An optical topography study of language recognition at birth. *Proceedings of the National Academy of Sciences, 100*(20), 11702–11705.

PENDERGAST, M. (1995). *Victims of memory: Sex abuse accusations and shattered lives.* Hinesburg, VT: Upper Access.

PENFIELD, W., & RASMUSSEN, T. (1950). *The cerebral cortex of man.* New York: Macmillan.

PENNEBAKER, J. W. (2004). Writing to heal: A guided journal for recovering from trauma and emotional upheaval. Oakland, CA: New Harbinger Press.

PENNISI, E. (2005). Strong personalities can pose problems in the mating game. *Science, 309,* 694–695.

PENTON-VOAK, I. S., & PERRETT, D. I. (2000). Female preference for male faces changes cyclically: Further evidence. *Evolution and Human Behavior, 21*(1), 39–48.

PEPLAU, L. A. (2003). Human sexuality: How do men and women differ? *Current Directions in Psychological Science, 12,* 37–40.

PEPLAU, L. A., & FINGERHUT, A. W. (2007). The close relationships of lesbians and gay men. *Annual Review of Psychology, 58,* 405–424.

PEPPERBERG, I. (1999). Rethinking syntax: A commentary on E. Kako's "Elements of syntax in the systems of three language-trained animals." *Animal Learning & Behavior, 27,* 15–17.

PERANI, D., PAULESCU, E., SEBASTIAN-GALLES, N., DUPOUX, E., DEHAENE, S., BETTINARDI, V., CAPPA, S., FAZIO, F., & MEHLER, J. (1998) The bilingual brain: Proficiency and age of acquisition of the second language. *Brain, 121,* 1841–1852.

PERDUE, C. W., DOVIDIO, J. F., GURTMAN, M. B., & TYLER, R. B. (1990). Us and them: Social categorization and the process of intergroup bias. *Journal of Personality and Social Psychology, 59,* 475–486.

PERKINS, D. N., & GROTZER, T. A. (1997). Teaching intelligence. *American Psychologist, 52,* 1125–1133.

PERLS, F. S. (1967). Group vs. individual therapy. *ETC, 24,* 306–312.

PERLS, F. S. (1969). *Gestalt therapy verbatim.* Moab, UT: Real People Press.

PERNER, J., & LANG, B. (1999). Development of theory of mind and executive control. *Trends in Cognitive Science, 6,* 337–344.

PERNER, J., & RUFFMAN, T. (2005). Infants' insight into the mind: How deep? *Science, 308,* 214–216.

PERROTT, D. A., GENTNER, D., & BODENHAUSEN, G. V. (2005). Resistance is futile: The unwitting insertion of analogical inferences in memory. *Psychonomics Bulletin & Review, 12,* 696–702.

PETERSON, C. (1999). Personal control and well-being. In D. Kahneman, E. Diener, & N. Schwarz (Eds.), *Well-being: The foundations of hedonic psychology* (pp. 288–301). New York: Russell Sage Foundation.

PETERSON, C. (2006). *A primer in positive psychology.* New York: Oxford University Press.

PETERSON, C., & MCCABE, A. (1994). A social interactionist account of developing decontextualized narrative skill. *Developmental Psychology, 30*(6), 937–948.

PETERSON, C., & PARK, C. (1998). Learned helplessness and explanatory style. In D. F. Barone, M. Hersen, & V. Van Hasselt (Eds.), *Advanced personality* (pp. 287–310). New York: Plenum.

PETERSON, C., & PARK, N. (2007). Explanatory style and emotion regulation. In J. Gross, *Handbook of emotion regulation* (pp. 159–179). New York: Guilford.

PETERSON, C., & SELIGMAN, M. E. P. (1984). Causal explanations as a risk factor for depression: Theory and evidence. *Psychological Review, 91,* 341–374.

PETERSON, C. T., & SELIGMAN, M. E. P. (2004). *Character strengths and virtues: A handbook and classification.* Washington, DC: APA Press and Oxford University Press.

PETERSON, C., SEMMEL, A., VON BAEYER, C., ABRAMSON, L. Y., METALSKY, G. I., & SELIGMAN, M. E. P. (1982). The Attributional Style Questionnaire. *Cognitive Therapy and Research, 6,* 287–299.

PETERSON, C., & VAIDYA, R. S. (2001). Explanatory style, expectations, and depressive symptoms. *Personality and Individual Differences, 31,* 1217–1223.

PETERSON, M. A., & ENNS, J. T. (2005). The edge complex: Implicit memory for figure assignment in shape perception. *Perception & Psychophysics, 67,* 727–740.

PETERSON, R. S., & BEHFAR, K. J. (2005). Leadership as group regulation. In D. M. Messick & R. M. Kramer (Eds.), *The psychology of leadership: New perspectives and research* (pp. 143–162). Mahwah, NJ: Erlbaum.

PETERSON, S. E., FOX, P. T., POSNER, M. I., MINTUN, M., & RAICHLE, M. E. (1988). Positron emission tomographic studies of the processing of single words. *Journal of Cognitive Neuroscience, 1,* 153–170.

PETRIDES, G., FINK, M., HUSAIN, M. M., KNAPP, R. G., RUSH, A. J., MUELLER, M., ET AL. (2001). ECT remission rates in psychotic versus nonpsychotic depressed patients: A report from CORE. *Journal of ECT, 17*(4), 244–253.

PETRILL, S. A., LUO, D., THOMPSON, L. A., & DETTERMAN, D. K. (2001). Inspection time and the relationship among elementary cognitive tasks, general intelligence, and specific cognitive abilities. *Intelligence, 29,* 487–496.

PETRY, N. M., TENNEN, H., & AFFLECK, G. (2000). Stalking the elusive client variable in psychotherapy research. In C. R. Snyder & R. Ingram (Eds.), *Handbook of psychological change: Psychotherapy processes and practices for the 21st century* (pp. 88–108). New York: Wiley.

PETTIGREW, T. F. (1998). Intergroup contact theory. *Annual Review of Psychology, 49.*

PETTIGREW, T. F., & TROPP, L. R. (2006). A meta-analytic test of intergroup contact theory. *Journal of Personality and Social Psychology, 90,* 751–783.

PETTITO, L. (1988). "Language" in the prelinguistic child. In F. S. Kessel (Ed.), *The development of language and language researchers: Essays in honor of Roger Brown* (pp. 187–222). Hillsdale, NJ: Erlbaum.

PETTY, R. E., & BRIÑOL, P. (2008). Persuasion: From single to multiple to metacognitive processes. *Perspectives on Psychological Science, 3*(2), 137–147.

PETTY, R. E., & CACIOPPO, J. T. (1985). The elaboration likelihood model of persuasion. In L. Berkowitz (Ed.), *Advances in experimental social psychology: Vol. 19.* New York: Academic Press.

PETTY, R. E., & CACIOPPO, J. T. (1986). Communication and persuasion: Central and peripheral routes to attitude change. New York: Springer-Verlag.

PETTY, R. E., WEGENER, D. T., & FABRIGAR, L. R. (1997). Attitudes and attitude change. *Annual Review of Psychology, 48,* 609–647.

PEZDEK, K. (2004). Event memory and autobiographical memory for the events of September 11, 2001. *Applied Cognitive Psychology, 14,* 1033–1045.

PEZDEK, K., BLANDON-GITLIN, I., & GABBAY, P. (2006). Imagination and memory: Does imagining implausible events lead to false autobiographical memories, *Psychonomic Bulletin & Review, 13,* 764–769.

PHAN, K. L., WAGER, T. D., TAYLOR, S. F., & LIBERZON, I. (2002). Functional neuroanatomy of emotion: A meta-analysis of emotion activation studies in PET and fMRI. *Neuroimage, 16,* 331–348.

PHELPS, E. A. (2006). Emotion and cognition: Insights from studies of the human amygdala. *Annual Review of Psychology, 57,* 27–53.

PHILIPS, M. F., MATTIASSON, G., WIELOCH, T., BJÖRKLAND, A., JOHANSSON, B. B., & TOMASEVIC, G. (2001). Neuroprotective and behavioral efficacy of nerve growth factor-transfected hippocampal progenitor cell transplants after experimental traumatic brain injury. *Journal of Neurosurgery, 94,* 765–774.

PHILLIPS, A. T., WELLMAN, H. M., & SPELKE, E. S. (2002). Infants' ability to connect gaze and emotional expression to intentional action. *Cognition, 85,* 53–78.

PHILLIPS, M. L., LADOUCEUR, C. D., & DREVETS, W. C. (2008). A neural model of voluntary and automatic emotion regulation: Implications for understanding the pathophysiology and neurodevelopment of bipolar disorder. *Molecular Psychiatry, 13,* 833–857.

PHILLIPS, P.E.M., STUBER, G. D., HEIEN, M. L.A.V., WIGHTMAN, R. M., & CARELLI, R. M. (2003). Subsecond dopamine release promotes cocaine seeking. *Nature, 422,* 614–618.

PIAGET, J. (1952). *The origins of intelligence in children.* New York: International University Press.

PICCINELLI, M., PINI, S., BELLANTUONO, C., & WILKINSON, G. (1995). Efficacy of drug treatment in obsessive-compulsive disorder: A meta-analytic review. *British Journal of Psychiatry, 166,* 424–443.

PILIAVIN, J. A., & CALLERO, P. L. (1991). Giving blood: The development of an altruistic identity. Baltimore, MD: Johns Hopkins University Press.

PINCUS, H., ZARIN, D., TANIELIAN, T., JOHNSON, J., WEST, J., PETTIT, A., ET AL. (1999). Psychiatric patients and treatments in 1997: Findings from the American Psychiatric Association Practice Research Network. *Archives of General Psychiatry, 56,* 441–449.

PINEL, J.P.J., ASSANAND, S., & LEHMAN, D. R. (2000). Hunger, eating, and ill health. *American Psychologist, 55,* 1105–1116.

PINKER, S. (1984). *Language learnability and language development.* Cambridge, MA: Harvard University Press.

PINKER, S. (1994). *The language instinct: How the mind creates language.* New York: HarperPerennial.

PINKER, S. (1995). Why the child holded the baby rabbits: A case study in language acquisition. In L. R. Gleitman & M. Liberman (Eds.), *Language: An invitation to cognitive science: Vol. 1* (2nd ed., pp. 107–133). Cambridge, MA: MIT Press.

PINKER, S. (1997). *How the mind works.* New York: Norton

PINKER, S. (1999a). *How the mind works.* New York: Norton.

PINKER, S. (1999b). *Words and rules: The ingredients of language.* New York: Basic Books.

PINKER, S. (2002). *The blank slate.* New York: Viking.

PINKER, S. (2003). The blank slate: The modern denial of human nature. *Skeptical Inquirer, 27,* 37–41.

PINKER, S., & ULLMAN, M. T. (2002). The past and future of the past tense. *Trends in Cognitive Sciences, 6*(11), 456–463.

PINTO, S., ROSEBERRY, A., LIU, H., DIANO, S., SHANABROUGH, M., CAI, X., ET AL. (2004). Rapid rewiring of arcuate nucleus feeding circuits by leptin. *Science, 304,* 110–115.

PIPE, M.-E., GOODMAN, G. S., QUAS, J., BIDROSE, S., ABLIN, D., & CRAW, S. (1997). Remembering early experiences during childhood: Are traumatic events special? In J. D. Read & D. S. Lindsay (Eds.), *Recollections of trauma: Scientific evidence and clinical practice* (pp. 417–423). New York: Plenum.

PIPE, M.-E., LAMB, M., ORBACH, Y., & CEDERBORK, A.-C. (EDS). (2007). *Child sexual abuse: Disclosure, delay, and denial.* Mahwah, NJ: Erlbaum.

PIPP, S., EASTERBROOKS, M. A., & BROWN, S. R. (1993). Attachment status and complexity of infants' self- and other-knowledge when tested with mother and father. *Social Development, 2,* 1–14.

PITTENGER, C., & KANDEL, E. R. (2003). In search of general mechanisms for long-lasting plasticity: Aplysia and the hippocampus. *Philosophical Transactions of the Royal Society London: B. Biological Science, 358,* 757–763.

PLATEK, S. M., BURCH, R. L., PANYAVIN, I. S., WASSERMAN, B. H., & GALLUP, JR., G. G. (2002). Reactions to children's faces: Resemblance affects males more than females. *Evolution and Human Behavior, 23,* 159–166.

PLATEK, S. M., RAINES, D., GALLUP, JR., G., MOHAMED, F., THOMSON, J., MYERS, T. ET AL. (2004). Reactions to children's faces: Males are more affected by resemblance than females are, and so are their brains. *Evolution and Human Behavior, 25,* 394–405.

PLOMIN, R., CORLEY, R., DEFRIES, J. C., & FULKER, D. W. (1990). Individual differences in television viewing in early childhood: Nature as well as nurture. *Psychological Science, 1,* 371–377.

PLOMIN, R., & DANIELS, D. (1987). Why are children from the same family so different from one another? *Behavioral and Brain Sciences, 10,* 1–16.

PLOMIN, R., & DEFRIES, J. C. (1985). A parent-offspring adoption study of cognitive abilities in early childhood. *Intelligence, 9,* 341–356.

PLOMIN, R., FULKER, D. W., CORLEY, R., & DEFRIES, J. C. (1997). Nature, nurture, and cognitive development from 1 to 16 years: A parent-offspring adoption study. *Psychological Science, 8,* 442–447.

PLOMIN, R., & MCGUFFIN, P. (2003). Psychopathology in the postgenomic era. *Annual Review of Psychology, 54,* 205–228.

PLOMIN, R., & SPINATH, F. M. (2004). Intelligence: Genetics, genes, and genomics. *Journal of Personality and Social Psychology, 86,* 112–129.

POEPPEL, D., & HACKL, M. (2007). The architecture of speech perception. In J. Pomerantz (Ed.), *Topics in integrative neuroscience: From cells to cognition.* Cambridge, England: Cambridge University Press.

POLDRACK, A., & WAGNER, A. (2004). What can neuroimaging tell us about the mind? Insights from prefrontal cortex. *Current Directions in Psychological Science, 13,* 177–181.

POLEY, W. (1974). Dimensionality in the measurement of authoritarian and political attitudes. *Canadian Journal of Behavioral Science, 6,* 83–94.

POLLACK, M. H. (2001). Comorbidity, neurobiology, and pharmacotherapy of social anxiety disorder [Suppl.]. *Journal of Clinical Psychiatry, 62*(12), 24–29.

POPE, H. G., GRUBER, A. J., & YURGELUN-TODD, D. (2001). Residual neuropsychologic effects of cannabis. *Current Psychiatry Report, 3,* 507–512.

POPE, H. G., HUDSON, J. I., BODKIN, J. A., & OLIVA, P. (1998). Questionable validity of "dissociative amnesia" in trauma victims. *British Journal of Psychiatry, 172,* 210–215.

PORSOLT, R. D., LePICHON, M., & JALFRE, M. (1977). Depression: A new animal model sensitive to antidepressant treatments. *Nature, 266,* 730–732.

PORTER, R., & SCHAAL, B. (1995). Olfaction and development of social preferences in neonatal organisms. In R. L. Doty (Ed.), *Handbook of olfaction and gustation* (pp. 229–321). New York: Marcel Dekker.

PORTER, S., BIRT, A. R., YUILLE, J. C., & LEHMAN, D. R. (2000). Negotiating false memories: Interviewer and rememberer characteristics relate to memory distortion. *Psychological Science, 11,* 507–510.

PORTER, S., & PEACE, K. A. (2007). The scars of memory: A prospective, longitudinal investigation of the consistency of traumatic and positive emotional memories in adulthood. *Psychological Science, 18,* 435–441.

POSNER, M. I., & ROTHBART, M. K. (2007). Research on attention networks as a model for the integration of psychological science *Annual Review of Psychology, 58,* 1–23.

POSNER, M., SNYDER, C., & DAVIDSON, B. (1980). Attention and the detection of signals. *Journal of Experimental Psychology: General, 109,* 160–174.

POSTHUMA, D., & deGEUS, E. (2006). Progress in the molecular-genetic study of intelligence, *Current Directions in Psychological Science, 15,* 151–155.

POULOS, C. X., & CAPPELL, H. (1991). Homeostatic theory of drug tolerance: A general model of physiological adaptation. *Psychological Review, 98,* 390–408.

POVINELLI, D. J. (2000). *Folk physics for apes: Tthe chimpanzee's theory of how the world works.* Oxford, England: Oxford University Press.

POVINELLI, D. J., BERING, J. M., & GIAMBRONE S. (2000). Toward a science of other minds: Escaping the argument by analogy. *Cognitive Science, 24,* 509–542.

POWDERLY, W. G., LANDAY, A., & LEDERMAN, M. M. (1998). Recovery of the immune system with antiretroviral therapy: The end of opportunism? *Journal of the American Medical Association, 280,* 72–77.

POWELL, H. A. (1969). Genealogy, residence, and kinship in Kiriwina. *Man, 4,* 177–202.

PRASADA, S., & PINKER, S. (1993a). Generalizations of regular and irregular morphology. *Language and Cognitive Processes, 8,* 1–56.

PRASADA, S., & PINKER, S. (1993b). Similarity-based and rule-based generalizations in inflectional morphology. *Language and Cognitive Processes, 8,* 1–56.

PREMACK, A., & PREMACK, D. (1983). *The mind of an ape.* New York: Norton.

PREMACK, D. (1965). Reinforcement theory. In D. Levine (Ed.), *Nebraska Symposium on motivation.* Lincoln: University of Nebraska Press.

PREMACK, D. (1976). *Intelligence in ape and man.* Hillsdale, NJ: Erlbaum.

PREMACK, D. (1978). On the abstractness of human concepts: Why it would be difficult to talk to a pigeon. In S. H. Hulse, H. Fowler, & W. K. Honig (Eds.), *Cognitive processes in animal behavior.* Hillsdale, NJ: Erlbaum.

PREMACK, D., & WOODRUFF, G. (1978). Does the chimpanzee have a theory of mind? *Behavioral and Brain Sciences, 4,* 515–526.

PRENTICE, D. A., & MILLER, D. T. (1993). Pluralistic ignorance and alcohol use on campus: Some consequences of misperceiving the social norm. *Journal of Personality and Social Psychology, 64,* 243–256.

PRESSMAN, S. D., & COHEN, S. (2005). Does positive affect influence health? *Psychological Bulletin, 131,* 925–971.

PRINCIPE, G., KANAYA, T., CECI, S., & SINGH, M. (2006). How rumors can engender false memories in preschoolers. *Psychological Science, 17,* 243–248.

PRINZ, J. J. (2002). *Furnishing the mind: Concepts and their perceptual basis.* Cambridge, MA: MIT Press.

PROCHASKA, J. O., & NORCROSS, J. C. (2007). *Systems of psychotherapy: A transtheoretical approach* (6th ed.). Pacific Grove, CA: Brooks/Cole.

PROVINE, W. B. (1971). *The origins of theoretical population genetics.* Chicago: University of Chicago Press.

PULLUM, G. K. (1991). *The great Eskimo vocabulary hoax and other irreverent essays on the study of language.* Chicago: University of Chicago Press.

PUTNAM, F. W., GUROFF, J. J., SILBERMAN, E. K., BARBAN, L., & POST, R. M. (1986). The clinical phenomenology of multiple personality disorder: Review of 100 recent cases. *Journal of Clinical Psychiatry, 47,* 285–293.

PUTNAM, K. E. (1979). Hypnosis and distortions in eye witness memory. *International Journal of Clinical and Experimental Hypnosis, 27,* 437–448.

PUTNAM, S. P., & Stifter, C. A. (2005). Behavioral approach-inhibition in toddlers: Prediction from infancy, positive and negative affective components, and relations with behavior problems. *Child Development, 76,* 212–226.

PYSZCZYNSKI, T., GREENBERG, J., SOLOMON, S., ARNDT, J., & SCHIMEL, J. (2004). Why do people need self-esteem? A theoretical and empirical review. *Psychological Bulletin, 130,* 435–468.

———

QUINE, W. (1960). *Word and object.* New York: Wiley.

QUINLAN, P. T. (2003). Visual feature integration theory: Past, present and future. *Psychological Bulletin, 129,* 643–673.

———

RADANT, A., TSUANG, D., PESKIND, E. R., McFALL, M., & RASKIND, W. (2001). Biological markers and diagnostic accuracy in the genetics of posttraumatic stress disorder. *Psychiatry Research, 102,* 203–215.

RAE, C., DIGNEY, A. L., McEWAN, S. R., & BATES, T. C. (2003). Oral creatine monohydrate supplementation improves brain performance: A double-blind, placebo-controlled, cross-over trial. *Proceedings of the Royal Society of London, Series B: Biological Sciences, 270,* 2147–2150.

RAFAL, R., & ROBERTSON, L. (1995). The neurology of visual attention. In M. Gazzaniga (Ed.), *The cognitive neurosciences* (pp. 625–648). Cambridge, MA: MIT Press.

RAINVILLE, P, DUNCAN, G., PRICE, D., CARRIER, B., & BUSHNELL, M. (1997). Pain affect encoded in human anterior cingulated but not somatosensory cortex. *Science, 277,* 968–971.

RAJARAM, S. (1993). Remembering and knowing: Two means of access to the personal past. *Memory & Cognition, 21,* 89–102.

RAKIC, P. (1995). Corticogenesis in human and nonhuman primates. In M. Gazzaniga (Ed.), *The cognitive neurosciences* (pp. 127–145). Cambridge, MA: MIT Press.

RAKIC, P. (2006). No more cortical neurons for you. *Science, 313,* 928–929.

RAMI-GONZALEZ, L., BERNARDO, M., BOGET, T., SALAMERO, M., GIL-VERONA, J. A., & JUNQUE, C. (2001). Subtypes of memory dysfunction associated with ECT: Characteristics and neurobiological bases. *Journal of ECT, 17,* 129–135.

RAMÓN Y CAJAL, S. (1913). *Degeneration and regeneration of the nervous system* (R. M. Day, Trans., 1928). London: Oxford University Press.

RAMÓN Y CAJAL, S. (1937). *Recollections of my life* (E. Horne-Craigie, Trans.). Philadelphia: American Philosophical Society.

RAMUS, F., NESPOR, M., & MEHLER, J. (1999). Correlates of linguistic rhythm in the speech signal. *Cognition, 73,* 265–292.

RANGANATH, C., YONELINAS, A. P., COHEN, M. X., DY, C. J., TOM, S., & D'ESPOSITO, M. (2003). Dissociable correlates for familiarity and recollection within the medial temporal lobes. *Neuropsychologia, 42,* 2–13.

RAPAPORT, M. H., & JUDD, L. L. (1998). Minor depressive disorder and subsyndromal depressive symptoms: Functional impairment and response to treatment. *Journal of Affective Disorders, 48,* 227–232.

RAPAPORT, M. H., PANICCIA, G., & JUDD, L. L. (1995). A review of social phobia. *Psychopharmacology Bulletin, 31,* 125–129.

RAPOPORT, J. L. (1989). *The boy who couldn't stop washing: The experience and treatment of obsessive-compulsive disorder.* New York: New American Library.

RAPPAPORT, Z. H. (1992). Psychosurgery in the modern era: Therapeutic and ethical aspects. *Medicine and Law, 11,* 449–453.

RASCH, B., & BORN, J. (2008). Reactivation and consolidation of memory during sleep. *Current Directions in Psychological Science, 17* (3), 188–192.

RASMUSSEN, S. A. (1993). Genetic studies of obsessive-compulsive disorder. *Annals of Clinical Psychiatry, 5,* 241–247.

RATEY, J., & JOHNSON, C. (1997). *Shadow syndromes.* New York: Pantheon.

RAUCH, S. L., & SAVAGE, C. R. (2000). Investigating cortico-striatal pathophysiology in obsessive-compulsive disorders: Procedural learning and imaging probes. In W. K. Goodman, M. J. Rudorfer, & J. D. Maser (Eds.), *Obsessive-compulsive disorder: Contemporary issues in treatment. Personality and clinical psychology series* (pp. 133–154). Mahwah, NJ: Erlbaum.

RAVEN, B. H., & RUBIN, J. Z. (1976). *Social psychology: People in groups.* New York: Wiley.

RAVUSSIN, E. (1994). Effects of a traditional lifestyle on obesity in Pima Indians. *Diabetes Care, 17,* 1067–1074.

Ravussin, E., & Bouchard, C. (2000). Human genomics and obesity: Finding appropriate drug targets. *European Journal of Pharmacology, 410*, 131–145.

Rayner, K., Carlson, M., & Frazier, L. (1983). The interaction of syntax and semantics during sentence processing: Eye movements in the analysis of semantically biased sentences. *Journal of Verbal Learning and Verbal Behavior, 22*, 358–374.

Rayner, K., Smith, T. J., Malcolm, G. L., & Henderson, J. M. (2009). Eye movements and visual encoding during scene perception. *Psychological Science, 20*, 6–10.

Reber, A. S. (1985). *The Penguin dictionary of psychology*. New York: Viking Penguin.

Reberg, D., & Black, A. H. (1969). Compound testing of individually conditioned stimuli as an index of excitatory and inhibitory properties. *Psychonomic Science, 17*, 3031.

Recanzone, G., Schreiner, C., & Merzenich, M. (1993). Plasticity in the frequency representation of primary auditory cortex following discrimination training in adult owl monkeys. *Journal of Neuroscience, 13*, 87–103.

Recht, D. R., & Leslie, L. (1988). Effect of prior knowledge on good and poor readers' memory of text. *Journal of Educational Psychology, 80*(1), 16–20.

Redelmeier, D. A., & Shafir, E. (1995). Medical decision making in situations that offer multiple alternatives. *Journal of the American Medical Association, 273*, 302–305.

Reed, M., & Roundtree, P. (1997). Peer pressure and adolescent substance abuse. *Journal of Quantitative Criminology, 13*, 143–180.

Reese, E., & Fivush, R. (1993). Parental styles of talking about the past. *Developmental Psychology, 29*(3), 596–606.

Rees, G. & Frith, C. (2007). Methodologies for identifying the neural correlates of consciousness. In M. Velmans. & S. Schneider (Eds.), *The Blackwell companion to consciousness* (pp. 553–566). Oxford, England: Blackwell.

Rees, G., Kreiman, G., & Koch, C. (2002). Neural correlates of consciousness in humans. *Nature Reviews Neuroscience, 3*(4), 261–270.

Reeves, L., & Weisberg, R. W. (1994). The role of content and abstract information in analogical transfer. *Psychological Bulletin, 115*(3), 381–400.

Regan, P. C., & Berscheid, E. (1999). *Lust: What we know about human sexual desire*. Thousand Oaks, CA: Sage.

Regier, D. A., Rae, D. S., Narrow, W. E., Kaelber, C. T., & Schatzberg, A. F. (1998). Prevalence of anxiety disorders and their comorbidity with mood and addictive disorders. *British Journal of Psychiatry, 34*(Suppl.), 24–28.

Regier, T., Kay, P., & Cook, R. S. (2005). Focal colors are universal after all. *Proceedings of the National Academy of Sciences, 102*(23), 8386–8391.

Reichenberg, A., & Harvey, P. D. (2007). Neuropsychological impairments in schizophrenia: Integration of performance-based and brain imaging findings. *Psychological Bulletin, 133*(5), 833–858.

Reid, D. H., Wilson, P. G., & Faw, G. D. (1991). Teaching self-help skills. In J. L. Matson & J. A. Mulick (Eds.), *Handbook of mental retardation* (pp. 436–450). New York: Pergamon.

Reiner, W. (2004). Psychosexual development in genetic males assigned female: The cloacal exstrophy experience. *Child and Adolescent Psychiatric Clinics of North America, 13*, 657–674.

Reisberg, D. (2010). *Cognition: Exploring the science of the mind* (4th ed.). New York: Norton.

Reisberg, D., & Hertel, P. (Eds.). (2004). *Memory and emotion*. New York: Oxford University Press.

Reisberg, D., & Heuer, F. (2004). Memory for emotional events. In D. Reisberg & P. Hertel (Eds.), *Memory and emotion* (pp. 3–41). New York: Oxford University Press.

Reisberg, D., & Heuer, F. (2005). Visuospatial images. In P. Shah & A. Miyake (Eds.), *The Cambridge Handbook of Visuospatial Thinking* (pp. 35–80). New York: Cambridge University Press.

Reisberg, D., Smith, J. D., Baxter, D. A., & Sonenshine, M. (1989). "Enacted" auditory images are ambiguous; "Pure" auditory images are not. *Quarterly Journal of Experimental Psychology, 41A*, 619–641.

Reisenzein, R. (1983). The Schachter theory of emotions: Two decades later. *Psychological Bulletin, 94*, 239–264.

Reiss, D., & Marino, L. (2001). Mirror self-recognition in the bottlenose dolphin: A case of cognitive convergence. *Proceedings of the National Academy of Science, 98*(10), 5937–5942.

Reiss, D., McCowan, B., & Marino L. (1997). Communicative and other cognitive characteristics of bottlenose dolphins. *Trends in Cognitive Science, 1*(2), 140–145.

Rensink, R. A. (2002). Change detection. *Annual Review of Psychology, 53*, 245–277.

Rentfrow, P. J., Gosling, S. D., & Potter, J. (2008). A theory of the emergence, persistence, and expression of regional variation in psychological characteristics. *Perspectives on Psychological Science, 3*, 339–369.

Repacholi, B. M., & Gopnik, A. (1997). Early reasoning about desires: Evidence from 14- and 18-month-olds. *Developmental Psychology, 33*(1), 12–21.

Resnick, S. M., Pham, D. L., Kraut, M. A., Zonderman, A. B., & Davatzikos, C. (2003). Longitudinal magnetic resonance imaging studies of older adults: A shrinking brain. *Journal of Neuroscience, 23*(8), 3295–3301.

Rescorla, R. A. (1967). Pavlovian conditioning and its proper control procedures. *Psychological Review, 74*, 71–80.

Rescorla, R. A. (1988). Behavioral studies of Pavlovian conditioning. *Annual Review of Neuroscience, 11*, 329–352.

Rescorla, R. A. (1991). Associative relations in instrumental learning: The eighteenth Bartlett Memorial lecture. *Quarterly Journal of Experimental Psychology, 43b*, 1–23.

Rescorla, R. A. (1993a). Inhibitory associations between S and R extinction. *Animal Learning and Behavior, 21*, 327–336.

Rescorla, R. A. (1993b). Preservation of response-outcome associations through extinction. *Animal Learning and Behavior, 21*, 238–245.

Rescorla, R. A., & Wagner, A. R. (1972). A theory of Pavlovian conditioning: Variations in the effectiveness of reinforcement and non-reinforcement. In A. H. Black & W. F. Prokasy (Eds.), *Classical conditioning II*. New York: Appleton-Century-Crofts.

Ressler, K. J., & Mayberg, H. S. (2007). Targeting abnormal neural circuits in mood and anxiety disorders: From the laboratory to the clinic. *Nature Neuroscience, 10*, 1116–1124.

Rest, J., Narvaez, D., Bebeau, M., & Thomas, J. (1999). *Postconventional moral thinking: A neo-Kohlbergian approach*. Mahwah, NJ: Erlbaum.

Reuter-Lorenz, P. A. (2002). New visions of the aging mind and brain. *Trends in Cognitive Science, 6*, 394–400.

Reveley, A. M., Reveley, M. A., Clifford, C. A., et al. (1982). Cerebral ventricular size in twins discordant for schizophrenia. *Lancet, 1*, 540–541.

Rey, G. (1996). Concepts and stereotypes. In E. Margolis & S. Laurence (Eds.), *Concepts: Core readings* (pp. 278–299). Cambridge, MA: MIT Press.

Reyna, V., & Farley, F. (2006). Risk and rationality in adolescent decision-making: Implications for theory, practice, and public policy. *Psychological Science in the Public Interest, 7*, 1–44.

Reynolds, C. R., Chastain, R. L., Kaufman, A. S., & McLean, J. E. (1987). Demographic characteristics and IQ among adults: Analysis of the WAIS-R standardization sample as a function of the stratification variables. *Journal of School Psychology, 25*(4), 323–342.

Rhodes, G. (2006). The evolutionary psychology of facial beauty. *Annual Review of Psychology, 57*, 199–226.

Rhodes, G., Proffitt, F., Grady, J. M., & Sumich, A. (1998). Facial symmetry and the perception of beauty. *Psychonomics Bulletin and Review, 5*, 659–669.

Rhodes, G., Sumich, A., & Byatt, G. (1999). Are average facial configurations attractive only because of their symmetry? *Psychological Science, 10*, 52–59.

Ribot, T. (1882). *Diseases of memory*. New York: Appleton.

Richards, J. M., & Gross, J. J. (2000). Emotion regulation and memory: The cognitive costs of keeping one's cool. *Journal of Personality and Social Psychology, 79*, 410–424.

Richards, J. M., & Gross, J. J. (2006). Personality and emotional memory: How regulating emotion impairs memory for emotional events. *Journal of Research in Personality, 79*(3), 410–424.

Rickard, T. C., Cai, D. J., Rieth, C. A., Jones, J., & Ard, M. C. (2008). Sleep does not enhance motor sequence learning. *Journal of Experimental Psychology: Learning, Memory, and Cognition, 34* (4), 834–842.

Rickels, K., & Rynn, M. A. (2001). What is generalized anxiety disorder? [Suppl.] *Journal of Clinical Psychiatry, 62*(11), 4–12.

Rieffe, C., Terwogt, M. M., Koops, W., Stegge, H., & Oomen, A. (2001). Preschoolers' appreciation of uncommon desires and subsequent emotions. *British Journal of Developmental Psychology, 19*, 259–274.

Riggio, R. E., & Murphy, S. E. (Eds.). (2002). *Multiple intelligences and leadership*. Mahwah, NJ: Erlbaum.

Rinck, M. (1999). Memory for everyday objects: Where are the digits on numerical keypads? *Applied Cognitive Psychology, 13*, 329–350.

Rincón-Limas, D. E., Lu, C. H., Canal, I., Calleja, M., Rodríguez-Esteban, C., Izpisúa-Belmonte, J. C. et al. (1999). Conservation of the expression and function of apterous orthologs in *Drosophila* and mammals. *Proceedings of the National Academy of Sciences, 96,* 2165–2170.

Ringelmann, M. (1913). Recherches sur les moteurs animés: Travail de l'homme. *Annales de l'institut National Agronomique* (Series 2), *12,* 1–40.

Rips, L. (1990). Reasoning. *Annual Review of Psychology, 41,* 321–353.

Risch, N., Herrell, R., Lehner, T., Liang, K.-Y., Eaves, L., Hoh, J., et al. (2009). Interaction between the serotonin transporter gene (5-HTTLPR), stressful life events, and risk of depression: A meta-analysis. *Journal of American Medical Association, 301,* 2462–2471.

Rizzolatti, G., & Craighero, L. (2004). The mirror-neuron system. *Annual Review of Neuroscience, 27,* 169–192.

Robbin, A. A. (1958). A controlled study of the effects of leucotomy. *Journal of Neurology, Neurosurgery and Psychiatry, 21,* 262–269.

Robbins, S. J. (1990). Mechanisms underlying spontaneous recovery in autoshaping. *Journal of Experimental Psychology: Animal Behavior Processes, 16,* 235–249.

Roberson, D., et al. (2005). Color categories: Evidence for the cultural relativity hypothesis. *Cognitive Psychology, 50,* 378–411.

Roberts, B. W., Kuncel, N., Shiner, R., N., Caspi, A., & Goldberg, L. R. (2007). The power of personality: The comparative validity of personality traits, socio-economic status, and cognitive ability for predicting important life outcomes. *Perspectives on Psychological Science, 2,* 313–345.

Roberts, B. W., Walton, K., & Bogg, T. (2005). Conscientiousness and health across the life course. *Review of General Psychology, 9,* 156–168.

Robertson, I. H., & Manly, T. (1999). Sustained attention deficits in time and space. In G. W. Humphreys & J. Duncan (Eds.), *Attention, space, and action: Studies in cognitive neuroscience* (pp. 297–310). New York: Oxford University Press.

Robertson, L., Treisman, A., Friedman-Hill, S., & Grabowecky, M. (1997). The interaction of spatial and object pathways: Evidence from Balint's syndrome. *Journal of Cognitive Neuroscience, 9*(3), 295–317.

Robins, L. N., & Regier, D. A. (Eds.). (1991). *Psychiatric disorders in America: The epidemiologic catchment area study.* New York: Free Press.

Robinson & Berridge, 2003

Robinson, L. A., Berman, J. S., & Neimeyer, R. A. (1990). Psychotherapy for the treatment of depression: A comprehensive review of controlled outcome research. *Psychological Bulletin, 108,* 30–49.

Rodin, J. (1990). Control by any other name: Definitions, concepts, and processes. In J. Rodin, C. Schooler, & K. W. Schaie (Eds.), *Self-directedness: Cause and effects throughout the life course* (pp. 1–17). Hillsdale, NJ: Erlbaum.

Rodin, J., & Langer, E. J. (1977). Long-term effects of a control-relevant intervention with the institutionalized aged. *Journal of Personality and Social Psychology, 35,* 897–902.

Rodman, H. R., Gross, C. G., & Albright, T. D. (1989). Afferent basis of visual response properties in area MT of the macaque: I. Effects of striate cortex removal. *Journal of Neuroscience, 9,* 2033–2050.

Rodriguez, M. L., Mischel, W., & Shoda, Y. (1989). Cognitive person variables in the delay of gratification of older children at risk. *Journal of Personality and Social Psychology, 57,* 358–367.

Roediger, H. L., III. (1980). Memory metaphors in cognitive psychology. *Memory and Cognition, 8,* 231–246.

Roediger, H., & McDermott, K. (1995). Creating false memories: Remembering words not presented in lists. *Journal of Experimental Psychology: Learning, Memory & Cognition, 21,* 803–814.

Roediger, H., & McDermott, K. B. (2000). Tricks of memory. *Current Directions in Psychological Science, 9,* 123–127.

Roffwarg, Muzio, & Dement, 1966

Rogers, C. R. (1951). *Client-centered therapy: Its current practice, implications, and theory* (2nd ed.). Boston: Houghton Mifflin.

Rogers, C. R. (1959). A theory of therapy, personality, and interpersonal relationships as developed in the client-centered framework. In S. Koch (Ed.), *Psychology: A study of a science: Vol. 3.* New York: McGraw-Hill.

Rogers, C. R. (1961). *On becoming a person: A therapist's view of psychotherapy.* Boston: Houghton Mifflin.

Rogers, C. R. (1980). *A way of being.* Boston: Houghton Mifflin.

Rogers, T. B., Kuiper, N. A., & Kirker, W. S. (1977). Self-reference and the encoding of personal information. *Journal of Personality and Social Psychology, 35,* 677–688.

Rogoff, B. (1990). *Apprenticeship in thinking.* New York: Oxford University Press.

Rogoff, B. (1998). Cognition as a collaborative process. In W. Damon (Ed.), *Handbook of child psychology, Vol. 2* (5th ed., pp. 679–744). New York: Wiley.

Rogoff, B. (2000). *Culture and development.* New York: Oxford University Press.

Rogoff, B., Paradise, R., Arauz, R. M., Correa-Chávez, M., & Angelillo, C. (2003). Firsthand learning through intent participation. *Annual Review of Psychology, 54,* 175–203.

Roland, P. E., Larsen, B., Lassen, N. A., & Skinhøj, E. (1980). Supplementary motor area and other cortical areas in organization of voluntary movements in man. *Journal of Neurophysiology, 43,* 539–560.

Rolls, E. J. (1978). Neurophysiology of feeding. *Trends in Neurosciences, 1,* 1–3.

Romanes, G. J. (1882). *Animal intelligence.* London: Kegan Paul.

Roopnarine, J. L., Johnson, J. E., & Hooper, F. H. (1994). *Children's play in diverse cultures.* Albany, NY: SUNY Press.

Roper, T. J. (1983). Learning as a biological phenomenon. In T. R. Halliday & P. J. B. Slater (Eds.), *Genes, development and behavior: Vol. 3. Animal Behavior* (pp. 178–212). Oxford, England: Blackwell.

Rorschach, H. (1921). *Psychodiagnostik.* Berne: Bircher.

Rosch, E. H. (1973a). Natural categories. *Cognitive Psychology, 4,* 328–350.

Rosch, E. H. (1973b). On the internal structure of perceptual and semantic categories. In T. E. Moore (Ed.), *Cognitive development and the acquisition of language.* New York: Academic Press.

Rosch, E. H. (1978). Principles of categorization. In E. Rosch & B. Lloyd (Eds.), *Cognition and categorization.* Hillsdale, NJ: Erlbaum.

Rosch, E. H., & Mervis, C. B. (1975). Family resemblances: Studies in the internal structure of categories. *Cognitive Psychology, 7,* 573–605.

Rosen, G. (1966). *Madness in society.* Chicago: University of Chicago Press.

Rosen, W. D., Adamson, L. B., & Bakeman, R. (1992). An experimental investigation of infant social referencing: Mothers' messages and gender differences. *Developmental Psychology, 28*(6), 1172–1178.

Rosenfeld, P., Giacalone, R. A., & Tedeschi, J. T. (1984). Cognitive dissonance and impression management explanations for effort justification. *Personality and Social Psychology Bulletin, 10,* 394–401.

Rosenstein, M. J., Milazzo-Sayre, L. J., & Manderscheid, R. W. (1989). Care of persons with schizophrenia: A statistical profile. *Schizophrenia Bulletin, 15,* 45–58.

Rosenthal, A. M. (1964). *Thirty-eight witnesses.* New York: McGraw-Hill.

Rosenthal, D. (1963). A suggested conceptual framework. In D. Rosenthal (Ed.), *The Genain quadruplets* (pp. 505–516). New York: Basic Books.

Rosenthal, D. (1970). *Genetic theory and abnormal behavior.* New York: McGraw-Hill.

Rosenthal, R. (1991). Teacher expectancy effects: A brief update 25 years after the Pygmalion experiment. *Journal of Research in Education, 1,* 3–12.

Rosenthal, R. (2002). Covert communication in classrooms, clinics, courtrooms, and cubicles. *American Psychologist, 57,* 839–849.

Rosenthal, R., Hiller, J. B., Bornstein, R. F., Berry, D.T.R., & Brunell-Neuleib, S. (2001). Meta-analytic methods, the Rorschach, and the MMPI. *Psychological Assessment, 13*(4), 449–451.

Rosenthal, R., & Jacobson, L. (1968). Pygmalion in the classroom: Teacher expectation and pupils' intellectual development. New York: Holt, Rinehart & Winston.

Rosenzweig, M. R., Leiman, A. K., & Breedlove, S. M. (1996). *Biological psychology.* Sunderland, MA: Sinauer.

Rosenzweig et al., 1999

Roser, M., & Gazzaniga, M. S. (2004). Automatic brains—interpretive minds. *Current Directions in Psychological Science, 13,* 56–59.

Ross, C. A. (1997). *Dissociative identity disorder: Diagnosis, clinical features, and treatment of multiple personality.* New York: Wiley.

Ross, C. A. (1999). Subpersonalities and multiple personalities: A dissociative continuum? In J. Rowan and M. Cooper (Eds.), *The plural self: Multiplicity in everyday life* (pp. 183–197). London: Sage.

Ross, D. F., Read, J. D., & Toglia, M. P. (Eds). (1994). *Adult eyewitness testimony: Current trends and developments.* New York: Cambridge University Press.

Ross, H. S., & Lollis, S. P. (1989). A social relations analysis of toddler peer relationships. *Child Development, 60*(5), 1082–1091.

Ross, J., & Lawrence, K. Q. (1968). Some observations on memory artifice. *Psychonomic Science, 13,* 107–108.

Ross, L. (1977). The intuitive psychologist and his short-comings: Distortions in the attribution process. In L. Berkowitz (Ed.), *Advances in experimental social psychology: Vol. 10.* New York: Academic Press.

Ross, L., Amabile, T. M., & Steinmetz, J. L. (1977). Social roles, social control, and biases in social perception processes. *Journal of Experimental Social Psychology, 35,* 817–829.

Ross, M., & Sicoly, F. (1979). Egocentric biases in availability and attribution. *Journal of Personality and Social Psychology, 37,* 322–336.

Roth, A., & Fonagy, P. (2004). *What works for whom? A critical review of psychotherapy research* (2nd ed.). New York: Guilford.

Rothbart, M. K., & Ahadi, S. A. (1994). Temperament and the development of personality. *Journal of Abnormal Psychology, 103,* 55–66.

Rothbart, M., & Bates, J. (1998). Temperament. In W. Damon & N. Eisenberg (Eds.), *Handbook of child psychology* (5th ed.): *Vol. 3. Social, emotional and personality development* (pp. 105–176). New York: Wiley.

Rothbart, M. K., & Bates, J. E. (2006). Temperament in children's development. In W. Damon, R. Lerner, & N. Eisenberg (Eds.), *Handbook of child psychology, Vol. 3: Social, emotional, and personality development* (5th ed., pp. 99–166). New York: Wiley.

Rothbaum, F., & Tsang, B. Y. P. (1998). Lovesongs in the United States and China: On the nature of romantic love. *Journal of Cross-Cultural Psychology, 29,* 306–319.

Rothbaum, F., Weisz, J., Pott, M., Miyake, K., & Morelli, G. (2000). Attachment and culture: Security in the United States and Japan. *American Psychologist, 55,* 1093–1104.

Rothchild, E. (1997). E-mail therapy. *American Journal of Psychiatry, 154,* 1476–1477.

Rouach, N. Koulakoff, A. Abudara, V., Willecke, K, & Giaume, C. (2008). Astroglial metabolic networks sustain hippocampal synaptic transmission. *Science, 322,* 1551–1555.

Rovee-Collier, C. (1999). The development of infant memory. *Current Directions in Psychological Science, 8*(3), 80–85.

Rovee-Collier, C. K. (1990). The "memory system" of prelinguistic infants. In A. Diamond (Ed.), *The development and neural bases of higher cognitive functions.* New York: New York Academy of Sciences.

Rovee-Collier, C., & Gerhardstein, P. (1997). The development of infant memory. In N. Cowan (Ed.), *The development of memory in childhood: Studies in developmental psychology.* Hove, England: Psychology Press.

Rovee-Collier, C. K., & Hayne, H. (1987). Reactivation of infant memory: Implications for cognitive develop-

ment. In H. W. Reese (Ed.), *Advances in child development and behavior: Vol. 20.* New York: Academic Press.

Rowe, A. D., Bullock, P. R., Polkey, C. E., & Morris, R. G. (2001). "Theory of mind" impairments and their relationship to executive functioning following frontal lobe excisions. *Brain, 124,* 600–616.

Rozin, E. (1973). *The flavor principle.* New York: Hawthorn Books.

Rozin, P. (1999). The process of moralization. *Psychological Science, 10,* 218–221.

Rozin, P., Dow, S., Moscovitch, M., & Rajaram, S. (1998). What causes humans to begin and end a meal? A role for memory for what has been eaten, as evidenced by a study of multiple meal eating in amnesic patients. *Psychological Science, 9,* 392–396.

Rozin, P., & Kalat, J. W. (1971). Specific hungers and poison avoidance as adaptive specializations of learning. *Psychological Review, 78,* 459–486.

Rozin, P., & Kalat, J. W. (1972). Learning as a situation-specific adaptation. In M. E. P. Seligman & J. L. Hager (Eds.), *Biological boundaries of learning* (pp. 66–96). New York: Appleton-Century-Crofts.

Rozin, P., Markwith, M., & Stoess, C. (1997). Moralization and becoming a vegetarian: The transformation of preferences into values and the recruitment of disgust. *Psychological Science, 8,* 67–73.

Rozin, P., & Schull, J. (1988). The adaptive-evolutionary point of view in experimental psychology. In R. C. Atkinson, R. J. Herrnstein, G. Lindzey, & R. D. Luce (Eds.), *Steven's handbook of experimental psychology: Vol. 1. Perception and motivation* (2nd ed., pp. 503–546). New York: Wiley.

Rubenstein, J. L., & Rakic, P. (1999). Genetic control of cortical development. *Cerebral Cortex, 9,* 521–523.

Rubin, H., Bukowski, W., & Parker, J. (1998). Peer interactions, relationships and groups. In W. Damon & N. Eisenberg (Eds.), *Handbook of child psychology* (5th ed.): *Vol. 3. Social, emotional and personality development* (pp. 619–700). New York: Wiley.

Ruderman, A. J. (1986). Dietary restraint: A theoretical and empirical review. *Psychological Bulletin, 99,* 247–262.

Ruffman, T., Perner, J., & Parkin, L. (1999). How parenting style affects false belief understanding. *Social Development, 8,* 395–411.

Rugg, M., & Curran, T. (2007). Event-related potentials and recognition memory. *Trends in Cognitive Sciences, 11,* 251–257.

Rumelhart, D. E. (1997). The architecture of mind: A connectionist approach. In J. Haugeland (Ed.), *Mind design 2: Philosophy, psychology, artificial intelligence* (2nd ed.). Cambridge, MA: MIT Press.

Rumelhart, D. E., & McClelland, J. L. (1986). On learning past tenses of English verbs. In J. L. McClelland & D. E. Rumelhart (Eds.), *Parallel distributed processing: Vol. 2* (pp. 216–271). Cambridge, MA: MIT Press.

Rushton, J. P., & Jensen, A. R. (2006). The totality of available evidence shows the race IQ gap still remains. *Psychological Science, 17,* 921–922.

Russek, M. (1971). Hepatic receptors and the neurophysiological mechanisms controlling feeding behavior. In S.

Ehrenpreis (Ed.), *Neurosciences research: Vol. 4.* New York: Academic Press.

Russell, J. A. (1980). A circumplex model of affect. *Journal of Personality and Social Psychology, 39,* 1161–1178.

Russell, J. A. (1983). Pan-cultural aspects of human conceptual organization of emotions. *Journal of Personality and Social Psychology, 45,* 1281–1288.

Russell, J. A. (1994). Is there universal recognition of emotion from facial expressions? A review of the cross-cultural studies. *Psychological Bulletin, 115,* 102–141.

Rutter, M. (2006). *Genes and behavior: Nature-nurture interplay explained.* Malden, MA: Blackwell.

Rutter, M., & O'Connor, T. G. (2004). Are there biological programming effects for psychological development? Findings from a study of Romanian adoptees. *Developmental Psychology, 40,* 81–94.

Rydell, R. J., McConnell, A. R., Mackie, D. M., & Strain, L. M. (2006). Of two minds: Forming and changing valence-inconsistent implicit and explicit attitudes. *Psychological Science, 17,* 954–958.

Ryff, C. D., Dienberg, L. G., Urry, H. L., Muller, D., Rosenkranz, M. A., Friedmann, E. M., et al. (2006): Psychological well-being and ill-being: Do they have distinct or mirrored biological correlates? *Psychotherapy and Psychosomatics, 75,* 85–95.

Ryff, C. D., & Singer, B. (1998). The contours of positive human health. *Psychological Inquiry, 9,* 1–28.

Sabini, J., Siepmann, M., & Stein, J. (2001). The really fundamental attribution error in social psychological research. *Psychological Inquiry, 12,* 1–15.

Sachs, G. S., & Thase, M. E. (2000). Bipolar disorder therapeutics: maintenance treatment. *Biological Psychiatry, 48*(6), 573–581.

Sackeim, H. A., Devanand, D. P., & Nobler, M. S. (1995). Electroconvulsive therapy. In F. E. Bloom & D. Kupfer (Eds.), *Psychopharmacology: The fourth generation of progress* (pp. 1123–1141). New York: Raven.

Sackeim, H. A., Prudic, J., Devanand, D. P., Kiersky, J. E., Fitzsimons, L., Moody, B. J., et al. (1993). Effects of stimulus intensity and electrode placement on the efficacy and cognitive effects of electroconvulsive therapy. *New England Journal of Medicine, 328,* 839–846.

Sackeim, H. A., Prudic, J., Devanand, D. P., Nobler, M. S., Lisanby, S. H., Peyser, S., et al. (2000). A prospective, randomized, double-blind comparison of bilateral and right unilateral electroconvulsive therapy at different stimulus intensities. *Archives of General Psychiatry, 57,* 425–434.

Sackett, D. L., Straus, S. E., Richardson, W. S., Rosenberg, W., & Haynes, R. B. (2000). *Evidence-based medicine: How to practice and teach EBM* (2nd ed.). London: Churchill Livingstone.

Sackett, P., Borneman, M., & Connelly, B. (2008). High-stakes testing in higher education and employment: Appraising the evidence for validity and fairness. *American Psychologist, 63,* 215–227.

Sacks, O. (1985). *The man who mistook his wife for a hat.* Simon & Schuster.

SADATO N., PASCUAL-LEONE, A., GRAFMAN, J., IBANEZ, V., DEIBER, M., DOLD, G., ET AL. (1996). Activation of the primary visual cortex by Braille reading in blind subjects. *Nature, 380,* 526–528.

SADLER, H., DAVISON, L., CARROLL, C., & KOUNTS, S. L. (1971). The living, genetically unrelated, kidney donor. *Seminars in Psychiatry, 3,* 86–101.

SAFFRAN, J. R. (2003). Statistical language learning: Mechanisms and constraints. *Current Directions in Psychological Science, 12,* 110–114.

SAFFRAN, J. R., ASLIN, R. N., & NEWPORT, E. L. (1996). Statistical learning by 8-month-old infants. *Science, 274*(5294), 1926–1928.

SAFFRAN, J. R., SENGHAS, A., & TRUESWELL, J. C. (2001). The acquisition of language by children. *PNAS, 98*(23), 12874–12875.

SAGHIR, M. T., & ROBINS, E. (1973). *Male and female homosexuality.* Baltimore: Williams & Wilkins.

SAGI, A., & HOFFMAN, M. L. (1976). Empathic distress in the newborn. *Developmental Psychology, 12,* 175–176.

ST. CLAIR, D., XU, M., WANG, P., YU, Y., FANG, Y., ZHANG, F., ET AL. (2005). Rates of adult schizophrenia following prenatal exposure to the Chinese famine of 1959–1961. *Journal of the American Medical Association, 294,* 557–562.

SALOVEY, P., & MAYER, J. D. (1990). Emotional intelligence. *Imagination, Cognition, and Personality, 9,* 185–211.

SALOVEY, P., ROTHMAN, A. J., DETWEILER, J. B., & STEWARD, W. T. (2000). Emotional states and physical health. *American Psychologist, 55*(1), 110–121.

SALTHOUSE, T. A. (1991). *Theoretical perspectives on cognitive aging.* Hillsdale, NJ: Erlbaum.

SALTHOUSE, T. A. (2000). Steps toward the explanation of adult age differences in cognition. In T. J. Perfect & E. A. Maylor (Eds.), *Models of cognitive aging.* New York: Oxford University Press.

SALTHOUSE, T. A. (2004). What and when of cognitive aging. *Current Directions in Psychological Science, 13,* 140–144.

SALTHOUSE, T. A. (2006). Mental exercise and mental aging: Evaluating the validity of the "use it or lose it" hypothesis. *Perspectives on Psychological Science, 1*(1), 68–87.

SALTHOUSE, T. A. (2007). Reply to Schooler: Consistent is not conclusive. *Perspectives on Psychological Science, 2*(1), 30–32.

SALTHOUSE, T. A., & PINK, J. (2008). Why is working memory related to fluid intelligence? *Psychonomics Bulletin & Review, 15,* 364–371.

SANFEY, A. G., RILLING, J. K., ARONSON, J. A., NYSTROM, L. E., & COHEN, J. D. (2003). The neural basis of economic decision-making in the Ultimatum Game. *Science, 300,* 1755–1758.

SANTARELLI, L., SAXE, M., GROSS, C., SURGET, A., BATTAGLIA, F., DULAWA, S., ET AL. (2003). Requirement of hippocampal neurogenesis for the behavioral effects of antidepressants. *Science, 301,* 805–809.

SANTINI, E., GE, H., REN, K., deORTIZ, S., & QUIRK, G. (2004). Consolidation of fear extinction requires protein synthesis in the medial prefrontal cortex. *Journal of Neuroscience, 24,* 5704–5710.

SAPOLSKY, R. M. (1998). *The trouble with testosterone.* New York: Simon & Schuster.

SATIR, V. (1967). *Conjoint family therapy* (rev. ed.). Palo Alto, CA: Science and Behavior Books.

SAVAGE-RUMBAUGH, E. S., & FIELDS, W. (2000). Linguistic, cultural and cognitive capacities of bonobos (*Pan paniscus*). *Culture & Psychology, 6,* 131–153.

SAVIN, H. B. (1973). Professors and psychological researchers: Conflicting values in conflicting roles. *Cognition, 2,* 147–149.

SAVIN-WILLIAMS, R. C. (2006). Who's gay? Does it matter? *Current Directions in Psychological Science, 15*(1), 40–44.

SAVOVA, V., ROY, D., SCHMIDT, L., & TENENBAUM, J. B. (2007). Discovering syntactic hierarchies. *Proceedings of the Twenty-Ninth Annual Conference of the Cognitive Science Society,* Nashville, TN.

SAWA, A., & SNYDER, S. H. (2002). Schizophrenia: Diverse approaches to a complex disease. *Science, 296,* 692–695.

SAWAMOTO, K., NAKAO, N., KAKISHITA, K., OGAWA, Y., TOYAMA, Y., YAMAMOTO, A., ET AL. (2001). Generation of dopaminergic neurons in the adult brain from mesencephalic precursor cells labeled with a nestin-GFP transgene. *Journal of Neuroscience, 21,* 3895–3903.

SAWYER, K. (2006). Explaining creativity: The science of human innovation. New York: Oxford University Press.

SAXE, G. (1981). Body parts as numerals: A developmental analysis of numeration among the Oksapmin in Papua, New Guinea. *Child Development, 52,* 306–316.

SAXE, R., CAREY, S., & KANWISHER, N. (2004). Understanding other minds: Linking developmental psychology and functional neuroimaging. *Annual Review of Psychology, 55,* 87–124.

SAXENA, S., BRODY, A. L., MAIDMENT, K. M., DUNKIN, J. J., COLGAN, M., ALBORZIAN, S., ET AL. (1999). Localized orbitofrontal and subcortical metabolic changes and predictors of response to paroxetine treatment in obsessive-compulsive disorder *Neuropsychopharmacology, 21,* 683–693.

SAYWITZ, K. J., & GEISELMAN, E. (1998). Interviewing the child witness: Maximizing completeness and minimizing error. In S. Lynn & K. McConkey (Eds.), *Truth in memory* (pp. 190–223). New York: Guilford Press.

SCAIFE, M., & BRUNER, J. S. (1975). The capacity for joint visual attention in the infant. *Nature, 253*(5489), 265–266.

SCARR, S. (1987). Distinctive environments depend upon genotypes. *Behavioral and Brain Sciences, 10,* 38–39.

SCARR, S. (1992). Developmental theories for the 1990s: Development and individual differences. *Child Development, 63,* 1–19.

SCARR, S. (1997). Why child care has little impact on most children's development. *Current Directions in Psychological Science, 6,* 143–148.

SCARR, S., & CARTER-SALTZMAN, L. (1982). Genetics and intelligence. In R. J. Sternberg (Ed.), *Handbook of human intelligence* (pp. 792–896). New York: Cambridge University Press.

SCARR, S., & WEINBERG, R. A. (1976). IQ test performance of black children adopted by white families. *American Psychologist, 31,* 726–739.

SCARR, S., & WEINBERG, R. A. (1983). The Minnesota adoption studies genetic differences and malleability. *Child Development, 54,* 260–267.

SCERIF, G., & KARMILOFF-SMITH, A. (2005). The dawn of cognitive genetics: Crucial developmental caveats. *Trends in Cognitive Science, 9,* 126–135.

SCHACTER, D. L. (1996). *Searching for memory: The brain, the mind and the past.* New York: Basic Books.

SCHACHTER, F. (1982). Sibling deidentification and split-parent identification: A family tetrad. In M. Lamb and B. Sutton-Smith (Eds.), *Sibling relationships: Their nature and significance over the lifespan.* Hillsdale, NJ: Erlbaum.

SCHACHTER, S., & SINGER, J. (1962). Cognitive, social and physiological determinants of emotional state. *Psychological Review, 69,* 379–399.

SCHACHTER, S., & SINGER, J. E. (1979). Comments on the Maslach and Marshall-Zimbardo experiments. *Journal of Personality and Social Psychology, 37,* 989–995.

SCHAFE, G., NADER, K., BLAIR, H., & LEDOUX, J. (2001). Memory consolidation of Pavlovian fear conditioning: A cellular and molecular perspective. *Trends in Neuroscience, 24,* 540–546.

SCHAIE, K. W. (1996). *Intellectual development in adulthood: The Seattle Longitudinal study.* New York: Cambridge University Press.

SCHAIE, K. W., & WILLIS, S. L. (1996). Psychometric intelligence and aging. In F. Blanchard Fields & T. M. Hess (Eds.), *Perspectives on cognitive change in adulthood and aging* (pp. 293–322). New York: McGraw-Hill.

SCHARFMAN, H., & HEN, R. (2007). Is more neurogenesis always better? *Science, 315,* 336–338.

SCHEFFLER, R. M., HINSHAW, S. P., MODREK, S., & LEVINE, P. (2007). The global market for ADHD medications. *Health Affairs, 26*(2), 450–457.

SCHER, C. D., & STEIN, M. B. (2003). Developmental antecedents of anxiety sensitivity. *Journal of Anxiety Disorders, 17,* 253–269.

SCHERER, K. R., SCHORR, A., & JOHNSTONE, T. (EDS.). (2001). *Appraisal processes in emotion: Theory, methods, research.* New York: Oxford University Press.

SCHILDKRAUT, J. J. (1965). The catecholamine hypothesis of affective disorders: A review of supporting evidence. *American Journal of Psychiatry, 122,* 509–522.

SCHEIER, M. F., & CARVER, C. S. (1985). Optimism, coping, and health: Assessment and implications of generalized outcome expectancies. *Health Psychology, 4,* 219–247.

SCHMIDT, C., COLLETTE, F., LECLERCQ, Y., STERPENICH, V., VANDEWALLE, G., BERTHOMIER, P., ET AL. (2009). Homeostatic sleep pressure and responses to sustained attention in the suprachiasmiatic area. *Science, 324,* 516–519.

SCHMIDT, F. L., & HUNTER, J. E. (1998). The validity and utility of selection methods in personnel psychology: Practical and theoretical implications of 85 years of research findings. *Psychological Bulletin, 124*(2), 262–274.

SCHMIDT, F. L., & HUNTER, J. E. (2004). General mental ability in the world of work: Occupational attainment and job performance. *Journal of Personality and Social Psychology, 86,* 162–173.

SCHMIDT, V., & GÖSELE, U. (2007). How nanowires grow. *Science, 316*(5825), 698–699.

SCHMITT, D. P. (2005). Fundamentals of human mating strategies. In D. M. Buss (Ed.), *The handbook of evolutionary psychology* (pp. 258–291). New York: Wiley.

SCHMITT, D. P., & BUSS, D. M. (2001). Human mate poaching: Tactics and temptations for infiltrating existing mateships. *Journal of Personality & Social Psychology, 80*(6), 894–917.

SCHNEIDER, B., ATKINSON, L., & TARDIF, C. (2001). Child-parent attachment and children's peer relations: A quantitative review. *Developmental Psychology, 37,* 86–100.

SCHNEIDER, B., & STEVENSON, D. (1999). *The ambitious generation: America's teenagers, motivated but directionless.* New Haven: Yale University Press.

SCHNEIDER, D. J. (1973). Implicit personality theory: A review. *Psychological Bulletin, 79,* 294–309.

SCHNEIDER, W., GRUBER, H., GOLD, A., & OPWIS, K. (1993). Chess expertise and memory for chess positions in children and adults. *Journal of Experimental Child Psychology, 56*(3), 328–349.

SCHOFIELD, W. (1964). *Psychotherapy: The purchase of friendship.* Englewood Cliffs, NJ: Prentice-Hall.

SCHOOLER, C. (2007). Use it—and keep it, longer, probably: A reply to Salthouse (2006). *Perspectives on Psychological Science, 2*(1), 24–29.

SCHOOLER, J. (2001). Discovering memories of abuse in the light of meta-awareness. *Journal of Aggression, Maltreatment & Trauma, 4,* 105–136.

SCHOOLER, J., OHLSSON, S., & BROOKS, K. (1993). Thoughts beyond words: When language overshadows insight. *Journal of Experimental Psychology: General, 122,* 166–183.

SCHRAW, G., DUNKLE, M., & BENDIXEN, L. (1995). Cognitive processes in well-defined and ill-defined problem solving. *Applied Cognitive Psychology, 9,* 523–538.

SCHROEDER, H. E. (1973). The risky shift as a general choice shift. *Journal of Personality and Social Psychology, 27*(2), 297–300.

SCHUL, Y., & VINOKUR, A. D. (2000). Projection in person perception among spouses as a function of the similarity in their shared experiences. *Personality and Social Psychology Bulletin, 26*(8), 987–1001.

SCHULTHEISS, O. C. (2008). Implicit motives. In O. P. John, R. W. Robins, & L. A. Pervin (Eds.), *Handbook of personality: Theory and research* (3rd ed., pp. 603–633). New York: Guilford.

SCHULTZ, W., TREMBLAY, L., & HOLLERMAN, J. R. (2000). Reward processing in primate orbitofrontal cortex and basal ganglia. *Cerebral cortex, 10*(3), 272–284.

SCHULZ-HARDT, S., FREY, D., LÜTHGENS, C., & MOSCOVICI, S. (2000). Biased information search in group decision making. *Journal of Personality and Social Psychology, 78,* 655–669.

SCHUNK, D. H. (1984). Self-efficacy perspective on achievement behavior. *Educational Psychologist, 19*(1), 48–58.

SCHUNK, D. H. (1985). Self-efficacy and classroom learning. *Psychology in the Schools, 22*(2), 208–223.

SCHWARTZ, S., & MAQUET, P. (2002). Sleep imaging and the neuropsychological assessment of dreams. *Trends in Cognitive Sciences, 6,* 23–30.

SCHWARTZ, B. (2004). *The paradox of choice: Why less is more.* New York: HarperCollins.

SCHWARTZ, B., WASSERMAN, E. A., & ROBBINS, S. (2002). *Psychology of learning and behavior* (5th ed.). New York: Norton.

SCHWARTZ, B. L. (1999). Sparkling at the end of the tongue: The etiology of tip-of-the-tongue phenomenology. *Psychonomics Bulletin & Review, 5,* 379–393.

SCHWARTZ, C. E., WRIGHT, C. I., SHIN, L. M., KAGAN, J., & RAUCH, S. L. (2003). Inhibited and uninhibited infants "grown up": Adult amygdalar response to novelty. *Science, 300,* 1952–1953.

SCHWARTZ, D., DODGE, K., PETTIT, G., BATES, J., & THE CONDUCT PROBLEMS PREVENTION RESEARCH GROUP. (2000). Friendship as a moderating factor in the pathway between early harsh home environment and later victimization in the peer group. *Developmental Psychology, 36,* 646–662.

SCHWARZ, N. (1999). Self-reports: How the questions shape the answers. *American Psychologist, 54,* 93–105.

SCHWARZER, R. (ED.). (1992). *Self-efficacy: Thought control of action.* Washington, DC: Hemisphere.

SCHWEDER, R. A. (1994). "You're not sick, you're just in love": Emotion as an interpretive system. In P. Ekman & R. J. Davidson (Eds.), *The nature of emotion* (pp. 32–47). New York: Oxford University Press.

SCHWEITZER, E., RICKELS, K., & UHLENHUTH, E. H. (1995). Issues in the long-term treatment of anxiety disorders. In F. E. Bloom & D. Kupfer (Eds.), *Psychopharmacology: The fourth generation of progress* (pp. 1349–1359). New York: Raven.

SCOTT, F. J., & BARON-COHEN, S. (1996). Imagining real and unreal things: Evidence of a dissociation in autism. *Journal of Cognitive Neuroscience, 8,* 371–382.

SCRIBNER, S. (1975). Recall of classical syllogisms: A cross-cultural investigation of error on logical problems. In R. J. Falmagne (Ed.), *Reasoning, representation and process in children and adults* (pp. 153–174). Hillsdale, NJ: Erlbaum.

SEDIKIDES, C., & GREGG, P. A. (2008). Self-enhancement: Food for thought. *Perspectives on Psychological Science, 3,* 102–116.

SEDIVY, J. C., TANENHAUS, M. K., CHAMBERS, C. G., & CARLSON, G. N. (1999). Achieving incremental sentence interpretation through contextual representation. *Cognition, 71*(2), 109–147

SEEMAN, M. V. (1997). Psychopathology in women and men: Focus on female hormones. *American Journal of Psychiatry, 154,* 1641–1647.

SEGAL, Z., PEARSON, J., & THASE, M. (2003). Challenges in preventing relapse in major depression: Report of a National Institute of Mental Health Workshop on state of the science of relapse prevention in major depression. *Journal of Affective Disorders, 77,* 97–108.

SEGALL, M. H., DASEN, P. R., BERRY, J. W., & POORTINGA, Y. H. (1999). *Human behavior in global perspective: An introduction to cross-cultural psychology* (2nd ed.). New York: Pergamon Press.

SEGERSTROM, S. C. (2000). Personality and the immune system: Models, methods, and mechanisms. *Annals of Behavioral Medicine, 22,* 180–190.

SEIDENBERG, M. (2005). Connectionist models of word reading. *Current Directions in Psychological Science, 14,* 238–242.

SEIDENBERG, M. S., & ZEVIN, J. D. (2006). Connectionist models in developmental cognitive neuroscience: Critical periods and the paradox of success. In Y. Munakata & M. Johnson (Eds.), *Processes of change in brain and cognitive development. Attention and Performance XXI.* Oxford, UK: Oxford University Press.

SELFRIDGE, O. G. (1959). Pandemonium: A paradigm for learning. In D. V. Blake & A. M. Uttley (Eds.), *Proceedings of the Symposium on the Mechanisation of Thought Processes.* London: HM Stationery Office.

SELIGMAN, M. E. P. (1970). On the generality of the laws of learning. *Psychological Review, 77,* 406–418.

SELIGMAN, M. E. P. (1971). Phobias and preparedness. *Behavior Therapy, 2,* 307–320.

SELIGMAN, M. E. P. (1975). *Helplessness: On depression, development, and death.* San Francisco: Freeman.

SELIGMAN, M. E. P. (1995). The effectiveness of psychotherapy: The Consumer Reports study. *American Psychologist, 50,* 965–974.

SELIGMAN, M. E. P., & CSIKSZENTMIHALYI, M. (2000). Positive psychology: An introduction. *American Psychologist, 55*(1), 5–14.

SELIGMAN, M. E. P., & GILLHAM, J. (2000). *The science of optimism and hope: Research essays in honor of Martin E. P. Seligman.* Philadelphia: Templeton Foundation Press.

SELIGMAN, M. E. P., & HAGER, J. L. (EDS.). (1972). *Biological boundaries of learning.* New York: Appleton-Century-Crofts.

SELIGMAN, M. E. P., KLEIN, D. C., & MILLER, W. R. (1976). Depression. In H. Leitenberg (Ed.), *Handbook of behavior modification and behavior therapy.* Englewood Cliffs, NJ: Prentice-Hall.

SELIGMAN, M. E. P., & MAIER, S. F. (1967). Failure to escape traumatic shock. *Journal of Experimental Psychology, 74,* 1–9.

SELIGMAN, M. E. P., MAIER, S. F., & SOLOMON, R. L. (1971). Unpredictable and uncontrollable aversive events. In F. R. Brush (Ed.), *Aversive conditioning and learning.* New York: Academic Press.

SELIGMAN, M. E. P., NOLEN-HOEKSEMA, S., THORNTON, N., & THORNTON, K. M. (1990). Explanatory style as a mechanism of disappointing athletic performance. *Psychological Science, 1,* 143–146.

SELIGMAN, M. E. P., STEEN, T., PARK, N., & PETERSON, C. (2005). Positive psychology progress: Empirical validation of interventions. *American Psychologist, 60,* 410–421.

SELIGMAN, M. E., & SCHULMAN, P. (1986). Explanatory style as a predictor of productivity and quitting among life insurance sales agents. *Journal of Personality & Social Psychology, 50,* 832–838.

SEMMLER, C., & BREWER, N. (2006). Postidentification feedback effects on face recognition confidence: Evidence for metacognitive influences. *Applied Cognitive Psychology, 20*, 895–916.

SENGHAS, A. (1995a). Conventionalization in the first generation: A community acquires a language. *Journal of Contemporary Legal Issues, 6*, 501–519.

SENGHAS, A. (1995b). The development of Nicaraguan Sign Language via the language acquisition process. In D. MacLaughlin & S. McEwen (Eds.), *Proceedings of the Boston University Conference on Language Development, 19*, 543–552.

SENGHAS, A., KITA, S., & ÖZYÜREK, A. (2004). Children creating core properties of language: Evidence from an emerging sign language in Nicaragua. Science, *305*(5691), 1779–1782.

SENGHAS, A., ROMÁN, D., & MAVILLAPALLI, S. (2006). *Simply unique.* London: Leonard Cheshire International.

SENKO, C., DURIK, A. M., & HARACKIEWICZ, J. M. (2008). Historical perspectives and new directions in achievement goal theory: Understanding the effects of mastery and performance-approach goals. In J. Y. Shah and W. L. Gardner (Eds.), *Handbook of motivation science* (pp. 100–113). New York: Guilford.

SERENO, A. B., & MAUNSELL, J. H. R. (1998). Shape selectivity in primate lateral intraparietal cortex. *Nature, 395*, 500–503.

SERPELL, R. (2000). Intelligence and culture. In R. J. Sternberg (Ed.), *Handbook of intelligence* (2nd ed., pp. 549–580). New York: Cambridge University Press.

SERVIN, A., NORDENSTROM, A., LARSSON, A., & BOHLIN, G. (2003). Prenatal androgens and gender-typed behavior: A study of girls with mild and severe forms of congenital adrenal hyperplasia. *Developmental Psychology, 39*(3), 440–450.

SETHI, A., MISCHEL, W., ABER, J. L., SHODA, Y., & RODRIGUEZ, M. L. (2000). The role of strategic attention deployment in development of self-regulation: Predicting preschoolers' delay of gratification from mother-toddler interactions. *Developmental Psychology, 36*, 767–777.

SHADER, R. I., & GREENBLATT, D. J. (1995). The pharmacotherapy of acute anxiety. In F. E. Bloom & D. Kupfer (Eds.), *Psychopharmacology: The fourth generation of progress* (pp. 1341–1348). New York: Raven.

SHADISH, W. R., MATT, G. E., NAVARRO, A. M., SIEGLE, G., CRITS-CHRISTOPH, P., HAZELRIGG, M., ET AL. (1997). Evidence that therapy works in clinically representative conditions. *Journal of Consulting and Clinical Psychology, 65*, 355–365.

SHAFFER, D. (2004). *Social and personality development* (5th ed.). New York: Wadsworth.

SHAFIR, E., SIMONSON, I., & TVERSKY, A. (1993). Reason-based choice. *Cognition, 49*, 11–36.

SHAH, A. M., & WOLFORD, G. (2007). Buying behavior as a function of parametric variation of number of choices. *Psychological Science, 18*, 369–370.

SHAM, P. V. C., O'CALLAGHAN, E., TAKEI, N., MURRAY, G. K., HARE, E. H., & MURRAY, R. M. (1992). Schizophrenia following pre-natal exposure to influenza epidemics between 1939 and 1960. *British Journal of Psychiatry, 160*, 461–466.

SHANAB, M. E., & YAHYA, K. A. (1977). A behavioral study of obedience in children. *Journal of Personality and Social Psychology, 35*, 530–536.

SHANNONHOUSE, R. (Ed.). (2000). *Out of her mind: Women writing on madness.* New York: Modern Library.

SHAPIRO, C. M., BORTZ, R., MITCHELL, D., BARTELL, P., & JOOSTE, P. (1981). Slow wave sleep: A recovery period after exercise. *Science, 214*, 1253–1254.

SHAVER, P., & CLARK, C. (1994). The psychodynamics of adult romantic attachment. In J. Masling & R. Bornstein (Eds.), *Empirical perspectives on object relations theory. Empirical studies of psychoanalytic theories: Vol. 5* (pp. 105–156). Washington, DC: American Psychological Association.

SHAVER, P., SCHWARTZ, J., KIRSON, D., & O'CONNOR, C. (1987). Emotion knowledge: Further exploration of a prototype approach. *Journal of Personality and Social Psychology, 52*, 1061–1086.

SHAVITT, S., SWAN, S., LOWREY, T. M., & WANKE, M. (1994). The interaction of endorser attractiveness and involvement in persuasion depends on the goal that guides message processing. *Journal of Consumer Psychology, 3*(2), 137–162.

SHEA, M. (1995). Interrelationships among categories of personality disorders. In W. J. Livesley (Ed.), *The DSM-IV personality disorders* (pp. 397–406). New York: Guilford.

SHEAR, M. K., PILKONIS, P. A., CLOITRE, M., & LEON, A. C. (1994). Cognitive behavioral treatment compared with nonprescriptive treatment of panic disorder. *Archives of General Psychiatry, 51*, 395–401.

SHEEHAN, P. W., GREEN, V., TRUESDALE, P. (1992). Influence of rapport on hypnotically induced pseudomemory. *Journal of Abnormal Psychology, 101* (4), 690–700.

SHELLEY, P. B. (1821). To a skylark. As published in A. T. Quiller-Couch (Ed.), *The Oxford book of English verse* (1900). Oxford, England: Clarendon.

SHEPARD, R. N., & COOPER, L. A. (1982). Mental images and their transformations. Cambridge, MA: MIT Press.

SHEPHERD, G. M. (1994). Discrimination of molecular signals by the olfactory receptor neuron. *Neuron, 13*, 771–790.

SHERIF, M. (1937). An experimental approach to the study of attitudes. *Sociometry, 1*, 90–98.

SHERIF, M. (1966). *The common predicament: Social psychology of intergroup conflict and cooperation.* Boston: Houghton Mifflin.

SHERIF, M., HARVEY, O. J., WHITE, B. J., HOOD, W. R., & SHERIF, C. W. (1961). *Intergroup conflict and competition: The Robbers Cave experiment.* Norman: University of Oklahoma Book Exchange.

SHERRINGTON, C. (1906). *The integrative action of the nervous system.* New Haven, CT: Yale University Press.

SHETTLEWORTH, S. J. (1972). Constraints on learning. In D. S. Lehrman, R. A. Hinde, & E. Shaw (Eds.), *Advances in the study of behavior: Vol. 4.* New York: Academic Press.

SHETTLEWORTH, S. J. (1983). Memory in food-hoarding birds. *Scientific American, 248*, 102–110.

SHETTLEWORTH, S. J. (1984). Learning and behavioral ecology. In J. R. Krebs & N. B. Davies (Eds.), *Behavioral ecology* (2nd ed., pp. 170–194). Oxford, England: Blackwell.

SHETTLEWORTH, S. J. (1990). Spatial memory in food-storing birds. *Philosophical Transactions of the Royal Society, Series B, 329*, 143–151.

SHI, R., MORGAN, J. L., & ALLOPENNA, P. (1998). Phonological and acoustic bases for earliest grammatical category assignment: A cross-linguistic perspective. *Journal of Child Language, 25*, 169–201.

SHIAH, I. S., & YATHAM, L. N. (2000). Serotonin in mania and in the mechanism of action of mood stabilizers: A review of clinical studies. *Bipolar Disorders, 2*, 77–92.

SHIH, M., PITTINSKY, T. L., & AMBADY, N. (1999). Stereotype susceptibility: Identity salience and shifts in quantitative performance. *Psychological Science, 10*, 80–83.

SHIPLEY, E. F., KUHN, I. F., & MADDEN, E. C. (1983). Mothers' use of superordinate category terms. *Journal of Child Language, 10*, 571–588.

SHOBE, K. K., & KIHLSTROM, J. F. (1997). Is traumatic memory special? *Current Directions in Psychological Science, 6*, 70–74.

SHODA, Y., MISCHEL, W., & PEAKE, P. K. (1990). Predicting adolescent cognitive and self-regulatory competencies from preschool delay of gratification: Identifying diagnostic conditions. *Developmental Psychology, 26*, 978–986.

SHORS, T. (2009). Saving new brain cells. *Scientific American, 300*, 47–54.

SHULMAN, S., ELICKER, J., & SROUFE, L. A. (1994). Stages of friendship growth in preadolescence as related to attachment history. *Journal of Social and Personal Relationships, 11*(3), 341–361.

SICOLY, F., & ROSS, M. (1977). Facilitation of ego-biased attributions by means of self-serving observer feedback. *Journal of Personality and Social Psychology, 35*, 734–741.

SIEGAL, M. (1997). *Knowing children: Experiments in conversation and cognition* (2nd ed.). New York: Psychology Press.

SIEGEL, A., & DEMETRIKOPOULOS, M. K. (1993). Hormones and aggression. In J. Schulkin (Ed.), *Hormonally induced changes in mind and brain* (pp. 99–127). San Diego, CA: Academic Press.

SIEGEL, J. M. (2003). Why we sleep. *Scientific American, 289*, 92–97.

SIEGEL, S. (1977). Morphine tolerance acquisition as an associative process. *Journal of Experimental Psychology: Animal Behavior Processes, 3*, 1–13.

SIEGEL, S. (1983). Classical conditioning, drug tolerance, and drug dependence. In Y. Israel, F. B. Slower, H. Kalant, R. E. Popham, W. Schmidt, & R. G. Smart (Eds.), *Research advances in alcohol and drug abuse: Vol. 7* (pp. 207–246). New York: Plenum.

SIEGEL, S., & ALLAN, L. G. (1998). Learning and homeostasis: Drug addiction and the McCollough effect. *Psychological Bulletin, 124*, 230–239.

SIEGEL, S., KIM, J. A., & SOKOLOWSKA, M. (2003). Situational-specificity of caffeine tolerance. *Circulation, 108*, E38.

Siegler, R. S. (1996). *Emerging minds: The process of change in children's thinking.* New York: Oxford University Press.

Siegler, R. S. (1998). *Children's thinking* (3rd ed.). Upper Saddle River, NJ: Prentice Hall.

Sigelman, C. K., Miller, T. E., & Whitworth, L. A. (1986). The early development of stigmatizing reactions to physical differences. *Journal of Applied Developmental Psychology, 7*(1), 17–32.

Silk, J. B. (1986). Social behavior in evolutionary perspective. In B. B. Smuts, D. L. Cheney, R. M. Seyfarth, R. W. Wrangham, & T. T. Struhsaker (Eds.), *Primate societies.* Chicago: University of Chicago Press.

Silverman, P., & Retzlaff, P. (1986). Cognitive state regression through hypnosis: Are earlier cognitive states retrievable? *International Journal of Clinical and Experimental Hypnosis, 34,* 192–204.

Simcock, G., & Hayne, H. (2002). Breaking the barrier? Children fail to translate their preverbal memories in language. *Psychological Science, 13,* 225–231.

Simner, M. L. (1971). Newborn's response to the cry of another infant. *Developmental Psychology, 5,* 136–150.

Simon, H. A. (1983). *Reason in human affairs.* Stanford, CA: Stanford University Press.

Simons, D. J. (2000). Attentional capture and inattentional blindness. *Trends in Cognitive Science, 4,* 147–155.

Simons, D. J., & Chabris, C. F. (1999). Gorillas in our midst: Sustained inattentional blindness for dynamic events. *Perception, 28*(9), 1059–1074.

Simonton, D. K. (2000). Creativity: Cognitive, personal, developmental, and social aspects. *American Psychologist, 55*(1), 151–158.

Simonton, D. K. (2003). Scientific creativity as constrained stochastic behavior: The integration of product, person, and process perspectives. *Psychological Bulletin, 129,* 475–494.

Simpson, E. L. (1974). Moral development research: A case of scientific cultural bias. *Human Development, 17,* 81–106.

Sims, E. A. (1986). Energy balance in human beings: The problems of plentitude. *Vitamins and Hormones: Research and Applications, 43,* 1–101.

Singer, W. (1996). Neuronal synchronization: A solution to the binding problem? In R. R. Llinas & P. S. Churchland (Eds.), *The mind-brain continuum: Sensory processes* (pp. 101–130). Cambridge, MA: MIT Press.

Singh, D. (1993). Adaptive significance of female physical attractiveness: Role of waist-to-hip ratio. *Journal of Personality and Social Psychology, 65,* 293–307.

Singh, D. (1994). Waist-to-hip ratio and judgment of attractiveness and healthiness of female figures by male and female physicians. *International Journal of Obesity and Related Metabolic Disorders, 18,* 731–737.

Singh, D., & Luis, S. (1995). Ethnic and gender consensus for the effect of waist-to-hip ratio on judgment of women's attractiveness. *Human Nature, 6,* 51–65.

Singleton, J. L., & Newport, E. L. (2004). When learners surpass their models: The acquisition of American Sign Language from inconsistent input. *Cognitive Psychology, 49,* 370–407.

Sinha, D. (1983). Human assessment in the Indian context. In S. H. Irvine & J. W. Berry (Eds.), *Human assessment and cultural factors* (pp. 17–34). New York: Plenum.

Sio, U. N., & Ormerod, T. C. (2009). Does incubation enhance problem solving? A meta-analytic review. *Psychological Bulletin, 135,* 94–120.

Skinner, B. F. (1938). *The behavior of organisms.* New York: Appleton-Century-Crofts.

Skotko, B. G., Kensinger, E. A., Locascio, J. J., Einstein, G., Rubin, D. C., Tupler, L. A., et al. (2004). Puzzling thoughts for H. M.: Can new semantic information be anchored to old semantic memories? *Neuropsychology, 18*(4), 756–769.

Sloane, R. B., Staples, F. R., Cristol, A. H., Yorkston, N. J., & Whipple, K. (1975). *Psychotherapy vs. behavior therapy.* Cambridge, MA: Harvard University Press.

Slobin, D. I. (1978) A case study of early language awareness. In A. Sinclair, R. Jarvella, & W.J.M. Levelt (Eds.), *The child's conception of language* (pp. 45–54). Heidelberg: Springer-Verlag.

Sloman, S. A. (1996). The empirical case for two systems of reasoning. *Psychological Bulletin, 119,* 3–22.

Slovic, P., Fischoff, B., & Lichtenstein, S. (1982). Facts versus fears: Understanding perceived risk. In D. Kahneman, P. Slovic, & A. Tversky (Eds.), *Judgment under uncertainty: Heuristics and biases.* New York: Cambridge University Press.

Smith, C. (1996). Women, weight and body image. In J. C. Chrisler, C. Golden, & P. D. Rozee (Eds.), *Lectures on the psychology of women.* New York: McGraw-Hill.

Smith, C., & Lloyd, B. (1978). Maternal behavior and perceived sex of infant: Revisited. *Child Development, 49,* 1263–1265.

Smith, E. E., & Medin, D. L. (1981). *Categories and concepts.* Cambridge, MA: Harvard University Press.

Smith, E. E., Osherson, D. N., Rips, L. J., & Keane, M. (1988). Combining prototypes: A selective modification model. *Cognitive Science, 12,* 485–527.

Smith, G. T., Spillane, N. S., & Annus, A. M. (2006). Implications of an emerging integration of universal and culturally specific psychologies. *Perspectives on Psychological Science, 1*(3), 211–233.

Smith, L. (2005). Psychotherapy, classism, and the poor: Conspicuous by their absence. *American Psychologist, 60,* 687–696.

Smith, L. B., & Thelen, D. (1993). *A dynamic systems approach to development: Applications.* Cambridge, MA: MIT Press.

Smith, L. B., & Thelen, E. (2003). Development as a dynamic system. *Trends in Cognitive Science, 7,* 343–348.

Smith, L. B., Thelen, E., Titzer, R., & McLin, D. (1999). Knowing in the context of acting: The task dynamics of the A-not-B error. *Psychological Review, 106,* 235–260.

Smith, L. B., & Yu, C. (2008). Infants rapidly learn word-referent mappings via cross-situational statistics. *Cognition, 106,* 333–338.

Smith, M. (1983). Hypnotic memory enhancement of witnesses: Does it work? *Psychological Bulletin, 94,* 387–407.

Smith, M. B. (1950). The phenomenological approach in personality theory: Some critical remarks. *Journal of Abnormal and Social Psychology, 45,* 516–522.

Smith, M. L., Glass, G. V., & Miller, R. L. (1980). *The benefits of psychotherapy.* Baltimore: Johns Hopkins Press.

Smith, P., & Dalish, L. (1977). Sex differences in parent and infant behavior in the home. *Child Development, 48,* 1250–1254.

Smith, P. B., & Bond, M. B. (1993). *Social psychology across cultures.* New York: Harvester Wheatsheaf.

Smith, P. B., Misumi, J., Tayeb, M., Peterson, M., & Bond, M. (1989). On the generality of leadership style measures across cultures. *Journal of Occupational Psychology, 62*(2), 97–109.

Smith, S. M. (1979). Remembering in and out of context. *Journal of Experimental Psychology: Human Learning and Memory, 5,* 460–471.

Smith, S. M., & Blankenship, S. E. (1989). Incubation effects. *Bulletin of the Psychonomic Society, 27*(4), 311–314.

Smith, S. M., & Vela, E. (2001). Environmental context-dependent memory: A review and meta-analysis. *Psychonomics Bulletin and Review, 8,* 203–220.

Smolensky, P. (1999). Grammar-based connectionist approaches to language. *Cognitive Science, 23,* 589–613.

Snedeker, J., Geren, J., & Shafto, C. (2007). Starting over: International adoption as a natural experiment in language development. *Psychological Science, 18*(1), 79–86.

Snedeker, J., & Gleitman, L. (2004). Why it is hard to label our concepts. G. Hall & S. Waxman (Eds.), *Weaving a lexicon* (pp. 207–294). New York: Cambridge University Press.

Snedeker, J., & Trueswell, J. (2003). Using prosody to avoid ambiguity: Effects of speaker awareness and referential context. *Journal of Memory and Language, 48,* 103–130.

Snibbe, A., & Markus, H. R. (2005). You can't always get what you want: Social class, agency, and choice. *Journal of Personality and Social Psychology, 88,* 703–720.

Snow, C., & Hoefnagel-Hohle, M. (1978). The critical period for language acquisition: Evidence from second language learning. *Child Development, 49,* 1114–1128.

Snow, R. E. (1994). Abilities in academic tasks. In R. J. Sternberg & R. K. Wagner (Eds.), *Mind in context: Interactionist perspectives on human intelligence* (pp. 3–37). Cambridge, England: Cambridge University Press.

Snow, R. E. (1996). Aptitude development and education. *Psychology, Public Policy, and Law, 2,* 536–560.

Snyder, D. K., Castellani, A. M., & Whisman, M. A. (2006). Current status and future directions in couple therapy. *Annual Review of Psychology, 57,* 317–344.

Snyder, M. (1987). *Public appearances/private realities.* New York: Freeman.

Snyder, M. (1995). Self-monitoring: Public appearances versus private realities. In G. G. Brannigan & M. R. Merrens (Eds.), *The social psychologists: Research adventures* (pp. 35–50). New York: McGraw-Hill.

Snyder, M., & Omoto, A. M. (1992). Who helps and why? The psychology of aids volunteerism. In S. Spacapan & S. Oskamp (Eds.), *Helping and being helped:*

Naturalistic studies (pp. 213–239). Thousand Oaks, CA: Sage.

SNYDER, M., TANKE, E. D., & BERSCHEID, E. (1977). Social perception and interpersonal behavior: On the self-fulfilling nature of social stereotypes. *Journal of Personality and Social Psychology, 44*, 510–517.

SNYDER, M. L., STEPHAN, W. G., & ROSENFIELD, D. (1976). Egotism and attribution. *Journal of Personality and Social Psychology, 33*, 435–441.

SNYDER, S. H. (1976). The dopamine hypothesis of schizophrenia. *American Journal of Psychiatry, 133*, 197–202.

SOJA, N. N., CAREY, S., & SPELKE, E. S. (1991). Ontological categories guide young children's inductions of word meaning: Object terms and substance terms. *Cognition, 38*, 179–211.

SOKOLOWSKA, M., SIEGEL, S., & KIM, J. A. (2002). Intraadministration associations: Conditional hyperalgesia elicited by morphine onset cues. *Journal of Experimental Psychology: Animal Behavior Processes, 28*(3), 309–320.

SORKHABI, N. (2005). Applicability of Baumrind's parent typology to collective cultures: Analysis of cultural explanation of parent socialization effects. *International Journal of Behavioral Development, 29*, 552–563.

SOTO, C. J., JOHN, O. P., GOSLING, S. D., & POTTER, J. (2008). The developmental psychometrics of Big Five self-reports: Acquiescence, factor structure, coherence, and differentiation from ages 10 to 20. *Journal of Personality and Social Psychology, 94*, 718–737.

SOX, H. C., JR., & WOOLF, S. H. (1993). Evidence-based practice guidelines from the U.S. Preventive Services Task Force. *Journal of the American Medical Association, 269*, 2678.

SPANOS, N. P. (1986). Hypnotic behavior: A social-psychological interpretation of amnesia, analgesia, and "trance logic." *Behavioral & Brain Sciences, 9* (3), 449–467.

SPANOS, N. P. (1996). *Multiple identities and false memories: A sociocognitive perspective.* Washington, DC: American Psychological Association.

SPANOS, N. P., BURGESS, C. A., BURGESS, M. F., SAMUELS, C., & BLOIS, W. O. (1999). Creating false memories of infancy with hypnotic and nonhypnotic procedures. *Applied Cognitive Psychology, 13*, 201–218.

SPANOS, N. P., & COE, W. C. (1992). A social-psychological approach to hypnosis. In E. Fromm & M. Nash (Eds.), *Contemporary hypnosis research* (pp. 102–130). New York: Guilford Press.

SPEAR, L. P. (2000). The adolescent brain and age-related behavioral manifestations. *Neuroscience and Biobehavioral Reviews, 24*, 417–463.

SPEARMAN, C. (1927). *The abilities of man.* London: Macmillan.

SPIEGEL, K., SHERIDAN, J. F., & VAN CAUTER, E. (2002). Reduced immune response to influenza virus vaccination in a state of sleep debt. *Journal of the American Medical Association, 288*(12), 1471–1472.

SPELKE, E. (2003). Core knowledge. In N. Kanwisher & J. Duncan (Eds.), *Attention and performance: Vol. 20. Functional neuroimaging of visual cognition.* New York: Oxford University Press.

SPELKE, E. S. (1994). Initial knowledge: Six suggestions. *Cognition, 50*(1–3), 431–445.

SPELKE, E. S. (2005). Sex differences in intrinsic aptitude for mathematics and science? A critical review. *American Psychologist, 60*(9), 950–958.

SPELKE, E. S., & NEWPORT, E. (1998). Nativism, empiricism, and the development of knowledge. In R. Lerner (Ed.), *Handbook of child psychology: Vol. 1. Theoretical models of human development* (5th ed.). New York: Wiley.

SPEMANN, H. (1967). *Embryonic development and induction.* New York: Hafner.

SPERBER, D., & WILSON, D. (1986). *Relevance: Communication and cognition.* Oxford, England: Blackwell.

SPERLING, G. (1960). The information available in brief visual presentations. *Psychological Monographs, 74*(Whole No. 11).

SPIRO, M. (1982). *Oedipus in the Trobriands.* Chicago: University of Chicago Press.

SPIRO, M. E. (1992). Oedipus redux. *Ethos, 20*, 358–376.

SPITZ, C. J., GOLD, A. R., & ADAMS, D. B. (1975). Cognitive and hormonal factors affecting coital frequency. *Archives of Sexual Behavior, 4*, 249–264.

SPITZ, H. H. (1999). Beleaguered Pygmalion: A history of the controversy over claims that teacher expectancy raises intelligence. *Intelligence, 27*, 199–234.

SPRINGER, S. P., & DEUTSCH, G. (1998). *Left brain, right brain: Perspectives from cognitive neuroscience* (5th ed.). New York: Freeman.

SQUIRE, L. R. (1977). ECT and memory loss. *American Journal of Psychiatry, 134*, 997–1001.

SQUIRE, L. R. (1986). Mechanisms of memory. *Science, 232*, 1612–1619.

SQUIRE, L. R. (1987). *Memory and brain.* New York: Oxford University.

SQUIRE, L. R., & COHEN, N. J. (1979). Memory and amnesia: Resistance to disruption develops for years after learning. *Behavioral Biology and Neurology, 25*, 115–125.

SQUIRE, L. R., & COHEN, N. J. (1982). Remote memory, retrograde amnesia, and the neuropsychology of memory. In L. S. Cermak (Ed.), *Human memory and amnesia* (pp. 275–304). Hillsdale, NJ: Erlbaum.

SQUIRE, L. R., & COHEN, N. J. (1984). Human memory and amnesia. In J. McGaugh, G. Lynch, & N. Weinberger (Eds.), *Neurobiology of learning and memory.* New York: Guilford.

SRIVASTAVA, S., & BEER, J. S. (2005). How self-evaluations relate to being liked by others: Integrating sociometer and attachment perspectives. *Journal of Personality and Social Psychology, 89*, 966–977.

SRIVASTAVA, S., JOHN, O. P., GOSLING, S. D., & POTTER, J. (2003). Development of personality in early and middle adulthood: Set like plaster or persistent change? *Journal of Personality and Social Psychology, 84*, 1041–1053.

SROUFE, L. A., EGELAND, B., CARLSON, E., & COLLINS, W. A. (2005). *The Development of the person: The Minnesota Study of Risk and Adaptation from Birth to Adulthood.* New York: Guilford.

STAKE, J., & NICKENS. S. (2005). Adolescent girls' and boys' science peer relationships and perceptions of the possible self as scientist. *Sex Roles, 52*, 1–11.

STANLEY, B. G., MAGDALIN, W., & LEIBOWITZ, S. F. (1989). A critical site for neuropeptide Y-induced eating lies in the caudolateral paraventricular/perifornical region of the hypothalamus. *Society for Neuroscience Abstracts, 15*, 894.

STANLEY, J. (1993). Boys and girls who reason well mathematically. In G. R. Beck & K. Ackrill (Eds.), *The origins and development of high ability.* Chichester, England: Wiley.

STANOVICH, K. E., & WEST, R. F. (1998). Who uses base rates and P(D|~H)? An analysis of individual differences. *Memory & Cognition, 26*, 161–179.

STANOVICH, K. E., & WEST, R. F. (2000). Individual differences in reasoning: Implications for the rationality debate. *Behavioral and Brain Sciences, 23*, 645–665.

STARKEY, P., SPELKE, E. S., & GELMAN, R. (1983). Detection of intermodal numerical correspondences by human infants. *Science, 222*, 179–181.

STARKEY, P., SPELKE, E. S., & GELMAN, R. (1990). Numerical abstraction by human infants. *Cognition, 36*, 97–127.

STEELE, C. M. (1998). Stereotyping and its threat are real. *American Psychologist, 53*, 680–681.

STEELE, C. M., & ARONSON, J. (1995). Stereotype threat and the intellectual test performance of African Americans. *Journal of Personality and Social Psychology, 69*(5), 797–811.

STEELE, C. M., & JOSEPHS, R. A. (1990). Alcohol myopia: Its prized and dangerous effects. *American Psychologist, 45*, 921–933.

STEELE, J. (2003). Children's gender stereotypes about math: The role of stereotype stratification. *Journal of Applied Social Psychology, 33*, 2587–2606.

STEFANSSON, H., RUJESCU, D., CICHON, S., PIETILÄINEN, O. P., INGASON, A., STEINBERG. S., ET AL. (2008). Large recurrent microdeletions associated with schizophrenia. *Nature, 455*(7210), 232–236.

STEIN, M. B., SCHORK, N. J., & GELERNTER, J. (2008). Interaction for anxiety sensitivity, an intermediate phenotype for anxiety disorders. *Neuropsychopharmacology, 33*, 312–319.

STEINBERG, L. (2001). We know some things: Adolescent-parent relationships in retrospect and prospect. *Journal of Research in Adolescence, 11*, 1–20.

STEINBERG, L. (2007). Risk taking in adolescence: New perspectives from brain and behavioral science. *Current Directions in Psychological Science, 16*(2), 55–59.

STEINBERG, L., ELKMAN, J. D., & MOUNTS, N. S. (1989). Authoritative parenting, psychosocial maturity, and academic success among adolescents. *Child Development, 60*(6), 1424–1436.

STEINBERG, L., & MORRIS, A. S. (2001). Adolescent development. *Annual Review of Psychology, 52*, 83–110.

STERN, J. A., BROWN, M., ULETT, G. A., & SLETTEN, I. (1977). A comparison of hypnosis, acupuncture, morphine, valium, aspirin, and placebo in the management of experimentally induced pain. In W. E. Edmonston (Ed.),

Conceptual and investigative approaches to hypnosis and hypnotic phenomena (Vol. 296, pp. 175–193). New York: Annals of the New York Academy of Sciences.

STERN, K., & MCCLINTOCK, M. (1998). Regulation of ovulation by human pheromones. *Nature, 392,* 177–179.

STERN, P. C., & CARSTENSEN, L. L. (2000). *The aging mind.* Washington, DC: National Academy Press.

STERNBERG, R. J. (1977). *Intelligence, information processing, and analogical reasoning: The componential analysis of human abilities.* Hillsdale, NJ: Erlbaum.

STERNBERG, R. J. (1985). General intellectual ability. In R. Sternberg (Ed.), *Human abilities: An information processing approach.* New York: Freeman.

STERNBERG, R. J. (1986). A triangular theory of love. *Psychological Review, 93,* 119–135.

STERNBERG, R. J. (1988). Triangulating love. In R. J. Sternberg & M. L. Barnes (Eds.), *The psychology of love* (pp. 119–138). New Haven, CT: Yale University Press.

STERNBERG, R. J. (1990). *Metaphors of mind.* New York: Cambridge University Press.

STERNBERG, R. J. (2000). The holey grail of general intelligence. *Science, 289,* 399–401.

STERNBERG, R. J. (2003). Our research program validating the triarchic theory of successful intelligence: Reply to Gottfredson. *Intelligence, 31,* 399–413.

STERNBERG, R. J. (2004). Culture and intelligence. *American Psychologist, 59,* 325–338.

STERNBERG, R. J., & DAVIDSON, J. E. (1983). Insight in the gifted. *Educational Psychologist, 18,* 51–57.

STERNBERG, R. J., & DESS, N. K. (Eds.). (2001). Creativity for the new millenium. *American Psychologist, 56*(4), 332–362.

STERNBERG, R., & GRIGORENKO, E. L. (2007). The difficulty of escaping preconceptions in writing an article about the difficult of escaping preconceptions: Commentary on Hunt & Carlson (2007). *Perspective on Psychological Science, 2,* 221–223.

STERNBERG, R. J., & KAUFMAN, J. C. (1998). Human abilities. *Annual Review of Psychology, 49,* 479–502.

STERNBERG, R. J., & WAGNER, R. K. (1993). The egocentric view of intelligence and job performance is wrong. *Current Directions in Psychological Science, 2,* 1–5.

STERNBERG, R. J., WAGNER, R. K., WILLIAMS, W. M., & HORVATH, J. A. (1995). Testing common sense. *American Psychologist, 50,* 912–927.

STEVENS, A., & COUPE, P. (1978). Distortions in judged spatial relations. *Cognitive Psychology, 10,* 422–437.

STEVENS, L., & JONES, E. E. (1976). Defensive attributions and the Kelley cube. *Journal of Personality and Social Psychology, 34,* 809–820.

STEVENS, S. S. (1955). The measurement of loudness. *Journal of the Acoustical Society of America, 27,* 815–819.

STEWART, T. D. (1957). Stone age surgery: A general review, with emphasis on the New World. *Annual Review of the Smithsonian Institution.* Washington, DC: Smithsonian Institution.

STICKGOLD, R. (2005). Why we dream. In M. H. Kryger, T. Roth, & W. C. Dement (Eds.), *Principles and practice of sleep medicine.* Philadelphia: Elsevier Saunders.

STICKGOLD, R., WHIDBEE, D., SCHIRMER, B., PATEL, V., & HOBSON J. A. (2000). Visual discrimination task improvement: A multi-step process occurring during sleep. *Journal of Cognitive Neuroscience, 12,* 246–254.

STOKOE, W. C., JR. (1960). Sign language structure: An outline of the visual communication systems. *Studies in Linguistics,* Occasional Papers 8.

STOLZ, J. A., & BESNER, D. (1999). On the myth of automatic semantic activation in reading. *Current Directions in Psychological Science, 8*(2), 61–65.

STOOLMILLER, M. (2001). Synergistic interaction of child manageability problems and parent-discipline tactics in predicting future growth in externalizing behavior for boys. *Developmental Psychology, 37*(6), 814–825.

STORMS, M. D. (1973). Videotape and the attribution process: Reversing actors' and observers' points of view. *Journal of Personality and Social Psychology, 27,* 165–175.

STOWE, L. (1987). Thematic structures and sentence comprehension. In G. Carlson & M. Tanenhaus (Eds.), *Linguistic structure in language processing.* Dordrecht: Reidel.

STRACK, F., MARTIN, L. L., & STEPPER, S. (1988). Inhibiting and facilitating conditions of the human smile: A nonobtrusive test of the facial feedback hypothesis. *Journal of Personality and Social Psychology, 54,* 768–777.

STRIANO T., & REID, V. M. (2006). Social cognition in the first year. *Trends in Cognitive Sciences, 10*(10), 471–476.

STRIANO, T., & ROCHAT, P. (2000). Emergence of selective social referencing in infancy. *Infancy, 1*(2), 253–264.

STRICKER, E. M., & ZIGMOND, M. J. (1976). Recovery of function after damage to catecholamine-containing neurons: A neurochemical model for the lateral hypothalamic syndrome. In J. M. Sprague & A. N. Epstein (Eds.), *Progress in psychobiology and physiological psychology: Vol. 6* (pp. 121–188). New York: Academic Press.

STRIEGEL-MOORE, R. H., DOHM, F. A., KRAEMER, H. C., TAYLOR, C. B., DANIELS, S., CRAWFORD, P. B., ET AL. (2003). Eating disorders in White and Black women. *American Journal of Psychiatry, 160,* 1326–1331.

STROBER, M., FREEMAN, R., LAMPERT, C., DIAMOND, J., & KAYE, W. (2000). A controlled family study of anorexia nervosa and bulimia nervosa: Evidence of shared liability and transmission of partial syndromes. *American Journal of Psychiatry, 157,* 393–401.

STROOP, J. R. (1935). Studies of interference in serial verbal reactions. *Journal of Experimental Psychology, 18,* 643–662.

STUMPF, H., & STANLEY, J. C. (1998). Stability and change in gender-related differences on the College Board Advanced Placement and Achievement tests. *Current Directions in Psychological Science, 7,* 192–198.

STUSS, D. T., & LEVINE, B. (2002). Adult clinical neuropsychology: Lessons from studies of the frontal lobes. *Annual Review of Psychology, 53,* 401–433.

STYRON, W. (1990). *Darkness visible: A memoir of madness.* New York: Random House.

SUE S. (1998). In search of cultural competence in psychotherapy and counseling. *American Psychologist, 53,* 440–448.

SUE, D. W., & KIRK, B. A. (1973). Psychological characteristics of Chinese-American college students. *Journal of Counseling Psychology, 19,*142–148.

SUE, S., & LAM, A.G. (2002). Cultural and demographic diversity. In J.C. Norcross (Ed.), *Psychotherapy: Relationships that work* (pp. 401–422). New York: Oxford University Press.

SUGRUE, K., & HAYNE, H. (2006). False memories produced by children and adults in the DRM paradigm. *Applied Cognitive Psychology, 20,* 625–631.

SULLIVAN, P. F., KENDLER, K. S., & NEALE, M. C. (2003). Schizophrenia as a complex trait: Evidence from a meta-analysis of twin studies. *Archives of General Psychiatry, 60,* 1187–1192.

SULLIVAN, P. F., NEALE, M. C., & KENDLER, K. S. (2000). Genetic epidemiology of major depression: Review and meta-analysis. *American Journal of Psychiatry, 157,* 1552–1562.

SULLOWAY, F. (1996). *Born to rebel.* New York: Pantheon Books.

SULLOWAY, F. J. (1979). *Freud, biologist of the mind: Beyond the psychoanalytic legend.* Cambridge, MA: Harvard University Press.

SULS, J. M. (1972). A two-stage model for the appreciation of jokes and cartoons: An information processing analysis. In J. H. Goldstein & P. E. McGhee (Eds.), *The psychology of humor* (pp. 81–100). New York: Academic Press.

SULS, J. M. (1983). Cognitive processes in humor appreciation. In P. E. McGhee & J. H. Goldstein (Eds.), *Handbook of humor research: Vol. 1* (pp. 39–58). New York: Springer.

SULS, J. M., & MILLER, R. L. (EDS.). (1977). *Social comparison processes: Theoretical and empirical perspectives.* New York: Washington Hemisphere.

SUNDET, J., ERIKSEN, W., & TAMBS, K. (2008). Intelligence correlations between brothers decrease with increasing age difference: Evidence for shared environmental effects in young adults. *Psychological Science, 19,* 843–847.

SUPALLA, I., & NEWPORT, E. L. (1978). How many seats in a chair? The derivation of nouns and verbs in American Sign Language. In P. Siple (Ed.), *Understanding language through sign language research.* New York: Academic Press.

SUPER, C. M. (1976). Environmental effects on motor development: A case of African infant precocity. *Developmental Medicine and Child Neurology, 18,* 561–567.

SUR, M., & RUBENSTEIN, J. L. R. (2005). Patterning and plasticity of the cerebral cortex. *Science, 310,* 805–810.

SURIAN, L., CALDI, S., & SPERBER, D. (2007). Attribution of beliefs by 13-month-old infants. *Psychological Science, 18*(7), 580–586.

SUROWIECKI, J. (2004). *The wisdom of crowds.* New York: Doubleday.

SUSMAN, E. J., DORN, L. D., & SCHIEFELBEIN, V. L. (2003). Puberty, sexuality, and health. In R. M. Lerner, M. A. Easterbrooks, & J. Mistry (Eds.), *Handbook of psychology,* Vol 6: *Developmental psychology.* New York: Wiley.

SUSSKIND, J. M., LEE, D. H., CUSI, A., FEIMAN, R., GRABSKI, W., ANDERSON, A. K., ET AL. (2008). Expressing fear enhances sensory acquisition. *Nature Neuroscience, 11,* 843–850.

SUTCLIFFE, J. S. (2008). Insights into the pathogenesis of autism. *Science, 321*(5886), 208–209.

SUTKER, P. B., ALLAIN, A. N., JR., & WINSTEAD, D. K. (1993). Psychopathology and psychiatric diagnoses of World War II Pacific Theater prisoner of war survivors and combat veterans. *American Journal of Psychiatry, 150,* 240–245.

SWANN, W. B., JR., RENTFROW, P. J., & GUINN, J. (2002). Self-verification: The search for coherence. In M. Leary and J. Tagney (Eds.), *Handbook of self and identity.* New York: Guilford.

SWEDO, S. E., PIETRINI, P., LEONARD, H. L., SCHAPIRO, M. B., RETTEW, D. C., GOLDBERGER, E. L., ET AL. (1992). Cerebral glucose metabolism in childhood-onset obsessive-compulsive disorder. Revisualization during pharmacotherapy. *Archives of General Psychiatry, 49,* 690–694.

SWETS, J. A., DAWES, R. M., & MONAHAN, J. (2000). Psychological Science can improve diagnostic decisions. *Psychological Science in the Public Interest, 1,* 1–26.

SWINGLEY, D., & FERNALD, A. (2002). Recognition of words referring to present and absent objects by 24-month-olds. *Journal of Memory and Language, 46,* 39–56.

SYMONS, D. (1979). *The evolution of human sexuality.* New York: Oxford University Press.

———

TAJFEL, H., & BILLIG, M. (1974). Familiarity and categorization in intergroup behavior. *Journal of Experimental Social Psychology, 10,* 159–170.

TAJFEL, H., BILLIG, M., BUNDY, R., & FLAMENT, C. (1971). Social categorization and intergroup behaviour. *European Journal of Social Psychology, 1,* 149–178.

TAKAHASHI, K. (1986). Examining the Strange-Situation procedure with Japanese mothers and 12-month-old infants. *Developmental Psychology, 22,* 265–270.

TAKATA, T. (1987). Self-deprecative tendencies in self-evaluation through social comparison. *Japanese Journal of Experimental Social Psychology, 27,* 27–36.

TALMI, D. GRADY, C. L., GOSHEN-GOTTSTEIN, Y., & MOSCOVITCH, M. (2005). Neuroimaging the serial position curve: A test of single-store versus dual-store models. *Psychological Science, 16,* 716–723.

TAN, H. Y., SUST, S., BUCKHOLTZ, J. W., MATAY, V. S., MEYER-LINDENBERG, A., EGAN, M. F., ET AL. (2006). Dysfunctional prefrontal region specialization and compensation in schizophrenia. *American Journal of Psychiatry, 163,* 1969–1977.

TANDON, R., & KANE, J. M. (1993). Neuropharmacologic basis for clozapine's unique profile [Letter]. *Archives of General Psychiatry, 50,* 158–159.

TANENHAUS, M. K., SPIVEY-KNOWLTON, M. J., EBERHARD, K. M., & SEDIVY, J. C. (1995). Integration of visual and linguistic information in spoken language comprehension. *Science, 268*(5217), 1632–1634.

TANENHAUS, M. K., & TRUESWELL, J. C. (2006). Eye movements and spoken language comprehension. In M. J. Traxler & M. A. Gernsbacher (Eds.), *Handbook of psycholinguistics* (2nd ed.). Amsterdam: Elsevier.

TANGNEY, J. P., BAUMEISTER, R. F., & BOONE, A. L. (2004). High self-control predicts good adjustment, less pathology, better grades, and interpersonal success. *Journal of Personality, 72,* 271–324.

TANNER, J. M. (1990). *Fetus into man: Physical growth from conception to maturity* (rev. ed.). Cambridge, MA: Harvard University Press.

TANNOCK, R. (1998). Attention deficit hyperactivity disorder: Advances in cognitive, neurobiological and genetic research. *Journal of Child Psychology and Psychiatry, 39,* 65–99.

TARBOX, S., & POGUE-GEILE, M. F. (2008). Development of social functioning in preschizophrenia children and adolescents: A systematic review. *Psychological Bulletin, 34*(4), 561–583.

TARR, M. J. (1995). Rotating objects to recognize them: A case study on the role of viewpoint dependency in the recognition of three-dimensional objects. *Psychonomic Bulletin & Review, 2,* 55–82.

TAYLOR, M., ESBENSEN, B. M., & BENNETT, R. T. (1994). Children's understanding of knowledge acquisition: The tendency for children to report that they have always known what they have just learned. *Child Development, 65*(6), 1581–1604.

TAYLOR, S. E. (2006). Tend and befriend: Biobehavioral bases of affiliation under stress. *Current Directions in Psychological Science, 15*(6), 273–277.

TAYLOR, S. E., & FISKE, S. T. (1975). Point of view and perceptions of causality. *Journal of Personality and Social Psychology, 32,* 439–445.

TAYLOR, S. E., KLEIN, L. C., LEWIS, B. P., GRUENEWALD, T. L., GURUNG, R.A.R., & UPDEGRAFF, J. A. (2000). Biobehavioral responses to stress in females: Tend-and-befriend, not fight-or-flight. *Psychological Review, 107*(3), 411–429.

TAYLOR, W. S., & MARTIN, M. F. (1944). Multiple personality. *Journal of Abnormal and Social Psychology, 39,* 281–300.

TEITELBAUM, P., & EPSTEIN, A. N. (1962). The lateral hypothalamic syndrome: Recovery of feeding and drinking after lateral hypothalamic lesions. *Psychological Review, 69,* 74–90.

TELLEGEN, A. & ATKINSON, G. (1974). Openness to absorbing and self-altering experiences ("absorption"), a trait related to hypnotic susceptibility. *Journal of Abnormal Psychology, 83,* 268–277.

TELLEGEN, A., LYKKEN, D. T., BOUCHARD, T. J., WILCOX, K. J., SEGAL, N. L., & RICH, S. (1988). Personality of twins reared apart and together. *Journal of Personality and Social Psychology, 54,* 1031–1039.

TERR, L. C. (1991). Acute responses to external events and posttraumatic stress disorders. In M. Lewis (Ed.), *Child and adolescent psychiatry: A comprehensive textbook* (pp. 755–763). Baltimore: Williams & Wilkins.

TERR, L. C. (1994). *Unchained memories: True stories of traumatic memories, lost and found.* New York: Basic.

TERRY, R., & COIE, J. D. (1991). A comparison of methods for defining sociometric status among children. *Developmental Psychology, 27*(5), 867–880.

TERVOORT, B. T. (1961). Esoteric symbolism in the communication behavior of young deaf children. *American Annals of the Deaf, 106,* 436–480.

TESSER, A., CAMPBELL, J., & SMITH, M. (1984). Friendship choice and performance: Self-evaluation maintenance in children. *Journal of Personality and Social Psychology, 46,* 561–574.

TETLOCK, P. E., PETERSON, R. S., MCGUIRE, C., CHANG, S.-J., ET AL. (1992). Assessing political group dynamics: A test of the groupthink model. *Journal of Personality and Social Psychology, 63*(3), 403–425.

THAPAR, A., & GREENE, R. (1994). Effects of level of processing on implicit and explicit tasks. *Journal of Experimental Psychology: Learning, Memory and Cognition, 20,* 671–679.

THARA, R. (2004). Twenty-year course of schizophrenia: The Madras Longitudinal Study. *Canadian Journal of Psychiatry, 49,* 564–569.

THELEN, E., SCHÖNER, G., SCHIER, C., & SMITH, L. B. (2001). The dynamics of embodiment: A field theory of infant perseverative reaching. *Behavioral & Brain Sciences, 24,* 34–86.

THEWISSEN, J.G.M., COOPER, L. N., CLEMENTS, M. T., BAJPAI, S., & TIWARI, B. N. (2009). Hippopotamus and whale phylogeny: Reply. *Nature, 458,* E5.

THIOUX, M., STARK, D. E., KLAIMAN, C., & SCHULTZ, R. T. (2006). The day of the week when you were born in 700 ms: Calendar computation in an autistic savant. *Journal of Experimental Psychology: Human Perception and Performance, 32,* 1155–1168.

THOMAS, A., & CHESS, S. (1977). *Temperament and development.* New York: Brunner/Mazel.

THOMAS, A., & CHESS, S. (1984). Genesis and evaluation of behavioral disorders: From infancy to early adult life. *American Journal of Psychiatry, 141,* 1–9.

THOMSEN, D. K., & BERNTSEN, D. (2009). The long-term impact of emotionally stressful events on memory characteristics and life story. *Applied Cognitive Psychology, 23,* 579–598.

THOMPSON, C. P., & COWAN, T. (1986). Flashbulb memories: A nicer recollection of a Neisser recollection. *Cognition, 22,* 199–200.

THOMPSON, M. M., ZANNA, M. P., & GRIFFIN, D. W. (1995). Let's not be indifferent about (attitudinal) ambivalence. In R. E. Petty & J. A. Krosnick (Eds.), *Attitude strength: Antecedents and consequences: Vol. 4* (pp. 361–386). Mahwah, NJ: Erlbaum.

THOMPSON, R. A. (1994). Emotion regulation: A theme in search of definition. In N. Fox (Ed.), *The development of emotion regulation and dysregulation: Biological and behavioral aspects. Monographs of the Society for Research in Child Development, 59*(240), 25–52.

THOMPSON, R. A. (1998). Early sociopersonality development. In W. Damon (Ed.), *Handbook of child psychology* (5th ed.): *Vol. 3. Social, emotional, and personality development* (N. Eisenberg, Vol. Ed.; pp. 25–104). New York: Wiley.

THOMPSON, R. A. (1999). Early attachment and later development. In J. Cassidy & P. Shaver (Eds.), *Handbook of attachment* (pp. 265–286). New York: Guilford.

THOMPSON, R. A. (2000). The legacy of early attachments. *Child Development, 71,* 145–152.

THOMPSON, R. A. (2006). The development of the person: Social understanding, relationships, self, conscience. In W. Damon & R. M. Lerner (Eds.), *Handbook of child psychology* (6th ed.): *Vol. 3. Social, emotional, and* personality development (N. Eisenberg, Vol. Ed.). New York: Wiley.

THOMPSON, R. A., LAIBLE, D., & ONTAI, L. (2003). Early understanding of emotion, morality, and the self: Developing a working model. In R. Kail (Ed.), *Advances in Child Development and Behavior: Vol. 31* (pp. 137–171). San Diego: Academic.

THOMPSON, W. L., & KOSSLYN, S. M. (2000). Neural systems activated during visual mental imagery: A review and meta-analyses. In J. Mazziotta & A. Toga (Eds.), *Brain mapping II: The applications.* New York: Academic Press.

THORNHILL, R., & GANGESTAD, S. G. (1999). Facial attractiveness. *Trends in Cognitive Science, 3,* 452–460.

TIERNEY, A. J. (2000). Egas Moniz and the origins of psychosurgery: A review commemorating the 50th anniversary of Moniz's Nobel Prize. *Journal of the History of Neuroscience, 9,* 22–36.

TIETJEN, A. M., & WALKER, L. J. (1985). Moral reasoning and leadership among men in a Papua New Guinea society. *Developmental Psychology, 21,* 982–989.

TIMBERLAKE, W. (1995). Reconceptualizing reinforcement: A causal system approach to reinforcement and behavior change. In W. O'Donohue & L. Krasner (Eds.), *Theories in behavior therapy* (pp. 59–96). Washington, DC: APA Books.

TIMBERLAKE, W., & ALLISON, J. (1974). Response deprivation: An empirical approach to instrumental performance. *Psychological Review, 81,* 146–164.

TODOROV, A., MANDISODZA, A., GOREN, A., & HALL, C. (2005). Inferences of competence from faces predict election outcomes. *Science, 308*(5728), 1623–1626.

TOLIN, D. F., & FOA, E. B. (2006). Sex differences in trauma and posttraumatic stress disorder: A quantitative review of 25 years of research. *Psychological Bulletin, 132*(6), 959–992.

TOLMAN, E. C. (1932). *Purposive behavior in animals and men.* New York: Appleton-Century-Crofts.

TOLMAN, E. C. (1948). Cognitive maps in rats and men. *Psychological Review, 55,* 189–208.

TOLMAN, E. C., & HONZIK, C. H. (1930). Introduction and removal of reward, and maze performance in rats. *University of California Publications in Psychology, 4,* 257–275.

TOLSTOY, L. (1868). *War and peace* (second epilogue). H. Gifford (Ed.), L. Maude & A. Maude (Trans.). New York: Oxford University Press, 1922.

TOMASELLO, M. (1994). Can an ape understand a sentence? A review of *Language comprehension in ape and child* by E. S. Savage-Rumbaugh et al. *Language & Communication, 14,* 377–390.

TOMASELLO, M. (2000). *The cultural origins of human cognition.* Cambridge, MA: Harvard University Press.

TOMASELLO, M. (2001). Perceiving intentions and learning words in the second year of life. In M. Bowerman & S. Levinson (Eds.), *Language acquisition and conceptual development.* New York: Cambridge University Press.

TOMASELLO, M. (2002). The social bases of language acquisition. *Social Development, 1*(1), 67–87.

TOMASELLO, M. (2003). *Constructing a language.* Cambridge, MA: Harvard University Press.

TOMASELLO, M. (2008). *Origins of human communication.* Cambridge, MA: MIT Press.

TOMASELLO, M., & FARRAR, M. J. (1986). Joint attention and early language. *Child Development, 57,* 1454–1463.

TOMASELLO, M., KRUGER, A., & RATNER, H. (1993). Cultural learning. *Behavioral and Brain Sciences, 16,* 495–552.

TOMASELLO, M., STROSBERG R., & AKHTAR, N. (1996). Eighteen month old children learn words in non-ostensive contexts. *Journal of Child Language, 23,* 157–176.

TOMKINS, S. S. (1962). *Affect, imagery, consciousness: The positive affects* (Vol. 1). New York: Springer.

TOMKINS, S. S. (1963). *Affect, imagery, consciousness: Vol. 2. The negative affects.* New York: Springer.

TONG, F., NAKAYAMA, K., VAUGHAN, J. T., & KANWISHER, N. (1998). Binocular rivalry and visual awareness in human extrastriate cortex. *Neuron, 21,* 753–759.

TONONI, G. (2004). An information integration theory of consciousness. *BMC Neuroscience 5*(42).

TOOBY, J., & COSMIDES, L. (1990). The past explains the present: Emotional adaptations and the structure of ancestral environments. *Ethology and Sociobiology, 11,* 375–424.

TORGERSEN, S. (1986). Genetic factors in moderately severe and mild affective disorders. *Archives of General Psychiatry, 43,* 222–226.

TORREY, E. F. (1983). *Surviving schizophrenia: A family manual.* New York: Harper & Row.

TORREY, E. F. (1992). *Freudian fraud: The malignant effect of Freud's theory on American thought and culture.* New York: HarperCollins.

TOURANGEAU, R., & ELLSWORTH, P. C. (1979). The role of facial response in the experience of emotion. *Journal of Personality and Social Psychology, 37,* 1519–1531.

TRACY, J. L., & ROBINS, R. W. (2008). The nonverbal expression of pride: Evidence for cross-cultural recognition. *Journal of Personality and Social Psychology, 94*(3), 516–530.

TREISMAN, A. M. (1986a). Features and objects in visual processing. *Scientific American, 255,* 114–125.

TREISMAN, A. M. (1986b). Properties, parts, and objects. In K. R. Boff, L. Kaufman, & J. P. Thomas (Eds.), *Handbook of perception and human performance: Vol. II* (Chapter 35). New York: Wiley.

TREISMAN, A. M. (1988). Features and objects: The Fourteenth Barlett Memorial Lecture. *Quarterly Journal of Experimental Psychology, 40A,* 201–237.

TREISMAN, A. M., & GELADE, G. (1980). A feature-integration theory of attention. *Cognitive Psychology, 12,* 97–136.

TREISMAN, A. M., & SOUTHER, J. (1985). Search assymetry: A diagnostic for preattentive processing of separable features. *Journal of Experimental Psychology: General, 114,* 285–310.

TREYNOR, W., GONZALEZ, R., & NOLEN-HOEKSEMA, S. (2003). Rumination reconsidered: A psychometric analysis. *Cognitive Therapy and Research, 27*(3), 247–259.

TRIANDIS, H. (1994). Major cultural syndromes and emotion. In S. Kitayama & H. R. Markus (Eds.), *Emotion and culture* (pp. 285–306). Washington, DC: American Psychological Association.

TRIANDIS, H. C. (1989). Cross-cultural studies of individualism and collectivism. *Nebraska Symposium on Motivation, 37,* 41–134. Lincoln: University of Nebraska Press.

TRIANDIS, H. C., & SUH, E. M. (2002). Cultural influences on personality. *Annual Review of Psychology, 53*(1), 133–160.

TRIMBLE, J. E. (1993). Cultural variations in the use of alcohol and drugs. In W. Lonner & R. Malpass (Eds.), *Readings in psychology and culture.* Boston, MA: Allyn & Bacon.

TRIPLETT, N. (1898). The dynamogenic factors in pacemaking and competition. *American Journal of Psychology, 9,* 507–533.

TRIVERS, R. L. (1972). Parental investment and sexual selection. In B. Campbell (Ed.), *Sexual selection and the descent of man* (pp. 139–179). Chicago: Aldine.

TROPP, L. R., & PETTIGREW, T. F. (2005). Relationships between intergroup contact and prejudice among minority and majority status groups. *Psychological Science, 16,* 951–957.

TRUE, W. R., RISE, J., EISEN, S., HEATH, A. C., GOLDBERG, J., LYONS, M., ET AL. (1993). A twin study of genetic and environmental contributions to liability for posttraumatic stress symptoms. *Archives of General Psychiatry, 50,* 257–264.

TRUESWELL, J. C., SEKERINA, I., HILL, N. M., & LOGRIP, M. L. (1999). The kindergarten-path effect: Studying on-line sentence processing in young children. *Cognition, 73*(2), 89–134.

TRUESWELL, J. C., & TANENHAUS, M. K. (1992). Consulting temporal context during reading. In *Proceedings of the 14th Annual Conference of the Cognitive Science Society* (pp. 492–497). Hillsdale, NJ: Erlbaum.

TRUESWELL, J. C., & TANENHAUS, M. K. (1994). Toward a lexicalist framework of constraint-based syntactic ambiguity resolution. In C. Clifton, Jr., & L. Frazier (Eds.), *Perspectives on sentence processing* (pp. 155–179). Hillsdale, NJ: Erlbaum.

TRUESWELL, J. C., TANENHAUS, M. K., & GARNSEY, S. M. (1994). Semantic influences on parsing: Use of thematic role information in syntactic ambiguity resolution. *Journal of Memory and Language, 33,* 285–318.

TSAI, J. L., & CHENTSOVA-DUTTON, Y. (2002). Different models of cultural orientation in American- and overseas-born Asian Americans. In K. Kurasaki, S. Okazaki, & S. Sue (Eds.), *Asian American mental health: Assessment theories and methods* (pp. 95–106). New York: Kluwer Academic/Plenum.

TSUANG, M. T., GILBERTSON, M. W., & FARAONE, S. V. (1991). The genetics of schizophrenia. *Schizophrenia Research, 4,* 157–171.

TUCKER, M., & ELLIS, R. (2001). The potentiation of grasp types during visual object categorization. *Visual Cognition, 8,* 769–800.

TUCKER, M., & ELLIS, R. (2004). Action priming by briefly presented objects. *Acta Psychologica, 116,* 185–203.

TULVING, E. (1985). How many memory systems are there? *American Psychologist, 40*, 385–398.

TULVING, E., & OSLER, S. (1968). Effectiveness of retrieved cues in memory for words. *Journal of Experimental Psychology, 77*, 593–606.

TULVING, E., SCHACTER, D. L., McLACHLAN, D. R., & MOSCOVITCH, M. (1988). Priming of semantic autobiographical knowledge: A case study of retrograde amnesia. *Brain and Cognition, 8*, 3–20.

TULVING, E., SCHACTER, D. L., & STARK, H. A. (1982). Priming effects in word-fragment completion are independent of recognition memory. *Journal of Experimental Psychology: Learning, Memory, and Cognition, 8*, 336–342.

TULVING, E., & THOMSON, D. M. (1973). Encoding specificity and retrieval processes in episodic memory. *Psychological Review, 80*, 352–373.

TUPES, E. C., & CHRISTAL, R. E. (1961, May). *Recurrent personality factors based on trait ratings (ASD-TR-61–97)*. Lackland Air Force Base, TX: Aeronautical Systems Division, Personnel Laboratory.

TURATI, C. (2004). Why faces are not special to newborns: An alternative account of the face preference. *Current Directions in Psychological Science, 13*, 5–8.

TURKHEIMER, E., HALEY, A., WALDRON, M., D'ONOFRIO, B., & GOTTESMAN, I. I. (2003). Socioeconomic status modifies heritability of IQ in young children. *Psychological Science, 14*, 623–628.

TURKHEIMER, E., & WALDRON, M. (2000). Nonshared environment: A theoretical, methodological, and quantitative review. *Psychological Bulletin, 126*(1), 78–108.

TURNER, J., BROWN, R., & TAJFEL, H. (1979). Social comparison and group interest in ingroup favouritism. *European Journal of Social Psychology, 9*, 187–204.

TVERSKY, A. (1977). Features of similarity. *Psychological Review, 84*(4), 327–352.

TVERSKY, A., & KAHNEMAN, D. (1973). Availability: A heuristic for judging frequency and probability. *Cognitive Psychology, 5*, 207–232.

TVERSKY, A., & KAHNEMAN, D. (1981). The framing of decisions and the psychology of choice. *Science, 211*, 453–458.

TWENEY, R. D., DOHERTY, M. E., & MYNATT, C. R. (1981). *On scientific thinking*. New York: Columbia University Press.

TYACK, P. (2000). Functional aspects of cetacean communication. In J. Mann, R. C. Connor, P. L. Tyack, & H. Whitehead (Eds.), *Cetacean societies* (pp. 270–307). Chicago: University of Chicago Press.

TYLER, L. K., BRIGHT, P., FLETCHER, P., & STAMATAKIS, E. A. (2004). Neural processing of nouns and verbs: The role of inflectional morphology. *Neuropsychologia, 42*(4), 512–523.

UNGERLEIDER, L. G., & HAXBY, J. V. (1994). "What" and "where" in the human brain. *Current Opinions in Neurobiology, 4*, 157–165.

UNGERLEIDER, L. G., & MISHKIN, M. (1982). Two cortical visual systems. In D. J. Ingle, M. A. Goodale, & R. J. W. Mansfield (Eds.), *Analysis of visual behavior* (pp. 549–586). Cambridge, MA: MIT Press.

U.S. DEPARTMENT OF HEALTH AND HUMAN SERVICES. (1999). *Mental health: A report of the surgeon general*. Rockville, MD: Author.

U.S. DEPARTMENT OF HEALTH AND HUMAN SERVICES. (2001). *Mental health: Culture, race, and ethnicity—A supplement to mental health: A report of the Surgeon General*. Rockville, MD: U.S. Department of Health and Human Services, Public Health Service, Office of the Surgeon General.

U.S. DEPARTMENT OF LABOR. (1995). *Marital and family characteristics of the labor force from the March 1994 Current Population Survey*. Washington, DC: Bureau of Labor Statistics.

URBERG, K. A., DEGIRMENCIOGLU, S. M., & PILGRIM, C. (1997). Close friend and group influence on adolescent cigarette smoking and alcohol use. *Developmental Psychology, 33*(5), 834–844.

URWIN, C. (1983). Dialogue and cognitive functioning in the early language development of three blind children. In A. E. Mills (Ed.), *Language acquisition in the blind child*. London: Croom Helm.

VAILLANT, G. E. (1974). Natural history of male psychological health: II. Some antecedents of healthy adult adjustment. *Archives of General Psychiatry, 31*, 15–22.

VAILLANT, G. E. (1976). Natural history of male psychological health: V: Relation of choice of ego mechanisms of defense to adult adjustment. *Archives of General Psychiatry, 33*, 535–545.

VAILLANT, G. E. (1977). *Adaptation to life*. Boston: Little, Brown.

VAILLANT, G. E. (1994). "Successful aging" and psychosocial well-being: Evidence from a 45-year study. In E. H. Thompson (Ed.), *Older men's lives: Vol. 6. Research on men and masculinities* (pp. 2–41). Thousand Oaks, CA: Sage.

VAILLANT, G. E., BOND, M., & VAILLANT, C. O. (1986). An empirically validated hierarchy of defense mechanisms. *Archives of General Psychiatry, 43*, 786–794.

VALENSTEIN, E. S. (1986). *Great and desperate cures*. New York: Basic Books.

VALENZUELA, M. (1990). Attachment in chronically underweight young children. *Child Development, 61*, 1984–1996.

VALENZUELA, M. (1997). Maternal sensitivity in a developing society: The context of urban poverty and infant chronic undernutrition. *Developmental Psychology, 33*, 845–855.

VAN DE VLIERT, E. (2006). Autocratic leadership around the globe: Do climate and wealth drive leadership culture? *Journal of Cross-Cultural Psychology, 37*(1), 42–59.

VAN DER LELY, H. K., & CHRISTIAN, V. (2000). Lexical word formation in Grammatical SLI children: A grammar-specific or input processing deficit? *Cognition, 75*, 33–63.

VAN ESSEN, D. C., & DeYOE, E. A. (1995). Concurrent processing in the primate visual cortex. In M. S. Gazzaniga (Ed.), *The cognitive neurosciences* (pp. 383–400). Cambridge, MA: MIT Press.

VAN GEERT, P. (2002). Developmental dynamics, intentional action, and fuzzy sets. In N. Granott & J. Parziale (Eds.), *Microdevelopment: Transition processes in development and learning*. New York: Cambridge University Press.

VAN GOOZEN, S., COHEN-KETTENIS, P., GOOREN, L., FRIJDA, N., & VAN DE POLL, N. (1995). Gender differences in behavior: Activating cross-sex hormones. *Psychoneuroendocrinology, 20*, 343–363.

VAN IJZENDOORN, M. (1997). Attachment, emergent morality and aggression: Toward a developmental socioemotional model of antisocial behaviour. *International Journal of Behavioral Development, 21*, 703–727.

VAN IJZENDOORN, M., SCHUENGEL, C., & BAKERMANS-KRANENBURG, M. (1999). Disorganized attachment in early childhood: Meta-analysis of precursors, concomitants, and sequelae. *Development and Psychopathology, 11*, 225–249.

VAN SICKLE, M., DUNCAN, M., KINGSLEY, P., MOUIHATE, A., URBANI, P., MACKIE, K., ET AL. (2005). Identification and functional characterization of brainstem cannabinoid CB2 receptors. *Science, 310*, 329–332.

VANDELL, D. L. (2000). Parents, peer groups, and other socializing influences. *Developmental Psychology, 36*(6), 699–710.

VANDELL, D. L., HENDERSON, V. K., & WILSON, K. S. (1988). A longitudinal study of children with day care experiences of varying quality. *Child Development, 59*, 1286–1292.

VAUGHN, B. E., EGELAND, B. R., SROUFE, L. A., & WATERS, E. (1979). Individual differences in infant-mother attachment at twelve and eighteen months: Stability and change in families under stress. *Child Development, 50*, 971–975.

VAULTIN, R. G., & BERKELEY, M. A. (1977). Responses of single cells in cat visual cortex to prolonged stimulus movement: Neural correlates of visual aftereffects. *Journal of Neurophysiology, 40*, 1051–1065.

VEIZOVIC, T., BEECH, J. S., STROEMER, R. P., WATSON, W. P., & HODGES, H. (2001). Resolution of stroke deficits following contralateral grafts of conditionally immortal neuroepithelial stem cells. *Stroke, 32*, 1012–1019.

VENTER, J. C., ADAMS, M. D., MYERS, E. W., LI, P. W., MURAL, R. J., SUTTON, G. G., ET AL. (2001). The sequence of the human genome. *Science, 291*, 1304–1351.

VERHAEGHEN, P., & SALTHOUSE, T. A. (1997). Meta-analyses of age-cognition relations in adulthood: Estimates of linear and nonlinear age effects and structural models. *Psychological Bulletin, 122*(3), 231–249.

VERKHRATSKY, A. (1998). Calcium signalling in glial cells. *Journal of Physiology, 506*, 15.

VERNON, P. A. (ED.). (1987). *Speed of information processing and intelligence*. Canada: Ablex.

VICKERS, J. C., DICKSON, T. C., ADLARD, P. A., & SAUNDERS, H. L. (2000). The causes of neural degeneration in Alzheimer's disease. *Neurobiology, 60*, 139–165.

VISSER, B., ASHTON, M., & VERNON, P. (2006). Beyond "g": Putting multiple intelligences theory to the test. *Intelligence, 34*, 487–502.

VITEVITCH, M. S. (2003). Change deafness: The inability to detect changes between two voices. *Journal of Experimental Psychology: Human Perception and Performance, 29*, 333–342.

VOLKMAR, F. R., SZATMARI, P., & SPARROW, S. S. (1993). Sex differences in pervasive developmental disorders. *Journal of Autism and Developmental Disorders, 23,* 579–591.

VONDRA, J., SHAW, D., SWEARINGEN, L., COHEN, M., & OWENS, E. (2001). Attachment stability and emotional and behavioral regulation from infancy to preschool age. *Development and Psychopathology, 13,* 13–33.

VRIJ, A. (2002). Deception in children: A literature review and implications for children's testimony. In H. Westcott, G. Davies, & R. Bull (Eds.), *Children's testimony: A handbook of psychological research and forensic practice* (pp. 175–194). New York: Wiley.

VUL, E., & PASHLER, H. (2007). Incubation benefits only after people have been misdirected. *Memory and Cognition, 35,* 701–710.

VUONG, Q. C., & TARR, M. J. (2004). Rotation direction affects object recognition. *Vision Research, 44,* 1717–1730.

VYGOTSKY, L. S. (1978). *Mind in society.* Cambridge, MA: Harvard University Press.

———

WACHTEL, P. L. (1977). *Psychoanalysis and behavior therapy: Toward an integration.* New York: Basic Books.

WACHTEL, P. L. (1982). What can dynamic therapies contribute to behavior therapy? *Behavior Therapy, 13,* 594–609.

WADDINGTON, J. L., TORREY, E. F., CROW, T. J., & HIRSCH, S. R. (1991). Schizophrenia, neurodevelopment, and disease. *Archives of General Psychiatry, 48,* 271–273.

WAGNER, A. D., KOUTSTAAL, W., & SCHACTER, D. L. (1999). When encoding yields remembering: Insights from event-related neuroimaging. *Philosophical Transactions of the Royal Society of London, Biology, 354,* 1307–1324.

WAGNER, A. D., SCHACTER, D. L., ROTTE, M., KOUTSTAAL, W., MARIL, A., DALE, A., ET AL. (1998). Building memories: Remembering and forgetting of verbal experiences as predicted by brain activity. *Science, 281,* 1188–1191.

WAGNER, A. D., SHANNON, B. J., KAHN, I., & BUCKNER, R. (2005). Parietal lobe contributions to episodic memory retrieval. *Trends in Cognitive Science, 9,* 445–453.

WAGNER, R. K. (1987). Tacit knowledge in everyday intelligent behavior. *Journal of Personality and Social Psychology, 52,* 1236–1247.

WAGNER, R. K. (2000). Practical intelligence. In R. J. Sternberg (Ed.), *Handbook of human intelligence* (pp. 380–395). New York: Cambridge University Press.

WAGNER, R. K., & STERNBERG, R. J. (1987). Tacit knowledge in managerial success. *Journal of Business and Psychology, 1,* 301–312.

WAKEFIELD, J. C. (1992). The concept of mental disorder: On the boundary between biological facts and social values. *American Psychologist, 47*(3), 373–388.

WALKER, E., GRIMES, K. E., DAVIS, D. M., & SMITH, A. J. (1993). Childhood precursors of schizophrenia: Facial expressions of emotion. *American Journal of Psychiatry, 150,* 1654–1660.

WALKER, E., KESTLER, L., BOLLINI, A., & HOCHMAN, K. (2004). Schizophrenia: Etiology and course. *Annual Review of Psychology, 55,* 401–430.

WALKER, E., SAVOIE, T., & DAVIS, D. (1994). Neuromotor precursors of schizophrenia. *Schizophrenia Bulletin, 20,* 441–452.

WALKER, L. J. (1984). Sex differences in the development of moral reasoning: A critical review. *Child Development, 55,* 677–691.

WALKER, L. J. (1989). Sex differences in the development of moral reasoning: A reply to Baumrind. *Child Development, 57,* 522–526.

WALKER, L. J. (1995). Sexism in Kohlberg's moral psychology. In W. M. Kurtines & J. L. Gewirtz (Eds.), *Moral development: An introduction.* Boston: Allyn & Bacon.

WALKER, L. J., & MORAN, T. J. (1991). Moral reasoning in a communist Chinese society. *Journal of Moral Education, 20,* 139–155.

WALKER, M. P., BRAKEFIELD, T., HOBSON, J. A., & STICKGOLD, R. (2003). Dissociable stages of human memory consolidation and reconsolidation. *Nature, 425,* 616–620.

WALKUP, J. T., ALBANO, A., PIACENTINI, J., BIRMAHER, B., COMPTON, S. N., SHERRILL, J. T., ET AL. (2008). Cognitive behavioral therapy, sertraline, or a combination in childhood anxiety. *New England Journal of Medicine, 359,* 2753–2766.

WALLACE, J., SCHNEIDER, T., & MCGUFFIN, P. (2002). Genetics of depression. In I. Gotlib & C. Hammen (Eds.), *Handbook of depression* (pp. 169–191). New York: Guilford.

WALLACE, P. (1977). Individual discrimination of humans by odor. *Physiology and Behavior, 19,* 577–579.

WALLACE, R. L., GILBERT, J. J., & KING, C. E. (2001). In memoriam: WT Edmondson (1916–2000). *Hydrobiologia, 446/447,* xv–xxi.

WALLAS, G. (1926). *The art of thought.* New York: Harcourt, Brace.

WALLER, N. G., & ROSS, C. A. (1997). The prevalence and biometric structure of pathological dissociation in the general population: Taxometric and behavior genetic findings. *Journal of Abnormal Psychology, 106,* 499–510.

WALSH, J. K., DEMENT, W. C., & DINGES, D. F. (2005). Sleep medicine, public policy, and public health. In M. H. Kryger, T. Roth, & W. C. Dement (Eds.), *Principles and practice of sleep medicine.* Philadelphia: Elsevier Saunders.

WALSTER, E., ARONSON, E., & ABRAHAMS, D. (1966). On increasing the persuasiveness of a low prestige communicator. *Journal of Experimental Social Psychology, 2,* 325–342.

WALSTER, E., ARONSON, E., ABRAHAMS, D., & ROTTMAN, L. (1966). The importance of physical attractiveness in dating behavior. *Journal of Personality and Social Psychology, 4,* 508–516.

WAMPOLD, B. E., MONDIN, G. W., MOODY, M., STICH, F., BENSON, K., & AHN, H. (1997). A meta-analysis of outcome studies comparing bona fide psychotherapies: Empirically, "all must have prizes." *Psychological Bulletin, 122,* 203–216.

WANG, P. S., BERGLUND, P., OLFSON, M., PINCUS, H. A., WELLS, K. B., & KESSLER, R. C. (2005). Failure and delay in initial treatment contact after first onset of mental disorders in the National Comorbidity Survey Replication. *Archives of General Psychiatry, 62*(6): 603–613.

WANG, P. S., LANE, M., OLFSON, M., PINCUS, H. A., WELLS, K. B., & KESSLER, R. C. (2005). Twelve-month use of mental health services in the United States: results from the National Comorbidity Survey Replication. *Archives of General Psychiatry, 62*(6): 629–640.

WAPNER, W. T., JUDD, T., & GARDNER, H. (1978). Visual agnosia in an artist. *Cortex, 14,* 343–364.

WARD, S. L., & OVERTON, W. F. (1990). Semantic familiarity, relevance, and the development of deductive reasoning. *Developmental Psychology, 26,* 488–493.

WARREN, S. L., HUSTON, L., EGELAND, B., & SROUFE, L. A. (1997). Child and adolescent anxiety disorders and early attachment. *Journal of the American Academy of Child & Adolescent Psychiatry, 36,* 637–644.

WARRINGTON, E. K., & WEISKRANTZ, L. (1978). Further analysis of the prior learning effect in amnesic patients. *Neuropsychologia, 16,* 169–176.

WASON, P. C. (1960). On the failure to eliminate hypotheses in a conceptual task. *Quarterly Journal of Experimental Psychology, 12,* 129–140.

WASON, P. C. (1966). Reasoning. In B. Foss (Ed.), *New horizons in psychology* (pp. 135–151). Middlesex, England: Penguin.

WASON, P. C. (1968). On the failure to eliminate hypotheses—A second look. In P. C. Wason & P. N. Johnson-Laird (Eds.), *Thinking and reasoning.* Harmondsworth, England: Penguin.

WASSERMAN, E. A., HUGART, J. A., & KIRKPATRICK-STEGER, K. (1995). Pigeons show same-different conceptualization after training with complex visual stimuli. *Journal of Experimental Psychology: Animal Behavior Processes, 21,* 248–252.

WATERHOUSE, L., FEIN, D., & MODAHL, C. (1996). Neurofunctional mechanisms in autism. *Psychological Review, 103,* 457–489.

WATERS, E., & CUMMINGS, E. M. (2000). A secure base from which to explore close relationships. *Child Development, 71*(1), 164–172.

WATERS, E., MERRICK, S., TREBOUX, D., CROWELL, J., & ALBERSHEIM, L. (2000). Attachment security in infancy and early adulthood: A twenty-year longitudinal study. *Child Development, 71,* 684–689.

WATERS, E., WIPPMAN, J., & SROUFE, L. A. (1979). Attachment, positive affect, and competence in the peer group: Two studies in construct validation. *Child Development, 50,* 821–829.

WATKINS, C. E., CAMPBELL, V. L., NIEBERDING, R., & HALLMARK, R. (1995). Contemporary practice of psychological assessment by clinical psychologists. *Professional Psychology: Research and Practice, 26,* 54–60.

WATKINS, M., WILSON, S., KOTZ, K., CARBONE, M., & BABULA, T. (2006). Factor structure of the Wechsler Intelligence Scale for Children—Fourth edition among referred students. *Educational and Psychological Measurement, 66,* 975–983.

WATSON, D., & CLARK, L. A. (1992). Affects separable and inseparable: On the hierarchical arrangement of the negative affects. *Journal of Personality and Social Psychology, 62,* 489–505.

WATSON, D., & CLARK, L. A. (1994). The vicissitudes of mood: A schematic model. In P. Ekman and R. Davidson

(Eds.), *The nature of emotion: Fundamental questions* (pp. 400–405). New York: Oxford University Press.

WATSON, J. B. (1925). *Behaviorism.* New York: Norton.

WATSON, J. B., & RAYNER, R. (1920). Conditioned emotional reactions. *Journal of Experimental Psychology, 3,* 1–14.

WATSON, J. S. (1967). Memory and "contingency analysis" in infant learning. *Merrill-Palmer Quarterly, 13,* 55–76.

WAUGH, N. C., & NORMAN, D. A. (1965). Primary memory. *Psychological Review, 72,* 89–104.

WEBB, W. B. (1972). Sleep deprivation: Total, partial, and selective. In M. H. Chase (Ed.), *The sleeping brain* (pp. 323–362). Los Angeles: Brain Information Service, Brain Research Institute.

WEBB, W. (1974). Sleep as an adaptive response. *Perceptual and Motor Skills, 38* (3), 1023–1027.

WEBB, W. (1994). Sleep as a biological rhythm: A historical review. *Sleep, 17* (2), 188–194.

WECHSLER, D. (1958). *The measurement and appraisal of adult intelligence* (4th ed.). Baltimore: Williams & Wilkins.

WECHSLER, D. (2003). *Wechsler intelligence scale for children—Fourth edition.* San Antonio, TX: Psychological Corporation.

WECHSLER, H., DAVENPORT, A., DOWDALL, G., MOEYKENS, B., & CASTILLO, S. (1994). Health and behavioral consequences of binge drinking in college: A national survey of students at 140 campuses. *Journal of the American Medical Association, 272,* 1672–1677.

WEEDEN, J., & SABINI, J. (2005). Physical attractiveness and health in Western societies: A review. *Psychological Bulletin, 131,* 635–653.

WEEKS, J. W., HEIMBERG, R. G., RODEBAUGH, T. L., & NORTON, P. J. (2008). Exploring the relationship between fear of positive evaluation and social anxiety. *Journal of Anxiety Disorders, 22*(3), 386–400.

WEGNER, D. M. (2002). *The illusion of conscious will.* Cambridge, MA: MIT Press.

WEINFIELD, N., SROUFE, L., & EGELAND, B. (2000). Attachment from infancy to early adulthood in a high-risk sample: Continuity, discontinuity, and their correlates. *Child Development, 71,* 695–702.

WEINGARTNER, H., & PARKER, E. S. (EDS.). (1984). *Memory consolidation: Psychobiology of cognition.* Hillsdale, NJ: Erlbaum.

WEISBERG, R. (1986). *Creativity: Genius and other myths.* New York: Freeman.

WEISKRANTZ, L. (1986). *Blindsight: A case study and implications.* Oxford, England: Clarendon.

WEISKRANTZ, L. (1997). *Consciousness lost and found.* New York: Oxford University Press.

WEISKRANTZ, L., & WARRINGTON, E. K. (1979). Conditioning in amnesic patients. *Neuropsychologia, 18,* 177–184.

WEISS, A., KING, J. E., & FIGUEREDO, A. J. (2000). The heritability of personality factors in chimpanzees (Pan troglodytes). *Behavior Genetics, 30,* 213–221.

WEISS, L. H., & SCHWARZ, J. C. (1996). The relationship between parenting types and older adolescents' personality, academic achievement, adjustment, and substance use. *Child Development, 67,* 2101–2114.

WEISS, Y., SIMONCELLI, E. P., & ADELSON, E. H. (2002). Motion illusions as optimal percepts. *Nature Neuroscience, 5*(6), 598–604.

WEISSMAN, M. M., & MARKOWITZ, J. C. (1994). Interpersonal psychotherapy: Current status. *Archives of General Psychiatry, 51,* 599–606.

WEISZ, J. R., DOSS, A., & HAWLEY, K. (2005). Youth psychotherapy outcome research: A review and critique of the evidence base. *Annual Review of Psychology, 56,* 337–364.

WEISZ, J. R., DOSS, A. J., & HAWLEY, K. M. (2006). Evidence-based youth psychotherapies versus usual clinical care: A meta-analysis of direct comparisons. *American Psychologist, 61,* 671–689.

WEISZ, J. R., HAWLEY, K., & DOSS, A. (2004). Empirically tested psychotherapies for youth internalizing and externalizing problems and disorders. *Child and Adolescent Psychiatric Clinics of North America, 13,* 729–815.

WELDON, M. S. (2001). Remembering as a social process. *Psychology of Learning and Motivation, 40,* 67–120.

WELLMAN, H., CROSS, D., & WATSON, J. (2001). Meta-analysis of theory-of-mind development: The truth about false belief. *Child Development, 72,* 655–684.

WELLMAN, H., & GELMAN, S. (1992). Cognitive development: Foundational theories of core domains. *Annual Review of Psychology, 43,* 337–375.

WELLMAN, H., & LAGATUTTA, K. H. (2000). In S. Baron-Cohen, H. Tager-Flusberg, & D. J. Cohen (Eds.), *Understanding other minds* (pp. 21–49). New York: Oxford University Press.

WELLMAN, H. M. (1990). *The child's theory of mind.* Cambridge, MA: MIT Press.

WELLMAN, H. M., & BARTSCH, K. (1988). Young children's reasoning about beliefs. *Cognition, 30,* 239–277.

WELLMAN, H. M., & WOOLEY, J. D. (1990). From simple desires to ordinary beliefs: The early development of everyday psychology. *Cognition, 35,* 245–275.

WELLS, G., & OLSON, E. (2002). Eyewitness identification. *Annual Review of Psychology, 54,* 277–295.

WELLS, G. L., OLSON, E. A., & CHARMAN, S. D. (2002). The confidence of eyewitnesses in their identifications from lineups. *Current Directions in Psychological Science, 11,* 151–154.

WENDER, P. H., KETY, S. S., ROSENTHAL, D., SCHULSINGER, F., & ORTMANN, J. (1986). Psychiatric disorders in the biological relatives of adopted individuals with affective disorders. *Archives of General Psychiatry, 43,* 923–929.

WEREBE, M. G., & BAUDONNIERE, P.-M. (1991). Social pretend play among friends and familiar preschoolers. *International Journal of Behavioral Development, 14*(4), 411–428.

WERKER, J. (1991). The ontogeny of speech perception. In I. G. Mattingly & M. Studdert-Kennedy (Eds.), *Modularity and the motor theory of speech perception: Proceedings of a conference to honor Alvin M. Liberman* (pp. 91–109). Hillsdale, NJ: Erlbaum.

WERKER, J. F. (1995). Exploring developmental changes in cross-language speech perception. In L. R. Gleitman & M. Liberman (Eds.), *An invitation to cognitive science: Vol. 1* (pp. 87–106). Cambridge, MA: MIT Press.

WERKER, J. F., & TEES, R. C. (1984). Cross-language speech perception: Evidence for perceptual reorganization during the first year of life. *Infant Behavior and Development, 7,* 49–63.

WERTHEIMER, M. (1912). Experimentelle Studien über das Gesehen von Bewegung. *Zeitschrift frPsychologie, 61,* 161–265.

WERTHEIMER, M. (1923). Untersuchungen zur Lehre von der Gestalt, II. *Psychologische Forschung, 4,* 301–350.

WEST, S. G., WHITNEY, G., & SCHNEDLER, R. (1975). Helping a motorist in distress: The effects of sex, race, and neighborhood. *Journal of Personality and Social Psychology, 31,* 691–698.

WESTCOTT, H. L., DAVIES, G. M., & BULL, R. H. C. (Eds.). (2002). *Children's testimony: A handbook of psychological research and forensic practice.* West Sussex, England: Wiley.

WESTEN, D. (1998). The scientific legacy of Sigmund Freud: Toward a psychodynamically informed psychological science. *Psychological Bulletin, 124,* 333–371.

WESTEN, D., & BRADLEY, R. (2005). Empirically supported complexity: Rethinking evidence-based practice in psychotherapy. *Current Directions in Psychological Science, 14,* 266–271.

WESTEN, D., NOVOTNY, C., & THOMPSON-BRENNER, H. (2004). The empirical status of empirically supported psychotherapies: Assumptions, findings, and reporting in controlled clinical trials. *Psychological Bulletin, 130,* 631–663.

WESTEN, D., & WEINBERGER, J. (2005). Clinical judgment in science. *American Psychologist, 60,* 659–661.

WESTERMEYER, J. (1987). Public health and chronic mental illness. *American Journal of Public Health, 77,* 667–668.

WETHINGTON, E. (2000). Expecting stress: Americans and the "midlife crisis." *Motivation & Emotion, 24,* 85–103.

WHEELER, L. R. (1942). A comparative study of the intelligence of East Tennessee mountain children. *Journal of Educational Psychology, 33,* 321–334.

WHITE, D. J., & GALEF, B. G. (1998). Social influence on avoidance of dangerous stimuli by rats. *Animal Learning and Behavior, 26*(4), 433–438.

WHITE, G. L. (1980). Physical attractiveness and courtship progress. *Journal of Personality and Social Psychology, 39,* 660–668.

WHITE, J. (1999). *Overcoming generalized anxiety disorder—client manual: A relaxation, cognitive restructuring, and exposure-based protocol for the treatment of GAD.* Oakland, CA: New Harbinger.

WHORF, B. (1956). *Language, thought, and reality: Selected writings of Benjamin Lee Whorf.* New York: Wiley.

WICKELGREN, W. A. (1974). *How to solve problems.* San Francisco: Freeman.

WIDAMAN, K. F. (2009). Phenylketonuria in children and mothers: Genes, environments, behavior. *Current Directions in Psychological Science, 18,* 48–52.

WIDIGER, T. A., & CLARK, L. A. (2000). Toward *DSM-V* and the classification of psychopathology. *Psychological Bulletin, 126*, 946–963.

WIDIGER, T. A., & SANDERSON, C. J. (1995). Toward a dimensional mode of personality disorders. In W. J. Livesley (Ed.), *The DSM-IV personality disorders* (pp. 433–458). New York: Guilford.

WIDIGER, T. A., & TRULL, T. J. (2007). Plate tectonics in the classification of personality disorder: Shifting to a dimensional model. *American Psychologist, 62*, 71–83.

WIEBE, R. P. (2004). Delinquent behavior and the Five Factor model: Hiding in the adaptive landscape? *Individual Differences Research, 2*, 38–62.

WIENS, A. N., & MENUSTIK, C. E. (1983). Treatment outcome and patient characteristics in an aversion therapy program for alcoholism. *American Psychologist, 38*, 1089–1096.

WIESENTHAL, D. L., ENDLER, N. S., COWARD, T. R., & EDWARDS, J. (1976). Reversibility of relative competence as a determinant of conformity across different perceptual tasks. *Representative Research in Social Psychology, 7*, 319–342.

WILCOXIN, H. C., DRAGOIN, W. B., & KRAL, P. A. (1971). Illness-induced aversions in rat and quail: Relative salience of visual and gustatory cues. *Science, 171*, 826–828.

WILEY, J. L. (1999). Cannabis: Discrimination of "internal bliss"? *Pharmacology, Biochemistry, & Behavior, 64*, 257–260.

WILHELM, F. H., TRABERT, W., & ROTH, W. T. (2001). Physiologic instability in panic disorder and generalized anxiety disorder. *Biological Psychiatry, 49*, 596–605.

WILLIAMS, G. C. (1966). *Adaptation and natural selection.* Princeton, NJ: Princeton University Press.

WILLIAMS, J. E., SATTERWHITE, R. C., & BEST, D. L. (1999). Pancultural gender stereotypes reivisited: The five factor model. *Sex Roles, 40*(7–8), 513–525.

WILLIAMS, L. (1994). Recall of childhood trauma: A prospective study of women's memories of child sexual abuse. *Journal of Consulting and Clinical Psychology, 62*, 1167–1176.

WILLIAMS, L. A., & DESTENO, D. (2009). Pride: Adaptive social emotion or seventh sin? *Psychological Science, 20*, 284–288.

WILLIAMS, W. M., & CECI, S. J. (1997). Are Americans becoming more or less alike? Trends in race, class, and ability differences in intelligence. *American Psychologist, 52*, 1226–1235.

WILLIAMS, H. L., TEPAS, D. I., & MORLOCK, J. H. C. (1962). Evoked responses to clicks and electroencephalographic stages of sleep in man. *Science, 138*, 685–686.

WILLIS, S. L., & REID, J. D. (EDS.). (1999). *Life in the middle: Psychological and social development in middle age.* San Diego: Academic Press.

WILSON, D. H., REEVES, A. G., GAZZANIGA, M. S., & CULVER, C. (1977). Cerebral commissurotomy for the control of intractable seizures. *Neurology, 27*, 708–715.

WILSON, G. T. (1991). Chemical aversion conditioning in the treatment of alcoholism: Further comments. *Behaviour Research and Therapy, 29*, 415–419.

WILSON, G. T. (1998). Manual-based treatment and clinical practice. *Clinical Psychology: Science and Practice, 5*, 363–375.

WILSON, G. T., & FAIRBURN, C. G. (2002). Treatments for eating disorders. In P. E. Nathan & J. M. Gorman (Eds.), *A guide to treatments that work* (2nd ed., pp. 559–592). New York: Oxford University Press.

WILSON, G. T., & PIKE, K. M. (2001). Eating disorders. In D. H. Barlow (Ed.), *Clinical handbook of psychological disorders* (3rd ed., pp. 332–375). New York: Guilford.

WILSON, J. Q. (1997). *Moral judgment: Does the abuse excuse threaten our legal system?* New York: Basic Books.

WILSON, T. D. (2002). *Strangers to ourselves: Discovering the adaptive unconscious.* Cambridge, MA: Harvard University Press.

WILSON, T. D., & DUNN, E. (2004). Self-knowledge: Its limits, value, and potential for improvement. *Annual Review of Psychology, 55*, 493–518.

WILSON, T. D., WHEATLEY, T. P., MEYERS, J. M., GILBERT, D. T., & AXSOM, D. (2000). Focalism: A source of durability bias in affective forecasting. *Journal of Personality and Social Psychology, 78*, 821–836.

WIMMER, H., & PERNER, J. (1983). Beliefs about beliefs: Representation and constraining function of wrong beliefs in young children's understanding of deception. *Cognition, 13*, 103–128.

WINNER, E. (2000). The origins and ends of giftedness. *American Psychologist, 55*(1), 159–169.

WINOGRAD, E., & NEISSER, U. (EDS.). (1993). *Affect and accuracy in recall: Studies of "flashbulb" memories.* New York: Cambridge University Press.

WINTER, D. G. (1999). Linking personality and "scientific" psychology: The development of empirically derived Thematic Apperception Test measures. In L. Gieser & M. I. Stein (Eds.), *Evocative images: The Thematic Apperception Test and the art of projection* (pp. 107–124). Washington, DC: American Psychological Association.

WIRSHING, W. C., MARDER, S. R., VAN PUTTEN, T., & AMES, D. (1995). Acute treatment of schizophrenia. In F. E. Bloom & D. Kupfer (Eds.), *Psychopharmacology: The fourth generation of progress* (pp. 1259–1266). New York: Raven.

WITHERINGTON, D. C., CAMPOS, J. J., & HERTENSTEIN, M. J. (2001). Principles of emotion and its development in infancy. In G. Bremner & A. Fogel (Eds.), *Blackwell handbook of infant development* (pp. 427–464). Malden, MA: Blackwell Publishing.

WITTENBRINK, B., JUDD, C. M., & PARK, B. (1997). Evidence for racial prejudice at the implicit level and its relationship with questionnaire measures. *Journal of Personality and Social Psychology, 72*(2), 262–274.

WITTGENSTEIN, L. (1953). *Philosophical investigations.* G. E. M. Anscombe (Trans.). Oxford, England: Blackwell.

WIXTED, J. T. (2004). The psychology and neuroscience of forgetting. *Annual Review of Psychology, 55*, 235–269.

WOHL, J. (1989). Cross-cultural psychotherapy. In P. B. Pedersen, J. G. Draguns, W. J. Lonner, & J. E. Trimble (Eds.), *Counseling across cultures* (pp. 79–113). Honolulu: University of Hawaii.

WOICIECHOWSKY, C., VOGEL, S., MEYER, B. U., & LEHMANN, R. (1997). Neuropsychological and neurophysiological consequences of partial callosotomy. *Journal of Neurosurgical Science, 41*, 75–80.

WOLF, M. E., & MOSNAIM, A. D. (1990). *Post-traumatic stress disorder: Etiology, phenomenology, and treatment.* Washington, DC: American Psychiatric Press.

WOLFE, J. M. (2003). Moving towards solutions to some enduring controversies in visual search. *Trends in Cognitive Science, 7*, 70–76.

WOLFE, J. M., & HOROWITZ, T. S. (2004). What attributes guide the deployment of visual attention and how do they do it? *Nature Reviews Neuroscience, 5*, 1–7.

WOLFE, J., KLUENDER, K., & LEVI, D. (2006). *Sensation and perception.* Sunderland, MA: Sinauer Associates.

WOLLEN, K. A., WEBER, A., & LOWRY, D. (1972). Bizarreness versus interaction of mental images as determinants of learning. *Cognitive Psychology, 3*, 518–523.

WOLPE, J. (1958). *Psychotherapy by reciprocal inhibition.* Stanford, CA: Stanford University Press.

WOLPE, J. (1996). *The practice of behavior therapy* (4th ed.). New York: Pergamon Press.

WOLPE, J., & LAZARUS, A. A. (1966). *Behavior therapy techniques: A guide to the treatment of neuroses.* Elmsford, NY: Pergamon.

WOLPE, J., & PLAUD, J. J. (1997). Pavlov's contributions to behavior therapy: The obvious and the not so obvious. *American Psychologist, 52*, 966–972.

WOOD, A. J., & GOODWIN, G. M. (1987). A review of the biochemical and neuropharmacological actions of lithium. *Psychological Medicine, 17*, 579–600.

WOOD, N., & COWAN, N. (1995). The cocktail party phenomenon revisited: How frequent are attention shifts to one's name in an irrelevant auditory channel? *Journal of Experimental Psychology: Learning, Memory and Cognition, 21*, 255–260.

WOOD, W. (2000). Attitude change: Persuasion and social influence. *Annual Review of Psychology, 51*, 539–570.

WOOD, W., & EAGLY, A. H. (2002). A cross-cultural analysis of the behavior of women and men: Implications for the origins of sex differences. *Psychological Bulletin, 128*(5), 699–727.

WOODRUFF, P. W. R., WRIGHT, I. C., BULLMORE, E. T., BRAMMER, M., HOWARD, R. J., WILLIAMS, S. C. R., ET AL. (1997). Auditory hallucinations and the temporal cortical response to speech in schizophrenia: A functional magnetic resonance imaging study. *American Journal of Psychiatry, 154*, 1676–1682.

WOODS, S. C., & RAMSAY, D. S. (2000). Pavlovian influences over food and drug intake. *Behavior and Brain Research, 10*, 175–182.

WOODWARD, A. L. (1998). Infants selectively encode the goal object of an actor's reach. *Cognition, 69*, 1–34.

WOODWARD, A. L. (2009). Infants' grasp of others' intentions. *Current Directions in Psychological Science, 18*, 53–57.

WOOLF, N. J. (1998). A structural basis for memory storage in mammals. *Progress in Neurobiology, 55*, 59–77.

WORLD FEDERATION FOR MENTAL HEALTH. (2005). *Without boundaries—challenges and hopes for living with ADHD: An international survey.* Retrieved Aug. 19, 2009, from Learning Disabilities Association of Alberta website, http://www.ldaa.ca/assets/pdfs/freeResources/ADHDWithoutBoundaries.pdf.

WORLD HEALTH ORGANIZATION (WHO). (1998). *The world health report 1998—Life in the 21st century: A vision for all.* Geneva: Author.

WORLD HEALTH ORGANIZATION (WHO). (2001). *Mental health: New understanding, new hope.* New York: Author.

WRIGHT, R. D., & WARD, L. M. (2008). *Orienting of attention.* New York: Oxford University Press.

WRZESNIEWSKI, A., MCCAULEY, C. R., ROZIN, P., & SCHWARTZ, B. (1997). Jobs, careers, and callings: People's relations to their work. *Journal of Research in Personality, 31*, 21–33.

WU, X., HART, C., DRAPER, T., & OLSEN, J. (2001). Peer and teaching sociometrics for preschool children: Cross-informant concordance, temporal stability, and reliability. *Merrill-Palmer Quarterly, 47*, 416–443.

WYNN, K. (1992). Addition and subtraction by human infants. *Nature, 358*, 749–750.

WYNN, K. (1995). Infants possess a system of numerical knowledge. *Current Directions in Psychological Science, 4*, 172–176.

XU, F. (2002). The role of language in acquiring object concepts in infancy. *Cognition, 85*, 223–250.

XU, F., & GARCIA, V. (2008). Intuitive statistics by 8-month-old infants. *Proceedings of the National Academy of Sciences, 105*, 5012–5015.

XU, F., & TENENBAUM, J. (2007). Word learning as Bayesian inference. *Psychological Review, 114*(2), 245–272.

YAMAGATA, S., SUZUKI, A., ANDO, J., ONO, Y., KIJIMA, N., YOSHIMURA, K., ET AL. (2006). Is the genetic structure of human personality universal? A cross-cultural twin study from North America, Europe, and Asia. *Journal of Personality and Social Psychology, 80*, 987–998.

YAN, L, DAVIGLUS, M., LIU, K., STAMLER, J., WANG, R. PIRZADA, A., ET AL. (2006). Midlife Body Mass Index and hospitalization and mortality in older age. *Journal of the American Medical Association, 295*, 190–198.

YANG, S.-H., CHENG, P.-H., BANTA, H., PIOTROWSKA-NITSCHE, K., YANG, J.-J., CHENG, E. C. H., et al. (2008). Towards a transgenic model of Huntington's disease in a nonhuman primate. *Nature, 453*, 921–924.

YANG, S.-Y., & STERNBERG, R. J. (1997). Taiwanese Chinese people's conceptions of intelligence. *Intelligence, 25*, 21–36.

YANIV, I., & MEYER, D. E. (1987). Activation and metacognition of inaccessible stored information: Potential bases for incubation effects in problem solving. *Journal of Experimental Psychology: Learning, Memory, and Cognition, 13*, 187–205.

YARMEY, A. (1973). I recognize your face but I can't remember your name: Further evidence on the tip-of-the-tongue phenomenon. *Memory & Cognition, 1*, 287–290.

YEHUDA, R. (1997). Sensitization of the hypothalamic-pituitary-adrenal axis in posttraumatic stress disorder. In R. Yehuda & A. C. McFarlane (Eds.), Psychobiology of posttraumatic stress disorder. *Annals of the New York Academy of Sciences, 821*, 57–75.

YEOMANS, M. R., & GRAY, R. (1996). Selective effects of naltrexone on food pleasantness and intake. *Physiology & Behavior, 60*, 439–446.

YONELINAS, A. (2002). The nature of recollection and familiarity: A review of 30 years of research. *Journal of Memory and Language, 46*, 441–517.

YOUNGSTEDT, S. D., O'CONNOR, P. J., & DISHMAN, R. K. (1997). The effects of acute exercise on sleep: a quantitative synthesis. *Sleep, 20*, 203–214.

YU, D., & SHEPARD, G. (1998). Is beauty in the eye of the beholder? *Nature, 396*, 321–322.

YUSSEN, S. R., & LEVY, V. M. (1975). Developmental changes in predicting one's own span of memory. *Journal of Experimental Child Psychology, 19*, 502–508.

ZAIDEL, E. (1976). Auditory vocabulary of the right hemisphere following brain bisection or hemidecortication. *Cortex, 12*, 191–211.

ZAIDEL, E. (1983). A response to Gazzaniga. Language in the right hemisphere, convergent perspectives. *American Psychologist, 38*(5), 542–546.

ZAIDI, L. Y., & FOY, D. W. (1994). Childhood abuse experiences and combat-related PTSD. *Journal of Traumatic Stress, 7*, 33–42.

ZAJONC, R. B. (1965). Social facilitation. *Science, 149*, 269–274.

ZAJONC, R. B. (1968). Attitudinal effects of mere exposure. *Journal of Personality and Social Psychology, 9*(Monograph suppl.), 1–27.

ZAJONC, R. B. (1980). Feeling and thinking: Preferences need no inferences. *American Psychologist, 35*, 151–175.

ZAJONC, R. B. (1984). On the primacy of affect. *American Psychologist, 39*, 117–123.

ZAJONC, R. B., ADELMANN, P. K., MURPHY, S. T., & NIEDENTHAL, P. M. (1987). Convergence in the physical appearance of spouses. *Motivation and Emotion, 11*, 335–346.

ZAJONC, R. B., HEINGARTNER, A., & HERMAN, E. M. (1969). Social enhancement and impairment of performance in the cockroach. *Journal of Personality and Social Psychology, 13*, 83–92.

ZAJONC, R. B., & MCINTOSH, D. N. (1992). Emotions research: Some promising questions and some questionable promises. *Psychological Science, 3*, 70–74.

ZAKRISKI, A., & COIE, J. (1996). A comparison of aggressive-rejected and non-aggressive-rejected children's interpretations of self-directed and other-directed aggression. *Child Development, 67*, 1048–1070.

ZARAGOZA, M. S., & MITCHELL, K. J. (1996). Repeated exposure to suggestion and the creation of false memories. *Psychological Science, 7*, 294–300.

ZARKIN, G. A., GRABOWSKI, H. G., MAUSKOPF, J., BANNERMAN, H. A., & WEISLER, R. H. (1995). Economic evaluation of drug treatment for psychiatric disorders. In F. E. Bloom & D. Kupfer (Eds.), *Psychopharmacology: The fourth generation of progress* (pp. 1897–1905). New York: Raven.

ZARZO, M., & STANTON, D. (2009). Understanding the underlying dimensions in perfumers' odor perception space as a basis for developing meaningful odor maps. *Attention, Perception & Psychophysics, 71*, 225–247.

ZELAZO, P. D. (2006). The dimensional change card sort (DCCS): A method of assessing executive function in children. *Nature Protocols, 1*, 297–301.

ZELAZO, P. D., & FRYE, D. (1998). Cognitive complexity and control: II. The development of executive function in childhood. *Current Directions in Psychological Science, 7*, 121–125.

ZENTALL, T. R. (2000). Symbolic representation by pigeons. *Current Directions in Psychological Science, 9*, 118–123.

ZENTALL, T. R. SUTTON, J., & SHERBURNE, L. (1996). True imitative learning in pigeons. *Psychological Science, 7*, 343–346.

ZHDANOVA, I. V., & WURTMAN, R. J. (1997). Efficacy of melatonin as a sleep-promoting agent. *Journal of Biological Rhythms, 12*(6), 644–650.

ZHONG, C., DIJKSTERHUIS, A., & GALINSKY, A. D. (2008). The merits of unconscious thought in creativity. *Psychololological Science, 19*, 912–918.

ZIGLER, E., & CHILD, I. L. (1969). Socialization. In G. Lindzey & E. Aronson (Eds.), *The handbook of social psychology: Vol. 3* (pp. 450–589). Reading, MA: Addison-Wesley.

ZIGLER, E. F., & CHILD, I. L. (1973). *Socialization and personality development.* Reading, MA: Addison-Wesley.

ZIHL, J., VON CRAMON, D., & MAI, N. (1983). Selective disturbance of movement vision after bilateral brain damage. *Brain, 106*, 313–340.

ZILBOORG, G., & HENRY, G. W. (1941). *A history of medical psychology.* New York: Norton.

ZILLMANN, D. (1989). Effects of prolonged consumption of pornography. In D. Zillmann & J. Bryant (Eds.), *Pornography: Research advances and policy considerations* (pp. 127–157). Hillsdale, NJ: Erlbaum.

ZILLMANN, D., & BRYANT, J. (1988). Pornography's impact on sexual satisfaction. *Journal of Applied Social Psychology, 18*, 438–453.

ZIMBARDO, P. G. (1969). The human choice: Individuation, reason, and order versus deindividuation, impulse and chaos. In W. J. Arnold & E. Levine (Eds.), *Nebraska Symposium on Motivation* (pp. 237–308). Lincoln: University of Nebraska Press.

ZIMBARDO, P. G. (1970). The human choice: Individuation, reason and order versus deindividuation, impulse and chaos. In W. J. Arnold & D. Levine (Eds.), *Nebraska Symposium on Motivation: Vol 18.* Lincoln: University of Nebraska Press.

ZIMBARDO, P. G. (1973). On the ethics of intervention in human psychological research: With special reference to the Stanford prison experiment. *Cognition, 2*(2), 243–256.

ZIMBARDO, P. G. (2005). Abu Ghraib: The evil of inaction, and the heroes who acted. *The Western Psychologist, 18*(1), 4–5.

ZIMBARDO, P. G. (2007). *The Lucifer effect: Understanding how good people turn evil.* New York: Random House.

ZIMMER, C. (2008). The search for intelligence. *Scientific American*, October, 68–75.

ZIMMERMAN, M., MATTIA, J. I., & POSTERNACK, M. A. (2002). Are subjects in pharmacological treatment trials of depression representative of patients in routine clinical practice? *American Journal of Psychiatry, 159,* 469–473.

ZORILLA, L.T. E., & CANNON, T. D. (1995). Structural brain abnormalities in schizophrenia: Distribution, etiology, and implications. In S. A. Mednick (Ed.), *Neural development in schizophrenia: Theory and research.* New York: Plenum Press.

ZUBIN, J., & SPRING, B. (1977). Vulnerability: A new view of schizophrenia. *Journal of Abnormal Psychology, 86,* 103–126.

ZUCKER, K. J. (2001). Biological influences on psychosexual differentiation. In R. K. Unger (Ed.), *Handbook of the psychology of women and gender.* New York: Wiley.

ZUCKER, K. J., BRADLEY, S. J., OLIVER, G., BLAKE, J., FLEMING, S., & HOOD, J. (1996). Psychosexual development of women with congenital adrenal hyperplasia. *Hormones and Behavior, 30,* 300–318.

ZUCKERMAN, M. (1979). *Sensation seeking: Beyond the optimum level of arousal.* Hillsdale, NJ: Erlbaum.

ZUCKERMAN, M. (1983). A biological theory of sensation seeking. In M. Zuckerman (Ed.), *Biological bases of sensation seeking, impulsivity, and anxiety.* Hillsdale, NJ: Erlbaum.

ZUCKERMAN, M. (1987a). All parents are environmentalists until they have their second child. Peer commentary on Plomin, R., & Daniels, D. Why are children from the same family so different from one another? *Behavioral and Brain Sciences, 10,* 38–39.

ZUCKERMAN, M. (1987b). A critical look at three arousal constructs in personality theories: Optimal levels of arousal, strength of the nervous system, and sensitivities to signals of reward and punishment. In J. Strelau & H. J. Eysenck (Eds.), *Personality dimensions and arousal: Perspectives on individual differences* (pp. 217–230). New York: Plenum.

ZUCKERMAN, M. (1990). The psychophysiology of sensation seeking [Special issue]. Biological foundations of personality: Evolution, behavioral genetics, and psychophysiology. *Journal of Personality, 58,* 313–345.

ZUCKERMAN, M. (1994). *Behavioral expressions and biosocial bases of sensation seeking.* New York: Cambridge University Press.

ZUGER, B. (1984). Early effeminate behavior in boys. *Journal of Nervous and Mental Disease, 172,* 90–96.

ZUMBAHLEN, M., & CRAWLEY, A. (1997). Infants' early referential behavior in prohibition contexts: The emergence of social referencing. *Infant Behavior and Development, 19*(1), 243–244.

Glossary

A-delta fibers One of the types of fibers crucial for perceiving pain. These fibers allow rapid transmission of pain signals. *See also* C fibers.

A-not-B effect The tendency of infants to reach for a hidden object where it was previously hidden (place A), rather than where it was hidden most recently while the child watched (place B).

absolute threshold The smallest quantity of a stimulus that an individual can detect.

accommodation In Piaget's theory, the developing child's process of changing his schemas based on his interactions with the environment. *See* assimilation.

achromatic colors Colors, such as black, white, and the neutral grays, that do not have the property of hue.

acquisition The processes of gaining new information and placing it in memory.

action potential A brief change in the electrical charge of a neuronal membrane; the physical basis of the signal that travels the length of the neuron.

activation-synthesis hypothesis The hypothesis that dreams may be just a byproduct of the sleeping brain's activities (activation), which are later assembled into a semicoherent narrative (synthesis).

activity dependence A property of neuronal plasticity such that changes in a neuron's functioning will occur only if that neuron is active (i.e., firing) at the same time as another neuron.

actual selves Self-schema for whom one is at the moment.

acuity The ability to distinguish between separate points projected on the retina. Acuity is greatest in the fovea, where the receptors are closely bunched together.

acute stress disorder A reaction sometimes observed in individuals who have experienced a trauma, characterized by flashbacks and recurrent nightmares.

ADHD *See* attention-deficit/hyperactivity disorder.

affective forecasting Predicting one's own emotional response to upcoming events.

affective neuroscience A field that uses cognitive neuroscience research methods to study emotion and related processes.

afferent neurons Nerves that carry messages inward toward the central nervous system.

aggressive-rejected The social status of children who are not respected or liked by peers and become aggressive as a result.

agonists Drugs that enhance a neurotransmitter's activity.

agoraphobia A fear of being in situations in which help might not be available or escape might be difficult or embarrassing. *See also* phobia.

all-or-none law The law that all action potentials have the same strength and speed regardless of the triggering stimulus.

allele An alternative form of a specific gene.

alpha rhythm A pattern of regular pulses, between 8 and 12 per second, visible in the EEG of a person who is relaxed but awake and typically has her eyes closed.

altruism Helping behavior that does not benefit the helper.

Alzheimer's disease A degenerative brain disorder characterized by memory loss followed by increasing disorientation and culminating in physical and mental helplessness.

American Sign Language (ASL) The manual-visual language used by most deaf persons in the United States.

amplitude The height of a wave crest, used (in the case of sound waves) as a measure of sound intensity.

amygdala An almond-shaped, temporal lobe structure that plays a central role in emotion and evaluating stimuli.

anal stage In psychoanalytic theory, the stage of psychosexual development during which the focus of pleasure is on activities related to elimination.

analogical representation An idea that shares some of the actual characteristics of the object it represents. *See also* symbolic representation.

analytic intelligence The ability typically measured by intelligence tests and crucial for academic success.

anecdotal evidence Evidence (usually just a few cases) collected informally, as in stories told by one person to another.

anorexia nervosa An eating disorder characterized by an extreme concern with being overweight and by compulsive dieting, sometimes to the point of self-starvation. *See also* bulimia nervosa.

antagonists Drugs that impede the activity of a neurotransmitter.

anterograde amnesia A memory deficit suffered after some kinds of brain damage, in which the patient seems unable to form new explicit memories; however, memories acquired before the injury are spared. *See also* retrograde amnesia.

antidepressants Medications designed to counteract depression.

ANS *See* autonomic nervous system.

antisocial personality disorder Also called psychopathy or sociopathy. The term describes persons who get into continual trouble with society, are indifferent to others, are impulsive, and have little concern for the future or remorse about the past.

anxiety disorders A group of disorders distinguished by feelings of intense distress and worry, and in many cases, disruptive and unsuccessful attempts to deal with these feelings.

anxiolytics Drugs that alleviate the symptoms of anxiety.

aphasia Any of a number of linguistic disorders caused by injury to or malformation of the brain. *See also* fluent aphasia, nonfluent aphasia.

apparent movement The perception of movement produced by stimuli that are stationary but are presented first at one positions and then, at an appropriate time interval, presented at a different position.

apraxia A serious disturbance in beginning or carrying out voluntary movements.

archetypes According to Carl Jung, the stories and images that constitute our collective unconscious.

ASL *See* American Sign Language.

assessment The set of procedures for gathering information about an individual's psychological state, sometimes leading to a diagnosis.

assimilation In Piaget's theory, the developing child's process of interpreting the environment in terms of the schemas he already has. *See* accommodation.

association A linkage between two psychological processes or representations as a result of past experience in which the two have occurred together.

associative links In network-based models of mental representation, connections between the symbols (or nodes) in the network.

attachment The strong, enduring, emotional bond between a child and its caregivers that some psychologists consider the basis for relationships later in life.

attention-deficit/hyperactivity disorder (ADHD) A disorder usually diagnosed in young children, and characterized by impulsivity, difficulty staying focused on a task, and a range of behavioral problems.

attitude A fairly stable evaluation of something as good or bad that makes a person think, feel, or behave positively or negatively about some person, group, or social issue.

attributional style The way a person typically explains the things that happen in his or her life.

atypical antidepressants A recently developed group of medications that work in varied ways on serotonin, norepinephrine, and dopamine systems to combat the symptoms of depression.

auditory canal The tube that carries sound from the outer ear to the eardrum.

auditory ossicles The three bones of the middle ear that transmit the vibrations of the eardrum to the oval window.

authoritarian parents One of the four types of parents; they adhere to strict standards about how children should behave, and attempt to mold their children's behavior accordingly.

authoritarian personality A cluster of personal attributes (e.g., submission to persons above and harshness to those below) and social attitudes (e.g., prejudice against minority groups) that is sometimes held to constitute a distinct personality.

authoritative parents One of the four types of parents; they exercise power over their children, but accept the reciprocal obligation to respond to their children's opinions and reasonable demands.

autism A disorder usually diagnosed in young children, and characterized by a wide range of developmental problems, including language and motor problems.

automaticity The ability to do a task without paying attention to it.

autonomic nervous system (ANS) The division of the peripheral nervous system that receives information from and controls the internal organs.

availability heuristic A strategy for judging how frequently something happens—or how common it is—based on how easily examples of it come to mind.

avoidant personality disorder A personality disorder characterized by social inhibition and social insecurity.

axon The part of a neuron that transmits impulses to glands, muscles, or other neurons.

axon terminals The knoblike swellings on the ends of an axon. The terminals contain the synaptic vesicles that are filled with neurotransmitters.

---

basic level A concept at some accessible, middling degree of abstractness or inclusiveness (e.g., *dog*, *spoon*). *See also* subordinates, superordinates.

basilar membrane A membrane running the length of the cochlea; sound waves cause a deformation of this membrane, bending the hair cells in the cochlea and thus stimulating the auditory receptors. *See also* cochlea.

behavioral contrast A response pattern in which an organism evaluates a reward relative to other available rewards or those that have been available recently.

behavioral data Data about a person based on direct observation of that person's actions or behavior.

belongingness in learning The fact that the ease of forming associations depends on the items to be associated. This holds for CS-US associations in classical conditioning and response-reinforcer associations in instrumental conditioning. *See also* biological constraints.

benzodiazepines A class of medications used to combat anxiety; the class includes Valium, Xanax, and Klonopin.

beta-blocker A medication intended to control autonomic arousal, and often used in the treatment of anxiety disorders.

beta rhythm The rhythmic pattern in the brain's electrical activity often observed when a person is actively thinking about some specific topic.

between-subject comparisons Within a study, comparing one group of individuals to a different group.

Big Five Five crucial dimensions of personality determined through factor analyses of trait terms: extroversion, neuroticism (or emotional instability), agreeableness, conscientiousness, and openness to experience.

binding problem The problem confronted by the brain of recombining the elements of a stimulus, given the fact that these elements are initially analyzed separately by different neural systems.

binge eating Eating a large amount of food within a brief period.

binocular disparity A depth cue based on the differences between the two eyes' views of the world. This difference becomes less pronounced the farther an object is from the observer.

binocular rivalry Either a perceptual phenomenon resulting from two separate images, one in front of each eye, or the procedure used to establish this phenomenon. The visual system is unable to interpret both stimuli at once or to fuse the stimuli into a single perception. Instead, the visual system alternates between the stimuli, so that the person is aware of one for a while and then the other.

biological constraints Principles governing what each species can learn easily and what it cannot learn at all. *See also* belongingness in learning.

biopsychosocial perspective A perspective on psychopathology that emphasizes the biological, psychological, and social factors that contribute to mental illness.

bipolar cells The intermediate neural cells in the eye that are stimulated by the receptors and excite the ganglion cells.

bipolar disorder A mood disorder in which the patient swings between emotional extremes, experiencing both manic and depressive episodes.

blind spot The region of the retina that contains no visual receptors and therefore cannot produce visual sensations.

blindsight The ability of a person with a lesion in the visual cortex to reach toward or correctly "guess" about objects in the visual field even though the person reports seeing nothing.

blocking effect A result showing that an animal learns nothing about a stimulus if the stimulus provides no new information.

blood-brain barrier Specialized membranes that surround the blood vessels within the brain and filter harmful chemicals out of the brain's blood supply.

Body Mass Index (BMI) The commonly-used measure of whether someone is at a healthy weight or not; BMI is calculated as weight in kilograms divided by the square of height in meters.

borderline personality disorder A personality disorder characterized by impulsive behavior and marked instability in relationships, self-concept, and affect.

brain lesion Damage to the brain cells, caused by injury or disease.

brain plasticity The capacity for the brain to alter its structure and function.

brain stem The brain region at the top of the spinal cord that includes the medulla and the pons.

brightness A perceived dimension of visual stimuli—an indication of how light or dark they appear.

brightness constancy The capacity to perceive an object as having an unchanging brightness, even though changes in illumination cause a change in how much light reflects off the object and reaches the eye.

brightness contrast The perceptual tendency to exaggerate the physical difference in the light intensities of two adjacent regions. As a result, a gray patch looks brighter on a black background and darker on a white background.

Broca's area A brain area in the frontal lobe crucial for language production. *See also* aphasia, nonfluent aphasia.

bulimia nervosa An eating disorder characterized by repeated binge-and-purge bouts. *See also* anorexia nervosa.

bystander effect One reason people fail to help strangers in distress: The larger the group a person is in, the less likely he is to help, partly because no one in the group thinks it is up to him to act.

C fibers One of the types of fibers crucial for perceiving pain. These unmyelinated fibers provide slow transmission of pain signals. *See also* A-delta fibers.

Cannon-Bard theory of emotion The theory that a stimulus elicits an emotion by triggering a particular response in the brain (in the thalamus) which then causes both the physiological changes associated with the emotion and the emotional experience itself.

case marker A word or affix that indicates the semantic role played by some noun phrase in a sentence. English case marks pronouns (e.g., *he* versus *him*) but usually marks semantic roles by word order, e.g., the first noun phrase in simple sentences usually plays the actor role. Many languages case mark all noun phrases and thus word order may be quite free in these languages.

case study An intensive study of one person.

causal attribution An inference about what caused a person's behavior.

cell body The portion of the neuron containing the metabolic machinery that keeps the cell alive and functional.

central fissure The anatomical "valley" that divides the frontal lobes on each side of the brain from the parietal lobes.

central nervous system (CNS) The brain and spinal cord.

central route to persuasion The process involved in attitude change when someone carefully evaluates the evidence and the arguments.

cerebellum The part of the brain that controls muscular coordination and equilibrium.

cerebral cortex The outermost layer of the forebrain.

cerebral hemisphere One-half (left or right) of the cerebrum, the topmost part of the brain.

cerebrospinal fluid A clear body fluid that surrounds and helps protect the brain.

character strengths Personal characteristics that contribute to a person's happiness without diminishing the happiness of others.

choice reaction time A measure of the speed of mental processing that takes place when someone must choose between several responses, depending on which stimulus is presented.

chromatic colors Colors that have a discernible hue. These are in contrast to the achromatic colors, which include black, the various shades of gray, and white.

chromosomes Structures in the nucleus of each cell that contain the genes, the units of hereditary transmission. A human cell has 46 chromosomes arranged in 23 pairs. *See also* gene.

chunking A process of reorganizing (or recoding) materials in working memory by combining a number of items into a single, larger unit.

classical antipsychotics Drugs (such as Thorazine and Haldol) that block dopamine receptors. These drugs seem to treat many positive symptoms of schizophrenia. *See* dopamine hypothesis.

classical conditioning A form of learning in which one stimulus is paired with another so that the organism learns a relationship between the stimuli.

client-centered therapy A form of humanistic therapy associated with Carl Rogers, in which the therapist's genuineness, unconditional positive regard, and empathic understanding are crucial to therapeutic success.

clinical utility Whether a therapeutic intervention works under real-world conditions.

CNS *See* central nervous system.

cochlea The coiled structure in the inner ear that contains the basilar membrane. *See also* basilar membrane.

cognitive-behavioral approach A hybrid form of psychotherapy focused on changing the patient's habitual interpretations of the world and ways of behaving.

cognitive dissonance An uncomfortable inconsistency among one's actions, beliefs, attitudes, or feelings. People attempt to reduce it by making their actions, beliefs, attitudes or feelings more consistent with one another.

cognitive reappraisal A form of emotion regulation in which an individual changes her emotional response to a situation by altering her interpretation of that situation.

cognitive restructuring A set of cognitive therapy techniques for changing a person's maladaptive beliefs or interpretations through persuasion and confrontation.

cognitive therapy An approach to therapy that tries to change some of the patient's habitual modes of thinking about herself, her situation, and her future.

cognitive unconscious The mental support processes outside our awareness that make our perception, memory, and thinking possible.

collective unconscious A set of primordial stories and images, hypothesized by Carl Jung to be shared by all of humanity, and which he proposed underlie and shape our perceptions and desires.

collectivistic cultures Cultures in which people are considered fundamentally interdependent and which emphasize obligations within one's family and immediate community. *See also* individualistic cultures.

comorbidity The tendency for different mental disorders to occur together in the same person.

companionate love An emotional state characterized by affection for those whose lives are deeply intertwined with one's own. *See also* romantic love.

comparative method A research method in which one makes systematic comparisons among different species in order to gain insights into the function of a particular structure or behavior, or the evolutionary origins of that structure or behavior.

compensatory behavior Actions taken to ensure that binge eating does not translate into weight gain (e.g., self-induced vomiting).

compensatory response A response that offsets the effects of the upcoming unconditioned stimulus.

complementary colors Two colors that, when additively mixed in the right proportions, produce the sensation of gray.

compliance A change in behavior in response to a request.

compulsions Repetitive or ritualistic acts that, in OCD, serve in some way to deal with the obsessions. *See* obsessions, obsessive-compulsive disorder.

computerized tomography scan *See* CT (computerized tomography) scan.

concept A mental category.

concordance rate The probability that a person with a particular familial relationship to a patient (e.g., an identical twin) has the same disorder as the patient.

concrete operational period In Piaget's theory, the period from about age 7 to about 12, in which the child is beginning to understand abstract ideas such as number and substance, but only as they apply to real, concrete events.

conditioned reinforcer An initially neutral stimulus that acquires reinforcing properties by pairing with another stimulus that is already reinforcing.

conditioned response (CR) A response elicited by an initially neutral stimulus—the conditioned stimulus (CS)—after it has been paired repeatedly with an unconditioned stimulus (US). *See also* conditioned stimulus (CS), unconditioned response (UR), unconditioned stimulus (US).

conditioned stimulus (CS) An initially neutral stimulus that comes to elicit a new response due to pairings with the unconditioned stimulus. *See also* conditioned response (CR), unconditioned response (UR), unconditioned stimulus (US).

cones Visual receptors that respond to greater light intensities and give rise to chromatic (color) sensations. *See also* rods.

confederate Someone who appears to be a research participant but actually is part of the research team.

confirmation bias (1) The tendency to seek evidence to support one's hypothesis rather than looking for evidence that will undermine it. (2) The tendency to take evidence that's consistent with your beliefs more seriously than evidence that's inconsistent with your beliefs.

confirmed hypothesis A hypothesis that has been tested many times and each time has made successful predictions.

conformity A change in behavior due to explicit or implicit social pressure.

conjunction search A search in which the target is defined by a combination of features.

consciousness Moment-by-moment awareness of ourselves, our thoughts, and our environment.

construal The way an individual makes sense of the world around him.

construct validity The attribute of truly reflecting the variable named in the researcher's hypothesis.

content morpheme A morpheme that carries the main semantic and referential content of a sentence. In English content morphemes are usually nouns, verbs, adjectives, or adverbs. *See also* function morpheme.

context reinstatement A way of improving retrieval by re-creating the state of mind that accompanied the initial learning.

contingency management A form of behavior therapy in which certain behaviors are reliably followed by well-defined consequences.

contralateral control The typical pattern in vertebrates in which movements of the right side of the body are controlled by the left hemisphere, while movements of the left side are controlled by the right hemisphere.

control group A group within an experiment that does not experience the experimental manipulation.

conventional reasoning According to Kohlberg, the third and fourth stages of moral reasoning, which are focused on social relationships, conventions, and duties.

convolutions The wrinkles visible in the cortex that allow the enormous surface area of the human cortex to be stuffed into the relatively small space of the skull.

cornea The eye's transparent outer coating.

corpus callosum The thick bundle of fibers connecting the cerebral hemispheres.

correct negative One of the four possible outcomes in a detection task. A response correctly indicating that no signal is present. *See also* miss.

correlation The tendency of two variables to change together. If one goes up as the other goes up, the correlation is positive; if one goes up as the other goes down, the correlation is negative.

correlation coefficient (*r*) A number that expresses both the size and the direction of a correlation, varying from +1.00 (perfect positive correlation) to −1.00 (perfect negative correlation).

correlational studies Studies in which the investigator analyzes the relationships among variables that were in place before the study, without manipulating those variables.

correspondence problem As your view changes, the perceptual task of determining which aspects of the current view correspond to which aspects of the view seen a moment ago.

counterirritation The phenomenon in which painful sensations from one part of the body trigger the gate neurons and so decrease the sensitivity to pain elsewhere in the body. *See also* gate control theory.

CR *See* conditioned response.

crib bilingual A prelinguistic infant who is exposed to two or more languages in the home environment.

crystallized intelligence Acquired knowledge, including the person's repertoire of verbal knowledge and cognitive skills. *See also* fluid intelligence.

CS *See* conditioned stimulus.

CT (computerized tomography) scan A technique for examining brain structure by constructing a composite of X-ray images taken from many different angles.

cultural competence An understanding of how a patient's cultural background shapes his beliefs, values, and expectations for therapy.

DBS *See* deep brain stimulation.

debriefing A step at the end of an experiment in which the researcher explains the study's purpose and design to each participant and undoes any manipulations to participants' beliefs or state.

decibels The logarithmic units used to describe sound intensity (or amplitude).

decision criteria An organism's rule for how much evidence it needs before responding.

declarative knowledge Knowledge of information that can be expressed in words.

deep brain stimulation (DBS) An emerging biomedical treatment for depression and OCD that involves stimulating specific parts of the brain with implanted electrodes.

deep processing An approach to memorization that involves focusing on the meaning of the stimulus.

defense mechanism A collective term for a number of reactions that try to ward off or lessen anxiety by various unconscious means.

definitional theory of word meaning The theory that mental representations of word meanings consist of a necessary and sufficient set of semantic features. The representation of *apple*, for example, might be [round], [edible], [sweet], [red], [juicy].

dehumanization of the victim Thinking about a potential victim in ways that make him seem inhuman (as vermin, for example, or as a mere number); this view makes aggression toward the victim more likely and less troubling to the aggressor.

deindividuation A state in which an individual in a group experiences a weakened sense of personal identity and diminished self-awareness.

deinstitutionalization A movement that began in the 1950s that aimed to provide better, less expensive care for chronically mentally ill patients in their own communities rather than at large, centralized hospitals.

delta rhythm The rhythmic pattern in the brain's electrical activity often observed when a person is in slow-wave sleep.

delusions Systematized false beliefs, often of grandeur or persecution.

demand characteristics The cues in a study that might tell a research participant what behaviors are expected or desirable in that setting.

dendrites The branched part of a neuron that receives impulses and conducts them toward the cell body.

dendritic spines Little knobs attached to the surface of the dendrites and serving as the "receiving stations" for most synapses.

deoxyribonucleic acid *See* DNA.

dependent personality disorder A personality disorder characterized by an excessive need to be taken care of by others.

dependent variable The variable that is measured or recorded in an experiment.

depolarize In the nervous system, to lose the charge that normally exists across the neuronal membrane.

depressants Drugs that diminish activity levels in the nervous system.

depression A mood disorder characterized by disabling sadness, hopelessness, and apathy; a loss of energy, pleasure, and motivation; and disturbances of sleep, diet, and other bodily functions. Also called major depression or unipolar depression.

depth cues Sources of information that signal the distance from the observer to the distal stimulus.

descriptive statistics Mathematical procedures that allow a researcher to characterize a data pattern; these procedures include measures of central tendency and of variability.

desensitization *See* in vivo desensitization.

Diagnostic and Statistical Manual for Mental Disorders (DSM) The manual that provides specific guidance on how to diagnose each of the nearly 200 psychological disorders; currently in its fourth edition, text revision (*DSM-IV-TR*).

diathesis-stress model A conception of psychopathology that distinguishes factors that create a risk of illness (the diathesis) from the factors that turn the risk into a problem (the stress).

DID *See* dissociative identity disorder.

difference threshold The smallest amount that a given stimulus must be increased or decreased so that an individual can detect the difference.

diffusion of responsibility *See* bystander effect.

directed thinking Thinking aimed at a particular goal.

disconfirmed hypothesis A hypothesis that has been tested but for which the data do not conform to the pattern it predicted.

discrimination An aspect of learning in which the organism learns to respond differently to stimuli that have been associated with a US (or reinforcement), and stimuli that have not.

discriminative stimuli In instrumental conditioning, a stimulus that signals a particular relationship between the instrumental response and the reinforcer. For example, if a pigeon gets a reinforcer (food) for hopping on a platform only while a green light is on, the green light is a positive discriminative stimulus. If a red light signals that hopping on the platform will not lead to a reinforcer, the red light is a negative discriminative stimulus.

disengaged parents One of the four types of parents; they provide few rules and demands and are relatively insensitive to their children's needs.

dishabituation An increase in responsiveness when something novel is presented, following a series of presentations of something familiar.

displacement A redirection of an impulse from a channel that is blocked into another, more available outlet.

display rules Cultural rules that govern the expression of emotion.

dispositional attributions Explanations of someone's behavior in terms of factors internal to the person, such as traits or preferences.

dissociation (1) A way of demonstrating that two brain functions can operate independently, by documenting cases in which one of the functions is impaired while the other is preserved. (2) In the stress disorders, the period of numbness immediately after the trauma in which the sufferer feels estranged, socially unresponsive, and oddly unaffected by the traumatic event. (3) A defense mechanism in which one seeks to create a sense of physical or psychological distance from a threatening event, person, or stimulus.

dissociative amnesia The inability of an individual to remember some period of her life, or even her entire past, including her identity; often understood as a way of coping with extremely painful events.

dissociative disorders Disorders in which a whole set of mental events seems to be stored out of ordinary consciousness. These include dissociative amnesia, fugue states, and, very rarely, cases of dissociative identity disorder.

dissociative fugue A state in which someone leaves home, then, days or months later, suddenly realizes he is in a strange place and doesn't know how he got there; often understood as a means of coping with (and escaping from) extremely painful events.

dissociative identity disorder (DID) A disorder that results in a person developing two or more distinct personalities.

distal stimulus An object or event in the outside world. *See also* proximal stimulus.

distance cues See depth cues.

dizygotic (DZ) twins Twins that develop from two different eggs that are simultaneously fertilized by two sperm. Like ordinary siblings, they share 50% of their genes. Also called fraternal twins. *See also* monozygotic (MZ) twins.

DNA (deoxyribonucleic acid) The complex molecule that is the constituent of genes.

dodo bird verdict An expression often used to summarize the comparison of the effectiveness of different forms of psychotherapy. According to the dodo bird in *Alice in Wonderland*, "Everyone has won and all must have prizes." Regarding psychotherapy, this statement is understood to mean that all the major forms of psychotherapy are equally effective.

dominant A term for a gene that directs the development of a particular characteristic even when the corresponding gene on the other chromosome is different, i.e. some other allele.

dopamine hypothesis Asserts that the brains of people with schizophrenia are oversensitive to the neurotransmitter dopamine. *See* classical antipsychotics.

double-blind design The technique of assigning participants to experimental conditions while keeping both the participants and the researchers unaware of who is assigned to which group.

drive A term referring to a state of internal bodily tension, such as hunger or thirst or the need for sleep.

DRM paradigm A common procedure for studying memory, in which participants read and then immediately recall a list of related words, but the word providing the "theme" for the list is not included.

drug tolerance The diminished response to a drug that results from extended use, so that over time the user requires larger doses to experience the drug's effects.

DSM See *Diagnostic and Statistical Manual for Mental Disorders*.

dual-center theory The hypothesis that one area in the lateral hypothalamus is the "on" center, the initiator of eating, while another area in the ventromedial hypothalamus is the "off" center, the terminator of eating. Current evidence indicates that although these brain regions are crucial for eating, the regulation of eating also involves other circuits.

dual-process theory The proposal that judgment involves two types of thinking: a fast, efficient, but sometimes faulty set of strategies, and a slower, more laborious, but less risky set of strategies.

DZ twins See dizygotic (DZ) twins.

---

eardrum The taut membrane that transmits the vibrations caused by sound waves from the auditory canal to the ossicles in the middle ear.

eclecticism An approach to treatment that deliberately weaves together multiple types and forms of therapy. Also called multimodal therapy.

ECT See electroconvulsive therapy.

edge enhancement A process that relies on brightness contrast and allows us to see the edges between objects more clearly.

EEA See environment of evolutionary adaptiveness.

EEG See electroencephalogram.

effect size The magnitude of the difference between groups in a study, often computed by subtracting the mean of one group's scores from mean the other's scores.

efferent neurons Nerves that carry messages outward from the central nervous system.

efficacy Whether a therapeutic intervention works under carefully controlled conditions.

ego In Freud's theory, a set of reactions that try to reconcile the id's blind pleasure strivings with the demands of reality. *See also* id, superego.

ego psychology A school of psychodynamic thought that emphasizes the skills and adaptive capacities of the ego.

Electra complex See Oedipus complex.

electroconvulsive therapy (ECT) A somatic treatment, mostly used for cases of severe depression, in which a brief electric current is passed through the brain to produce a convulsive seizure.

electroencephalogram (EEG) A record of the brain's electrical activity recorded by placing electrodes on the scalp.

embryonic stage The third through eighth week of prenatal development.

emotion regulation The ability to influence one's emotions.

emotional intelligence The ability to understand your own and others' emotions and to control your emotions appropriately.

emotional support Social support focused on emotional needs.

emotions Affective responses (such as joy, sadness, pride, and anger), which are characterized by loosely linked changes in behavior (how we act), subjective experience (how we feel), and physiology (how our bodies respond).

empirical claims Claims that can be true or false depending on the facts.

empirically supported treatments (EST) Clinical methods that research has shown to be effective for treating a given disorder.

empiricism A school of thought holding that all knowledge comes by way of the senses.

empty chair technique A therapeutic technique associated with Gestalt therapy in which the patient imagines he is seated across from another person, and then tells her honestly what he feels.

encoding specificity The hypothesis that when information is stored in memory, it is not recorded in its original form but translated ("encoded") into a form that includes the thoughts and understanding of the learner.

endocrine system The system of glands that release secretions directly into the bloodstream and affect organs elsewhere in the body.

environment of evolutionary adaptiveness (EEA) The environment that was in place when a trait was evolving.

episodic memory Memory for specific events and experiences.

ERP *See* event-related potential.

EST *See* empirically supported treatments.

estrogen A female sex hormone that dominates the first half of the female cycle through ovulation.

estrus In mammals, the period in the cycle when the female is sexually receptive (in heat).

event-related potential (ERP) Electrical changes in the brain that correspond to the brain's response to a specific event; measured with EEG.

excitation threshold The voltage difference between a neuron's interior and exterior that, if exceeded, causes the neuron to fire.

executive control Processes such as making plans or overriding habitual responses that let the brain direct its own cognitive activities.

experiential therapies A family of therapies that seek to create an empathic and accepting therapeutic atmosphere, while challenging the patient to deepen his experience.

experiment A study of causal relationships in which the researcher manipulates an independent variable to examine its effect on a dependent variable.

experimental group The group within an experiment that experiences the researcher's manipulation of the independent variable.

experimental manipulation The deliberate alteration of the independent variable in an experiment in order to learn about its effects on the dependent variable.

explanatory style A person's characteristic way of explaining his experiences. Consistently attributing bad experiences to internal, global, and stable causes may increase vulnerability to depression.

explicit memory Conscious memories that can be described at will and can be triggered by a direct question. *See also* implicit memory.

exposure therapy A behavior therapy that aims to remove the anxiety connected to a feared stimulus by gradually conditioning relaxed responses to the stimulus.

external validity The degree to which a study's participants, stimuli, and procedures adequately reflect the world as it actually is.

extinction The weakening of a learned response that is produced if a conditioned stimulus is now repeatedly presented without the unconditioned stimulus, or if a previously reinforced operant behavior is no longer reinforced.

extrinsically rewarding An activity or object that is pursued because of rewards that are not an inherent part of the activity or object.

---

factor analysis A statistical method for studying the interrelations among various tests. The goal is to discover whether the tests are all influenced by the same factors.

false alarm One of the four possible outcomes in a detection task. A response indicating that a signal is present when it actually is not. *See also* hit.

familiarity A general sense that a certain stimulus has been encountered before.

family resemblance structure An overlapping set of semantic features shared by members of a category, such that no members of the category need to have all of the features but all members have at least one of them.

feature detectors Neurons in the retina or brain that respond to specific attributes of the stimulus, such as movement, orientation, and so on.

feature net A model of pattern recognition involving a network of detectors and having feature detectors as the network's starting point.

Fechner's law The observation that the strength of a sensation is proportional to the logarithm of physical stimulus intensity.

fetal alcohol syndrome A developmental disorder that affects children whose mothers consumed alcohol during pregnancy. Its effects include a range of psychological problems and physical abnormalities.

fetal stage The prenatal period from the ninth week until birth.

figure The object focused on; the rest of the stimulus input is considered merely as "background." *See also* ground.

flashbulb memories Vivid, detailed memories said to be produced by unexpected and emotionally important events.

fluent aphasia A syndrome, derived from a specific form of brain damage, in which the person seems able to produce speech but is unable to understand what is said to her. In most cases, the sentences she produces make little sense, consisting instead of "word salad."

fluid intelligence The ability to deal with new and unusual problems. *See also* crystallized intelligence.

Flynn effect A worldwide increase in IQ scores over the last several decades, at a rate of about 3 points per decade.

fMRI *See* functional MRI (fMRI) scan.

forebrain In mammals, the bulk of the brain. Its foremost region includes the cerebral hemispheres; its rear includes the thalamus and hypothalamus.

forgetting curve The graphic pattern representing the relationship between measures of learning and the length of the retention interval: As the retention interval gets longer, memory decreases.

formal operational period In Piaget's theory, the period from about age twelve on, in which a child can think abstractly and consider hypothetical possibilities.

fovea The area roughly at the retina's center where cones are plentiful and visual acuity is greatest.

fragment-completion task A procedure sometimes used for testing implicit memory; the participant is given a fragment of a word (C__O__O__I__E) and has to fill in the missing letters to complete an actual word (CROCODILE).

framing The way a decision is phrased or the way options are described. Seemingly peripheral aspects of the framing can influence decisions by changing the point of reference.

fraternal twins *See* dizygotic (DZ) twins.

free association Method used in psychoanalytic therapy in which the patient is to say anything that comes to her mind, no matter how apparently trivial, unrelated, or embarrassing.

free recall A test of memory that asks for as many items in a list as a research participant can recall, regardless of order.

frequency The number of wave peaks per second. In sound, frequency governs the perceived pitch of the sound.

frequency distribution An arrangement for tabulating data values based on how often they occur in a data set.

frequency estimates A person's estimates of how often he has encountered a particular event or object.

frontal lobe The area at the front of each cerebral hemisphere; includes tissue crucial for many aspects of planning and controlling thoughts and behavior.

function morpheme A morpheme that, while adding such content as time, mode, individuation, and evidentiality, also serves a grammatical purpose (e.g., the suffixes *–s* and *–er*, or the connecting words *and* or *if*). *See also* content morpheme.

functional MRI (fMRI) scan A technique for examining brain function by measuring blood flow and oxygen use within the brain.

fundamental attribution error The tendency to attribute behaviors to a person's internal qualities while underestimating situational influences.

---

g *See* general intelligence.

GAD *See* generalized anxiety disorder.

ganglion cells In the retina, one of the intermediate links between the receptor cells and the brain. The axons of the ganglion cells converge into a bundle of fibers that leave the eyeball as the optic nerve. *See also* bipolar cells.

garden path A premature, false syntactic analysis of a sentence as it is being heard or read, which must be mentally revised when later information within the sentence falsifies the initial interpretation, as in, e.g., *Put the ball on the floor into the box.*

gate control theory The proposal that pain sensations must pass through a neural "gate" in order to reach the brain and can be blocked at that gate by neurons that inhibit signals from the nociceptors.

gene A section of a DNA molecule that contains instructions for how and when to assemble a protein. Genes are located on chromosomes. *See also* chromosomes.

general intelligence (*g*) A mental attribute that is hypothesized as contributing to the performance of virtually any intellectual task.

generalization gradient The curve showing the relationship between the tendency to respond to a new stimulus and its similarity to the original conditioned stimulus (CS).

generalized anxiety disorder (GAD) A disorder characterized by pervasive, free-floating anxiety.

generativity versus stagnation According to Erikson, a major developmental task of later adulthood is finding meaning in one's work, which produces a sense of generativity. Failure leads to a sense of stagnation.

generic memory *See* semantic memory.

geniculate nucleus *See* lateral geniculate nucleus.

genital stage In psychoanalytic theory, the stage of psychosexual development reached in adult sexuality in which sexual pleasure involves not only one's own gratification but also the social and bodily satisfaction brought to another person.

genome The complete set of a species' genes.

genotype The complete set of an organism's genes. *See also* phenotype.

geons (geometric ions) Simple geometric figures, such as cubes, cylinders, and pyramids, that can be combined to create all other shapes. An early (and crucial) step in some models of object recognition is determining which geons are present.

Gestalt psychology A theoretical approach that emphasizes the role of organized wholes in perception and other psychological processes.

Gestalt therapy A form of humanistic therapy associated with Fritz Perls that aims to help the patient integrate inconsistent aspects of herself into a coherent whole by increasing self-awareness and self-acceptance.

glia A type of cell in the nervous system long believed to provide a "support" function for neurons; recent research indicates that glia provide many other functions as well.

global workspace hypothesis A hypothesis about the neural basis of consciousness. It proposes that specialized neurons, called workspace neurons, give rise to consciousness by allowing us to link stimuli or ideas in dynamic, coherent representations.

glomeruli Sites in the brain's olfactory bulb where signals from the smell receptors converge.

glove anesthesia A loss of feeling in the entire hand that does not extend above the wrist. This symptom makes no organic sense given the arrangement of the nerves, which indicates that it has a psychological basis.

glucoreceptors Receptors in the brain (in the area of the hypothalamus) that detect the amount of glucose in the bloodstream.

goal maintenance The mental process of keeping one's goal in mind to guide the selection of the next actions.

goal state The situation one is trying to reach when solving a problem.

good continuation A factor in visual grouping; we tend to perceive contours in a way that alters their direction as little as possible.

grammar *See* rules of syntax (or grammar).

grasp reflex An infantile reflex in which an infant closes her hand into a fist when her palm is touched.

gray matter The tissue of the brain that appears gray. It consists of the cell bodies, dendrites, and unmyelinated axons that comprise the nervous system's microcircuitry.

ground The backdrop against which a figure is viewed. *See also* figure.

group polarization A pattern in group discussions in which each member's attitudes become more extreme, even though the discussion draws attention to arguments that could have moderated their views.

groupthink A pattern of thinking that occurs when a cohesive group minimizes or ignores members' differences of opinion.

H *See* heritability ratio.

habituation A decline in the response to a stimulus once the stimulus has become familiar.

habituation procedure A method for studying infant perception. After some exposure to a stimulus, an infant becomes habituated and stops paying attention to it. If the infant shows renewed interest when a new stimulus is presented, this reveals that the infant regards the new stimulus as different from the old one.

hair cells The auditory receptors in the cochlea, lodged between the basilar membrane and other membranes above.

hallucinations Perceived experiences that occur in the absence of actual sensory stimulation.

hallucinogens Drugs that powerfully change perception and can trigger sensory experiences in the absence of any inputs.

halo effect The tendency to assume that people who have one good trait also have other good traits.

heritability ratio (*H*) A measure that describes, for a given population in a given environment, what proportion of the variance of a trait is due to genetic differences.

hertz (**Hz**) A measure of the frequency of a sound wave in number of cycles per second.

heuristics A strategy for making judgments quickly, at the price of occasional mistakes.

hierarchy of needs The theory that people will strive to meet their higher-order needs, such as love, self-esteem, and self-actualization, only when their lower, more basic needs like food and safety have been met. *See also* self-actualization.

hippocampus A temporal lobe structure that plays a pivotal role in learning and forming new memories.

histrionic personality disorder A personality disorder characterized by an unusual degree of attention seeking and emotionality.

hit One of the four possible outcomes in a detection task. A response correctly indicating that a signal is present. *See* false alarm.

homeostasis The body's tendency to maintain the conditions of its internal environment by various forms of self-regulation.

homogamy The tendency of like to mate with like.

hormone A chemical released by a gland. Hormones travel through the bloodstream and influence functions such as metabolic rate, arousal level, and the liver's sugar output.

hue A perceived dimension of visual stimuli whose meaning is close to the term color (e.g., red, blue).

human sexual response cycle A sequence of four stages that characterizes the sexual response in both men and women: excitement, plateau, orgasm, and resolution.

humanistic approach An approach to therapy centered around the idea that people must take responsibility for their lives and actions.

hypnosis A highly relaxed, suggestible state of mind in which a person is likely to feel that his actions and thoughts are happening to him rather than being produced voluntarily.

hypnotic analgesia A reduction in pain produced through hypnotic suggestion.

hypomania A mild manic state in which the individual seems infectiously merry, extremely talkative, charming, and tireless.

hypothalamus A subcortical structure that plays a vital role in controlling many motivated behaviors, like eating, drinking, and sexual activity.

hysteria An older term for a group of presumably psychogenic disorders that included a wide variety of physical and mental symptoms.

Hz *See* hertz.

---

id In Freud's theory, a term for the most primitive reactions of human personality, consisting of blind striving for immediate biological satisfaction regardless of cost. *See also* ego, superego.

ideal self The concept that each person holds of the self that she would most like to be.

identical twins *See* monozygotic (MZ) twins.

identity versus role confusion According to Erikson, the major developmental task of adolescence is developing a stable ego identity, or sense of who one is. Failure results in developing a negative identity or in role confusion.

ill-defined problem A problem for which the goal state is defined only in general terms, so the steps toward a solution are unclear.

illumination The third of Wallas's four stages of problem solving. In his theory, this is the stage in which new insights suddenly arrive. *See also* incubation, preparation, verification.

illusory conjunction A pattern of errors in which observers correctly perceive the features present in a display, such as color and shape, but misperceive how they were combined. For example, they might report seeing a green O and a red X when a green X and red O were presented.

implicit memory Memories that we may not recall consciously, but that are still demonstrable through an indirect test. *See also* explicit memory.

implicit theories of personality Beliefs about what kinds of behaviors are associated with particular traits and which traits usually go together; used to develop expectations about people's behavior.

imprinting In many species, the learned attachment that is formed at a particular early period.

impulsivity A tendency to act without reflecting on one's actions.

in vivo desensitization One key step in the behavioral treatment of a phobia in which the patient is gradually exposed to the phobic stimulus.

incidental learning Learning without trying to learn, and often without awareness that learning is occurring.

incubation The second of Wallas's four stages of problem solving. In his theory, this is the stage in which new ideas emerge through unconscious thought. *See also* illumination, preparation, verification.

independent variable The variable that the experimenter manipulates as a basis for making predictions about the dependent variable.

individualistic cultures Cultures in which people are considered fundamentally independent and which value standing out by achieving private goals. *See also* collectivistic cultures.

induced motion Perceived movement of a stationary stimulus, usually caused by movement of a surrounding framework or nearby objects.

induced motion of the self A pattern in which surrounding objects that are moving are misperceived as stationary, and the self is therefore misperceived as moving. An example occurs in traffic, when a neighboring car rolls forward but appears stationary, and one's own car momentarily seems to roll backward.

inferential statistics Mathematical procedures that allow a researcher to draw further claims from a data pattern, including claims about whether the pattern observed in the sample is likely to be observed in other samples.

informant data Data about a person derived from others who know the person well.

informational influence A reason for conformity based on people's desire to be correct.

informed consent A research participant's agreement to take part in the study, based on full information about what the experiment will involve.

inhibited temperament A personality style associated with introversion and neuroticism, and characterized by a fear of novelty that is evident early in life.

inhibitor A stimulus signaling that an event is not coming, which elicits a response opposite to the one that the event usually elicits.

initial state The status of a person at the start of her attempts to solve a problem. *See also* goal state.

inner ear The internal portion of the ear in which the transduction of sound takes place.

inspection time The time someone needs to make a simple discrimination between two stimuli.

instrumental conditioning A form of learning in which the participant receives a reinforcer only after performing the desired response, and thereby learns a relationship between the response and the reinforcer. Also called operant conditioning.

integrity versus despair According to Erikson, the major developmental task of older age is finding meaning in the life that one has led. Success gives rise to a sense of integrity, whereas failure leads to despair.

intentional learning Placing new information into memory in anticipation of being tested on it later.

inter-rater reliability A measure of the agreement among several independent observers of an event or stimulus.

internal validity The characteristic of a study that allows us to conclude that the manipulation of the independent variable caused the observed changes in the dependent variable.

internal working model A set of beliefs and expectations about how people behave in social relationships, and also guidelines for interpreting others' actions, and habitual responses to make in social settings.

interneurons Neurons that are neither afferent nor efferent, but instead carry information from one neuron to another.

interpersonal therapy (IPT) A form of therapy focused on helping the patient understand how she interacts with others and then learn better ways of interacting and communicating.

interposition A monocular cue to distance that relies on the fact that objects farther away are blocked from view by closer objects.

interval schedule A pattern of delivering reinforcements only after a certain amount of time has passed.

intimacy versus isolation According to Erikson, a major developmental task of early adulthood is developing an intimate relationship. Failure to do so may lead to isolation.

intrinsically rewarding An activity or object that is pursued for its own sake.

introspection The process of "looking within" to observe one's own thoughts, beliefs, and feelings.

intrusion errors Memory mistakes in which elements that were not part of the original information get mixed into ("intrude" into) someone's recall.

inverted spectrum The notion that if someone had inverted color vision, there would be no way to determine that his color perceptions differed from the norm. Philosophers use this hypothetical situation to convey the impossibility of knowing another person's subjective experience.

ion channels Biochemical "windows" in a cell wall that allow ions to flow in or out of the cell.

ion pumps Biochemical mechanisms that use energy to move ions either into or out of the cell.

IPT *See* interpersonal therapy.

iris The smooth circular muscle in the eye that surrounds the pupil and contracts or dilates under reflex control to govern the amount of light entering.

James-Lange theory of emotion The theory that the subjective experience of emotion is the awareness of one's own bodily reactions in the presence of certain arousing stimuli.

jnd *See* just-noticeable difference.

judgment The process of extrapolating from evidence to draw conclusions.

just-noticeable difference (jnd) The smallest difference that an organism can reliably detect between two stimuli.

---

kinesthesis The sensations generated by receptors in the muscles, tendons, and joints that inform us of our skeletal movement.

Korsakoff's syndrome A brain disorder characterized by serious memory disturbances. The most common cause is extreme and chronic alcohol use.

---

latent content In psychoanalytic interpretation, the anxiety-inducing wishes and concerns that a dream or behavior expresses in disguised form; usually contrasted with manifest content.

latent learning Learning that occurs without a corresponding change in behavior.

lateral fissure The deep indentation that runs horizontally across each hemisphere of the brain and separates the frontal lobe (above the fissure) from the temporal lobe (below).

lateral geniculate nucleus (LGN) An important neural way station on the path from the eye to the brain; ganglion neurons on the retina send their signals to the lateral geniculate nucleus; from there, other neurons carry the signal to the visual cortex in the occipital lobe.

lateral inhibition The pattern of interaction among neurons in the visual system in which activity in one neuron inhibits adjacent neurons' responses.

lateralization Functional differences between the two cerebral hemispheres. E.g., in most right-handers, the left hemisphere is specialized for language, while the right hemisphere is better at some visual and spatial tasks.

law of effect Thorndike's theory that a response followed by a reward will be strengthened, whereas a response followed by no reward (or by punishment) will be weakened.

learned helplessness A condition of passivity apparently created by exposure to inescapable aversive events. This condition inhibits or prevents learning in later situations in which escape or avoidance is possible.

learning model The hypothesis that mental disorders result from some form of faulty learning.

learning theorists Researchers who argued that most learning can be understood in terms of a small number of principles that apply to all organisms and all situations.

lens The portion of the eye that bends light rays and thus can focus an image on the retina.

leptin A chemical produced by the adipose cells that seems to signal that plenty of fat is stored and that no more fat is needed. This signal may diminish eating.

LGN *See* lateral geniculate nucleus.

life data Data about a person concerning concrete, real-world outcomes.

lifetime prevalence The percentage of people in a certain population who will have a given disorder at any point in their lives.

liking The pleasure that follows receipt of a reward.

limbic system A group of interconnected structures (including the hypothalamus, the amygdala, and others) that are crucial for emotion, motivation, and many aspects of learning and memory.

linear perspective A cue for distance based on the fact that parallel lines seem to converge as they get farther away from the viewer.

literature review A summary of research findings on a particular topic; literature reviews are available in scientific journals.

lock-and-key model The theory that neurotransmitter molecules will affect the postsynaptic membrane only if their shape fits into that of certain synaptic receptor molecules.

long-term memory The vast memory depository containing all of an individual's knowledge and beliefs—including all those not in use at any given time.

long-term potentiation (LTP) A long-lasting increase in a neuron's response to specific inputs, caused by repeated stimulation. *See also* activity dependence.

longitudinal fissure The front-to-back cleavage dividing the left and right hemispheres of the brain.

loss aversion The strong tendency to regard losses as considerably more important than gains of comparable magnitude—and, with this, a tendency to take steps (including risky steps) to avoid possible loss.

LTP *See* long-term potentiation.

M *See* mean.

Mach bands The accentuated edges between two adjacent regions that differ in brightness. This sharpening is maximal at the borders, where the distance between the two regions is smallest and the contrast most striking.

magnetic resonance imaging *See* MRI.

magno cells Ganglion cells that, because of their sensitivity to brightness changes, are particularly suited to perceiving motion and depth. *See also* parvo cells.

maintenance rehearsal Mechanical repetition of material without thinking about its meaning or patterns.

mania A state characterized by racing thoughts, pressured speech, irritability or euphoria, and impaired judgment. *See also* bipolar disorder.

manifest content In psychoanalytic interpretation, the visible, surface content of a dream or behavior. This content is hypothesized to be a means of disguising the latent content, to protect against the anxiety associated with the latent content.

manualized therapy A form of therapy, often used in research, in which a manual describes a set course of therapy, indicating what steps the therapist should take, what instructions to offer, and so on.

mastery orientation A learning orientation characterized by a focus on gaining new knowledge or abilities and improving.

maximum variation sampling A strategy of deliberately seeking out for study the unusual or extreme cases.

mean (M) A measure of central tendency computed by calculating the sum of all the observations, then dividing by the number of observations.

means-end analysis A problem-solving strategy in which you continually evaluate the difference between your current state and your goal, and consider how to use your resources to reduce the difference.

measure of central tendency A single number intended to summarize an entire distribution of experimental results. Two commonly used measures of central tendency are the mean and the median.

median A measure of central tendency taken by putting the data values in order and finding the value that divides the distribution in half.

medulla The lower part of the brain stem that controls respiration, circulation, and balance.

memory consolidation The biological process through which memories are transformed from a transient and fragile status to a more permanent and robust state; according to most researchers, consolidation occurs over the course of several hours.

memory trace The physical record in the nervous system that preserves a memory.

mental images Mental representations that resemble the objects they represent by directly reflecting the perceptual qualities of the thing represented.

mental maps An internal representation of the spatial layout of a scene.

mental representations Contents in the mind that stand for some object, event, or state of affairs.

mental set The perspective that a person takes and the assumptions he makes in approaching a problem.

mere presence effect Changes in a person's behavior due to another person's presence.

meta-analysis A statistical technique for combining the results of many studies on a particular topic, even when the studies used different data collection methods.

method of loci A mnemonic technique that requires the learner to visualize each of the items she wants to remember in a different spatial location (locus). Recall requires that each location be mentally inspected for the item placed there.

midbrain The portion of the brain between hindbrain and forebrain that is involved in arousal, the sleep-wake cycle, and auditory and visual targeting.

middle ear An antechamber to the inner ear; it amplifies the sound-produced vibrations of the eardrum and transfers them to the cochlea. *See also* cochlea.

midlife transition A period of time proposed by many authors in which individuals reappraise what they have done with their lives thus far and may reevaluate their marriage and career.

mind-body problem The difficulty in understanding how the mind and body influence each other—so that physical events can cause mental events, and so that mental events can cause physical ones.

mirror neurons Neurons that fire whenever an animal performs an action, such as stretching out its arm or reaching toward a target, and also whenever the animal watches another performing the same action.

misinformation effect The result of a procedure in which, after an experience, people are exposed to questions or suggestions that misrepresent what happened. The term refers to people's tendency to include the misinformation as part of their recall of the original experience.

miss One of the four possible outcomes in a detection task. A response indicating that a signal is not present when it actually is. *See also* correct negative.

mixed states A pattern sometimes observed with bipolar disorder in which the person displays a combination of manic and depressive symptoms.

mnemonics Deliberate techniques people use to memorize new materials.

monocular depth cues Features of the visual stimulus that indicate distance even if the stimulus is viewed with only one eye.

monogamy A mating pattern in which one male and one female form an enduring reproductive partnership.

monozygotic (MZ) twins Twins that develop from a single fertilized egg that then splits in half. These twins are genetically identical. *See also* dizygotic (DZ) twins.

mood disorders A group of disorders distinguished primarily by changes in positive and negative affective state.

mood stabilizers Medications that treat bipolar disorder, such as lithium.

moods Affective responses that are typically longer-lasting than emotions, and less likely to have a specific object.

morbid obesity The level of obesity at which someone's health is genuinely at risk, usually defined as a BMI over 40.

morpheme The smallest significant unit of meaning in a word (e.g., the word *boys* has two morphemes, *boy* and *-s*).

motion detectors Cells in the visual cortex that are sensitive to an image moving in a particular direction across the retina.

motion parallax A depth cue based on the fact that, as an observer moves, the retinal images of nearby objects move more rapidly than do the retinal images of objects farther away.

motivated social cognition Thinking about the social world in ways that serve an emotional need, such as when people hold beliefs that help them feel less anxious.

motivational-enhancement therapy A brief, nonconfrontational, client-centered therapy designed to change specific problematic behaviors such as alcohol or drug use.

MRI (magnetic resonance imaging) A neuroimaging technique that documents the effects of strong magnetic pulses on the molecules that make up brain tissue. A computer then assembles this information into a picture of brain structure.

MS *See* multiple sclerosis.

multi-unit recording A procedure that uses microelectrodes to simultaneously record the activity of individual cells in the nervous system.

multicausal model A conception of how mental disorders arise that emphasizes the roles played by many different factors.

multiple intelligences In Howard Gardner's theory, the six essential, independent mental capacities (linguistic, logical-mathematical, spatial, musical, bodily-kinesthetic, and personal intelligence).

multiple sclerosis (MS) A progressive neurological disease wherein the immune system mistakenly destroys the myelin sheaths that comprise the brain's white matter, producing manifestations such as numbness, blindness, and paralysis.

mutations Errors in the replication of DNA.

myelin A fatty substance that makes up some types of glial cells; these cells wrap around the axon of some neurons, providing an insulating myelin sheath around these neurons. *See also* myelin sheath, nodes of Ranvier.

myelin sheath The series of fatty wrappers, formed by special glial cells, that surrounds the axon of a neuron that communicates over a long distance in the nervous system; the sheath helps speed the propagation of action potentials along the axon. *See also* nodes of Ranvier.

MZ twins *See* monozygotic (MZ) twins.

─────────────────

narcissistic personality disorder A personality disorder characterized by grandiosity, lack of empathy, and a need for the attention and admiration of others.

national character The idea that people in different cultures have different personalities.

natural selection The mechanism that drives biological evolution. It refers to the greater likelihood of successful reproduction for organisms whose attributes are advantageous in a given environment.

naturalistic fallacy The (mistaken) idea that anything "natural" must be "good."

negative afterimage In color vision, the persistence of an image that possesses the hue complementary to that of the stimulus (e.g., seeing a yellow afterimage after staring at a blue lamp) due to the operation of opponent processes.

negative cognitive schema According to Aaron Beck, the core cognitive component of depression, consisting of an individual's automatic negative interpretations concerning himself, his future, and the world. *See also* explanatory style.

neglect syndrome The result of certain right parietal lobe lesions that leave a patient completely inattentive to stimuli to her left, including the left side of her own body.

neural correlates of consciousness Specific brain states that seem to correspond to the content of someone's conscious experience.

neural synchrony A pattern of firing in the nervous system in which neurons in different brain areas fire at the same rate and at the same time; this seems to be a cue within the nervous system that links processing in distinct areas.

neural tube The tubular structure formed early in the embryonic stage from which the central nervous system (brain and spinal cord) develops.

neurodevelopmental disorder A disorder that stems from early brain abnormalities.

neurogenesis The process through which the nervous system grows and develops, which includes cellular signaling, differentiation, migration and proliferation.

neuroimaging techniques Methods that permit noninvasive study and depiction of brain structure or function. *See also* CT scan, MRI, functional MRI scan, PET scan.

neuron A specialized cell in the nervous system that accumulates and transmits information.

neuropeptide Y (NPY) A chemical found widely in the brain and periphery. In the brain, it acts as a neurotransmitter; when administered at sites in and near the hypothalamus, it is a potent elicitor of eating.

neuropsychology The study of brain-damaged individuals with the aim of learning how brain function makes psychological processes possible.

neuroscience A multidisciplinary field—drawing on psychology, biology, and chemistry—focused on learning how the nervous system functions.

neurotransmitters Chemicals released by one neuron (usually the presynaptic neuron), which trigger a response in another neuron (usually the postsynaptic neuron); the chief means of communication among neurons.

niche construction The process in which organisms, through their own behaviors, alter the environment and create their own circumstances.

nociceptors Receptors in the skin that give rise to the sense of pain; they respond to various forms of tissue damage and to temperature extremes.

node In network-based models of mental representation, a "meeting place" for the various connections associated with a particular topic.

nodes of Ranvier The gaps between the glial-cell wrappers that form the myelin sheath surrounding many kinds of axons. The nodes help speed the propagation of action potentials along the axon. *See also* myelin, myelin sheath.

nonfluent aphasia Speech disorder in which the main difficulty is in speech production, often involving damage to Broca's area in the frontal lobe.

norm of reciprocity The social standard that suggests that a favor must be repaid.

normative influence A reason for conformity based on people's desire to be liked (or not appear foolish).

NPY *See* neuropeptide Y.

nucleus accumbens A dopamine-rich area in the forebrain that is critical in the physiology of reward.

---

obedience A change in behavior in response to an instruction or command from another person.

object permanence The conviction that an object exists even when it is out of sight. Piaget believed infants didn't develop this level of understanding until the age of at least eight months.

object relations A school of psychodynamic thought that emphasizes the real (as opposed to fantasized) relations an individual has with others.

observational learning The process of watching how others behave and learning from their example.

obsessions Recurrent unwanted or disturbing thoughts. *See also* compulsions, obsessive-compulsive disorder.

obsessive-compulsive disorder (OCD) A disorder whose symptoms are obsessions and compulsions, which seem to serve as defenses against anxiety.

obsessive-compulsive personality disorder A personality disorder characterized by a preoccupation with orderliness, perfection, and control.

occipital lobe The rearmost area of each cerebral hemisphere; includes tissue crucial for processing visual information.

OCD *See* obsessive-compulsive disorder.

odorants Airborne molecules that can produce a response in the olfactory receptor neurons in the epithelial tissue of the nasal cavity.

Oedipus complex In psychoanalytic theory, a general term for the cluster of impulses and conflicts hypothesized to occur during the phallic phase, at around age five. In boys, a fantasized form of intense, possessive sexual love is directed at the mother, which is soon followed by hatred for and fear of the father. As the fear mounts, the sexual feelings are pushed underground and the boy identifies with the father. An equivalent process is hypothesized in girls and is called the Electra complex.

olfactory epithelium A mucous membrane at the top of the nasal cavity; contains the olfactory receptor neurons that respond to airborne molecules called odorants.

one-trial learning In classical conditioning, the establishment of a conditioned response after only one pairing of the conditioned stimulus and the unconditioned stimulus.

operant In Skinner's system, an instrumental response that is defined by its effect (the way it operates) on the environment. *See* instrumental conditioning.

operant conditioning *See* instrumental conditioning.

operational definition A definition that translates the variable we want to assess into a specific procedure or measurement.

opponent-process theory A theory of color vision that proposes three pairs of color antagonists: red-green, blue-yellow, and white-black. Excitation of neurons sensitive to one member of a pair automatically inhibits neurons sensitive to the other member.

optic flow The phenomenon wherein an object's retinal image enlarges as we approach the object and shrinks as we retreat from it. The visual system uses optic flow as a depth cue.

optic nerve The bundle of fibers that proceeds from each retina to the brain.

oral stage In psychoanalytic theory, the earliest stage of psychosexual development during which the primary source of bodily pleasure is stimulation of the mouth and lips, as in sucking at the breast.

orienting The tendency of an organism to shift its attention and sensory surfaces (e.g., by moving the eyes or turning the ears) to inspect a stimulus.

ought self The concept that each person holds of the self that she should be.

out-group homogeneity effect The tendency for a member of a group (the in-group) to view members of another group (the out-group) as "all alike" or less varied than members of his or her own group.

outcome expectations A set of beliefs, drawn from experience, about what the consequences (rewards or punishments) of certain actions are likely to be.

outer ear The external structures of the ear; these include the pinna, the auditory canal, and the outer surface of the eardrum.

oval window The membrane separating the middle ear from the inner ear.

---

p-value The probability of getting a particular data pattern purely by accident.

pain matrix A distributed network of brain regions, including the thalamus and anterior cingulate cortex, thought to respond to many types of pain.

panic attack A sudden episode of terrifying bodily symptoms such as labored breathing, choking, dizziness, tingling hands and feet, sweating, trembling, heart palpitations, and chest pain.

panic disorder An anxiety disorder characterized by repeated or disabling panic attacks. *See also* anxiety disorders, panic attack.

papillae Structures on the tongue that contain the taste buds, which in turn contain taste receptors.

paranoid personality disorder A personality disorder characterized by widespread suspiciousness and mistrust of others.

parasympathetic branch The division of the autonomic nervous system that restores the body's normal resting state and conserves energy.

parietal lobe The area in each cerebral hemisphere that lies between the frontal and occipital lobes; includes tissue crucial for receiving information from the skin senses.

parsing The perceptual process of determining which parts of a figure belong together as aspects of a whole.

partial reinforcement A learning condition in which only some of the organism's responses are reinforced.

parvo cells Ganglion cells that, because of their sensitivity to differences in hue, are particularly suited to perceiving color and form. *See also* magno cells.

pattern theory The proposal that different sensory qualities are encoded by specific patterns of firing among the relevant neurons.

payoff matrix The pattern of benefits and costs associated with certain types of responses.

peer review A procedure that provides the main "quality control" within the scientific community; in this procedure, other investigators (presumably the peers of the initial study's authors) evaluate the methods and interpretation of the data in a paper that has been submitted for publication.

penis envy In psychoanalytic theory, the wish for a penis that is assumed to ensue normally in females as part of the Electra complex.

perceptual constancy The accurate perception of certain attributes of a distal object, such as its shape, size, and brightness, despite changes in the proximal stimulus caused by variations in our viewing circumstances.

perceptual sensitivity An organism's ability to detect a signal.

performance orientation A learning orientation characterized by a focus on presenting oneself well and appearing intelligent to others.

period A measure of how much time elapses between one crest of a wave (e.g., a sound wave) and the next.

peripheral nervous system (PNS) The afferent and efferent nerves that extend from the brain and spinal cord to connect them with the organs and muscles.

peripheral route to persuasion The process involved in attitude change when someone relies on superficial factors, such as the appearance or charisma of the person presenting the argument.

permissive parents One of the four types of parents; they set few explicit dos and don'ts for their children, and try not to assert their authority.

perseveration The tendency to repeat a response inappropriately; often a result of deficits in executive control caused by prefrontal lesions.

personal constructs The dimensions used by a person to organize his or her experience.

personal myths The personal narratives or stories that provide a person with a sense of direction and meaning.

personality disorders Relatively stable, pervasive patterns of behavior and inner experience that are culturally discrepant and lead to distress or impairment; noted on Axis II of the DSM.

personality paradox The idea that people seem to behave much less consistently than a trait conception would predict.

PET (positron emission tomography) scan A technique for examining brain function by observing the amount of metabolic activity in different brain regions.

phallic stage In psychoanalytic theory, the stage of psychosexual development during which the child begins to regard his or her genitals as a major source of gratification.

phenomenology The study of individuals' own unique, first-person, conscious experience.

phenotype The overt characteristics and behaviors of an organism. *See also* genotype.

phenylketonuria (PKU) A condition in which a person lacks the gene that enables him to metabolize the anino acid phenylalanine. If detected early, this condition can be treated by means of a special diet. If not detected early, it can cause a severe form of retardation.

pheromones Biologically produced odorants that convey information to other members of the species.

phobia An anxiety disorder characterized by an intense and, at least on the surface, irrational fear.

phoneme The smallest significant unit of sound in a language. Alphabetic characters roughly correspond to phonemes (e.g., *apt*, *tap*, and *pat* are all made up of the same phonemes).

photopigment A chemical in the photoreceptors that changes its form in response to light, producing an electrical change that signals to the nervous system that light is present.

photoreceptor A light-sensitive cell located on the retina that converts light energy into neural impulses.

phrase structure description A tree diagram or labeled bracketing that shows the hierarchical structure of a sentence.

physiological data Data about a person derived from measurement of biological structures and processes.

pictorial cues Patterns that can be represented on a flat surface in order to create a sense of a three-dimensional object or scene.

PKU *See* phenylketonuria.

place theory A proposal about pitch perception stating that regions of the basilar membrane respond to particular sound frequencies, and the nervous system interprets the excitation from different basilar regions as different pitches.

placebo A chemically inert substance that produces real medical benefits because the patient believes it will help her.

pleasure principle One of two major principles that Freud held governed psychological life. This principle is thought to characterize the id, which seeks to reduce tensions generated by biological urges. *See also* reality principle.

pluralistic ignorance A type of misunderstanding that occurs when members of a group don't realize that the other members share their perception (often, their uncertainty about how to react to a situation). As a result, each member wrongly interprets the others' inaction as reflecting their better understanding of the situation.

PNS *See* peripheral nervous system.

point prevalence The percentage of people in a given population who have a given disorder at any particular point in time.

polygamy Any mating system in which a member of one sex mates with several members of the opposite sex.

polygenic inheritance A pattern in which many genes all influence a single trait.

pons The upper part of the brain stem that coordinates facial sensations and muscular actions and regulates sleep and arousal.

population The entire group about which the investigator wants to draw conclusions. *See also* sample.

position constancy The capacity to perceive an object as having an unchanging location in space, even though changes in the viewer's position cause a change in the spatial position of the retinal image cast by the object.

positive psychology A research movement that emphasizes factors that make people psychologically healthy, happy, or able to cope well with their life circumstances.

positron emission tomography scan *See* PET (positron emission tomography) scan.

possible selves Self-schemas for whom one may be in the future; these include the ideal self and the ought self.

post-traumatic stress disorder (PTSD) A chronic, sometimes lifelong disorder that may follow a traumatic experience. Symptoms include dissociation, recurrent nightmares, flashbacks, and sleep disturbances.

postconventional reasoning According to Kohlberg, the fifth and sixth stages of moral reasoning, which are focused on ideals and broad moral principles.

posthypnotic amnesia The situation a hypnotist can produce by instructing a person to forget certain events that took place during his or her hypnosis.

posthypnotic instructions Various directions given to a person under hypnosis, telling the person specifically how he or she should behave after the hypnosis is done.

postsynaptic neuron The cell receiving a neural message at the synapse.

power of the situation The notion that our behavior often depends more on the setting we are in than on who we are in terms of traits.

practical intelligence The ability to solve everyday problems through skilled reasoning that relies on tacit knowledge.

preconventional reasoning According to Kohlberg, the first and second stages of moral reasoning, which are focused on getting rewards and avoiding punishments.

predicate verb phrase The verb phrase immediately descending from the root of the sentence tree. In simple English sentences, this verb phrase usually expresses the action or state of the agent or actor.

predictive validity An assessment of whether a test measures what it's intended to measure, based on whether the test score correlates with another relevant criterion measured later.

prefrontal area The frontmost portion of the frontal lobes, involved in working memory, strategy formation, and response inhibition.

prejudice A negative attitude toward another person based on that person's group membership.

preoperational period In Piaget's theory, the period from about ages 2 to 7, in which a child can think representationally, but can't yet relate these representations to each other or take a point of view other than her own.

preparation The first of Wallas's four stages of problem solving. In his theory, this is the stage in which the person works on the problem but makes little progress. *See also* incubation, illumination, verification.

prepared learning Learning that occurs without extensive training because of an evolved predisposition to the behavior.

presynaptic facilitation A process, documented in studies of Aplysia, that underlies many kinds of learning. It occurs when learning results in an increased release of neurotransmitter into the synapse.

presynaptic neuron The cell that releases a neurotransmitter across the synaptic gap.

prevalence For a particular illness or condition, the number of active cases in a population at any point in time.

prevention focus An orientation to avoid doing harm thought to arise when we compare our actual self to our ought self.

primacy effect In free recall, the tendency to recall the first items on the list more readily than those in the middle. *See also* recency effect.

primary attachment figure The main person with whom an infant forms a strong, enduring, emotional bond.

primary reinforcers Stimuli that serve as reinforcers because of their immediate biological significance; e.g., food, water, or escape from the scent of a predator.

primary sexual characteristics Bodily structures directly related to reproduction.

primary somatosensory projection area Areas of the cortex that are the initial "receiving stations" for sensory information.

priming The process through which a detector or portion of the nervous system is prepared for an upcoming input, making it easier for the participant to recognize that input.

procedural knowledge Knowledge of how to do something, such as riding a bike; expressed in behaviors rather than in words.

progesterone A female sex hormone that dominates the latter phase of the female cycle during which the uterine walls thicken to receive the embryo.

prognosis The forecast of how a situation (including an illness) will improve or fail to improve in the future.

projection A mechanism of defense in which various forbidden thoughts and impulses are attributed to another person rather than the self.

projection areas Areas in which the brain tissue seems to form a "map" of sensory information.

promotion focus An orientation to actively pursue valued goals thought to arise when we compare our actual self to our ideal self.

propagation The spread of the action potential down an axon, caused by successive changes in electrical charge along the length of the axon's membrane.

proposition (1) A statement relating a subject and a claim about that subject. (2) A predicate-argument structure. In a sentence, the verb is the predicated act or state and the noun phrases are its arguments, playing various semantic roles.

prosopagnosia The inability to recognize faces; this disorder is usually produced by lesions in the parietal lobes.

prototype The typical or most familiar example of a category (e.g., a robin is a prototypical bird for many Americans but an auk might be the prototype for Laplanders). *See also* prototype theory.

prototype theory A theory in which concepts and word meanings are formed around average or typical values. Some prototype theories comprise feature representations, but without the necessary and sufficient conditions of definitional theory, but some are exemplar representations. In both cases, centrality in the category is measured by closeness to an ideal or average. *See also* prototype.

proximal stimulus The energies from the outside world that directly reach our sense organs. *See also* distal stimulus.

proximate cause The influences within an organism's lifetime that led to its particular traits or behaviors.

proximity In perception, the closeness of two figures. The closer together they are, the more we tend to group them together perceptually.

psychoanalysis A theory of human personality development formulated by Freud, based on assertions about unconscious conflict and early psychosexual development; also the method of therapy that draws heavily on this theory.

psychodynamic approaches Approaches to personality and/or therapy that are derived from psychoanalytic theory, which asserts that clinical symptoms arise from unconscious conflicts rooted in childhood.

psychogenic hypothesis The hypothesis that mental disorders result from psychological causes.

psychogenic symptoms Symptoms believed to result from some psychological cause rather than from tissue damage.

psychological intensity The magnitude of a stimulus as it is perceived, rather than in terms of its physical attributes.

psychometric approach to intelligence An attempt to understand the nature of intelligence by studying the pattern of results obtained on intelligence tests.

psychopathology The study of mental disorders, or a term for the mental disorder itself.

psychopathy *See* antisocial personality disorder.

psychophysics An approach to perception that relates the characteristics of physical stimuli to the sensory experiences they produce.

psychosis Loss of contact with reality, most often evidenced as delusions or hallucinations.

psychosurgery Neurosurgery performed to alleviate manifestations of mental disorders that cannot be alleviated using psychotherapy, medication, or other standard treatments.

psychotropic drugs Medications that control, or at least moderate, the manifestations of some mental disorders.

PTSD *See* post-traumatic stress disorder.

puberty The period of physical and sexual maturation in which the child's body begins to assume develop into its adult form.

---

quasi-experiment A comparison that relies on already-existing groups (i.e., groups the experimenter did not create).

---

r *See* correlation coefficient.

random assignment In an experimental design, the random placement of participants in either the experimental or control groups, ensuring that the groups are matched at the outset of the experiment.

random sampling A procedure in which every member of the population has an equal chance of being picked to participate in a study.

randomized clinical trial (RCT) A procedure for evaluating the outcome of therapy, usually involving random assignment of participants to one or more treatment groups or a no-treatment control group.

ratio schedule A pattern of delivering reinforcements only after a certain number of responses.

rational emotive behavioral therapy A form of cognitive therapy associated with Albert Ellis, in which the therapist actively challenges the patient's irrational beliefs.

rationalization A mechanism of defense by means of which unacceptable thoughts or impulses are reinterpreted in more acceptable and, thus, less anxiety-arousing terms.

RCT *See* randomized clinical trial.

reaction formation A mechanism of defense in which a forbidden impulse is turned into its opposite.

reality principle One of two major principles that Freud held governed psychological life. This principle is thought to characterize the ego, which is satisfied by finding strategies that work in the real world. *See also* pleasure principle.

reasoning The process of figuring out the implications of particular beliefs.

recall A type of retrieval that requires you to produce an item from memory in response to a cue or question. *See also* recognition, recollection.

recency effect In free recall, the tendency to recall items at the end of the list more readily than those in the middle. *See also* primacy effect.

receptive field For a particular cell in the visual system, the pattern of retinal stimulation that most effectively causes the cell to fire. For some cells, this pattern is defined solely in terms of a retinal location; for others, the most effective input has a particular shape, color, or direction of motion.

recessive A term for a gene that directs the development of a particular characteristic only if the corresponding gene on the other chromosome matches it—i.e., is the same allele.

recognition A type of retrieval that requires you to judge whether you have encountered a stimulus previously. *See also* recall, recollection.

recollection Recall of the context in which a certain stimulus was encountered. *See also* recall.

reconditioning In classical conditioning, the presentation of further reinforced conditioning trials after a conditioned response (CR) has been extinguished.

reflex A simple, stereotyped reaction in response to a stimulus (e.g., flexing a limb in withdrawing from pain).

refractory period The time after an action potential during which a neuron's cell membrane is unprepared for the next action potential.

reinforcement schedule *See* schedule of reinforcement.

reinforcer A stimulus delivered after a response that makes the response more likely in the future.

reliability The degree of consistency with which a test measures a trait or attribute. *See also* test-retest reliability.

REM rebound The tendency to spend more time in REM sleep if deprived of it on previous nights. REM rebound often occurs during withdrawal from drugs that suppress REM sleep (e.g., barbiturates or alcohol).

REM sleep Sleep characterized by rapid eye movements, EEG patterns similar to wakefulness, speeded heart rate and respiration, near-paralysis of skeletal muscles, and highly visual dreams.

repetition priming An increase in the likelihood that an item will be identified, recognized, or recalled; caused by recent exposure to that item, which may occur without explicit awareness.

repetitive transcranial magnetic stimulation (rTMS) An emerging biomedical treatment for depression that involves applying rapid pulses of magnetic stimulation to the brain from a coil held near the scalp.

replication A repetition of an experiment that yields the same results.

representativeness heuristic A strategy for judging whether an individual, object, or event belongs in a certain category based on how typical of the category it seems to be.

repression In psychoanalytic theory, a mechanism of defense by means of which thoughts, impulses, or memories that give rise to anxiety are pushed out of consciousness.

resistance In psychoanalysis, a term describing the patient's failure to associate freely and say whatever enters her head.

response rate The number of responses per unit of time; one way to measure of the strength of an operant response.

resting potential The voltage difference between the inside and the outside of a neuronal membrane when the neuron is not firing.

restructuring A reorganization of a problem that can facilitate its solution; a characteristic of creative thought.

retention interval The time that elapses between learning and retrieval.

retinal image The image of an object that is projected on the retina. Its size increases with the size of that object and decreases with the object's distance from the eye.

retrieval The process of searching for a memory and finding it.

retrieval cue A hint or signal that helps one to recall a memory.

retrieval failure The inability to access a memory, often due to poor encoding; an alternative to erasure as an explanation for forgetting.

retrieval paths The mental connections linking one idea to the next that people use to locate a bit of information in memory.

retrograde amnesia A memory deficit, often suffered after a head injury, in which the patient loses memory for events that occurred before the injury. *See also* anterograde amnesia.

reversible figure A visual pattern that easily allows more than one interpretation, in some cases changing the specification of figure and ground, in other cases changing the perceived organization in depth.

rhodopsin The photopigment used in the rods within the retina.

risky shift A pattern in which a group appears more willing to take chances or to take an extreme stance than any individual members would have been on their own.

rods Photoreceptors in the retina that respond to lower light intensities and give rise to achromatic (colorless) sensations. *See also* cones.

romantic love An emotional state characterized by idealization of the beloved, obsessive thoughts of this person, and turbulent feelings. *See also* companionate love.

Romeo-and-Juliet effect The intensification of romantic love that can occur when the couple's parents oppose relationship.

rooting reflex In an infant, the sucking elicited by stroking applied on or around the lips; the reflex aids breast-feeding.

rules of syntax (or grammar) The regular principles governing how words can be assembled into sentences.

rTMS *See* repetitive transcranial magnetic stimulation.

---

sample The subset of the population that the investigator studies in order to learn about the population at large. *See also* population.

satisfice In decision making, seeking a satisfactory option rather than spending more time and effort to locate and select the ideal option.

saturation A perceived dimension of visual stimuli that describes the "strength" of a color—the extent to which it appears rich or pale (e.g., light pink versus hot pink).

savant syndrome A syndrome in a developmentally disabled person who has some remarkable talent that contrasts with his low level of general intelligence.

scatter plot A graph depicting the relationship between two variables, in which each axis represents one variable; often used to graph correlation data.

Schachter-Singer theory of emotion The theory that emotional experience results from the interpretation of bodily responses in the context of situational cues.

schedule of reinforcement The rules about how often and under what conditions a response will be reinforced. *See also* interval schedule, ratio schedule.

schema An individual's mental representation that summarizes her knowledge about a certain type of event or situation.

schizoid personality disorder A personality disorder characterized by a striking detachment from others.

schizophrenia A group of severe mental disorders characterized by at least some of the following: marked disturbance of thought, withdrawal, inappropriate or flat emotions, delusions, and hallucinations.

schizotypal personality disorder A personality disorder characterized by discomfort with close relationships, cognitive or perceptual distortions, and odd behavior.

SD *See* standard deviation.

second-order conditioning A form of learning in which a neutral stimulus is first made meaningful through classical conditioning. Then, that stimulus (the CS) is paired with a new, neutral stimulus until the new stimulus also elicits the conditioned response.

secondary sexual characteristics Bodily structures that change with sexual maturity but are not directly related to reproduction.

secure base According to John Bowlby, the relationship in which the child feels safe and protected.

selection task A task used in research on reasoning, in which participants are presented with four cards (each showing one side) and a rule about what appears on each side of them. Participants must decide which cards to turn over to determine whether the rule has been followed.

selective serotonin reuptake inhibitors (SSRIs) Medications such as Prozac, Zoloft, and Paxil that increase serotonin turnover in the brain and find wide use as treatments for depression, obsessive-compulsive disorder, panic disorder, and many other disorders.

self-actualization According to Abraham Maslow and some other adherents of the humanistic approach to personality, the full realization of one's potential. *See also* hierarchy of needs.

self-control The ability to pursue a goal while adequately managing internal conflicts about it, or to delay pursuing a goal because of other considerations or constraints.

self-efficacy The sense a person has about what things he can plausibly accomplish.

self-esteem The relative balance of positive and negative judgments about oneself.

self-fulfilling prophecies Beliefs about how a person will behave that actually make the expected behavior more likely.

self-handicapping A self-protective strategy of arranges for an obstacle to one's own performance, so that failure can be attributed to the obstacle instead of one's own limitations.

Self-Monitoring Scale A personality measure that seeks to determine the degree to which a person alters or adjusts their behavior in order to act appropriately in new circumstances.

self-perception theory The theory that we know our own attitudes and feelings only by observing our own behaviors and deciding what probably caused them, just as we do when trying to understand others.

self-report data Data supplied by the research participant describing herself (usually, ratings of attitudes or moods, or tallies of behavior), rather than that collected by the experimenter.

self-schema An organized body of knowledge about the self and that shapes one's behaviors, perceptions, and emotions.

self theory Carl Rogers's theory of personality, which emphasizes the individual's active attempts to satisfy his needs in a manner that is consistent with his self-concept.

semantic feature A basic semantic category or concept that cannot be decomposed into smaller or less inclusive categories. According to several strict theories (e.g., Hume, 1739), the basic features are all sensory-perceptual.

semantic memory Memory for facts (including word meanings); these memories are not tied to any specific time or place.

semantic role The part that each phrase plays in the "who did what to whom" drama described by a sentence. One word takes the role of being the cause of the action, another, its effect, and so on.

semicircular canals Structures in the inner ear that contain the receptors for the vestibular sense.

semistructured interview An interview in which questions are posed in a standardized yet flexible way.

sensation seeking A predisposition to seek novel experiences, look for thrills and adventure, and be highly susceptible to boredom.

sensitive period An early period during the development of an organism when it is particularly responsive to environmental stimulation. Outside of this period, the same environmental events have less impact and may yield imperfect learning even after lengthy exposure and practice.

sensorimotor period In Piaget's theory, the period of cognitive development from birth to about 2 years, in which the child has not yet achieved object permanence.

sensory adaptation The process by which the sensitivity to a stimulus declines if the stimulus is presented for an extended period of time.

sensory coding The process through which the nervous system represents the qualities of the incoming stimulus—whether auditory or visual, for example, or whether a red light or a green one, a sour taste or a sweet taste.

sensory memory A type of memory included in early stage models, preserving sensory in "raw" form. Iconic memory holds onto visual inputs; echoic memory holds onto auditory inputs.

sensory projection area *See* primary somatosensory projection area.

sensory quality A distinguishing attribute of a stimulus (e.g., brightness, hue, or pitch).

separation anxiety A pattern of emotions and behaviors that reflect a child's fear when her mother (or other caregiver) leaves the room; usually observed in children 6 to 8 months of age.

set point A general term for the level at which negative feedback tries to maintain stability.

shallow processing An approach to memorization that involves focusing on the superficial characteristics of the stimulus, such as the sound of a word or the typeface in which it's printed.

shape constancy The tendency to perceive objects as retaining their shapes despite changes in our angle of regard that produce changes in the image projected on the retina.

shaping The process of eliciting a desired response by rewarding behaviors that are increasingly similar to that response.

short-term memory *See* stage theory of memory.

signal-detection theory The theory that perceiving or not perceiving a stimulus is actually a judgment about whether a momentary sensory experience is due to background noise alone or to the background noise plus a signal.

signs In psychopathology, what the clinician observes about a patient's physical or mental condition. *See also* symptoms.

similarity In perception, a principle by which we tend to group like figures, especially by color and orientation.

simple reaction time A measurement of how quickly someone can respond to a stimulus.

simultaneous color contrast The effect produced because any region in the visual field tends to induce its complementary color in adjoining areas. For example, a gray patch will tend to look bluish if surrounded by yellow and yellowish if surrounded by blue.

sine waves Waves (e.g., sound waves or light waves) that correspond to the plot of the trigonometric sine function.

single-cell recording A procedure of monitoring the moment-by-moment electrical activity of an individual cell in the nervous system.

situational attributions Explanations of someone's behavior in terms of the circumstances rather than aspects of the person.

size constancy The tendency to perceive objects as retaining their size, despite the increase or decrease in the size of the image projected on the retina caused by moving closer to or farther from the objects. *See also* unconscious inference.

skin senses The group of senses, including pressure, warmth, cold, and pain, through which we gain information about our immediate surroundings.

slow-wave sleep A term used for both Stage 3 and Stage 4 sleep; characterized by slow, rolling eye movements, low cortical arousal, and slowed heart rate and respiration.

smooth muscles The nonstriated muscles controlled by the autonomic nervous system. Smooth muscles constrict the blood vessels to help regulate blood pressure, and they line many internal organs.

social facilitation The tendency to perform simple or well-practiced tasks better in the presence of others than alone.

social inhibition The tendency to perform complex or difficult tasks more poorly in the presence of others.

social loafing A pattern in which people working together on a task generate less total effort than they would have if they had each worked alone.

social referencing A process of using others' facial expressions as a cue about the situation.

sociometric data Data that describe how individuals in a group interact.

sociopathy *See* antisocial personality disorder.

somatic nervous system (SNS) The division of the peripheral nervous system that controls the skeletal muscles and transmits sensory information.

somatogenic hypothesis The hypothesis that mental disorders result from organic (bodily) causes.

somatosensory area *See* primary somatosensory projection area.

sound waves Successive pressure variations in the air that vary in amplitude and wavelength.

species general Pertaining to all organisms in a species.

species specific Pertaining to just one species.

Specific Language Impairment (SLI) A syndrome of unknown etiology in which the course of development of a first language is unusually protracted despite otherwise normally developing cognitive functions. The language problems may eventually diminish or disappear but sometimes persist throughout life.

specific phobias Any of the disorders characterized by extreme and irrational fear of a particular object or situation.

specificity theory The proposal that different sensory qualities are signaled by different quality-specific neurons. This theory is correct in only a few cases (e.g., pain)

spontaneous recovery The reappearance of an extinguished response after a period in which no further conditioning trials have been presented.

spreading activation The process through which activity in one node in a network flows outward to other nodes through associative links.

SSRIs *See* selective serotonin reuptake inhibitors.

stage theory of memory An approach to memory that proposes a short-term memory store, which holds small amounts of information for fairly short intervals, and a long-term memory store, which can hold vast amounts of information for extended periods. According to the theory, information can be transferred to long-term memory only if it has first been in short-term memory.

stages of psychosexual development The sequence of four developmental stages from infancy through the attainment of adult sexuality that is considered universal in psychoanalytic theory: the oral stage, the anal stage, the phallic stage, and the genital stage.

standard deviation (SD) A measure of the variability of a data set, calculated as the square root of the variance (V).

Stanford Prison Experiment Philip Zimbardo's study of the effect of roles on behavior. Participants were randomly assigned to play either prisoners or guards in a mock prison. The study was ended early because of the "guards'" role-induced cruelty.

states Temporary patterns of thought, feeling, or behavior.

statistical significance A calculation central to inferential statistics that describes the likelihood that the results of a study happened by chance.

stem cells Cells that are found in early stages of an organism's development and are the precursors for all the other cells; stem cells have not begun to specialize or differentiate.

stereotype threat A mechanism through which a person's performance is influenced by her perception that her score may confirm stereotypes about her group.

stereotypes Schemas that are often negative and are used to categorize complex groups of people.

stimulants Drugs that have activating or excitatory effects on brain or bodily functions.

stimulus generalization The tendency for stimuli similar to those used during learning to elicit a reaction similar to the learned response.

strange situation An experimental procedure for assessing attachment, in which the child is allowed to explore an unfamiliar room with the mother present before the mother leaves for a few minutes, and then returns.

stress disorders Anxiety disorders that develop after experiencing a traumatic stressor.

Stroop effect A marked decrease in the speed of naming the colors of ink in which various color names are printed when the color words themselves don't match the ink colors. An effect of the automatization of reading.

subject noun phrase The noun phrase immediately descending from the root of the sentence tree. In simple English sentences, this noun phrase usually plays the semantic role of actor or agent of the action.

subjective contours Perceived contours that do not exist physically. We tend to complete figures that have gaps in them by perceiving a contour as continuing along its original path.

subordinates Concepts that are less abstract or more particular than basic-level concepts (e.g., *poodle, soup spoon*). *See also* basic level, superordinates.

subroutines In problem solving, specific procedures for solving familiar, well-defined problems.

subsyndromal disorder An instance of a mental disorder in which someone does show symptoms, but not at a level of intensity, frequency, or duration that would justify a formal diagnosis.

successive approximations A learner's responses during instrumental conditioning that are rewarded for being increasingly similar to the desired response. *See also* shaping.

sucking reflex An infantile reflex in which an infant sucks on whatever is placed in his mouth.

superego In Freud's theory, reaction patterns that emerge from within the ego, represent the internalized rules of society, and come to control the ego by punishment with guilt. *See also* ego, id.

superordinates Concepts that are more abstract or inclusive than basic-level concepts (e.g., *animal, utensil*). *See also* basic level, subordinates.

supertasters People who are extremely sensitive to certain tastes, probably because they have more papillae than other people do.

suppression A form of emotion regulation that involves inhibiting emotion-expressive behavior.

syllogism A logic problem containing two premises and a conclusion; the syllogism is valid if the conclusion follows logically from the premises.

symbolic representation A mental representation that stands for some content without sharing any characteristics with the thing it represents. *See also* analogical representation.

sympathetic branch The division of the autonomic nervous system that mobilizes the organism for physical exertion

symptoms In psychopathology, what the patient reports about his physical or mental condition. *See also* signs.

synapse The small gap between two adjacent neurons, consisting of the presynaptic and postsynaptic neurons' membranes and the space between them.

synaptic reuptake The presynaptic neuron's process of reabsorbing its own neurotransmitters after signaling so that they can be released again the next time the neuron fires.

synaptic vesicles Tiny sacs within a presynaptic membrane that contain the neurotransmitter; when the presynaptic neuron fires, some of these vesicles burst and eject their contents into the synaptic gap.

syntax *See* rules of syntax (or grammar).

System 1 In dual-process models of judgment, the fast, efficient, but sometimes faulty type of thinking.

System 2 In dual-process models of judgment, the slower, more effortful, and more accurate type of reasoning.

---

tabula rasa Latin for "blank slate"; a reference to the idea that people are born without innate knowledge—so that all knowledge must be gained from experience.

tacit knowledge Practical "how-to" knowledge accumulated from everyday experience.

tangible support Social support focused on practical or material needs.

tastants Molecules that can trigger a response by the neural receptors within the sense of taste.

taste aversion learning A form of learning in which an organism learns to avoid a taste after just one pairing of that taste with illness.

temperament A person's characteristic level of reactivity and energy; often thought to be constitutional.

temporal lobe The areas in each cerebral hemisphere lying below the temples; includes tissue crucial for hearing and many aspects of language use.

teratogens Environmental factors that can disrupt healthy neural development. These include lead, alcohol, and cigarette smoke.

test-retest reliability An assessment of whether a test is consistent in what it measures, determined by asking whether the test results on one occasion are correlated with the results from the same test (or a close variant on it) on another occasion.

testable hypothesis A prediction that has been formulated specifically enough so that it is clear what observations would confirm the prediction and what observations would challenge it.

testosterone The principal male sex hormone in mammals.

texture gradient A depth cue based on changes in surface texture that depend on how far away the observer is.

thalamus The part of the brain that serves as a major relay and integration center for sensory information.

that's-not-all technique A sales method that starts with a modest offer, then improves on it. The improvement seems to require reciprocation, which often takes the form of purchasing the item.

theory of mind The set of interrelated concepts we use to make sense of our own thoughts, feelings, and behaviors, as well as those of others.

therapeutic alliance The relationship between therapist and patient that helps many patients feel hopeful and supported.

thermoregulation The process by which organisms maintain a constant body temperature.

third-variable problem The possibility that two correlated variables may be changing together only due to the operation of a third variable.

timbre The quality of a sound apart from its pitch or loudness; timbre enables us to distinguish a clarinet from an oboe, or one person's voice from another.

tip-of-the-tongue (TOT) effect The condition in which one remains on the verge of retrieving a word or name but continues to be unsuccessful.

TMS *See* transcranial magnetic stimulation.

token economy A behavioral therapy technique based on operant conditioning in which patients' positive behaviors are reinforced with tokens that they can exchange for desirable items.

tonotopic map A map organized on the basis of tone.

TOT effect *See* tip-of-the-tongue (TOT) effect.

traits Relatively stable patterns of thought, feeling, or behavior that characterize an individual.

transcranial magnetic stimulation (TMS) The technique of applying repeated magnetic stimulation at the surface of the skull to temporarily stimulate or disable a target brain region.

transduction The process through which a physical stimulus is converted into a signal within the nervous system.

transection Surgical cutting of a nerve tract or brain region, performed to functionally isolate the regions on either side.

transference A patient's tendency to respond to the analyst or therapist in ways that re-create her responses to major figures in her life.

tree diagram A geometric representation of the structure of a sentence. Its nodes are labeled with phrase- (e.g., noun phrase) and word-class (e.g., adjective) category names, and the descending branches indicate relationships among these categories.

trichromatic color vision The principle underlying human color vision. Color vision occurs through the operation of three sets of cones, each maximally sensitive to a different wavelength of light.

---

ultimate cause The reasons why, over many years of evolution, a particular trait or behavior helped members of a population to survive and reproduce.

unconditioned response (UR) A response elicited by an unconditioned stimulus without prior training. *See also* conditioned response (CR), conditioned stimulus (CS), unconditioned stimulus (US).

unconditioned stimulus (US) A stimulus that reliably triggers a particular response without prior training. *See also* conditioned response (CR), conditioned stimulus (CS), unconditioned response (UR).

unconscious inference A process postulated by Hermann von Helmholtz to explain certain perceptual phenomena such as size constancy. For example, an object is perceived to be at a certain distance and this is unconsciously taken into account in assessing its retinal image size, with the result that size constancy is maintained. *See also* size constancy.

UR *See* unconditioned response.

US *See* unconditioned stimulus.

---

vagal nerve stimulation An emerging biomedical treatment for depression that involves electrically stimulating the vagus nerve with a small battery-powered implant.

validity The extent to which a method or procedure measures what it is supposed to measure. *See also* construct validity, external validity, internal validity, predictive validity.

variability The degree to which scores in a frequency distribution depart from the central value.

variable Any characteristic whose values can change.

verification The last of Wallas's four stages of problem solving. In his theory, this is the stage in which the person confirms that the ideas that emerged in the illumination stage actually solve the problem. *See also* illumination, incubation, preparation.

vestibular senses The sensations generated by receptors in the semicircular canals of the inner ear that inform us about the head's orientation and movements.

vicarious conditioning A form of learning in which the learner acquires a conditioned response merely by observing another participant being conditioned.

visible spectrum The range of wavelengths that our visual system can respond to; extends from about 400 (the wavelength usually perceived as the color violet) to 750 nanometers (the wavelength usually perceived as the color reddish orange).

visual agnosia The inability to recognize a visual stimulus despite the ability to see and describe it.

visual perspective A depth cue in which—due to the principles of optics—parallel lines appear to converge as they recede into the distance, and objects cast smaller images if they are farther away from the viewer.

visual search A task in which participants are asked to determine whether a specified target is present within a field of stimuli.

---

wait-list control In randomized clinical trials, a control condition in which patients receive delayed treatment rather than no treatment. Before being treated, they are compared to patients treated earlier.

wanting An organism's motivation to obtain a reward.

wavelength The distance between the crests of two successive waves and the major determinant of pitch (for sound) and hue (for light).

Weber fraction In Weber's law, the fraction given by the change in stimulus intensity (D I) divided by the standard intensity (I) required to produce a just-noticeable difference: D I/I = C.

Weber's law The observation that the size of the difference threshold is proportional to the intensity of the standard stimulus.

well-defined problem A problem for which there's a clear-cut way of deciding whether a proposed solution is correct.

Wernicke's area A brain area in the temporal lobe and adjacent to the auditory projection area, damage to which leads to deficits in understanding word meaning. *See also* aphasia, fluent aphasia.

"what" system The visual pathway leading from the visual cortex to the temporal lobe; especially involved in identifying objects.

"where" system The visual pathway leading from the visual cortex to the parietal lobe; especially involved in locating objects in space and coordinating movements.

white matter Whitish-appearing brain tissue that is composed of myelinated axons.

Whorfian hypothesis The proposal that the language one speaks determines or heavily influences the thoughts one can think or the saliency of different categories of thought.

withdrawal A consequence of drug dependence that occurs when the drug is withheld, such that the person feels strong drug cravings and psychological and medical distress.

withdrawn-rejected The social status of children who are not respected or liked by peers and become anxious as a result.

within-subject comparisons Within a study, comparing the data about each participant in one situation to data about the same participant in another situation.

working memory A term describing the status of thoughts in memory that are currently activated.

Young-Helmholtz theory A theory of color vision holding that each of the three receptor types (short-wave, medium-wave, and long-wave) gives rise to the experience of one basic color (blue, green, or red).

---

zone of proximal development The range of accomplishments that are beyond what the child can do on her own, but that she can achieve with help or guidance.

zygote The fertilized egg, formed by the union of sperm and egg.

Name Index

Bandura, A., 290, 623, 690
Banich, M., 435
Banks, C., 530
Banks, W. P., 231
Bannerman, H. A., 706
Bantick, R. A., 696
Barban, L., 671
Barber, J. P., 704, 711
Barcklay, J. R., 317
Bargh, J., 225
Bargh, J. A., 368, 512
Barkley, R. A., 668
Barlow, D. H., 647, 648, 711
Barnes, M. F., 78, 482
Barnes, V. A., 247
Barnet, R. C., 274
Barnier, A. J., 245
Baron-Cohen, S., 549, 667
Barrett, H. C., 369
Barrett, L. F., 493, 496
Barrouillet, P., 434
Barry, H. I., 602
Barselou, I. W., 388
Bartell, P., 238
Barth, H., 559
Bartholomew, K., 614
Bartlett, F. C., 321
Bartlett, J. R., 701
Bartlett, M. Y., 79
Bartol, C. R., 600
Bartoshuk, L. M., 151, 152
Bates, E., 386, 396
Bates, J., 567, 573
Bates, T. C., 433
Bateson, G., 665
Batson, C. D., 533
Battle, Y. L., 663
Baudonniere, P. -M., 572
Baumeister, R. F., 36, 476, 481, 483
Baumrind, D., 44, 569, 575, 581
Baup, N., 703
Bayer, E., 470
Baynard, M. D., 236
Beach, F. A., 76
Bear, M. F., 121
Beauchamp, G., 151
Bebeau, M., 575
Bechara, A., 438
Beck, A. T., 641, 653, 657, 691, 692
Beckers, T., 275
Becklen, R., 211
Bédard, J., 373
Beech, J. S., 128
Beecher, M. D., 291
Beedle, D., 703
Beehner, J., 414
Beers, M., 438
Beethoven, Ludwig van, 372
Begg, I., 336, 370
Behrmann, M., 344
Beier, M. E., 436
Beitman, B. D., 692
Belin, D., 601
Bell, A. P., 483
Bell, S. M., 565
Bellugi, U., 410

Bem, D. J., 517
Benbow, C., 452
Benbow, C. P., 452
Bendixen, L., 366
Benet-Martínez, V., 598
Bengel, D., 58
Ben Hamida, S., 290, 651
Benjet, C., 576
Bennett, C., 530
Bennett, R., 530
Benson, H., 707
Benson, K., 711
Berens, M. S., 408
Bergbower, K., 627
Bergen, J. R., 204
Bergen, S. E., 73
Berger, S., 330
Bergin, A. E., 711
Berglas, S., 627
Berglund, P., 649, 682
Bergman, T., 414
Bergson, C., 664
Berkeley, George, 135, 135, 260
Berkeley, M. A., 204
Berman, J. S., 710
Bermant, G., 481
Bernard, V. W., 526
Bernardo, M., 702
Berndt, T. J., 572, 574, 582
Bernstein, D., 325
Bernstein, D. A., 477
Bernstein, D. M., 320, 332
Berntsen, D., 330
Berrettini, W. H., 655
Berridge, K. C., 490
Berry, D. T. R., 642
Berscheid, E., 535, 536, 537, 539
Bersoff, D. M., 534
Berthomier, P., 238
Besner, D., 368
Bessenoff, G. R., 535
Betancourt, T. S., 658
Bever, T., 392
Bhardwaj, R. D., 127
Bialystok, E., 409, 584
Biederman, Irving, 191
Biello, S.M., 251
Bigelow, B., 582
Bihrle, A., 410
Bijl, R. V., 644
Billings, F. J., 320
Binder, E. B., 650, 713
Binet, A., 426, 426, 427, 441
Birmaher, B., 705
Birnbaum, M., 360
Bitterman, M. E., 295
Bittigau, P., 549
Björk-Eriksson, T., 127
Bjorklund, D. F., 35, 78, 475, 483
Björklund, L., 128
Black, D. N., 700
Black, D. W., 649, 650, 655, 661, 665, 671, 701
Black, J. B., 321
Blackwell, L., 624

Blair, H., 312
Blair, I., 322
Blair, N. J., 275
Blake, R., 230
Blanchette, I., 370
Blandon-Gitlin, I., 332
Blankenship, S. E., 372
Blascovich, J., 456
Blatt, S. J., 682
Blehar, M. C., 565, 614
Bleuler, M., 638
Blier, P., 697
Blin, O., 650
Bliss, E. L., 671
Bliss, T. V. P., 297
Block, J., 595, 613
Block, J. H., 613
Block, N., 233, 256
Blois, W. O., 325
Bloom, B. S., 486
Bloom, P., 396, 401
Blumberg, S. J., 361
Bodenhausen, G. V., 237, 370, 456
Bodkin, J. A., 330
Bogen, J. E., 117
Boget, T., 702
Bogg, T., 598
Bohus, M., 693
Bolland, S. W., 334
Bolles, R. C., 291, 294
Bollini, A., 661, 663
Bolnick, D. I., 63
Bolton, P., 658
Bond, M., 613
Bond, R., 510, 522
Bonnet, M. H., 236
Boodoo, G., 455
Book, A. S., 476
Boone, A. L., 36
Bootzin, R. R., 238
Bordone, Paris, 136
Boring, E. G., 197
Borkenau, P., 599
Born, J., 238
Bornstein, M. H., 551
Bornstein, R. F., 642
Bortz, R., 238
Both, S., 482
Botvinick, M. M., 435
Bouchard, C., 471
Bouchard, T. J., 599, 603
Bouchard, T. J., Jr., 444, 455, 472
Bourdon, K. H., 645
Bouret, S. G., 468
Bouton, M. E., 274
Bowen, M., 694
Bower, G. H., 284, 311, 321
Bower, J. M., 115
Bowerman, M., 417
Bowker, A., 574
Bowmaker, J. K., 169
Boyd, J. H., 645
Brabeck, M., 575
Brackett, M. A., 438, 439
Bradley, G. W., 626
Bradley, R., 708

Bradley, R. G., 650
Bradshaw, J. L., 124
Braffman, W., 245
Brailowsky, S., 698
Brainerd, C., 322
Brambrilla, P., 656
Brandone, A. C., 560
Brannan, S. K., 656, 703
Brannon, E., 559
Bransford, J. D., 309, 310, 317
Braswell, L., 690
Brauer, M., 530
Brawman-Mintzer, O., 699
Brechbühl, J., 150
Breedlove, S. M., 476, 480, 549
Brendgen, M., 574
Brennan, K. A., 614
Brennen, T., 314
Brenner, L., 362
Breslau, N., 644
Bretherton, I., 566
Breuer, A., 252
Breuer, J., 606
Brewer, J., 309
Brewer, N., 325
Brewer, W. F., 321
Brewin, C. R., 330
Brickman, J. S., 656, 703
Brickman, P., 620
Bridgeman, B., 206, 453
Bridges, M., 571
Bridges, P., 701
Bright, J., 314
Britton, W. B., 331
Broadbent, D. E., 304
Brobeck, J. R., 465
Broca, Pierre-Paul, 123
Brody, G. H., 570
Brody, N., 438, 452, 454
Broillet, M.-C., 150
Bronfenbrenner, U., 442
Brooks, K., 373
Brooks-Gunn, J., 448, 578
Brown, A., 313
Brown, B. B., 582
Brown, C. M., 383
Brown, E., 324
Brown, G., 58
Brown, G. K., 641
Brown, H. E., 313
Brown, M. W., 323
Brown, N., 12
Brown, P., 395
Brown, R., 313, 329, 385, 403, 405, 453
Brown, S. A., 249
Brown, T., 650
Browning, P., 435
Bruce, C., 177
Bruce, V., 314
Bruck, M., 320, 321
Brunell-Neuleib, S., 642
Bruner, J. S., 510
Bryant, G. A., 79
Bryant, J., 482
Brzustoski, P., 456
Buchanan, D. R., 535

Miller, S. D., 704
Miller, T. E., 573
Miller, W. R., 289, 686
Mills, B., 322
Milner, A. D., 194, 224
Milner, B., 124, 333
Mineka, S., 290, 294, 651
Minsky, M., 228
Minuchin, S., 694
Mischel, H. N., 629
Mischel, W., 510, 596, 597, 624, 628,
    629, 630
Miselis, R. R., 468
Mishkin, M., 194
Mishler, E. G., 666
Mistlberger, R. E., 233
Mita, T. H., 536
Mitchell, D., 238
Mitchell, J., 323, 566, 711
Miyake, A., 396
Modrek, S., 668
Moen, P., 442
Modahl, C., 667
Moffat, S., 453
Moffitt, T. E., 58, 655
Moghaddam, F., 522
Mohamed, F., 80
Mohyde, M., 582
Molden, D. C., 624
Molinari, L., 237
Moloney, D. P., 603
Monahan, J., 142
Mondin, G. W., 7111
Monroe, S. M., 656
Montagu, A., 442
Montague, D., 562
Montague, P., 672
Montgomery, S. A., 698
Moody, M., 711
Moore, B., 629
Moore, J., 59
Moore, M. K., 290
Moorhead, G., 531
Moos, R. H., 481
Mora, F., 470, 695
Moran, T. J., 575
Moray, M., 582
Moray, N., 214
Moreland, R. L., 530, 536
Moreno, C., 654
Morewedge, C., 240
Morewedge, C. K., 361
Morgan, B., 102
Morgan, C. P., 530
Morgan, J. L., 382, 399
Morgan, M. J., 251
Morgan, R. F., 446
Morris, A. S., 578
Morris, E. K., 320
Morris, H., 102
Morris, P. G., 660
Morrison, F. J., 568
Morrison, S. L., 665
Morse, H. M., 595
Morse, R., 446
Moscovici, S., 355, 530

Moscovitch, M., 313, 325
Moser, M. B., 125, 297
Mosher, D. L., 482
Moskovitch, M., 4
Mosnaim, A. D., 647
Motohashi, K., 148
Mottolese, C., 231
Mounts, N. S., 574
Mozel, M., 150
Mullen, M. K., 569
Müller, H. J., 196
Müller, Johannes, 143
Mulrow, C. D., 697
Munafo, M. R., 58, 657
Munnich, E., 418
Mural, R. J., 54
Murphy, B. C., 573
Murphy, F. C., 496
Murphy, G. L., 387
Murray, C., 428
Murray, C. A., 442
Murray, S. R., 696
Murray, T. H., 44
Murre, J. M. J., 312
Musch, J., 356
Mussell, M., 711
Myers, B., 325
Myers, E. W., 54
Myers, T., 80
Mynatt, C. R., 355

Nadel, L., 238, 313, 331
Nader, K., 312
Nagel, T., 256
Naigles, L. G., 403
Nakagawa, S., 493
Nakamura, J., 372
Nakayama, K., 229
Nappa, R., 403
Narvaez, D., 575
Nash, M. R., 245, 246
Nasser, M., 670
Nathan, P. E., 708, 711, 712
National Research Council and Institute
    for Medicine, 571
Naumer, B., 356
Nauta, W. J. H., 88
Navarro, A. M., 709
Nazzi, T., 398
Neale, M. C., 484, 650, 655, 662
Neck, C. P., 531
Needham, D., 370
Neimeyer, G., 539
Neisser, U., 12, 211, 330, 442, 446, 447,
    449, 455
Nelson, C. A., 572
Nelson, E. S., 575
Nelson, K., 569
Nemeth, C., 522
Neria, Y., 656
Nespor, M., 382, 399
Nettelbeck, T., 439
Neumann, C., 447
Newcomb, A. F., 572, 573, 574
Newcomb, T., 529

Newcombe, F., 195
Newcombe, N., 453
Newcombe, N. S., 2002
Newell, A., 366
Newell, L., 573
Newman, E. A., 92
Newport, E. L., 400, 406, 410, 412, 413
Nezworski, M. T., 642
Nich, C., 686
NICHD Early Child Care Research
    Network, 570
Nichols, K. E., 601
Nicholson, R. A., 710
Nickens, S., 453
Nickerson, R. A., 308
Nickerson, R. S., 446
Nicolelis, M., 106
Nida, S. A., 533
Nieberding, R., 642
Nilsson, M., 64
Nimmo-Smith, I., 496
Nisbett, R., 358
Nisbett, R. E., 224, 225, 226, 285, 352,
    353, 357, 440, 477, 507, 508, 596
Nitsch, K., 317
Nobler, M. S., 701, 702
Nolen-Hoeksema, S., 628, 652
Noll, J., 432
Nopoulos, P., 659, 665
Norbury, H. M., 419
Norcross, J. C., 692, 711
Norenzayan, A., 534, 602
Norman, D. A., 304
Norman, W. T., 593
Norton, M. I., 240
Noseck, B. A., 523
Nosek, B. A., 512
Novak, M. A., 571
Novick, J. M., 410
Novotny, C., 708
Noyes, R., 650
Nurnberger, J. I., 655
Nyberg, L., 124
Nystrom, L., 3

Oakes, M. A., 612
Oberman, L. M., 667
Obhi, S., 231
Ochsner, K. N., 493, 499, 612
O'Connor, T. G., 572
Odbert, H. S., 593
Odiorne, J. M., 474
Oesterman, K., 35, 476
Ofshe, R., 332
Ohlsson, S., 373
Öhman, A., 290, 294, 646, 651
Okamoto, S., 62
Okasha, A., 636
Okasha, T., 636
Olff, M., 649
Olfson, M., 682, 697
Oliva, P., 330
Oliver, L. M., 357
Ollendick, T. H., 706, 712
Olsen, J., 573
Olsen, S., 573

Olson, A., 122
Olson, D. J., 295
Olson, E. A., 325
Olson, M., 334
Omoto, A. M., 534
O'Neal, J., 659
Ones, D. S., 427
Oomen, A., 561
Opie, M., 386
Orbach, Y., 331
Ordóñez, L., 360
Orne, M. T., 244
Ortmann, J., 655
Orwoll, E. S., 453
Osherson, A., 670
Osherson, D. N., 388
Osler, S., 317
Ost, L. G., 646
Oster, H., 491
Ottenberg, P., 526
Oviatt, S. K., 453
Owens, E., 566
Ozer, E. J., 598
Özyürek, A., 407

Pacifici, R., 251
Packer, D. J., 531
Palmer, S. E., 186
Pals, J. L., 617
Panksepp, J., 668
Pantev, C., 126
Panyavin, I. S., 80
Panzarella, R., 524
Papafragou, A., 395, 403, 416, 421
Paradiso, M. A., 121
Paris, J., 671
Park, B. G., 660
Park, C., 627
Park, M., 628
Parker, E. S., 313
Parker, G., 663
Parker, J., 573, 574
Parson, L. M., 115
Parsons, J. E., 453
Pascual-Leone, A., 126
Pashler, H., 368, 372
Pasupathi, M., 587
Patnoe, S., 516
Pattee, L., 574
Patterson, B. W., 245
Patterson, D., 245
Pauls, D. L., 650
Paulus, M. P., 711
Pavlov, Ivan Petrovich, 263–64, 263
Payne, D. G., 325
Payne, J. D., 331
Peabody, D., 595
Peace, K. A., 330
Peake, P. K., 629
Pearce, J. M., 274
Pearlmutter, N. J., 392, 396
Pearson, J., 656
Pedersen, N., 72
Pederson, E., 419
Pekkarinen, T., 452
Pemberton, M., 663

Subject Index

compensatory, 669
consciousness and, 221
consistency in, 595–97
evolution and, 66, 79
expressions and, 66–69
genetic influence on, 79
hormonal changes and, 480
instrumental (operant) conditioning and, 281, 299
natural selection and, 59–60
niche construction and, 66
sexual, 478–85
see also social behavior
behavioral contrast, 285–86, 299
behavioral data, 597
behaviorism, 623
behavior modification, 281, 283–85, *284,* 287, 687–90, 714
vs. acquired knowledge, 287–89
behavior therapy, 687–90, *687,* 714
belongingness, 291–94
Bem, Daryl, 517
benzodiazepines, 248, 249, 698–99
Berkeley, George, 135, *135,* 260
Bernard, Claude, 463–64
Bernard, Luther, 463
beta-blockers, 698
beta rhythm, 234–35, *235*
between-subject comparisons, 41
bias, confirmation, 354–55, *355,* 376, 530–31
see also prejudice; stereotypes
bidirectional activation, 189–90, *190*
Biederman, Irving, 191
Big Five, 591, 593–98, *599,* 602, 604, 605, 632
bilingualism, 408–10
cognitive flexibility of, 409
crib, 408
executive control and, 409
rate of learning and, 408–9
binding problem, 195–96, 210, 216
Binet, Alfred, 426, *426,* 428, 458
binge eating, 669
binocular cues, 200
binocular disparity, 200, *200,* 203
binocular rivalry, 229, *230*
biological constraints, on conditioning, 291–94
biology, biological factors:
behavior and, *599*
depression and, 638
in learning, 291–94
in personality, 598–601, *599,* 632
in psychopathology, 638–39
race and, 442
see also brain; nervous system; neurons; *specific organs*
biomedical factors, psychopathology and, 638–39
biomedical treatments, 694–703
for psychopathology, 694–703, 714

biopsychosocial perspective, of psychopathology, 638–39, 674
bipolar cells, *162, 163*
bipolar disorder, 58, 635–36, 653–55, 674, 677–78, 692, 698
medication for, 698
suicide and, 654–55
bisexuality, 484
"black box" warning, 699, *700*
Bleuler, Eugen, 658
blindsight, 223
blind spot, *163,* 164, *164*
blocking effect, 274–75, 298
blood-brain barrier, 102
blood circulation, 130
blood-injury-injection phobia, 645–46
bloodletting, 694
blood-oxygenation-level-dependent signal (BOLD), 111
bloodstream, communication through, 103–5
bodily-kinesthetic intelligence, 439
Body Mass Index (BMI), 471, *471,* 473
body temperature, 464–66, *465,* 478
"Bonnie Earl O'Murray," 182
borderline personality disorder, 672, 693
Bordoni, Paris, *136*
bottom-up processing, 189–90, *190*
Bowlby, John, 566–67, 613–14
Bowlby's theory of attachment, 563–65, 588
brain:
activity of, 3, *3,* 6, 8–9, *9,* 65, 229–31, *230,* 233, 234, 238, 241–43, *242,* 247, 248, *248,* 309, *345,* 433, 488, *488,* 650, 656
amygdala of, 116
antipsychotics and, 695–96
autism and, 667
blood-brain barrier of, 102
chemical signals of, 97
consciousness and, 227–29, *228*
decision making and, 4–6
depression and, 703
development of, 57, 90, *550*
EEG and, 109
ERP and, 109
executive control in, 435, *435*
of fruit flies, 238
gray matter in, 91, *91*
hemispheres of, 116–18, 120
hippocampus of, 116
imaging, 2
lateralization of, 116–18, *117*
lesions of, 106–7, *106*
localization of function in, 131
major structures of, 87–94, *115*
manipulation of, 106–7
maturation of, 588
meditation and, 247–48, *248,* 257
mental disorders and, 680
mental retardation and, 57

morality and, 2–3, *3,* 4
nervous system and, 85–131
neuroimaging of, 110–11
parts of, *see specific parts*
plasticity of function in, 125–28, 296–97
prenatal development of, *547*
psychotherapy and function of, 700–701
recording electrical activity of, 109, *109*
schizophrenia and development of, 661–63
schizophrenia and structural defects in, 664–65, *665*
structure of, *9,* 112, 126
subcortical structures of, 89, *116*
THC and, 252
in visualization, 344
visual processing in, 192–95, *193*
white matter in, 91, *91*
brain damage, 85–86, 106–8, 121–25, *124,* 130
agnosias and, 95, 122, 131
amnesias and, *313,* 333
to amygdala, 9, 10
aphasias and, 123
apraxias and, 121, 131
consciousness and, 229, 256
effects of, 106–9
episodic memory and, 328
to frontal lobe, 124–25
goal maintenance and, 435
of H.M., *333, 333*
to hypothalamus, 469
memory loss and, 4
neglect syndrome caused by, 122
neuroimaging and, 112
of Phineas Gage, 26–27, 107, *107*
to prefrontal cortex, *124*
repair of, 127–28, *128*
unconscious functioning and, 223–24
vision and, 376
brain stem, 114, *115*
breeding, 61, 63, 75, *77*
Breuer, Joseph, 606
brightness, 161, 164
amplification of, 165
of color, 168, *168*
of light, 161, 164, *165, 166*
perceived, *166*
physical, *166*
brightness contrast, 165–68, *165, 166*
Broca's area, 123, *123*
Brunn Natural History Society, 56
Brunn Society's Proceedings, 56
Buddhism, 247
bulimia nervosa, 668, 669–70, *669,* 699, 712
Bush, George W., 12, *12,* 128
BuSpar, 699
Buss, David, 78
bystander effect, 532–33, *533,* 543

caffeine, 250, *250, 251*

competencies, self-regulatory plans and, 625–26, 633

complementary hues, 170–71

complex waves, 155, *155*

compliance, 526–27, 542
  reciprocity and, 526–27
  that's-not-all technique and, 527, 542

compulsions, 648

computerized axial tomography (CAT) scan, 110, *110*

computerized tomography (CT) scan, 100

concepts, 346

conciliatory signals, 478, *478*

concordance rate, 650

concrete operations, 552, *553*, 556, 578, 588, 589

conditional statements, 291

conditioned reflex, 263–69

conditioned reinforcement, 282–85

conditioned reinforcer, 284–85, 299

conditioned responses, 263–78, *267, 268,* 274, 298

conditioned stimulus, 268, 273, 274

conditioning:
  biological constraints on, 291–94
  classical, *see* classical conditioning
  contiguity in, 270
  contingency in, 270–71, 287–89
  extinction in, 266–68, *267,* 278
  generalization and discrimination in, 268–69, 278, 282–83, 298
  instrumental (operant), *see* instrumental conditioning
  Pavlovian, 651
  second-order, 265
  vicarious, 290, 651

cones, *162,* 163, *163,* 170
  day vision served by, 164
  pattern of response of, 169–70, *169*
  in trichromatic vision, 169
  visual pigments in, 164–65

confederates, 496

confirmation bias, 25, 354–55, *355,* 356, 376, 530–31

conflict, and defense, 608–9

conformity, 519–22, *521,* 542
  causes of, 520–21
  culture and, 522
  minority influence vs., 522, *522*
  psychological distance and, 525

conjunction search, 209

conscience, 576, 589
  parent-child relationships and, 576
  punishment and, 576

conscientiousness, 593

conscious level, *607*

consciousness, 219–57
  automatic processes and, 226, *226*
  behavior and, 221
  brain activity and, 229–31, *230*
  brain areas needed for, 228–29, *228*

cognitive unconscious and, 222–23, 256

dreams and, *see* dreams, dreaming

drug-induced changes in, 248–55

executive control and, 226–27

"free will" and, 230–31, *231,* 257

function of, 226–27, 231

global workspace hypothesis and, 231–33, 257

honest reporting and, 220–21, *221*

hypnosis and, 243–46

implicit memory and, 223

ineffable experiences of, 221

introspection and functions of, 220–27, 256

inverted spectrum in, 221, *221*

meditation and, 247–48

memory and, 223, 224

mind-body problem of, 227–28, 255, 256

neural basis for, 227–33, 256–57

neural correlates of, 229–31, 257

perception and, 222, 224

readiness potential and, 231, *231*

religious states of, 247–48

sleep and, *see* sleep

translating thoughts into words and, 220–22

two aspects of, 228–29, *229*

unconscious attributions and, 224–25

unconscious functioning and, 223–24

varieties of, 233–55

conservation, failure of, 555–56, *556*

consistency, cultural differences in, 598

consolidation, 498

constancy, perceptual, 196–99, *196*
  brightness and, 196
  of position, 205
  of shape, 196, *196,* 198
  of size, 196, *197,* 198

construals, 632

construct validity, 24

contact comfort, 563–64, *564,* 588

content morphemes, 382–83, 422

context reinstatement, 315–16, *316,* 339

contingency management, 689

contralateral control, 119, 120, 131

contrast effects, 165–68, *165, 166*

control, 625–26, *626,* 633

control groups, 38–40, 44, 48

conventional reasoning, 574

conversational inference, 395

conversational patterns, 568–69

conversion disorder (hysteria), 606, 637, 643

Copland, Aaron, 484

copulation, 481

cornea, *162, 162*

corpus callosum, 117, *117*

correlation coefficient, 31, 32

correlations, correlational studies, 31–33, 37–38, *37,* 48, 112, 427–28, 458, 459
  causation and, 3
  reliability and, 32–33

twin studies and, 70
  see also statistics

correspondence problem, 207–8, *207*

cortex:
  development of, *550*
  parallel processing and visual, 192–94
  structure of, *115,* 131

cortical reorganization, 126

Cosmides, Leda, 357

counterirritation, 148

counting, 559

couples therapy, 694, *694*

Creedence Clearwater Revival, 181

crib bilingualism, 408

critical thinking, 375

Crow, Sheryl, 673

crowd behavior, bystander effect and, 532–33, *533*

Crucible, The (Miller), 355

crystallized intelligence, 432, 459, 583–84, 589

CT (computerized tomography) scan, 100

cultural competence, 682–83, 714

culturally appropriate therapy, 682

culture:
  childhood socialization and, 589
  collectivistic, 543, 627
  conformity and collectivistic, 522
  conversational patterns and, 568–69
  depression and, 657–58, *658*
  individualistic, 543 love in, 540
  influence of, on cognition, 568
  intelligence and, 440–41, 450–51
  language learning and, 396, 422
  love in collectivistic, 540
  mate choice and, 78
  moral reasoning and, 575
  parenting and, 571–72
  perception shaped by language in, 417–21
  personality and, 602–3
  personality trait taxonomy and, 595, 632
  psychotherapy and, 714
  romantic love and, 539–40, *540,* 543
  slow pace of human growth and, 550, *550*

Curie, Marie, 371

d-amphetamine, 250

Darkness Visible (Styron), 652–53

Darley, John, 532

Darwin, Charles, 52, 59, 61, 64, 68, 81, 278–79, 371, 372, 380, 491
  on evolution, 59–61, 278–79

data:
  collecting of, 25, *25,* 26
  correlations in, 31–33
  demand characteristics' influence on, 28
  descriptive statistics and, 28, 29
  frequency distribution and, 29, 30, *30*
  means and variability of, 29–31
  scatter plots and, 31, *31*
  standard deviation and, 30

data (*cont.*)
testing differences and, 34–36
variability and, 30, 34
working with, 28–36
data-driven processing, 189–90, *190*
day vision, 164
deafness, language learning and, 406
debriefing, 44
decibels, 154
decision criteria, 140
decision making, 4–6, 341, 348, 358–64, 376–77
affective forecasting in, 360–61, 364, 376
excessive options in, 361–63, *361*, 376
framing effects and, 5, *5*, 359–61, *360*, 364
in groups, 530–31
influences on, 5, 6
justifications of decisions in, 364
loss aversion in, 360
morals and, 2–3
predictions of outcomes and, 361, 363, 364, 376, 377
process of, 364, 377
reason-based choices of, 363–64, *363*
satisfice and, 363, 364, 377
declarative knowledge, 334
deductive reasoning, 354, *356*
deep brain stimulation (DBS), 702, *702*, 714
deep processing, 309, 338
defense, conflict and, 608–9
defense mechanisms, 608–9, 612–13, *613*, 632
definitional theory of word meaning, 386–87, *386*
dehumanization, of victims, 526, 542
deindividuation, 529–30, *529*, 542
deinstitutionalization, 696, *696*, 714
delta-9–tetrahydrocannabinol (THC), 251, 252
delta rhythm, 235, *235*
delusions, 659–60, 674
depression and, 653
of reference, 660
demand characteristics, 27–28
dendrites, 88–89, *88*, *90*, 92
spines, *125*, 130, 297
dependent personality disorder, 672
dependent variables, 24, *24*, 33, 35, 36, 39, 42, 48
depolarization, 95
depressants, 248–49, 257
depression, 37, 636, 638, 652–53, *652*, 669, 673, 674, 677, 691–92, 701, 703, 707
anxiety and, 653
bipolar disorder and, 653–55
childhood, 653
cognitive deficits and, 653
cognitive theory of, 657
culture and, 657–58, *658*
delusions and, 653
electroconvulsive therapy for, 701–2, *701*
genetic components of, 638
genetic factors of, 655
helplessness and hopelessness and, 657
learned helplessness and, 289

major, 652
medication for, 103, 696–98, 701, 714
neurochemical malfunction and, 656
obsessive-compulsive disorder and, 648
predictors for, 628
social support vs., 657
socioeconomic status and, 658
stress and, 656–57
subsyndromal, 711
suicide and, 654–55
war and, 657–58, *658*
Depression and Bipolar Support Alliance, 678
deprivation, social, 571–72, *572*
depth cues, 200, *202*, *203*
depth perception:
binocular disparity, 200, *200*, 203
monocular cues for, 200–202, *203*
through motion, 202
pictorial cues for, 201, *201*
redundancy in, 203
Descartes, René, *86*, 227–28, *228*, 379
on reflexes, 87, 96
descriptive statistics, 28, *29*
desensitization, 688
despair, integrity versus, 586, 589
detectors:
activation and inhibition of, 189–90, *190*
complex, 174
feature, 174–75, 182, 191, 209
motion, 204
development, 545–89
adult, 582–87
childhood, 550–76
after childhood, 589
cognitive, 552–62
conversational patterns and, 568–69
fluid and crystallized intelligence throughout, 432, 459
genetic transmission and, *54*, 55–56
as growth, 546–50
growth of brain throughout, *550*
human physical, 546–50
language learning throughout, 343–45, 396, *411*
of manual skills, 550–51, *551*
of memory, 568
milestones of, *552*
newborn's capacities and, 550–51
of personal identity, 581–82
Piaget's stages of, 552–56
prenatal, 546–49, *547*
proximal, 568
psychosexual, Freud's theories of, 609–10, 632
representational thought in, 555
sexual, 589
social cognition and, 559–62
spatial knowledge and, 557–58
see also cognitive development; social development
developmental disorders, 666–68, 675

attention-deficit/hyperactivity disorder (ADHD), 250, 636, 667–68, *667*, 675, 699, 714
autism, 666–67, *666*, 675, 689
dhat, Indian illness, 643
diabetes, 473
diagnosis, assessment vs., 643
Diagnostic and Statistical Manual of Mental Disorders (DSM-IV-TR), 639, 640, 643, 650, 668, 669, 674
dialectical behavior therapy (DBT), 692–93
Diana, Princess of Wales, *669*
diathesis-stress models, 638, *638*, 674
difference threshold, 137–39, 178
diffusion of responsibility, 532, *533*, 543
digital representations, *see* symbolic representations
Dimensional Change Card Sorting Task, 408–9
dimples, 57, *57*
directed thinking, 348
direction specific cells, 204
disengaged parents, 570, 589
dishabituation, 261, 298
disorders:
of action, 121
of language, 123–24
of memory, 333
mental, *see* mental disorders
of perception, 122
of planning and social cognition, 124–25
disorganized children, 614
disorganized schizophrenia, 660, *660*
displacement, 609, 632
display rules, 492–93, 500
dispositional attribution, 507, 509, 510, 541
dissociation, 649, 670–71
in infant cognition, *554*
dissociative amnesia, 670, 671, 675
dissociative fugue, 670, 671, 675
dissociative identity disorder (multiple personality disorder), 658n, 670–71, *671*, 675
distal stimulus, 135, *135*
distance, psychological, 525, 542
distance cues, *136*, 197
see also depth cues
distance perception, 200–203
divorce, domestic conflict and, 571
Dix, Dorothea, 679–80
dizygotic twins, *see* fraternal twins
DNA (deoxyribonucleic acid), 52–53, *53*, *54*, 82
mutations in, 61
paternity testing of, 80, *80*
doctrine of specific nerve energies (specificity theory), 144
dodo bird verdict, 712–13, *712*, 715
dominant genes, 57
dopamine (DA), 100, 103, 490, 600, 655, 695–96, 697
dopamine hypothesis, 644, *664*
double-blind design, 28, *28*, 43

downward drift, 665
dreams, dreaming, 239–43, *239*
  activation-synthesis hypothesis of, 241, 242, 243
  brain activity during, 238, 241–43, *242*
  consciousness and, 229
  emotions within, 240
  Freudian view of, 241, *241*
  Freud's theories on, 611, 632
  interpretation of, 240–41, *241*
  latent content of, 241, 611, 632
  manifest content of, 241, 611, 632
  reasons for, 240–43
  reports of, 239–40
  themes in, 240
drive, 464, 485–90, 500–501, 502
drive-reduction, 464, 485, 487
DRM paradigm, 322, *322*, 339
drugs, 248–55, 257, 325
  abuse of, 654
  addiction to, 253–54, 257
  agonists vs. antagonists, 101–3
  conditioning and use of, 276–78, *277*
  depressants, 248–49
  difference among people and, 254–55
  "gateway," 252
  genetics and, 255
  hallucinogens, 251, 252–53
  mental disorders and, 635
  mind-altering, 257
  in nervous system, 101–3
  psychoactive drugs, 699
  psychotropic, 683, 714
  side effects, 249, 251, *251*
  stimulants, 250–51
  tolerance for, 249, 253
  withdrawal from, 249, 250, 253–54
  see also medication
drug therapy, 710
DSM-IV-TR (Diagnostic and Statistical Manual of Mental Disorders), 639, 643, 640, 650, 668, 669
dual-center theory, 469
dual-process systems, 353
dual-process theories, 352–54, 376
duplex theory of vision, 164
Dweck, Carol, 624

ear, 145–46, *146*, 156, *157*
eardrum, 133, *157*, *159*
eating, 466–73, *466*, 501–2
  cognitive control over, 471
  control signals for, 468–69
  cultural influences on, 470, *471*
  disorders, 668–70, *669*
  memory and, 471
  physiological aspects of, 467–70
  poverty and, 471
  social influences on, 470, *470*, 502

Ebbinghaus, Hermann, 318
Eber papyrus, 636
eclecticism, 692–93
ecstasy (MDMA), 250
ECT (electroconvulsive therapy), 701–2, *701*, 703, 714
ectotherms, 464
EEG (electroencephalogram), 109, 111, 234–35, *235*, 247–48, *248*, 257
efferent nerves, 113
efferent neurons, 89, *90*
Effexor, 697
efficacy, 709, 714
  utility vs., 708–9
egg cells, 55–56, *56*, 69–70, *70*, 546, 588
ego, 607–8, 611, 612–13, 632
ego identity, 580, 589
ego psychology, 612–13, 632
Egyptian art, 215, *215*
Eichmann, Adolf, 523–24, *524*
eight ages of man, Erikson on, 580, *580*, 589
8–stage model, 579
Einstein, Albert, 440
Electra complex, 610, *612*, 632
electroconvulsive therapy (ECT), 701–2, *701*, 703, 714
electroencephalogram (EEG), 109, 111, 131, 234–35, *235*, 247–48, *248*, 257
electroencephalography (EEG), 111
electromagnetic spectrum, 161
Ellis, Albert, 690–91, 692, 714
Ellsworth, Phoebe, 341
embryo, 480, 546, 547, 548, 588
emotion, 490–500, *493*, 502–3
  behavioral aspects of, 491–93
  Cannon-Bard theory of, 494, 496, 502
  cognitive reappraisal and, 498–99, *499*, 500, 503
  cultural perspective of, 491, 493, *494*
  dimensions of, 493, *493*
  display rules of, 492–93, *492*, 500, 502
  experiential aspects of, 493
  facets of, 490–96
  facial expressions and, 491–93, *499*, 502
  functions of, 497–98
  James-Lange theory of, 494, 495–96, 502
  of jealousy, 79–80
  of love, 537–40
  memory and, 329–32, 497–98
  models of, *495*
  mood vs., 491
  motivation and, 461–503
  perception of, 492
  perceptual effects of, 497, *497*
  physiological aspects of, 494–96
  regulation of, 498–500
  Schachter-Singer theory of, 496, 502, 538
  in sleep, 240–41, *241*
  suppression of, 498–99, 503

emotional experience, 493
emotional intelligence, 438–39, 459
emotional memory, *9*
  active interpretation of, 11, 18
  children and, 14
  cognitive influences on, 11–12, 14
  cultural setting of, 13–14, *13*
  developmental perspective on, 14–15
  disorders of, 15–16, *15*
  evolutionary basis for, 9–11
  genetic heritage and, 9–11, 17
  neural basis of, 8–9
  painful, 15–16
  PTSD and, 16, 18
  recorded information in, 11
  sharing of, 12–13
  social influences on, 12–13, 14
  survival advantage to, 10
  as unreliable, 12, 13
emotional support, 486, 502
empirical claims, 46
empirically supported treatments (EST), 706, 714
empiricism, 135–36
empty chair technique, 687
encoding of memories, 303–4, 309
  context of, 315–16
  retrieval and, 315–16
encoding specificity, 317, 339
endocrine glands, *104*, 130
  functions of, *104*
endocrine system, 103–4, 130
endorphins, 102, *102*, 148, 490
endotherms, 464, 501
entity view, 624–25, *625*
environment:
  external, 463–64
  intelligence and, 445–48, *446*, 450–51
  internal, 463–64, 501
  IQ and, 445–48
  language learning and, 404–10, 423
  prenatal, 548
  vs. genetics, 446–47, 450–51, 602–3
environment of evolutionary adaptiveness (EEA), 73
epilepsy, 119, 701
epinephrine (adrenaline), 103, 474, 495, 496
episodic memory, 328–29, 331, 339, 583, 661
Erikson, Erik, 579, 582, 585–86
  on eight ages of man, 580, *580*, 589
ERP (event-related potential), 109
estrogen, 479, 480
estrus cycle, 479, 481, 502
ethics, in scientific research, 14, 43–45, 48–49, 106–7, 128, 289*n*
euphoria, *102*, 103
European Americans, IQ scores of, 450
event-related potential (ERP), 109
evolution, 51–83, 481, 483, 497
  adaptive specializations of, 294–95

evolution (*cont.*)

of behavior and genetics, 65–81

broken-wing display and, 62, *62*

Darwin's theory of, 59–61, 278–79

EEA and, 73

emotional remembering and, 9–11, *10*

finches and, 59, 65

fossils and, 63, *63*

genes and, 61–62

of intelligence, 73–75

learning and, 294–95

of mating patterns, 75–81

natural selection and, 58–65

proximate causes and, 58

sexual behavior and, 479

as "survival of the fittest," 61–62

ultimate causes and, 58

unity of life and, 64–65, *65*

evolutionary psychology, 77

excitation threshold, of neurons, 93, 106

excitement phase, of sexual response, 481, 502

executive control, 124, 226–27, 409, 434–36, *435*, *436*

exercise, 585

exogenous agents, 102

expectations, surprise and, 273, *274*, 298

experiential therapies, 687, 712

experimental groups, 39, 40, 48

experimental manipulation, 39, 40, 41, 47, 48

experimental studies, 38–43, 108

animals in, 65, 106, *106*

groups of, 38, 40, 48

internal validity of, 41–42

manipulation of, 41, 47

quasi-, 36, 44

random assignment in, 41, 47

replication of, 42

scientific process and, 42

signal-detection, 140, *140*

see also research methods

experts, 367

explanatory style, 657, 674

explicit memory, 327, 328, 334, 336, 337, 339

exposure therapy, 267–77, 688, *688*, 714

Expression of the Emotions in Man and Animals (Darwin), 68

expression rules, 658

external environment, 463–64

external validity, 27, *27*, 47, 48

extinction procedures, *267*, 688

extraversion, 593, 594, 599, 600, 632

extrinsic rewards, 489

eye, 162–63, *162*

see also vision

eye movements, 209, 211

in motion perception, 205–6, *205*

eyewitness testimony, false memories in, *11*, 320, *320*, 324, *324*, 325

Eysenck, Hans, 593, 600, 706

facial expressions, 491–93, *492*, *499*

facial recognition, 562, *562*

facilitation, social, 528, 542

factor analysis, 430, 458

false-belief tests, 561, *561*, 588

false memories:

in eyewitness testimony, *11*, 320, *320*

hypnosis and, 324–25

leading questions and, 320–21

recovery of repressed memories and, 331–32

schemas and, 321

source confusion and, 256–57

familiarity, 322–24, *323*, 339, 536, *536*

family environment, and schizophrenia, 665–66

family resemblance structure, 388, *388*

family therapy, 694, 714

fear conditioning, 10, *10*

feature detectors, 174–75, 182, 191, 209

feature nets, 188–91, *189*, 216

features, 182–83

geons and, 191, *191*

hidden figures and, *184*

parsing and, *185*

Fechner, Gustav Theodor, 139

Fechner's law, 139, 178

feelings:

conscience and, 576

see also emotion

Festinger, Leon, 516–17

fetal alcohol syndrome, 549, *549*

fetal stage, 548

fetus, 548, 588

fidelity, emotional vs. sexual, 79–80

figure, in form perception, 185

figures, impossible, *188*

Fillmore, Kaye, 21–22

finches, 59, 65

firstborns, 604, *604*, 632

Fischer, Bobby, *620*

Fisher, Carrie, *653*

fixed-interval (FI) schedule, 286, *287*

fixed-ratio (FR) schedule, 286, *286*

flashbulb memories, 329–30, *329*, 339

flow states, *620*

fluid intelligence, 432, 459, 583–84, 589

Flynn effect, 447, *447*

fMRI (functional magnetic resonance imaging), 2, 3, *9*, 48, 112, 230, *230*, 4999

folk theories, 389

follicles, 479–80

Food and Drug Administration (FDA), U.S., 108, 128, 699, *700*, 702

foot-in-the-door technique, 517–18

forebrain, *115*

see also cortex

forgetting, 318–19

forgetting curve, 318, *318*

formal operational period, 578, 589

formal operations, 552, *553*

form perception:

Biederman's model of, 191

figure and ground in, 186–88, *187*

nervous system and, 192

of partially occluded figures, *183*

variability of stimuli and, *183*, 835

visual processing in, 192

fossils, 63, *63*

Fourier, Joseph, 155–56

fovea, *162*, 163, *163*, 164, 165

Fox, Michael J., *128*

fragment-completion tasks, 335

Franklin, Eileen, *332*

Franklin, George, Sr., *332*

fraternal (dizygotic) twins, 70–71, *70*, *71*, 73, 444, *444*, 448, 484, 599, 650, 652, 655

free association, 606

free recall, 304, *304*

frequency, light, *see* wavelengths, of light

frequency, sound, 154, *154*, 158, *159*

frequency distributions, *30*

frequency estimates, 349

frequency theory, 158

Freud, Sigmund, 17, 222, 241, *241*, 614, 674, 680, 684–85, 687, 712, 714

on adolescence, 632

case studies of, 26

on dreams, 611, 632

on mythology, 611, *612*

psychoanalysis and, 606–15, *606*, 632, *687*

psychopathology of everyday life and, 610–11

on slips of the tongue, 610–11, *611*

on stages of psychosexual development, 609–10, 632

Freudian slips, 610–11, *611*

friendships, 572–74, 589

frontal cortex, 489

frontal lobe, 119, 124, 700

functional magnetic resonance imaging (fMRI), 2, 3, *9*, 111, *111*, 112, 230, *230*, 489

function morphemes, 382–83, 391–92, 422

fundamental attribution error, 509–10, *509*, 541

fusiform face area (FFA), 229, *230*, 499

g (general intelligence), 431–32, *431*, 433, 435, 458–59

GABA (gamma-amino butyric acid), 100, 698

Gage, Phineas, 26–27, 107, *107*, 124

Galapagos Islands, 59

Gale, Crystal, 181

Galileo Galilei, 86, 87

gamma-amino butyric acid (GABA), 100, 698

ganglion cells, *162*, 163–64, 192

see also magno cells; parvo cells

garden path, 392–93, 422

Gardner, Howard, on multiple intelligences, 439–40

gate control theory, 148

gender:

agreeableness differences of, 604, *604*

autism and, 666
development of, 589
genetic determination of, 43, *54*
intelligence differences of, 452–54
moral reasoning and, 574–75, 589
personality and, 604
stereotypes of, *453*
suicide and, 655
see also sex, sexuality
general intelligence (*g*), 431–32, *431*, 433, 435,
    458–59
generalization gradient, 268, *268*, 282, *282*
generalized anxiety disorder, 647–48, 698
general paresis, 637
generativity versus stagnation, 586, 589
generic knowledge and memory, 268, 321
genes, genetics, 51–83
    alleles and, 57, 61, 69, 81
    anorexia nervosa and, 669
    attention-deficit/hyperactivity disorder
        (ADHA) and, 668
    bulimia nervosa and, 670
    codominance in, 57, 82
    concordance rate and, 650
    depression and, 638
    development and, 548
    dimples and, 57, *57*
    DNA and, 52–53
    dominance in, 57, 82
    drug dependence and, 255
    earlobes and, 74–75, *75*
    emotional remembering and, 9–11, 17
    environment vs., 446–47, 450–51, 602–3
    evolution and, 61–62
    evolution of behavior and, 65–81
    gender determination and, *54*
    gene expression and, 54–55, 79
    genes and, 53–54
    gene transmission and, 55–56
    genome and, 54, 61, 64, 69, 70, 73, 74, 75, 81
    genotype of, 55, 57, 66, *70*, 73, 81, 82, 443–45,
        484
    incomplete dominance in, 57, 82
    of intelligence, 69–75, *71*
    intelligence and, 443–45, *444*, 450, 454
    interactions among, 56–58
    IQ and, 443–45
    learning capacity and, 445
    malfunctioning, 57
    mental disorders and, 647–48, 655, 661–63,
        662, 674
    pattern of, 58, 81
    personality traits and, 598–601
    phenotype of, 55, 57, 61, 65, 72, 73, 81
    polygenic inheritance and, 58
    recessive, 82
    SES and IQ interaction with, 447–48
    set point and, 620
    sexual orientation and, 484

survival of, 62
    taste and, 133, 152
genetic survival, 79–80
Genghis Khan, 301–2
geniculate nucleus, 163
Genie, 405–6
genital stage, 609
genome, human, 55, 61, 64, 69, 70, 73, 74, 75, 81,
    548, 588
genotype, 55, 57, 66, *70*, 73, 81, 82, 443–45, 484
Genovese, Kitty, 532, *532*
geons, 191, *191*, 216
Gestalt psychology, 184–85, *186*
Gestalt therapy, 686, 714
gestural language, 406–7, *407*
ghost sickness, Native American, 643
Gilligan, Carol, on moral reasoning, 574–75
glia, 548
glial cells, 90–92, *90*, 130
global workspace hypothesis, 231–33, 257
glomeruli, 149, *149*, 178
glove anesthesia, 606, *606*
glucoreceptors, 468, 469, 501
glucose, 467–68
glutamates, schizophrenia and transmission
        dysfunction of, 664, 675
glycogen, 467
goal maintenance, 435
goal neglect, 435
goal state, in problem solving, 365–66, 377
good continuation, 186, *186*
Good Samaritan, 533
Good Samaritan, The (Bassano), *534*
grasp reflex, 551, *551*, 588
gratification, delay of, 629–30, *629*, 633
ground, in form perception, 186–88
group dynamics, 527–31
    deindividuation in, 529–30, 542
    mere presence effects and, 527–28, *527*, 542
group inhibition, 533
group polarization, 530–31, 542
group therapy, 693–94, *693*, 714
groupthink, 531, *531*, 542
growth, developmental, 546–50, *550*
guilt, survival, 649

habituation, 259, 261–62, 298
habituation procedures, 557, 588
hair cells, as auditory receptors, 134, *157*
Haldol, 696
hallucinations, 660, 674
hallucinogens, 251, 252–53, 257
halo effect, 535
Harlow, Harry, 563
Harman, Sabrina, 505
Harper's Weekly, 182
Harvard College, 613
Hawn, Goldie, *389*
hearing (audition), 118, 143, 153–60

absolute threshold of, *138*
decline of, *583*
frequency theory in, 158
language in absence of, 406, *407*
loss of, *158*
nervous system and, 158–59
place theory in, 158
sound as stimulus for, 153–60, *153*
tonotopic map and, 159–60, *160*
transduction in, 156–58
Weber fraction for, *139*
Helmholtz, Hermann von, 158, *158*, 169
    on unconscious inference, 197–98
helping, 532, *534*, 543
    costs of, 533–34
helplessness, learned, *see* learned helplessness
Hering, Ewald, 172
heritability, intelligence and, 71–73, 75, 448–50,
    450, 451
heritability ratio (H), 72, 73, 83, 448–50, 459
heroin, 102, 253, 254, 276–78, *277*
Herrnstein, Richard J., 442
hertz, 154, *155*
Hertz, Heinrich, 154
heterosexuality, 483–85
heterozygous, 57
heuristics, 348, 349–52, 376
    availability, 348–49, 376
    judgment, 348
    representativeness, 348–49
hierarchical conception, of intelligence, 431–32,
    431, 458–59
hierarchy of needs, 487, *487*, 502, 615
Higgins, E. Tory, 617
Hilgard, Ernest, 246
Hinduism, 247
hippocampus, 9, *9*, 116, 126, 223, 309
histrionic personality disorder, 672
H.M., 26, 333, *333*
homelessness, 696, *696*
homeostasis, 464, *464*, 474, 478, 501
    internal, 276
homogamy, 537
homosexuality, 483–85
homozygous, 57
Horemhab offering wine to Annubis, 215
horizontal cells, *162*
hormonal cycles, 479–80
hormones, 103–5, 234, 238, 453, 475–76, 479
    aggression and, 502
    changing of, 480
    prenatal, 484, 549
    secretion of, *104*
    sexuality and, 481
horse racing, predicting outcome of, *437*
hospitals, mental, 679, *679*, 696, *696*
Hubel, David, 175, *175*
hue, 168, *168*, 169
hue pairs, 172, *172*

internal environment, 463–64, 473, 501
internal homeostasis, 276
internal validity, 34, 41–42
internal working model, 566–67
International Classification of Disease System
    (ICD-10), 642
interneurons, 89
interpersonal intelligence, 439
interpersonal therapy (IPT), 685, 712
interposition, 201, 217
Interpretation of Dreams (Freud), 241
interpretations, illogical, *215*
inter-rater reliability, 32
intimacy, 537, 543
    isolation vs., 585, *586*, 589
intrapersonal intelligence, 439
intrinsically rewarding, 489, 620
intrinsic motivation, 285–86, 299
introspection, 256
    cognitive unconscious and, 222–23
    communication of, 225
    functions of consciousness and, 220–27
    honest reporting and, 220–21, *221*
    mistaken, 225–26
    translating thoughts into words and, 220–22
introversion, 600, 632
intrusion:
    memory, 319–25
    semantic memory and, 322
intrusion errors, 319, 321, 339
intuition, vs. reasoning, 352
inverted spectrum, 221, *221*
in vivo desensitization, 688, *688*
ion channels, 94
ion pump, 94
IPT (interpersonal therapy), 685
IQ, as measure, *see* intelligence quotient (IQ), as
    measure
iris, 138, *162*
Isabelle (code name), 405
isolated children, 405–6, 423
isolation, intimacy versus, 585, *586*, 589
Iyengar, Sheena, 626

Jamadi, Manadel al-, 505
James, William, 220, 463, 494, 616, *616*
James-Lange theory of emotion, 494, 495–96,
    502
Jameson, Dorothea, 172
Jamison, Kay Redfield, 653–54
jealousy, 79–80
Jefferson, Thomas, 615, *615*
jet lag, *234*
J.S., 86
judgment, 348–54, 376
    heuristics, 348–49, 376
    moral, 574–75
    reasoning and, 358
    training and, 358

Jung, Carl, on collective unconscious, 611, *611*
justification:
    of effort, 516–17, *516*, *517*
    insufficient, 517
just-noticeable difference (jnd), 137, 178

Kahneman, Daniel, 348–49, *349*
Kamala (wild girl), 405
Kant, Immanuel, 136, *136*
Kanzi (chimpanzee), 414
Kelley, Harold, 507–8
Kelly, George, 624
Kennedy, John F., 329
Kepler, Franz, 86
kinesthesis, 145
    Weber fraction for, *139*
King, Coretta Scott, *522*
King, Martin Luther, Jr., *522*
Kinsey, Alfred, 485
Kluver-Bucy syndrome, 9
knowledge:
    declarative, 334
    expert, 367
    fluid vs. crystallized intelligence and, 432, 459
    perception and, 215
    procedural, 334
    tacit, 438
knowledge acquired, vs. behavior modification,
    287–89
knowledge-driven processing, 189–90, *190*
Knowles, Beyoncé, 440
Kohlberg, Lawrence, on stages of moral reasoning,
    574–75, *575*, 589
Korsakoff's syndrome, 333
Kraepelin, Emil, 637, *637*
Krafft-Ebbing, Richard von, 637

labeling, of mental illnesses, pros and cons, 644
Lake Washington, 63–64, *64*
Lamb, Fred and Don, *599*
Lamictal, 678
Lange, Carl, 494
language, 379–423
    accents and, 396
    adult, progression to, 403–4, 423
    ambiguity in, 391
    basic-level words and, 401–2, 422
    basic units of, 380–85
    bilingualism and, 408–10
    building blocks of, 397–98, 422
    child, 401–3, 422–23
    color perception and, 417
    combining definitional and prototype theories
        of, 388–89, *389*, 422
    comprehension of, 395–96
    cultural perceptions and, 417–21
    and definitional theory of word meaning,
        386–87, *386*, 422
    disorders of, 123–24

    environment and growth of, 404–10, 423
    foreign, *399*
    frequency sensitivity in infants, 399–400, 422
    gestural, 406–7, *407*, 423
    hierarchical nature of, 380–81, *381*, 422
    late exposure to, 405–6, 413, 423
    learning and, 396–404, 422–23
    meaning conveyed by, 385–96, 422
    without models, 406–7, 423
    morphemes and words in, 314–17, 422
    in nonhumans, 413–15, *414*, 423
    phrases and sentences in, 383–85, 389–91,
        390, *393*, *395*, 422
    phrase structure organization in, 384–85, *384*,
        385, 422
    prototype theory of meaning of, 387–88, 422
    rhythm of, 381–82, 398–99
    rules of syntax in, 383, 422
    and second-language learning, 412–13, *412*
    sensitive period hypothesis of, 410–15, *411*, 423
    social origins in learning of, 396, *396*
    social origins of word learning in, 400–401
    without sound, 406, 423
    sound units in, 380–82, 399
    of spatial position and direction, 417–21, *418*,
        419
    spatial thinking and Tzeltal, 419–21
    stages of development and growth of,
        396–404, 422
    subordinates and, 403, 422
    superordinates and, 403, 422
    syntax rules of, 391
    thought and, 415–21, 423
    understanding, 391–96
    see also sign language
larynx, *381*
Latané, Bibb, 532
latent content, of dreams, 611, 632
latent learning, 287, 299
lateral geniculate nucleus, 163, 241–42, *242*
lateral hypothalamus, 469
lateral inhibition, 166, *167*
lateralization, 116–18, *117*
Law and Order: Criminal Intent, 7
law of effect, 278–81, *280*, 299
leading questions, 320–21
learned helplessness, 299
    depression and, 289
learning, 259–99
    associative, 273
    biological constraints on, 291–94
    brain activity during, 309
    classical conditioning in, 259
    empiricist view of, 136
    evolution and, 294–95
    incidental, 338
    intentional, 303
    language and, 262, 396–404, 406–7, 422–23
    latent, 287

procedural, 334, 335, 339
recall and, 303, 319, 322, 336
recency effects in, 304–5, *304, 305*
recoding in, 306–7
recognition and, 303
recollection and, *308,* 314, 322–23, 339, 498
recovered, 332, *332*
rehearsal, *305,* 306–7
repression of, 331–32, 339
retrieval, *see* retrieval, memory
schemas and, 321, 339
selective, 25
semantic, 328, 583
short-term, *see* working memory
stage theory of, 304
storage, 245, 302–3
storage capacity, 304
storage of, 338
as supplemented, 11–12
thinking and, 373–74, *374*
trauma and, 330–32, *330*
types of, 327–37, *327*
as unreliable, *5,* 11–12, 25
witnesses and testimony and, 320, *320,* 324, 325
working, *see* working memory
see also false memories
memory failure, 583
decay as, 318–19
forgetting in, 318–19
interference and, 319, *319*
retention intervals and, 318–19
retrieval failure in, 338–39
memory span, 304
memory trace, 303, 312, 338
menarche, 577
Mendel, Gregor, 56–57, *56*
menopause, 586
menstruation, 480, 481, 577
mental disorders, 636–52, *673*
alcohol consumption and, 635
anxiety, 644–52, 674
assessment of, 640–42
biological factors of, 680
biomedical treatments, 694–703
biomedical treatments for, 680, 702–3
causal models of, 674
clinical interviews, 640–41
cognitive-behavioral approaches to treatment of, 690–92, 714
comorbidity and, 650
cultural considerations in treatment for, 682–83
current treatments for, 680–83
defined, 639–40
dissociative, 670–71, 675
drug use and, 635
early conceptions of, 637, 674
early treatments of, 694–95, *695*

evaluating treatments of, 705–13
genetic factors in, 647–48, 655, 661–63, *662,* 674
humanistic approaches to treatment of, 685–87
medication for, 680, 695–700, 714
misdiagnosis of, 677
modern conceptions of, 638–39, 674
mood, 652–58, 674
multicausal models of, 638–39
nonpharmalogical treatments for, 700–703, *700*
overprescribed medication for, 699, *699*
past treatments for, 678–80, *679*
psychodynamic approaches to treatment of, 684–85
as psychological illness, 638–39
psychological risk factors for, 656–57
psychological treatments for, 680, 683–94
psychotherapy for, 714
schizophrenia, 644, 674–75
signs of, 641, 674
social support for, *639,* 652, 681
stress, 649, 674
subsyndromal, 673, 682, 711–12
symptoms of, 640–41
treatment of, 677–715
treatment providers for, 681–82, *681*
treatment recipients for, 682
see also psychopathology
mental exercise, 585
mental hospitals, 679, *679,* 696, *696*
mental images, imagery, 343–45, *345,* 376
mental representations, 342, 376, 588, 617
mental retardation:
autism and, 667, 675
PKU and, 449
mental rotation, 452, *452*
mental sets, 368–69, 377
mental speed, 433
mental testing, 458
see also intelligence testing
mere presence effects, 527–28, *527,* 542
mescaline, 251, *252*
Mesmer, Franz, 243–44, *244*
meta-analysis, 42, 709–10, 713, 715
methamphetamine, 250, *251*
method of loci, 309, 311
methodological eclecticism, 46–47
methylenedioxymethamphetamine (MDMA; ecstasy), 250, 251
midbrain, 115, *115*
middle age, 582
middle ear, 156
midlife transition (midlife crisis), 586, *587*
Milgram, Stanley, studies of, 524–26, *524,* 542
Miller, Arthur, *355*
mind-body connection, 228, *228*
mind-body problem, 227–28, 255, 256

Minnesota Multiphasic Personality Inventory (MMPI), 641–42, *642*
minorities, 522
mirror neurons, 290, *290*
Mischel, Walter, 596, 624, 628, 630
misinformation effect, 320–21, 339
mixed states, depression and mania as, 653
MMPI (Minnesota Multiphasic Personality Inventory), 641–42, *642*
mnemonics, 302, 310–11, *311,* 338
modeling, as behavior therapy, 690, *690,* 714
mondegreen, 181–82
monoamine oxidase (MAO) inhibitors, 696–97, *697*
monocular depth cues, 200–202, *203*
monocular distance cues, 217
monogamy, 75, 79–80
monosodium glutamate (MSG), 151
monozygotic twins, *see* identical twins
mood disorders, 652–58, 674
explanatory style, 657
negative cognitive schema and, 567
risk factors for, 656–57
roots of, 655–58
moods, 491
mood stabilizers, 698
moral development:
conscience and, 576, 589
prosocial behavior and, 589
morality, 2–3, 4
making decisions and, *2, 3*
moral judgment, 574–76
moral reasoning, 574–76, *575,* 589
morbid obesity, 471, 473
morphemes, 382–83, 391, 399, 406, 422
morphine, 102, 148, 245, *246*
motion detectors, 204, 208
motion parallax, 202, *203,* 217
motion perception, 202, 203–8, *204, 205,* 217
motivated social cognition, 523
motivation, motives, 485–90, 502
diversity of, 487–90, 502
drive and, 464
drive-based, 500–501
emotion and, 461–503
hierarchy of needs and, 487, *487,* 502
motivational states, 462–64, 501
motive to achieve, 486, *486,* 502
motive to belong, 485–86, *485,* 502
motivational-enhancement therapy, 686
motor areas, 118
motor cortex, 242
motor neurons, 89
motor projection area, primary, 119, *119,* 121
MRI (magnetic resonance imaging), 83–84, 110, *110, 111*
MSCEIT (Mayer-Salovey-Caruso Emotional Intelligence Test), 438–39, *438*
MSG (monosodium glutamate), 151

Müller, Johannes, 143–44
multicausal model of mental disorders, 674
multimodal therapy, 693, 705
multiple intelligences, 439–40, 459
multiple personality disorder (dissociative identity disorder), 658n, 670–71, 671, 675
    women and, 670
multiple sclerosis (MS), 96, 107
multi-unit recording, 105
Murray, Charles, 442
muscular action, 119–20, 119
musical intelligence, 439
mutations, in DNA, 61
myelin, 88, 91, 91, 96
My Fair Lady, 397
myths, psychoanalytic theory of, 611–12, 612

Nagel, Thomas, 256
narcissistic personality, 672
Nardil, 696
national character, 602, 632
National Highway Traffic Safety Administration, 249
National Science Foundation, 452
Native Americans, 440
naturalistic fallacy, 60, 60, 82
naturalistic intelligence, 439
natural selection, 10, 58–65, 64, 66, 69, 73, 74, 76, 77, 79, 81, 82, 152, 278, 280–81, 475, 478, 483, 651
nature vs. nurture, problems with, 443
Navratilova, Martina, 485
Nazi Germany, 523, 526, 526
Nebuchadnezzar, King of Babylon, 636, 636
Necker cube, 187, 187
needs, hierarchy of, 615
negative afterimage, 171, 171
negative cognitive schema, 657, 674
negative identity, 580, 589
negative symptoms, 660–61, 674
neglect syndrome (left neglect), 122, 122
neocortex, see cortex
nerve cells, interaction between, 88–89, 113
nerve impulses, 88–89
nervous system:
    adolescent changes of, 578
    architecture of, 112–18, 131
    autonomic (ANS), 113, 133, 131, 464–65, 474, 501, 502, 650
    brain and, 85–130
    central (CNS), 90, 112–13, 113, 127
    chemical signals of, 97, 103
    communication of, 103, 195–96
    communication within, 91–103, 113
    contralateral quality of, 119, 120, 131
    depressant drugs and, 248
    development of, 549
    effect of drugs on, 101–3
    endocrine system and, 103–4
    form perception and, 192

functional specialization of, 112
hearing and, 158–59
memory traces in, 303
pattern coding and, 170
peripheral, 112–13, 113, 127
PGO waves of, 242
plasticity of, 125–28
pre-natal development of, 547–48
repairing damage to, 127–28, 127
role of neurotransmitters in, 130
senses and, 142
sleep and, 238–39, 241–42, 242
somatic, 113, 113
stimulant drugs and, 250
structure of, 88–92, 112–18, 113
study of, 85–131
sympathetic, 474–75, 497, 499
neural correlates, 229–31, 257
neural plasticity, 125–28, 296
neural synchrony, 195–96
neural tube, 547
neurochemical malfunction, 656
neurodevelopmental disorder, 663, 675
neurogenesis, 127
neuroimaging, 110–11, 344
    see also CT scan, fMRI
neuroleptics, see antipsychotics
neurons, 88, 88, 105, 195
    afferent, 90
    chemical signals between, 92
    communication among, 92, 109, 232
    development of, 548
    efferent, 90
    electrical activity of, 92–95
    electrical signals within, 92, 109
    excitation threshold of, 99
    firing synchrony of, 195–96
    function of, 88–89
    interaction among, 88–89, 296–97
    learning and function of, 296–97
    mirror, 290, 290
    motor, 89
    new, 126–27
    parts of, see specific parts
    postsynaptic, 98–99
    potentiation of, 297
    presynaptic, 98–99, 100
    projection, 89
    protomaps and, 549
    recording from, 105
    in sensory coding, 143
    sleep deprivation and, 238
    sound frequency and, 158
    structure of, 88–89, 99, 130, 189
    types of, 89
    workspace, 232
neuropeptide-Y (NPY), 468–69, 472
neuropsychology, 107–8
neuroscience, 88, 192–96, 216
    affective, 496, 503

neuroscience approach, see perception, neuroscience approach
neurosis, 643
neurosurgery, 700
neuroticism, 593, 599, 602
neurotransmission, 148
neurotransmitters, 98–99, 100, 103, 104, 105, 130, 252, 257
    depression and, 655–56
    effect of drugs on, 101–3, 697, 697, 698
    lock-and-key model of, 101, 130
    in schizophrenics, 664
    in sensation seeking personalities, 600
newborns, 550–51, 562, 562
New Freedom Commission on Mental Health, 673
New Guinea, 67
Newton, Isaac, 87, 635
Nicaragua, deaf children in, 407, 407
niche construction, 66
night vision, 164
nine-dot problem, 366, 371
9/11 terrorist attack, 12, 12, 13–14, 329, 329, 518–19, 534
No Child Left Behind (NCLB), 452
nociceptors, 147–48
nodes, 346–48, 376
nodes of Ranvier, 88, 91, 91, 95
non-primary areas (association areas), 121
norepinephrine (NE), 100, 103, 105, 474, 655, 697, 697
normative influence, 521, 542
norm of reciprocity, 526, 542
noun phrases, 384, 384
novocaine, 250
NPY (neuropeptide-Y), 468–69, 472
nucleus accumbens, 489, 490

Obama, Barack, 128
obedience, 523–26, 523, 542
    psychological distance and, 525
obesity, 37, 81–82, 471–73, 501–2, 692
    environmental factors and, 473
    genetic roots of, 472–73
    morbid, 471, 473
    twin studies of, 472, 472
object permanence, 553–54, 553, 555, 558, 588
object relations, and attachment theory, 613–14, 632
objects, and space in infancy, 557–58
observational learning, 289–90, 299, 477, 514–15
observational studies, 36–38, 47
    see also case studies; correlations, correlational studies
observations, 22–28
    behavior changes during, 27–28
    clinical, 107–8
obsessive-compulsive disorder (OCD), 648, 648, 650, 672, 674, 701
occipital cortex, 118, 242, 242
occipital lobe, 86, 120

research methods (*cont.*)
  effect size and, 34
  ethics in, 43–45, 48–49, 289*n*
  experiments and, 36, 38–43
  explicit measures and, 512
  implicit measures and, 512
  maximum variation sampling, 26
  observational studies in, 36–38
  observations and, 22–28
  operational definitions in, 24
  outside the lab, 45–46, *45*
  testable hypotheses and, 23–24, *23*
  testing differences and, 31–36
  working with data and, 28–36
resilience, 621
resistance, 606
resolution phase, of sexual response, 481, 502
respiratory system, 88
response control, 280, *280*
responses, to stimuli:
  conditioned, 263–78, 298
  unconditioned, 198–202, 298
resting potential, of neurons, 93, *94*, 98
restructuring, in problem solving, 377
retention interval, 318, 339
reticular activating system, 229
reticular formation, 228
retina, 135, *162*, 163, *163*, 164, 165, 196
  color receptors in, 169, *169*, 172, *172*
  ganglion cells in, 192; *see also* magno cells;
    parvo cells
  in perception of movement, 204, *205*
retinal image, *145*, 162, 197–98, *197*, *198*, 205, 206
retinal motion, 204
retrieval, memory, 302–3, 310–11, 313–16, 338,
    372–73
  context reinstatement and, 315–16, 338
  cues for, 310–11, 314–16, 338–39
  encoding and, 315–16
  failure, 338
  partial, 313–14
  paths, 310, 314, 339
retrograde amnesia, 312–13, *313*, 338
reversible figures, 187, *187*
rewards:
  intrinsic vs. extrinsic, 285
  and punishment, 576
rhodopsin, 164–65
rhythm, 381–82, 398
Ribot's law, 313
Rico (comprehending dog), *414*
risk factors, psychopathology, 638–39
risky shift, 530
Risperdal, 696
Ritalin, in attention-deficit/hyperactivity disorder,
    667–68
rods, *162*, 163, *163*
  night vision served by, 164
  visual pigment in, 164–65
  as visual receptors, 164

Rogers, Carl, 616, 619, 622, 631, 686, *686*, 714
romantic love, 537–39, *538*, *540*, 543
Romeo-and-Juliet effect, 538–39, *538*
Roosevelt, Eleanor, 615, *615*
rooting reflex, 551, 588
Rorschach inkblot technique, *643*
Rozin, Paul, 462
Ruffini endings, 147, *147*
rules, expression, 658
Rush, Benjamin, 694

——————

sample selection, 25–26
satisfice, 363, 364, 377
saturation, color, *168*, 169
Saul, King of Judea, 636
savant syndrome, 439, 459
scatter plots, 31, *31*
Schachter-Singer theory of emotion, 496, 502, 538
schedules of reinforcement, 286, 299
schemas, 321, 339
  cognitive, 554–55, 657, 674
schematic knowledge, 510, 511
schizoid personality disorder, 672
schizophrenia, 58, 103, 636, 644, 658–66, 673,
    674–75, 692, 701
  behavioral disorder in, 660
  brain defects and, 664–65, *665*
  brain development and, 661–63
  catatonic, 660, *661*
  cognitive symptoms of, 661
  cultural sensitive treatment for, 683
  disorganized, 660, *660*
  disorganized speech in, 660
  electroconvulsive therapy (ECT) for, 701–2, *701*
  family environment and, 665–66
  glutamate transmission dysfunction and, 664,
    675
  hallucinations in, 660
  heredity and, 661–63, *662*
  homelessness and, 696, *696*
  medication for treatment of, 103, 695–96
  negative symptoms of, 660–61
  neurotransmitter malfunctioning in, 664
  painting by sufferers of, *659*
  personal contact loss in, 660–61
  positive symptoms of, 659–60
  precursors of, 663, *663*, 675
  prenatal environment and, 675
  prenatal factors of, *663*
  signs and symptoms of, 659–61, 674
  social and psychological environment and,
    665–66
  social realities of treating, 695–96
  socioeconomic status and, 665, *665*, 675
  structural defects in, 664–65
  viral infection and, 662–63
schizotypal personality disorder, 672
Scholastic Aptitude Test (SAT), 452
scientific method, *see* research methods
Scream, The (Munch), *647*

secondary sexual characteristics, 577, 589
second-order conditioning, 265–66, *266*, 298
secure attachment, 566–67, *567*
secure base, 564, 566, 588
securely attached children, 588, 614
segmentation, *382*
selection, perceptual:
  central, 209–11
  eye movements and, *209*, 211
  in hearing, 213
  through orientation, 209
  in vision, 209–11
selection task, 356–57, *356*, *357*
selective serotonin reuptake inhibitors (SSRIs),
    697, 699, *700*, 714
self, 616–19
  actual, 617, *617*
  culture and, 618–19
  in humanistic psychology, 616
  ideal, 617, *617*
  ought, 617, *617*
  possible, 617
  theory, 616, 633
self-actualization, 487, 615–16, *615*, 622, 632
self-concept, 616
self-consistency, 598
self-control, 36, 500, 625–26, 628–30, *628*
self-descriptions, 618–19, *619*
self-efficacy, 623, 633
self-enhancement, 617–18
self-esteem, 476, 486, 617–18, *618*, 619, 633
self-fulfilling prophecies, 513, 541
self-handicapping, 627
self-identity, 580
self-interest, altruism and, 534
self-monitoring scale, 597, *598*, 632
self-perception theory, 517
self-promotion, 619
self-punishment, 576
self-regulation, 499, 578, 630
self-regulatory plans, competencies and, 625–26,
    633
self-report data, 594
self-schema, 616–17, *616*, 618, 633
self theory, 616, 633
Seligman, Martin, 289, 621, 657
semantic features, 386, 422
semantic memory, 328, 583
semantic roles, 389–90
semistructured interview, 640
senescence, 587
sensation, 133–79
  detection and, 137
  detection and decision of, 139–42
  detection for complex forms and, 176–77
  empiricist view of, 136
  genetics and, 133, 152
  hearing as, 129–36
  kinesthesis and, 145
  of pain, 147–48, 178

sensory adaptation and, 144–47, *145*
sensory thresholds and, 137–39
of skin, 146–47, *147*, 178
of smell, 148–50, 178
supertasting and, 133–34, 152
of taste, 151–53, *151*, 178
vestibular, 143, 145–46, 178
vision as, 160–77
see also senses; sensory processes
sensation seeking, 476
sensation seeking personalities, 600, *600*, 632
senses, 142–53
kinesthesis, *139*, 145
pain, *139*, 147–48, 178
pressure, *139*
see also hearing (audition); skin senses; smell;
taste; vision
sensitive period hypothesis, 410–15, *411*, 423
sensorimotor capacities, of newborns, 550–51
sensorimotor period, 552–55, *553*, 588
sensory adaptation, 144–45, *145*, 178
sensory areas, 118
sensory coding, 143–44
for psychological intensity, 143, 178
sensory perception, 96–97, 118, *119*
see also perception
sensory processes, 133–79
active perceiver in, 136, 168, 214
coding in, 143–44
decision and detection in, 139–40, *140*, *141*
empiricist view of, 136, 178
hearing as, 153–60, 178–79
intensity of sensation in, 137–39
passive perceiver in, 135–36
pattern theory of, 144
perceptual sensitivity in, 140
psychological intensity in, 143, 178
quality in, 143–44, 178
signal-detection in, 140–42, *140*, *141*, 178
specificity theory of, 144, 178
transduction in, 143, 156–58
vision in, 160–77, 179
sensory projection areas, primary, 118–19, *119*, 120
sentences, 383–85, 422
meanings of, 389–91, *390*, *393*, *394*
phrase structure description of, 383–85, *384*, *385*
predicates of, 389, 422
separation anxiety, 563
Seroquel, 696
serotonin (5HT), 100, 655, 697, *697*
serotonin transporter gene, 57–58
Serzone, 697
set point, 467, 501, 620
sex, sexuality, 83, 478–85, 502
and advertising for a mate, 70–71
animal, 70–71
attraction and, 483
cultural and cognitive aspects of, 482–83, 502

estrus cycle and, 479, 481, 502
hormones and, 481
human response cycle of, 481, *481*, 502
mate choice and, 78, 482–83, *482*
physiological aspects of, 479–81
situational determinants of, 482
see also gender
sexual abuse, repressed memories of, 331
sexual aggression, 482
sexual arousal, 482
sexual development, 589
sexual orientation, 483–85, *483*
attraction and, 483
genetic influence on, 484
sexual reproduction, 56, 66
shading, as depth cue, *203*
Shakespeare, William, 79, 538, 546
shallow processing, 309, 338
shape constancy, 196, *196*, 198
shape perception, 174
see also form perception
shaping, 283–84
shared-problem groups, 693
Shaver, Phillip, 493
shenjing shauiro, Chinese illness, 643
Sherif, Muzafer, 519–20
shock treatment, *see* electroconvulsive therapy
short-term memory, *see* working memory
side effects:
of drug treatment, 698, 699
of lobotomy, 700
sight, *see* vision
signal-detection analysis, 141–42, *141*
medicine and, 141–42, *141*
signal-detection theory, 140–42, 178
analysis, 141–42, *141*
implications of, 141–42
procedures, 140–41
sign language, American Sign Language (ASL), 406, 413, *413*, 423
signs, *see* symptoms and signs
similarity, 536–37, *536*, 543
principle of, 185, *186*
simple reaction time, 433
simultaneous color contrast, 170, *171*
sine wave, 154, *154*
single-case experiments, *see* case studies
single-cell recording, 105, 130
situational attributions, 507, 509, 510, 541
size constancy, 196, *196*, 198
Skinner, B. F., 17
on operant behavior, 281, *281*
Skinner box, 281, *281*
skin senses, 143, 146–47, *147*, 178
absolute threshold of touch and, *138*
sleep, 229, 233–43
alpha rhythm of, 234, *235*
beta rhythm of, 234–35, *235*
brain activity during, 233, 234–35

circadian rhythm of, 233, 239
delta rhythm of, 235, *235*
deprivation of, 236–38, *236*, *238*, 239
dreams and, *see* dreams, dreaming
function of, 238–39, *239*
hypnagogic imagery of, 234
insomnia and, 237
lateral geniculate nucleus and, 241–42, *242*
need for, 236–38, *237*
neural communication during, 233
paradoxical, 235
paralysis of, 235
REM, 235–36, *235*, 237, 238, 239, 243, 257
slow-wave, 235, *235*, 236, 237, 238, 239, 257
spindles of, 235
stages of, 234–35
wake cycles and, 234–36
slippery slope, 526
slow-wave sleep, 235, *235*, 236, 237, 238, 239, 257
smell, 148–50, *149*, 178
absolute threshold of, *138*
communication based on, 150
decline in, *583*
flavor and, 149–50
menstrual synchrony and, 150
pheromones and, 150
sensation of, Weber fraction for, *139*
smiling, 67–69, 83
biological roots of, 67
crow's feet and, 68, *68*
expressive, 68, *68*
origins of, 67–68, 69
polite, 68, *68*
as species general, 68–69
smooth muscles, 113
"Snow White and the Seven Dwarfs," *612*
Snyder, Mark, 597
social aggression, 36, 476, *476*
social animal, man as, 531
social behavior, 7–8
brain damage affecting, 124–25
conformity in, 519–22
false confessions and, 7
helping in, 532
obedience in, 523–26, *523*
police interrogations and, 7–8, *7*
social class, and schizophrenia, 665
social cognition, 506–19, 541–42
attribution, 507–10, 541
cognitive dissonance and, 516, *516*
development and, 559–62
disorders of, 124–25
motivated, 523
person perception and, 510–14
social-cognitive approach to personality, 622–31, 633
social-cognitive approach to psychology, origins of, 623–25, 633
social contact, 486

of schizophrenia, 659–61
synapses, 96–100, *99, 100,* 130, 296–97
  communication between, 97
  communications across, 97
  mechanism of, 97–100, *98, 99, 101*
  vesicles of, *98, 100*
synaptic gap, *99*
synaptic reuptake, 100, 101–3, 130, *697*
synchrony, neural, 195–96
syntax, rules of, 324–25, 383, *390, 391,* 414, 422
syphilis, 637
systematic desensitization, 688

———

tabula rasa, 135
tacit knowledge, 438
talent, intelligence vs., 440
talking cures, *see* psychotherapy
tangible support, 486, 502
Taoism, 247
task model, 434–36
tastants, 151
taste, 151–53, *152*
  absolute threshold of, *138*
  age and, 151
  genetics and, 133, 152
  papillae and, 151, *151, 152,* 178
  as sensation, Weber fraction for, *139*
  supertasting and, 133–34, 152
taste aversion, learned, 152, 292–94, *292, 293,* 299
TAT (Thematic Apperception Test), 642, *642*
temperament, 6, 599, 632
  among children, 567, *567,* 589
  inhibited, 601, *601,* 632
temperature, body, 464–66, *465,* 478
temporal cortex, 118, 194
temporal lobe, 86, 120
temptation, *577*
tending, 474, *474*
tension-reduction, 485
teratogens, 549, 588
testable hypothesis, 23–24, *23*
testosterone, 453, 476, 502
test-retest reliability, 32, 458
tests, testing:
  culture and, 440–41, *440*
  false-belief, 561, *561*
  Implicit Association Test (IAT), 512
  intelligence, *see* intelligence testing
  Mayer-Salovey-Caruso Emotional Intelligence Test (MSCEIT), 438–39, *438*
  mental, *see* mental testing
  personality, 641–42
  projective, 642
  Raven's Progressive Matrices, 427, *427,* 433, 441, 455
  reliability and validity of, 427, 458
  stereotypes and, *457,* 512
  Thematic Apperception Test (TAT), 642, *642*

Wechsler Adult Intelligence Scale (WAIS), 427, *427, 458*
Wechsler Intelligence Scale for Children (WISC), 426
  see also statistics
texture gradients, 202, *202, 203*
thalamus, 115, *115,* 116, 163–64, *163,* 228, 229, 257, 488, 548, 700
that's-not-all technique, 527, 542
THC (tetrahydrocannabinol), 251, 252
Thematic Apperception Test (TAT), 642, *642*
theory of mind, 545, 560–61, *562,* 588
therapeutic alliance, 704, 715
thermal stimulation, 488, *488*
thermoregulation, 464–66, 473, 478, 501
thinking, 341–77
  creative, 371–73
  critical, 375
  directed, 348
  dual-process theories of, 352–54
  in groups, 530–31
  heurisitics and, 348–49, 376
  illumination and, 372
  images and symbols in, 343
  incubation and, 372
  judgment in, 348–54, 376
  language and, 415–21, 423
  mental representations, 342, 376
  preparation and, 372
  problem-organization and, 365–69
  problem solving and, 365–75, 377
  problem-solving obstacles and, 368–70
  problem-solving process of, 365–75
  reasoning and decision making in, 341, 354–58, 376–77
  spatial, *see* spatial thinking
  symbolic, 346–48
  symbolic elements and, 346–48
  types of, 353
  verification and, 372
third-variable problem, 37, *38,* 40, 48
Thorazine, 696
Thorndike, Edward L., *279*
  on learning, 278–80, *279, 280,* 281, 297
threat, 473–78, *478,* 502
  cultural and cognitive aspects of, 476–78
  "fight or flight" response and, 474–75
  physiological aspects of, 474–76
Three Faces of Eve, The, 671, *671*
"thrifty gene" hypothesis, 473
timbre, 158
tip-of-the-tongue (TOT) effect, 313–14, 338
Toastmasters, 693
Tofranil, 696
token economies, 689, 714
Tolman, Edward, C., 287, *287*
tone, 382
Tong et al. procedure, 230
tonotopic map, 159–60, *160*

Tooby, John, 357
top-down processing, 189–90, *190*
touch, *see* skin senses
trait approach, personality and, 592–93, 632
traits, personality, 592–93, 632
  and biology, 598–601, *599*
  cultural taxonomy differences in, 595, 632
  taxonomy of, 632
  vs. situations, 596, 632
tranquilizers, *see* anxiolytics
tranquilizers, major, *see* antipsychotics
transcranial magnetic stimulation (TMS), 108–9, *108,* 112, 131, 345
transduction, 89
  of stimuli, 143, 156–58
transference, 684, 687, 714
traumatic events, 330–32, *330*
tree diagram, 384, *384,* 422
trephining, 694, *694*
trichromatic vision, 169
tricyclic antidepressants, 696
Triplett, Norman, 527
Turing, Alan, 485
Turner, Amanda, 591–92
Tversky, Amos, 348–49, *349*
twins:
  fraternal, 70–71, *70, 71,* 73, 444, *444,* 448, 484, 599, 650, 652, 655
  identical, 70–71, *70, 71,* 73, 444, *444,* 448, 472, *472,* 484, 599, *599,* 603, 632, 650, 652, 655, *665*
twin studies, 6, 69–71, *70, 71,* 73, 444, *444,* 448, 472, *472,* 484, 599, *599,* 603, 632, 650, 655, 661–62, *665*
Tzeltal (language), 419–21

———

ultimate causes, 58, 73, 74, 75
umami, 151
umbilical cord, 547
unconditional positive regard, 633
unconditioned reflex, 263–69
unconditioned response, 263–69, 276–78, 298
unconditioned stimulus, 268, 273, 274
unconscious, 607, *607,* 611
unconscious attributions, 224–25
unconscious conflict, 608–9
unconscious functioning, brain damage and, 223–24
unconscious inference, 197–98, 216, 222
unconscious processes, 226, *226*
understanding, language, 391–96
unique colors, 168, *168*
uterus, 480
utility:
  clinical, 709
  efficacy vs., 708–9

———

vagal nerve stimulation, 702, 714
vagus nerve, 97, 702